TEXAS
WRITE
SOURCE

Grade 11

TEACHER'S EDITION

Authors
Dave Kemper, Patrick Sebranek, and Verne Meyer

Consulting Author
Gretchen Bernabei

Illustrator
Chris Krenzke

GREAT
SOURCE®

HOUGHTON MIFFLIN HARCOURT

TEXAS
WRITE
SOURCE
Online

www.hmheducation.com/tx/writesource

Printed in the U.S.A.

ISBN-13 978-0-547-39487-9

2 3 4 5 6 7 8 9 10 0914 19 18 17 16 15 14 13 12 11 10

TEXAS WRITE SOURCE

Reviewers

Kim Brody
Lindale Independent School District
Lindale, Texas

Laurie Coker
Round Rock Independent School District
Austin, Texas

Rita Curington
Athens Independent School District
Athens, Texas

Sandy Emmerson
Midland Independent School District
Midland, Texas

Paula Jay
Fort Bend Independent School District
Missouri City, Texas

Lou Ann Kemper
Lewisville Independent School District
Flower Mound, Texas

Shelli Shaw
Katy Independent School District
Katy, Texas

Valerie Taylor
Eanes Independent School District
Austin, Texas

Table of Contents

Program Overview

Teacher Resources

The Writing Process

USING THE WRITING PROCESS

UNDERSTANDING THE TEXAS TRAITS

EXPLORING THE WRITING PROCESS

The Forms of Writing

NARRATIVE WRITING

EXPOSITORY WRITING

PERSUASIVE WRITING

How Does *Texas Write Source* Work?

Texas Write Source is a complete language arts curriculum focused on writing and grammar in print and digital formats.

With writing instruction at the core, all TEKS and ELPS are taught in an authentic writing context.

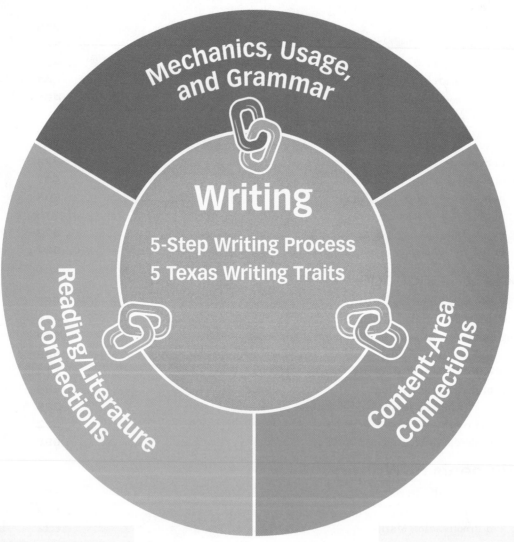

Mechanics, Usage, and Grammar

Writing
5-Step Writing Process
5 Texas Writing Traits

Reading/Literature Connections

Content-Area Connections

The Texas Traits

- Focus and Coherence
- Organization
- Development of Ideas
- Voice
- Conventions

Steps of the Writing Process

- Prewrite
- Draft
- Revise
- Edit
- Publish

Introduce the writing form:

- Analyze a model paragraph.

- Preview the form by responding to questions about the model or by writing a new paragraph.

 Students reflect on how revising for the Texas traits and editing for **mechanics, usage, and grammar** can improve their writing.

Each core writing unit follows the same instructional path— a consistent writing curriculum across all grade levels.

Explore the writing form:*

- Analyze a model essay or story.

 Students see how the author of the model essay or story used the steps of the writing process.

- Use the writing process to write an essay or story.

 Students revise their work using the Texas traits, and edit for **mechanics, usage, and grammar.**

*Repeat these steps based on an additional writing model as an enrichment activity.

Write for assessment:

- Write a piece in the same writing form for assessment.

 Students read essays and responses that model the appropriate form.

 Texas Write Source prepares students for success in the 21st century.

Write in other content areas:

- Write a piece in the same writing form for assessment.

 Students write in a variety of forms across the **major content areas—Science, Social Studies, Math, and the Arts.**

How is *Texas Write Source* Organized?

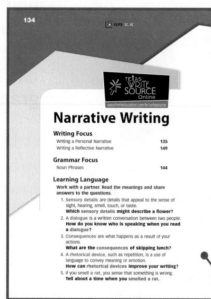

The Forms of Writing

The core units focus on instruction in the following writing forms:

- Narrative Writing
- Expository Writing
- Persuasive Writing
- Interpretitive Response
- Creative Writing
- Research Writing
- Writing Across the Curriculum (Grades 9–12)

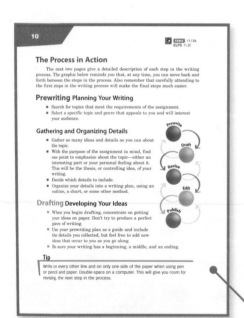

The Writing Process

This unit introduces students to the steps in the writing process and integrates instruction on the five Texas traits of writing.

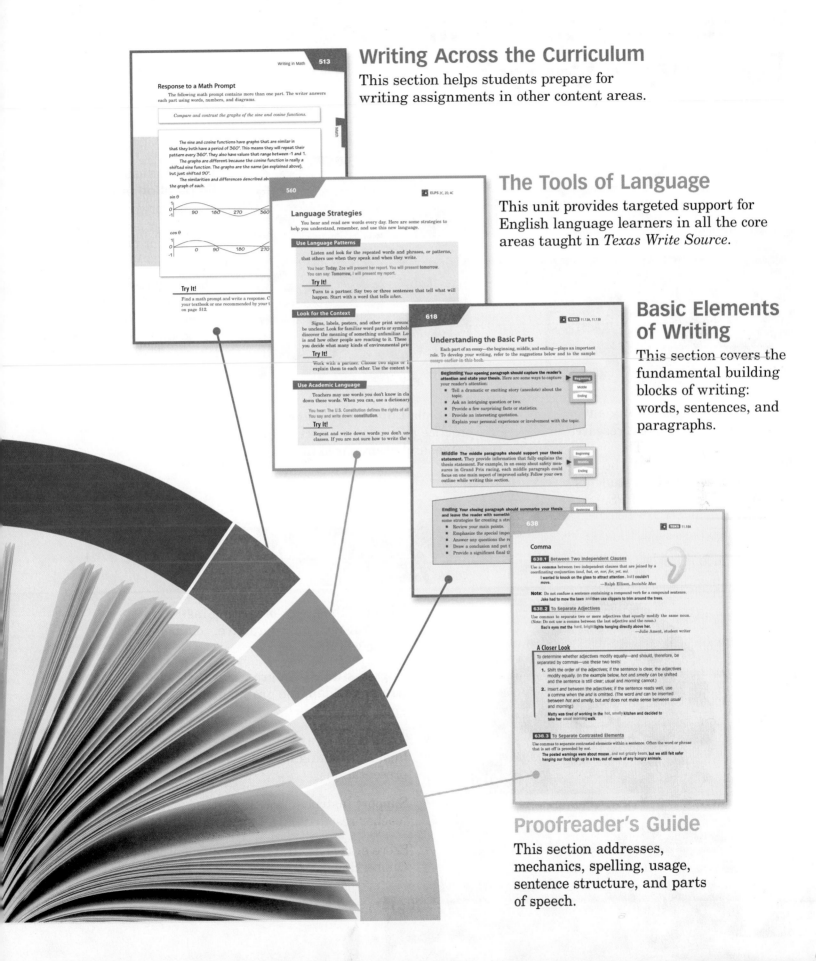

Writing Across the Curriculum

This section helps students prepare for writing assignments in other content areas.

The Tools of Language

This unit provides targeted support for English language learners in all the core areas taught in *Texas Write Source*.

Basic Elements of Writing

This section covers the fundamental building blocks of writing: words, sentences, and paragraphs.

Proofreader's Guide

This section addresses, mechanics, spelling, usage, sentence structure, and parts of speech.

What are the main components in Texas Write Source?

The *Texas Write Source* **Student Edition** reflects the latest research on writing instruction. The **Teacher's Edition** has all the support you need to help students master the TEKS and ELPS.

The **SkillsBook** helps students practice and improve mechanics, usage, and grammar skills.

Texas Assessment Preparation provides a pretest, progress tests, a post-test, and Texas assessment preparation.

The **Daily Language Workouts** build student grammar skills through quick, daily editing and proofreading activities.

Write Source Online
www.hmheducation.com/tx/writesource

- Discover the power of writing instruction with **Net-text**, an interactive, collaborative online worktext.

- Engage students in grammar through **GrammarSnap**, the grammar practice web application.

- Transform writing instruction through high-functioning **Interactive Whiteboard** presentations.

- Support instruction with a searchable teacher resource **File Cabinet**.

- Score essays accurately and efficiently with **Online Essay Scoring**.

How does the Teacher's Edition support instruction?

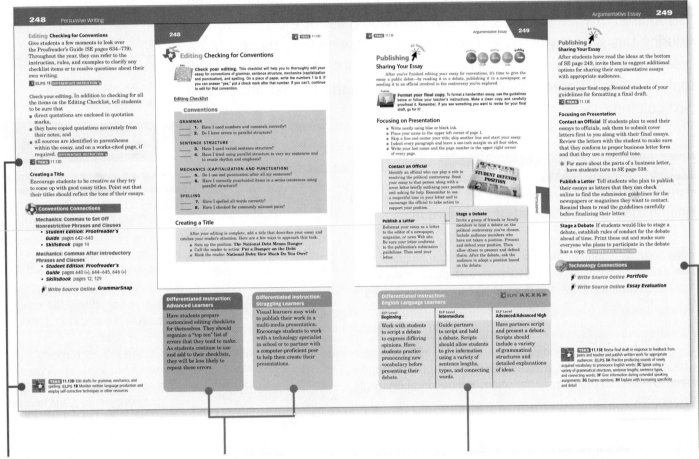

The Teacher's Edition has all the support you need to help students master the **TEKS and ELPS.**

Differentiated Instruction for advanced learners and struggling learners appears throughout the core instructional units.

The Teacher's Edition provides consistent support for **English language learners at all proficiency levels**.

Conventions Connections support grammar, usage, and mechanics instruction.

Additional Resources

- Texas Standards Correlations
- Yearlong Timetable
- Professional Development
- Language Transfer Support
- Reading–Writing Connection
- Benchmark Papers
- Copy Masters Resources

Texas Essential Knowledge and Skills for English Language Arts

The Texas Essential Skills for English Language Arts and Reading indicate the skills students need to master by the end of English III. To remind you what is required of your students, we have provided a list of the skills you will cover during this school year. The second column shows where these TEKS are addressed in this program. As students master the TEKS, they will also practice and apply the Texas Career and College Readiness Standards that are listed in the third column.

TEKS 11.13 Writing/Writing Process

Students use elements of the writing process (planning, drafting, revising, editing, and publishing) to compose text. Students are expected to:

A plan a first draft by selecting the correct genre for conveying the intended meaning to multiple audiences, determining appropriate topic through a range of strategies (e.g., discussion, background reading, personal interests, interviews), and developing a thesis or controlling idea

pages 2–4, 8, 9, 10, 12, 14–17, 52, 92–98, 138, 139, 152, 158–162, 164–168, 202, 203, 209, 216, 222, 260, 261, 267, 280, 333, 344, 345, 396–398, 406, 512, 516, 518, 535, 618, 620, 630, 631.

B structure ideas in a sustained and persuasive way (e.g., using outlines, note taking, graphic organizers, lists) and develop drafts in timed and open-ended situations that include transitions and rhetorical devices to convey meaning

pages 9, 12, 18, 98, 100–106, 140, 153, 159–162, 170–174, 204, 210, 211, 230, 232, 262, 268, 269, 332, 333, 335, 346, 485, 506, 512, 516, 518, 520, 535, 612–616, 618, 621–624.

C revise drafts to clarify meaning and achieve specific rhetorical purposes, consistency of tone, and logical organization by rearranging the words, sentences, and paragraphs to employ tropes (e.g., metaphors, similes, analogies, hyperbole, understatement, rhetorical questions, irony), schemes (e.g., parallelism, antithesis, inverted word order, repetition, reversed structures), and by adding transitional words and phrases

pages 9, 11, 12, 20–25, 108–112, 114, 141–143, 154, 176–184, 205, 212, 234–242, 263, 270, 292, 294–300, 321, 336, 347, 478, 506, 612–616, 623, 624.

D edit drafts for grammar, mechanics, and spelling

pages 9, 12, 26, 27, 122–126, 144, 145, 186, 187, 190, 206, 212, 244–248, 264, 270, 302–306, 322.

E revise final draft in response to feedback from peers and teacher and publish written work for appropriate audiences

pages 9, 12, 22, 23, 28–31, 116–120, 128–133, 155, 191, 206, 249, 307, 322, 431.

Texas Career and College Readiness Standards

ENGLISH/LANGUAGE ARTS STANDARDS

Writing:

1. Determine effective approaches, forms, and rhetorical techniques that demonstrate understanding of the writer's purpose and audience.

2. Generate ideas and gather information relevant to the topic and purpose, keeping careful records of outside sources.

3. Evaluate relevance, quality, sufficiency, and depth of preliminary ideas and information, organize material generated, and formulate a thesis.

4. Recognize the importance of revision as the key to effective writing. Each draft should refine key ideas and organize them more logically and fluidly, use language more precisely and effectively, and draw the reader to the author's purpose.

5. Edit writing for proper voice, tense, and syntax, assuring that it conforms to standard English, when appropriate.

CROSS-DISCIPLINARY STANDARDS

Foundational Skills B:

1. Write clearly and coherently using standard writing conventions.

2. Write in a variety of forms for various audiences and purposes.

3. Compose and revise drafts.

*Page References in *Teacher's Edition*
*Page References in *SkillsBook*

TEKS 11.14 Writing/Literary Texts

Students write literary texts to express their ideas and feelings about real or imagined people, events, and ideas. Students are responsible for at least two forms of literary writing. Students are expected to:

A write an engaging story with a well-developed conflict and resolution, complex and non-stereotypical characters, a range of literary strategies (e.g., dialogue, suspense) and devices to enhance the plot, and sensory details that define the mood or tone

pages 135–143, 145, 150–154, 340, 344, 345, 346, 608.

B write a poem that reflects an awareness of poetic conventions and traditions within different forms (e.g., sonnets, ballads, free verse)

pages 362, 363, 364, 365, 366, 367, 368, 369, 370, 371, 372, 373.

C write a script with an explicit or implicit theme, using a variety of literary techniques

pages 353, 354, 355, 356, 357, 358, 358, 360, 488, 489, 490, 491, 492.

ENGLISH/LANGUAGE ARTS STANDARDS

Writing:

1. Determine effective approaches, forms, and rhetorical techniques that demonstrate understanding of the writer's purpose and audience.

CROSS-DISCIPLINARY STANDARDS

Foundational Skills B:

2. Write in a variety of forms for various audiences and purposes.

⭐ (TEKS) 11.15 Writing/Expository and Procedural Texts

Students write expository and procedural or work-related texts to communicate ideas and information to specific audiences for specific purposes. Students are expected to:

A   write an analytical essay of sufficient length that includes:

   (i)   effective introductory and concluding paragraphs and a variety of sentence structures

   (ii) rhetorical devices, and transitions between paragraphs

   (iii) a clear thesis statement or controlling idea

   (iv) a clear organizational schema for conveying ideas

   (v) relevant and substantial evidence and well-chosen details

   (vi) information on multiple relevant perspectives and a consideration of the validity, reliability, and relevance of primary and secondary sources

pages 158, 165–168,170–174, 176–183, 203, 204, 210, 476–478, 516–519, 535, 536, 609, 610, 625, 628, 629.

B   write procedural or work-related documents (e.g., resumes, proposals, college applications, operation manuals) that include:

   (i)   a clearly stated purpose combined with a well-supported viewpoint on the topic

   (ii) appropriate formatting structures (e.g., headings, graphics, white space)

   (iii) relevant questions that engage readers and consider their needs

   (iv) accurate technical information in accessible language

   (v) appropriate organizational structures supported by facts and details (documented if appropriate)

pages 481, 482, 538, 539, 540, 541, 542, 543, 544, 545, 546, 547, 548, 549.

C   write an interpretation of an expository or a literary text that:

   (i)   advances a clear thesis statement

   (ii) addresses the writing skills for an analytical essay, including references to and commentary on quotations from the text

   (iii) analyzes the aesthetic effects of an author's use of stylistic or rhetorical devices

   (iv) identifies and analyzes the ambiguities, nuances, and complexities within the text

   (v) anticipates and responds to readers' questions or contradictory information

pages 282–284, 286, 287, 289, 290, 293–300, 304, 314, 318–320, 326–328, 332, 333, 335.

D   produce a multimedia presentation (e.g., documentary, class newspaper, docudrama, infomercial, visual or textual parodies, theatrical production) with graphics, images, and sound that appeals to a specific audience and synthesizes information from multiple points of view:

pages 432, 464, 465, 466, 467, 484, 493, 534.

⭐ Texas Career and College Readiness Standards

ENGLISH/LANGUAGE ARTS STANDARDS

Writing:

1.   Determine effective approaches, forms, and rhetorical techniques that demonstrate understanding of the writer's purpose and audience.

CROSS-DISCIPLINARY STANDARDS

Key Cognitive Skills B:

2.   Construct well-reasoned arguments to support positions.

3.   Gather evidence to support arguments, findings, or lines of reasoning.

Foundational Skills B:

2.   Write in a variety of forms for various audiences and purposes.

CROSS-DISCIPLINARY STANDARDS

Foundational Skills E:

3.   Use technology to communicate and display findings in a clear and coherent manner.

4.   Use technology appropriately.

*Page References in Teacher's Edition
*Page References in SkillsBook

★ (TEKS) 11.16 Writing/Persuasive Texts

Students write persuasive texts to influence the attitudes or actions of a specific audience on specific issues. Students are expected to write an argumentative essay (e.g., evaluative essays, proposals) to the appropriate audience that includes:

A a clear thesis or position based on logical reasons supported by precise and relevant evidence, including facts, expert opinions, quotations, and/or expressions of commonly accepted beliefs
pages 216–220, 223, 224, 229, 234, 235, 238, 239, 261, 268, 269, 508, 510, 511, 521, 611.

B accurate and honest representation of divergent views (i.e., in the author's own words and not out of context)
pages 217–220, 224, 225, 230, 232, 238–241, 268, 269, 508, 510, 511, 521.

C an organizing structure appropriate to the purpose, audience, and context
pages 218–220, 226, 232, 236, 237, 262, 263, 509–511.

D information on the complete range of relevant perspectives
pages 223, 224, 225, 231, 238–241, 508, 510, 511.

E demonstrated consideration of the validity and reliability of all primary and secondary sources used
pages 223, 234, 235, 509–511.

F language attentively crafted to move a disinterested or opposed audience, using specific rhetorical devices to back up assertions (e.g., appeals to logic, emotions, ethical beliefs)
pages 231, 238, 239, 240, 241, 268, 269.

ENGLISH/LANGUAGE ARTS STANDARDS

Writing:

1. Determine effective approaches, forms, and rhetorical techniques that demonstrate understanding of the writer's purpose and audience.
2. Generate ideas and gather information relevant to the topic and purpose, keeping careful records of outside sources.
3. Evaluate relevance, quality, sufficiency, and depth of preliminary ideas and information, organize material generated, and formulate a thesis.

CROSS-DISCIPLINARY STANDARDS

Key Cognitive Skills B:

1. Consider arguments and conclusions of self and others.
2. Construct well-reasoned arguments to support positions.
3. Gather evidence to support arguments, findings, or lines of reasoning.

Foundational Skills B:

2. Write in a variety of forms for various audiences and purposes.

★ (TEKS) 11.17 Oral and Written Conventions/Conventions

Students understand the function of and use the conventions of academic language when speaking and writing. Students will continue to apply earlier standards with greater complexity. Students are expected to:

A use and understand the function of different types of clauses and phrases (e.g., adjectival, noun, adverbial clauses and phrases)
pages 144, 426, 430, 530, 728, 760, 761, 762, 763.
pages 9, 10, 14, 15, 126–136.

B use a variety of correctly structured sentences (e.g., compound, complex, compound-complex)
pages 427, 430, 756–759, 764–769.
pages 137–144, 155–159, 161–166, 173.

ENGLISH/LANGUAGE ARTS STANDARDS

Writing:

5. Edit writing for proper voice, tense, and syntax, assuring that it conforms to standard English, when appropriate.

⭐ TEKS 11.18 Oral and Written Conventions/Handwriting, Capitalization, and Punctuation

Students write legibly and use appropriate capitalization and punctuation conventions in their compositions. Students are expected to:

A correctly and consistently use conventions of punctuation and capitalization

pages 26, 28, 155, 428, 430, 530, 635–679.
pages 3, 5, 6, 41–46, 68.

⭐ TEKS 11.19 Oral and Written Conventions/Spelling

Students spell correctly. Students are expected to spell correctly, including using various resources to:

A determine and check correct spellings

pages 26, 429, 430, 556, 557, 680–683, 690, 691, 694, 695, 702–721.
pages 51, 55–60, 196.

⭐ TEKS 11.20 Research/Research Plan

Students ask open-ended research questions and develop a plan for answering them. Students are expected to:

A brainstorm, consult with others, decide upon a topic, and formulate a major research question to address the major research topic

pages 378, 379, 396–398, 406, 494, 524.

B formulate a plan for engaging in in-depth research on a complex, multi-faceted topic

pages 378, 379, 398, 494, 524.

Texas Career and College Readiness Standards

CROSS-DISCIPLINARY STANDARDS

Foundational Skills B:
1. Write clearly and coherently using standard writing conventions.

CROSS-DISCIPLINARY STANDARDS

Foundational Skills B:
1. Write clearly and coherently using standard writing conventions.

ENGLISH/LANGUAGE ARTS STANDARDS

Research A:
1. Formulate research questions.
2. Explore a research topic.
3. Refine research topic and devise a timeline for completing work.

CROSS-DISCIPLINARY STANDARDS

Foundational Skills C:
1. Understand which topics or questions are to be investigated.
2. Explore a research topic.

*Page References in *Teacher's Edition*
*Page References in *SkillsBook*

⬥ Texas Career and College Readiness Standards

⭐ TEKS 11.21 Research/Gathering Sources

Students determine, locate, and explore the full range of relevant sources addressing a research question and systematically record the information they gather. Students are expected to:

A follow the research plan to gather evidence from experts on the topic and texts written for informed audiences in the field, distinguishing between reliable and unreliable sources and avoiding over-reliance on one source

pages 376, 377, 380–384, 399–401, 405, 435–437, 440, 495, 524.

B systematically organize relevant and accurate information to support central ideas, concepts, and themes, outline ideas into conceptual maps/timelines, and separate factual data from complex inferences

pages 377, 402, 403, 458, 459, 499, 525, 619.

C paraphrase, summarize, quote, and accurately cite all researched information according to a standard format (e.g., author, title, page number), differentiating among primary, secondary, and other sources

pages 399, 400, 402, 413, 435–440, 442–454, 526.

ENGLISH/LANGUAGE ARTS STANDARDS

Research B:

1. Gather relevant sources.
2. Evaluate the validity and reliability of sources.

CROSS-DISCIPLINARY STANDARDS

Key Cognitive Skills B:

2. Construct well-reasoned arguments to support positions.
3. Gather evidence to support arguments, findings, or lines of reasoning.

Key Cognitive Skills F:

3. Include the ideas of others and the complexities of the debate, issue, or problem.

⭐ TEKS 11.22 Research/Synthesizing Information

Students clarify research questions and evaluate and synthesize collected information. Students are expected to:

A modify the major research question as necessary to refocus the research plan

pages 404, 434, 499, 525.

B differentiate between theories and the evidence that supports them and determine whether the evidence found is weak or strong and how that evidence helps create a cogent argument

pages 404, 405, 406, 499, 525, 526.

C critique the research process at each step to implement changes as the need occurs and is identified

pages 398, 404, 407, 423, 434.

ENGLISH/LANGUAGE ARTS STANDARDS

Research B:

3. Synthesize and organize information effectively.
4. Use source material ethically.

CROSS-DISCIPLINARY STANDARDS

Key Cognitive Skills F:

2. Evaluate sources for quality of content, validity, credibility, and relevance.

Foundational Skills C:

3. Refine research topic based on preliminary research and devise a timeline for completing work.
4. Evaluate the validity and reliability of sources.
5. Synthesize and organize information effectively.

⊞ TEKS 11.23 Research/Organizing and Presenting Ideas

Students organize and present their ideas and information according to the purpose of the research and their audience. Students are expected to synthesize the research into an extended written or oral presentation that:

A provides an analysis that supports and develops personal opinions, as opposed to simply restating existing information — pages 409, 410, 412, 420–423, 463, 500, 502, 526, 531.

B uses a variety of formats and rhetorical strategies to argue for the thesis — pages 409, 410, 412, 418, 419, 422, 423, 460, 462, 500, 502, 529, 531.

C develops an argument that incorporates the complexities of and discrepancies in information from multiple sources and perspectives while anticipating and refuting counter-arguments — pages 416, 417, 422, 423, 456, 457, 502, 527, 529, 531.

D uses a style manual (e.g., Modern Language Association, Chicago Manual of Style) to document sources and format written materials — pages 394, 413, 418, 442–454, 501, 502, 528, 531.

E is of sufficient length and complexity to address the topic — pages 461, 463, 501, 502, 528, 531.

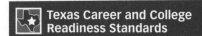

Texas Career and College Readiness Standards

ENGLISH/LANGUAGE ARTS STANDARDS

Research C:
1. Design and present an effective product.
2. Use source material ethically.

CROSS-DISCIPLINARY STANDARDS

Key Cognitive Skills F:
1. Attribute ideas and information to source materials and people.

Foundational Skills C:
6. Design and present an effective product.
7. Integrate source material.
8. Present final product.

Foundational Skills E:
3. Use technology to communicate and display findings in a clear and coherent manner.
4. Use technology appropriately.

English Language Proficiency Standards

The English Language Proficiency Standards (ELPS) outline expectations for students who are learning English. The chart below includes descriptions of activities and interactions that will help students develop their knowledge of English. It also provides you with information on where these skills are specifically addressed in this program.

⭐ ELPS 1 Cross-curricular Second Language Acquisition/Learning Strategies

The ELL uses language learning strategies to develop an awareness of his or her own learning processes in all content areas. In order for the ELL to meet grade-level learning expectations across the foundation and enrichment curriculum, all instruction delivered in English must be linguistically accommodated (communicated, sequenced, and scaffolded) commensurate with the student's level of English language proficiency. The student is expected to:

A use prior knowledge and experiences to understand meanings in English;

pages 3, 15, 134, 149, 164, 165, 275, 279, 349

B monitor oral and written language production and employ self-corrective techniques or other resources;

pages 9, 51, 74, 81, 83, 109, 112, 129, 131, 148, 177, 181, 190, 191, 198, 205, 233, 235, 248, 257, 263, 271, 291, 293, 301, 315, 328, 337, 351, 357, 395, 411, 412, 413, 419, 423, 430, 439, 441, 458, 461, 465, 467

C use strategic learning techniques such as concept mapping, drawing, memorizing, comparing, contrasting, and reviewing to acquire basic and grade-level vocabulary;

pages 81, 89, 121, 134, 141, 157, 171, 198, 203, 209, 217, 225, 257, 227, 267, 269, 299, 315, 339, 340, 341, 353, 355, 365, 390, 394, 397, 437, 559

D speak using learning strategies such as requesting assistance, employing non-verbal cues, and using synonyms and circumlocution (conveying ideas by defining or describing when exact English words are not known);

pages 379, 394, 395, 558, 561

E internalize new basic and academic language by using and reusing it in meaningful ways in speaking and writing activities that build concept and language attainment;

pages 3, 9, 32, 49, 69, 70, 71, 93, 97, 102, 109, 111, 119, 121, 131, 139, 141, 143, 148, 153, 155, 159, 198, 205, 211, 237, 225, 245, 257, 263, 269, 285, 307, 327, 331, 333, 339, 348, 350, 373, 390, 402, 403, 406, 407, 423, 439, 443

F use accessible language and learn new and essential language in the process;

pages 3, 47, 69, 267, 333, 345, 348, 415, 451

G demonstrate an increasing ability to distinguish between formal and informal English and an increasing knowledge of when to use each one commensurate with grade-level learning expectations; and

pages 5, 14, 15, 19, 22, 23, 24, 25, 79, 111, 129, 133, 142, 154, 183, 184, 185, 243, 352, 357, 465, 467

H develop and expand repertoire of learning strategies such as reasoning inductively or deductively, looking for patterns in language, and analyzing sayings and expressions commensurate with grade-level learning expectations.

pages 23, 32, 57, 71, 75, 77, 86, 87, 97, 141, 153, 171, 177, 209, 235, 259, 261, 271, 327, 357, 358, 561

*Page References in *Teacher's Edition*
*Page References in *SkillsBook*

⭐ ELPS 2 Cross-curricular Second Language Acquisition/Listening

The ELL listens to a variety of speakers including teachers, peers, and electronic media to gain an increasing level of comprehension of newly acquired language in all content areas. ELLs may be at the beginning, intermediate, advanced, or advanced high stage of English language acquisition in listening. In order for the ELL to meet grade-level learning expectations across the foundation and enrichment curriculum, all instruction delivered in English must be linguistically accommodated (communicated, sequenced, and scaffolded) commensurate with the student's level of English language proficiency. The student is expected to:

A distinguish sounds and intonation patterns of English with increasing ease;

pages 47, 214, 245, 272, 351, 357, 373, 375, 461, 550, 576

B recognize elements of the English sound system in newly acquired vocabulary such as long and short vowels, silent letters, and consonant clusters;

pages 47, 156, 214, 245, 338, 550

C learn new language structures, expressions, and basic and academic vocabulary heard during classroom instruction and interactions;

pages 4, 24, 47, 63, 67, 72, 86, 87, 93, 94, 173, 209, 245, 267, 348, 353, 365, 447, 581, 582, 593

D monitor understanding of spoken language during classroom instruction and interactions and seek clarification as needed;

pages 25, 74, 134, 353, 395, 437, 470, 471, 554, 560, 561, 563, 567, 586

E use visual, contextual, and linguistic support to enhance and confirm understanding of increasingly complex and elaborated spoken language;

pages 97, 165, 437, 441, 443, 451

G understand the general meaning, main points, and important details of spoken language ranging from situations in which topics, language, and contexts are familiar to unfamiliar;

pages 75, 79, 117, 159, 173

H understand implicit ideas and information in increasingly complex spoken language commensurate with grade-level learning expectations; and

pages 167, 173, 233, 359, 435

I demonstrate listening comprehension of increasingly complex spoken English by following directions, retelling or summarizing spoken messages, responding to questions and requests, collaborating with peers, and taking notes commensurate with content and grade-level needs.

pages 69, 72, 93, 94, 141, 190, 233, 395

⭐ ELPS 3 Cross-curricular Second Language Acquisition/Speaking

The ELL speaks in a variety of modes for a variety of purposes with an awareness of different language registers (formal/informal) using vocabulary with increasing fluency and accuracy in language arts and all content areas. ELLs may be at the beginning, intermediate, advanced, or advanced high stage of English language acquisition in speaking. In order for the ELL to meet grade-level learning expectations across the foundation and enrichment curriculum, all instruction delivered in English must be linguistically accommodated (communicated, sequenced, and scaffolded) commensurate with the student's level of English language proficiency. The student is expected to:

A practice producing sounds of newly acquired vocabulary such as long and short vowels, silent letters, and consonant clusters to pronounce English words in a manner that is increasingly comprehensible;

pages 156, 191, 245, 272, 338, 351, 461, 705, 713, 717, 747, 757

B expand and internalize initial English vocabulary by learning and using high-frequency English words necessary for identifying and describing people, places, and objects, by retelling simple stories and basic information represented or supported by pictures, and by learning and using routine language needed for classroom communication;

pages 81, 159, 245, 345, 415, 439, 465, 467, 559

C speak using a variety of grammatical structures, sentence lengths, sentence types, and connecting words with increasing accuracy and ease as more English is acquired;

pages 63, 67, 89, 191, 406, 407, 461

D speak using grade-level content area vocabulary in context to internalize new English words and build academic language proficiency;

pages 69, 77, 299, 348, 402, 403, 415

E share information in cooperative learning interactions;

pages 71, 133, 148, 233, 279, 301, 315, 365, 375, 394, 395, 581

F ask and give information ranging from using a very limited bank of high-frequency, high-need, concrete vocabulary, including key words and expressions needed for basic communication in academic and social contexts, to using abstract and content-based vocabulary during extended speaking assignments;

pages 191, 213, 249, 379, 467

G express opinions, ideas, and feelings ranging from communicating single words and short phrases to participating in extended discussions on a variety of social and grade-appropriate academic topics;

pages 4, 12, 32, 69, 111, 133, 148, 177, 183, 235, 261, 279, 315, 366, 403, 406, 407, 553, 554, 559, 563, 565, 567, 572, 573, 578, 579, 581, 582, 584, 585, 587, 590, 591, 593, 594, 596, 597, 600, 602, 603, 709, 713, 747, 757, 765

H narrate, describe, and explain with increasing specificity and detail as more English is acquired;

pages 43, 106, 114, 177, 191, 235, 249, 297, 407, 421, 456, 457, 461, 465, 467, 595, 553, 563, 567, 568, 569, 570, 571, 572, 573, 575, 576, 577, 578, 579, 580, 581, 583, 584, 585, 586, 587, 588, 590, 591, 593, 595, 596, 597, 599, 601, 602, 603, 709, 717, 721, 735, 743, 747, 765

I adapt spoken language appropriately for formal and informal purposes; and

pages 197, 457, 462, 467, 553

J respond orally to information presented in a wide variety of print, electronic, audio, and visual media to build and reinforce concept and language attainment.

pages 77, 92, 139, 307, 331, 378, 379

⭐ ELPS 4 Cross-curricular Second Language Acquisition/Reading

The ELL reads a variety of texts for a variety of purposes with an increasing level of comprehension in all content areas. ELLs may be at the beginning, intermediate, advanced, or advanced high stage of English language acquisition in reading. In order for the ELL to meet grade-level learning expectations across the foundation and enrichment curriculum, all instruction delivered in English must be linguistically accommodated (communicated, sequenced, and scaffolded) commensurate with the student's level of English language proficiency. For kindergarten and first grade, certain of these student expectations apply to text read aloud for students not yet at the stage of decoding written text. The student is expected to:

A learn relationships between sounds and letters of the English language and decode (sound out) words using a combination of skills such as recognizing sound-letter relationships and identifying cognates, affixes, roots and base words;

pages 156, 272, 339, 375

B recognize directionality of English reading such as left to right and top to bottom;

pages 431, 557, 571, 577, 583, 589, 595, 601

C develop basic sight vocabulary, derive meaning of environmental print, and comprehend English vocabulary and language structures used routinely in written classroom materials;

pages 55, 71, 120, 121, 134, 194, 335, 447, 470, 471, 449, 556, 557, 562, 563, 566. 567, 568, 569, 570, 574, 575, 580, 581, 586, 587, 592, 593, 598, 599, 600, 705, 709, 713, 717, 721, 735, 743

D use prereading supports such as graphic organizers, illustrations, and pretaught topic-related vocabulary and other prereading activities to enhance comprehension of written text;

pages 141, 143, 203, 351

E read linguistically accommodated content area material with a decreasing need for linguistic accommodations as more English is learned;

pages 139, 163, 281

F use visual and contextual support and support from peers and teachers to read grade-appropriate content area text, enhance and confirm understanding, and develop vocabulary, grasp of language structures, and background knowledge needed to comprehend increasingly challenging language;

pages 19, 49, 57, 69, 81, 120, 121, 139, 141, 143, 152, 155, 159, 173, 259, 291, 301, 441, 447

G demonstrate comprehension of increasingly complex English by participating in shared reading, retelling or summarizing material, responding to questions, and taking notes commensurate with content area and grade level needs;

pages 134, 225, 275, 331, 439

H read silently with increasing ease and comprehension for longer periods;

pages 12, 13, 288, 289

I demonstrate English comprehension and expand reading skills by employing basic reading skills such as demonstrating understanding of supporting ideas and details in text and graphic sources, summarizing text and distinguishing main ideas from details commensurate with content area needs;

pages 119, 181, 191, 285, 407, 439

J demonstrate English comprehension and expand reading skills by employing inferential skills such as predicting, making connections between ideas, drawing inferences and conclusions from text and graphic sources, and finding supporting text evidence commensurate with content area needs; and

pages 57, 59, 75, 377, 397

K demonstrate English comprehension and expand reading skills by employing analytical skills such as evaluating written information and performing critical analyses commensurate with content area and grade level needs.

pages 19, 49, 57, 75, 111, 198, 259, 291, 423, 458

⚅ ELPS 5 Cross-curricular Second Language Acquisition/Writing

The ELL writes in a variety of forms with increasing accuracy to effectively address a specific purpose and audience in all content areas. ELLs may be at the beginning, intermediate, advanced, or advanced high stage of English language acquisition in writing. In order for the ELL to meet grade-level learning expectations across foundation and enrichment curriculum all instruction delivered in English must be linguistically accommodated (communicated, sequenced, and scaffolded) commensurate with the student's level of English language proficiency. For kindergarten and first grade, certain of these student expectations do not apply until the student has reached the stage of generating original written text using a standard writing system. The student is expected to:

A learn relationships between sounds and letters of the English language to represent sounds when writing in English;

pages 206, 264, 265

B write using newly acquired basic vocabulary and content-based grade-level vocabulary;

pages 70, 71, 133, 205, 245, 263, 275, 357, 365, 373, 402, 403, 406, 407, 411, 439, 563, 567, 569, 575, 581, 593, 705, 721, 735, 743, 747, 757, 765

*Page References in *Teacher's Edition*
*Page References in *SkillsBook*

C spell familiar English words with increasing accuracy, and employ English spelling patterns and rules with increasing accuracy as more English is acquired;

pages 84, 85, 126, 127, 206, 264, 337, 429, SB-51, SB-55, SB-57, SB-58, SB-59, SB-60

D edit writing for standard grammar and usage, including subject-verb agreement, pronoun agreement, and appropriate verb tenses commensurate with grade-level expectations as more English is acquired;

pages 145, 212, 245, 270, 328, 336, 367

E employ increasingly complex grammatical structures in content area writing commensurate with grade level expectations, such as:
(i)   using correct verbs, tenses, and pronouns/antecedents;
(ii)   using possessive case (apostrophe -s) correctly;
(iii)   using negatives and contractions correctly;

pages 123, 124, 144, 145, 155, 187, 227, 245, 430

F write using a variety of grade-appropriate sentence lengths, patterns, and connecting words to combine phrases, clauses, and sentences in increasingly accurate ways as more English is acquired; and

pages 70, 86, 87, 89, 173, 184, 185, 205, 227, 243, 261, 263, 271, 328, 357, 419, 430

G narrate, describe, and explain with increasing specificity and detail to fulfill content area writing needs as more English is acquired.

pages 81, 133, 141, 143, 153, 173, 174, 181, 184, 185, 205, 211, 217, 233, 243, 261, 263, 269, 293, 365, 411, 412, 413, 419, 423, 439, 563, 567, 569, 575, 581, 587, 593

Yearlong Timetable

This suggested yearlong timetable presents one possible sequence of writing and language skills units based on a five-days-per-week writing class. There is a logical sequence of units and lessons built into the timetable. This logical sequence from personal to more challenging forms can also support an existing writing curriculum or integrated reading/language arts program.

First Six Weeks

Week	Writing Lessons	*Write Source*	Grammar and Writing Skills
1	**Understanding the Writing Process**	1–12	Correcting common errors, commas, transitions, parts of speech, sentence types
2	**One Writer's Process**	13–32	Verb tenses, subject-verb agreement, end punctuation, apostrophes, abbreviations, commonly misspelled words
3	**Basic Elements of Writing**	605–616	Drafting paragraphs, sentence and paragraph structure, transitions, comparison-contrast
4	**Writing a Personal Narrative** (Model, Prewriting, Drafting)	135–139	Personal pronouns, narrative mapping
5	**Writing a Personal Narrative** (Revising, Editing, Publishing, Evaluating)	140–148	Noun phrases, forms of verbs, antecedents, using commas correctly
6	**Portfolio Review** *SkillsBook* Posttests		

Second Six Weeks

Week	Writing Lessons	*Write Source*	Grammar and Writing Skills
1	**Writing an Informative Article** (Writing an Informative Paragraph, Model, Prewriting, Drafting)	157–168	Unparallel construction, sentence combining
2	**Writing an Informative Article** (Revising, Editing, Publishing, Evaluating)	169–198	Subject-verb agreement, semicolons, colons, capitalization
3	**Expository Writing: Writing a Comparison–Contrast Essay** (Model, Guidelines)	199–206	Shifts in verb tense, linking verbs
4	**Writing for Assessment: Responding to Expository Prompts**	207–213	Sentence rhythm, sentence types, adverbs, adjectives
5	**Argumentative Essay** (Model, Prewriting, Drafting)	215–232	Using the right word, commas to set off nonrestrictive phrases and clauses, numbers, commas with introductory phrases and clauses
6	**Argumentative Essay** (Revising, Editing, Publishing, Evaluating) **Portfolio Review** *SkillsBook* Posttests	233–273	Commonly misused pairs, numbers and numerals, varying sentence structure, parallel structure

Third Six Weeks

Week	Writing Lessons	*Write Source*	Grammar and Writing Skills
1	**Responding to Persuasive Prompts**	265–271	Transitions, conjunctions, sentence lengths, end punctuation, using the right word, capitalization (proper nouns), run-on sentences, spelling
2	**Interpretive Response: Interpreting a Theme** (Model, Prewriting, Writing)	273–290	Direct quotations, paraphrasing
3	**Interpretive Response: Interpreting a Theme** (Revising, Editing, Publishing)	291–307	Punctuating dialogue, prepositions and interjections, nouns, verbs modeling sentences, sentence problems review, subject-verb agreement, pronouns (shifts and indefinite)
4	**Responding to Prompts About Literature**	329–338	Punctuating dialogue, pronouns review, using the right word, commas (dates, addresses, nouns of direct address, interjections)
5	**Narrative Writing: Writing a Reflective Narrative**	149–156	Verb forms, subject-verb agreement, end punctuation, apostrophes, capitalization, homophones
6	**Tools of Language: Listening and Speaking, Using Reference Materials** **Portfolio Review** *SkillsBook* Posttests	551–558	Spelling and capitalization

Fourth Six Weeks

Week	Writing Lessons	Write Source	Grammar and Writing Skills
1	**Creative Writing: Writing Stories** (Model, Prewriting, Drafting)	339–346	Parts of speech review, adjectives and adverbs, subjects and predicates, phrases, spelling, commas in nonrestrictive phrases and clauses
2	**Creative Writing: Writing Stories** (Revising, Editing)	347–348	Passive voice, action verbs, personal pronouns
3	**Creative Writing: Writing Plays** (Model, Prewriting, Drafting)	349–356	Dialogue, using modifiers, apostrophes
4	**Creative Writing: Writing Plays** (Revising, Editing)	357–360	Dialogue, interjections, spelling
5	**Writing Across the Curriculum: Writing in the Workplace**	537–550	Proper nouns, capitalization, linking verbs
6	**Persuasive Writing: Writing an Editorial** **Portfolio Review** *SkillsBook* Posttests	257–264	Active and passive verbs, mood of verbs, clauses (adjective and adverb), colons and semicolons, sentence review, brackets, ellipses, parentheses

Fifth Six Weeks

Week	Writing Lessons	*Write Source*	Grammar and Writing Skills
1	**Writing Across the Curriculum** (Teacher's Choice)		
2	**Creative Writing: Writing Poetry** (Writing Process, Sonnet)	361–374	Subject-verb agreement, pronouns, antecedents
3	**Creative Writing: Writing Poetry** (Writing Process, Quatrain)	361–374	Checking punctuation, parentheses
4	**Interpreting a Story** (Sample, Model, Guidelines)	323–328	Quotation marks, subject-verb agreement
5	**Interpreting a Poem** (Sample, Model, Guidelines)	315–322	Quotation marks, sentence structure, capitalization
6	**Writing Across the Curriculum** (Teacher's Choice) **Portfolio Review** *SkillsBook* Posttests		

Sixth Six Weeks

Week	Writing Lessons	*Write Source*	Grammar and Writing Skills
1	**Research Writing Skills**	375–384	Primary sources, using reference materials
2	**MLA Research Report** (Model, Prewriting)	385–407	Outlines, spacing, underlining
3	**MLA Research Report** (Drafting, Revising)	408–423	Citations, alphabetizing, transitional words and phrases
4	**MLA Research Report** (Editing, Publishing)	424–432	Parallel structure, compound-complex sentences
5	**Making Oral Presentations**	455–464	Pacing, sentence structure, creating note cards
6	**Creating a Multimedia Presentation** **Portfolio Review** *SkillsBook* Posttests	465–467	Incomplete sentences, auxilliary verbs, spelling rules

TEXAS
WRITE
SOURCE

Authors
Dave Kemper, Patrick Sebranek, and Verne Meyer

Consulting Author
Gretchen Bernabei

Illustrator
Chris Krenzke

GREAT
SOURCE®

HOUGHTON MIFFLIN HARCOURT

Copyright © 2012 by Houghton Mifflin Harcourt Publishing Company

Printed in the U.S.A.

ISBN-13   978-0-547-39501-2

1 2 3 4 5 6 7 8 9 10 0914 19 18 17 16 15 14 13 12 11 10

Quick Guide

A Quick Tour of *Texas Write Source*

Write Source contains many key features that will help you improve your writing and language skills. Once you become familiar with this book, you will begin to understand how helpful these features can be.

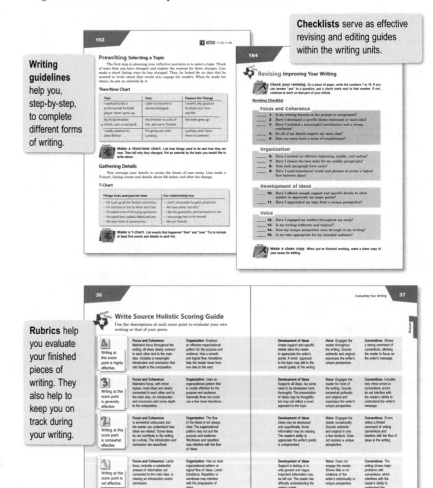

Checklists serve as effective revising and editing guides within the writing units.

Writing guidelines help you, step-by-step, to complete different forms of writing.

Rubrics help you evaluate your finished pieces of writing. They also help to keep you on track during your writing.

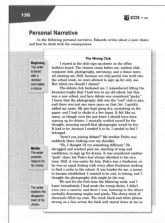

The **writing samples** will stimulate you to write your own effective essays.

Graphic organizers show you how to organize your ideas for writing.

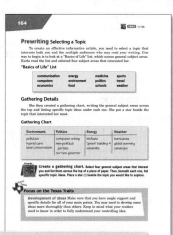

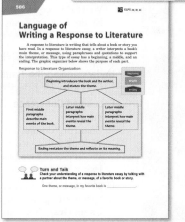

Links to the traits help you appreciate the importance of different traits at different points in the writing process.

EXPLORING THE WRITING PROCESS

viii

contents

The Forms of Writing

NARRATIVE WRITING

x

contents

PERSUASIVE WRITING

RESPONSE TO LITERATURE

CREATIVE WRITING

RESEARCH WRITING

xiv

contents

contents

The Tools of Language

xviii

contents

Proofreader's Guide

1

Why Write?

The very best answer to that question is this: Write to know yourself. Aside, perhaps, from professional analysis, no other activity allows you to explore your thoughts and feelings and then express them as a unique part of you. This personal exploration occurs every time you write something, whether it's a journal entry, a poem, or a personal essay.

Write every day, preferably at a set time. Some writers do their personal writing early in the morning when they are fresh and alert. Others record their thoughts at the end of the day. Write when and where it feels comfortable for you—during your study hall, on the bus, at a coffee shop, while taking a bath.

Meaning will come if you make the effort and stick to it. You'll enter the world of your inner thoughts and soon feel a little sharper, as if your senses had been fine-tuned. Your writing will give you the special opportunity to "taste life twice," as writer Anaïs Nin has so aptly stated.

- Using a Writer's Notebook
- Sample Notebook Entries

"Writing is a long process of self-understanding."

—Edwidge Danticat

Why Write?

If students are not already writing regularly, now is the time for them to start. Encourage students to ease into a routine by writing just two or three times a week, with writing every day as the ultimate goal.

To get students started, guide them in determining appropriate topics by giving them something specific to write about. For example:

- Share an interesting quotation every day and encourage students to explore the quotation in their writer's notebooks.
- Ask students to write about background reading they have done or about personal interests.
- Read examples of personal writing by favorite authors and discuss why professional writers share their personal thoughts and feelings in writing. ✓ DIFFERENTIATE INSTRUCTION

⭐ **TEKS** 11.13A

TEKS 11.13A Determine appropriate topics through a range of strategies; **ELPS** 1E Internalize new basic language by using and reusing it/writing; **1F** Use accessible language and learn new and essential language in the process; **5B** Write using newly acquired basic and content-based grade-level vocabulary; **5G** Describe and explain with increasing specificity and detail

Using a Writer's Notebook

Help students organize their writer's notebook. Offer these tips:

- A three-ring binder allows them to insert, remove, and rearrange pages.
- Lined paper keeps their writing neat, and blank paper provides space for illustrating their ideas.
- An additional small notebook is extremely useful for jotting down ideas and observations on the go.

Ensuring Success

As you discuss the quantity, quality, and variety of entries in a writer's notebook, point out that some students may prefer to use a computer to note ideas and appropriate writing topics. An electronic notebook is intrinsically neat and organized and allows for easy insertion, deletion, and reorganization of ideas. Remind students that if they keep their writer's notebook on a computer that has more than one user, they can password-protect their files so that no one else can access them. **DIFFERENTIATE INSTRUCTION** ↘

 TEKS 11.13A

TEKS 11.13A

Using a Writer's Notebook

Your most powerful writing tool can be a notebook reserved exclusively for daily writing. A writer's notebook (also called a journal) is a place to record your thoughts on any topic. As you do so, you will make countless discoveries about your world. You may also find yourself inspired to create more polished forms of writing—poems, stories, and narratives.

In her book of autobiographical essays, *Something to Declare,* Julia Alvarez writes: "The writing life is a life with all the windows and doors opened." That's exactly what a writer's notebook does! It opens all the windows and doors to your world.

Ensuring Success

To make sure that your writer's notebook is a success, consider the quantity, quality, and variety of your entries.

- **Quantity:** Approach each entry with a high level of enthusiasm. Write about things that matter to you, and develop your ideas fully.
- **Quality:** Focus on exploring and developing your ideas, not on producing perfect copy. Some of your entries are bound to be messy. Your notebook is your place to experiment, take risks, and make mistakes.
- **Variety:** Write some of your entries from different points of view. For example, after a disagreement with a family member, write about the experience from the other person's point of view, or from the perspective of someone who overheard the discussion.

Suggestions for Notebook Writing

1. Date each entry. The date on an entry helps you find it later and places it in a context with other entries and experiences.
2. Write freely. Push to keep your pen moving or your fingers keyboarding. Continuous writing helps you make new discoveries.
3. Write regularly. Develop the habit of writing daily. Then reread your entries to consider what you've discovered. Those ideas may prompt additional writing.

Differentiated Instruction: Struggling Learners

Students who lack confidence in their writing may resist maintaining a writer's notebook. To encourage these students, stress that their writer's notebook will not be graded for content or correctness. Their goal is to record ideas and observations that will help them determine appropriate writing topics.

TEKS 11.13A

TEKS 11.13A

> "You write down a few sentences in your journal and sigh. This exhalation is not exhaustion but anticipation at the prospect of a wonderful tale exposing a notion that you still only partly understand."
>
> —Walter Mosley

Writing

Writing About Anything—and Everything

There are no limits to what you can write about—just as long as each of your entries connects with you personally. Write about people, places, and things; delve into your hopes and dreams; explore snippets of conversations that you overhear or expand on ideas that come up in a discussion among friends. Your notebook is the perfect place to explore these topics and form new understandings in the process.

Refer to the following questions for ideas about writing topics.

- **Observations:** What is happening around you? Have you done any background reading to learn more? What are your thoughts about it?

- **Memories:** What was the best moment of your day? The week? The year? What was the worst moment?

- **Hopes and dreams:** What do you want in life? What do you hope for in the future? What personal interests do you hope to explore?

- **People:** What person means the most to you? What person would you most want to interview? What sort of person do you think you are or wish you were?

- **Places:** Where are you right now? Where do you wish you were? Where do you never want to be again?

- **Things:** What is your favorite possession? Your least favorite? What one thing most closely links you to your past?

- **Thoughts:** What is the most peculiar thing you've learned recently? What is the best piece of advice you've given or received?

 Find inspiration. Write freely for 8 to 10 minutes. The topic is *you*. Begin with *I am . . .* and see where your writing takes you. Afterward, underline at least two discoveries that you made in this writing.

Write About Anything—and Everything

If students are setting up a writer's notebook for the first time, encourage them to copy the seven bulleted ideas for getting started on the first page of their notebooks. Then they can easily refer to this page whenever they need ideas or are determining appropriate topics to write about.

Ask students to give examples of writing topics that might come up through the use of strategies such as discussion, background reading, personal interests, or interviews. ✔ **DIFFERENTIATE INSTRUCTION**
TEKS 11.13A

Find inspiration

Encourage students to use prior experiences as a springboard for their writing. Point out that their reactions and responses to these experiences will help them to make discoveries about themselves.
ELPS 1A

Differentiated Instruction: English Language Learners

ELPS 1A, 1E, 1F

ELP Level **Beginning**	ELP Level **Intermediate**	ELP Level **Advanced/Advanced High**
Begin a dialogue journal in which you respond to students' writing and provide English models. As needed, allow students to use their primary language and translate periodically.	Have students write about prior experiences with writing. Point out and discuss the basic language involved to help students internalize the words.	Have students use familiar language to describe prior experiences with writing. Guide them to brainstorm synonyms and higher level terms to discuss the experience.

 TEKS **11.13A** Determine appropriate topics through a range of strategies; **ELPS** **1A** Use prior experiences; **1E** Internalize new and essential basic language by using and reusing it/ writing; **1F** Use accessible language and learn new language in the process

Taking It Personally

Discuss each of the bulleted objectives for the sample notebook entry. As needed, discuss and explain any new vocabulary in the entry.

Sample Notebook Entry

Then have students use new vocabulary to point out how the writer accomplishes the four bulleted objectives in the entry. Ask them to use specific details from the entry to support their explanations.

- *captures a time in the writer's life* (Saturday, cleaning out grandmother's attic, finding an old photo album, and realizing a connection to all the generations that came before)
- *describes something that is of personal interest to the writer* (the writer's connection to the people in his or her family tree)
- *starts with a "seed idea"* (looking at a family photo album)
- *reflects on the writer's insight, thoughts, and feelings* (details students may point out include the "treasure" photo album; *face of a stranger*; reflections of the writer's physical appearance and personality found in the family photos; no longer lonely after viewing the album)

TEKS 11.13A; **ELPS** 2C

Try It!
Answers

Encourage students to include these four bulleted objectives in their freewrite for the **Try It!** activity. Suggest that these objectives can also serve as the basis for their group discussion of their opinions, ideas, and feelings.

ELPS 3E, 3G

Taking It Personally

Here is a page from a student writer's notebook. This entry focuses on an old photo album and does several important things. It . . .

- captures a time in the writer's life,
- describes something that is of personal interest to the writer,
- starts with a "seed idea" (an old photo album), and
- reflects on the writer's insight, thoughts, and feelings.

Sample Notebook Entry

February 28, 2011

Last Saturday, I found a treasure. It wasn't gold or precious stones, nor was it a bundle of bills or a sack of coins. The treasure was an old photo album. Glued to the yellowing pages were pictures of my ancestors: grandparents, great-aunts and -uncles, and distant cousins. I found the album as I helped my mom clean out Abuelita's attic. I knew that in my hands I held branches from our family tree.

I sat on a rickety chair and opened the dusty, brittle cover. The face of a stranger stared back at me. She looked somewhat familiar. As I gazed into her eyes, I saw my mother's eyes, and then my eyes. The words under the photo read, "Gloriosa Rey Acevedo." She was my great-great-grandmother.

Slowly, I turned the pages, looking carefully at every photograph. In each of my ancestors, I saw a part of myself. There was my smile, my naturally curly hair, my short (and, in my opinion, too round) body. I caught glimpses of my personality in the faces of the people—a pout, a mischievous twinkle in the eyes, a look of loneliness (perhaps a need to feel wanted and loved).

After closing the album's cover, I felt different. The loneliness that has been with me for a while now is gone. I know that I belong, not only to my immediate family, but also to all the generations that came before me.

Note: Keeping a writer's notebook lets you look at ordinary things in a new way, talk about your feelings, use descriptive language, and simply practice writing.

Try It!

Write freely for 10 minutes about your family or friends. What did you learn? Share your ideas and opinions in a small group.

TEKS **11.13A** Determine appropriate topics through a range of strategies; **ELPS** **2C** Learn new basic vocabulary; **3E** Share information in cooperative learning interactions; **3G** Express opinions, ideas, feelings

Sample Notebook Entries

A journal can be a useful tool for sorting out your thoughts. Below are samples that show how three different students use their journals.

Writing

Working Out a Problem

This student uses her journal to explore and sort out her feelings.

> I just don't know if I should keep seeing Michael. I mean, I really like having someone who's always there. But that's just it. He's always there. Like today, I really wanted to get to know the new exchange student. So we were talking, and I guess I was flirting. Anyway, Michael came right up and totally wrecked the moment. I just wanted to get to know Georg, without Michael hanging around. I like Ben in my physics class, too. Maybe I do want to go out with other people. . . .

Reliving an Experience

Here the student shows how an informal style is appropriate in a journal.

> Awesome concert! Music pulsing, crowd cheering. Man, the band was flying! Light sticks, stripes of green and purple neon, streaks against the night. There were strangers around me, but we felt like one. We linked elbows and swayed together. We all sang. The lights, the sound! I could feel the music like it went through me. It filled me and I thought I would burst. I was connected with everyone there. We were like one giant family. I just want to remember that feeling forever.

Questioning/Solidifying a Belief

This student explores her disappointment in an effort to understand herself better.

> When I saw Ms. Harris yelling at her poor dog I couldn't believe it. She sounded so confident when she said she'd help me train my new puppy. Is this what she meant—screaming for the whole neighborhod to hear? Why should I feel so betrayed? It's not like she's a criminal. I guess I idealize people, and then I feel disappointed when they turn out to be human. Why can't I just accept people for who they are? Why do I always put them on a pedestal? I have to stop trying to make everyone perfect. . . .

Sample Notebook Entries

After students have a chance to read and discuss the sample notebook entries, discuss the writers' use of informal English. Ask them to explain how the notebook entries would be different if the writers used formal English.

◢ DIFFERENTIATE INSTRUCTION

ELPS 1G

Then outline your requirements for maintaining a writer's notebook.

- Distribute a printed copy of your writer's notebook guidelines and requirements or post them on the class Web site.
- If you will be examining individual notebooks, provide students with a review schedule and explain how you will assess the notebook.
- Since students are encouraged to explore not only their observations but also their feelings, hopes, and dreams, they may be reluctant to share their notebook with you. Assure them that you will respect their privacy. You may wish to suggest that students select and mark pages for you to read, or you can assign the entries that you will review.

Differentiated Instruction: English Language Learners

ELPS 1G

ELP Level **Beginning**	ELP Level **Intermediate**	ELP Level **Advanced/Advanced High**
Use visuals, gestures, and modeling to define and explain idioms such as *seeing, the band was flying,* and *up on a pedestal,* as well as other examples of informal English in the samples.	Have students work with a partner to discuss the meanings of idioms such as *seeing, the band was flying,* and *up on a pedestal.* Tell them to use each idiom in a sentence.	Have students suggest more formal synonyms for idioms such as *seeing, the band was flying,* and *up on a pedestal.* Ask them to identify situations in which each idiom might be used.

 ELPS 1G Demonstrate ability to distinguish between formal and informal English

Using the Writing Process

Understanding the Writing Process (pages 7–12)

Students learn how the steps of the writing process work together and about the consistent effort it takes to become good writers.

One Writer's Process (pages 13–32)

Students explore the steps in the writing process through a student writer's development of an expository essay.

Evaluating Your Writing (pages 33–45)

Students learn to understand a holistic scoring guide and review four model essays to see how the writing traits work together in the development of a piece of writing. Students then use the holistic scoring guide to assess a model expository essay.

Using the Writing Process Unit Scope and Sequence

| Day | Writing and Conventions Instruction | Write Source Student Edition | | | Daily Language Workouts | Skills-Book | Write Source Online |
		Core Unit	Tools of Language	Resource Units			
1	**Why Write?**	1	**TL** 560–565		6-9		
2–3	**Understanding the Writing Process**	7–12					
4	**One Writer's Process**	13–32					
5	**Evaluating Your Writing**	33–45					

(Left margin: WEEK 1)

Resource Units referenced above are located in the back of the *Student Edition* and *Teacher's Edition*
TL *"The Tools of Language"* **BEW** *"Basic Elements of Writing"* **PG** *"Proofreader's Guide"*

Writing Focus

- Understanding the Writing Process
- One Writer's Process
- Evaluating Your Writing

Learning Language

Read aloud the basic and academic terms, as well as the descriptions and questions. Model for students how to read one question and answer it. For example, *It says that a holistic view looks at the whole rather than the parts, and it asks if I enjoy food in a holistic way. When I eat a pizza, I don't think about the dough, the sauce, or the cheese. I think about how good the whole thing tastes. That's a holistic view!* Have partners monitor their understanding of the terms by working through the meanings and questions together. DIFFERENTIATE INSTRUCTION ⬎

⭐ ELPS 1F, 2C, 4G

Minilessons

Springing Poetry   Understanding Writing

- Have students **CREATE** a springboard poem that describes their writing process. Provide the sentence starter "I am a _____ writer who _____."

Advice Column   One Writer's Process

- Have students **WORK** with a partner (or small group) to **REVIEW** Lakendra's revising on pages 20–21 and 24–25. Then ask them to **WRITE** 10 statements of advice based on her decisions. For example, *Cut unnecessary words, or be sure each paragraph has a topic sentence and sufficient details.* Allow time for partners or groups to **SHARE** results.

⭐ ELPS 11.1F, 11.2C, 11.4G

www.hmheducation.com/tx/writesource

Using the Writing Process

Writing Focus

Learning Language

Work with a partner. Read the meanings and share answers to the questions.

1. Writing nonstop about a topic is freewriting.
   Tell about a time you used freewriting to find a writing topic.

2. Transitions are words or phrases that connect one idea to another.
   What transitions would you use to tell about events that happened over a week-long period?

3. A holistic view looks at the whole rather than parts.
   Do you enjoy food in a holistic way, or do you notice all the ingredients?

4. Writer's block occurs when a writer has no ideas to start or continue writing.
   What kind of assignment might give you writer's block?

🏴 **ELPS 1F** Use accessible language and learn new and essential language in the process; **2C** Learn new basic vocabulary; **4G** Demonstrate comprehension of increasingly complex English/ responding to questions

Understanding the Writing Process

A process is a series of actions resulting in a desired end product. Think of the process of baking bread, changing a tire, or painting a model aircraft. One action or step follows another until the bread is cooling, the tire is replaced, or the model is drying. To write an essay, however, you may not always move in such a linear fashion. As you reach one step in the process *(writing the first draft),* you may see the need to return to the previous step *(prewriting).* This interplay between the steps often continues until the essay is complete.

There is nothing "instant" about effective writing. Working with a computer does, of course, speed up the process; but when it comes to writing, speed doesn't count for much. What really counts is your ability to stay with a piece of writing until it says exactly what you want it to say. Each time you start a new writing project, keep this thought by Dr. Samuel Johnson in mind: "What is written without effort is in general read without pleasure."

- **Writing Is Discovering**
- **Understanding the Writing Process**
- **The Process in Action**
- **A Closer Look at the Process**

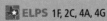
"My method is one of continuous revision. While writing a long novel, every day I loop back to earlier sections to rewrite, in order to maintain a consistent, fluid voice."
—Joyce Carol Oates

Understanding the Writing Process

Objectives
- learn what makes writing a process of discovery
- demonstrate an understanding of the five steps in the writing process
- learn the five traits of effective writing

Discuss the Joyce Carol Oates quotation, which emphasizes the point that the writing process is not a series of isolated steps. Point out the following:
- Students should always be prepared to "loop back" to an earlier step in order to complete an assignment effectively.
- Students should think of "looping back" as an indication that they understand the goals of the assignment and that they know what they need to do to achieve those goals.
- Assure students that you will extend assignment deadlines if they demonstrate that they have a genuine and sincere need to continue developing their writing.

Differentiated Instruction: English Language Learners

⭐ **ELPS** 1F, 2C, 4A, 4G

ELP Level **Beginning**	ELP Level **Intermediate**	ELP Level **Advanced/Advanced High**
Use gestures and simplified language to model terms and their meanings. Point out sound-letter relationships and practice saying each term with students.	Point out sound-letter relationships and have partners practice saying terms aloud. Then have them make a web for each term using key words that tell about its meaning.	Invite partners to clarify word meanings for each other. Students can complete sentence stems or respond in complete sentences to describe their experiences.

ELPS 1F Use accessible language and learn new and essential language in the process; **2C** Learn new basic vocabulary; **4A** Learn relationships between sounds and letters of English and decode using a combination of skills; **4G** Demonstrate comprehension of increasingly complex English/responding to questions

Writing Is Discovering

As needed, review and discuss the meaning of *writer's block* provided on SE page 6.

Setting the Stage

Tell students that, with each writing assignment they complete, they will learn much more about the points listed in this section. At the same time, they will

- build good writing habits,
- improve their writing skills, and
- discover their own writing style and voice, which will make their writing unique.

DIFFERENTIATE INSTRUCTION ↘

Tip

Point out that regular reading helps students see how professional writers apply the traits of writing to hold a reader's interest. Regular reading will also help students build an extensive vocabulary that is essential for writers.

Try It!
Answers

As students reflect on a prior writing experience, explain that they will be asked to reflect on writing assignments throughout the year. Encourage them to add their paragraph from the **Try It!** activity to a special section in their writer's notebook that is set aside for reflections. Tell students to date the paragraph and all future reflections. Explain that this will help them monitor their progress as writers.

TEKS 11.13A; **ELPS** 1A

TEKS 11.13A
ELPS 11.1A

Writing Is Discovering

Writing is not trying to figure out everything you want to say *before* you put pen to paper or fingers to the keyboard. Overplanning in this way will almost certainly result in writer's block. (Ever heard of it?) Writing will spring from the discoveries you make *during* the writing process.

Setting the Stage

Before you use the writing process, it's important that you understand these points about writing:

- **Experience shapes writing.** Each of your experiences becomes part of what you know, what you think, and what you have to say. Writing is the process of capturing the essence of your experience in words.
- **Writing seldom follows a straight path.** Writing is a backward as well as a forward activity, so don't expect to move neatly through the steps in the process. You may start with one thesis, or controlling idea, and end with a very different one. By its very nature, writing includes detours, wrong turns, and repeat visits.
- **Each assignment presents special challenges.** For one assignment, you may search high and low for an appropriate topic. For another, you may do a lot of prewriting and planning. For still another, you might be ready to write your first draft right away.
- **Each writer works differently.** Some writers work more in their heads, while others work more on paper. Some writers need to talk about their writing early on, while others would rather keep their ideas to themselves. As you continue to use the writing process, your unique writing personality will develop.

Tip

You are sure to improve your writing ability if you (1) become a regular reader, (2) write every day, (3) write about topics that truly interest you, and (4) experiment with different forms of writing. Remember: Writing is like any other skill. It takes practice and patience to become good at it.

Try It!

Write a brief paragraph, answering the following questions about a recent writing assignment that challenged you: *Why was it so challenging? What did you do to complete the assignment? Were you satisfied with the finished product? Why or why not?*

Differentiated Instruction: Advanced Learners

Students who are gifted in math and logical reasoning may have difficulty with the nonlinear process of writing. Point out that it is somewhat like going back to check math work or to check assumptions in logic problem. Explain that sometimes one goes backward in order to move forward.

TEKS 11.13A–E
ELPS 11.1F

Why Write? **9**

Understanding the Writing Process

Before you share a piece of writing, you should take it through a series of steps called the *writing process*. This page briefly describes these steps.

Writing

The Steps in the Writing Process

Prewriting

The first step in the writing process involves selecting a specific topic and genre, and gathering details. Developing a thesis, or controlling idea, and thinking about the audience for a piece of writing helps to organize those details into a writing plan.

Drafting

During this step, the writer completes a first draft, using the prewriting plan as a guide. This draft is a writer's *first* chance to get everything on paper.

Revising

During revising, the writer reviews the draft for four key traits: *focus and coherence, organization, development of ideas,* and *voice.* After deciding what changes to make, the writer deletes, moves, adds to, and rewrites parts of the text.

Editing

Then the writer edits the revised draft for the **conventions** of punctuation, capitalization, spelling, and grammar and proofreads the final copy before sharing it.

Publishing

Finally, the writer publishes the work by preparing a final copy and sharing it with others.

Analyze your own process. Which steps in the process explained above do you use regularly? Which ones should you use more often?

Understanding the Writing Process

Remind students that a process is a series of steps taken to achieve a particular goal, which in this case is a thoughtful and clearly written piece of writing.

The Steps in the Writing Process

Review the individual steps in the writing process together. While most students will be familiar with the process, many of them may not utilize each step effectively.

■ Tell students that they will be guided through the five steps of the writing process for each assignment in this book.

■ Explain that because they will have many opportunities to practice the process, the steps will soon become an automatic part of their writing routine.

TEKS 11.13A–E

Analyze your own process

Have students reflect in their writer's notebook on which step or steps they should address more thoroughly. Explain that this type of monitoring of their written language will help to show them when self-correcting techniques are necessary.

✔ DIFFERENTIATE INSTRUCTION

ELPS 1B

Differentiated Instruction:
English Language Learners

ELPS 1E, 1F

Refer to the Tools of Language for additional language support for steps in the writing process.

ELP Level **Beginning**	ELP Level **Intermediate**	ELP Level **Advanced/Advanced High**
Clarify each step. Have students write each term and use their home language or drawings to help them understand each step.	Clarify each step. Provide sentence stems such as *In prewriting, I ____* for students to complete to write about each step.	Have students use complete sentences to tell about the steps of the writing process they have used and to note which steps they should monitor.
Use pages 550–567	Use pages 550–567	Use pages 550–567

TEKS **11.13A** Plan a first draft; **11.13B** Develop drafts; **11.13C** Revise drafts; **11.13D** Edit drafts; **11.13E** Revise final draft in response to feedback; **ELPS** **1B** Monitor written language production and employ self-corrective techniques or other resources; **1E** Internalize new basic language by using and reusing it/ writing; **1F** Use accessible language and learn new and essential language in the process

The Process in Action

Point out and discuss the writing process graphic with students.

Prewriting Planning Your Writing

Tell students that they will use a variety of prewriting activities including freewriting, clustering, making lists, brainstorming, and discussing. They will also generate topic ideas by looking through their writer's notebooks, personal journals, reading and learning logs, and personal collections. Point out that the interests of their audience are an important consideration at this stage.

Prewriting Gathering and Organizing Details

Display a variety of graphic organizers and invite students to tell which ones they think work best for specific genres of writing or types of assignments and why. Reproducible copy masters for a variety of graphic organizers are available on TE pages 828–834.

TEKS 11.13A

Drafting Developing Your Ideas

Point out the expression "getting your ideas on paper" and elicit its meaning from students. Explain to students that even after developing a prewriting plan, professional writers sometimes have trouble getting started with writing their first draft. This may be because they are not sure of where to begin.

ELPS 2C

 TEKS 11.13A
ELPS 11.2C

The Process in Action

The next two pages give a detailed description of each step in the writing process. The graphic below reminds you that, at any time, you can move back and forth between the steps in the process. Also remember that carefully attending to the first steps in the writing process will make the final steps much easier.

Prewriting Planning Your Writing

- Search for topics that meet the requirements of the assignment.
- Select a specific topic and genre that appeals to you and will interest your audience.

Gathering and Organizing Details

- Gather as many ideas and details as you can about the topic.
- With the purpose of the assignment in mind, find one point to emphasize about the topic—either an interesting part or your personal feeling about it. This will be the thesis, or controlling idea, of your writing.
- Decide which details to include.
- Organize your details into a writing plan, using an outline, a chart, or some other method.

Drafting Developing Your Ideas

- When you begin drafting, concentrate on getting your ideas on paper. Don't try to produce a perfect piece of writing.
- Use your prewriting plan as a guide and include the details you collected, but feel free to add new ideas that occur to you as you go along.
- Be sure your writing has a beginning, a middle, and an ending.

Prewrite
Draft
Revise
Edit
Publish

Tip

Write on every other line and on only one side of the paper when using pen or pencil and paper. Double-space on a computer. This will give you room for revising, the next step in the process.

 TEKS 11.13A Plan a first draft by selecting a genre and determining appropriate topics; **ELPS** 2C Learn new expressions

TEKS 11.13C
ELPS 11.4G, 11.5D

Writing

Revising Improving Your Writing

- Set aside your first draft for a while so you can return to it with a fresh perspective.
- Read your draft, looking for places where you can clarify meaning.
- Use these questions as a revising guide:
  - Is my topic interesting for the reader?
  - Does the beginning catch the reader's attention?
  - Do the ideas have a logical order that is easy to understand?
  - Are there enough details to support my thesis, or controlling idea?
  - Does the ending leave the reader with something to think about?
  - Do I sound interested in and knowledgeable about the topic?
  - Are the nouns specific and the verbs active?
  - Are the modifiers (adjectives and adverbs) clear and descriptive?
  - Does the whole piece read smoothly?
- Ask at least one person to review your writing and offer suggestions.
- Make as many changes as necessary to improve your writing.

Editing Checking for Conventions

- Check for errors in punctuation, capitalization, spelling, and grammar.
- Have another person check your writing for errors.
- Prepare a neat final copy and proofread it before publishing.

Publishing Sharing Your Writing

- Using feedback from others, create a final draft to share with friends.
- Consider submitting your writing to a newspaper or other publication.
- Include the writing in your portfolio.

Tip

For assignments, save all your work. Refer to the earlier drafts and to the teacher's comments on each graded piece for ideas and inspiration for future writing projects.

Learning Language

When you summarize, you give the most important ideas on a topic in your own words. Discuss the writing process with a partner to decide what those key ideas are. Share your summary with the class.

Revising Improving Your Writing

When writers revise, they need to be willing to do the following:

- Identify the parts of a draft that could be improved. The questions provided here and in the revising checklists for each core writing assignment can help students do this.
- Recognize when a piece of writing is finished (writers can become obsessive about rewording their drafts). An assignment deadline will help students declare their piece of writing finished.

TEKS 11.13C

Editing Checking for Conventions

Students may want to use the same editing partner for every writing assignment. This can be helpful because, after one or two assignments, editors are likely to be alert for the specific kinds of mistakes their partner tends to repeat.

TEKS 11.13D; **ELPS** 5D

Publishing Sharing Your Writing

Ask students to suggest ways to share their writing online.

Tip

Suggest that students create a folder to save their work. Point out that electronic folders are available for those who store their work on a computer.

Learning Language

Have partners analyze one another's summaries of the writing process to determine if all of the stages have been addressed. If either student feels that a key point has been omitted, ask him or her to explain their thinking.

☑ **DIFFERENTIATE INSTRUCTION**

ELPS 4G

Differentiated Instruction: English Language Learners

ELPS 2C, 4G

Refer to the Tools of Language for additional language support for steps in the writing process.

ELP Level **Beginning**	ELP Level **Intermediate**	ELP Level **Advanced/Advanced High**
Have students repeat each step in the writing process. Have them write each word and practice reading them aloud with a partner.	Have partners create a web for each step of the writing process, and complete each web by writing key words about each concept.	Have partners discuss each step of the writing process. Then have them write a sentence or two that summarizes each step.
Use pages 550–567	Use pages 550–567	Use pages 550–567

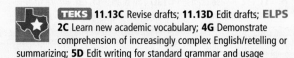

TEKS **11.13C** Revise drafts; **11.13D** Edit drafts; **ELPS** **2C** Learn new academic vocabulary; **4G** Demonstrate comprehension of increasingly complex English/retelling or summarizing; **5D** Edit writing for standard grammar and usage

A Closer Look at the Process

Ask students to share tips about the writing process that have worked for them. For example, students may have

- created scheduling charts to manage their writing assignments;
- developed methods for determining if a topic is too broad or too narrow;
- identified useful search engines to research topics and gather information; or
- identified specific Web sites that provide links to reliable source information.

TEKS 11.13A, 11.13B, 11.13C, 11.13D, 11.13E

Try It!
Answers

Select one or two of the articles students have chosen for a class discussion. Have the class read the articles silently. Then encourage students to share their opinions, ideas, and feelings about the articles to demonstrate their comprehension.

DIFFERENTIATE INSTRUCTION ↘

ELPS 3G, 4H

 **TEKS** 11.13A, 11.13B, 11.13C, 11.13D, 11.13E
ELPS 11.3G

A Closer Look at the Process

Although writing is a complex process, there are ways to have a meaningful experience whenever you write.

Keep time on your side. Effective writing requires a lot of searching, planning, reflecting, and revising, so give yourself plenty of time. Follow the timetable your teacher provides, or create your own. And always reserve enough time for revising. As you probably know, waiting until the last minute takes all the fun out of writing.

Remember: Good writing takes time.

Limit your topic. It would be almost impossible to write an effective essay or report about a general subject like photography. You wouldn't know where to begin or end. But if you narrowed this subject to the use of photography by investigative reporters, for instance, you would find it much easier to manage your writing.

Remember: Good writing has a focus.

Work from a position of authority. The more you know about your topic, the easier it is to write about it. You can collect plenty of information by tapping into your own knowledge and thoughts, asking others about the topic, consulting print material, surfing the Web, and so on.

Remember: Good writing requires good information.

Pace yourself when you revise. Many professional writers believe that the real writing happens when they add, cut, rearrange, and rewrite different parts of their first drafts. They do not rush these changes or make them all at once. Instead, they pace themselves, patiently and methodically revising until the entire piece is clear and complete.

Remember: Good writing usually requires numerous changes.

Take some risks. Don't be afraid to experiment. Share a personal anecdote in an essay or develop an interview report in a question-and-answer format, much as you would find in many magazine articles. Rearrange the events of a narrative to add suspense. If one experiment doesn't work out, try another.

Remember: Good writing is a process of discovery.

Try It!

Find an article in a magazine or newspaper that seems well-written. Express your opinions, ideas, and feelings about the article with your class, pointing out the features that demonstrate what makes it outstanding.

Differentiated Instruction:
English Language Learners

 ELPS 2I, 4H

Provide students with magazines at their reading level and allow time to choose and examine an article.

ELP Level **Beginning**	ELP Level **Intermediate**	ELP Level **Advanced/Advanced High**
Have partners answer yes/no questions to demonsrate understanding of the directions. Have them point out useful visuals.	Have partners use sentence stems to tell about the article. Provide a word bank of adjectives that students can choose to express their ideas and opinions.	Have partners read the article independently. Then have them compare their ideas about the article and identify elements that are effective.

13

One Writer's Process

As you know, there are many ways to share ideas electronically. When you text or send an instant message, you can take shortcuts to write some words or phrases. However for longer or more formal pieces of writing, it's a good idea to draft and store your files in a computer that has writing and editing tools to help you develop, refine, and finalize your writing.

This chapter shows how one student, Lakendra Harris, used the writing process to develop an expository essay in her history class. She first previewed the goals for the assignment. Then she selected an appropriate topic—the Cuban Missile Crisis—to write about. After gathering information about her topic, Lakendra wrote her first draft. She then made a series of changes in her writing until she felt it was ready to share.

- **Previewing the Goals**
- **Prewriting**
- **Drafting**
- **Revising**
- **Editing**
- **Publishing**
- **Assessing the Final Draft**
- **Evaluating and Reflecting on Your Writing**

"Writing is an exploration. You start from nothing and learn as you go."

—E. L. Doctorow

One Writer's Process

Objectives

- examine the goals for expository writing
- evaluate one writer's work step-by-step through the writing process
- review one writer's final essay, self-assessment, and reflection

Give students time to skim SE pages 14–32. Then ask them what writing assignments they are working on in other curriculum areas. For each of those assignments, have them tell which stage they have reached in the writing process. Discuss how using the writing process for academic writing will help them complete those assignments successfully.

Ask students what they think the benefits of this section will be and how it can help them complete their assignments more successfully. Possible responses:

- Students can compare their writing process to a model.
- They can improve their writing style.
- They will learn to use a peer response sheet.
- They will learn to assess their writing.

Resources

Copy Masters

- 5 W's and H chart (TE p. A94)

Previewing the Goals

Have students preview the holistic scoring guide on SE pages 36–37. If a majority of students are unfamiliar with the use of such guides, skip ahead to the Holistic Scoring Guide section on SE pages 33–45 and introduce that information before students answer the **Review the traits** questions.

Traits of Expository Writing

Explain to students that for their major assignment in each of the core writing units, they will be provided with a goals chart like the Traits of Expository Writing chart shown here. The chart will help them get started and guide them through the writing process. Discuss the terms used to describe each of the traits to help students learn the new academic vocabulary.

TEKS 11.13A; **ELPS** 2C

 Review the traits.

Answers

- Focus and Coherence and Organization are useful traits for planning a first draft.
- An essay for a history class generally explores or analyzes an event or situation, so a factual, informed voice is appropriate. Language should be specific and formal.

Learning Language

Remind students that their way of speaking to friends and family tends to be informal, while a presentation or speech to a group is usually formal. As needed, model and discuss the use of formal and informal language with students. You may wish to use the following statements: *The Cuban Missile Crisis created worldwide panic. The Cuban Missile Crisis was a big mess.* Have partners report on their own examples of formal and informal tone.

ELPS 1G

 TEKS 11.13A Plan a first draft; **ELPS 1G** Demonstrate ability to distinguish between formal and informal English; **2C** Learn new academic vocabulary

---

 TEKS 11.13A
ELPS 11.2C

 Previewing the Goals

Before Lakendra began writing her essay, she previewed the goals for expository writing, which are shown below. She also looked over the holistic scoring guide on pages 198–199. Both of these activities helped her get started.

36–37

Traits of Expository Writing

- **Focus and Coherence**
  Identify an interesting topic that suits your assignment. Create a clear thesis statement to explore an important aspect of the topic. Maintain your focus on the topic throughout your essay.

- **Organization**
  Organize your essay's ideas into three main parts—beginning, middle, and ending—and use transitions to connect them smoothly.

- **Development of Ideas**
  Gather information from several sources, and identify evidence and quotations that support your thesis.

- **Voice**
  Use language that fits the audience and purpose of your writing. Maintain a formal tone but show your unique perspective and ideas.

- **Conventions**
  Use correct punctuation, capitalization, spelling, and grammar.

 Review the traits. Which trait would be useful to plan a first draft? What voice would suit an essay for a history class?

Learning Language

Explore the idea of a "formal tone" with a partner. Practice how it would sound and decide which words should or should not be used.

Differentiated Instruction: Struggling Learners

Display a variety of organizers and discuss their usefulness for particular types of topics. Ask students why Lakendra used a 5 W's and H chart. Point out that to explain a historical event, Lakendra needs to present a variety of facts, much like a news report. She chose a format that would help her gather basic facts about the topic.

★ **TEKS** 11.13A

Writing

Prewriting Selecting a Topic

Lakendra's assignment was to write an essay explaining a major event in twentieth-century United States history. Keeping in mind the genre she would use to convey her ideas, Lakendra listed topics and underlined the one she liked most.

Topics List

> the use of the atom bomb   Prohibition
> <u>Cuban Missile Crisis</u>   Watergate

Gathering Your Thoughts

Lakendra knew that listing the 5 W's and H—*who? what? where? when? why?* and *how?*—about her topic would help her gather her initial thoughts.

5 W's and H Chart

Who?	John F. Kennedy and Nikita Khrushchev
What?	a nuclear missile confrontation
Where?	in Cuba
When?	October 1962
Why?	the two countries were involved in an arms race
How?	Soviets built nuclear missile bases near the U.S.

Lakendra then did some freewriting about the event to gather more of her initial thoughts. Here is a part of her freewriting.

Freewriting

> I know about the Soviet bases in Cuba. Did the U.S. have any bases close to the Soviet Union? It's hard to believe that almost half a century ago, countries were involved in an arms race. I think it even continues today, unfortunately. Even though the Cuban Missile Crisis ended peacefully, it resulted only in an agreement to ban nuclear testing—not on the nukes . . .

Prewriting Selecting a Topic

Ask students to jot down the first thing they would do to find a topic for an essay explaining a major event in twentieth-century United States history. Invite students to read aloud their responses. Then discuss the variety of approaches students can take to generate appropriate topics for any assignment. Suggestions may include

- creating a topics list (shown),
- clustering,
- brainstorming,
- asking family members and teachers for ideas, and
- looking through history texts, news magazines, and on-line history sites.

★ **TEKS** 11.13A

Topics List

Review Lakendra's list of topic with students to determine their familiarity with each one.

Prewriting Gathering Your Thoughts

Provide photocopies of the reproducible 5 W's and H chart (TE page A102). Ask students to choose another topic for a U.S. history essay and have them practice filling in the 5 W's and H chart to gather their thoughts on the topic. Students can use one of the topics in the Topics List on this page or they can choose a familiar topic of their own. Allow them to work with a partner.

↙ **DIFFERENTIATE INSTRUCTION** ↙ **DIFFERENTIATE INSTRUCTION**

5W's and H Chart

Discuss the ideas in the chart, prompting students to suggest other ideas to include.

Freewriting

Ask students to comment on why freewriting is a useful technique.

Differentiated Instruction: English Language Learners

★ **ELPS** 1A, 1G

If they prefer, allow students to base their topic ideas on historical events in their country of origin.

ELP Level **Beginning**	ELP Level **Intermediate**	ELP Level **Advanced/Advanced High**
Provide visuals and other support to help students gather information for the 5 W's and H chart.	Students can complete sentence frames to identify information for the 5 W's and H chart. Use simplified language to help students express their ideas.	Have students use informal language to complete their charts. Have them explain how their language will change when they write their essay.

TEKS **11.13A** Plan a first draft by determining appropriate topics; **ELPS** **1A** Use prior knowledge; **1G** Demonstrate ability to distinguish between formal and informal English and knowledge of when to use formal and informal English

Prewriting Gathering Details

Many students use computers to gather and store information, lessening the need to use note cards. With computers, students can bookmark Web sites, making it easy to return to resources. They can also copy, cut, and paste selected sections of texts they plan to quote. However, caution students that computer files can become corrupted or accidentally deleted. Emphasize that when using a computer for research and for gathering and storing information, it is important to

- save files frequently,
- make back-up copies of files on CDs, and
- keep up-to-date lists of sources.

Sources of Information

Point out that whatever method students use to gather information, keeping track of their sources is necessary to prove the credibility of the facts or details they use.

DIFFERENTIATE INSTRUCTION ↘

★ TEKS 11.13A

Quotations and Paraphrases

Explain that a paraphrase is a type of summary that rephrases the key points of a passage.

✱ For more about writing a paraphrase, see SE pages 401 and 438–439.

Try It!
Answers

Check that students are able to correctly differentiate between a quotation and a paraphrase. Remind them to cite their sources for both.

★ ELPS 2C

Prewriting Gathering Details

Lakendra next went to the library to find resources about the Cuban Missile Crisis; she also searched for reliable Internet Web sites. She searched for secondary sources such as books and encyclopedias, but she also looked for primary sources such as diaries and journals.

Sources of Information

She recorded her source information on note cards and in an electronic file.

> Stern, Sheldon M. *The Week the World Stood Still: Inside the Secret Cuban Missile Crisis.* Stanford University Press: Palo Alto, 2005.

> Kennedy, Bruce. "The Birth of the Hotline." *CubaNet.com* Cuba News Network. 6 April 2009. Web. 10 April 2011.

Quotations and Paraphrases

Lakendra also used note cards to record quotations and paraphrases. The source of the information is listed at the bottom of each card.

Quotation

> "Sensing an opportunity to gain a strategic foothold in America's backyard, Khrushchev eagerly extended an offer of assistance to the desperate Cuban general."
>
> Source: Goldman and Stein

Paraphrase

> Today electronic transmissions are achieved via two satellite systems, but they are still written rather than verbal to reduce the chance of an incorrect translation.
>
> Source: Kennedy

Try It!

Find at least one book or magazine and one Web site containing information about the Cuban Missile Crisis. Write down one quotation and one paraphrase from either source of information.

Differentiated Instruction: Struggling Learners

Offer these tips for sifting through the Web's vast amounts of information to find reliable sources.

- Look for Web sites that end in *.gov* or *.org* or *.edu*.
- Before reading an article, assess whether it is too complex or technical.
- Check the date of publication to ensure current information.

Forming a Thesis Statement

Once Lakendra had enough information, she was ready to write a *thesis statement* for her essay. (A thesis statement identifies the focus of the writing.) An effective thesis statement consists of two parts: a specific topic plus a particular feeling or opinion about it. Lakendra wrote this thesis statement:

Lakendra's Thesis Statement

> The Cuban Missile Crisis of October, 1962 (specific topic), was the closest the United States and the Soviet Union ever came to a nuclear war (particular feeling).

Organizing the Essay

Next, Lakendra created an organized list, arranging the main points and details that support her thesis statement. (An organized list is a modified form of outlining.)

Lakendra's Organized List

Thesis statement: The Cuban Missile Crisis of October, 1962, was the closest the United States and the Soviet Union ever came to a nuclear war.

+ Background
  - The Soviets were losing the arms race.
  - The Cubans were fearful of a U.S. invasion.
  - The Soviets constructed missile bases in Cuba.

+ The Impending Crisis
  - Kennedy discovered the secret base.
  - He ordered a blockade and a dismantling of the bases.
  - Khrushchev authorized use of force.

+ Crisis Averted
  - Khrushchev proposed an exchange.
  - Kennedy agreed to the first part of the proposal.
  - Khrushchev announced plans to dismantle the bases.

+ Outcomes
  - Reliable communication was established.
  - Both sides signed a nuclear test ban agreement.

Prewriting Forming a Thesis Statement

Review with students that a thesis statement
- states the main idea and focus of an essay,
- controls the direction of the writing, and
- determines what kinds of details to include.

✓ DIFFERENTIATE INSTRUCTION

Lakendra's Thesis Statement

Provide other examples of thesis statements or ask students to share ones they have written. Break down each thesis statement using the two-part formula *(specific topic + particular feeling or opinion)*. If a thesis statement doesn't follow this formula, ask students to revise it so that it addresses both parts.

TEKS 11.13A

Prewriting Organizing the Essay

Explain that gathering information is an important first step, but organizing that information is necessary to clearly communicate the ideas. Encourage students to use an organized list to arrange main ideas and details for the next essay they write.

Lakendra's Organized List

Point out that an organized list creates categories of information, making it easier to see where new ideas will fit, and showing places where additional information may be needed. Explain that an organized list can guide students through the drafting stage. It can also easily be turned into a sentence outline to provide even greater guidance.

Differentiated Instruction: English Language Learners

 ELPS 2C

ELP Level **Beginning**	ELP Level **Intermediate**	ELP Level **Advanced/Advanced High**
Use examples and visuals to help students learn the term *thesis statement*. Using topic ideas from SE page 15, work together to form possible thesis statements.	Have partners work together to form thesis statements for their topic ideas on SE page 15. Have them use academic vocabulary to label the two parts of their thesis statements.	Have students write thesis statements for their topic ideas on SE page 15. Then have them use academic vocabulary to share their statements with a partner.
Use pages 559–567	**Use pages 559–567**	**Use pages 559–567**

 TEKS 11.13A Plan a first draft by developing a thesis or controlling idea; **ELPS** 2C Learn new academic vocabulary

Drafting Developing Your Ideas

Have students evaluate Lakendra's first draft and determine whether she achieves the writer's goals set out in the Traits of Expository Writing chart on SE page 14. Remind them to look for ways in which Lakendra structured her ideas in a sustained and persuasive way. **DIFFERENTIATE INSTRUCTION** ↘

TEKS 11.13B

Lakendra's First Draft

Record observations on chart paper so that students can compare their evaluation with Lakendra's revisions on SE pages 20–26 and page 27. Students may make the following points and suggestions. **DIFFERENTIATE INSTRUCTION** ↘

Goals Achieved

- The thesis consists of two parts.
- The details support the thesis.
- The writer uses sources of information about the topic.

Goals Not Achieved

- More details are needed to explain some ideas.
- Some ideas seem out of order.
- The level of language is often too informal and colloquial (for example, *big-time, jumped on, payback, hot heads*).
- The term *boondoggle* is misused.
- Mistakes in conventions include spelling errors, a run-on sentence, and a sentence fragment.

 TEKS 11.13B

Drafting Developing Your Ideas

Lakendra referred to her organized list as she wrote her first draft. At this point, she just needed to get all her ideas on paper in a sustained and persuasive way. She also rephrased her thesis statement to fit the flow of her ideas.

Lakendra's First Draft

The Cuban Missile Crisis

Beginning
The first paragraph ends with the thesis statement.

Both the United States and the Soviet Union have had nuclear capability since the early 1940s. The closest the cold war ever came to a nuclear war was the Cuban Missile Crisis of October, 1962.

The Soviet Union was losing the arms race big-time. They knew that the U.S. had more missiles than they did. And they knew that some of these missiles were based in Turkey, only 150 mi. from the Soviet border.

In an effort to even things out, the Soviets wanted to be friends with Cuba in order to "gain a strategic foothold in America's backyard" (Goldman and Stein 15). Cubas leader, Fidel Castro, believed Cuba would be attacked again by the U.S. He jumped on an offer from Nikita Khrushchev, leader of the Soviet Union, to protect Cuba from the U.S.

Middle
The middle paragraphs describe the crisis.

By October of 1962, the construction of a missile base was well under way. The U.S., which was under the leadership of John F. Kennedy at the time, discovered the secret while checking out some reconaissance photos. Kennedy demanded that the Soviets dismantle the base and ordered a navel blockade of Cuba. Khrushchev, in turn, authorized payback if U.S. forces invaded.

For 5 days, neither side backed down. Then Khrushchev made a written proposal. Soviet missiles would be removed from Cuba in exchange for a guarantee that the U.S. would not invade Cuba. A day later, he put his foot down and demanded removal of U.S. missiles from Turkey. Kennedy ignored this second proposal but agreed to the first, Khrushchev backed down and announced plans to dismantle the base.

One Writer's Process **19**

TEKS 11.13B

Writing

> The crisis had another result, too. The lack of a reliable form of communication meant a delay of several hours between the two world powers when sending messages. So a set of teletype machines linked the Kremlin and the White House, allowing the leaders to communicate directly. Today the electronic transmissions are achieved via two satellite systems, but they are still written rather than verbal to reduce the chance of an incorrect translation (Kennedy).
>
> Nine months later, Kennedy and Khrushchev signed an agreement to ban nuclear testing in the atmosphere. The world's relief was clear at having avoided this war. Many praised Kennedy's calm in the matter, for if he had authorized an invasion, the Soviets may well have evened the score with their nuclear weapons. And the U.S., of course, would follow with their own ("Cuban" 43). The willingness of the two world leaders to compromise, avoiding such a boondoggle, was a welcome sign. That they knew the prevention of nuclear war was not only possible but necessary. Kennedy and Khrushchev agreed on that—and their pact was the most obvious outcome of the crisis.
>
> Tensions between world leaders will probably always prevent world peace. However, the actions of two opposing forces in October 1962 showed the world that cool heads beat hot heads. They gave the world hope.

A paraphrase explains an important concept.

Sources of information are given in parentheses.

Ending
The ending paragraph sums up the topic and provides a final thought.

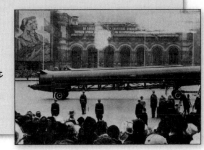

Try It!

Look through Lakendra's planning list and first draft. Does her first draft contain all the details from her organized list (page **17**)? Does she add any new details? If so, what are they?

Try It!
Answers

Lakendra's first draft uses all of the details from her outline.

Lakendra adds new details to support main points and to explain other details. New details include the following:

- U.S. and Soviet Union nuclear capability since early 1940s
- location of U.S. missiles in Turkey
- Fidel Castro, leader of Cuba
- reconnaissance photos
- number of days the crisis lasted—5 days
- description of Khrushchev's written proposal
- Khrushchev's demand that the United States remove missiles from Turkey
- explanation of what might have happened if the crisis had not been averted

TEKS 11.13B

TEKS **11.13B** Structure ideas in a sustained and persuasive way; ELPS **1G** Demonstrate knowledge of when to use formal and informal English; **4F** Use support from peers and teachers to develop vocabulary and background knowledge; **4K** Demonstrate English comprehension and expand reading skills by employing analytical skills

Revising Improving the Writing

Point out to students that revising takes a great deal of effort, but it can be the most rewarding step in the process. Ask students to express their feelings about revising a piece of writing.
⭐ **ELPS** 3G

Tell students that in order to improve a draft, they must be willing to make meaningful—even drastic—changes. If they are serious about improving their writing, they will set aside ample time for revising. (DIFFERENTIATE INSTRUCTION ↘)

Development of Ideas

Explain that setting her draft aside for a day helped Lakendra to recognize that it needed more background information to help readers understand her ideas.

Organization

Tell students that changes in organization are among the most useful revisions a writer can make. Rearranging paragraphs or adding transitions help to make the writer's main points clearer to readers.

Lakendra's First Revision

Explain that Lakendra understood that revising requires

- a careful analysis of the first draft;
- an understanding of the initial goals of writing;
- an understanding of the traits of writing; and, above all,
- a willingness to invest time and effort in making the changes that result in a solid piece of writing.

⭐ **TEKS** 11.13C

 ⭐ **TEKS** 11.13C

Revising Improving the Writing

Lakendra set her first draft aside for a day. Then she rechecked the traits on page 14 before reviewing her first draft. Lakendra's thoughts below reveal the changes she planned to make.

Development of Ideas

"I need to add more background details to lead up to my thesis statement. I could also explain some parts better."

Organization

"I should change the order of the fifth and sixth paragraphs for a more logical organization. I need to add some transition words to make the connections between ideas clearer."

Lakendra's First Revision

Here are the revisions that Lakendra made in the first part of her essay.

> The U.S. was a pal of the Soviet Union during World War II, but tensions between the two countries began to mount following the war. These tensions led to a period of time known as the cold war.
>
> ~~Both the United States and the Soviet Union have had nuclear capability since the early 1940s.~~ The closest the
> conflict
> ~~cold war~~ ever came to a nuclear war was the Cuban Missile Crisis of October, 1962.
>
>   at the time
> The Soviet Union was losing the arms race ~~big time~~.
>
> They knew that the U.S. had more missiles than they did. And they knew that some of these missiles were based in Turkey, only 150 mi. from the Soviet border. ↩
>
> In an effort to even things out, the Soviets wanted to be friends with Cuba in order to "gain a strategic

More background information is added in the first paragraph.

Organization is improved by combining two paragraphs.

---

foothold in America's backyard" (Goldman and Stein 15).

Cubas leader, Fidel Castro, believed Cuba would be attacked

eagerly accepted

again by the U.S. He jumped on an offer from Nikita

Khrushchev, leader of the Soviet Union, to protect Cuba from

the U.S.

By October of 1962, the construction of a missile base

was well under way. The U.S., which was under the leadership of

through careful analysis of

John F. Kennedy at the time, discovered the secret ∧

while checking out some reconaissance photos. Kennedy

demanded that the Soviets dismantle the base and ordered a

navel blockade of Cuba. Khrushchev, in turn, authorized

retaliation in the event that

∧ payback if U.S. forces invaded.

For 5 days, neither side backed down. Then

Khrushchev made a written proposal. Soviet missiles would

be removed from Cuba in exchange for a guarantee that the

also

U.S. would not invade Cuba. A day later, he put his foot

down and demanded removal of U.S. missiles from Turkey.

Kennedy ignored this second proposal but agreed to the

first, Khrushchev backed down and announced plans to

dismantle the base.

The crisis had another result, too. The lack of a

reliable form of communication meant a delay of several

hours between the two world powers when sending

To improve the situation

messages. So a set of teletype machines linked the Kremlin

and the White House, allowing the leaders . . .

Margin notes (left column):

- Necessary background details are added and explained.
- Details that clarify meaning are added.
- Unnecessary details are deleted.
- Paragraphs are rearranged for a more logical organization.

Remind students that for each of their main writing assignments they will have a traits chart that lists well-defined goals. In addition, the holistic scoring guide contains information for analyzing drafts for the five traits of writing. They can use these tools to revise and improve their writing.

Have students evaluate Lakendra's revisions, or changes, in small groups. Tell them to use the margin notes and the following questions to guide their discussion.

- How does each change improve the development of ideas or organization?
- Do any changes create additional problems?
- What other changes could Lakendra still need?
  TEKS 11.13C

Ask students to keep track of their responses so that they can compare them to the comments and suggestions on the peer response sheet on SE page 22 and to help them complete the **Try It!** activity on that page.

Display the chart of students' evaluation of Lakendra's first draft (TE page 18) and have students compare their ideas and opinions with Lakendra's revisions.

ELPS 3G

Differentiated Instruction: English Language Learners

ELPS 3C, 3D, 3G, 3J

ELP Level **Beginning**	ELP Level **Intermediate**	ELP Level **Advanced/Advanced High**
Point out the connecting words and phrases Lakendra adds. Have students repeat them with you. Help students use the connecting words in their own sentences.	Use yes/no questions to have students explore revisions to the essay. Have students point out new transition words and tell how they improve the writing.	Have students point out revisions that they think improve the writing and explain their opinions.

 TEKS **11.13C** Revise drafts to clarify meaning and achieve logical organization; **ELPS** **3C** Speak using a variety of connecting words; **3D** Speak using grade-level content-area vocabulary in context/new English words and academic language; **3G** Express opinions and ideas; **3J** Respond orally to information presented/concept and language attainment

Revising Using a Peer Response Sheet

Help students understand the purpose of the two parts of the **Peer Response Sheet**. For more about peer responding, see SE pages 115–120.

`DIFFERENTIATE INSTRUCTION ⭧`

Try It!
Answers

Have students refer to their evaluation of Lakendra's revision (TE page 21) as they complete the **Try It!** activity.

Possible answers: Explaining why Cuba needed protection seems to be the most important suggestion because it will provide vital background information for the reader about what led to the Cuban Missile Crisis.

Other Possible Improvements

■ **Development of Ideas:** Add details about how the public responded to the end of the crisis.
■ **Organization:** The connection between the paragraph that ends with *to protect Cuba from the U.S.* and the next paragraph would be stronger if the writer added the term *missile base* to the first of the two paragraphs. For example, end the paragraph with the words *by building a missile base on Cuban soil.*
■ **Voice:** *Pal* is too informal. Use a more formal, serious term, such as *ally.*

⭐ **TEKS** 11.13C, 11.13E

⭐ **ELPS** 1G

 **TEKS** 11.13C, 11.13E

Revising Using a Peer Response Sheet

Ashley evaluated Lakendra's essay using a scoring guide like the one on pages 36–37. Her suggestions on the response sheet below showed Lakendra where she could revise to achieve specific rhetorical purposes, like adding clear transitions.

Peer Response Sheet

Writer: <u>Lakendra Harris</u>   Responder: <u>Ashley Wright</u>

Title: <u>The Cuban Missile Crisis</u>

What I liked about your writing:

<u>You chose an interesting topic, and you cover it well—from</u>

<u>background info to the outcome of the crisis.</u>

_____

Changes I would suggest:

<u>Could you add more details about the following?</u>

   • <u>the cold war</u>

   • <u>why Cuba needed protection</u>

   • <u>the purpose for the blockade</u>

<u>Also, could you check the ending? It seems to end too suddenly.</u>

_____

_____

_____

Try It!

Review Ashley's suggestions for improvements above. Which suggestion seems to be the most important? Explain why. Add at least one new suggestion to improve Lakendra's writing. Look at the explanations of development of ideas, organization, and voice on page 14 to help you make your suggestions.

⭐ **TEKS** **11.13C** Revise drafts to clarify meaning and achieve logical organization; **11.13E** Revise drafts in response to feedback from peers; **ELPS** **1G** Demonstrate ability to distinguish between formal and informal English

★ TEKS 11.13C, 11.13E

Lakendra's Revision Using a Peer Response

Using Ashley's comments, Lakendra revised her essay again. Some of the changes that she made are shown here.

Writing

> **Transitional phrase added to achieve rhetorical purpose.**

The U.S. was a pal of the Soviet Union during World War II, but tensions between the two countries began to mount following the war. These tensions led to a period of time ∧*beginning in the late 1940s* known as the cold war. ∧*Each country perceived the other as hostile.* The closest the conflict ever came to a nuclear war was the Cuban Missile Crisis of October, 1962.

> **New details explain why Cuba needed protection.**

The Soviet Union at the time was losing the arms race. They knew that the U.S. had more missiles than they did. And they knew that some of these missiles were based in Turkey, only 150 mi. from the Soviet border. In an effort to even things out, the Soviets wanted to be friends with Cuba in order to "gain a strategic foothold in America's backyard" (Goldman and Stein 15). Cubas leader, Fidel Castro, believed Cuba would be attacked again by the U.S. ∧*following the 1961 Bay of Pigs invasion ("Cuban 44").* He eagerly accepted an offer from Nikita Khrushchev, leader of the Soviet Union, to protect Cuba from the U.S.

> **More details about the purpose of the blockade are added.**

By October of 1962, the construction of a missile base was well under way. The U.S., which was under the leadership of John F. Kennedy at the time, discovered the secret through careful analysis of reconaissance photos. Kennedy demanded that the Soviets dismantle the base and ordered a navel blockade of Cuba. ∧*to prevent any more supply deliveries* Khrushchev, in turn, authorized retaliation in the event that U.S. forces invaded.

Lakendra's Revision Using a Peer Response

Have students point out the specific changes Lakendra made to her essay based on Ashley's responses.

★ TEKS 11.13C, 11.13E

Remind students that as writers, they are in control of the content and style of their writing.

- If they do not understand a responder's comment or suggestion, they should ask for clarification.
- If they do not agree with a comment or suggestion, they should seek a second opinion or request a conference with you.
- The final decision about making changes is in their hands, but if more than one person suggests a change, they should strongly consider making that change.

Differentiated Instruction: English Language Learners

★ ELPS 1G, 1H

ELP Level **Beginning**	ELP Level **Intermediate**	ELP Level **Advanced/Advanced High**
Explain that Ashley thinks the essay needs more details. Use gestures and visuals to explain the concept of adding details to fill out a picture or idea.	Ask yes/no questions to gauge students' understanding of Ashley's comments. Have students form questions using the bulleted details, such as *What was the Cold War?*	Have students review the essay to discuss Lakendra's use of formal and informal language. Have them compose a suggestion on how she might address this.

★ TEKS **11.13C** Revise drafts to clarify meaning and achieve logical organization; **11.13E** Revise drafts in response to feedback from peers; ELPS **1G** Demonstrate ability to distinguish between formal and informal English; **1H** Develop and expand repertoire of learning strategies/looking for patterns in language

Revising **Focusing on Voice**

Remind students that a writer's authentic and original voice shows his or her unique perspective on a topic.

Voice

Discuss Lakendra's comment about the revisions she intends to make, and guide students to understand why a more formal tone is appropriate for her topic. **DIFFERENTIATE INSTRUCTION** ↘

⭐ **ELPS** 1G

Lakendra's Improvements in Voice

Focus attention on the revisions Lakendra makes to achieve a more formal tone, such as changing "be friends with" to "actively sought an alliance." Then point out that combining some sentences also contributes to a more formal tone. Direct attention to the sentences that Lakendra combines at the beginning of the sample, one of which begins with the word *and*.

- Point out that although beginning a sentence with *and* isn't incorrect, it is generally not done in formal, serious writing.
- Remind students that *and* is a conjunction used to combine words, phrases, and clauses that are related in meaning. If students have begun a sentence with *and, but,* or *or,* the sentence is likely to be related to an idea in the sentence that comes before it, so they should consider combining these sentences.
- Have students explain how the ideas in the sentences that Lakendra combines are related. (They both relate to what the Soviet Union knew about U.S. missiles.)

⭐ **TEKS** 11.13C; **ELPS** 2C

⭐ **TEKS** 11.13C

Revising **Focusing on Voice**

Lakendra next reviewed her writing for its voice. Her thoughts below tell what changes she planned to make.

Voice

"I need a more formal voice. There are places where I need to use different words to reflect a more serious tone."

Lakendra's Improvements in Voice

After reviewing the style and sound of her writing, Lakendra focused on improving her voice and sentence structure. Even though she intends to use a more formal tone, she hopes to engage her readers with language that sounds authentic and original, and she wants sentences to flow together more naturally. Lakendra also plans to express her unique perspective on this historical event.

> **Combining sentences clarifies the idea.**
>
> **Verb choice is improved, and more formal wording is used.**
>
> The Soviet Union at the time was losing the arms race. They knew ~~that~~ the U.S. had more missiles than they did. ~~And they knew~~ that some of these missiles were based in Turkey, only 150 mi. from the Soviet border. In an effort to even things out, the Soviets ~~wanted to be friends~~ actively sought an alliance with Cuba in order to "gain a strategic foothold in America's backyard" (Goldman and Stein 15). Cubas leader, Fidel Castro, believed Cuba would be attacked again by the U.S. following the 1961 Bay of Pigs invasion ("Cuban" 44). He eagerly accepted an offer from Nikita Khrushchev, leader of the Soviet Union, to protect Cuba from the U.S.
>
> By October of 1962, the construction of a missile base was well under way. The U.S., ~~which was~~ under the

---

★ TEKS 11.13C

Writing

> leadership of John F. Kennedy ~~at the time~~, discovered the
>
> secret through careful analysis of reconaissance photos.
>
> Kennedy demanded that the Soviets dismantle the base and
>
> ordered a navel blockade of Cuba to prevent any more supply
>
> deliveries. Khrushchev, in turn, authorized retaliation in the
>
> event that U.S. forces invaded.
>
>   For 5 days, neither side backed down. Then Khrushchev
>
> made a written proposal. Soviet missiles would be removed
>
> from Cuba in exchange for a guarantee that the U.S. would
>
>   In a surprise move
> not invade Cuba. A day later, he also demanded removal
>
>   viewed
> of U.S. missiles from Turkey. Kennedy ~~ignored~~ this second
>
>   as a bluff
> proposal but agreed to the first, Khrushchev backed down and
>
> announced plans to dismantle the base.
>
>   With the news that war had been avoided, a sense of great
> ~~The world's relief was clear at having avoided this war.~~
> relief spread from capital cities to small villages around the world.
> Many praised Kennedy's calm in the matter, for if he had
>
> authorized an invasion, the Soviets may well have retaliated
>
> with their nuclear weapons. And the U.S., of course, would
>
> follow with their own ("Cuban" 43). The willingness of the two
>
>   catastrophe
> world leaders to compromise, avoiding such a ~~boondoggle~~, was
>
> a welcome sign. That they knew the prevention of nuclear war
>
> was not only possible but necessary. Kennedy and Khrushchev
>
> agreed on that—and 9 months later, they signed an
>
> agreement to ban nuclear testing in the atmosphere (although
>
> underground testing continued). This pact was the most
>
> obvious outcome of the crisis.

Unnecessary words are deleted.

A colon is used to introduce an important point.

Language that engages the reader is added.

Revision shows the writer's authentic view.

Word choice is improved, and a fragment is fixed.

Point out that one of the best ways for writers to identify problems with voice is to read their writing aloud or to ask someone else to read it aloud to them. When a piece is read aloud, problems with tone and style often stand out. Some problems that students can listen for in their own writing include the following:

- words that the writer is unlikely to use or seems unfamiliar with
- casual or informal words or words with the wrong connotation
- overuse of quotations
- short, choppy sentences that could be combined

Have students take turns reading aloud paragraphs in Lakendra's draft before and after she revised it for voice. Tell students that although they may not have made the same changes that Lakendra made, they should be able to hear why she made these changes.

★ TEKS 11.13C

Differentiated Instruction: English Language Learners

★ ELPS 1G, 2D

ELP Level **Beginning**	ELP Level **Intermediate**	ELP Level **Advanced/Advanced High**
Use simplified examples to demonstrate how voice can be formal or informal, such as *Two people are friends. Two countries are allies.*	Read aloud the original and the revised sentences in the essay's first paragraph. Have students ask questions to monitor their understanding about voice.	Have students read aloud the revisions in the essay's third paragraph. Have them use the call-outs to monitor their understanding or seek clarification about language structures.

 TEKS 11.13C Revise drafts to clarify meaning and achieve consistency of tone; **ELPS 1G** Demonstrate knowledge of when to use formal and informal English; **2D** Monitor understanding of spoken language and seek clarification as needed

Editing Checking for Conventions

Give students a few minutes to look at the Proofreader's Guide on SE pages 634–781 and preview the conventions that are addressed in that section. Encourage them to think about how they can use the Proofreader's Guide when they edit their own writing.

Conventions

Relate Lakendra's comment to the checklist below as you discuss each type of convention. Then ask students to suggest the resources Lakendra can use to check her writing for spelling errors.

★ **TEKS** 11.19

Try It!
Answers

Possible answers:

- mi. (miles)
- Cubas (Cuba's) **DIFFERENTIATE INSTRUCTION ↘**
  DIFFERENTIATE INSTRUCTION ↘
- reconaissance (reconnaissance)
- navel (naval)
- 5 (five)
- comma splice (Kennedy ignored this second proposal but agreed to the first. Khrushchev backed down. . .)
- sentence begins with *and* (The U.S., of course, would follow with their own ("Cuban").
- 9 (nine)

✳ For more on writing numerals, see SE pages 245 and 686.

★ **TEKS** 11.13D, 11.18A

 ★ **TEKS** 11.13D, 11.18A, 11.19

Texas Traits

Editing Checking for Conventions

Lakendra's last step in the process was to check her draft for punctuation, capitalization, spelling, and grammar errors. She used the "Proofreader's Guide" in the back of her *Write Source* textbook and the checklist below.

Conventions

"I'll look carefully at my essay for grammar, sentence structure, capitalization, punctuation, and spelling errors."

GRAMMAR

_____ 1. Do I use the proper tense and voice for my verbs?

_____ 2. Do my subjects and verbs agree in number?

_____ 3. Do my pronouns clearly agree with their antecedents?

SENTENCE STRUCTURE

_____ 4. Do I use a variety of correctly structured sentences that clearly communicate ideas?

MECHANICS (CAPITALIZATION AND PUNCTUATION)

_____ 5. Have I capitalized all the proper nouns and adjectives?

_____ 6. Do I use end punctuation correctly?

_____ 7. Do I use commas correctly?

_____ 8. Do I correctly italicize or use quotation marks for titles?

_____ 9. Do I use apostrophes correctly?

_____ 10. Are sources properly presented and documented?

SPELLING

_____ 11. Have I spelled words correctly?

_____ 12. Have I used the spell-checker on my computer?

Try It!

Find three or four errors in Lakendra's revised draft on pages 24–25. Did you find the same errors as she found (on page 27)?

Differentiated Instruction: Struggling Learners

Review with students the use of apostrophes to show possession (a correction Lakendra made in her essay). Write the following sentence on the board: *The cats food dish was empty, so it ate from the dogs bowl.*

Ask how students would show possession in this sentence for one cat and one dog (cat's, dog's). Then ask how they would change the sentence to show possession for two cats and two dogs. (The *cats'* food dish was empty, so *they* ate from the *dogs'* bowl.)

★ TEKS 11.13D

Writing

Lakendra's Editing

Here is a sample of Lakendra's editing. (See the inside back cover of this textbook for common editing and proofreading marks.)

> United States
> The U.S. was an ally of the Soviet Union during World
> War II, but tensions between the two countries began to
> mount following the war. These tensions led to a period of
> time beginning in the late 1940s known as the cold war. Each
> country perceived the other as hostile. However, the closest
> the conflict ever came to a nuclear war was the Cuban
> Missile Crisis of October, 1962.
>
> The Soviet Union at the time was losing the arms race.
> They knew not only that the U.S. had more missiles than
> they did, but also that some of these missiles were based
> miles
> in Turkey, only 150 mi. from the Soviet border. In an effort
> to even things out, the Soviets actively sought an alliance
> with Cuba in order to "gain a strategic foothold in America's
> backyard" (Goldman and Stein 15). Cuba's leader, Fidel Castro,
> believed Cuba would be attacked again by the U.S. following the
> 1961 Bay of Pigs invasion ("Cuban" 44). He eagerly accepted
> an offer from Nikita Khrushchev, leader of the Soviet Union, to
> protect Cuba from the U.S.
>
> By October of 1962, the construction of a missile base
> was well under way. The U.S., under the leadership of John F.
> Kennedy, discovered the secret through careful analysis of
> reconnaissance
> reconaissance photos. Kennedy demanded that the Soviets . . .

The first instance of an abbreviated term is spelled out.

An incorrectly placed comma is deleted, and an abbreviation is replaced.

An apostrophe is added to indicate possession.

A spelling error is corrected.

Editing Lakendra's Editing

If students need a refresher on editing and proofreading marks, refer them to the inside back cover of the book. Encourage them to use these marks whenever they edit.

Have students explain why Lakendra deleted the comma between *October* and *1962*. Then ask them to use the Index to find the page in their Proofreader's Guide that lists rules for using commas to set off dates. Have students point out the specific rule that supports Lakendra's editing. (SE page 644, item 644.1)

★ TEKS 11.13D

TEKS **11.13D** Edit drafts for grammar, mechanics, and spelling; ELPS **5E** Employ increasingly complex grammatical structures/possessive case

Publishing Sharing Your Writing

Explain that incorporating your feedback into a final draft shows that students have understood your comments well enough to apply them, and it demonstrates awareness of all aspects of the writing process.

Ask students why it is important to produce "a clean copy" of their final work. Students may suggest the following ideas.

- A clean copy reflects the writer's pride in his or her work and shows respect for the reader.
- A clean, neat paper with correct capitalization and punctuation is easy to read, so readers can focus on the ideas.

 TEKS 11.18A

Tips for Handwritten Copies

Discuss your formatting requirements for submission of final copies. Explain to students that you post these requirements in the classroom, or upload them to the class Web site, if that is available.

Tips for Computer Copies

Many teachers require computer-generated copies and some accept on-line submissions of final student writing. Before establishing such a standard, make sure all students have access to computers and can meet these requirements.

 TEKS 11.13E

Publishing Sharing Your Writing

Lakendra used feedback from her teacher to revise her essay. Then she used these tips to produce a clean copy of her final essay to show her classmates.

Tips for Handwritten Copies

- Use blue or black ink and write clearly.
- Write your name according to your teacher's instructions.
- Center your title on the first page; skip another line and begin your essay.
- Indent each paragraph.

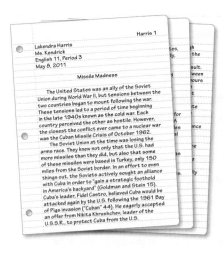

Tips for Computer Copies

- Use an easy-to-read font set at a 12-point type size.
- Double-space the text and set your margins so that you have a one-inch space around the outside of each page.

Lakendra's Final Draft

Lakendra submitted her final draft with confidence. She felt that her writing met her goals and satisfied the terms of the assignment.

Writing

Harris 1

Lakendra Harris
Ms. Kendrick
English 11, Period 3
May 8, 2011

Missile Madness

The United States was an ally of the Soviet Union during World War II, but tensions between the two countries began to mount following the war. These tensions led to a period of time beginning in the late 1940s known as the Cold War. Each country perceived the other as hostile. However, the closest the conflict ever came to a nuclear war was the Cuban Missile Crisis of October 1962.

The Soviet Union at the time was losing the arms race. They knew not only that the U.S. had more missiles than they did, but also that some of these missiles were based in Turkey, only 150 miles from the Soviet border. In an effort to even things out, the Soviets actively sought an alliance with Cuba in order to "gain a strategic foothold in America's back yard" (Goldman and Stein 15). Cuba's leader, Fidel Castro, also believed Cuba would be attacked again by the U.S. following the 1961 Bay of Pigs invasion ("Cuban" 44). He eagerly accepted an offer from Nikita Khrushchev, leader of the Soviet Union, to protect Cuba from the U.S.

By October of 1962, the construction of a missile base was well under way. The U.S., under the leadership of John F. Kennedy, discovered the secret through careful analysis of reconnaissance photos. Kennedy demanded that the Soviets dismantle the base and ordered a naval blockade of Cuba to prevent any more supply deliveries. Khrushchev, in turn, authorized retaliation in the event that U.S. forces invaded.

Publishing Lakendra's Final Draft

Discuss Lakendra's final essay with the class. Use the goals on SE page 14 and the holistic scoring guide on SE pages 36–37 to evaluate the writing and help students recognize why it is a good example of an expository essay.

◤ DIFFERENTIATE INSTRUCTION

Include the following points in the discussion.

Focus and Coherence

- The essay begins with a clearly worded thesis statement.
- The essay maintains its focus throughout.
- The essay has a strong introduction and conclusion that add depth to the essay.

Organization

- The essay has a clear beginning, middle, and ending.
- The writer uses strong transitions that help show the chronological organization.

Development of Ideas

- The writer has selected a topic that interests her and provides the background necessary for readers to understand it.
- The topic and thesis are clearly stated.
- The writer has supported her thesis with evidence.

TEKS 11.13E

**Differentiated Instruction:
English Language Learners**

ELPS 4D, 4F

Before reading the final essay, use prereading supports to develop vocabulary and enhance comprehension.

ELP Level **Beginning**	ELP Level **Intermediate**	ELP Level **Advanced/Advanced High**
Use visuals, gestures, and simplified language to clarify the meaning of challenging language such as *hostile* (angry) and *sought* (looked for).	Have partners work together to clarify the meaning of challenging language such as *tensions, alliance,* and *willingness.*	Have students share ideas about the meaning of words such as *diplomacy, retaliated,* and *catastrophe.* Then have partners discuss the meanings.

 TEKS **11.13E** Publish written work; ELPS **4D** Use prereading supports to enhance comprehension of written text; **4F** Use support from peers and teachers to develop vocabulary

Continue to evaluate Lakendra's final essay with students, focusing on voice and conventions.

Voice

- *The writer creates a knowledgeable voice by using proper names, places, and dates.*
- *The language is serious and appropriate for an essay on an important event in U.S. history.*

Conventions

- *The essay is free of errors in grammar, sentence structure, capitalization, punctuation, and spelling.*
- *The writer shows source information in parentheses.*

⭐ **TEKS** 11.13E

⭐ **TEKS** 11.13E

Harris 2

For five days, neither side backed down. Then Khrushchev made a written proposal: Soviet missiles would be removed from Cuba in exchange for a guarantee that the U.S. would not invade Cuba. In a surprise move a day later, he also demanded removal of U.S. missiles from Turkey. Kennedy viewed this second proposal as a bluff but agreed to the first. Khrushchev backed down and announced plans to dismantle the base.

With the news that war had been avoided, a sense of great relief spread from capital cities to small villages around the world. Many praised Kennedy's calm in the matter, for if he had authorized an invasion, the Soviets may well have retaliated with their nuclear weapons. The U.S., of course, would have followed with their own ("Cuban" 43). The willingness of the two world leaders to compromise, avoiding such a catastrophe, was a welcome sign that they knew the prevention of nuclear war was not only possible but necessary. Kennedy and Khrushchev agreed on that—and nine months later, they signed an agreement to ban nuclear testing in the atmosphere (although underground testing continued). This pact was the most obvious outcome of the crisis.

The confrontation, however, had another result. The lack of a reliable form of communication between the two world powers meant a delay of several hours when sending messages—not a good thing when tensions are high. To improve the situation, a set of teletype machines linked the Kremlin and the White House, allowing the leaders to communicate directly. Today the electronic transmissions are achieved via two satellite systems, but they are still written rather than verbal to reduce the chance of an incorrect translation (Kennedy).

Tensions between world leaders will probably always be an obstacle to world peace. However, the actions of two opposing forces in October 1962 showed the world that diplomacy and compromise can work. The government leaders involved in the Cuban Missile Crisis weighed their options carefully and, in the end, made hard choices. Fortunately, their decisions under duress ultimately led to increased cooperation of governments the world over.

TEKS 11.13E
ELPS 11.2C, 11.3E

Assessing the Final Draft

Lakendra's teacher used a scoring guide like the one found on pages **36–37** to assess her final draft. A 4 is the very best score that a writer can receive for each trait. The teacher also included comments under each trait.

Holistic Scoring Guide: Score Point 4

Title: Missile Madness

Writer: Lakendra Harris

Focus and Coherence
You maintained your focus throughout and you made it clear how ideas connect to one another.

Organization
You wrote a solid beginning, middle, and ending, and each paragraph is well developed.

Development of Ideas
You supported your thesis statement with details and examples, but I think that your essay would have been better if you included more quotations.

Voice
The voice is much improved from the first draft. It's more formal and knowledgeable.

Conventions
Your writing is free of careless errors.

Learning Language

Do you agree with the scores and comments made by Lakendra's teacher? Why or why not? In a small group, discuss your reaction to Lakendra's essay and how you would evaluate it. Talk about each trait and cite evidence that supports your evaluation.

Assessing the Final Draft

If possible, have students assess the essay on their own before they read the sample teacher assessment.

- Have students create their own assessment sheets by listing each of the five writing traits on a sheet of paper, leaving space between each trait for comments. Discuss how to fill in the assessment sheet using descriptions provided in the Holistic Scoring Guide on SE pages 36–37. For detailed directions, turn to SE pages 34–35.
- Have students work independently or with a partner to fill in the assessment sheet.
- Then tell students to use the sample teacher assessment and their own assessment sheet to complete the **Learning Language** activity at the bottom of the page.

TEKS 11.13E

Learning Language

Before beginning the activity, review the five traits of writing and have students explain their understanding of each one. Tell students to demonstrate their understanding of the new academic vocabulary by using the terms in their discussion of the essay. ✔DIFFERENTIATE INSTRUCTION

ELPS 2C, 3E

Differentiated Instruction:
English Language Learners **ELPS** 4G, 4K

ELP Level **Beginning**	ELP Level **Intermediate**	ELP Level **Advanced/Advanced High**
Have students repeat the names of traits as you use simplified language to discuss the Holistic Scoring Guide and the teacher's comments on Lakendra's essay.	Lead a shared reading to support understanding of the scoring guide. Have students complete sentence stems to provide their own assessments of the essay.	Have partners do a shared reading of the teacher's assessment of the essay. Have students use complete sentences to analyze and evaluate the essay.

 TEKS **11.13E** Publish written work; **ELPS** **2C** Learn new academic vocabulary; **3E** Share information in cooperative learning interactions; **4G** Demonstrate comprehension of increasingly complex English/shared reading; **4K** Demonstrate English comprehension and expand reading skills by employing analytical skills

Evaluating and Reflecting on Your Writing

Provide students with motivation for using the reflecting process to become better writers.

- Ask students to explain how Lakendra could use her completed reflection sheet to become a better writer. (Possible responses: She could use it to see where she needs to focus attention the next time she writes. She could monitor her growth as a writer by comparing it to previous and later reflections.)
- Ask students to offer reasons why Lakendra, or any other writer, may be reluctant to complete a reflection sheet like this after finishing a piece of writing. (Possible responses: ran out of time; inability to recognize strengths and weaknesses)
- Invite students to explain how they can make reflecting a natural part of their writing. (Possible responses: They could attach a copy of their reflections to their finished writing when they turn it in. They could think of reflecting as the sixth step in the writing process.)

DIFFERENTIATE INSTRUCTION ⬎

32

Evaluating and Reflecting on Your Writing

After the whole process was finished, Lakendra filled out a reflection sheet. This helped her think about the assignment and plan for future writing. (Complete a reflection sheet like this right after you finish your writing.)

Lakendra Harris
Ms. Kendrick
English 11, Period 3
May 8, 2011

Expository Essay: Missile Madness

1. The best part of my essay is . . .
   my beginning. It gives needed background information and leads up to the thesis statement.

2. The part that still needs work is . . .
   my use of sources. Maybe I should have used more quotations to support the main idea of each paragraph.

3. The most important part of my prewriting and planning was . . .
   listing the 5 W's and H and using freewriting to gather my thoughts.

4. During revising, I spent a lot of time dealing with . . .
   adding more details to support my main points.

5. What I've learned about this type of essay is . . .
   that it is important to start with plenty of information. I also learned that using a formal voice for my essay makes it seem more authoritative.

6. Here is one question I still have . . .
   What are some good transitions I can use to connect paragraphs smoothly?

Differentiated Instruction: English Language Learners

🏫 ELPS 1E, 1H, 3G

ELP Level **Beginning**	ELP Level **Intermediate**	ELP Level **Advanced/Advanced High**
Use gestures and simplified language to explore ideas about reflecting and evaluating. Have students repeat these terms as you discuss them.	Use simplified language to discuss evaluating and reflecting on one's writing. Provide sentence frames using these terms for students to share their ideas orally.	Have partners discuss Lakendra's reflections. Invite them to express ideas, opinions, and feelings about how reflecting on one's writing can be useful.

ELPS 1E Internalize new basic and academic language by using and reusing it/speaking; **1H** Develop and expand repertoire of learning strategies; **3G** Express opinions, ideas, and feelings

Evaluating Your Writing

Imagine a high jumper studying the crossbar he must leap over. Think of a long jumper pacing along the sand pit where she will land. Envision a weight lifter examining the bar that holds a gold medal winning weight. From start to finish, each of these athletes is focused on a specific, measurable mark for excellence.

When you write, you do the same thing. A writing scoring guide sets the standard to judge the focus and coherence of your writing, its organization, the development of your ideas, and the authenticity of your voice, as well as the correctness of every last punctuation mark.

This chapter will show you how to use a scoring guide throughout the writing process to ensure your best possible score at the end. Like a great athlete, you'll learn to focus on the scoring guide not just when your work is assessed but from start to finish.

- ■ **Understanding a Holistic Scoring Guide**
- ■ **Write Source Holistic Scoring Guide**
- ■ **Evaluating an Essay**
- ■ **4-Point Model**
- ■ **3-Point Model**
- ■ **2-Point Model**
- ■ **1-Point Model**
- ■ **Assessing an Expository Essay**

"Either write something worth reading or do something worth writing."

—Benjamin Franklin

Evaluating Your Writing

Give students time to familiarize themselves with the holistic scoring guide on SE pages 36–37. Suggest that students bookmark these pages when they begin a writing assignment for a particular form of writing. During the writing process, they can refer to the holistic scoring guide to check the goals and to read the trait descriptions.

Understanding a Holistic Scoring Guide

Point out to students that people in the workplace are rated on performance. Performance ratings are usually based on a set of established standards that are meant to provide guidance and to encourage people to perform at the highest level of competence in their fields. People who care about what they do usually strive to get the best possible ratings from their superiors and their peers. In the arts and entertainment fields, performing at the highest level results in awards, acclaim, and often financial success. In the business world, performing at the highest level results in promotions and pay increases.

Evaluation Guide

Discuss the purpose of the holistic scoring guide by telling students that for people to do their best, they have to know the standards by which they will be evaluated so that they can apply those standards to their work. For students to achieve the highest scores for their writing, they have to know and understand the traits of writing and then apply them to all their writing assignments. The more they practice, the better they will understand the traits, and the higher their scores and rewards (grades) will be.

Understanding a Holistic Scoring Guide

When you see a movie, chances are you come away with an overall impression—you really liked it, you thought it was OK, or you didn't like it very much. There might be one aspect of the movie that you found especially strong (car chases, anyone?) but your opinion is based on some combination of the acting, the story, and the way the film was put together.

Holistic scoring for writing is similar in that it is based on the idea that the whole is greater than the sum of its parts.

A **holistic scoring guide** provides a way to evaluate the overall quality of writing on the basis of five traits: *focus and coherence, organization, development of ideas, voice,* and *conventions.* (For an introduction to these traits, see pages **46–89.**) With a scoring guide, you can rate your level of expertise—or mastery—as a writer on a scale of 4 to 1.

Evaluation Guide

A holistic scoring guide uses a 4-point system to evaluate writing. Scores of 4 or 3 indicate strong levels of mastery in most aspects of writing. Scores of 2 or 1 show that the writer has not yet mastered many aspects of writing.

 A **4** means that the writing is **highly effective.**
It shows an overall master of the five writing traits.

 A **3** means that the writing is very **generally effective.**
It clearly shows some master of most of the five traits.

 A **2** means that the writing is **somewhat effective.**
It shows that the writer has little mastery of most traits.

 A **1** means that the writing is **not effective.**
It indicates that the writer needs to work to master most of the traits.

Reading a Scoring Guide

Scoring guides in this book are color coded. Traits describing a score of *4* appear in a blue strip, a score of *3* in a green strip, and so forth. There is a description for each score to help you assess your writing for a particular trait.

Scoring Guide for Expository Writing

Writing at this score point is highly effective.

Focus and Coherence
Maintains focus throughout the writing; all ideas clearly connect to each other and to the main idea. Includes a meaningful introduction and conclusion that add depth to the composition.

Organization Employs an effective organizational pattern for the purpose and audience. Has a smooth and logical flow; transitions help the reader move from one idea to the next.

Writing at this score point is generally effective.

Focus and Coherence
Maintains focus, with minor lapses; most ideas are clearly connected to each other and to the main idea. An introduction and conclusion add some depth to the composition.

Organization Uses an organizational pattern that is mostly effective for the purpose and audience. Generally flows but could use a few more transitions.

Guiding Your Writing

A scoring guide helps you . . .

- **plan your work**—knowing what is expected,
- **create a strong first draft**—focusing on *organization, development of ideas,* and *voice,*
- **revise and edit your work**—considering each trait, and
- **assess your final draft**—rating the whole piece of writing based on the traits.

Think about the scoring guide. Read the descriptions above and consider what they have to say about organization, development of ideas, and voice. What should the essay include in addition to the thesis statement? What needs to be used to help with organization? How should the writer sound?

Reading a Scoring Guide

To help students better understand the role of the different traits, use this analogy to compare writing and building a house:

- When writers focus on organization and development of ideas, they are like architects creating a blueprint, or plan, for the design of a house.
- When writers focus on the other three traits—focus and coherence, voice, and conventions—they are like the contractors who carry out the details, bringing the architect's ideas together to construct a functional, solidly built house.

Scoring Guide for Expository Writing

Work with students to analyze the descriptions for Focus and Coherence, and guide them to note the differences for a score of 4 and a score of 3. Follow a similar procedure for the descriptions for Organization. **DIFFERENTIATE INSTRUCTION**

Guiding Your Writing

Ask students to explain the value of knowing what is expected when they are writing. Discuss with them the scoring guide's usefulness at each stage of the writing process.

Think about the scoring guide.

Answers

- **Focus and Coherence** In addition to a thesis statement the essay should also include supporting evidence that relates to the thesis.
- **Organization:** Strong transitions help to clarify the organizational pattern.
- **Voice:** The writer should sound knowledgeable about the topic.

Differentiated Instruction: English Language Learners		**ELPS** 3B, 3D, 4F
ELP Level Beginning	**ELP Level Intermediate**	**ELP Level Advanced/Advanced High**
Use visuals, gestures, and simplified language to explain scores and how a score of 4 is different from a score of 3 and so on.	Use visuals and contextual supports to explain terms such as *effective, highly, generally,* and *somewhat.* Have student repeat these terms with you and use them in sentences.	Invite students to expand their understanding of terms such as *effective, highly, generally,* and *somewhat* by sharing examples of ways to solve a problem.

 ELPS 3B Expand vocabulary/learning and using routine language needed for classroom communication; **3D** Speak using grade-level content-area vocabulary in context/academic language; **4F** Use visual and contextual support and support from peers and teachers to read content-area text

Write Source Holistic Scoring Guide

Remind students that holistic scoring examines the overall quality of the writing. Point out that a piece of writing that receives a score of 4 is probably not perfect. For example, it might have some minor errors in conventions or other traits. Similarly, writing that receives a score 1 or 2 might be correct for all conventions, but not have well-developed ideas that are presented in a logical way. **DIFFERENTIATE INSTRUCTION ↘**

Discuss the descriptions for each trait at the score of 4. Ask students to explain why writing that receives this score is considered highly effective. Follow a similar procedure for scores of 3, of 2, and of 1. **DIFFERENTIATE INSTRUCTION ↘**

36

Write Source Holistic Scoring Guide

Use the descriptions at each score point to evaluate your own writing or that of your peers.

 Writing at this score point is highly effective.

Focus and Coherence Maintains focus throughout the writing; all ideas clearly connect to each other and to the main idea. Includes a meaningful introduction and conclusion that add depth to the composition.

Organization Employs an effective organizational pattern for the purpose and audience. Has a smooth and logical flow; transitions help the reader move from one idea to the next.

 Writing at this score point is generally effective.

Focus and Coherence Maintains focus, with minor lapses; most ideas are clearly connected to each other and to the main idea. An introduction and conclusion add some depth to the composition.

Organization Uses an organizational pattern that is mostly effective for the purpose and audience. Generally flows but could use a few more transitions.

 Writing at this score point is somewhat effective.

Focus and Coherence Is somewhat unfocused, but the reader can understand how ideas are related. Some ideas do not contribute to the writing as a whole. The introduction and conclusion are superficial.

Organization The flow of the ideas is not always clear. The organizational pattern may not suit the purpose and audience. Wordiness and repetition may interfere with the flow of ideas.

 Writing at this score point is not effective.

Focus and Coherence Lacks focus; includes a substantial amount of information not connected to the main idea. Is missing an introduction and/or conclusion.

Organization Has no clear organizational pattern or logical flow of ideas. Lacks transitions. Repetition or wordiness may interfere with the progression of ideas.

Differentiated Instruction: Struggling Learners

Some students are reluctant to write due to spelling or grammar problems. Point out one advantage of holistic scoring is that other traits of writing are equally important in getting a high score. Guide students to focus on the development of their ideas and organization, while seeking help from a peer or teacher to address conventions.

Writing

Development of Ideas Ample support and specific details allow the reader to appreciate the writer's points. A novel approach to the topic may add to the overall quality of the writing.

Voice Engages the reader throughout the writing. Sounds authentic and original; expresses the writer's unique perspective.

Conventions Shows a strong command of conventions, allowing the reader to focus on the writer's message.

Development of Ideas Supports all ideas, but some need to be developed more thoroughly. The presentation of ideas may be thoughtful but may not reflect a novel approach to the topic.

Voice Engages the reader for most of the writing. Sounds somewhat authentic and original and expresses the writer's unique perspective.

Conventions Includes only minor errors in conventions; errors do not interfere with the reader's ability to understand the writer's message.

Development of Ideas Ideas may be developed only superficially. Some information may be missing. The reader's ability to appreciate the writer's points is compromised.

Voice Engages the reader occasionally. Sounds authentic and original in only a few sections. Does not express a unique perspective.

Conventions Errors reflect a limited command of writing conventions and interfere with the flow of ideas in the writing.

Development of Ideas Support is lacking or is only general and vague. Important information may be left out. The reader has difficulty understanding the writer's points.

Voice Does not engage the reader. Shows little or no evidence of the writer's individuality or unique perspective.

Conventions The writing shows major problems with conventions, which interferes with the reader's ability to understand the message.

Point out that it would be extremely difficult to keep all of the features of each trait in mind constantly while writing. Explain that for this reason, good writers tend to focus on certain traits during a particular stage of the writing process. Work with students to decide which traits are likely to be useful at each stage, using the following as a guide:

- Prewriting: organization and development of ideas
- Drafting: organization, development of ideas, and voice
- Revising: focus and coherence, organization, development of ideas, and voice
- Editing: conventions
- Publishing: voice and conventions

Differentiated Instruction: English Language Learners

ELPS 3D, 4D, 4F, 4G, 4I

ELP Level **Beginning**	ELP Level **Intermediate**	ELP Level **Advanced/Advanced High**
Simplify language and ideas to describe attributes of scores and traits. Have students repeat descriptors such as *highly effective* as you use them.	Focus on one trait at a time. Read descriptions for each score together and ask yes/no questions to develop and assess comprehension.	Allow time for students to read and examine the scoring guide. Encourage them to ask questions. Have partners summarize each trait's key ideas.

ELPS 3D Speak using grade-level content-area vocabulary in context/academic language; **4D** Use prereading supports to enhance comprehension of written text; **4F** Use support from peers and teachers to read content-area text and to enhance and confirm understanding/develop vocabulary; **4G** Demonstrate comprehension of increasingly complex English/responding to questions; **4I** Demonstrate English comprehension by employing basic reading skills

Evaluating an Essay

To support understanding of the following four sample essays—one sample essay for each possible score point—refer to the holistic scoring guide on pages 36–37 and to key instruction from the expository writing chapter.

Score Point 4: Highly Effective

Work through this sample essay with students, pointing out the qualities that earn it an overall score point of 4. In addition to the call-outs on the student pages, use the following questions to facilitate analysis: DIFFERENTIATE INSTRUCTION ↘

- What scientific discovery does this essay describe? *(the discovery of Pluto)*
- Which aspects of the writing make the writer's voice original and authentic? *(The writer presents facts and details in an interesting way by personifying Pluto and by including details about the people involved in its initial discovery.)*

Evaluating an Essay

To learn how to evaluate an essay, you'll use the scoring guide on pages **36–37** and the essays that follow. These essays about scientific discoveries are examples of writing for each score on the scoring guide.

Notice that this first essay received a score of 4. Read the description for a score of 4 on pages **36–37**. Then read the essay. Use the same steps to study the other examples. Always remember to think about the overall quality of the writing.

Writing that fits a score of 4 is very strong.

A Space Oddity?

August 24, 2006: Schoolteachers everywhere awoke to a new directive. Thanks to a vote by the members of the International Astronomic Union, our solar system now consists of not nine planets, but just eight.

Poor, distant Pluto had gotten the boot. Demoted, declassified, and probably demoralized, Pluto was now just a "dwarf planet." However, the story of Pluto's discovery is far too compelling and entertaining to be swept into the cosmos's historical dustbin.

Pluto's tale began with an eccentric Boston aristocrat, Percival Lowell. A skilled mathematician and world traveler, Lowell also held romantic notions about distant worlds. His ideas about the "canals" of Mars and their possible creation by intelligent alien beings attracted some enthusiastic followers, but primarily earned him little more than disdain from serious academics and scholars. Undeterred, he established the Lowell Observatory in Flagstaff, Arizona in 1894 to conduct serious research.

Lowell's unusual ideas also included pursuing the existence of another planet, which he dubbed "Planet X." For eleven years Lowell and his associates toiled fruitlessly in their search. New photographic techniques allowed them to systematically observe the region where Lowell's mathematical calculations led him to believe Planet X would be located. Lowell's death in 1916 stalled the progress of the search, as his widow waged costly legal battles for control of his estate and threatened the future of the observatory.

Introduction clearly states the essay's focus; voice is immediately distinct.

Organizational strategy allows ideas to flow naturally.

Progression of thought is smooth and controlled; voice is confident and assured.

Writing

Transitions are meaningful and strengthen the progression of ideas, which are thorough and specific.

Errors in conventions are few.

Strong details support ideas and retain reader's interest.

Ending is complete; hearkens back to opening ideas but shows implications for the future.

Family ties, however, saved the day. Percival's younger brother happened to also be the president of Harvard University. Through his influence, a new refractor telescope dedicated to the search for Planet X was installed at Lowell Observatory. In a highly unusual move, the director of the observatory hired a farm boy and astronomy fan from Kansas, one Clyde Tombaugh, to man the telescope and continue the search.

Largely self-educated, Tombaugh, just 22, had an impressive bank of astronomical knowledge, and took his job to search for Planet X very seriously. Day in and day out, he compared photographic plates that would show movement that might indicate a planetary body—by his own estimate, Tombaugh had scanned more than 1,500,000 stars before February 18, 1930, when he found what he had been searching for. Planet X did indeed exist!

Announced to the world on March 13, 1930 (not coincidentally also the birthday of Pervical Lowell), Planet X was an immediate sensation, and the name "Pluto" was offered by an 11-year-old girl from England (besting the suggestion of Lowell's widow to use her own name, Constance). The name of the Greek god of the underworld seemed a fitting moniker for the cold, distant planet. The planet's symbol, ♇, happily intertwined Percival Lowell's initials.

And so Pluto enjoyed its new rank for the next 76 years, until it was summarily stripped of its planetary status as being too small, too icy, and too odd, with its orbit tipped out of the plane of the solar system. The IAU determined that because Pluto looks much like other neighboring bodies in the Kuiper belt where it resides, it cannot be rightly classified as a planet.

In 2006, NASA's New Horizons mission launched into space with the express purpose of visiting Pluto and the rest of the Kuiper belt. Set to reach its destination in 2015, New Horizons ensures that Pluto's tumultuous story is far from over.

- What unusual situations does the writer describe in paragraphs 4–6? How do these details engage the reader? *(The writer describes the impact of Mrs. Lowell's "costly legal battles," the influence of "family ties," and the hiring of a "largely self-educated" man to search for Planet X. The details reveal the human side of a scientific discovery.)*

- In what way does the writer connect the essay's conclusion to its introduction? *(The conclusion returns to the idea that despite its interesting discovery, Pluto is no longer considered a planet.)*

Score Point 3: Generally Effective

Work through this sample essay with students, pointing out the qualities that earn it an overall score point of 3. In addition to the call-outs on the student pages, use the following questions to facilitate analysis: **DIFFERENTIATE INSTRUCTION ↘**

- How might the writer have revised the essay's thesis to be less broad than "The contributions of Pierre and Marie Curie … cannot be overstated"? *(The writer could have focused on a single discovery, or on the applications of the Curies' discoveries.)*

- Why is the background information provided in the second paragraph important? *(The background helps readers to understand the state of scientific knowledge at the time and explains why the Curies' discoveries were important.)*

Writing that fits a score of 3 is generally effective.

Focus clearly stated; topic seems a bit broad.

Details provide important background information.

Organization is consistent; writer emphasizes ideas well.

Clear progression of ideas.

Pioneers in Science: Marie and Pierre Curie

The contributions of Marie and Pierre Curie to our understanding of physics and chemistry cannot be overstated. Their work in radiation studies opened doors to new areas of study and knowledge in physics and chemistry. With their colleague, Antoine Henri Becquerel, they received the Nobel Prize in physics in 1903 for their studies in radiation phenomena. In 1911, Marie Curie won the Nobel Prize in chemistry for the discovery of two new elements, radium and polonium.

Advances in science are often built on the work of others, and the Curies were no exception. In December of 1895, a German physicist made the astonishing discovery that what he called X-rays ("X" means "unknown") could move through solid materials and produced the first photographs of living people's bones. Only a few months later, Becquerel made a related discovery and found that uranium compounds also emitted rays, although they were much weaker.

Fascinated by this discovery about uranium compounds, Marie Curie focused her attention on learning more about their rays. She found that the form of the compound didn't matter, that the electrical effects of the rays were always the same. Her findings supported Becquerel's work and went even farther: she suggested that the emission of rays could be an atomic property of the element uranium. This was a shocking idea, because at the time, scientists believed that the atom could not be divided, that it was the primary building block of the universe.

After a long process of testing all the elements, Curie concluded that only certain compounds, like those of uranium, gave off the Becquerel rays. To describe this, she came up with the word "radioactivity." Together, she and Pierre began an ardous process of tracking down radioactive elements. They finally isolated two new elements, radium and polonium, both of which were strong in radioactivity. They then had to present detailed evidence about these elements to the scientific community.

Writing

> **Voice is consistent and authentic; details engage reader.**

That the Curies, while working tirelessly on their projects under extremely difficult circumstances, were also busy teaching and raising a family makes their discoveries all the more remarkable. Their work and schedules did not permit them to attend the 1903 Nobel awards ceremony. Pierre grew increasingly ill as time went on, and then, in 1906, he was killed by a wagon as he was crossing a street.

> **Some ideas not as well developed as others.**

Undaunted by this tragedy, Marie carried on and was granted a position as the first female professor at the Sorbonne in Paris. She also, under nearly unbeatable odds, finally isolated the elements polonium and radium, which in 1911 earned her a second Nobel prize.

> **Use of conventions strong overall; ending includes important ideas but seems rushed.**

The far-ranging applications of the Curies's work are numerous. During World War I, Marie Curie realized the lifesaving possibilities of X-rays during wartime and established mobile radiology units to help doctors treat wounded soldiers. Today, the medical community depends on X-rays in countless settings. Later discoveries about isotopes, the half-life of elements, and even determining the age of the world would not have been possible without the groundbreaking work of Marie and Pierre Curie.

- Why do details about the Curies's family life engage the reader? *(The details about the Curies' family life show some of the challenges they faced at the same time they were conducting their research. Such details help readers to identify with the Curies and allow readers to more fully appreciate their accomplishments.)*

- Do you agree that the writer tried to include too many details in the concluding paragraph? Explain your thinking. *(Possible answer: Yes. Going from World War I to modern day in one sentence is too confusing, and the discoveries cited seem vague.)*

Differentiated Instruction: English Language Learners

⭐ **ELPS** 3J, 4D, 4F, 4K

Before reading the sample essay, provide or elicit background information on basic ideas involved in chemistry and physics.

ELP Level **Beginning**	ELP Level **Intermediate**	ELP Level **Advanced/Advanced High**
Use gestures and visuals such as photographs and objects to make the writing model comprehensible.	Work with students to analyze idioms such as *built on the work of others* and cultural or historical references such as *the Nobel Prize* and *World War I.*	Explain unfamiliar cultural references and complex ideas. Have students analyze how the author organizes the essay.

ELPS 3D Speak using grade-level content area vocabulary in context/new English words; **4D** Use prereading supports to enhance comprehension of written text; **4F** Use visual and contextual supports to read content area text; **4K** Demonstrate English comprehension by employing analytical skills

Score Point 2: Somewhat Effective

Work through this sample essay with students, pointing out the qualities that earn it an overall score point of 2. In addition to the call-outs on the student pages, use the following questions to facilitate analysis: **DIFFERENTIATE INSTRUCTION ↘**

- The writer uses forms of the word *surprise* multiple times in the first two paragraphs. What might the writer have done to avoid this problem? *(The writer could have used synonyms, or combined sentences to avoid some of the repetition.)*
- What organizational pattern might the writer have used to better highlight key ideas in the essay? *(A clear chronological pattern about the discovery and the sequence of events that led to it would highlight key ideas.)*

Writing that fits a score of 2 is somewhat effective.

Icy Surprises

The Census of Marine Life began in 2000. Some scientists working on the Census came back from a 30-day trip recently. They went to study the Arctic Ocean. The scientists were from places like Russia, China, Canada, and the United States. This is a world effort. They were surprised to find that these dark, icy waters have lots of life deep in them. They found new types of jellyfish and worms in this ocean. This was a suprise. They were also surprised to see squid and octopuses. They live in warmer waters.

> *Focuses on one idea, but sentences are not well-developed.*

Why were the researchers surprised? Because this ocean is covered by ice all year and doesn't get much light for a long time. They thought there wouldn't be enough plant life for seafloor animals. Seafloor animals are things like rays and anemones. They thought that a small food supply in the ocean would make it hard for seafloor animals to live. This doesn't seem to be the case.

> *Presents important ideas, but these are impeded by awkward sentences; voice inconsistent.*

The scientists lived in an American icebreaker ship called the Healy. Robot submarines helped them check out the deep waters. These robot submarines were developed to deal with the cold water. They also could deal with the pressure of the deep ocean. They also used sonar to find out the water depth and to find things.

> *Organization needs improvement; needs clearer link to earlier paragraphs.*

The trip was paid for by both government and non-government sources. The scientists learned a lot, especially there is a great deal of life in the icy Artic Ocean! That researchers are learning so much about it is amazing.

> *Ending is contrived; errors in conventions weaken writer's ideas.*

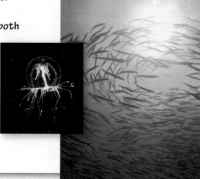

Evaluating Your Writing **43**

Writing

Writing that fits a score of 1 is ineffective.

1

Focus is unclear.

Progression of ideas is unclear; weak connection to prompt.

Gaps in information and errors in conventions make ideas hard to follow or understand.

Ideas seem superficial and are not clearly connected.

Little coherence; errors in conventions and poor organization seriously weaken writing.

Nanotechnology

Around 1950, Buckminster Fuller coined the term geodesic dome for spheres that are made up of many shapes next to each other. Several years later, the chemistry Professor Richard Smalley at Rice Univeristy in Texas won a nobel prize in 1996 when he discovered "fullerenes", which is a new form of carbon. Smalley and his fellow researchers named them after Buckminster Fuler, because they look like his domes.

Today, fullerenes are in what is called nanotechnology. Nano-techmology is making very very small things. They are so small that you can't even see them. They are not atoms. They say a nanometer is about 1/100,000 the with of a human's hair.

But nanotechnology is a hugely growing field today. It can be used in fields like healing cancer. Lots of computers need nanotechnology. Things called nanomateriales are very very strong used in things like bicycles and tennis rackets. They make nanos lightweight and with technologogy.

The states of California, New York, Massachusets and Texas are the leaders using working on nanotechnology all across the USA. Scientists say that nanotechnology was used way back in the 10st century. You couldn't see it, but it was in things like stain glass and other small objects such as like in glass.

Some people are afraid of nanotechnology, because they think it can be harmful to humans. Can you breath in these tiny things? Can they get into humans because they are so small? We don't know for sure yet, so science has to be carful, otherwise humans could lose the battle—not the war. I think nanotechnology is amazing. It will change our city andworld. Doctors will be able to use it to help fight diseases. They can make paper batterys with them, like "fuellerenes." There are to many great things to list!

Score Point 1: Ineffective

Work through this sample essay with students, pointing out the qualities that earn it an overall score point of 1. In addition to the call-outs on the student pages, use the following questions to facilitate analysis:

- Based on the information in the essay, do you think the writer's thesis statement should have focused on the uses of nanotechnology or its discovery? Why? *(Responses will vary. Ask students to explain their thinking.)*

- Which ideas in the essay are most interesting to you? What supporting details might the writer have included to better develop these ideas? *(Possible answer: The use of nanotechnology to heal cancer is interesting. The writer could have developed this idea by explaining a specific treatment as an example, or by citing evidence of lives saved or prolonged through the use of nanotechnology.)*

Differentiated Instruction: English Language Learners

⚡ **ELPS** 3D, 3H, 4F, 4K

Before reading, provide background as needed. Make sure students understand that these essays are examples of ineffective writing.

ELP Level **Beginning**	ELP Level **Intermediate**	ELP Level **Advanced/Advanced High**
Use gestures and visuals such as photographs and objects to make the sample comprehensible. Highlight errors as appropriate.	Use gestures and visuals. Explain unfamiliar idioms (*coined the term*) and cultural references. Encourage students to point out areas that are confusing.	Explain unfamiliar cultural references (*stain glass*). Invite students to explain why the sentences in the first paragraph of "Icy Surprises" are not well developed.

⭐ **ELPS 3D** Speak using grade-level content area vocabulary in context/new English words; **3H** Explain with increasing specificity and detail; **4F** Use visual and contextual supports to read content-area text; **4K** Demonstrate English comprehension by employing analytical skills

Assessing an Expository Essay

Prior to reading the essay, remind students that they will use a holistic scoring guide to give an overall assessment of the writing. Tell students to read the essay through from beginning to end and then jot down any initial impressions. Then list of the five traits of writing—*focus and coherence, organization, development of ideas, voice,* and *conventions*—on the board, and ask students to reread the essay with the traits in mind. DIFFERENTIATE INSTRUCTION ↘

NOTE: In each core unit (narrative, expository, persuasive, and response to literature) there are additional writing models that can be used with students for further assessment practice. Genre-specific checklists allow you and students to rate the writing samples.

Assessing an Expository Essay

Read the essay below, focusing on its strengths and weaknesses. Then follow the directions at the bottom of page 45. **(The essay contains errors.)**

Jim Hamar
Mr. Fremont
English III
November 17, 2011

Ebola: The Scourge of Africa

In 1976, 318 people in one area of the Democratic Republic of the Congo were stricken with a horrific illness; it progressed so rapidly that it had killed 280 of the victims within a few weeks. Scientists named the virus causing the disease after the Ebola River, near where the outbreak occurred. Today, Ebola is known as a deadly viral illness that has no known source and no known cure.

Once a person becomes infected with the virus, there is nothing doctors can do except offer pain relief and life support. In addition, family members caring for the sick person are likely to become ill, too. Direct contact with virus-infected blood or other body fluid leads to contraction of the disease. Unless caretakers take strict precautions, such contact may be hard to avoid; vomiting, diarrhea, and internal and external bleeding are common secondary symptoms. Death is usually 7 to 10 days after symptoms begin: In more than 80 percent of confirmed Ebola cases, the sufferers have died ("Ebola" 36). Four countries in Central Africa have had outbreaks of Ebola (affecting not only human populations but gorilla and chimpanzee populations, as well.) Local health practitioners have had to learn to control the epidemics through the use of basic hygiene practices including masks, goggles, and gloves. Sterilization of needles is, of course, paramount to preventing the spread of the disease. Patients are kept in isolation, and precautions are continued as a corpse is readied for burial.

Differentiated Instruction: Struggling Learners

To support students who find the **Exercise** activity challenging, have them assess the essay with a partner. Have them begin by analyzing the essay for each trait. For example:
"The writer could have developed ideas better by providing more detail about some of the medical terms, such as *contraction* and *sterilization*."

After their review, have partners discuss their comments and decide on an overall score.

Hamar 2

Although the origin of the virus is indefinite, researchers believe that its natural host is an animal native to Africa. How it gets from animal to human is still a mystery, but one hypothesis is that the initial transmission occurs via ingestion—that is, the virus is present in an animal that the victim eats. Some people in central Africa regularly eat fruit bats, and scientists have recently discovered that three species of fruit bats in the region carry the Ebola virus despite showing no symptoms (Lovgren 7). This research is the latest step in understanding of this lethal disease.

Other viral diseases are fatal, too; but what makes Ebola so remarkable is its speed of destruction. It seems to come from nowhere and then just annihilates some small population.

The only hope to avoid more suffering is that science can develop a vaccine or determine the source—and the cure.

Exercise

Assess this expository essay, using the scoring guide on pages **36–37** as your guide. To get started, review the description of holistic scoring on page **34**. *Remember:* Evaluate each trait, and then identify a score that reflects the essay as a whole.

Exercise Answers

To be sure students get the most out of the **Exercise** activity, have them expand their comments with examples from the essay. For example, instead of "The topic is interesting," they might write, "The writer creates interest in the topic, especially at the beginning where he explains how Ebola began." ✔ **DIFFERENTIATE INSTRUCTION**

Have students share their assessments with the class so that you can evaluate how well individual students have grasped the purpose and benefits of holistic scoring.

Differentiated Instruction: English Language Learners

⚡ **ELPS** 3D, 3E, 3G, 4D, 4F, 4K

Before reading the sample essay, provide background information as needed. Make sure students understand that they will evaluate this essay.

ELP Level **Beginning**	ELP Level **Intermediate**	ELP Level **Advanced/Advanced High**
Use gestures and visuals to make the sample comprehensible. Ask yes-no questions as you work together to score the essay.	Use gestures and visuals. Explain unfamiliar idioms and cultural references. Ask for student input as you work together to score the essay.	Explain unfamiliar cultural references. Have students score the essay independently. Then have them share ideas and opinions with a partner.

ELPS 3D Speak using grade-level content area vocabulary in context/ new English words; **3E** Share information in cooperative learning interactions; **3G** Express ideas and opinions; **4D** Use prereading supports to enhance comprehension of written text; **4F** Use visual and contextual supports to read content area text; **4K** Demonstrate English comprehension by employing analytical skills

Understanding the Texas Traits

Understanding the Traits of Writing (pages 47–50)

Students explore the five writing traits and how they work together in the writing process.

Focus and Coherence (pages 51–58)

Students learn how creating a thesis and connecting details to that thesis will make their writing more effective.

Organization (pages 59–66)

Students explore basic methods of organization.

Development of Ideas (pages 67–74)

Students learn how focusing on the best main ideas and details is a key to effective writing.

Voice (pages 75–82)

Students develop an understanding of voice and the practices that will lead to the natural development of their own unique writer's voice.

Conventions (pages 83–89)

Students understand how the proper tools will help them ensure they have the correct grammar, sentence structure, mechanics, and spelling in their writing.

Understanding the Texas Traits Unit Scope and Sequence

| Day | Writing and Conventions Instruction | Write Source Student Edition | | | Daily Language Workouts | Skills-Book | Write Source Online |
		Core Unit	Tools of Language	Resource Units			
1–5	**Understanding the Traits of Writing**	47–50	**TL** 566–567		10–13		
	Focus and Coherence	51–58					
	Organization	59–66					
	Development of Ideas	67–74					
	Voice	75–82					
	Conventions	83–89		**PG** 634–695			

(Week 1)

Resource Units referenced above are located in the back of the *Student Edition* and *Teacher's Edition*
TL *"The Tools of Language"*   **BEW** *"Basic Elements of Writing"*   **PG** *"Proofreader's Guide"*

Writing Focus

- Understanding the Traits of Writing
- Focus and Coherence
- Organization
- Development of Ideas
- Voice
- Conventions

Learning Language

Read aloud the basic and academic terms, as well as descriptions and questions. Model for students how to read one question and answer it. For example, *It says that effective ideas work out as planned, and it's asking what makes a joke effective. Jokes are supposed to be funny, so if a joke is effective, listeners will laugh at it.* Have partners monitor their understanding of the terms by working through the meanings and questions together. **DIFFERENTIATE INSTRUCTION ↘**

ELPS 1F, 2C, 4G

Minilessons

Set the Standard Understanding the Traits of Writing

- Have students **THINK** about a skill, sport, or game that they know well. Ask them to **WRITE** a description of the qualities or traits that make somone good at the skill, sport, or game. Be sure to they **CONSIDER** the mental as well as physical traits involved.

Beyond the Words Voice

- Have students **FIND** a passage from an interesting article, a favorite story, or a play. Ask them to **DECIDE** how the passage would sound if it were read by someone who was bored with it, by someone who thought it was funny, or by someone who was confused by it. Have them **SHARE** their reading with a partner or the class. **ASK** them to suggest the word the describes each reader's "voice."

www.hmheducation.com/tx/writesource

Understanding the Texas Traits

Writing Focus

Learning Language

Work with a partner. Read the meanings and share answers to the questions.

1. **Effective** ideas or plans work as intended.
   What makes a joke effective?
2. A **method** is a plan.
   Describe a studying method.
3. Something **appropriate** fits or seems right.
   What is an appropriate way to act on the bus?
4. Stories with **coherence** are told in a way that makes sense.
   What would a story without coherence be like?
5. When ideas **pan out**, they succeed.
   Tell about an idea that panned out for you.

47

Understanding the Traits of Writing

What makes a great piece of pizza? First of all, it needs to look good, with a golden crust, bubbly cheese, and colorful toppings. Then it needs to smell wonderful: yeasty crust, Italian spices, fragrant cheese . . . Of course, the pizza should be hot and baked to perfection. And last, but certainly not least, it should taste delicious! A great piece of pizza has many traits, but it takes just one bite to discern the quality.

Writing works the same way. A great piece of writing exhibits many essential traits, which a careful reader can recognize after a few paragraphs. These traits include obvious focus and coherence, logical organization, powerfully developed ideas, engaging voice, and clear, correct copy. Skillful writers pay attention to all these traits, just as skillful chefs worry about the look, smell, and taste of their creations.

In this chapter, you'll get a quick overview of the traits of writing, and you'll see how these traits fit into the writing process.

- **Understanding the Traits**
- **Using the Traits**
- **Checklist for Effective Writing**

"I have an 'ideas' file full of newspaper clippings of scientific facts and human interest stories."

—Monica Hughes

Understanding the Traits of Writing

Objectives

- demonstrate an understanding of each of the five traits of effective writing
- apply the concepts of the traits to writing

Point out to students that the ultimate goal of the writer is to communicate effectively with the reader. The traits are the tools they need to succeed. Although some astute readers may be able to recognize the individual writing traits, most readers aren't aware of the attention to detail that goes into producing a successful piece of writing.

Readers simply want a piece of writing to do what it's supposed to do. For example, if it's an explanation, the writing should explain the topic in a clear, interesting, and informative way. Reading a poorly constructed piece of writing is as unsatisfying as listening to a disorganized speaker. Using the five traits of effective writing is the best way to meet readers' expectations.

Differentiated Instruction: English Language Learners

 ELPS 1F, 2A, 2B, 2C

ELP Level **Beginning**	ELP Level **Intermediate**	ELP Level **Advanced/Advanced High**
Provide synonyms or phrases, such as *effective: works well,* and *appropriate: seems right.* Have partners practice pronouncing and writing each term.	Have students listen for long, short, and schwa vowel sounds as you read each term aloud. Then have partners practice pronouncing the terms.	Invite partners to clarify word meanings for each other. Students can complete sentence stems or use complete sentences in their responses.

 ELPS 1F Use accessible language and learn new and essential language in the process; **2A** Distinguish sounds and intonation patterns of English; **2B** Recognize elements of the English sound system in newly acquired vocabulary; **2C** Learn new basic and academic vocabulary

Understanding the Traits

Give students time to read the trait descriptions. Answer any questions that they have and assure them that they will receive extensive instruction and practice in using the traits.

Focus and Coherence

Ask what problems unnecessary or irrelevant details in writing might cause.

Organization

Elicit students' ideas about ways to organize a piece of writing.

Development of Ideas

Draw attention to the phrase "heart of writing" and ask students to explain what it means.

Voice

Discuss the differences in voice that might be found in funny story and an essay for a history class.

Conventions

Ask students why conventions are usually addressed at the end of the writing process.

Try It!
Answers

Before asking students to do the **Try It!** activity, encourage them to recall specific feedback that they have received from teachers and peers about their writing.

Suggest that students write their reflection for the **Try It!** activity in their writer's notebook. Tell them to bookmark the page, and suggest that they return to it throughout the year to see if they would answer these questions differently as they explore more types of writing.

`DIFFERENTIATE INSTRUCTION ↘`

Understanding the Traits

Throughout this book, you'll use certain traits to make your writing the best it can be. Here is a brief description of each of those traits. As you read, think about how each trait can help to contribute to the overall impression that you make in a piece of writing.

Focus and Coherence

Writing that has **focus and coherence** has a thesis, or controlling idea. All of the main supporting points and details relate to this thesis. No extraneous or unnecessary information is included.

Organization

Organization refers to the way your writing begins, the order of the ideas in the middle, and the way your writing ends. By using logic and transitions, you can lead your reader step by step through your ideas.

Development of Ideas

The **development of ideas** in your writing is the way you present supporting points and clarifying details to help readers understand the point you want to make. These ideas are the heart of writing—the message you want to communicate to your reader.

Voice

Your writing **voice** reflects your personality, your feelings about the topic, your purpose in writing, and your relationship with the reader. Voice can be bubbly or angry, hopeful or sarcastic, formal or casual.

Conventions

Conventions are the rules of punctuation, capitalization, spelling, and grammar. Once upon a time, the rules of writing were taught as writing itself. Now, the rules are a separate consideration, especially important near the end of the writing process.

Try It!

Reflect on the traits by answering the following questions:

1. Which trait is strongest in my writing? Explain.
2. Which trait is weakest in my writing? Explain.

Using the Traits

Since no one can focus on all of the traits at once, different traits are important at different stages in the writing process.

Prewriting

Focus and Coherence	Select a topic, gather details, choose your focus (thesis), and decide on main points.
Organization	Write your thesis statement and topic sentences, decide on a method of organization, and create a list or an outline.

Drafting

Development of Ideas	Connect all your ideas and details.
Organization	Write a beginning, a middle, and an ending, using the plan you have made.
Voice	Use a voice appropriate to your personality, topic, purpose, and reader.

Revising

Focus and Coherence	Make sure your introduction and conclusion introduce and reinforce your thesis. Remove unnecessary details.
Organization	Check the order and unity of your paragraphs.
Development of Ideas	Add details that clarify your meaning or provide background information.
Voice	Adjust your voice as needed.

Editing, Proofreading, and Publishing

Conventions	Edit your work for punctuation, capitalization, spelling, grammar, and format.

Try It!

Answer the following questions:

1. Which traits get the most attention early in the process? Why?
2. Which traits get the most attention later in the process? Why?

Traits

Using the Traits

Make sure students understand that although they may focus on a few traits during each step of the writing process, this doesn't mean that they should completely ignore the other traits. For example, although the chart shows that it is important to check for focus and coherence during revising, it is still important to pay attention to focus and coherence during the drafting stage. However, at that point, they shouldn't agonize over focus and coherence to such a degree that it inhibits the flow of ideas.

Try It!
Answers

1. Development of ideas, organization, and voice are applied early in the process because these traits help the writer communicate ideas about the topic.
2. Focus and coherence and conventions get more attention later in the process to ensure that main points have been made in a clear and accurate way. These traits help the writer present ideas in the most understandable way for the reader.

Differentiated Instruction: English Language Learners

ELPS 1B, 1E, 4F, 4K

ELP Level **Beginning**	ELP Level **Intermediate**	ELP Level **Advanced/Advanced High**
Focus on one trait at a time, using simplified language, gestures, and objects. Have students confirm understanding by completing oral sentences.	Ask yes/no questions to discuss each trait. Have students describe their writing strengths and weaknesses as well as self-correcting techniques by completing sentence frames.	Provide sentence stems for students to discuss their own writing. Tell them to save their sentences as way to monitor their writing production.

 ELPS 1B Monitor written language production and employ self-corrective techniques or other resources; **1E** Internalize new basic and academic language by using and reusing it/speaking; **4F** Use visual and contextual support to enhance and confirm understanding; **4K** Demonstrate English comprehension and expand reading skills by employing analytical skills

Checklist for Effective Writing

Encourage students to bookmark this page and to use it to check the effectiveness of all their writing.

Traits Checklist

Point out that throughout the book, students will be using revising and editing checklists similar to this one. Although the questions in the checklists are phrased for "yes" or "no" answers, the checklists are helpful only if students

- give each question careful thought,
- respond honestly,
- can support their "yes" answers with clear examples from their writing, and
- use the "no" answers to improve their writing.

DIFFERENTIATE INSTRUCTION ⟩

✱ Have students turn to SE pages 143 and 145 in the Narrative unit to see an example of a revising checklist and an editing checklist.

50

Checklist for Effective Writing

If a piece of writing meets the following standards, it exhibits the traits of effective writing. Check your work using these standards.

Traits Checklist

Focus and Coherence

_____ 1. Is there a thesis, or controlling statement?
_____ 2. Is there a specific focus and purpose throughout?
_____ 3. Do all of details support the thesis?

Organization

_____ 4. Is there a clear beginning, middle, and ending?
_____ 5. Are the details arranged in the best order to support the focus?
_____ 6. Do transitions and key words connect the ideas?

Development of Ideas

_____ 7. Is the topic interesting?
_____ 8. Are ideas described with unique and thoughtful details?
_____ 9. Do a variety of details support the focus?

Voice

_____ 10. Does the writing sound natural?
_____ 11. Does the voice fit the topic and the purpose?
_____ 12. Is the voice appropriate for the audience?

Conventions

_____ 13. Does the work follow the rules of punctuation, capitalization, spelling, and grammar?
_____ 14. Is the work presented in a clear, correct format?

51

Focus and Coherence

Imagine that a friend is telling you that she just saw a great new movie. She begins to describe the characters and the story but then explains that she encountered an awfully long line at the theater's snack counter. She gets back to telling you about the movie but is soon sidetracked with details about a TV show that one of the movie's stars appeared in. She finishes by pointing out that she didn't really enjoy the movie. At this point, you're totally confused! Did she like it or didn't she? Which events were part of the movie, and which are part of the TV show or your friend's experience at the theater?

Your confusion is understandable because your friend's story did not focus on her main point. Many of the details she included did not relate to her main idea—her opinion of the movie. The same types of problems can happen when you are writing if you are not careful. The information in this chapter will help you learn to focus on the controlling idea, or thesis, of your writing and make sure that all the details you include are connected to that main idea.

- **Focusing**
- **Ensuring Completeness**
- **Writing a Focused Introduction**
- **Writing a Focused Conclusion**
- **Using Effective Support**

"Say all you have to say in the fewest possible words, or your reader will be sure to skip them."

—John Ruskin

Focus and Coherence

Objectives
- learn how to respond to a writing prompt in a focused way
- understand the importance of ensuring completeness in writing
- learn how to write a strong introduction and conclusion

Write the expression "Less is more" on the board, and then have a student read aloud the quotation by John Ruskin. Discuss why readers might be inclined to skip sections of piece of writing if a writer doesn't make his or her point in "the fewest possible words."

Ask students if they have ever felt the need to "pad" a piece of writing with additional sentences or paragraphs to fill a page or to reach an assigned length. Point out that unless such additions add depth or dimension to the piece of writing, they only serve to confuse or bore readers.

The **Try It!** activities on SE pages 52–58 will help your students consider the elements that give their writing focus and coherence.

Differentiated Instruction: English Language Learners

ELPS 1B, 4I

ELP Level **Beginning**	ELP Level **Intermediate**	ELP Level **Advanced/Advanced High**
Focus on one trait at a time. Read aloud each question and clarify its meaning. Invite students to demonstrate comprehension by answering each question with you.	Have students read the questions aloud. Guide them to see that they can monitor their writing production by using the questions to help them self-correct a piece of writing.	Have partners read aloud the questions. Then have them use complete sentences to discuss what they can do to self-correct if they answered *no* to any of the questions.

ELPS 1B Monitor written language production and employ self-corrective techniques or other resources; **4I** Demonstrate English comprehension by employing basic reading skills and expanding reading skills

Focusing

Lead students to understand that the time to start thinking about how to give their writing focus and coherence is before they write a single word. Explain that when they are planning a first draft, analyzing a given prompt and developing a thesis statement will provide the criteria that will help them decide what does and doesn't belong in a piece of writing.

DIFFERENTIATE INSTRUCTION ⟍

⭐ TEKS 11.13A

Try It!
Answers

Remind students to use the questions provided on page 52 to analyze the prompt before creating a thesis statement. After partners have had a chance to discuss and analyze the prompt, have them share their ideas and opinions with the class. As needed, point out that a variety of genres might be appropriate for the prompt, including a personal reflection, a narrative, or a persuasive essay.

⭐ ELPS 3E, 3G

52

⭐ TEKS 11.13A
ELPS 3E, 3G

"Words—so innocent and powerless as they are, as standing in a dictionary, how potent for good and evil they become in the hands of one who knows how to combine them."

—Nathaniel Hawthorne

Focusing

There are times when it's appropriate to freewrite about a topic using any idea that comes into your head. There are times when you can explore your feelings, figuring out those feelings as you write. Both can be appropriate, depending on your purpose for writing. However, for a writing assignment with a specific prompt, different rules apply. For that kind of writing you need to focus.

What is focus? When you write with focus, you zero in on a main idea, and every detail you include has a clear connection to that main idea. You might compare focused writing to a bicycle wheel—it has a hub (or main idea) at the center, with spokes (or details) connecting the hub to the outer rim and the tire. The parts work together to allow a bicycle to move (or to get your writing where it needs to go). The following guidelines will help you learn about focusing.

Study the prompt. Look at the specifics in your writing assignment:

- Are you given a topic, or can you make a choice?
- What genre will you write? Is it a story, an essay, or another type?
- What verbs are used? Should you explain, describe, or convince?

FYI

You often have choices to make when you are given a writing prompt, so read with an open mind, knowing there are many ways to respond correctly. Look for the "must-haves" in the prompt before you make your choices.

Develop a thesis, or controlling idea. Decide on the main point you want to make, or how you will answer the question in the prompt. Each sentence that you write should contribute to making that main point or answering that question.

Try It!

Think about this prompt: What is the best possible way to spend a summer day? Analyze the prompt with a partner, using the guidelines above. Then agree on a thesis on which to base a response. Be prepared to explain your choices.

Differentiate Instruction: Advanced Learners

Direct students' attention to the quotation by Nathaniel Hawthorne. Ask them to discuss how it relates to the concept of focus and coherence in writing. Suggest that they write a short response in their writer's notebooks about the power of words "in the hands of one who knows how to combine them."

Think about what fits. As you gather information and ideas for your writing, consider how each new idea connects to your thesis. Look for background information that readers might need to understand your main point. Consider whether each new piece of information is logically connected to your thesis or whether it is simply something you find interesting, funny, or alarming.

Connect the puzzle pieces. You may know that all the puzzle pieces in a box fit together, but the puzzle is far from finished until you actually link those pieces correctly. It's the same with your writing. A list of details is a start, but once you have gathered all that information and all those ideas, you need to put them together in a way that makes sense.

Introduce the idea. The introduction to a piece of writing is the key to capturing a reader's interest, but it is also the place to show a reader that you have a point to make and are knowledgeable about the topic.

Have a strong conclusion. Writing with a strong finish makes an impression on readers. It is the writer's last chance to restate to the main point, to summarize the main idea, to highlight why all the details lead inescapably to the writer's thesis.

Traits

Try It!

Look at the prompt in the Try It! activity on page 52. Work with a partner to brainstorm details to include, and discuss how to present those details.

"A strange thing happens when you write: you discover what you truly think; you find out what your heart means."

—Shirley Rousseau Murphy

Point out that the introduction and conclusion of a good piece of writing are like bookends that hold the middle paragraphs together. Discuss with students the role of a clear, focused introduction and a strong conclusion in giving a piece of writing coherence.

TEKS 11.13A

Try It!
Answers

Tell students to review the genre and thesis statement they chose for the prompt on SE page 52. Give partners time to brainstorm ideas, and then remind them to choose those that are most closely related to their thesis statement. Point out that if they are not able to explain how a detail relates to the thesis, that detail should not be included. Invite partners to share their ideas with the class. DIFFERENTIATE INSTRUCTION

ELPS 3E, 3G

Differentiated Instruction: English Language Learners		ELPS 3E, 3G, 4F
ELP Level Beginning	**ELP Level Intermediate**	**ELP Level Advanced/Advanced High**
Read the prompt aloud and have students repeat it with you. Use photos and other visuals to generate and label ideas and details they could use.	Use photos and other visuals to generate ideas and details. Provide sentence stems to help students express their opinions, ideas, and feelings	Have partners work together to create a graphic organizer that looks like a bike wheel, with the main idea at the hub, and details radiating out, like spokes.

TEKS **11.13A** Plan a first draft by developing a thesis or controlling idea; ELPS **3E** Share information in cooperative learning interactions; **3G** Express opinions, ideas, and feelings; **4F** Use visual and contextual support and support from peers and teachers to develop vocabulary

Ensuring Completeness

Tell students that in order to structure their ideas in a sustained and persuasive way, they need to be sure they have included all of the information readers need. Explain that one typical problem happens when a writer assumes that readers have all of the same background knowledge as he or she does. This might happen when a writer has done extensive research on a topic and has become so familiar with the basics that he or she forgets to define terms or explain connections or relationships. When writers assume these types of prior knowledge, readers are left with a feeling that information is missing.

TEKS 11.13B

Learning Language

Point out that an apple may seem complete without its stem or core, since most people focus on the parts that can be eaten. Write the words *part* and *whole* on the board and encourage partners to use them as they discuss other examples. Students may suggest other whole/part examples such as a *book* (*pages, words, chapters, covers*); *school* (*floor, roof, stairs, classrooms, gym, library*); and *park* (*trees, grass, bushes, benches, walking paths, swings, slides*).

DIFFERENTIATE INSTRUCTION ↘

ELPS 4C

Ensuring Completeness

You notice it when it feels like something is missing in your day. Do you feel like a meal is not complete until you have bite of something sweet? Are you one of those people who has to begin the day by reading a newspaper or by watching the morning news on TV? Does your day not seem quite right unless you take an early-morning run, or perhaps check in with friends online?

Good writing also needs a sense of completeness. Writing should present a complete whole in which all ideas clearly connect to each other and to the main idea. Use these hints to ensure completeness in your writing.

Sleep on it. One of the best ways to review your writing is to leave it alone—but just overnight. When you reread your writing after you have been away from it for a day you are more likely to notice that key pieces of information are missing or that the connections between ideas are unclear.

Check with peers. Your favorite books and stories didn't go directly from the author's desk to your library shelf. Authors almost always get comments on their writing from friends, family members, or editors. When you ask someone to read over a piece of writing, their questions will help you figure out if you have been successful in linking ideas in a clear and coherent way or if you have left anything out.

Read it out loud. Become an audience of one as you read your piece of writing aloud. Listen for gaps, or bits of information that you thought you had included but didn't. Try to imagine the questions you would ask or what you would want to know more about. Your questions are clues that the writing may not have a sense of completeness.

Learning Language

One way to understand the idea of completeness is to think about the idea of a whole and its parts. For example, an apple is a whole. Its parts are the core, stem, skin, and flesh. Work with a partner to discuss whether the apple would seem complete if any parts were missing. Then brainstorm other examples of a whole and its parts.

TEKS **11.13B** Structure ideas in a sustained and persuasive way; **ELPS** **4C** Develop basic sight vocabulary and comprehend English vocabulary

TEKS 11.13B

Writing a Focused Introduction

The introduction to a piece of writing has a big job to do. It must capture the readers' interest, make the subject and purpose of the writing clear, and establish that the writer has an important point to make. These suggestions will help you to write a focused introduction:

Capture Readers' Interest

- Begin with an intriguing question that has no obvious answer. Make readers want to continue reading to discover your answer.
- Start with a brief anecdote that describes an unusual situation or a complex issue.
- Make a startling or unexpected statement.

Make the Subject and Purpose Clear

- Include a thesis statement that makes your main idea clear.
- Let readers know in the middle section of your piece of writing what you intend to do. Make it clear if you intend to
  —explain why something happened,
  —describe how something came to be,
  —compare and contrast ideas,
  —or persuade readers to share your opinion.
- Use transitional words and phrases to connect the sentences in your introduction. This kind of coherent writing will help readers move smoothly from one thought to the next and prepare them to follow the ideas that are in the middle section of your piece of writing.

Establish the Writer's Main Point

- Position your thesis statement near the beginning or end of your introduction to highlight its importance.
- Repeat key words at the beginning and end of the introduction to emphasize your main point.

Try It!

Look back at the introductions you wrote for your last few writing assignments. Choose one that you think could be improved and use the hints on this page to rewrite it.

Traits

Writing a Focused Introduction

Select, or have students select, examples of introductions in a variety of writing forms. In addition to fiction and nonfiction literature, look for interesting introductions in newspaper and magazine articles and on a variety of Web sites. Analyze the examples to see which of the hints provided on SE page 55 have been applied.

Capture Readers' Interest

Encourage students to use the hints to suggest ways that one or more of the examples might be improved.

Make the Subject and Purpose Clear

Explain that clarity in the introduction engages readers by letting them know what to expect.

Establish the Writer's Main Point

Tell students that a clear thesis statement shows that a writer is aware of and focused on the topic.

 TEKS 11.13B

Try It!
Answers

Have students share the before-and-after versions of their writing and explain how they decided which hints were most useful for a particular piece of writing. Have them provide examples of combined sentences and transitions.

ELPS 5F

Differentiated Instruction:
English Language Learners

ELPS 4C, 4F

ELP Level **Beginning**	ELP Level **Intermediate**	ELP Level **Advanced/Advanced High**
Use a classroom example, such as a clock, to guide students to identify a whole and its parts. Have students point to the different parts and name them with you.	Invite students to generate ideas of classroom- or school-related examples of a whole and its parts. Provide sentences frames for students to record the examples.	Have partners examine a class text or reference book and work together to identify its parts. Have them describe their ideas to the class.

 TEKS **11.13B** Structure ideas in a sustained and persuasive way; **ELPS** **4C** Develop basic sight vocabulary and comprehend English vocabulary and language structures; **4F** Use visual and contextual support to develop vocabulary; **5F** Write using a variety of grade-appropriate sentence lengths, sentence patterns, and connecting words

Writing a Focused Conclusion

Explain that in order for the conclusion of a piece of writing to connect with rest of the text, it needs a clear link to what came before it. Work with students to brainstorm transition words and phrases for each of the following types of writing.

- a story or essay about a sequence of events
- a cause-effect essay
- a problem-solution essay
- a descriptive essay about a work of art

 11.13B

Try It!
Answers

1. b (These transitions are used to show how things are alike.)
2. a (These transitions are used to show chronological order, often used in personal narratives.)
3. d (These transitions are used to show order of importance, an organizing plan frequently used to build an argument in persuasive writing.)
4. c (These transitions show position or placement of things when using spatial order.)

DIFFERENTIATE INSTRUCTION ⬊

Writing a Focused Conclusion

In a focused conclusion you can restate your thesis and explain why the details you've presented support it. To do that, your conclusion should flow logically from the ideas presented in the introduction and in the middle of your writing. In other words, your writing needs coherence that allows readers to move smoothly from the early sections to the conclusion. These ideas will help you maintain focus and coherence in your writing.

Transitional words and phrases can connect the middle section of your piece of writing to the conclusion, as shown by the words in blue in these examples.

> Jack's cause in *The Lord of the Flies* is a noble one: to purify the world of evil. However, as the details presented in this paper show, he goes about looking for the beast in all the wrong places.

> Early in the summer, the first sign of the oil crisis appeared. It showed up in the front windows of gasoline stations across the land: "Closed." And they were...

> Later in the year, the reality of the crisis really hit home. A mandatory fuel allocation program was announced to take effect within 30 days. It called for ...

> By the end of 1973, even a six-gallon ration was too much to expect. It was in November that Arab oil-producing nations cut off oil...

Repeating a key word is another way to make clear connections between ideas.

> ... Most farmers in the market for new irrigation equipment are buying efficient, environmentally friendly systems.

> These systems have done much to reduce the amount of water used by wheat farmers....

Try It!

Review the following sets of related transitions. Identify which set of transitions you would use to connect ideas in the essays listed below.

a. First   Then   Next   In the end

b. In the same way   Also   Similarly

c. Above   Below   To the left   To the right

d. First of all   Additionally   Most importantly

_____**1.** Comparing two unique polititians

_____**2.** Sharing a life-changing experience

_____**3.** Arguing for a remodeled school theater

_____**4.** Describing a striking new monument

Using Effective Support

There are many types of details you can include in your writing. Your main idea, or thesis, plus the genre you are writing determines which details will maintain your focus. The key types are explained below and on the following page.

Facts are *details* that can be proven.

> The construction of the Panama Canal greatly decreased the number of cargo ships that traveled around Cape Horn.
>
> *The Jazz Singer,* which opened on October 6, 1927, in New York, was the first motion picture to use dialogue as part of the movie's action.

Statistics present *numerical information* about a specific topic.

> According to the American Academy of Allergy, Asthma, and Immunology (AAAAI), 12.8 million school days are missed annually due to asthma.
>
> Russ McCurdy, the coach with the most wins in NCAA Women's Ice Hockey, holds a record of 264 wins, 36 losses, and 10 ties in 15 years of coaching for New Hampshire.

Examples are *statements that illustrate a main point.*

> Different breeds of horses exhibit distinct characteristics, developed either purposefully or randomly through generations (main point). For example, Morgan horses are known for their power and stamina in either working or racing, and Arabians are prized for their graceful, arched necks and delicately shaped heads. While these characteristics were carefully cultivated in the breeds, no one really knows where the Bashkir Curly got its distinctive curly coat.

Anecdotes are *brief stories* that help to make a point about a topic. Because they are usually very engaging, they are much more effective than a matter-of-fact list of details.

> It's difficult to pigeonhole gender roles in today's world, and even more so when both partners have powerhouse careers. Bob Dole was an important and powerful senator from Kansas when, in 1985, his wife, Elizabeth, was appointed secretary of transportation in President Reagan's cabinet. Magazines had a field day following the pair, and one ran a photo of them working together to make their bed at home. Afterward, the senator received a humorous letter from a man complaining that he should stop doing work around the house, as he was creating some problems for men around the country.
>
> "You don't know the half of it," Senator Dole wrote back. "The only reason she was helping was because they were taking pictures."

Traits

Using Effective Support

Tell students they will learn how to select appropriate supporting details later in this unit. Their book also provides instruction for using graphic organizers to gather details for every type of writing. These organizers help writers to structure their ideas in a sustained and persuasive way.

⭐ **TEKS** 11.13B

Explain that even though the anecdote about Bob and Elizabeth Dole is factual, the writer applies narrative techniques to tell the story. Have students point out the elements used in the anecdote that help make it an engaging story. (Possible responses: interesting characters, dialogue, humorous, unexpected ending)

Point out that the need for examples or anecdotes that will clarify meaning often becomes apparent during the revising stage of writing. Ask students to suggest examples of this situation from their own writing experiences.

⭐ **TEKS** 11.13C

Differentiated Instruction: English Language Learners

⭐ **ELPS** 1H, 4F, 4J, 4K

ELP Level **Beginning**	ELP Level **Intermediate**	ELP Level **Advanced/Advanced High**
Use gestures and visuals to help students see how the words in each set of transitions are related. Have them practice saying and writing transition words.	Guide students to read aloud each set of transition words and infer how they are related. Provide sentence stems to help students complete the activity.	Have partners analyze how the transition words in each set are related. Then have students use complete sentences to connect the words to the essay ideas.

TEKS **11.13B** Structure ideas in a sustained and persuasive way; **11.13C** Revise drafts to clarify meaning; **ELPS1H** Expand repertoire of learning strategies; **4F** Use visual and contextual support to develop grasp of language structures; **4J** Demonstrate English comprehension and expand reading skills by employing inferential skills; **4K** Demonstrate English comprehension by employing analytical skills

Try It!
Answers

Suggest that to find examples, students should refer to the table of contents. Possible answers:

- **Facts:** On December 7, 1941, Japan attacked the U.S. naval base at Pearl Harbor. (p. 219)
- **Statistics:** By late 2006, the national debt had risen to almost $9 trillion . . . (p. 230)
- **Examples:** Some designs for green homes and businesses incorporate on-site energy generation technologies such as solar panels or windmills. (pp. 172–173)
- **Anecdote:** One day in second grade, Harpo got thrown out the window and simply walked away, never returning to school again. (p. 308)
- **Quotation:** "And the rock gym is a great way to get a taste of the thrills of ice climbing without so much risk." (p. 161)
- **Definition:** The national debt is the difference over the years between the money the government collects in taxes and the money it spends. (p. 229)
- **Reason:** A high debt makes the United States less economically competitive. (p. 231)
- **Comparison:** Gasoline-electric hybrids and fuel-cell cars have a number of structural and operational similarities. (p. 200)

DIFFERENTIATE INSTRUCTION ↘

Quotations are *people's statements* repeated word for word. Quotations can provide powerful supporting evidence.

> Sometimes a funny statement can also be a chilling wake-up call. For example, comedian Robert Orben once observed, "There's so much pollution in the air now that if it weren't for our lungs there'd be no place to put it all." We laugh at this idea, but when we actually think about it, the statement is downright frightening.

Definitions give the *meaning* of unfamiliar terms. Definitions of technical terms are especially important for the reader. Defining such terms makes your writing clear.

> **Casein paint,** a milk-based artist's medium, **was used by early Egyptians and was even found in 9,000-year-old cave drawings.**

Reasons answer *why* and can explain or justify ideas.

> **We need to preserve the South American rain forest.** The rain forest is home to many unusual species of animals, birds, and insects that could become extinct if the forest is destroyed. In addition, the rain forest prevents the land from eroding away and also plays a vital role in human health. **Many medicines are continually being discovered or developed from the forest's plants and animals.** Most importantly, the rain forest plays an important role in maintaining the delicate ecological balance of the world. **Without the oxygen and water produced by the rain forest, weather patterns will probably change, wreaking havoc around the globe.**

Comparisons address the *similarities* or *differences* between two things. It is especially helpful to compare something new or unknown to something your reader understands.

> Not all vegetarians are alike. While ovo-lacto vegetarians and vegans may seem the same, they have some differences. Those who follow an ovo-lacto diet avoid eating meat or meat products, although they do include dairy products and eggs in their diets. Vegans not only skip the meat, they also avoid dairy products and eggs. While ovo-lacto vegetarians will use animal products such as leather, vegans avoid anything made from or by an animal, including leather, silk, or even honey. Both groups maintain the philosophy of animal dignity, but their approach to the subject varies.

Try It!

Find examples of writing in this book that show four of the detail types explained on the previous two pages. On your own paper, write the examples and the pages on which you found them.

Organization

Organization becomes important when, and only when, you have an intriguing idea that prompts you to write. Writers and teachers Dan Kirby and Tom Liner state, "A subject often seeks its own form," meaning that once you have a writing idea in mind, a method of organization often becomes clear early in the writing process.

For example, when you have a personal story to tell, you will naturally recall the key details chronologically. Or when a short story idea pops into your head, you will almost automatically envision the main character and establish his or her conflict. This is the way writing should work: You start out, knowing you will find an appropriate structure or shape for your ideas.

On the other hand, you don't want to become trapped by a basic structure or pattern of organization. According to Kirby and Liner, that makes writing a "cookie cutter operation." Formulas and patterns are indispensable for mathematicians; not so for writers. Writing is often more engaging or compelling when it blazes an unpredictable path.

This chapter provides background information about the basic methods of organization. Use this information as a helpful starting point when you develop different types of writing.

- **Understanding the Big Picture**
- **Following the Thesis Statement's Lead**
- **Using a Logical Progression of Ideas**
- **Using Graphic Organizers**
- **Transitions**

"Good writing cannot be a cookie cutter operation."
—Dan Kirby and Tom Liner

Objectives
- demonstrate an understanding of the basic structure of an essay
- identify organizing patterns
- create a logical progression of ideas
- learn about using graphic organizers
- identify transitions that support organizing patterns

Emphasize that whenever students are assigned writing such as an article, an essay, or a research report, the guidelines for the assignment will probably indicate its organization.

Understanding the Big Picture

The remaining pages in this section focus on applying the trait of organization to informational writing. Lead students to explain how understanding organizational patterns will help them to write in a sustained way. Explain that while there are many organizing patterns, most writing forms include a beginning, a middle section, and an ending.

TEKS 11.13B

Try It!
Answers

You may wish to model finding the beginning, middle, and ending of an essay for the class. Then have small groups or partners follow a similar procedure with an essay of their own choosing. **DIFFERENTIATE INSTRUCTION ↘**

60

TEKS 11.13B

Understanding the Big Picture

The basic structure of informational writing is quite simple. Essays, articles, and reports contain three main parts: the *beginning,* the *middle,* and the *ending.* Each part plays an important role in an effective piece of writing.

> **Beginning** The opening paragraph should capture the reader's attention and state your thesis. Here are some ways to capture your reader's attention.
> - Tell a dramatic or exciting story (anecdote) about the topic.
> - Ask an intriguing question or two.
> - Provide a few surprising facts or statistics.
> - Introduce an interesting quotation.
> - Explain your personal experience or involvement with the topic.

> **Middle** The middle paragraphs should support your thesis statement. For example, in an essay about improved safety in Grand Prix racing, each middle paragraph would focus on one main aspect of improved safety. (An outline will help you write this section. See pages **174, 230,** and **591.**)

> **Ending** The closing paragraph should summarize your thesis and leave the reader with something to think about. Here are some strategies for creating a strong closing.
> - Review your main points.
> - Emphasize the special importance of one main point.
> - Answer any questions the reader may still have.
> - Draw a conclusion and put the information in perspective.
> - Provide a final significant thought for the reader.

Try It!

As a class or in a small group, discuss one of the essays in this book. Focus your remarks on the development of the three main parts.

Following the Thesis Statement's Lead

Once you have a thesis statement, a logical pattern of organization for writing usually reveals itself. As the chart below shows, some of these patterns are specific and others are more general. Knowing how these patterns work will help you plan and organize your essays.

Using Organizing Patterns

Essay Types	Organizing Patterns
Process How something works	Chronological order
Narrative How something happened	Chronological order
Description How something/someone appears	Spatial order
Comparison How two things are alike/different	Whole vs. whole/point by point
Cause-effect How one thing affects something else	Identify cause/explore effects Identify effect/explore causes
Problem-solution How a problem can be solved	Study the problem/solutions
Classification How something can be categorized	Name categories/examine each one
Argumentation How a position or an opinion can be asserted and supported	State an opinion/support it/ consider the opposing point of view/restate the opinion

Traits

Try It!

For each assignment listed below, identify the organizing pattern that you would use to develop your writing.

1. A history paper pointing out the results of the Missouri Compromise
2. An economics paper arguing for or against a flat tax
3. An art paper describing a Van Gogh painting
4. A personal narrative detailing a life-changing experience
5. A science paper explaining how a tsunami develops

Following the Thesis Statement's Lead

Work with students to brainstorm examples of each essay type shown in the chart on SE page 61. Have students explain why the suggested organizing pattern is appropriate for each example.

⭐ **TEKS** 11.13B

Using Organizing Patterns

Before assigning the **Try It!** activity, work as a class to discuss the organizing pattern students would use to develop a piece of writing for each of the topics listed on SE page 69 under the "Expository" and "Persuasive" heads.

Try It!
Answers

1. cause-effect
2. argumentation
3. description
4. narrative
5. process

⭐ **TEKS** **11.13B** Structure ideas in a sustained and persuasive way; **ELPS** **2C** Learn new academic vocabulary; **3D** Speak using grade-level content area vocabulary in context/academic language; **3J** Respond orally to information presented/concept attainment

Differentiated Instruction: English Language Learners

⭐ **ELPS** 2C, 3D, 3J

ELP Level **Beginning**	ELP Level **Intermediate**	ELP Level **Advanced/Advanced High**
Choose an essay, and point out and describe the beginning, the thesis statement, the middle, and the ending. Have students repeat these terms with you.	Help students choose an essay. Provide sentence stems to help students discuss its organization and practice using content-area vocabulary.	Help students choose an essay. Have partners identify how it is organized and identify the beginning, the thesis statement, the middle, and the ending.

Using a Logical Progression of Ideas

Tell students that the chart on SE page 61 is useful for choosing an overall pattern of organization. Explain that the ideas presented on SE pages 62–63 offer more specific descriptions for organizing a piece of writing.

What's the Point?

As you discuss each description, ask students to give examples of writing assignments for which they used that progression of ideas. Have them explain whether the piece of writing was effective, and describe why.

Timing Is Everything

Ask students to suggest why the use of chronological order was one of the first organizing patterns they learned when they began to write.

Just the Facts

Remind students that the main idea of a paragraph is often stated in the first sentence. Prompt students to suggest why that placement results in a logical progression of ideas.

Problem-Solving Skills

Have students explain why the description of a problem helps readers to understand possible solutions.

What You See Is What You Get

Ask students to describe a flower, a building, and a person, using each of the strategies suggested. Discuss what makes each description effective.

TEKS 11.13B

Using a Logical Progression of Ideas

Good writers use a logical arrangement of ideas so that each sentence and each paragraph builds on the one before it. Each new idea lays the groundwork so that later ideas make sense. This logical progression of ideas allows readers to follow the ideas in a piece of writing, but it can also help you as a writer by providing a template or outline for your writing.

What's the Point?

You have a point to make with your thesis statement. How will you make that point? What will your starting point be, and where will you go from there? Use the following hints to create a logical progression of ideas in your writing.

Timing Is Everything

When you have a story or a series of events to describe, it usually makes sense to start at the beginning and tell the events in the order that they happen. Similarly, if you are describing a process—how to do something or how something works—it is best to state what happens first, next, and so on, until the final step.

Just the Facts

Much of the writing you do in school involves stating a main idea and explaining the details that support that main idea. When all of your details are of roughly equal importance, introduce them in an order that makes sense to you, and help readers understand your choices by using transition words and phrases that link the details.

Problem-Solving Skills

Have you ever been given the solution on a math test and been told to figure out what the problem was? It's tough! To prevent that problem when writing, it makes sense to state the problem before you begin describing a solution.

What You See Is What You Get

When you write a description, whether of a flower, a building, or a person, you become the readers' eyes. What do you want them to see? When do you want them to see it?

- Describe the view from afar, and then zoom in on the details, starting at the top and moving toward the bottom, or moving left to right.
- Focus on specific parts, and then show how they contribute to an overall impression.
- Explore the senses: sights, sounds, sensations, smells, or tastes.

TEKS 11.13B

Traits

Make a Pyramid

Whether you want to persuade readers to share your opinion about an issue or explain a situation, build your case logically.

- Start with the most important idea or reason, and progress to the least important.
- Conversely, you can begin with the least important idea and build on it to end with a bang as you state your most important idea.

Alike, but Different

When you discuss similarities and differences, organize your ideas in a way that will be apparent to readers.

- List all of the similarities, and then move on to discuss all of the differences.
- Look at an individual feature or aspect, and discuss its similarities and differences. Repeat the process for another feature or aspect.

Why's That?

When you write to tell what happened and why it happened, you are writing about causes and effects.

- Describe many causes, and then explain how they lead to a single effect.
- Describe one cause, and show how it led to several different effects.

Try It!

Review some recent writing assignments with a partner. Discuss the pattern of organization that was best suited to each assignment, and explain the reasons for your choices.

Make a Pyramid

Have students suggest topics for which each organization makes sense. For example, you might begin with the most important reason when asking to change a school policy, but you might build toward the most important reason when seeking classmates' votes.

Alike, but Different

Ask students to compare and contrast two types of fruit, or two sports using the methods described.

Why's That?

Discuss examples of multiple causes (a war might have several causes) and multiple effects (a change to the school schedule may impact teachers and students in different ways).

 TEKS 11.13B

Try It!
Answers

Encourage partners to consider writing assignments for several school subjects to see whether a particular progression of ideas is best suited to a certain curriculum.

☑ **DIFFERENTIATE INSTRUCTION**

 TEKS **11.13B** Structure ideas in a sustained and persuasive way; **ELPS** **2C** Learn new language structures, expressions, basic vocabulary, and academic vocabulary; **3C** Speak using a variety of grammatical structures, sentence lengths, sentence types, and connecting words

Using Graphic Organizers

Point out to students that graphic organizers can help them see how the facts and details they have gathered are related to the topic and to each other. A graphic organizer can help writers figure out a reasonable and sensible organizing plan for writing and form the basis of an organized list. Ask students to explain why a graphic organizer might also be useful for revising a draft. (Possible answer: It shows how ideas are connected at a glance, which would help a writer incorporate better transitions.)

TEKS 11.13C

Give students time to look over the organizers. Encourage them to ask questions about the design and use of any organizer that is new to them. Ask partners to ask and answer questions about how each organizer is used.

ELPS 2E

TEKS 11.13C

Using Graphic Organizers

Graphic organizers can help you gather and organize your details for writing. Clustering is one method (see page 92); the next two pages list other useful organizers. (Re-create the organizer on your own paper to gather details for an essay.)

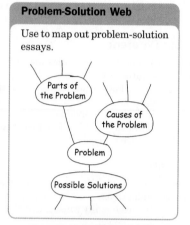

Cause-Effect Organizer

Use to collect and organize details for cause-effect essays.

Cause · Effects

Causes · Effect

Problem-Solution Web

Use to map out problem-solution essays.

Parts of the Problem · Causes of the Problem · Problem · Possible Solutions

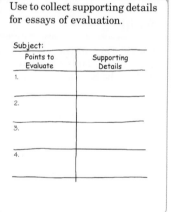

Time Line

Use for personal narratives to list actions or events in the order they occurred.

Subject:
(Chronological Order)
① ② ③ ④ ⑤

Evaluation Collection Grid

Use to collect supporting details for essays of evaluation.

Subject:

Points to Evaluate	Supporting Details
1.	
2.	
3.	
4.	

TEKS 11.13C

Organization **65**

Traits

Venn Diagram

Use to collect details to compare and contrast two topics.

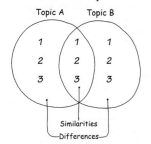

Line Diagram

Use to collect and organize details for academic essays.

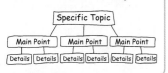

Process (Cycle) Diagram

Use to collect details for science-related writing, such as how a process or cycle works.

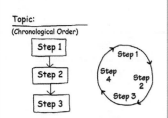

5 W's Chart

Use to collect the *Who? What? When? Where?* and *Why?* details for personal narratives and news stories.

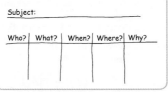

Definition Diagram

Use to gather information for extended-definition essays.

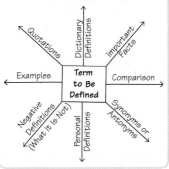

Sensory Chart

Use to collect details for descriptive essays and observation reports.

Subject: _____

Sights	Sounds	Smells	Tastes	Textures

Have students suggest topics for use with each of the graphic organizers shown. They can use the list of writing ideas on SE page 69, the list of assignments in the **Try It!** activity on SE page 61, and ideas from their own current and past writing assignments.

Ask students to make connections between specific topics and organizers by explaining why they match up to create a logical organization in their writing. You may also wish to have partners give one another directions to complete a graphic organizer for a chosen topic to demonstrate understanding.

✔ **DIFFERENTIATE INSTRUCTION**

TEKS 11.13C; **ELPS** 2I, 4J

Reproducible copy masters for some graphic organizers are provided on TE pages A101–A107. If you maintain a class Web site, ask interested students to re-create the organizers from SE pages 64–65 that are not included on TE pages A101–A107

Differentiated Instruction: English Language Learners

ELPS 4D, 4F

ELP Level **Beginning**	ELP Level **Intermediate**	ELP Level **Advanced/Advanced High**
Provide a sample topic for which each organizer would be well suited. As you model, have students repeat the words that name the sections of each organizer.	Suggest a variety of topics and discuss which organizer would be best for each. Have partners work together to create and complete model organizers.	Provide a list of potential topics. Have students work independently to decide which organizer to use for each topic. Then have partners share their ideas.

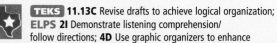

TEKS 11.13C Revise drafts to achieve logical organization; **ELPS** 2I Demonstrate listening comprehension/ follow directions; **4D** Use graphic organizers to enhance comprehension of written text; **4F** Use visual and contextual support and support from peers and teachers to enhance and confirm understanding and to develop vocabulary; **4J** Demonstrate English comprehension and expand reading skills by employing inferential skills

Transitions

Point out that transitions may also be thought of as signal words that tell readers what to expect from a piece of writing.

Match Transitions to Writing Type

Assign each writing type to partners or a small group. Tell them to brainstorm words and phrases to expand each list of transitions.

DIFFERENTIATE INSTRUCTION ↘

TEKS 11.13B, 11.13C

Try It!
Answers

As needed, suggest historical events that students are currently studying. It may also be useful to assign one historical event to two or more groups to elicit ideas for multiple organizing patterns. **DIFFERENTIATE INSTRUCTION ↘**

 **TEKS** 11.13B, 11.13C

Transitions

With so many organizing options available to writers, readers need some signals that will help them recognize the writer's progression of ideas. Transitions are words and phrases that connect ideas, and they help readers to recognize whether a writer is explaining events chronologically, is comparing and contrasting, is describing, or is using some other organizing principle.

Match Transitions to the Writing Type

The chart shows some common transitions that are often used with particular patterns of organization. Use these transitions as a start, and add more of your own.

Sequence of Events	Comparison	Contrast	Cause-Effect	Description
first	likewise	however	because	beneath
second	similarly	although	as a result	on top
third	both	but	since	in back of
finally	also	yet	for this reason	in front of
eventually	in the same way	on the other hand	therefore	next to
before			accordingly	above
during		even though		beside
after				

Try It!

Work with a partner to brainstorm a list of transition words and phrases for a piece of writing that tells about a historical event. Decide on the type of organization you will use, and choose transitions accordingly. Be prepared to explain your choices.

Differentiated Instruction: Advanced Learners

Refer students back to the quotation from Dan Kirby and Tom Liner on SE page 59.

- Have students work with a partner or small group to create guidelines to help avoid "cookie cutter" writing.
- Provide an opportunity for students to share and discuss their guidelines with the class.

Development of Ideas

In his book *Breathing In, Breathing Out,* Ralph Fletcher talks about the "food chain" of writing ideas. High on the food chain are the main ideas (the meat or protein) that prompt you to write. Lower on this chain are the details (the fruits and vegetables, the fiber) that you include in your writing to support or explain the main idea. You need only one main idea (topic) to get started on an essay or an article, but you need many details to develop the idea.

Of course, the key to effective writing is identifying a writing idea that truly interests you. If you have strong feelings about a topic, you will naturally put more effort into your writing right from the start. As writer and philosopher Lancelot Law Whyte once said, "There are few experiences quite so satisfactory as getting a good idea. . . . You're pleased with it, and feel good [about getting started]." The information in this chapter will help you focus on the best main ideas and details for your writing. You will also learn about developing and presenting your ideas.

- **Starting with a Strong Main Idea**
- **Reviewing Possible Starting Points**
- **Developing Your Ideas**
- **Presenting Your Ideas**
- **Avoiding Gaps**

"You don't write because you want to say something, you write because you've got something to say."

—F. Scott Fitzgerald

Development of Ideas

Objectives
- learn how to find writing ideas in life experiences
- understand the importance of a strong main idea
- learn how to develop and present ideas

For many students, feeling confident enough to share ideas on topics of their own choosing may be the most difficult part of writing. Students often prefer assigned topics, at least until they feel more confident in the value of their ideas.

The Try It! activities on SE pages 68–74 will help your students explore and develop their ideas, express their unique perspective, and build a reservoir of writing possibilities.

Differentiated Instruction: English Language Learners

ELPS 2C, 3C

ELP Level **Beginning**	ELP Level **Intermediate**	ELP Level **Advanced/Advanced High**
Explain that a paper on a historical event might be organized by sequence of events. Read aloud the connecting words and have students repeat them with you.	Explain that a paper on a historical event could use a sequence of events or a cause-effect organization. Have students read aloud those transition words.	Have partners identify which methods of organization might work best. Invite partners to think of more transition words and share them with a larger group.

ELPS 2C Learn new language structures and academic vocabulary; **3C** Speak using a variety of grammatical structures and connecting words

Starting with a Strong Main Idea

If possible, meet with teachers from other curriculum areas early in the year to discuss the kinds of writing assignments they have planned and to determine how often students will be dealing with specific teacher-supplied topics.

- Depending on the purpose of the writing assignments, suggest that teachers allow students to "customize" topics in order to encourage them to do their best writing.
- If possible, provide time for students to discuss their assignments with classmates to find ways to customize the topics and make them their own.

If you are presenting this unit at the start of the school year, ask students to recall assignments from the previous year in order to respond to the italicized questions at the bottom of the page.

68

Starting with a Strong Main Idea

Writing is hard work, but trying to write about something that doesn't really interest you can be pure torture. That is why it is important to select writing ideas carefully. The following tips will help you connect with effective topics.

Be receptive. Interesting writing ideas will find you if you think and act like a writer, but you have to set the stage and take advantage of the ideas when they occur to you. Writing regularly in a writer's notebook is a great source of ideas. It will keep you thinking, and give you new writing ideas. Record images you encounter, experiences you have, and ideas from your reading.

Test an idea. Whenever you feel like writing, don't hesitate. Put pen to paper or fingers to the keyboard and see what develops. Even if this writing doesn't pan out, it may give you other ideas.

Make an assignment your own. Some writing assignments are open-ended, allowing you to choose your own topic. Others are very specific, with your teacher supplying the topic. When this happens, try to "customize" the topic so it becomes your own.

For example, let's say that you are asked to classify the different types of microbes. While the overall assignment may seem "blah" to you, one type of microbe, a nasty little cold or flu virus that has recently paid you a visit, may "fascinate" you. Perhaps your teacher would allow you to write about how this virus operates.

Show restraint. Don't settle for your first or even your second writing idea if neither one interests you. Remember: You can do your best writing only when you care about the topic.

Use selecting strategies. When you need help to come up with a writing idea, try a selecting strategy such as clustering or brainstorming. (See page **92**.) Recall your best writing idea this year. Discuss this idea in a brief paragraph, considering these questions: *What was the assignment? How did you come across this topic? Why was it enjoyable? How did the finished piece turn out?*

Differentiated Instruction: Advanced Learners

Students often prefer the one writing mode that is most comfortable for them. For the **Try It!** activity, have students categorize the three writing ideas they chose as expository, persuasive, narrative, or descriptive.

Then ask: "Do you find that one form of writing appeals to you more than the others?" If necessary, have them brainstorm ideas for all forms of writing. Gaining experience in all forms will help students grow and develop into skilled, successful writers.

Reviewing Possible Starting Points

You come across many people, places, experiences, concepts, trends, and beliefs during the school year, all of which may lead to interesting writing ideas. Listed below are a number of starting points for the basic modes of writing. Considering subjects you are studying currently, recent experiences, and so on, you can translate the ideas below into writing topics of your own.

Expository

- Discuss the impact of the Magna Carta on modern government.
- Select one character (including Willy) in the play *Death of a Salesman*, and analyze that character's role in Willy Loman's downfall and death.
- What one thing would you change in the world?
- Explore the evolution of the modern-day trumpet.
- Explain why the F-11 is virtually invisible to radar.

Persuasive

- Persuade the school board to add a class you would like to take.
- Identify America's greatest poet, and defend your choice.
- Pretend you are the lawyer for Dred Scott. Defend him in his case before the Supreme Court.
- Persuade your school board to include vegetarian meals in the cafeteria.

Narrative

- Tell about a time you were frightened by something or someone.
- Write about the love story of Elizabeth Barrett and Robert Browning.
- Write about meeting your first girlfriend/boyfriend.
- Write about the moment you discovered life isn't always fair.

Descriptive

- Describe the most beautiful/unusual sight you have ever seen.
- Describe the school building a half hour after school ends.
- Describe your best friend's hands.
- Describe your favorite store on a Saturday afternoon.
- Describe the Mars landscape.

Try It!

Identify three writing ideas that truly interest you by reviewing your writer's notebook (if you keep one), your class notes, your textbooks, and the Internet.

Traits

Differentiated Instruction: English Language Learners

ELPS 1H, 3D, 3G, 4F

ELP Level **Beginning**	ELP Level **Intermediate**	ELP Level **Advanced/Advanced High**
Use simplified language, gestures, and visuals to discuss the possible starting points. Use yes/no questions to elicit writing topics that interest students.	Use the listed starting points as a springboard. Provide sentence frames to help students express ideas for writing topics that interest them.	Have students work independently to identify a possible writing topic for the four writing modes. Have them share their ideas with a partner or a small group.

Reviewing Possible Starting Points

As you discuss each mode of writing, invite volunteers to suggest additional examples. Encourage students to repeat the terms to name each type of writing as they discuss it and to use accessible language to describe each one.

ELPS 1E, 1F

Expository

Remind students that expository writing informs readers. Discuss the types of information each idea would include.

Persuasive

Review that the purpose of persuasive writing is to convince readers to share the writer's idea. Have students suggest ideas that might be developed for each topic.

Narrative

Point out that narrative writing tells a story. Ask students to suggest some storytelling techniques for each idea.

Descriptive

Descriptive writing "paints a picture." Discuss images to make each description effective.

Try It!
Answers

The **Try It!** activity will benefit students who aren't sure how to adapt the starting points into writing topics of their own. It can also give students concrete writing ideas based on topics they are currently studying or on school-related experiences, such as discussing world events or defending a position. ✔ DIFFERENTIATE INSTRUCTION

Remind students that they will be writing paragraphs and essays in each of the basic modes of writing (expository, persuasive, narrative, and descriptive). Encourage them to jot down in their writer's notebook any ideas from the list and from the class discussion that they would like to explore. ✔ DIFFERENTIATE INSTRUCTION

ELPS 2I

 ELPS **1E** Internalize new basic and academic language by using and reusing it/speaking; **1F** Use accessible language and learn new and essential language in the process; **1H** Develop and expand repertoire of learning strategies; **2I** Demonstrate listening comprehension/taking notes; **3D** Speak using grade-level content area vocabulary in context/academic language; **3G** Express opinions, ideas, and feelings; **4F** Use support from peers and teachers to enhance and confirm understanding and to develop vocabulary and background knowledge

Developing Your Ideas

As a class, have students brainstorm a definition for the word *unique*. You may also wish to have students check a print or online thesaurus for synonyms. Use the definition and synonyms to inform your discussion of developing ideas.

Your Unique Perspective

Choose one or two fairly mundane topics, such as school furniture or windows. Use the topics to discuss each of the bulleted points, suggesting ways to write about each one with a unique perspective. (For example, a writer might be concerned about the comfort of school chairs, with a goal of encouraging more movement during the school day, and give clear suggestions to facilitate the idea.)

Try It!
Answers

Provide time for partners to compare their rewritten passages and then report to the class on what made each perspective unique.

> DIFFERENTIATE INSTRUCTION ↘

 ELPS 1E, 5B, 5F

Developing Your Ideas

You buy your clothes in the same stores as a lot of other people, yet the way you put those clothes together is uniquely yours. Your hair may be cut in the same way as many others, but its color, texture, and style are yours alone. Your writing should be the same. You may use a lot of the same words as another writer, but your own unique perspective on the topic makes it all yours.

Your Unique Perspective

Strangely enough, you don't have to put a lot of effort into making your writing reflect you and your views. It happens quite naturally. Trying to reflect someone else and his or her views—now *that* might take some work! Choose a topic that interests you, think about your "take" on that topic, and let your views shine through. Keep the following ideas in mind to help you share ideas with your own unique perspective.

- **Care about your topic.** Focus on ideas that matter to you, and you will have little difficulty communicating that concern to readers and saying what you think. Even when a topic is assigned, find a way give it a "spin" that makes it your own.

- **Have a goal.** If you know what you want to say about your chosen topic, you will be able to choose specific supporting details and write more effectively. Readers are more likely to recognize and appreciate what you have to say.

- **Be clear.** Writing that is direct and simply stated sends a strong message that the writer knows his or her topic. Ideas are not hidden or confused with flowery language or vague explanations. This doesn't mean that your writing should be devoid of descriptive language or imagery. It means that your writing should clearly convey your view of those images.

Try It!

Revise the following passages in a way that gives each one your own unique perspective.

> The sun rose. It filled the sky with light. A new day began.
>
> It was nearly the end of the game. The score was tied. The home team had one last chance to score.
>
> You are very hungry. The school cafeteria is serving your favorite dish. There is only one serving remaining when you arrive for lunch.

ELPS 1E Internalize new basic and academic language by using and reusing it/speaking and writing; **5B** Write using newly acquired basic vocabulary; **5F** Write using a variety of grade-appropriate sentence lengths, sentence types, and connecting words

What Makes Your Writing Unique?

What makes your writing unique is not necessarily the ideas you choose to include. It's what you have to say about those ideas. It's the chance you have to prompt readers to think about those ideas in a way that they hadn't considered before. It's the descriptive picture you create that allows readers to look at something through your eyes, to see it in the same way you do.

Try It!

Each of the following writers has a decidedly different perspective on school elections. Work with a partner to discuss what makes each piece of writing unique. How do the writers let their views be known?

When this election is over, when the last ballot has been cast, when the campaign signs no longer adorn every available space, when the class officers have been sworn in, take a moment to ask yourself, "Whose ideas won my vote? Why did I vote as I did?" I know I'll be proud of my answers. Will you?

A month of campaigning will end when class elections are held on Friday, October 6, during the lunch hour. Results will be announced before the end of the school day—probably in hopes that it will all be forgotten by Monday. For all the hoopla about democracy in action, does any of it really matter? In truth, this is little more than a school-sponsored popularity contest.

Red, white, and blue signs shout, "Vote for me!" Each campaign slogan, carefully crafted to draw voters' attention, pleads, "Vote for me!" A thirty-minute debate, preceded by weeks of study and preparation, begs, "Vote for me!" Elections are part business and part pep rally, but above all, elections are the candidates' hope that others see them as they see themselves.

71

Traits   1

What Makes Your Writing Unique?

Invite students to share their rewritten passages from the **Try It!** activity on SE page 70 with the class. Discuss the similarities in ideas, and highlight what made each one unique.

Try It!
Answers

Have partners create a list or chart to show the similarities (a school election, campaigning, candidates) and the unique perspectives (Passage 1: a reflection on the choices and how they were made; Passage 2: a cynical view of the futility of the process; Passage 3: a focus on the emotional aspects of campaigning) of each passage.

Differentiated Instruction: English Language Learners

⭐ ELPS 1E, 1H, 3E, 4C, 5B

ELP Level **Beginning**	ELP Level **Intermediate**	ELP Level **Advanced/Advanced High**
Use gestures and visuals to help students describe the unique perspective of one of the passages. Have students practice writing and reading new words.	Have students list words and phrases about one of the passages. Provide sentence frames with transition words to help them express their own unique ideas.	Have students work independently to revise one of the passages to show their unique perspective. Have partners exchange their writing and share their ideas.

ELPS 1E Internalize new basic and academic language by using and reusing it/speaking and writing; **1H** Develop and expand repertoire of learning strategies; **3E** Share information in cooperative learning interactions; **4C** Comprehend English vocabulary and language structures; **5B** Write using newly acquired basic vocabulary

Presenting Your Ideas

Ask students to explain the idiom *train of thought*. Guide them to suggest examples of situations in which one might lose a train of thought.

⭐ ELPS 2C

Following a Train of Thought

As you discuss each bulleted point with students, ask them to explain the point in the writing process when they would be likely to address each one. (Possible answer: Most students will say that the tips are most useful during prewriting and revising.)

Try It!
Answers

Have partners collaborate to present their ideas to the class and to demonstrate comprehension by explaining how they would present their choices in a logical sequence.

DIFFERENTIATE INSTRUCTION ↘

⭐ ELPS 2I

Presenting Your Ideas

You are describing your weekend to friends, and suddenly your mind goes blank. "Where was I?" you ask. "I've completely lost my train of thought!" Your baffled friends suggest all sorts of ideas until one of them reminds you what you intended to say next.

In speaking, "losing your train of thought" happens because you think faster than you speak or because your mind gets distracted. Your brain shuts down for a moment to sort out the jumble of thoughts, words, and outside influences.

The same kind of thing can happen when you are writing. Perhaps you get so caught up in relating an anecdote that you don't explain how it connects with the ideas you are writing about. Maybe your clever play on words makes your ideas difficult to follow. Whatever the cause, giving the reader that "where was I?" feeling is something you want to avoid in your writing.

Following a Train of Thought

Your mind works much faster than you can possibly write or type, so sometimes the connections in your train of thought get lost. Use the following hints to present your ideas in a thoughtful and logical way.

- **Your thesis statement rules.** Your main point or controlling idea gives you an overall guide to the ideas that belong in your writing. Information that doesn't relate to your thesis statement will disrupt your train of thought.

- **You can't get there from here.** Even the most beautifully written sentence or paragraph doesn't belong in an essay if it doesn't clearly connect to the ideas before it and after it.

- **Plan the route.** When you map out a route, you highlight the roads you plan to take and indicate where you move from one highway to another. You need to do the same in your writing by using words and phrases that link ideas. If you are unable to connect the ideas, then you may need to rethink the logical progression in your writing.

Try It!

Work with a partner to decide how you would present the following ideas about a perfect Saturday. In what order would you write about them? Which would you omit?

seeing a movie with friends	going to a soccer game
a run in the park	playing in a soccer game
sleeping late	reading a good book

Adding a Spark

You have examined the idea of following your train of thought through your thesis statement and supporting details. Once you have established which details belong in your writing and have figured out how to connect those details to one another, one part of your writing task is done.

However, another important aspect of presenting your ideas is the overall impression or insight you want to share in your writing. To spark readers' interest, you need to present your ideas in a way that gives them something to wonder about and return to that notion again and again. Consider the following ideas and examples:

Traits

- Build your writing around a question or comment that will lead readers into your topic, making them wonder how you will explain or clarify it.

    How weird is it to feel completely lost in a place filled with road signs that tell you exactly where you are and exactly where you're headed? That's the situation I found myself in during my family's last road trip.

- Keep that train of thought going by reminding readers of your question or comment periodically as you present your ideas.

    My "deer in the headlight" feeling continued as we headed down the highway, passing sign after sign that suggested possible destinations. With each sign I'd wonder, "Could this be the place?"

- Return to your question or comment in your conclusion, showing readers how you've answered or explained it.

    Like so many before me, I knew I'd found my way "home" immediately when I saw it. As we drove across the campus, I knew I'd found the place where I would begin my journey to adulthood.

Try It!

Look at the ideas you decided to present when writing about a perfect Saturday. What overall impression or insight would you want to give in that essay? What questions or comments might help you to share that impression or insight with readers?

Adding a Spark

Give students time to read the suggestions and examples. Have them explain what they found intriguing or interesting about the passages and why.

Try It!
Answers

Have partners work together to choose an overall impression for the "perfect Saturday" essay and to brainstorm some techniques they could use to give that impression.

Avoiding Gaps

Discuss the types of gaps that might occur in different forms of writing. As need, point out the following possibilities:

- Narrative: missing events in a series
- Expository: missing facts or details
- Persuasive: unclear connections between reasons, evidence, or statistics
- Descriptive: unclear transitions

Buddy Readers

Students may be reluctant to have peers review writing that is "unfinished." Take time to discuss and model the use of positive feedback along with constructive criticism.

Self-Review

Suggest self-corrective techniques that students can use to monitor their writing. For example, students who do a self-review can make use of prewriting notes and graphic organizers. Looking back at intial ideas and connections can help to make gaps in writing more apparent.

ELPS 1B

Try It!
Answers

Remind students to seek clarification if they do not understand a partner's comments. After partners review one another's writing, ask them to categorize the types of gaps they found. Suggest that they list some examples in their writer's notebooks as reminders for future writing assignments. **DIFFERENTIATE INSTRUCTION ↘**

ELPS 2D

Avoiding Gaps

If you have ever had to work with an incomplete set of directions, you know how frustrating it can be to deal with missing information. The same is true for writing. When writers omit information or key ideas, they create significant gaps between ideas. These gaps prevent the readers from clearly understanding the writer's ideas and usually make the writing ineffective.

Buddy Readers

One of the best ways to avoid gaps in your writing is also one of the easiest. Ask a classmate, friend, teacher, or family member to read your draft, and think about the questions they ask. Questions like these are clues that there are gaps in your writing.

Missing idea: How did your class get the money to pay for those repairs?

Missing transition: What came first—the principal's meeting or the school assembly?

Missing information: Who made the repairs—students or someone else?

Self-Review

When a buddy reader is not an option, avoiding gaps becomes a do-it-yourself operation. However, no one knows what you intend to write better than you, so a self-review is an excellent alternative. Focus on looking for gaps in your writing. As much as possible, read as if you have never seen the piece of writing before. Use the margins of your draft to make note of questions that suggest missing ideas or information. Look for places where transitions will help to make the writing more effective.

FYI

Reviewing your draft a day or more after it is written gives you a fresh perspective that is almost as good as a "second pair of eyes."

Try It!

Review a narrative or essay you wrote in the last month or so. Try to identify gaps that would make it difficult for readers to understand the ideas. Then exchange your writing with a partner, and examine that piece of writing for gaps. Discuss whether your partner identified the same gaps as you.

 ELPS 1B Monitor written language production and employ self-corrective techniques or other resources; **2D** Monitor understanding of spoken language during classroom instruction and interactions and seek clarification as needed

Voice

Objectives

- develop a natural writing voice
- demonstrate an understanding of how purpose and audience affect voice
- demonstrate an understanding of two basic levels of diction: formal and informal English
- experiment with voice

Writer and teacher Dan Kirby says, "Voice is the aspect of writing closest to the writer." Voice tags you like a thumbprint, establishing your special place among all other writers. As the quotation below states, however, finding your natural voice may take time. That is, you may not automatically write with a distinctive voice. Reading, writing regularly in a journal, tuning in to the language—these are the practices that will help you develop your natural writing voice.

How do you know if your writing has voice? First of all, it should communicate to the reader something authentic and unique about you as an individual. Secondly, it should engage the reader, making him or her feel that you sincerely care about what you say—and how you say it. Lastly, it should establish a meaningful connection between you and the reader. The purpose of this chapter is to help you better understand voice, one of the most important, yet least understood, traits of writing.

- Developing Voice
- Knowing Your Purpose
- Identifying Your Audience
- Understanding Diction
- Using Effective Modifiers
- Including Sensory Details
- Choosing Vivid Verbs

"All of us who write need a certain amount of time, often quite a lot of time, to relax and find our natural voice."

—William Zinsser

Tell students that of the three ways listed to determine if their writing has voice, the first (it should communicate something authentic and unique about you as an individual) may be the most difficult to achieve, especially in informational writing. That is why it is so important for students to choose topics that they are interested in, believe in, or have strong and definite opinions about.

Work with students to develop a list of possible topics of interest. Ask partners to choose two topics from the list and analyze how they might communicate something authentic and unique.

ELPS 1H, 4K

Differentiated Instruction: English Language Learners

ELPS 2G, 4J, 4K

ELP Level **Beginning**	ELP Level **Intermediate**	ELP Level **Advanced/Advanced High**
Read aloud a brief narrative in which a key event is missing. Ask yes/no questions to assess comprehension and that help students identify what is missing.	Present a brief narrative that omits a key event or information. Have partners read it aloud and work together to identify what is missing.	Present a brief narrative that omits two pieces of information. Have students infer what has been left out. Then have partners discuss their ideas.

ELPS 1H Develop and expand repertoire of learning strategies; **2G** Understand general meaning, main points and important details of spoken language; **4J** Demonstrate English comprehension and expand reading skills by employing inferential skills; **4K** Demonstrate English comprehension and expand reading skills by employing analytical skills

Developing Voice

Remind students that a writer's voice is the way his or her writing sounds to readers. Emphasize that a natural voice is not the same thing as using a casual or informal voice.

Sample Notebook Entry

Use the sample notebook entry to discuss with students how reading, personal journaling, or notebook writing can help them develop voice for informational writing. Explain that what makes a writer's voice sound natural is the unique way of presenting ideas that belongs to the writer alone. Assure students that the more they read and write, the stronger their voice will become.

Exercise
Answers

1. Yes. The author uses personification in a unique way, comparing the craft to the prancing and rearing of a wild animal.
2. Yes. The author again personifies the boat, this time comparing it to a wild horse trying to jump over an outrageously high fence. The reader senses the impossible task confronting the men in the boat.
3. Yes. The author's use of parallel structure heightens the effectiveness and originality of this line and helps the reader feel the up-and-down motion of the boat.
4. Yes. The adjectives used in the first sentence mount in intensity and mirror the growing intensity of the stormy sea. The structure of the two sentences—the first moving toward a crescendo and the second almost matter-of-fact in comparison, work very well together to create the feeling that the men are helpless as they face the storm. **DIFFERENTIATE INSTRUCTION ↘**

⭐ ELPS 4J

Developing Voice

Your natural voice will begin to develop once you reach a certain comfort level with writing. Writing regularly in a notebook or journal will help you reach that level. (See pages 1–5.)

Read the following notebook entry. It shows someone who writes regularly in action. This entry reflects the writer's personality and personal viewpoint.

Sample Notebook Entry

> **March 3**
> It happened again today. At the mall someone yelled, "Katie!" to me, or actually to my identical twin sister. For some reason, people think of us as "the twins," almost as if we are not separate beings. I love my sister and all, but I get so mad when people call me Katie. Listen everyone! I'm Cali: I play center field on Park's softball team. Katie plays third base. I'm good at running down fly balls; she's good at keeping ground balls in the infield. I'm fast on the base paths; she's a big bopper, with three home runs this year.

Exercise

Decide whether or not each of the following passages exhibits voice. Be able to explain your answers.

1. The craft pranced and reared, and plunged like an animal.
2. As each wave came, and she rose for it, she seemed like a horse making at a fence outrageously high.
3. As the boat bounced from the top of each wave, the wind tore through the hair of hatless men, and then as the craft plopped her stern down again the spray slashed past them.
4. The huge wave moved forward, huge, furious, and implacable. It fairly swallowed the dingy, and almost simultaneously the men tumbled into the sea.

—Stephen Crane, *The Open Boat*

Differentiated Instruction: Struggling Learners

The **Try It!** activity may be difficult for some students. Encourage them to check a dictionary for difficult or unfamiliar terms. Suggest that they use their own words to describe what is happening in each passage, and then reread the author's description.

Knowing Your Purpose

Once your natural voice has had a chance to develop, you'll be ready and able to adjust it depending on the purpose of your writing. (The purpose is your specific reason for writing.)

Identifying Reasons for Writing

Purpose: To share an experience
Voice: Engaging and personal

I had to get back to class as fast as I could. First graders follow rules in a serious way, and the first rule of order is to be on time, always. Once I got into class, I rubbed my chin and noticed blood on my hand. Mrs. Gehring said my chin just looked skinned. I personally thought it was more serious than that, but I didn't say anything. The second rule of order in first grade is to listen to your teacher.

Purpose: To express an opinion
Voice: Convincing and informed

The school board should realize just how necessary art really is for student success. First of all, art improves visual literacy. According to the International Visual Literacy Association, visual literacy is fundamental to normal human learning.

Purpose: To share information
Voice: Interesting and knowledgeable

Safety wasn't always a primary concern on the Formula One racing circuit. When the Grand Prix began in 1906, the race ran on city streets and country roads, and accidents involving drivers and spectators were common.

Exercise

Identify the purpose and appropriate voice for the passages below. Use the information above as a guide.

1. Unlike the typical ocean waves caused by storms, a tsunami begins with a fault line in the seabed. Faults occur when two or more of the earth's tectonic plates meet and rub against each other.
2. The rain hit my helmet lightly, like a soft tapping on a door. I pulled my chin strap across my chin and snapped it on the other side. Forty-three teammates standing beside me started to jog, workhorses on the move.
3. Upper-level students in McKinley High School need access to work-study programs. Studies have shown that students retain new information more effectively if they experience it.

Traits

Knowing Your Purpose

Elicit from students some common purposes for writing, such as to inform, to entertain, to persuade, or to reflect.

Identifying Reasons for Writing

Have students point out specific details in each sample passage that help the writer achieve an appropriate voice. Possible choices:

- Engaging and personal: *as fast as I could, in a serious way, the first rule of order is, I rubbed my chin, I personally thought, the second rule of order is*
- Convincing and informed: *The school board should, According to the International Visual Literacy Association*
- Interesting and knowledgeable: *When the Grand Prix began in 1906, the race ran on city streets and country roads*

✔ DIFFERENTIATE INSTRUCTION

Exercise
Answers

1. Purpose: To share information;
   Voice: interesting and knowledgeable
2. Purpose: To share an experience;
   Voice: Engaging and personal
3. Purpose: To express an opinion;
   Voice: Convincing and informed

ELPS 1H Develop and expand repertoire of learning strategies; **3D** Speak using grade-level content area vocabulary/academic language in context; **3J** Respond orally to information presented/concept and language attainment

Identifying Your Audience

Ask students to read each passage carefully and pay attention to how the voice changes for the different audiences. After students have had a chance to read and discuss the voice of each passage, ask what details writers need to know about their audiences to help them adjust their writing voice.

Possible responses:

- It is important to know the age of the audience. (Young children don't have the same vocabulary or comprehension level as high school students or adults.)
- It is important to recognize the position and authority of the audience. (School board members have authority to make changes, while classmates do not.)
- It is important to know the interest level and the extent of knowledge of the audience. (School board members do not need to have specific terms such as *bullying* or *vandalism* explained, while younger students will probably need to have terms clarified.)

 11.13A

Try It!
Answers

Suggest that students choose one of the audiences listed at the top of SE page 78.

 11.13A

Identifying Your Audience

Your writing voice will change depending on whom you are addressing. The three passages below demonstrate this principle.

> **Possible Audiences**
> – Classmates
> – School board members
> – Grade school students
> – Grandparents
> – Community members
>
> **Audience: school board members**
>
> The problem of disruptive behavior on our school buses is everyone's concern. During the last few weeks there have been reports of bullying, fights, and vandalism. Unless we deal with this problem now, someone may get seriously hurt. Students, administrators, school board members, and bus drivers need to get together and establish a workable safety plan for the buses.
>
> **Audience: grade school students**
>
> It's really important that you follow the rules on the bus. If you get out of your seat or act rowdy, someone might get hurt. Also, if someone is bothering you, make sure to report this person to the bus driver. Everyone must work together to keep our buses safe.
>
> **Audience: classmates**
>
> We need to set a better example on the school buses. Grade school kids look up to us, and they try to copy our behavior. If we act like jerks on the bus, the younger students are going to do the same thing. Someone is going to get hurt if things don't change. We are the young adults. Let's act like it.

Try It!

Rewrite a paragraph in one of your essays so that it speaks to a different audience. Discuss your rewrite with your classmates.

Understanding Diction

Diction is the level of language that you use based on the purpose and intended audience for a piece of writing. Here are the two basic levels of diction that you will use for most of your assigned writing.

Formal English

Your essays, research papers, and business letters should meet the standards of formal English. This level of language pays careful attention to word choice, follows the conventions for grammar and usage, and maintains a serious, objective (factual) tone throughout.

> Shakespeare lived in a rough-and-tumble world. He began his career as a poor actor in a traveling troupe, much like one of the "Rustics" in *A Midsummer Night's Dream*. Once in London, Shakespeare became a poor playwright, struggling to win audiences away from "bear baiting"—staged fights between bears and dogs.

Tip

Generally, avoid using *I, we,* and *you* in academic writing. Instead, focus on the topic itself and let your attitude be revealed indirectly.

Informal English

For many other pieces, such as personal narratives and feature articles, you may use a more informal level of language. Informal English usually includes some personal references, a few popular expressions, and shorter sentences.

> On Friday, I took my girlfriend, Tasha, to see *The Complete Works of William Shakespeare (Abridged)*. She loves Shakespeare, but I thought I'd just thrown away my Saturday night. The curtain opened, and out came three actors who said they were going to do all of Shakespeare's plays in an hour and a half. They started with *Romeo and Juliet*, with one of the guys in a dress.

Other Forms of Diction

- **Colloquial language** refers to expressions that are accepted in informal situations: **I'll just hang out since I've got nothing better to do.**
- **Slang** is language used by a particular group of people among themselves: **Arissa drove to the hoop, got huge air, and slammed it for two.**
- **Jargon** (technical diction) is the specialized language used by a specific group, such as those who use computers: **The initialism PCMCIA means Peripheral Component Micro-Channel Interconnect Architecture.**

Traits

Understanding Diction

Have students suggest examples of situations in which formal and informal English are appropriate. ✔ DIFFERENTIATE INSTRUCTION

Formal English

Discuss why formal English is used for most school assignments, pointing out as needed that most writing in school is intended to demonstrate understanding of subject matter details.

Informal English

Make sure students know that the conventions of grammar apply to informal English. In other words, *informal* does not imply that it is acceptable to relax the rules of grammar. Students can, however, relax the level of language to make it more personal and less serious, as the sample passage illustrates.

Other Forms of Diction

Review the list of other forms of diction and point out that colloquial language and slang are usually acceptable only in story dialogue and when quoting someone directly.

Differentiated Instruction: English Language Learners

⭐ ELPS 1G

ELP Level **Beginning**	ELP Level **Intermediate**	ELP Level **Advanced/Advanced High**
Present statements that include examples of formal and informal English. Use simplified language to examine each statement and its possible audiences.	Present examples of formal and informal English. Use sentence stems to help students identify the features and make inferences about possible audiences.	Have partners write formal and informal versions of news about an upcoming school event. One version should be for fellow students; the other should be for a local newspaper.

ELPS 1G Demonstrate ability to distinguish between formal and informal English and demonstrate knowledge of when to use formal and informal English

Using Effective Modifiers

As needed, review that an adjective describes a noun or a pronoun, while an adverb modifies a verb, an adjective, or another adverb.

Selecting Specific Adjectives

Have students list overused modifiers on a chart.

- They can start by listing the overused adjectives on the SE page (*neat, big, pretty, small, cute, fun, bad, nice, good, great, funny*).
- Then have them add other meaningless modifiers to the list, such as *really* and *totally*.
- Students can continue to add to the list throughout the year. They can also make their own list in their writer's notebook under the heading "Words to Avoid."

Choosing Specific Adverbs

Discuss why the addition of the adverb *reluctantly* changes the meaning of the sentence.

Try It!
Answers

Possible revision:
It was three o'clock in the morning when my mother frantically rushed down the hall and pulled us out of our beds. She told us to grab the dog and to get out of the house right away. The temperature began to rise as I rushed down the dark, winding stairs. I was hit with a blast of hot air and the crashing sound of breaking glass when I opened the side door. The first thing I saw was my neighbor's motorcycle exploding into tiny pieces that flew in all directions. Then I saw a blinding blaze engulf our new Honda.

Using Effective Modifiers

The two main types of modifiers, adjectives and adverbs, can establish your voice as they create colorful word pictures for the reader. Just as fresh seasonings and sauces are essential to delicious entrées, specific modifiers are essential to clear writing.

Selecting Specific Adjectives

Follow these guidelines to choose strong adjectives that will clarify the nouns in your writing.

- Use adjective to create a clear picture for your reader.

  Unclear: My neighbor drove up in his convertible.

  Clear: My neighbor drove up in his *sleek, red* convertible.

- Avoid using adjectives that carry little meaning: *neat, big, pretty, small, cute, fun, bad, nice, good, great, funny,* and so on.

  Overused adjective: His old roadster is in storage.

  Specific adjective: His classic roadster is in storage.

- Use adjectives selectively so they don't lose their effectiveness.

  Too many adjectives: A tall, narrow column of thick, yellow smoke marked the exact spot where the unexpected explosion occurred.

  Selective use: A column of thick, yellow smoke marked the spot where the explosion occurred.

Choosing Specific Adverbs

Sometimes, adverbs are needed to describe the action in a sentence.

Okay: Mayor Meyer agreed to meet the protesters.

Better: Mayor Meyer reluctantly agreed to meet the protesters.

Try It!

Revise the following passage. You may substitute specific adjectives for overused ones, delete adjectives when too many are used, and add an adverb to describe the action.

It was three o'clock when my mother rushed down the hall waking us up. She told us to grab the dog and to get out of the house. The temperature began to rise as I ran down the steep, dark, winding stairs, and I was hit with a blast of hot air and the sound of breaking glass when I opened the wooden, paneled, decorative side door. The first thing I saw was my neighbor's nice red motorcycle explode with pieces flying in all directions, and I saw a bright blaze engulf a neat Honda.

Including Sensory Details

Sensory details are details that are experienced through the senses. They help a reader to see, feel, smell, taste, and hear what is being described. Here is a passage from a descriptive essay that contains sensory details:

> I stood backstage, surrounded by giggles and rustling gowns. The smell of talcum powder, hair spray, and rosin rolled in from the stage, and a familiar bitter taste filled my mouth. The music rose, and the dancers swept onto the stage in a frothy swirl of pink and blue.

Charting Your Senses

You can use a graphic organizer to collect sensory details for your writing. The chart below includes some of the sensory details one writer used in a personal narrative about his last football game. (Whether or not a writer covers all of the senses depends on the chosen topic.)

Sensory Chart

sights	sounds	smells	tastes	textures
the packed bleachers, bursting onto the field	rain tapping on my helmet, clip-clopping of our spikes	fresh popcorn, wet cut grass	plastic mouthpiece	chin strap tight across chin, spikes sinking in the muddy field

FYI

Keep in mind that different senses have different effects on the reader. For example, smells may be positive or negative. The smell of fresh popcorn suggests something good to the reader, while the stink of burning tires suggests something bad.

Try It!

Evaluate one of your personal narratives by filling in a chart like the one above with the sensory details you used. Then answer these questions: *Did you include enough sensory details? Which senses did you cover? Where could you use more sensory details?*

Including Sensory Details

Have students point out the sensory details in the passage at the top of the page and tell what senses these details appeal to.
- sight: dancers in a frothy swirl of pink and blue
- sound: giggles and rustling gowns; music rose
- smell: talcum powder, hair spray, rosin
- taste: bitter taste

Have partners work together to brainstorm other familiar words that might be used to describe and express opinions about the scene.
ELPS 3B

Charting Your Senses

Draw attention to the parenthetical statement about not covering all senses for certain topics. Ask students to suggest examples, such as omitting sounds when describing a flower.

Sensory Chart

Ask students to suggest additional sensory details that could be added to the chart.

Try It!
Answers

Distribute photocopies of the reproducible sensory chart (TE page A105) for students to use for the **Try It!** activity.

Tell students that they will most often use sensory details in their writing to enrich personal narratives, short stories, descriptive passages, and poems. However, students may also use sensory details in news articles and reviews, persuasive pieces, and research reports.

DIFFERENTIATE INSTRUCTION

ELPS 5G

Differentiated Instruction: English Language Learners

ELPS 1B, 1C, 4F

ELP Level **Beginning**	ELP Level **Intermediate**	ELP Level **Advanced/Advanced High**
Provide visuals or objects to prompt students to describe a seasonal event for a sensory chart. Have students repeat the sensory words with you.	Provide and discuss visuals or objects related to a seasonal event. Ask yes/no questions to determine appropriate sensory details for the chart.	Have partners create a sensory chart that describes a seasonal event and share them with the group. Discuss words that they ultimately chose not to include.

ELPS 1B Monitor written language production and employ self-corrective techniques or other resources; **1C** Use strategic learning strategies to acquire basic and grade-level vocabulary; **3B** Express opinions; **4F** Use support from peers and teachers to develop vocabulary; **5G** Narrate with increasing specificity and detail

Choosing Vivid Verbs

Some students have a tendency to latch on to a few favorite verbs and use them over and over in their writing. Point out that overusing any word—even the most vivid, colorful verb—will have a negative effect on their writing. Readers are likely to think that they (the student writers) are unimaginative and are too lazy to search for other suitable words.

Focus attention on the third tip, which encourages writers to use active rather than passive verbs. Explain that while active verbs are always preferred, there will be instances when using passive verbs makes more sense. Tell students they should always read aloud their writing to check the sense and sound of the verbs they decide to use.

Make sure students understand the concept of showing rather than telling, which can be a difficult concept to grasp. Encourage them to listen to a radio broadcast of an exciting event such as a baseball game. Tell students to pay particular attention to how the announcers help listeners visualize what is happening.

ELPS 2F

Revising for Vivid Verbs

Emphasize that vivid verbs can help to clarify a writer's meaning. Discuss the example sentences, focusing on how the revised version sends a much clearer message.

Try It!
Answers

Ask students to share examples of the verbs they changed. Have them explain how the changes affect the narrative. **DIFFERENTIATE INSTRUCTION**

Choosing Vivid Verbs

Like nouns, verbs that are too general will not create a clear word picture. For example, the verb *looked* does not say the same thing as *stared, glared, glanced, peeked,* or *inspected*. The statement "Officer Shaw *inspected* the crime scene" is more specific than "Officer Shaw *looked* at the crime scene." The tips that follow will help you choose the best verbs for your writing.

- Whenever possible, use a verb that is strong enough to stand alone without the help of an adverb.

  Verb and adverb: Mr. Walters fell down in the hospital.

  Vivid verb: Mr. Walters collapsed in the hospital.

- Don't overuse the "be" verbs *(is, are, was, were, . . .)*. Also avoid overusing *would, could,* or *should*. Often a better verb can be made from another word in the same sentence.

  A "be" verb: Yolanda is someone who plans for the future.

  A stronger verb: Yolanda plans for the future.

- Include active rather than passive verbs as much as possible.

  Passive verb: Another deep pass was launched by Geraldo.

  Active verb: Geraldo launched another deep pass.

- Work with verbs that show rather than tell.

  A verb that tells: Greta is very tall.

  A verb that shows: Greta towers over her teammates.

Revising for Vivid Verbs

When you revise a first draft for verbs, use the information above as a basic guide. Also remember that making every verb vivid and colorful may result in a forced, unnatural style. Instead, change only those verbs that you know will improve your writing.

First draft sentence: Mr. Gardner talked to us about the exit exam, saying our futures depend on it.

Revised version: Mr. Gardner warned us about the exit exam, saying our futures depend on it.

Try It!

Review the personal narrative you analyzed in the Try It! activity on the previous page. Change at least four or five verbs that are too general.

 ELPS 2F Listen to and derive meaning from a variety of media/ concept and language attainment

Conventions

Effective writing is edited with care to ensure that the work is clear and correct. It follows the conventions of our language, the accepted standards of punctuation, mechanics, spelling, and grammar. To check your own writing for conventions, it's important to have the proper editing tools on hand—including the "Proofreader's Guide" in this book (pages **634–783**), a dictionary, a thesaurus, a computer spell-checker, and so on.

Like other aspects of writing, the best way to learn about the conventions is to pay attention to them—in conversations, in reading, and in writing. As writer Dr. Samuel Johnson says, "Grammar is the art of using words properly." The grammar work that you do in your English classes adds to your understanding of the language in two basic ways. It helps you (1) to recognize and name the different parts of the language and (2) to know what to look for when you edit your writing. The pages that follow serve as a helpful guide for checking the conventions in your writing.

- Spelling
- Punctuation
- Varying Sentences
- Combining Sentences
- Expanding Sentences
- Checking for Sentence Problems

"I really never knew what editing was until I started reading my own stuff and thinking about it and listening to it."

—Sandra Belton

Conventions

Conventions

Objectives
- know when to check for conventions
- recognize errors in conventions

If students haven't already reviewed the contents of the Proofreader's Guide (SE pages 634–779), or the Editing and Proofreading Marks on the inside back cover, encourage them to take time to do that now.

Differentiated Instruction: English Language Learners

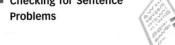 **ELPS 1B**

ELP Level **Beginning**	ELP Level **Intermediate**	ELP Level **Advanced/Advanced High**
Use gestures and visuals to replace general verbs such as *walk, ask,* and *eat* with more vivid verbs. Have students repeat and act out the verbs with you.	Work together to write vivid verbs that are more specific than verbs such as *ran, laughed,* and *took.* Have students monitor their writing and self-correct by using vivid verbs.	Have partners replace verbs such as *said, asked,* and *walked* with more vivid verbs. Tell partners to monitor their writing and use a thesaurus to find vivid verbs.

 ELPS 1B Monitor written language production and employ self-corrective techniques or other resources

Spelling

Ask students to cite other instances when a computer spell-check is unable to recognize an error, such as an incorrect word (*tow* instead of *two*, or *shed* instead of *she'd* for example).

Commonly Misspelled Words

Suggest that students begin a list of commonly misspelled words in their writer's notebook. You may also wish to refer them to Using the Right Word on SE pages 702–721.

ELPS 5C

Using a Dictionary

Some students believe that dictionaries are not useful for checking spelling because "you need to know how to spell the word before you look it up." Point out that the dictionary is, in fact, ideal for making sure the written word matches the intended definition.

Try It!
Answers

Tell students to use a dictionary to check their work. DIFFERENTIATE INSTRUCTION ↘

Rewritten paragraph:

   I think it's really fun to have a dog for a pet. Our neighbors have a dog, but their dog is not well trained. Your dog fetches and comes when it's called. Does he do tricks too? Of the two dogs, I'll bet that your dog is smarter.

TEKS 11.19; **ELPS** 5C

 TEKS 11.19

Spelling

   If you write on a computer, using its spell-check feature is a good way to find spelling errors. However, spell check is not perfect. If you write *to* when you mean *two*, it can't tell. In fact, if you use any of the commonly misspelled words below incorrectly, spell check may not flag it as an error.

Commonly Misspelled Words

   Words that sound alike, or nearly alike, but have different meanings are commonly misspelled. Here are some words that sound alike but have different spellings and different meanings.

> its — a possessive pronoun meaning *of it* or *belonging to it*
> it's — a contraction for *it is* or *it has*
>
> their — a possessive pronoun meaning *belonging to them*
> they're — a contraction for *they are*
> there — an adverb referring to place
>
> your — a possessive pronoun meaning *belonging to you*
> you're — a contraction for *you are*
>
> to — a preposition or part of the infinitive form of a verb
> too — an adverb meaning *also* or *very*
> two — the number that is the sum of one plus one

Using a Dictionary

   To determine whether or not you have used the correct spelling for these commonly misspelled words, check the word you are unsure about in the dictionary. Make sure that the word, as you have used it in your writing, matches its definition in the dictionary.

Try It!

Rewrite the following passage, correcting the commonly misspelled words.

   I think its really fun to have a dog for a pet. Our neighbors have a dog, but there dog is not well trained. You're dog fetches and comes when its called. Does he do tricks to? Of the two dogs, I'll bet that you're dog is smarter.

Punctuation

Using a speaker's exact words can add color and life to your writing. A direct quotation is the exact words that a person or character says.

- Use quotation marks to set the speaker's words apart from the rest of the sentence.
- Begin the direct quotation with a capital letter.
- Use a comma to separate the quotation from the rest of the sentence.

Incorrectly Punctuated: "I really hope we win tonight Manny said.

Correctly Punctuated: "I really hope we win tonight," Manny said.

Incorrectly Punctuated: "Who is pitching tonight" asked Elena?

Correctly Punctuated: "Who is pitching tonight?" asked Elena.

Punctuating a Divided Quotation

One way to vary your sentence structure or to add emphasis, is to divide a direct quotation. The example below shows how to punctuate a divided quotation that is part of the same sentence. Notice that the first letter of the second part of the quotation is not capitalized.

One Sentence: "There's Alex," Carmella said, "getting ready to play right now."

You can also divide a quotation into two separate sentences. In this case, you must capitalize the first word in the second sentence.

Two Sentences: "We're in trouble if Jason's pitching tonight," Rafael said. "He's just impossible to hit."

Try It!

Rewrite each of the following sentences, correcting errors in punctuation and capitalization.

1. Let's try out for the school play, Dan suggested.
2. "Oh, I don't know" Benito said. "what if I stink?"
3. "Yeah, but what if you don't stink" Dan asked?
4. "I'm afraid I'll get up on the stage and just freeze", Benito said.
5. "No, you won't." Dan said. "When you gave your class report last week you were great."

Traits

Punctuation

Point out to students that correctly punctuating a quotation signals readers that the words are not those of the writer. Incorrectly punctuated quotations can lead to misunderstandings and miscommunications.

Punctuating a Divided Quotation

Guide students to note the differences in punctuation between a one- and a two-sentence quotation.

Try It!
Answers

Rewritten sentences:
1. "Let's try out for the school play," Dan suggested.
2. "Oh, I don't know," Benito said. "What if I stink?"
3. "Yeah, but what if you don't stink?" Dan asked.
4. "I'm afraid I'll get up on the stage and just freeze," Benito said.
5. "No, you won't," Dan said. "When you gave your class report last week you were great."

TEKS 11.18A; **ELPS** 5E

TEKS **11.18A** Correctly and consistently use conventions of punctuation and capitalization; **ELPS** 5C Spell familiar English words and employ English spelling patterns and rules with increasing accuracy; **5E** Employ increasingly complex grammatical structures

Varying Sentences

Remind students that varying sentence structure and length adds interest to their writing and engages readers.

Varying Sentence Beginnings

To make sure students can recognize sentences that lack variety, do the following:

- Read aloud the original version of the first sample passage and ask students to listen for the dull, almost mechanical quality of the writing.
- Read aloud the revised version and ask students to listen for the smooth flow of sentences created by varied beginnings.

Varying Sentence Lengths

Follow a similar procedure to highlight the need to vary sentence lengths. **DIFFERENTIATE INSTRUCTION ↘**

Try It!
Answers

Have students rewrite the passages they identify to create better variety. Tell partners to check each other's work to be sure that compound, complex, and compound-complex sentences are written correctly.

Encourage students to make a practice of reading aloud their writing during the revising process. If their sentences sound repetitive or short and choppy, they should check whether too many begin the same way or are too similar in length.

★ TEKS 11.17B; **ELPS** 1H, 2C, 5F

Varying Sentences

According to author William Zinsser, writing in which "all the sentences move at the same plodding gait" is deadly. Such writing lacks sentence variety.

Varying Sentence Beginnings

If all of your sentences begin in the same way, they will sound stilted and robotic. To avoid this problem, vary your beginnings.

Starting with the Main Subject

Original version: The U.S.S. *Constitution,* known as Old Ironsides, is a famous United States sailing ship that workers began building in 1794. Old Ironsides was one of six ships approved by Congress to fight piracy. This ship helped defeat the Barbary pirates during its years of service.

Varied Beginnings

Revised version: In 1794, workers began to build the famous U.S.S. *Constitution* sailing ship later known as Old Ironsides. This ship was one of six approved by Congress to fight piracy. During its years of service, Old Ironsides helped defeat the Barbary pirates.

Varying Sentence Lengths

A series of sentences that are similar in length may also sound robotic. To avoid this problem, write sentences of different lengths.

Similar Lengths

Original version: Amateur photographers once relied on film for taking pictures. In recent years, however, that has all changed. Today's amateurs are replacing film cameras with digital ones. Consumers are gleefully embracing changes in this industry.

Varied Lengths

Revised version: Amateur photographers once relied on film for taking pictures. That has all changed. Today's amateurs, gleefully embracing changes in the industry, are replacing film cameras with digital ones.

Try It!

Find a passage in something you have written in which all (or most) of the sentences begin with the main subject. Rewrite this passage, varying the sentence beginnings. Then do the same for a passage in which all (or most) of the sentences are similar in length.

★ TEKS **11.17B** Use a variety of correctly structured sentences; **ELPS** **1H** Develop and expand repertoire of learning strategies; **2C** Learn new language structures; **5F** Write using a variety of grade-appropriate sentence patterns

Traits

> "Have something to say and say it as clearly
> as you can. That is the only secret of style."
> —Matthew Arnold

Combining Sentences

Sentence combining, which can be done in a variety of ways, can help you improve fluency. By combining a series of short, choppy sentences, you create a smooth-reading, longer sentence.

Combining Shorter Ideas

Suppose you were writing about a tornado that struck a small town without warning, causing extensive damage, a number of serious injuries, and several deaths. You wouldn't put each idea into a separate sentence. Instead, you would combine the ideas in a variety of ways.

- Use a **series** to combine three or more similar ideas.
  The tornado struck the small town, causing extensive damage, numerous injuries, **and** several deaths.

- Use a **relative pronoun** *(who, whose, that, which)* to link two related ideas.
  The tornado, which was completely unexpected, **swept through the small town.**

- Use an **introductory phrase** or **clause** to link two related ideas.
  Because the tornado was unexpected, **it caused extensive damage, numerous injuries, and several deaths.**

- Use a **participial phrase** *(-ing, -ed)* to begin or end a sentence.
  The tornado swept through the town, leaving a trail of death and destruction.

- Use an **appositive** to emphasize a key point.
  A single incident, a tornado that came without warning, **changed the face of a small town forever.**

- Repeat a **key word** or phrase to emphasize an idea.
  The unexpected tornado left a permanent scar **on the small town, a** scar **of destruction, injury, and death.**

Try It!

Consider these ideas: Several students have volunteered for a six-month period to clean and paint homes owned by older people in your neighborhood. Compose at least four sentences, combining these ideas in different ways.

Combining Sentences

Remind students that as they combine sentences they should remember that it's important to vary their sentence lengths within a passage. Provide opportunities for partners to work together to combine sentences.

Combining Shorter Ideas

Help students understand how using appositives and repeating key words for emphasis differs from redundancy and repetition. Point out that appositives and repeated key words add emphasis and clarity to sentences, while redundancy and unnecessary repetition sound as though the writer has run out of ideas.

⭐ **ELPS** 2C, 5F

Try It!
Answers

Possible answers:
1. For the next six months, a group of student volunteers will clean and paint homes owned by older people in our neighborhood.
2. A group of students who have volunteered their time for the next six months will be cleaning and painting homes owned by older people in my neighborhood.
3. A group of students, volunteers from the local school, will spend the next six months cleaning and painting homes owned by older people in my neighborhood.
4. Volunteering their time for the next six months, a group of local students will clean and paint homes owned by older people in my neighborhood.

⭐ **TEKS** 11.17B

TEKS **11.17B** Use a variety of correctly structured sentences; **ELPS** **1H** Develop and expand repertoire of learning strategies; **2C** Learn new language structures; **5F** Write using a variety of grade-appropriate sentence patterns

Expanding Sentences

Have students rewrite the passages they identify to create better variety. Tell partners to check each other's work to be sure that compound, complex, and compound-complex sentences are written correctly.

Try It!
Answers

Possible answers:

1. Toshi entered the store, whistling his favorite song, blissfully unaware that his life was about to take a detour.
2. Dressed as clowns, Albert and Benito ran onto the field when halftime began.
3. Demonstrating his expertise, Mr. Gardner talked to the student about multiple career choices.
4. The car squealed around the corner, smoke rising from its back tires, disturbing the peace of the quiet neighborhood.
5. With a forlorn look in his big brown eyes, our dog Max watches us eat, silently begging for some scraps. **DIFFERENTIATE INSTRUCTION ↘**

DIFFERENTIATE INSTRUCTION ↘

⭐ **TEKS** 11.17B

⭐ **TEKS** 11.17B

Expanding Sentences

Experienced writers often expand a basic idea by adding engaging details. A sentence that expands an idea in this way is called a *cumulative sentence*. The main idea is modified by words, phrases, or clauses. In the following sentence, the main clause (in blue) precedes the modifying phrases.

Maly was studying at the kitchen table, **memorizing a list of vocabulary words, completely focused, intent on acing tomorrow's Spanish quiz.**

In the cumulative sentence that follows, modifiers are placed before and after the main clause (in blue):

Before every practice, Kesha Sims and Tonya Harper work on free throws, **taking 50 shots each.**

FYI

There are five basic ways to expand upon a main clause:

Individual words: Jose prepared his breakfast *quickly.*

Prepositional phrases: Jose ate *with his cat on his lap.*

Participial (-*ing* or -*ed*) phrases: *Looking at the clock,* Jose gobbled his first piece of toast.

Subordinating clauses: Jose was still eating *when his mother left for work.*

Relative clauses: The cat, *who loves leftovers,* purred for a treat.

Try It!

Expand each of these main clauses by adding at least two modifying words, phrases, or clauses.

1. Toshi entered the store.
2. Alberto and Benito ran onto the field.
3. Mr. Gardner talked to the student.
4. The car squealed around the corner.
5. Our dog Max watches us eat.

Differentiated Instruction: Advanced Learners

After students have completed the Try It! activity, have them go through some of their own writing and identify sentences that can be expanded to include more engaging details. Have students revise at least three of their own sentences and share their revisions with partners.

⭐ **TEKS** 11.17B

Checking for Sentence Problems

Complete, correct sentences can contain several ideas. The trick is getting those ideas to work and make sense. The most common errors writers make are fragments, run-ons, and rambling sentences.

Watching for Fragments

A sentence fragment lacks a subject, a verb, or some other essential part. Because of the missing part, the thought is incomplete.

Fragment: Spaghetti all over the table. (This fragment lacks a verb.)

Corrected: Spaghetti slipped all over the table.

Fragment: When Aneko opened the box. (This fragment does not express a complete thought. We need to know what happened "when Aneko opened the box.")

FYI

You can use fragments if you have a good reason. Dialogue, for example, often contains fragments.

Revising Run-On Sentences

A run-on is two or more sentences joined without adequate punctuation or a connecting word. To correct this error, turn the run-on into two sentences or into a compound sentence.

Run-On: I thought the ride would never end my eyes were crossed, and my fingers were numb.

Corrected: I thought the ride would never end. My eyes were crossed, and my fingers were numb.

Try It!

Rewrite the following passage, correcting any sentence problems you find.

> As I tripped and fell. I must have tried to brace myself. Spikes of pain up my left arm as I tried to stand. Feeling woozy, I sat back down and rested and I got back on my feet and I tried to walk.

Traits

Checking for Sentence Problems

As needed, review basic sentence structure. You may wish to refer students to Understanding Sentences on SE pages 756–779.

Watching for Fragments

Make sure students are aware of your policy regarding use of sentence fragments. If students use fragments intentionally, tell them that they must have good reasons for them. When they submit their final copies, ask them to flag any intentional sentence fragments they have written.

Revising Run-On Sentences

Help students understand that run-on sentences lead to boredom and confusion for readers.

Try It!
Answers

Possible rewrite:

When I tripped and fell, I must have tried to brace myself. Looking over my shoulder, I spotted the problem. A root the color of the ground had ruptured the earth and created a bump in the road. Spikes of pain shot up my left arm as I tried to stand. Feeling woozy, I sat back down. After resting a bit, I tried again to get back on my feet.

Advise students that during revision they can inadvertently introduce new problems when they try to improve fluency by varying, combining, and expanding sentences. Caution them to reread their revisions carefully to make sure that they haven't introduced errors.

⭐ **TEKS** 11.17B

TEKS **11.17B** Use a variety of correctly structured sentences; **ELPS** **1C** Use strategic learning strategies to acquire grade-level vocabulary; **3C** Speak using a variety of connecting words; **5F** Write using a variety of grade-appropriate connecting words

Exploring the Writing Process

11.13A Plan a first draft by determining appropriate topics through a range of strategies and developing a thesis or controlling idea; **11.13B** Structure ideas in a sustained and persuasive way and develop drafts in a timed situation that include transitions and rhetorical devices to convey meaning; **11.13C** Revise drafts to clarify meaning and achieve specific rhetorical purposes, consistency of tone, and logical organization by rearranging the words, sentences, and paragraphs to employ tropes, schemes, and by adding transitional words and phrases; **11.13D** Edit for grammar, mechanics, and spelling; **11.13E** Revise final draft in response to feedback from peers and teachers and publish written work for appropriate audiences

1B Monitor written language production and employ self-corrective techniques or other resources; **1C** Use strategic learning strategies to acquire basic and grade-level vocabulary; **1E** Internalize new basic and academic language by using and reusing it/speaking and writing; **1F** Use accessible language and learn new and essential language in the process; **1G** Demonstrate ability to distinguish between and knowledge of when to use formal and informal English; **1H** Develop and expand repertoire of learning strategies; **2C** Learn new expressions, basic and academic vocabulary; **2D** Monitor understanding of spoken language and seek clarification as needed; **2G** Understand the general meaning, main points, and important details of spoken language/topics, language, and contexts; **2I** Demonstrate listening comprehension by following directions, retelling or summarizing, responding to questions and requests, collaborating with peers, and taking notes; **3B** Expand vocabulary/learning and using routine language needed for classroom communication; **3C** Speak using a variety of grammatical structures, sentence lengths, sentence types, and connecting words; **3D** Speak using grade-level content-area vocabulary in context/new English words; **3E** Share information in cooperative learning interactions; **3F** Ask for/give information during extended speaking assignments; **3G** Express opinions, ideas, and feelings; **3H** Narrate, describe, and explain with increasing specificity and detail; **3I** Adapt spoken language for informal purposes; **3J** Respond orally to information presented/concept and language attainment; **4A** Decode using a combination of skills and learn relationship between sounds and letters of English; **4C** Derive meaning of environmental print; **4D** Use prereading supports to enhance comprehension of written text; **4F** Use visual and contextual support and support from peers and teachers to read content area text and to enhance and confirm understanding; **4G** Demonstrate comprehension of increasingly complex English; **4I** Demonstrate English comprehension by employing basic reading skills and expanding reading skills; **4K** Demonstrate English comprehension and expand reading skills by employing analytical skills; **5B** Write using newly acquired basic and content-based grade-level vocabulary; **5C** Spell familiar English words and employ English spelling patterns and rules with increasing accuracy; **5D** Edit writing for standard grammar and usage; **5E** Employ increasingly complex grammatical structures; **5G** Narrate, describe, and explain with increasing specificity and detail

Prewriting (pages 91–98)

Students explore prewriting and its importance as a solid foundation for the other steps in the writing process.

Drafting (pages 99–106)

Students learn to develop their prewriting into a complete unit of writing.

Revising (pages 107–114)

Students gain a deeper understanding of basic revising techniques as well as more advanced strategies.

Peer Response (pages 115–120)

Students learn about the value of peer feedback in the writing process.

Editing (pages 121–126)

Students work on improving their editing skills through the use of resources such as "The Proofreader's Guide" and technology tools.

Publishing (pages 127–133)

Students explore options for sharing their completed writing.

Exploring the Writing Process Unit Scope and Sequence

Day	Writing and Conventions Instruction	Write Source Student Edition			Daily Language Workouts	Skills-Book	Write Source Online
		Core Unit	Tools of Language	Resource Units			
1–5	Prewriting	91–98	TL 562–565		14–17		
	Drafting	99–106					
	Revising	107–114					
	Peer Response	115–120					
	Editing	121–126					
	Publishing	127–133					

(Week 1)

Resource Units referenced above are located in the back of the *Student Edition* and *Teacher's Edition*
TL "*The Tools of Language*" BEW "*Basic Elements of Writing*" PG "*Proofreader's Guide*"

Exploring the Writing Process

- Prewriting
- Drafting
- Revising
- Peer Responding
- Editing
- Publishing

Learning Language

Read aloud the basic and academic terms, as well as the descriptions and questions. Model for students how to read one question and answer it. For example, *It says that writing someone else's words as though they were yours is plagiarism, and it asks if you can commit plagiarism by mistake. I think that could happen if someone forgot that they copied some words and didn't use quotation marks.* Have partners monitor their understanding of the terms by working through the meanings and questions together.

DIFFERENTIATE INSTRUCTION ↘

 ELPS 1F, 2C, 3D, 3E, 4G

Minilessons

Learn the Basics	Prewriting

- Have students **TURN** to the "Basics of Life" list on page 93 and **CHOOSE** one item from each column. Tell them to **MAKE UP** one character associated with each of their four "basics of life" and **WRITE** a story about the characters. Have them **FREEWRITE** for 5 to 8 minutes.

For Example	Drafting

- Have students **READ** "Developing the Middle" (pages 102–105) to learn about ways to support a thesis. Ask them to **THINK** or **READ** about a current event or a classic children's story. Tell them to **WRITE** a sentence or two that models each support strategy

The End	Revising

- Explain that Ernest Hemingway is said to have rewritten one of his endings 27 times. Have students **CHOOSE** a short story and **REWRITE** its ending. Tell them to **IMITATE** the author's voice to make the new ending appear seamless.

 ELPS 1F Use accessible language and learn new and essential language in the process; **2C** Learn new basic and academic vocabulary; **3D** Speak using grade-level content-area vocabulary in context/new English words; **3E** Share information in cooperative learning interactions; **4G** Demonstrate comprehension of increasingly complex English/responding to questions

---

www.hmheducation.com/tx/writesource

Exploring the Writing Process

Learning Language

Work with a partner. Read the meanings and share answers to the questions.

1. The major point you are trying to make is your controlling idea.
   Name the controlling idea in an essay you wrote.

2. If your writing is succinct, it is clear and briefly stated.
   What are some things you can do to make your writing more succinct?

3. If you write someone else's ideas or words as if they were your own, you have committed plagiarism.
   Could you commit plagiarism by mistake? Explain.

4. If you draw a blank, you are suddenly unable to remember or think of something.
   Tell about a time when you drew a blank.

Minilessons (cont.)

Do You See What I See?	Peer Responding

- Have a small group **CHOOSE** an illustration from a textbook. Tell each student to **WRITE** for 5 to 10 minutes about it. Then have the group **RESPOND** to each person's work using the response sheet on page 22.

Prewriting

91

Writer and teacher James Burke says, "Good writing is built, not born. It requires time." Approaching writing as a process allows for effective "building" to take place. As you know, prewriting is the first step in the writing process. During prewriting, you (1) select a specific topic, (2) gather information about it, (3) establish a thesis to guide your writing, and (4) organize the details that support your thesis. Prewriting also refers to any additional research and planning that you may do after you've begun to write.

The amount of prewriting you do depends on the writing project. If you are writing about a personal experience, you may do very little planning. On the other hand, if you are developing a complex persuasive essay, you may do a great deal of research and planning. Whatever the case, giving prewriting the proper attention will lay a solid foundation for all the other steps in the writing process.

- Selecting a Topic
- Gathering Details
- Finding Additional Information
- A Closer Look at Prewriting
- Forming Your Thesis Statement
- Organizing Your Details

"Good writing is clear thinking made visible."
—Bill Wheeler

Prewriting

Objectives

- recognize the importance of the prewriting stage in the writing process
- learn strategies for selecting an effective topic
- learn strategies for gathering and organizing details
- understand the function and form of a thesis statement

Ask students if they have ever tried to write an essay without doing any prewriting. Discuss the results of this approach.

- Were they able to develop their first drafts in an efficient manner?
- Was the revising process focused and easy?

Most students will conclude that skipping the prewriting step in the writing process is likely to result in disorganized drafts that require a good amount of revision.

Differentiated Instruction: English Language Learners

 ELPS 4A

ELP Level **Beginning**	ELP Level **Intermediate**	ELP Level **Advanced/Advanced High**
Use gestures and simplified language to explain the terms and their meanings. Point out sound-letter relationships and have partners practice saying each term.	Have students practice saying terms aloud. Have them write each term and underline important letters and sounds that can help them decode each word.	Have students note suffixes like *-ism* that can help them decode words and their meanings. Have partners use reference tools to help them clarify word meanings.

 ELPS **4A** Decode using a combination of skills and learn relationships between sounds and letters of English

Selecting a Topic

Point out to students that the scope (the size and complexity) of a topic they choose to write about will depend on the writing assignment. For example, when they are asked to write only one or two paragraphs, their topic must be small enough to be supported by only a few important details. On the other hand, when they are asked to write a longer essay or a research report, their topic should be much broader in scope and will require much more support.

DIFFERENTIATE INSTRUCTION ↘

Keeping a Writer's Notebook

Remind students that in addition to providing daily writing opportunities, a writer's notebook is also a good place to list topics of interest.

Developing a Cluster

Have students examine the topic ideas in the sample cluster. Point out that the broadest topic in the cluster—*U.S. Constitution*—is at the center, or nucleus, of the cluster. The terms that radiate from the nucleus become more specific. Ask students to point out the most specific topics in the cluster. (states' rights, free press, freedom of speech, freedom to assemble, freedom to worship, and executive, legislative, judicial) Encourage students to look through their social studies or history texts for similar topic ideas. Have partners work together to discuss how to explore one topic of their choosing in a cluster.

★ TEKS 11.13A; **ELPS** 3J

Making a List

Tell students each word or term they list will prompt them to think of other words and terms, and may eventually lead to a writing topic.

★ TEKS 11.13A

Selecting a Topic

Your teacher may provide you with a general subject and ask that you narrow it to a specific topic

> **General Subject:** Abolitionist movement
> **Specific Topic:** Siege of fort at Harper's Ferry

As you plan your first draft, decide the genre you will use. Then, depending on the assignment, use one of the following strategies to select an effective, specific writing topic.

Keeping a Writer's Notebook

Write on a regular basis in a personal notebook (journal), exploring your experiences and thoughts. Review your entries on occasion and underline ideas that you could explore in writing assignments. (See pages **1–5** for more information.)

Developing a Cluster

Begin a cluster with a nucleus word, usually a general term or idea related to your writing assignment. Then cluster related words around it.

Sample Cluster

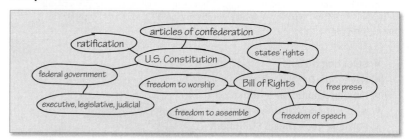

Note: After 3 or 4 minutes, scan your cluster for a word or an idea that interests you. Write nonstop about that idea for 5 to 8 minutes. A few writing topics should begin to occur to you.

Making a List

Begin with a thought or a key word related to your assignment, and simply start listing words and ideas. Listing ideas with a group of classmates (brainstorming) is also an effective way to search for writing topics.

TEKS 11.13A Plan a first draft by determining appropriate topics through a range of strategies; **ELPS 3J** Respond orally to information presented/concept and language attainment

Trying Freewriting

Begin writing with a particular focus in mind—one that is related to your assignment. Write nonstop for 5 to 10 minutes to discover possible writing topics.

- Don't stop to judge, edit, or correct your writing.
- Keep writing even when you seem to be drawing a blank. If necessary, write "I'm drawing a blank" until a new idea comes to mind.
- Review your writing and underline ideas you like.
- Continue freewriting about ideas you want to explore further.

Sample Freewriting

Unlike the citizens of a lot of other countries, we have the freedom of assembly. Our Constitution guarantees that. That means students or teachers or any group can get together to talk about our country. We can debate the work of the government and ask questions. We don't have to worry about being arrested. Our first political thinkers, who helped . . .

Considering the "Basics of Life" List

Below you will find a list of essential elements in our lives. The list provides an endless variety of topic possibilities. For example, the category *education* led to the following writing ideas:

- internships for high school students
- community service requirements
- open campus vs. closed campus

Basics of Life

clothing	education	love	entertainment
communication	machines	rules/laws	health/medicine
exercise/training	faith/religion	science/technology	recreation
housing	family	energy	literature/books
community	trade/money	land/property	tools/utensils
food	agriculture	work/occupation	freedom/rights
arts/music	heat/fuel	water	clean air

Try It!

List four or five possible writing ideas for any two categories in the "Basics of Life" list. (For your next writing assignment, use one of the strategies above to identify possible topics.)

Process

Trying Freewriting

Provide an opportunity for students to practice the freewriting technique described. Suggest a general topic and tell students you will freewrite along with them. Discuss and compare the ideas that are generated.

Considering the "Basics of Life" List

Have student examine and discuss the list. Challenge them to think of any topics that are not covered by the list.

Try It!
Answers

To generate enough topic ideas for all students, do the **Try It!** activity in class. Encourage students to suggest a variety of related topics for as many categories in the Basics of Life list as possible. Ask two or three volunteers to record the ideas that students suggest. Later, these volunteers can cross-check their lists and create a master list of topics that can be entered on a classroom or school computer. Students can print out the list and add it to their writing notebooks.

★ TEKS 11.13A

★ TEKS 11.13A Plan a first draft by determining appropriate topics through a range of strategies; ELPS 1E Internalize new basic language by using and reusing it/writing; 2C Learn new expressions, basic and academic vocabulary; 2I Demonstrate listening comprehension/collaborating with peers

Gathering Details

Guide students to see that gathering details is a key step during prewriting because it allows them to know whether enough ideas and information are available before they have invested significant time in a piece of writing.

Gathering Your Thoughts

As needed, have partners collaborate to define or explain the term *freewriting*, as well as *who, what, when, where,* and *why.*

⭐ **ELPS** 2C, 2I

Students can demonstrate their understanding by combining the two strategies—focused freewriting and the 5 W's—to explore a topic. Have students begin by writing *Who?* at the top of their papers and then write freely for several minutes to answer that question about their topics. Then they can continue this process for the remaining questions. If they are unable to answer any of the questions, students will want to select other topics. **DIFFERENTIATE INSTRUCTION ↘**

⭐ **TEKS** 11.13A; **ELPS** 2I

Try It!
Answers

Have students report on which of the strategies was most useful for them in gathering their thoughts.

94

⭐ **TEKS** 11.13A

Gathering Details

Once you've selected a specific topic, you need to gather details for writing. In most cases, it's a good idea to first collect your initial thoughts about the topic, including personal experience and past knowledge. Then, if necessary, do research to find more information.

Gathering Your Thoughts

The following strategies will help you to recall what you already know and establish how you feel about your topic.

- **Freewriting:** At this point, you can approach freewriting in two ways. (1) You can do a focused freewriting, exploring your topic from a number of different angles. (2) You can approach your freewriting as if it were a quick version of the actual paper.
- **5 W's:** Answer the 5 W questions—*who? what? when? where?* and *why?*—to identify basic information about your topic. Add *how?* to the list for even better coverage.
- **Audience appeal:** Address a specific audience as you write about your topic. Consider a group of parents, a live television audience, or the readers of a popular teen magazine.
- **Directed writing:** Write whatever comes to mind about your topic, using the questions listed below.

Describe it.	What do you see, hear, feel, smell, or taste?
Compare it.	What is it similar to? What is it different from?
Apply it.	What can you do with it? How can you use it?
Associate it.	What connections between this and something else come to mind?
Analyze it.	What parts does it have? How do they work together?
Argue for or against it.	What do you like about it? What don't you like about it? What are its strengths and its weaknesses?

- **Directed dialoguing:** Create a dialogue between two people in which your specific topic is the focus of the conversation. This writing will help you explore differing opinions about the topic.

Try It!

Gather your initial thoughts. Use one of these strategies when you are ready to collect your own thoughts about a writing topic.

Differentiated Instruction:
Struggling Learners

To help students gather their thoughts on a topic, have them work with a partner to explore the topic orally, using the directed-writing questions on this page. Once they have generated some details orally, it will be less overwhelming for students to write about their topics.

TEKS 11.13A

Prewriting **95**

Finding Additional Information

For most writing assignments, it won't suffice to simply gather your own thoughts about a topic. Expository and persuasive essays, for example, will almost always require that you consult other sources for information. These sources can be divided into two categories—*primary* and *secondary*.

Exploring a Variety of Sources

- **Primary sources** include interviews, personal observations, firsthand experiences, surveys, experiments, and so on. A primary source informs you directly, not through another person's explanation or interpretation.
- **Secondary sources** include periodicals, books, references, Web sites, and so on. A secondary source is one that contains information other people have gathered and interpreted. It is at least once removed from the original.

Process

Tips for Researching

Follow these guidelines when gathering information:

- Whenever possible, use both primary and secondary sources to get a thorough understanding of your topic.
- Read secondary sources with a critical eye, always evaluating the quality and the purpose of the information. (See page **377**.)
- Take careful notes, writing down important facts, opinions, and quotations. Record any source information you will need to cite. (See page **401**.)
- Consider using a graphic organizer such as a gathering grid (page **398**) to keep track of the facts and details your research uncovers.
- Consult librarians and teachers if you have trouble finding useful sources of information.

Try It!

Identify the best resources. List at least one or two primary sources and one or two secondary sources that you could use to gather information for each of the following writing assignments:

- an article about a high school basketball game
- an editorial about cutting park jobs for students
- an essay about the quality of medical care during the Civil War
- a research paper exploring some aspect of U.S. immigration policy

---

Finding Additional Information

Encourage students to develop and practice research skills to gather information.

Exploring a Variety of Sources

List the kinds of sources you want students to use and show them how to evaluate the validity and reliability of these primary and secondary sources. ✔ DIFFERENTIATE INSTRUCTION

Tips for Researching

For more information on research skills, including how to evaluate source information, encourage students to read SE pages 376–384.

Try It!
Answers

Possible answers:
- basketball game—primary: interview basketball player, team video of the game; secondary: a newspaper article about the game, a television report about the game
- cutting park jobs—primary: the park finance manager, personal experience working in the park; secondary: magazine article about state budget, Web site on student job programs
- medical care during the Civil War—primary: diaries of Civil War soldiers or medical personnel, medical and military reports of the period; secondary: history books, biographies of wounded soldiers and caregivers
- U.S. immigration policy—primary: State Department regulations on immigration, interview with immigration official; secondary: books about the current immigration policies, magazine articles

 TEKS 11.13A

 TEKS **11.13A** Plan a first draft by determining appropriate topics through a range of strategies; **ELPS** **4K** Demonstrate English comprehension and expand reading skills by employing analytical skills

A Closer Look at Prewriting

Direct attention to the quotation from Rachel Carson at the top of the page. Discuss what the steps involved in prewriting might "tell" a writer about his or her subject.

Taking Inventory of Your Thoughts

Admitting that a topic is not a good match is difficult for student writers for the following reasons.

- Students may feel that they have already invested a lot of time, energy, and thought on the topic.
- Students may feel pressured by deadlines. Choosing a new topic, or even shifting the focus of the original topic, usually requires additional research and preparation. This can put even the most conscientious students behind schedule.
- If students had a difficult time selecting a topic to begin with, they may think they can't choose another topic that will work any better than the original.

You can support students who must change topics by extending deadlines and reworking schedules for submissions. You can also remind students that choosing a new topic can make the difference between an enjoyable writing experience and a disappointing one.

DIFFERENTIATE INSTRUCTION ↘

⭐ **TEKS** 11.13A

96

⭐ **TEKS** 11.13A

"The discipline of the writer is to learn to be still and listen to what his subject has to tell him."
—Rachel Carson

A Closer Look at Prewriting

After you've selected a topic and gathered details about it, you can plan and write your first draft, or you can consider how well you match up with your topic before you go any further.

Taking Inventory of Your Thoughts

After carefully considering the questions that follow, you will be ready to (1) move ahead with your writing or (2) change your topic.

Purpose
- Does my topic meet the requirements of the assignment?
- Am I writing to explain, persuade, describe, entertain, or retell?

Self
- How do I feel about the topic? Have I made a personal connection with it?
- Do I have enough time to develop it?

Topic
- How much more do I need to know about this topic?
- Has my research changed my thinking about the topic?
- What part of the topic will I focus on?

Audience
- Who are my readers?
- How much do they already know about my topic?
- How can I keep them interested in my ideas?

Form
- How should I present my ideas—in a story, an essay, a report, a multimedia presentation?
- What form of writing should I use—narrative, descriptive, persuasive, expository?

Differentiated Instruction: Struggling Learners

To avoid wasted time and energy, require that students submit two or three possible writing topics before starting their research. Work with students to choose the best topic for the assignment, for their personal enjoyment, and for ease of finding adequate research material.

Differentiated Instruction: Advanced Learners

To extend their experience with thesis statements, have students read op-ed pieces in several newspapers and underline each writer's thesis statement. Ask students to demonstrate how each thesis statement fits into the formula on this page.

TEKS 11.13A Plan a first draft by determining appropriate topics through a range of strategies

Forming Your Thesis Statement

After you have explored the topic and collected information, you should begin to develop a more focused interest in your topic. If all goes well, this interest will become the thesis, or controlling idea, of your writing. **A thesis statement identifies the focus of an academic essay.** It usually highlights a particular condition, feature, or feeling about the topic or takes a stand.

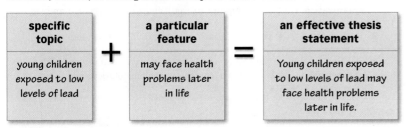

specific topic		a particular feature		an effective thesis statement
young children exposed to low levels of lead	**+**	may face health problems later in life	**=**	Young children exposed to low levels of lead may face health problems later in life.

Sample Thesis Statements

Writing Assignment: Essay about opportunities in education
Specific Subject: High school internships
Thesis Statement: Internship programs (**specific topic**) give students real-world experiences (**particular feature**).

Writing Assignment: Essay on the Civil War
Specific Subject: General George McClellan
Thesis Statement: General George McClellan's overcautious tactics (**specific topic**) prolonged the war (**particular feeling**).

Try It!

Rewrite each of the following thesis statements on your own paper. Circle the specific topic. Then underline the part of the statement that identifies the feature, feeling, or stand that will be developed.

1. The new graduated licensing laws have had a positive effect on young drivers.
2. Students should be allowed to leave campus during lunch.
3. The pressures of being the best can overload some students.
4. Practicing conflict resolution reduces violence in schools.

Process

Forming Your Thesis Statement

Throughout this book, students will be encouraged to use the formula shown here for writing thesis statements. Encourage them to take the time now to understand how to use the formula. ✔ **DIFFERENTIATE INSTRUCTION**

Try It!
Answers

Have students share their responses for the **Try It!** activity with the class. If the majority of students cannot recognize how the formula applies to the thesis statements, provide additional instruction and practice before moving on. ✔ **DIFFERENTIATE INSTRUCTION**

★ **TEKS** 11.13A

✱ For more on forming thesis statements, see SE page 620.

Topics are shown in boldface type.
1. The **new graduated licensing laws** have had a positive effect on young drivers.
2. **Allowing students to leave campus at lunch time** shows respect for their maturity and sense of responsibility.
3. The **pressures of being the best** can overload some students.
4. **Practicing conflict resolution** reduces violence in schools.

★ **TEKS** 11.13A Plan a first draft by developing a thesis statement; **ELPS** 1E Internalize new academic language by using and reusing it/speaking; 1H Develop and expand repertoire of learning strategies; 2E Use visual support, contextual support, and linguistic support to confirm understanding of spoken language

Organizing Your Details

Have students recall what they learned about selecting appropriate organizing patterns for different types of assignments. Suggest that they turn back to SE page 61 to review these different patterns. Provide opportunities for students to use appropriate vocabulary to describe and explain the graphic organizers.

DIFFERENTIATE INSTRUCTION ↘

 ELPS 3B

Sample Brief List

Invite students to compare and contrast the content and level of detail in the brief list and in the sentence outline that follows.

Sample Sentence Outline

Remind students that they can use a variety of graphic organizers (SE pages 64–65) to gather and organize their ideas before they create a list or a detailed sentence outline.

TEKS 11.13A, 11.13B

✴ For more on creating a sentence outline, see SE pages 403 and 619.

Organizing Your Details

After forming a thesis statement, you may need to design a writing plan before you start your first draft. Your plan can be anything from a brief list of ideas to a detailed sentence outline. Use the guidelines that follow to help organize your details for writing.

1. Study your thesis statement. Select a structure, or method of organization, that will communicate your ideas in a sustained and persuasive way.
2. Review the details you have gathered. Be sure all of them support your thesis.
3. Decide which basic pattern of organization fits your essay topic— chronological, spatial, compare-contrast, problem-solution, and so on. (See pages **612–616**.)

Sample Brief List

> Topic: Freedom of Assembly
> • Opposition to citizen assemblies
> • Opportunities for debate
> • Concerns about society and government
> • Suggestions for change

Sample Sentence Outline

> Topic: Freedom of Assembly
> I. Tyrants or dictators oppose citizen assemblies.
>   A. Dictators know it is easier to control people who are uninformed.
>   B. People might learn that many oppose certain policies.
>   C. Such meetings might lead to the overthrow of the dictator.
> II. Citizens have the right to assemble for any number of purposes.
>   A. Government cannot restrict who may or may not assemble.
>   B. United States citizens have a right to decide . . .

Drafting

Once you have collected and organized your details, you're ready to write your first draft. Note the word "first." This is your first chance to develop your prewriting into a complete, cohesive unit of writing.

There can be a great satisfaction in writing a first draft, an excitement at seeing your initial thinking about a topic take shape. Write your first draft freely without being overly concerned about correctness. Your goal is to get all your ideas on paper in a form that is easy to follow. Use the planning you've done (outline) as a basic guide, but be open to new ideas that come to mind as you write.

If you are writing an essay or a research paper, develop each main point in a separate paragraph. Also connect the paragraphs with linking words or transitions. The information in this chapter provides many additional drafting tips and strategies.

- Considering the Big Picture
- Drafting the Beginning
- Developing the Middle
- Drafting the Ending

"If you want to write, you must begin by beginning, continue by continuing, finish by finishing. This is the great secret."

—Jack Heffron

Drafting

Objectives
- learn strategies for drafting a beginning paragraph
- learn the types of support to include in middle paragraphs
- learn to use different levels of detail in middle paragraphs
- understand the purpose of an ending paragraph

Call attention to the Jack Heffron quotation. Encourage students to make this quotation their writing motto, to copy it onto a bookmark for their writer's notebook or journal, and to refer to it before they begin their next writing assignment.

Ask students to share their opinions, based on personal experience, on which part of writing is the most difficult—beginning, continuing, or finishing. Ask them to defend their opinion in their journals by telling about their experiences.

⭐ ELPS 3G, 5G

Differentiated Instruction: English Language Learners

⭐ ELPS 3G, 5G

ELP Level **Beginning**	ELP Level **Intermediate**	ELP Level **Advanced/Advanced High**
Using an example thesis statement generated from TE page 97, guide students to decide which pattern of organization would be best suited for an essay on the topic.	Choose an example thesis statement from TE page 97. Review patterns of organization and ask students to give opinions about which pattern would work best and why.	Have partners choose an example thesis statement generated from TE page 97 and write a few sentences to explain which pattern of organization they would use and why.

 ELPS 3G Express opinions; **5G** Narrate with increasing specificity and detail

Considering the Big Picture

The information on this page summarizes what students have learned so far about using the Texas traits of focus and coherence, organization, and development of ideas, and about creating a first draft.

Drafting Hints

Suggest that students add the drafting hints to their writer's notebooks.

Remembering the Parts of Writing

This page also reinforces the information presented in the Big Picture chart on SE page 60, which students can look at now to refresh their memories. Have students review the chart and summarize the features of the beginning, the middle, and the ending of a piece of writing.

TEKS 11.13B; **ELPS** 4G

Tell students that for each essay in this book, there will be a Big Picture chart that shows them how all the elements of the assigned essay should fit together. The pages on which these big picture charts appear are the following:

- Personal narrative, SE page 140
- Informative article, SE page 170
- Argumentative essay, SE page 228
- Theme interpretation, SE page 286

Try It!
Answers

Invite students to share their self-assessments in small groups.

Considering the Big Picture

As you prepare to write a first draft, keep in mind these three traits of good writing: *focus and coherence, organization,* and *development of ideas.*

Focus and Coherence Respond directly to the assignment. Decide what your controlling idea is. Check that all of your details support that idea.

Organization Using your planning notes, organize your ideas so that your sentences are logically linked. Exclude ideas that are unrelated to your controlling idea.

Development of Ideas As you write your first draft, concentrate on fleshing out ideas so that each sentence adds meaning to the sentence that came before it.

Drafting Hints

- *Review your prewriting materials before you begin.*
- *If you are drafting by hand, write on every other line; if you are drafting on a computer, double-space so you will have room to revise.*
- *Don't be overly concerned about being neat and avoiding errors. You can make corrections later on.*

Remembering the Parts of Writing

As you draft, keep in mind the three parts of any writing: the beginning, the middle, and the ending.

The Beginning

- gets the reader's attention
- identifies the controlling idea of your writing

The Middle

- presents the main points that support the controlling idea
- includes details that develop the main points

The Ending

- restates the controlling idea
- wraps up the paper

Try It!

Before you write your next first draft, review this page. Then, assess your results. Did you get all your relevant ideas on paper? Did you include a beginning, middle, and ending?

TEKS **11.13B** Develop drafts in which ideas are structured in a sustained and persuasive way; **ELPS** **4G** Demonstrate comprehension of increasingly complex English/retelling or summarizing

Drafting the Beginning

Your opening paragraph should "hook" the reader with its interesting information. Here are some ways to attract the reader's interest.

Grabbing Your Reader's Attention

- Give a surprising fact or statement.
  The Bushmen of Kalahari face extinction; yet, ironically, it is modern tourism that might save them.

- Ask a question.
  With the world rapidly changing, how is it that one group of people has survived without modern conveniences?

- Use a relevant quotation.
  "If the government has its way, my people will be gone," says a member of the once proud Bushmen tribe.

- Present an interesting detail about the topic.
  In the wild, inhospitable Kalahari Basin, a hardy people live much as their ancestors did 30,000 years ago.

Shaping Your Beginning Paragraph

The first part of your opening paragraph should identify your topic and hook the reader. Follow with any necessary background information. End with your controlling idea, identifying the specific part of the topic you plan to emphasize.

Sample Beginning Paragraph

Attention-getting opening	*"If the government has its way, my people will be gone," says a member of the once proud Bushmen tribe.* **Although**
Background information	**the tribe has lived in the African Kalahari Basin for more than 30,000 years, its members are now being relocated and modernized by the government. Soon the remaining members of the tribe will have either died out or become assimilated.**
Thesis statement	*Because of modernization and greed, the lifestyle of the Kalahari Bushmen is in jeopardy.*

Try It!

Analyze the opening paragraph of one of the essays in this book. Using the information above as a guide, explain how the opening accomplishes its purpose.

Process

Drafting the Beginning

Ask students to suggest why it is considered important to "hook" readers at the beginning of a piece of writing.

Grabbing Your Reader's Attention

Sometimes students get so involved in trying to write imaginative beginnings that they cannot move on. Tell students that if they are still not satisfied after trying all four opening strategies (surprising fact, question, relevant quotation, and interesting detail), they should settle on one of their attempts for the time being, finish their opening paragraphs, and move on. Reassure them that during revising they can refocus their attention on improving their beginnings. They may also find that as they are developing the middle of their essays, their ideas about the beginning may crystallize.

Shaping Your Beginning Paragraph

Guide students through the three elements of the beginning paragraph, asking them to explain the purpose of each one.

TEKS 11.13B

Try It!
Answers

Before asking students to do the **Try It!** activity on their own, select one or two opening paragraphs from essays in the book and work together as a class to analyze how well each opening accomplishes its purpose of attracting the reader's interest, providing relevant background information, and stating the thesis.

☑ DIFFERENTIATE INSTRUCTION

Differentiated Instruction: English Language Learners

ELPS 4F, 4G, 4K

ELP Level **Beginning**	ELP Level **Intermediate**	ELP Level **Advanced/Advanced High**
Use gestures, simplified language, and visuals to help students comprehend the ideas in the examples you choose. Point out how each topic is introduced.	Provide sentence stems for students to summarize the topic of each sample essay. Ask yes/no questions to help students infer how each topic is introduced.	Have partners summarize the topic of each sample essay and analyze how each topic is introduced. Have students share their work with another pair.

TEKS **11.13B** Develop drafts in which ideas are structured in a sustained and persuasive way; ELPS **4F** Use support from peers and teachers to read content area text and to enhance and confirm understanding; **4G** Demonstrate comprehension of increasingly complex English/retelling or summarizing; **4K** Demonstrate English comprehension and expand reading skills by employing analytical skills

Developing the Middle

Explain to students that the guidelines of their writing assignments will usually indicate what types of support they should gather during prewriting and what types of support they should use in their middle paragraphs.

Using Various Types of Support

Point out that essay assignments and writing prompts always contain one or more signal words (*explain, define, describe*, and so on) that indicate how the thesis statements should be supported.

- Read aloud past writing assignments and test writing prompts. Some of the topic ideas listed on SE page 69 can easily be turned into writing prompts.
- Have students identify the signal word or words in each prompt you read and tell what types of support they would provide to support the thesis.
  ★ ELPS 1E
- To extend this activity, have students tell what type of graphic organizer they would use to gather details for different types of support.

★ TEKS 11.13B

Developing the Middle

After you have written a strong opening paragraph that clearly states your thesis, or controlling idea, you need to support that idea with details in a sustained and persuasive way. This is the purpose of your middle paragraphs.

What will determine the success of your writing is not how many details you include, but how well those details support your controlling idea. Look back at your prewriting ideas. Select details that persuasively support your thesis and use clear transitions to show how they are linked. Eliminate weak or unrelated details.

Most essays, articles, and research papers require various types of support. Details that explain, narrate, describe, summarize, define, argue, compare, analyze, and reflect can all be used to support your controlling idea. As you decide which details and what type of details to use, ask yourself, *Which details do the best job of persuasively supporting my thesis statement, or controlling idea?*

FYI

Most essays, articles, and research papers require a number of these methods to thoroughly develop their theses. For example, an essay of definition may contain two or more definitions, a comparison, a brief story, and so on.

Using Various Types of Support

Below and on the next page are some examples of how one student used various types of support in his paper about the Bushmen of the Kalahari.

Define: Identify or clarify the meaning of a specific term or idea.

> The people of the Kalahari go by several names, depending on the regional language. Some call the natives "San," a Khoi word that means "outsider," or "Basarwa," a Herero word meaning "person who has nothing." Understandably, the Kalahari people themselves prefer to be called, simply, "Bushmen."

Explain: Provide important facts, details, and examples.

> The drive to relocate the Bushmen is just one more—perhaps the last—chapter in a story of cultural annihilation. For more than 30,000 years, the Bushmen lived as peaceful hunter-gatherers until they were made slaves by Afrikaner farmers to the south and the Tswana tribes to the north. In the 1960s, the Central Kalahari Game Reserve was established to preserve their way of life, but in the 1980s, the Botswana government, embarrassed by the backward image projected by the Bushmen, decided to bring them into the present. The natives were forcibly resettled in the city, into a life of squalor and humiliation.

TEKS 11.13B   Drafting 103

Compare: Show how two things are alike or different.

Botswana's treatment of this indigenous people can be compared with the United States' treatment of Native Americans. In 2002, the Botswana government began relocating the native Bushmen to "settlements" in much the same way that Native Americans were placed on reservations by the United States government. Both groups have suffered a loss of their culture through the insensitivity of the ruling government. Unfortunately, the transplanted Bushmen battle alcoholism and poverty in much the same way as Native Americans have done in this country. The Bushmen, like Native Americans, are also beginning to use the courts to reclaim their land. In both cases, the government has insisted that relocation is actually good for the people.

Analyze: Examine the parts of something to better understand the whole.

The reasons given for the relocation are suspect when examined closely. The government cites environmental reasons, stating that the growth of farming in the area has lowered the water table. This provides the financial reason for resettlement: the expense of bringing in water for the Bushmen's use. Finally, the government alleges that the change is for the people's own good, that their archaic culture must adapt to a changing society so they can live better lives. Despite all this rhetoric, it is interesting to note that the Bushmen's territory is a valuable diamond area. Moving the native peoples opens the way for extensive—and lucrative—mining.

Summarize: Present only the most important details.

The encroaching modern world threatens the entire Kalahari as ever-expanding diamond mines threaten the environment, bit by bit devouring the land in the quest for riches. Even as it enriches the country, the greed of industry destroys a way of life. Today, in the shadow of the modern city of Gaborone, the proud Bushmen, dressed in secondhand clothing rather than their traditional breechcloths, dance their ancient dances. They cling to the thread of their ancestry even as the door to the past slams shut in their faces.

Try It!

Analyze the middle paragraphs in one of the essays in this book. Tell which method of support is used to develop each main point (explaining, comparing, analyzing, and so on).

Process

Using Various Types of Support (cont'd)

After students have had time to read all of the examples, discuss how the information in each one provides the type of support required.

☑ DIFFERENTIATE INSTRUCTION

Try It!
Answers

Have students work in small groups to complete the **Try It!** activity. Students who don't feel confident about analyzing text on their own will benefit from the insights and critical reading skills of their classmates.

Assure students that they will receive ample practice and instruction to help them determine what kind of support to use, how to gather support, and how to use that support to develop their middle paragraphs for each essay they will write this year.

TEKS 11.13B; ELPS 4K

Differentiated Instruction: English Language Learners

ELPS 4D

Before reading the sample essay, use prereading supports to develop vocabulary and enhance comprehension.

ELP Level **Beginning**	ELP Level **Intermediate**	ELP Level **Advanced/Advanced High**
Use visuals, gestures, and simplified language to clarify the meaning of challenging language such as *relocate, reclaim,* and *devouring.*	Have partners work together to clarify the meaning of challenging language such as *humiliation, insensitivity,* and *extensive.*	Have students discuss the meaning of words such as *annihilation, squalor,* and *encroaching.* Then have partners work together to clarify meanings.

TEKS **11.13B** Develop drafts in which ideas are structured in a sustained and persuasive way; **ELPS 4D** Use prereading supports to enhance comprehension of written text; **4K** Demonstrate English comprehension and expand reading skills by employing analytical skills

Developing the Middle
Using Different Levels of Detail

Make sure students understand that a paragraph may contain several Level 2 and Level 3 sentences. Provide students with an example of a well-written paragraph. Ask them to mark

- the topic sentence with a *1*,
- the sentences that provide main supporting points with a *2*, and
- the sentences that use rhetorical devices to convey meaning with a *3*.

Discuss how each level of detail helps to create a complete picture about the topic.

DIFFERENTIATE INSTRUCTION ↘

TEKS 11.13B

Try It!
Answers

Possible answers:

- The struggle between the Bushmen and the government is rooted in modern changes in the area. Level 1
- The Botswana government claims that the Bushmen do not always stick to the ancient practices. Level 2
- Since that time, however, the government has continued to make it difficult—if not impossible—for the Bushmen to return to their ancestral land. Level 3

Developing the Middle Using Different Levels of Detail

In most cases each main point is developed in a separate paragraph. Remember that specific details add meaning to your writing and make it worth reading, while writing that lacks effective detail leaves the reader with an incomplete picture and questions about the topic. In general, a well-written paragraph often contains three levels of detail.

Level 1: A controlling sentence names the topic.

"If the government has its way, my people will be gone," says a member of the once proud Bushmen tribe.

Level 2: Clarifying sentences provide relevant supporting details.

Although the tribe has lived in the African Kalahari Basin for more than 30,000 years, its members are now being relocated and modernized by the government.

Level 3: Rhetorical devices convey meaning by adding emphasis or evoking emotional responses.

The drive to relocate the Bushmen is just one more—perhaps the last—chapter in a story of cultural annihilation.

Try It!

Identify sentences that show the three levels of detail in the paragraph below. Label each sentence after writing it down.

The struggle between the Bushmen and the government is rooted in modern changes in the area. The Botswana government claimed that the Bushmen did not always stick to the ancient practices, nor have they maintained their isolated, nomadic existence. Instead, they have created settlements and are using modern implements, such as guns and trucks. The government believes that relocating the tribe will help preserve the delicate ecological balance in the Kalahari area. The Bushmen do not agree. Backed by Survival International, the Bushmen took their case to the courts. In 2006, the high court ruled that the eviction of the Bushmen was "unlawful and unconstitutional." Since that time, however, the government has continued to make it difficult—if not impossible—for the Bushmen to return to their ancestral land.

Differentiated Instruction: Struggling Learners

Stress that it is not necessary to be able to categorize levels of detail in order to write good paragraphs. Students only need to remember that good paragraphs should contain a topic sentence and two or more main supporting details.

Integrating Quotations

Always choose quotations that are appropriate for your writing. Quotations should support your ideas, not replace them.

Strategies for Using Quotations

Use the strategies below to make the most effective use of quoted material in your writing.

- **Use quotations to support your main points.**
  Effective quotations can back up your key ideas or support your arguments.

  > For many, the destruction of the environment in remote regions is far removed from daily life. Yet, as John C. Sawhill, president of the Nature Conservancy, once said, "In the end, our society will be defined not only by what we create, but by what we refuse to destroy." In other words, man's legacy is tied directly to the management or mismanagement of the land.

- **Use quotations to lend authority to your writing.**
  Quoting an expert shows that you have researched your topic and understand its significance.

  > The nations of the world must band together to make sure that we never reach the point of using nuclear weapons in war. Perhaps it was put best by General Omar Bradley, first chairman of the Joint Chiefs of Staff, when he said, "The way to win an atomic war is to make certain it never starts." With this type of "victory," everyone wins.

- **Use quotations that are succinct and powerful.**
  Distinctive quotations add value to your writing.

  > Pianist Benny Green defines a jazz musician as "a juggler who uses harmonies instead of oranges." The test of jazz is how these harmonies, tossed about seemingly at random, actually hold together in a smooth, if loosely defined, pattern.

Common Quotation Problems to Avoid

Avoid these problems as you choose quotations.

- **Plagiarism**
  Cite sources for all quotations (and paraphrases).
- **Long quotations**
  Keep quotations brief and to the point.
- **Overused quotations**
  Use a quotation only when you cannot share its message as powerfully or effectively in another way.

Process

Integrating Quotations

Remind students that a quotation should only be used when your own words are not as effective.

Strategies for Using Quotations

Give students time to read each example. Have them explain why each example is effective in presenting the writer's ideas.

 DIFFERENTIATE INSTRUCTION

TEKS 11.13B

Common Quotation Problems to Avoid

After you have discussed the common problems, offer students these additional tips and guidelines for using quotations effectively and correctly.

- **Know your source.** If you are copying a quotation from a resource, make sure the resource is reliable.
- **Be exact.** Copy the quotation exactly and double-check to make sure it is correct. If you are handwriting your notes, make sure you copy the quotation correctly into your first draft.
- **Be fair.** If you are using a quotation from an interview, have the interviewee review the quotation before you prepare your final copy to make sure you have not misquoted the person.
- **Use correct punctuation.** Be sure to enclose the entire quotation in quotation marks and use correct end punctuation.

✱ For more on punctuating quotations, see SE pages 660–663.

 TEKS 11.13B Develop drafts in which ideas are structured in a sustained and persuasive way; **ELPS** 2G Understand the main points and important details of spoken language/topics

Drafting the Ending

Point out that some writers actually write their beginning and ending paragraphs first so that they know where to start and where they're going to end up. If students want to try this strategy, tell them to keep their overall writing plan in mind and to use their outline to make sure that they construct an ending that logically follows their middle paragraphs.

Sample Closing Paragraph

Discuss the elements of a strong ending shown in the sample closing paragraph.

Forming a Final Thought

Encourage students to experiment with all three ways (call to action, lingering question, good or bad conclusion) to form a final thought for their ending paragraph. Point out that one way may be more effective than another for a particular form of writing. For example, using a call to action is an effective way to end a persuasive essay.

DIFFERENTIATE INSTRUCTION ↘

Try It!
Answers

Have students work in small groups to complete the **Try It!** activity. Students who don't feel confident about analyzing text on their own will benefit from the insights and critical reading skills of their classmates. Elicit examples of the three ways of forming a final thought.

TEKS 11.13B

Drafting the Ending

Your ending paragraph allows you to tie up all the ideas in your essay. It should do at least two of the following things.

- **Restate the thesis of your paper.**
- **Review the main points.**
- **Leave the reader with something to think about.**

Sample Closing Paragraph

Restatement of the thesis	
Review of a main point	The Bushmen of the Kalahari are in danger of extinction as a separate cultural entity. The government of Botswana has moved them from their tribal lands. It has taken away their means of self-support as it tries to include them in a society for which they are neither eager nor equipped. Whether the Bushmen can survive as a people in such a world is yet to be seen. Perhaps the government's relocation plan is a positive, inevitable move, or perhaps it is simply a form of legalized elimination.
A final thought	

Forming a Final Thought

Here are three different ways to form a final thought.

A call to action often directs the reader to do something.

If you see litter on the street, don't just shake your head in disgust. Pick it up and toss it away. If everyone acted in this way, we would have a cleaner town.

A lingering question encourages the reader to further examine the subject.

People may be threatened by the very water they drink. Can they live with that?

A good or bad conclusion suggests that your topic poses a possible benefit or threat the reader should be aware of.

Using aromatherapy to manage stress, heal tired bodies, and simply feel good is cheap, safe, and enjoyable.

Try It!

Analyze the ending paragraph of one of the essays in this book. Using the information above, tell what the paragraph has accomplished.

Differentiated Instruction: English Language Learners

ELPS 3G, 3H, 4K

ELP Level **Beginning**	ELP Level **Intermediate**	ELP Level **Advanced/Advanced High**
Choose an ending example and use gestures, simplified language, and visuals to help students comprehend the ideas. Point out how the draft is concluded.	Select an ending example. Provide sentence stems for students to explain the ideas with detail. Ask yes/no questions to help students analyze how the writer concludes the draft.	Have partners select an ending example and summarize its ideas. Then have them analyze how the writer concludes the draft and whether it is effective.

 TEKS **11.13B** Develop drafts in which ideas are structured in a sustained and persuasive way; **ELPS** **3G** Express ideas; **3H** Explain with increasing specificity and detail; **4K** Demonstrate English comprehension and expand reading skills by employing analytical skills

107

Revising

Experienced writers have an extensive working knowledge of the revising process. More specifically, with a first draft in hand, they know just how much work is ahead of them. They will continue to work with a piece of writing until it says what they want it to say from start to finish. They also know the importance of setting aside the first draft for a reasonable length of time before they begin making changes. As writer Kenneth Atchity says, "It would be crazy to begin revising immediately after finishing the first draft, and counter to the way the mind likes to create."

This chapter will help you gain a better understanding of the revising process. It covers everything from a review of basic revising guidelines to an explanation of a valuable revising strategy. As you go through this material, remember that revising may be the most important step in the writing process, because when you revise, you improve the thoughts and details that carry your message.

- **Understanding the Basics**
- **Using a Strategy That Works**
- **A Closer Look at Revising**
- **Revising Checklist**
- **Revising in Action**
- **Checking for Snapshots**

"The first draft reveals the art; revision reveals the artist."

—Michael Less

Revising

Objectives
- practice a strategy for revising a timed writing
- learn a strategy for in-depth revising
- practice evaluating a passage for revising

Ask students to describe in their writer's notebook their strategy for revising. Tell them to date and bookmark the page. Have them turn to this page before and after they revise any piece of writing from this point forward. Encourage students to reflect on their revising skills periodically. As the year progresses, students will recognize the great benefits of meaningful revision.

Resources

Copy Masters

- Sensory chart, 5 W's chart (TE page 114)

Understanding the Basics

Discuss each bulleted point, eliciting students' ideas about why the strategy is useful for revising. Ask them to give examples of instances when they have used each strategy to see where they need to clarify meaning, to achieve better consistency of tone, or to add transitional phrases.

TEKS 11.13C

Revising a Timed Writing

Tell students that in a timed-writing situation, it is a good idea to review the writing prompt before beginning to revise. Explain that ensuring that they are addressing all elements of the prompt will help them to focus their effort where it is most needed.

Try It!
Answers

To stimulate a real test situation, for the Try It! activity, remind students to use the 30 minutes of response time wisely. They should use the first 5–10 minutes for planning and the remaining 20 minutes for writing. Allow 10–15 minutes for students to revise their drafts.

DIFFERENTIATE INSTRUCTION ↘

TEKS 11.13B, 11.13C

Understanding the Basics

No writer gets it right the first time. Few writers even get it right the second time. In fact, professional writers almost always carry out many revisions before they are satisfied with their work. As writer Virginia Hamilton says, "The real work comes in the rewriting stage." The following guidelines will help you make the best revising moves.

- **Set your writing aside.** Get away from it for a day or two. This will help you see your first draft more clearly when you are ready to revise.
- **Carefully review your draft.** Read it at least two times: once silently and once aloud. Also ask another person to react to your writing—someone whose opinion you trust.
- **Consider the big picture.** Decide if you've effectively developed your thesis.
- **Look at the specific parts.** Rewrite any parts that aren't clear or effective. Cut information that doesn't support your thesis, and add ideas if you think your reader needs more information.
- **Assess your opening and closing paragraphs.** Be sure that they effectively introduce and wrap up your writing.

Revising a Timed Writing

When you have little time to make changes, writer Peter Elbow recommends "cut and paste revising." For example, if you are responding to a writing prompt on a test or for an in-class assignment, you may have just 10 to 15 minutes to revise your writing. The steps that follow describe this quick revising strategy.

1. Don't add any new information.
2. Cut unnecessary details.
3. Check for basic organization.
4. Do whatever rewriting is necessary.

Try It!

Take 30 minutes to respond to the prompt below. Then spend 10 to 15 minutes revising your writing with the cut-and-paste strategy.

Write about a time in which you either gained someone's respect or came to respect someone else.

Differentiated Instruction: Struggling Learners

To help students reduce their stress levels when taking exams, provide regular practice with timed writing prompts. This will help them learn to budget their time appropriately and to develop their own systems of revision based on their individual writing styles.

 TEKS **11.13B** Develop drafts in timed situations; **11.13C** Revise drafts to clarify meaning, to achieve consistency of tone, or by adding transitional phrases

Using a Strategy That Works

The strategy below covers everything from reading the first draft to improving specific ideas. Use this strategy when you have time for in-depth revising.

Read: Keep an open mind when you read your first draft.

- Whenever possible, put your writing aside for a day or two.
- When you return to it, read your first draft aloud.
- Ask others (peers, family members) to read it aloud to you.
- Listen to your writing: What does it say? How does it sound?

React: Use these questions to help you react to your writing:

- What parts of my writing work for me?
- Do all of the parts work together, and are they arranged in the best order?
- Could I use a trope, such as a fresh and original metaphor or simile, to clarify and add color to my writing?
- What other revising should I do?

Rework: As you revise, think of places where using a scheme (such as inverted word order, rhetorical questions, or parallelism) would help emphasize important ideas. Continue making changes until all parts of your writing work equally well.

Reflect: Write comments in the margins of your paper (or in a notebook) as you revise. Here are some guidelines for reflecting:

- Explore your reactions freely. Be honest about your writing.
- Note what you plan to cut, move, explain further, and so on.
- Reflect on the changes you make. (How do they work?)
- If you are unsure of what to do, write down a question to answer later.

Refine: Refining is checking specific ideas for logic, readability, and balance. Use these questions to help you refine your ideas:

- Will the reader be able to follow my train of thought from idea to idea?
- Do I use transitional words or phrases to link ideas?
- Have I overdeveloped or underdeveloped certain points?

Tip

Remember that revising is the process of improving the ideas and the details that carry the message in your writing. Don't pay undue attention to conventions too early in the process; just concentrate on improving your message.

Process

Using a Strategy That Works

Ask students if they've ever felt so attached to their words and ideas that they couldn't bear to cut or change them. Point out that a writer's attachment to her or his own writing can make revising difficult. Tell students that a good way to solve this problem is to set aside a piece of writing for a day or two. This "cool-down" period will help them acquire some objectivity about their work.

When returning to the piece of writing, the writer is less emotionally involved or attached to it, making it easier to look at the work objectively and begin to make the necessary revisions to improve it. To encourage students to take this time off from their writing, set a date for students to turn in their first draft and a date for them to begin revising.

As you review the steps of the strategy with students, discuss why the revising stage is a good time for writers to incorporate tropes and rhetorical devices. (Possible answer: After major points have been incorporated into a draft, it is easier for writers to see the most effective places to use such devices.)

Discuss how each step of the strategy can help students identify where they need to clarify meanings; rearrange words, sentences, or paragraphs to achieve a more logical organization; or add transitional words or phrases. ⟋DIFFERENTIATE INSTRUCTION

TEKS 11.13C

A Closer Look at Revising

Have students record each bulleted question in their writer's notebook in a section titled *Revising Help*. Have them use these questions as a guide the next time they work alone or with a writing partner to revise a piece of writing to clarify meaning, achieve specific rhetorical purposes, or achieve consistency of tone.

Try It!
Answers

Possible answers:

- **Is your topic worn out?** Revise the title to attract the reader's attention.
- **Is your approach stale?** Add details that will evoke a response in readers, especially about how McCarthy's campaign ruined people's careers and lives.
- **Do you sound uninterested or unnatural?** The voice is natural and knowledgeable.
- **Do parts of your writing seem boring?** Vary some of the sentences for interest.
- **Does your writing seem to jump around?** Ideas are logically connected..
- **Is your writing choked by an overly tight organization?** Add some transitions to improve the flow of ideas.

DIFFERENTIATE INSTRUCTION ↘

 TEKS 11.13C

 TEKS 11.13C

A Closer Look at Revising

The later stage of revising allows you to deal with parts of your writing that seem boring or unclear. Use the questions that follow to check for any uninspired "badlands" in your writing.

- **Is your topic worn out?** An essay entitled "Lead Poisoning" sounds uninteresting. Enliven it with a new twist: "Get the Lead Out!"
- **Is your approach stale?** Are you writing primarily to please your teacher? If so, start again. Try to trigger your readers' emotions.
- **Do you sound uninterested or unnatural?** If you do, try another approach that shows your individual voice.
- **Do parts of your writing seem boring?** Maybe those parts don't say enough; possibly, they say too much. To rework these parts, think of them as a series of snapshots, with each word picture achieving the proper balance between ideas and the supporting details.
- **Does your writing seem to jump around?** Add transitions between paragraphs, and be sure to logically link your sentences to each other.
- **Is your writing choked by an overly tight organization?** The structure of an essay provides you with a frame to build on. However, if you follow the frame too closely, your writing may become predictable and boring. If the "formula" is obvious when you read your draft, change the structure in order to more freely present your ideas.

Try It!

As a class (or in a small group) evaluate this paragraph using the questions above as a guide.

McCarthyism

MaCarthyism is associated with Joseph McCarthy, a Wisconsin resident who served from 1947–1957 as a United States senator. On February 20, 1950, McCarthy spoke for six hours on the senate floor, arguing that there was a large foreign espionage ring operating within the United States government. He accused the Truman administration of dismissing the entire issue. This criticism came at a time of strong anticommunist sentiments in the United States. There was anxiety that communists were quietly penetrating the government and the culture. People from all walks of life were accused of being communists—often without evidence. This anticommunist movement was called McCarthyism. Some writers used their craft to protest McCarthy. Arthur Miller, for example, wrote *The Crucible* in which the Salem witch trials serve as a metaphor for McCarthyism.

 TEKS **11.13C** Revise drafts to clarify meaning and to achieve specific rhetorical purposes and consistency of tone

TEKS 11.13C Revising **111**

"I rush through a first draft, and then I go back and rewrite because I can usually see what the problems are going to be. Rewriting is more fun to me than the writing is."

—Walter Dean Myers

Revising Checklist

Use this checklist as a guide when you revise your writing. Remember: When you revise, you improve the thoughts and details that carry your message.

Focus and Coherence

_____ **1.** Is my writing focused on the prompt or assignment?
_____ **2.** Have I developed a specific thesis statement, or controlling idea?
_____ **3.** Do all the parts of my writing support my thesis, or controlling statement?
_____ **4.** Does my writing as a whole have a sense of completeness?

Organization

_____ **5.** Is each sentence logically linked to the previous sentence?
_____ **6.** Do effective transitions link my paragraphs?
_____ **7.** Do I need to reorder or revise any parts?

Development of Ideas

_____ **8.** Have I layered, or fleshed out, my details so that each sentence adds meaning to the sentence that came before it?
_____ **9.** Have I approached my topic from a unique perspective?
_____ **10.** Have I made interesting connections between ideas?

Voice

_____ **11.** Have I tried to make a meaningful connection with my readers?
_____ **12.** Is my writing authentic and original?
_____ **13.** Will my writing engage readers?
_____ **14.** Does my unique perspective and personality come through?

Process

Revising Checklist

Take a survey to find out how many students share Walter Dean Myers's opinion about rewriting. Ask students to review what they wrote earlier in their writer's notebook about revising. Did they use the word *fun* anywhere? The quotation and the survey can provide you with a good springboard for a discussion about ways students have made the revising process less painful, if not fun.

ELPS 3G

Go over the Revising Checklist with students. Point out that they will use a revising checklist for each core unit writing assignment in this book. Each checklist will include questions related to their specific goals for that assignment. The pages on which these revising checklists appear are the following:

- Personal narrative, SE page 143
- Informative article, SE page 205
- Argumentative essay, SE page 242
- Theme interpretation, SE page 300

TEKS 11.13C

Differentiated Instruction:
English Language Learners

ELPS 1E, 1G, 4D, 4K

Provide support as needed by preteaching vocabulary from the paragraph in the Try It! activity.

ELP Level **Beginning**	ELP Level **Intermediate**	ELP Level **Advanced/Advanced High**
Use simplified language to present the ideas in the paragraph. Then use sentence stems to help students identify parts or ideas that are confusing or unclear.	Work together to note aspects of the paragraph that could be improved by revising. Provide stems for students to write a sentence about one aspect to revise.	Have partners analyze the paragraph and write ideas about aspects that could be revised. Ask students to determine whether the voice sounds formal or informal.

TEKS **11.13C** Revise drafts to clarify meaning and to achieve specific rhetorical purposes and consistency of tone; **ELPS** **1E** Internalize new academic language by using and reusing it/writing; **1G** Demonstrate ability to distinguish between formal and informal English; **3G** Express opinions; **4D** Use prereading supports to enhance comprehension of written text; **4K** Demonstrate English comprehension and expand reading skills by employing analytical skills

Revising in Action

Explain that each method of improving a draft is shown in the Sample Revision on SE page 113. Guide students to identify each of the following methods in the sample.

- Adding Information
- Deleting Information
- Moving Material
- Reworking Material

Point out that sometimes a revised hard copy can become too messy to read or understand when it's time to make the final copy. Share these tips.

- One way to avoid this problem is for students to write on every other line if they handwrite their draft, or to double- or triple-space if they write on a computer.
- Students should make it a habit to use standard editing marks when they revise so it will be easy to understand what they want to change.
- If students have to add a single word or short phrase, they can write it in the available space. If they want to rework an entire part, they can rewrite on a new piece of paper and mark the revised part as an insert. They need to be sure to mark where to insert the revised text.
- Students who are revising on a computer should create a new file for each revision and print out a copy. Then they can easily track their changes.

Being Your Own Critic

Ask students to review each of the suggestions for improving a draft at the top of the page and each question at the bottom of the page. Discuss which suggestions would help to clarify meaning, achieve consistency of tone, or achieve specific rhetorical purposes.

TEKS 11.13C **ELPS** 1B

TEKS 11.13C

Revising in Action

When you revise a first draft, focus on improving the writing overall. You can improve a piece by adding, deleting, moving, or reworking information. (See the next page for examples.)

Adding Information

Add new information to your writing if you feel you need to . . .

- share more details to make a point,
- clarify or complete an interesting idea, or
- use transitions to link sentences and paragraphs to improve clarity and flow.

Deleting Information

Delete material from your draft if the ideas . . .

- do not support your focus or
- are redundant or repetitious.

Moving Material

Move material in your writing in order to . . .

- create a clear flow of ideas,
- present points in order, or
- make a dramatic impact.

Reworking Material

Rework material in your writing if it . . .

- is confusing or unclear,
- does not maintain the proper voice, or
- needs to be simplified.

Being Your Own Critic

When revising, try to anticipate your reader's concerns. Doing so will help you determine what changes to make. Here are some questions and concerns a reader may have:

- What is the main point of this essay?
- Is the writer's voice interested and authoritative?
- Can I follow the writer's ideas smoothly?
- Does the ending wrap up the essay in a clear way?

★ TEKS 11.13C   Revising **113**

Sample Revision

The writer of this essay improved the piece by moving, adding, deleting, and reworking parts.

Process

Playing with Fire

The most exciting moment of any Olympic opening

ceremony is the lighting of the flame. A torchbearer sprints

into the stadium, flaming torch in hand. Anticipation builds.

The runner's torch ignites a roaring fire in a huge cauldron,

symbolizing the official opening of the games. *The flame has*

already traveled a great distance and has been carried by

many people to get to its destination.

The Olympic Torch Relay begins with the lighting of the

torch. This happens at the site of the first Olympic Games in

Olympia, Greece. From there, torchbearers carry the torch *from country to country* until

it reaches the site of the host city where that year's games

are being held.

Running isn't the only way the flame is moved from

place to place. It can be carried by other forms of

"transportation". ~~In the past, it has been transported by plane,~~

car, boat, bicycle, horse, even dogsled! In places where open

flames are not allowed, the flame is stored in a special enclosed

lamp.

The Olympic Games Organizing Committee (OCOG)

is responsible for planning how the torch will travel from Greece

~~determines the route and forms of transportation that will~~

to the host city. ~~convey the flame from Greece to the host location.~~ The torch

travels through many places on its way to the games. . . .

A sentence is moved for clarity.

A key detail is added.

An unnecessary detail is cut.

A passage is reworded for appropriate voice.

Sample Revision

Have students read through the sample revision. Point out that the margin notes explain the purpose of each change. Then ask students to explain how each of these changes improves the writing for readers. Tell students to be specific.

- The sentence about the distance the flame has traveled should follow the sentence that tells about the torchbearer sprinting into the stadium because the ideas are so closely related.
- Adding the detail about carrying the torch from country to country is important to provide background information for readers who may not know about the Olympics and the tradition of bringing the torch from Greece to the host country.
- Cutting the unnecessary detail about the past makes the writing tighter and to the point.
- The rewording sounds more like the natural voice of the rest of the writing.

↙ DIFFERENTIATE INSTRUCTION

★ TEKS 11.13C

Differentiated Instruction:
English Language Learners   ⚙ ELPS 3F, 4K

Provide background information to help students understand cultural traditions associated with the Olympic Games.

ELP Level **Beginning**	ELP Level **Intermediate**	ELP Level **Advanced/Advanced High**
Use simplified language and gestures to clarify the revisions and show how they improve the writing. Ask yes/no questions to confirm understanding.	Work together to analyze the revisions and their effects on the writing. Ask questions to have students explain and assess each revision.	Using questions like *What is this revision? How does it improve the writing?*, have partners analyze and discuss the revisions.

TEKS **11.13C** Revise drafts to clarify meaning and achieve specific rhetorical purposes; **ELPS** **3F** Ask for/give information during speaking assignments; **4K** Demonstrate English comprehension and expand reading skills by employing analytical skills

Checking for Snapshots

Remind students that writers use specific nouns, vivid verbs, and sensory details to *show* readers something rather than *telling* them about it.

Creating a Snapshot Moment

Have students point out details the writer uses in the sample snapshot to *show* the torchbearer's actions. (Possible choices: sprints, flaming torch in hand, flame struggles in the wind, flares up, hush falls over the stadium, only sound is the torchbearer's footsteps, slowly and ceremoniously) **DIFFERENTIATE INSTRUCTION ↘**

Try It!
Answers

Distribute photocopies of the reproducible sensory chart (TE page A105) and the 5 W's chart (TE page A102) to help students generate details for the **Try It!** activity.

Invite students to read aloud their snapshots. Have them point out the details that *show* the reader what is happening and suggest tropes, such as similes or metaphors, that could enhance the descriptions while achieving consistency of tone. **DIFFERENTIATE INSTRUCTION ↘**

TEKS 11.13C; **ELPS** 3G, 3H

 TEKS 11.13C

Checking for Snapshots

One way of improving your writing is to check for places where you can show instead of tell. Writer Barry Lane suggests thinking in terms of "snapshots."

Creating a Snapshot Moment

1. Choose one important "moment" from your essay or story.
2. Imagine that you are viewing it through a camera lens. Zoom in, and take a picture.
3. Write about the snapshot.
4. Make your snapshot sparkle by using a trope, such as a unique metaphor or simile.

The writer of "Playing with Fire" (see page 113) decided to improve her writing by creating a snapshot of the torchbearer. Here is the result.

> The torchbearer sprints toward the platform, flaming torch in hand. The flame struggles in the wind for a split second; then it flares up in defiance. A hush falls over the stadium. The only sound is the torchbearer's footsteps. He stops. Slowly and ceremoniously, he touches the flame to the base of a thick, glass column. It shoots up the column. Whoosh! Fire explodes in a giant, silver cauldron towering over the stadium. The Olympic Games have begun!

Try It!

Write two snapshot moments—first, of a person you know very well, and second, of a place. Remember to focus on just one small part and zoom in on the details. Show the reader what is happening.

Tip

If you get stuck, try asking yourself the 5 W and H questions *(who? what? when? where? why?* and *how?)* about the moment: *Who* is this? *What* is she or he doing? *When* and *how* did this happen? *Why* is the person doing this? *Where* is this person?

Differentiated Instruction: Advanced Learners

Have students check for "snapshots" in writing assignments they have completed. Encourage them to work in small groups to discuss ways to incorporate "snapshots" into all forms of writing—including expository and persuasive writing.

115

Peer Response

Good friends constantly ask for and provide feedback: "Does this top look good on me?" "I'm not sure that red is really your color." "How did we sound?" "You guys nailed every song." Sharing opinions and considering the opinions of others enhances life. It helps you to see things from different perspectives. You may even decide to change your mind on occasion—a prerogative.

You already know the value of listening with an open mind to feedback you receive from your teacher. Listening to your writing peers is different, but not that different. Your writing peers aren't teachers, but they are real-life readers and, as such, can provide you with important information.

Writing peers also share their opinions, letting each other know what makes sense and what could be clearer in a piece of writing. In this chapter, you will learn how to conduct peer-responding sessions. At first, you may be reluctant to have your classmates respond to your writing; however, once you realize how helpful their feedback can be, you'll come to appreciate the importance of this activity. Your peers' feedback is especially helpful for evaluating a first draft during the early stages of revising.

- **Peer-Response Guidelines**
- **Using the Traits to Respond**
- **Trying a New Strategy**

"Criticism, like rain, should be gentle enough to nourish a man's growth without destroying his roots."

—Frank A. Clark

Peer Response

Objectives

- demonstrate an understanding of the role of the writer and the role of the responder in peer responding
- learn how to give helpful responses
- learn a four-step strategy for peer responding

Ask students to share their experiences and feelings about peer responding.

- Have they ever participated in peer responding sessions? If so, when and for what purpose?
- Were they ever reluctant about having classmates read and respond to their writing? Why? How did they overcome this reluctance?
- What negative feelings do they have about peer responding, if any?
- What benefits have they derived from peer responding, as writers and as responders?
- How has peer responding helped them improve as writers?

Differentiated Instruction: English Language Learners

ELPS 3C, 3G

ELP Level **Beginning**	ELP Level **Intermediate**	ELP Level **Advanced/Advanced High**
After students have written their snapshots, have them read one aloud. Guide students, using language supports, to discuss their ideas about their writing.	Invite students to read one of their snapshots aloud. Provide support as needed to help them express their opinions, ideas, and feelings about their writing.	Have partners read aloud one of their snapshots. Have the listener use a variety of sentence types and lengths to point out the details that show rather than tell.

 TEKS **3C** Speak using a variety of grammatical structures, sentence lengths, sentence types, and connecting words; **3G** Express opinions, ideas, and feelings

Peer-Response Guidelines

Use what you know about your students' preferences, as well as their writing strengths and weaknesses, to select students for peer response sessions.

The Writer's Role

As needed, discuss the guidelines provided for writers. Observe students to be sure they have understood and implemented the guidelines.

Seeking Constructive Criticism

Explain to students that constructive criticism recognizes the strengths in a piece of writing and also offers ideas for improving weaker parts.

Try It!
Answers

Tell students that depending on the type of feedback they are seeking, they may want to ask more than one *W* or *H* question in each category.

⭐ **TEKS** 11.13E

⭐ **TEKS** 11.13E

Peer-Response Guidelines

The guidelines below will help you participate in peer response sessions. (If you're just starting out, work in small groups of two or three classmates.)

The Writer's Role

Come to the session with a meaningful piece of your writing—a recently completed first draft, or even a final written draft that you want feedback on. Make a copy for each member of the group (if this is what the group usually does).

- **Introduce your writing.** Give a brief explanation of what your piece is about without going into too much detail.
- **Read your writing aloud.** However, if you don't feel comfortable reading aloud, ask group members to read your piece silently.
- **Ask for feedback.** Listen carefully and consider all suggestions. Don't be defensive, since this will stop some members from commenting honestly.
- **Take notes.** Record your classmates' comments on your copy so you can decide later what to change.
- **Answer questions.** If you're unsure of an answer, it's okay to say, "I don't know" or "I'll look into that."
- **Seek assistance.** If you have trouble with a specific part of your writing, ask for help.

Seeking Constructive Criticism

To get constructive criticism, you may need to ask the responders some direct questions. Consider your purpose, your intended audience, and the focus of your writing. Knowing these three things will help you form your questions.

Try It!

Choose one piece of writing to review with your peers. Using the 5 W and H questions *(who? what? when? where? why?* and *how?),* form questions that will help the group provide constructive criticism. Sample questions follow:

1. Who will be most interested in my story?
2. What is the strongest or the weakest part of my essay?
3. When do you seem to lose interest?
4. Where do I need more detail?
5. Why will the reader appreciate the beginning?
6. How can I change the ending to make it more effective?

The Responder's Role

You need to be honest in your feedback without hurting the writer's feelings. Your comments should always be polite and constructive.

Giving Constructive Criticism	
Don't make demands . . . "Change the ending so the reader has something to think about."	**DO make suggestions . . .** "The ending could be stronger if you leave the reader with a question to think about."
Don't focus on the writer . . . "Nobody understands what you're trying to say in the middle part."	**DO focus on the writing . . .** "Don't you think your ideas would be easier to follow if you switched paragraphs two and three?"
Don't focus on the problem . . . "The beginning paragraph is boring."	**DO focus on the solution . . .** "Descriptive details might make the beginning more interesting."
Don't give general comments . . . "Your sentences aren't very interesting."	**DO give specific advice . . .** "Changing from passive to active voice in a few places could liven things up."

Process

Responding Tips

- Listen carefully to the writer's reading and questions.
- Take notes in the margins of your copy so you can show the writer where changes need to be made.
- Ask questions. If you are not sure of something, ask for clarification.

Try It!

Read the following paragraph. Write three strong, constructive criticisms about the writing, using the tips above.

Dr. Condoleezza Rice is a native of Birmingham, Alabama. She was born in 1954, one year before Emmett Till was murdered and Rosa Parks refused to give up her seat on the bus. As a child, she was an excellent student and a gifted musician who played the piano. Her plan was to become a concert pianist. Along the way, she became interested in politics. She ended up working at the White House as Secretary of State under President George W. Bush. Most people don't know that she didn't give up playing the piano. In 2002, she performed a concert in Washington, D.C., with cellist Yo-Yo Ma.

The Responder's Role

Emphasize the importance of being polite and constructive when giving feedback. Tell students to put themselves in the writer's position and think about how a comment or question will affect the writer.

Responding Tips

Have students read the tips in the Giving Constructive Criticism chart to learn ways to rephrase comments so that the writer will be receptive to them. Remind students that as responders, their purpose is to help a writer recognize problems in a piece of writing and to offer reasonable suggestions for addressing those problems. Tell students to be sure they understand comments, and to seek clarification as needed.

⭐ **ELPS** 2D

Try It!
Answers

Possible answers:
1. Varying your sentence beginnings and using different sentence lengths might make the writing sound more lively and interesting.
2. The detail about Rice playing the piano is surprising. Moving it to the beginning of the paragraph would capture the reader's interest right away.
3. Explaining who Emmet Till and Rosa Parks were would help readers understand the connection between Rice and these two people.

✔ **DIFFERENTIATE INSTRUCTION**

⭐ **TEKS** 11.13E

Differentiated Instruction: English Language Learners   ⭐ **ELPS** 2G, 2I, 3G, 3I

Before starting the Try It! activity, clarify for students that their job will be to make informal suggestions on how to strengthen the sample.

ELP Level **Beginning**	ELP Level **Intermediate**	ELP Level **Advanced/Advanced High**
Use visuals and simplified language as you read the paragraph aloud. Ask yes/no questions to help students make specific suggestions.	Provide question frames to help students express their ideas and opinions. Have students write notes about questions and suggestions as they listen.	Have students write notes about questions and suggestions as they listen. Then have them adapt their notes to express their ideas as questions.

TEKS **11.13E** Revise final draft in response to feedback from peers; **ELPS** **2D** Monitor understanding of spoken language and seek clarification as needed; **2G** Understand the general meaning, main points, and important details of spoken language/topics, language, and contexts; **2I** Demonstrate listening comprehension by following directions, retelling or summarizing, responding to questions and requests, collaborating with peers, and taking notes; **3G** Express opinions and ideas; **3I** Adapt spoken language for informal purposes

Using the Traits to Respond

Some students will find it helpful to review the five traits, and to discuss the sorts of revisions that might be needed to address each one.

Addressing Focus and Coherence, Organization, and Development of Ideas

Suggest that students choose one or two traits (focus and coherence, organization, or development of ideas) early in the revising process. As responders focus on these traits, they become more familiar with them and can offer more constructive criticism. The writer benefits by receiving more helpful and thoughtful responses.

 TEKS 11.13E

Try It!
Answers

Possible answers:

- **Development of Ideas:** It feels to me that this sentence has so many scientific words that they detract from the main idea. Is it possible to find a simpler way to express this idea?
- **Voice:** It would be good to know what audience you had in mind when you wrote this. It sounds extremely formal.

 TEKS 11.13E

Using the Traits to Respond

Responders help writers rethink, refocus, and revise their writing. As a responder, you may find it helpful to base your responses on the traits of writing.

Addressing Focus and Coherence, Organization, and Development of Ideas

Focus and Coherence: Help the author address focus and coherence.
- Can you tell us the prompt or assignment you're writing about?
- It seems like your main idea is . . . Is that right?
- Your strongest and most convincing details are . . .
- A few details like . . . may make this part more interesting.
- In my opinion, details like . . . may distract from your main idea.
- The point you're making in your ending is . . . Is that right?
- Your writing left me thinking . . . Is that what you intended?

Organization: Help the author focus on organization.
- You got my attention right away and made me want to read more.
- I'm wondering if you need the . . . sentence in the . . . paragraph. In my opinion, you covered that earlier. What do you think?
- Are there some details missing from . . . ?
- Why did you place the information about . . . in the fourth paragraph?
- I wonder if a transition is needed between the second and third paragraphs?
- I think I might move paragraph . . . so that it comes earlier. What do you think?

Development of Ideas: Help the author focus on development of ideas.
- It seems like you're trying to say . . . Is that right?
- A more unique approach to this topic might be . . .
- Could you explain more about the idea that . . . ?
- What sorts of connections do you see between this idea and that one?

Try It!

Read the following sentence, and write two constructive criticisms: one about the quality of the ideas and one about the voice.

The investigative nature of a forensic pathologist's personality provides a foundation for detecting microscopic details to explain a crime.

Addressing Voice

Voice: **Help the author focus on voice.**
- The sentences that most clearly show your personality are . . .
- How would you describe how you feel about this topic?
- What audience did you have in mind when you wrote this?
- The third paragraph sounds too formal to me. Do you think it fits in with the rest of your writing?
- I love the image that you used to describe . . . It's original and shows your unique perspective.
- The overall feeling I get from your writing is . . .
- The middle part of your essay might be too subjective.
- I like your conclusion. It sounds authentic, the way you speak to me all the time . . .

Try It!

Read the following paragraph. Then write some constructive criticisms about the author's voice.

> At Christmas time, it was Aunt Anne who always brought a bunch of cookies over to our house for the annual tree-trimming party. It was Anne who did most of the tree trimming. It was Anne who would some years disappear with my shopping list entitled "I Have No Idea What to Get for So and So," and she'd come back several hours later with the perfect gift. She asked only that I make her a cup of coffee while she wrapped it for me. We always knew we could crash at Aunt Anne's house. She wouldn't mind if her house got messy; she had all the time in the world to clean it.

Reacting to Criticism

You don't have to incorporate all of your classmates' suggestions. The following tips will help you get the most out of response sessions.

- Trust your own judgment about your writing.
- Determine which issues are most important.
- Pay attention to comments made by more than one responder.
- Get another opinion if you are not sure about something.
- Be patient. Focus on one problem area at a time.

Process

Addressing Voice

When addressing voice, responders should also help the writer focus on problems related to consistency of
- tone,
- mood, and
- style.

Try It!
Answers

Possible answers:
- The word *bunch* doesn't sound quite right to me. You could use a more specific word or words, like *dozens and dozens.* I think it would also add interest if you told what kind of cookies Aunt Anne brought, like chocolate chip with almonds.
- Check your sentences at the beginning of the paragraph. Do you think too many of them begin with *it was Anne?* Or is that a style you want to emphasize? ✔ DIFFERENTIATE INSTRUCTION

⭐ **TEKS** 11.13E

Reacting to Criticism

Remind students that in the end, they have ownership of their writing and are responsible for monitoring their written language production. Point out that peers' suggestions are just one of the resources they can use.

⭐ **ELPS** 1B

Differentiated Instruction: ⭐ **ELPS** 1E, 4I, 4K
English Language Learners

Before reading the sample, provide background support to help students understand cultural traditions that are mentioned.

ELP Level **Beginning**	ELP Level **Intermediate**	ELP Level **Advanced/Advanced High**
Use gestures and visuals as you read the paragraph aloud. Ask yes/no questions to help students form criticisms about the writer's voice.	Have partners read the paragraph aloud together. Have them complete sentence stems to analyze and make suggestions about the writer's voice.	Have students read the paragraph independently and write two suggestions or questions about the writer's voice. Then have partners discuss their analysis and ideas.

⭐ **TEKS** 11.13E Revise final draft in response to feedback from peers; **ELPS** 1B Monitor written language production and employ self-corrective techniques or other resources; **1E** Internalize new basic language and new academic language by speaking and writing; **4I** Demonstrate English comprehension and expand reading skills by employing basic reading skills; **4K** Demonstrate English comprehension and expand reading skills by employing analytical skills

Trying a New Strategy

Point out that peer responders have a lot of advice and information to keep in mind. Explain that the OAQS strategy is a good guide to help them internalize the process.

DIFFERENTIATE INSTRUCTION ⬎

Minding Your OAQS

Create a poster for classroom display that is divided into four sections, with the headings *Observe, Appreciate, Question,* and *Suggest.* To help students derive meaning from environmental print, in each section, write the meaning of each word as shown in boldface. Suggest that students make a copy of the poster in their writer's notebook. Encourage them to refer to the poster or to their notebook page during peer response sessions to remind them of this simple, effective four-step strategy for peer responding. **DIFFERENTIATE INSTRUCTION ⬎**

ELPS 4C, 4F

Try It!
Answers

Possible answers:
- Positive comment: I really like the way the author describes how the humorous story is spun out, wanders around, arrives nowhere, and bubbles gently.
- Question: I wonder why the author thinks a comic or witty story requires no art in telling.

TEKS 11.13E

Trying a New Strategy

Here's a simple and effective four-step strategy that you can use in peer-response sessions.

Minding Your OAQS

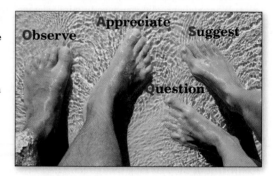

Observe means to notice what another person's writing is designed to do. Then you can say something about the design or purpose. For example, "Even though you mean to write objectively about the November election, your political opinions come through."

Appreciate means to identify something in the writing that impresses or pleases you. Positive comments are important to a writer. As a responder, it's important to balance your criticism. For example, you could say, "I really like the way you . . ." or "The best part of your essay is . . ."

Question means to ask whatever you want to know after you have read the writing. You can ask for background information, a definition, an interpretation, or an explanation. For example, "Could you tell us more about how you felt when you found the letter?"

Suggest means to give helpful advice about possible changes. Offer advice honestly and courteously. Be specific and positive. For example, "If you add a few details about what happened in the second paragraph, maybe what you heard and felt, I think your essay will be perfect!"

Try It!

Read this excerpt from Mark Twain's *How to Tell a Story and Others.* Write one positive comment and one question about the writing.

The humorous story may be spun out to great length, and may wander around as much as it pleases, and arrive nowhere in particular; but the comic and witty stories must be brief and end with a point. The humorous story bubbles gently along, the others burst. The humorous story is strictly a work of art—high and delicate art—and only an artist can tell it; but no art is necessary in telling the comic and the witty story; anybody can do it.

Differentiated Instruction: Struggling Learners

Encourage students to create their own, personalized, writer's handbook (perhaps in a separate section in their writer's notebook). In this handbook, they should note new vocabulary words, words that they commonly misspell or confuse with other words, grammar rules that trip them up, and so on.

They can use this handbook as reference when writing and editing their own work.

Editing

Two hundred years ago, Thomas Jefferson gave his daughter this advice: "Take care that you never spell a word wrong. Always before you write a word, consider how it is spelled, and, if you do not remember, turn to a dictionary." Editing was just as important back then as it is now. A good writer is also a skillful editor, fully versed in the conventions of the language.

Editing is the process of checking your revised writing for spelling, mechanics, and grammar errors. Unfortunately, few people know *all* of the rules for conventions. That's why spell-checkers, grammar checkers, dictionaries, thesauruses, and writing handbooks are important editing tools. This chapter, along with the "Proofreader's Guide" on pages **634–783**, will help you improve your editing skills.

- Checklist for Editing and Proofreading
- Editing in Action
- Errors to Watch For
- Special Editing and Proofreading Strategies

"Good writers are those who keep the language efficient. That is to say, keep it accurate, keep it clear."

—Ezra Pound

Editing

Objectives

- demonstrate an understanding of editing symbols
- know what errors to look for during editing
- learn three special editing and proofreading strategies

Encourage students to keep a dictionary and the Proofreader's Guide on SE pages 634–779 on hand as they edit. If they need to check spelling or find a specific rule or example, they can quickly look it up.

Make sure that all the tools mentioned here (spell-checker, grammar-checker, dictionary, thesaurus, and writing handbook) are available in the classroom or the school library for students to use when they edit.

↙ DIFFERENTIATE INSTRUCTION

Checklist for Editing and Proofreading

Review the Checklist for Editing and Proofreading with students. By now, they should be familiar with the checklist format and understand how to use it. Tell students they will use an Editing Checklist to check for conventions for each core unit writing assignment in this book. The pages on which these editing checklists appear are the following:

- Personal narrative, SE page 145
- Informative article, SE page 206
- Argumentative essay, SE page 248
- Theme interpretation, SE page 306

TEKS 11.13D

 TEKS 11.13d

"In writing, punctuation plays the role of body language. It helps readers hear you the way you want to be heard."
—Russell Baker

Checklist for Editing and Proofreading

Use this checklist as a guide when you edit and proofread your revised writing. Also refer to "Errors to Watch For" on pages **124–125**.

Tip

Always have a trusted friend or peer serve as a second editor. You're too close to your work to catch every error.

Conventions

LOOK AT GRAMMAR . . . (See pages 727–759.)
_____ **Do** the subjects and verbs agree in my sentences?
_____ **Do** my sentences use correct and consistent verb tenses?
_____ **Do** my pronouns agree with their antecedents?
_____ **Have** I avoided any other usage errors?

LOOK AT MECHANICS . . . (See pages 676–699.)
_____ **Do** my sentences end with the proper punctuation?
_____ **Do** I use commas correctly in compound sentences?
_____ **Do** I use commas correctly in a series and after long introductory phrases or clauses?
_____ **Do** I use apostrophes correctly?
_____ **Do** I punctuate dialogue correctly?
_____ **Do** I start my sentences with capital letters?
_____ **Do** I capitalize proper nouns?

LOOK AT SPELLING . . . (See pages 692–697.)
_____ **Have** I checked for spelling errors (including those the spell-checker may have missed)?

 TEKS **11.13D** Edit for grammar, mechanics, and spelling

Editing in Action

Have students practice using editing symbols. Prepare a passage that contains grammar, capitalization, punctuation, and spelling errors. Give students time to correct the passage using the editing symbols. Then have partners compare their work to see if they caught the same mistakes and used the correct editing symbols.

↙ DIFFERENTIATE INSTRUCTION

⭐ **TEKS** 11.13D

⭐ **TEKS** 11.13d

Editing in Action

Note the editing corrections made in these paragraphs from a student essay. See the inside back cover of this book for an explanation of the editing symbols used.

Process

Gender Equality

Should young women be grateful for their education? Absolutely. According to the <u>united</u> <u>nations</u> (UN), two-thirds of the world's illiterate people are female. Just as shocking is that two-thirds of the world's children who don't go to school are female. In point of fact, females in developing countries are disadvantaged in many aspects of life.

In September 2000, the UN set specific goals for the twenty-first century to address this problem. Eight goals were outlined in a resolution called the ⌄United Nations Millennium Declaration.⌄ Two of the goals directly address promoting gender equality and primary education worldwide. The UN believes that placing more emphasis on educating girls in developing countries will have significant economic benefits. The organization⌄s hope is that educated women will participate more fully in public and political life and break the cycle of poverty. A 2006 UN report shows the effort is slowly succeeding, but there is much more to be done.

The UN wants to eliminate gender ⟨discrimenation⟩ *discrimination* in all levels of education no later than 2015. The declaration states that "by 2015 children everywhere, boys and girls alike, will be able to complete a full c̶o̶a̶r̶s̶e̶ *course* of primary schooling and that girls and boys will have equal access to all levels of education."

A proper noun is capitalized.

A comma is placed after a transition.

A title is punctuated.

An apostrophe is added to show singular possession.

A spelling error is corrected.

A usage error is corrected.

Differentiated Instruction:
English Language Learners

⭐ **ELPS** 5D, 5E

Turn to the Appendix of the Teacher's Edition for information on language transfer issues with grammar, punctuation, and mechanics.

ELP Level **Beginning**	ELP Level **Intermediate**	ELP Level **Advanced/Advanced High**
Guide students to understand the editing symbols and the notes that explain each edit. Have students repeat terms such as *proper noun* and *comma* with you.	Review each edit and editing symbol with students. Ask yes/no questions to enhance and confirm understanding.	Have partners cover the callout notes and examine each edit. Have them identify each symbol and tell why it appears.

TEKS **11.13D** Edit for grammar, mechanics, and spelling;
ELPS **5D** Edit writing for standard grammar and usage/subject-verb agreement, pronoun agreement, and verb tenses;
5E Employ increasingly complex grammatical structures

Errors to Watch For

The errors on these pages focus on grammar and punctuation problems commonly found in students' writing. Tell students that if they cannot understand any of the problems by reading the solution and consulting the Proofreader's Guide (SE pages 634–779), they should come to you for extra help.

Many writers have problems with confusing pronoun references. Call attention to the example for item 2 and ask students to explain why the writer deleted the pronoun *she* and repeated the name *Angel*. (The pronoun reference was unclear. Readers could not know whether *she* referred to *Angel* or *Samantha*.) Follow a similar procedure with the remaining items on SE pages 124–125.

 **TEKS** 11.13D; **ELPS** 5D, 5E

Errors to Watch For

These two pages show 10 common errors to check for in your writing.

1. **Problem:** **Missing Comma After Long Introductory Phrases**
   Solution: Place a comma after a long introductory phrase.

   > Because of the snowstorm⌄school was canceled for the day.

2. **Problem:** **Confusing Pronoun Reference**
   Solution: Be sure the reader knows whom or what your pronoun refers to.

   >   Angel
   > When Angel talked with Samantha, ~~she~~ said she would drive.

3. **Problem:** **Missing Comma in Compound Sentence**
   Solution: Use a comma between two independent clauses joined by a coordinating conjunction—*and, but, or, nor, so, for,* or *yet.*

   > I tried to call Jake this morning⌄but his cell phone was turned off.

4. **Problem:** **Missing Comma(s) with Nonrestrictive Phrases or Clauses**
   Solution: Use commas to set off a phrase or clause that is not needed to understand the sentence. (See page **642**.)

   > I gave five dollars to my little brother⌄who gave me a big smile.

5. **Problem:** **Comma Splices**
   Solution: When only a comma separates two independent clauses, add a conjunction or create two sentences.

   >   so
   > Javon is graduating from college on Sunday,⌄we're having a family party.

6. **Problem:** **Subject-Verb Agreement Error**
   Solution: Verbs must agree in number with their subjects.

   > The ballots list~~s~~ four candidates for class president.

TEKS 11.13d

Editing 125

7. Problem: Missing Comma in a Series
Solution: Use commas to separate individual words, phrases, or clauses in a series.

> Our van was cluttered with CD's˄garbage˄and empty water bottles.

8. Problem: Pronoun-Antecedent Agreement Errors
Solution: A pronoun must agree in number with the word that the pronoun refers to. (See page **786**.)

> Either Rose or Emily brought ~~their~~ her DVD's to Adrian's house.

9. Problem: Missing Apostrophe to Show Ownership
Solution: Use an apostrophe after a noun to show possession.

> Jorge's dream is to attend a World Series game.

10. Problem: Misusing *Its* and *It's*
Solution: *Its* is a possessive pronoun meaning "belonging to it." *It's* is a contraction of "it is" or "it has."

> It's a fact that the distance from earth's surface to its center is about 3,963 miles.

Try It!

Copy the paragraph below on your own paper, exactly as it appears. Then find and correct the eight errors it contains. Use the correction symbols on the inside back cover of this book.

Almost 60,000 teens participated in *USA Weekend Magazine*s recent music survey. The magazine published the results on it's Web page. One of the findings which was a big surprise to everyone showed that teens often borrowed and listened to their parents CD's. In the final analysis it remains clear that teens need their tunes, their favorite types of music include hip-hop, rap pop and punk rock.

Process

Focus attention on the problem of misusing *its* and *it's*. Ask students what other words they frequently misuse that have similar spellings or that sound alike. (Possible answers: *their, there,* and *they're; to, too,* and *two*)

✱ For an extensive list of commonly misused words that students can check for during editing, see SE pages 702–721.

Try It!
Answers

(**Red** = insert **Green** = delete)

Almost 60,000 teens participated in *USA Weekend Magazine's* recent music survey. The magazine published the results on it's Web page. One of the findings, which was a big surprise to everyone, showed that teens often borrowed and listened to their parents' CD's. In the final analysis, it remains clear that teens need their tunes,. Their favorite types of music include hip-hop, rap, pop, and punk rock.

✔ DIFFERENTIATE INSTRUCTION

TEKS 11.13D

TEKS 11.13D Edit for grammar, mechanics, and spelling; **ELPS 5D** Edit writing for standard grammar and usage/subject-verb agreement and pronoun agreement; **5E** Employ increasingly complex grammatical structures

Special Editing and Proofreading Strategies

Tell students that the first time they try editing from the bottom to the top, it may seem confusing because they are subconsciously trying to read the text for meaning instead of focusing on the separate words. Assure students that the more they practice this strategy for checking spelling, the easier it will become to focus on the individual words and find errors.

ELPS 5C

Try It!
Answers

Answers for both Try It! activities are shown below. (**Red** = insert **Green** = delete)

The wind meandered through the ancient trees, methodically shakeing loose the ~~the~~ thick armor of ice that encrusted the rigid branches. Icicles plunged like swords from the sky, pieircing (piercing) snowdrifts caught silent and unaware. Oh, that it were only rain falling gently through leafves (leaves) onto the mossy forest floor. **DIFFERENTIATE INSTRUCTION ↘**

TEKS 11.13D

 TEKS 11.13d

Special Editing and Proofreading Strategies

The following three strategies will help you become a more efficient and effective editor and proofreader. Professional editors and proofreaders employ these types of strategies.

1. **Read from the bottom to the top.** Begin at the end of your writing and work back through your paper, word by word and line by line. This will help you focus on spelling errors, repeated words, and so on.

2. **Know your most common errors.** If spelling is your most frequent mistake, always check your writing for that problem first. After that, go back and proofread for other types of errors, one at a time if necessary.

Try It!

Read this passage backward. See if you can find three errors.

The wind meandered though the ancient trees, methodically shakeing loose the the thick armor of ice that encrusted the rigid branches.

Tip

Some editors like to place a ruler under each line of text as they read it. Focusing on a small amount of text at a time results in fewer missed errors.

3. **Use editing and proofreading marks.** Editing and proofreading marks (see the inside back cover of this book) offer a uniform way of marking the errors in your writing.

Try It!

Copy the following passage. Use the editing and proofreading marks to correct the mistakes.

The wind meandered though the ancient trees, methodically shakeing lose the the thick armor of ice that encrusted the rigid branches. Icicles plunged like swords from the sky peircing snowdrifts caught silent and unaware. Oh that it were only rain falling gently through leafs onto the mossy forest floor.

Note: Be careful when using grammar checkers and spell-checkers on your computer. Although these programs are helpful, they aren't foolproof. They can easily misread your intentions and give you bad advice. The best editors are human editors.

 TEKS **11.13D** Edit for grammar, mechanics, and spelling; **ELPS** **5C** Spell familiar English words and employ English spelling patterns and rules with increasing accuracy

Publishing

Writing becomes real when you publish it. Publishing is to a writer what a live performance is to a musician or an exhibit is to an artist. It is why you have worked so hard in the first place—to share a finished piece of writing that expresses your thoughts and feelings. It makes all of your prewriting, drafting, and revising worth the effort.

The most helpful form of publishing is sharing a finished project with one or more of your classmates. As writer Tom Liner states, "You learn ways to improve your writing by seeing its effect on others."

You can also select a piece of writing for your classroom portfolio or submit something to your school newspaper or literary magazine. If you're really adventurous, you may even want to submit your writing outside of school. This chapter will help you with all your publishing needs.

- **Preparing to Publish**
- **Places to Publish**
- **Preparing a Portfolio**
- **Parts of a Portfolio**
- **Creating Your Own Web Site**

"To make your unknown known—that's the important thing."
—Georgia O'Keeffe

Publishing

Objectives
- learn how to format and design writing for publication
- demonstrate an understanding of types of portfolios
- demonstrate an understanding of parts of portfolios
- learn how to create a Web site

Discuss when and how students would like to share their writing with their classmates. Some students might prefer exchanging with a writing partner. Some might like to share in small discussion groups. Others might feel comfortable reading their writing aloud to the whole class or to a larger school audience. Provide several options for sharing so that students can choose the one that suits them best.

Each core writing unit in this book provides several different publishing options at the end of the main writing assignment. Encourage students to consider these options when it is time for them to decide how to publish their writing.

✓ DIFFERENTIATE INSTRUCTION

Differentiated Instruction: English Language Learners

✦ ELPS 5C

ELP Level **Beginning**	ELP Level **Intermediate**	ELP Level **Advanced/Advanced High**
Read the passage aloud once while students follow along, and then work together to identify the errors. Have students write each misspelled word correctly.	Guide students to identify and correct errors. Elicit spelling rules and patterns that students know, such as dropping final *e* when adding *-ing* to verbs.	Have students complete the activity independently. Then have partners discuss their responses and share spelling rules and patterns they used.

ELPS 5C Spell familiar English words and employ English spelling patterns and rules with increasing accuracy

Preparing to Publish

Most students appreciate the publishing stage in the writing process, mainly because it signifies that they have finished an assignment. Advise students to store a copy of their finished writing assignments in a personal portfolio. This way they can access the writing anytime for ideas, sources, further revision, and reflection.

Publishing Tips

In addition to the tips shown on SE page 128, review any additional guidelines or requirements that you have set for preparing a neat final copy.

Try It!
Answers

Discuss any questions students may have about the publishing process. Be sure students understand that they are not expected to publish every piece of writing they work on.

TEKS 11.13E

> "A writer is unfair to himself when he is unable to be hard on himself."
> —Marianne Moore

Preparing to Publish

Publishing is the final step in the writing process, offering that "other audience"—your readers—a chance to enjoy your writing. The following guidelines will help you prepare your writing for publishing.

Publishing Tips

- **Work with your writing** until you feel good about it from start to finish. If any parts still need work, then it isn't ready to publish.

- **Ask for input and advice** from your teacher and writing peers during the writing process. Your writing should answer any questions your teacher and writing peers may have about your topic.

- **Save all drafts for each writing project** so you can keep track of the changes you have made. If you are preparing a portfolio, you may be required to include early drafts as well as finished pieces. (See pages **130–132.**)

- **Check for the traits of writing** to be sure that you have effectively addressed focus and coherence, organization, development of ideas, and voice in your work. (See pages **46–89.**)

- **Carefully edit and proofread for conventions** after you have completed all of your revisions. (See pages **83–89.**)

- **Prepare a neat final copy** to share with the reader. Use pen (blue or black ink) and one side of the paper if you are writing by hand. If you are using a computer, avoid fancy, hard-to-read fonts and odd margins.

- **Know your publishing options,** since there are many ways to publish. (See page **129.**)

- **Follow the requirements** indicated by the publisher. Each publisher has its own set of requirements, which must be followed exactly.

Try It!

Use these guidelines once you decide to publish a piece of writing. Be sure to ask your teacher for help if you have any questions about the publishing process.

Places to Publish

Think back to the day you started writing a particular piece. You decided what you would write about with two fundamental ideas in mind: a topic that interested you and a thesis, or controlling idea, about that topic. At this point, you've done a lot of work—prewriting, drafting, revising, and editing—to perfect your writing. Peers and teachers probably reviewed it as you went along. Now it's time to share the finished product with a variety of readers by publishing your work.

School Days

If you have written about a topic that interests or affects others in your age group, school publications provide some good publishing options.

- Your school's newspaper is a good choice for expository or persuasive writing about school-related topics.
- A student literary magazine might offer publishing opportunities for a variety of writing forms.
- There may be a page for student writing on your school's Web site.

Your Own Backyard

The people in a community generally share some interests or background—that's what brought them together as a community in the first place. You may find that local publications are interested in publishing your writing.

- A local newspaper or newsletter may be interested in an insider's view of school events or a young person's opinions on current issues.
- Look for clubs and organizations that have a connection to your writing topic.

Explore the Possibilities

You can also look in the *Writer's Market*—available in most libraries—for more places to publish. You might consider publishing your writing on a blog. Some blogs are personal diaries, some focus on creative writing, while others deal with commentary about a particular area or topic. By posting comments, readers can interact with other writers on the blog.

Tip

Before submitting your work to a publication, check the submission guidelines to be sure your writing is in an acceptable form and style. Include a self-addressed stamped envelope (SASE) when submitting your work to help ensure that you receive a response and that your work will be returned if that's what you want.

Process

Places to Publish

Some students may not think that their writing is good enough to submit to a publication or to enter a contest. They may worry about how they will feel if their writing is rejected. Tell students that most professional writers experienced rejection at different points during their careers. If these writers had never risked rejection, they would never have been discovered or achieved success. ✔ DIFFERENTIATE INSTRUCTION

School Days

Remind students to use the appropriate voice (respectful and courteous) when submitting a piece of writing to a school publication. Have students give examples of formal and informal English and discuss when the use of each is appropriate.

ELPS 1G

Your Own Backyard

Tell students that the local library is a good place to investigate community publications that may have an interest in printing their writing.

Explore the Possibilities

Point out that writing a blog creates the potential that anyone with Internet access can read a piece of writing. Suggest that students consider carefully whether this type of publishing is appropriate for them.

TEKS 11.13E

Differentiated Instruction: English Language Learners

ELPS 1B, 1G

ELP Level **Beginning**	ELP Level **Intermediate**	ELP Level **Advanced/Advanced High**
Together, investigate places to publish student work. Guide students to review their work to correct any errors and prepare a final copy.	Have partners investigate places to publish their work and share their findings. Guide students to correct any errors and prepare a final copy.	Have partners investigate places to publish their work. Have students review their work for appropriate voice and for the use of formal and informal English.

TEKS **11.13E** Publish written work for appropriate audiences; ELPS **1B** Monitor written language production and employ self-corrective techniques or other resources; **1G** Demonstrate ability to distinguish between formal and informal English and knowledge of when to use formal and informal English

Preparing a Portfolio

Make sure students understand your specific requirements for preparing and maintaining a portfolio.

Working Smart

Review the guidelines to address any questions students may have. In addition to a *showcase portfolio*, students may be interested in knowing about these other kinds of portfolios:

- Personal portfolios contain writing that students want to keep for themselves.
- Growth portfolios contain writing assignments that show writing progress.
- Electronic portfolios are any kind of portfolio that is available online. **DIFFERENTIATE INSTRUCTION ↘**

Try It!
Answers

Students may find it helpful to review the forms of writing they have worked on recently. Discuss recent writing assignments in several subject areas before students make their choices.

DIFFERENTIATE INSTRUCTION ↘

TEKS 11.13E

Preparing a Portfolio

A writing portfolio is a collection of your work that shows your skill as a writer. It is different from a writing folder that contains writing in various stages of completion. Your teacher will probably ask you to compile a *showcase portfolio*—a collection of your best writing for a quarter or a semester. Compiling a showcase portfolio allows you to participate in the assessment process. You decide which writing samples to include, and you reflect upon your writing progress.

Working Smart

Use the following information as a guide when you compile a showcase portfolio. There are no shortcuts when it comes to putting together an effective portfolio, so don't skip any of these suggestions.

1. Organize and keep track of your writing (including planning notes and drafts). Then, when it comes to compiling your portfolio, you will have all the pieces to work with.
2. Make sure that you understand all of the requirements for your portfolio. If there's something you're unsure of, ask your teacher for help.
3. Keep your work in a safe place. Use a good-quality, expandable folder for your portfolio to avoid dog-eared or ripped pages.
4. Maintain a regular writing/compiling schedule. It will be impossible to create an effective portfolio if you approach it as a last-minute project.
5. Develop a feeling of pride in your portfolio. Make sure that it reflects a positive image of yourself. Look your best! (Remember that your teacher will be reviewing your portfolio for assessment.)

FYI

A showcase portfolio may follow you into the next school year. Next year's teacher may use the portfolio to assess your competencies and weaknesses as a writer. Of special interest will be your personal reflections on your writing progress.

Try It!

Imagine that you are compiling a showcase portfolio. List at least two or three pieces that you would include. Explain in a brief paragraph why you think these three pieces represent your best work.

Differentiated Instruction: Struggling Learners

Artistic students may already have portfolios of their artwork. Invite these students to share their portfolios with the class and discuss the similarities and differences between visual art portfolios and writing portfolios.

Parts of a Portfolio

Check with your teacher about specific requirements for your portfolio. Most showcase portfolios contain the following parts.

- **A table of contents** listing the pieces included in the portfolio.
- **An opening essay or letter** detailing the story behind your portfolio (how you organized it, what it represents to you, and so on).
- **Specific finished pieces** representing your best writing. (Your teacher may ask you to include all of the planning, drafting, and revising for one or more of your writing samples.)
- **A best "other" piece** related to your work in another content area.
- **A cover sheet** attached to each piece of writing, discussing the reason for its selection, the work that went into it, and so on.
- **Evaluation sheets or checklists** charting the basic skills you have mastered as well as the skills you still need to work on. (Your teacher will supply these sheets.)

Writing Your Opening Pages

The first two pages of a showcase portfolio are shown here.

Process

Table of Contents

Showcase Portfolio
Chantele Barnes

Table of Contents

Opening Letter

Dear Mr. _____

I'm pleased with my writing progress this semester. My goal was to write about topics that were important to me, in hopes that I would enjoy writing more. I think I succeeded. I really felt connected to the topics in my main writing projects. I did some of my best writing this semester because I seemed to care so much about what I was saying. I still have a long way to go, but I now feel much more confident about my writing ability.

My first piece is a personal narrative about a memorable experience. Picking a topic was easy because my sophomore trip to Italy was the most memorable thing that has ever happened to me. I was part of the All-City Choir that had the privilege of singing in Rome. My challenge was to select only the most important things to say about the experience. At first I just went on and on ("First, I did this . . . Then I did . . .), but then I figured out that I could only focus on the most important details. I enjoyed finding just the right words to capture the feeling of the time.

I also included a response to *The Great Gatsby*. It was easier to analyze Jay Gatsby than I thought it would be. That may be because I plan to study psychology in college. It was interesting to explore Gatsby's personality.

My favorite selection is "Seashells, Sparks, and Stars." I liked playing with alliteration in this poem, which is a playful ode to summer. I hope you enjoy reading it as much as I enjoyed writing it.

This summer my goal is to become a regular reader and a regular writer. I plan to keep a writer's notebook and write some more poems.

Sincerely,
Chantele Barnes

Parts of a Portfolio

Be sure students are aware of any differences between your requirements and those listed on SE page 131.

Writing Your Opening Page

Provide additional samples of opening letters for students to use as models when preparing their own opening letters for their portfolios.

If you plan to review and assess portfolios regularly throughout the year, tell students

- the schedule for their individual reviews, including date, time, and place;
- what materials they should have in their portfolios at the time of their review; and
- how their portfolios will be part of their overall grade for the course.

★ **TEKS** 11.13E

TEKS **11.13E** Publish written work for appropriate audiences; **ELPS** **1B** Monitor written language production and employ self-corrective techniques or other resources; **1E** Internalize new basic language and new academic language by using and reusing it/writing

Creating a Cover Sheet

Encourage students to review the following items for each piece of writing they choose for their portfolios before they write a cover sheet.

- all prewriting materials, including notes, freewriting, lists, clusters, gathering grids, other graphic organizers, and outlines
- first draft
- revised draft(s)
- completed revising and editing checklists
- final copy
- reflection sheet
- peer-responding sheet(s)
- self-assessment sheet
- teacher assessment

Reviewing these materials will remind students of the writing experience and help them recognize the reasons they chose different pieces of writing.

Try It!
Answers

Ask several students to read their cover sheets, and address classmates' questions about how and why they selected the piece of writing they decided to include. Discuss the appropriate audiences for each piece. **DIFFERENTIATE INSTRUCTION ⇘**

TEKS 11.13E

Creating a Cover Sheet

When you create your showcase portfolio, you should attach a cover sheet to each writing project you include. (See the sample below written for a student essay about *The Great Gatsby*.) Your cover sheet should do one or more of the following things:

- Explain why you chose the piece for your portfolio.
- Tell about the process of writing you used, including problems you encountered.
- Describe the strong points and the weak points in the writing.
- Reflect on the writing's importance to you.

Sample Cover Sheet

> Our assignment was to write a literary response about *The Great Gatsby*. We had several topic choices, but I chose to analyze the main character, Jay Gatsby.
>
> Because Gatsby is such a complex character, I didn't know where to start. Using the webbing and freewriting techniques we practiced early in the year helped me dig into his character. In addition, what I learned about writing a thesis statement made it easier to put my essay together and organize the different parts.
>
> I think my voice is a strong feature of my analysis. My interest in people and their actions really comes through. Throughout my analysis, I kept my classmates in mind. I wanted them to share my fascination with Gatsby and his flawed character. I think that my analysis would have been more effective if I had included a few more direct quotations from the novel. I also appreciate the importance of asking a trusted peer to edit my work. I can't find all of the errors on my own.
>
> This writing project taught me to look beyond the surface in a novel. The truth is often hidden. I think authors do that on purpose. They want the reader to enjoy the story, but they also want the reader to think about the characters' actions, to look deep into their souls, and to discover their secrets.

Try It!

Write a cover sheet for a piece of writing that you would like to include in your portfolio.

Creating Your Own Web Site

Creating a Web site is one way to showcase your work. Use a social-networking site or check with your Internet service provider to find out how to get started. If you are designing your page at school, ask your teacher for help. The questions and answers below will help you get started.

Q. **How do I begin planning my site?**

A. Who do you think will want to visit your site? Keep that audience in mind as you plan your site. Then, decide the number of pages you want. Do you want just one page, or do you want multiple pages (a home page, a page of poetry, a short story, a page of favorite links, and so on)? Check out other students' Web pages for ideas. Then, sketch out your pages. Note how the pages will be linked by marking the "hot spots" on your sketches.

Q. **How do I make the pages?**

A. Each page is created as a separate file. Many word-processing programs let you save a file as a Web page. Otherwise, you may have to learn HTML (hypertext markup language). This is a code that allows you to add text and graphics to a page. Your teacher may be able to help you with it. If not, you can find instructions on the Internet. (See the "Web Design" page on our Web site at *www.thewritesource.com* for help.)

Q. **How do I know if my pages work?**

A. You should always test your pages. Using your browser, open your first page. Then follow the links to make sure they work correctly.

Q. **How do I get my pages on the Web?**

A. Ask your Internet provider how to upload finished pages to your provider's computer. (If you're working on your home computer, get a parent's approval. If you're using a school computer, work with your teacher.) Your provider will tell you how to access the pages later, in case you want to make changes. After you upload a page, visit your site and make sure it still works.

Try It!

Get the word out about your site. E-mail your friends and ask them to visit your site. Link to other sites you find interesting. Check to see how your site appears in search engines.

Process

Creating Your Own Web Site

Students will benefit from their classmates' experiences with creating Web sites.

- Invite students who have created their own Web sites to share their experiences with the class.
- Ask students to explain how they solved any problems they had with designing and creating their Web sites, as well as any problems they had uploading their finished designs onto the Internet provider's computer.
- Ask students to provide Web addresses for instruction sites they used to create their Web sites, especially if they found the instructions easy to follow and apply.

Try It!
Answers

Invite students to brainstorm ideas for getting their Web sites noticed by appropriate audiences.

TEKS 11.13E

When they have completed their cover sheets, have students share them with a larger group.

ELP Level **Beginning**	ELP Level **Intermediate**	ELP Level **Advanced/Advanced High**
Prepare a formatted cover sheet and guide students to complete statements to explain why they chose the piece and what they learned.	Work together to create a formatted cover sheet and guide students to complete statements to explain why they chose the piece and what they learned.	Students should include ideas about using formal and informal English, explain why they chose the piece, and describe what they learned.

TEKS **11.13E** Publish written work for appropriate audiences; ELPS **1G** Demonstrate ability to distinguish between formal and informal English and knowledge of when to use formal and informal English; **3E** Share information in cooperative learning interactions; **3G** Express ideas; **5B** Write using newly acquired basic vocabulary and content-based grade-level vocabulary; **5G** Narrate, describe, and explain with increasing specificity and detail

Narrative Writing

11.13A Plan a first draft by determining appropriate topics through a range of strategies; **11.13B** Develop drafts that structure ideas in a sustained way; **11.13C** Revise drafts to clarify meaning and achieve specific rhetorical purposes, consistency of tone, and logical organization by rearranging the words, sentences, and paragraphs to employ tropes, schemes, and by adding transitional words and phrases; **11.13D** Edit drafts for grammar, mechanics, and spelling; **11.13E** Publish written work for appropriate audiences; **11.14A** Write an engaging story with a well-developed conflict and resolution using a range of literary strategies and devices to enhance the plot, and sensory details that define the mood or tone

 UNIT ELPS

1A Use prior knowledge and experiences; **1B** Monitor written language production; employ self-corrective techniques or other resources; **1C** Use strategic learning strategies to acquire basic and grade-level vocabulary; **1E** Internalize new basic language and academic language by using and reusing it; **1F** Use accessible language; learn new and essential language in the process; **1G** Demonstrate ability to distinguish between formal and informal English; **1H** Develop and expand repertoire of learning strategies; **2C** Learn new basic and academic vocabulary; **2D** Monitor understanding of spoken language; **2I** Demonstrate listening comprehension; **3E** Share information in cooperative learning interactions; **3G** Express ideas; **3J** Respond orally to information presented; **4C** Comprehend English vocabulary; **4D** Use prereading supports to enhance comprehension of written text; **4E** Read linguistically accommodated content area material with a decreasing need for linguistic accommodations; **4F** Use visual/contextual support to enhance and confirm understanding and to develop vocabulary; use support from peers and teachers to develop grasp of language structures and to develop vocabulary; **4G** Demonstrate comprehension of increasingly complex English/responding to questions; **4K** Demonstrate English comprehension and expand reading skills by employing analytical skills; **5D** Edit writing for standard grammar and usage; **5E** Employ increasingly complex grammatical structures; **5G** Narrate, describe, and explain with increasing specificity and detail

Personal Narrative (pages 135–148)

Students share a conflict created by a choice they made through a personal narrative.

Reflective Narrative (pages 149–155)

Students create a reflective narrative about a change they have gone through.

 Technology Connections

⚡ *Write Source Online* www.hmheducation.com/tx/writesource
- ***Net-text***
- ***Writing Network***
- ***Portfolio***
- ***GrammarSnap***
- ***Essay Scoring***
- ***File Cabinet***

⚡ *Interactive Whiteboard Lessons*

Narrative Writing Unit Scope and Sequence

Day	Writing and Conventions Instruction	Core Unit	Tools of Language	Resource Units	Daily Language Workouts	Skills-Book	Write Source Online
		Write Source Student Edition					
1	**Personal Narrative** Model, Prewriting	135–139	**TL** 568–573		18–21		Interactive Whiteboard Lesson
2	Drafting	140		**BEW** 617–631			Net-text
3	Revising	141–143					Net-text
	Skills Activities: •Specific Nouns			**PG** 723–725		72–74, 76, 77	GrammarSnap
	•Verbs (transitive, intransitive)			**PG** 736–737		91, 97, 98	GrammarSnap
	•Adjectives and Adverbs			**PG** 748–749, 750–751		105, 111	GrammarSnap
	•Pronouns			**PG** 730–731, 732–733		80–82	GrammarSnap
4	Editing and Publishing	144–145					Net-text
	Skills Activities: •Punctuating Dialogue			**PG** 646, 660–661		30	GrammarSnap
	•Pronoun-Antecedent Agreement			**PG** 726–727, 774–775		79, 151, 153	GrammarSnap
	•Apostrophes			**PG** 656–657, 658–659		25–29	
5	Evaluating a Personal Narrative	146–147					Net-text
	Evaluating and Reflecting on Your Writing	148					Net-text
6–10	**Reflective Narrative** Model	149–151	**TL** 568–573		22–25		Net-text
	Prewriting	152					Net-text
	Drafting	153		**BEW** 617–631			Net-text
	Revising	154					Net-text
	Editing and Publishing	155					Net-text
	Skills Activities: •End Punctuation			**PG** 635–637		5	
	•Using the Right Word			**PG** 702–703, 704–705, 706–707		62	
	•Capitalization (Proper Nouns)			**PG** 674–675, 676, 678		43	GrammarSnap
	•Spelling			**PG** 690–695		55	

Week 1 spans Days 1–5; Week 2 spans Days 6–10.

Resource Units referenced above are located in the back of the *Student Edition* and *Teacher's Edition*
TL *"The Tools of Language"* **BEW** *"Basic Elements of Writing"* **PG** *"Proofreader's Guide"*

Writing Focus
- Writing a Personal Narrative
- Writing a Reflective Narrative

Grammar Focus
- Noun Phrases

Learning Language

Read aloud the basic and academic terms, as well as the descriptions and questions. Model for students how to read one question and answer it. For example, *It says that consequences are what happen as a result of something you do, and it's asking about the consequences of skipping lunch. When I skip lunch my stomach growls and I get sleepy in the afternoon.* Have partners monitor their understanding of the terms by working through the meanings and questions together.

DIFFERENTIATE INSTRUCTION ↘

⭐ **ELPS** 2C, 4C, 4G

Minilessons

Wasn't That a Time?   Writing a Personal Narrative

- Have students freewrite about a time in their lives that proved challenging. Tell them to **CONSIDER** the following questions: *Why was this event challenging? How did it change you? What would be different about your life if this hadn't happened to you?* Suggest that they **KEEP** their freewriting in their journal or notebook to use as a source of ideas for future narrative assignments.

Changes   Writing a Reflective Narrative

- Have students **LIST** five ways in which they are different than they were five years ago or longer. Tell them to **CHOOSE** a change that resulted from a decision they made. (For example, deciding to use a formal given name instead of a nickname.) Ask them to **WRITE** a paragraph about why they made the change and explain why the change is important to them.

⭐ **ELPS** **1A** Use prior experiences; **1C** Use strategic learning strategies to acquire grade-level vocabulary; **2D** Monitor understanding of spoken language; **2C** Learn new basic and academic vocabulary; **4C** Comprehend English vocabulary; **4G** Demonstrate comprehension of increasingly complex English/responding to questions

---

Narrative Writing

Writing Focus

Grammar Focus

Learning Language

Work with a partner. Read the meanings and share answers to the questions.

1. **Sensory details** are details that appeal to the sense of sight, hearing, smell, touch, or taste.
   Which sensory details might describe a flower?

2. A **dialogue** is a written conversation between two people.
   How do you know who is speaking when you read a dialogue?

3. **Consequences** are what happens as a result of your actions.
   What are the consequences of skipping lunch?

4. A **rhetorical device**, such as repetition, is a use of language to convey meaning or emotion.
   How can rhetorical devices improve your writing?

5. If you **smell a rat**, you sense that something is wrong.
   Tell about a time when you smelled a rat.

Differentiated Instruction: English Language Learners

⭐ ELPS 1A, 1C, 2D

ELP Level **Beginning**	ELP Level **Intermediate**	ELP Level **Advanced/Advanced High**
Use gestures, visuals, and simplified language to model terms and their meanings. Have students practice saying and writing each term with you.	Have partners practice saying terms aloud. Provide sentence stems to help students share their prior knowledge and experiences.	Invite partners to describe their experiences for each other. Students can monitor their understanding by completing a web for each term.

135

Narrative Writing
Writing a Personal Narrative

Everyone makes a bad decision occasionally, and every bad decision usually results in conflict—the key to a good narrative. What makes a narrative engaging is how the writer deals with the conflict.

A personal narrative is a true story told from the writer's point of view. It is more than just an entertaining tale. It is the retelling of an event or experience that has affected the writer's life. The story should be real and natural, allowing readers to experience the event for themselves.

In this chapter, you will write a personal narrative about a difficult—and bad—decision. You will examine why you made the choice and reflect on how you felt about it—then and later. Include complex characters, a well-developed conflict and resolution, literary strategies (such as dialogue and suspense), literary devices (such as figurative language and foreshadowing), and sensory details to bring the event to life.

Writing Guidelines

Subject:	**A bad decision**
Purpose:	**To share an important experience**
Form:	**Personal narrative**
Audience:	**Classmates**

"Our deeds determine us, as much as we determine our deeds."

—George Eliot

Writing a Personal Narrative

Objectives

- understand the purpose, content, and form of a personal narrative
- choose a topic (a bad decision) to write about
- plan, draft, revise, and edit a personal narrative

A **personal narrative** is a piece of writing in which the writer shares a personal experience.

- It uses narrative elements (setting, characters, conflict, and dialogue) to tell a story.
- It uses sensory details to help readers visualize the experience.
- It provides the writer with an opportunity to reflect on the experience and share what was learned from it.

Have students discuss the quotation by George Eliot at the bottom of the page. Do they agree or disagree with Eliot? Why?

Ask students to freewrite for five minutes about how the quotation applies to their lives. This will help them begin to think about choices and decisions they have made and how these choices have affected their lives.

 Technology Connections

Use the Interactive Whiteboard lessons to introduce narrative writing.

 Interactive Whiteboard Lesson

Resources

Copy Masters

- Sensory chart (TE p. 141)

Benchmark Papers

- Happy Days (strong)
  TE Appendix
- My First Skateboard (poor)
  TE Appendix

Personal Narrative

Work through the model essay with students, pointing out the elements that make it a good personal narrative. **DIFFERENTIATE INSTRUCTION** ↘

⭐ TEKS 11.14A

Focus and Coherence

■ The writer addresses a single controlling idea: his decision to join the photography club.

■ All of the details provided give information about and expand on the controlling idea.

Organization

■ A strong beginning draws the reader in.

■ Dialogue, actions, and details tell the story in chronological order and help build suspense.

■ The ending explains what the writer learned.

Development of Ideas

■ The writer explains a bad choice and the consequences of that choice.

■ The writer's reasons for making his choice are presented clearly and logically.

■ Sensory details help re-create the experience.

Voice

■ The writer uses a natural narrative voice.

■ Dialogue creates interest and spontaneity.

DIFFERENTIATE INSTRUCTION ↘

 ⭐ TEKS 11.14A

Personal Narrative

In the following personal narrative, Eduardo writes about a poor choice and how he dealt with the consequences.

The Wrong Club

Beginning
The writer is faced with a decision and makes a choice.

I stared at the club sign-up sheets on the office bulletin board. The choices swam before me: outdoor club, computer club, photography, astronomy, and a dozen more, all enticing me. Still, because our club period was built into the school week, we were allowed to sign up for only one. But which one should I choose?

The debate club beckoned me. I remembered lifting the forensics trophy that I had won in my old school, but this was a new school, and here debate was considered "geeky." I knew that the photography club was the "cool" club to join, and there was just one more space on that list. I quickly added my name. My pen kept going dry, scratching on the paper, and I had to shake it a few times. It felt like an omen, as though even the pen knew I should have been signing up for debate. I mentally scolded myself for the thought, assuring myself that photography would be fun. It had to be, because I needed it to be. I needed to feel I belonged.

"Aren't you joining debate?" My brother Pedro was suddenly there, looking over my shoulder.

Middle
The writer presents reasons for his choice.

"No, I thought I'd try something different." He shrugged and reached past me, smelling of soap and confidence, to sign up for drama. It was considered another "geek" class, but Pedro had always whistled to his own tune. Still, it was easier for him. Pedro was a freshman, so he was on equal footing with every other freshman seeking to find a niche in the school. It was harder for me, a junior, to become established. I wanted to be cool, to belong, and I thought the photography club might be the way.

The writer explains the disappointment of his choice.

We met for the first time the following week, and I knew immediately I had made the wrong choice. I didn't even own a camera, and there I was, listening to the others excitedly discussing angles and pixels. The sharp stink of chemicals filled my nose. The stark black-and-white photos strung on a line across the back wall stared down at me as

Differentiated Instruction: Advanced Learners

Working in pairs, have students identify three examples of dialogue in Eduardo's narrative. Then have them rewrite each set of sentences, eliminating the dialogue. Ask volunteers to read aloud the sentences—both with and without the dialogue. Discuss what the dialogue adds to the narrative.

if I didn't belong. It was like picking the wrong chocolate from an assortment—bitter and hard instead of sweet and chewy.

> I asked to leave to get a drink, but I really slipped down the hall to the room where the debate team was meeting. I stopped outside the door to hear Mrs. Holmes, the advisor, discussing the various issues they would be debating. I was a statue, still, listening to her explanation of the structure of a debate, and words like "rebuttal" and "logical argumentation." This was what I wanted, what I needed, where I belonged. Finally, I could stand it no more. I stepped inside; heads turned, and a sea of faces stared at me.
>
> "Excuse me, Mrs. Holmes," I gulped. "I was wondering if I could still join the team."
>
> She shook her head. "I'm afraid we have a full team already." I must have looked pathetic, because she smiled. "If you like, you can be an alternate, taking the place of anyone who can't make it to a meet. You'd have to learn to argue both sides of an issue."
>
> "I can do that," I grinned broadly. "I'll be right back."
>
> I explained my situation to the photography advisor. I was so convincing, he agreed immediately that I should be in debate. Then I practically skipped down the hall to Mrs. Holmes's room.
>
> No one on our team missed a meet, so I didn't get to debate that season. It was hard going to all the meets and not being able to participate. But at least I realized it was more important to be myself than to be popular. In fact, being myself was the only way to "be cool."

An attempt to remedy the situation is shared.

Ending The writer reveals the consequences of his choice and the lesson learned.

Narrative

 Respond to the reading. Answer the following questions.

Focus and Coherence (1) Is the writing focused on telling about a bad decision or choice? (2) What is the narrative's controlling, or main, idea?

Organization (3) How is the narrative organized? (4) How is each paragraph linked to the previous paragraph?

Development of Ideas (5) How has the author layered his ideas so that each sentence adds meaning to the sentence that comes before it?

Voice (6) Find examples where the author's individual and unique voice comes through. (7) How does the author's voice keep the reader engaged?

Differentiated Instruction: English Language Learners

ELPS 3J, 4D, 4G, 4K

Before reading the writing model, turn to the Tools of Language for additional language support for narrative writing.

ELP Level **Beginning**	ELP Level **Intermediate**	ELP Level **Advanced/Advanced High**
Use simplified language and visuals to help make the writing model comprehensible. Ask yes/no questions about the choices the writer faced and made.	Ask simple questions to help students comprehend the concept of school clubs and idiomatic language such as *sign up* and *be cool*.	Ask questions to have students analyze the choices the writer faced and made. Have students respond in complete sentences.

Point out the simile *It was like picking the wrong chocolate from an assortment.* Explain that Eduardo uses the simile to show he was keenly aware he had made the wrong choice.

Ask students if they can name other kinds of figurative language Eduardo uses in his narrative. (metaphor: *I was a statue; a sea of faces;* personification: *choices swam; debate club beckoned; even the pen knew; photos stared*) Encourage them to use their own words to describe the mental image created by each example.

 Respond to the reading.

Answers

Focus and Coherence 1. Yes. It focuses on Eduardo's decision to join the photography club instead of the debate team. **2.** Eduardo made a bad choice because he was more concerned about what others might think than about his own needs and interests.

Organization 3. Events are organized in chronological order. **4.** The writer uses appropriate transitions to signal time changes throughout the narrative.

Development of Ideas 5. He explains and builds on his misgivings through the use of dialogue and sensory images.

Voice 6. Possible choices: The debate club was considered "geeky." This was what I wanted, what I needed, where I belonged. **7.** The writer keeps readers engaged with strong imagery that reflects the emotional toll his bad decision is taking on him.

TEKS 11.14A

TEKS **11.14A** write an engaging story with a well-developed conflict and resolution, complex and non-stereotypical characters, a range of literary strategies, and sensory details that define the mood or tone; **ELPS 3J** Respond orally to information presented/concept attainment; **4D** Use prereading supports to enhance comprehension of written text; **4G** Demonstrate comprehension of increasingly complex English/responding to questions; **4K** Expand reading skills by employing analytical skills

Prewriting Planning Your Writing

Have students review the holistic scoring guide (SE pages 36–37) *before* they begin their assignment. This will help them remind them of the traits of good writing.

Topic Web

Review the sample topic web with students and discuss potential consequences of each decision.

Planning your writing. Remind students that they will be sharing their writing with you and with their classmates. To help students select an appropriate topic, ask them to submit their ideas for your approval.

 TEKS 11.13A

Focus on the Texas Traits

Focus and Coherence
Remind students to analyze the bad decision they select for their topic.

- It should involve true conflict, not just regret that making a different decision would have resulted in a more positive outcome.
- Students should be able to identify a series of events leading to an important life lesson that they learned as a result of coping with difficult consequences.

DIFFERENTIATE INSTRUCTION ↘

TEKS 11.14A

---

138  **TEKS** 11.13A, 11.14A

Prewriting Planning Your Writing

To select a topic for his personal narrative, Eduardo created a web showing bad decisions he had made at school, at home, and out with friends. He was trying to remember a choice that had brought difficult consequences and taught him an important lesson. After creating the web, he put an asterisk next to the topic he wanted to write about.

Topic Web

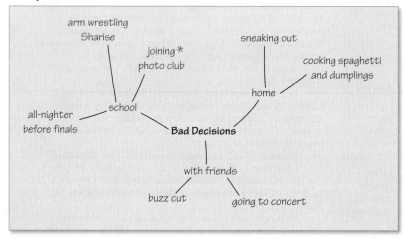

 Planning your writing. Create a web, writing "Bad Decisions" in the center, and "school," "home," and "with friends" beyond it. Write down bad decisions you made in each situation. Think of consequences and lessons learned for each decision. Put an asterisk (*) next to the topic you will write about.

 Focus on the Texas Traits

Focus and Coherence Your personal narrative will focus on the conflict created by the choice you made. Individual paragraphs should focus on that controlling idea and help the reader understand what you eventually learned from the experience. Your closing paragraph should be meaningful and add depth to your composition.

Differentiated Instruction: Struggling Learners

Point out that in the student model, the writer's bad decision was rectified in the end—Eduardo was able to change his decision. Tell students that because many poor decisions cannot be undone, they should focus on ones that taught them important lessons, rather than on problems that were ultimately solved.

TEKS 11.13A, 11.14A

Writing a Personal Narrative **139**

Mapping your Narrative

Your personal narrative begins with the bad decision you made, tells why you made it, and reveals its consequences. The natural order of such events is *chronological*. That means you write about what happened in the order that it occurred. Eduardo used a narrative map to plan his narrative.

Narrative Map

> **Narrative Map**
>
> Decision: __I signed up for photography club instead of debate team.__
>
> Reasons: __I thought photography was "cool" and debate was "geeky."__
>
> **Consequences:**
>
> First: __Pedro questioned me, showing how confident he was.__
>
> Next: __I went to photography club and didn't even have a camera.__
>
> Then: __I sneaked away to listen to debate team.__
>
> After: __I asked to join debate team and got an alternate position.__
>
> What I learned: __It's more important to be myself than to be popular.__

Prewrite

Map your narrative. Create a narrative map like the one above, listing the bad decision, your reasons for making it, the consequences in chronological order, and what you learned.

Focus on the Texas Traits

Organization One way to connect sentences and paragraphs is to use transitional words and phrases, such as *finally* and *in the end*. There are, however, other ways to move logically from one idea to the other:

■ End a paragraph with a question and answer it in the next.
  But which one should I choose? . . . The debate club beckoned me . . .

■ Repeat key ideas within a paragraph or between paragraphs.
  Still, it was easier for him. Pedro was a freshman. . . . It was harder for me, a junior . . .

Prewriting Mapping Your Narrative

Explain that a narrative map is similar to an outline. It is a plan students will follow to write their narratives.

Narrative Map

Discuss how the sample narrative map would be useful for the writer.

Map your narrative. As students create their narrative maps, remind them to do the following:

■ List consequences in the order in which they happened. These consequences will make up the middle part of their narratives and provide the main action of their stories.

■ Check each consequence to make sure it is a direct result of the bad decision and that it relates to the lesson learned.

✔ **DIFFERENTIATE INSTRUCTION**

TEKS 11.13A

Focus on the Texas Traits

Organization

Point out that simply using time-order words such as *first, next, then,* and *last* will make a narrative seem more like a recipe than a story. Explain that using the question-answer technique or making connections between key ideas creates transitions that keep readers interested and engaged.

TEKS 11.14A

Differentiated Instruction: English Language Learners

ELPS 1E, 1F, 3J, 4E, 4F

Before students begin their own narrative maps, present an adapted version of Eduardo's map that uses simplified language.

ELP Level **Beginning**	ELP Level **Intermediate**	ELP Level **Advanced/Advanced High**
Together, read aloud the adapted map. Ask yes/no questions to confirm students' understanding of Eduardo's ideas and narrative events.	Examine the adapted map together. Have students use sentence stems to discuss Eduardo's ideas and the events in his narrative.	Have students use complete sentences to orally summarize Eduardo's ideas and the events in his narrative.

TEKS **11.13A** Plan a first draft by determining appropriate topics; **11.14A** Write an engaging story using a range of literary strategies and devices to enhance plot; **ELPS** **1E** Internalize new basic language and new academic language by using and reusing it/speaking; **1F** Use accessible language and learn new and essential language in the process; **3J** Respond orally to information presented/concept attainment; **4E** Read linguistically accommodated content area material with a decreasing need for linguistic accommodations; **4F** Use visual and contextual support to enhance and confirm understanding

Drafting
Creating a Beginning, a Middle, and an Ending

Before they begin drafting their narrative, remind students that a paragraph has three parts:

- a topic sentence that tells what the paragraph is mainly about,
- body sentences that help explain the main idea expressed in the topic sentence, and
- a closing sentence that wraps up the paragraph or provides a link to the next paragraph.

✱ For more about basic paragraph skills, see SE pages 605–607. For specific instruction about writing a narrative paragraph, see SE page 608. **DIFFERENTIATE INSTRUCTION** ↘

 TEKS 11.13B

Develop your first draft. Remind students to keep prewriting notes handy as they write.

Focus on the Texas Traits

Voice

Explain to students that the best way to tell if their narrative sounds natural is to read their draft aloud. They can listen for parts that sound stiff or awkward. They can also read it to friends and family members and ask for feedback.

TEKS 11.14A

Drafting Creating a Beginning, a Middle, and an Ending

A personal narrative is basically a true story that relates and reflects on a pivotal moment in the writer's life. All narratives have a beginning, a middle, and an ending.

Beginning Catch the reader's interest. The beginning should introduce the situation and the people involved and convince the reader to continue reading.

- Start with a rhetorical question, one not meant to be answered, to intrigue the reader.
- Start with a rhetorical device, such as dialogue, to pull the reader into the action.
- Start with a statement that piques the reader's curiosity.

Eduardo chose the third technique. *I stared at the club sign-up sheets on the office bulletin board.* Immediately, the reader is compelled to wonder why the writer was staring and what was on the board.

> Beginning
> Middle
> Ending

Middle Build suspense through action and sensory details. The middle presents the details that support the narrative's main idea. In the sample essay, Eduardo uses his conversation with his brother, his own thoughts, and the description of the photography club meeting to illustrate the idea that he had made the wrong choice.

> Beginning
> **Middle**
> Ending

Ending Explain what the writer learned from the situation. The ending is the writer's chance to reflect on the situation and on the lesson learned. Eduardo's ending reveals how he learned the importance of being true to himself.

> Beginning
> Middle
> **Ending**

 Develop your first draft. Catch your reader's interest, build suspense through action and details, and reveal the lesson you learned.

 Focus on the Texas Traits

Voice A personal narrative should sound natural, as though you are talking to the reader. Use dialogue to create interest and achieve a spontaneous voice.

Differentiated Instruction: Advanced Learners

Lead a discussion about the ways narrative endings differ from the endings of other types of writing. Have students compare the ending of a persuasive essay (usually a call to action) and an expository essay (may sum up or repeat the main ideas) to the ending of Eduardo's essay on SE page 137. Point out that in addition to revealing the lesson the writer learned, a narrative ending may

- add a new insight,
- resolve a conflict, or
- surprise the reader.

Challenge students to add interest to their ending by using one of these strategies in addition to revealing the lesson learned.

TEKS 11.13C, 11.14A

Revising Using Sensory Details to Create Different Effects

Writing about what you see, hear, smell, taste, and touch lets the reader experience the event with you. Each sensory category you use will help to define the mood or tone of your narrative. Each one impacts the reader differently.

- **Sight:** "Seeing is believing." Sight is connected to truth. Give sensory details such as shape, size, and color to help the reader believe something is true.
  The stark black-and-white photos strung on a line across the back wall stared down at me as if I didn't belong.

- **Sound:** "I heard it through the grapevine." Hearing relates to communication and community. Let the reader hear dialogue to understand how people relate to each other.
  She shook her head. "I'm afraid we have a full team already."

- **Smell:** "I smell a rat." Smell depicts positive or negative feelings. Use pleasant smells to describe good situations and unpleasant smells to describe bad ones.
  He reached past me, smelling of soap and confidence.
  The sharp stink of chemicals filled my nose.

- **Taste:** "It's all a matter of taste." Taste tells the exact quality of something. Use *sweet, sour, tangy, spicy, salty, bitter,* and other taste words to capture quality.
  It was like picking the wrong chocolate from an assortment—bitter and hard instead of sweet and chewy.

- **Touch:** "Your words touched me." Touch is connected to emotion. Use touch words such as *warm, sharp, rough, shivering,* and *prickly* to show how you feel.
  My pen kept going dry, scratching on the paper, and I had to shake it a few times. It felt like an omen . . .

Narrative

Revise

Check your sensory details. Create a sensory chart, checking how often you include each type of sensory detail. If necessary add more details, considering the information above.

See	Hear	Smell	Taste	Touch
✓	✓	✓	✓	✓

Revising
Using Sensory Details to Create Different Effects

Point out that the sample sentence for **Sight** (*The stark black-and-white . . .*) is from the writing model on SE page 136. Have students turn to the writing model and read the fifth paragraph. Then have them read it again, replacing the sample sentence with this one, which does not include sensory details: *The photos made me feel out of place.*

- Ask students to compare the two sentences. (The original is lively and colorful. The replacement is dull.)
- Ask what Eduardo's sentence adds to the narrative. (Readers see the room through Eduardo's eyes, conveying his feelings.)

ELPS 2I

Check your sensory details. Distribute photocopies of the reproducible sensory chart (TE page A105) for students to use as they check their draft for sensory details. They can also use the chart to jot down sensory details they'd like to add to their narrative. DIFFERENTIATE INSTRUCTION

TEKS 11.13C, 11.14A

Conventions Connections

Grammar: Specific Nouns
- ***Student Edition: Proofreader's Guide*** pages 723–725
- ***SkillsBook*** pages 72, 73, 74, 76, 77

Write Source Online **GrammarSnap**

Grammar: Transitive and Intransitive Verbs
- ***Student Edition: Proofreader's Guide*** pages 736–737
- ***SkillsBook*** pages 91, 97, 98

Write Source Online **GrammarSnap**

Grammar: Adjectives and Adverbs
- ***Student Edition: Proofreader's Guide*** pages 748–749, 750–751
- ***SkillsBook*** pages 105, 111

Differentiated Instruction: English Language Learners

ELPS 1C, 1E, 1H, 4D, 4F, 5G

Work together to create a "five senses" chart to discuss and examine sensory details.

ELP Level **Beginning**	ELP Level **Intermediate**	ELP Level **Advanced/Advanced High**
Use visuals and gestures to discuss each sense. Have students repeat terms with you. Use details from the student essay and elicit additional examples.	Use visuals and gestures to generate examples of each sense. Ask questions to have students categorize sensory details from the student essay.	Have students identify and categorize examples from the student essay. Have partners generate and record additional examples for each sense.

TEKS **11.13C** Revise drafts to achieve consistency of tone by using tropes; **11.14A** Write an engaging story with a range of literary devices; ELPS **1C** Use strategic learning strategies to acquire basic vocabulary; **1E** Internalize new basic language and new academic language by using and reusing it/speaking and writing; **1H** Expand repertoire of learning strategies; **2I** Demonstrate listening comprehension/responding to questions and requests; **4D** Use prereading supports to enhance comprehension of written text; **4F** Use visual and contextual support to enhance and confirm understanding and to develop vocabulary; **5G** Narrate, describe, and explain with increasing specificity and detail

Revising Adjusting for Mood and Tone

Discuss sensory details that would help to create each of the following moods:

- gloomy
- bright
- peaceful
- zany

Using the example provided, ask students to describe Eduardo's tone as formal or informal. Have them explain their choice.

ELPS 1G

Check for mood and tone. Discuss each of the questions with students. Ask them to suggest how readers are likely to respond to writing in which the mood and tone are not consistent.

 DIFFERENTIATE INSTRUCTION ↘

TEKS 11.13C, 11.14A

TEKS 11.13C, 11.14A

Revising Adjusting for Mood and Tone

Mood is the overall feeling that a piece of writing produces in a reader. The mood may be gloomy or bright, peaceful or zany, depending on the writer's intent. **Tone** describes the feelings a writer or speaker conveys about his or her subject. In writing, tone is expressed through the writer's choice of details, sentence length and structure, and word choice.

A writer's choice of sensory details, in particular, defines the mood and tone of his or her writing. In his description of the room where the photography club met, Eduardo carefully chose sensory details that conveyed his discomfort and feeling that he did not belong.

The sharp stink of chemicals filled my nose. The stark black-and-white photos strung on a line across the back wall stared down at me as if I didn't belong. It was like picking the wrong chocolate from an assortment—bitter and hard instead of sweet and chewy.

Revise

Check for Mood and Tone. Reread your personal narrative. Does it create the mood that you want it to have? Look for parts you could improve by making your tone clearer and more consistent. Use the following questions as a guide.

- Am I clear about how I feel about my subject? If so, does this feeling come through in my writing?
- Have I chosen adjectives and adverbs carefully, making sure that the feeling they convey matches my intended tone?
- Do my sensory details and figurative language support my tone?
- Does my sentence length and structure add emphasis where it is needed and thus contribute to the tone I want to create?
- Have I included transitional words and phrases, when needed, to help achieve consistency of tone?

TEKS **11.13C** Revise drafts to achieve consistency of tone by using tropes and schemes; **11.14A** Write an engaging story with a range of literary strategies and devices; **ELPS** **1G** Demonstrate ability to distinguish between formal and informal English

Revising Improving Your Writing

Use a checklist. On your own paper, write the numbers 1 to 12. Put a check next to the number if you can answer "yes" to that question. If not, go back and revise that part of your personal narrative.

Revising Checklist

Focus and Coherence

____ **1.** Do I respond to the assignment or prompt?

____ **2.** Do I have a clearly stated controlling, or main, idea?

____ **3.** Do all my paragraphs support, or contribute to, that controlling idea?

Organization

____ **4.** Are my actions and details arranged chronologically?

____ **5.** Is each paragraph linked to the paragraph that precedes it?

____ **6.** Have I fixed parts of my composition that are unnecessarily wordy or repetitious?

Development of Ideas

____ **7.** Have I arranged my ideas so that each sentence adds meaning to the sentence that comes before it?

____ **8.** Has each idea been developed thoroughly? Am I missing important details?

____ **9.** Have I made interesting connections between ideas?

Voice

____ **10.** Does my voice reflect my feelings about the event?

____ **11.** Will my voice keep the reader interested and engaged?

____ **12.** Have I used unique literary strategies and devices to showcase my personal voice?

Make a clean copy. After you've finished your revisions, make a fresh copy of your narrative to edit.

Narrative

Revising Improving Your Writing

Use a checklist. Remind students to give careful thought to each question on the revising checklist.

Revising Checklist

Have students review their checklist answers with a partner.

- If writers answer "yes" to questions, tell them to provide clear examples from their drafts that support "yes" answers.
- If writers answer "no" to questions, tell them to explain how they plan to improve those parts of their writing.

If students feel that they have not developed ideas well enough (item 8 in the checklist), encourage them to review the sensory details examples on SE page 141. Advise students to develop ideas by incorporating sensory details.
⭐ **TEKS** 11.13C, 11.14A

Make a clean copy. Tell students that leaving space between lines will help to make the editing process easier.

⭐ **Conventions Connections**

Grammar: Indefinite Pronouns
- ***Student Edition: Proofreader's Guide*** pages 730–731, 732–733
- ***SkillsBook*** pages 80–81, 82

💥 ***Write Source Online* GrammarSnap**

⭐ **TEKS** 11.13C Revise drafts to achieve consistency of tone by using tropes and schemes; **11.14A** Write an engaging story with a range of literary strategies and devices; **ELPS 1E** Internalize new basic and academic language by using and reusing it/speaking and writing; **4D** Use prereading supports to enhance comprehension of written text; **4F** Use visual and contextual support to develop vocabulary; **5G** Narrate with increasing specificity and detail

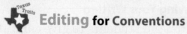

Editing for Conventions

Before students work on the Grammar Exercise, review the meaning and use of noun phrases in the writing model on SE pages 136–137.

Grammar Exercise
Answers

1. younger people

2. colorful, intricate maps, every part of the world

3. the many painful choices, the coming year

4. my youngest brother, the very competitive oratory club

5. the familiar comforting smell of oil paint, an old friend

TEKS 11.13D, 11.17A; **ELPS** 5E

 **TEKS** 11.13D, 11.17A

Editing for Conventions

When you edit for conventions, you check grammar, sentence structure, punctuation, capitalization, and spelling. One aspect of grammar is the use of noun phrases. Use the following activity to improve your use of noun phrases.

A **noun phrase** consists of a noun and its modifiers. In the example below, Eduardo uses two noun phrases as objects of the preposition. Notice that his noun phrases add important sensory details to his writing. Noun phrases function as nouns in a sentence, that is, as subjects, direct and indirect objects, and objects of a preposition.

I stared at the club sign-up sheet on the office bulletin board.

Grammar Exercise

Write the noun phrases in the sentences below. Notice the detail noun phrases add to each sentence.

1. Only younger people attended the event.
2. Mrs. Hanlon decorated her classroom with colorful, intricate maps from every part of the world.
3. Of the many painful choices she had to make, choosing her classes for the coming year was the most difficult.
4. My youngest brother tried out for the very competitive oratory club.
5. The familiar, comforting smell of oil paint greeted me like an old friend.

Differentiated Instruction: Struggling Learners

To help students check subject-verb agreement, provide this example sentence: *The article about the soldiers was riveting.* Point out that the plural noun *soldiers* is part of a phrase; it is not the subject of the sentence, so it does not determine whether the verb is singular or plural in this sentence.

TEKS **11.13D** Edit drafts for grammar; **11.17A** Use and understand the function of noun phrases; **ELPS 5E** Employ increasingly complex grammatical structures

★ **TEKS** 11.13D, 11.14A

Writing a Personal Narrative **145**

Editing Checking Your Writing

 Use a checklist. On your own paper, write the numbers 1 to 12. Put a check by the number if you can answer "yes" to that question. If not, go back and edit your narrative for that convention.

Editing Checklist

Conventions

GRAMMAR

____ **1.** Do I use correct forms of verbs?

____ **2.** Do my pronouns agree with their antecedents?

____ **3.** Do my verbs agree with their subjects?

SENTENCE STRUCTURE

____ **4.** Do I use a variety of correctly structured sentences that clearly communicate my ideas?

MECHANICS (CAPITALIZATION AND PUNCTUATION)

____ **5.** Do I use punctuation after all my sentences?

____ **6.** Do I use commas after long introductory word groups?

____ **7.** Do I use commas correctly in compound and complex sentences?

____ **8.** Do I punctuate dialogue correctly?

____ **9.** Do I begin all my sentences with capital letters?

____ **10.** Do I capitalize all proper nouns?

SPELLING

____ **11.** Have I spelled all my words correctly?

____ **12.** Have I checked for words my spell-checker might miss?

Publishing Sharing Your Writing

Here are several ways to publish your personal narrative.

- Read your narrative out loud to the class.
- Send the narrative to a local newspaper.
- Send your narrative to a student-writing magazine.

Differentiated Instruction:
English Language Learners   ★ **ELPS** 5D, 5E

Turn to the Appendix of the Teacher's Edition for information on language transfer issues with grammar, usage, and mechanics.

ELP Level **Beginning**	**ELP Level** **Intermediate**	**ELP Level** **Advanced/Advanced High**
Work together to guide students to review their narratives for conventions and edit their work.	Pair students with a language-proficient peer to review and edit their narratives for conventions.	Have students review and edit their narratives for conventions and then review their narratives a second time with a partner.

Editing Checking Your Writing

Use a checklist. Remind students to give careful thought to each question on the editing checklist.

Editing Checklist

Give students a few moments to skim the Proofreader's Guide (SE pages 634–779). Tell them that they can refer to the guidelines, rules, and examples to clarify any items on their checklist or to resolve questions about their writing. ✔ **DIFFERENTIATE INSTRUCTION**

✔ **DIFFERENTIATE INSTRUCTION**

Remind students to pay special attention to conventions that often give them problems. For example, if they frequently neglect to capitalize proper nouns (item 10), they should check to see that these words are capitalized correctly.

✱ For more about proper nouns and capitalization, see SE pages 674–679 and 723.

★ **TEKS** 11.13D, 11.14A

Publish Sharing Your Writing

If students choose to submit their narrative to the school newspaper or a magazine that solicits writing, have them first check the submission requirements and deadlines for the publication. Most commercial publications post their submission requirements online.

★ **Conventions Connections**

Mechanics: Punctuating Dialogue
- ***Student Edition: Proofreader's Guide*** pages 646(+), 660–661
- ***SkillsBook*** page 30

Grammar: Pronoun-Antecedent Agreement
- ***Student Edition: Proofreader's Guide*** pages 726–727, 774–775
- ***SkillsBook*** pages 79, 151, 153

☀ *Write Source Online* **GrammarSnap**

Mechanics: Apostrophes
- ***Student Edition: Proofreader's Guide*** pages 656–657, 658–659
- ***SkillsBook*** pages 25, 26, 27, 28, 29

 TEKS **11.13D** Edit drafts for grammar, mechanics, and spelling; **11.14A** Write an engaging story with a range of literary strategies and devices; **ELPS 5D** Edit writing for standard grammar and usage/subject-verb agreement, pronoun agreement, verb tenses; **5E** Employ increasingly complex grammatical structures

Narrative

Evaluating a Personal Narrative

To support understanding of the overall score that the sample essay received, review the holistic scoring guide on SE pages 36–37.

Work through the sample essay with students, pointing out the qualities that earn it an overall score point of 4. In addition to the call-outs on the student pages, make the following points.

DIFFERENTIATE INSTRUCTION ↘

Focus and Coherence—The controlling idea and details in the essay all relate to the day the writer got her license.

Organization—The writer does a good job of tying the ending to the beginning by thinking back on all the years she'd wanted to drive.

Development of Ideas—Including at least one good reason at the beginning will help readers better understand why the writer so willfully ignored the law.

Voice—Using natural-sounding dialogue at important moments in the story gives readers a first-hand sense of the writer's experience and how she felt.

Conventions—The writer should add commas after introductory phrases and clauses, and between clauses in compound and complex sentences.

146

Evaluating a Personal Narrative

As you read the narrative below, focus on the overall quality of the writing. Look for the writer's strengths and weaknesses. Notice that the essay received a score of 4. (**The essay contains a few errors.**)

Writing that fits a score of 4 is very strong.

Driving into Trouble

Ever since I was a kid I wanted to drive. While other girls dressed their dolls, I drove mine around in my brother's toy trucks. While other girls spent hours in front of a mirror, styling their hair, my favorite style came from rolling down the window and letting the wind tousle my hair. I grabbed every chance I could to go somewhere in the car, and as the years went by, I couldn't wait to be in charge, just me and the road. After 16 years of waiting I was about to get my license and my freedom!

Flash! The camera caught my grin as I stood in front of the blue screen. The clerk at the DMV took my license from the laminating machine and slid it across the counter toward me. I grabbed at it—still hot—but the clerk didn't let go. "You realize this is a graduated license," she said, peering over her reading glasses. "Until you're eighteen, you can't drive more than one teenaged friend at a time and you can't use a cell phone while driving."

"Right, I know. Thanks!" I said. Glancing at my photo, I noticed that my eyes looked wide and round. I was a little disappointed that I didn't look quite as relaxed and mature as I had imagined, but it didn't dampen my bliss.

My dad said he'd walk back to work just up a few blocks, so I had the car all to myself. I jumped in, fired up the engine, and peeled confidently out of the parking lot. Pulling out onto the main drag, I lowered the windows all the way, cranked up the radio and flipped open my cell phone. "Jenna! It's me! I got it! I'm a driver! Yeah, I'm coming to pick you up, like I promised. See ya. Bye."

Voice presents unique perspective, is engaging, and sounds real.

Organization is strong; ideas flow logically and events are easy to follow.

Resources

Benchmark Papers

- Happy Days (strong)
  TE Appendix

- My First Skateboard (poor)
  TE Appendix

To give students additional practice with evaluating narrative essays, use one or both of the **benchmark papers** listed in the Resources box on page 146.

Narrative

Sensory details develop ideas and make them come alive.

The light in front of me went red. I slammed on the brakes. The smell of burning rubber wafted through the open windows. Behind me, I could see black skids on the road. Harsh but cool, I thought. I used the time at the light to call Ashley and Jarisse. We had planned that I would pick them up and we'd all go cruising.

Except that there were blue lights flashing in my rearview mirror. When the traffic light turned green, I edged through the intersection, hoping the policeman would turn after some real criminal. He was after me. I pulled over to the curb and the steel-blue sedan slid in behind me. I heard the crunch of gravel, as the policeman approached my car. My heart started to pound.

As the officer walked up, light glinted off the lenses of his sunglasses. I lowered my head. "May I see your license?"

I nodded silently and handed it to him. He glanced at it. "You just got it today? It's practically still warm!"

"Yes, sir," I said.

"Didn't they tell you about cell phone calls?"

Dialogue sharpens focus and adds depth to essay's ideas.

"Yes," I murmured. I stared down at my black wallet with its hot pink stripe, feeling like I was seeing it for the first time.

"Not a great way to start your driving career. It's going on your record as a warning. I'm sorry."

I still couldn't lift my head. "I understand. Sir, since the engine's off, is it all right if I make another call?" He nodded. A tear plopped onto my wallet's pink stripe and I flicked it away.

While the officer went back to his car, I called Jenna, Ashley, and Jarisse and told them I didn't feel like celebrating.

After I hung up I thought back on all those years I'd wanted to drive. I had dreamed about this day for so long—the bright blue sky, laughing with my friends, breezes whipping our hair as we zipped down the road! Now I had a mark on my record and my license wasn't even an hour old.

Ideas are presented clearly and thoughtfully and add depth.

My fantasies about driving had a collision with reality that day. I've been careful to follow the rules and I've not gotten stopped again. Driving is still a joy, but I've learned that freedom and responsibility go hand in hand.

Evaluating and Reflecting on Your Writing

Remind students to date their reflections so that they can easily monitor their progress by comparing them to other narrative writing they produce throughout the school year.

Before students write their reflections, be sure that they have had a chance to

- share their narratives with writing partners and get their feedback, and
- read any comments or remarks you have provided on assessment sheets and on their final copies.

Tell students to use all of the above resources to help identify the strengths and weaknesses of their writing. DIFFERENTIATE INSTRUCTION ↘

148

Evaluating and Reflecting on Your Writing

You've worked hard to write a personal narrative that your classmates will enjoy. Now take some time to think about your writing. Finish each of the sentence starters below on your own paper. Thinking about your writing will help you see how you are growing as a writer.

My Narrative

1. The strongest part of my personal narrative is . . .

2. The part that still needs work is . . .

3. The main thing I learned about writing a personal narrative is . . .

4. In my next personal narrative, I would like to . . .

5. One question I still have about writing personal narratives is . . .

Differentiated Instruction:
English Language Learners   ⭐ ELPS 1B, 1E, 3E, 3G

Have students add this sentence starter to their reflections and complete the statement: *One new concept I learned about English writing is . . .*

ELP Level **Beginning**	ELP Level **Intermediate**	ELP Level **Advanced/Advanced High**
Guide students to complete their reflections by focusing on the five traits.	Have students complete their reflections and then discuss their responses in a group.	Have students complete their reflections and then discuss their responses with a partner.

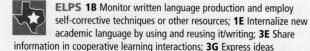
ELPS 1B Monitor written language production and employ self-corrective techniques or other resources; **1E** Internalize new academic language by using and reusing it/writing; **3E** Share information in cooperative learning interactions; **3G** Express ideas

Writing a Reflective Narrative

A mirror reflects the person you are on the outside: the color of your eyes, shape of your nose, and clothes you wear. But what reflects the person you are on the inside: your personality, hopes, fears, and experiences?

Writing is a powerful mirror. When you write a reflective narrative, you explore who you are now and who you were "back then." A reflective narrative focuses on a change you have experienced and reflects on how that change makes you unique.

In this chapter, you will read a personal narrative in which the writer recalls his changing relationship with his younger brother. Then you will write a reflective narrative of your own.

Writing Guidelines

Subject: **A change in your life**
Purpose: **To reflect on the impact of the change**
Form: **Reflective narrative**
Audience: **Classmates**

"They always say time changes things, but you actually have to change them yourself."
—Andy Warhol

Resources

Materials

• Details chart, T-chart (TE p. 152)

Writing a Reflective Narrative

Objectives

• choose a topic for a reflective narrative
• create a then/now chart to organize the narrative
• write, revise, and edit a reflective narrative

A **reflective narrative** tells the story of a life-changing experience in the writer's life.

Explain to students that all personal narratives are, by nature, introspective. The narrative they will write now will focus on a change that took place over an extended period of time. Discuss how it will differ from the narrative they wrote about making a bad decision. (That narrative focused on one experience at a specific moment in time; this narrative will cover a longer period of time.) Ask students to explain how they can make use of prior knowledge and experience to write a reflective narrative.

 ELPS 1A

ELPS **1A** Use prior knowledge and experiences

Reflective Narrative

Have students read the model narrative, paying particular attention to

- how Linc captures the reader's attention at the beginning of the essay;
- specific details that explain and clarify Linc's feelings, before and after the change he experiences;
- the dialogue that helps to bring the characters to life; and
- the reflective, or thoughtful, quality of the language—especially in the last three paragraphs—that conveys Linc's deep interest in his topic. **DIFFERENTIATE INSTRUCTION ↘**

DIFFERENTIATE INSTRUCTION ↘

⭐ **TEKS** 11.14A

Reflective Narrative

A reflective narrative looks back at a change in the writer's life. Linc wrote about his changing relationship with his little brother.

Not Taken for Granted

Beginning
The beginning provides background and introduces the topic.

I guess I was spoiled. At first, I was an only child, cuddled and cooed over by parents, grandparents, aunts, and uncles. Up until I was eight years old, life was sweet. Then along came Grant, and everything changed.

Grant is my little brother. I don't remember all the details, but he was born a month prematurely, so he needed a lot of extra attention, especially from Mom. My mom and dad didn't ignore me, but I was no longer the center of their universe, and I resented the change in dynamics. And at first, I also resented Grant.

Middle
The middle provides details and events leading up to the change.

Fortunately, Grant's early birth didn't cause any real problems in his growth, and he crawled, toddled, and talked pretty much on schedule. My parents were still somewhat protective of him, but as he got older, he developed the obnoxious habit of attaching himself to me, following my every move. My parents warned me to be nice to him, but I found him totally annoying. By the time I became a teenager, he was, at five, my shadow, following me around, copying my every move, asking questions, and generally being a pest.

The writer comes to a realization.

Still, despite my irritation, I began to enjoy him. He was a funny little guy, and I began to find his hero-worship endearing. He copied the way I walked, the way I talked, and even the way I ate.

I remember one time we were eating jelly sandwiches, and he was humming away as he ate.

"Grant, why are you humming?" I asked.

He looked genuinely surprised. "You do it, too."

"Do not," I growled. I took a bite then and realized I had been humming! Apparently, I hummed a lot and never even knew. I looked at Grant and the delighted little smirk on his face and had to laugh. He laughed, too, although I don't think he understood exactly why. Still, from then on, whenever one of us hummed, we both burst into laughter.

Differentiated Instruction: Struggling Learners

Have small groups meet to discuss the model narrative, paragraph by paragraph, focusing on these questions:

- How does the writer introduce the topic?
- Where does he use dialogue?
- Which details help you visualize the story?

The writer reflects on the way the realization affected him.

As we got older, we established boundaries and alliances, becoming more considerate of each other. Grant stopped asking to go along on dates with me, and I set aside time to go fishing with him. He cheered me on at my soccer games, and I volunteered to coach his T-ball team. I taught him to moonwalk, and he taught me to laugh at myself.

I wonder if the transition happened because as he grew older he became less annoying and more of a buddy. Or was it because I had done the growing, becoming more patient, more able to share, more receptive to the unconditional love he offered? Looking back, I have come to the conclusion that maybe it was a combination of both.

Ending
The ending sums up the writer's reflection about the change.

Today, I am happy to say that after a rocky beginning, Grant and I are a team. We've already talked about how he'll come visit me when I am in college. It will be hard to be separated, but I know that we will always be close, if not in age or distance, then in that love shared by brothers.

Narrative

Respond to the reading. Answer the following questions about the sample reflective narrative.

Focus and Coherence (1) What is the author's controlling, or main, idea? (2) Name three details that contribute to that main idea.

Organization (3) How is the narrative organized? (4) How is the first paragraph linked to the second paragraph?

Development of Ideas (5) What details does the author include to develop the idea that when Grant was young he annoyed the author? (6) What details illustrate how the author's attitude toward Grant changed?

Voice (7) Find two examples in the reflective narrative that show the author's unique voice.

Respond to the reading.

Answers

Focus and Coherence
1. Linc resented his younger brother at first, but came to love and respect him eventually. **2.** Linc was an only child for eight years; Grant followed Linc everywhere, and imitated him; Grant begins to find humor in the fact that he and his brother hum.

Organization
3. The narrative is organized chronologically. **4.** The first paragraph names Grant but doesn't identify him; the second paragraph explains who Grant is.

Development of Ideas
5. Grant's premature birth took their parents' attention away from Linc; Grant imitated and followed Linc, which was annoying for Linc. **6.** Linc realizes that Grant is imitating him by humming, and the realization leads Linc to begin to accept Grant; the brothers begin to do some activities together and to support each other.

Voice
7. Possible choices: delighted little smirk; burst into laughter; more considerate of each other; set aside time; cheered me on; laugh at myself

TEKS 11.14A

TEKS **11.14A** Write an engaging story with a well-developed conflict and resolution; ELPS **3J** Respond orally to information presented/concept attainment; **4D** Use prereading supports to enhance comprehension of written text; **4G** Demonstrate comprehension of increasingly complex English/responding to questions; **4K** Expand reading skills by employing analytical skills

Prewriting Selecting a Topic

Before asking students to make a then/now chart, brainstorm a list of areas of life in which people often experience change, such as the following:

- relationships (family and friends)
- goals (academic, career, athletic)
- interests and hobbies
- hopes and dreams
- fears

Then/Now Chart

Encourage students to focus on these prior experiences as they try to think of ways they have changed over the years. Then review Linc's Then/Now Chart together.

Make a then/now chart. Distribute photocopies of the reproducible details chart (TE page A106) for students to use for their then/now chart.

DIFFERENTIATE INSTRUCTION ↘

TEKS 11.13A, 11.14A; **ELPS** 1A

Prewriting Gathering Details

Students may have explored their topic in other personal writing. Suggest that they look through their personal journals, writer's notebooks, old letters, and e-mails to find details that may help them recall their feelings before and after the change.

T-Chart

Discuss Linc's T-chart together, focusing on how his feelings changed over time. Ask questions to confirm students' understanding.

Make a T-chart. Distribute photocopies of the reproducible T-chart (TE page A103) for students to use to gather details for their narrative.

TEKS 11.13A, 11.14A; **ELPS** 4F

Prewriting Selecting a Topic

The first step in planning your reflective narrative is to select a topic. Think of ways that you have changed and explore the reasons for those changes. Linc made a chart listing ways he has changed. Then, he looked for an idea that he wanted to write about that would also engage his readers. When he made his choice, he put an asterisk by it.

Then/Now Chart

Then	Now	Reason for Change
I wanted to be a professional football player when I grew up.	I plan to become a marine biologist.	I wasn't any good at football, but I love sea life.
*My little brother, Grant, was a real pest.	My brother is a lot of fun, and we're friends.	We both grew up.
I really wanted to date Bette.	I'm going out with Lyndsey.	Lyndsey and I have more in common.

Make a then/now chart. List how things used to be and how they are now. Then tell why they changed. Put an asterisk by the topic you would like to write about.

Gathering Details

Now arrange your details to create the frame of your essay. Linc made a T-chart, listing events and details about life before and after the change.

T-Chart

Things that annoyed me then	Our relationship now
– He took up all the family's attention.	– I don't mind when he gets attention.
– He tattled on me to Mom and Dad.	– We have some "secrets."
– He asked a lot of annoying questions.	– I like his questions, and he listens to me.
– He copied how I walked, talked, and ate.	– I encourage him to be himself.
– We were kind of adversaries.	– We are friends.

Make a T-chart. List events that happened "then" and "now." Try to include at least five events and details in each list.

Differentiated Instruction: Struggling Learners

To help them select a topic, have students meet with you to discuss changes in their lives that have helped them to grow as students. The discussion will help students formulate their ideas before they begin to write.

TEKS **11.13A** Plan a first draft by determining appropriate topics through a range of strategies; **11.14A** Write an engaging story with a well-developed conflict and resolution; **ELPS** **1A** Use prior experiences; **4F** Use visual and contextual support to enhance and confirm understanding

 TEKS 11.13B, 11.14A

Writing a Reflective Narrative **153**

Drafting Revisit Your Prewriting Notes

When you think you are ready to begin drafting, review and evaluate your prewriting notes. Consider whether you have what you need to draft an engaging narrative. Use the questions below to guide you as you revise or add to your prewriting notes.

- Do I have the details I need to describe a well-developed conflict and resolution?
- Do I have the details I need to create complex, non-stereotypical characters?
- Have I carefully chosen my sensory details to match the mood and tone I would like to create?
- Have I thought of literary strategies and devices that would enhance the plot of my narrative?

Creating Your First Draft

Use the chart below as a framework to write your first draft. If you think of new ideas, go ahead and add them. You'll be able to revise and rearrange ideas as needed later in the writing process. Write freely, and don't worry about spelling or grammar at this time.

Narrative

Beginning	Middle	Ending
Provide background details and events that build your narrative and lead up to the change.	Include an anecdote that helps demonstrate the change. Remember to show readers what is happening and use dialogue.	Reflect on events after the change and think about how your life was different.

Write your first draft. Be sure to include a beginning, a middle, and an ending. Use all of your planning notes as a guide, and remain open to new ideas as you write.

Drafting Revisit Your Prewriting Notes

Allow time for students to rework their prewriting notes as needed.

⤷ **DIFFERENTIATE INSTRUCTION**

Creating Your First Draft

Before students create their first draft, suggest that they read the descriptions in the Beginning, Middle, and Ending graphic at the bottom of the page to help them structure their ideas in a sustained way. Explain that these descriptions summarize the kinds of details and information that they should use in each part of their narratives. Tell students to refer to their T-charts for specific details that relate to each part of the narrative.

Write your first draft. Advise students to scan the Revising Checklist on SE page 154 before they begin to write. The list of goals for each trait on the checklist will help guide them with writing their draft as well as with revising it.

⭐ TEKS 11.13B, 11.14A

✱ For more information about the basic parts of any narrative or essay, see SE page 618.

TEKS **11.13B** Develop drafts that structure ideas in a sustained way; **11.14A** Write an engaging story with well-developed conflict and resolution; ELPS **1E** Internalize new basic language by using and reusing it/writing; **1H** Expand repertoire of learning strategies; **5G** Narrate with increasing specificity and detail

Revising Improving Your Writing

When students use the Revising Checklist on their own, they may have a tendency to zip through the questions, answering "yes" to all of them. Caution students not to minimize this important step in the process.

Revising Checklist

Encourage a more thoughtful revising process.

- Have students exchange papers with a partner. After the partner reads the essay, have the writer ask the checklist questions in a way that elicits specific and useful feedback. For example, instead of "Is the change that I write about interesting?" the writer could ask "What is the change that I write about? What is interesting about this change?"
- Encourage partners to give thoughtful and constructive responses.
- Point out to students that although they may use informal language in discussions with their partner, their writing is more formal. Ask students to distinguish between formal and informal language.

ELPS 1G

Revise your first draft. Explain that although the process described above may take longer than simply reading down the checklist, it can provide writers with a more accurate assessment of where they are in the revising stage.

TEKS 11.13C, 11.14A

TEKS 11.13C, 11.14A

Revising Improving Your Writing

Use the following checklist to decide how to improve your writing. Number your paper from 1 to 12. If you can answer "yes" to a question, place a check next to the number. If not, go back and revise your paper for that trait.

Revising Checklist

Focus and Coherence

_____ 1. Do I respond to the assignment or the prompt?
_____ 2. Do I have a clearly stated controlling, or main, idea?
_____ 3. Do all my details support or contribute to that main idea?

Organization

_____ 4. Does my beginning provide background and introduce the topic?
_____ 5. Do the middle paragraphs show how I changed?
_____ 6. Does the ending reflect how my life was altered by the experience?

Development of Ideas

_____ 7. Have I arranged ideas so that each sentence adds meaning to the sentence that comes before it?
_____ 8. Has each idea been developed thoroughly? Am I missing important ideas?
_____ 9. Have I made interesting connections between ideas?

Voice

_____ 10. Is the change I write about interesting?
_____ 11. Does my dialogue sound natural?
_____ 12. Will my voice keep the reader interested and engaged?

Revise your first draft. Use the checklist above to revise your first draft. When you are finished, make a clean copy to edit.

TEKS **11.13C** Revise drafts to clarify meaning and achieve specific rhetorical purposes, consistency of tone, and logical organization by rearranging the words, sentences, and paragraphs to employ tropes, schemes, and by adding transitional words and phrases; **11.14A** Write an engaging story with a well-developed conflict and resolution; **ELPS 1G** Demonstrate ability to distinguish between formal and informal English

TEKS 11.13D, 11.13E, 11.18A

Editing Checking for Conventions

Once you have revised your reflective narrative, you're ready to edit your writing for conventions. Use the following checklist to review your writing for grammar, sentence structure, capitalization, punctuation, and spelling errors.

Editing Checklist

Conventions

GRAMMAR

_____ **1.** Have I used the correct forms of verbs (*I saw*, not *I seen*)?

_____ **2.** Do my subjects and verbs agree in number (*We were going*, not *We was going*)?

_____ **3.** If words sound alike, have I used the right words?

SENTENCE STRUCTURE

_____ **4.** Do I use a variety of correctly structured sentences that clearly communicate my ideas?

MECHANICS (CAPITALIZATION AND PUNCTUATION)

_____ **5.** Have I used end punctuation correctly?

_____ **6.** Have I used apostrophes to show possession (*Grant's smile*)?

_____ **7.** Have I capitalized each speaker's first word in dialogue?

SPELLING

_____ **8.** Have I checked my spelling?

_____ **9.** Have I checked for words that my spell-checker might miss?

Edit your narrative. Use the checklist above to find and correct any errors. Then ask someone else to check your work. Create a neat final copy and proofread it.

Publishing Sharing Your Writing

When you publish something, you make it public. By sharing your reflective narrative with an appreciative audience, you can let them know more about who you are.

Share your reflective narrative. Ask a friend or family member to read your narrative, or read it aloud to the person.

Narrative

Editing Checking for Conventions

Suggest that students use a different color to edit their hand-written narratives. If they are using a computer, have them highlight and save their changes. Using color will help students easily see changes when they write their final copy.

Edit your narrative. Remind students to refer to the writing conventions in the Proofreader's Guide at the back of the book (SE pages 634–779) as they edit. ✔ DIFFERENTIATE INSTRUCTION

TEKS 11.13D, 11.18A

Publishing Sharing Your Writing

Some students may want to create an illustrated version of their narrative using photographs or original drawings. Explain that the photos or illustrations should show how they and others in the story have changed.

Share your reflective narrative. Point out that classmates and teachers are also good audiences with whom to share the narratives.

TEKS 11.13E

Conventions Connections

Mechanics: End Punctuation
- *Student Edition: Proofreader's Guide* pages 635–637
- *SkillsBook* page 5

Using the Right Word
- *Student Edition: Proofreader's Guide* pages 702–703, 704–705, 706–707
- *SkillsBook* page 62

Mechanics: Capitalization
- *Student Edition: Proofreader's Guide* pages 674–675, 676(+), 678(+)
- *SkillsBook* page 43

Run-On Sentences
- *Student Edition: Proofreader's Guide* pages 756, 758
- *SkillsBook* page 161

Spelling
- *Student Edition: Proofreader's Guide* pages 690–695
- *SkillsBook* page 55

TEKS **11.13D** Edit drafts for grammar, mechanics, and spelling; **11.13E** Publish written work for appropriate audiences; **11.18A** Correctly and consistently use conventions of punctuation and capitalization; **ELPS 1E** Internalize new academic language by using and reusing it/writing; **4F** Use support from peers and teachers to develop grasp of language structures; **5E** Employ increasingly complex grammatical structures

Expository Writing

UNIT TEKS

11.13A Plan first draft by selecting the correct genre for conveying the intended meaning to multiple audiences, determining appropriate topics through a range of strategies, developing a thesis/controlling idea; **11.13B** Structure ideas in a sustained, persuasive way; develop drafts in timed/open-ended situations that include transitions, rhetorical devices to convey meaning; **11.13C** Revise drafts to clarify meaning, achieve specific rhetorical purposes, consistency of tone, logical organization; **11.13D** Edit drafts for grammar, mechanics, spelling; **11.13E** Revise final draft in response to feedback from peers/teacher; publish written work for appropriate audiences; **11.15A** Write an analytic essay of sufficient length that includes **(i)** effective introductory, concluding paragraphs, a variety of sentence structures; **(ii)** rhetorical devices, transitions between paragraphs; **(iii)** a clear thesis statement/controlling idea; **(iv)** a clear organizational schema for conveying ideas; **(v)** relevant, substantial evidence, well-chosen details; **(vi)** information on multiple perspectives

UNIT ELPS

1A Use prior knowledge, experiences; **1B** Monitor oral, written language production; employ self-corrective techniques; **1C** Use strategic learning strategies to acquire basic vocabulary; **1E** Internalize new basic, academic language by using, reusing it; **1F** Use accessible language; **1G** Demonstrate ability to distinguish between formal, informal English; **1H** Develop/expand repertoire of learning strategies; **2B** Recognize elements/English sound system in newly acquired vocabulary; **2C** Learn new language structures, expressions, vocabulary; **2E** Use support to confirm understanding of spoken language; **2F** Listen to/derive meaning from a variety of media; **2G** Understand general meaning, main points, important details of spoken language; **2H** Understand implicit ideas, information in spoken language; **2I** Demonstrate listening comprehension; **3A** Practice producing sounds of vocabulary to pronounce English words; **3B** Expand vocabulary; **3C** Speak using a variety of grammatical structures, sentence lengths/types, connecting words; **3D** Speak using content-area vocabulary in context; **3E** Share information in cooperative learning interactions; **3F** Give information during extended speaking assignments; **3G** Express opinions, ideas, feelings; **3H** Explain with increasing specificity, detail; **3I** Adapt language for formal, informal purposes; **3J** Respond orally to information presented; **4A** Learn relationships between sounds, letters of English; decode using a combination of skills; **4C** Comprehend English vocabulary, language structures; **4D** Use prereading supports to enhance comprehension; **4E** Read linguistically accommodated content area material; **4F** Use visual/contextual support, support from peers/teachers to enhance/confirm understanding; **4G** Demonstrate comprehension of increasingly complex English; **4I** Demonstrate English comprehension by employing basic reading skills; **4K** Demonstrate English comprehension by employing analytical skills; **5A** Learn relationships between sounds, letters to represent sounds when writing in English; **5B** Write using basic, content-based vocabulary; **5C** Spell familiar English words; employ English spelling patterns, rules; **5D** Edit writing for standard grammar, usage; **5E** Employ increasingly complex grammatical structures; **5F** Write using a variety of sentence lengths, patterns, connecting words; **5G** Explain with increasing specificity, detail

Informative Paragraph

(pages 157–159)

Students share an anecdote about a class they attend through writing an informative paragraph.

Informative Article

(pages 160–198)

Following the steps of the writing process, students learn to develop a well-organized and entertaining article that contains timely information.

Comparison-Contrast Essay

(pages 199–206)

Students show the differences and similarities between two technologies through their creation of this essay.

Writing for Assessment

(pages 207–213)

Using the STRAP questions as a guide, students respond to a timed-writing prompt.

 Literature Connections

- **"The Next Frontier"** by S. C. Gwynne

 Technology Connections

 Write Source Online
www.hmheducation.com/tx/writesource
- **Net-text**
- **Writing Network**
- **Portfolio**
- **GrammarSnap**
- **Essay Scoring**
- **File Cabinet**

 Interactive Whiteboard Lessons

Expository Writing Unit Scope and Sequence

Day	Writing and Conventions Instruction	Write Source Student Edition			Daily Language Workouts	Skills-Book	Write Source Online
		Core Unit	Tools of Language	Resource Units			
WEEK 1 1–3	**Informative Paragraph** Model	157–159	**TL** 574–579	**BEW** 610	26–29		Interactive Whiteboard Lesson
	Skills Activities: •Verbs			**PG** 734–745		88–97	GrammarSnap
	•Using the Right Word			**PG** 702–721		61–66	GrammarSnap
4–5	**Informative Article** Model, Prewriting Literature Connection "The Next Frontier" by S.C. Gwynne	160–168		**BEW** 617–620			Net-text
WEEK 2 6–8	Drafting	169–174	**TL** 574–579	**BEW** 621–631	30–33		Net-text
9–10	Revising	175–184					Net-text
	Skills Activities: •Verbals			**PG** 746–747		99, 127	GrammarSnap
	•Clauses and Phrases			**PG** 640–641, 762–763		126–136	GrammarSnap
WEEK 3 11–13	Editing, Publishing	185–191	**TL** 574–579	**BEW** 632–633	34–37		Net-text
	Skills Activities: •Subject-Verb Agreement			**PG** 770–773		145–149	GrammarSnap
	•Pronoun-Antecedent Agreement			**PG** 774–775		150–154	GrammarSnap
14–15	Evaluating an Informative Article	192–198					
WEEK 4 16–18	**Comparison-Contrast Essay** Model, Prewriting	199–203	**TL** 574–579	**BEW** 613	38–41		Net-text
	Drafting, Revising	204–205		**BEW** 621–631			Net-text
	Editing, Publishing	206		**BEW** 632–633			Net-text
	Skills Activities: •Parallel Structure					170–172	GrammarSnap
	•Sentence Combining					155–158	GrammarSnap
	•Semicolons, Colons			**PG** 648–649, 650–651		19–21	GrammarSnap
19–20	**Writing for Assessment**	207–213					

Resource Units referenced above are located in the back of the *Student Edition* and *Teacher's Edition*
TL *"The Tools of Language"* **BEW** *"Basic Elements of Writing"* **PG** *"Proofreader's Guide"*

Writing Focus

- Writing an Informative Article
- Writing a Comparison-Contrast Essay
- Responding to Expository Prompts

Grammar Focus

- Subject-Verb Agreement
- Pronouns

Learning Language

Read aloud the basic and academic terms, as well as the descriptions and questions. Model for students how to read one question and answer it. For example, *It says that a periodical is a magazine, so it's asking me about magazine I enjoy reading. I enjoy a periodical that has articles about the newest electronic products.* Have partners monitor their pronunciation and understanding of the terms by working through the meanings and questions together.

DIFFERENTIATE INSTRUCTION ⟍

 ELPS 1F, 2C, 4G

Minilessons

Did You Know . . . ?   Writing an Informative Article

- Have students interview a classmate. Tell them to **ZERO IN** on an individual issue in the classmate's life, such as whether he or she has visited an unusual place, lived in another country, etc. Have them **TAKE** notes and **GATHER** facts and details. Then ask them to **EXCHANGE** roles. Allow time to **SHARE** the interviews orally

Right Around the Corner   Writing an Informative Article

- Have students **RESEARCH** the history of a building, company, church, store, or restaurant and **WRITE** the findings in a feature article. Invite them to **PRESENT** the topic in an unusual or interesting light.

ELPS 1F Use accessible language and learn new and essential language in the process; **2B** Recognize elements of the English sound system in newly acquired vocabulary; **2C** Learn new language structures, expressions, basic and academic vocabulary; **3A** Practice producing sounds of newly acquired vocabulary to pronounce English words; **4A** Learn relationships between sounds and letters of English and decode using a combination of skills; **4G** Demonstrate comprehension of increasingly complex English/shared reading

---

156

⭐ ELPS 1F, 2C, 4G

www.hmheducation.com/tx/writesource

Expository Writing

Writing Focus

Grammar Focus

Learning Language

Work with a partner. Read the meanings and share answers to the questions.

1. Periodical is another name for a magazine or journal. **Name a periodical you enjoy reading.**
2. Evidence is information that proves something is true. **What evidence would prove a sport is dangerous?**
3. A provocative statement is meant to excite or anger. **When might a provocative statement be useful?**
4. To live on the edge is to do dangerous activities. **Name someone you know who lives on the edge.**

Differentiated Instruction: English Language Learners

⭐ ELPS 2B, 3A, 4A

ELP Level **Beginning**	ELP Level **Intermediate**	ELP Level **Advanced/Advanced High**
Say *periodical, evidence,* and *provocative* aloud and have students repeat them with you. Guide students to note and pronounce the vowel sounds in each word.	Pronounce *periodical, evidence,* and *provocative* together. Have partners divide each word into syllables and identify the vowel sounds.	Pronounce *periodical, evidence,* and *provocative* together. Have students divide each word into syllables and discuss the vowel sounds.

157

Expository Writing
Writing an Informative Article

When you pick up a newspaper or magazine, you are entering a world of information. It's almost impossible to read a periodical and not learn something new. Informative articles in newspapers or magazines cover every topic under the sun, from aardvarks to zoology.

These articles share common characteristics. They are created to inform and entertain. They contain timely information, even when the topic is historical. They employ a lively writing style to hook the reader, present information in a logical sequence, and explain a topic clearly.

The best way to learn about article writing is to read articles in your favorite periodicals. Pay careful attention to the topic and focus, the way in which the writer hooks the reader, the development of the middle part, and so on. Later, incorporate some of these techniques in your own writing.

In this chapter, you'll learn how to develop a well-organized, entertaining informative article suitable for publication in a newspaper or magazine.

Writing Guidelines

Subject: A timely topic
Purpose: To engage and inform
Form: Informative article
Audience: Local or school newspaper or magazine readers

"All glory comes from daring to begin."
—Eugene F. Ware

Writing an Informative Article

Objectives
- demonstrate an understanding of the purpose and focus of an informative article
- choose a topic and identify relevant and substantial details
- plan, draft, revise, edit, and publish an informative article

Remind students that expository writing *explains* a topic. As a group, discuss the meaning of the term *article* when applied to writing. Responses may include the following:
- Articles discuss nonfiction topics.
- Articles usually appear in magazines, newspapers, or on Web sites.
- Articles usually strive to present information objectively.

Share with students articles from various periodicals or Web sites. Point out any writing techniques in the articles that students may want to try.

ELPS 1C

 Technology Connections

Use the Interactive Whiteboard lessons to introduce expository writing.

 Interactive Whiteboard Lesson

Resources

**Benchmark Papers
(see Appendix)**

- Hot Dogs: This is No Bologna! (strong)
- Recycling (poor)

 ELPS 1C Use strategic learning strategies to acquire basic and grade-level vocabulary

Expository Writing Warm-Up
Processing Information

Discuss each type of information, and ask students to demonstrate their understanding by citing examples they have encountered.

 ELPS 2G, 3B

Try It!
Answers

Suggest that students use a details chart to organize the information they find for the Try It! activity. Their chart should include four columns: *Facts, Statistics, Quotations,* and *Anecdotes.* Encourage students to try to fill in more than one detail per column. Explain that doing so will give them more information to work with as they begin their first draft. **DIFFERENTIATE INSTRUCTION ↘**

TEKS 11.13A, 11.15A(v)

 Writer's Craft

Remind students that each type of information they uncover will provide a different type of support for their main idea:

- Facts create clarity and a knowledgeable voice.
- Statistics create precision.
- Quotations give voice to people particularly knowledgable about the topic.
- Anecdotes help readers make a personal connection to the topic.

Conventions Connections

Grammar: Verbs
- *Proofreader's Guide* pages 734–735
- *SkillsBook* pages 89–90

Using the Right Word
- *Proofreader's Guide* pages 708–709, 710–711
- *SkillsBook* page 63

 TEKS **11.13A** Plan first draft; **11.15A(v)** Use relevant and substantial evidence and well-chosen details; **ELPS** **2G** Understand the important details of spoken language/topics, language, and contexts; **3B** Expand vocabulary/retelling simple stories and basic information

---

Expository Writing Warm-Up Processing Information

As a student you need to be an expert at handling the information you hear, see, write down, and discuss every day in class. This means recognizing evidence that is relevant and substantial and details that are persuasive and to the point. Here are examples of the many types of information you process every day.

> **Facts:** Things that can be proven
>
> The great American author William Faulkner had a tough time making enough money in his early years.

> **Statistics:** Facts that give precise numerical values
>
> Faulkner wrote his novel *As I Lay Dying* in only six weeks while working the night shift at a local power plant, making less than seventy cents an hour.

> **Quotations:** The exact words of a speaker
>
> "Everything goes by the board: humor, pride, decency . . . to get the book written. If a writer has to rob his mother, he will not hesitate; the *Ode on a Grecian Urn* is worth any number of old ladies."
> —William Faulkner

> **Anecdotes:** Little stories that give insight
>
> Faulkner hired himself out to write screenplays but hated living and working in Hollywood. Once when he struggled over a tough screenplay in his office, he asked his boss if he could go home to work on it. The boss agreed, thinking Faulkner was heading back to his Hollywood apartment. Instead, he headed back to Mississippi.

Try It!

Think about the classes you have had so far today. Which was most memorable? Choose one class period and write down the relevant facts, statistics, quotations, or anecdotes that came from that class period. You will be using these details as you begin writing an informative paragraph on the next page.

Differentiated Instruction: Advanced Learners

Analyzing informative articles on a regular basis can help students become better writers. Have partners read and discuss short articles in other content areas, looking at organization, tone, and development of the main ideas in each one. What techniques might they emulate? Have them record their insights in a writer's notebook.

TEKS 11.13A, 11.13B

Writing an Informative Paragraph

An informative paragraph focuses on one main idea, supporting it with different types of details. Alex wrote the following informative paragraph about the money troubles of William Faulkner. Remember that a paragraph has three parts.

- The **topic sentence** introduces the thesis, or controlling idea, of the paragraph.
- The **body sentences** use details to support the thesis.
- The **closing sentence** restates the thesis in an interesting way.

Topic Sentence

Body Sentences

Closing Sentence

Writing on a Dime

Though William Faulkner became one of the most famous American writers of the twentieth century, he had to struggle to make enough money. After publishing his classic novel *The Sound and the Fury,* Faulkner wrote the novel *Sanctuary* just to make money, but his publisher rejected it. Desperate, he took a night-shift job at a factory, making less than seventy cents an hour. Over a six-week period, while working at the factory, he spent his days writing the classic *As I Lay Dying.* Later, Faulkner hired himself out to write screenplays, but he hated working in Hollywood. Once he asked his boss if he could go home to work on a screenplay, and the boss agreed—not realizing Faulkner was heading all the way back to Mississippi. Faulkner had a sense of humor about his money troubles: "If a writer has to rob his mother, he will not hesitate; the *Ode on a Grecian Urn* is worth any number of old ladies." Luckily for his mother, Faulkner never stooped so low, and luckily for modern readers, he kept writing, even when he wasn't getting paid.

Expository

Draft

Write your own informative paragraph. Write about an interesting class period you had today. Create a topic sentence that presents a controlling idea about the class. Include a variety of details to support your topic sentence.

Writing an Informative Paragraph

Discuss the sample paragraph. How does each type of detail support the main idea? Encourage students to use the terms *facts, statistics, quotations,* and *anecdotes* in their responses to help them internalize the new vocabulary. Responses may include the following:

- The <u>facts</u> give background information about Faulkner, the subject of the article.
- The <u>statistic</u> supports the main idea of the article.
- The <u>anecdote</u> illustrates the writer's focus with a humorous account.
- The <u>quotation</u> uses a revealing exaggeration to make a memorable point. **✔ DIFFERENTIATE INSTRUCTION**

ELPS 1E

Write your own informative paragraph. Remind students to include a topic sentence that introduces the thesis, body sentences, and a closing sentence. Point out that the prompt says to write about an interesting class period, but this does not mean students should explain *why* the class was interesting. Instead, their task is to inform the reader about the class or explain a topic covered in the class. It is the writer's job to engage the reader's interest by using well-chosen details and clearly written explanations.

TEKS 11.13A, 11.13B

✽ For Basic Paragraph Skills, see SE pages 605–616; for more about writing an Expository Paragraph, see SE page 610.

TEKS **11.13A** Plan first draft; **11.13B** Structure ideas in a sustained and persuasive way; **ELPS 1E** Internalize new basic language and academic language by using and reusing it/ writing; **2G** Understand the important details of spoken language/topics, language, contexts; **3B** Expand vocabulary/retelling simple stories and basic information; **4F** Use support from peers and teachers to enhance and confirm understanding and to develop background knowledge

Understanding Your Goal

Review the goals of this unit with students, focusing on how each of the five traits relates to writing an informative article. To reinforce understanding, ask questions such as *Why is it important to include only details that support your thesis statement?* and *How will writing a clear beginning, middle, and end make your article stronger?* Revisit SE pages 566–567 to support English language learners' understanding of the Texas traits.

TEKS 11.13A, 11.13B

Connecting to the Scoring Guide

Before reviewing the sample essay, take a few minutes to connect the goals of this unit to those detailed in the holistic scoring guide on SE pages 36–37. Note that this scoring guide provides a trait-centered description of the qualities of strong writing in general, not just expository writing.

Literature Connections

In the informative article, "The Next Frontier," S.C. Gwynne explains how one of the most well-known ranches in Texas is managing not only to survive but also to thrive. (If this article is not available to you, comparable ones are included in your literature anthology.) With students, locate the beginning, middle, and closing paragraphs. Find the thesis, or controlling idea, of the article. Discuss how relevant details support the author's thesis. For additional expository writing models, see SE pages 192–197.

TEKS 11.13A, 11.13B

TEKS **11.13A** Plan first draft; **11.13B** Structure ideas in a sustained and persuasive way

---

160

 **TEKS** 11.13A, 11.13B

Understanding Your Goal

Your goal in this chapter is to write a well-organized informative article that engages and informs the reader. The traits listed in the chart below will help you plan and write your article.

Traits of Expository Writing

- **Focus and Coherence**

  Choose a topic that addresses the prompt or assignment, write a clear thesis statement, and include only details that support that thesis statement.

- **Organization**

  Start with a hook that captures the reader's attention. Expand the main focus in the middle paragraphs. Sum up the topic in the closing paragraph.

- **Development of Ideas**

  Layer or "flesh out" your ideas so that each sentence adds meaning to the sentence that comes before it.

- **Voice**

  Use an engaging voice that shows *your* interest in and knowledge of the topic.

- **Conventions**

  Be sure that your punctuation, capitalization, spelling, and grammar are correct.

Literature Connection. You can find an example of an informative article in S. C. Gwynne's "The Next Frontier."

> "There are a thousand ways to write, and each is as good as the other if it fits you."
> —Lillian Hellman

Informative Article

An informative article provides information in the form of statistics, anecdotes, quotations from experts, and even the writer's own experiences. In this sample, a student presents information about the high-risk sport of ice climbing.

Beginning
The beginning introduces the topic and presents the thesis statement (underlined).

Middle
The first middle paragraph uses a personal example to explain the sport's popularity.

The second middle paragraph explains how many ice climbers get their start.

Life on Ice

For most people, walking across an icy sidewalk is enough danger for one day. The thought of scaling a frozen waterfall with ropes and an ice ax might seem like a sure shortcut to the intensive-care unit, but for many high school students, the thrill of ice climbing is irresistible. More and more young outdoor enthusiasts are discovering the sport of ice climbing—and living on the edge.

Ice climbing isn't for everyone, but it's attracting a steady stream of newcomers. Danielle Harris is typical of the new breed of ice climbers. She's a high school senior who is tired of "ordinary" recreational pursuits like in-line skating and cycling. So last winter, Harris headed to New Hampshire's White Mountains to give ice climbing a try. "I was terrified at first," Harris says. "It looked just plain crazy." Once she was on the ropes, however, she discovered that while physically and mentally demanding, the sport was far from impossible. "I was able to do some good climbing on that first day," says Harris. "And from then on, I was hooked." She isn't alone. The number of high school students who have tried ice climbing continues to grow.

Believe it or not, many ice climbers get their start indoors—and for good reason. Indoor rock gyms have become increasingly popular as training grounds for inexperienced climbers ("Ice Geeks"). The gyms consist of vertical walls studded with hundreds of plastic handholds of various sizes and shapes. The handholds simulate the holds a climber might find on a real rock face, from large, chunky handles to tiny nubs of rock. Steve Carstens, a high school junior who has been ice climbing for two years in New York's Adirondack Mountains, got his start at an indoor rock gym. "Ice climbing isn't for everyone," Carstens points out. "And the rock gym is a great way to get a taste of the thrills of ice climbing without so much risk."

Expository

Informative Article

Work through the sample essay with the class, pointing out the elements that make it a good example of an informative article

✔ DIFFERENTIATE INSTRUCTION

TEKS 11.13A, 11.13B

Focus and Coherence

- The thesis statement clearly identifies the topic and the focus of the essay.
- The article opens with an attention-grabbing paragraph that includes a clearly worded thesis statement.

Organization

- The beginning captures readers' attention by using a familiar example.
- The middle paragraphs provide interesting and relevant details, including quotes from sports enthusiasts.
- The details in each paragraph clearly support the topic sentence of the paragraph and the main idea of the essay.

Development of Ideas

- The essay includes a variety of detail types.
- All details provide solid and substantive support for the main idea.
- The essay provides a unique perspective on the topic.

Voice

- The writer's voice is authentic and original.
- The writer engages the reader throughout the essay.
- The tone of the essay suits its purpose and audience.

 TEKS 11.13A Plan first draft by developing a thesis or controlling idea; **11.13B** Structure ideas in a sustained and persuasive way; **ELPS 4F** Use support from peers and teachers to develop vocabulary and background knowledge and a grasp of language structures

Respond to the reading

Answers

Focus and Coherence 1. Answers will vary but should focus on specific examples of young outdoor enthusiasts discovering the sport.

Organization 2. to give the topic of the paragraph **3.** It sums up the feelings and experiences of people who participate in the sport.

Development of Ideas 4. Answers will vary but should include specific sentences that flesh out or build on the preceding sentence.

Voice 5. Answers will vary but should include examples of the effective use of quotations, relevant and engaging details, and words that show enthusiasm. **DIFFERENTIATE INSTRUCTION ↘**

TEKS 11.13A, 11.13B; **ELPS** 4K

The third middle paragraph provides important safety information.

Because ice climbing is so risky, many first-time climbers find an experienced instructor to guide them. Every year, dozens of deaths and serious injuries happen to careless or unprepared rock and ice climbers (Brown and William 32). Falling, avalanches, and even hypothermia (a dangerously low body temperature caused by overexposure to cold weather) are all dangers of ice climbing. Guides can help beginning climbers follow safety rules and avoid taking unnecessary risks. "We have a saying in this business," says Ellen Gustafson, a veteran ice-climbing guide in Colorado. "There are old climbers. And there are bold climbers. But there are no old, bold climbers" ("Ice Forum").

The fourth middle paragraph gives the reader a feel for the experience of climbing.

If the risks of ice climbing are greater than in other sports, so are the thrills. From a hundred feet up a massive blue-green wall of ice, the view is breathtaking, and getting there means a physical and mental challenge that few have experienced. From the bottom of a wall, it's a constant battle of mind and muscle, as the climber chooses a viable route and uses a combination of poise and power to get to the top. "There's no workout like it," says Danielle Harris, "and there's no gym in the world as beautiful as an ice wall" ("Ice Forum").

Ending
The ending summarizes the article's main ideas and gives the reader something to think about.

Boosted by the enthusiasm of new participants such as Danielle Harris, the sport of ice climbing is growing, drawing climbers to ice walls from Alberta's Jasper National Park to the Bitterroot Mountains of Montana and New Hampshire's White Mountains. Ice climbing's unique combination of challenging workouts and heart-racing thrills is part of the draw. The feeling of accomplishment is no doubt another attraction for participants. After all, few individuals can show up at school on Monday morning and talk about scaling a 100-foot tower of ice over the weekend.

Respond to the reading. Answer the following questions.

Focus and Coherence (1) List three details that support the thesis statement of this essay.

Organization (2) What is the purpose of the first sentence of each paragraph? (3) How does the last paragraph summarize the main idea?

Development of Ideas (4) Find three examples of sentences that add meaning to the preceding sentence.

Voice (5) How does the writer show interest in the topic? Explain.

Writing an Informative Article **163**

Prewrite — Revise — Publish

Draft — Edit

Prewriting

All effective writing begins with prewriting. In the prewriting stage, you'll choose a topic, do some research, gather details, and organize your ideas.

Keys to Effective Prewriting

1. Choose a topic that you know well or would like to know more about. Focus on finding a topic that will interest your reader as well.

2. Identify sources of information and begin your research.

3. Gather a variety of interesting details about your topic.

4. Write a thesis statement and topic sentences.

5. Plan your essay using an outline or an organized list.

Expository

Prewriting

Keys to Effective Prewriting

Remind students of the purpose of the prewriting stage of the writing process: It is when the writer selects a topic, gathers details, and decides how to organize those details.

The Keys to Effective Prewriting list explains the process students will be guided through on SE pages 164–168.

Remind students that during the prewriting stage they will figure out what they intend to say in their writing. For this reason, they should always budget a generous amount of time for this stage of the process.

- Rushing through topic selection might result in settling for a topic that they aren't really interested in or one that isn't appropriate for the project at hand.
- Rushing through the gathering and organizing stages will leave gaps in their drafts that they'll have to work harder to fill later on during the revising stage. ✔ **DIFFERENTIATE INSTRUCTION**

Writing Workshop

Note that the pages in the prewriting, drafting, revising, and editing sections can function as minilessons. Each assignment focuses on an important skill, explains and models it, and asks students to apply the skill to their own writing.

Differentiated Instruction: English Language Learners

⭐ ELPS 2E, 3C, 4E

ELP Level **Beginning**	ELP Level **Intermediate**	ELP Level **Advanced/Advanced High**
Point to and read aloud the article's thesis statement. Provide a simplified paraphrase. Guide students to identify details that support the thesis to confirm understanding.	Present paraphrases of the first sentence of each paragraph and read them aloud together. Examine how each sentence is related to paragraph content to confirm understanding.	Ask students to explain how they know that a writer is interested in a topic. Have partners confirm understanding by finding examples in the article.

ELPS 2E Use contextual support to confirm understanding of spoken language; **3C** Speak using a variety of grammatical structures, sentence lengths, sentence types, and connecting words; **4E** Read linguistically accommodated content material with a decreasing need for linguistic accommodations

Prewriting Selecting a Topic

Explain that this page provides some strategies for selecting a topic.

"Basics of Life" List

Suggest that students use the "Basics of Life" list as a starting point for choosing a topic. If students prefer, have them select a topic that interests them from a general subject area they have studied or that you assign. Alternately, suggest that students brainstorm a list of possible topics generated by the model article.

Gathering Details

Point out that the goal of the gathering chart is to narrow the scope of the topic.

Gathering Chart

Examine each column of the chart and discuss why the topics "fit" in each category.

Create a gathering chart. Tell students to select four subject areas that interest them and list them across the top of the chart. Have them complete a gathering chart based on their own prior knowledge.  DIFFERENTIATE INSTRUCTION ↘

★ **TEKS** 11.13A; **ELPS** 1A

Focus on the Texas Traits

Development of Ideas

Suggest that students test possible topics by making a small cluster diagram. They should put their topic in the center circle and brainstorm three to five different aspects of the topic that could be addressed in their article.

- Remind students that if they can't come up with at least three branches for the diagram, their topic may be too narrow.
- If students' diagrams have too many branches, their topic may be too broad.
- Students may need to do some basic research before brainstorming ideas for their topic.

 TEKS **11.13A** Plan a first draft by selecting the correct genre, determining an appropriate topic, and developing a thesis or controlling idea; **ELPS** **1A** Use prior knowledge and experiences

---

Prewriting Selecting a Topic

To create an effective informative article, you need to select a topic that interests both you and the multiple audiences who may read your writing. One way to begin is to look at a "Basics of Life" list, which names general subject areas. Karla read the list and selected four subject areas that interested her.

"Basics of Life" List

communication	energy	medicine	sports
computers	environment	politics	travel
economics	food	schools	weather

Gathering Details

She then created a gathering chart, writing the general subject areas across the top and listing specific topic ideas under each one. She put a star beside the topic that interested her most.

Gathering Chart

Environment	Politics	Energy	Weather
pollution	computer voting	biofuels	hurricanes
hybrid cars	new political	"green" building ✱	global warming
land conservation	parties	windmills	raindrops
	our new governor		

 Create a gathering chart. Select four general subject areas that interest you and list them across the top of a piece of paper. Then, beneath each one, list specific topic ideas. Place a star (✱) beside the topic you would like to explore.

 Focus on the Texas Traits

Development of Ideas Make sure that you have ample support and specific details for all of your main points. You may need to develop some ideas more thoroughly than others. Keep in mind what your readers need to know in order to fully understand your controlling idea.

Differentiated Instruction: Advanced Learners

Students may propose several topics in which they are already well versed. Encourage students to choose a topic that interests them but about which they need more information for their article. This will make the assignment more of a challenge—and more of an opportunity for learning and personal growth.

Researching Your Topic

To create an informative article that engages and informs, you'll need to research the most current information possible. The following strategies can help.

- **Begin with your own experience.** What about the topic interests you? What connection do you have to the topic? What personal experiences or anecdotes can you share?
- **Search sources.** Visit a library and search for primary sources—original or firsthand accounts of an event or time period. Also, consult secondary sources—documents that analyze and interpret primary sources. Look through the *Readers' Guide* to find recent magazine articles. Search for books related to your topic with recent copyright dates. Surf the Internet, but carefully evaluate each Web page: Is it current? Is it balanced and not biased? Is the source reliable?
- **Do some investigating.** Experts surround you. Think of teachers in your school who know about your topic or people in your community involved with the issue. Arrange interviews or find other ways to gather firsthand information.

Listing Your Sources

Karla made a list of sources of information about "green" building practices.

Sources List

Personal Experience:
    Encouraged neighbors to recyle.
    Parents bought an energy-efficient refrigerator.

Traditional Sources:
    Save Money by Going Green magazine
    Building the Natural Way by Bill Kosonen
    International Green Building Board Web site

Experts and Special Sites:
    Manuel Johnson, Green City Advocates
    Eileen McCoy, Medford City Council

Prewrite

List sources and begin your research. Write down the personal experiences, primary and secondary sources, and experts and special sites you can investigate. Then conduct your research.

Expository

Prewriting Researching Your Topic

Encourage students to use the strategies to choose a topic that interests them and about which they have some prior knowledge.

DIFFERENTIATE INSTRUCTION

ELPS 1A

If students plan to do computer research, offer them these tips:

- Check your library's online catalog to quickly determine what books and resources their library owns.
- Check your library's electronic resources. For example, many libraries have the *Readers' Guide*, encyclopedias, and other resources online that offer relevant and substantial evidence on many topics.
- Web sites of governmental organizations (ending in *.gov*) and educational institutions (ending in *.edu*) are generally reliable sources.
- Interviews can be conducted online via e-mail. This expands the possibilities for communicating with experts on a topic to gain multiple relevant perspectives. Suggest that students also look for experts at their school or in their own community.

TEKS 11.13A, 11.15A(v), 11.15A(vi); **ELPS** 2F

Listing Your Sources

Remind student to keep an accurate record of the sources they use. Tell students to sort their sources by type of source: personal experiences, traditional sources (books, magazines, web sites), and experts and special sites.

Sources List

Discuss each example in the list.

List sources and begin your research. Remind students to keep their source information on notes cards, in a notebook, or in a special file on their computer.

Prewriting Gathering Different Types of Details

Remind students to record their details and source information carefully. Suggest that they take extra care copying numbers correctly, especially with statistical information. Stress the importance of developing a reliable system for indicating whether they are quoting directly from their research or paraphrasing it. This will prevent them from accidentally failing to acknowledge a source.

✻ For more information on using note cards, see SE pages 400–401.

Gather different types of details. Remind students as they research and gather details, to make sure they have details that reflect multiple relevant perspectives. Also, suggest that they note the details they think are strongest and will best support their thesis.

 TEKS 11.13A, 11.15A(v), 11.15A(vi)

Focus on the Texas Traits

Organization
Suggest that students develop topic headings for their details as they research. Remind them that as they do more research, these headings may change and evolve.

 **TEKS** 11.13A, 11.15A(v), 11.15A(vi)

Prewriting Gathering Different Types of Details

An informative article should be filled with different types of details and include both primary and secondary sources.

- **Facts** are details that can be proven. Facts provide strong support for the main points of your essay.

  The generous use of foam insulation provides protection from summer heat and winter cold, thus reducing both heating and air-conditioning costs.

- **Statistics** present numerical data and make your information precise and quantifiable.

  Because of the weak economy, oil prices dropped during the first half of 2009. Once the economy improves, however, oil prices are expected to rise.

- **Quotations** are the exact words of someone knowledgeable about your topic. They provide important opinions or information about your topic.

  Manuel Johnson of Green City Advocates says, "People understand that they'll be paying utility bills on a new home or business for a long time. That's why more and more of them are asking us to make energy efficiency a part of our plans."

- **Examples** are representative ideas that illustrate a main point and show an abstract idea in a concrete way.

  Other designs may include alternative heating technologies, such as furnaces that burn wood pellets, wood chips, or even corn stalks.

- **Anecdotes** are stories that help prove your point. Use anecdotes from your life or the lives of others. Make sure that each demonstrates a specific point about your topic.

  Green building can also be expressed in small ways. When my family's refrigerator broke down, we bought a new one that was thirty percent more efficient.

 Prewrite

Gather different types of details. As you research, gather a variety of details that will explain your topic and strengthen your essay.

Focus on the Texas Traits

Organization As you gather details, make sure they all support your organizational pattern and the purpose of your writing. Also, remember to note your sources. If your teacher requires you to include parenthetical references and a works-cited page, see pages **441–454** and **413** for help.

Differentiated Instruction: Advanced Learners

Suggest that students generate several thesis statements for their own articles and survey their peers to determine which is the most compelling.

TEKS 11.13A

 TEKS **11.13A** Plan a first draft by selecting the correct genre, determining an appropriate topic, and developing a thesis or controlling idea; **11.15A(v)** Use relevant and substantial evidence and well-chosen details; **11.15A(vi)** Include information reflecting multiple relevant perspectives

Writing a Thesis Statement

After completing her research, Karla was ready to write her thesis statement. She used the following formula:

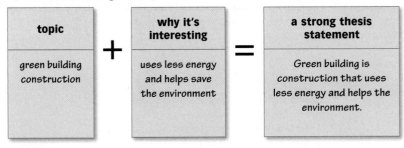

topic		why it's interesting		a strong thesis statement
green building construction	+	uses less energy and helps save the environment	=	Green building is construction that uses less energy and helps the environment.

Write your thesis statement. Use the model above to create a thesis statement for your essay. Try different versions until you are satisfied.

Writing Topic Sentences

Every thesis needs the support of three or more main points. Karla reviewed her research, listed main points, and wrote a topic sentence for each.

Main Points List

1. Energy problems make green building important.	Topic sentence 1: Problems with energy are changing people's ideas about building construction.
2. Green buildings use energy efficiently.	Topic sentence 2: Green buildings are designed to use less energy.
3. Some green buildings generate energy.	Topic sentence 3: Green building practices not only save energy, but can also generate more energy.
4. Location and materials also are important.	Topic sentence 4: Builders of green structures also pay attention to where they build and what materials they use.

Write topic sentences. List main points that will support your thesis statement. Then, for each main point, write a topic sentence.

Expository

Prewriting **Writing a Thesis Statement**

Suggest that as students research their topic, they jot down ideas or questions about the topic to use later as a possible thesis statement. Tell students they can keep a list of ideas and questions with their research notes and consult it when they are ready to write a thesis statement. Remind students that the thesis they choose during prewriting can be adjusted and improved as they write and edit their drafts.
✔ DIFFERENTIATE INSTRUCTION

Write your thesis statement. Remind students that their thesis statement will serve as a road map for their entire essay and that, for this reason, they need to take time to make sure that it is clear and focused.

★ **TEKS** 11.13A, 11.15A(iii)

Writing Topic Sentences

To help students decide on the main points associated with their topics, suggest that they

- sort their research note cards into related groups, and
- review the notes and cluster they made for the **Focus on the Texas Traits** activity on TE page 164 to remind themselves of the points they intended to pursue before they began researching.

Main Points List

Reviewing the main points may give students ideas for individual paragraphs—and, thus, for topic sentences. **✔ DIFFERENTIATE INSTRUCTION**

Write topic sentences. Remind students that a topic sentence should not only state the main idea of the paragraph, but also establish a logical connection to the paragraph that precedes it.

Differentiated Instruction:
English Language Learners

★ **ELPS** 2H

ELP Level **Beginning**	ELP Level **Intermediate**	ELP Level **Advanced/Advanced High**
Use students' topic ideas to develop examples of a main points list. Generate and display possible topic sentences, and have students read them aloud.	Guide students to share their topic ideas. Discuss implicit main ideas and possible topic sentences. Help students clarify and communicate challenging ideas.	Have partners share their topic ideas and the research they have gathered. Have students work together to identify implicit main points and possible topic sentences.

TEKS **11.13A** Plan a first draft by selecting the correct genre, determining an appropriate topic, and developing a thesis or controlling idea; **11.15A(iii)** Write a clear thesis statement or controlling idea **ELPS** **2H** Understand implicit ideas and information in spoken language

Prewriting Outlining Your Paper

Talk with students about using outlines to organize ideas, and provide them helpful tips as appropriate. **DIFFERENTIATE INSTRUCTION ⬎**

Sentence Outline

Use the sample outline to provide visual and contextual support as you make the following points. Ask questions to allow students to confirm their understanding

- Remind students that a sentence outline is made up of complete sentences, while a topic outline uses words and phrases to remind the writer what he or she plans to write.
- Many students will have used outlines in the past. Ask them, *Did you find the outlines helpful? Which style do you prefer? Why?*
- Note that outlines generally cover only the middle paragraphs in detail, not the introduction and conclusion. However, students may outline these paragraphs, if they find it helpful. Review the use of Roman numerals and letters in outlines.
- Point out that supporting details are indicated by letters and indented beneath the main points, which are indicated by Roman numerals. This system helps to visually differentiate each point on the outline.

TEKS 11.13A, 11.15A(iv); **ELPS** 2E

Create an outline. Circulate to provide help as needed while students work on their outlines.

✴ For more about Outlining Your Ideas, see SE page 619.

168

 **TEKS** 11.13A, 11.15A(iv)

Prewriting Outlining Your Paper

Before writing your informative article, organize your ideas and details in an outline. Include topic sentences and supporting points. Karla wrote a sentence outline, but your teacher may prefer a topic outline.

Sentence Outline

I. Problems with energy are changing people's ideas about building construction.
  A. Over time, as oil reserves are exhausted, oil prices are expected to rise.
  B. Demand for electricity causes blackouts and brownouts.
  C. People are more aware of the value of energy efficiency and want energy-efficient homes.

II. Green buildings are designed to use energy efficiently.
  A. Building sites make use of natural sunlight.
  B. Efficient materials and appliances are built in.
  C. Designs save water as well as energy.

III. Green building practices not only save energy, but can also generate it.
  A. Some designs use solar panels and windmills.
  B. Other designs use furnaces that burn wood chips or other biofuels.
  C. Some designs even use fuel cells.

IV. Builders of green structures also pay attention to where they build and what materials they use.
  A. Green builders chose sites to minimize dependence on cars.
  B. Green builders recycle building sites and use materials that have low environmental impact.

Prewrite

Create an outline. Use the example above as your guide to create a sentence outline, or create a topic outline if your teacher prefers. (See page 619.)

Differentiated Instruction: Struggling Learners

Visual and spatial learners may benefit more from using a cluster diagram or other type of organizer than from writing a traditional outline. This will help them visualize the topics and details in a spatially differentiated format.

✴ For examples of types of organizers to use, refer students to SE page 209.

 TEKS **11.13A** Plan a first draft by selecting the correct genre, determining an appropriate topic, and developing a thesis or controlling idea; **11.15A(iv)** Include information reflecting multiple relevant perspectives **ELPS** **2E** Use visual, contextual, and linguistic support to confirm understanding of spoken language

Writing an Informative Article **169**

Drafting

You have identified a topic, done some research, and created an outline with main ideas and details. Now you are ready to draft your informative article. Remember, you can also use these guidelines for timed writing assignments.

Keys to Effective Writing

1. Use your outline as a writing guide.

2. Write on every other line or double-space if you are using a computer. This will allow room for changes.

3. Introduce the topic and state your thesis in the first paragraph.

4. Include your topic sentences in your first draft.

5. Use specific details to support your topic sentences.

6. Restate your thesis at the end.

Expository

Drafting

Keys to Effective Writing

Remind students that the drafting stage is when they get their ideas on paper.

The Keys to Effective Writing list explains the process students will be guided through on SE pages 170–174.

Note that after gathering and organizing information, students can prepare mentally for the task.

- Encourage students to seek out good places where they can write. They may prefer the silence of a library, the comfort of their home workspace, or the bustle of the cafeteria. They may find it helpful to spread their papers out on a table or even on the floor.

- Urge students to set aside enough time to write—they should plan to spend at least an hour or two at each sitting. Point out that they won't be able to create a unified work if they try to patch together the results of brief work sessions.

- Remind students that their goal at this point is to get their ideas on paper—the draft doesn't have to be perfect. They will be able to revise and edit later.

Writing Workshop

Model writing for your students. When students see you writing, they will be more ready to try it on their own. ✔ **DIFFERENTIATE INSTRUCTION**

Differentiated Instruction: English Language Learners

🏴 ELPS 2E

Provide support as needed to help students understand the features of an outline.

ELP Level **Beginning**	ELP Level **Intermediate**	ELP Level **Advanced/Advanced High**
Use visuals and simplified language to discuss the outline's ideas and details. Ask yes/no questions to confirm understanding.	Use visuals and simplified language to highlight the outline's main ideas and details. Ask questions to confirm understanding.	Read aloud the main ideas in the outline and ask questions to confirm students' understanding. Use a similar process for the details.

 ELPS 2E Use visual, contextual, and linguistic support to confirm understanding of spoken language

Drafting Seeing How the Parts Fit Together

As students review the page, note that the writer made use of the thesis statement and topic sentences she crafted during prewriting to develop a clear organizational scheme to convey ideas in her essay. The only part of the article she has not yet focused on is the ending, though she has noted a general idea of what should be included.

- Ask students to spend a few minutes thinking over their topic and looking at their outlines.
- Do they have any ideas yet for a closing sentence? Assure them that they will be guided through the process of crafting a closing sentence and that their thoughts at this point can be general, rather than specific.
- Have students jot down notes about their ideas for closing sentences that they can keep with their planning notes.

⭐ **TEKS** 11.13B, 11.15A(iv); **ELPS** 2I

Drafting Seeing How the Parts Fit Together

The graphic below shows how the elements of an informative article should fit together. Use this graphic as a guide to help you write your first draft. (The examples are from the student essay on pages **171–174**.)

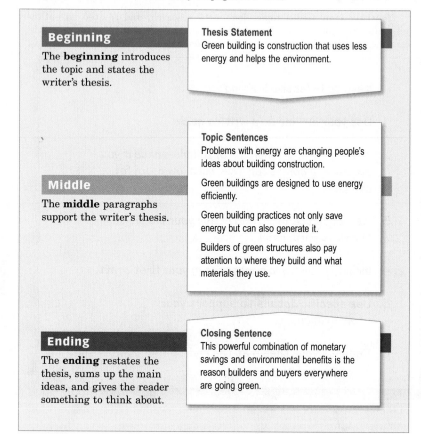

Beginning

The **beginning** introduces the topic and states the writer's thesis.

Thesis Statement
Green building is construction that uses less energy and helps the environment.

Topic Sentences
Problems with energy are changing people's ideas about building construction.

Green buildings are designed to use energy efficiently.

Green building practices not only save energy but can also generate it.

Builders of green structures also pay attention to where they build and what materials they use.

Middle

The **middle** paragraphs support the writer's thesis.

Ending

The **ending** restates the thesis, sums up the main ideas, and gives the reader something to think about.

Closing Sentence
This powerful combination of monetary savings and environmental benefits is the reason builders and buyers everywhere are going green.

⭐ **TEKS** **11.13B** Structure ideas in a sustained and persuasive way; **11.15A(iv)** Use a clear organizational scheme for conveying ideas; **ELPS 2I** Demonstrate listening comprehension/responding to questions and requests and taking notes

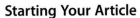

Starting Your Article

The beginning paragraph of your informative article should engage the reader, introduce your topic, and provide a thesis statement. Here are three strategies for engaging the reader:

Beginning
Middle
Ending

- **Make a startling statement.**
  Just because oil prices have gone down in recent months does not mean there is no energy crisis.

- **Ask a provocative question.**
  How can consumers fight high energy costs?

- **Begin with a strong quotation.**
  According to Alan Davidson of the Energy Council, "The secret to solving the energy crisis is not to use less energy, but to make better use of the energy."

- **Use a rhetorical device, such as a common metaphor or idiom, in a new or surprising way.**
  Faced with high energy costs, owners of homes and businesses are taking the heat.

Beginning Paragraph

Karla began her essay by using a common metaphor or idiom *(taking the heat)* in a new and surprising way. She then introduced the topic and presented her thesis statement.

The writer engages the reader and states her thesis (underlined).

> Faced with high energy costs, owners of homes and businesses are taking the heat. They're paying more to heat and cool the buildings they own, and they're spending more to run appliances and office machines, too. On a positive note, a fairly new trend in building construction, called green building, is making things easier on homeowners, business owners, and the environment. <u>Green building is construction that uses less energy and helps the enrvironment.</u>

Draft

Write a beginning paragraph. Use the guidelines above to help you begin your informative article. (Also refer to the sample beginning on page **161**.)

Expository

Drafting Starting Your Article

Explain that in the vocabulary of journalism, the beginning of an article is called the *lead*. The lead may be either the first sentence or the first paragraph. Helpful advice for writing a lead includes the following:

- To grab readers' attention, make the lead fast-paced and lively. This means avoiding complex sentence structures and overly descriptive language.
- If you're having trouble writing your opening sentence, try writing a three-word newspaper-style headline for the article. This can serve as inspiration for your lead.
- When applying the questions *Who?, What?, When?, Where?, Why?,* and *How?* to your topic, decide which questions are the most important. Consider making those details the focus of your lead. ✔ **DIFFERENTIATE INSTRUCTION**

⭐ **TEKS** 11.13B, 11.15A(i); **ELPS** 1C, 1H

Beginning Paragraph

Have students comment on the sample beginning paragraph. Does it grab their attention? Do they have suggestions for how the lead could be improved?

Write a beginning paragraph. Suggest that students experiment with their opening paragraphs. Have them try two or three different ways to begin and choose the one that works best.

Differentiated Instruction:
English Language Learners   ⭐ **ELPS** 1C, 1H

Point out the idiom *taking the heat*, and guide students to explain its meaning and use as a strategy to start an article.

ELP Level **Beginning**	ELP Level **Intermediate**	ELP Level **Advanced/Advanced High**
Display a chart of the possible strategies for beginning an article. Use simplified language and ask yes/no questions to discuss each example.	Work together to create a chart of the possible strategies to start an article. Have students complete sentence stems to discuss each example.	Have students make a chart of the possible strategies to start an article. Have partners discuss why Karla used an idiom to begin her essay.

⭐ **TEKS** **11.13B** Structure ideas in a sustained and persuasive way; **11.15A(i)** Write an analytical essay that includes effective introductory paragraphs **ELPS** **1C** Use strategic learning strategies to acquire basic and grade-level vocabulary; **1H** Develop and expand repertoire of learning strategies

Drafting Developing the Middle

Suggest that students gather their prewriting outlines and other notes to review the ideas they will write about in their middle paragraphs.

Middle Paragraphs

After students have read the sample, have them employ analytical skills to discuss the paragraphs in detail. Ask questions to help guide their responses. For example:

- What clear organizational scheme does the writer use in the middle paragraphs? (The writer uses logical order, first explaining why green construction is popular and then describing three different aspects of the practice.)
- How does the quotation in the first middle paragraph contribute to the article? (It shows the writer is providing information from multiple perspectives; it provides confirmation from an expert that the writer's assertion about green construction is correct.)
- What specialized terms related to the topic does the writer use and define? (*brownouts, blackouts*)

TEKS 11.13B, 11.15A(iii), 11.15A(iv), 11.15A(v), 11.15A(vi); **ELPS** 4K

✱ For information about Developing the Middle Part, see SE page 622.

 **TEKS** 11.13B, 11.15A(iii) 11.15A(iv), 11.15A(v), 11.15A(vi)

Drafting Developing the Middle

The middle part of your informative article adds ideas and details that expand upon your thesis statement. Begin each paragraph with a topic sentence. Add a variety of supporting details. Use transitional words and phrases to link sentences and paragraphs. Use your outline (see page **168**) as a guide.

Beginning

Middle

Ending

Middle Paragraphs

This is the middle part of Karla's informative article on green building practices. Read it carefully, noticing how she used topic sentences, facts, statistics, examples, quotations, and transitional words and phrases to build her paragraphs.

> The topic sentence offers a main point (underlined).

> The body includes facts, statistics, examples, and quotations that expand on the topic sentence.

> Sentences are linked with transitional words and phrases (underlined).

<u>Problems with energy are changing people's ideas about building construction.</u> With the economy in slow mode and wages stagnant, most homeowners worry about paying bills, especially home heating in the winter and home cooling in the summer. If you live in an urban area, you are probably all too familiar with brownouts and blackouts—partial and total losses of electricity during the summer. These and other problems, says Manuel Johnson, president of Green City Contractors, have made people more aware of the importance of energy-efficient building. "People understand that they'll be paying utility bills on a new home or business for a long time," Johnson says. "That's why more and more of them are asking us to make energy efficiency a part of our plans."

<u>Green buildings are designed to use energy efficiently.</u> <u>To begin,</u> builders use materials that increase energy efficiency. <u>For example,</u> the generous use of foam insulation provides protection from summer heat and winter cold, thus reducing both heating and air-conditioning costs. <u>In addition,</u> using light-colored exterior paints and roofing materials that reflect sunlight, can cut cooling costs. Carefully placed windows will take advantage of natural lighting and save money. <u>Similarly,</u> motion-detecting light switches that turn lights on when people enter and off when they leave a room lower electricity bills. Water costs can be reduced as well by using low-flow water fixtures and high-efficiency water heaters.

Differentiated Instruction: Struggling Learners

Remind students of the purpose of transition words and phrases—to logically connect ideas and create a smooth flow of prose. Have students identify some of the transition words in the model paragraphs on this page (*To begin, For example, In addition, Similarly*).

TEKS **11.13B** Structure ideas in a sustained and persuasive way; **11.15A(iii)** Include clear thesis statement or controlling idea; **11.15A(iv)** Use clear organizational scheme for conveying ideas; **11.15A(v)** Use relevant substantial evidence and well-chosen ideas; **11.15A(vi)** Include information on multiple relevant perspectives; **ELPS** **4K** Demonstrate English comprehension and expand reading skills by employing analytical skills

★ **TEKS** 11.13B, 11.15A(i),
11.15A(ii), 11.15A(iii),
11.15A(iv), 11.15A(v)

Rhetorical devices (the repetition of words at the beginning of successive sentences) add emphasis and rhythm (underlined).

Longer, more complex and shorter, simpler sentences add a variety of sentence structures (underlined).

> Green building practices not only save energy but can also generate it. <u>Some designs</u> for green homes and businesses incorporate on-site energy generation technologies such as solar panels or windmills. <u>Other designs</u> include alternative heating technologies such as furnaces that burn wood pellets, wood chips, or even corn stalks. <u>Still other designs</u> featuring the use of fuel cells have found their way into green building (Stratt 263). In the long run, all these technologies will help building owners cut energy costs and save money.
>
> Builders of green structures pay attention to where they build and the materials they use. Whenever possible, they recycle building sites instead of carving up untouched land. <u>In addition, green builders frequently choose sites near city centers, where access to public transportation can decrease residents' and workers' dependence on cars.</u> <u>Green builders also prefer recycled building materials.</u> If new materials are used, green builders most often opt for those that have a minimal environmental impact, such as bamboo flooring and low-vapor paint.

Draft

Write your middle paragraphs. Create middle paragraphs that expand upon your thesis statement. Start each paragraph with a topic sentence. Then follow with explanations and details that support the topic sentence.

Expository

Focus on the Texas Traits

Organization As you write, remember to connect your ideas by repeating key words from one sentence to the next.

To begin, builders <u>use</u> materials that increase energy efficiency. For example, the generous <u>use</u> of foam insulation provides protection from summer heat and winter cold.

Connect ideas by using transition words and phrases like these:

for example	to begin	in addition	as well
whenever possible	similarly	in the long run	

Point out that the writer does a very good job of writing fluent sentences with appropriate language structures. She uses a variety of beginnings, structures, and lengths. To help demonstrate this, have volunteers read the paragraphs aloud to classmates. Ask the listeners to identify the varied beginnings and the way the ideas connect from one sentence to the next. Be sure that students demonstrate understanding of the implicit idea that well-constructed sentences are easy to read aloud.

★ **TEKS** 11.13B, 11.15A(i), 11.15A(v); **ELPS** 2C, 2G, 2H, 4F

Write your middle paragraphs. Tell students to check that each topic sentence supports their thesis and that each sentence within individual paragraphs builds on the sentence that precedes it to present relevant evidence.

✔ DIFFERENTIATE INSTRUCTION

★ **TEKS** 11.13B, 11.15A(iii), 11.15A(v); **ELPS** 2C, 5F, 5G

 Focus on the Texas Traits

Organization

When reviewing the information about repeating key words, discuss the difference between purposeful repetition that connects ideas and excessive repetition that can weigh the writing down. ✔ DIFFERENTIATE INSTRUCTION

★ **TEKS** 11.13B, 11.15A(ii), 11.15A(iv); **ELPS** 2C

**Differentiated Instruction:
English Language Learners**   ★ **ELPS** 5F, 5G

As you review the sample, point out the variety of sentence lengths and patterns and connecting words the writer uses.

ELP Level **Beginning**	ELP Level **Intermediate**	ELP Level **Advanced/Advanced High**
Work with students to generate a middle paragraph for their article. Model using connecting words and phrases to add details.	Pair students with an English-proficient peer. Have them use connecting words and phrases to add details.	Have students work independently to write a middle paragraph. Have partners discuss the types of sentences used.

★ **TEKS** **11.13B** Structure ideas in a sustained and persuasive way; **11.15A(i)** Write an analytical essay that includes effective introductory paragraphs; **11.15A(ii)** Use rhetorical devices and transitions between paragraphs; **11.15A(iii)** Include a clear thesis statement or controlling idea; **11.15A(iv)** Use a clear organizational scheme for conveying ideas; **11.15A(v)** Use relevant substantial evidence and well-chosen ideas; **ELPS** **2C** Learn new language structures; **2G** Understand general meaning of spoken language/topics, language, and contexts; **2H** Understand implicit ideas and information in spoken language; **4F** Use support from peers and teachers to develop a grasp of language structures; **5F** Write using a variety of grade-appropriate sentence lengths, sentence patterns, and connecting words; **5G** Explain with increasing specificity and detail

Drafting Ending Your Article

Suggest that students take a break before writing their ending paragraph. This will allow them to approach it with a fresher outlook. During this time, they can think about ideas for endings. (Encourage them to keep their writer's notebook handy, in case a great ending idea suddenly comes to them.) **DIFFERENTIATE INSTRUCTION ↘**

Ending Paragraph

Discuss the student writer's use of the dash in her ending paragraph.

- Note that this dash could be replaced with a comma, but the dash adds more emphasis.
- Dashes should be used sparingly because (1) using too many reduces their impact, and (2) they are eye-catching and can interrupt the reading.
- Remind students using a computer to type two hyphens to make a dash. (Most word-processing programs change them to a dash automatically, but it's fine to use two hyphens.)

✳ For more about using dashes, see SE pages 668–669.

Write the ending paragraph. Have students reread their opening and middle paragraphs to be sure they have used a clear organizational scheme, included substantial evidence, and presented multiple relevant perspectives. Remind them to be sure that their endings restate their thesis and sum up their major points.
DIFFERENTIATE INSTRUCTION ↘

★ **TEKS** 11.13B, 11.15A(iii), 11.15A(iv), 11.15A(v), 11.15A(vi); **ELPS** 5G

Prepare a copy of your entire article. Suggest that students make an extra copy of their article to save for future reference.

174

★ **TEKS** 11.13B, 11.15A(iii)–11.15A(vi)

Drafting Ending Your Article

The ending paragraph needs to effectively wrap up your essay. The following guidelines will help.

| Beginning |
| Middle |
| **Ending** |

- **Restate your thesis.**
  Green building has found new ways to apply the old maxim "Reduce, reuse, and recycle."
- **Summarize the main ideas of your article.**
  Due to increased energy demand, dwindling supply, and higher prices, builders are designing dwellings that use less energy and even generate their own.
- **Make the reader think.**
  By building more efficient homes and using the free energy supplied by the sun and the wind, green builders are constructing the future, one house at a time.

Ending Paragraph

Karla's ending paragraph restates her thesis and supports it with a powerful example and a final insight.

> The thesis is powerfully restated.
>
> The essay ends with a final insight.

With energy prices predicted to rise again, it looks like green building is here to stay—and for good reason. According to the U.S. Green Building Council, building green admittedly adds about 2 percent to the initial construction cost of an average home. But, over a 20-year period, the energy savings will replace 20 percent of the construction cost and additionally benefit the environment. This powerful combination of monetary savings and environmental benefits is the reason builders and buyers everywhere are going green.

Draft

Write the ending paragraph. Restate your thesis in the topic sentence, summarize the supporting ideas, and leave your reader something to think about.

Texas Traits

Prepare a copy of your entire article. Double-space on a computer or write on every other line. This gives you room to revise.

Differentiated Instruction: Advanced Learners

To give students more experience with strong endings, have them choose several articles they have recently enjoyed. Ask them to read the last paragraph of each article to assess the strength of the ending. Students may model their own endings after a piece of writing they have found particularly effective.

TEKS **11.13B** Structure ideas in a sustained and persuasive way; **11.15A(iii)** Include clear thesis statement or controlling idea; **11.15A(iv)** use clear organizational scheme for conveying ideas; **11.15A(v)** include relevant substantial evidence and well-chosen ideas; **11.15A(vi)** use information on multiple, relevant perspectives
ELPS 5G Explain with increasing specificity and detail

Writing an Informative Article **175**

Revising

Revision improves your work in many ways. When you revise, you may add or delete details, rearrange parts of your writing, or create a more engaging, informative voice. You will also check for varied sentence structures, consistency of tone, and the effective use of rhetorical devices and transitional words and phrases.

Keys to Effective Revising

1. Read your essay aloud to yourself or to a friend.

2. Be sure you have provided engaging, accurate information about your topic.

3. Check your topic sentences to confirm that you have followed your outline.

4. Be sure you have included a variety of details—facts, statistics, quotations, and examples.

5. Check that you have used a variety of sentence structures and that your ideas are linked by transitional words and phrases.

6. To mark revisions on your first draft, use the editing and proofreading marks found on the inside back cover of this book.

Expository

Revising

Keys to Effective Revising

Remind students that the revising stage is when writers have an opportunity to make improvements to their first drafts. At this stage they can think about refinements they might not have considered when they were drafting.

The Keys to Effective Revising list explains the process students will be guided through on SE pages 176–184.

Have students work with a writing partner or small group as they revise their drafts. This will provide them with helpful feedback on the areas they need to improve.

Peer Response

A constructive peer response at the beginning of the revision stage can help students discover what is working—and what is not—in their writing. (See pages 115–120 for a closer look at peer response.)

ELPS 3E ✔ DIFFERENTIATE INSTRUCTION

Armed with a thoughtful response, students can decide which revising strategies on the next pages will make the biggest improvement to their work.

Differentiated Instruction: English Language Learners

ELPS 2G, 5G

ELP Level Beginning	ELP Level Intermediate	ELP Level Advanced/Advanced High
Work with students to develop an ending for their articles. Then, in a group, guide students to share and discuss their topics.	Guide students to develop an ending for their articles. Then pair students with an English-proficient peer, and have them discuss their topics and the types of details they used.	Have students work independently to write an ending. In a group, invite students to share their topics and answer questions about the types of details they used.

ELPS 2G Understand the main points of spoken language/topics, language, contexts; **3E** Share information in cooperative learning interactions; **5G** Explain with increasing specificity and detail

Revising **for** Focus and Coherence

Remind students that maintaining focus and coherence means making sure that all of their ideas and details relate to their thesis.

Have I maintained my focus?

Suggest the students read their essay or parts of it to a classmate. If their classmate has a hard time following their ideas, it may be because the writing is off the topic.

Have I included a meaningful introduction and conclusion?

Have students ask themselves the following questions as they revise.

- Is my introduction interesting enough to make others want to read more?
- Does my introduction give necessary background information?
- Does my introduction include a clearly worded thesis statement?
- Does my conclusion restate my thesis and sum up my major points?
- Does my conclusion leave readers with something interesting to think about?

TEKS 11.13C, 11.15A(i)

Exercise
Answers

After students have completed the **Exercise** activity, have them identify which sentences they deleted (4 and 9) and explain why. Then ask students to identify the detail they added and explain why. Students' explanations will vary but should mention why the sentences don't support the topic sentence. **DIFFERENTIATE INSTRUCTION** ↘

Check the details in your introduction. Remind students that details that support their thesis offer facts, statistics, expert opinions, or quotations directly related to their major points.

TEKS **11.13A** Plan a first draft by developing a thesis or controlling idea; **11.13C** Revise drafts to clarify meaning; **11.15A(i)** Write an analytical essay that includes effective introductory and concluding paragraphs and a variety of sentence structures

---

Revising **for** Focus and Coherence

When you revise for *focus and coherence*, you make sure that you have maintained your focus through your essay, that all your ideas are clearly connected to each other, that you have included a meaningful introduction and conclusion, and that your overall essay has a sense of completeness.

Have I maintained my focus?

Make sure that all of your details support your main idea. Delete irrelevant details. Add additional support to weak details.

Have I included a meaningful introduction and conclusion?

Make sure that your introduction is engaging and makes your readers want to read on. Your conclusion should sum up your main points and leave your readers with something to think about.

Exercise

Read the following introduction to an article about candidates for mayor in a city election. Underline the thesis statement. Then rewrite the paragraph, omitting any details that do not support the thesis statement. Add at least one more supporting detail.

> The city's upcoming mayoral election pits three seasoned politicians against one another. Steven Johnson is a six-term city councilor who has deep roots in the community. Like his father and his grandfather before him, he has played various roles in city government for most of his adult life. Mr. Johnson's previous jobs ranged from sales representative to police officer. Regina Suarez lacks that sort of longevity in the city, but she was active in community events for nearly 20 years before winning a seat on the city council in 2007. She cites her business success as evidence of her fiscal responsibility and promises to use that experience to balance the city's budget. Jane Hargrove began her political career with a 2002 come-from-behind victory to win a seat on the school board, a seat she has never relinquished. She credits family support in helping her win her first election. Ms. Hargrove has promised to make educational funding a priority if she is elected mayor.

Check the details in your introduction. Make sure the details all support your thesis.

Differentiated Instruction: Advanced Learners

Encourage students who complete the **Exercise** activity quickly to extend the assignment to include the introductory paragraphs of their own essays. Have them make sure that their thesis statement is stated clearly and that all details support that thesis statement.

TEKS 11.13A

Does my essay have an overall sense of completeness?

Make sure that your essay is finished, that all of your main points are well-developed, and that you have deleted any irrelevant or distracting details.

Exercise

Copy each main idea below. Beside each, write the detail that best supports the idea. Explain why you excluded the other two details.

1. Scientists are working to help people live longer and healthier lives.
   a. Everyone wants to live longer.
   b. Scientists have developed gene therapies that they hope will slow the aging process.
   c. Scientists are working hard to discover things.
2. Engaging in regular exercise promotes both physical and mental health.
   a. Physical activity stimulates brain chemicals that often leave you feeling happier and more relaxed.
   b. Many people need to be pushed to exercise.
   c. Too many people in the United States have unhealthy lifestyles and diets.

Revise

Maintain your focus. Check that all of your details are relevant and clearly support your main idea.

Focus and Coherence
Include a meaninful introduction with relevant supporting details.

> Faced with high energy costs, owners of homes and businesses are taking the heat. ~~Food costs have skyrocketed as well.~~
>
> They're paying more to heat and cool the buildings . . .

Expository

Does my essay have an overall sense of completeness?

Have students work with a partner to check that they have a well-developed beginning, middle, and end for their essay and that each of the parts of their essay are supported by relevant details.

★ TEKS 11.13C, 11.15A(i); **ELPS** 1B

Exercise
Answers

1. **Main idea:** Scientists are working to help people live longer and healthier lives. **Supporting detail:** Scientists have developed gene therapies that they hope will slow the aging process.
2. **Main idea:** Engaging in regular exercise promotes both physical and mental health. **Supporting detail:** Physical activity stimulates brain chemicals that often leave you feeling happier and more relaxed.

Students' explanations for the answers will vary but should mention how effectively the detail supports the main idea. ✔DIFFERENTIATE INSTRUCTION
★ **ELPS** 1H, 3G

Maintain your focus. Suggest to students that they reread their essay as someone who knows nothing about the topic would read it. Have them ask themselves: *Have I provided enough details for my readers to understand my thinking?*

★ TEKS 11.13C

Focus and Coherence Ask students to explain why the writer deleted the sentence.

★ TEKS **11.13C** Revise drafts to clarify meaning; **11.15A(i)** Write an analytical essay that includes effective introductory and concluding paragraphs and a variety of sentence structures; **ELPS 1B** Monitor written language production and employ self-corrective techniques or other resources; **1H** Develop and expand repertoire of learning strategies; **3G** Express ideas; **3H** Explain with increasing specificity and detail

Revising **for** Organization

Point out that beginning with the basics and adding increasingly complex details should be a familiar sequence for students. It is the way nearly everything they've learned has been explained. It makes sense, therefore, that this would be the best way to order information in expository writing.

Have I chosen the best order for my paragraphs?

Have students work with a partner to check the order of information in their articles.

- Ask students to read their partner's draft.
- Are there gaps or confusing parts of the article?
- Are any specialized terms left undefined?
- Is information out of order?
- Remind writers to take notes on their partner's comments and to keep these comments in mind as they revise.

TEKS 11.13C, 11.15A(iv); **ELPS** 3E, 4F

Exercise
Answers

1. The first law of black holes is. . .
2. As the star shrinks. . .
3. If the force of gravity . . .
4. When a massive star runs out of fuel . . .

TEKS 11.15A(iv)

Check the order of your paragraphs. Suggest that students exchange papers with a partner. Each partner should check that paragraphs are in an order that makes sense.

Revising **for** Organization

When you revise for *organization,* you check the structure of your essay. Make sure the paragraphs are in order, have a smooth and logical flow, and are connected by transitional words and phrases.

Have I chosen the best order for my paragraphs?

You have chosen the best order for your paragraphs if you begin with basic information and advance toward the more-complicated ideas. Ask yourself these questions:

- What **background information** does my reader need to know?
- What **basic information** should I provide next?
- Do I adequately prepare readers for any **complex ideas** I present?

Exercise

The topic sentences below are out of order. Read the main idea, and then use the questions above to decide how to order the topic sentences.

Main idea: A black hole seems to break all the laws of physics, but actually those laws demonstrate that black holes exist.

If the force of gravity is powerful enough to overcome both electron degeneracy and neutron degeneracy, the star shrinks until all its mass takes up no more space than a pinpoint.

The first law of black holes is gravity—the force that forms and feeds a black hole.

As the star shrinks, it reaches the point where the electrons are pressing upon each other—a phase called *electron degeneracy.*

When a massive star runs out of fuel, it may explode, becoming a supernova, or implode, becoming a black hole.

Check the order of your paragraphs. Make sure that you have begun with background and basic information and progress to more complex issues.

TEKS **11.13C** Revise drafts to achieve logical organization by rearranging the words, sentences, and paragraphs; **11.15A(iv)** Use a clear organizational scheme for conveying ideas; **ELPS** **3E** Share information in cooperative learning interactions; **4F** Use support from peers and teachers to read content area text and to enhance and confirm understanding

TEKS 11.13C, 11.15A(iv)

Writing an Informative Article   **179**

Does each paragraph have unity?

A paragraph has unity if each of its details clearly supports the topic sentence of the paragraph and the main idea of the essay. Unified paragraphs also include transitional words and phrases that create a logical flow between ideas.

Exercise

The following paragraph includes details that do not support the topic sentence. Indicate which sentences should be eliminated to create unity.

1. Not all salamanders that begin the annual migration finish it. That's because
2. they face a number of hazards along the way. At road crossings, automobiles take
3. a heavy toll on the tiny amphibians. Birds, which migrate by air, do not face this
4. particular hazard. Raccoons are always on the look out for salamanders, which
5. make an easy meal. But owls are no threat because they eat rodents instead. And
6. even curious humans can harm salamanders by picking them up with dry hands,
7. which can transmit diseases.

Organization
Any detail that does not support the topic sentence is cut, giving the paragraph unity.

Green building practices not only save energy but also generate it as well. Some designs for green homes and businesses incorporate on-site energy generation technologies such as solar panels or windmills. ~~Both of these technologies have been around for decades.~~ Other designs may include alternative heating technologies . . .

Expository

Does each paragraph have unity?

Explain that sometimes a sentence doesn't support the paragraph's topic sentence, yet it contains interesting information. Tell students that before they delete a sentence, they should evaluate the information it contains. How does the information contribute to the main idea? Perhaps the sentence, or a revised version of it, would work in a different paragraph—either an already-existing paragraph or a new one.

Exercise
Answers

1. Birds, which migrate by air, . . .
2. But, owls are no threat . . .

After students complete the **Exercise,** have partners explain their choices to each other. Students should note that the migration of birds does not support the topic sentence, which is about the migration of salamanders. They should indicate that the predatory habits of owls do not relate to or support the topic sentence.

✔ DIFFERENTIATE INSTRUCTION
★ ELPS 3E, 4I

Organization Remind students to check their own essays to make sure that they have deleted any details in a paragraph that do not support the topic sentence.

★ TEKS 11.13C, 11.15A(iv)

Differentiated Instruction:
English Language Learners   ★ ELPS 2G, 4F, 4I

ELP Level **Beginning**	ELP Level **Intermediate**	ELP Level **Advanced/Advanced High**
Use simplified language as you read aloud the paragraph. Then ask yes/no questions to help students identify the main ideas and unnecessary details.	Have students follow as you read aloud the paragraph. Ask yes/no questions to have students identify main ideas and unnecessary details.	Have students read the paragraph independently. Then have partners summarize the main ideas and identify unnecessary details.

TEKS 11.13C Revise drafts to achieve logical organization by rearranging the words, sentences, and paragraphs; **11.15A(iv)** Use a clear organizational scheme for conveying ideas **ELPS 2G** Understand the main points and important details of spoken language; **3E** Share information in cooperative learning interactions; **4F** Use support from peers and teachers to read content area text and to enhance and confirm understanding; **4I** Demonstrate English comprehension and expand reading skills by employing basic reading skills

Revising for Development of Ideas

Tell students that they will check that they have enough details and that all of their details support major points.

Have I included a variety of details?

Tell students that they can use a details grid to analyze their writing.

Details Grid

Point out that the design of the details grid—showing types of details within individual paragraphs—can help students determine whether they have placed details fairly evenly throughout the draft, even if they did not use all types of details.

Explain that if the pattern of check marks shows large blank spaces—or if a paragraph doesn't have any check marks—the grid can help students decide what type of detail would fill the gap.

Exercise
Answers

Facts— ✓ ✓ ✓ (*One study conducted on mice . . . ; Another study, performed on fruit flies . . . ; After a few generations . . .*)

Statistics— ✓ (*Flies, whose normal life spans were 35 days . . .*)

Quotations—none

Examples— ✓ ✓ ✓ (*One study conducted on mice . . . ; Another study, performed on fruit flies . . . ; Of course, most people faced . . .*)

Anecdotes—none

ELPS 4I

Check the variety of your details. Point out that if students need to add more details and can't find the relevant and substantial evidence they need in their research notes, they may need to do additional research. Remind them to use tropes and schemes and to add transitions as needed.

DIFFERENTIATE INSTRUCTION ↘

TEKS 11.13C, 11.15A(v)

 **TEKS** 11.13C, 11.15A(v)

Revising for Development of Ideas

When you revise for *development of ideas*, you offer enough support and specific details to allow the reader to appreciate your major points. As much as possible, you bring a unique approach to your topic, an approach that adds to the overall quality of your writing. Ask yourself the following questions.

Have I included a variety of details?

You have included a variety of details if you have used facts, statistics, quotations, examples, and anecdotes to develop your ideas in depth. Use a details grid to check your details.

Details Grid

	Facts	Statistics	Quotations	Examples	Anecdotes
Beginning Paragraph 1	✓ ✓		✓		
Paragraph 2	✓	✓		✓	✓

Exercise

Create a details grid for the following paragraph. Make a check mark for each kind of detail you find.

1   Scientists have made many recent discoveries that indicate life spans could
2 be lengthened—possibly indefinitely. One study conducted on mice showed that a
3 low-calorie diet caused a "survival gene" to trigger, making the mice superefficient
4 at using energy and repairing damage to their bodies. Another study, performed on
5 fruit flies, indicated that reproduction was the key to longevity. Flies, whose normal
6 life spans were 35 days, were prevented from reproducing until much later. After a
7 few generations, the life spans reached 70 days. Of course, most people faced with
8 the option of eating very little and not reproducing until late in life may wonder if it
9 just seems that you live longer!

Revise

Check the variety of your details. Create a details grid and check the types of details you used in each paragraph.

TEKS **11.13C** Revise drafts to employ tropes and schemes, and by adding transitional words and phrases; **11.15A(v)** Write an analytical essay that includes relevant and substantial evidence and well-chosen details; **ELPS 4I** Demonstrate English comprehension by employing basic and expanding reading skills

TEKS 11.13C, 11.15A(v)

Writing an Informative Article **181**

Have I provided enough and the right kind of support? Have I left out any important details?

- Check that all of your details relate to your main idea.
- Check that all of your details provide solid and substantial support for your main idea.
- Reread your essay as if you were someone who knows nothing about the topic. Make sure that you have supplied such readers with all the information they need to understand your essay.

Have I presented a unique perspective on my topic?

Is there a unique angle or perspective you can bring to your writing in order to make it fresh or more interesting?

Exercise

Read the following opening sentences to an informative essay about medieval jousting. Which set of sentences provides the more interesting perspective? Explain your answer.

1. A joust, an organized fight between knights on horseback wearing armor, attracted large crowds during the medieval times. Jousting was an exciting, but dangerous sport.
2. Are you an extreme-sports enthusiast? If so, and if you had lived during the 15th century, you would have probably loved the exciting and often dangerous sport of jousting.

Revise

Make your writing original. Use your own ideas and perspective to engage readers and help you develop your main ideas in depth.

> **Development of Ideas**
> Your own perspective gives the reader a better sense of your ideas.

With energy prices predicted to rise again, it looks like green building ~~is a good idea.~~
    ⌃ is here to stay—and for good reason

Expository

Have I provided enough and the right kind of support? Have I left out any important details?

Suggest that students exchange papers with a partner. Have partners indicate where they think relevant or substantial evidence has been omitted. Partners should also tell each other when they think a detail does not support the main idea.

TEKS 11.13C, 11.15A(v); **ELPS** 1B, 5G

Have I provided a unique perspective on my topic?

Have students reread their papers to check that they have offered a new and unique perspective on their topic. Remind them that it is not enough to restate existing information and perspectives. Suggest that they think back about what first interested them in the topic. Recalling this may help them formulate their unique perspective.

Exercise
Answers

The second answer provides the more interesting perspective. Students' explanations may vary but might include: The author's opening sentence, comparing jousters to contemporary sports enthusiasts, is a unique approach to the topic.

Make your writing original. Suggest that students consider using a rhetorical device—a startling figure of speech, a rhetorical question, deliberate repetition, or parallel structure—to give their writing an original flair.

TEKS 11.13C; **ELPS** 1B

Development of Ideas Working with a partner, ask students to explain how the revision improves the sentence. (Students should mention that the revision, particularly the use of the dash and last phrase, clearly indicates the writer's personal perspective on the topic.)

TEKS **11.13C** Revise drafts to employ tropes and schemes, and by adding transitional words and phrases; **11.15A(v)** Write an analytical essay that includes relevant and substantial evidence and well-chosen details; **ELPS 1B** Monitor written language production and employ self-corrective techniques or other resources; **4I** Demonstrate English comprehension and expand reading skills by employing basic reading skills; **5G** Explain with increasing specificity and detail

Revising for Voice

Remind students that a **thesaurus** can be a very helpful tool for a writer who knows what he or she wants to say but isn't sure which word best expresses it.

Have I engaged my readers throughout my writing? Point out to students that one of the best ways to check the voice in your essay is to ask a partner to read it aloud. This leaves the writer free to listen to how the words sound and decide whether the organizational scheme clearly conveys the ideas. The writer should make a copy of the draft and highlight any parts where the reader sounds confused or begins to speak in a tone that isn't consistent. Before making any changes, the writer should ask a second partner to read the highlighted areas.

TEKS 11.13C , 11.15A(iv)

Does my writing sound authentic and original? Tell students that their essays will be more interesting and convincing if their own authentic voice comes through. **DIFFERENTIATE INSTRUCTION** ↘

Exercise
Answers

The first set of sentences better conveys an original and unique voice appropriate to the audience. Students' explanations will vary but should include examples of a unique voice, such as *It's about the glory and about being the best; If you know anything about competitive pumpkin growing, then . . .*

ELPS 3G

Express your unique voice. Suggest that students consider how they would present their articles to an audience during a speech.

Revising for Voice

When you revise for *voice*, you make sure that you have engaged the reader throughout your writing, that your voice sounds authentic and original, that your writing expresses your unique perspective, and that you have used a tone appropriate for your audience. Ask yourself the following questions.

Have I engaged my readers throughout my writing?

If you are bored or distracted rereading your essay, chances are that your readers will be too. Think about what interested you in the topic to begin with. Imagine yourself telling someone about your topic and trying to keep his or her attention. Revise your essay to keep your readers interested and engaged.

Does my voice sound authentic and original?

Your writing needs to sound original and authentic. Readers should be able to hear you and your unique personality in your writing. Revise your writing to be sure it conveys your voice.

Exercise

The following sentences address the topic of growing pumpkins. The audience is fellow students. Pick out the passage that conveys the more original and unique voice and is appropriate for an audience of fellow students. Explain your answer.

1. For thousands of gardeners growing pumpkins is not about producing a perfect jack-o-lantern. It's about glory and about being the best. If you know anything about competitive pumpkin growing, then you know the term *heavyweights*. These are gigantic pumpkins grown specifically to win against other large-size pumpkins.

2. Growing pumpkins, whether big or small, requires knowledge about some basic planting principles. You must know about fertilizing, planting and space requirements, irrigation, insects and diseases, pollination, and harvesting and storing.

Express your unique voice. Try to engage the reader with your own perspective. Use words and phrases that would catch your own interest if you were the first person to read this.

Differentiated Instruction: Struggling Learners

Some students feel that using more words adds emphasis to their ideas. Make sure students understand that when writing to inform, it is best to use concise, direct language. Have students work in pairs and exchange drafts. They should look for places where words can be cut.

Is the tone of my essay appropriate for my intended audience?

Whether you are writing for a timed test, your teacher, or your fellow classmates, you need to use language that is courteous and shows your interest in the topic. If you are writing for your classmates, you may use language that is less formal than that which you might use for a timed test. Avoid using words that sound sarcastic, flippant, or bored.

Create a voice that sounds . . . interested	Avoid a voice that sounds . . .		
	sarcastic	flippant	bored
unique	weird	wacky	odd
gigantic	bloated	puffy	fat
microscopic	insignificant	wee	puny

Exercise

Read the following paragraph from an informative article about growing giant pumpkins. The tone should be friendly and interested, but it currently sounds hostile. For each underlined word or phrase, write a replacement that would make the tone more appropriate.

1   It's important, says Smith, to keep your pumpkin patch weed free. To do this,
2   he uses some <u>disgusting-looking</u> composted manure. The compost attracts <u>these</u>
3   <u>nasty little</u> bugs that help to <u>slaughter</u> garden pests like hornworms. If this doesn't
4   work, Smith uses <u>deadly</u> natural pesticides. These chemicals come from plants and
5   so won't <u>kill or maim</u> humans.

Check your tone. Watch for words and phrases that create an inappropriate tone. Replace them with synonyms that show your interest in the topic in a courteous way.

Voice
The writer improves the language level and tone of the essay.

> The generous use of foam insulation
> ~~Builders squirt all this foamy junk in the walls to~~ provide
> protection from summer heat and winter cold, ~~so these dudes~~
> ~~at the gas company don't wind up with so much cash.~~
> thus reducing both heating and air-conditioning costs.

Expository

Is the tone of my essay appropriate for my intended audience?

Remind students to keep their audience in mind as they check their essay for consistent tone and voice—the appropriate tone and voice for a formal or timed essay would be different from what you would use if your essay was intended for your classmates only. Tell students that even if they don't particularly like an assignment, they should avoid letting their attitude influence the way they complete the assignment or answer the prompt.

⭐ **TEKS** 11.13C

Exercise
Answers

Students' answers will vary. Sample answers shown below.
1. disgusting-looking: dark
2. these nasty little: tiny
3. slaughter: kill
4. deadly: lethal, but
5. kill or maim: harm ✔ **DIFFERENTIATE INSTRUCTION**

Check your tone. Tell students to carefully check their word choice. Remind them that some words may create a tone other than what they intend. Caution them to maintain a clear organizational scheme that conveys their ideas as they revise.

⭐ **TEKS** 11.13C, 11.15A(iv)

Voice Have students work in pairs and explain how the revisions improve the tone of the essay. (Students' explanations will vary but should note that the revisions incorporate language appropriate for an informative essay.)

TEKS **11.13C** Revise drafts to achieve consistency of tone by employing tropes and schemes, and by adding transitional words and phrases; **11.15A(iv)** Use a clear organizational scheme for conveying ideas; **ELPS** **1G** Demonstrate ability to distinguish between formal and informal English and knowledge of when to use formal and informal English; **3G** Express ideas

Revising Improving Your Writing

Check your revising. Tell students that if they have carefully revised for all the traits, they should be able to place a check mark next to each item on the list. DIFFERENTIATE INSTRUCTION ↘

Revising Checklist

Depending on the needs of the class, you may want to focus on the questions for a particular trait during a whole group discussion. For example, you might focus on the need for additional detail, or on the appropriate use of formal and informal English.

 TEKS 11.13C; **ELPS** 1G, 5F, 5G

Make a clean copy. Point out that students' clean copy should be double spaced for use during the editing stage.

Conventions Connections

Grammar: Verbals
- *Proofreader's Guide* pages 746–747
- *SkillsBook* pages 99, 127

☀ *Write Source Online* **GrammarSnap**

Grammar: Clauses and Phrases
- *Student Edition: Proofreader's Guide* pages 640–641, 762–763
- *SkillsBook* page 133

☀ *Write Source Online* **GrammarSnap**

184

 TEKS 11.13C

Revising Improving Your Writing

Check your revising. On a piece of paper, write the numbers 1 to 15. If you can answer "yes" to a question, put a check mark next to that number. If not, continue to work on that part of your article.

Revising Checklist

Focus and Coherence

_____ 1. Is my writing focused on the prompt or assignment?
_____ 2. Have I developed a specific thesis statement or main idea?
_____ 3. Have I included a meaningful introduction and a strong conclusion?
_____ 4. Do all of my details support my main idea?
_____ 5. Does my essay have a sense of completeness?

Organization

_____ 6. Have I created an effective beginning, middle, and ending?
_____ 7. Have I chosen the best order for my middle paragraphs?
_____ 8. Does each paragraph have unity?
_____ 9. Have I used transitional words and phrases to create a logical flow between ideas?

Development of Ideas

_____ 10. Have I offered enough support and specific details to allow readers to appreciate my major points?
_____ 11. Have I approached my topic from a unique perspective?

Voice

_____ 12. Have I engaged my readers throughout my essay?
_____ 13. Is my writing authentic and original?
_____ 14. Does my unique perspective come through in my writing?
_____ 15. Is my tone appropriate for my intended audience?

Make a clean copy. When you've finished revising, make a clean copy of your essay for editing.

TEKS **11.13C** Revise drafts to clarify meaning and achieve specific rhetorical purposes, consistency of tone, and logical organization by rearranging the words, sentences, and paragraphs to employ tropes, schemes, and by adding transitional words and phrases; **ELPS 1G** Demonstrate ability to distinguish between formal and informal English; **5F** Write using a variety of grade-appropriate sentence lengths, sentence patterns, and connecting words; **5G** Explain with increasing specificity and detail

Writing an Informative Article **185**

Editing

Now that you have finished revising your essay, you are ready to edit for conventions: grammar, sentence structure, mechanics (punctuation and capitalization), and spelling.

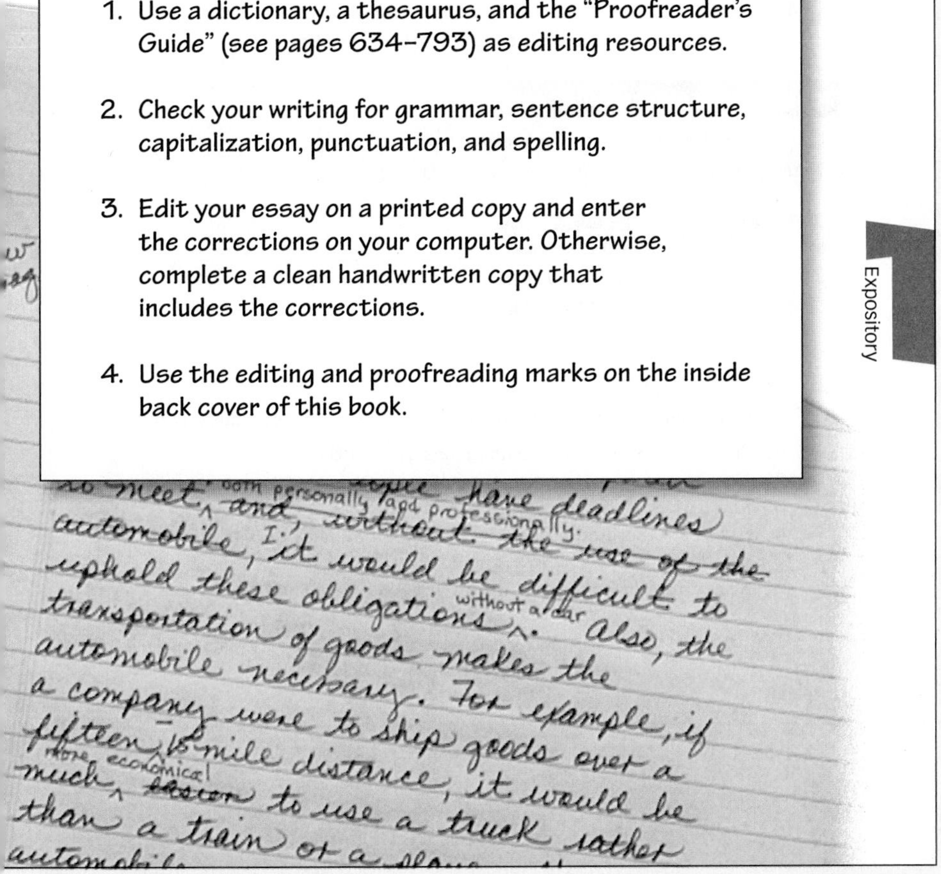

Keys to Effective Editing

1. Use a dictionary, a thesaurus, and the "Proofreader's Guide" (see pages 634–793) as editing resources.

2. Check your writing for grammar, sentence structure, capitalization, punctuation, and spelling.

3. Edit your essay on a printed copy and enter the corrections on your computer. Otherwise, complete a clean handwritten copy that includes the corrections.

4. Use the editing and proofreading marks on the inside back cover of this book.

Expository

[handwritten draft text]

to meet. both personally and professionally (and) have deadlines automobile, it would be difficult to uphold these obligations without a car. Also, the transportation of goods makes the automobile necessary. For example, if a company were to ship goods over a fifteen-mile distance, it would be much easier to use a truck rather than a train or a plane...

Differentiated Instruction:
English Language Learners

⭐ **ELPS** 1G, 5F, 5G

ELP Level **Beginning**	ELP Level **Intermediate**	ELP Level **Advanced/Advanced High**
Work individually with students to complete the revising checklist and make suggestions for improvement to sentence lengths, patterns, and connecting words.	Have partners review each other's articles and make suggestions about ideas that could use more specificity and detail. Have students incorporate the ideas in their revisions.	Have partners review each other's articles to identify use or formal and informal English, and to look for a variety of sentence lengths, patterns, and connecting words.

Editing

Keys to Effective Editing

Remind students that during the editing stage they should check to find and correct errors in grammar, sentence structure, mechanics (capitalization and punctuation), and spelling.

The Keys to Effective Editing list explains the process students will be guided through on SE pages 186–190.

To prepare students for proofreading their work, focus on familiarizing them with how to mark editing and proofreading changes:

- Review each of the editing and proofreading marks shown on SE page 633.
- Make an overhead transparency of a sample text with errors, and have students point out the mistakes.
- Distribute photocopies of the sample paragraph with errors. Have students edit to correct the mistakes.
- Ask students to choose a pen or pencil in a different color than they use for writing, and reserve it specially for editing and proofreading. Using a contrasting color for noting changes on the draft will make the marks stand out and ensure that all edits are made on the final copy. ✔ **DIFFERENTIATE INSTRUCTION**

ELPS 1G Demonstrate ability to distinguish between formal and informal English; **5F** Write using a variety of grade-appropriate sentence lengths, patterns, and connecting words; **5G** Explain with increasing specificity and detail

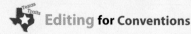 **Editing** for Conventions

Grammar

How can I check my subject-verb agreement?

Discuss the idea of "notional agreement" of subject and verb. Explain that notional agreement refers to a word that may be singular in form but plural in meaning (or vice versa) and, therefore, will take a verb form that matches the meaning. For example:

- Collective nouns, words that describe a group (such as *group, family,* or *pair*), are usually treated as singular. However, if the focus is on individuals in the group, a plural verb can work better: *Her family constantly interrupt each other.*
- Some combinations of words that are grammatically plural are considered a single unit: *Steak and eggs is my favorite breakfast.*

Review and discuss both types of compound subjects with students.

Grammar Exercise
Answers

1. Both Saturn and Jupiter have . . .
2. The rings around Saturn are . . .
3. The Kuiper Belt contains . . .
4. Halley's comet or other occasional visitors fly . . .
5. Either Jupiter or Saturn is . . .

Check your subject-verb agreement. Remind students to pay particular attention to compound subjects, collective nouns, and groups of words that are grammatically plural but generally considered a single unit. **DIFFERENTIATE INSTRUCTION ↘**

TEKS 11.13D; **ELPS** 5D

⭐ **Conventions Connections**

Grammar: Subject-Verb Agreement
- **Student Edition: Proofreader's Guide** pages 770–771, 772–773
- **SkillsBook** page 146

⚡ **Write Source Online GrammarSnap**

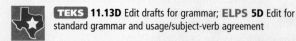 **TEKS** 11.13D Edit drafts for grammar; **ELPS** 5D Edit for standard grammar and usage/subject-verb agreement

---

 **Editing** for Conventions

Grammar

When you edit for *grammar,* make sure that you have used nouns, verbs, pronouns, and other parts of speech correctly. In particular, check that the subjects and verbs in your sentences always agree.

How can I check my subject-verb agreement?

You can check your subject-verb agreement by making sure singular subjects have singular verbs and plural subjects have plural verbs. (Remember that a singular verb often ends in *s,* and a plural verb often does not.)

The planet Mercury orbits nearest the sun, but Venus is the hottest planet.
The terrestrial planets include Mercury, Venus, Earth, and Mars.

Compound Subjects with *and*

Compound subjects connected with *and* require a plural verb.
Mercury, Venus, Earth, and Mars have solid surfaces.

Compound Subjects with *or*

If the subjects are joined by *or,* the verb must agree with the subject nearest to it.
Either Pluto or Uranus is farthest from the sun at any given time, due to Pluto's elliptical orbit.

Grammar Exercise

Rewrite each sentence below to correct subject-verb agreement errors.

1. Both Saturn and Jupiter has rings around them.
2. The rings around Saturn is much more spectacular.
3. The Kuiper Belt contain billions of asteroids.
4. Halley's comet and other occasional visitors flies into view every few decades or so.
5. Either Jupiter or Saturn are almost massive enough to become a star.

 Check your subject-verb agreement. Make sure that singular subjects have singular verbs and plural subjects have plural verbs.

Differentiated Instruction: Struggling Learners

For students who need more practice with subject-verb agreement, focus on nouns that are the same in the singular and plural (such as *fish* or *deer*) or irregular plural forms (such as *data* or *alumnae*). Remind students to use the sentence context to determine whether a noun is singular or plural.

Are my pronouns clearly linked to their antecedents?

Your pronouns are clearly linked to their antecedents if the pronoun clearly refers to the most recent noun with the same number and gender.

Galileo discovered four moons of Jupiter with his homemade telescope.

If another noun intervenes, the antecedent may be unclear. The pronoun should be replaced or the sentence should be rewritten.

Galileo's discovery showed that not all things revolved around Earth, and it angered many people.

Galileo's discovery showed that not all things revolved around Earth, and this idea angered many people.

Grammar Exercise

Rewrite each of the following sentences to clear up the antecedent problems.

1. Maria called Eva after she had finished her exam questions.
2. They learned that Galileo challenged the theories of Copernicus and that he was forced to recant.
3. Linda told Beth that her brother had won the science contest.

Check your antecedents. Make sure each pronoun refers to the last noun that agrees with it in number and gender.

Conventions
A sentence is rewritten because of an unclear pronoun.

Green builders also most often opt for recycled building materials. ~~When they choose new materials, they use~~ If new materials are used, builders prefer those that have a minimal environmental impact, such as bamboo flooring . . .

Learning Language

Readers may have a difficult time understanding your writing if your pronouns are not clearly connected to their antecedents—the nouns that the pronouns are replacing. Look at some of your recent writing. Circle all the pronouns you use. Check that your pronouns are clearly connected to their antecedents. Explain to a partner how the pronouns you use are clearly connected to their antecedents.

Expository

Are my pronouns clearly linked to their antecedents?

Focus on a common trouble spot: using *they* or *their* with a singular antecedent (*Everyone wishes they had more free time*). Acknowledge that this is common in conversation, but urge students to avoid it in writing. Explain that often, it is better to rewrite to avoid the pronoun: *Everyone wants more free time.*

Grammar Exercise
Answers

Possible answers:
1. After Eva had finished her exam, Maria called her.
2. They learned that after Galileo challenged the theories of Copernicus, he was forced to recant.
3. Linda found out that her brother won the science contest when Beth told her.

Check your antecedents. Tell students to check for use of the correct pronoun for each antecedent.

TEKS 11.13D

Conventions To encourage students to use grade-level content-area vocabulary in context, have partners discuss how the revision clarifies and improves the grammatical structures.

ELPS 3C, 3D

Learning Language

Suggest that partners check for sentences in which the subject and the verb are separated by a prepositional phrase. One of the girls left *her* purse behind. (not *their*) ⟋DIFFERENTIATE INSTRUCTION

ELPS 5E

Grammar: Pronoun-Antecedent Agreement
- **Student Edition: Proofreader's Guide** pages 774 (+)
- **SkillsBook** page 152

⚡ *Write Source Online* **GrammarSnap**

**Differentiated Instruction:
English Language Learners**

ELPS 5D, 5E

Turn to the Appendix of the Teacher's Edition for information on language transfer issues with subject-verb agreement and pronouns.

ELP Level **Beginning**	ELP Level **Intermediate**	ELP Level **Advanced/Advanced High**
Provide additional examples to use in guiding students to practice editing writing for standard grammar usage such as correct pronoun agreement.	Provide additional examples. Have students correct the pronoun agreement independently and then discuss their edits together.	Provide additional examples. Have students correct the pronoun agreement independently and then discuss the correct usage with a partner.

TEKS **11.13D** Edit drafts for grammar; **ELPS** **3C** Speak using a variety of grammatical structures; **3D** Speak using grade-level content-area vocabulary in context/new English words; **5D** Edit writing for standard grammar and usage/pronoun agreement; **5E** Employ increasingly complex grammatical structures

Sentence Structure

Have students work with partners to check their essays for sentence lengths and structures.

Have I used varied sentence structures?

Suggest that each partner read the other's essay aloud. The listening partner should pay close attention to how his or her essay sounds. Have students ask themselves the following questions:

- Do my sentences all sound the same?
- Do I have an interesting combination of long and short sentences?
- Are there places I could combine sentences or parts of sentences to vary sentence length and pattern?

 ELPS 5F

Exercise
Answers

Possible answers:

1. Although green buildings can be expensive, later they will save the owner money.
2. Because using natural lighting saves money and energy, green builders use natural light whenever possible.
3. Architects should seek the advice of green professionals who will help them develop an environmentally-friendly vision for their their building.

Reread your essay aloud. As they revise their essays for sentence length and structure, suggest that students ask for feedback from you or from a classmate.

188

Sentence Structure

When you edit for *sentence structure*, make sure that you are using a variety of sentences. Look for ways to combine simpler sentences into more complex sentences, to use inverted order, or to interject rhetorical devices.

Have I used varied sentence structures?

Read your essay aloud. If your sentences all sound alike, you probably have not varied your sentence structure. Varying your sentence structure will make your essay more interesting to read and will help you emphasize important ideas. If most of your sentences are structured subject, verb, object (*Architects design buildings.*), you need to add some varied structures. Try the ideas below.

Combine two simple sentences to form a compound sentence.
Construction had gone on for two years. Finally their home was complete.
Construction had gone on for two years, but finally their new home was complete.

Compound Subjects with *and*
Compound subjects connected with *and* require a plural verb.
Mercury, Venus, Earth, and Mars have solid surfaces.

Compound Subjects with *or*
If the subjects are joined by *or*, the verb must agree with the subject nearest to it.
Either **Pluto** or **Uranus** is farthest from the sun at any given time, due to Pluto's elliptical orbit.

Exercise

Rewrite the sentences below to vary their sentence structure.

1. Green buildings can be expensive. Later they will save the owner money.
2. Green builders use natural light whenever possible. Using natural lighting saves money and energy.
3. Architects should seek the advice of green professionals. Green professionals will help architects develop an environmentally friendly vision for their building.

 Reread your essay aloud. Make sure that it sounds interesting. If it sounds flat and boring, try revising your sentence structure.

Writing an Informative Article **189**

Mechanics

When you edit for *mechanics,* you check for correct punctuation and capitalization. Make sure that any changes in sentence structure are done with correct punctuation and capitalization.

Are my revised sentences correctly punctuated?

Changing the structure of sentences will affect how you punctuate and use capitalization. Check the sentences you revise to make sure they use correct punctuation and capitalization.

Compound sentences A compound sentence expresses two or more complete ideas. Compound sentences are connected by a conjunction, such as *and, but,* or *or.* Use a comma between the sentences. You can also use a semicolon alone to join the two sentences.

Construction had gone on for two years, but **finally their new home was complete.**

Complex sentences A clause is a group of words that include a subject and a predicate. A complex sentence is made up of an independent clause (a clause that expresses a complete thought) and a dependent clause (a clause that does not express a complete thought). Connect the independent and dependent clause with a subordinating conjection such as *when, although,* or *because.* Always use a comma with a dependent clause that begins a sentence. No comma is needed for a dependent clause that comes after the independent clause.

When he was just a young boy, **Daniel discovered his passion for architecture.**

Inverted order sentences The natural order of a sentence is a subject followed by a verb or the predicate. A sentence with inverted order shifts that order, usually to the predicate followed by its subject.

Onto the flower flew **a gorgeous** butterfly.
     Predicate   *Subject*

Exercise

Rewrite each of the following sentences with correct punctuation and capitalization.

1. Although he worked very hard with his garden all of Alex's plants died.
2. The tomatoes were hardy and strong. But many of the cucumbers died.
3. Alex got help with his spring planting, because this year he wanted a healthy crop.

Expository

Mechanics

Remind students that using correct capitalization and punctuation helps readers focus on and understand their main points.

Are my revised sentences correctly punctuated?

Have students work in pairs to check for correct punctuation of their revised sentences. Have them do the following.

- Find any compound sentences. Check that there is a comma after the first sentence and before the conjunction connecting the two sentences: *Alice was invited to the party, but she decided she didn't want to go.*
- Find any compound elements within sentences. If there are three or more compound elements, check that there are commas separating the elements: *Aaron, Raphael, and Joaquin all competed in the race.*
- Find any complex sentences. Look for dependent clauses that begin a sentence. Make sure there is a comma after the dependent clause and before the independent clause: *Because the trainer was so skilled, she got the dog under control in minutes.*
- Make sure that all sentences begin with a capital letter and have correct end punctuation.

 ELPS 5F

Exercise
Answers

1. Although he worked very hard with his garden, all of Alex's plants died.
2. The tomatoes were hardy and strong, but many of the cucumbers died.
3. Alex got help with his spring planting because this year he wanted a healthy crop.

✔ DIFFERENTIATE INSTRUCTION

 ELPS 5F Write using a variety of grade-appropriate sentence lengths, patterns, and connecting words

Editing
Checking for Conventions

Check your editing. Use this activity to help students demonstrate listening comprehension of increasingly complex English by collaborating with peers.

After students have completed the checklist for their own articles, have them trade papers with a partner and read each other's work aloud, carefully listening for stray errors.

ELPS 1B, 2I

Editing Checklist

Remind students that they can use the Proofreader's Guide (SE pages 634–779) for instruction, rules, and examples to resolve conventions questions about their own writing.

Creating a Title

If students created a three-word headline for their article when they first began writing (see TE page 171), have them refer to it. The headline might give them additional ideas for a title now.

 TEKS 11.13D

Editing Checking for Conventions

 Check your editing. On a piece of paper, write the numbers 1 to 8. If you can answer "yes" to a question, put a check mark after that number. If you can't, continue to edit for that convention.

Editing Checklist

Conventions

GRAMMAR

_____ **1.** Do my subjects and verbs agree in number?

_____ **2.** Are my pronouns clearly linked to their antecedents?

SENTENCE STRUCTURE

_____ **3.** Have I varied my sentence structure by writing different types of sentences?

MECHANICS (CAPITALIZATION AND PUNCTUATION)

_____ **4.** Do I use end punctuation after all my sentences?

_____ **5.** Have I correctly punctuated compound and complex sentences?

_____ **6.** Have I cited sources correctly in my essay? (See pages **441–454**.)

SPELLING

_____ **7.** Have I spelled all words correctly?

_____ **8.** Have I double-checked words my spell-checker may have missed?

Creating a Title

After your editing is complete, add a title that engages your reader and sums up your article. Here are a few ways to approach this task.

- **Be creative: Building Green and Saving Green**
- **Use a line from the article: Maximum Efficiency and Minimum Impact**
- **Use a saying: It *Is* Easy Being Green**

TEKS 11.13E

Writing an Informative Article **191**

Publishing

Sharing Your Essay

The purpose of an informative article is to engage and inform your reader. After preparing a final copy of your essay, consider reaching the public with your ideas in one of the ways presented below.

Format your final copy. To format a handwritten essay, use the guidelines below or follow your teacher's instructions. Remember, revising is an ongoing process. If you see something that needs revising, do it. Make a clean copy and carefully proofread it.

Focusing on Presentation

- Write neatly using blue or black ink.
- Place your name in the upper left corner of page 1.
- Skip a line and center your title; skip another line and start your essay.
- Indent every paragraph and leave a one-inch margin on all four sides.
- Write your last name and the page number in the upper right corner of every page.

Publish Your Article

Use e-mail or the postal service to send your article to a local or school-based magazine or newspaper. Before sending your article, make sure it conforms to the publication's submission guidelines.

Publish It Yourself

With today's desktop publishing software, you can easily format and print copies of your article. Depending upon the topic you've chosen, you may even be able to add your own photographs or illustrations. Once you've printed your article, you can give it to members of your audience or post it on a bulletin board or other prominent site. Be sure to get permission before posting.

Give a Public Reading

Another way to share your article is to give a public reading to classmates, friends, or family. Schedule a time that is convenient for you and your audience. Practice reading your article in advance to ensure a smooth, clear presentation.

Expository

Publishing

Sharing Your Essay

Consider having students create a class Web site or Web log (blog) for publishing their articles. Depending on students' interests, programming abilities, and available time, the Web site can do the following:

- allow writers to embellish their essays with photos and other illustrations.
- let students organize the topics by theme and provide space for readers' comments.
- make the writing available to the district.

✱ For more about Creating Your Own Web Site, see SE page 133.

Format your final copy. Remind students to keep an extra copy of their final essays for themselves for future reference.

Focusing on Presentation

Have students work in pairs to check that the final copies of their essays are correct, especially in terms of form.

TEKS 11.13E

Publish Your Article

Suggest that partners check the other's work to be sure the essays conform to publication guidelines.

Publish It Yourself

Suggest that students share addresses of organizations, Web sites, or blogs that might be interested in an informative article.

Give a Public Reading

Have students who plan to give a public reading work in pairs to practice their tone and volume.

DIFFERENTIATE INSTRUCTION

 Technology Connections

📐 *Write Source Online* **Portfolio**

📐 *Write Source Online* **Essay Evaluation**

TEKS 11.13E Revise final draft in response to feedback from peers and publish for appropriate audience; **ELPS 1B** Monitor written language production and employ self-corrective techniques or other resources; **3A** Practice producing sounds of newly acquired vocabulary to pronounce English words; **3C** Speak using a variety of grammatical structures, sentence lengths, sentence types, and connecting words; **3F** Give information during extended speaking assignments; **3H** Explain with increasing specificity and detail

---

Differentiated Instruction: English Language Learners

ELPS 1B, 3A, 3C, 3F, 3H

ELP Level **Beginning**	ELP Level **Intermediate**	ELP Level **Advanced/Advanced High**
Have students read their articles with a small group and employ self-corrective techniques. Allow time to practice producing sounds of new vocabulary with you in advance.	Pair students with an English-proficient partner. Tell each partner to practice his or her article's grammatical structures. Then have them read their articles to a small group.	Have students present their articles as an extended speaking assignment. Then have them respond to questions with specificity and detail.

Evaluating an Informative Article

To support understanding of the following four sample essays—one sample essay for each possible score point—refer to the holistic scoring guide on SE pages 36–37 and to key instruction from the expository writing unit.

DIFFERENTIATE INSTRUCTION ⬎

Score Point 4: Highly Effective

Work through this sample essay with students, pointing out the qualities that earn it an overall score point of 4. In addition to the call-outs on the student pages, use the following questions to facilitate analysis:

- How does the opening paragraph grab the reader's attention? *(It helps draws the reader in by beginning with something most people have experienced: the common cold.)*
- What background details does the writer give in the second paragraph? *(how long people have been battling colds, cures for the cold, and causes of the cold)*
- What vivid, energetic words does the writer use in the third paragraph? *(grabs, injects, hijacks, explodes, battled)*

⭐ **ELPS** 4K

Evaluating an Informative Article

To learn how to evaluate an informative article, you will use the holistic scoring guide on pages **36–37** and the articles that follow. These informative articles are examples of writing for each score on the scoring guide (1–4).

Notice that the first article received a score of 4. Read the description for a score of 4 on page **36**. Then read the narrative. Use the same steps to study the other examples. As you read, concentrate on the overal quality of the writing in each example.

Writing that fits a score of 4 is highly effective.

Strong introduction draws readers in and clearly identifies ideas to be discussed.

Background details set the stage to develop ideas.

Voice is energetic; vivid words create effective images.

A Good Cold Is Hard to Beat

If you're like most people, you catch a cold two to four times each year. Each cold means a week or two of sneezing, sniffling, and misery, and while you're feeling so lousy, you may be doing some thinking. How is it that scientists can discover new treatments for all sorts of serious diseases, but they can't find a cure for the common cold? The answer is both simple and complex—the cold is an extremely difficult bug to beat.

People have been battling colds for thousands of years. In fact, the ancient Egyptians even had a hiroglyphic that represented the illness (Paris 328). Over that long time, people have tried any number of cures—from medicinal herbs to vitamins to antibiotics—with little success. For the longest time, people didn't know what caused a cold—or even how people got them. That changed in 1914, when scientists learned that colds were caused by tiny disease-carrying microbes called viruses. Unfortunately, discovering the cause of the colds didn't make curing it any easier.

One reason for this is that viruses can reproduce very quickly. Here's how they work to make you sick: A virus comes along and grabs one of your cells. It injects the cell with genetic information. The genetic information hijacks the cell and reprograms it to make more viruses. The cell gets so full of viruses that it explodes, sending its deadly cargo out to invade even more cells. Your body's immune system tries to ward off the attack with white blood cells, but these warriors are only

> effective if they've battled this particular virus before. Not giving up easily, your immune system works even harder, and soon, the sneezing, sniffling, and misery begin.
>
> Another reason cold viruses are hard to stop is that there are many different kinds of them. Over 200 different viruses can cause a cold ("Cold"). In order to stop people from getting sick, scientists would have to invent a treatment that works on every one of them. A tall order! Even now, medical science has a hard time just keeping up with the flu virus, which only has about half a dozen different varieties.
>
> Another factor that makes the "common cold" difficult to beat is that viruses can mutate quickly. Each year, scientists prepare a vaccine to deal with the influenza virus, but that vaccine won't work the following year, because the virus will have mutated. Cold viruses do the same things, very quickly. Even if scientists found a treatment that would kill most of the cold viruses in your body, it probably wouldn't kill all of them. Some would be resistant to the treatment, and those would survive too quickly multiply. In no time, an individual's body would be full of viruses again.
>
> The good news is that even if people can't beat a cold, they can try to make cold symptoms less severe. You can help your body during its battle by drinking lots and lots of fluids, and getting plenty of rest. (On a preventative note, experts say that people who get less than seven hours of sleep each night are three times as likely to get colds!) Gargling with salt water or using throat lozenges will ease a sore throat. Antibiotics, however, won't do a thing to help a cold. That's because antibiotics kill bacteria, not viruses. When a person gets a cold, he or she is not alone. We all get them—and we all feel miserable when it happens!

Transitions are smooth; ideas progress logically.

Voice is assured and authentic throughout.

Few errors in conventions; individual paragraphs are focused and show depth of understanding.

Expository

? Review the essay with a partner. Discuss what makes it a 4-point essay.

- What transition words and phrases does the writer use to keep the writing smooth and the flow logical? (*Another reason, Even now, Another factor, In no time, On a preventative note, however*)
- What examples can you find of the author's assured and authentic voice? (*A tall order!; Cold viruses do the same things, very quickly; The good news is . . .*)

? Review the essay with a partner

As they review the essay, suggest that students consider the writer's focus, development of ideas, organization, and voice.

Differentiated Instruction: English Language Learners

⭐ ELPS **3E, 4D, 4F, 4K**

Refer to pages 574–579 for an example of a shared reading of an informative article.

ELP Level **Beginning**	ELP Level **Intermediate**	ELP Level **Advanced/Advanced High**
Preteach vocabulary such as *misery* and *lousy* to enhance comprehension. Use visuals and gestures to develop vocabulary and grasp of language structures.	Before reading, have students complete sentence stems to explain what having a cold feels like. Discuss new vocabulary and language structures.	Before reading, have partners share experiences with the common cold. After reading, have them analyze new information from the article.

ELPS 3E Share information in cooperative learning interactions; **4D** Use prereading supports to enhance comprehension of written text; **4F** Use support from peers and teachers to develop vocabulary and grasp of language structures; **4K** Demonstrate English comprehension and expand reading skills by employing analytical skills

Score Point 3: Generally Effective

Work through this sample essay with students, pointing out the qualities that earn it an overall score point of 3. In addition to the call-outs on the student pages, use the following questions to facilitate analysis:

- Find the awkward phrasing in the opening paragraph. (*Scientists can put people on the moon—and on the bottom of the ocean.*) How could the writer have revised this sentence to make it less awkward?

- How could the writer have given more emphasis to the phrase "a tall order" in paragraph 4? (*Possible answer: The writer could have used it as an interjection: A tall order! Using the exclamation point instantly emphasizes the point and shows the writer's voice clearly.*)

- What errors in conventions can you find? (*Students should note the misspelling of* hieroglyphic, *the unclear pronoun antecedents, and lapses in verb tenses.*)

DIFFERENTIATE INSTRUCTION ⇘

⭐ **ELPS** 4C

Writing that fits a score of 3 is generally effective.

A Good Cold Is Hard to Beat

> Opening is fairly strong, but awkward phrasing is a little distracting.

Most people catch a cold 2–4 times each year. Each cold means one 1–2 weeks of sneezing and sniffling. You may be doing some thinking. Science can put people on the moon—and on the bottom of the ocean. It has discovered new treatments for all sorts of serious diseases. But why can't doctors find a cure for one of the most common diseases—the cold? The answer is that the cold is an extremely difficult bug to beat.

People have been battling colds for thousands of years. In fact, the ancient Egyptians even had a hiroglyphic that represented the illness (Paris 328). Over those thousands of years, people have tried any number of cures with little success. For the longest time, people didn't know what caused a cold—or even how people got them, but that changed in 1914, when scientists learned that colds were caused by viruses. Unfortunately, discovering the cause of colds hasn't made things easier.

> Ideas in sentences and in paragraphs generally flow smoothly.

One reason for this is that viruses can reproduce very quickly. Here's how they work to make a person sick. A virus invades a cell and injects the cell with genetic information. The genetic information reprograms the cell to make more viruses. The cell gets so full of viruses that it explodes. Even more cells get invaded. Soon, they are throughout the body and the person is sneezing and sniffling. But why is this so hard to stop?

Another reason cold viruses are hard to stop is that there are so many different kinds of them. Over 200 different viruses can cause a cold ("Cold"). It would probably be impossible for scientists to invent a treatment that works on every one of them, a tall order. Even now, medical science has a hard time just keeping up with the flu virus, which has about only half a dozen different varieties.

Each paragraph develops a specific idea; beginning paragraph sentences could use more variety.

Another reason makes the cold virus hard to stop. Viruses can mutate quickly. Each year, scientists prepare a vaccine to deal with the influenza virus, but that vaccine won't work for the following year, because the virus has mutated. So even if scientists found a treatment that would kill most of the cold viruses a person has, it probably wouldn't kill all of them. Some would be resistent to the treatment, and they would quickly multiply. An individual's body would be full of viruses again very quickly.

Many other reasons make cold viruses hard to stop. Often people are not aware that they have a cold virus, and they spread the virus without knowing it. Cold viruses can also live for several hours and can be found wherever people are present. Schools, stores, and restaurants are breeding grounds for all types of cold viruses. Cold viruses can also spread in enclosed places where people gather, such as on buses, trains, and airplanes. It's impossible to avoid these types of places, but there are some things people can do. Experts say that washing your hands frequently and throughly is a good idea. Many schools and businesses have installed hand wipes to lessen the spread of cold viruses, and these can also be useful.

Focus is generally strong, but strays a bit from the topic toward the end.

Can antibiotics stop viruses from spreading? Antibiotics are not recommended by doctors because they kill bacteria, not viruses. So don't bother asking your doctor for a prescription for an antibiotic—it won't help.

Voice is engaging and consistent.

Even if people can't beat a cold, they can try to make cold symptoms less severe. Warm fluids and rest will help. Gargling with salt water or using throat lozenges will make a sore throat that accompanies a cold feel better. Cold medicines sold in drugstores will not "cure" a cold, but they can make a person's cold symptoms less uncomfortable. The thing to remember is that when a person gets a cold, he or she is not alone. All people get them—and they all feel miserable when it happens!

Expository

- How would you add more sentence variety to the first paragraph? *(combining some sentences and tightening up others)*
- Where in the second paragraph does the writer's focus stray? *(Many schools and businesses . . .)*
- Find examples of the writer's engaging voice. *(Possible answers: difficult bug to beat, a tall order, breeding grounds)*

Differentiated Instruction: English Language Learners

⚡ **ELPS** 3B, 4C, 4K

ELP Level **Beginning**	ELP Level **Intermediate**	ELP Level **Advanced/Advanced High**
Read the sample article together. Simplify the call-out notes to discuss traits like *focus and coherence* and *voice*. Have students repeat each trait with you.	Read the sample article together and guide students to examine traits. Have students analyze the language structures that begin the middle paragraphs.	Have students read the sample independently. Then have them demonstrate comprehension by analyzing the sample's strengths and weaknesses.
Use pages 574–579	Use pages 574–579	Use pages 574–579

ELPS **3B** Expand vocabulary/learning and using routine language needed for classroom communication; **4C** Comprehend English vocabulary and language structures; **4K** Demonstrate English comprehension and expand reading skills by employing analytical skills

Score Point 2: Somewhat Effective

Work through this sample essay with students, pointing out the qualities that earn it an overall score point of 2. In addition to the call-outs on the student pages, use the following questions to facilitate analysis:

- How could the writer have made the introduction stronger? *(The writer could have included more details to make the writing easier to follow.)*
- What convention errors should the writer have corrected on this page? *(Possible answers: reporduce, Another reason cold viruses are hard to stop?, servere, Another reason that cold viruses are hard to stop., probaly, symtoms, misrable; inconsistent verb tenses in paragraph 2; the shift in voice in paragraph 4)*
- Is the sentence "A virus grabs a cell" an appropriate voice for an informational article? Explain why or why not. *(Accept responses students can support.)*
- Where does the writer's organizational pattern begin to break down? *(paragraphs 5 and 6)*

DIFFERENTIATE INSTRUCTION ⟩

Writing that fits a score of 2 is somewhat effective.

What Causes a Cold?

You may be wondering, why can't doctors find a cure for the cold? The answer is that there are a lot of reasons.

For a long time, people didn't know what caused a cold. That changed in 1914. Scientists learned that colds were caused by viruses. They also discovered that that viruses can reporduce very quickly. Here's what happens: A virus grabs a cell. It takes over the cell and makes more. Soon, they've invaded your system.

Another reason cold viruses are hard to stop? There are over 200 of them ("Cold"). There's no way scientists could invent a treatment that works on every one of them. A tall order.

Another reason the cold virus is hard to stop? Because viruses mutate quickly. So even if scientists could kill most of the cold viruses in your body, it probaly wouldn't kill all of them. Soon, a person's body would be full of viruses again.

So even if people can't beat a cold, they can make cold symtoms less servere. Get rest and drink lots of fliuds. Can antibiotics stop viruses from spreading? The answer is no. That's because antibiotics kill bacteria, not viruses. So don't bother asking for antibiotics.

Another reason that cold viruses are hard to stop. People may not know that they have them, and they spread them without knowing it! Experts say washing your hands is a good idea to avoid cold viruses.

The thing to remember is that when a person gets a cold, you are not alone. All people get them, and they all feel misrable when it happens!

Call-outs:

- Voice sounds natural, and introduction indicates clear focus, but some of the ideas lack details.
- A number of ideas are presented, but are not developed in depth.
- Organizational logic breaks down toward end of essay.
- Errors in conventions detract from ideas and weaken writing.

Writing an Informative Article **197**

Writing that fits a score of 1 is ineffective.

1

The Common Cold

    Why can't doctors find a cure for the common cold? Everyone gets them. As you will see, there are a lot of reasons why they can't cure the common cold.

    The cold is caused by what is known as a virus. It can envade your body at any time, because it can live for sevral hours. Sceintists learned that colds were caused by viruses in 1914. This was not known before. The cold and the flu are not the same thing, the cold virus is seperate from the flu virus. Most people are confused by this and think the cold and the flu are the same thing. They are not. They are both viruses, but they are two different things. It is important to remember.

    Doctors say to rest and drink lots of fliuds. Can antibotics stop viruses from spreading? The answer is no. That's because antibotics kill bacteria. Not viruses. So don't bother asking for antibotics.

    There are more reasons cold viruses are hard to cure. They seem to change in a short amount of time quickly. There's just no way we could stop every one of them. A tall order. Even if they could stop most of them, they would find new kinds of cold viruses and they would take over your body in no time. Another reason that cold viruses are hard to stop. People need to wash there hands more, experts say. They say that washing your hands is a good idea to avoid cold viruses.

    Just remember that there are a lot of reasons why sceince can't cure the the common cold. When a person gets a cold, you are not alone. Even tho they can't be cured, all people get them.

Topic is stated, but voice is unoriginal.

Ideas are disconnected and are not always related to the topic.

Lack of organization makes the writing hard to follow.

Numerous errors in conventions add to overall lack of coherence and fluency.

Expository

Score Point 1: Ineffective

Work through this sample essay with students, pointing out the qualities that earn it an overall score point of 1. In addition to the call-outs on the student pages, use the following questions to facilitate analysis:

- What could the writer have done to improve the last sentence in the first paragraph? (*It is too vague, so any additional details would improve it.*)
- Find and explain convention errors in this paper. (*envade, sevral, Sceintists, there (for their), Another reason that cold viruses are hard to stop., tho; students may also note incorrect verb tenses and punctuation errors.*)
- How could the organization of the article be improved? (*The fourth paragraph should be moved to be the third paragraph.*)

Differentiated Instruction: English Language Learners

★ **ELPS** 3G, 3I, 4K

Before reading, explain that these two articles show a lack of mastery of the five traits, which makes the writing difficult to understand.

ELP Level **Beginning**	ELP Level **Intermediate**	ELP Level **Advanced/Advanced High**
Discuss the articles by focusing on one trait, such as organization. Create a web to help students "see" the lack of organization.	Point out examples of inconsistent or inappropriate voice. Have students give examples of adapting the language for formal or informal purposes.	Have each student analyze the articles to decide which traits are weakest. Have them discuss their opinions, ideas, and feelings with a partner.

ELPS **3G** Express opinions, ideas, and feelings; **3I** Adapt spoken language for formal and informal purposes; **4K** Demonstrate English comprehension and expand reading skills by employing analytical skills

Evaluating and Reflecting on Your Writing

Have students use the analyses they did of the sample essays in this chapter as a guide for helping them to reflect on and evaluate their own essays. Tell them to be as honest as possible in their reflections. Remind them that a carefully completed evaluation and reflection sheet can help them monitor their language production and guide their next writing assignment. It can also help them internalize the new basic and academic vocabulary they have learned. Remind them also to include the date and title of the article on their evaluation and reflection sheet.

DIFFERENTIATE INSTRUCTION ↘

Encourage students to keep their reflection with their essay. Their notes can be very helpful in reminding students of

- writing techniques that worked well for them and that they should use again,
- areas that caused them trouble and might need more work, and
- ideas for future expository writing projects in this class and others.

ELPS 1B, 1C, 1E, 4K

Writer's Craft

Reflection: Different writers have different experiences when they reflect on their works:

"I am very foolish over my own book. I have a copy which I constantly read and find very illuminating. Swift confesses to something of the sort with his own compositions."

—J. B. Yeats in a letter to his son, W. B. Yeats

"If there is a special Hell for writers it would be in the forced contemplation of their own works, with all the misconceptions, the omissions, the failures that any finished work of art implies."

—John Dos Passos

ELPS 1B Monitor written language production and employ self-corrective techniques or other resources; **1C** Use strategic learning strategies to acquire basic and grade-level vocabulary; **1E** Internalize new basic and academic language by using and reusing it/ writing; **4K** Demonstrate English comprehension and expand reading skills by employing analytical skills

198

Evaluating and Reflecting on Your Writing

Now that you have completed your informative article, take some time to reflect on your writing experience. On a separate sheet of paper, complete each sentence below. As you evaluate and reflect, think about how well you achieved focus and coherence, organization, development of ideas, and voice. This reflective writing will help reinforce what you've already learned and what you would like to learn about writing an informative article.

My Informative Article

1. The strongest part of my article is . . .

2. The part that still needs work is . . .

3. The prewriting activity that worked best for me was . . .

4. The main thing I learned about writing an informative article is . . .

5. In my next informative article, I would like to . . .

6. One question I still have about writing an informative article is . . .

Differentiated Instruction: English Language Learners

ELPS 1B, 1C, 1E, 4K

ELP Level **Beginning**	ELP Level **Intermediate**	ELP Level **Advanced/Advanced High**
Guide students to reflect on their writing. Review new basic and academic language related to five traits in context and have students repeat these terms with you.	Guide students as they write their reflections. Have them use new basic and academic language related to the five traits as they analyze their work.	Have students focus on the five traits as they write their reflections. Have them highlight two areas they will monitor in future writing tasks.

199

Expository Writing
Writing a Comparison-Contrast Essay

A DVD player and an MP3 player have some things in common. Both are digital technologies, both can be portable, and both are quite popular. They are, however, different in some ways, too. A DVD player does not store digital files; it only plays files stored on a disk. However, an MP3 player can store thousands of songs, offering users the ability to take hours of music with them wherever they go.

In a comparison-contrast essay, a writer takes a close look at two separate ideas—technologies, cultures, people, events, and so on. Then he or she explains the ways in which the two are similar and the ways in which they are different. A well-written comparison-contrast essay provides the reader with fresh insight into two topics by examining how they relate to each other.

In this chapter, you'll read a sample comparison-contrast essay about gasoline-electric hybrid cars and fuel-cell cars. Then you'll write your own comparison-contrast essay that shows the similarities and differences between two other technologies.

Writing Guidelines

Subject: **Two technologies**
Purpose: **To show how two topics are the same and different**
Form: **Comparison-contrast essay**
Audience: **Classmates**

"Shall I compare thee to a summer's day?
Thou art more lovely and more temperate."

—William Shakespeare

Writing a Comparison-Contrast Essay

Objectives
- demonstrate an understanding of what a comparison-contrast essay is
- use what has been learned about expository writing to create a comparison-contrast essay
- plan, draft, revise, edit, and share a comparison-contrast essay

Before reading this chapter, enhance students' understanding of the term *comparison-contrast essay* by discussing the etymologies of the words *compare* and *contrast*.

- *Compare* is made up of the prefix *com-* (with) and the root *par* (equal). To compare, the writer should show how two things are "equal with," or similar to each other.
- *Contrast* comes from the Latin word *contrastare*, which contains the prefix *contra-* (against) and the root *stare* (stand). To contrast, the writer should show how two things "stand against" each other, or differ.

As needed, guide students to learn and practice the letter-sound relationships in the words *compare* and *contrast*.

★ **ELPS** 4A, 4D

Resources

Copy Masters
- Venn diagram (TE p. 202)

ELPS 4A Learn relationships between sounds and letters of English; **4D** Use prereading supports to enhance comprehension of written text

Comparison-Contrast Essay

After students read the model essay, have them assess it using the traits of writing (there are no conventions errors). Responses may include:

Focus and Coherence

The topic is clearly stated and numerous details help to explain how the cars are similar and different.

Organization

The compare-contrast pattern is clear, and the paragraphs provide good transitions between ideas.

Development of Ideas

- The writer uses facts, statistics, and examples, but not quotations or anecdotes. He could consider adding either kind of detail.
- The writer could have provided a short explanation of terms such as *fuel cell, internal combustion,* and *hydrogen.*

Voice

The voice sounds knowledgeable and appropriate for an informative piece. DIFFERENTIATE INSTRUCTION ↘

DIFFERENTIATE INSTRUCTION ↘

200

Comparison-Contrast Essay

In the following essay, Ang looks at the similarities and differences between hybrid and fuel-cell cars.

Cars of Today—and Tomorrow

Beginning
The writer clearly identifies the topics and provides a thesis statement (underlined).

For many years, people have understood the main problem with the internal-combustion gasoline engine. This engine, which powers most American cars, burns gasoline for fuel, a process that releases many pollutants into the air. Today's carmakers have developed two similar—yet ultimately different—solutions to the car pollution problem. Hybrid and fuel-cell cars both battle pollution, but one is the car of today, and the other is the car of the future.

Middle
The first middle paragraph presents the major similarities.

Gasoline-electric hybrids and fuel-cell cars have a number of structural and operational similarities. Both vehicles look and handle like regular cars. They come equipped with the features common to all automobiles—tires, steering wheels, brakes and signals, safety features like air bags and seat belts, and even optional features like air conditioning and CD players. To the people who drive them, both hybrid and fuel-cell vehicles seem like regular cars.

The second middle paragraph details one major difference.

Look under the hood, however, and the differences between the two cars begin to emerge. A hybrid car has two motors. The first is a standard internal-combustion motor that runs on gasoline. It drives the car at high speeds, during acceleration, or with heavy loads that require hauling power. The second motor is electric, powered by a battery, and it drives the car at low speeds, during stops and starts, and with light loads. The battery is charged using a system called regenerative braking—the force that slows the car also runs a generator that charges the battery ("How it Works"). In contrast, a fuel-cell car has an electric motor, too, but this single motor drives the car at all times. The fuel cell is powered by a chemical process that extracts electrons from hydrogen. The only emission from this process is water (Davidson 132).

Another major difference is explained.

The differences in the drive systems mean differences in the amount of emissions created by each. Both hybrid and fuel-cell cars pollute less than traditional gasoline engines, but the fuel-cell car is potentially cleaner. The

---

Differentiated Instruction: Struggling Learners

Have students identify words in the model essay that signal comparisons and contrasts. Explain that they will need to use these words in their essays.

✳ For a list of words used to compare and contrast, refer students to SE pages 623–624.

Differentiated Instruction: Advanced Learners

Encourage students to bring in examples of comparative writing they have found in their own reading, such as in specialty magazines or on informational Web sites. Have them analyze the presentation of ideas, organization, voice, and word choice in their selected articles.

Writing a Comparison-Contrast Essay **201**

hydrogen needed to run a fuel cell can be extracted from water using solar or wind power ("Fuel"). Fuel produced in this way would make a fuel-cell car pollution free. Hybrid cars, on the other hand, run on gasoline, so they always produce some pollution, no matter what. Still, the hybrids generally produce 30 to 50 percent fewer pollutants than gasoline engines do (Clark 17).

The most critical difference is explained.

Perhaps the most critical difference between the two car types is availability. Ten different hybrid models are on the market today, and buyers have purchased more than 200,000 of them (Clark 23). With current trends, as many as 780,000 may be purchased in 2012 ("Hybrids on the Rise"). Unfortunately, today's fuel-cell cars are mostly experimental and might not be available to consumers for years. One reason for this is that there are very few fueling stations that can dispense hydrogen. In order for fuel-cell cars to become popular, a network of fueling stations must be available (Davidson 135).

Ending
The ending summarizes the writer's thesis.

Hybrid and fuel-cell cars look alike and operate in similar ways, but the differences between the two are substantial. While the fuel-cell car offers the potential of pollution-free operation, mainstream production is still years away. Hybrids, on the other hand, offer both significant pollution reduction and current availability. These differences make hybrids the high-tech model for today, and fuel-cells the cars of the future.

Expository

Respond to the reading. Answer the following questions.

Focus and Coherence (1) How does the writer's first middle paragraph support or contribute to the main idea? (2) How does the concluding paragraph provide a meaningful summary of the essay?

Organization (3) How does the writer organize the presentation of similarities and differences?

Development of Ideas (4) What supporting details does the writer provide for the main similarities between hybrid and fuel-cell cars? (5) What supporting details does the writer provide for their differences? (6) What novel approach does the writer use?

Voice (7) Find a sentence that you think best expresses the author's unique voice. Explain your choice.

 Respond to the reading

Answers

Focus and Coherence 1. The first middle paragraph presents the similarities among fuel-cell, hybrid, and regular cars. **2.** The conclusion summarizes the major similarities and differences between fuel-cell and hybrid cars and states why these features support the thesis.

Organization 3. Similarities are described in the first middle paragraph; differences are addressed in the three paragraphs that follow.

Development of Ideas 4. They look like regular cars and operate the same way. **5.** Power source (fuel-cell cars use hydrogen-powered electricity but hybrids use both gas and electricity); number of engines (fuel-cell cars have one but hybrids have two); emissions (fuel-cell cars create no pollution but hybrids create less than half the pollution of conventional cars); stages of development (fuel-cell cars are experimental but hybrids are on the market) **6.** The author uses the differences between the two kinds of high-tech cars to show how one is an appropriate solution for today while the other is a solution for the future.

Voice 7. Possible response: *Look under the hood, however, . . .* in third paragraph 3; this phrase is informal and friendly; it shows knowledge and is inviting to the reader.

✔ **DIFFERENTIATE INSTRUCTION**

Prewriting Selecting the Topics

Explain that the reason for beginning by listing tasks and related technologies is to ensure that the topic pairs have a fundamental similarity.

Tasks and Technologies List

Remind students that they must consider both their audience's interest and their own knowledge and ideas in order to choose suitable topics for expository writing. Informational writing is most successful when both the writer and the audience are engaged in the subject matter. **DIFFERENTIATE INSTRUCTION ↘**

Select the topics. Students may need to add to their knowledge or do some additional information gathering before choosing their topics. See the Development of Ideas box below for suggestions.

 TEKS 11.13A

Focus on the Texas Traits

Development of Ideas

Distribute Venn diagrams (TE page A98) to help students decide whether potential topics have a good balance of similarities and differences. Have them do some basic research to gain a better sense of the details involved. If students cannot identify at least two strong similarities and two major differences, they should try a different topic.

 TEKS 11.13A

Prewriting Selecting the Topics

The purpose of your comparison-contrast essay is to take a closer look at two technologies and explain their similarities and differences. To find topics for his essay, Ang made a list of tasks and related technologies.

Tasks and Technologies List

Tasks	One Technology	Another Technology
send messages	e-mail	telephone
travel on land	gas-electric hybrid car*	fuel-cell car*
travel in the air	propeller-driven plane	jet plane
play music	DVD player	MP3 player
cook food	microwave oven	gas oven

At first, Ang thought he might write a comparison-contrast essay about microwave and gas ovens. He then thought about his readers and decided they might be more interested in the similarities and differences between hybrid and fuel-cell automobiles. He chose automobiles as his topics.

 Prewrite

Select the topics. Make a three-column chart. In the first column, list tasks that can be performed using technology. In the other columns, list technologies for accomplishing the tasks. Consider your own interests and those of your audience before choosing your topics.

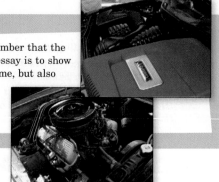

Hybrid engine

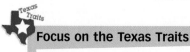 **Focus on the Texas Traits**

Development of Ideas Remember that the goal of a comparison-contrast essay is to show not only how things are the same, but also how they are different. Make sure your paragraphs have a balance of similarities and differences.

Gasoline engine

Differentiated Instruction: Struggling Learners

Give students ample time to find sources and take notes. Remind them that *paraphrasing* means writing research information in one's own words. When taking notes, students should paraphrase or jot down information in incomplete sentences to ensure that they will use their own words when writing their essays.

 TEKS 11.13A Plan a first draft by selecting the correct genre for conveying the intended meaning to multiple audiences and determining appropriate topics through a range of strategies

Gathering and Organizing Details

After you choose two topics for your comparison-contrast essay, you need to gather and organize details about them. Ang did this with a T-chart.

T-Chart

Hybrid Car	Fuel-Cell Car
– Operates and has features like a regular gas car	– Operates and has features like a regular gas car
– Has two motors; one is gas powered and the other runs on batteries that recharge by braking	– Has one motor powered by an electric fuel cell that uses hydrogen
– 30 to 50 percent cleaner than gas engine	– Potential to be 100 percent pollution free
– Available today; more than 200,000 on the road	– May take years before widely available

Prewrite

Gather your details. Make your own T-chart. On each side, list characteristics of one of the technologies you will write about.

Writing a Thesis Statement

A thesis statement states the main idea of your essay. For a comparison-contrast essay, the thesis statement should name the two topics and sum up the comparison and contrast. Ang used this formula to develop his thesis statement.

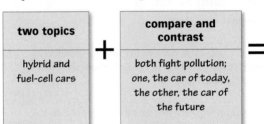

two topics		compare and contrast		thesis statement
hybrid and fuel-cell cars	**+**	both fight pollution; one, the car of today, the other, the car of the future	**=**	Hybrid and fuel-cell cars both battle pollution, but one is the car of today, and the other is the car of the future.

Prewrite

Write your thesis statement. Name the two technologies and sum up the comparison and contrast between them. Try two or three versions of your thesis statement until you are satisfied with it.

Expository

Gathering and Organizing Details

Ask students to name the types of details from outside sources that an effective informative essay includes (facts, statistics, examples, quotations, and, if appropriate, anecdotes). Then have them analyze the T-chart Ang made.

T-Chart

Point out that Ang's T-chart lists only basic facts, but the writer also collected the specific details used in the sample on SE pages 200–201. For their research, encourage students to

- use books and periodicals, as well as the Internet;
- evaluate sources to be sure they are reliable;
- use note cards to collect specific details; and
- always keep full, accurate bibliographic information on all sources consulted.

✻ For more about research skills, see SE pages 375–384.

Gather your details. Students may benefit from sharing their charts for reactions and feedback.

⏎ DIFFERENTIATE INSTRUCTION

Writing a Thesis Statement

If students have trouble getting started, suggest that they use the same sentence structure as in the writing model (*Topic 1 and topic 2 both . . . but . . .*), and then revise the sentence to make it their own.

Write your thesis statement. Encourage students to try out a few versions of their thesis statements with a partner or small group.

TEKS 11.13A, 11.15(v)

✻ Have students refer to SE page 620 for more information on thesis statements.

Differentiated Instruction:
English Language Learners   ELPS 1C, 4D

ELP Level **Beginning**	ELP Level **Intermediate**	ELP Level **Advanced/Advanced High**
Use visuals and gestures to explain vocabulary in the list. Have students repeat terms with you as you model completing a basic Venn diagram about each idea.	Use visuals and gestures to explain the ideas in Ang's list as you work together to complete a basic Venn diagram about each idea.	Have partners use basic and grade-level vocabulary to complete a Venn diagram that shows how two technologies in Ang's list are alike and different.

TEKS **11.13A** Plan a first draft by selecting the correct genre for conveying the intended meaning to multiple audiences, determining appropriate topics through a range of strategies, and developing a thesis or controlling idea; **11.15A(v)** Write an analytical essay of sufficient length that includes relevant and substantial evidence and well-chosen details ELPS **1C** Use strategic learning strategies to acquire basic and grade-level vocabulary; **4D** Use prereading supports to enhance comprehension of written text

Drafting Creating Your First Draft

Before students begin drafting, suggest that they use their prewriting notes to create an outline. Point out that their outline can be either a sentence outline or a topic outline. Refer students to SE pages 168 and 619 if they need to review the two types. **DIFFERENTIATE INSTRUCTION ⬊**

Writing Your Beginning Paragraph

Remind students that a beginning paragraph introduces the topic in an interesting way and states the thesis. A brief description of the topic and a few explanatory details should lead directly to a strong thesis statement.
DIFFERENTIATE INSTRUCTION ⬊

Creating Your Middle Paragraphs

The middle paragraphs support the thesis with clear similarities and differences organized in a compare-contrast structure. Suggest that students share their ideas to get feedback about which ideas are the most compelling.

Finishing with a Strong Ending Paragraph

The ending paragraph returns to the thesis, connecting it to the information presented.

Write your first draft. Before students begin, tell them to read the page carefully and to keep the tips in mind as they write.
TEKS 11.13B, 11.15A(i)

✱ For more about the basic parts of an essay, see SE page 618.

Writing Workshop

The guidelines on this page can provide scaffolding for students during individual writing time. You can also use each section of this page (beginning, middle, and ending) for small-group minilessons.

Drafting Creating Your First Draft

The following tips will help you to write your comparison-contrast essay. Use your prewriting as a guide.

Writing Your Beginning Paragraph

The **beginning** paragraph should include a clear thesis statement.

■ **Present your thesis statement.**
Hybrid and fuel-cell cars both battle pollution, but one is the car of today, and the other is the car of the future.

Creating Your Middle Paragraphs

The **middle** paragraphs explain how your topics are similar and different.

■ **Start each paragraph with a topic sentence that indicates the similarity or difference that will be addressed.**
Gasoline-electric hybrids and fuel-cell cars have a number of structural and operational similarities.

■ **Include examples to support each topic sentence.**
They come equipped with the features common to all automobiles—tires, steering wheels, brakes and signals, safety features like air bags and seat belts, . . .

■ **Vary your sentence structure.**
Look under the hood, however, and the differences between the two cars begin to emerge. A hybrid car has two motors.

Finishing with a Strong Ending Paragraph

The **ending** paragraph restates your thesis.

■ **Take a final look.**
While the fuel-cell car offers the potential of pollution-free operation, mainstream production is still years away. Hybrids, on the other hand, offer both significant pollution reduction and current availability.

■ **Restate your thesis.**
These differences make hybrids the high-tech model for today, and fuel-cells the cars of the future.

Draft

Write your first draft. Use the guidelines above, your prewriting work, and the sample essay to help you write a first draft of your comparison-contrast essay.

Differentiated Instruction: Struggling Learners

Remind students that a *thesis statement* states the purpose of the essay and directs every detail. Tell students that their thesis statements should answer these questions:

• What is my point or purpose for writing this essay?
• What details do my readers need to understand my message?

TEKS **11.13B** Structure ideas in a sustained and persuasive way; **11.15A(i)** Write an analytical essay of sufficient length that includes effective introductory and concluding paragraphs

Revising Improving Your First Draft

As you revise, use the checklist below to polish your first draft.

Revising Checklist

Focus and Coherence

_____ **1.** Is my writing focused on the prompt or assignment?

_____ **2.** Do I have a clearly stated thesis statement, or main idea, that names the topics and sums up the comparison and contrast?

_____ **3.** Are all my ideas clearly connected to each other?

_____ **4.** Have I included a strong introduction and conclusion?

Organization

_____ **5.** Does my essay have a strong beginning, middle, and ending?

_____ **6.** Have I presented my points in a logical order?

_____ **7.** Have I used transitional words and phrases effectively?

Development of Ideas

_____ **8.** Have I included specific supporting details?

_____ **9.** Have I approached my topic from a unique perspective?

Voice

_____ **10.** Have I engaged my readers throughout my essay?

_____ **11.** Is my voice confident and convincing?

_____ **12.** Is my writing authentic and original?

Revise your first draft. Read your essay carefully. Then use the checklist above to help you revise your first draft.

Creating a Title

- Draw on your thesis: **Cars of Today—and Tomorrow**
- Ask a question: **Can Hybrids and Fuel Cells Save Earth?**
- Appeal to your reader's interest: **Your Future Car**

Expository

Revising Improving Your First Draft

Have students set their drafts aside for a day or two before revising them.

Revising Checklist

Suggest that students check their entire response for one trait at a time. Once students have completed their revisions, discuss their thoughts on taking a break before revising.

- Did taking a break help them approach their draft with fresh eyes?
- Ask students if taking a break helped them resolve any specific problems they had during the writing stage.

Most students should agree that taking a break helped. Encourage students to do this whenever possible for future writing projects.

Revise your first draft. After their own review, suggest that students exchange drafts with a partner to get feedback and the benefit of another point of view.

TEKS 11.13C **ELPS** 1B

Creating a Title

Have students read the possible titles and discuss which ones they think work best and why. Encourage students to come up with two or three title ideas for their own essays as well.

★ Conventions Connections

Grammar: Parallel Structure
- *SkillsBook* page 170

✦ *Write Source Online* **GrammarSnap**

Grammar: Sentence Combining
- *Student Edition: Proofreader's Guide* pages 764–766
- *SkillsBook* page 156

Differentiated Instruction: English Language Learners

ELPS 1E, 5B, 5F, 5G

ELP Level **Beginning**	ELP Level **Intermediate**	ELP Level **Advanced/Advanced High**
Focus on guiding students to draft their beginning paragraphs. Provide sentence stems to help them form a clear thesis statement.	Focus on guiding students to draft the middle paragraphs. Present sentence frames that include basic vocabulary such as comparison/contrast signal words and transitions.	After students draft a middle paragraph, have them share their work with a partner to discuss and strengthen their use of specific details and variety of sentence structures.

TEKS 11.13C Revise drafts to clarify meaning; **ELPS** 1B Monitor written language production and employ self-corrective techniques or other resources; **1E** Internalize new basic and academic language by using and reusing it/writing; **5B** Write using newly acquired basic and content-based grade-level vocabulary; **5F** Write using a variety of grade-appropriate sentence lengths, patterns, and connecting words; **5G** Explain with increasing specificity and detail

Editing Checking for Conventions

Editing Checklist

Suggest that students address each question by checking their entire response before moving on to the next question.

Edit your essay. Suggest that students proofread their final copy as follows:

- Set the revised draft and final copy side by side, placing the final copy on their writing-hand side, so that it's easier to mark any errors.
- Compare the two versions word for word.
- Check the parts that weren't changed during revising. They may find an error that they overlooked, or they may find problems that slipped in when they made corrections.
- Focus only on the conventions at this point, not substantive changes in the content.

 **TEKS** 11.13D **DIFFERENTIATE INSTRUCTION** ↘

Publishing **Sharing Your Work**

Publish your essay. You may wish to suggest that students adapt their essays as multimedia presentations to share with classmates.

 TEKS 11.13E

✳ For more about multimedia presentations, see SE pages 464–467.

Conventions Connections

Grammar: Subject-Verb Agreement
- ***Student Edition: Proofreader's Guide*** pages 756–757, 758–759, 770(+)
- ***SkillsBook*** page 148

 *Write Source Online* **GrammarSnap**

Punctuation: Semicolons, Colons
- ***Student Edition: Proofreader's Guide*** pages 648–649, 650–651
- ***SkillsBook*** pages 19–20

Capitalization
- ***Student Edition: Proofreader's Guide*** pages 674 (+), 676 (+), 678 (+)
- ***SkillsBook*** page 45

 TEKS **11.13D** Edit drafts for grammar, mechanics, and spelling; **11.13E** Revise final draft in response to feedback from peers and teacher and publish written work for appropriate audiences; **ELPS 5A** Learn relationships between sounds and letters to represent sounds when writing in English; **5C** Spell familiar English words with increasing accuracy, and employ English spelling patterns and rules with increasing accuracy

---

 TEKS 11.13D, 11.13E

 Editing Checking for Conventions

After revising your essay, you can use the following checklist to edit your writing for grammar, sentence structure, mechanics, and spelling errors.

Editing Checklist

Conventions

GRAMMAR
_____ 1. Do my subjects and verbs agree in number?
_____ 2. Do my pronouns agree with their antecedents?

SENTENCE STRUCTURE
_____ 3. Do I use a variety of correctly structured sentences?

MECHANICS (CAPITALIZATION AND PUNCTUATION)
_____ 4. Have I ended my sentences with the correct punctuation?
_____ 5. Have I used commas, semicolons, and colons correctly?
_____ 6. Have I punctuated quotations correctly?
_____ 7. Do I capitalize the first word in every sentence?
_____ 8. Do I capitalize all proper nouns and adjectives?

SPELLING
_____ 9. Do I spell all my words correctly?
_____ 10. Have I double-checked for easily confused words that my spell-checker would miss?

 Edit your essay. Use the checklist above to edit for conventions. Ask a partner to help you review your essay, too. Then prepare a final copy and proofread it.

Publishing **Sharing Your Work**

You can share your comparison-contrast essay by having your teacher read it, by reading it aloud in the classroom, or by posting it on a bulletin board. If you present your essay, consider taking questions from your audience as a follow-up.

 Publish your essay. Give your writing to your teacher, to classmates, or to family members to read. Also, consider presenting it as a speech, posting it on a bulletin board, or uploading it to a Web site.

Differentiated Instruction:
English Language Learners   **ELPS** 5A, 5C

Turn to the Appendix of the Teacher's Edition for information on language transfer issues with grammar, usage, and mechanics.

ELP Level **Beginning**	ELP Level **Intermediate**	ELP Level **Advanced/Advanced High**
Pair students with an English-proficient peer to check for spelling. Have students speak and write to explore relationships between sounds and letters.	Pair students with an English-proficient peer to check spelling. Have them note spelling patterns and rules that help them spell with greater accuracy.	Have partners use spelling patterns and rules to check each other's work for spelling. Have them consult a dictionary to confirm correct spellings.

Writing for Assessment
Responding to Expository Prompts

In expository writing, you share your knowledge about a topic by explaining or informing your reader about it. Depending upon the topic and approach you've chosen for your essay, you might summarize, illustrate, analyze, classify, or compare. Sometimes, you'll be given days to complete an expository essay. Other times, you'll be given minutes to respond to an expository prompt. In such a situation, you'll need to quickly plan, draft, revise, and proofread your writing.

Many high school exit exams and college entrance exams include timed-writing components. This chapter will show you how to respond to an expository prompt with a well-organized, powerful essay within minutes—your ticket out of high school or into college.

Writing Guidelines

Subject: Expository prompt
Purpose: To demonstrate competence
Form: Response essay
Audience: Instructor

"If you can't explain it simply, you don't understand it well enough."

—Albert Einstein

Objectives

- demonstrate an understanding of the elements of an expository prompt
- practice analyzing an expository prompt, and then plan, write, revise, and edit the response
- practice writing for assessment

Assure students that when they write expository essays for assessment, they won't be asked to explain topics for which they haven't had the chance to prepare.

- Some essays, such as the response on SE page 208, do not require outside study.
- For others, students will have been told what to study in advance of the test.
- Still other assessments, such as document-based essays, provide all the background information that is needed.

✳ For more about document-based essays, see SE pages 494–504.

Resources

Copy Masters

- Quick list (TE p. 209)
- Time line (TE p. 209)
- T-chart (TE p. 209))
- Venn diagram (TE p. 209)

Prewriting Analyzing an Expository Prompt

Analyze the sample prompt with students. Point out that some prompts may not include answers to every STRAP question. Students should approach an incomplete prompt as follows:

- Do *not* skip any STRAP questions. An effective essay addresses all five STRAP items.
- Plan answers to "missing" questions that make sense in the context of the prompt.

Explain that answering all five questions every time makes it less likely that students will overlook or misinterpret part of the prompt.

DIFFERENTIATE INSTRUCTION ↘

Point out that **role** and **audience** are the questions most likely to be left up to the writer. Role and audience affect the voice of a response, so it is important to answer these questions even if the prompt does not specify them.

Ask students to do the **Try It!** activity on their own and then compare their answers.

Try It!
Answers

1. **Subject:** freedom of expression; **Type:** essay; **Role:** citizen or student; **Audience:** teacher; **Purpose:** explain
2. **Subject:** two modes of transportation; **Type:** essay; **Role:** traveler; **Audience:** fellow travelers; **Purpose:** compare and contrast

DIFFERENTIATE INSTRUCTION ↘

Reinforce students' familiarity with the STRAP strategy, using these tips:

- Display the STRAP questions on a poster or chart in a readily visible place in the room.
- Have students write the strategy in their notebooks.

208

Prewriting Analyzing an Expository Prompt

In order to respond effectively to an expository prompt, you need to read and analyze the prompt. To analyze a prompt effectively, use the **STRAP questions:**

Subject: What topic should I write about?

Type: What form of writing should I create (essay, letter, editorial, article, report)?

Role: What role should I assume as the writer (student, son or daughter, friend, employee, citizen)?

Audience: Who am I writing to (teacher, parents, classmates, employer, official)?

Purpose: What is the goal of my writing (inform, summarize, illustrate, analyze, classify, compare)?

Subject
Type
Role
Audience
Purpose

Holiday celebrations are important in most families. Yet each family has its own traditions that make the celebration of a holiday unique. Choose a holiday that your family celebrates. *As a member of your family,* write an <u>article</u> informing your classmates about the family traditions that make your celebration of that holiday unique.

Try It!

Analyze these prompts by answering the STRAP questions. (Some answers may be implied or left open. Use your best judgment.)

1. The First Amendment to the Constitution guarantees freedom of expression. The framers of the Constitution believed this freedom essential to a strong democracy. Write an essay that explains how freedom of expression contributes to democracy.
2. People travel by many different means, each with advantages and disadvantages. Choose two of the following modes of transportation and write an essay comparing and contrasting them: walking, bicycling, driving a car, taking a train, flying, and sailing by ship.

Differentiated Instruction: Struggling Learners

Provide practice for analyzing prompts in which students need to infer STRAP components. Use this sample prompt: *What steps can your community take to make people more aware of—and responsible for—their impact on the environment?* Discuss which STRAP questions can be answered from the prompt and which need to inferred.

Differentiated Instruction: Advanced Learners

Some students will want to dive into the writing process without a clear plan. Remind them that in a standardized test, they will be judged, in part, on the organization of their essay. Emphasize the importance of using prewriting time to create a thesis statement and an outline or other organizer.

Planning Your Response

Provide photocopies of the reproducible time line, T-chart, Venn diagram, and quick list (TE pages A95, A97, A98, A101) for students to consult as they organize their responses. Remind them, however, that in a test situation they will not have access to photocopies of graphic organizers.

Encourage students to try out different graphic organizers as they complete regular class writing assignments. This will help them decide which ones to use with different forms of writing. Once they are familiar with the organizers they use most, they will quickly be able to reproduce these organizers when they take a test.

✔ DIFFERENTIATE INSTRUCTION

Use a graphic organizer. Give students about five minutes to complete planning and organizing their response. Announce the halfway point to help students estimate their time.

⭐ TEKS 11.13A

Tip

Draw students' attention to the suggested time-management plan in the tip. Suggest that as they practice timed writing, they may need to adjust these times to accommodate their own style of working.

Planning Your Response

After answering the STRAP questions, you need to begin planning your expository response. Graphic organizers are wonderful tools for planning and organizing an effective response.

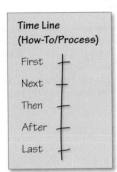

Quick List (Any Essay)
1. First Point
   —Detail 1
   —Detail 2
2. Second Point
   —Detail 1
   —Detail 2
3. Third Point
   —Detail 1
   —Detail 2

Time Line (How-To/Process)
First
Next
Then
After
Last

T-Chart (Two-Part Essay)
Topic:
Part A	Part B
*	*
*	*
*	*
*	*

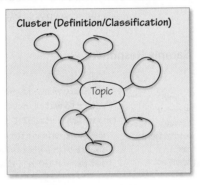

Venn Diagram (Compare-Contrast)
Topic A   Topic B
Similarities
Differences

Cluster (Definition/Classification)
Topic

Prewrite

Use a graphic organizer. Reread the expository prompts on page **208**. Choose one prompt, and then use a graphic organizer to plan and organize your response. Keep the STRAP questions in mind as you work.

Tip

Be sure to manage your time carefully. For example, if you have 45 minutes to respond to a prompt, use the first 5 minutes to analyze the prompt and plan your response, the last 5 minutes to revise and edit your response, and the 35 minutes in between for writing your response.

Differentiated Instruction: English Language Learners   **⭐ ELPS** 1C, 1H, 2C

Explain unfamiliar terms and concepts related to the Constitution of the United States.

ELP Level **Beginning**	ELP Level **Intermediate**	ELP Level **Advanced/Advanced High**
Have students repeat basic and academic words and phrases as you model using the STRAP strategy to analyze the prompts.	Work together to analyze the prompts. Have students answer yes/no questions and use sentence stems to apply the STRAP strategy.	Have partners work together to apply the STRAP strategy to analyze the prompts and write their responses. Discuss their responses in a larger group.

 TEKS 11.13A Plan a first draft by selecting the correct genre for conveying the intended meaning to multiple audiences and determining appropriate topics through a range of strategies
ELPS 1C Use strategic learning strategies to acquire basic and grade-level vocabulary; **1H** Develop and expand repertoire of learning strategies; **2C** Learn new expressions and basic and academic vocabulary

Expository

Drafting Responding to a Prompt

Discuss with students how the prompt relates to the sample essay.

Sample Expository Prompt

Consider having small groups of students analyze the sample prompt together, using the STRAP strategy. Provide a time limit and a reminder of the limit when about half of the time has elapsed.

Try It!
Answers

Subject: two ways of watching movies;
Type: brief essay; **Role**: moviegoer;
Audience: fellow moviegoers;
Purpose: compare and contrast

Sample Response

Have students compare their STRAP answers together. Then ask them to analyze the response to see how well it develops each aspect of the prompt. As needed, provide these observations.

- Note that the writer echoes selected phrases from the prompt in the beginning paragraph of the essay (*millions of Americans, advantages and disadvantages*) so that the response is closely tied to the question.
- More specifically, note that the writer adapts the phrase *advantages and disadvantages* so that it appears in both the thesis statement and the first line of the ending paragraph.

Encourage students to look for phrases in prompts that they can use as stepping stones at the beginning of their own essays. These will demonstrate their close reading of the test question and help them to get started.

★ **TEKS** 11.13B, 11.15A(i), 11.15A(ii)

★ **TEKS** 11.13B, 11.15A(i), 11.15A(ii)

Drafting Responding to a Prompt

Once you have answered the STRAP questions and planned your response using a graphic organizer, you can begin writing.

Sample Expository Prompt

Millions of Americans enjoy movies. Today's technology offers people the option of viewing movies in the theater or watching them at home on DVD. Both of these viewing choices have advantages and disadvantages. Write a brief essay comparing and contrasting the experience of watching a movie at home on DVD and watching it in a theater.

Try It!

Answer the STRAP questions for the sample expository prompt above.

Sample Response

Beginning
The beginning paragraph gives the thesis statement (underlined).

Every weekend, millions of Americans travel to their local theater to watch movies, and millions of others stay at home and watch rented DVD's. Some viewers wouldn't trade the movie theater experience for anything. Others wouldn't give up the pleasure of enjoying a film in the comfort of their own home. For most people, though, the choice isn't as clear. <u>While the movie and "home theater" experiences are similar, each offers unique advantages and disadvantages.</u>

Movie theaters and home theaters have a lot in common. Both offer the opportunity to watch a range of current films. Both also offer comfortable settings, a range of snacking options, and the chance to share quality time with family members or friends. With advances in video and audio technology, a home theater can deliver both picture and sound that rival those at a movie theater. Yet the differences between the two viewing options are significant.

★ **TEKS** **11.13B** Structure ideas in a sustained and persuasive way and develop drafts in timed and open-ended situations that include transitions and the rhetorical devices used to convey meaning; **11.15A(i)** Write an analytical essay of sufficient length that includes effective introductory and concluding paragraphs and a variety of sentence structures; **11.15A(ii)** Write an analytical essay of sufficient length that includes rhetorical devices and transitions between paragraphs

One major difference between watching a movie in a theater and watching one at home is comfort. While newer movie theaters offer more comfortable seats, many home cinema fans argue that nothing beats the opportunity to curl up on the sofa in one's home. In addition, while the movie theater offers a range of snacks, they are usually limited to sweets, popcorn, and soda. At home, it's possible to watch a movie while enjoying healthful snacks like fruit, or even a full meal.

Middle
Each middle paragraph supports and explains the thesis.

Cost is another major difference between going to a movie theater and watching a movie at home. Movie tickets for a family of four can cost $40 or more, and that's before the expense of concession-stand snacks, which can easily add another $25. In contrast, a current-run DVD can be rented for about $5. And snacking at home is a lot cheaper than eating at the movie theater. So the total cost of the home-theater experience is usually much less—provided, of course, that the viewer returns the video on time, thus avoiding late fees.

So far, it may sound like home theater is a hands-down winner, yet one main difference remains—the opportunity to see a film on the first run. Many movie buffs don't want to wait for the film to come out on DVD—they want to see it as soon as possible. They also want to see the movie with an eager crowd. Theaters make movies into events.

Ending
The ending sums up the comparison and contrast.

The similarities and differences between watching a movie in a theater and watching one at home provide choices for everyone. Most people who prefer the movie-theater experience probably rent DVD's on occasion. And most people who prefer renting movies will occasionally find their way to the movie theater. Diehard film fans, however, continue to flock to the movie theaters.

Expository

Draft

Respond to an expository prompt. Review the prompt you chose on page 208. Then use your answers to the STRAP questions and your graphic organizer to write a response within the time limit set by your teacher.

Discuss how the first four writing traits apply to the sample (there are no errors in conventions). Ask students to tell which STRAP question relates to each comment. Possible responses:

Focus and Coherence
- The writer addresses the topics specified. (Subject)
- The essay focuses on the thesis, with no deviation. The central, controlling idea is clear and sustained throughout the essay.

Organization
- The writer compares and contrasts the topics in sentences that flow smoothly (for example, in paragraph 1: *Some viewers . . . Others . . . For most people, though.*) (Purpose)
- The first middle paragraph compares; the next three paragraphs contrast. The ending sums up the beginning and provides a final interesting idea.

Development of Ideas
- A good number of details are provided to support the subject.
- Experiences are compared and contrasted based on the same aspects—comfort, snacks, quality of viewing, cost.
- The vocabulary is suitable for the topic and uses many comparing and contrasting words.

Voice
- The voice is that of someone who enjoys movies, addressing someone who has a general familiarity with movies. (Role and Audience)

Respond to an expository prompt. Guide students as they write by reminding them of the elapsed time based on the time limit you have established. ✔ DIFFERENTIATE INSTRUCTION
★ TEKS 11.13B

Differentiated Instruction:
English Language Learners

⚞ ELPS 1E, 5G

ELP Level **Beginning**	ELP Level **Intermediate**	ELP Level **Advanced/Advanced High**
Have students write their own copy as you work together to write a response to the prompt. Ask yes/no questions to confirm and generate ideas and details.	Have partners use their graphic organizers to compare and discuss ideas and details. Then have them work together to write a response to the prompt.	Have partners discuss their graphic organizers to review their ideas and details. Then have students work independently to write a response to the prompt.

TEKS 11.13B Structure ideas in a sustained way and develop drafts in timed situations that include transitions and the rhetorical devices used to convey meaning; **ELPS 1E** Internalize new basic and academic language by using and reusing it/ writing; **5G** Explain with increasing specificity and detail

Revising
Improving Your Response

Remind students that by using the STRAP questions both to analyze a prompt and to review the written essay, they ensure that their work is on target. A well-written essay that is off topic or that does not accomplish the purpose will not score highly.

If students discover a deficiency, they should devise a quick solution. For example, the prompt on page 210 says, "Both of these viewing choices have advantages and disadvantages." If the student had not addressed disadvantages, adding a paragraph to focus on this part of the prompt could result in a higher score on the assessment.

Revise your work. Tell students that if they focus on developing their ideas and organization during prewriting and drafting, then they can devote their revising time to improving focus and coherence and voice.

⭐ **TEKS** 11.13C

Editing Checking Your Response

Remind students that the more familiar they become with the conventions, the more likely they are to get them right the first time around. For example, as students check their spelling, help them recognize patterns and rules that will help them improve their accuracy.

⭐ **TEKS** 11.13D **ELPS** 5C

Editing Checklist

Review subject-verb agreement with students, using examples that show some common errors. Then suggest that students address each checklist question by checking their entire response before moving on to the next question.

⭐ **TEKS** 11.13D **ELPS** 5D

Check your conventions. Tell students to watch for the types of errors that they often find in their writing.

⭐ **TEKS** **11.13C** Revise drafts to clarify meaning; **11.13D** Edit drafts for grammar, mechanics, and spelling; **ELPS 5C** Spell familiar English words and employ English spelling patterns and rules with increasing accuracy; **5D** Edit writing for standard grammar and usage/subject-verb agreement

---

212

⭐ **TEKS** 11.13C, 11.13D

Revising Improving Your Response

Before you begin a writing test, find out whether you will be allowed to make revisions to your response or not. If changes are allowed, make them as neatly as possible. Use the **STRAP questions** to guide your revisions.

> **S**ubject: Have I developed ideas to respond to the topic of the prompt? Do my main points support my thesis?
>
> **T**ype: Have I responded in the correct form (essay, letter, article)?
>
> **R**ole: Have I assumed the role called for in the prompt?
>
> **A**udience: Have I used appropriate language and voice for my audience?
>
> **P**urpose: Does my response accomplish the goal outlined by the prompt?

Revise your work. Read your response carefully. Use the STRAP questions above as your guide to revise your response within the allotted time period.

Editing Checking Your Response

Be sure to check your expository response and correct any errors in grammar, sentence structure, capitalization, punctuation, and spelling.

Editing Checklist

Conventions

_____ 1. Have I made sure my subjects and verbs agree?

_____ 2. Have I capitalized all proper nouns and the first word of every sentence?

_____ 3. Have I used end punctuation for every sentence?

_____ 4. Have I spelled all words correctly?

_____ 5. Have I used the right words (*their, they're, there*)?

Check your conventions. Review your response for any errors in grammar sentence structure, capitalization, punctuation, and spelling. Make neat corrections within the allotted time.

Differentiated Instruction: Advanced Learners

For more practice, encourage students to locate copies of writing tests or SATs from past years at the school or local library. Ask students to copy two or three challenging writing prompts and bring them to class. Then have small groups share the prompts and discuss strategies to answer them in a timed setting.

Expository Writing on Tests

Use the following tips when you respond to an expository writing prompt.

Before you write . . .

- **Analyze the prompt.**
  Use the STRAP questions. Remember that an expository prompt asks you to explain or inform.
- **Budget your time carefully.**
  Be sure to spend several minutes planning and organizing your response before beginning to write. Use a graphic organizer to gather details and organize your response.

As you write . . .

- **Provide a clear thesis statement in your opening paragraph.**
  Keep your main idea and purpose in mind.
- **Include examples.**
  Choose examples that support and clarify your focus.
- **End by restating your thesis.**
  In the final paragraph, summarize your explanation.

After you've written a first draft . . .

- **Revise and edit.**
  Use the STRAP questions to guide your revision.
- **Check conventions.**
  Check your grammar, sentence structure, capitalization, punctuation, and spelling.

Learning Language

When you are trying to remember things, especially when you have a limited amount of time, it often helps to take notes. On your own paper, write notes that will help you remember these tips for expository writing on tests. Your notes are for you, so put them in words that you will easily understand when you reread them.

Work with a partner. Read your notes and explain to your partner how these notes will help you to remember the tips.

Expository

Expository Writing on Tests

Point out that students must approach writing-on-demand assignments differently from open-ended writing assignments. To provide practice, allow students the same amount of time to write their response essay as they will be allotted on school, district, or state assessments.

Start the assignment at the top of the hour or at the half-hour to make it easier for students to keep track of the time. Announce when time is up for each section. ✔ **DIFFERENTIATE INSTRUCTION**

Before you write...

Tell students that you will break down each part of the process into chunks of time. You might give students 5–10 minutes for note taking and planning, 25–30 minutes for drafting, and 5 minutes for revising, editing, and proofreading.

As you write...

Tell students that they will have about 25–30 minutes for drafting. If your state, district, or school requires students to use and submit a graphic organizer as part of their assessment, refer students to SE pages 612–615.

After you've written a first draft...

Tell students that they will have about 5 minutes for revising, editing, and proofreading.

Learning Language

Tell student partners to quiz one another about any unfamiliar terms, making sure that they address terms such as *analyze* and *time limit*. Then have them write their own notes about the terms and use them to explain the steps they would follow during a timed-writing assignment.

ELPS 1C, 1E, 4F, 4G ✔ **DIFFERENTIATE INSTRUCTION**

Differentiated Instruction: **English Language Learners**		⭐ **ELPS** 2I, 3B, 3D, 3F, 3H, 3J

Turn to the Appendix of the Teacher's Edition for information on language transfer issues with grammar, usage, and mechanics.

ELP Level **Beginning**	ELP Level **Intermediate**	ELP Level **Advanced/Advanced High**
Provide sentence stems that include academic language as you guide students to write their notes. Then have students take turns reading their notes aloud.	Provide sentence stems that include academic language to help students write their notes. Ask questions as partners explain and discuss their notes.	Have students work independently to write their notes. Then have students use complete sentences to explain their notes to a partner.

⭐ **ELPS 1C** Use strategic learning strategies to acquire basic and grade-level vocabulary; **1E** Internalize new academic language by using and reusing it/writing; **2I** Demonstrate listening comprehension/collaborating with peers, taking notes; **3B** Expand vocabulary/retelling simple stories and basic information; **3D** Speak using grade-level content area vocabulary in context/new English words, academic vocabulary; **3F** Give information during speaking assignments; **3H** Explain with increasing specificity and detail; **3J** Respond orally to information presented/concept and language attainment; **4F** Use support from peers and teachers to read content area text, to enhance and confirm understanding, and to develop vocabulary; **4G** Demonstrate comprehension of increasingly complex English/taking notes

Persuasive Writing

Argumentative Paragraph (pages 215–217)

Students learn to state their opinion of a controversy in a concise and organized way.

Argumentative Essay (pages 218–256)

Through the creation of an argumentative essay, students explore a political topic and convince others to adopt their viewpoint.

Writing an Editorial (pages 257–264)

Students learn to create an effective editorial using their own unique perspective and voice.

Writing for Assessment

(pages 265–271)

Using the STRAP questions as a guide, students respond to a timed-writing prompt.

Literature Connections

- **"Martin Luther King, Jr.: He Showed Us the Way"** by César Chávez

Technology Connections

 Write Source Online
www.hmheducation.com/tx/writesource

- **Net-text**
- **Writing Network**
- **Portfolio**
- **GrammarSnap**
- **Essay Scoring**
- **File Cabinet**

Interactive Whiteboard Lessons

Persuasive Writing Unit Scope and Sequence

		Write Source Student Edition					
Day	Writing and Conventions Instruction	Core Unit	Tools of Language	Resource Units	Daily Language Workouts	Skills-Book	Write Source Online
1–2	**Argumentative Paragraph** Model	215–217	**TL** 580–585	**BEW** 611	42–45		Interactive Whiteboard Lesson
	Skills Activities: • Shifts in Verb Tenses					176–178	GrammarSnap
3–5	**Argumentative Essay** Model, Prewriting ⏺ Literature Connection "Martin Luther King, Jr."	218–226		**BEW** 617–620			Net-text

 Resource Units referenced above are located in the back of the *Student Edition* and *Teacher's Edition*
TL *"The Tools of Language"* **BEW** *"Basic Elements of Writing"* **PG** *"Proofreader's Guide"*

Day	Writing and Conventions Instruction	Write Source Student Edition			Daily Language Workouts	Skills-Book	Write Source Online
		Core Unit	Tools of Language	Resource Units			
WEEK 2 6–7	Drafting	227–232	**TL** 580–585	**BEW** 621–631	46–49		Net-text
8–10	Revising	233–242					Net-text
	Skills Activities: •Sentence Types			**PG** 764–767		138–140	GrammarSnap
	•Adverbs			**PG** 750–751		109–113	
	•Adjectives			**PG** 638, 640, 748–749		8, 104–108	
WEEK 3 11–13	Editing, Publishing	243–249	**TL** 580–585	**BEW** 632–633	50–53		Net-text
	Skills Activities: •Using the Right Word			**PG** 702–721		61–66	
	•Numbers and Numerals			**PG** 684–685		47–48	
	•Parallel Structure					170–172	GrammarSnap
	•Commas/Nonrestrictive Phrases and Clauses			**PG** 642–643		14–15	GrammarSnap
	•Commas/Introductory Phrases and Clauses			**PG** 640–641, 644–645, 646		9–12, 129	GrammarSnap
14–15	Evaluating an Argumentative Essay	250–256					Net-text
WEEK 4 16–19	**Writing an Editorial** Model, Prewriting, Drafting	257–262	**TL** 580–585	**BEW** 617–631	54–57		Net-text
	Revising	263					Net-text
	Skills Activities: •Sentence Combining					155–158	
	Editing, Publishing	264		**BEW** 632–633			Net-text
	Skills Activities: •Tenses and Irregular Verbs			**PG** 738–739, 740–741		93–95, 100–101	GrammarSnap
	•Hyphens, Dashes			**PG** 652–655, 668–669		22–24	GrammarSnap
	•Plurals, Spelling			**PG** 680–683, 690, 692–694		53, 54, 55–60	
20	**Writing for Assessment**	265–271					

Resource Units referenced above are located in the back of the *Student Edition* and *Teacher's Edition*
TL *"The Tools of Language"*   **BEW** *"Basic Elements of Writing"*   **PG** *"Proofreader's Guide"*

Writing Focus

- Argumentative Essay
- Writing an Editorial
- Writing for the Texas Assessment

Grammar Focus

- Commonly Misused Words
- Numbers and Numerals

Learning Language

Read aloud the basic and academic terms, as well as the descriptions and questions. Model for students how to read one question and answer it. For example, *Sometimes* position *means the place where something is, as in the position of a star, but this meaning is different. It says that a position is an opinion or belief, and asks for my position on cell phone use in cars. My position is that cell phones should not be used by people who are driving.* Have partners monitor their understanding of the terms by working through the meanings and questions together.

DIFFERENTIATE INSTRUCTION ↘

ELPS 1F, 2C, 3E, 4G

Minilessons

Tall-Tale Defense   Argumentative Essay

- Have students **CHOOSE** an impossible position to defend. For example, *to end pollution, people should return to horse-and-buggy transportation.* Or, *to end war, no more guns or bombs should be produced.* Tell students to **WRITE** a defense of the position in tall-tale style.

I Object!   Responding to Persuasive Prompts

- Explain that in any argument, there are bound to be objections. Have students **BRAINSTORM** a list of as many objections to this stand as possible: *All cars should be banned from cities with a population over 250,000. People should only rely on public transportation.*

ELPS 1F Use accessible language and learn new and essential language in the process; **2A** Distinguish sounds of English; **2B** Recognize elements of the English sound system in newly acquired vocabulary; **2C** Learn new language structures, expressions, and basic and academic vocabulary; **3E** Share information in cooperative learning interactions; **4A** Learn relationships between sounds and letters of English and decode using a combination of skills; **4G** Demonstrate comprehension of increasingly complex English/responding to questions

www.hmheducation.com/tx/writesource

Persuasive Writing

Writing Focus

Grammar Focus

Learning Language

Work with a partner. Read the meanings and share answers to the questions.

1. An objection is a statement of doubt or disagreement.
   What is an objection to a longer school day?
2. A position is an opinion or belief.
   What is your position on cell phone use in cars?
3. Relevant ideas have a strong connection to a topic.
   Name some relevant topics for discussing music.
4. To take sides is to choose one view in a disagreement.
   When do you take sides in an argument between friends?

Differentiated Instruction:
English Language Learners   ⭐ **ELPS** 2A, 2B, 4A

ELP Level **Beginning**	ELP Level **Intermediate**	ELP Level **Advanced/Advanced High**
Have students repeat the words after you pronounce them. Point out the *-ion* ending and the schwa sound that *objection* and *position* share.	Practice saying the words together. Point out the *-ion* and the schwa sound in *objection* and *position*, and compare this sound to the same letters in the familiar word *question*.	Point out the *-ion* and the schwa sound in *objection* and *position*, and compare it to *question*. Have students name other words that end in *-ion* and compare their sounds.

Persuasive Writing
Argumentative Essay

Political controversies force people to take sides. For example, you may favor legislation aimed at curbing global warming, or you may oppose the rising cost of higher education. Whatever position you take, someone else will take the opposite viewpoint. In order to convince others to adopt your position, you'll need to defend it with a solid, well-organized argument.

One way to convince people to accept your side of a controversial issue is to write an argumentative essay. Writing an argumentative essay means more than just airing your opinions. It means organizing your ideas, supporting your viewpoint with facts and persuasive arguments, and answering objections that others may have.

In this chapter, you'll write an argumentative essay about a national or international political topic. You'll consider a range of controversies, choose one, and then decide your position, gather evidence, and explore opposing viewpoints. Finally, you will write an essay to convince others that your arguments have merit.

Writing Guidelines

Subject: A national or international political controversy

Purpose: To convince people to accept your argument

Form: Argumentative essay

Audience: Classmates and community members

"I'm a controversial figure. My friends either dislike me or hate me."

—Toni Morrison

Argumentative Essay

Objectives
- take a position on a controversial issue
- conduct research to identify solid reasons for the position
- write a beginning that states a position, a middle that provides support, and an ending that restates the position

An **argumentative essay** states the writer's stand on a controversial issue and includes specific reasons in defense of that position.

In this unit, students will read sample passages about controversial issues and they will select a controversial topic to write about. Discussions about these issues are likely to ensue, so before beginning the unit, establish ground rules for expressing opinions. Emphasize that students should focus discussions on the issues and refrain from making comments about those who hold different opinions. Tell students that the best way for them to justify their positions, whether in discussion or in writing, is to be well informed and prepared for counterarguments.

 Technology Connections

Use the Interactive Whiteboard lessons to introduce persuasive writing.

 Interactive Whiteboard Lesson

Resources

Copy Masters
- T-Chart (TE p. 216)

Benchmark Papers
- Secondhand Smoke: A Silent Killer (strong) TE Appendix
- High Insurance for Teens (poor) TE Appendix

Persuasive Writing Warm-Up
Understanding Controversy

Be sure students understand that while a controversy may foster strong opinions and one point of view may eventually prevail, no position is necessarily right or wrong.

T-Graph

Explain that analyzing the arguments for and against an idea is a good way to think through an issue and decide on a position for which they can write a thesis statement.

Try It!
Answers

Students who are not involved in school or community affairs will need guidance in identifying and selecting a controversy for their paragraphs.

- Provide students with current editions of school and local newspapers. Have students skim the headlines and the editorial and op-ed pages to identify current community controversies.
- Caution students to avoid selecting issues that are based on someone's personal agenda.
- Suggest that students select a controversy that may potentially affect them or people they know. This will help them feel motivated to delve into the issue.

Provide photocopies of the reproducible T-chart (TE page A97) and have students use it to list arguments for and against the issue. Tell students they can model their opinion statement on the one at the bottom of the sample T-graph, making sure to include a reason that they are for or against the issue. **DIFFERENTIATE INSTRUCTION** ↘
DIFFERENTIATE INSTRUCTION ↘ **DIFFERENTIATE INSTRUCTION** ↘

TEKS 11.13A, 11.16A

 **TEKS** 11.13A, 11.16A

Persuasive Writing Warm-Up Understanding Controversy

Some people think that *controversy*—an issue that invites divergent or opposing points of view—is what makes life interesting. Discussing ideas related to a controversy is a way to learn about yourself and others.

One way to examine a controversy is to use a T-graph. Elisa wrote a controversy at the top of a piece of paper. Then she created a T-graph that listed arguments for and against the idea. At the bottom, she wrote her opinion.

T-Graph

Controversy: The state is considering requiring each senior to take one online class before graduating.

Arguments for . . .	Arguments against . . .
• Students can take specialty classes—like Russian or computer animation—that the school doesn't offer. • Our generation will take more and more classes online and should get used to it. • Online classes let students from our town study beside students from Argentina, India, and other countries.	• Some students don't have home computers with high-speed Internet access. • Some online classes have little value; don't really teach much. • Seniors often are working jobs after school, and online courses would only overload them.

My Opinion: I'm in favor of the state's proposal because I would enjoy getting some of my credits online instead of in the classroom.

Try It!

Create a T-graph. Think about controversies in your school or community—any issue about which people tend to have strong and often opposed viewpoints. Write the controversy at the top of a piece of paper. Then use your T-graph to list arguments for and against the idea. Last, write your own opinion about the issue.

Differentiated Instruction: Struggling Learners

To help students understand the purpose of a persuasive essay, prompt them to connect persuasion to their own lives. Have they tried to convince a friend to see a particular movie, written a letter of request, or considered a product because of an advertisement?

Differentiated Instruction: Advanced Learners

Encourage students to spend some time every day reading newspaper editorials, listening to talk radio programs, or reading magazine opinion pieces. Expanding their exposure to persuasive writing or speaking in this way will prepare them to form and support their own opinions.

 TEKS **11.13A** Plan a first draft by determining appropriate topics through a range of strategies; **11.16A** Write an argumentative essay that presents a clear thesis or position based on logical reasons

Drafting an Argumentative Paragraph

Sample Position Paragraph

An argumentative paragraph states your opinion about a controversy, argues for your position, and answers an important objection raised against it. An argumentative paragraph has three main parts.

- The **thesis** clearly states the argument.
- The **body sentences** support the argument and respond to an objection.
- The **closing sentence** restates the argument.

Elisa wrote the following argumentative paragraph, using the details from her T-graph on page **216**.

The **thesis** cleary states the position.

The **body sentences** argue for the position and respond to divergent views.

The **closing sentence** restates the position.

Being Brave in a New World

The state should require each senior to take at least one online course before graduation. For one thing, this generation will be learning more and more online—in high school, college, on the job, and even after retirement. Also, online classes offer many subjects that the school can't provide—such as computer animation, music composition, paleontology, and Native American languages. Most importantly, though, online courses move students into the larger world. They can take classes with people from Pakistan or Zimbabwe and become citizens not just of our city or state but of the world. Some people worry about whether students have enough after-school time or have access to high-speed Internet at home. If the online courses are offered through the school, however, those difficulties are solved. If the state requires each student to take an online course, a whole new world will open for schools and for students.

Persuasive

Draft

Write an argumentative paragraph. Review the T-graph you created on the previous page. Write an argumentative paragraph with a clear thesis statement, precise and relevant arguments for your position, an answer to an objection, and a closing sentence.

Drafting an Argumentative Paragraph

Review the three main parts of an argumentative paragraph. Remind students that in addition to stating the writer's opinion on an issue, an argumentative paragraph also tries to persuade readers to support that position and responds to possible objections to the position.

✳ For more about basic paragraph skills and the construction of an effective persuasive paragraph, see SE pages 605–607 and 611.

Sample Position Paragraph

Discuss the organization of reasons from least to most important in the body sentences of the sample position paragraph.

Point out the play on words (reference to Aldous Huxley's *Brave New World*) in the title of Elisa's paragraph.

Write an argumentative paragraph. Have students use their T-graphs to identify an objection or divergent view that they should answer in their position paragraph. Tell them to choose the most significant argument that they listed for the opposing side of the issue. This is the argument they will need to address.

TEKS 11.16A, 11.16B

★ Conventions Connections

Grammar: Shifts in Verb Tenses
- ***Student Edition: Proofreader's Guide*** pages 738, 740, 742
- ***SkillsBook*** page 176

TEKS 11.16A Write an argumentative essay that presents a clear thesis or position based on logical reasons; **11.16B** Write an argumentative essay that presents an accurate and honest representation of divergent views; **ELPS 1C** Use strategic learning strategies to acquire basic and grade-level vocabulary; **5G** Explain with increasing specificity and detail

---

Differentiated Instruction: English Language Learners

★ ELPS 1C, 5G

ELP Level **Beginning**	ELP Level **Intermediate**	ELP Level **Advanced/Advanced High**
Suggest topics of controversy with which students will be familiar. Ask yes/no questions to help students generate vocabulary and details as you model creating a T-graph.	Identify a topic of controversy. Make a T-graph together and have students create their own copy. Provide sentence stems to help students explain details.	Choose a topic of controversy together. Have partners use complete sentences as they create a T-graph together. Then have students compare and explain their graphs.

Understanding Your Goal

Review the goals of this unit with students, focusing on how each of the five traits relates to writing an argumentative essay. To reinforce understanding, ask questions such as *What are some ways to identify a position or thesis statement? Why is it important to represent divergent points of view?* and *What organizational pattern is most appropriate for your audience and purpose?* Revisit SE pages 566–567 to support English language learners' understanding of the Texas traits. DIFFERENTIATE INSTRUCTION ↘

⭐ **TEKS** 11.16A, 11.16B, 11.16C

Connecting to the Scoring Guide

Before reviewing the sample essay, take a few minutes to connect the goals of this unit to those detailed in the holistic scoring guide on SE pages 36–37. Note that this scoring guide provides a trait-centered description of the qualities of strong writing in general, not just persuasive

Literature Connections

Students may not yet have studied the controversies surrounding the struggle for civil rights in the United States. Explain that the argumentative essay "Martin Luther King, Jr.: He Showed Us the Way" was written after Martin Luther King, Jr.'s death. In it, Chávez argues in support of nonviolent protest as the only means for achieving fair treatment for migrant farm workers. Chávez reiterates King's points that violence undermines their cause.

TEKS **11.16A** Write an argumentative essay that presents a clear thesis or position based on logical reasons; **11.16B** Write an argumentative essay that presents an accurate and honest representation of divergent views; **11.16C** Write an argumentative essay that presents an organizing structure appropriate to the purpose, audience, and context

---

⭐ **TEKS** 11.16A, 11.16B, 11.16C

Understanding Your Goal

Your goal in this chapter is to write a well-organized argumentative essay that effectively states and defends a position. The traits listed in the chart below will help you plan and write your argumentative essay.

Traits of Persuasive Writing

■ **Focus and Coherence**

Choose a topic that addresses the prompt or assignment. Next, write a clear thesis statement. Use only precise and relevant details that support that thesis statement. Include an introduction that clearly states your thesis and a conclusion that sums up your arguments.

■ **Organization**

Use an effective organizational pattern: the beginning states your thesis; the middle arranges your arguments logically; the ending restates your position. Use transitions to create a smooth, logical flow.

■ **Development of Ideas**

Use evidence (facts, expert opinions, quotations) to support your thesis. Provide information on multiple relevant perspectives, including divergent points of view. Show that you have considered the reliability and validity of the primary and secondary sources you use.

■ **Voice**

Engage the reader throughout your writing. Use language that shows that your care about your position but are also respectful of opposing viewpoints. Let your unique voice come through.

■ **Conventions**

Check your writing for errors in grammar, sentence structure, mechanics (capitalization and punctuation), and spelling.

 Literature Connection. You can find an argumentative essay in César Chávez's essay "Martin Luther King, Jr.: He Showed Us the Way."

Differentiated Instruction: Struggling Learners

To help students follow the arguments and the organization of ideas in the model, create an outline of the essay. First make sure students understand the meaning of economic sanctions. Then help students identify the main ideas of the essay. Tell them to use the call-out notes to analyze how the writer organized the essay.

Argumentative Essay

An argumentative essay identifies an issue and clearly states and defends a position on it. In this essay, the writer defends her position on economic sanctions.

TEKS 11.16A, 11.16B, 11.16C

Beginning
The beginning introduces the topic and states the thesis or position (underlined).

Middle
The first middle paragraph provides a logical and relevant reason why sanctions do not work.

The second middle paragraph includes expressions of commonly held beliefs to support the argument.

The third middle paragraph provides precise and relevant facts to support the argument.

Sanctions Won't Solve Political Problems

In July of 1941, the United States imposed economic sanctions against Japan, banning exports to the country and freezing any of its assets that were under U.S. control. These sanctions were meant to stop Japanese military aggression in Asia. On December 7, 1941, however, Japan attacked the U.S. naval base at Pearl Harbor. Instead of reducing aggression, the sanctions had helped push both nations into a war. Though economic sanctions appear to be a powerful peacetime weapon, they actually do more harm than good.

To begin with, economic and political sanctions often prolong bad situations rather than end them. They create a stalemate. Political sanctions usually come about when an international dispute cannot be resolved by discussion and compromise. In order to get what it wants, one nation reduces or stops trade with another nation. It may also freeze any assets the "offending" nation has invested in the country. In 1962, for example, Communist leader Fidel Castro took power in Cuba. His government took control of U.S. businesses there. The United States imposed sanctions, cutting trade with Cuba, hoping the action would speed the fall of Castro's government ("United States Sanctions"). More than 40 years later, the sanctions were still in place, and Castro was still in power.

One reason that sanctions are ineffective is that they often reduce dialogue between disputing nations. Instead of searching for common ground, sanctions rely on unilateral force and provoke anger, which only makes matters worse. For the duration of the sanctions, talks are focused almost exclusively on their removal instead of on the common ground the parties may be able to find.

Another reason for the ineffectiveness of sanctions is that they often harm innocent victims while doing little or nothing to affect the lives of those in power. In August of 1990, the United Nations imposed sanctions on Iraq

Persuasive

Argumentative Essay

Work through the model essay with the class, pointing out the elements that make it a good argumentative essay. ✔ DIFFERENTIATE INSTRUCTION

TEKS 11.16A, 11.16B, 11.16C

Development of Ideas

- The thesis states the position that economic sanctions do more harm than good.
- The writer supports the position with four solid reasons that strengthen the writer's argument.
- The writer counters an important objection with a reasonable defense.

Organization

- The middle paragraphs build the argument with strong reasons that are presented in order of importance, from least important to most important.
- Each paragraph has a clear topic sentence, and additional sentences provide details that support the topic sentence.
- The last middle paragraph states and responds to a divergent point of view.
- The ending restates the position and adds a final insight for the reader.

Voice

- The use of specific facts and examples creates a persuasive and reasonable voice.
- The writer avoids using language that triggers negative feelings.

ELPS 4D, 4F

Differentiated Instruction:
English Language Learners

Before reading the sample essay, turn to the Tools of Language, pages 580–585, for additional language support for persuasive writing.

ELP Level **Beginning**	ELP Level **Intermediate**	ELP Level **Advanced/Advanced High**
Use visuals such as maps to enhance comprehension. Provide support to develop vocabulary and background knowledge	Before reading, define terms such as *sanctions* and *diplomacy*. Use simplified language and visuals to enhance comprehension.	Before reading, define words such as *stalemate* and *compromise*. Have students share knowledge about U.S. relations with Japan and Cuba.

TEKS **11.16A** Write an argumentative essay that presents a clear thesis or position based on logical reasons; **11.16B** Write an argumentative essay that presents an accurate and honest representation of divergent views; **11.16C** Write an argumentative essay that presents an organizing structure appropriate to the purpose, audience, and context; **ELPS 4D** Use prereading supports to enhance comprehension of written text; **4F** Use support from peers and teachers to develop vocabulary and develop background knowledge

Be sure students note the use of in-text citations where information from sources is paraphrased in the essay.

✱ For more about formatting in-text citations, see SE pages 442–444.

 Respond to the reading.

Answers

Focus and Coherence 1. Accept any three: Sanctions create a stalemate, reduce dialogue, harm innocent victims, and can isolate the sanctioning nation from the rest of the world.

Organization 2. The writer first states her position, or thesis, in the last sentence of the first paragraph.

Development of Ideas 3. Sanctions against Japan resulted in the 1941 bombing of Pearl Harbor. Sanctions against Cuba failed to remove Castro from power and led to an increase in Cuba's trade with Mexico, Canada, and the Soviet Union. Sanctions against Iraq led to the near collapse of its economy and the death of hundreds of thousands of Iraqis. **DIFFERENTIATE INSTRUCTION** ↘

⭐ **TEKS** 11.16A, 11.16B, 11.16C

---

following its invasion of Kuwait. The sanctions shut off the sale of broad categories of goods to Iraq and prohibited Iraq from selling its oil on the international market. In place for more than 10 years, the sanctions led to a near collapse of the Iraqi economy ("Iraq"). Hundreds of thousands of Iraqis died because of malnutrition or because of lack of medical care. Meanwhile, Iraqi president Saddam Hussein and other Iraqi leaders lived in luxury, unaffected by the embargo. There was no reason for Hussein to bend to international will because he and those closest to him were not suffering.

> *The fourth middle paragraph presents the writer's most important reason. A transitional phrase links this reason with the previous reasons.*

The most important reason a country should think twice before applying sanctions is that they may backfire. For example, when the United States sanctioned Cuba, Cuba simply increased its trade with Mexico, Canada, and the Soviet Union (Smith 238). Thus, the United States lost out. This pattern is especially common when the international community disagrees with the sanctions. The sanctioning nation may find itself isolated from the rest of the world.

> *The last middle paragraph presents an honest and accurate representation of a divergent view.*

Those who support sanctions insist that they represent a useful tool in international diplomacy that is preferable to war. The real truth is that sanctions are ineffective and that they often succeed in hastening war, not preventing it. If the efforts made to impose sanctions were redirected toward finding common ground and dialoguing to solve problems, wars may more often be avoided.

> **Ending**
> *The ending restates the thesis and offers a commonly held belief as a final argument.*

When two friends disagree, they can negotiate, or they can use manipulative games to try to "win" the argument. The latter passive-aggressive behavior doesn't work for friends, and it doesn't work for nations, either. In international disputes, economic sanctions all too often put nations on a "peaceful" path to war.

 Respond to the reading. Answer the following questions about the sample essay.

Focus and Coherence (1) List three reasons the writer gives for opposing sanctions.

Organization (2) What organizational pattern does the author use?

Development of Ideas (3) What evidence supports the writer's thesis?

⭐ **TEKS** **11.16A** Write an argumentative essay that presents a clear thesis or position based on logical reasons; **11.16B** Write an argumentative essay that presents an accurate and honest representation of divergent views; **11.16C** Write an argumentative essay that presents an organizing structure appropriate to the purpose, audience, and context

Prewriting

Argumentative Essay **221**

In prewriting, you will select a political controversy of national or international importance. You'll decide your position, gather reasons and facts to support it, and organize your ideas.

Keys to Effective Prewriting

1. Choose a political controversy that affects people in the United States or in the international community. Form your position on the controversy.

2. Gather the most precise and relevant reasons and details to support your position.

3. Identify an important objection to your position.

4. Create a clear thesis statement to guide your writing.

5. Use a list or an outline as a planning guide.

Persuasive

Prewriting

Keys to Effective Prewriting

Remind students of the purpose of the prewriting stage in the writing process: It is when the writer selects a topic, gathers details, and decides how to organize those details.

The Keys to Effective Prewriting list explains the process students will be guided through on SE pages 222–226. ☑ DIFFERENTIATE INSTRUCTION

Keep in mind that while some students will demonstrate an acute awareness of political controversies and have passionate opinions about these issues, other students may be uninformed and not ready to form thoughtful opinions. Be prepared to supply possible topics for students who think they have no positions on current issues. Engage these students in debates by presenting position statements on both sides of controversial issues. When engaged, students may be surprised to learn that they have formed an opinion that can be supported as they gain more knowledge about the topic.

Writing Workshop

The activities on the following pages teach key prewriting strategies and are perfect to use as minilessons in a writing workshop. Present the material to the whole class or to a small group.

Differentiated Instruction: English Language Learners

⭐ ELPS 3C, 4K

ELP Level **Beginning**	ELP Level **Intermediate**	ELP Level **Advanced/Advanced High**
Work together to discuss focus and coherence. Restate ideas in the essay and have students say *yes* if each idea is used as a reason for opposing sanctions.	Analyze the development of ideas with students. Have students restate the author's evidence in the third paragraph, using a variety of grammatical structures.	Work together to analyze organization. Review the call-out notes together. Then have students use complete sentences to restate these ideas using a variety of sentence types.

ELPS 3C Speak using a variety of grammatical structures, sentence lengths, sentence types, and connecting words; **4K** Demonstrate English comprehension and expand reading skills by employing analytical skills

Prewriting Selecting a Political Controversy

Provide students with current editions of major newspapers and weekly news magazines, and encourage them to skim the headlines for topics that interest them. Suggest that students listen to and derive meaning from a variety of media, such as NPR (National Public Radio) and CNN (Cable News Network). Ask them to take notes about topics from these national news broadcasts to demonstrate their language and concept attainment. You may also wish to ask the debate club for a list of controversies that they have debated.

 ELPS 2F, 2I

List of Political Controversies

Work together to develop a list of political controversies. Students can also include the non-starred issues in the sample List of Political Controversies.

List controversies. Check that students' position statements reflect careful thought on the issues.

DIFFERENTIATE INSTRUCTION ↘

TEKS 11.13A,

Focus on the Texas Traits

Development of Ideas

Most students will need to do some preliminary research to find solid reasons to defend their positions. Suggest that students have back-up topics in case they cannot identify enough sources.

Prewriting Selecting a Political Controversy

A political controversy is a disagreement about a political issue. To find a writing topic, Lee, a student, answered some key questions about national or international political controversies.

List of Political Controversies

> In the recent past, what political disagreements have made headlines in national newspapers, on news shows, and on Internet sites?
> - political campaign contributions
> - health care
> - the war in Afghanistan
> - the rising national debt *
>
> What national or international political controversies have we discussed recently in class?
> - controlling international pollution
> - providing health care in Africa
> - stopping genocide

After Lee chose her controversy, she wrote a sentence that summarized her position.

The rapidly growing national debt is bad for the United States.

 Prewrite

List controversies. On your own paper, answer the two key questions above. Try to come up with at least three controversies that answer each question. Then place an asterisk (*) beside a controversy you feel strongly about. Write a sentence that summarizes your position on it.

 Texas Traits

Focus on the Texas Traits

Development of Ideas Make sure that you have ample support and specific details for all of your main points. Keep in mind what your readers need to know in order to fully understand your argument. A unique approach may add to the overall effectiveness of your writing.

Differentiated Instruction: Struggling Learners

Students must be informed on issues before they can articulate clear positions on them. Tell students that once they choose controversial issues that interest them, they should read about them and do some research before writing position statements. This will ensure that their positions are valid.

Differentiated Instruction: Struggling Learners

Help students get started on their research. In one-on-one conferences, give specific suggestions and guidance in how to find appropriate periodicals, books, and Web sites students should consult first. Then conduct an online search together to demonstrate how to access reliable sites.

Conducting Research

A position is only as strong as the reasons and details that support it. Here are tips for researching the controversy you have chosen.

- **Consult both primary and secondary sources.** Scan the opinion and editorial pages of large newspapers such as the *New York Times* and the *Chicago Tribune*. Use the *Readers' Guide* to find recent articles and first-person accounts related to your topic.
- **Find timely books.** Use only books that have the latest information on your topic.
- **Search Web sites.** Carefully evaluate each site, making sure the information is current, correct, reliable, and balanced.
- **Ask an expert.** Find a politician who takes part in the debate and interview him or her in person, on the phone, or by e-mail.
- **Gather many types of support.** Write down facts, statistics, examples, quotations, and anecdotes and keep track of where you find the information. (If your teacher requires parenthetical citations or a works-cited page, see page **413**.)
- **Find details that support and oppose your opinion.** Your argumentative essay will be stronger if you include an honest and accurate representation of divergent views.

Lee used note cards to keep track of the information she gathered. At the top of each card, she wrote a question. Then she wrote answers to the question and, at the bottom, noted the source. Here is an example note card.

Note Card

> Why can't we just cut the budget?
>
> Budget cuts take away vital programs. Taxes would
>
> have to be raised to keep those services.
>
> * Raising taxes would hurt people already
>
> struggling with the economic downturn.
>
> * Cutting services could affect education, child-
>
> support enforcement, and elder-care benefits.
>
> Source: The Houston Messenger online

Draft

Conduct research. Read articles in national newspapers and magazines, find timely books and Web sites, and gather supporting details.

Persuasive

Conducting Research

Review the research tips with the class, making sure students are aware that they should consult both primary and secondary sources.

✔ **DIFFERENTIATE INSTRUCTION**

Note Card

Remind them to make note of divergent views as they conduct their research, so that those ideas can be represented in their essays.

Point out that biased sources present information that favors one side of an issue in a highly subjective, unbalanced way. Encourage students to think critically when conducting their research to assess the validity and reliability of the information they find. To help them recognize biased information, provide the following tips:

- Evaluate the use of language devices such as emotionally charged words or exaggeration, which are intended to manipulate or present opinion as fact.
- Verify facts and make sure an erroneous judgment or assumption is not included.
- Identify the background and purpose of the writer or group that produced the information. Try to determine the intended use of the information and its potential audience.

Remind students that talk shows are generally not the most reliable or valid sources of information for political controversies and should not be used as primary resources for information.

Conduct research. Tell students to use both print and online resources to conduct their research.

✔ **DIFFERENTIATE INSTRUCTION**

★ **TEKS** 11.16A, 11.16D, 11.16E

Differentiated Instruction: English Language Learners

★ **ELPS** 2I, 4G, 4I, 4J

Hold "research clinics" for small groups to provide practice in various aspects of conducting research.

ELP Level **Beginning**	ELP Level **Intermediate**	ELP Level **Advanced/Advanced High**
Model locating a primary source on a particular topic and read it together. Have students use sentence stems to take notes and restate ideas.	Model locating a primary source and taking notes. Read the source aloud and have students take notes as you model the process.	Have partners locate a variety of web sites on a particular topic. Then have them tell about how they inferred whether each site was useful and reliable.

TEKS **11.16A** Write an argumentative essay to the appropriate audience that includes a clear thesis or position based on logical reasons supported by precise and relevant evidence, including facts, expert opinions, quotations, and/or expressions of commonly accepted beliefs; **11.16D** Write an argumentative essay to the appropriate audience that includes information on the complete range of relevant perspectives; **11.16E** Write an argumentative essay to the appropriate audience that includes demonstrated consideration of the validity and reliability of all primary and secondary sources used; **ELPS** **2I** Demonstrate listening comprehension/taking notes; **4G** Demonstrate comprehension of increasingly complex English/taking notes; **4I** Demonstrate English comprehension and expand reading skills by employing basic reading skills; **4J** Demonstrate English comprehension and expand reading skills by employing inferential skills

Prewriting
Listing Reasons That Support Your Position

Explain that creating a "Why" chart will help students analyze and organize the information they have found in their research.

"Why" Chart

Tell students that each of the "because" sections in their "Why" chart will become a separate paragraph in their essays. Remind them that using different levels of detail in a paragraph adds meaning and deeper interest for the reader.

- In the first row of the sample "Why" chart, the reason in the second column can be a topic sentence for the first middle paragraph.
- In the third column, the first bulleted item provides a general detail that supports the reason, and the next two items are examples.
- Students can turn to SE page 230 to see how the writer uses these different levels of detail to write the first middle paragraph.

Create a "why" chart. Tell students to create their chart and then rank the reasons.

`DIFFERENTIATE INSTRUCTION ↘`

★ **TEKS** 11.16A, 11.16B, 11.16D

★ Focus on the Texas Traits

Organization

If students can't decide how to rank their reasons, suggest that they review their notes to see how experts on the issue rank the reasons. Experts often present their strongest argument last to leave the reader with a powerful reason to ponder.

★ **TEKS** 11.16A, 11.16B, 11.16D

Prewriting Listing Reasons That Support Your Position

After conducting research, think about your position. Do you still have the same opinion? Adjust your thesis statement as necessary. Then decide on the main reasons that support your position. Lee used a "why" chart to list her main arguments.

"Why" Chart

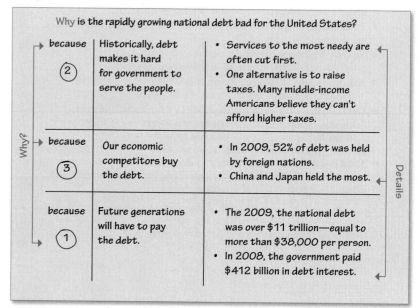

Why is the rapidly growing national debt bad for the United States?		
because ②	Historically, debt makes it hard for government to serve the people.	• Services to the most needy are often cut first. • One alternative is to raise taxes. Many middle-income Americans believe they can't afford higher taxes.
because ③	Our economic competitors buy the debt.	• In 2009, 52% of debt was held by foreign nations. • China and Japan held the most.
because ①	Future generations will have to pay the debt.	• The 2009, the national debt was over $11 trillion—equal to more than $38,000 per person. • In 2008, the government paid $412 billion in debt interest.

Create a "why" chart. On top, write your position in the form of a "why" question. In the middle sections, write three reasons that answer the question. Then provide details that support each reason.

Focus on the Texas Traits

Organization Argumentative essays are often organized by order of importance, with transitional words and phrases creating a logical flow. After you have finished your chart, rank your reasons—1, 2, 3—from least to most important.

Differentiated Instruction: Advanced Learners

To demonstrate the importance of presenting valid reasons on an issue, have students work in pairs to create scenarios for several controversial issues. For each scenario, have them create one reason that uses emotional language, and one reason that uses logic. For example:

- Emotional—"Recycling is crucial to our quality of life. Do you want to live on a huge landfill of trash?"
- Logical—"Recycling helps not only to save precious resources, but also to reduce the amount of trash that must be disposed of in landfills."

★ **TEKS** 11.16A

★ TEKS **11.16A** Write an argumentative essay to the appropriate audience that includes a clear thesis or position based on logical reasons supported by precise and relevant evidence, including facts, expert opinions, quotations, and/or expressions of commonly accepted beliefs; **11.16B** Write an argumentative essay to the appropriate audience that includes accurate and honest representation of divergent views; **11.16D** Write an argumentative essay to the appropriate audience that includes information on the complete range of relevant perspectives

TEKS 11.16B, 11.16D

Identifying Objections

In order for your essay to be effective, you need to present accurate and honest objections to your argument. If you can do this, your argument will be stronger, and you'll be more likely to convince people to accept your position. Start by identifying objections.

- **Check news sources,** including newspapers, magazines, television news, and Internet news sites. Editorials are a great place to start.
- **Try to recall classroom discussions** or conversations with your peers about your topic. What were the objections to your position?
- **Ask the opinions of your friends,** family, or others you respect. Identify their objections and think about ways to counter them.

After researching opposing arguments, Lee listed the following objections to her position on the federal debt.

> Position: The rapidly growing national debt is bad for the United States.
> Objections:
> The government can always find the money it needs.
> The debt is necessary to keep the government running. *
> We have more important problems than the national debt.

Prewrite

Gather objections. Use the strategies above to gather and list three objections to your position. Put an asterisk (*) next to the strongest objection.

Countering an Objection

Countering an objection means simply arguing against it. Lee listed three reasons why she disagreed with the strongest objection to her position.

> The debt is necessary to keep the government running.
> 1. Some debt is necessary, but this debt is too big.
> 2. Borrowing money is a bad way to run a business.
> 3. Cutting wasteful spending is better than more borrowing.

Prewrite

Counter an important objection. Write down the strongest objection to your argument. List several reasons why you disagree with it.

Persuasive

Identifying Objections

Remind students that their argumentative essay should include a range of relevant perspectives, and that a controversy always has at least two sides. If students can't identify valid and reasonable objections to their positions, then perhaps their topics aren't truly controversial. They can do additional research, revisit the list on SE page 222, or ask you or a writing partner for topic ideas. **✔ DIFFERENTIATE INSTRUCTION**

Gather objections. Remind students to note the sources for any divergent views they list.

Countering an Objection

Explain to students that thoughtful objections point out real consequences. The strongest objection identifies the most important consequence. To counter an objection successfully, students must prove that the negative consequence is not as important as what will happen if the writer's position is not supported.

Counter an important objection. Point out that the use of facts, examples, and statistics are excellent tools to counter an objection.

TEKS 11.16B, 11.16D

TEKS **11.16B** Write an argumentative essay to the appropriate audience that includes accurate and honest representation of divergent views; **11.16D** Write an argumentative essay to the appropriate audience that includes information on the complete range of relevant perspectives; **ELPS** **1C** Use strategic learning strategies to acquire basic and grade-level vocabulary; **1E** Internalize new basic and academic language by using and reusing it/ writing; **4G** Demonstrate comprehension of increasingly complex English/ taking notes

Prewriting Outlining Your Argument

Discuss the organization of information in the outline. Point out that one of the benefits of writing a sentence outline is that it provides a solid framework for constructing each paragraph in the essay.

Create an outline. Remind students to use their "why" charts to help them create an outline.

DIFFERENTIATE INSTRUCTION ↘ DIFFERENTIATE INSTRUCTION ↘

⭐ TEKS 11.16C

✴ For more about creating a topic outline or a sentence outline, see SE page 619.

Prewriting Outlining Your Argument

Before writing your argumentative essay, organize your information in an outline. The main points will become the topic sentences in the body paragraphs of your essay. The supporting points will become details in each paragraph. (Lee's outline uses complete sentences, though your teacher may let you use phrases.)

Sentence Outline

<u>Position Statement:</u> The rapid growth of the national debt is bad for the United States' future.

I. First of all, a high national debt makes it difficult for the government to serve its people effectively.
   A. In late 2009, the national debt topped $11 trillion.
   B. The president decided to reform the health care system to reduce the national debt.
   C. Another alternative is to raise taxes, but most middle-income Americans feel they can't afford a tax hike.
   D. Cutting services could save money, but needy people suffer.
II. A high national debt passes a burden on to future generations.
   A. The government sells bonds to raise money.
   B. It must pay interest on these bonds.
   C. In 2008, the government paid more than $412 billion in interest on the debt.
III. Perhaps most important, a high debt makes the United States less economically competitive.
   A. Foreign nations hold 52% of our national debt.
   B. China and Japan hold the most.
IV. Some people argue that the federal government needs more money and must take on debt in order to function.
   A. This is true, but only to a point.
   B. Much of the debt is due to wasteful spending.

Prewrite

Create an outline. Using the example above, create an outline for your position essay. Organize your reasons by order of importance. At the end, answer an important objection to your opinion.

Differentiated Instruction: Struggling Learners

If students need help organizing their topic outline, provide an outline framework such as the following:

Position Statement: _____
I. Supporting reason #1: _____
   A. Detail that illustrates reason #1: _____
   B. Detail that illustrates reason #1: _____

Differentiated Instruction: Advanced Learners

Have partners exchange outlines and evaluate the organization. Partners should note which details seem most convincing and whether the ordering of ideas effectively supports the writer's position

TEKS 11.16C Write an argumentative essay to the appropriate audience that includes an organizing structure appropriate to the purpose, audience, and context

Drafting

Argumentative Essay **227**

You have researched a political controversy, chosen a position, developed reasons for its support, and have given an accurate and honest representation of a divergent view. You have also organized your ideas in an outline. Now you are ready to begin drafting your argumentative essay.

Keys to Effective Writing

1. Use your outline as a writing guide.

2. To allow room for changes, write on every other line, or double-space if you are using a computer.

3. In the first paragraph, introduce the controversy and state your position.

4. Write topic sentences that give your supporting reasons. Include a variety of details in each middle paragraph.

5. In the last middle paragraph, respond to an important objection.

6. In your closing paragraph, restate your position and leave your reader with something to think about.

Persuasive

Drafting

Keys to Effective Writing

Remind students that the drafting stage is when they get to write, or draft, their ideas on paper.

The Keys to Effective Writing list explains the process students will be guided through on SE pages 228–232.

Encourage students to review their outlines and other prewriting materials to make sure they are complete.

- Do they have three logical reasons that defend their position? Have they ranked the reasons in order of importance?
- Have they gathered compelling facts, statistics, examples, expert opinions, quotations, and anecdotes to support their reasons?
- Have they proposed a valid argument to counter an important objection?

If students answer "no" to any of these questions, encourage them to return to the prewriting stage to address any problem areas before they begin drafting. ✔ **DIFFERENTIATE INSTRUCTION**

Differentiated Instruction: English Language Learners

ELPS 1C, 5E, 5F

Guide students to use a variety of sentence lengths, patterns, and connecting words as they create their outlines.

ELP Level **Beginning**	ELP Level **Intermediate**	ELP Level **Advanced/Advanced High**
Work with students to create their outlines. To reinforce strategic learning, have students highlight basic and grade-level vocabulary.	Have students work on one section of their outlines at a time, using grade-level vocabulary. Review each one with them before they begin a new section.	Have students use grade-level vocabulary to create their outlines independently. Then have them share and discuss their work with a partner.

 ELPS 1C Use strategic learning strategies to acquire basic and grade-level vocabulary; **5E** Employ increasingly complex grammatical structures; **5F** Write using a variety of grade-appropriate sentence lengths, patterns, and connecting words

Drafting
Getting the Big Picture

Encourage students to skim SE pages 229–232 to see how this graphic reflects the organization of ideas in the student writer's essay.

When students have finished their first drafts, they can return to this page and work with a partner to prepare a similar graphic, using ideas from their own papers. This can help them to confirm their understanding and to identify any flaws in their draft's organization and structure, which they can address when they revise.

ELPS 4F

Point out that the topic sentences for the middle section of the graphic come from the student writer's sentence outline on SE page 226.

Writer's Craft

Writing freely: The drafting step in the process should be done freely. Prewriting is work, and revising is work, but drafting should be more akin to play. The student's main job is to pour the prewriting ideas onto paper. The British writer John Boyton Priestly put it this way:

> "Most writers enjoy two periods of happiness—when a glorious idea comes to mind and, secondly, when a last page has been written and you haven't had time to know how much better it ought to be."
>
> —J. B. Priestly

228

Drafting Getting the Big Picture

The graphic below shows how the elements of an argumentative essay should fit together. Use it to guide your writing. (The examples are from the student essay on pages 229–232.)

Beginning

The **beginning** introduces the controversial issue and includes a clear thesis statement.

Thesis Statement
The rapid growth of the national debt is bad for the United States' future.

Middle

Each **middle** paragraph includes logical reasons supported by precise and relevant evidence.

The last middle paragraph gives an accurate and honest representation of a divergent view.

Topic Sentences
First of all, a high national debt makes it difficult for the government to serve its people effectively.

In addition, a high national debt passes a burden on to future generations.

Perhaps most important, a high debt makes the United States less economically competitive.

Some people argue that the federal government needs more money and must take on debt in order to function.

Ending

The **ending** restates the argument, sums up the reasons, and offers the reader something to think about.

Closing Sentence
Reducing the national debt will put our nation on a more secure path to the future.

 ELPS 4F Use visual and contextual support and support from peers and teachers to read grade-appropriate content area text, enhance and confirm understanding, and develop vocabulary

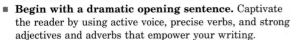

Starting Your Essay

The beginning paragraph of your argumentative essay should capture the reader's attention, introduce the controversy, and state your position clearly.

> Beginning
>
> Middle
>
> Ending

- **Begin with a dramatic opening sentence.** Captivate the reader by using active voice, precise verbs, and strong adjectives and adverbs that empower your writing.

  The growth of the national debt threatens the ability of our nation to function and to compete effectively in the international economy.

- **Provide important background information.** Give basic information about the controversy.

  The national debt is the difference over the years between the money the government collects in taxes and the money it spends.

- **Build powerfully toward your position statement.** All sentences in your beginning paragraph should lead the reader toward your thesis statement.

  The rapid growth of the national debt is bad for the United States' future.

Beginning Paragraph

The writer introduces the controversy. (underlined).

The growth of the national debt threatens the ability of our nation to function and to compete effectively in the international economy. The national debt is the difference over the years between the money the government collects in taxes and the money it spends. Today, the national debt is skyrocketing. The growth of the debt is reducing the ability of the government to provide necessary services. It's creating a staggering financial burden for future generations, and it's even weakening the economic competitiveness of our nation. The rapid growth of the national debt is bad for the United States' future.

The writer gives a thesis statement (underlined).

Persuasive

Draft

Write a beginning paragraph. Create your essay's opening and read it to a friend. Is your friend interested in what you've written? If not, write another version. Keep trying until you have your reader hooked.

Starting Your Essay

Before students write their beginning paragraph, suggest that they look at the opening paragraphs of several of the articles they used when researching their topic. As they review these materials, they should ask themselves these questions.

- Which opening sentence grabs my attention most effectively?
- What words or phrases in the sentence have the greatest impact on me?
- Which beginning pulled me in, made me want to read on, or evoked a response from me?
- Which beginning stated a valid position in the most powerful language?

Recognizing what works to capture their interest as readers can help students write effective beginnings that will capture their own readers' interest.

Beginning Paragraph

Guide students to relate the bulleted tips at the top of the page with the writer's sample.

✔ DIFFERENTIATE INSTRUCTION

Write a beginning paragraph. You may wish to have students share their beginning paragraphs in a writing group. Determine whether or not each one contains a dramatic opening sentence, background information, and a position or thesis statement.

★ TEKS 11.16A; ELPS 3E

TEKS 11.16A Write an argumentative essay to the appropriate audience that includes a clear thesis or position; **ELPS 3E** Share information in cooperative learning interactions; **4F** Use visual and contextual support and support from peers and teachers to read grade-appropriate content area text, enhance and confirm understanding, and develop vocabulary; **4I** Demonstrate English comprehension and expand reading skills by employing basic reading skills; **4J** Demonstrate English comprehension and expand reading skills by employing inferential skills

Drafting

Developing the Middle

Explain that in addition to providing logical reasons and precise and relevant evidence for their position, the middle paragraphs of an argumentative essay also present and respond to divergent viewpoints.

Using Transitions

Review the transitions shown in the chart and invite students to suggest additional examples.

DIFFERENTIATE INSTRUCTION ↘

Middle Paragraphs

Have students find the sentences in the beginning paragraph on the preceding page that present the order of the reasons for the middle paragraphs (sentences 4 and 5). Ask students to explain where the writer should present divergent viewpoints. (after the three reasons)

⭐ **TEKS** 11.13B, 11.16B

 **TEKS** 11.13B, 11.16B

Drafting Developing the Middle

The middle part of your essay uses logical reasons and precise and relevant evidence to support your position. Write a topic sentence for each paragraph and additional sentences that include supporting details. Address a divergent view in the last middle paragraph. Use your outline (page **226**) as your guide.

Beginning
Middle
Ending

Using Transitions

Transitions help your reader move easily from one idea to the next. They also help you arrange your ideas in order of importance. The following chart includes transitions that could connect your middle paragraphs.

Paragraph 1	Paragraph 2	Paragraph 3
First of all, ⟶	Also, ⟶	The best reason . . .
One reason . . . ⟶	In addition, ⟶	Finally,
To begin with, ⟶	Another reason . . . ⟶	Most importantly,

Middle Paragraphs

A topic sentence (underlined) introduces each reason.

> First of all, a high national debt makes it difficult for the government to serve its people effectively. By late 2009, the national debt had risen to almost $11 trillion, or more than $38,000 for every man, woman, and child in the U.S. That was up from $9 trillion in 2006. With these conditions, programs related to education and elder-care were endangered. Faced with mounting debts and under pressure to reduce spending, President Obama proposed sweeping heath care reform as a way of cutting the national debt over the long term. While many agreed that such reform was long overdue, legislators disagree as to whether or not the proposed bill will actually reduce the deficit ("Swimming in Debt").

The body sentences include compelling details that support each topic sentence.

> In addition, a high national debt poses another threat: it places a huge financial burden on future generations. When the government spends more than it collects in taxes, it makes up the difference by selling bonds. Investors buy these bonds for a certain amount, and the U.S. promises to pay that money back

---

Differentiated Instruction: Struggling Learners

Have students analyze the sample middle paragraphs for transition words that add or clarify information, show a comparison or contrast, or emphasize a point (*in fact, in comparison, but, at least*).
* Refer students to SE pages 623–624 for more examples of transition words to use in body paragraphs.

Differentiated Instruction: Advanced Learners

Ask students to revise these statements, using fair language:

- Anyone who disagrees with this position is pathetically misinformed. (not fully aware of the issue)
- The project won't be approved because the mayor is cheap. (concerned about the budget)

 TEKS **11.13B** Structure ideas in a sustained and persuasive way; **11.16B** Write an argumentative essay to the appropriate audience that includes accurate and honest representation of divergent views

along with interest at a later date. This interest burden only increases the amount of debt. In fact, in 2008, the government paid more than $412 billion in interest on the federal debt. With more and more interest, the debt will continue to skyrocket.

> Perhaps most important, a high debt makes the United States less economically competitive. That's because the buyers of bonds that finance the debt are economic competitors of the United States. As of December 2008, about 52 percent of the national debt was held by foreign nations. Japan and China held the most (Brighton Watchdog). Being in debt to these nations only increases our dependence on them as well as their power over our economy.

> Some people argue that the federal government needs more money and must take on debt in order to function. They say this is how government meets its obligations while keeping taxes low. This may be true, but the amount of debt now has reached staggering proportions. At least some of this debt results from government waste.

The middle paragraphs build to the most important reason.

The fourth middle paragraph counters an objection.

Draft

Write your middle paragraphs. Create middle paragraphs that support your position. Start each paragraph with a topic sentence. Then follow with details that support the topic sentence. Your final middle paragraph should respond to a significant objection.

Tip

- **Build your paragraphs** using your outline as a guide.
- **Use transitions between paragraphs** to show the order of importance.
- **Include logical reasons to support your position;** avoid overly emotional language.
- **Answer a divergent view** with logical, reasonable ideas.

Persuasive

Write your middle paragraphs. Remind students to include a range of relevant perspectives, and to craft their language to appeal to those with opposing views. Point out that the last middle paragraph should present and respond to a divergent viewpoint. ☑ DIFFERENTIATE INSTRUCTION

⭐ TEKS 11.16D, 11.16F

Tip

Focus on the third bulleted tip at the bottom of the page. Point out that emotional language often includes implicit ideas or information that provoke an impulsive reaction to a situation instead of prompting a reasoned, thoughtful response. Two examples of overly emotional words are *pathetic* and *heartbreaking*.

Have the class suggest and discuss other kinds of language that can weaken one's argument:

- **inflammatory words** such as *stupid, foolish, disgusting,* and *greedy* that assign blame to a particular person or group
- **sarcasm,** which means the opposite of what the writer is really saying and is usually intended to mock or deride an opponent's position or beliefs
- **overused qualifiers** such as *always, never, really, seems, appears, somewhat, totally, maybe, might* ☑ DIFFERENTIATE INSTRUCTION

Encourage students to develop their own vocabularies and to seek help from peers so that they can use more effective language to identify and describe their ideas.

⭐ ELPS 2H, 3B, 3D, 4F

TEKS **11.16D** Write an argumentative essay to the appropriate audience that includes information on the complete range of relevant perspectives; **11.16F** Write an argumentative essay to the appropriate audience that includes language attentively crafted to move a disinterested or opposed audience, using specific rhetorical devices to back up assertions; **ELPS 2H** Understand implicit ideas and information in spoken language; **3B** Expand vocabulary/learning and using high-frequency words for identifying and describing; **3D** Speak using grade-level content area vocabulary in context/new English words and academic language; **4F** Use support from peers and teachers to develop vocabulary and grasp of language structures; **5B** Write using newly acquired basic vocabulary and content-based grade-level vocabulary; **5F** Write using a variety of grade-appropriate sentence lengths, patterns, and connecting words

---

Differentiated Instruction: English Language Learners

⭐ ELPS 4F, 5B, 5F

Before students begin writing, examine the language structures used in the sample's topic sentences together.

ELP Level **Beginning**	ELP Level **Intermediate**	ELP Level **Advanced/Advanced High**
Review the outlines students created. Then guide students to write a topic sentence for a first middle paragraph.	Guide students to write a middle paragraph using appropriate sentence lengths and patterns. Then have partners share their writing.	Have students write a middle paragraph. Have partners examine their sentence construction and use of connecting words.

Drafting
Ending Your Essay

Remind students that the ending paragraph is their final chance to show readers that it is in their best interest to embrace and enthusiastically support the writer's position. Review the guidelines for ending an essay effectively.

Ending Paragraph

- Have students compare the restatement of the position in the sample Ending Paragraph to the position statement at the end of the sample Beginning Paragraph on SE page 229. Students should note that both statements use the word *future,* but in the ending the writer adds power by connecting the threat to "all of us."
- Point out that the third sentence in the sample Ending Paragraph summarizes the main reasons stated in the topic sentences of the first three middle paragraphs on SE pages 230–231. Tell students that to summarize the main reasons in their ending, they can restate and combine the ideas in their topic sentences.

✳ For more about how to shape great endings, see SE page 625.

Draft your ending paragraph. Suggest that students model their ending paragraph on the sample to be sure it is organized in a persuasive way that includes divergent views.

Prepare a complete first draft. Explain that a complete first draft will serve as the basis for the revising and editing stages.

⭐ **TEKS** 11.13B, 11.16B, 11.16C

⭐ **TEKS** 11.13B, 11.16B, 11.16C

Drafting Ending Your Essay

So far, your essay has identified a political controversy, taken a position, defended the position using solid reasons, and responded to a significant objection. Now you are ready to write your ending paragraph. To do the job effectively, use the following guidelines.

Beginning
Middle
Ending

- Restate your position clearly and powerfully.
- Summarize the main reasons that support your position.
- Summarize your response to the objection.
- Add a final insight that makes the reader think.

Ending Paragraph

The position is powerfully restated.

The writer sums up support for her position.

The essay ends with a final insight.

<u>The rising national debt threatens the United States' future—and that's a concern for all of us.</u> In order for the federal government to meet the needs of Americans now and in the future, it must practice fiscal responsibility. By balancing taxes and spending, politicians can cut the national debt, thus preserving necessary services, reducing the burden on future generations, and keeping this country competitive. Reducing the national debt will put our nation on a more secure path to the future.

Draft your ending paragraph. Draft the ending paragraph of your essay. Restate your position and summarize the reasons that support it. Finally, leave your reader something to think about.

Prepare a complete first draft. Write a copy of your entire essay. Double-space if you use a computer, or write on every other line if you write by hand. Double-spacing gives you room to revise.

⭐ **TEKS** **11.13B** Structure ideas in a sustained and persuasive way; **11.16B** Write an argumentative essay to the appropriate audience that includes accurate and honest representation of divergent views; **11.16C** Write an argumentative essay to the appropriate audience that includes an organizing structure appropriate to the purpose, audience, and context

Argumentative Essay **233**

Prewrite · Draft · **Revise** · Edit · Publish

Revising

Revision fine-tunes your writing in many ways. When you revise, you add or delete details, rearrange parts of your writing, and create a more powerful, persuasive voice.

Keys to Effective Revising

1. Read your essay aloud and decide whether it sounds convincing.

2. Make sure you have clearly explained the controversy and your position.

3. Check your topic sentences to make sure they follow your outline.

4. Make sure all of your details support your topic sentences. If necessary, add or delete details.

5. Check your draft for convincing reasons, relevant facts, and language carefully crafted to convince a disinterested or opposing audience.

6. To mark revisions on your draft copy, use the editing and proofreading marks found on the inside back cover of this book.

Persuasive

Revising

Keys to Effective Revising

Remind students that the revising stage is when writers have an opportunity to monitor their written language production and make improvements to their first drafts. At this stage they can think about refinements they might not have considered when they were drafting.

The Keys to Effective Revising list explains the process students will be guided through on SE pages 234–242.

Tell students to read their drafts from beginning to end, paying attention to their own reactions to the ideas. Tell them to make mental notes of what ideas work well and what ideas seem unclear or weak. Then tell students to put their essays aside for a day or two before they begin to revise. During this time away from their essays, students should think about different ways to tackle the problems that they identified. When they return to their essays, they will be refreshed and prepared to employ self-corrective techniques that will improve their writing.

Peer Responding

Writers need the perspective of readers, so make sure that students have a chance to get (and give) peer responses in cooperative learning interactions. These conversations with peers will also help students to develop their ability to understand implicit ideas and information in spoken language.

ELPS 1B, 2H, 3E

Differentiated Instruction: English Language Learners

ELPS 2I, 5G

ELP Level **Beginning**	ELP Level **Intermediate**	ELP Level **Advanced/Advanced High**
Before students write their endings, review the sample. Use simplified language to read it aloud. Ask yes/no questions to help them summarize the ideas.	Guide students to write their ending paragraphs. Have students discuss their work with a partner to check that it summarizes their ideas with specificity and detail.	Have students write their ending paragraphs. Then have them discuss their work with a partner. Have them identify and assess their final insights.

ELPS 1B Monitor written language production and employ self-corrective techniques or other resources; **2H** Understand implicit ideas and information in spoken language; **2I** Demonstrate listening comprehension/retelling or summarizing and by collaborating with peers; **3E** Share information in cooperative learning interactions; **5G** Explain with increasing specificity and detail

Revising for Focus and Coherence

Explain that like puzzle pieces, the ideas in an argumentative essay should fit together in a way that makes sense.

Do I have a clearly stated thesis statement?

Remind students that their thesis statement should clearly establish their position.

Have I maintained my focus throughout my essay?

Suggest that students first delete irrelevant or unnecessary details, and then look for places where additional support, reasons, or evidence is needed. DIFFERENTIATE INSTRUCTION ➘

Exercise
Answers

Students should delete the second sentence (*Some accidents...cell phone use*). Students may use a primary source such as an interview to give examples of driver frustration or road rage. Students may use a secondary source such as a newspaper article to provide details about the annual cost of gas, maintenance, and parking. Students should be able to describe the reliability and validity of any sources they use.

★ **TEKS** 11.13C, 11.16A, 11.16E

Check your thesis statement. Remind students that their thesis statements should be based on logical reasons, supported by precise and relevant evidence from valid and reliable sources.

★ **TEKS** 11.13C, 11.16A

Revising for Focus and Coherence

When you revise for *focus and coherence*, you make sure that you have maintained your focus throughout your essay, that your ideas are clearly connected to each other and to your thesis, that you have included a meaningful introduction and conclusion, and that your essay has an overall sense of completeness. Ask yourself the following questions.

Do I have a clearly stated thesis statement?

The first step in writing a focused argumentative essay is to create a clearly stated thesis statement that directly addresses the prompt or writing assignment. If your thesis is fuzzy and not worded clearly, chances are the rest of your essay will be unfocused.

Have I maintained my focus throughout my essay?

Every one of your details needs to support and develop your thesis. Delete any irrelevant or weak details. Consider whether additional details are needed to support your arguments, and if so, use appropriate primary and secondary resources to locate relevant facts. Check that your details are clearly connected to each other and to your thesis statement.

Exercise

Read the following introduction to an argument about the need for public transportation. Then rewrite the paragraph, omitting any details that do not support the thesis statement. Use a reliable primary or secondary source to add at least one detail that supports the argument.

> Another day, another traffic jam. Every day in our city, cars and trucks inch along amid delays, breakdowns, and accidents. Some accidents are caused by cell phone use. The frustrations of these drivers and passengers are well-known, and in fact, may contribute to some accidents. The cost of gas, upkeep on the vehicles, and parking is enormous. Providing convenient and affordable public transportation would not only make financial sense, but would also improve our quality of life.

Revise

Check your thesis statement. Make sure that it addresses the prompt and that it clearly expresses your main argument.

TEKS **11.13C** Revise drafts to clarify meaning and achieve specific rhetorical purposes, consistency of tone, and logical organization; **11.16A** Write an argumentative essay to the appropriate audience that includes a clear thesis or position based on logical reasons supported by precise and relevant evidence, including facts, expert opinions, quotations, and/or expressions of commonly accepted beliefs; **11.16E** Write an argumentative essay to the appropriate audience that includes demonstrated consideration of the validity and reliability of all primary and secondary sources used

Argumentative Essay **235**

⭐ **TEKS** 11.13C, 11.16A, 11.16E

Have I included a meaningful introduction and conclusion?

Make sure that your introduction includes a clearly worded thesis statement and makes your readers want to read on. Consider the use of rhetorical devices to appeal to readers through logic, emotions, or ethical beliefs. Your conclusion should sum up your arguments and leave readers with something to think about.

Does my essay have an overall sense of completeness?

Check that your essay is finished. This means that you have a strong introduction and conclusion and that all of your arguments are well developed and supported by precise and relevant details from reliable primary and secondary sources.

Exercise

Read the following introduction to an argumentative essay on the importance of wearing seatbelts. Underline the thesis statement. Explain how you could determine the reliability of the sources used for the facts provided.

1 "I can't move with the seat belt on. It's too uncomfortable." Are you serious?
2 That's your reason for refusing to do the one thing that could save your life in a car
3 accident? Seat belts prevent ejection, protect against load and spread crash forces,
4 and defend the head, neck, chest and spinal column from serious injury. With what we
5 know these days about car accidents, there is no excuse for refusing to buckle up.

Revise

Check your sources. Examine the facts you used in your argumentative essay, and explain how you determined the reliability of your sources.

Focus and Coherence

Changes clarify a key point to give readers background.

The national debt is the difference ~~over the years~~ ⸜

between the money the government collects in taxes and the

         This debt accumulates from year to year.

money it spends. ⋀

Persuasive

Have I included a meaningful introduction and conclusion?

Suggest that students review the ideas and tips on SE pages 229 and 232 before analyzing their essay's introduction and conclusion.

Does my essay have an overall sense of completeness?

Have partners work together to analyze each other's essays. Ask them to point out each essay's thesis statement, list reasons supported by facts, statistics, or expert opinions, and identify a response to divergent viewpoints.

⭐ **TEKS** 11.13C, 11.16A

Exercise
Answers

Students should underline *With what we know these days about car accidents, there is no excuse for refusing to buckle up.* They may suggest that they can check the reliability of the information on the effectiveness of seat belts by verifying it on the National Transportation Safety Board's (NTSB) web site. Accept other valid responses.

Check your sources. Have students create a list of their sources and explain how they determined the validity and reliability of each one. Remind them to pay particular attention to the validity and reliability of online sources.

⭐ **TEKS** 11.16E

Focus and Coherence
Discuss how the revisions clarify a key point for readers.

Differentiated Instruction:
English Language Learners

🔲 **ELPS** 1B, 1H, 3G, 3H

ELP Level **Beginning**	ELP Level **Intermediate**	ELP Level **Advanced/Advanced High**
In a small group, read aloud and discuss students' introductions and conclusions. Have them employ self-corrective techniques as they discuss revision ideas.	Have partners read each other's essays and make suggestions to improve focus and coherence. Provide sentence stems students can use to express opinions.	Have partners monitor written language by reading each other's essays. Discuss the elements that make the essay complete or identify elements that need strengthening.

🔲 **TEKS** **11.13C** Revise drafts to clarify meaning and achieve specific rhetorical purposes, consistency of tone, and logical organization; **11.16A** Write an argumentative essay to the appropriate audience that includes a clear thesis or position based on logical reasons supported by precise and relevant evidence, including facts, expert opinions, quotations, and/or expressions of commonly accepted beliefs; **11.16E** Write an argumentative essay to the appropriate audience that includes demonstrated consideration of the validity and reliability of all primary and secondary sources used; **ELPS** **1B** Monitor written language production and employ self-corrective techniques or other resources; **1H** Develop and expand repertoire of learning strategies; **3G** Express opinions; **3H** Explain with increasing specificity and detail

Revising for Organization

Point out that clarifying the organization of an argumentative essay allows readers to focus on its substance.

How can I make the order of my reasons clear?

Suggest that students highlight transitions in their work by underlining or circling them with a red pencil. This will help them assess their transitions.

✱ For more about using transitions, see SE pages 623–624.

Exercise
Answers

Possible answers:

1. First of all, seat-belt laws are easy to enforce.
2. In addition, seat-belt laws save drivers and insurance companies millions of dollars per year.
3. Most importantly, seat-belt laws save 4,000 American lives each year.
4. Some people say that they should be free to decide whether or not to wear seat belts.

The preservation of 4,000 lives each year is the most important reason because saving lives is more important than the ability to enforce the law or save money. DIFFERENTIATE INSTRUCTION ↘

Check your transitions. Suggest that students review the transitions in the chart at the top of the page and compare to be sure that the transitions they used are as effective.

⬤ TEKS 11.13C, 11.16C

 TEKS 11.13C, 11.16C

Revising for Organization

When you revise for *organization,* you make sure that the order of your reasons is clear and that the ideas in your sentences are connected.

How can I make the order of my reasons clear?

You can make the order of your reasons clear by using transitional words and phrases to connect your reasons as well as your answer to an objection. Here are some transitional words and phrases to try:

Reason 1	Reason 2	Reason 3	Objection Answer
First of all To begin For starters	In addition For that matter Besides	Most importantly The strongest reason Fundamentally	Some people say . . . Opponents argue . . . Though some say . . .

Exercise

Read the following topic sentences for an argumentative essay. Decide on a logical order for the topic sentences (either most important topic sentence first or most important topic sentence last) and rewrite them. Add transitional words and phrases to connect the topic sentences. Explain how you chose the most important reason.

1. Seat-belt laws save 4,000 American lives every year.
2. Seat-belt laws are easy for police to enforce.
3. People should be free to decide whether or not to wear seat belts.
4. Seat-belt laws save drivers and insurance companies millions of dollars per year.

Revise

Check your transitions. Make sure you have ordered your reasons clearly and indicated which is most important. Also introduce your answer to an objection.

How can I connect the ideas in my sentences?

You can connect the ideas in your sentences by repeating a key term from one sentence in the next. The repeated term makes the sentences interlock like puzzle pieces.

Nice Visual

| In most states, troopers do not pull over a vehicle for a seat-belt **violation** alone. | The **violation** is cited only if the driver is stopped for other **reasons**. | The **reason** for seat-belt laws, obviously, is not to hamper drivers, but to keep them safe. |

Exercise

In the following paragraph, find the key words or phrases that are repeated to connect the sentences.

1   A seat belt helps its wearer survive the tremendous forces involved in an
2 accident. The force of a 150-pound body moving at 45 miles an hour cannot be stopped
3 merely by bracing against the dashboard. The unbelted rider will strike the dashboard
4 or go through the windshield. A rider with a belt will stay in the seat and benefit from all
5 the crumple zones designed to absorb the tremendous impact forces.

Revise

Connect your ideas. Read your essay and watch for places where the ideas are disconnected. Rewrite sentences, using key words to connect the ideas.

Organization
Changes introduce and clarify the most important reason.

Perhaps most important,
A high debt makes the United States less economically
                                    that finance the debt
competitive. That's because the buyers of bonds are economic

competitors of the United States. As of December . . .

Persuasive

How can I connect the ideas in my sentences?

Point out that while repetition can make the connection of ideas clear, too much repetition can make writing seem clumsy and lazy.

- Emphasize the importance of repeating only key words and phrases from one sentence to the next.
- Encourage students to read aloud their paragraphs after they revise to make sure that they haven't repeated too many words.

Exercise
Answers

(line 1) forces; (line 2) force; (line 5) forces
(line 3) dashboard/dashboard
(line 3) unbelted rider; (line 4) rider with a belt

Connect your ideas. Students may benefit from working with a partner to identify places where ideas need better connections.

TEKS 11.13C, 11.16C

Organization
Discuss how the addition of a transitional phrase highlights the most important reason.

TEKS 11.13C Revise drafts to clarify meaning and achieve specific rhetorical purposes, consistency of tone, and logical organization; **11.16C** Write an argumentative essay to the appropriate audience that includes an organizing structure appropriate to the purpose, audience, and context; **ELPS 1E** Internalize new basic and academic language by using and reusing it/writing

Revising for Development of Ideas

Point out that many argumentative essays suffer from redundancy and circuitous reasoning.

- In a redundant argument, the writer offers several reasons in support of a position, but the reasons are not really different, just reworded.
- Circuitous reasoning, as the word *circuitous* suggests, goes in circles. The writer's argument tends to be lengthy and indirect, repeating many words and phrases to make a point.

Do I have enough support for my position?

Stress that using three distinct reasons to support a position, and presenting the reasons clearly and succinctly, will help to avoid problems of redundancy and circuitous reasoning.

DIFFERENTIATE INSTRUCTION ↘

"Rule of Threes" Table

Be sure students understand that each of the three arguments is connected to a set of three details.

Check your support. If students find their ideas need additional support, suggest that they check the "why" charts they created during the Prewriting stage. Remind students that their language should be crafted to appeal to a disinterested or opposed audience.

TEKS 11.13C, 11.16A, 11.16D, 11.16F

TEKS **11.13C** Revise drafts to clarify meaning and achieve specific rhetorical purposes, consistency of tone, and logical organization; **11.16A** Write an argumentative essay to the appropriate audience that includes a clear thesis or position based on logical reasons supported by precise and relevant evidence, including facts, expert opinions, quotations, and/or expressions of commonly accepted beliefs; **11.16D** Write an argumentative essay to the appropriate audience that includes information on the complete range of relevant perspectives; **11.16F** Write an argumentative essay to the appropriate audience that includes language attentively crafted to move a disinterested or opposed audience, using specific rhetorical devices to back up assertions

TEKS 11.13C, 11.16A, 11.16D, 11.16F

Revising for Development of Ideas

When you revise for *development of ideas*, you check that you have offered enough support and specific and relevant details to allow the reader to understand your major arguments. As much as possible, you bring an individual perspective to the topic, a perspective that adds to the overall quality of your writing. You use rhetorical devices that appeal to logic, emotions, or ethical beliefs to back up your statements of fact. Ask yourself the following questions.

Do I have enough support for my position?

You have enough support if you have provided at least three main arguments, which in turn are supported by three or more relevant details. This is called the "rule of threes." Use a table like the one below to graph your support.

"Rule of Threes" Table

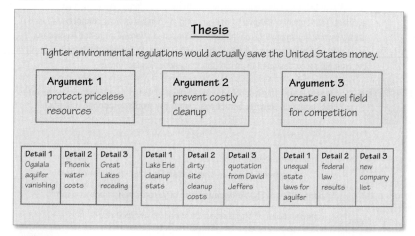

Check your support. Create your own "rule of threes" table. If you need more arguments or details, add them. (You may not always be able to include three supporting details for each reason.)

Differentiated Instruction: Struggling Learners

Tell students to make sure they back up their position with facts and not opinions. Remind students that facts are statements that can be proven with evidence, while opinions are personal statements that describe what someone feels or believes.

Ask students which of the following sentences includes a statistic that can be verified.

- Less than 10 percent of public school funding comes from the federal government. (fact)
- The federal government should give more money to schools. (The writer's opinion is unsupported.)

Have I effectively answered a significant objection?

You have answered a significant objection—or divergent view—if you have honestly represented the objection and provided facts to refute it. Answer the following questions to evaluate how well you have fulfilled this requirement.

1. Does my last middle paragraph answer an objection?
2. What is the main point of the objection? Do I address it?
3. Do I use clear facts to refute the objection?
4. Do I back up my facts with appeals to logic, emotions, or beliefs?

Exercise

Read the following answer to an objection and use the questions above to analyze it. Make suggestions to improve the paragraph.

1   Owners of power plants say pollution controls will cost them money. "And
2 besides," says Electric Board President William Samuels, "we haven't completed
3 testing the equipment." Plants, however, already have to pay fines for breaking
4 pollution laws. In addition, they regularly spend money to fight off civil suits.
5 Installation of pollution-control devices will not only prevent pollution, but may
6 also save power plants money in the long run.

Development of Ideas
Changes make the main point of an objection clear.

> Some people argue that the federal government needs ~~and must take on debt in order to function.~~ more money. They say this is how government ~~can keep on going.~~ meets its obligations while keeping taxes low. This may be true, but the amount of debt now has . . .

Persuasive

Revise
Check your response to an objection. Examine your argumentative essay to evaluate your response to an objection. Consider whether appeals to logic or emotion will strengthen your response.

Have I effectively answered a significant objection?

Remind students that their response to a divergent viewpoint should be both honest and accurate. However, explain that they can use the techniques mentioned in question 4 to craft language in a way that will appeal to a reader with an opposing view, and perhaps move that reader to change his or her opinion.

★ TEKS 11.13C, 11.16A, 11.16B, 11.16D, 11.16F

Exercise
Answers

Possible answers:
1. Yes.
2. The main point of the objection is that owners of power plants are worried that pollution controls will cost them money.
3. Yes. The writer explains that power plant owners already spend money on fines and on fighting civil suits. The writer suggests that installing pollution-control devices can be done easily and quickly, and it will provide more jobs.
4. No. Facts and statistics should be added. The writer could provide specific dollar amounts spent on fines and damages and compare the legal fees to the cost of installing pollution-control devices. ✔ **DIFFERENTIATE INSTRUCTION**

★ **ELPS** 4K

Development of Ideas
Discuss why the revisions make the main point clear.

Check your response to an objection. After students evaluate how effectively they have answered an objection, suggest that they exchange papers with a classmate for a peer review of their answer.

Revising for Voice

Point out that if a writer feels strongly about his or her position, an authentic and original voice is likely to come through naturally.

Have I engaged my readers throughout my writing?

As needed, discuss examples of rhetorical devices that can capture and keep readers' interest.

How can I show that I care about my position on the topic?

Tell students to pay particular attention to the tone of the paragraph in which they answer an objection. This is where their zeal may lead them to use sarcasm, overstatements, and extreme language. Emphasize that they will weaken their argument if they show a lack of respect toward people who hold opposing positions.

Exercise
Answers

Possible answers:
1. When it comes to energy consumption, businesses are using more and more of a diminishing resource.
2. Though a single business computer uses little energy, a thousand computers displaying a thousand screen savers on a thousand desks consume a tremendous amount of energy that is needed elsewhere.
3. In search of low-cost real estate, downtown businesses move to quiet suburbs.
4. Inadequate public transportation forces workers to drive vehicles that consume valuable fuel and release harmful gases into the air.

Check your voice. Tell students to practice pronouncing any new vocabulary as they read their essays aloud. Remind them that engaging and persuasive writing is not necessarily informal. Point out that their goal is to sound thoughtful, respectful, and well informed.
TEKS 11.13C, 11.16B, 11.16D, 11.16F; **ELPS** 3A

 **TEKS** 11.13C, 11.16B, 11.16D, 11.16F

240

 Revising for Voice

When you revise for *voice*, you make sure that you convey that you care about your topic and that you are fair in dealing with divergent viewpoints. Also, check that you have engaged the reader throughout your writing, provided a unique perspective, and expressed a voice that sounds like you—authentic and original. Ask yourself the following questions.

Have I engaged my readers throughout my writing?

As you reread your essay, notice if you find yourself bored or distracted. Chances are if you are bored, your readers will be as well. Try to find the parts of your essay that sound dull. Think about varying your sentence structures or adding rhetorical devices that appeal to emotions to make your writing more interesting.

How can I show that I care about my position on the topic?

You can show that you care about your position by following these tips.

- **Use serious language.** Avoid sarcasm, overstatement, slang, cliches, and jargon.
- **Use specific details.** Show that you are well informed about the situation.
- **Use a moderate tone.** Avoid the extremes—sounding either flat or overly emotional.

Exercise

In each of the following sentences, the underlined words and phrases create an inappropriate tone. Use the tips above and your imagination to rewrite each sentence so that it sounds serious, specific, and moderate.

1. When it comes to energy consumption, businesses are <u>pigs feeding at an ever-shrinking trough</u>.
2. Though a single business computer uses little energy, a thousand computers displaying a thousand screen savers on a thousand desks <u>send out a pretty glow that dooms the world</u>.
3. In search of <u>dirt-cheap</u> real estate, downtown businesses move to <u>Hicksville</u>.
4. Providing inadequate public transportation, city officials force <u>wage slaves</u> to drive <u>gas-guzzling SUV's</u>.

 Revise
Check your voice. Read your essay aloud. Notice parts that fail to convey your interest in the topic and rewrite to make them more engaging and persuasive.

 TEKS **11.13C** Revise drafts to clarify meaning and achieve specific rhetorical purposes, consistency of tone, and logical organization; **11.16B** Write an argumentative essay to the appropriate audience that includes accurate and honest representation of divergent views; **11.16D** Write an argumentative essay to the appropriate audience that includes information on the complete range of relevant perspectives; **11.16F** Write an argumentative essay to the appropriate audience that includes language attentively crafted to move a disinterested or opposed audience; **ELPS** **3A** Practice producing sounds of newly acquired vocabulary to pronounce English words

TEKS 11.13C, 11.16B,
11.16D, 11.16F

How can I sound fair when I answer an objection?

You can sound fair when answering an objection by following these tips.

- **Focus on the issue.** Do not comment on the people who oppose your position.
- **Keep your voice "cool."** Don't use emotional language when dealing with an opposing viewpoint.
- **Use solid logic.** Avoid misrepresenting the other position, ridiculing it, or using other forms of fuzzy logic.

Exercise

Notice the underlined voice error in each sentence below. Then, using the tips above, rewrite each sentence to correct the problem.

1. Some people think that businesses naturally try to conserve energy, but <u>those people are stupid and don't know what they're talking about.</u>
2. People who are in favor of big business are <u>just slaves to the establishment.</u>
3. Those who oppose government regulations of energy consumption <u>just want to rob homeowners.</u>

Voice
Changes improve the voice, making it serious, specific, and moderate in tone.

> In addition, a ~~gianormous~~ ^high national^ debt passes a ~~plague on~~ ^burden^ to future generations. When the government, ~~run by fat-cat politicians,~~ spends more than it collects in taxes, it makes up the difference by selling bonds. Investors buy these bonds for a certain amount, and the U.S. promises to pay...

 Revise

Check your logic. Look over your answer to an objection to find places where you can back up your assertions with an appeal to the reader's sense of logic.

Persuasive

How can I sound fair when I answer an objection?

Explain to students that fuzzy logic is reasoning that is based on inexact, partial, or incorrect information. This type of logic often includes assumptions that are made as a result of incomplete research or biased information. Tell students they can avoid fuzzy logic by conducting extensive research, using reliable sources, and reporting all facts, statistics, and details accurately and objectively.

 TEKS 11.13C, 11.16B, 11.16D, 11.16F

Exercise Answers

Possible answers:
1. Some people believe that businesses naturally try to conserve energy, but this is not always true.
2. People who support big business may overlook the contributions small companies make to the nation's economy.
3. Those who oppose government regulations of energy consumption argue that deregulation will lead to higher levels of production and greater distribution of energy.

☑ DIFFERENTIATE INSTRUCTION

Voice
Discuss how the changes affect the writer's voice in the passage.

Check your logic. Tell students that the best way to appeal to a reader's sense of logic is with solid facts, statistics, and expert opinions.

Differentiated Instruction:
English Language Learners

 ELPS 4K, 5E, 5F

ELP Level **Beginning**	ELP Level **Intermediate**	ELP Level **Advanced/Advanced High**
Use intonation to demonstrate inappropriate voice. Use more appropriate language and have students read revised sentences with you.	Work together to craft a more appropriate voice for each sentence. Analyze voice by having students read the existing and revised sentences aloud.	Have partners work together to complete the exercise. Encourage them to revise sentence structures and transition words as they see fit.

 TEKS **11.13C** Revise drafts to clarify meaning and achieve specific rhetorical purposes, consistency of tone, and logical organization; **11.16B** Write an argumentative essay to the appropriate audience that includes accurate and honest representation of divergent views; **11.16D** Write an argumentative essay to the appropriate audience that includes information on the complete range of relevant perspectives; **11.16F** Write an argumentative essay to the appropriate audience that includes language attentively crafted to move a disinterested or opposed audience; **ELPS** **4K** Demonstrate English comprehension and expand reading skills by employing analytical skills; **5E** Employ increasingly complex grammatical structures; **5F** Write using a variety of grade-appropriate sentence lengths, patterns, and connecting words

Revising Improving Your Writing

Check your revising. Remind students to carefully evaluate their writing as they answer each question.

 TEKS 11.13C

Revising Checklist

Note that most of the items on this checklist connect directly to the revising strategies provided on pages 234–241. The checklist, therefore, can help students pinpoint which strategies they need to use to complete their revisions. A student who can honestly answer "yes" to an item does not need to employ the revision strategy that connects to that item.

DIFFERENTIATE INSTRUCTION ↘

Writing Workshop

The revising checklist can help guide students during individual work time. You can assign each student to use the checklist to determine what areas need revision, and then choose two or three of the items to revise for. You can also use the checklist to identify and group students who would benefit from separate minilessons on development of ideas, organization, and so forth.

Make a clean copy. Tell students that a clean copy of their revised essays will make the next stage of the writing process, editing, easier.

 Conventions Connections

Grammar: Sentence Types
- *Student Edition: Proofreader's Guide* pages 764–765
- *SkillsBook* page 138

Grammar: Adverbs
- *Student Edition: Proofreader's Guide* pages 750
- *SkillsBook* pages 109, 112

Grammar: Adjectives
- *Student Edition: Proofreader's Guide* pages 638, 748
- *SkillsBook* pages 8, 107

 TEKS 11.13C

 Revising Improving Your Writing

 Check your revising. On a piece of paper, write the numbers 1 to 15. If you answer "yes" to a question, put a check mark next to that number. If not, continue to work on that part of your essay.

Revising Checklist

Focus and Coherence

_____ **1.** Is my writing focused on the prompt or assignment?
_____ **2.** Have I written a clearly stated thesis?
_____ **3.** Do all of my details support my main idea?
_____ **4.** Have I included a strong introduction and conclusion?
_____ **5.** Does my argumentative essay have a sense of completeness?

Organization

_____ **6.** Have I created an effective beginning, middle, and ending?
_____ **7.** Have I chosen a logical order for my main arguments?
_____ **8.** Have I used transitional phrases to connect my arguments?

Development of Ideas

_____ **9.** Have I offered enough support and specific details to allow readers to appreciate my major arguments?
_____ **10.** Have I effectively answered a significant objection?
_____ **11.** Have I brought a unique perspective to my topic?

Voice

_____ **12.** Have I engaged my readers throughout my writing?
_____ **13.** Does my writing show that I care about the topic?
_____ **14.** Have I been fair in answering objections to my arguments?
_____ **15.** Is my writing authentic and original?

 Make a clean copy. When you are finished with your revision, make a clean copy of your essay for editing.

TEKS **11.13C** Revise drafts to clarify meaning and achieve specific rhetorical purposes, consistency of tone, and logical organization

Editing

Editing

You have finished revising your argumentative essay. Now you are ready to edit for *conventions:* grammar, sentence structure, mechanics (capitalization and punctuation), and spelling.

Keys to Effective Editing

1. Use a dictionary, a thesaurus, and the "Proofreader's Guide" in the back of this book to check your writing.

2. Mark corrections using the editing and proofreading marks in the back of this book.

3. Edit your essay on a printed copy and enter the corrections on your computer. Otherwise, complete a clean handwritten copy that includes the corrections.

4. Check for commonly misused words to be sure you have made the correct choice.

5. Check your writing for grammar, sentence structure, mechanics (capitalization and punctuation), and spelling.

Persuasive

Editing

Keys to Effective Editing

Remind students that during the editing stage, they have a chance to find and correct errors in

- grammar,
- sentence structure,
- punctuation,
- capitalization,
- and spelling.

The Keys to Effective Editing list explains the process students will be guided through on SE pages 244–248.

- If students are using a computer, suggest that students make their edits on a printed copy. In either case—handwritten or printed first draft—have students edit with a colored pen or pencil. This will make the corrections easier to see as they enter them on the computer or make their final handwritten copy.
- After they make a correction, tell students to make a check mark on their drafts next to the lines in which edits appear. This way they can see they have made the changes on their final copies.

Peer Responding

Suggest that each student find a peer editor—preferably a person who is good at spotting conventions errors.

Differentiated Instruction: English Language Learners

⭐ ELPS 1G, 5F, 5G

ELP Level **Beginning**	ELP Level **Intermediate**	ELP Level **Advanced/Advanced High**
Work with students to check their work for major issues. Point out areas for revision to add detail and specificity.	Work with students to check their work for major issues. Encourage them to revise sentence structures to improve clarity and add more variety.	Have students share their essays with a partner. Have partners pay close attention to voice and the use of formal and informal English.

ELPS 1G Demonstrate ability to distinguish between formal and informal English; **5F** Write using a variety of grade-appropriate sentence lengths, patterns, and connecting words; **5G** Explain with increasing specificity and detail

 **Editing for Conventions**

Grammar

How can I check for commonly misused pairs?

Point out that errors with commonly misused pairs of words are usually caused by carelessness or haste during drafting and editing. Emphasize the importance of reading carefully when checking for commonly misused words.

✻ For more instruction and practice with using the right word, see SE pages 702–721.

Grammar Exercise
Answers

Many people who don't vote claim **it's** not in **their** best interest to get involved in politics. Think twice, however, before you surrender **your** franchise. A number of elections have been decided by just one vote. Imagine that a candidate you supported lost by only one vote, and you didn't take the time to go **to** the polls. Fortunately, **there** is a simple way to avoid this. On election day, make sure **your** vote counts, **too**!

Watch for commonly misused words Suggest that students use a print or electronic dictionary to check any words about which they have questions.

⭐ **TEKS** 11.13D; **ELPS** 5D

⭐ **Conventions Connections**

Grammar: Using the Right Word
- **Student Edition: Proofreader's Guide** pages 712–713, 718–719, 720–721
- **SkillsBook** page 64

244

 TEKS 11.13D

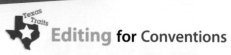 **Editing for Conventions**

Grammar

When you edit for *conventions,* you correct grammar, sentence structure, mechanics (capitalization and punctuation), and spelling errors.

How can I check for commonly misused pairs?

You can check for commonly misused pairs by watching for words that sound the same but are spelled differently. Here are the most commonly misused pairs:

- **it's, its** ■ *It's* is the contraction of "it is." *Its* is the possessive form of "it."
- **their, there, they're** ■ *Their* is a possessive personal pronoun. *There* is an adverb used to point out location. *They're* is the contraction for "they are."
- **to, too, two** ■ *To* is a preposition that can mean "in the direction of." *To* is also used to form an infinitive. *Too* means "also" or "very," and *two* is the number.
- **your, you're** ■ *Your* is a possessive pronoun. *You're* is the contraction for "you are."

Grammar Exercise

Find the commonly misused words in this paragraph. Correct them as you rewrite the paragraph.

1   Many people who don't vote claim its not in there best interest to get involved
2   in politics. Think twice, however, before you surrender you're franchise. A number of
3   elections have been decided by just one vote. Imagine that a candidate you supported
4   lost by only one vote, and you didn't take the time to go two the polls. Fortunately, their
5   is a simple way to avoid this. On election day, make sure you're vote counts, to!

 Watch for commonly misused words. Read your essay, looking for words that have the same sound but different spellings. Make sure each word is used correctly.

 TEKS **11.13D** Edit drafts for grammar; **ELPS** **5D** Edit writing for standard grammar and usage

Have I used numbers and numerals correctly?

You have used numbers and numerals correctly if you follow these simple rules:

1. Write out numbers one to nine.

one	three	five	seven	nine

2. Use numerals for 10 and above.

10	43	695	1,432	10,000

3. Use numbers and numerals together for very large amounts.

35 billion	3.4 trillion	253 million

4. Use numerals for decimals, percentages, dates, and statistics.

26.2	82 percent	July 22, 1966	a vote of 4 to 6

Grammar Exercise

Identify the number errors in the following paragraph.

1   In the Obama-McCain presidential race in two thousand eight, Senator Barack
2 Obama received fifty-two point nine percent of the popular vote, whereas Senator
3 John McCain received forty-five point six percent. Voters above forty-five years of
4 age had the highest voter turnout, above sixty-nine percent. Sixty-six percent of
5 voters from the age of eighteen to twenty-four voted for Barack Obama. Although
6 the percent of younger voters increased slightly in the 2008 elections, younger
7 voters still remained at the low voting rate of forty-nine percent.

Use numbers correctly. Review your essay to correct your use of numbers. Follow the rules above.

Learning Language

With only a letter or two difference among them, the words *million, billion,* and *trillion* are similar enough to potentially cause confusion. Work with a partner to connect each word to the numeral it represents. Put the numerals in order according to their value. Then develop a prompt that will help you to remember the value of each number. You might try making a rhyme that uses the words in sequence, or use the numerals in an image such as a pyramid

Persuasive

Have I used numbers and numerals correctly?

Most argumentative essays about a political controversy include references to dates, statistics, and other relevant numbers.

■ Have students turn back to the model Argumentative Essay on SE pages 219–220 to look for different kinds of numbers.

■ Ask students to explain the rule for each number they find.

Grammar Exercise
Answers

line 1: two thousand eight—2008
line 2: fifty-two point nine percent—52.9 percent
line 3: forty-five point six percent—45.6 percent; forty-five—45
line 4: sixty-nine percent—69 percent
line 5: eighteen to twenty-four—18 to 24
line 7: forty-nine percent—49 percent
Note: In line 4, "Sixty-six percent" remains in words because it begins the sentence.

Use numbers correctly. Encourage students to copy examples for writing numbers in their writer's notebook and bookmark the page for later reference.

⭐ TEKS 11.13D; ELPS 5D, 5E

✱ For more about writing numbers, see SE page 684.

Learning Language

As partners work, be sure they pronounce the words *million, billion,* and *trillion* aloud in order to distinguish each beginning sound or blend.

✔ DIFFERENTIATE INSTRUCTION
⭐ ELPS 2A, 2B

  Conventions Connections

Grammar: Numbers and Numerals
- *Student Edition: Proofreader's Guide* pages 684–685
- *SkillsBook* page 47

✱ *Write Source Online* **GrammarSnap**

Sentence Structure

How can I add variety to my sentence structures?

Ask students to discuss the examples shown on the SE page. Have students describe what is the same about each word, phrase, or clause in each example. Explain that this sameness is what creates the parallel structure of each sentence.

Ask students to explain the effect that parallel structure has for the reader. If they have difficulty describing the effect, ask them to write the information from the first sentence in a different way. Help them realize that the example sentence communicates its information clearly and concisely.

✱ For more about understanding and using a variety of sentences, see SE pages 756–775.

Exercise
Answers

1. The committee debated the humane, political, and **rising-costs** aspects of the problem.

2. Nick spent the afternoon studying Spanish, practicing his wrestling, and **working at the hardware store**.

3. Most Americans are concerned about jobs, health care, and **the environment**.

4. Rafael's coach said that he had made important plays, **supported the team, and helped boost team spirit.** DIFFERENTIATE INSTRUCTION ↘

Check for the correct use of parallel structure. Guide students to identify any examples of parallel structure in their writing, and to correct it as needed.
⭐ TEKS 11.13D ELPS 5E, 5F

⭐ **Conventions Connections**

Grammar: Parallel Structure

Student Edition: Proofreader's Guide pages 770–773
- ***SkillsBook*** pages 170, 171

🖊 ***Write Source Online GrammarSnap***

⭐ TEKS **11.13D** Edit drafts for grammar; ELPS **5E** Employ increasingly complex grammatical structures; **5F** Write using a variety of grade-appropriate sentence lengths, patterns, and connecting words

---

⭐ TEKS 11.13D

Sentence Structure

How can I add variety to my sentence structures?

When you edit for *sentence structure*, you look for ways to add variety to your writing. One way to do that is to use parallelism with words, phrases, or clauses. Parallelism, or parallel structure, happens when you repeat similar word patterns—or grammatical structures—for clarity, rhythm, or emphasis.

Parallel structure with words

Martino likes hiking, swimming, and wrestling.

Parallel structure with phrases

The coach wanted Elisa to exercise regularly, to get enough sleep, and to practice every day.

Parallel structure with clauses

Alex expected that he would present his paper, that he would show his slides, and that his audience would ask questions.

Remember, once you decide to use parallel structure, you have to keep your grammatical constructions—whether with words, phrases, or clauses—the same.

Exercise

Rewrite each sentence, correcting errors in parallel structure.

1. The committee debated the humane, political, and the rising costs aspects of the problem.
2. Nick spent the afternoon studying Spanish, practicing his wrestling, and he worked at the hardware store.
3. Most Americans are concerned about jobs, health care, and that we need to do something to fix the environment.
4. Rafael's coach said that he had made important plays, he had supported the team, and that he had helped boost team spirit.

Edit

Check for the correct use of parallel structure. Make sure that if you use three or more words, phrases, or clauses in a series that the word pattern, or grammatical structure, is the same for each.

Mechanics: Punctuation

How do I punctuate in parallel structures?

When you edit for *mechanics*, you check for correct use of capitalization and punctuation. If you use three or more words, phrases, or clauses in a sentence that have the same grammatical construction, you need to use commas to separate each of the three items.

- Notice the correct use of commas in these parallel structures.

    Incorrect: The most important political issues are the economy, health care and the national debt.

    Correct: The most important political issues are the economy, health care, and the national debt.

    Incorrect: Anya's aunt advised her to study hard to get involved in sports and to help out at home.

    Correct: Anya's aunt advised her to study hard, to get involved in sports, and to help out at home.

Exercise

Rewrite each sentence, correcting punctuation errors with the use of parallel structure.

1. Manuel's dream was to study architecture, to start his own business and to help his community.
2. My dog loves running barking and chasing balls.
3. My dad told me that I had to bring up my grades, that I had to spend less time on the computer and that I had to develop a better attitude.
4. Pedro's shopping list included fruit rice, milk, lettuce and beans.

Check for punctuation in parallel structures. Make sure that you have used commas to separate the elements in any series of three items in your essay.

Persuasive

Mechanics: Punctuation

How do I punctuate in parallel structures?

Point out to students that creating parallel structure in their sentences won't help their readers if they haven't punctuated the sentences clearly as well. Have students discuss the example sentences shown. Ask them to explain the parallel structure of each sentence and why the commas increase the clarity of each one.

Have partners work together to write three sentences showing parallel structure—one with parallel words, one with parallel phrases, and one with parallel clauses. Then have them exchange sentences with another pair and read through them together.

Exercise
Answers

1. Add a comma after *business* in first line.

2. Add a comma after *running* and after *barking*.

3. Add a comma after *computer* in second line.

4. Add a comma after *fruit* and after *lettuce*.

Check for punctuation in parallel structures. Guide students to identify any examples of parallel structure in their writing, and to correct its punctuation as needed.

 TEKS 11.13D; **ELPS** 5E, 5F

Differentiated Instruction: **ELPS** 5E, 5F
English Language Learners

Turn to the Appendix section of the Teacher's Edition for information on language transfer issues with sentence structure.

ELP Level **Beginning**	ELP Level **Intermediate**	ELP Level **Advanced/Advanced High**
Write sentences, such as *Nick studied Spanish. He practiced wrestling. He worked at the store.* Guide students to combine them into one long sentence.	Have partners examine the word patterns in each example and work together to correct the parallel structure. Discuss their work as a group.	Have partners complete the exercise. Then challenge students to revise the examples to include a variety of sentence structures and connecting words.

TEKS **11.13D** Edit drafts for mechanics **ELPS** **5E** Employ increasingly complex grammatical structures; **5F** Write using a variety of grade-appropriate sentence lengths, patterns, and connecting words

Editing Checking for Conventions

Give students a few moments to look over the Proofreader's Guide (SE pages 634–779). Throughout the year, they can refer to the instruction, rules, and examples to clarify any checklist items or to resolve questions about their own writing.

 **ELPS** 1B **DIFFERENTIATE INSTRUCTION ↘**

Check your editing. In addition to checking for all the items on the Editing Checklist, tell students to be sure that
- direct quotations are enclosed in quotation marks,
- they have copied quotations accurately from their notes, and
- all sources are identified in parentheses within the essay, and on a works-cited page, if required. **DIFFERENTIATE INSTRUCTION ↘**

 TEKS 11.13D

Creating a Title

Encourage students to be creative as they try to come up with good essay titles. Point out that their titles should reflect the tone of their essays.

 **Conventions Connections**

Mechanics: Commas to Set Off Nonrestrictive Phrases and Clauses
- *Student Edition: Proofreader's Guide* pages 642–643
- *SkillsBook* page 14

Mechanics: Commas After Introductory Phrases and Clauses
- *Student Edition: Proofreader's Guide* pages 640 (+), 644–645, 646 (+)
- *SkillsBook* pages 12, 129

✳ *Write Source Online* **GrammarSnap**

Texas Traits

Editing Checking for Conventions

Check your editing. This checklist will help you to thoroughly edit your essay for conventions of grammar, sentence structure, mechanics (capitalization and punctuation), and spelling. On a piece of paper, write the numbers 1 to 8. If you can answer "yes," put a check mark after that number. If you can't, continue to edit for that convention.

Editing Checklist

Conventions

GRAMMAR
_____ 1. Have I used numbers and numerals correctly?
_____ 2. Do I have errors in parallel structure?

SENTENCE STRUCTURE
_____ 3. Have I used varied sentence structure?
_____ 4. Have I tried using parallel structure to vary my sentences and to create rhythm and emphasis?

MECHANICS (CAPITALIZATION AND PUNCTUATION)
_____ 5. Do I use end punctuation after all my sentences?
_____ 6. Have I correctly punctuated items in a series (sentences using parallel structure)?

SPELLING
_____ 7. Have I spelled all words correctly?
_____ 8. Have I checked for commonly misused pairs?

Creating a Title

After your editing is complete, add a title that describes your essay and catches your reader's attention. Here are a few ways to approach this task.
- Sum up the position: **The National Debt Means Danger**
- Call the reader to action: **Put a Damper on the Debt**
- Hook the reader: **National Debt: How Much Do You Owe?**

Differentiated Instruction: Advanced Learners

Have students prepare customized editing checklists for themselves. They should organize a "top ten" list of errors that they tend to make. As students continue to use and add to their checklists, they will be less likely to repeat these errors.

Differentiated Instruction: Struggling Learners

Visual learners may wish to publish their work in a multi-media presentation. Encourage students to work with a technology specialist in school or to partner with a computer-proficient peer to help them create their presentations.

Publishing

Sharing Your Essay

After you've finished editing your essay for conventions, it's time to give the essay a public debut—by reading it in a debate, publishing it in a newspaper, or sending it to an official involved in the controversy you've explored.

Format your final copy. To format a handwritten essay, use the guidelines below or follow your teacher's instructions. Make a clean copy and carefully proofread it. Remember, if you see something you want to revise for your final draft, go for it!

Focusing on Presentation

- Write neatly using blue or black ink.
- Place your name in the upper left corner of page 1.
- Skip a line and center your title; skip another line and start your essay.
- Indent every paragraph and leave a one-inch margin on all four sides.
- Write your last name and the page number in the upper right corner of every page.

Contact an Official

Identify an official who can play a role in resolving the political controversy. Send your essay to that person along with a cover letter briefly outlining your position and asking for help. Remember to use a respectful tone in your letter and to encourage the official to take action to support your position.

Publish a Letter

Reformat your essay as a letter to the editor of a newspaper, magazine, or news Web site. Be sure your letter conforms to the publication's submission guidelines. Then send your letter.

Stage a Debate

Invite a group of friends or family members to hold a debate on the political controversy you've chosen. Include audience members who have not taken a position. Present and defend your position. Then allow others to present and defend theirs. After the debate, ask the audience to adopt a position based on the debate.

Persuasive

Publishing

Sharing Your Essay

After students have read the ideas at the bottom of SE page 249, invite them to suggest additional options for sharing their argumentative essays with appropriate audiences.

Format your final copy. Remind students of your guidelines for formatting a final draft.

TEKS 11.13E

Focusing on Presentation

Contact an Official If students plan to send their essays to officials, ask them to submit cover letters first to you along with their final essays. Review the letters with the student to make sure that they conform to proper business letter form and that they use a respectful tone.

✳ For more about the parts of a business letter, have students turn to SE page 538.

Publish a Letter Tell students who plan to publish their essays as letters that they can check online to find the submission guidelines for the newspapers or magazines they want to contact. Remind them to read the guidelines carefully before finalizing their letter.

Stage a Debate If students would like to stage a debate, establish rules of conduct for the debate ahead of time. Print these out and make sure everyone who plans to participate in the debate has a copy. ✔ DIFFERENTIATE INSTRUCTION

Technology Connections

✳ *Write Source Online* **Portfolio**

✳ *Write Source Online* **Essay Evaluation**

Differentiated Instruction: English Language Learners

ELPS 3A, 3C, 3F, 3G, 3H

ELP Level **Beginning**	ELP Level **Intermediate**	ELP Level **Advanced/Advanced High**
Work with students to script a debate to express differing opinions. Have students practice pronouncing new vocabulary before presenting their debate.	Guide partners to script and hold a debate. Scripts should allow students to give information using a variety of sentence lengths, types, and connecting words.	Have partners script and present a debate. Scripts should include a variety of grammatical structures and detailed explanations of ideas.

TEKS 11.13E Revise final draft in response to feedback from peers and teacher and publish written work for appropriate audiences; **ELPS 3A** Practice producing sounds of newly acquired vocabulary to pronounce English words; **3C** Speak using a variety of grammatical structures, sentence lengths, sentence types, and connecting words; **3F** Give information during extended speaking assignments; **3G** Express opinions; **3H** Explain with increasing specificity and detail

Evaluating an Argumentative Essay

To support understanding of the following four sample essays—one sample essay for each possible score point—refer to the scoring guide on SE pages 36–37 and to key instruction from the persuasive writing unit.

Score Point 4: Highly Effective

Work through this sample essay with students, pointing out the qualities that earn it an overall score point of 4. In addition to the callouts on the student pages, use the following questions to facilitate analysis.

- What position does the writer defend? (...*a strong dollar can also be responsible for many of our country's economic problems, and... Americans need to make better buying choices if they want to strengthen our economy.*)
- What ideas argue that a strong dollar is not always good for the U.S. economy? (*Visitors to the U.S. receive fewer dollars for their own currency and are less likely to visit the U.S.; U.S. products are more expensive in foreign markets, so fewer U.S. products are sold, manufacturing declines, and the U.S. economy gets weaker.*) **DIFFERENTIATE INSTRUCTION ↘**

250

Evaluating an Argumentative Essay

To evaluate the argumentative essays that follow, use the scoring guide on pages **36–37**. The essays are examples of writing for each score on the guide. Always remember to think about the overall quality of the writing. (**The essays may contain some errors.**)

Writing that fits a score of 4 is highly effective.

A Strong Dollar Weakens America

Position is clearly stated; voice is forceful.

The prevailing wisdom is that a strong dollar is good for the U.S. economy. When the dollar rises against the currencies of others, such as the European Union, China, or Japan, it generally indicates that our country's resources and labor market are in good shape and that inflation is under control. In short, when the dollar is strong, so is our economy. However, a closer look reveals that a strong dollar can also be responsible for many of our country's economic problems, and that Americans need to make better buying choices if they want to strengthen our economy.

When people think about whether the dollar is strong, they point to travel. A strong dollar means that U.S. tourists get more for their money when they spend it in other countries. This is true, but the U.S. tourism industry can also be hit hard by a strong dollar. When tourists visit the United States, they trade their currency for U.S. dollars. If the dollar is strong, these visitors receive fewer dollars in trade for their own currency. This makes a visit to the U.S. more expensive, and tourists may be less likely to visit. Expanding this thinking down the line, this will result in fewer jobs and less pay for people in the tourism industry here at home.

Shows strong organization; each idea flows smoothly to the next.

A strong dollar makes it difficult for U.S. firms to compete in foreign markets. Products made here are usually priced in U.S. dollars, so when a computer made in the U.S. is sold in another country, it costs more compared to products made in places with weaker currencies. As a result, fewer products made by U.S. companies are sold in foreign markets (Gilliam). This inevitably leads to a decline in manufacturing jobs in the United States, which then contributes to a weaker economy.

Resources

Benchmark Papers

- Secondhand Smoke: A Silent Killer (strong) See TE Appendix

- High Insurance for Teens (poor) See TE Appendix

Complex ideas are developed thoroughly.

Perhaps the worst problem with the strong dollar is that it makes it harder for U.S. companies to compete on our own shores. As noted earlier, when the dollar is stronger, products made in the U.S. tend to be more expensive than products made in countries with weaker currencies. Here's an illustration of the process and its consequences: a frugal American consumer chooses to purchase a television made in Japan because its price is significantly lower than the price of a similar unit made in the U.S. Such consumers are not aware of how the strong dollar may affect their buying decisions; they are just looking for the biggest bang for their hard-earned bucks. This kind of thinking ends up weakening our economy, because it will, down the line, result in fewer U.S.-made products and fewer U.S. workers who will be needed to make those products.

Counters opposing argument effectively.

Some economists argue that a strong dollar is beneficial because it provides Americans with more buying power. In a sense, this is true. The strong dollar makes the cost of imported goods cheaper, but the far-ranging results of their choices need to be made clearer to the buying public: When people in this country buy foreign-made goods, U.S. dollars flow out of our economy and into the coffers of the nations that produce them. China's economy is growing at a phenomenal rate, thanks in part to (and at the expense of) our strong U.S. dollar (Allain). Every time an American consumer chooses to buy a Japanese car that is flashier and less expensive then its American counterpart, it strengthens Japan's economy, it hurts U.S. workers, and is weakens our economy.

Focus is clear and sustained; overall firm grasp of conventions enhances writing.

A strong dollar can mean some advantages for consumers now, but it tends to hurt the U.S. economy in the long run. Fewer exports for American businesses, fewer jobs for Americans, and lower pay for American workers are the result. If, as Americans, we truly want to do the best we can to strengthen our nation's economy, we need to adjust our thinking about a strong dollar and take it to the marketplace the next time we go shopping.

Persuasive

 Review your essay. Discuss the essay with a partner to determine why it is considered a 4-point essay.

- Why is the writer's analysis of the "worst problem with the strong dollar" in Paragraph 4 effective? *(Possible response: The writer builds a logical, progressively detailed case to support an idea that might seem illogical at first reading.)*
- How does the use of an expert citation strengthen the counter-argument in Paragraph 5? *(Possible response: It provides a source of concrete information, showing the reader that this argument is supported and verified with significant financial data.)*
- What makes the final paragraph an effective ending for the essay? *(Possible response: It restates both the writer's position and the call to action from the first paragraph.)*

 Review your essay. Use the holistic scoring guide to frame the discussion for why the essay received a score of 4.

**Differentiated Instruction:
English Language Learners**

⭐ **ELPS** 3E, 4D, 4F, 4K

Refer to pages 582–583 for a reminder of how to do a shared reading of a persuasive essay.

ELP Level **Beginning**	ELP Level **Intermediate**	ELP Level **Advanced/Advanced High**
Preteach terms and vocabulary such as *a strong dollar* and *economy*. Use simplified language to make the sample comprehensible.	Preteach terms and vocabulary such as *economy, products,* and *consumers*. After reading, provide sentence stems to help students share what they learned.	Ask students to share what they know about trade and the economy. After reading, have them analyze new information from the essay.

ELPS **3E** Share information in cooperative learning interactions; **4D** Use prereading supports to enhance comprehension of written text; **4F** Use support from peers and teachers to develop vocabulary; **4K** Demonstrate English comprehension and expand reading skills by employing analytical skills

Score Point 3: Generally Effective

Work through this sample essay with students, pointing out the qualities that earn it an overall score point of 3. In addition to the callouts on the student pages, use the following questions to facilitate analysis.

- How effective is the title of the essay? Why? (*Possible response: Equation format establishes focus on statistical information while signaling a somewhat informal approach to the content; students will have varying ideas about effectiveness.*)

- How does the accumulation of information about teen debt in Paragraphs 2 and 3 help the reader understand the writer's position? (*It creates an image of piled up teen debt threatening to topple the country's economy.*)

- What errors in conventions are present in the essay? Do they distract from the writer's main points? (*Possible responses: The use of the word* right *rather than* rite *in Paragraph 1; the use of* faze *rather than* phase *in Paragraph 2; the use of* fairing *rather than* faring *in Paragraph 3. Most students will find that the errors are relatively minor and generally do not distract from the writer's main points.*)

DIFFERENTIATE INSTRUCTION ↘

252

Writing that fits a score of 3 is generally effective.

Teens + Easy Credit = Bad Idea!

There's no question that teens are a powerful part of our nation's economy. Teenagers spend billions of dollars annually, and businesses spend untold marketing bucks courting teenagers and their cash. If you spend a day at a mall, you'll see hordes of teenagers wielding credit cards in the clothing stores and food courts. As about a third of all high school seniors use a credit card (Goodman), it's not surprising that many more teenagers think they deserve credit cards. Some say it's a right of passage! This trend is a major problem, however, and it has long-term consequences.

> **Organizational strategy is effective, uses examples to illustrate points.**

Here's another familiar scene: Swarms of first-year college students descend on campuses across the country, excited and enthusiastic to begin this new faze in their lives. At the same time, they get bombed with offers for credit cards, and many eagerly sign up. Soon, many students find themselves over their heads in debt, and what do they do? They turn to their parents to bail them out. The average college student racks up more than $3,000 in credit card debt by the time they graduate (Marks). This makes it obvious that many teenagers need more education than they're getting about how to manage their money.

> **Strong details support writer's position.**

Recent studies and surveys show some eye-opening news about how young adults (those ages 19 to 35) are fairing in today's economic climate. It doesn't look good. About a third of young adults say they are burdened with over $10,000 in credit card debt. More than half of them pay just the minimum amount on their credit cards each month. Three out of 20 young adults report having their credit taken away (Meegan). Again, these statistics make it crystal clear that too many young people don't have a clue about how to handle money, and if these trends continue, our country will be facing severe economic ruin down the road.

Voice is generally authentic, but writer uses a few too many informal, overused phrases.

Each paragraph has a clear focus and develops ideas.

A few spelling errors are distracting, but writer's command of conventions is generally good.

Parents need to do a better job preparing their kids to be financially-savvy as adults. Too many parents hand off their credit cards to their teens. This easy access to credit doesn't teach teenagers about how to pay for that new must-have. While a number of students have their own debit cards, these don't build a credit history for the owner, and teens can run into trouble if they overdraw their accounts. Other credit options for young people like prepaid or stored-value cards can be useful, but most of these have built-in fees, they also don't help teens build a credit history. The bottom line is that parents need to take the time to educate their kids about credit and explore the options.

A national group, called Jump$tart, has formed a coaltion of all 50 states to advocate for educating teens and young adults about their finances. Jump$tart reports that a few states right now require a course in personal finances, and many more, such as New York, Texas, North Carolina, and Illinois, require personal finance instruction to be built into other classes. These efforts will go a long way to helping our nation's economic picture. So on the plus side, it seems that more grownups are paying attention!

Lawmakers have also recognized that easy access to credit for young people is not good for the economy either. Under a law that takes affect in 2010, applicants under 21 will no longer be eligible for a credit card unless they can prove they are able to prepay debt, or unless a parent co-signs the card. While some teenagers may complain that this is harsh or unfair, at the end of the day, it's really for our own good.

This isn't to say that teens are financially irresponsible, that learning about credit is rocket science. Experts agree that high school students can and should learn to use a checking account wisely, and many do (Booth). However, students need to become educated credit users, for their own good, and for the good of our country's economy.

Persuasive

■ How would you describe the tone of this essay? What words and phrases in the essay establish this tone? *(Possible responses: Informal or familiar, but knowledgeable. First page: Title equation, "there's no question," "hordes of teenagers," "another familiar scene"; second page: "hand off," "paying attention," "rocket science.")*

■ What changes could the writer make to strengthen the position and the conclusion of the essay? *(Possible response: Including a statement at the beginning about students' need to learn more about credit and how to handle money would strengthen the overall focus and coherence of the essay.)*

Differentiated Instruction: English Language Learners

ELPS 3B, 4F

ELP Level **Beginning**	ELP Level **Intermediate**	ELP Level **Advanced/Advanced High**
Read the sample essay together. Simplify the callout notes to discuss traits like organization and voice. Have students repeat each trait with you.	Read the sample essay together and guide students to examine traits. Provide sentence stems to help students discuss new ideas in the content area text.	Have students read the sample independently. Then have them use complete sentences to discuss new ideas in the content area text.

ELPS 3B Expand vocabulary/learning and using routine language needed for classroom communication; **4F** Use support from peers and teachers to read content area text

Score Point 2: Somewhat Effective

Work through this sample essay with students, pointing out the qualities that earn it an overall score point of 2. In addition to the callouts on the student pages, use the following questions to facilitate analysis.

- What information does the writer provide to support the position that people should "shop locally"? (*Possible responses: The writer provides quite a bit of local information, including quotations from local business owners and personal observations. However, there is only one piece of specific statistical data cited to support the assertions.*)

- What are some ways that the writer could have developed the idea that buying locally improves the *national* economy? (*Possible response: The writer could have described the connections of one local business to the larger economy, for example, jobs it provides, suppliers it does business with, taxes it pays.*)

- How might the writer have made better use of the ideas in the final paragraph? (*Possible response: The writer might have placed this paragraph earlier in the essay and then supported each stated reason in subsequent paragraphs.*)

Writing that fits a score of 2 is somewhat effective.

2

Why Buying Local is *Good for Our Economy*

One way to boost our national economy can be found in the slogan, "Shop Locally." This means that people should spend more of their money in their own home towns, rather than ordering items from the Internet or from other countries. This is a good idea for many reasons.

> Writer states focus clearly; voice sounds authentic.

When people spend their money by buying things off the Internet, they think it is easier and quicker. This may be true. But it hurts the local business owners. Lots of whom have been in business for awhile and have seen their business drop off in recent times. As one local business owner says, "People who used to shop here think it's easier to just order something off the Internet. They don't realize that they are shutting down businesses like mine." What they also don't realize is that people often end up paying more because they have to pay for the extra shipping and handing costs, too.

> Ideas in second and third paragraphs not developed or are too similar.

Another local shop owner states that "I try to provide extra services to my customers, such as doing special orders. This helps, but I've seen my business drop twenty percent in the last two years." She feels that people don't understand that when local stores close, it hurts the town's economy.

> Ideas do not progress smoothly.

You can walk down the streets in this town and you will see a lot of store fronts for rent. Others are struggling just to stay open. Some hold big sales or give big markdowns to intice customers in. There are also states that have "state tax holidays" when people don't have to pay the sales tax. These ideas can all help, but they won't solve the problem long-turn.

> Developing an important idea— how businesses support towns— would add depth to reader's understanding.

What are some reasons to buy local? One, it makes your town's economy stronger. Town businesses support things like the police, schools and roads by paying taxes. So when you buy local, you support your town. Two, it leads to a stronger economy for our country as a whole.

Argumentative Essay **255**

Writing that fits a score of 1 is ineffective.

Too many ideas are presented in one paragraph; writing lacks cohesion and organization.

Outsourcing and Our Econmy

A big problem with our country's econmy today is what is called outsourcing. This is when jobs are taken from the US to other places because the labor is cheaper in other countries. This is a bad idea and it hurts our country's econmy. Some jobs are in manfacturing, such as in the car industry. Other places that have been hurt by outsourcing are in fields like customer service industrys. Places like Detroit, Michigan were for a long time the center of manfacturing for cars. Then businesses decided that they could have the cars made in other countries and it would be less expensive to make them because they could pay them less. This is an example of outsourcing. This was good for the car companies but it was bad for places like Detroit, Michigan. As a result lots of people in Detroit lost there jobs and the econmy suffered. Companies like computer companies realized that they could pay workers in other countries to do there customer service. So now when you call customer service with a problem your having with your computer you might talk to someone in places like India. Many customers are disatissfied with this outsourcing because they have to stay on hold for a long time and then when they answer they still don't get there problems fixed.

Some ideas veer off-topic; errors in conventions make writing hard to follow.

Many people are out of work right here in the US. They need jobs to help support there families and not live paycheck-to-paycheck. Too many families are struggling hard to put food on the table. Just because labor is cheaper in other countries doesn't make it alright. Businesses can do without a little bit extra profit, they make enough profit as it is!

Conclusion is one long run-on sentence. The essay is incomplete and unfocused.

Unemployment is up due to outsourceing and businesses need to change this cuz unemployment hurts our countrys' econmy and our country has a lot of people out of work right here at home, so its best that we go back to the US way of doing business—the US way.

Persuasive

Score Point 1: Ineffective

Work through this sample essay with students, pointing out the qualities that earn it an overall score point of 1. In addition to the callouts on the student pages, use the following questions to facilitate analysis.

- How might the writer reorganize the ideas in the first paragraph? (*Possible responses: The ideas about manufacturing could be one paragraph; the ideas about customer service could be another paragraph.*)
- Why is Paragraph 2 considered off-topic? (*The writer discusses unemployment in the U.S. without clearly connecting this problem to the main issues of outsourcing; the implied connection is distracting and confusing to the reader.*)
- What opposing arguments could the writer have addressed? (*Possible responses: The advantages of outsourcing outweigh its disadvantages, both to individual businesses and to the economy as a whole; therefore, its use is not likely to decrease in the future.*)

Student Self-Assessment

To give students additional practice with evaluating argumentative essays, use one or both of the **Benchmark Papers** (see Resources box, TE page 250). ✔ DIFFERENTIATE INSTRUCTION

 ELPS 4K Demonstrate English comprehension and expand reading skills by employing analytical skills

Evaluating and Reflecting on Your Writing

It is important for students to have an opportunity to evaluate and reflect on their writing experience. Yet many students are reluctant to engage in this process, partially because they have difficulty identifying their own strengths and weaknesses, and partially because it may feel like just another writing assignment. To help students benefit from the reflective process, provide alternatives to written responses.

- They can share reflections in one-on-one discussions with you.
- They can work with classmates to record their reflections in a writer's blog.

DIFFERENTIATE INSTRUCTION ↘

A Writer's Blog

Most students are probably familiar with blogs. The term *blog* is an abbreviation for *Web log*. Here are some of its features.

- A blog is an online journal or diary that one person or several people contribute to on a regular basis.
- It is available for reading by the general public.
- Blogs can be established for many different purposes. A writer's blog could be used to reflect on writing successes and problems.
- Readers can leave comments and feedback for the "bloggers."

Students can find information about setting up a blog by typing a key phrase, such as "create a blog," in the entry box of their search engine.

Evaluating and Reflecting on Your Writing

After you finish your argumentative essay, take some time to reflect on your essay and your writing experience. On a separate sheet of paper, complete each sentence below. This activity will reinforce what you've learned and help you to apply it to future assignments.

My Argumentative Essay

1. The strongest part of my essay is . . .

2. The part that still needs work is . . .

3. The prewriting activity that worked best for me was . . .

4. The main thing I learned about providing precise and relevant evidence in an argumentative essay is . . .

5. In my next argumentative essay, I would like to . . .

6. One question I still have about writing an argumentative essay is . . .

Persuasive Writing
Writing an Editorial

Persuasive writing can take many forms. An argumentative essay, a letter to the editor, an editorial, and a satire are all examples of persuasive writing. Editorials often appear in newspapers and magazines. These articles present an opinion, an idea, or a solution. Much of what you have learned about writing an agumentative essay applies to writing an editorial as well. A good editorial will have a clearly stated thesis based on logical reasons and supported by precise and relevant details. Like a well-written argumentative essay, an effective editorial will have a clear organizational structure and a tone appropriate for the intended audience. Finally, a well-written editorial will express the author's unique perspective and voice.

In this chapter, you'll read a sample of an editorial that argues for the creation of a youth recreational center in the town of Harriston. You will then write your own editorial about a topic you feel strongly about.

Writing Guidelines

Subject:	A school or community issue
Purpose:	To make a point
Form:	Editorial
Audience:	Classmates

"Our opinions do not really blossom into fruition until we have expressed them to someone else."

—Mark Twain

Writing an Editorial

Objectives

- recognize an editorial as a form of persuasive writing
- use what was learned about persuasive writing to write an editorial
- plan, draft, revise, edit, and share an editorial

An **editorial** is a brief piece of writing in which the writer shares an opinion, idea, or solution about a topic or problem.

- An editorial states a position that is strongly felt as well as clearly reasoned and supported.
- The writer's goal is to help readers see an issue from his or her particular perspective, which may or may not be different from their own.

Editorials can be written for different purposes. The most common purposes are the following:

- to explain or interpret a situation;
- to criticize an action, decision, or situation;
- to persuade readers to take a specific, positive action; or
- to praise people or organizations for doing something well.

Explain that students will be focusing on writing a persuasive editorial. Encourage them to review examples of editorials from several different sources (local and national newspapers, magazines, and other publications, both in print and on the internet) as references for writing their own editorials.

Differentiated Instruction: English Language Learners

ELPS 1B, 1C, 1E

ELP Level **Beginning**	ELP Level **Intermediate**	ELP Level **Advanced/Advanced High**
Guide students to reflect on their writing. Review the five traits in context and have students repeat these terms with you.	Guide students as they write their reflections. Have them focus on the five traits and identify one area they will monitor in future writing tasks.	Have students focus on the five traits as they write their reflections. Have them identify two areas they will monitor in future writing tasks.

ELPS 1B Monitor written language production and employ self-corrective techniques or other resources; **1C** Use strategic learning strategies to acquire basic and grade-level vocabulary; **1E** Internalize new basic and academic language by using and reusing it/ writing

Editorial

After students read the editorial on SE pages 258–259, ask what they notice about the editorial that makes it similar to the argumentative essay they wrote earlier. Students may notice the following characteristics:

- The editorial states a position about a controversial issue.
- It builds the argument with three supporting reasons.
- It counters an objection.
- It encourages the audience to take a specific, positive action.

Ask students to describe what makes this editorial a persuasive one. Discuss whether it includes elements of other types of editorials in addition to its persuasive focus. Students may point out the last sentence in the first paragraph, for example, where the writer states a critical opinion of the council's decision not to fund the youth center. **DIFFERENTIATE INSTRUCTION** ↘

Editorial

In the following editorial, Julia shares her opinion that her town needs a recreation center. Like an argumentative essay, the editorial presents the writer's position, provides details to support that position, and addresses the objections of those who have divergent views.

Say Yes to the Future

Beginning
The beginning introduces the issue with a real-life anecdote to engage readers and provides a clear thesis statement.

Recently, a group of teens spoke before the city council to support a proposed youth recreational center for the city of Harriston. The teens, many of who were joined by their parents, asked voters to provide $100,000 to convert the old Elm Street Gym into a place where young people could go to play basketball, lift weights, enjoy a game of chess, or just hang out with their friends. City council members listened politely, but in the end decided the city had better ways to spend its money. The council's priorities are skewed, and their decision is wrong-headed. For the sake of everyone in Harriston, the new youth recreational center must be funded.

Middle
The middle paragraphs provide precise and relevant evidence that support the writer's thesis.

The issue is not just about providing funding for something the youth of Harriston want. The issue is about providing funding for something the youth of Harriston desperately need. The medical community has already sounded the alarm. Physically, America's teens are in worse shape, much worse shape, than they were twenty years ago. Fifty percent of teenagers are not getting the exercise they need to develop healthy hearts and lungs, and are gaining weight. Overweight teens will likely become overweight adults who will experience myriad health problems: heart disease, diabetes, and arthritis.

Many teens spent far too much time involved in sedentary activities. They watch endless TV re-runs, spend hours playing computer games, or chat and text on their phones. A recent study conducted by the University of Memphis found that watching TV slows metabolism—the rate at which the body burns calories—down to a crawl. A person watching TV actually burns fewer calories than a person sitting still and doing nothing. Most teens watch an average of 30 hours of television a week. We must offer them more life-enhancing alternatives for their spare time.

Writing an Editorial **259**

Finally, we need to consider the well-documented social and psychological benefits of exercise, sports, and spending time with friends. Physical activity is good not only for the body but for the mind. Physically active teens have higher self-esteem and experience less anxiety than inactive teens. Team or individual sports help teens set goals, improve self-discipline, and develop social skills.

Some will argue that schools already provide physical education programs or that it is the responsibility of parents to provide opportunities for their children. In fact, economic constraints have forced our high school to cut back dramatically its physical education program, paring it down to minimum standards. In addition, most parents in our town simply cannot afford sports club memberships.

Building a youth recreational center is something we must find the money and the will to do. The physical, social, and psychological benefits for teens are undeniable. Investing in a youth recreational center is an investment in the future—an investment in the health and well-being of the young people of our town. We must not fail to do this.

Middle
The fourth middle paragraph provides an honest and accurate representation of divergent views.

Ending
The ending restates the writer's position and leaves the reader something to think about.

Persuasive

 Respond to the reading. Answer the following questions.

Focus and Coherence (1) How do the middle paragraphs support the writer's thesis?

Organization (2) What organizational pattern does the writer use?

Development of Ideas (3) Name three specific details that support the writer's main ideas.

Voice (4) Find an example of the writer's unique and authentic voice.

 Respond to the reading

Answers

Focus and Coherence 1. The middle paragraphs argue that teens need the youth center to counteract the effects of sedentary activities and to promote good physical and mental habits.

Organization 2. The beginning states the thesis, the middle presents the evidence in a logical sequence, and the ending restates the writer's position. Smooth transitions provide a clear, logical flow of information and ideas.

Development of Ideas 3. Possible details include 1) America's teens are in much worse shape than 20 years ago, 2) teens spend too much time in sedentary activities, and 3) physically active teens experience less anxiety.

Voice 4. *We must offer them more life-enhancing alternatives* states a strong opinion about the low value of watching TV and other sedentary activities when contrasted with the benefits of physical and social activity; this language provides a clear view of the writer's thoughts and ideas about the topic.

Differentiated Instruction: English Language Learners

ELPS 1H, 4F, 4K

Before reading the sample editorial, turn to TE pages 580–585 for additional language support for persuasive writing.

ELP Level Beginning	**ELP Level Intermediate**	**ELP Level Advanced/Advanced High**
Use visuals and gestures to preteach terms such as *recreational center* and *exercise* to help make the writing sample comprehensible.	Preteach terms such as *funding* and *sedentary*. Guide students to sort and analyze related terms about health and fitness.	Have students use the call-out notes to analyze how well the details support the writer's thesis statement.

 ELPS 1H Develop and expand repertoire of learning strategies; **4F** Use visual and contextual support to read content area text; **4K** Demonstrate English comprehension and expand reading skills by employing analytical skills

Prewriting Selecting a Topic

Work together to brainstorm a list of topics for students' editorials.

■ Create a chart on the board like the one shown, or provide photocopies of the reproducible T-chart (TE page A97) for students.

■ Distribute local and school newspapers. Have students skim feature articles and op-ed sections for topic ideas to list in their charts.

■ Encourage students to select issues that truly interest them and that they think they can discuss with clarity and strong feeling.

Choose your topic. Use brainstorming sessions to generate topic ideas. When you generate ideas together, some students are likely to choose the same issues. This has two benefits: Students can offer each other helpful advice and insights during the writing and revising stages. Later, students can compare their editorials to see how their individual perspectives affected how and what they wrote about the topics.

TEKS 11.13A

Focus on the Texas Traits

Development of Ideas

Remind students that they should try not to use overstatements or extreme language, which could weaken their ideas and their position. Any strongly critical statements they write must be balanced and supported by relevant, compelling details that will be convincing to readers.

Prewriting Selecting a Topic

The purpose of your editorial is to express an opinion about an issue you care about in your community or school. To find a topic for her editorial, Julia checked local newspapers and made a list of issues that were being discussed.

In the Community	At School
lack of support for senior center	unhealthful cafeteria food
cutting trees in city park	restrictions on student parking
teen recreation center *	elimination of gymnastic team

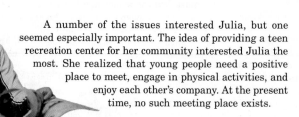

A number of the issues interested Julia, but one seemed especially important. The idea of providing a teen recreation center for her community interested Julia the most. She realized that young people need a positive place to meet, engage in physical activities, and enjoy each other's company. At the present time, no such meeting place exists.

 Prewrite

Choose your topic. In a chart like the one above, list timely issues in your community and in your school. Then put an asterisk (*) next to the issue you want to write about.

Focus on the Texas Traits

Development of Ideas Remember that the purpose of an editorial is to give an opinion and support it with enough relevant details to convince readers to support your position.

 TEKS 11.13A Plan a first draft by determining appropriate topics through a range of strategies

Gathering and Organizing Details

After you choose an issue, gather your thoughts about it. In a detail chart, Julia first listed serious arguments in favor of a recreation center. Then, for each serious point, she listed supporting facts and details.

Details Chart

Youth Recreation Center in Harriston	
Serious Arguments in Favor	Supporting Facts and Details
Teenagers need more opportunities for physical exercise.	50% of teenagers are not getting the exercise they need.
Teenagers spend too much time watching TV.	Watching TV slows metabolism down to a crawl.
Social and psychological benefits of a youth recreation center	Physically active teens have higher self-esteem

Writing a Thesis Statement

An editorial needs a strong thesis statement. Make sure that your thesis is clear and to the point. You can add supporting details and facts later. Here's how Julia created her thesis statement.

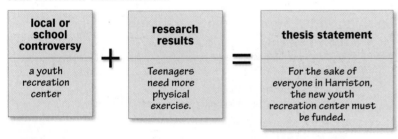

local or school controversy

a youth recreation center

+

research results

Teenagers need more physical exercise.

=

thesis statement

For the sake of everyone in Harriston, the new youth recreation center must be funded.

Persuasive

Prewrite

Write a thesis statement. Be sure that your thesis statement is a clear and concise representation of your opinion on the topic.

Gathering and Organizing Details

Ideally, students have chosen an issue that they care about and one that they can easily generate several positive, action-oriented statements about in their editorial. Keep in mind that students may decide to argue a position *against* a local decision or situation; guide them to alter their details charts as needed to help them support their thesis with a clear, positive approach. Students may benefit from working in groups and sharing ideas for reactions and feedback.

⟋ DIFFERENTIATE INSTRUCTION

Writing a Thesis Statement

Remind students that an editorial balances the writer's forceful opinion with evidence that will be persuasive to readers. Both the issues students choose and the research they decide to rely on need to be compelling to readers; balancing these two pieces will enable them to create a strong thesis statement for their editorial.

Write a thesis statement. Guide students to write a statement that accurately reflects their views on the topics they have chosen.

TEKS 11.13A, 11.16A

TEKS **11.13A** Plan a first draft by developing a thesis or controlling idea; **11.16A** Write an argumentative essay to the appropriate audience that includes a clear thesis or position based on logical reasons supported by precise and relevant evidence, including facts, expert opinions, quotations, and/or expressions of commonly held beliefs; **ELPS 1H** Develop and expand repertoire of learning strategies; **3G** Express opinions; **5F** Write using a variety of grade-appropriate sentence lengths, patterns, and connecting words; **5G** Explain with increasing specificity and detail

Drafting

Creating Your First Draft

Support students as they begin drafting each part of their editorials.

Writing Your Beginning Paragraph

Remind students that a beginning paragraph introduces the topic in an interesting way and states the thesis. A brief description of the topic and a few explanatory details should lead directly to a strong thesis statement that moves the reader forward to the supporting arguments.

Writing Your Middle Paragraphs

Tell students that the middle paragraphs of an editorial support the thesis with reasons, facts, and details that are appropriate to the purpose, audience, and content. Remind students to present and refute a view that is contrary to their own argument. Suggest that they share their ideas with others to get feedback about which evidence is the most compelling.

Finishing with a Strong Ending Paragraph

The ending paragraph summarizes ideas and leaves the reader with one final thought about the topic.

Write your first draft. Before students begin their drafts, tell them to read the page carefully and to keep the tips in mind as they write. Remind them to use transitions and rhetorical devices to clarify and enhance their argument.

TEKS 11.13B 11.16C

✱ For more about the basic parts of an essay, see SE page 618.

Drafting Creating Your First Draft

The following tips will help you to write an effective editorial. Also refer to the planning you did on the previous page.

Writing Your Beginning Paragraph

The **beginning** paragraph will introduce the topic and present your thesis statement.

- Open by clearly identifying the topic.

   Recently, a group of teens spoke before the city council in support of a youth recreation center for the city of Harriston.

- Present some details that explain the topic.

   The teens, many of whom were joined by their parents, asked voters to provide $100,000 to convert the old Elm Street Gym . . .

- End with your thesis statement.

   For the sake of Harriston, the new youth center . . .

Writing Your Middle Paragraphs

The **middle** paragraphs support your argument.
- Supply a main point, or argument, in each middle paragraph.
- Support each main point with solid and relevant evidence.
- Give an accurate and fair representation of a divergent view and present facts to explain why you disagree with that view.

Finishing with a Strong Ending Paragraph

- Restate your position.

   Building a youth recreation center is something we must find the money and the will to do.

- Give your reader food for thought.

   Investing in a youth recreation center is an investment in the future . . .

- Close with a powerful persuasive statement.

   We must not fail to do this.

Write your first draft. Use the guidelines above and your prewriting work as you develop your editorial.

TEKS **11.13B** Structure ideas in a sustained, persuasive way and develop drafts that include transitions and the rhetorical devices used to convey meaning; **11.16C** Write an argumentative essay that includes an organizing structure appropriate to the purpose, audience, and context

TEKS 11.13C, 11.16C

Writing an Editorial **263**

Revising Improving Your First Draft

After you have completed your first draft, it's time to do some revising. Use the guidelines below to help you revise.

Revising Checklist

Focus and Coherence

_____ **1.** Do I have a thesis that clearly states my position on the topic?

_____ **2.** Are all of my ideas connected to each other and to my thesis?

_____ **3.** Do I have a strong introduction and a meaningful conclusion?

_____ **4.** Does my editorial have an overall sense of completeness?

Organization

_____ **5.** Have I presented my points in a logical order, appropriate to my purpose and audience?

_____ **6.** Have I used transitional words and phrases to connect ideas?

Development of Ideas

_____ **7.** Have I offered enough support and specific details to allow readers to appreciate my major points?

_____ **8.** Have I approached my topic from a unique perspective?

Voice

_____ **9.** Have I engaged my reader throughout my editorial?

_____ **10.** Is my voice confident and convincing?

_____ **11.** Is my writing authentic and original?

 Revise your first draft. Read your editorial carefully. Then use the checklist above to help you improve your first draft.

Creating a Title

A good title catches the reader's interest and helps introduce your topic. Here are some examples of titles for an editorial.

- Ask a question: **Where Are Our Priorities?**
- State your case: **Support a Youth Recreation Center**
- Call for action: **Say Yes to the Future**

Persuasive

Revising Improving Your First Draft

Tell students to keep these additional points about editorials in mind as they look for ways to improve their drafts. A good editorial . . .

- represents an opposing position fairly and with accurate research;
- relies on compelling data to reveal weaknesses of the opposing point of view;
- has as its ultimate goal the improvement of a particular situation and the overall improvement of the human condition. **✔ DIFFERENTIATE INSTRUCTION**

Revise your first draft. After their own review, suggest that students exchange drafts with a partner to get feedback that will help them revise for clarity, and to be sure that their argument is appropriate for their purpose, audience, and content.

 TEKS 11.13C, 11.16C

Creating a Title

Encourage students to experiment with a variety of titles. If they cannot decide which one they like best, they can ask for advice. Partners can read each other's essays and suggest the titles that best capture the tone and topic of the editorials as well as catch a reader's interest.

⭐ Conventions Connections

Grammar: Sentence Combining
- **Student Edition: Proofreader's Guide** pages 760 (+), 762 (+), 766 (+)
- **SkillsBook** page 158

Grammar: Adjectives
- **Student Edition: Proofreader's Guide** page 748 (+)
- **SkillsBook** page 106

Differentiated Instruction: English Language Learners

ELPS 1B, 1E, 5B, 5F, 5G

Have students monitor their writing to be sure that they have supported their ideas with specificity and detail.

ELP Level **Beginning**	ELP Level **Intermediate**	ELP Level **Advanced/Advanced High**
Review drafts with students and have them note new, academic, and content-based vocabulary they have used in their writing.	Focus on organization as you review drafts together. Discuss areas that could be strengthened by including connecting words.	Have students review their drafts with a partner to monitor that they have used a variety of sentence lengths, patterns, and connecting words.

 TEKS **11.13C** Revise drafts to clarify meaning; **11.16C** Write an argumentative essay that includes an organizing structure appropriate to the purpose, audience, and context **ELPS 1B** Monitor written language production and employ self-corrective techniques or other resources; **1E** Internalize new basic and academic language by using and reusing it/writing; **5B** Write using newly acquired basic vocabulary and content-based grade-level vocabulary; **5F** Write using a variety of grade-appropriate sentence lengths, patterns, and connecting words; **5G** Explain with increasing specificity and detail

Editing Checking for Conventions

Point out to students that following grammar and mechanics rules in their editorials will enable readers to concentrate on the arguments they present. If necessary, remind students of the following issues. DIFFERENTIATE INSTRUCTION ↘

■ Review the rules for presenting numbers and numerals correctly; a consistent presentation of numerical data makes it easier for the reader to understand the editorial content.

■ Check for parallel structures with words, phrases, or clauses in a series. Parallellism provides rhythm and emphasis that allows readers to quickly absorb and retain information.

Edit your editorial. Remind students to answer the checklist questions carefully and honestly.

TEKS 11.13D

Publishing Sharing Your Work

Review the publishing options with students.

Publish your editorial. Remind students to review submission guidelines before submitting their essays to a school or local newspaper. If students plan to post their essays on a school or class Web site or blog, advise them to follow the proper instructions for uploading files.

Conventions Connections

Grammar: Tenses and Irregular Verbs
- *Student Edition: Proofreader's Guide* pages 738–739, 740–741
- *SkillsBook* page 93–94, 100–101

Mechanics: Hyphens, Dashes
- *Student Edition: Proofreader's Guide* pages 652–653, 654–655, 668–669
- *SkillsBook* page 22–23, 24

Plurals, Spelling
- *Student Edition: Proofreader's Guide* pages 680–681, 682–683, 690, 692–694
- *SkillsBook* page 53, 54, 58, 59–60

Editing Checking for Conventions

After revising your editorial, be sure to edit for grammar, sentence structure, mechanics (capitalization and punctuation), and spelling errors.

Editing Checklist

Conventions

GRAMMAR
_____ 1. Have I used numbers and numerals correctly?
_____ 2. Do I have errors in parallel structure?

SENTENCE STRUCTURE
_____ 3. Have I used varied sentence structures?
_____ 4. Have I tried using parallel structures to vary my sentences and to create rhythm and emphasis?

MECHANICS (CAPITALIZATION AND PUNCTUATION)
_____ 5. Do I use end punctuation after all of my sentences?
_____ 6. Have I correctly punctuated items in a series?

SPELLING
_____ 7. Have I spelled all my words correctly?
_____ 8. Have I checked for commonly misused pairs?
_____ 9. Have I double-checked words my spell-checker would miss?

Edit your editorial. Use the checklist above to edit for conventions. You may want to ask a partner to check your work, too. Then prepare a final copy and proofread it.

Publishing Sharing Your Work

It's time to make your ideas public—by publishing them.

Publish your editorial. Choose one of the following methods.
■ Read your work aloud to your teacher, classmates, or family.
■ Submit your editorial to a school or local newspaper.
■ Post your editorial on a Web site.

TEKS **11.13D** Edit drafts for grammar, mechanics, and spelling

265

Writing for Assessment
Responding to Persuasive Prompts

Sometimes you have the luxury of taking your time to develop a persuasive argument. If you receive a writing assignment with a one-week deadline, for example, you have time to do some research, write a draft, revise it carefully, and even ask a friend to help you test your argument. Other times, you need to organize and present a persuasive argument quickly. For example, if you're trying to convince a friend to let you borrow her tennis racket for the weekend, you need to come up with some good reasons on the spot.

Writing tests may also require you to present a persuasive argument quickly. After reading a prompt, you need to choose a position, structure your argument, and present it in a logical manner. And you need to do all this within a strict time limit. This chapter will show you how to use the writing process to create an effective persuasive response to a prompt.

Writing Guidelines

Subject: Persuasive prompt
Purpose: To demonstrate competence
Form: Response essay
Audience: Instructor

"Opinions cannot survive if one has no chance to fight for them."

—Thomas Mann

Responding to Persuasive Prompts

Objectives
- apply what has been learned about persuasive writing
- practice writing for assessment

Remind students that the writer's interest is key to effective persuasive writing. Most writing tests offer students a choice of prompts. Impress on students that they should always choose the prompt that interests them most. This will ensure that they can quickly choose a position and structure a solid argument.

ELPS 5A Learn relationships between sounds and letters to represent sounds when writing in English; **5C** Employ English spelling patterns and rules with increasing accuracy

Prewriting Analyzing a Persuasive Prompt

Remind students that, in addition to identifying key words in a prompt, they also need to pay attention to its overall focus. For example, the sample prompt asks students to choose between two specific class trips, but this is fundamentally a prompt to persuade others to make the same choice.

Review the acronym and questions of the STRAP strategy with students. Review each question and have students apply it to the sample prompt shown. Be sure students understand that the information in parentheses contain some, but not all, possible responses for each STRAP question. Their analysis of a specific prompt will reveal the information they need to fully respond to it.

Try It!
Answers

Ask students to underline the key words in the **Try It!** activity in addition to applying the STRAP questions.

1. **Subject:** sports funding cuts **Type:** letter **Role:** concerned student **Audience:** school board **Purpose:** persuade
2. **Subject:** town building plan for affordable housing on town park land **Type:** editorial **Role:** concerned town resident **Audience:** members of the community **Purpose:** persuade DIFFERENTIATE INSTRUCTION ↘

Tip

Remind students to use the STRAP questions as support for answering a prompt. When the questions are not useful, students should not waste time trying to address them.

266

Prewriting Analyzing a Persuasive Prompt

The first step in responding to a persuasive prompt is to carefully analyze the prompt. What topic should you write about? What form should your response take? To whom should you address your response? To analyze a prompt effectively, use the **STRAP questions**:

> Subject: What topic should I write about?
> Type: What form of writing should I create (essay, letter, editorial, article, report)?
> Role: What position should I assume as the writer (student, son or daughter, friend, employee, citizen)?
> Audience: To whom am I writing (teacher, parents, classmates, employer, official)?
> Purpose: What is the goal of my writing (persuade, respond, evaluate, tell, describe)?

Subject
Type
Role
Audience
Purpose

> **Imagine that your class must vote between two choices for a class trip—the Museum of Fine Arts or the Oak Beach Aquarium. As a student of the junior class, write a letter to the school newspaper that will persuade your classmates to vote for one of these choices.**

Try It!

Analyze these prompts by answering the STRAP questions. (Some answers may be implied or left open. Use your best judgment.)

1. Your school board has announced plans to cut funding for sports teams. As a concerned student, write a letter to the school board airing your opinion about funding cuts.
2. You have recently learned that your town is planning to use 10 acres of the 100-acre town park to build affordable housing for low-income families. Write an editorial supporting or opposing the building plan.

Tip

Some prompts may not include answers for every STRAP question. Use your judgment to answer those questions.

Differentiated Instruction: Struggling Learners

Many students have problems with time management. Draw students' attention to the Tip on page 267.

- Provide a visual timeline on the board that represents 45 minutes, with markings at 5-minute intervals.
- Bracket the first 5-minute interval, the next 35-minute interval, and the last 5-minute interval.

- Have students label each bracketed area with the task they should be focusing on during that time.
- When students practice timed writing, use this visual to track their progress.

Planning Your Response

After answering the STRAP questions, you can use these graphic organizers to plan your response quickly.

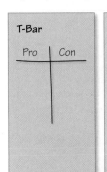

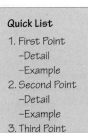

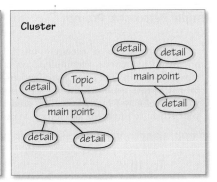

Looking at Both Sides

Some prompts ask you to look at two sides of an argument and write persuasively in support of the stronger argument. First you'll need to consider both sides carefully and then choose the side that is more reasonable.

A pro-con chart is a great tool for thoroughly examining both sides of an argument. Placing the "pros" and "cons" side by side will make it easier for you to choose the stronger side.

Looking at both sides of an argument will also prepare you to respond to the weaker side. Explaining an important objection as flawed can strengthen your argument.

Prewrite

Use a graphic organizer. Reread the persuasive prompts on page 266. Use a graphic organizer to plan your response to one of the prompts.

Tip

In a timed writing test, be sure to manage your time carefully. For example, if you have 45 minutes to respond to a prompt, use the first 5 minutes to analyze the prompt and plan your response, the last 5 minutes to revise and edit your response, and the 35 minutes in between for writing.

Persuasive

Planning Your Response

Ask volunteers to share their experiences in using each type of graphic organizer to plan their writing.

After the discussion, have students generate their own graphic organizers as they plan their responses to the prompts. Few on-demand writing tests provide ready-made graphic organizers for students to use. By creating their own organizers, students are practicing a crucial skill for test day.

Looking at Both Sides

Discuss the content on the SE page with students. Then work with the group as follows:
- Brainstorm "pros" and "cons" for both sides of the issues raised in the persuasive prompts on SE page 266 (the **Try It!** activity).
- List students' suggestions on the board.
- Suggest that students choose from these ideas to plan a response to one of the prompts.

Use a graphic organizer. Elicit from students that the graphic organizer they use should be guided by the genre in which they are asked to write. Point out to students that for all written tests, creating and using graphic organizers will help them quickly plan their response.

 TEKS 11.13A

Tip

Explain that the times provided in the tip should be used as a guide rather than a hard-and-fast rule. **✔ DIFFERENTIATE INSTRUCTION**

TEKS 11.13A Plan a first draft by selecting the correct genre for conveying the intended meaning to multiple audiences and determining appropriate topics through a range of strategies; **ELPS 1C** Use strategic learning strategies to acquire basic and grade-level vocabulary; **1F** Use accessible language and learn new and essential language in the process; **2C** Learn new expressions, basic vocabulary, and academic vocabulary

Drafting Responding to a Prompt

Give students a time limit (perhaps 5 minutes) to read and analyze the prompt, as if they were going to write the response themselves. Suggest that students list the key words and answers to the STRAP questions.

Once students finish individually, work as a class to compare answers to the STRAP questions for the sample persuasive prompt.

Try It!
Answers

Subject: charity organizations' need for volunteers **Type:** letter **Role:** concerned student **Audience:** fellow high school students **Purpose:** persuade DIFFERENTIATE INSTRUCTION ↘

DIFFERENTIATE INSTRUCTION ↘

Sample Response

Review the Traits of Persuasive Writing chart on SE page 218. Then ask students to look at how the writer structured ideas in a sustained and persuasive way in the sample response:

- a beginning paragraph with a clearly stated position,
- middle paragraphs with compelling reasons that support the position and help build the argument,
- a final middle paragraph that counters an objection with language crafted to move an opposed audience, and
- a strong ending that restates the position, summarizes the argument, and compels readers to act.

Discuss students' analyses of the sample response together. Ask them to compare the response to the answers to the STRAP questions to evaluate how well the response meets the requirements of the prompt.

 TEKS 11.13B, 11.16A, 11.16B, 11.16F

 TEKS 11.13B Structure ideas in a sustained and persuasive way and develop drafts in timed and open-ended situations that include transitions and the rhetorical devices used to convey meaning; **11.16A** Write an argumentative essay to the appropriate audience that includes a clear thesis or position based on logical reasons supported by precise and relevant evidence; **11.16B** Write an argumentative essay to the appropriate audience that includes accurate and honest representation of divergent views; **11.16F** Write an argumentative essay to the appropriate audience that includes language attentively crafted to move a disinterested or opposed audience, using specific rhetorical devices to back up assertions

---

Drafting Responding to a Prompt

Once you have answered the STRAP questions and planned your response using a graphic organizer, you can begin writing.

Sample Persuasive Prompt

> According to a recently published newspaper article, charity organizations in your community have been experiencing a severe shortage of volunteers. In fact, some organizations may be forced to shut down if they cannot attract more volunteers. As a high school student, write a letter to your school newspaper persuading students at your school to volunteer for charity work.

Try It!

Answer the STRAP questions for the above prompt. (See page **266**.)

Sample Response

Beginning
The beginning paragraph states the opinion (underlined).

Dear Editor:

Read about the early days of almost any town, and you'll see that volunteers played a critical role in its history. From organizations like the Red Cross to community libraries, from school tutors to people working on local committees, volunteers have made a tremendous impact. Sadly, it appears that the times are changing. Recently, a number of local charity organizations have announced they may no longer be able to carry on their missions. They lack the volunteers they need to get the job done. <u>Students at Harris High should step up and volunteer—not only for the good of the community but also for their own benefit.</u>

One reason to volunteer is to help keep local taxes low. Volunteers provide necessary services that local governments could not afford. Most libraries, for example, could not provide a sufficient level of service without volunteer help. Hiring more workers would increase local taxes. People who volunteer at

---

Differentiated Instruction: Struggling Learners

Emphasize the importance of taking the time to prewrite and organize one's thoughts when responding to a test prompt. Assure students that most people feel pressured when writing under a time constraint. Guide students to concentrate on completing an organizer to get their thoughts down on paper.

Differentiated Instruction: Advanced Learners

Have partners analyze the Sample Response. Ask these questions:

1. What is the main idea? How does that idea relate to the prompt?
2. What facts, examples, or other support backs up the main idea?
3. What transitions or repetitions help keep the prose smooth and clear?

schools, senior centers, and food pantries provide free services that help keep taxes low.

Middle
The middle paragraphs express reasons for supporting the position.

Volunteering also benefits the volunteer. When you volunteer to support a community organization, you gain friends and learn new skills, as you enjoy the good feeling of helping people in need. At a time when many people suffer from a lack of physical exercise and personal interaction, volunteering offers a chance to exercise your body and your mind.

The most important reason for becoming a community volunteer is that no matter what skills you have, the need for help is real. From young children who need help with studying and learning to senior citizens who need help with getting to appointments, community volunteers get important jobs done. Spending an hour or two a week as a volunteer, you could make a positive difference in people's lives.

The final middle paragraph addresses an objection.

Those who don't take the time to volunteer may think that someone else will do the job—or even that their skills are not useful. Nothing could be further from the truth. As last week's newspaper article pointed out, some of our vital community organizations are in danger of shutting their doors due to lack of volunteer help. When it comes to volunteering, even something as simple as talking and listening can be life changing.

Ending
The ending restates the writer's position and makes a call to action.

In conclusion, if you've thought about volunteering but put it off, now is the time to step forward. And if you've never considered volunteering, now is the time to try it. You'll benefit the community, you'll benefit yourself, and most of all, you'll benefit the people who need help. Volunteer today, and you'll be glad you did.

Sincerely,

Nick DiCarlo

Persuasive

Draft

Respond to a persuasive prompt. Use the prompt you chose on page 266, your answers to the STRAP questions, and your graphic organizer to draft a response. Be sure to finish your response in the time allotted.

During the discussion of the Sample Response, highlight the similarities between the argumentative essay students wrote earlier (see SE pages 218–249) and the Sample Response on these pages, as follows.

In students' argumentative essays:

- The goal was to persuade readers to agree with their positions on controversial issues.
- They stated their positions in beginning paragraphs.
- In the middle paragraphs, they built their arguments with compelling reasons organized according to order of importance, and they countered significant objections.
- At the end of their essays, they restated their positions, summarized their arguments, and left the reader with something to think about.

In the Sample Response:

- The writer's goal is to persuade classmates to volunteer.
- The writer states his position clearly at the end of the beginning paragraph.
- The writer builds a strong argument in the middle paragraphs, presenting reasons in order of importance.
- The writer answers an objection in the last middle paragraph.
- The writer concludes the essay by restating his position and ending with a final insight.

Respond to a persuasive prompt. Give students a time limit in which to complete their responses. Remind them that they are well prepared to write this type of response to a prompt, given their earlier experiences with argumentative essays and editorials. ✔DIFFERENTIATE INSTRUCTION
TEKS 11.13B, 11.16A, 11.16B, 11.16F

TEKS **11.13B** Structure ideas in a sustained and persuasive way and develop drafts in timed and open-ended situations that include transitions and the rhetorical devices used to convey meaning; **11.16A** Write an argumentative essay to the appropriate audience that includes a clear thesis or position based on logical reasons supported by precise and relevant evidence; **11.16B** Write an argumentative essay to the appropriate audience that includes accurate and honest representation of divergent views; **11.16F** Write an argumentative essay to the appropriate audience that includes language attentively crafted to move a disinterested or opposed audience, using specific rhetorical devices to back up assertions; **ELPS 1C** Use strategic learning strategies to acquire basic and grade-level vocabulary; **1E** Internalize new basic and academic language by using and reusing it/writing; **5G** Explain with increasing specificity and detail

Revising Improving Your Response

Point out to students that in normal test situations, they are not likely to have the time or the writing space to make major revisions. This is why it is important to write out the answers to the STRAP questions before they even begin to plan their responses. These answers will help them keep their responses on target, and they can also be used during revision as the basis for a quick final check.

Improve your work. Tell students that if they concentrate on developing their subject ideas and organization during prewriting and drafting, then they can devote their revising time to improving how well they state and support their thesis and establish the voice in their response.
TEKS 11.13C

Editing Checking Your Response

Suggest that students try reading their response backward from the end to the beginning to find mistakes in capitalization, end punctuation, and spelling. When students are not distracted by the meaning of their words, they are more likely to spot certain errors.
ELPS 5C

Editing Checklist

Suggest that students address each question by checking their entire response before moving on to the next question.

Check your conventions. Tell students to watch for the types of errors that they often find in their writing, including standard grammar and usage.
TEKS 11.13D; **ELPS** 5D

Revising Improving Your Response

Some writing tests allow you to make changes in your writing; others don't. Before you begin a writing test, find out whether you will be allowed to make changes or not. If changes are allowed, make them as neatly as possible. Use the STRAP questions to guide your revisions.

> **Subject:** Have I developed ideas to respond to the topic of the prompt? Do all my main points support my persuasive argument?
>
> **Type:** Have I used the form requested in the prompt (essay, letter, editorial, article, report)?
>
> **Role:** Does my voice reflect the role called for in the prompt?
>
> **Audience:** Have I addressed the audience named in the prompt?
>
> **Purpose:** Does my response accomplish the goal indicated in the prompt?

Improve your work. Reread your response, using the STRAP questions above as your guide. Within the time allowed, make neat changes to your response.

Editing Checking Your Response

After revising, you should read through your response one final time. As you read, check for and correct any errors in grammar, sentence structure, capitalization, punctuation, and spelling.

Editing Checklist

Conventions

_____ **1.** Have I used varied sentence structures?

_____ **2.** Have I capitalized all proper nouns and the first word of every sentence?

_____ **3.** Have I used end punctuation for every sentence?

_____ **4.** Have I spelled all words correctly?

_____ **5.** Have I used the right words (their, there, they're)?

Check your conventions. Read through your response one final time. In the time allowed, neatly correct any errors in grammar, sentence structure, capitalization, punctuation, and spelling.

TEKS **11.13C** Revise drafts to clarify meaning; **11.13D** Edit drafts for grammar, mechanics, and spelling **ELPS** **5C** Spell familiar English words; **5D** Edit writing for standard grammar and usage

Persuasive Writing on Tests

Use this guide when preparing to respond to a persuasive writing prompt.

Before you write . . .

- **Understand the prompt.**
  Use the STRAP questions, and remember that a persuasive prompt asks you to use facts and logical reasons to persuade or convince.
- **Plan your time wisely.**
  Spend 5 to 10 minutes planning before starting to write.

As you write . . .

- **Decide on a focus for your essay.**
  Keep your main idea or purpose in mind as you write. Be sure all your points clearly support your argument.
- **Be selective.**
  Use examples that directly support your opinion.
- **End in a meaningful way.**
  Remind the reader about the topic and your point of view.

After you've written a first draft . . .

- **Check for completeness and correctness.**
  Use the STRAP questions to revise your work. Then check for errors in grammar, sentence structure, capitalization, punctuation, and spelling.

Learning Language

One way to be persuasive is to assume the role of a leader and tell your readers what you expect them to do. In other words, you include some imperative sentences that give directions or commands. You can see some examples of imperative sentences in the Sample Response on pages **268–269.** The writer strengthened his argument with commands such as "Read about the early days…" and "Volunteer today…" Work with a partner to review your draft to identify places where an imperative sentence would add emphasis to your argument.

Persuasive

Persuasive Writing on Tests

Point out to students that they must approach timed writing assignments differently than open-ended writing assignments and that timed writing creates pressures for everyone. To give them practice, provide the same amount of time to write their responses as they will be allotted for school, district, or state assessments.

Before you write...

Tell students you will break down each part of the process into clear chunks of time. For example, you might give students 5–10 minutes for note taking and planning.

As you write...

Tell students that they will have about 25–30 minutes for drafting. If your state, district, or school requires students to use and submit a graphic organizer as part of their assessment, refer students to SE pages 612–615.

After you've written a first draft...

Tell students that they will have about 5 minutes for revising, editing, and proofreading. Indicate when time is up for each section. Start the assignment at the top of the hour or at the half-hour to make it easier for them to keep track of the time.

Learning Language

Tell student partners to make sure that they understand the terms *imperative, directions,* and *commands* by locating the examples in the Sample Response and also stating examples of their own. Then, as they identify places to add imperatives, have them take notes to provide suggestions for their partner.

☑ DIFFERENTIATE INSTRUCTION

ELPS 1C, 1E, 4F, 4G

Differentiated Instruction: English Language Learners

ELPS 1B, 1H, 5F

Present and discuss sample imperative sentences that give directions and commands.

ELP Level **Beginning**	ELP Level **Intermediate**	ELP Level **Advanced/Advanced High**
Model monitoring written work by pointing out opportunities to include imperative sentences. Revise sentences and read them aloud together.	Have students self-correct by pointing out opportunities for imperative sentences. Have students revise the sentences and read them aloud.	Have students review their drafts and self-correct to include imperative sentences. Have partners share their work and identify the variety of sentence patterns.

ELPS **1B** Monitor written language production and employ self-corrective techniques or other resources; **1C** Use strategic learning strategies to acquire basic and grade-level vocabulary; **1E** Internalize new academic language by using and reusing it/writing; **1H** Develop and expand repertoire of learning strategies; **4F** Use support from peers and teachers to read content area text, to enhance and confirm understanding, and to develop vocabulary; **4G** Demonstrate comprehension of increasingly complex English/taking notes; **5F** Write using a variety of grade-appropriate sentence patterns

Interpretive Response

Interpreting a Theme (pages 273–275)

Students choose a biographical article and write a one-paragraph resonse to analyze the article.

Response Essay (pages 276–314)

Through their analysis of biographies and autobiographies, students explore real-life stories and interpret themes.

Interpreting a Poem (pages 315–322)

Students learn to break down a poem's elements and see how they fit together.

Interpreting a Short Story

(pages 323–328)

Through careful examination of the elements of a short story, students learn to find the meaning of a story and an appreciation of the author's craft.

Writing for Assessment

(pages 329–337)

Using the writing process, students learn to respond to fiction in a timed-writing situation.

Literature Connections

- **The Autobiography of Benjamin Franklin**

Technology Connections

 Write Source Online
www.hmheducation.com/tx/writesource
- **Net-text**
- **Writing Network**
- **Portfolio**
- **GrammarSnap**
- **Essay Scoring**
- **File Cabinet**

Interactive Whiteboard Lessons

Interpretive Response Unit Scope and Sequence

| Day | Writing and Conventions Instruction | Write Source Student Edition | | | Daily Language Workouts | Skills-Book | Write Source Online |
		Core Unit	Tools of Language	Resource Units			
1–3	**Interpreting a Theme** Model	273–275	TL 586–591		58–61		Interactive Whiteboard Lesson
	Skills Activities: • Punctuating Titles			PG 662–663, 664–665		32	
4–5	**Response Essay** Model ⓛ Literature Connection *The Autobiography of Benjamin Franklin*	276–278					Net-text
	Prewriting	279–284		BEW 617–620			Net-text

WEEK 1

Resource Units referenced above are located in the back of the *Student Edition* and *Teacher's Edition*
TL *"The Tools of Language"*   BEW *"Basic Elements of Writing"*   PG *"Proofreader's Guide"*

	Day	Writing and Conventions Instruction	Write Source Student Edition			Daily Language Workouts	Skills-Book	Write Source Online
			Core Unit	Tools of Language	Resource Units			
WEEK 2	6–7	Drafting	285–290	TL 586–591	BEW 621–631	62–65		Net-text
	8–10	Revising	291–300					Net-text
		Skills Activities: •Misplaced and Dangling Modifiers					167–168	
		•Pronouns			PG 726–733, 772		78–87	GrammarSnap
WEEK 3	11–12	Editing, Publishing	301–307	TL 586–591	BEW 632–633	66–69		Net-text
		Skills Activities: •Adjectives			PG 748–749		104–108	GrammarSnap
		•Tense Shifts			PG 738–742		93–95, 175–178	GrammarSnap
		•Punctuating Compound and Complex Sentences			PG 648–651, 762–763, 766-767		7, 10, 13, 140	GrammarSnap
		•Punctuating Quotations			PG 660		31	GrammarSnap
	13	Evaluating a Response to Literature	308–314					
	14–15	**Interpreting a Poem** Model, Prewriting	315–319		BEW 617–620			Net-text
		Drafting, Revising	320–321		BEW 621–631			Net-text
WEEK 4	16	Editing, Publishing	322	TL 586–591	BEW 632–633	70–73		Net-text
		Skills Activities: •Subject-Verb Agreement			PG 770–773		145–149	GrammarSnap
		•Quotation Marks			PG 660		30–33	GrammarSnap
		•Punctuation			PG 635–673		3–40	GrammarSnap
	17–19	**Interpreting a Short Story** Model, Prewriting	323–326		BEW 617–620			Net-text
		Drafting, Revising, Editing	327–328		BEW 621–633			Net-text
	20	**Writing for Assessment**	329–337					

 Resource Units referenced above are located in the back of the *Student Edition* and *Teacher's Edition*
TL "The Tools of Language"   BEW "Basic Elements of Writing"   PG "Proofreader's Guide"

Writing Focus

- Interpreting a Theme
- Interpreting a Poem
- Interpreting a Short Story
- Responding to Prompts About Literature

Grammar Focus

- Comparative and Superlative Adjectives
- Compound Adjectives

Learning Language

Read aloud the basic and academic terms, as well as the descriptions and questions. Model for students how to read one question and answer it. For example, *It says that a quotation is someone's exact words and it asks where I might see quotations. I often see quotations in newspaper and magazine articles.* Have partners monitor their understanding of the terms by working through the remaining meanings and questions together. **DIFFERENTIATE INSTRUCTION ↘**

 ELPS 1F, 2C, 3E, 4G

Minilessons

Building a Case
Interpreting a Theme

- Have students **TEST** a theme by pretending to be an attorney who must defend the theme in court. Ask them to use these suggestions to **FIND** as much solid evidence in the text as they can to support the theme: **LOOK** for testimony of what characters have to say. **FIND** events or incidents that support the theme. **CONNECT** all the facts and circumstances to build a convincing closing argument.

A Common Thread
Interpreting a Theme

- Tell students to **NAME** five favorite books. Ask them to **THINK** of a common element that two or more of the books share (for example, two books focus on what leads to success, or three books describe how the main character must decide whether to act courageously to protect the vulnerable or go along with the crowd). This practice can help them identify literary themes.

 ELPS 1F Use accessible language and learn new and essential language in the process; **2A** Distinguish sounds of English; **2C** Learn new basic and academic vocabulary; **3A** Practice producing sounds of newly acquired vocabulary to pronounce English words; **3E** Share information in cooperative learning interactions; **4A** Learn relationships between sounds and letters of the English language and decode words using a combination of skills; **4G** Demonstrate comprehension of increasingly complex English/responding to questions

---

 ELPS 1F, 2C, 3E, 4G

Interpretive Response

Writing Focus

Grammar Focus

Learning Language

Work with a partner. Read the meanings and share answers to the questions.

1. A theme is an idea or lesson about life.
   What is the theme of your favorite book or movie?
2. A quotation is a person's exact words.
   Where are you likely to see a quotation?
3. To summarize a story, only tell the important parts.
   Summarize what you did yesterday after school.
4. When you take time for something, you do not rush.
   Why do you need to take time to do homework?

Differentiated Instruction:
English Language Learners
 ELPS 2A, 3A, 4A

Turn to the Teacher's Edition Appendix for information on language transfer issues with consonants, digraphs, and vowels.

ELP Level **Beginning**	ELP Level **Intermediate**	ELP Level **Advanced/Advanced High**
Have students repeat the words after you pronounce them. Guide them to distinguish sounds and learn relationships between sounds and letters.	Display the words and practice saying them together. Point to the vowels and consonants in each word and have students identify the sounds they make.	Guide students to identify a combination of skills they can use to decode the words, such as silent *e* and the endings *-tion* and *-ize*.

273

Response to Literature
Interpreting a Theme

One thing that's just as enjoyable as reading a good fictional story is reading a good *true* story. As amazing as it may be to read about a character such as Captain Ahab or Huck Finn, it's just as amazing to read about the lives of real people.

Biographies, autobiographies, and other works that tell about real-life people and events all explore themes that enrich our understanding about who we are. While we may find these real-life accounts fascinating, troubling, entertaining, or inspiring, they are always thought-provoking and instructive.

Themes in biographies, autobiographies, and other works about real people and events are especially powerful because they come from actual individuals, their lives, and their experiences. These books prove that truth can be just as forceful as fiction—and just as enjoyable to read.

Writing Guidelines

Subject:	A nonfiction book that tells a story
Purpose:	To interpret a main theme
Form:	Literary interpretation
Audience:	Classmates

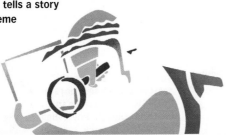

"Whenever you say 'well that's not convincing' the author tells you that's the bit that wasn't made up. This is because real life is under no obligation to be convincing."

—Neil Gaiman

Interpreting a Theme

Objectives
- demonstrate an understanding of the content and form of an essay that interprets a theme
- plan, draft, revise, edit, and publish an interpretation of a theme in a nonfiction book

Brainstorm a list of recommended biographies, autobiographies, memoirs, and narrative nonfiction books. Check online reading lists such as those on the American Library Association Web site: http://www.ala.org. You may also wish to review the table of contents from your literature anthology for nonfiction excerpts that interest students and encourage them to read the full-length book. Save the list for when students select a book (SE page 280).

 Technology Connections

Use the Interactive Whiteboard lessons to introduce interpretive response.

 Interactive Whiteboard Lesson

Resources

Copy Masters
- 5 W's chart (TE p. 275)
- T-chart (TE pp. 280, 282)
- Time line (TE p. 281)

Benchmark Papers
- The Source of Horror in "The Lottery" (strong) TE Appendix
- O Sweet Spontaneous (poor) TE Appendix

Writing Warm-Up Thinking About Amazing Lives

Review the categories listed and invite students to suggest the names of people who fit in each one. **DIFFERENTIATE INSTRUCTION ↘**

Amazing People Chart

Discuss any names with which students are unfamiliar, leading them to see why the name appears on the chart.

Create an amazing people chart. Students may benefit from working with partners or small groups to brainstorm names for their charts.

Finding a Biographical Article

Students will gain the most from this assignment if the biographical article they choose to analyze has both literary and factual merit. Remind students to choose an article from a reliable source. Provide recommendations such as the following:

- The Notable American Women series of biographical dictionaries, published by Harvard University Press
- *The Dictionary of Literary Biography,* published by the Gale Group, and *American National Biography,* published by H. W. Wilson (both are multivolume library references, which may be available online through your public library's Web site)
- *The Scientific 100: A Ranking of the Most Influential Scientists, Past and Present,* by John Galbraith Simmons
- *Life Stories: Profiles from the New Yorker,* edited by David Remnick

Search for a biographical article about the person you chose. You may wish to review students' choices before going any further.

274

Writing Warm-Up Thinking About Amazing Lives

As a warm-up, you'll write a paragraph response to a biographical article. Begin by considering the types of interesting people you could write about:

activists	astronauts	explorers	musicians
actors	athletes	inventors	scientists
artists	business people	leaders/rulers	writers

One student chose three categories from the list above and listed people who interested her. Then she chose one person to write about.

Amazing People Chart

Business People	Leaders/Rulers	Writers
Bill Gates Oprah Winfrey ✳	Benazir Bhutto Nelson Mandela	Maya Angelou John Neihardt

 Prewrite

Create an amazing people chart. Choose three categories of people from the list above and write these categories at the top of a piece of paper. Then, under each category, list famous people. Put an asterisk (*) next to the one you would like to write about.

Finding a Biographical Article

After choosing Oprah Winfrey, the student searched for articles about Oprah. She checked the *Readers' Guide to Periodical Literature* and the Internet. Once she found a well-documented article from a reliable source, she read it and prepared her response.

 Prewrite

Search for a biographical article about the person you chose. Be sure the article contains enough interesting information to write about in a response paragraph. Then carefully read the article.

Differentiated Instruction: Struggling Learners

To help students connect to the nonfiction genre, help them brainstorm a list of movies based on nonfiction such as *The Pianist, A League of Their Own, Apollo 13, Gorillas in the Mist, Cinderella Man, Antwone Fisher,* or *Schindler's List.* If students enjoyed one of these movies, suggest that they look for an article about the main character.

Interpreting a Theme 275

Writing a Paragraph Analysis

You can analyze the article you chose by following these guidelines:

- In the **opening sentence,** name the article, author, and subject.
- In the **body sentences,** briefly summarize the article and provide insight into its main idea.
- In the **closing sentence,** restate the main theme of the article.

Sample Paragraph Analysis

In the following paragraph, a student writer analyzes a biographical article about Oprah Winfrey.

The **opening sentence** names the article, the writer, and the subject.

The **body sentences** summarize the article and its main idea.

The **closing sentence** restates the main theme of the article.

An Uncommon Woman

In "The Life and Times of O," Sarah Williams shows how Oprah Winfrey used her "common touch" to become a most uncommon woman. Born in Mississippi, Oprah did most of her growing up in Milwaukee. At age 13, she suffered abuse and went to live in Nashville with her father. He was strict but expected Oprah to make something of herself. At 17, she got a job at a radio station, and at 19, she became a TV news anchor. After college, she landed the position as host of *AM Chicago* and turned it into the number one talk show in the nation—*The Oprah Winfrey Show.* Oprah next appeared in the movie *The Color Purple,* and its success allowed her to set up her own production company, called Harpo (Oprah backward). In time, she became the first female African American billionaire. Oprah may have had a humble start and faced many challenges, but she also learned to believe in herself—and in other people. She used her common touch to build an entertainment empire and inspire millions of people around the world.

Response

Draft an analysis paragraph. Read the biographical article you selected on the previous page. Then draft a response paragraph in which you summarize the article and provide insight into its main theme.

Writing a Paragraph Analysis

Discuss the challenges of condensing a response to an article into a single analytical paragraph. Share these tips:

- Read the article through twice carefully.
- Determine what overall message the author conveys.
- Freewrite your thoughts about the most important point of the article. Use what you freewrite to gather details for your analysis paragraph. ✔ DIFFERENTIATE INSTRUCTION

Sample Paragraph Analysis

Review the blue callout boxes to point out the writer's opening, body, and closing sentences. Remind students to restate the article's main point in their own words when summarizing.

✱ For details about paragraph skills, see SE pages 605–607.

Draft an analysis paragraph. To help students with the summary portion of their paragraphs, distribute photocopies of the 5 W's chart (TE page A96). Remind students that they must analyze as well as summarize the article.

⭐ **Conventions Connections**

Grammar: Punctuating Titles

- ***Proofreader's Guide*** pages 662–663, 664–665
- ***SkillsBook*** page 32

Differentiated Instruction: English Language Learners

⭐ ELPS 1A, 4G, 5B

ELP Level **Beginning**	ELP Level **Intermediate**	ELP Level **Advanced/Advanced High**
Before reading the sample, use visuals and sentence stems to guide students to share prior knowledge about terms such as *radio station* and *news anchor.*	Have students share prior knowledge about terms such as *radio station* and *news anchor.* Ask yes/no questions to help students summarize the sample.	After reading the sample, have students write a brief summary of the passage's main ideas and identify the theme the writer discusses.

ELPS 1A Use prior knowledge and experiences; **4G** Demonstrate comprehension of increasingly complex English/ retelling or summarizing; **5B** Write using newly acquired basic vocabulary and content-based grade-level vocabulary

Understanding Your Goal

Review the goals of this unit with students, focusing on how each of the five traits relates to writing an essay that interprets a theme. To reinforce understanding, ask questions such as *Why should your essay provide insight into the importance of the theme? How do paraphrases and quoted passages help to support an interpretation of a theme?* Revisit SE pages 566–567 to support English language learners' understanding of the Texas traits.

Connecting to the Scoring Guide

Before reviewing the sample essay, take a few minutes to connect the goals of this unit to those detailed in the holistic scoring guide on SE pages 36–37. Note that this scoring guide provides a trait-centered description of the qualities of strong writing in general, not just interpretive writing.

Literature Connections

In *The Autobiography of Benjamin Franklin*, the author looks back on his life, including his efforts to achieve moral perfection. Discussing this theme as well as others in the autobiography will serve as a guide for students as they plan their interpretations. For additional writing models, see pages 308–311.

`DIFFERENTIATE INSTRUCTION ↘` `DIFFERENTIATE INSTRUCTION ↘`

Understanding Your Goal

Your goal in this chapter is to write an essay that interprets the theme of a nonfiction book that tells a story. The chart below lists the key traits of a literary interpretation essay, with specific suggestions for this assignment.

> ### Traits of a Response to Literature
>
> ■ **Focus and Coherence**
> Write a thesis statement that explains one main theme of the book. Make sure that your writing stays focused on this topic throughout your essay. Your closing should provide some insight into the importance of the book's theme.
>
> ■ **Organization**
> Write clear beginning, middle, and ending parts. Use transitions to effectively connect ideas, sentences, and paragraphs.
>
> ■ **Development of Ideas**
> In each paragraph, present your ideas about the book's theme, and flesh them out. Paraphrase and quote passages that summarize or support your ideas and the book's theme.
>
> ■ **Voice**
> Sound interested in and knowledgeable about the book you have read. Engage readers with your unique perspective on the book as you explain why it affected you as it did.
>
> ■ **Conventions**
> Check your writing for grammar, sentence structure, mechanics (capitalization and punctuation), and spelling errors.

Literature Connection. You can find an example of autobiographical writing to interpret in Part One of *The Autobiography of Benjamin Franklin.*

Differentiated Instruction: Struggling Learners

To help students understand the term *theme*, explain that it is the author's "overall meaning" or "message." Point out that the theme is often about living in society or learning an important lesson about human nature. As a class, practice identifying themes of familiar nonfiction books or films.

Differentiated Instruction: Advanced Learners

Ask students to create examples of literary devices (such as simile or hyperbole) or to recall examples of books that use various literary devices (such as irony).

✳ Have students review and discuss SE pages 626–629 for a refresher on literary terms.

Response Essay

In the following essay, Tyrell interprets a main theme in the book *Walden, or Life in the Woods*, by Henry David Thoreau.

Beginning
The beginning names the book and author and states the main theme (underlined).

A Search for Harmony

On July 4, 1845, Henry David Thoreau moved into a cabin he had built by himself near Walden Pond in Concord, Massachusetts. During the two years he lived there, he wrote about his experiences, and published these writings several years later. Seen today as a classic work of American literature, Thoreau's *Walden, or Life in the Woods* provides insights into the life and mind of a man who decided to explore the choices he could make and the way he could live his life. A saying about individuality that is familiar to many comes from the pages of *Walden*: "If a man does not keep pace with his companions, perhaps it is because he hears a different drummer. Let him step to the music which he hears, however measured or far away." (311)

Thoreau was born in Concord in 1817 into a family of modest means. After graduating from Harvard College, Thoreau tried out different vocations and jobs, but found most were not satisfying. He developed a long friendship with Ralph Waldo Emerson, the American philosopher and poet, who encouraged Thoreau in his writings. Thoreau kept personal journals and wrote essays and reviews for a magazine called *The Dial*, which promoted the ideals of what was known as the Transcendentalist movement. Thoreau was drawn to these complicated ideas, which valued personal truth over everything else.

Middle
The middle paragraphs discuss the meaning of the events in the book.

Thoreau begins *Walden* by explaining at length why he chose to forego traditional paths in society, stating that "the mass of men lead lives of quiet desperation." (11) Believing that most people, whether farmers or merchants or business owners, ended up chained to a life they did not choose but entered into without deep thought, Thoreau decided he would live simply, economically, and with purpose at Walden.

Thoreau deeply valued all the opportunities that life at Walden brought. With no neighbor closer than a mile away, he spent many hours alone and writes fondly of the gifts that solitude brings him.

Storms and snowfalls that sometimes kept him inside his small dwelling for hours

Response

Response Essay

Work through the model essay with the class, pointing out the elements that make it a good response to literature. ✔ DIFFERENTIATE INSTRUCTION

Focus and Coherence

- The writer presents a thesis statement in the beginning of the essay.
- The middle paragraphs explain and support the thesis statement.

Organization

- The first paragraph tells the book's title and author, and then briefly describes its premise (the circumstances that lead to the writer's experience) and the theme.
- The middle paragraphs summarize the events and tell how they relate to the theme.

Development of Ideas

- The writer identifies a major theme from the book (exploring individual choices).
- Examples and quotations from the book support the theme.

Voice

- The writer sounds interested and knowledgeable.
- The writer chooses quotations that give a sense of the voices of the author.

ELPS 4F Use support from peers and teachers to develop vocabulary and background knowledge

Respond to the reading

Answers

Focus and Coherence 1. The writer explores the theme that there is value is living a simple life with purpose. **2.** The writer is focused on the theme throughout, giving examples of Thoreau's experiences with living a simple life at Walden and the far-reaching lessons he learned; the writer provides well-known quotations from the book ("a different drummer," "lives of quiet desperation") to support the theme.

Development of Ideas 3. The quotations support the writer's ideas by illustrating what Thoreau learned in living his simple life at Walden: his observations about nature, his own life, and the lives of others. **4.** Responses will vary, but most will say that the writer's ideas are well-developed with examples and quotations from the book.

Voice 5. Yes. The writer uses numerous examples and quotations from the book. ine.

DIFFERENTIATE INSTRUCTION ↘ DIFFERENTIATE INSTRUCTION ↘

or even days were not a problem: "Shall I not have intelligence with the earth? Am I not partly leaves and vegetable mould myself?" (136)

While living his simple, self-reliant life at Walden, Thoreau was also a keen observer of nature. *Walden* is filled with detailed descriptions and musings on what trees, plants, loons, and even ants can tell us, and how humans affect their existence. It is difficult to read Thoreau's pages of descriptions of Walden Pond and not be drawn into a calmer, slower, more reflective state.

Much of *Walden* examines the choices people make and whether these are useful, pointless, or even damaging. For example, a train's whistle leads Thoreau to ponder whether what we consider to be progress is moving forward at all, since people seem to just want things that travel brings and don't consider whether we actually need these things.

Ending
The ending paragraph reflects on the main theme of the book.

In the chapter of *Walden* called "Where I Lived and What I Lived For," Thoreau sums up his reasoning: "I went to the woods because I wished to live deliberately, to front only the essential facts of life, and see if I could not learn what it had to teach, and not, when I came to die, discover that I had not lived." (89) Thoreau left his cabin in September, 1847, confident that his "experiment" was a great personal success. While *Walden* did not achieve financial success, it has inspired generations of readers to consider Thoreau's theme of living simply and with purpose. *Walden* remains an invitation and a challenge to us all.

 Respond to the reading. Answer the following questions about the essay:

Focus and Coherence (1) What main theme does the writer interpret? (2) Does the writer stay focused on this theme? Explain.

Development of Ideas (3) Do the quotations from the book support the writer's ideas? Explain. (4) Do you think the writer's ideas are well-developed? Tell why or why not.

Voice (5) Does the writer sound knowledgeable about the book? Explain.

Interpreting a Theme **279**

Prewriting

If you've ever had writer's block, prewriting can help. Step-by-step, you'll find the ideas you need to fill those blank pages. Listed below are prewriting guidelines for planning your interpretation.

Keys to Effective Prewriting

1. Select an interesting nonfiction book that tells a story.

2. Summarize major events in the book.

3. Review the major events to decide what themes they point to.

4. Write a clear thesis statement stating a main theme.

5. Decide how to organize the information in your middle paragraphs.

6. Write a topic sentence for each middle paragraph.

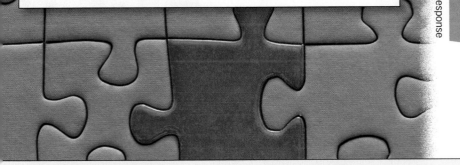

Response

Differentiated Instruction: English Language Learners

 ELPS 3G

ELP Level **Beginning**	ELP Level **Intermediate**	ELP Level **Advanced/Advanced High**
Have students repeat short phrases about the theme, such as *living simply*. Guide students to examine how these ideas appear in the essay.	Focus on voice. Provide sentence stems to help students express their ideas and opinions about the writer's voice in the essay.	Guide an extended discussion to help students express their ideas and opinions about the meaning and use of the quotations the writer includes.

Prewriting
Keys to Effective Prewriting

Remind students of the purpose of the prewriting stage in the writing process: It is when the writer selects a topic, gathers details, and decides how to organize those details.

The Keys to Effective Prewriting list explains the process students will be guided through on SE pages 280–284.

Ask students to share experiences they have had with writer's block.
- What were they trying to write at the time?
- What caused the block? (For example, anxiety, or an uninteresting or difficult topic)

⚡ ELPS 1A, 3E

Share your own experiences of writer's block and suggest helpful actions students can take to keep themselves writing.
- Skipping over troublesome parts and coming back to them later when they've built up more momentum.
- Freewriting—improvising on paper, using the topic as a starting point.
- Pretending they're telling their best friend about the topic, making it funny, tragic, or a huge secret.
- Setting a time to meet with a friend who also has a project deadline.

Writing Workshop

The activities in the prewriting, writing, revising, and editing sections of this chapter can function as minilessons to teach specific skills. These activities work for whole-class instruction, small-group lessons, or scaffolding for individual students.

ELPS 1A Use prior experiences; **3E** Share information in cooperative learning interactions; **3G** Express opinions and ideas

Prewriting Selecting a Book

Invite students who have already selected books to share their choices and to give reasons for the choices.

Topic List

Provide photocopies of the reproducible T-chart (TE page A97) for students to use when making their topics list.

TEKS 11.13A

Brainstorm a topics list. You may wish to have partners work together to brainstorm lists.

Searching the Library Catalog

Emphasize that students should look for a work of *literary nonfiction;* that is, a work that is factual and that presents the facts creatively and well. To find the best possible book about their topic, students can do the following:

- Ask a teacher or a librarian.
- Search the Web sites of libraries, newspapers' book review sections, or booksellers for titles.
- Refer to the book list the class compiled (TE page 273).

Remind students that the public library's interlibrary loan program may make it possible for them to get a book that isn't in their branch library's regular collection.

Search for a book. As an alternative to choosing a topic and then choosing the book, you may wish to allow some students to browse the available literary nonfiction titles to look for a book that engages their interest. **DIFFERENTIATE INSTRUCTION** ↘

---

280 **TEKS** 11.13A

Prewriting Selecting a Book

You may already have read a nonfiction book that you would like to analyze. Otherwise, follow the directions on this page. Biographies and autobiographies work well for this assignment, as do other nonfiction books. One way to find a book is to brainstorm a list of people, events, and animals that interest you. Malaya brainstormed the following list.

Topics List

People	Events/Animals
Katharine Hepburn	the fall of the Berlin wall
Frederick Douglass *	Koko the gorilla
Jane Austen	September 11, 2001
Mahatma Gandhi	bald eagles

 Brainstorm a topics list. Write "People" in one column and "Events/Animals" in another column. Write down topics you'd like to read about. Put an asterisk (*) next to the topic you choose.

Searching the Library Catalog

Once you've chosen a subject, do a subject search in your library's computer catalog to find *nonfiction* books about the subject. Tammy found more than one book on Frederick Douglass. She chose his autobiography. You may want to review each actual book.

 Search for a book. Perform a subject search and select a nonfiction book that is appropriate for your reading level. Take time to read it.

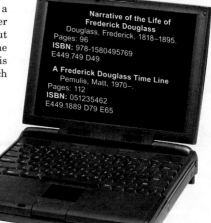

Narrative of the Life of Frederick Douglass
Douglass, Frederick, 1818–1895.
Pages: 96
ISBN: 978-1580495769
E449.749 D49

A Frederick Douglass Time Line
Pemulis, Matt, 1970–.
Pages: 112
ISBN: 051235462
E449.1889 D79 E65

Differentiated Instruction: Struggling Learners

Choosing a book will seem daunting to some students, but choosing a book, rather than having one assigned, will keep students more invested in their analysis. To motivate students, remind them that nonfiction novels and biographies cover just about anything in any time period—from the world's first Olympic games to becoming a basketball star. To generate topic ideas, create a display of nonfiction books and give short book talks. Encourage students to make a list of key words to use in searching the library's catalogs for books. Suggest that they also browse the library's nonfiction and biography aisles for books.

Writing Down Main Events

After reading the book you selected, take some time to think about its main events. A time line can help you focus on the main events. Here is the time line that Tammy created for the autobiography *Narrative of the Life of Frederick Douglass, an American Slave:*

Time Line

1818	Douglass is born (month and date unknown) at a farm in Maryland to Harriet Bailey, a slave. Father is unknown; may have been his master, Aaron Anthony. He is separated from his mother as an infant.
1819	Raised as a slave to be a companion to his master's son; witnesses
1825	many beatings and whippings of other slaves; his mother dies.
1826	Sent to Baltimore to serve the Auld family; endures beatings but
1833	also learns to read and write; is rented out to Edward Covey.
1834	Covey beats him until Douglass finally resists and is not beaten again.
1836	Plans escape with five other slaves, but they are betrayed and jailed; is returned to the Aulds. He is later beaten by white apprentices.
1837	Makes plan to escape from slavery forever. On 9/3/1838, he escapes
1838	and travels to New York; is aided there by David Ruggles.
1838	Marries Anna Murray; he takes Douglass as his new last name. They
1839	move to New Bedford, MA; he finds work as a free man and takes up cause of anti-slavery.

Create a time line. After you finish reading the book, page through it, writing down important events in the order that they occurred.

Focus on the Texas Traits

Voice When you review the book to write down main events, you will become more familiar with ideas and events. You may also notice some things you had missed on your first reading. By the time you start drafting, you will be comfortable with the book, which will help make your voice confident and authentic.

Response

Writing Down Main Events

Discuss the following strategies students can use to improve their comprehension. During reading, ask them to

- keep a notebook nearby for recording thoughts and questions,
- use sticky notes to mark pages that contain important information or good quotations, and
- keep a running list of words they need to look up, as well as technical words that may help them establish a knowledgeable tone.

✔ DIFFERENTIATE INSTRUCTION

Time Line

Provide photocopies of the reproducible time line (TE page A95) for students to use when writing down main events.

Create a time line. Remind students that an accurate time line will be a useful guide when they begin drafting.

Focus on the Texas Traits

Voice
Tell students that their time lines can help them to maintain an authentic voice in their essays. Explain that sounding knowledgable about the book helps to convince readers of the validity of their ideas.

**Differentiated Instruction:
English Language Learners**

ELPS 2I, 4E, 4F, 4G

Use visuals to provide background knowledge about Frederick Douglass and his life.

ELP Level **Beginning**	ELP Level **Intermediate**	ELP Level **Advanced/Advanced High**
Point out features of a time line. Use simplified language to explain the types of events the writer includes.	Use simplified language to discuss the events the writer includes in the time line. Have students summarize the events orally.	Have students examine the time line and take notes about the types of events the writer includes. Invite students to share their notes.

ELPS **2I** Demonstrate listening comprehension/retelling or summarizing; **4E** Read linguistically accommodated content area material with a decreasing need for linguistic accommodations; **4F** Use visual and contextual support to develop vocabulary and background knowledge; **4G** Demonstrate comprehension of increasingly complex English/taking notes

Prewriting Considering Themes

Review and discuss themes from books and selections the class has read recently. Be sure students understand that there is no single "correct" theme for works of literature.

DIFFERENTIATE INSTRUCTION ↘

Quotation Chart

Distribute photocopies of the reproducible T-chart (TE page A97) and ask students to make a quotation chart. Emphasize the importance of including the page number with each quotation.

■ Ask students to review the model essay on SE pages 277–278 and notice that each long quotation is followed by a page citation. Remind them that they will be expected to provide citations.

■ Point out that recording the page numbers in their notes will help them locate the quotations later to double-check them for accuracy. (It is always a good idea to double-check quotations during proofreading.)

■ Require at least four quotations, but encourage students to record favorites as they read. This should provide an abundance of quotations to choose from when writing their drafts.

■ Point out that students may collect more than one quotation in support of each event.

★ TEKS 11.15C(ii)

Create a quotation chart. Suggest that students use their time lines as a guide for identifying quotations about important events.

DIFFERENTIATE INSTRUCTION ↘

Prewriting Considering Themes

Study your time line of the book's major events to identify a theme, or major lesson about life. Tammy thought about themes by creating a quotation chart. On the left, she listed major events from the story, and on the right, she listed quotations about the importance of these events. (For each quotation, she noted a page number in parentheses.)

Quotation Chart

Major Events	What Frederick Douglass Wrote
Douglass's mother dies.	"Never having enjoyed…her tender and watchful care, I received the tidings of her death with much the same emotions I should probably have felt at the death of a stranger." (16)
His master orders an end to Douglass's reading lessons.	"In learning to read, I owe almost as much to the bitter opposition of my master, as to the kindly aid of my mistress. I acknowledge the benefit of both." (38)
He fights back during a beating by his master Mr. Covey.	"My long-crushed spirit rose . . . however long I might remain a slave in form, the day had passed forever when I could be a slave in fact." (65)
He and other slaves plan a secret escape.	". . . we did more than Patrick Henry, when he resolved upon liberty or death. . . . For my part, I should prefer death to hopeless bondage." (74)

Prewrite

Create a quotation chart. List the book's major events. Then gather quotations in which the writer reflects on the meaning of the events. Note in parentheses the page on which each quotation appears. Afterward, write down possible themes. Here are Tammy's ideas.

> Themes: hope and faith
> know your enemy
> the injustice of slavery

Differentiated Instruction: Struggling Learners

Students may need additional tools to help identify the theme. Suggest that they think about or freewrite about one thing they learned from reading their book and why it mattered to them. Point out that often, what they learn is connected to the author's intended theme, so their personal response can guide them to the book's meaning.

Differentiated Instruction: Advanced Learners

As students create their quotation charts, encourage them to start quotation books. Suggest that they use a spiral notebook or blank book. As they create their charts, they can record their favorite quotations in their books. Then whenever they read, they can copy quotations into their books, noting author, title, and page number.

Writing a Thesis Statement

Your thesis statement identifies the book or writer and introduces the theme you want to explore. The following formula can help you.

book/author		theme		thesis statement
Narrative of the Life of Frederick Douglass, an American Slave by Frederick Douglass	**+**	hope and faith can help us endure and overcome	**=**	In his autobiography, the author tells how hope and faith helped him endure years of slavery and eventually overcome its bonds.

Prewrite

Form a focus. Write a thesis statement for your response essay using the formula above.

Organizing the Middle Paragraphs of Your Essay

The first few middle paragraphs should focus on the main events of the book. The later paragraphs should focus on the meaning of the events—demonstrating the theme. Tammy wrote the following topic sentences for her middle paragraphs.

Topic Sentence 1 (First middle paragraph)

Born in 1818, Douglass never learned who his father was.

Topic Sentence 2 (Second middle paragraph)

Even as a child, Douglass was aware of the soul-threatening nature of slavery.

Topic Sentence 3 (Third middle paragraph)

Throughout his life, Douglass felt the power of education an invaluable aid on the path to freedom.

Topic Sentence 4 (Fourth middle paragraph)

After an unsuccessful attempt to escape in 1836, Douglass continued his plans, and escaped forever on September 3, 1838.

Topic Sentence 5 (Fifth middle paragraph)

By clinging to hope, Douglass could continue to fight for his life and his freedom.

Prewrite

Create topic sentences. Write topic sentences for your middle paragraphs. The first paragraphs should focus on the main events of the book. The later paragraphs should focus on the theme you wish to explore.

Response

Writing a Thesis Statement

Before students write their thesis statements, point out that effective thesis statements list the points the writer will address in order to convince the reader that the thesis is accurate. For example, the analysis of *Narrative Life of Frederick Douglass, an American Slave* must

- faithfully convey the ideas expressed by the author, *Frederick Douglass;*
- explain how Douglass used *hope and faith to endure and overcome;* and
- show how Douglass *used hope and faith to endure and overcome the bonds of slavery.*

Form a focus. Remind students that the writer states and supports the thesis in order to reveal the theme of the book.

TEKS 11.15C(i)

Organizing the Middle Paragraphs of Your Essay

If students find it difficult to create finished topic sentences at this stage, allow them to simply use words and phrases to indicate the important points in their thesis statements that they plan to address in each middle paragraph. Point out that they are creating a topic outline to organize their essay. ✓ DIFFERENTIATE INSTRUCTION

✱ For more about outlining ideas, see SE page 619.

Create topic sentences. Explain that the topic sentences that students write now can be revised later to better fit into the flow of the response.

Prewriting Including Paraphrases and Quotations

Point out that, in general, writers use paraphrases to explain the author's ideas and use quotations to provide clear support for their main points.

Try It!
Answers

Possible paraphrase:

The phone rang as the narrator was working hard to complete his project. He was annoyed as he answered the phone. It was his friend Steve, telling him to turn on the television. The scene that he saw—smoke and burning skyscrapers—was strange. "Somebody's flown planes into the World Trade Center," Steve explained. Suddenly he forgot all about his pressing deadline. The whole world was changing forever. Just then, one of the towers started to collapse.

DIFFERENTIATE INSTRUCTION ↘

⭐ **TEKS** 11.15C(ii)

Focus on the Texas Traits

Development of Ideas
Suggest that students think of quotations as a support system that emphasizes and highlights their main points. Explain that the quotations they choose will also help them to identify and confirm their main points.

Prewriting Including Paraphrases and Quotations

Most of your responses about the book should be paraphrases—ideas expressed in your own words. However, when the author's exact words are especially concise and powerful, you will want to quote the author. An effective quotation allows you to showcase the author's writing voice. The exercise below will help you learn when to paraphrase and when to include a quotation.

Try It!

Read the passage below. Then write a paragraph that paraphrases *most* of the information. Also include a concise, powerful quotation to demonstrate the author's writing voice.

> I was in the thick of my latest project when the phone rang: the blasted phone. Telemarketers were the bane of my existence. Still, this could be my boss.
>
> I lifted the receiver and barked, "What?"
>
> "Turn on the TV," came the voice on the other end—a man's voice, grave and slightly trembling. Even as I staggered to the TV and punched the "on" button, I realized it was the voice of my friend Steve.
>
> The screen brightened, and the scene that appeared was strange—two great glass towers, straight and smooth, with two columns of black smoke pouring and twisting sideways from them.
>
> "Somebody's flown planes into the World Trade Center," Steve explained.
>
> I stood there gaping, unsure of what I was seeing, torn between the deadline that a moment ago had seemed of ultimate significance and this terrible sight, which meant the whole world was changing forever.
>
> "What?" I repeated stupidly.
>
> Before Steve could answer, one of the towers began to fall.

Focus on the Texas Traits

Development of Ideas Paraphrasing and including quotations can help you add depth to an idea you want to develop. Try to avoid the mistake of using them simply to add length to your essay. A paraphrase or a quotation should be used to support an idea you're trying to set forth, not to repeat the idea in another way or restate it.

 ⭐ **TEKS** **11.15C(ii)** Write an interpretation that includes references to and commentary on quotations from the text

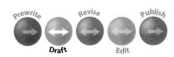

Drafting

Now that you have finished prewriting, you are ready to write the first draft of your response. At this stage, focus only on getting your ideas on paper. You can make improvements later.

> ### Keys to Effective Drafting
>
> 1. Write on every other line so that you have room to make changes later.
>
> 2. Use your thesis statement and topic sentences to guide your writing.
>
> 3. Support your topic sentences with paraphrased information and direct quotations.
>
> 4. In your first middle paragraphs, summarize important events from the book; then interpret the main theme in the later paragraphs.
>
> 5. Tie your ideas together with transitions.

Response

Drafting

Keys to Effective Drafting

Remind students that the drafting stage is when they get to write, or draft, their ideas on paper.

The Keys to Effective Drafting list explains the process students will be guided through on SE pages 286–290.

Discuss different approaches to the task of drafting an essay.

- At one end of the spectrum are writers who prefer to work slowly and methodically, creating a polished first draft.
- At the other end of the spectrum are writers who work fast, pouring out their ideas quickly to create a rough first draft.
- Most writers fall somewhere in the middle of this range.

Assure students that whatever their preferred method of creating a first draft, they will find that conscientiously following the steps in this and the next section (revising) will improve their work.

Writing Workshop

Model drafting for your students. If your students see you composing sentences as examples, they will recognize you as a fellow writer and facilitator. This is a key concept for the writing workshop approach.

Drafting Getting the Big Picture

Ask students to gather their planning notes, thesis statement, quotation chart, and topic outline for the book they will analyze. Then encourage them to create an organizer like the one shown to chart their big picture.

DIFFERENTIATE INSTRUCTION ↘

Remind students, as they work, to step back from time to time and review their organizer to help them keep the big picture in mind and to be sure they are advancing a clear thesis statement. They should also confirm that they are using and providing commentary on quotations from the work.

TEKS 11.15C(i), 11.15C(ii)

Drafting Getting the Big Picture

Remember that an essay includes three parts—the beginning, the middle, and the ending. You are ready to begin drafting your response if you have . . .

1. written a clear thesis statement that identifies the theme,
2. gathered events and quotations that reveal the theme, and
3. written topic sentences to organize your paragraphs.

The chart below shows how the three parts of a theme interpretation fit together. The examples are from the essay on pages **287–290**.

Beginning

The **beginning** names the book and the author, tells what the story is about, and states the thesis.

Thesis Statement
First published in 1845, the autobiography *Narrative of the Life of Frederick Douglass, an American Slave* shines a bright light on the pain Douglass and countless others endured, and highlights the idea that without hope and faith, escape and freedom would have been impossible.

Topic Sentences
Even as a child, Douglass was aware of the soul-threatening nature of slavery.

Throughout his life, Douglass felt the power of education an invaluable aid on the path to freedom.

Douglass's turning point came in 1834, when he found himself "broken in body, mind, and spirit" at the hands of a cruel master, Edward Covey.

Throughout his years in slavery, Douglass experienced prolonged periods of deep despair and self-doubt.

Middle

The **middle** paragraphs summarize the important events and analyze the main theme.

Ending

The **ending** paragraph reemphasizes the main theme.

Closing Sentences
The greatest lesson we can take from his words and life is that Douglass's belief in himself and his worth as a human being was sparked, and never extinguished, as long as hope and faith still burned.

Differentiated Instruction: Struggling Learners

Students should be able to organize their topic sentences if they have a firm grasp of the time line of events in their books. At this point, suggest that students refer to the time lines they created for SE page 281. Once they have reviewed them, suggest that they refer to the time lines as they chart their big pictures.

TEKS **11.15C(i)** Write an interpretation of an expository text that advances a clear thesis statement; **11.15C(ii)** Write an interpretation that includes references to and commentary on quotations

⭐ **TEKS** 11.15C(i),
11.15C(ii)

Starting Your Essay

The opening of your essay grabs the reader's interest and
should include . . .

- **the title and author of the book,**
- **background information about people and events,
  and**
- **your thesis statement.**

Beginning
Middle
Ending

Beginning Paragraph

Tammy places Frederick Douglass's life story in its historical context.

The first part introduces the book and gives the thesis statement (underlined).

> Slavery casts a long shadow across our nation's history,
> but our understanding of slavery can be illuminated by the
> words of those who lived through this dark time. First published
> in 1845, the autobiography *Narrative of the Life of Frederick
> Douglass, an American Slave*, shines a bright light on the pain
> Douglass and countless others endured and highlights the idea
> that without hope and faith, escape and freedom would have been
> impossible.

Draft

Draft your beginning. As you develop your beginning paragraph, include
the title and author of the book, background information that introduces the
story, and your thesis statement. Write as many versions as it takes to compose
a beginning that says what you want it to say.

Tip

If you have trouble getting started, review these tips to trigger your thinking.

- **Talk about your story with a classmate** before you begin to write.
- **Write freely** without worrying about producing a perfect essay on your
  first try. First drafts are often called *rough drafts* for a reason.
- **Review the book** to find supporting details for your thesis statement.
- **Show your personal interest** in the autobiography and in your
  interpretation by using natural, sincere, though careful language.
- **Focus on these key traits of writing:** focus and coherence, organization,
  development of ideas, and voice.

Response

Starting Your Essay

Discuss the three elements that should be
included in the beginning of the essay, and have
students explain why each one is necessary.

↙ **DIFFERENTIATE INSTRUCTION**

Beginning Paragraph

Point out that in the sample beginning
paragraph, putting the topic into historical
context makes for a strong opening. Explain that
there are many other ways to grab a reader's
attention. Invite students to share and comment
on ideas for opening strategies before they begin
writing. Ideas might include the following:

- Begin with an attention-getting quotation.
  ⭐ **TEKS** 11.15C(ii)
- Start in the middle of an exciting bit of action,
  and then circle back and explain it in the
  context of the book.
- Ask a thought-provoking question.
- Reveal something surprising about the topic.

Draft your beginning. After students have drafted
an opening, encourage those who would like
feedback to read aloud their paragraphs to a
small group of peers. Invite students to comment
on the following:

- whether or not the opening includes all the
  necessary elements, including a clear thesis
  statement,
- whether or not it grabs the reader's interest,
  and
- possible ways to improve the opening.
  ⭐ **TEKS** 11.15C(i)

Tip

Discuss the tips, asking students to evaluate the
usefulness of each one.

Differentiated Instruction:
English Language Learners

🎧 **ELPS** 3B, 3E, 5B

ELP Level **Beginning**	ELP Level **Intermediate**	ELP Level **Advanced/Advanced High**
Guide students to learn and use new vocabulary by generating words, phrases, and ideas about their topic. Have students create a list of these describing words.	Have student share information about their topic with an English-proficient peer and create a web or chart of vocabulary they can use in their beginnings.	Have students answer questions such as *How is my topic important to others?* Then have students share and discuss their responses with a partner.

TEKS **11.15C(i)** Write an interpretation of an expository
text that advances a clear thesis statement; **11.15C(ii)** Write
an interpretation that includes references to and commentary
on quotations; **ELPS 3B** Expand vocabulary/learning and using routine
language needed for classroom communication; **3E** Share information in
cooperative learning interactions; **5B** Write using newly acquired basic
vocabulary and content-based grade-level vocabulary

Drafting Developing the Middle Part

Before students analyze the middle paragraphs in the essay, discuss each element the writer should include: a summary of the book, followed by paragraphs that detail how events contribute to and support the theme.

Middle Paragraphs

Analyze how the writer organizes details in the sample middle paragraphs. Ask students to identify the main purpose of each middle paragraph.

- Middle paragraph 1 summarizes major events in Douglass's early life.
- Middle paragraph 2 discusses Douglass's awareness of his plight as a slave.
- Middle paragraph 3 describes the role of education in Douglass's life.
- Middle paragraph 4 explains the turning point in Douglass's mindset, as it applies to the main theme.
- Middle paragraph 5 relates specific examples (Douglass's escape and life after slavery) to the theme.
- Middle paragraph 6 refocuses attention on the theme.

Point out that the writer reveals details from the book in chronological order. Explain to students that if they can support their thesis more effectively (without confusing readers) by mentioning events in order of importance, they should do so.

288

Drafting Developing the Middle Part

Beginning
Middle
Ending

Your first job is to summarize the story's events. Afterward, you'll shift your focus to the main theme. Begin each middle paragraph with one of your topic sentences. Supply support for each topic sentence with paraphrases and quotations.

Middle Paragraphs

In the middle paragraphs, Tammy begins by recounting important events in Douglass's life as a slave. She then shifts her focus to the main theme.

> The first middle paragraphs summarize the main events in the book.

Born in 1818, Douglass never learned who his father was, although he suggests that it was his then-master, Aaron Anthony. Douglass only rarely saw his mother, a slave named Harriet Bailey. He goes on to relate that "Never having enjoyed... her tender and watchful care, I received the tidings of her death with much the same emotions I should probably have felt at the death of a stranger" (16). Douglass endured his early life as a slave under a number of masters, and witnessed and was himself subject to numerous savage beatings and whippings. He describes how even initially kind masters, such as Sophia Auld, became corrupted by "the fatal poison" of slave-owning and its "irresponsible power" (37).

> The writer includes some quotations from the author to support her ideas.

Even as a child, Douglass was aware of the soul-threatening nature of slavery. Speaking to white children on a farm, he tells them, "You will be free as soon as you are twenty-one, *but I am a slave for life!*" (41). Deep within him, however, the flame of hope was ever-present. He possessed "a deep conviction that slavery would not always be able to hold me within its foul embrace" (36).

Throughout his life, Douglass felt the power of education an invaluable aid on the path to freedom. Until she was ordered to stop, Sophia Auld taught Douglass to read, and he later ingeniously learned to write by challenging young white children that he knew more letters and words than they—through "winning," those children unknowingly taught Douglass to write more letters and words. At times, however, Douglass found himself tormented by education's power, that "it had given me

The middle paragraphs include paraphrased and quoted material.

a view of my wretched condition, but without the remedy" (42). Douglass's education also involved learning all that he could about his masters and sharing nothing with them about himself. A keen observer of his masters and fellow slaves, Douglass believed that conventions such as "holidays" and "wages" led to contentment, which only served to keep the chains of slavery strong, tight, and intact.

Douglass's turning point came in 1834, when he found himself "broken in body, mind, and spirit" at the hands of a cruel master, Edward Covey. Facing another beating for running away, Douglass fought back, for "nearly two hours" (64) and afterwards experienced a "glorious resurrection," resolving "that however long I might remain a slave in form, the day had passed forever when I could be a slave in fact" (65).

After an unsuccessful attempt to escape in 1836, Douglass continued his plans, and escaped forever on September 3, 1838, when he fled to Wilmington, and from there to New York. He married and hired himself out for work of all kinds, experiencing "the starting-point of a new existence" (95). Encouraged by the work and words of others, he became a ceaseless and devoted voice for abolition and freedom.

The later middle paragraphs use events and quotations to demonstrate the main theme.

Throughout his years in slavery, Douglass experienced prolonged periods of deep despair and self-doubt. Evoking Patrick Henry's famous words, "Give me liberty, or give me death!" Douglass argues that "for my part, I should prefer death to hopeless bondage" (74). In those words we can find the key to Douglass's survival—by clinging to hope, however faint, however dimmed, Douglass could continue to fight for his life and his freedom.

Response

Draft

Draft your middle paragraphs. Use your topic sentences, time line, and quotations chart to guide your writing. Anticipating readers' questions will also help you develop your essay. Try to include strong quotations that help reveal the author's voice or that could help clear up contradictory information in the book.

Before students begin writing, point out a few of the stylistic conventions in the sample paragraphs:

- The writer uses the present tense to describe events in the first middle paragraph. This is because each reader experiences events in a book as if they are happening in the present.
- The writer uses figurative language such as metaphors (*"the fatal poison" of slave-owning, flame of hope*) to engage readers.
- Quotations from the book are cited with page references noted in parentheses.

TEKS 11.15C(ii)

- Appositive phrases (as in *a cruel master, Edward Covey*) provide useful information and emphasize key points.

✱ For more about appositive phrases, see SE pages 87 and 760.

Draft your middle paragraphs. Tell students to be sure to consult their prewriting notes and charts as they are writing. Remind them that each middle paragraph should advance their thesis.

✔ DIFFERENTIATE INSTRUCTION

TEKS 11.15C(i)

**Differentiated Instruction:
English Language Learners**

ELPS 4H, 4I, 5B

ELP Level **Beginning**	ELP Level **Intermediate**	ELP Level **Advanced/Advanced High**
Preteach words like *master* and *slave* before reading the sample paragraphs. Then use simplified language to read the paragraph together.	Preteach words and phrases like *endured* and *turning point*. Read each paragraph aloud and pause to ask yes/no questions to gauge comprehension.	Have students read the paragraph silently, and write questions about vocabulary or concepts that confuse them. Discuss the questions as a group.

TEKS **11.15C(i)** Write an interpretation of an expository text that advances a clear thesis statement; **11.15C(ii)** Write an interpretation that includes references to and commentary on quotations; **ELPS 4H** Read silently with increasing ease and comprehension; **4I** Demonstrate English comprehension by employing basic reading skills and expanding reading skills; **5B** Write using newly acquired basic vocabulary and content-based grade-level vocabulary

Drafting Ending Your Essay

Suggest that before writing their endings, students try some or all of the following strategies:

- Carefully reread what they have written so far.
- Review their big picture charts to remind themselves of their initial ideas for closing sentences.
- Take a little time away from their writing to think about their main themes.
- Show the writing to an outside reader and discuss ideas for effective endings.

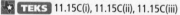
DIFFERENTIATE INSTRUCTION ↘

Ending Paragraph

Discuss the writer's choice of strategy for ending the essay. Ask students to explain whether they find the ending effective.

Draft your ending and form a complete first draft. Remind students that they should reiterate their thesis statement in the ending. Ask them to consider whether a quotation or an analysis of the the author's use of rhetorical or stylistic devices will make the ending more effective. Be sure students understand that completing their first draft marks a milestone in the writing process.

TEKS 11.15C(i), 11.15C(ii), 11.15C(iii)

Drafting Ending Your Essay

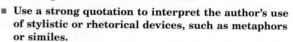

The ending of your response reflects on the main theme. Here are some strategies for an effective conclusion:

- **Use a strong quotation to interpret the author's use of stylistic or rhetorical devices, such as metaphors or similes.**
  Comparing himself to an "unarmed mariner" who gets "rescued by a friendly man-of-war from the pursuit of a pirate," Douglass aptly describes his complicated feelings when he found himself in a free state. (89)
- **Refer to ideas in the beginning of your essay.**
  Douglass's words will shine forever to focus light on this dark corner of our country's history.
- **Include historical context for the theme.**
  Those who believe that the effects of slavery ended with the Emancipation Proclamation are sorely mistaken and misguided.

Ending Paragraph

In the final paragraph, Tammy returns to ideas and images she presented in the beginning of her essay.

> The ending applies the theme to life in general.

> In his autobiography, Douglass forces readers of all hues and backgrounds to confront this shameful period in our country's history. We must never forget or ignore how slavery dimmed or ended the lives of so many; Douglass's words will shine forever to focus light on this dark corner of our country's history. The greatest lesson we can take from his words and life, however, is that Douglass's belief in himself and his worth as a human being was sparked, and never extinguished, as long as hope and faith still burned.

Draft

Draft your ending and form a complete first draft. Develop the last paragraph of your essay, using one or more of the suggestions listed above. Make a complete copy of your essay. Double-space or write on every other line so that you have room for revising.

TEKS **11.15C(i)** Write an interpretation of an expository text that advances a clear thesis statement; **11.15C(ii)** Write an interpretation that includes references to and commentary on quotations; **11.15C(iii)** Write an interpretation that analyzes the aesthetic effects of an author's use of stylistic or rhetorical devices

Revising

You've written a first draft, pouring your ideas onto the page. Now it's time to revise, making whatever changes are necessary to improve the content of your essay.

Keys to Effective Revising

1. Make sure that your writing achieves its purpose of interpreting a theme in a work of nonfiction.

2. Read your essay aloud to see whether it is focused and holds together from start to finish.

3. Check to confirm that your essay has a strong beginning and an effective conclusion.

4. Be sure that your middle paragraphs are organized logically and that they develop your main idea.

5. Revise your voice to make it confident and engaging.

6. Use the editing and proofreading marks inside the back cover of this book.

Response

Revising
Keys to Effective Revising

Remind students that the revising stage is when writers have an opportunity to make improvements to their first drafts. At this stage they can think about refinements they might not have considered when they were drafting.

The Keys to Effective Revising list explains the process students will be guided through on SE pages 292–300.

Point out that a common error when responding to literature is to become too involved in retelling the story. When this happens, the interpretation of the work will suffer. Encourage students to keep this pitfall in mind as they review their drafts.

Ask students to respond to each other's essays using appropriate vocabulary to discuss concepts. A constructive peer response helps the writer know just what needs to be improved in an essay. For more on peer responding, see pages 115–120.

⭐ **ELPS** 4F

Differentiated Instruction:
English Language Learners

⭐ **ELPS** 1B, 4K

ELP Level **Beginning**	ELP Level **Intermediate**	ELP Level **Advanced/Advanced High**
Use questions such as *What do I want readers to remember about my topic?* to help students construct their endings.	Have students reread and analyze the last sentence of the sample ending. Then have them construct their endings to describe a lesson to share with readers.	Have students work to write their endings. Then have partners share their work and make suggestions to help strengthen their ideas.

 ELPS 1B Monitor written language production and employ self-corrective techniques or other resources; **4F** Use support from peers and teachers to develop vocabulary and grasp of language structures; **4K** Demonstrate English comprehension and expand reading skills by employing analytical skills

Revising for Focus and Coherence

Suggest that students begin the revision process by reading their introduction and conclusion. Have them analyze whether these sections of their essays relate to and support their thesis statement. **DIFFERENTIATE INSTRUCTION** ↘

Have I maintained focus throughout my essay and within each paragraph?

Explain that students should be able to explain how each each paragraph in the beginning, middle, and ending of the essay relates to their thesis statement.

Exercise
Answers

Students should delete "A number of these virtues would be named differently today."

Students should revise the last sentence which, as written, is vague. Possible revision: For example, Virtue 9 on the list, "Moderation. Avoid Extremes. Forbear resenting injuries so much as you think they deserve" suggests that a measured response to an injury or slight is always better than extreme anger or violence.

Review your essay. Tell students to be prepared to share an example of a detail they deleted or clarified. Ask them to how the revision clarifies their meaning.

⭐ **TEKS** 11.13C

292

⭐ **TEKS** 11.13C

Revising for Focus and Coherence

When you revise for *focus and coherence*, you make sure that your writing stays focused on your thesis statement. All of your paragraphs and sentences should relate to that single idea, and your writing should make clear connections between and among the ideas presented. Your essay should include a meaningful introduction and conclusion. Each paragraph of your essay should add depth to your interpretation and give your essay a sense of completeness.

Have I maintained focus throughout my essay and within each paragraph?

Review your essay and make sure that each of your paragraphs clearly relates to your thesis statement. Look for places in the essay where you need to clarify your meaning, or perhaps make your point in a more specific way. Then review each paragraph in your essay. Make sure that the ideas within each paragraph support your thesis statement and are clearly connected to one another. Delete details that stray from your thesis statement and weaken your focus.

Exercise

Read the paragraph and determine its thesis statement. Then identify two details that should be deleted or revised to more clearly connect to the thesis, and explain why.

1   In the second section of his *Autobiography*, Benjamin Franklin includes a list
2   of thirteen virtues that every person should strive to develop. A number of these
3   virtues would be named differently today. While Franklin's wry tone indicates that
4   attempting to uphold all of these virtues is an impossible task, his inclusion of them
5   in his autobiography reveals his sincere belief that humans have the power to better
6   themselves. Virtue 9 on the list, "Moderation. Avoid Extremes. Forbear resenting
7   Injuries so much as you think they deserve" is puzzling but clearly important.

Review your essay. Read through your draft to be certain that all the paragraphs relate to the focus of your essay. Check each paragraph. Delete irrelevant details, and revise those that need a clearer connection.

Differentiated Instruction: Struggling Learners

Explain that it is natural for writers to become so attached to their words that they are reluctant to change them, even when they know they need to revise. Point out that in the exercises on this and the following pages, students will have an opportunity to practice revising on words that are not their own. This will help them see how small changes can lead to dramatic improvements in quality.

How do I know if my introduction is strong?

Your introduction is strong if it engages the reader's attention and presents your topic clearly. Have a classmate read your essay's introduction and answer these questions.

- What is the theme that this essay will interpret?
- How does the introduction focus my attention?
- What makes me want to keep reading?

 Review your introduction. Make revisions that will help draw your audience in and help them better understand what your essay will be about.

How do I know if my conclusion adds depth to my interpretation?

Your conclusion adds depth if it ties to your introduction and says something more for your audience to consider. Give your readers something to think about! Try to provide a deeper insight that ties your interpretation to an idea common to many people.

 Review your conclusion. Does it leave the reader with something to think about? If your conclusion only restates the main idea of your essay, revise your ending to prompt readers to consider a new idea or viewpoint.

Focus and Coherence
The writer adds depth by addressing the audience and suggesting a deeper idea to think about.

In his autobiography, Douglass forces readers of all hues and backgrounds to confront this shameful period in our country's history. ∧ We must never forget or ignore how Slavery dimmed or ended the lives of so many; Douglass's words will shine forever to focus light on this dark corner. ∧ The greatest lesson we can take from his words and life, however, is that Douglass's belief in himself and his worth as a human being was sparked, and never extinguished, as long as hope and faith still burned.

Response

How do I know if my introduction is strong?

Assign partners to read each other's essays and discuss their answers to the three questions. Encourage them to discuss ideas for any necessary revisions.

Review your introduction. As needed, refer students to the strategies on SE page 295.

How do I know if my conclusion adds depth to my interpretation?

Discuss the writer's revisions to the conclusion of the essay about Frederick Douglass's autobiography. Ask them to explain how the revisions add depth, and gives the audience something to think about. ✔DIFFERENTIATE INSTRUCTION

Review your conclusion. Remind students that their conclusion should connect to their thesis statement. Suggest that they complete the following statement about their conclusion: *The idea that I want the audience to give more thought to is _____.*

⭐ TEKS 11.15C(i)

Focus and Coherence

Read the passage once without the revisions, and then a second time with the writer's revisions. Discuss how the changes improve the conclusion.

Differentiated Instruction: English Language Learners

⭐ ELPS 1B, 5G

ELP Level **Beginning**	ELP Level **Intermediate**	ELP Level **Advanced/Advanced High**
Work with students to review their introductions and conclusions. Point out opportunities to narrate, describe, or explain in more detail.	Pair students with an English-proficient peer to review their introductions and conclusions. Have them use self-corrective techniques to make revisions as needed.	Partners can work together to review their conclusions. Have them identify a lesson or idea for readers to think about, and revise their writing to include it.

 TEKS **11.15C(i)** Write an interpretation of an expository or a literary text that advances a clear thesis statement; ELPS **1B** Monitor written language production and employ self-corrective techniques or other resources; **5G** Narrate, describe, and explain with increasing specificity and detail

Revising for Organization

Remind students that if their essay is organized in a logical way, readers will clearly understand how one idea is connected to the next. For example, commentary that explains a quotation would immediately follow the quotation itself.

How do I check my organization?

Refer students back to Big Picture chart on SE page 286 as they analyze the beginning, middle, and ending paragraphs in their essays.

Exercise
Answers

Students will likely note that Paragraph 4 should be moved to be the first paragraph of the essay. If students suggest other ideas for rearranging the plan, ask them to explain their thinking.

Review your essay. You may wish to suggest that students annotate their essays to identify transitions and to show how paragraphs and ideas are connected. Remind students that transitions can also connect relevant commentary to the appropriate quotation.

TEKS 11.13C, 11.15C(ii)

 **Revising** for Organization

When you revise for *organization,* you make sure your essay is easy to follow from beginning to end. Your thoughts should move smoothly from sentence to sentence and from paragraph to paragraph. Transitional words and phrases should guide readers in understanding your organizational strategy. The strategies you choose to organize your essay should help you present your ideas in a way that is both clear and effective.

How do I check my organization?

The steps you followed while drafting your essay included some effective organization strategies: Your beginning introduces the book and the theme you will interpret. In the middle paragraphs, you discuss important events and analyze how those events both reveal and emphasize the theme. In the ending, you restate and reflect on the theme.

Exercise

Read one student's plan for organizing an essay that interprets a theme in *The Autobiography of Benjamin Franklin.* Then identify how the student could make the ideas flow more logically by moving one paragraph.

Paragraph 1: Introduce topic and theme of self-improvement; provide historical context.

Paragraph 2: Discuss Franklin's life and his efforts at self-improvement.

Paragraph 3: Discuss ideas about self-improvement from *Part 2* of autobiography.

Paragraph 4: Discuss how autobiography is organized in three parts.

Paragraph 5: Discuss what Franklin accomplished through self-improvement.

Paragraph 6: Conclude with ideas about how self-improvement is considered an American trait/goal.

 Revise

Review your essay. Make sure that you have organized your paragraphs in a logical sequence. Identify the paragraphs that make up the beginning, the middle, and the end of your essay. Then check that you have used transitional words and phrases to connect the ideas in each section of your essay.

TEKS **11.13C** Revise drafts to clarify meaning by adding transitional words and phrases; **11.15C(ii)** Write an interpretation of an expository or a literary text that addresses the writing skills for an analytical essay, including commentary on quotations from the text

Have I used strategies to organize my sentences and paragraphs?

The following strategies and rhetorical devices can help you get readers' attention as well as organize your writing.

1. **Make a startling claim.**
   The modern masterpiece *In Cold Blood* succeeds in part because it portrays the full personality of a cold-blooded killer.

2. **Ask an intriguing question.**
   What modern masterpiece is hailed as both horrifying and hypnotically beautiful?

3. **Begin with an anecdote.**
   When Truman Capote first laid eyes on Perry Smith, a cold-blooded killer, the writer seemed to fall under a terrible spell.

4. **Use a quotation from the book.**
   "Until one morning in mid-November of 1959, few Americans—in fact, few Kansans—had ever heard of Holcomb" (5).

5. **Use transitional words and phrases to show time order or to move from event to event.**
   During his travels, Capote gathered chilling facts and details about the case.

Revise

Review your organization. Use strategies that will make your writing flow more smoothly. Look for places where a rhetorical device can add interest while maintaining your organizational structure.

Organization
The writer revises sentences to include transitional words and phrases that improve organization.

> After an unsuccessful attempt to escape in 1836,
> ∧Douglass continued his plans, and escaped forever on
>   when
> September 3, 1838. He fled to Wilmington, and from there to
>   ∧
> New York.

Response

Have I used strategies to organize my sentences and paragraphs?

Review each strategy with students, and invite volunteers to share examples from their writing that illustrate one or more of the strategies.

Focus attention on the use of quotations and point out that this strategy can be especially effective when interpreting a literary work. Point out that the use of quotations provides validity to their commentary, and helps readers recognize them as knowledgable writers.

After students have reviewed the strategies, extend the discussion with the following:

- Ask students to vote for the strategy they think is most effective.
- Invite one or two students to explain their preference.
- Finally, encourage the writers to consider this feedback when they revise their beginning paragraphs. (Remind them that the final decision about which strategy to use is always theirs to make.)

Review your organization. Remind students that the use of rhetorical devices is not an end in itself, but a means of enhancing their writing. Point out that they should carefully choose the place in their essays where such devices will be most useful and use transitions where appropriate. ✔DIFFERENTIATE INSTRUCTION

TEKS 11.13C, 11.15C(ii)

Organization
Point out that the transitional words and phrases in the revision help to provide clarity for the reader.

ELP Level **Beginning**	ELP Level **Intermediate**	ELP Level **Advanced/Advanced High**
Work with students to review their organization, and suggest revisions as needed. Point out opportunities to revise to add variety to sentence patterns.	Pair students with an English-proficient peer, and have them collaborate to review their essays for organization. Have them take notes about suggestions for revisions.	Have partners read each other's essays and employ inferential skills to decide how they are organized. Partners can discuss rhetorical devices that could add interest.

TEKS **11.13C** Revise drafts to clarify meaning by adding transitional words and phrases; **11.15C(ii)** Write an interpretation of an expository or a literary text that addresses the writing skills for an analytical essay, including commentary on quotations from the text; **ELPS 2I** Demonstrate listening comprehension/collaborating with peers; **4J** Demonstrate English comprehension and expand reading skills by employing inferential skills; **5F** Write using a variety of grade-appropriate sentence patterns

Revising for Development of Ideas

Explain that for readers to understand and appreciate their ideas, writers must go beyond an overview of the book they are interpreting to develop and support ideas that are unique.

Have I developed my ideas fully?

Discuss how each suggestion could enhance an interpretation of a literary work.

Exercise
Answers

Students' response will vary. They will likely note that examples or quotations from the book would enhance and clarify the writer's claims in both paragraphs.

Review your essay's main ideas. Tell students to identify at least one place in their essays where a quotation, an analysis of a rhetorical or stylistic device, or example would more fully develop an idea. Remind them to use transitions as appropriate. **DIFFERENTIATE INSTRUCTION ↘**

TEKS 11.13C, 11.15C(iii)

Revising for Development of Ideas

When you revise for *development of ideas*, you make sure you have included enough information so that readers can understand and appreciate your ideas. Try to incorporate details that add depth to your thoughts, or that indicate your understanding of the author's writing and ideas.

Have I developed my ideas fully?

Simply presenting an idea is not enough to help your readers gain a full understanding of your topic. You can develop your ideas in a number of ways:

- Include details such as facts, examples, and statistics that support your ideas.
- Choose quotations that illustrate your understanding of the author's ideas and stylistic devices.
- Provide a fresh insight or a unique perspective.

Exercise

Each paragraph below interprets a theme in Truman Capote's *In Cold Blood*. Read each one and tell how effectively the ideas are developed.

> Capote delves deeply into who Perry Smith was and what shaped him. A fearless writer, Capote takes great pains in presenting this killer as a full, complex human being. Before *In Cold Blood*, no one had written an account like it; the book remains in a class by itself.

> Capote is unflinching in portraying the humanity of criminals as well as that of their victims. This is a lesson that we still need to learn—that villains are as human as their victims. Even today, individuals who commit acts of terrorism are still simply demonized. Capote would say that by taking away their humanity, we take away the hope of ever understanding the source of their terrible acts.

 Revise

Review your essay's main ideas. Make sure that you have included enough details to develop them fully.

TEKS **11.13C** Revise drafts to clarify meaning by adding transitional words and phrases; **11.15C(iii)** Write an interpretation of an expository or a literary text that analyzes the aesthetic effects of an author's use of stylistic or rhetorical devices

Interpreting a Theme **297**

★ **TEKS** 11.13C,
11.15C(iii)

Does my writing show that I understand the author's ideas?

One way to show that you understand an author's ideas is by including quotations that help to present the ideas more fully. Don't go overboard and stuff your essay with quotations, however. Readers will find too many quotations distracting, and that will make it difficult for them to follow your thinking. Select quotations strategically and use only those that help to illustrate your point about the author's ideas.

Another way to show that you understand the author's ideas is by analyzing stylistic devices that she or he uses. Consider how those stylistic devices strengthen the author's message. You can develop your ideas by describing how any of the following elements add to your understanding.

- the author's tone
- the mood or feeling the author creates
- the author's writing style
- the author's craft in using rhetorical devices such as similes or metaphors

Revise

Check your ideas. Be sure that your writing shows that you understand the author's ideas. Consider whether the use of quotations from the book or an analysis of stylistic devices will enhance your development of ideas.

Development of Ideas
The writer adds details that highlight her understanding of the author's ideas.

Evoking Patrick Henry's famous words, "Give me liberty, or give me death!" Douglass argues that "for my part, I should prefer death to hopeless bondage." (74) In those words we can find the key to Douglass's survival—

∧ By clinging to hope, however faint, however dimmed,

Douglass could continue to fight for his life and his freedom.

Response

Does my writing show that I understand the author's ideas?

Have students suggest guidelines for the appropriate use of quotations in an interpretive response. Then discuss why an analysis of the author's use of stylistic devices would enhance their essays.

Check your ideas. Have students explain their choices regarding the use of quotations or analysis of stylistic devices. Remind them to use transitions as appropriate.

★ **TEKS** 11.13C, 11.15C(iii)

Development of Ideas

Elicit from students and discuss the similarities and differences between the context of Patrick Henry's quotation (the American Revolution) and Douglass' situation as a slave. Discuss why the two quotations strengthen the interpretation.

Differentiated Instruction:
English Language Learners

★ **ELPS** 3H, 5G

ELP Level Beginning	**ELP Level** Intermediate	**ELP Level** Advanced/Advanced High
Work with students to review their development of ideas. Point out opportunities to describe and explain their ideas with more specificity.	Guide students to summarize their ideas orally. Then point out and discuss opportunities to describe and explain their ideas with more specificity.	Have students describe and explain their main ideas to a partner. Have partners look for opportunities to describe and explain their ideas more fully.

★ **TEKS** **11.13C** Revise drafts to clarify meaning by adding transitional words and phrases; **11.15C(iii)** Write an interpretation of an expository or a literary text that addresses the writing skills for an analytical essay, including references to quotations from the text and analyzes the aesthetic effects of an author's use of stylistic or rhetorical devices **ELPS** **3H** Describe and explain with increasing specificity and detail; **5G** Describe and explain with increasing specificity and detail

Revising for Voice

Tell students that using strong verbs and nouns and vivid modifiers will help them achieve an engaging voice. However, if they pack every sentence with feeling, their voice will sound forced and unnatural. Explain that variation and balance is key. Encourage students to vary sentences to achieve a balance.

Does my writing voice sound engaging?

Read the two examples aloud to illustrate the differences in voice. After students revise the **Exercise** sentences, have them follow a similar procedure.

Exercise
Answers

Possible answers:

1. Fred was a perfectionist who practiced for hours at a time.
2. He was never satisfied with a dance on the first try and urged his directors to film it again and again.
3. Fred insisted that every dance number had to be captured on film in one single shot, from start to finish.
4. For Fred Astaire, life without dancing wasn't life at all!
5. Dancers today still study and practice his moves in hopes of absorbing a little of his magic.

Check your voice. Suggest that students try reading their essays aloud to identify sections that could be more engaging with tropes or schemes. Remind students to rearrange words, sentences, and paragraphs as needed to highlight commentary on quotations.

 **TEKS** 11.13C, 11.15C(ii)

298

 **TEKS** 11.13C, 11.15C(i)

 **Revising for Voice**

When you revise for *voice,* make sure you sound engaging and authentic as a writer. You want your unique perspective on the piece of literature to shine through. You should also show an understanding of the author's voice in the piece of literature you are responding to.

Does my writing voice sound engaging?

Your writing voice sounds engaging when your words show strong feeling about the events you are describing. Note the difference between the following two passages.

A Flat Voice
Fred Astaire started out as a tap dancer in vaudeville **before he** appeared in his first movie, *Flying Down to Rio.*

An Engaging Voice
Fred Astaire tapped his way across thousands of vaudeville stages **before he** got his big break in the film *Flying Down to Rio.*

Exercise

Rewrite any two of the flat sentences below, replacing the underlined words with new ones that say the same thing *with feeling.*

1. Fred practiced a lot.
2. He asked his directors to film each dance many times.
3. Fred wanted each number filmed from start to finish without breaks.
4. For Fred Astaire, dancing was important.
5. Dancers today still try to learn something from his moves.

Revise

Check your voice. Read through your first draft and underline words and phrases that sound flat. Rewrite them to show your feeling about the subject.

Differentiated Instruction: Struggling Learners

To help students recognize how just one word can clearly communicate an author's voice, ask them to focus on the word *keen* in the edited passage at the bottom of page 299. Read aloud the sentence with and without the word *keen* and discuss the difference. Then ask the class to brainstorm a list of words, such as *passionate, obsessed,* or *determined,* that can describe how an author might feel about a subject. Suggest that students write down any descriptive words that they think of in connection with their authors and then work these words into their essays.

TEKS **11.13C** Revise drafts to achieve specific rhetorical purposes, consistency of tone, and logical organization by rearranging the words, sentences, and paragraphs to employ tropes/schemes; **11.15C(ii)** Write an interpretation of an expository or a literary text that addresses the writing skills for an analytical essay, including commentary on quotations from the text

How can I describe the author's voice?

You can describe the author's voice by using adjectives that show the writer's personality, feeling about the topic, and relationship with the reader.

- **Writer's personality:** Meticulous, lazy, capricious, caustic, stoic, compassionate, aggressive
- **Feeling about the topic:** Enthusiastic, hopeful, sarcastic, amazed, sympathetic, ambiguous
- **Relationship with the reader:** Welcoming, formal, informative, antagonistic, friendly, gruff

Exercise

Read the following paragraph and write down adjectives that describe the voice of the author.

> Fred Astaire's autobiography, *Steps in Time,* exhibits the same graceful ease as the man himself. His words are gentle and smiling, reflecting the same light step of his dancing style. His writing, like his moves on the stage, embodies this autobiography's theme: grace.

Check your understanding of the author's voice. Brainstorm a list of adjectives that describe the voice of the author and consider using some of them in your essay.

Voice	
Adjectives make the writing more engaging and reveal the author's voice	Douglass's education also involved learning all that he could A keen observer of his masters and fellow slaves, about his masters and sharing nothing with them about himself. ∧ Douglass believed that conventions such as "holidays" and "wages" led to contentment∧ , which only served to keep the chains ∧of slavery strong, tight, and intact.

Response

Differentiated Instruction: English Language Learners

ELPS 1C, 3D

ELP Level **Beginning**	ELP Level **Intermediate**	ELP Level **Advanced/Advanced High**
Read aloud the sample passage. Guide students to identify and define adjectives that tell about the author's voice. Have them repeat these words with you.	Have students read aloud the sample passage. Work together to create a web to identify and define adjectives that tell about the author's voice.	Have partners read the sample passage and identify adjectives that describe the author's voice. Have them discuss how the words relate to the essay's subject.

How can I describe the author's voice?

Remind students that well chosen quotations will provide examples of the author's voice.

Have students look back at the sample ending on SE page 296 and identify how the author's voice is described. Students should note that one sentence describes the voice (*Capote is unflinching in portraying . . .*). The entire second paragraph gives a strong sense of the voice in the way it uses strong nouns and verbs to explain Capote's reasons for writing the book.

Exercise Answers

Possible answers: *graceful, welcoming, simple, down-to-earth, gentle, smiling, light*
✓ DIFFERENTIATE INSTRUCTION

Check your understanding of the author's voice. Suggest that students use a print or online thesaurus to develop their lists of adjectives.

TEKS 11.13C, 11.15C(ii)

Voice

Have students identify the adjectives and explain how they reveal the author's voice.
✓ DIFFERENTIATE INSTRUCTION

TEKS **11.13C** Revise drafts to achieve specific rhetorical purposes, consistency of tone, and logical organization by rearranging the words, sentences, and paragraphs to employ tropes/schemes; **11.15C(ii)** Write an interpretation of an expository or a literary text that addresses the writing skills for an analytical essay, including commentary on quotations from the text; **ELPS 1C** Use strategic learning strategies to acquire basic and grade-level vocabulary; **3D** Speak using grade-level content-area vocabulary in context/new English words, academic language

Revising Improving Your Writing

Check your revising. Have students work with a partner to complete the checklist. Remind them that, as peer responders, it is their responsibility to be polite and honest in giving constructive criticism.

- Ask each student to read aloud his or her essay.
- After the first essay reading, allow a few minutes for the partner to make notes about the essay's analysis of the author's use of stylistic or rhetorical devices.
- Have them change roles for the second essay.
- Ask partners to go through the checklist together and apply it to each essay.

DIFFERENTIATE INSTRUCTION ↘

TEKS 11.13C, 11.15C(iii)

Make a clean copy. Before they make a clean copy, remind writers that they must decide whether they will make any suggested change. When they are uncertain about making a change, encourage them to talk to the responder to pinpoint why there was a concern.

✱ For more about peer responding, see SE pages 115–120.

Conventions Connections

Grammar: Misplaced and Dangling Modifiers
- *SkillsBook* pages 167–168

Grammar: Pronouns (relative, indefinite, interrogative, demonstrative)
- *Student Edition: Proofreader's Guide* pages 726, 728–729, 772
- *SkillsBook* pages 83, 84, 85, 86

 **TEKS** 11.13C, 11.15C(ii

Revising Improving Your Writing

Check your revising. On a piece of paper, write the numbers 1 to 13. If you can answer "yes" to a question, put a check mark after that number. If not, continue to work with that part of your essay.

Revising Checklist

Focus and Coherence

_____ **1.** Does my essay interpret a theme from a work of nonfiction?

_____ **2.** Is the focus of my essay clear?

_____ **3.** Have I maintained that focus within paragraphs and throughout my essay?

_____ **4.** Have I included a meaningful introduction and a strong conclusion?

_____ **5.** Does my essay feel complete?

Organization

_____ **6.** Have I used effective strategies to organize my essay?

_____ **7.** Do my paragraphs flow in a logical order?

_____ **8.** Have I used rhetorical devices and transitional words to help my ideas flow within paragraphs?

Development of Ideas

_____ **9.** Have I used a variety of strategies to fully develop my ideas?

_____ **10.** Have I included strong quotations that show I understand the author's ideas?

_____ **11.** Do I show an understanding of the author's stylistic devices?

Voice

_____ **12.** Does my voice sound engaging?

_____ **13.** Have I shown an understanding of the author's voice?

Make a clean copy. When you finish revising your essay, make a clean copy before you begin to edit.

TEKS **11.13C** Revise drafts to clarify meaning; **11.15C(iii)** Write an interpretation of an expository or a literary text that analyzes the aesthetic effects of an author's use of stylistic or rhetorical devices

Editing

Now that you have improved the content of your essay, it's time to edit for conventions: grammar, sentence structure, mechanics (capitalization and punctuation), and spelling.

Keys to Effective Editing

1. Use a dictionary, a thesaurus, and the "Proofreader's Guide" in the back of this book (pages 634–793).

2. Check your use of any comparative and superlative modifiers.

3. Check your writing for grammar, sentence structure, mechanics (capitalization and punctuation), and spelling errors.

4. If you use a computer, edit on a printed copy and enter your changes on the computer.

5. Use the editing and proofreading marks inside the back cover of this book.

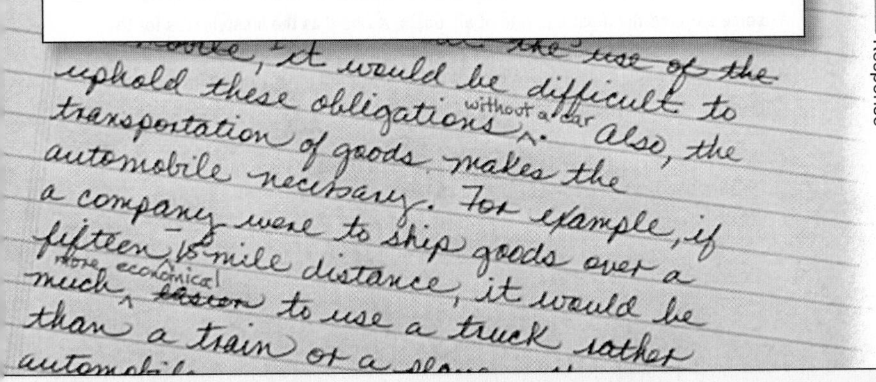

Response

[handwritten text]
...the use of the mobile, it would be difficult to uphold these obligations without a car. Also, the transportation of goods makes the automobile necessary. For example, if a company were to ship goods over a fifteen-mile distance, it would be much easier to use a truck rather than a train or a plane...

Editing

Keys to Effective Editing
Remind students that during the editing stage, they have a chance to find and correct errors in
- grammar,
- sentence structure,
- capitalization,
- punctuation, and
- spelling.

The Keys to Effective Editing list explains the process students will be guided through on SE pages 301–306.

Review the editing and proofreading marks shown on the inside back cover of the book. You may want to provide practice with sample sentences that contain errors and have students use the editing and proofreading marks to correct the errors.

Suggest that students use a different color ink to mark editing changes on their work so their corrections are clearly visible.

Differentiated Instruction: English Language Learners

⭐ **ELPS** 1B, 3E, 4F

ELP Level **Beginning**	ELP Level **Intermediate**	ELP Level **Advanced/Advanced High**
Work with students to assess their essays and guide them to employ self-corrective techniques. Make sure students to understand and make revisions.	Have partners read each other's essays and summarize the main ideas to confirm their understanding. Then guide students to make revisions.	Have partners read each other's essays and make suggestions for revisions and about ways to employ self-corrective techniques.

ELPS 1B Monitor written language production and employ self-corrective techniques or other resources; **3E** Share information in cooperative learning interactions; **4F** Use support from peers and teachers to enhance and confirm understanding

Editing for Conventions

Grammar

Explain that editing for grammar helps to remove minor problems that could distract readers from the ideas in students' writing.

How should I form comparative and superlative adjectives?

Encourage students to consult a dictionary if they are uncertain about adjective forms. Most dictionaries list the comparative and superlative forms of adjectives.

✴ For more about adjectives, see SE page 748.

Grammar Exercise
Answers

line 1: most brave—bravest
line 3: least stablest—least stable
line 4: most bad—worst
line 5: more hard—harder
line 7: more risky—riskier

Check comparatives and superlatives. Remind students to use the comparative form to discuss two things and the superlative form to discuss three or more.

 **TEKS** 11.13D

Conventions Connections

Grammar: Adjectives
- ***Student Edition: Proofreader's Guide***
  page 748
- ***SkillsBook*** page 106
- ✦ ***Write Source Online GrammarSnap***

 TEKS 11.13D

Editing for Conventions

Grammar

When you edit for *grammar*, you make sure that you have used all of the parts of speech correctly and that the subjects and predicates of your sentences agree in number.

How should I form comparative and superlative adjectives?

Comparative and superlative adjectives are formed using the following rules. (Also see page **758**.)

- For one-syllable adjectives, use *-er* (comparative) or *-est* (superlative).

fast	faster	fastest
high	higher	highest

- For most adjectives of two or more syllables, use *more* or *less* (comparative) or *most* or *least* (superlative).

courageous	more courageous	most courageous
successful	less successful	least successful

- Watch for *irregular* forms, such as the following:

good	better	best
bad	worse	worst

Grammar Exercise

Correct the errors in the use of comparative and superlative adjectives in the following paragraph.

1 In *The Right Stuff,* Tom Wolfe tells the story of the most brave test pilots of
2 the last century. They flew the toughest missions of any Air Force fliers, climbing
3 into the least stablest aircraft. Many of the test pilots suffered serious injuries, and
4 some suffered the most bad fate of all: death. As hard as the lifestyle was for the
5 pilots, it was even more hard for their wives, who waited fearfully to hear the bad
6 news. But the pilots who survived had the "right stuff" to take the controls of an
7 even more risky type of machine: a spacecraft.

 Check comparatives and superlatives. Read your essay and make sure you have correctly formed comparative and superlative adjectives.

TEKS 11.13D
ELPS 3C

When should I hyphenate compound adjectives?

Hyphenate compound adjectives when they appear just before the nouns they modify.

DO hyphenate: Thrilled, wide-eyed spectators watched John Glenn blast off.

DON'T hyphenate: The spectators, thrilled and wide eyed, watched John Glenn blast off.

Grammar Exercise

In the following paragraph, indicate where compound adjectives should be hyphenated.

1 During his flight, Glenn saw a swarm of free floating lights around his
2 capsule. He thought they were beautiful, but mission control knew they were
3 friction-generated. Engineers feared a heat shield failure. Upon reentry, these
4 fairy fire sparks could turn into an all encompassing inferno that would burn up
5 the capsule and John Glenn inside it. Mission control told him the news, though
6 there wasn't much he could do about it. John Glenn began his nail biting descent,
7 and the world nervously watched a piloting feat that was awe-inspiring.

Edit for grammar. Read through your essay and watch for compound adjectives. Make sure you have correctly hyphenated them.

Learning Language

For most single-syllable words, form the comparative by adding *-er*. For most adjectives with two or more syllables, form the superlative by adding *-est*. Use the comparative form when you compare two things. Use the superlative form when you compare three or more things.

Write sentences using these adjectives.

longest   smarter   cleverest   younger

Share your sentences with a partner. Explain why your use of the comparative or superlative form of the adjective is correct.

Response

When should I hyphenate compound adjectives?

For additional guidance with compound adjectives consider these points:

- Remind students to use as many hyphens as needed to connect a phrase (He gave her an oh-my-gosh-what-should-I-do-now look).
- Note that some compound adjectives have evolved into a single word, for example, *straightforward* or *firsthand*. Encourage students to consult the dictionary or their word processing program for guidance.
- If the first word is an adverb ending in *ly*, do not use a hyphen (a beautifully drawn portrait).

✱ For more about compound adjectives, see SE pages 652–653.

Grammar Exercise
Answers

line 1: free-floating
line 3: friction generated; heat-shield
line 4: fairy-fire; all-encompassing
line 6: nail-biting
line 7: awe inspiring

Edit for grammar. Tell students to check the form of each adjective in their essays.

TEKS 11.13D

Learning Language

Before students begin the activity, model several examples of sentences in which comparative and superlative adjectives are used correctly.

DIFFERENTIATE INSTRUCTION

Possible sentences:
This is the longest walk I have ever taken.
My dog is smarter than your dog.
Of all my friends, Sam has the cleverest ideas for projects.
My younger sister and I both enjoy swimming.

ELPS 3C

Differentiated Instruction: **English Language Learners**		**ELPS** 3C, 3D, 3G, 3J, 4A
ELP Level **Beginning**	**ELP Level** **Intermediate**	**ELP Level** **Advanced/Advanced High**
Have students repeat the adjectives with you. Point out and explain the affixes *-er* and *-est* to help students learn sound-letter relationships. Have them decode similar words.	Have students read the adjectives with you. Have partners write sentences together and explain the use of the comparative or superlative forms they used.	Have partners discuss their sentences, using complete sentences to explain their ideas and tell about the comparative or superlative forms they used.

TEKS 11.13D Edit drafts for grammar; **ELPS** 3C Speak using a variety of grammatical structures; **3D** Speak using grade-level content area vocabulary in context to internalize new English words and build academic language proficiency; **3G** Express ideas; **3J** Respond orally to information presented/concept and language attainment; **4A** Learn relationships between sounds and letters of the English language and decode words using a combination of skills

Sentence Structure

Remind students that readers often have different responses to literature, in part because writers purposely leave some ideas open to interpretation. Point out that one way authors add complexity, nuance, or ambiguity to their writing is through varied sentence structures. Remind students to address such techniques in their interpretations.

TEKS 11.15C(iv)

Explain that like anything else that is done repeatedly, sentence structure that never varies becomes boring. Tell students that a good time to introduce a variety of sentence types is during the editing stage of the writing process.

Have I used a variety of sentence types?

Have a volunteer read aloud the incorrect and then the correct example. Discuss with students how sentence variety improves the passage.

Exercise
Answers

Possible revision:
Because David wanted to become a writer, he made it a point to read books, poetry, and short stories. He also kept a journal in which he noted ideas for writing topics. Unfortunately, the only thing David didn't do was to actually write!

DIFFERENTIATE INSTRUCTION ↘

ELPS 5F

Check sentence structures. As needed, review the use of clauses and adjectival phrases.

TEKS 11.13D; **ELPS** 5F

 **TEKS** 11.13D, 11.15C(iv)

Sentence Structure

When you edit for *sentence structure*, you check that you have varied the length and type of your sentences enough to make your essay interesting and engaging. You also make sure that all of your sentences are complete, that is, that each one contains a subject and a predicate.

Have I used a variety of sentence types?

You have used a variety of sentence types if your sentences vary in length and structure and in the way they begin. The sample sentences below show a paragraph with no sentence variety and a paragraph revised to vary sentence structure.

Incorrect: Joseph Conrad became an orphan at the age of eleven. He lived in Russia, He served as a seaman on French and British ships. He served from 1874 to 1894. He was twenty when he began his career as a seaman. Later, he would become a famous writer. He used what he had experienced as a seaman. He used it in many novels and short stories.

Correct: Orphaned at the age of eleven, Joseph Conrad had few ties to his home in Russia. At the age of twenty, he decided to become a seaman and for the next twenty years served on French and British ships. Later, when he began writing, he used his experiences as a seaman as the basis for many of his novels and short stories.

Exercise

Revise the following paragraph to vary its sentence structure. Add extra words and information as needed to write complete sentences with more varied structures.

1   David wanted to become a writer. He read books. He also ready poetry and
2 short stories. He payed careful attention in class. He also kept a journal. He wrote
3 down many ideas for topics. They only thing he didn't do was actually write.

 Check sentence structures. Review your writing, looking for a variety of sentence structures. Look for places where you might begin with a clause or an adjectival phrase.

⭐ **TEKS** 11.13D

Mechanics: Punctuation

Are my revised sentences correctly punctuated?

When you edit for *mechanics*, you check for correct use of capitalization and punctuation. Changing the structure of sentences will affect how you punctuate these sentences. Often, you will need to use commas to punctuate the phrases or clauses you add. Check the sentences you revise to make sure they use correct punctuation.

Use commas after words, phrases, and clauses that come at the beginning of a sentence.

- **Introductory word**

    Incorrect: Yes that sounds like a great idea.
    Correct: Yes, that sounds like a great idea.

- **Introductory phrase**

    Incorrect: In the middle of the game Greg remembered something he had forgotten to do.
    Correct: In the middle of the game, Greg remembered something he had forgotten to do.

- **Introductory clause**

    Incorrect: When he realized his mistake Jorge apologized.
    Correct: When he realized his mistake, Jorge apologized.

Exercise

Rewrite each sentence by adding correct punctuation.

1. In the evening I like to spend time with friends
2. So what do you think?
3. While Sal put on his overcoat I looked for my purse.
4. During the lecture Marlene fell asleep.
5. As soon as we finished dinner we went out for a walk.

 Check your use of commas. Read your essay to be sure you have correctly used commas to punctuate your writing.

Response

Mechanics: Punctuation

Tell students that when they edit for punctuation, they should check their use of end punctuation, quotation marks, and commas.

Are my revised sentences correctly punctuated?

Draw attention to the use of the blue comma in each correct example. Point out that adding commas aids understanding by signaling readers to pause momentarily.

Exercise
Answers

1. In the evening, I like to spend time with friends.
2. So, what do you think?
3. While Sal put on his overcoat, I looked for my purse.
4. During the lecture, Marlene fell asleep.
5. As soon as we finished dinner, we went out for a walk.

Check your use of commas. Suggest that students read their essays aloud to help them notice where pauses should occur.

⭐ **TEKS** 11.13D

 TEKS **11.13D** Edit drafts for mechanics; **ELPS** **5C** Spell familiar English words; **5F** Write using a variety of grade-appropriate sentence lengths and patterns

Editing Checking for Conventions

Suggest that students skim the Proofreader's Guide (SE pages 634–779). Throughout the year, they can refer to the guidelines, rules, and examples whenever they need help to resolve questions about their own writing.

Check your editing. Remind students to check their spelling and sentence structure.

TEKS 11.13D; **ELPS** 5C, 5F

Editing Checklist

In addition to the checklist, advise students to learn spelling rules. These will help them whenever they write and will make proofreading easier and quicker. Point out, however, that there are many exceptions to the rules. The key is to

- become familiar with words so that they can recognize correct spellings,
- memorize exceptions to the rules,
- use the rules to guess correct spelling, and
- check the dictionary to see if their guesses are correct.

✱ For details about spelling rules, see SE pages 690–695.

Creating a Title

Have students use the three strategies and spend 5 to 10 minutes brainstorming possible titles.

 Conventions Connections

Grammar: Tense Shifts
- *Student Edition: Proofreader's Guide* pages 738, 742, 744–745
- *SkillsBook* pages 95, 177–178

Grammar: Punctuating Compound and Complex Sentences
- *Student Edition: Proofreader's Guide* pages 638–639, 648, 762, 766, 778–779
- *SkillsBook* pages 7, 13, 110, 140

 ⚡ *Write Source Online* **GrammarSnap**

Grammar: Punctuating Quotations
- *Student Edition: Proofreader's Guide* pages 646, 660
- *SkillsBook* page 31

 ⚡ *Write Source Online* **GrammarSnap**

TEKS **11.13D** Edit drafts for grammar, mechanics, and spelling; **ELPS** **5C** Spell familiar English words; **5F** Write using a variety of grade-appropriate sentence lengths, sentence patterns, and connecting words

---

  Editing Checking for Conventions

Check your editing. This checklist will help you to thoroughly edit your essay for conventions of grammar, sentence structure, mechanics (capitalization and punctuation) and spelling. On a piece of paper, write the numbers 1 to 9. If you can answer "yes," put a check mark after that number. If you can't, continue to edit for that convention.

Editing Checklist

Conventions

GRAMMAR
_____ **1.** Have I used the correct comparative and superlative forms?
_____ **2.** Have I used correct verb tenses throughout?

SENTENCE STRUCTURE
_____ **3.** Have I used varied sentence structures?
_____ **4.** Have I varied the way I begin my sentences?

MECHANICS (CAPITALIZATION AND PUNCTUATION)
_____ **5.** Do I use end punctuation after all of my sentences?
_____ **6.** Have I correctly hyphenated compound adjectives?
_____ **7.** Have I used quotation marks and correctly cited direct quotations?

SPELLING
_____ **8.** Have I spelled all words correctly?
_____ **9.** Have I double-checked the spelling of names and terms from the book?

Creating a Title

- Engage the reader: **A Lesson in History: A Lesson on Life**
- Draw on your thesis: **Faith and Hope: The Life of Frederick Douglass**
- Use words from the biography: **Glorious Resurrection: The Life of Frederick Douglass**

Publishing

Sharing Your Essay

After all the work of writing, revising, and editing your essay, you should share it with others. See the suggestions in the boxes below for a variety of ways to present your essay.

Make a final copy. Follow your teacher's instructions or use the guidelines below to format your paper. Prepare a final copy of your essay and proofread it for errors.

Focusing on Presentation

- Use blue or black ink and write neatly.
- Write your name in the upper left corner of page 1.
- Skip a line and center your title; skip another line and start your essay.
- Indent every paragraph and leave a one-inch margin on all four sides.
- Write your last name and the page number in the upper right-hand corner of every page.

Create a Multimedia Presentation
Convert your essay into a speech, scan in photos from the book or from the time period, and gather other visual aids to highlight your work.

Submit to a Newspaper
Check the submission guidelines for your local newspaper, write a cover letter introducing your response essay, and send it in.

Post Your Essay on a Bookseller's Site
Check out bookselling Web sites to determine how to submit your writing. Upload your essay to the site.

Response

Publishing **Sharing Your Essay**

Remind students to incorporate teacher and peer feedback in their final drafts. After students have read the ideas at the bottom of SE page 307, invite them to suggest additional options for sharing their interpretive response essays with appropriate audiences. ☑ **DIFFERENTIATE INSTRUCTION**

Make a final copy. Remind students of your guidelines for formatting a final draft.
⭐ **TEKS** 11.13E

Focusing on Presentation

If students decide to post their work as a review on a bookseller's Web site, tell them the following:

- They will need to follow the site's guidelines for submissions.
- They may need to condense their essay to meet length requirements.
- Although their full-length essay is an analysis, the shorter version will be a review. Students will need to avoid giving details (such as the ending of a novel) that readers should discover for themselves.
- Students must never allow their real name, e-mail address, or other personal details to appear with the review (most sites will allow them to post under a pseudonym).
- Some sites allow readers to add comments or indicate whether they found a review helpful. After posting, students should check back occasionally to see if they have received feedback.

Technology Connections

⭐ *Write Source Online* **Portfolio**

⭐ *Write Source Online* **Essay Evaluation**

Differentiated Instruction:
English Language Learners

⭐ **ELPS** 1E, 3J

Have students prepare a multimedia presentation. After each presentation, have them respond orally to the concepts presented.

ELP Level **Beginning**	ELP Level **Intermediate**	ELP Level **Advanced/Advanced High**
After each presentation, guide students to identify new language and concepts. Guide them to ask questions about new ideas.	After each presentation, have students complete sentence and question frames to discuss new concepts and ideas.	After each presentation, have students respond orally by asking questions about the concepts and ideas.

TEKS 11.13E Revise final draft in response to feedback from peers and teacher and publish written work for appropriate audiences; **ELPS** **1E** Internalize new basic and academic language by using and reusing in speaking and writing; **3J** Respond orally to information presented in a wide variety of media to build and reinforce concept and language attainment

Evaluating a Response to Literature

To support understanding of the following four sample essays—one sample essay for each possible score point—refer to the scoring guide on SE pages 36–37 and to key instruction from the Response to Literature unit.

Score Point 4: Highly effective

Work through this sample essay with students, pointing out the qualities that earn it an overall score point of 4. In addition to the callouts on the student pages use the following questions to facilitate analysis.

- What theme does the writer interpret? (*In Harpo Speaks!, Harpo tells how he found fun in little things.*)
- What details suggest that Harpo loved the life of a performer? (*He slept peacefully wherever they happened to be; he didn't mind not having amenities.*) **DIFFERENTIATE INSTRUCTION ↘**

Evaluating a Response to Literature

To learn how to evaluate a response to literature that interprets a theme in a work of nonfiction, you will use the holistic scoring guide on pages 36–37 and the essays that follow. These essays are examples of writing for each score on the scoring guide (1–4).

Notice that the first article received a score of 4. Read the description for a score of 4 on page 36. Then read the essay. Use the same steps to study the other examples. As you read, concentrate on the overall quality of the writing in each example.

Writing that fits a score of 4 is highly effective.

Playing with Nothing

Anyone who has ever seen a Marx Brothers movie must wonder what was going on beneath Harpo's mop of curly red hair and behind his wide, innocent eyes. In all of their movies, such as "Duck Soup" and "A Night at the Opera," Harpo often wears a mischievous smile, but he never speaks. In his autobiography, *Harpo Speaks!*, Harpo does speak, telling how he spent his life finding fun in little things.

Adolph "Harpo" Marx grew up poor in a Jewish neighborhood of New York City. His father was a bad tailor, so the family never had much money, but he was a wonderful cook who delighted his family at mealtimes. Harpo began his education at a local Catholic school, where one bully was in the habit of throwing him out the first floor window. One day in second grade, after getting thrown out the window yet another time, Harpo simply got up, walked away, and never returned to school again.

A veritable force of nature, Harpo's mother Minnie strong-armed her sons Adolph, Julius, Leonard, and Milton into a stage career. Performing in a vaudeville act called "The Four Nightingales," the boys often didn't have enough money for a room, but Harpo loved the lifestyle. "I can't remember ever having a poor night's sleep. . . . I've slept on pool tables, dressing-room tables, piano tops, bathhouse benches, in rag baskets and harp cases." Harpo relates how, during a card game on the road, each of the brothers got their famous stage names: Julius became Groucho because he carried his money in what was called a "grouch bag," Leonard became Chico because he chased "chicks," Adolph

Writer's voice is relaxed and confident.

Quotations and details support the writer's ideas.

Resources

Benchmark Papers

- The Source of Horror in "The Lottery" (strong) TE Appendix
- O Sweet Spontaneous (poor) TE Appendix

Transitions between and within paragraphs are smooth and logical. Writer shows strong command of conventions.

Maintains focus throughout essay.

Conclusion includes insightful ideas.

became Harpo because he'd taught himself to play the harp, and Milton's habit of sneaking up on people like a gumshoe made him Gummo. As their acts and their talents developed, the four boys took to ditching the script and breaking into ad-libbed comedy.

The words of one critic created the Harpo that the world knows and loves: "Adolph Marx performed beautiful pantomime which was ruined whenever he spoke." From then on, Harpo didn't say a word and kid with a second-grade education, a beat-up trench coat, a smashed top hat, a red wig, and no voice soon became an international sensation. He became fast friends with Alexander Woollcott, drama critic for *The New Yorker*, and thereby became part of the "Algonquin Round Table" with authors like Dorothy Parker and Robert Benchley. When asked how he fit in among so many intellectuals, Harpo simply said that he "listened."

Harpo Speaks! is the story of a playful man creating delight out of very little. When he was a child, he had only a single ice skate, and says he became the best single-skate skater in the world. He taught himself to play harp and became so good that trained harpists wanted to learn his techniques. He once took his trench coat and a bunch of butter knives to Soviet Russia and did a pantomime act that tore down barriers between east and west.

Toward the end of *Harpo Speaks!*, Harpo tells how a series of heart attacks forced him to slow down; he was ordered by his doctor to even stop playing the harp, because it was too strenuous. He complied for a time, but concludes his autobiography by explaining that he cannot live to simply wait quietly for death; life is for the living.

The stereotype that within every great clown exists a sad human cannot be applied to Harpo. Once dubbed "the most normal man in Hollywood," his autobiography reveals a person who loved nearly everything about his life, from his chaotic beginnings to the unfettered freedom that his professional successes afforded him. Harpo Marx truly spent his life making joy out of nothing.

Response

Review the essay. With a partner, discuss why this essay is considered a 4-point essay.

■ Why is the quotation from a critic in Paragraph 4 effective? (*Possible response: It answers a question readers might have had about why Harpo was a silent performer.*)

■ How might Harpo's act in Soviet Russia have torn down barriers? How does this detail support the writer's thesis? (*Possible response: He made people laugh, and in doing so, created a positive connection between Soviet and American people. The event supports the idea that Harpo found fun in little things, such as butter knives.*)

Review the essay. Use the holistic scoring guide on SE pages 36–37 to frame the discussion for why the essay received a score of 4.

Score Point 3: Generally Effective

Work through this sample essay with students, pointing out the qualities that earn it an overall score point of 3. In addition to the callouts on the student pages use the following questions to facilitate analysis.

- What details suggest that Grimes's encounter with the Chicken was unusual? (*Possible responses: The Chicken appeared in a big-city setting; it wasn't bothered by other animals.*)
- How does the writer's question-and-answer format in Paragraph 4 help to create a unique voice? (*It develops a rhythm and adds humor.*)
- What errors in conventions are present in the essay? Do they distract from the writer's main points? (*Possible responses: The use of* wondered *rather than* wandered *in Paragraph 1, inconsistent verb tenses in Paragraph 3; Most students will find that the errors are relatively minor and do not distract from the writer's main points.*) **DIFFERENTIATE INSTRUCTION** ⌄

310

Writing that fits a score of 3 is generally effective.

A Chicken in the City

People love animals, there's no question about that. We love having them as a part of our lives and our families. Almost everyone enjoys watching animals on a farm or in a zoo. *My Fine Feathered Friend* by William Grimes tells about the unusual creature—a chicken—that wondered into his yard and life.

It was an odd enough thing to have a chicken show up out of nowhere in Grimes's yard. It was even odder is that it happened in New York City, in the Queens neighborhood where Grimes lives. Although *My Fine Feathered Friend*, from 2002, is a short book, it brings up a number of themes and ideas that are common to all people—and to many animals, too!

The chicken shows up one day out of the blue in the middle of winter. Needless to say, Grimes was pretty surprised to see this healthy-looking black bird scratching around in his yard. Grimes was fascinated because, believe it or not, the chicken just hangs around and doesn't take off. The neighborhood cats don't scare it away. If anything, they seemed to be a little afraid of the chicken! The chicken seems perfectly content to stick around even on snowy days, pecking, scratching, and eating dry cat food from the bowls on Grimes's patio. As you might imagine, Grimes really doesn't know what to think about this chicken.

This is quite a really enjoyable book, partly because Grimes is a great writer, he's both funny and curious. In the book, he tells about all the questions that the chicken's appearance brings up for him and his wife. Is it a rooster or a chicken? (It's a chicken.) What does a chicken eat? (It turns out that chickens can eat almost anything, including rocks. Which they need to help them digest food.) Where could it have come from? (He never finds out.) What type of chicken is it? (He figures out through research it's a Black Australorp.) What should they name it? (They finally decide to just call it the Chicken.)

Callouts:

Writer introduces the book and his or her ideas clearly.

Some convention errors are present; verb tense is not consistent.

Writer's voice expresses individuality.

Sentences in each paragraph support each topic sentence.

Writing maintains focus; conclusion adds depth.

The Chicken kind of takes over Grimes's life but Grimes doesn't seem to mind that. He tells about all the research he did to find out more about the Chicken. He tells how him and his wife, once they find out that the Chicken is laying eggs, cook them and compare them to two different kind of store-bought eggs. (The Chicken's eggs win.) Later on, when he's worried about whether he needs to give the Chicken better food, he calls his mother in Texas for advice and she gets chicken food from a local feed store and sends it to him in shipments.

Grimes writes in a humorous way about his life with the Chicken. For example, when early on he's wondering if it's OK for the Chicken to eat the cat food, he says, "It might be like giving a child a steady diet of Slim Jims." He tells about how one time he thinks the Chicken is having some kind of attack, and all of the cats are watching it roll around, "their faces a study in wonderment and concern." It turns out that the Chicken was just enjoying a dustbath, which apparantly chickens like to do. It's not really a surprise when the reader finds out that Grimes is a writer for a living and is a restaurant critic for the New York Times. In fact, this just makes the book more interesting!

I won't tell what happens to the Chicken, because I think everyone should read it and I don't want to spoil it for anyone. But I will say this: The book leaves you thinking about questions and ideas such as, How much are animals like us? Or we, like them? How are animals and people different? Why do we like to take care of creatures? People care about animals, but do the animals care about people? These are all questions that lots of people wonder about, and *My Fine Feathered Friend* makes you think about them.

Response

- What does Grimes's interest in and concern for the Chicken reveal about him? (*Possible responses: He is kind and has an unusual outlook on life; he is curious.*)
- Do you agree that the conclusion adds depth to the essay? Why or why not? (*Some students may say that questions in the concluding paragraph provide explicit examples of giving readers something to think about; others may point out that the conclusion is somewhat vague.*)

Differentiated Instruction: English Language Learners

⭐ **ELPS** 5D

ELP Level **Beginning**	ELP Level **Intermediate**	ELP Level **Advanced/Advanced High**
Use visuals, simplified language, and gestures to help make the sample comprehensible. Guide students to identify examples of inconsistent verb tenses.	Use visuals, simplified language, and gestures. Work together to identify examples of inconsistent verb tenses and to rewrite sentences.	Explain unfamiliar cultural references and idioms. Have students rewrite sentences to correct inconsistent verb tenses and share their revisions.

ELPS 5D Edit writing for standard grammar and usage/verb tenses

Score Point 2: Somewhat Effective

Work through this sample essay with students, pointing out the qualities that earn it an overall score point of 2. In addition to the callouts on the student pages use the following questions to facilitate analysis.

- What details does the writer provide to support the idea that Kahlo put the tragedies of her life into her art? (*Possible responses: The writer provides few examples. She describes Kahlo's injuries and her difficult marriage, but doesn't provide specific examples of paintings that relate to these events.*)

- How might the writer have provided more detail in Paragraph 3? (*Possible response: The writer might have discussed one or two specific self-portraits as examples of "a bad dream or a nightmare" or of "painfull things" that "are not pretty to look at."*)

- What errors in conventions are present in the essay? (*Possible responses: The book title is not italicized, the use of 3rd, 4, and 6 rather than spelling out the words, misspellings such as unfaithfull and painfull, and other errors in grammar, usage, and mechanics.*)

- What details could have been added to make the ending of the essay less abrupt? (*Possible responses: The writer could have described "The Frame" and explained what made the artwork so compelling. The writer might also have explained what the Louvre is, and why it was an accomplishment for Kahlo's work to appear there.*) **DIFFERENTIATE INSTRUCTION ↘**

312

Writing that fits a score of 2 is somewhat effective.

Callouts:

Introduction is somewhat brief but states focus clearly.

Ideas are introduced but writing is not well-organized; errors in convention are present throughout essay.

An important idea in last sentence is stated but not developed.

Essay seems to end abruptly.

The Life and Art of Frida Kahlo

The Mexican artist Frida Kahlo lived from 1907–1954. Her life was full of tragedies and she put those tragedies in her artwork. The book Frida Kahlo: A Modern Master, by Terri Hardin describes what her life was like and what her art was like. She had a really unbelievable life even though she only lived for 47 years.

Kahlo was born into a wealthy family in Mexico, she was the 3rd of 4 children, all girls. First, when she was 6 she got polio and it effected her right leg. Next, when she was a teenager, she got in the middle of a horrible accident between a trolley and a bus, she was "pierced through" by the bus's guardrail. She also fractured her right leg and collerbone. Her right foot was also injured. She spent a long time in the hospital, and she had pain from the accident for the rest of her life. She began painting while she was in the hospital. Kahlo also met a famous painter when she was young named Diego Rivera. He was a well known painter, a large man, and very attractive to woman even though he was not very attractive to himself. He was much older than she but they fell in love, and they later got married. Rivera was unfaithfull many times to her and she was deeply hurt by this. She showed this theme in her own paintings.

Many of her paintings are self portraits, she did over 200 of them. Some of her paintings tell stories about painfull times in her life. Others of them look like she is having a bad dream or a nightmare. But they also seem very truthful in many ways and sometimes painfull things are not pretty to look at.

Hardin says that Kahlo's paintings helped her get through the many difficult times in her life. She tells that her painting called "The Frame" which she painted in 1938, "was the first painting by a Mexican artist to be purchased by the Louvre."

Writing that fits a score of 1 is ineffective.

1

Ideas in introduction are not focused.

Example from text supports idea, but idea is repeated over and over.

Writing strays from topic; ideas are unoriginal.

Overall lack of effort is compounded by numerous errors in conventions.

Angela's Ashes by Frank McCourt

The book Angela Ashes is the story of Fran McCourt's life. He had a very poor upbringeing in Ireland and then moved to the United States in the hopes that he would improve his live. He became a school teacher in New York City for manny years. This book was an instant over night best-seller and it won him awards such as the Pulizer Prize in 97. It made him a very sucessful writer.

The McCourt family was very poor in Ireland. They never had enough to eat and they had to move all the time. Some people called the author's father "useless," but he told his children lots of stories about the history of famous people in Ireland. In Angela's Ashes, Frank McCourt tells many funny stories about his family life that are very funny even though they are sad, too. One example of this theme is when he tells a story about the time his family moves again and his father tries to hang up one picture on the wall. It is their only picture, of a pope. He doesn't even have a hammer so he bangs the nail with a glass jar and it breaks and he cuts himself and he gets blood on the picture and the mother is all upset about this. It is very funny but also sad and amazing.

When u read Angela's Ashes u r amaze that he survived all the brokenness and hard life that he had, which is another theme in the book. Lots of them over the years have been moving from Ireland to the United States in the hopes that they would improve thier lives and most of them have. Many people here have relatives orginally from Ireland so you can see that lots of people can survive poverty and live through very very hard times.

The mane reason Frank Mccourt wanted to come to live in the Untied States was because he had such a hard life in Ireland and felt he could find a better life in the the United States. You can see, from the sucess he had with his book, Angelas Ashes that he was able to over come a very poor start in life, and could wind up being a world famous arthur. It is a very funny boook but it it is very very inspiring to. The End.

Response

Score Point 1: Ineffective

Work through this sample essay with students, pointing out the qualities that earn it an overall score point of 1. In addition to the callouts on the student pages use the following questions to facilitate analysis.

- How might a quotation from *Angela's Ashes* have improved Paragraph 2? (*Possible responses: A quotation might have better illustrated the family's poverty or have shown why the incident involving the picture of a pope was "very funny but also sad and amazing."*)

- Why is Paragraph 3 considered off-topic? (*The writer discusses Irish immigration in general, rather than the reasons for the McCourt family's immigration.*)

- What questions might the writer have addressed to anticipate information readers would wonder about? (*Possible responses: Why was the book titled* Angela's Ashes? *Who was Angela? Who were the other members of the McCourt family?*)

Differentiated Instruction: English Language Learners

⭐ ELPS 3B, 3D

Before reading, explain to students that these two essays indicate a lack of mastery of the five traits, which may make the writing difficult to understand.

ELP Level **Beginning**	ELP Level **Intermediate**	ELP Level **Advanced/Advanced High**
Discuss the essays by focusing on development of ideas. Create a chart to help students see repeated and undeveloped ideas.	Provide sentence stems that include high-frequency words to help students identify and describe weaknesses in the sample essays.	Have students use academic language to discuss the lack of mastery of the traits that lead to weaknesses in the sample essays.

 ELPS 3B Expand vocabulary/learning and using high-frequency words for identifying and describing; **3D** Speak using grade-level content-area vocabulary in context/new English words, academic language

Evaluating and Reflecting on Your Writing

Have students complete their reflections before you return their marked essays to them. Then ask them to compare what they wrote with the comments you made about their essays. Do their thoughts correspond to your assessments as an informed outside reader? **DIFFERENTIATE INSTRUCTION ↘**
DIFFERENTIATE INSTRUCTION ↘

Invite students to schedule a conference with you if they find discrepancies between their impressions and yours.

Hold a group discussion in which students share what they learned about anticipating and responding to readers' questions (item 4) and about analyzing the author's use of rhetorical and stylistic devices (item 5). Encourage a free exchange of ideas, insights, and advice. End the discussion by allowing students five minutes of freewriting time to add further thoughts to their reflections, based on the exchange of ideas.

★ **TEKS** 11.15C (iii), 11.15C(v)

★ **TEKS** 11.15C(iii), 11.15C(v)

Evaluating and Reflecting on Your Writing

Reflect on your finished essay by completing each starter sentence below. These comments will help you monitor your progress as a writer.

My Theme Interpretation Essay

1. The strongest part of my interpretation is . . .

2. The part that most needs change is . . .

3. The main thing I learned about writing an interpretation of a theme is . . .

4. In my next response to literature, I can better anticipate and respond to questions by . . .

5. Here is one question I still have about analyzing an author's use of stylistic and rhetorical devices:

6. Right now I would describe my writing ability as (excellent, good, fair, poor) because . . .

Differentiated Instruction: Struggling Learners

As students reflect on how to improve their essays, help them focus on some positive feedback to balance out the self-critique. Suggest that they identify a favorite sentence they wrote. Then ask students to trade papers with partners. Students should also find favorite sentences or ideas in each other's essays.

Differentiated Instruction: Advanced Learners

If possible, have students form a poetry exchange for the duration of the poetry unit. Choose a favorite poem and ask students to bring their own favorite, short poems. First share your poem and tell why you like it. Then have students read their poems aloud. Invite them to share what makes their poems meaningful.

Response to Literature
Interpreting a Poem

Robert Frost once said, "Like a piece of ice on a hot stove, the poem must ride on its own melting." When you interpret a poem, you "melt" it, looking at the parts that make up the whole. By close examination of the elements that make up the poem—theme, structure, and language—you can find more meaning in the poem and develop a deeper appreciation of the author's craft.

In this chapter, you will learn how to interpret a poem: how to break it down into its various elements and see how they fit together. You will read a sample poem and see how a student writer organizes his interpretation. Then you will read a second poem and write your own interpretation of the poem's content and message.

Writing Guidelines

Subject: **Poem**
Purpose: **To explore meaning**
Form: **Interpretation**
Audience: **Instructor**

"Genuine poetry can communicate before
it is understood."

—T. S. Eliot

Interpreting a Poem

Objectives

- apply what has been learned about interpreting literature to responding to poetry
- demonstrate an understanding of the form and content of an essay in response to a poem
- plan, draft, revise, edit, and publish an interpretation of a poem

To begin thinking about interpreting poetry, focus on what others have said about reading poems.

- Discuss the quotations by Frost and Eliot that are on the page.
- Ask students to find quotations about poetry to share with the class. (The topic is well covered in references such as *Bartlett's Familiar Quotations*.)
- Have students explain why they chose their quotations—do they represent the way they read and understand poetry?
- Have students recall and express opinions, ideas, and feelings about poems that they particularly enjoyed or that made connections to their own lives. ✓ **DIFFERENTIATE INSTRUCTION**

✪ **ELPS** 3G

ELPS **1B** Monitor written language production and employ self-corrective techniques or other resources; **1C** Use strategic learning strategies to acquire basic and grade-level vocabulary; **3E** Share information in cooperative learning interactions; **3G** Express opinions, ideas, and feelings

Sample Poem

Before discussing the poem, emphasize that it is important to read a poem several times to fully appreciate and understand it.

- Invite students to read the poem quietly.
- Then ask two or three volunteers to read it aloud.
- Suggest that as students listen to the different voices reading the poem, different ideas about its meaning may come to them.
- Suggest that students read with a partner whenever they analyze poems.

DIFFERENTIATE INSTRUCTION ↘   DIFFERENTIATE INSTRUCTION ↘

Sample Poem

Read the poem below and think about its content, theme, organization, and use of poetic techniques. Then read student writer Stefano Giangregorio's interpretation on the next two pages. The margin comments point out important elements of that interpretation.

I AM THE PEOPLE, THE MOB
By Carl Sandburg

I AM the people—the mob—the crowd—the mass.
Do you know that all the great work of the world is
   done through me?
I am the workingman, the inventor, the maker of the
   world's food and clothes.
I am the audience that witnesses history. The Napoleons
   come from me and the Lincolns. They die. And
   then I send forth more Napoleons and Lincolns.
I am the seed ground. I am a prairie that will stand
   for much plowing. Terrible storms pass over me.
   I forget. The best of me is sucked out and wasted.
   I forget. Everything but Death comes to me and
   makes me work and give up what I have. And I
   forget.
Sometimes I growl, shake myself and spatter a few red
   drops for history to remember. Then—I forget.
When I, the People, learn to remember, when I, the
   People, use the lessons of yesterday and no longer
   forget who robbed me last year, who played me for
   a fool—then there will be no speaker in all the world
   say the name: "The People," with any fleck of a
   sneer in his voice or any far-off smile of derision.
The mob—the crowd—the mass—will arrive then.

Response Essay

As you read the essay on this page and the next, consider how Stefano's ideas compare with your own ideas about "I Am the People, the Mob."

Beginning
The thesis (underlined) states the writer's main idea.

Middle
The middle supports the thesis statement with specific examples.

Verse quotations of more than one line include slashes to show line breaks.

The writer shows how stylistic and rhetorical devices help make this poem a powerful statement.

Identifying with the Masses

Carl Sandburg was a poet "of the people," and his working-class background and socialist leanings are reflected in his writing. Sandburg believed that the common people had great potential, but that too often that potential was wasted. He admired the people's strength and endurance but grieved over their suffering and complacency. <u>The poem "I Am the People, the Mob" illustrates Sandburg's mixed and nuanced feelings toward the masses.</u>

The poem opens with positive thoughts about the people, then transitions to negative images, and finally returns to a hopeful conclusion. Sandburg begins with the affirming question, "Do you know that all the great work of the world is / done through me?" (2–3) and supports this idea with specific examples in the next two lines. He then describes the mob's more passive role as the "audience that witnesses history" (6). Still, he says, it is from this passive soil that heroes (Lincolns) and villains (Napoleons) come forth. This soil is repeatedly plowed, bears many storms, and has its best "sucked out and wasted" but again and again forgets the abuse (10–14). Occasionally, like a beast, the mob is briefly roused to anger, to "spatter a few red / drops for history to remember" but then sinks into forgetfulness again (15-16). Sandburg uses the image of the people rising up, however briefly, to transition to the hope that the people may someday "learn to remember" (17). He says, "The mob —the crowd—the mass—will arrive then," at last attaining its destiny (23).

In addition to imagery, Sandburg uses other stylistic and rhetorical devices to make this a powerful poem. Throughout the poem, he uses personification to make the abstract concept of "the people" more immediate and concrete (the narrator says, "I AM the people"). Sandburg uses repetition and parallelism, repeating the opening words, "I am," five times in all. He also repeats "I forget" four times, further emphasizing this sad theme. However, even as he repeats "I forget," Sandburg plants the word

Response

Response Essay

Discuss the essay with the class, commenting on various points as follows:
- Note that the citations in the essay refer to lines of the poem.
- The writer uses the first middle paragraph to summarize the entire poem. Point out that this can be a useful way for students to structure their analyses (although, as always, they should use the organization that best supports their thesis).
- In the closing paragraph, the writer uses repetition for emphasis: *Clearly, Sandburg believes* and *Clearly, he wishes for.* There are two reasons the writer might have used this technique: (1) repetition for emphasis, and (2) the writer is saying, "This is what the *poet* thinks, and it is important."

Differentiated Instruction: English Language Learners

⭐ **ELPS** 2I, 4F

ELP Level **Beginning**	ELP Level **Intermediate**	ELP Level **Advanced/Advanced High**
Before reading the poem aloud, use visuals to preteach words such as *witnesses* and *prairie*. Read the poem aloud. Use simplified language to discuss its ideas.	Before reading the poem aloud, use gestures to preteach words such as *sneer* and *derision*. Have students define words such as *growl* and *spatter*.	Read the poem aloud. Have partners identify and discuss its ideas, and share ideas about new vocabulary and meanings.

ELPS 2I Demonstrate listening comprehension/collaborating with peers; **4F** Use visual and contextual support and support from peers and teachers to develop vocabulary

Respond to the reading.

Possible Answers

Focus and Coherence 1. The closing is effective in returning to the thesis presented in the introduction, and in giving readers something to consider.

Organization 2. The writer uses the poem's organization as a framework for addressing the techniques of imagery, repetition, and parallelism. He also explains the significance of Sandburg's use of free verse.

Development of Ideas 3. The writer included relevant quotations from the poem and an analysis of rhetorical and stylistic devices.

Voice 3. He sounds authentic and knowledgeable, as indicated by

- the generous number of supporting details;
- the use of confident declarative sentences, such as *The poem . . . illustrates Sandburg's mixed feelings . . . ;*
- approving references to the poem, such as *powerful poem, message of hope and challenge, inspire the people to greatness.*

★ **TEKS** 11.15C(iii)

Prewriting Selecting a Topic

Encourage students to choose their own poems. This will allow them to focus on works that have personal meaning—and during their search, they may be exposed to a range of poems.

Select a poem. Provide poetry anthologies and other sources to aid students in identifying a poem. **DIFFERENTIATE INSTRUCTION ↘**

DIFFERENTIATE INSTRUCTION ↘

"remember" (16) and expands it to "learn to remember" one line later (17), ending the poem with his hope for the future. That this message of hope and challenge is intended for the common people themselves is shown in Sandburg's choice of form—free verse rather than a formal structure—and by his use of commonplace language.

Ending
The ending restates the thesis and leaves the reader with something to think about.

Clearly, Sandburg believes that the people have a tremendous potential, but that they fall short due to forgetfulness and lack of motivation. Clearly, he wishes for a better future in which the people take responsibility for their own welfare instead of blindly following heroes and villains. By identifying with the masses and speaking frankly to them in this poem, Sandburg hopes to inspire the people to the greatness they are capable of achieving.

Respond to the reading. On your own paper, reflect on the focus, organization, ideas, and voice of Stefano's interpretation of Carl Sandburg's poem.

Focus and Coherence (1) Evaluate the effectiveness of Stefano's concluding paragraph.

Organization (2) How has Stefano organized his essay?

Development of Ideas (3) What specific and relevant support does Stefano offer in his middle paragraphs to support his thesis?

Voice (4) Does Stefano's writing sound authentic? Explain with examples.

Prewriting Selecting a Topic

If your instructor does not assign a poem for you to interpret, you need to find one yourself or interpret the brief poem provided here.

Select a poem. Search your library and your literature book, looking for poems that interest you. Select one to interpret—or interpret the poem on this page.

Fire and Ice
By Robert Frost

Some say the world will end in fire,
Some say in ice.
From what I've tasted of desire
I hold with those who favor fire.
But if it had to perish twice,
I think I know enough of hate
To say that for destruction ice
Is also great
And would suffice.

Differentiated Instruction: Struggling Learners

Students may find a poem that inspires them by visiting the Web site of The Favorite Poem Project, founded by former Poet Laureate Robert Pinsky, at www.bu.edu/favoritepoem/ The site includes favorite poems chosen by everyday people and videos of the volunteers reading their poems.

Considering the Elements

The various elements of a poem can give you a clue to its purpose and meaning. Ask yourself the following questions and note the answers.

- Does the poem have a specific shape? What meaning does this organization suggest?
- What images does the poem contain?
- Is the meaning of any image left deliberately ambiguous so as to suggest several interpretations? How does this make the meaning of the poem more nuanced?
- What poetic techniques (pages **368–369**) does the poet use? How do they affect the reader?
- Who is the probable audience for this poem? Why?
- What is the writer's purpose for writing this poem?

 Consider the elements. Use the questions above to think deeply about your poem. Write down your answers for reference as you write your essay.

Writing Your Thesis Statement

Once you have thought deeply about the elements and purpose of the poem, it's time to write a thesis statement. An effective thesis statement names the poem and indicates a strong feeling about it. Here is the pattern Stefano used to write his thesis statement.

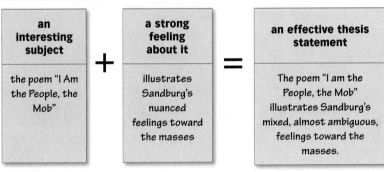

an interesting subject		a strong feeling about it		an effective thesis statement
the poem "I Am the People, the Mob"	**+**	illustrates Sandburg's nuanced feelings toward the masses	**=**	The poem "I am the People, the Mob" illustrates Sandburg's mixed, almost ambiguous, feelings toward the masses.

Response

 Develop a thesis statement. Follow the example above as you create a thesis statement for your interpretive essay. Try two or three versions until you feel satisfied.

Considering the Elements

Remind students that reading aloud the poem can help them think about it. Emphasize the importance of listening to the poem and suggest that students approach this in a variety of ways. For example:

- Read the poem at different volumes and with different expressions—loud and soft, dramatic and reserved.
- Exaggerate the punctuation and line breaks as they read.
- Ask friends and family members to read the poem to them.
- Seek out audio recordings, if possible. Check the audio section of the library or search online collections such as www.loc.gov/poetry/180.

Consider the elements. Point out that students' ability to answer questions about rhetorical or stylistic devices or about ambiguities, nuances, and complexities in the text is a good indication of a poem's impact on them. Point out that these elements may also help them identify quotations to analyze.

TEKS 11.15C(ii), 11.15C(iii), 11.15C(iv)

Writing Your Thesis Statement

Review and discuss the elements of an effective thesis statement. Remind students that a strong thesis statement will guide and inform their writing.

Develop a thesis statement. Point out that it is not necessary to use the same order of information as in the sample (first the subject, then the feeling). This could, for example, be reversed: *Sandburg confronts his mixed feelings about the masses in his poem "I Am the People, the Mob."*

TEKS 11.15C(i)

TEKS **11.15C(i)** Write an interpretation of an expository or a literary text that advances a clear thesis statement; **11.15C(ii)** Write an interpretation of an expository or a literary text that addresses the writing skills for an analytical essay, including references to quotations from the text; **11.15C(iii)** Write an interpretation of an expository or a literary text that analyzes the aesthetic effects of an author's use of stylistic or rhetorical devices; **11.15C(iv)** Write an interpretation of an expository or a literary text that identifies and analyzes the ambiguities, nuances, and complexities within the text; **ELPS** **2E** Use contextual and linguistic support to confirm understanding of spoken language; **2F** Listen to and derive meaning from a variety of media/concept and language attainment; **4F** Use support from peers and teachers to develop vocabulary, grasp of language structures, and background knowledge

Drafting Getting Your Ideas Down

Point out that with prewriting notes in mind, students can begin drafting to get ideas on paper and fine-tune their ideas later in the process.

DIFFERENTIATE INSTRUCTION ↘ **DIFFERENTIATE INSTRUCTION** ↘

Beginning

Suggest that students underline their thesis statement as a way to focus their writing.

Middle

Remind students to support their thesis with appropriate quotations from the poem. Then draw students' attention to the tip for the Middle part. Note that it is always a good idea, when they analyze a poem, to

- do some basic research about the poet,
- determine whether the poem is associated with a particular literary style of the time, and
- consider whether historical and political context might be relevant to its meaning.

This background information may or may not support their thesis—but if students don't do the research, they may miss out on important aspects of the poem's meaning.

Ending

Remind students that their interpretation must include their own unique perspective on the effects of the author's use of rhetorical and stylistic devices in the poem, and that the ending of the essay is a good place to highlight that perspective.

✳ For more information about the basic parts of an essay, see SE page 618.

Develop your first draft. Suggest that students reread their poem before they begin drafting so that it is fresh in their minds.

⭐ **TEKS** 11.15C(i), 11.15C(ii), 11.15C(iii)

320

⭐ **TEKS** 11.15C(i), 11.15C(ii), 11.15C(iii)

Drafting Getting Your Ideas Down

Your first draft is your chance to get all your ideas on paper. Start by reading through your prewriting and getting your main ideas firmly in your mind. Then start writing. Don't be concerned with spelling or mechanics yet. (You can fix problems when you revise.) If new ideas come to you as you write, go ahead and add them. Below is a brief guide to writing your first draft.

Beginning

- Write your introductory paragraph.
- Include your thesis statement.

Tip

Include the name of the poem and the author's name in your opening paragraph.

> **Beginning**
> Middle
> Ending

Middle

- Use a separate paragraph for each of your main points.
- Support the topic sentence of each paragraph with details from the poem.
- Include quoted words and phrases and specific examples from the poem to support your ideas.

Tip

If the information helps support your thesis, include anything you might know about the author, his or her other works, or the time period in which the poem was written.

> Beginning
> **Middle**
> Ending

Ending

- Restate your thesis statement and sum up your main points.
- Leave your reader with something to think about.

Tip

Because your reader comes to your ending with a deeper understanding of your topic, you can end with a more thoughtful point about the topic.

> Beginning
> Middle
> **Ending**

Draft

Develop your first draft. Use your prewriting and the guidelines above as you create the first draft of your interpretive essay.

Differentiated Instruction: Struggling Learners

Students may have limited experience relating to poetry. To help them feel comfortable with interpreting their poems, and to provide them with another tool for finding their meaning, remind students that poetry is often as much an emotional experience as it is an intellectual one.

Then ask students to freewrite in their personal journals about how their poem makes them feel, which lines move them the most, and why. When they finish, ask students to review what they wrote to see if their response gives them insights into the poetry.

⭐ **TEKS** **11.15C(i)** Write an interpretation of an expository or a literary text that advances a clear thesis statement; **11.15C(ii)** Write an interpretation of an expository or a literary text that addresses the writing skills for an analytical essay, including references to quotations from the text; **11.15C(iii)** Write an interpretation of an expository or a literary text that analyzes the aesthetic effects of an author's use of stylistic or rhetorical devices;

Revising Improving Your Writing

After you have written a first draft, take some time away from your essay to get some perspective. Use the guidelines below to help you revise.

Revise your interpretation. Use the checklist below to guide your revision. Number a paper from 1 to 11, and when you can answer any of the following questions "yes," check off the number. Keep revising until you can check off all the numbers.

Revising Checklist

Focus and Coherence

_____ **1.** Do I have a thesis that clearly states my interpretation of the poem?

_____ **2.** Are all of my ideas connected to each other and to the main idea?

_____ **3.** Have I included a strong introduction and a meaningful conclusion?

_____ **4.** Does my interpretive essay have an overall sense of completeness?

Organization

_____ **5.** Does my interpretive essay have a smooth and logical flow?

_____ **6.** Have I used transitional words and phrases to connect ideas?

Development of Ideas

_____ **7.** Have I offered enough support and specific details from the poem to allow readers to appreciate my major points?

_____ **8.** Have I approached my topic from a unique perspective?

Voice

_____ **9.** Have I engaged my reader throughout my interpretive essay?

_____ **10.** Is my voice confident and convincing?

_____ **11.** Is my writing authentic and original?

Response

Tell students that taking time away from a piece of writing before revising gives them a "fresh set of eyes," almost as if they are seeing the writing for the first time.

Revise your interpretation. Remind students to answer the checklist questions honestly and sincerely so that they can do a good job of revising for clarity and to achieve rhetorical purposes.

TEKS 11.13C

Revising Checklist

Focus attention on the idea of "unique perspective," mentioned in item 8 on the checklist. Tell students that an interpretation of a poem can be intensely personal, and that their writing should reflect that. Emphasize that there are no right or wrong interpretations, as long as they can support their views with examples.

TEKS 11.13C Revise drafts to clarify meaning and achieve specific rhetorical purposes; **ELPS 5B** Write using newly acquired basic vocabulary and content-based grade-level vocabulary; **5G** Describe with increasing specificity and detail

Editing Checking for Conventions

Suggest that when editing and proofreading, students should double-check *everything* they're not completely certain about. They should

- read slowly and carefully to avoid glossing over errors,
- investigate anything that they wrote in haste, and
- familiarize themselves with the Proofreader's Guide on SE pages 634–779.

Edit for conventions. Remind students to use the checklist questions as a guide when they edit for grammar, mechanics, and spelling.

DIFFERENTIATE INSTRUCTION ↘
 TEKS 11.13D

Publishing Sharing Your Interpretation

Consider having interested students form poetry reading groups. Meeting regularly to talk about poetry will allow students to

- hear poems read aloud,
- respond to poetry,
- keep up with new works by present-day poets,
- become familiar with classic poems from the past, and share their own poems.

Publish your interpretation. Some students may be interested in compiling the classmates' interpretations into a book for future reference.

TEKS 11.13E

⭐ Conventions Connections

Grammar: Subject-Verb Agreement
- *Student Edition: Proofreader's Guide*
  pages 756, 758, 770

☀ *Write Source Online* **GrammarSnap**

Mechanics: Quotation Marks
- *Student Edition: Proofreader's Guide*
  page 660

Mechanics: Punctuation
- *Student Edition: Proofreader's Guide*
  pages 635–647

Editing Checking for Conventions

After you have made major improvements to your work by revising, you need to edit your work to make sure the grammar, sentence structure, mechanics (capitalization and punctuation), and spelling are correct.

 Edit for conventions. Use the following conventions checklist to guide your editing. Write the numbers 1 to 5 on a piece of paper. When you can answer a given question "yes," place a check mark beside the number. Keep editing until you can answer all the questions "yes."

Editing Checklist

Conventions

_____ **1.** Have I varied my sentence structure?

_____ **2.** Have I used correct punctuation throughout?

_____ **3.** Have I placed quotation marks around exact words I quoted from the poem?

_____ **4.** Have I included line numbers in parentheses for these quotations?

_____ **5.** Have I spelled everything correctly and checked any words that I'm not sure of?

Publishing Sharing Your Interpretation

An interpretive essay of this kind is a great way to get other people interested in a poem you have enjoyed or in a poet you admire. So, let your written interpretation have a life beyond the classroom. This sort of writing is perfect for a Web log or Internet message board entry. If you don't have a blog or Web space of your own, you may find sites devoted to the poet, maintained by fans or literary societies. You can also share print copies of your own essay with friends and family members. You may be surprised at the conversation it spawns.

 Publish your interpretation. Choose a way to share your work—with family and friends, with your school or community, or with the world—and publish your interpretive essay.

323

Response to Literature
Interpreting a Short Story

One of the masters of the short story, Flannery O'Connor, once said, "I find that most people know what a story is until they sit down to write one." Great short story writers make their craft look effortless, but writing a good short story is anything but easy. When you interpret a short story, you explain why and how the story works. You carefully examine its elements—character, setting, plot, point of view, images, themes, and style—in order to find more meaning in the story and to develop a deeper appreciation of the author's craft.

In this chapter, you will learn how to interpret a short story by breaking it into its various elements and explaining how these elements fit together. You will first study a student writer's interpretation of a short story, and then you will write your own interpretation of a short story.

Writing Guidelines

Subject: **Short Story**
Purpose: **To explore meaning**
Form: **Interpretation**
Audience: **Instructor**

"Don't tell me the moon is shining; show me a glint of light on broken glass."
—Anton Chekhov

Interpreting a Short Story

Review the elements of a short story that are noted in the introduction. Invite students to define, discuss, and give examples of the following elements from familiar short stories:

- Characters
- Setting
- Plot
- Point of view
- Theme

Differentiated Instruction:
English Language Learners   **ELPS** 5F

Turn to the Appendix of the Teacher's Edition for information on language transfer issues with grammar, usage, and mechanics.

ELP Level **Beginning**	ELP Level **Intermediate**	ELP Level **Advanced/Advanced High**
Work with students to assess their work for any major issues. Model how to revise the writing to add variety to the sentence patterns.	Have students work with an English-proficient peer to assess their work. Tell partners to look for ways to add variety to the sentence patterns.	Have students work with a partner to assess their work for any major issues. Have them make sure that they have used a variety of sentence patterns.

 ELPS 5F Write using a variety of grade-appropriate sentence patterns

Response Essay

Discuss the essay with the class, commenting on various points as follows:

- Note the strong connections to the thesis statement throughout the essay.
- The writer uses selected quotations from the short story to emphasize and clarify points.

Discuss the writer's use of variations on the phrase "romantic notions of war." Have students explain or infer the meaning of the phrase, and discuss whether the phrase has positive or negative connotations in the essay.

DIFFERENTIATE INSTRUCTION ↘

Response Essay

As you read the response essay about a short story on this page and the next, consider how the writer interprets the story's content, theme, and use of stylistic devices. The margin comments point out important elements of the interpretation.

No Vulgar Assassin

Beginning
The thesis (underlined) states the writer's main idea.

At first glance, Ambrose Bierce's chilling short story, "Occurrence at Owl Creek Bridge," might strike readers as little more than a horrific account of a man's death by hanging. A closer reading, however, reveals a story of considerably more depth. <u>In "Occurrence at Owl Creek Bridge," Ambrose Bierce provides a powerful illustration of the disastrous and senseless consequences of romantic notions of war.</u>

Middle
Writer notices and points out an example of nuance in the story. (underlined)

The story's main character, Peyton Farquhar, a respected southern planter and slave owner, is about to be hanged by the Union Army for sabotage. <u>For reasons deliberately left ambiguous, Farquhar has not joined the Confederate Army.</u> Nonetheless he harbors a deep desire to assist the South, believing that there was "no adventure too perilous for him to undertake."

Farquhar knows nothing of the horrors that the men who fight in war experience. He is, in fact, an armchair warrior, disappointed that he had never had the opportunity to display his courage on the battlefield. When a soldier approaches Farquhar and his wife outside their home, Farquhar, sensing his opportunity, suggests he would be willing to volunteer to blow up the bridge at Owl Creek. It never occurrs to Farquhar, wrapped up as he is in his own heroic vision of "an opportunity for distinction," that the soldier is a Union spy.

Middle
The middle supports the thesis with specific and relevant examples from the story.

Farquhar's romantic view of war persists right until the very end. Unable to accept that he is about to be hanged for an incredibly stupid act, he constructs an elaborate fantasy of escape. Farquhar's denial contrasts sharply with realistic acceptance of real soldiers who treat death as a "dignitary" whose arrival "is to be received with . . . respect."

Interpreting a Short Story   **325**

The writer cites rhetorical and literary devices that help convey the theme of the story.

Bierce points his critique at readers as well. Just as Farquhar hopes wildly for a happy ending, so do readers. How else can one explain the surprise of the ending? At the end of the first section, the narrator informs readers the execution has taken place with the simple statement, "The sergeant stepped aside." Images of the inevitable passing of time (and death)—the loudly ticking watch and the swinging pendulum—further alert readers as to what is actually happening. To the extent that readers refuse to acknowledge Farquhar's death and vainly hope for his escape, they also participate in a romantic view of war.

Ending
The ending restates the thesis and leaves the reader with something to think about.

Having fought in the Civil War himself, Bierce was no armchair warrior. Bierce was well ahead of his time in his grim assessment of the damage done by romantic notions of war. As he so eloquently illustrates in this story, boys go into war dreaming of heroism and emerge from it dead or forever hardened men. Those who have no first-hand experience perpetuate the romantic vision of war. His tale is a cautionary warning to all of us: romanticize war at your peril.

Respond to the reading. On your own paper, reflect on the focus, organization, ideas, and voice of the writer's interpretation of "Occurrence ar Owl Creek Bridge."

Focus and Coherence (1) Evaluate the effectiveness of the writer's opening paragraph.

Organization (2) Find examples of the use of repetition to create a smooth and logical flow.

Development of Ideas (3) What evidence does the writer give to show that Farquhar is an "armchair warrior"?

Voice (4) Find three examples of an authentic and original voice. Explain your choices.

Response

Respond to the reading.
Possible answers:

Focus and Coherence 1. Most students will find the opening paragraph effective in that it highlights the central event in the short story and definitively states the writer's thesis. It also engages readers by suggesting it will reveal a deeper meaning in story events.

Organization 2. The writer repeats the name *Farquhar* in the first sentences of Paragraphs 2, 3, 4, and 5.

Development of Ideas 3. Evidence that Farquhar is an "armchair warrior" include the fact that he offers to blow up the bridge as an "opportunity for distinction," and he remains in denial about his execution, in contrast to real soldiers who see death as a "dignitary . . . to be received with respect."

Voice 4. Possible responses: "It never occurrs to Farquhar, wrapped up as he is in his own heroic vision …," "Unable to accept that he is about to be hanged for an incredibly stupid act …," "His tale is a cautionary warning to all of us."

Differentiated Instruction:
English Language Learners

★ **ELPS** 4F, 4G

Before reading the sample essay, use visuals to develop historical context about the Civil War.

ELP Level **Beginning**	ELP Level **Intermediate**	ELP Level **Advanced/Advanced High**
Use simplified language to preteach terms such as *battlefield* and *spy*. Have students repeat these terms with you to help them develop vocabulary.	Model the meaning of terms such as *armchair warrior* and *fantasy*. Ask yes/no questions to confirm understanding of language structures.	Pause while reading to have students demonstrate comprehension by summarizing events and ideas. Discuss language structures the writer uses.

 ELPS **4F** Use visual and contextual support and support from peers and teachers to read content area text, enhance and confirm understanding, and develop vocabulary and grasp of language structures; **4G** Demonstrate comprehension of increasingly complex English/retelling or summarizing and responding to questions

Prewriting

You may wish to point out that your literature anthology includes a variety of short stories that students may want to interpret.

Select a short story. Remind students to select a short story that interests or intrigues them, since that will help them to write a more dynamic interpretation.

Selecting a Topic

Explain that taking time to analyze elements of the short story during prewriting will help the drafting stage flow more readily.

Consider the elements. Point out that in order to interpret the short story effectively, students should focus on story elements about which they feel strongly.

Writing Your Thesis Statement

Remind students that in addition to the title and author, an effective thesis statement reflects the writer's strong feeling about the short story.

TEKS 11.15C(i)

Choosing quotations for commentary. Suggest that students look at what the author chose to describe, at characters' dialogue, and at the story's narrator as they look for relevant quotations.

TEKS 11.15C(ii)

Anticipating Readers' Concerns

While there are no right or wrong interpretations of a short story, tell students to have a plan to address potential disagreements that others might have.

TEKS 11.15C(v)

 **TEKS** 11.15C(i), 11.15C(ii), 11.15C(v)

Prewriting

If your instructor does not assign a short story for you to interpret, you need to find one yourself or interpret one of the short stories suggested here.

"A Rose for Emily," William Faulkner   "The Story of an Hour," Kate Chopin

"The Rockpile," James Baldwin   "The Pit and the Pendulum," Edgar Allan Poe

"In the Sky Ball," Joyce Carol Oates

 Select a short story. Search your library, the Internet, and your literature book, looking for short stories that interest you. Select one to interpret—or interpret one of the stories suggested on this page.

Selecting a Topic

Before you begin prewriting, be sure that you have read the story carefully. Underline key phrases or take notes as you read. Think about the elements of a story story—character, setting, plot, point of view, images, themes, and style. Decide which two of these elements you think are especially important to the story and tailor your note taking and use of graphic organizers to fit those elements.

 Consider the elements. Consider the elements. Think deeply about your short story. Write down two elements you think are particularly important to the meaning of the story.

Writing Your Thesis Statement

Once you have thought deeply about the elements of your short story, it's time to write a thesis statement. An effective thesis names the short story and states your interpretation of it. A strong thesis will be a roadmap for your essay.

 Choosing Quotations for Commentary. Choose lines from the story that will best support your thesis. Scan for images and rhetorical devices, and for nuanced text that adds depth to the short story.

Anticipating Readers' Concerns

What parts of your interpretation might readers not agree with? Anticipate those objections and plan to address them either directly or indirectly in your essay.

TEKS **11.15C(i)** Write an interpretation of an expository or a literary text that advances a clear thesis statement; **11.15C(ii)** Write an interpretation of an expository or a literary text that addresses the writing skills for an analytical essay, including references to and commentary on quotations from the text; **11.15C(v)** Write an interpretation of an expository or a literary text that anticipates and responds to readers' questions or contradictory information

Drafting

Your first draft is your chance to get your ideas on paper. Start by reading through your prewriting notes and getting your main ideas firmly in your mind.

Analyze the Author's Style

In writing, style is not *what* an author says, but *how* she or he says it. An author's style is intimately connected to the mood and tone created by the writing. Ask yourself these questions as you analyze an author's style.

- Does the the author write using as few words as possible?
- Is the author's writing concrete and direct?
- How does the author's word choice affect mood and tone?
- Does the author often use figurative language?
- Does the author include many sensory details or very few?
- How would you describe the author's use of specific sentences?

Here are some words and phrases you might use to describe an author's style.

flowery	aloof	straightforward	evocative
jarring	distant	rich in sensory details	matter-of-fact

Analyze the Complexity of the Story

When you have a hard time figuring out what the author means in a particular passage, it may be because the author intends to imply several meanings simultaneously. This is important because, in life, the meaning of events is often complex and cannot be reduced to one simple statement. Locating passages in which the author communicates a nuanced, ambiguous, or complex idea—perhaps through rhetorical devices such as figurative language—can provide an important key to understanding the deeper meanings of a story. Look at this example. Think about the complex ideas Welty conveys about her character.

> "She was very old and small and she walked slowly in the dark pine shadows, moving a little from side to side in her steps, with the balanced heaviness and lightness of a pendulum in a grandfather clock."
>
> —Eudora Welty, "A Worn Path"

Draft

Develop your first draft. Use your prewriting and the guidelines above as you create the first draft of your interpretation.

Response

Drafting

Remind students to have prewriting notes as well as a copy of the short story nearby as they begin creating their first draft

Analyze the Author's Style

Use examples from several familiar short stories to prompt students to think about the authors' style. Use works by authors with distinctive or contrasting styles, such as O. Henry and Tim O'Brien, or Mark Twain and Edgar Allan Poe. Ask students to identify rhetorical and stylistic devices used by the authors you discuss.

Analyze the Complexity of the Story

Point out that the best writers tend to include layers of complexity in their stories. In their stories, the basic elements of a plot serve as a foundation on which the author may build subtleties and nuances about the events or characters or deliberate ambiguities about reactions or responses. Remind students to look for these nuances, ambiguities, and complexities as they interpret their short story.

Develop your first draft. Tell students to develop a first draft that gets their major points on paper. Remind them that they will have an opportunity to revise and edit their work.

✔ **DIFFERENTIATE INSTRUCTION**

★ **TEKS** 11.15C(iii), 11.15C(iv)

★ **TEKS** **11.15C(iii)** Write an interpretation of an expository or a literary text that analyzes the aesthetic effects of an author's use of stylistic or rhetorical devices; **11.15C(iv)** Write an interpretation of an expository or a literary text that identifies and analyzes the ambiguities, nuances, and complexities within the text; **ELPS** **1E** Internalize new basic and academic language by using and reusing it/writing; **1H** Develop and expand repertoire of learning strategies

Revising Improving Your First Draft

Point out that students should take some time away from their interpretations before beginning the revision process.

Revising Checklist

Explain that as part of the revision process, students should reevaluate the effectiveness and clarity of their thesis statements, and determine whether they have adequately presented information about the author's use of rhetorical and stylistic devices.

Revise your first draft. After students have answered the checklist questions, have them work with partners to plan the revisions they will make. DIFFERENTIATE INSTRUCTION ↘

TEKS 11.15C(i), 11.15C(iii)

Editing Checklist

Suggest that when editing and proofreading, students should double-check *everything* they're not completely certain about. This means that they should

- read slowly and carefully to avoid glossing over errors,
- investigate anything that they wrote in haste, and
- familiarize themselves with the Proofreader's Guide on SE pages 634–779.

328

 TEKS 11.15C(i), 11.15C(iii)

Revising Improving Your First Draft

After you have written a first draft, it's time to do some revising. Use the guidelines below to help you revise.

<u>Revising Checklist</u>

Focus and Coherence

____ **1.** Does my thesis clearly state my interpretation of the story?
____ **2.** Are all of my ideas connected to each other and to the thesis?
____ **3.** Have I included a strong introduction and a meaningful conclusion?

Organization

____ **5.** Does my essay have a smooth, logical flow?
____ **6.** Have I used transitions and the repetition of key words and ideas to move smoothly from one idea to the next?

Development of Ideas

____ **7.** Have I used relevant and specific details to support my ideas?
____ **8.** Have I approached my topic from a unique perspective?

Voice

____ **9.** Have I engaged my reader throughout my interpretation?
____ **10.** Is my writing authentic and original?

 Revise

Revise your first draft. Read your interpretation carefully. Then use the checklist above to help you improve your first draft.

<u>Editing Checklist</u>

Conventions

____ **1.** Do my subjects and verbs agree in number?
____ **2.** Have I used quotation marks correctly?
____ **3.** Have I checked the spelling of any words I'm not sure of?

TEKS **11.15C(i)** Write an interpretation of an expository or a literary text that advances a clear thesis statement; **11.15C(iii)** Write an interpretation of an expository or a literary text that analyzes the aesthetic effects of an author's use of stylistic or rhetorical devices; ELPS **1B** Monitor written language production and employ self-corrective techniques or other resources; **5D** Edit writing for standard grammar and usage/subject-verb agreement; **5F** Write using a variety of grade-appropriate sentence lengths, patterns, and connecting words

Differentiated Instruction: ELPS 1B, 5D, 5F
English Language Learners

Turn to the Appendix of the Teacher's Edition for information on language transfer issues with grammar, usage, and mechanics.

ELP Level **Beginning**	ELP Level **Intermediate**	ELP Level **Advanced/Advanced High**
Work with students to assess their work. Guide students to revise and edit their final drafts, focusing on the use of connecting words.	Pair students with an English-proficient peer to check for subject-verb agreement, and for varied sentences lengths and patterns.	Have students check for subject-verb agreement, and revise as needed to use connecting words to vary sentence lengths and patterns.

Writing for Assessment
Responding to Prompts About Literature

Your response to a literature prompt on an assessment test will show how well you understand the literature. For responses to fiction, you should focus on *plot, character, theme, setting,* and *style.* For responses to nonfiction, you should focus on the writer's ideas and how he or she conveys them. Responding to such prompts reveals how well you've analyzed the literature, as well as the prompt.

This chapter will help you respond effectively to literature prompts in timed writing situations. You will use the writing process in practice test situations to respond to fiction. Your goal is to produce a focused, clear response that discloses your own insights into the reading.

Writing Guidelines

Subject: **Literature prompt**
Purpose: **To demonstrate competence**
Form: **Response essay**
Audience: **Instructor**

"In a real sense, people who have read good literature have lived more than people who cannot or will not read."
—S. I. Hayakawa

Responding to Prompts About Literature

Objectives
• demonstrate an understanding of the elements of a literature prompt
• analyze a literature prompt
• plan, write, revise, and edit a response to a literature prompt
• practice writing for timed-writing situation

Even if students will not be tested on the response to literature form this year, consider working through this section if your schedule permits. Practicing this skill will help students as they respond to both fiction and nonfiction literature prompts during in-class and placement examinations throughout their academic careers. The skills used when responding to literature (thoughtful analysis and explanation) are useful in other timed-writing situations as well.

Prewriting

Analyzing a Literature Prompt

Remind students that, in addition to identifying key words in a prompt, they also need to pay attention to the overall focus of the prompt. For example, the sample prompt asks specifically how Elie Wiesel's personality affected his choices, but generally this is a question about cause and effect.

Sample Prompt

One way to analyze the prompt is to answer the STRAP questions. Review these questions and have students apply them to the sample prompt:

- **S**ubject (What is the topic?): Elie Wiesel's memoir
- **T**ype (What writing form is it?): essay
- **R**ole (What position should I write from?): reader of the memoir *Night*
- **A**udience (Who is the intended reader?): test evaluators
- **P**urpose (What is the goal of the writing?): to explain

Ask students to apply the STRAP questions in the **Try It!** activity in addition to underlining the key words.

Try It!
Answers

Possible answers:
1. became the leader of the Catholic church; what characteristics contributed to his rise
2. image of a military jet; evolves into a description of a typical spring day; how the author ties the two ideas together and why; personification of the season

---

"In the highest civilization, the book is still the highest delight. He who has once known its satisfactions is provided with a resource against calamity."

—Ralph Waldo Emerson

Prewriting Analyzing a Literature Prompt

A prompt about literature asks you to respond to specific characteristics of a story, a poem, a novel, or a nonfiction selection. As you read a prompt, look for key words that tell you exactly what the prompt requires. In the sample prompt below, key words and phrases are underlined. The word *explain* gives the main direction or focus for the response.

Sample Prompt

> In Elie Wiesel's memoir *Night*, a teenage boy deals with his guilt at having survived the Holocaust. <u>Write an essay</u> in which you <u>explain how his despair leads him first to question his faith</u> and then to <u>make sure that the world never forgets this evil</u>. How do his personal characteristics affect him and the way he resolves his crisis? Support your thesis with <u>evidence from the story</u>.

Try It!

Copy the following sample prompts on a sheet of paper. Underline key words and phrases in each prompt and make notes about the kinds of supporting information that you would need for a response.

1. Joseph Ratzinger, the subject of Paul Elie's article "Behind the Scenes at the Vatican," became the leader of the Catholic church after the death of Pope John Paul II. In an essay, explain what characteristics contributed to Ratzinger's rise. Include specific examples to support your ideas.
2. "In Late Spring," by Ted Kooser, is a poem that opens with an image of a military jet but evolves into a description of a typical spring day. In an essay, discuss how the author ties the two ideas together and why he might have done so. What does his personification of the season say about his feelings for it?

Planning Your Response

Once you analyze and understand a prompt, you are ready to plan your response. If a reading selection is provided, read it with the prompt in mind, picking out the information you need for your response. Then form your topic sentence and organize the details.

Sample Prompt and Selection

> *In the following excerpt from Lafcadio Hearn's "Fuji-No-Yama," the author describes Mt. Fuji. In a paragraph, discuss the comparison created by the author. What details create the comparison?*
>
> From "Fuji-No-Yama" by Lafacadio Hearn
> You can <u>seldom distinguish</u> the snowless base, which remains <u>the same color</u> as the sky: you <u>perceive</u> only the white cone <u>seeming to hang in heaven</u>. . . . Even lighter than a fan <u>the vision appears</u>—rather <u>the ghost or dream of a fan</u>—yet the <u>material reality a hundred miles away</u> is grandiose among the mountains of the globe.

The underlined words refer to the mountain's ghost-like qualities.

Writing a Topic Sentence

After reading the prompt and selection, one student wrote this topic sentence.

> **Hearn's description of Mt. Fuji** (specific topic) **compares it to an apparition** (particular focus related to the prompt).

Creating a Graphic Organizer

The student also used a graphic organizer to gather details.

Response

Planning Your Response

Remind students always to read a prompt twice: once quickly to get the overall idea, and a second time to note key words and answer the STRAP questions.

Sample Prompt and Selection

Have a volunteer read aloud the prompt and the selection. Discuss each underlined element and ask students to explain why each was chosen.

Writing a Topic Sentence

Ask students to comment on whether the sample topic sentence reflects the idea they would convey in their own response to the prompt. (Some students might say they would pick up on the idea of the mountain being compared to the dream of a fan, an object strongly associated with Japanese culture.) Invite students to create their own topic sentences in response to the prompt.

Creating a Graphic Organizer

Have students identify the graphic organizer shown (cluster diagram or topic web). Distribute photocopies of other graphic organizers students might find useful, for example,

- quick list, or brief outline (TE page A101), and
- T-chart (TE page A97)—students could use one column for the description of the vision and one for the reality.

Remind students that they will have to generate their own graphic organizers during a timed writing assignment.

Drafting Responding to a Fiction Prompt

Explain that the sample prompt and selection provide a model for responding to a fiction prompt.

Sample Prompt and Selection

Give students a time limit (perhaps 10 minutes) to read and analyze the prompt and excerpt as if they were going to write the response themselves. Suggest that students list the key words and answers to the STRAP questions.

- Key words: *describes a future civilization and his thoughts about it; foreshadows disturbing events to come despite the seemingly ideal conditions described*
- **S**ubject: the time traveler's description of a future culture
- **T**ype: response essay
- **R**ole: reader of the excerpt
- **A**udience: teacher/evaluator of test
- **P**urpose: to explain

Ask students to make their own notes about the stylistic and rhetorical devices in the excerpt to supplement the sample margin notes shown. Suggest that they use abbreviations so they can get their ideas down quickly in a timed situation. (They can practice doing this in their class notes so that it will come easily during a test.) Share some common abbreviations, such as

- *w/ (with)* and *w/o (without),*
- *& or + (and),*
- *no. or # (number),*
- initials instead of the names of major people mentioned, and
- numerals instead of words.

✱ For other common abbreviations, see SE page 687.

When the time is up, discuss students' notes as a group. Have them compare their answers to the STRAP questions and talk about the stylistic and rhetorical devices they identified as important.

TEKS 11.13B, 11.15C(iii)

Drafting Responding to a Fiction Prompt

The following prompt and fiction selection show how a student underlined key words and phrases and added some notes on a copy of the selection to address the focus of the prompt.

Sample Prompt and Selection

Many science fiction writers have described future scenarios in their stories. In the following excerpt from The Time Machine, *a time traveler describes a future civilization and his thoughts about it. In an essay, explain how the narrator foreshadows disturbing events to come, despite the seemingly ideal conditions described in this excerpt. What feeling does the author convey about the culture he encounters?*

From *The Time Machine* by H. G. Wells

> The air was <u>free from gnats</u>, the earth from <u>weeds or fungi</u>; <u>everywhere were fruits</u> and sweet and <u>delightful flowers</u>; brilliant butterflies flew hither and thither. The <u>ideal of preventive medicine was attained.</u> Diseases had been stamped out. I saw no evidence of any contagious diseases during all my stay. And I shall have to tell you later that even the processes of putrefaction and decay had been profoundly affected by these changes.
>
> <u>Social triumphs</u>, too, had been effected. I saw mankind housed in <u>splendid shelters, gloriously clothed,</u> and as yet I had found them engaged in no toil. There were <u>no signs of struggle, neither social nor economical</u> struggle. The shop, the advertisement, traffic, all that commerce which constitutes the body of our world, was gone. It was natural on that golden evening that I should jump at the idea of a social paradise. The difficulty of increasing population had been met, I guessed, and <u>population had ceased to increase.</u>
>
> <u>But</u> with this change in condition comes inevitably adaptations to the change. What, unless biological science is a mass of errors, is the <u>cause of human intelligence and vigour?</u> Hardship and freedom: conditions under which the <u>active, strong, and subtle</u>

At first the narrator describes the future world using words such as "ideal," "triumphs," and "paradise."

The word "but" signals the narrator's change in focus.

 TEKS 11.13B Develop drafts in timed situations; **11.15C(iii)** Write an interpretation of an expository or a literary text that analyzes the aesthetic effects of an author's use of stylistic or rhetorical devices

> survive and the weaker go to the wall; conditions that put a premium upon the loyal alliance of capable men, upon self-restraint, patience, and decision. And the institution of the family, and the emotions that arise therein, the fierce jealousy, the tenderness for offspring, parental self-devotion, all found their justification and support in the imminent dangers of the young. *Now, where are these imminent dangers?*

Writing a Thesis Statement

After reading the excerpt and making notes, the student wrote the following thesis statement for his response essay.

> The narrator's reservations about the future utopian civilization (specific topic) **seem to foreshadow** events that will later reveal this civilization's true nature (particular focus related to the prompt).

Creating a Graphic Organizer

The student also created a T-graph, listing the good aspects of the utopian society and the author's fears for the future.

Good Aspects	Fears for the Future
no bugs or weeds	adaptations not best for species
much natural beauty	hardship needed for intelligence
no social struggle	no "vigour"
no economic struggle	freedom connected to risk
fine clothes and shelter	danger needed for family strength
no overpopulation	emotions not natural
no disease	

Response

Writing a Thesis Statement

In reviewing the sample thesis statement, focus on the writer's use of *seem* (*seem to foreshadow*).

- Point out that in some essays, using *seem* would inject an undesirable hint of uncertainty into the author's voice.
- In this case, however, as with many prompts accompanied by excerpts, students are being asked to use only the information they can gather from the excerpt, which only hints at dangers to come; it doesn't describe them.
- Note that if students have read the book from which the excerpt was taken and know the ending, they may make use of their knowledge. However, they must keep the main focus on the information they've been provided in the selection and avoid using many details from other parts of the book. ✔DIFFERENTIATE INSTRUCTION

⭐ **TEKS** 11.13A

Creating a Graphic Organizer

Remind students that there are several graphic organizers to choose from, and they should always use the graphic organizer that best fits the task and that they find most helpful. Suggest that they use a graphic organizer that will allow them to note examples of the author's use of rhetorical and stylistic devices as well as to identify and analyze complexities, nuances, and ambiguities within the text.

⭐ **TEKS** 11.13B, 11.15C(iii), 11.15C(iv)

TEKS **11.13A** Plan a first draft by developing a thesis or controlling idea; **11.13B** Structure ideas in a sustained way; **11.15C(iii)** Write an interpretation of an expository or a literary text that analyzes the aesthetic effects of an author's use of stylistic or rhetorical devices; **11.15C(iv)** Write an interpretation of an expository or a literary text that identifies and analyzes the ambiguities, nuances, and complexities within the text; **ELPS** **1E** internalize new basic and academic language by using and reusing/writing; **1F** Use accessible language and learn new and essential language in the process

Drafting Student Response

After students have had time to read and consider the model response, ask them to apply the traits of writing (there are no errors in conventions). What are the essay's strong points? For example:

Focus and Coherence—The writer uses the important details provided in the excerpt to support his thesis.

Organization—The writer uses an effective transition between the two middle paragraphs, ending the first paragraph with a question and answering it in the second paragraph. Transitional words (such as *however, despite, although*) show the contrast between the apparent utopia and the writer's sense of danger.

Development of Ideas—The writer uses the important details provided in the excerpt to support his thesis.

✱ For more about effective transitions see SE pages 623–624.

Voice—The writer's use of the specialized terms *utopian* and *foreshadow* help him to sound knowledgeable and confident.

Drafting Student Response

In this student response to the excerpt from *The Time Machine*, note how the writer uses details from the story to support the thesis statement.

Storm Clouds in Paradise

Beginning
The first paragraph leads up to the thesis statement (underlined).

The excerpt from The Time Machine by H. G. Wells begins with a description of a utopian civilization that the narrator, a time traveler, has encountered. Following his glowing review, however, he expresses misgivings about it. The narrator's reservations about the future utopian civilization seem to foreshadow events that will later reveal this civilization's true nature.

Middle
One paragraph focuses on the "perfect" society.

The future world the narrator travels to is, at first glance, a paradise. There are no nasty bugs, only butterflies. There are no weeds, only "sweet and delightful flowers." Disease has been wiped out, and overpopulation is no longer a concern. Despite a lack of commerce or, indeed, any work being done by the inhabitants, they are well clothed and live in "splendid shelters." The narrator observes no apparent competition or strife between people. What could possibly be wrong with such a picture?

The next paragraph focuses on the narrator's reservations about the society.

The first clue that the narrator is, perhaps, uncomfortable with what he sees is the word but beginning the third paragraph: "But with this change in condition comes inevitably adaptations to the change." It's as if he is warning against feeling too smug about achieving the ideal he previously described. He continues to express his reservations, discussing the lack of "hardship and freedom—conditions under which the active, strong, and subtle survive." He is implying, of course, that the paradise fosters passive, weak, and unperceptive beings. His sense that there is no danger to the young leads him to believe that the ability to feel emotions—"the fierce jealousy, the tenderness for offspring, parental self-devotion"—has died, as has the concept of family.

> Although Wells's time traveler does not come right out and say that there is trouble within the society he's witnessed, he certainly conveys a feeling of distrust. His description of the paradise followed by his qualms about it give the reader a sense of foreboding. The last paragraph of the excerpt suggests that the narrator's suspicions will play a role later in the novel.

Ending
The closing reiterates the thesis.

Response

⭐ **Respond to the reading.** Answer the following questions about the student response.

Focus and Coherence (1) What is the focus of the student writer's thesis statement? (2) Does the thesis statement accurately reflect the prompt? Explain.

Organization (3) How does the writer organize the middle part of the response?

Voice (4) Which words or phrases quoted from the story are the most effective? Name two and explain your choices.

 Respond to the reading.

Answers

Focus and Coherence 1. The writer focuses on the idea that the narrator's feeling of foreboding foreshadows later events in the book.
2. Yes, the student writer answers the question asked in the prompt.

Organization 3. The first middle paragraph summarizes the positive aspects of the culture. The second middle paragraph traces the narrator's transition to the negative aspects of the culture and summarizes his fears for the future.

Voice 4. Possible answers:
- "But with this change" (shows the point where the tone of the piece changes)
- "conditions under which the active, strong, and subtle survive" (illustrates the author's voice and expresses the idea more powerfully than a paraphrase could)
- "the fierce jealousy, the tenderness for offspring" (uses the author's vivid words as an appositive phrase to expand on *emotions*)

✓ DIFFERENTIATE INSTRUCTION

⭐ **TEKS** 11.13B, 11.15C(iii); **ELPS** 4K

⭐ **TEKS** **11.13B** Structure ideas in a sustained way; **11.15C(iii)** Write an interpretation of an expository or a literary text that analyzes the aesthetic effects of an author's use of stylistic or rhetorical devices; **ELPS** **4C** Comprehend English vocabulary and language structures; **4F** Use visual and contextual support to read content area text and to enhance and confirm understanding; **4K** Demonstrate English comprehension and expand reading skills by employing analytical skills

Revising Improving Your Response

Point out that during timed-writing exercises, students must create a relatively polished first draft because their revising time is limited. Tell students to ask themselves the questions shown with each trait.

Improve your work. Tell students that if they focus on developing their ideas and logical organization during prewriting and drafting, then they can devote their revising time to clarifying meaning, consistency of tone, and the use of tropes and schemes to improve focus and coherence and voice.

TEKS 11.13C

Editing Checking Your Response

Remind students that the more familiar they become with the conventions, the more likely they are to get them right the first time around. This will free them up to
- spend more time on planning, writing, and revising; and
- focus on finding subtle errors, rather than spending time on basic conventions such as capitalization and end punctuation.

Editing Checklist

Suggest that students address each question by checking their entire response before moving on to the next question.

Check your response. Tell students to watch for the types of errors that they often find in their writing, including subject-verb agreement.

ELPS 5D

336

 TEKS 11.13C

Revising Improving Your Response

Always review your response at the end of a writing test. Make any changes and corrections as neatly as possible. Use the following questions to help you revise your response.

- **Focus and Coherence** Does my thesis statement address the focus of the prompt? Do the details relate to and support the thesis?
- **Organization** Have I included a beginning, a middle, and an ending? Does each paragraph have a focus? Do I conclude with an insight about the literature selection?
- **Development of Ideas** Are my ideas fully developed and given ample support? Have I presented my ideas in a thoughtful way? Have I taken an unusual approach?
- **Voice** Do I sound confident and clear? Does my writing reflect my unique perspective and authentic voice?

 Revise

Improve your work. Reread your practice response, asking yourself the questions above. Make any changes neatly.

Editing Checking Your Response

In your final read, check your grammar, sentence structure, punctuation, capitalization, and spelling.

Editing Checklist

Conventions

____ 1. Have I made sure my subjects and verbs agree?
____ 2. Have I put quotation marks around the exact words that I quoted from the selection?
____ 3. Have I used end punctuation for every sentence?
____ 4. Have I capitalized all proper nouns and first words of sentences?
____ 5. Have I checked my spelling in either a print or electronic dictionary?

 Edit

Check your response. Read over your work, looking for errors in grammar, sentence structure, punctuation, capitalization, and spelling. Make corrections neatly.

TEKS 11.13C Revise drafts to clarify meaning and achieve specific rhetorical purposes, consistency of tone, and logical organization by rearranging the words, sentences, and paragraphs to employ tropes, schemes, and by adding transitional words and phrases; **ELPS 5D** Edit writing for standard grammar and usage/subject-verb agreement

Responding to Literature on Tests

Use the following tips as a guide whenever you respond to a prompt about literature. These tips will help you respond to both fiction and nonfiction selections.

Before you write . . .

- **Be clear about the time limit.**
  Plan enough time for prewriting, writing, and revising.
- **Understand the prompt.**
  Be sure that you know what the prompt requires. Pay special attention to the key word that tells you what you need to do.
- **Read the selection with the focus of the prompt in mind.**
  Take notes that will help you form your thesis. If you're working on a copy of the selection, underline important details.
- **Form your thesis statement.**
  The thesis statement should identify the specific topic plus the focus of the prompt.
- **Make a graphic organizer.**
  Jot down main points and possible quotations for your essay.

As you write . . .

- **Maintain the focus of your essay.**
  Keep your thesis in mind as you write.
- **Be selective.** Use examples from your graphic organizer and the selection to support your thesis.
- **End in a meaningful way.**
  Start by revisiting the thesis. Then try to share a final insight about the topic with the reader.

After you've written a first draft . . .

- **Check for completeness and correctness.**
  Use questions like those on page **336** to revise your essay. Then check for errors in punctuation, capitalization, spelling, and grammar.

Learning Language

On a separate piece of paper, write notes in your own words that will help you remember the tips for responding to literature on tests. Write down any words that are confusing or that you don't understand. Share and discuss your list with a partner, checking a print or electronic dictionary as need for unfamiliar terms.

Response

Responding to Literature on Tests

Point out to students that they must approach timed-writing assignments differently from open-ended writing assignments. To give them practice, provide the same amount of time to write their responses as they will be allotted for school, district, or state assessments.

Tell students when time is up for each section. Start the assignment at the top of the hour or at the half-hour to make it easier for them to keep track of the time.

Before you write...

Tell students you will break down each part of the process into clear chunks of time. For example, you might give students 5–10 minutes for note taking and planning.

As you write...

Tell students that they will have about 25–30 minutes for drafting. If your state, district, or school requires students to use and submit a graphic organizer as part of their assessment, refer students to SE pages 612–615.

After you've written a first draft...

Tell students that they will have about 5 minutes for revising, editing, and proofreading.

Learning Language

Tell student partners to quiz one another about any unfamiliar terms, making sure that they address terms such as *prompt* and *time limit*. Then have them write their own notes about the terms and use them to explain the steps they would follow during a timed-writing assignment.

✔ DIFFERENTIATE INSTRUCTION

ELPS 1C, 1E, 4G

Differentiated Instruction: English Language Learners		ELPS 1B, 5C
ELP Level **Beginning**	**ELP Level** **Intermediate**	**ELP Level** **Advanced/Advanced High**
Work together to create a list or chart of tips. Have students generate and write a spelling list or word bank. Point out spelling patterns and rules.	Have partners create a list of tips. Together, compile a list of essential vocabulary for prompts. Guide students to identify spelling patterns and rules.	Discuss students' responses as a group. Together, compile a list of essential vocabulary and have students identify spelling patterns and rules.

 ELPS 1B Monitor written language production and employ self-corrective techniques or other resources; **1C** Use strategic learning strategies to acquire basic and grade-level vocabulary; **1E** internalize new basic and academic language by using and reusing it/speaking and writing; **4G** Demonstrate comprehension of increasingly complex English/taking notes; **5C** Spell familiar English words and employ English spelling patterns and rules with increasing accuracy

Creative Writing

Writing Stories (pages 339–348)

Students learn to create an engaging story with a well-developed conflict and a resolution that changes the main character.

Writing Plays (pages 349–360)

While exploring this collaborative medium, students will write a play about a person facing a dilemma.

Writing Poetry (pages 361–373)

Students learn about poetic conventions and create their own free-verse poem to reflect on a relationship.

Technology Connections

Write Source Online www.hmheducation.com/tx/writesource
- **Net-text**
- **Writing Network**
- **Portfolio**
- **GrammarSnap**
- **Essay Scoring**
- **File Cabinet**

Interactive Whiteboard Lessons

Creative Writing Unit Scope and Sequence

	Day	Writing and Conventions Instruction	Core Unit	Tools of Language	Resource Units	Daily Language Workouts	Skills-Book	Write Source Online
			Write Source Student Edition					
WEEK 1	1	**Writing Stories** Model	339–343	TL 592–597		74–77		Interactive Whiteboard Lesson
	2–3	Prewriting	344–345					Net-text
	4–5	Drafting	346					Net-text
WEEK 2	6–9	Revising, Editing	347	TL 592–597		78–81		Net-text
		Skills Activities: •Punctuating Dialogue			PG 660		30	
		•Prepositions, Conjunctions, Interjections			PG 752–753, 754–755		114–118	GrammarSnap
	10	Elements of Fiction	348					Net-text
WEEK 3	11	**Writing Plays** Model	349–352	TL 592–597		82–85		Net-text
	12–13	Prewriting	353–355					Net-text
	14–15	Drafting	356					Net-text
WEEK 4	16–19	Revising, Editing	357	TL 592–597		86–89		Net-text
		Skills Activities: •Commas			PG 638–647		7–18	GrammarSnap
	20	Writing an Advertising Script	358–360					
WEEK 5	21	**Writing Poetry** Model, Prewriting	361–363	TL 592–597		90–93		Net-text
	22	Drafting	364–365					Net-text
	23	Revising, Editing, Publishing	366–367					Net-text
		Skills Activities: •Prepositions/Prepositional Phrases; Phrases			PG 752–753, 760–761, 762		128	GrammarSnap
		•Parts of Speech Review; Adjectives and Adverbs			PG 722, 723–755		108, 113, 119–120	GrammarSnap
		•Subjects and Predicates			PG 756–759		123–125	
		•Spelling			PG 690–695		55–59	
	24–25	Using Poetic Conventions and Techniques	368–369					Net-text
		Writing a Shakespearean Sonnet	370–371					Net-text
		Poetic Form: Quatrains	372–373					Net-text

Resource Units referenced above are located in the back of the *Student Edition* and *Teacher's Edition*
TL *"The Tools of Language"*   BEW *"Basic Elements of Writing"*   PG *"Proofreader's Guide"*

Writing Focus

- Writing Stories
- Writing Plays
- Writing Poetry

Learning Language

Read aloud the basic and academic terms, as well as the descriptions and questions. Help students recognize and practice producing the sounds of each word, such as the consonant clusters *fl* and *pl* in *conflict* and *complex*. Then model for students how to read one question and answer it. For example, *It says that a* conflict *is a problem that you have to solve, and it's asking about a conflict I've had with someone I care about. I'll tell about a time my friend Jorge forgot to bring lunch for our hike.* Have partners monitor their understanding by working through the meanings and questions together.

 ELPS 1F, 2B, 2C, 3A, 3E, 4G DIFFERENTIATE INSTRUCTION ↘

Minilessons

Once Upon a Time   Writing Stories

- **CHOOSE** a classic fairy tale or well-known short story. Have students **CREATE** a plot line for it by labeling each element along the graphic plot line. Have them **SHARE** their work with the class.

Wow! Oh, no! Look out!   Writing Plays

- Have students **WRITE** two versions of a dialogue— one with stage directions and another without—between two characters who only use interjections. Have them **GIVE** the version without stage directions to another person to see if he or she can figure out what's happening.

Poetry Partner   Writing Poetry

- Have partners **EXCHANGE** copies of original poems. Tell them to **CIRCLE** the words in the poem that are especially vivid, descriptive, sensory-based, or onomatopoeic in construction. **ASK** volunteers to share their best words with the class.

ELPS 1F Use accessible language and learn new and essential language in the process; **2B** Recognize elements of the English sound system in newly acquired vocabulary; **2C** learn new language structures, expressions, and basic and academic vocabulary; **3A** Practice producing sounds of newly acquired vocabulary to pronounce English words; **3E** Share information in cooperative learning interactions; **4G** Demonstrate comprehension of increasingly complex English/responding to questions

---

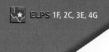
www.hmheducation.com/tx/writesource

Creative Writing

Writing Focus

Learning Language

Work with a partner. Read the meanings and share answers to the questions.

1. A conflict is a problem a person has to solve.
   Tell about a time you had a conflict with someone you care about. What made the conflict end?

2. A resolution is how a conflict is solved.
   Tell how you felt about the resolution of the conflict you had.

3. Something that is complex is not easy to understand.
   What is a subject in school that you think is complex? Why?

4. To face a challenge means to do something difficult.
   Tell about a character in a story who faced a challenge. What did the character want to do? Why was this difficult to do?

Writing Stories

It seems that everybody wants something. That "thing" might be as huge as to be accepted into a prestigious college or as small as wanting to buy a certain pair of shoes. What is true in life is also true in stories. A story becomes interesting only when the main character wants something that is difficult to obtain. That's called conflict, and it's what makes fiction—and life—interesting.

Someone once described a story as getting your main character up in a tree, throwing rocks at him, and then getting him down again. The tree is your conflict; the rocks are complications or rising action. Resolving the conflict gets the character out of the tree. Developing a story means fitting your ideas into this pattern in your own way so the story is yours alone.

In this chapter you will write a story about someone facing a life challenge. You will learn how to build an engaging story with a well developed conflict and a resolution that changes the main character.

Writing Guidelines

Subject: A life challenge
Purpose: To engage and entertain
Form: Short story
Audience: Classmates

"There have been great societies that did not use the wheel, but there have been no societies that did not tell stories."

—Ursula K. LeGuin

Writing Stories

Objectives
- understand the content and structure of a short story
- choose a topic (a life challenge) to write about
- plan, draft, revise, and edit a short story

A **short story** is a piece of creative writing that often focuses on a conflict or problem that the characters need to overcome. Explain to students that they are going to write a short story that focuses on a life challenge as its central conflict.

Discuss what is meant by a *life challenge* (an experience in which a person must overcome an obstacle). Explain that a life challenge doesn't have to be large scale or life threatening to create an interesting conflict. Many great stories center on subtle conflicts. However, to hold the readers' attention, the conflicts should create strong feelings in the characters.

Invite students to suggest conflicts they could base stories on. Sample conflicts may center on
- someone who must leave her school and her friends because her family is moving;
- someone who wants to go out with friends but has been left in charge of his little brother; or
- someone who gets lost in the woods during a snowstorm.

Talk about these examples together, discussing in what ways each one would be interesting to readers. Encourage students to use terms such as *conflict* and *resolution*.

⭐ELPS 1E

 Technology Connections

Use the Interactive Whiteboard lessons to introduce creative writing.

 Interactive Whiteboard Lesson

The Shape of Stories

Explain that fragments of ideas for a story may come to a writer at different times, and not necessarily in chronological order. For example, a writer may first decide what the climax of the story should be and then figure out what events will lead to that point. Eventually, however, a writer usually combines these fragments into a classic story structure, called a plot line.

Plot Line

Review the diagram of a plot line with students. Ask them to describe its shape; discuss how this shape helps them understand how a good story builds complex characters, events, and details into a strong, engaging story. Then have students discuss each term shown in the diagram, explaining them in their own words.

⭐ **TEKS** 11.14A **DIFFERENTIATE INSTRUCTION** ⬎

Encourage students to be open to the idea that inspiration can arrive piecemeal and that a plot line can emerge from these pieces over time. Suggest that they jot down in their writer's notebook any details or ideas that occur to them, such as a great character or a humorous predicament for the characters. Over time, they can determine how these ideas fit into the arc of their story.

✱ For more about writer's notebooks, see SE pages 2–5.

Try It!
Answers

1–5. Answers will vary. Have students discuss their answers together, using the terms that describe each element of a plot line.

DIFFERENTIATE INSTRUCTION ⬎

⭐ **TEKS** 11.14A **ELPS** 1C

 TEKS 11.14A

The Shape of Stories

As a child, you probably wrote stories that simply gave one event after another: "And then . . . and then . . . and then . . . " Now you should write stories in which events build upon each other, using the classic plot line.

Plot Line

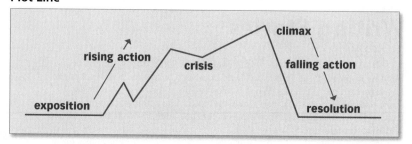

The **exposition** gives background information the reader needs to understand the story. It introduces the main characters, the setting, and the conflict.

The **rising action** is a series of events, called *complications,* that build suspense. Each event develops the story line. During the rising action, the stakes increase as the character faces complications that block his or her way.

The **crisis** is a moment of realization for the main character, when he or she comes to some decision or does something that will determine the outcome of the story. The crisis is not the climax but will lead to it.

The **climax** is the moment of truth, or the emotional high point of the story, when the main character either triumphs or fails. The climax should also somehow cause a change, either obvious or subtle, in the main character.

The **falling action** shows how the main character adjusts to the change.

The **resolution,** also called the *denouement,* is the ending. The falling action and the resolution should be short, bringing the story to a satisfying close.

Try It!

Think about a short story or novel you have recently read and answer the following questions.

1. Who was the main character, and what was the conflict? (exposition)
2. What challenges did the main character face? (rising action)
3. When did the main character make a difficult decision? (crisis)
4. What was the high point of the story? (climax)
5. What happened afterward? (falling action and resolution)

Differentiated Instruction: Struggling Learners

For the **Try It!** activity, have students work with a partner or in a small group. Ask them to fill in a story map for a work of fiction that was read in class. Afterward, work with students one-on-one to make sure they undersand the elements of plot and to answer the Try It! questions for stories of their own choosing.

Differentiated Instruction: Advanced Learners

Invite students to compare plot lines of some of their stories to the sample story. Ask them to analyze the organization and language from story to story and to note similarities and differences they find.

Have students add to their notebook any new ideas or techniques they learn from their analysis.

 TEKS **11.14A** Write an engaging story with a well-developed conflict and resolution and complex characters; **ELPS** **1C** Use strategic learning strategies to acquire basic and grade-level vocabulary

Sample Story

In her story, Chandra examined a conflict between a young woman and her father. Note how the use of a flashback helps establish the main character's motivation for her feelings. (See page **345**.)

The **exposition** introduces the main character, sets the scene, and provides the conflict.

The **rising action** elevates the conflict.

A **flashback** helps the reader understand the conflict.

Small Steps

Hannah sat sullenly, watching the unfamiliar desert landscape glide by the truck window. Her father drove silently, his fingers beating a little pattern on the wheel to the rhythm of the music from the CD player. *His* music. *His* truck. *His* home. It all used to be *us* and *we*. Now it was only *him.*

At the airport, he had tossed her suitcase and backpack into the back of the truck, as carelessly as he had tossed her from his life nearly a year ago. That was when he had left her and her mother to "find himself" in this sagebrush and saguaro wasteland. And now he expected her to forget all the hurt!

"Almost there." He smiled at her.

"Whoopee," Hannah growled, and he looked at her sadly.

"Look, Pooh, I—"

"Don't call me that," Hanna snapped at the pet name her father had given her as a child. He had no right anymore. "This was Mom's idea, not mine. She seems to think I need to spend time with my—dad!" The word was bitter, and she almost spat it out.

"I'm sorry. Hannah, I know I can never make up the lost time, but you've got to believe how sorry I am. I love you, Honey, and I missed you. Couldn't you understand, and maybe forgive me?"

Understand and forgive. Those had been her mother's words when Hannah had asked why her father left.

"He's not running away from us, Hannah," Mom had said sadly. "He's running toward something, and we just can't go with him. I understand, and I can forgive him."

Hannah didn't understand, and she didn't forgive. As he looked at her hopefully, she felt herself boiling inside.

"You were only thinking of yourself!" Hannah exploded. "I needed you, and you weren't there! Where were you when my cat got run over? Or when I sprained my

Creative Writing

Sample Story

Work through the model story with students, pointing out the elements that make it good short story. ✔ **DIFFERENTIATE INSTRUCTION**

★ **TEKS** 11.14A

Focus and Coherence

- The writer addresses a single controlling conflict: her difficult and changing relationship with her father.
- All the story events provide context and information that support the central conflict.

Organization

- The rising action leads logically to the obstacle that Hannah must overcome.
- The last sentence (information about *bitter words*) refers back to metaphorical language used early in the story (paragraph 6).

Development of Ideas

- The characters are portrayed as real, complex people.
- The conflict is believable and is explained both in the story events and in the flashback (paragraphs 8 and 9).

Voice

- The narration and dialogue sound natural.
- The writer's choice of words helps to express the characters' thoughts and feelings effectively.

TEKS 11.14A Write an engaging story with a well-developed conflict and resolution and complex characters; **ELPS** 1C Use strategic learning strategies to acquire basic and grade-level vocabulary

Point out to students how using certain parts of speech purposefully can improve sentence fluency. For example:

- Adverbs help show how the characters feel (her father said *softly, miserably;* Hannah eyed him *coldly*).
- Prepositions define the relationship between objects (tossed her suitcase . . . *into* the back *of* the truck; eggs sizzled *in* a skillet; affidavits clutched *under* his arm; the office was squeezed *between* a coffee shop and a souvenir shop).
- Conjunctions connect ideas (understand *and* forgive; popped her head up *and* smiled; so relaxed *and* happy).

Ask individual students to choose a sentence from the story and explain which adverbs, prepositions, or conjunctions help improve its overall meaning and fluency. Then have them alter the sentence's meaning by changing one or more of these words. **DIFFERENTIATE INSTRUCTION** ↘

✱ For information about adverbs, prepositions, and conjunctions, see SE pages 750, 752, and 754.

ankle? Or when I didn't make the volleyball team? I needed you then!"

"I know," her father said softly, miserably. "I wasn't there. But I want to be there for you now."

His voice, which had always been sharp and hurried, was softer somehow, sad and pleading, not at all as she remembered it. Hannah eyed him coldly. "You're too late. I don't need you anymore."

He flinched, and she thought, "Good." Now you know how it feels to be rejected. She turned back to the window, and they finished the ride in silence.

The next morning Hannah followed her nose out of her room toward the smell of fresh coffee. She found her father at the stove, where bacon and fried eggs sizzled in a cast-iron skillet.

"Since when do you cook?" Hannah asked, surprised.

"Since I had to," her father replied simply, setting a glass of orange juice in front of her. The only times she had seen him in the kitchen at home was late at night when he got home from work and sat down to eat some warmed-over dinner.

"Listen, I thought maybe we'd go hiking today," he said. "But I've got to go into the office for a little while first. Want to come?"

The office. She knew he couldn't have changed. It had always been work first, family second. While Hannah's mom rushed to get her fed and off to school, Hannah's dad rushed out the door in suit and tie, affidavits clutched under his arm. "All right, I guess." Hannah grabbed a book out of her backpack, figuring that once he got to work it would be a long time before they got out again.

"Let's go," he called from the door.

"Like that?" she said, surprised that he was still in his T-shirt and jeans.

"They've seen me in worse," he laughed.

"Aren't you still a lawyer?"

"Yeah, but not the same kind of lawyer as I was. People around here don't care if I wear a suit and tie, as long as I help them. And that's what I try to do."

His tiny office was squeezed between a coffee shop and a souvenir shop that boasted "genuine hand-polished native

Hannah notices a difference in her father.

Past information is given to help the reader understand Hannah's feelings.

Another complication occurs as Hannah notices another difference in her father.

Differentiated Instruction: Struggling Learners

With students, fill in a story map or outline showing the organization and structure of each part of the plot of the sample story. Then have students reread the story and afterward discuss the plot structure.

Differentiated Instruction: Advanced Learners

To explore point of view further, have students choose a section of the sample story to rewrite from the first-person point of view. Encourage them to share their new versions, and hold a discussion about the advantages of each point of view.

stones." He checked the messages on his desk, then sat down to make some calls. Hannah settled down in the small reception area near the desk of a pleasant-looking woman who was going through some papers with a highlighter. She tried to read her book, but couldn't help overhearing some of his conversation.

"Can we meet next week to settle this, Bob? My daughter's visiting—yeah, from St. Louis. Sixteen. Rough, but that's why—Thanks. Sure, Monday's fine. Thanks." He punched in another call. "Mrs. Whitefern? John Kirk. They've accepted our offer. You'll be getting a check later this week. No, thank YOU for the cactus jelly." Hannah was curious.

"Was that payment? The cactus jelly?"

The woman at the desk popped her head up and smiled. "Oh, partially. Most of our clients are pretty poor. They pay what they can, and sometimes they like to throw in a little extra to make up the difference. Your dad's always so gracious about it!" Shaking her head, she chuckled and went back to work.

Hannah had never seen her father so relaxed and happy. Before he left, he had usually been surly or silent. He hung up the phone and smiled at her.

"All done?" she asked, surprised.

"All done and ready to go hiking." He thought a moment. "We do have some big hills to climb, don't we?"

"Yes, we do," she considered this idea. "And they're pretty steep. It'll probably take a long time to reach the top."

Hannah understood exactly how high those hills were—but she also knew that every climb begins with small steps. She saw the hopeful look on his face.

"I'm willing to try," she said, and added, "Dad." She tasted the word on her tongue and found it was not bitter at all.

A secondary character is used to present new information.

The climax occurs when Hannah decides to try to get along with her father.

The resolution lets us know that Hannah has changed.

Respond to the reading Answer the following questions.

Focus and Coherence (1) What is the conflict in the story?

Organization (2) How do events in the rising action lead to the climax?

Development of Ideas (3) How does Hannah's relationship with her father develop and change?

Creative Writing

Respond to the reading

Answers

Focus and Coherence 1. Hannah, who is 16, is angry with her father for leaving their family and must resolve her feelings about him.

Organization 2. Story events are organized in chronological order, with one flashback (SE page 341) that provides background information.
✔ **DIFFERENTIATE INSTRUCTION**

Development of Ideas 3. At first, Hannah is hurt, angry, and focused on her own feelings. As she begins to listen more closely to her father and to understand his new life, she realizes that she is still important to her father and that she wants to help repair their relationship.

After students respond to the reading, have them read about point of view on SE page 348. Then ask students to identify the point of view of the narrator in the sample story (limited omniscient), and to support their choice.
- The writer uses a narrator to tell Hannah's story.
- The narrator uses third-person pronouns.
- The narrator focuses on what Hannah experiences and how she perceives her father.

✔ **DIFFERENTIATE INSTRUCTION**

Differentiated Instruction:
English Language Learners

ELPS 2D, 3B

Use page 560 of the Tools of Language to support students' use of language patterns and pages 752–753 for practice with prepositions.

ELP Level **Beginning**	**ELP Level** **Intermediate**	**ELP Level** **Advanced/Advanced High**
Write prepositions on index cards. Have partners read each card and use objects to show each meaning.	Have partners write prepositional phrases and use objects or drawings to demonstrate each meaning.	Have individuals write prepositional phrases, exchange with a partner, and show the meaning of each phrase.
Use pages 560 and 752–753.	Use pages 560 and 752–753.	Use pages 560 and 752–753.

 ELPS 2D Monitor understanding of spoken language; **3B** Expand vocabulary/learning and using high-frequency words for identifying and describing

Prewriting Planning Your Writing

Remind students that their goal is to write a story about people facing life challenges. The topic they choose may be rooted in their own experience, but it doesn't have to be. Provide students with support as needed.

Creating Characters

Emphasize to students that because they are writing short stories, they must limit their scope. Tell them to limit the number of characters to the protagonist and one or two minor characters.

Creating Conflict

Encourage students to limit the number of events in the rising action to keep things moving at a quick pace and to prevent the story from getting too drawn out. Point out that the conflict should be direct and dramatic. A complex problem may require too much explanation.

Establishing a Setting

Tell students to be selective, finding just the right setting to highlight story events.

Planning Action and Dialogue

Remind students that, in short stories in particular, every action and interaction of their characters must be focused on moving the plot action forward.

Plan your story. Encourage students to share their ideas for a well-developed plot and complex, non-stereotypical characters with other students for feedback and advice.

 TEKS 11.13A, 11.14A

Prewriting Planning Your Writing

Stories focus on people (characters) who face a problem (conflict) in a certain place and time (setting). The story shows what the people do (action) and say (dialogue) to resolve the conflict. Plan each of these elements before you begin.

Creating Characters

Your main character is called the **protagonist**. He or she should be likable—but not perfect, or there would be nothing to learn or change, and no real story. Work to create complex and non-stereotypical characters that seem real and authentic.

> Sometimes a minor character can add insight to the story. Chandra used the secretary to tell Hannah something that helped her understand her father better.

Creating Conflict

The protagonist must want something that is blocked by an obstacle—the antagonist. This obstacle creates the **conflict** that the character must overcome.

> The antagonist may be a physical barrier, an idea, or another person. Hannah's antagonist was her own hurt and anger, which kept her from forgiving her father.

Establishing a Setting

The setting might be relatively unimportant, or it might actually be the antagonist, as in a story about someone trying to find a way out of a forest. The setting can also help establish a character or a story's mood or tone.

> Use sensory details to describe the setting and help set a mood. Chandra chose a dry, barren desert setting to reflect Hannah's feelings about her father.

Planning Action and Dialogue

Let readers see what your characters are doing and hear what they are saying. Action and dialogue help you show instead of tell.

> Instead of writing that a character is angry, show the person ripping open a bag of chips. Don't tell the reader that a character yelled at his brother; let the reader hear the character shout, "Get out of my room, Henry!"

 Prewrite

Plan your story. Create characters, a conflict, and a setting that sets a mood. Plan action and dialogue to move the story along.

TEKS **11.13A** Plan a first draft by determining appropriate topics; **11.14A** Write an engaging story with well-developed conflict, resolution, and non-stereotypical characters

Mapping Your Plot

The plot is the series of events that build from exposition to climax and end in resolution. In any plot, the climax occurs when the main character confronts the conflict head-on and learns something or changes. You can map your story by creating a plot graph.

Plot Graph

				She is touched that he shows that she is more important than his work.	
			She notices he doesn't worry only about money anymore.		
		She observes that he doesn't worry about his outward appearance.			
	She is surprised that he has learned to cook.				
At first, Hannah hates her father because he left.					At the end of the story, she resolves to try to repair their relationship.

Prewrite **Create a plot graph.** Write events and discoveries that build toward the climax of your story and end in your resolution.

Using Flashbacks

Writers use flashbacks to show events that occurred at an earlier time. A flashback is a literary device that is used to show how the character got into the present situation or to contrast current events with previous ones.

In the sample story, Chandra used a flashback to show how Hannah ended up in the truck with her father. Another flashback showed how her father had left Hannah and her mother earlier.

> At the airport, he had tossed her suitcase and backpack into the back of the truck, as carelessly as he had tossed her from his life nearly a year ago. That was when he had left her and her mother to "find himself" in this sagebrush and saguaro wasteland. And now he expected her to forget all the hurt!

Later on, flashbacks help show how Hannah's father has changed.

Prewrite **Plan flashbacks.** Review your plot graph, looking for places in which flashbacks might provide context for your story.

Creative Writing

Mapping Your Plot

Have students compare the plot graph on this page and the plot line on SE page 340, reviewing the definition of each part. Guide them to understand that

- the first box of the graph corresponds to the exposition and describes the conflict;
- boxes 2–4 describe events that make up the rising action;
- box 5, the highest point on the graph, is the moment of truth, the climax; and
- box 6 describes the resolution.

✔ DIFFERENTIATE INSTRUCTION

Create a plot graph. Suggest that students use note cards to make their plot graphs, writing one item on each card, with as much detail as they like. Then students can arrange and rearrange the cards until they have them the order they think works best. ✔ DIFFERENTIATE INSTRUCTION

Using Flashbacks

Explain that literary devices and strategies such as flashbacks can provide necessary information that moves a plot forward, even though the reference is to past events. The information writers provide in flashbacks gives readers context for what is happening in the present; a story doesn't have to start "at the beginning" of the characters' lives for readers to understand who the characters have become in the present.

Plan flashbacks. Remind students that any flashbacks they decide to use should be written on note cards and added to their plot graphs where appropriate. ✔ DIFFERENTIATE INSTRUCTION

★ TEKS 11.13A, 11.14A

TEKS **11.13A** Plan a first draft by determining appropriate topics; **11.14A** Write an engaging story with a range of literary strategies and devices; **ELPS** **1F** Use accessible language and learn new and essential language in the process; **3B** Expand vocabulary/learning and using high-frequency words for identifying and describing, retelling simple stories and basic information

Drafting Creating Your First Draft

Discuss ways students can create an engaging story from beginning to end.

Starting Strong

Explain that natural and energetic dialogue is one strong way to begin a story. Dashes and ellipsis points are two ways to indicate natural, meaningful pauses in dialogue.

A dash can speed up the action and increase the tension. It indicates a sharp break, as follows:

■ A character interrupts the speaker:
"Sarah, I want to tell you—"
"That you're sorry?"

■ The speaker has a sudden realization: "I'll go look for Jordan—oh, wait, here he is."

An ellipsis slows dialogue by indicating a long pause or a fade to silence. It often suggests uncertainty or sadness.

■ uncertainty: "Is that . . . Jordan?"

■ sadness: "Oh, Sarah, I really am sorry . . ."

✳ For information about using dashes and ellipsis points, see SE pages 668 and 670.

Building the Action

Talk with students about how the strategies suggested help to create rising action and show how their characters change throughout the story. Remind them that including details and dialogue can get the reader involved in the story.

Bringing the Story to a Close

Discuss how an effective closing helps readers feel a sense of satisfaction.

Write your first draft. Students may want to add more detail to their note cards as they write; this will help them keep track of ideas they have used and ideas they might want to consider when they revise their drafts.

Drafting Creating Your First Draft

Every story has a beginning, a middle, and an ending. Follow these guidelines as you develop each part of your story.

Starting Strong

Use one of the following strategies to capture your reader's attention and get your story started. (Chandra used strong imagery.)

■ **Begin with dialogue.**
"He's not running away from us, Hannah," Mom had said sadly. "He's running toward something, and we just can't go with him."

■ **Begin with action.**
Hannah's father carelessly tossed her suitcase and backpack into the back of his truck, as carelessly as he had tossed her from his life nearly a year ago.

■ **Use strong imagery to set a mood.**
Hannah watched the desert glide by the truck window. Her father drove silently, his fingers beating a little pattern on the wheel to the rhythm of the music from the CD player. *His* music. *His* truck. *His* home.

After capturing the reader's attention, get your story underway by introducing the characters, setting, and conflict.

Building the Action

Increase the seriousness of the problem, leading the protagonist toward a direct confrontation with the conflict. Follow these tips:

■ Use **action** that shows what the protagonist is experiencing.
■ Use devices like **flashbacks** to help provide conflict.
■ Use **natural-sounding dialogue** to help establish and develop realistic, complex characters.
■ Include **sensory details,** allowing the reader to participate in the story.

Bringing the Story to a Close

Show how the character is changed by the climax. Then, in the falling action and resolution, indicate how life will be different.

 Draft

Write your first draft. Use your planning from page 344 and the information above as a general guide to your writing.

Revising Improving Your Writing

Revise your writing. Use the following checklist to guide your revision. Make changes until you can answer every question "yes."

Revising Checklist

Focus and Coherence

_____ **1.** Does my exposition introduce the main characters and the conflict?

_____ **2.** Do all of the events relate to the story's conflict?

_____ **3.** Does my resolution make the story complete?

Organization

_____ **4.** Does my story include exposition, rising action, crisis, climax, and resolution?

_____ **5.** Do I use flashbacks that help provide context?

Development of Ideas

_____ **6.** Do I present my characters as real and complex individuals?

_____ **7.** Does my main character undergo a change?

_____ **8.** Do I include a setting that establishes a mood?

Voice

_____ **9.** Does my dialogue sound natural?

Editing Checking for Conventions

Edit your writing. When you edit, check your grammar, sentence structure, mechanics (capitalization and punctuation), and spelling.

Editing Checklist

Conventions

_____ **1.** Have I used commas after introductory word groups and in series?

_____ **2.** Have I correctly punctuated dialogue?

Creative Writing

Differentiated Instruction: English Language Learners

ELPS 2E, 5B

ELP Level **Beginning**	ELP Level **Intermediate**	ELP Level **Advanced/Advanced High**
• Guide students through each checklist. • Have students show how they will check their work using the checklists and editing marks.	• Have partners or small groups show and explain how to use the checklists. • Have partners do the same with the chart of editing and proofreading marks.	• Have students explain how they will use each checklist. • Ask them what items, if any, they might add to a personal checklist.
Use pages 632–633.	Use pages 632–633.	Use pages 632–633.

Revising Improving Your Writing

Before students begin their revisions, ask them to review the sample story on SE pages 341–343 and find examples where the writer uses details to *show* instead of *tell*. Possible responses include:

- The opening shows Hannah's feelings without saying she's angry. She sits *sullenly*, and the repetition of *his*, in her thoughts, reveals her resentment (SE page 341).
- The fact that Hannah's father cooks is revealed by describing the kitchen smells (SE page 342).
- The work Hannah's father does is revealed in conversations with clients (SE page 343).

Revise your writing. As students revise, remind them that it is more effective to *show* what's happening rather than *tell* readers about it.
TEKS 11.13C

Revising Checklist
Suggest that students check their entire story for one trait at a time.

Editing Checking for Conventions
Edit your writing. After students have checked their own work for conventions errors, have them exchange papers with a partner.
✔ DIFFERENTIATE INSTRUCTION
TEKS 11.13D

Editing Checklist
Suggest that students address each question by checking their entire response before moving on to the next question.

★ Conventions Connections

Mechanics: Punctuating Dialogue
- ***Student Edition: Proofreader's Guide*** pages 646(+), 660(+)

✎ ***Write Source Online* GrammarSnap**

Grammar: Prepositions, Conjunctions, Interjections
- ***Student Edition: Proofreader's Guide*** pages 752–753, 754(+)
- ***SkillsBook*** pages 115, 116, 117

TEKS 11.13C Revise drafts to clarify meaning and achieve specific rhetorical purposes, consistency of tone, and logical organization; **11.13D** Edit drafts for grammar, mechanics, and spelling; **ELPS 2E** Use visual, contextual, and linguistic support to enhance and confirm understanding of spoken language; **5B** Write using newly acquired basic and content-based grade-level vocabulary

Elements of Fiction

Encourage students to learn the terms on the page and to make them a part of their working vocabulary related to writing. Point out to students that becoming familiar with the elements of fiction can help them analyze, appreciate, and understand movies, narrative poetry, and plays, as well as stories they read.

Ask students to think about a book or short story they've recently read as a class (or a movie that students have seen). Have them work together in pairs or small groups to describe each of its elements, using the terms shown here. Then have the whole class discuss it together. **ELPS** 1E, 1F, 2C, 3D

Note that as with other types of writing, the 5 W and H questions can be applied to short stories. Ask students to identify how the questions correspond to the story elements (some might correspond to more than one element). For example:

- Who—protagonist, antagonist, narrator, character
- What—conflict, rising action, plot, climax
- When, where—setting
- Why—theme
- How—point of view, tone

To help students express themselves clearly when talking and thinking about writing, make a point of using these and other specialized terms frequently in class discussions.

DIFFERENTIATE INSTRUCTION ↘

✳ For more literary terminology, see SE pages 626–631.

348

Elements of Fiction

Antagonist	The person or force that works against the hero of the story (See *protagonist*.)
Character	A person or an animal in a story
Climax	The moment of change when the protagonist either succeeds or fails and is somehow changed by the action
Conflict	A problem or clash between two forces in a story ■ **Person vs. person** A problem between characters ■ **Person vs. self** A problem within a character's own mind ■ **Person vs. society** A problem between a character and society, the law, or some tradition ■ **Person vs. nature** A problem with an element of nature, such as a blizzard or a hurricane ■ **Person vs. destiny** A problem or struggle that appears to be beyond a character's control
Mood	The feeling that is aroused in a reader (such as happiness, anger, bitterness, hopefulness) by the story's setting, characters, or events
Narrator	The person or character who tells the story, gives background information, and fills in details between dialogue
Plot, Plot Line	See page **340**.
Point of View	The angle from which a story is told ■ In **first-person point of view,** one character is telling the story. ■ In **third-person point of view,** someone outside the story, a narrator, is telling it.
Protagonist	The main character or hero in a story (See *antagonist*.)
Rising Action	A series of events that propel the protagonist toward the climax
Setting	The place and time period in which a story takes place
Theme	The author's message about life or human nature
Tone	The writer's attitude toward his or her subject (*angry, humorous,* and so on)

Differentiated Instruction: English Language Learners

ELPS 1E, 1F, 2C, 3D

ELP Level **Beginning**	ELP Level **Intermediate**	ELP Level **Advanced/Advanced High**
• Use visuals and gestures whenever possible to explain the terms. • Have students repeat each term after you.	• Use visuals and gestures as needed to explain the terms. • Provide sentence stems for students to demonstrate understanding.	• Have partners discuss the terms. • Ask them to work together to annotate a plot graphic like the one shown on page 340 to show how the terms are connected.

ELPS 1E Internalize new academic language by using and reusing it/speaking; **1F** Use accessible language and learn new and essential language in the process; **2C** Learn new academic vocabulary; **3D** Speak using grade-level content area vocabulary in context/ new English words and academic language

Writing Plays

Most writers work alone, getting help from a peer only during revising or editing. However, playwrights create works that are truly collaborative. In a sense, a play is not a play until actors perform it in front of an audience.

Plays engage sight and sound, creating the illusion that real events are unfolding before the viewers. Sets, props, lighting, and sound help playwrights transport their audiences across space and time.

This powerful medium has been used for centuries to explore broad themes about the nature of humanity and to address social problems such as racism or injustice. In this chapter, you will read a brief play about a student faced with the prospect of cheating to help a friend. Then, following the guidelines, you'll write your own play about a person facing a dilemma.

Writing Guidelines

Subject:	**Facing a personal dilemma**
Purpose:	**To entertain and enlighten**
Form:	**Brief play**
Audience:	**Classmates**

"The play's the thing wherein I'll catch the conscience of the king."

—William Shakespeare

Resources

Copy Masters

- T-chart (TE p. 354)

Objectives

- understand the content and structure of a play, including stage directions and stage terminology
- choose a topic (a personal dilemma) to write about
- plan, draft, revise, and edit a play
- write an ad script for a commercial

Ask students to share their experiences related to a theatrical performance.

- What element was most memorable (acting, costumes, sets, lighting, sound, musical score, the story itself)?
- How was the theme conveyed?
- Afterward, were you more or less likely to attend or read another play by the same playwright, or read about the playwright?

Invite students to talk about their experiences as audience members. Ask them to briefly describe the plays and tell how they affected them. Were they transported into the world that the playwright imagined? If so, how do they think this was achieved?

ELPS 1A

Note that the noun *playwright* is sometimes misspelled as *playwrite*. Have students look up *wright* (a skilled maker or manufacturer of something). Together discuss the spelling and meaning of each word, explaining that a *playwright* is a practitioner of *playwriting*.

Sample Play

Point out that a play includes the same elements of fiction as those listed on SE page 348, with the exception of elements related to narration. Ask students to identify the applicable elements in the sample play. **DIFFERENTIATE INSTRUCTION**

- Setting: classroom
- Protagonist: Missy
- Antagonist: Cali
- Characters: James, Steve, Mr. Day, unnamed students
- Conflict (person vs. person): Cali wants Missy to help her cheat on a test, but Missy refuses.
- Rising Action: Cali tries to persuade Missy; Steve tries to support Missy; Cali flirts with Steve to try to win his support; Missy gives Cali a paper during the test; the teacher accuses the girls of cheating.
- Climax: Missy reveals the trick she played.
- Theme: It is wrong to cheat on tests.
- Tone: Realistic

ELPS 1E

Sample Play

In the following play by student writer Jamie Lin, Missy faces the problem of "helping" a friend on a test. The side notes identify key points in the development of the play.

The Test

Characters:
Missy, a high school student
Cali, Missy's self-absorbed friend
Steve, Missy's friend
James, Cali's friend
Mr. Day, their social studies teacher
Other students in the class

Scene 1

Stage Directions The opening scene is described.

(The curtain rises on a classroom with desks arranged in rows. A teacher's desk is set at an angle stage left, where Mr. Day is seated grading papers. A bell rings, and students start to file in and take their places, chatting about the day. James, Missy, Cali, and Steve come in and take their places, in that order, in the front row.)

MR. DAY: Okay, everyone, we'll start the test as soon as the bell rings.

CALI: Oh no! Missy, I forgot all about the test!

MISSY: Cali, I reminded you about it yesterday.

Beginning The characters are introduced and the problem is presented.

CALI: Hey, who listens? I've been *totally* thinking about the pom routine we're doing for homecoming.

MISSY: Well, you are *totally* out of luck now!

CALI: Listen, no problem. You can just kind of slip me your pages as you finish.

MISSY: You want to *copy* mine?

JAMES: What's the dif?

Background information is given.

MISSY: Who asked you, James?

CALI: If I mess up my grade in here, I won't be on the pom squad.

MISSY: Not my problem.

JAMES: Come on, Missy, be a bud.

STEVE: Hang in there, Missy. Don't let them bully you.

JAMES: *(Sneering)* Listen to Mr. Good Guy.

STEVE: Yeah? Well, maybe I'll just let Mr. Day know about your little plan.

Middle Complications are introduced as rising action.

CALI: Steve, you are such a jer—*(A thought hits her, and she is suddenly very cute.)* Aw, come on,

ELPS 1E Internalize new basic and academic language by using and reusing it/speaking

Stevey. Be a good sport. Hey, have you got a date for the homecoming dance yet?

STEVE: *(Taken off guard)* Uh—no, but—*(Looking at Missy)*

CALI: How would you like to go with me? Hmmm?

STEVE: *(Flustered)* Well, I mean, sure, but . . .

CALI: Just keep quiet about this little—um—arrangement, and you can go out with a homecoming queen.

STEVE: Uh—sure.

(Cali flashes him a megawatt smile and then turns and exchanges glances with James. Missy looks at Steve, disgusted. The bell rings.)

MR. DAY: All right, everyone, everything off your desks.

(He hands a pile of papers to a student in the back, who takes a packet and passes it on, moving the papers around the class.)

CALI: *(Whispering to Missy)* So, you in?

MISSY: *(Taking her test papers)* Just shut up.

(The students begin writing, and Mr. Day stands at his desk for a moment, then goes to sit down. The lights go down.)

Scene 2

(The lights come up again. Mr. Day is seated at his desk, working on some papers, and the class is frantically writing. Cali looks up, glances at Mr. Day, and then nudges Missy, who ignores her. Cali nudges her harder, and Missy passes a paper over to her. James notices and grins. Steve glances over at the action and scowls. The lights go down.)

Scene 3

(The lights come up. It is the end of the class. The bell rings.)

MR. DAY: All right, everyone, hand in your papers.

(There are some groans. Students begin filing out, handing in their papers as they go.)

MR. DAY: Oh, Missy and Cali, would you two please stay after class a moment?

(James shakes his head with a laugh, and Steve gives the girls a sympathetic look.)

CALI: Uh-oh. He knows!

MISSY: *(Feigning innocence)* What do you mean?

Different scenes are used to allow for the passing of time.

Creative Writing

Ask students to examine the sample play and point out the special formatting used for play scripts.

- The characters are listed and briefly described at the beginning.
- Stage directions—descriptions of the setting, characters' actions, lighting directions, or other instructions—are enclosed in parentheses and set in italics.
- Each scene begins with a paragraph of stage directions that describes the setting.
- The scene is indicated by the words *Scene X*, set in bold type and centered.
- Stage directions are also placed in the middle of dialogue, if necessary. These directions do not have end punctuation.
- Each speaker's name is given in all capital letters. A colon separates the speaker's name from his or her dialogue.

Have students read aloud the first scene of the play. Ask them to pay particular attention to the stage directions, including those that describe how certain characters are meant to speak their lines—the emotions, intonation, and informal language of the characters. Encourage students to experiment with their speaking voices to create just the right effects for the scene. Continue with the rest of the play as time permits.

⭐ **ELPS** 1B, 2A, 3A

Differentiated Instruction: English Language Learners

⭐ **ELPS** 4D

Before reading the sample play, turn to the Tools of Language for additional language support and/or review.

ELP Level **Beginning**	ELP Level **Intermediate**	ELP Level **Advanced/Advanced High**
• Display a generic plot-line diagram. • As you read the play aloud, have students use the diagram to identify each plot stage.	• Have pairs or small groups review plot terms together. • Then help students use the side notes as they read the play together.	• Have students create a generic plot-line diagram. • As they read the play individually, have them identify each plot stage.
Use pages 592–593.	Use pages 592–593.	Use pages 592–593.

⭐ **ELPS 1B** Monitor oral language production and employ self-corrective techniques or other resources; **2A** Distinguish intonation patterns of English; **3A** Practice producing sounds of newly acquired vocabulary to pronounce English words; **4D** Use prereading supports to enhance comprehension of written text

Respond to the reading

Answers

Organization 1. The three separate scenes indicate the passage of time; the scenes divide the play into action that takes place before, during, and after the test.

Development of Ideas 2. Cali wants to copy Missy's test, but Missy doesn't want to cheat.

Voice 3. The writer uses realistic-sounding sentence fragments and pauses and chooses words that help express the characters' personalities. Examples include the following:
- MISSY: Well, you are *totally* out of luck now.
- MISSY: Who asked you, James?
- MISSY: Not my problem.
- CALI: Steve, you are such a jer—

Discuss with students why the use of sentence fragments sounds natural in this play. Talk with them about the difference between formal and informal English, and ask them to identify uses of both informal and formal English in the play. Have them explain why each use sounds natural and makes the play realistic and believable.

DIFFERENTIATE INSTRUCTION ↘

⭐ **ELPS** 1G

MR. DAY:	You girls know the school policy about cheating. I'm going to have to report you.
MISSY:	For what?
MR. DAY:	Missy, I saw you pass that paper to Cali.
MISSY:	I did give her a paper, but I didn't pass her any answers.
MR. DAY:	Give me that paper, Cali. *(Reading and looking confused.)* For the question, "Whose faces are on Mt. Rushmore?" you wrote, David Crosby, Stephen Stills, Graham Nash, and Neil Young."
MISSY:	*(Smiles)* I took two tests and answered one just as a joke to ease my nerves. Here's my real test.

(She hands him the other paper.)

CALI: A joke?

(Mr. Day takes it from her and reads it.)

MR. DAY: I don't think Cali realized it was a joke. Well, Missy, I'm not sure how to handle this one, but it certainly doesn't look like you were trying to help Cali, so I won't turn you in.

MISSY: Thank you.

MR. DAY: As for you, Cali, it looks like your failing grade will be punishment enough!

CALI: *(Turning toward Missy)* You rat!

(Cali starts to stomp out, but is stopped by Steve.)

STEVE: We're still on for homecoming, right, Cali?

(Cali just stares at him, makes a little screech, and goes out.)

STEVE: Guess not.

MISSY: Come on, Steve, let's get to class. Maybe I'll go to homecoming with you if you don't think you'll be cheating on Cali!

(They go out. The lights go down.)

Climax
The problem is solved.

Falling Action
Results of the action are given.

Resolution
Two characters set a new course of action.

Respond to the reading. Answer the following questions about the play.

Organization (1) What is the purpose of having three separate scenes?

Development of Ideas (2) What is the problem Missy faces?

Voice (3) How does the writer make the dialogue sound realistic? Give three examples.

ELPS 1G Demonstrate ability to distinguish between formal and informal English and knowledge of when to use formal and informal English

Prewriting Creating a Protagonist

Your first step in writing a play is choosing a main character or protagonist, a word that means literally "first contender." Your protagonist can be very much like you *(a high school student)* or very different *(a nursing-home resident),* likeable *(a friendly aunt)* or dislikable *(Scrooge).* One way to quickly develop a protagonist is to create a character grid.

Character Grid

Gender	Age	Strength	Weakness	Name
female	6	imagination	afraid of dogs	Amelia
male	73	singing	loneliness	Chester
female	17	"A" student	peer pressure	Missy*

Prewrite

Create a character grid. Write "gender, "age," and so forth across the top. Beneath each heading, list vital statistics for four characters and give each a name. Put an asterisk (*) next to the character you'd like to write about.

Choosing a Theme and Conflict

You will need to choose one of five basic types of conflict. Will your character face a problem with himself or herself, with another person, with society, with an element of nature, or with destiny? In the sample play, Missy has a conflict with her friend, Cali, who pressures her to pass answers on a test.

To help you make this decision, think about the theme, or larger message, that you would like to convey. What idea do you want your audience to appreciate or think about? Will your play have an explicit or implicit theme? An explicit theme is stated directly in a script. An implicit theme is not spelled out directly, but is an idea that can be "read between the lines." Jamie Lin decided on an implicit theme to show that people can remain true to themselves and successfully resist peer pressure.

Once you are clear about a theme, and whether you will approach it explicitly or implicitly, you can decide on the type of conflict that will best test your main character's strengths and weaknesses.

Prewrite

Determine the conflict and theme. Decide which of the five basic types of conflict would best test your character. Write down your theme and the specific conflict the protagonist will have to overcome. (Tip: Use a character grid to generate an antagonist and other characters for your play.)

Creative Writing

Prewriting Creating a Protagonist

Tell students that they don't necessarily have to plan their play in the sequence described here. If they already have an idea for one or more of the elements (character, conflict, tone, or setting), they should write down any details they've worked out and use these details as starting points for developing the elements.

Character Grid

Suggest that students insert another column in their character grid called *Other* to allow them to include any personality-defining details that occur to them, such as

- information about the character's family,
- his or her favorite book or musician,
- how the character dresses, or
- other defining characteristics.

⭐ **ELPS** 1C

Create a character grid. If students have a particular setting or conflict in mind, remind them to think about choosing characters who will fit well into that setting or conflict.

Choosing a Theme and Conflict

Suggest that students spend a few minutes imagining the protagonist they have chosen. What likely conflicts could the character become involved in? Have students spend 5 or 10 minutes freewriting about this question to see if it yields usable ideas that would suggest the theme they want to convey.

⭐ **TEKS** 11.14C

Determine the conflict and theme. Suggest that students list the five basic types of conflict and then see which of these their characters might fit with best.

Differentiated Instruction:
English Language Learners ⭐ **ELPS** 2C, 2D

Use the Tools of Language to support students as they monitor their understanding of spoken language.

ELP Level **Beginning**	ELP Level **Intermediate**	ELP Level **Advanced/Advanced High**
Read Scene 3 aloud. Ask students to raise a hand when they hear a sentence fragment. Discuss why this technique works well here.	Read Scene 1 and/or 3 aloud. Guide students to explain each dialogue technique used and to tell why it works well here.	Have students read Scenes 1 and/or 3 aloud. Ask them to explain each dialogue technique and to tell why it works well here.
Use pages 560–561.	Use pages 560–561.	Use pages 560–561.

⭐ **TEKS** **11.14C** Write a script with an explicit or implicit theme, using a variety of literary techniques; **ELPS** **1C** use strategic learning techniques to acquire basic and grade-level vocabulary; **2C** Learn new language structures; **2D** Monitor understanding of spoken language and seek clarification as needed

Prewriting Deciding on a Tone

If students are interested in using a satirical tone in their writing, discuss satire a little further with them.

- Note that satire is intended as humorous exaggeration, often by treating a situation with less seriousness than might occur in real life.
- Because satire uses humor to make its point, it can be comedic.

If some students plan to write in this genre to convey their theme, advise them to read several short satires and discuss them with each other and with you before attempting their own.

 TEKS 11.14C

Choose a tone. Students may find that they are ambivalent about their character or conflict. If so, suggest that perhaps they should revise one or both to create stronger tension in their story.

DIFFERENTIATE INSTRUCTION ↘

Selecting a Setting

If students have difficulty listing or choosing settings for their plays, suggest that they

- Brainstorm with a partner or small group to come up with some ideas;
- Think carefully about the tone of the play and choose settings that support that tone.

Setting T-Graph

Suggest that students connect the places and times of day on their T-graph (using leader lines) to help strengthen the sense of where and when the action will unfold.

Select a setting. Students may want to add a column to their T-graph to list more details.

 TEKS 11.14C

Prewriting Deciding on a Tone

The tone of your play reflects your feelings about the character and conflict. Any adjective that describes emotions can also describe tone:

joyful	smug	petulant	serious	paranoid	capricious
angry	hopeful	giddy	annoyed	patient	resigned

Most often, the tone of a play should express your true feelings about the character and the conflict. However, sometimes playwrights adopt a satirical tone—using an opposite feeling than the one they truly have. For example, if characters break into song about the fun of appendicitis, the playwright is being satirical.

Prewrite
Choose a tone. Ask yourself "How do I feel about this character and conflict?" Write down three adjectives that describe your feeling. Choose one to represent your tone—or choose an opposite feeling for a satirical tone.

Selecting a Setting

The setting is the place and time of the play. You may have two or three locations, each one suggesting a different time in the action, or you could focus the action in one main location. Setting can also be used to support the theme, such as a subway station for a character who has to make choices. To decide on the setting for her play, Jamie created a T-graph listing places and times.

Setting T-Graph

Settings	
Places	Times
the football field	during poms practice
the hallway	before the test*
the history classroom*	during the test*
Missy's locker	after the test*

Prewrite
Select a setting. Make a T-graph, listing places and times where your character could deal with the conflict. Then choose one or more locations and times. Think about how to suggest the settings with furniture, props, and lighting.

Differentiated Instruction: Struggling Learners

Remind students that *tone* can be conveyed in very subtle ways. If the overall tone of a play is joyful, for example, colorful scenery or bright lighting support the feeling. Also, the individual characters may add to the play's tone.

For example, a protagonist may present a straightforward attitude toward the conflict (like Missy), whereas the antagonist may be manipulative (like Cali), creating a tone of discord.

 TEKS 11.14C Write a script with an explicit or implicit theme, using a variety of literary techniques

Mapping Your Plot

A play generally follows the standard plot line, shown below. The beginning introduces the characters and setting and initiates the conflict. The middle builds tension to a climax in which the protagonist faces the conflict head-on. The ending resolves the conflict one way or another. Jamie used a plot chart to map out her play. She also divided the action into scenes.

Plot Chart

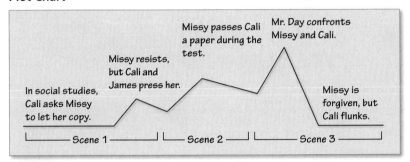

In social studies, Cali asks Missy to let her copy.

Missy resists, but Cali and James press her.

Missy passes Cali a paper during the test.

Mr. Day confronts Missy and Cali.

Missy is forgiven, but Cali flunks.

— Scene 1 —   — Scene 2 —   — Scene 3 —

Prewrite

Map your plot. Create a plot chart like the one above. Introduce the characters and situation, start the conflict, build tension to a climax, and resolve the conflict. If possible, also divide up the action into at least two scenes.

Learning Stage Terminology

As you write stage directions, use stage shorthand to indicate the acting areas.

Stage Diagram

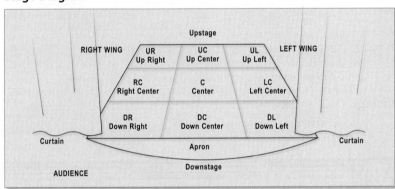

Upstage

RIGHT WING   UR Up Right   UC Up Center   UL Up Left   LEFT WING

RC Right Center   C Center   LC Left Center

DR Down Right   DC Down Center   DL Down Left

Curtain   Apron   Curtain

AUDIENCE   Downstage

Creative Writing

Mapping Your Plot

Discuss various ideas to consider when dividing the action into scenes.

- A scene is like a chapter in a book; it can show the passage of time or take the audience to a different character or place.
- A scene change can create suspense by building up to an important event and ending just before the event occurs. The audience must wait to learn the outcome.
- A scene change can also deal with an event that's too complicated to show onstage. The event can happen offstage, and the next scene can show the characters' reactions.
- Shifting from one location to another can provide a new angle on the characters (many behave differently in different circumstances) and help to convey the theme.

 ★ TEKS 11.14C

Plot Chart

Have students discuss Jamie's plot chart and how it connects to the scene breaks. Ask students whether the scene breaks are effective or not.

Map your plot. Encourage students to consult each other as they plot their plays.

Learning Stage Terminology

Guide students to connect each stage area to its abbreviation, as shown in the diagram.

Stage Diagram

Point out that the stage areas are named from the point of view of the actors, not the audience. This is because the stage directions are written for the actors, and the actors face the audience.

Encourage students to visualize the costumes, sets, and actors' movements on the stage. To help students see the relationship between the plot and the visual and spatial effects of a play, read a scene from a well-known play and then show students a videotape of it. ✔ DIFFERENTIATE INSTRUCTION

Differentiated Instruction: English Language Learners
★ ELPS 1C

ELP Level **Beginning**	ELP Level **Intermediate**	ELP Level **Advanced/Advanced High**
Provide blank stage diagrams. Have small groups name each stage area. Guide them to fill in the terms and abbreviations.	Provide blank stage diagrams. Have small groups fill in the terms and abbreviations. Then have them give each other stage directions to act out.	Have students compare and contrast *scenes* with a standard plot line. Then have them create a plot graph, with scenes, for a short video they know well.

TEKS **11.14C** Write a script with an explicit or implicit theme, using a variety of literary techniques; **ELPS** **1C** Use strategic learning strategies to acquire basic and grade-level vocabulary

Drafting Creating Your First Draft

Point out that writing a play involves weaving together two types of writing that have different purposes. Remind students to use narrative voice to write realistic, natural-sounding dialogue, and to use an expository voice for stage directions.

Writing Stage Directions

Ask students to compare the specific and general stage directions shown. Point out that even though the "general" stage direction leaves more choices up to the director, it still uses specific language to guide him or her. Ask students to analyze the specific language in the General Stage Direction. Possible responses:

- The name of the family is mentioned.
- The setting is one room.
- The living room is creatively described so the set can be easily produced.

Provide examples of stage directions written by well-known playwrights as models for students. Examples include George Bernard Shaw, Samuel Beckett, Anton Chekhov, Lillian Hellman, Henrik Ibsen, Eugene O'Neill, and Tennessee Williams.

Developing the Three Main Parts

Point out that playwrights often use sensory details convey their theme and to enhance the experience for the audience. In addition to audio and visual effects, a play can include smells (if, for example, someone snuffs out a candle). Ask students to consider, as they write their drafts, how audiences will experience the action through their senses.

⭐ **TEKS** 11.14C

✱ For more about sensory details, see SE page 81.

Draft your play. Remind students to review this page carefully before and as they write.

Drafting Creating Your First Draft

Follow the guidelines below as you develop your play.

Writing Stage Directions

Some playwrights describe the exact placement of every piece of furniture and prop. Others present general ideas, giving directors complete freedom.

Specific Stage Direction

> *(The scene is the Howells' living room. A worn, stained green love seat is set stage right at an angle. A ratty, multi-colored throw has been tossed carelessly across its back. An orange-plaid wingback chair with torn cushions is set stage center.)*

General Stage Direction

> *(The general wear of the Harris' living room creates an aura of a stuffed animal that has been handed down generation after generation.)*

Developing the Three Main Parts

Beginning

1. **Give your opening stage directions.** Set the scene with any information that you feel is necessary. (See above.)
2. **Introduce your characters and conflict.** Include any background information necessary for the audience to understand how the characters got to the opening point.
3. **Start in the middle of the action.** The reader should immediately understand what the conflict is.

Middle

4. **Use dialogue and action to move the play along.** Include complications (difficulties) to add suspense.
5. **Divide your play into scenes.** Use scenes to condense time.
6. **Present the climax.** Make the protagonist face the conflict head-on.

Ending

7. **Resolve your action.** Show the results of the climax.
8. **End your play.** Close with a final exchange of dialogue.

Draft your play. Draft your play, using your prewriting as a guide. Include at least two scenes. Add any new ideas that come to you as you write.

Writing Plays **357**

Revising Improving Your Writing

Revise your writing. Read your play out loud or have someone read it to you. Change any lines that sound forced. Use these questions as a revising guide.

Revising Checklist

Focus and Coherence

_____ **1.** Is the conflict in my play clear?

_____ **2.** Is my theme clear? Is the theme explicit or implicit?

Organization

_____ **3.** Does my play build to a climax?

_____ **4.** Do my stage directions clearly explain the action?

Development of Ideas

_____ **5.** Have I created tension and suspense?

_____ **6.** Do the characters seem real?

Voice

_____ **7.** Does the dialogue sound natural?

_____ **8.** Does the tone help convey my ideas?

Editing Checking for Conventions

Edit your writing. Use the following checklist as a guide when you check your play for proper formatting and for conventions.

Editing Checklist

Conventions

_____ **1.** Does the play follow correct script form?

_____ **2.** Have I checked for punctuation and capitalization?

_____ **3.** Have I checked for spelling errors?

Creative Writing

Differentiated Instruction: English Language Learners

ELPS 5B, 5F

ELP Level **Beginning**	ELP Level **Intermediate**	ELP Level **Advanced/Advanced High**
• Choose a short scene from among students' drafts. • Work together to revise dialogue and stage directions, using a variety of sentence lengths and patterns.	• Ask small groups to choose one scene from among their drafts. • Have each group revise the scene, using a variety of sentence lengths and patterns.	• Pair each student with an English proficient student. • Partners revise one scene from each of their drafts, using a variety of sentence lengths and patterns.

Revising Improving Your Writing

Have small groups choose parts and read all the scripts aloud. Playwrights should listen carefully and take notes. After each reading, groups can give feedback on whether the dialogue improves the overall formal or informal tone and direction of the play.

ELPS 1B, 1G, 1H, 2A

Revise your writing. Suggest that students focus on one trait at a time as they revise their drafts

✔ DIFFERENTIATE INSTRUCTION

TEKS 11.14C

Editing Checking for Conventions

Remind students that using correct punctuation helps actors understand how the lines should sound. (Actors will add their own interpretation and emphasis to the lines.) Review punctuation rules that are essential. Students should . . .

■ use exclamation marks to show strong emotion,

■ use commas to set off interjections, and

■ use commas for direct address.

ELPS 1B, 1H, 2A

Edit your writing. Suggest that students exchange drafts with a partner for a second review.

✱ For information on publishing, see SE pages 128–129.

Conventions Connections

Mechanics: Punctuating Dialogue

• **Student Edition: Proofreader's Guide** pages 646 (+), 660 (+)

⚡ **Write Source Online** *GrammarSnap*

Mechanics: Commas

• **Student Edition: Proofreader's Guide** pages 644 (+), 646–647

• **SkillsBook** page 16

⚡ **Write Source Online** *GrammarSnap*

TEKS 11.14C Write a script with an explicit or implicit theme, using a variety of literary techniques; **ELPS 1B** Monitor oral and written language production; **1G** Demonstrate ability to distinguish between formal and informal English; **1H** Develop and expand repertoire of learning strategies; **2A** Distinguish intonation patterns of English; **5B** Write using newly acquired basic and content-based grade-level vocabulary; **5F** Write using a variety of grade-appropriate sentence lengths and sentence patterns

Writing an Advertising Script

Ask students to describe and discuss some of their favorite, memorable advertisements. Help them discover how each ad achieves its purpose. Use these questions.

- How does the ad attract your attention?
- What does the ad say about why you need the product or service it sells?
- How does the ad convince you to keep buying the product or service?

Encourage students to write down some of these techniques in their writer's notebook.

DIFFERENTIATE INSTRUCTION ⌄

⭐ **ELPS** 1H

Explicit and Implicit Themes in Advertising

Discuss the difference between explicit and implicit themes. Ask students to sort the advertisements discussed earlier into those with explicit and those with implicit themes. Discuss which ones students think work best and why.

⭐ **TEKS** 11.14C

Select a theme for your advertising script.

As students begin choosing their imaginary products or services, remind them to think about what features of their creation will make it a good subject for a strong advertisement. Encourage them to decide whether they will use an explicit or implicit theme as part of their ad campaign.

⭐ **TEKS** 11.14C

Writing an Advertising Script

"Be a part of it!" "Say goodbye to your worries!" "You can do it, too!" Advertisements are everywhere, and they can influence how we think, act, and behave. The purpose of an advertisement is to sell you a product, whether it's a type of jeans, a brand of shampoo, a vacation package, or a particular university or college.

An advertisement script is carefully developed to make a product appealing to its intended audience. Every advertisement you see, whether it is on television, in print media, on the radio, or on the Internet, carries a particular message in hopes of attracting your attention to a specific product. The aims of an advertisement are to attract your attention, show you why you need the product or service, and convince you to keep "buying" that product or service, whatever it might be.

Explicit and Implicit Themes in Advertising

Advertisements may use explicit or implicit themes. Some television commercials state their message directly, such as "Dazzle will brighten your smile!" An advertisement that uses an explicit theme is forthright about why you should buy a specific product or service.

Other commercials employ implicit themes, which means that they are not stated directly. Implicit themes in advertisements and commercials appeal to basic human desires, such as wanting to belong to an "exclusive" group or improving some part of our appearances, personalities, or lives.

Many commercials use both explicit and implicit themes in order to have the greatest impact on their intended audiences: "Drink LimeGreen to quench your thirst and join the Green Generation!"

Advertisements can be persuasive and powerful. To write a television advertisement, you'll need to create an imaginary product or service for a specific audience. To make your advertisement effective, you'll need to explore ways you could present the product or service to make the maximum impact on your intended audience.

Types of Themes in Ad Slogans	
Explicit Theme	**Implicit Theme**
"Brayniac will make you smarter!"	"Where are you shredded?"
"Never worry about sore feet—with Heelers!"	"Papaya skateboard decks: Feel the chill..."

Prewrite

Select a theme for your advertising script. After you create an imaginary product to advertise, make a T-graph and list possible slogans.

Differentiated Instruction: Advanced Learners

Have small groups perform the commercials. The writers should be the directors, telling actors what to do during each part of the script. Students may wish to videotape their commercials, adding music and other effects, to present to the class.

TEKS 11.14C Write a script with an explicit or implicit theme, using a variety of literary techniques; **ELPS** 1H Develop and expand repertoire of learning strategies

Sample Advertising Script

Every commercial you see on TV comes from a script. One way to write a commercial is to include columns for both the audio (what you hear) and the video (what you see). The sample below is a brief commercial "spot."

	Video	Audio
The **beginning** establishes a mood.	1. A boy and a girl stroll in slow motion on a city street.	1. (Slow, romantic music)
The **middle** uses a voice-over to give the message.	2. Close-up of boy and girl, obviously in love, smiling, sweet innocence.	2. (Announcer) Ah, love! Time frozen in one sweet instant.
	3. Suddenly, slow motion goes to normal time. Close-up of girl's face as she winces.	3. (Music turns sharp and out of tune.) Would you want this perfect moment spoiled because of . . .
The **problem** is established.	4. Girl limps and reaches down to her foot.	4. . . . sore feet?
The **product** is introduced.	5. Sparks fly as her shoes become Heelers.	5. Avoid foot pain with new Heelers, the world's most comfortable shoes.
The **ending** suggests the problem is solved by the product.	6. Close-up of girl's feet, with animation of clouds floating around the foot.	6. Heelers cushion your feet in comfort with built-in air pockets. You'll be walking on air!
	7. Long shot of girl and boy, who start to dance.	7. So enjoy every moment, and never worry about sore feet—with Heelers.

Try It!

Write an ad script. Think of a product or service to promote—or satirize. You can address themes explicitly, implicitly, or both ways. Create a commercial using images and words to convey your point.

Creative Writing

Sample Advertising Script

Note that all advertisements involve persuasive writing. The writer's goal is to persuade potential buyers that they need the product—the call to action is "Buy this!" Ask students to describe TV or magazine ads they have seen.

- What is the "plot" of each ad? Can students identify each part of a plot line, as described on SE page 340?
- What is the message of each ad?

ELPS 2F, 2H

Provide guidance as students plan and write their ads.

- Give them time to decide what their products will be. If the products are imaginary, encourage students to make sketches of them.
- Who would use the products? Have students make character grids to decide on specific groups.
- The general complication is that the main character in each play needs the product but doesn't have it. How can students flesh out this statement with details so that it grabs viewers' interest?
- Students might find it useful to transcribe a television or radio advertisement and use the transcription as a model for their own scripts.

Try It!
Answers

Remind students to review these pages as they write their ads. ✔DIFFERENTIATE INSTRUCTION

TEKS 11.14C

TEKS 11.14C Write a script with an explicit or implicit theme, using a variety of literary techniques; **ELPS 2F** Listen to and derive meaning from a variety of media/language attainment; **2H** Understand implicit ideas and information in spoken language

Drafting Your Script

Review the literary techniques students have pointed out so far in their discussions of advertisements. Then discuss hyperbole, symbolism, and using sensory details in more detail, as follows.

Using Hyperbole

Discuss with students why hyperbole might work best in a humorous or entertaining advertisement, rather than a serious or dramatic one. Ask them to provide examples or descriptions of their ideas.

Using Symbolism

Ask students to describe other uses of symbols they have seen or read. Remind students of symbols they use in other subjects areas, such as math, which are widely understood by most people. Encourage them to brainstorm some ideas for symbolism they might use in their ads.

Using Sensory Details

Ask students to consider, as they write their drafts, how audiences will experience the advertisement through their senses.

✱ For more about sensory details, see SE page 81.

Draft your advertisement. Encourage students to ask for feedback if they are having difficulty drafting a script with an explicit or implicit theme, or want a fresh reaction to their ideas.

DIFFERENTIATE INSTRUCTION ⟍

✪ **TEKS** 11.14C **ELPS** 5B, 5G

Drafting Your Script

Advertisements use a variety of literary techniques to get their themes across. Some literary techniques make messages come in loud and clear, while others produce more subtle and seductive messages. Try using one or more of the following literary techniques to draft your advertisement script.

Using Hyperbole

Hyperbole is an exaggeration or overstatement. Some advertisements use hyperbole to make outrageous or unbelievable claims: "A Dazzle smile will get you a date every Saturday night!" Most often, hyperbole in advertising is used for a humorous or entertaining effect: "Dazzle brightens every smile—hmm, maybe Fido could be a Dazzle dog!"

Using Symbolism

Symbolism is the use of a person, a place, a thing, or an event to represent something else. For example, our flag is a symbol that stands for our country. For many citizens, the flag also symbolizes ideas such as freedom, liberty, and justice. In a literary text, a storm might symbolize unrest or impending trouble. Advertisers often use their own products as symbols. A mouthwash advertisement might show someone in a social situation enjoying a garlic-filled meal visualizing the mouthwash he or she will need later. Symbolism in advertisements can be a very effective way to promote a product without saying a word.

Using Sensory Details

Sensory details appeal to the senses of sight, sound, touch, hearing, and taste. Advertisements make great use of sensory details to make an audience crave a product—think of commercials that show a close-up of a mouth-watering meal or the leather interior of a new car. Other commercials may use musical elements that grab our attention. Sensory details used in advertisements can override our sense of logic by appealing to our many appetites.

Draft your advertisement. Draft your advertising script. Include at least two literary techniques to support your explicit or implicit theme.

TEKS **11.14C** Write a script with an explicit or implicit theme, using a variety of literary techniques; **ELPS** **5B** Write using newly acquired basic and content-based grade-level vocabulary; **5G** Describe with increasing specificity and detail

361

Writing Poetry

Poetry is often considered the language of feelings, from the smiles of a summer morning to the cry of a breaking heart. The compact form and precise use of words is the perfect frame for exploring emotions, expressing beauty, or questioning the unfairness of the world.

The goal of the poet is to share intensely personal emotions that the reader can relate to his or her own life. You have probably read a poem and thought, "Yeah, that's right." It's that ability to read someone else's feelings and recognize them in your own experience that makes poetry universal. Poetry reaches across barriers of age, race, and nationality to touch a shared part of the human soul.

In this chapter, you will write a free-verse poem in which you reflect on a relationship. It could be a family relationship or a connection with a teacher, a classmate, someone you love, or even a pet. You will also explore the use of poetic conventions such as rhythm and rhyme patterns and learn about two other distinct forms of poetry and their traditions.

Writing Guidelines

Subject: **A relationship**
Purpose: **To entertain**
Form: **Free-verse poem**
Audience: **Friends, family, and classmates**

"Poetry is language at its most distilled and most powerful."

—Rita Dove

Writing Poetry

Objectives

- demonstrate an understanding of the content and structure of a free-verse poem and other forms of poetry
- choose a topic (a relationship) to inspire a poem
- use poetic techniques, including rhythm and line breaks
- plan, draft, revise, edit, and share original poems

A week or so before students begin writing poetry, present a new poem at the beginning of each class (write it on the board or distribute individual photocopies).

- Take a few minutes to tell students why you chose the poem (it is a good idea to share poems you feel strongly about), who wrote it, and what style of poetry it represents.
- After a few days, begin asking students to contribute poems and to be prepared to talk about them.
- Continue having students bring poems to class, at least while they are writing poetry.

Differentiated Instruction: English Language Learners

ELPS 2H, 5B, 5G

Have students listen to a television or radio advertisement that has an implicit theme. Discuss the ad with them.

ELP Level **Beginning**	ELP Level **Intermediate**	ELP Level **Advanced/Advanced High**
• Ask students to draw or act out the implicit message. • Guide students to write the implicit message together.	• Guide a discussion of the ad's message. • Have small groups work together to write the implicit message of the ad.	• Have students discuss how the ad supports its implicit message. • Have individuals write the implicit message of the ad.

 ELPS 2H Understand implicit ideas and information in spoken language; **5B** Write using newly acquired basic and content-based grade-level vocabulary; **5G** Describe with increasing specificity and detail

Sample Free-Verse Poem

After students read "Windows and Doors" silently, invite a volunteer to read it aloud. Ask the reader to speak clearly, observing the pauses indicated by the punctuation and line breaks.

Ask students what they notice about the line that is repeated at the end of each stanza.

- internal rhyme (*mine, nine*) ;
- alliteration (*size, seven*);
- assonance (*mine, size, nine*);
- the depth of the writer's knowledge of her friend—she knows her shoe size;
- the information is expressed with very few words and the two ideas are linked with a semicolon. **DIFFERENTIATE INSTRUCTION ↘**

DIFFERENTIATE INSTRUCTION ↘

 For more about using semicolons, see SE page 648.

Respond to the reading

Answers

You may wish to have students work with a partner or small group to answer the questions.

Focus and Coherence 1. The poem is held together by the presence and absence of braces on the two girls' teeth.

Organization 2. The relationship changes between the two stanzas. After their braces are removed, the girls make new friends. One moves on without looking back, but the speaker still misses their friendship.

Development of Ideas 3. Friends laugh and dream together; time changes friendships and friends don't always stay friends.

Voice 4. nostalgia and sadness

TEKS 11.14B **ELPS** 4F

Sample Free-Verse Poem

Free-verse poems are not usually restricted to a specific rhythm or rhyme scheme, although they usually have within them their own distinct pattern. Student writer Nina Whitefeather wrote the following free-verse poem examining changes in her relationship with her friend Marla. As you read, watch for the subtle rhythm and rhyme within the poem.

Windows and Doors

Wire-bound in the Sisterhood of Braces
   (and of giggles secretly shared),
We gazed through open summer windows,
And dreamed the same dreams,
Of princes who would love us
   (gap-toothed and freckled).
Do you remember the window we broke,
Playing baseball in my neighbor's yard?
We ran, laughing, tumbling, scared,
Two pairs of feet matching step for step
   (Mine, size nine; yours, size seven).

Then our braces were gone,
And with no gated guardians,
Our secrets escaped
   (Couldn't you hear the pain?)
Our feet turned toward different doors,
   (Different faces, different places).
Our smiles stretched to others,
And our friendship lay in brittle shards,
   (Like that long-ago window)
Perfect, empty smiles beneath our feet
   (Mine, size nine; yours, size seven).

Respond to the reading. Use the following questions to guide your reflection on the free-verse poem above.

Focus and Coherence (1) What image holds this poem together?

Organization (2) Where and how does the relationship change?

Development of Ideas (3) What ideas about friendship does the poet develop?

Voice (4) How would you describe the writer's feelings about this particular friendship?

Differentiated Instruction: Advanced Learners

Encourage students to note the poem's emotional language and sensory imagery. Ask students to identify examples and to explain what the words convey. (*Sisterhood, giggles, gap-toothed,* and *freckled* evoke carefree, youthful joy. *Pain, different faces, brittle shards,* and *empty smiles* evoke sadness, discomfort, and loss.)

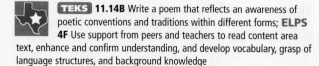

Prewriting Choosing a Topic and a Focus

Your challenge is to write a poem about a relationship. First you must choose a relationship, and then decide on your focus—the one aspect of the relationship that you want to write about. Nina listed the various relationships she had had in her life.

Topic List

> **Family members:** mother, father, my brother John, Grandpa George, Aunt Lucy
> **Friends:** boyfriend Bobby, former best friend Marla, friend Kristi
> **Other people:** teacher Ms. Friedman, boss Mr. Tortelli, neighbor Mrs. Konjak
> **Pets:** dog Heinz, guinea pig Rags

Nina decided to write about her best childhood friend, Marla, and chose to focus on how their relationship changed as they grew older.

Find a topic and a focus. Make a list of the various relationships you have had in your life. Select one you would like to write about and choose a focus.

Gathering Images

Writing a poem about a relationship is an emotional exercise. You can express your feelings by finding a metaphor to represent them. How do you decide which image, or metaphor, to use? Nina did a little freewriting.

Freewriting

> What images would represent my friendship with Marla? We were the best of friends, and we did a lot of fun and stupid stuff together, like the time we broke my neighbor's window and ran away. Boy, did we laugh about that, but we were so scared! We were equal when we both had braces, but things changed when she got hers off first. She thought she was better than me, just because she was tiny and cute. She made different friends and left me to find my own. That really hurt. A sharp hurt, like broken glass. Windows. Glass. Broken glass looks like teeth. I can use the image of windows and broken glass.

Gather images. Ask yourself what metaphors or images represent the relationship you are writing about. Freewrite for 5 to 10 minutes to discover metaphors you can use.

Creative Writing

Prewriting Choosing a Topic and a Focus

Review the range of choices open to students. Their poems could tell stories (as the sample does) or create single images, like portraits. The sample poem focuses on a relationship that went wrong. Students might also choose to

- tell the story of a good relationship,
- tell how an important relationship evolved,
- describe a transitional moment (such as a change from friends to best friends, adversary to ally, or stranger to friend),
- create a snapshot of a relationship, or
- focus on a temporary relationship, such as a conversation with a stranger on a bus.

Topic List

Have students generate a topic list of their best ideas and discuss it with a partner.

 TEKS 11.14B ELPS 4F

Find a topic and a focus. Have students narrow their list and choose their strongest idea.

Gathering Images

Ask students to identify the central metaphor in the sample poem. (The braces are what held the girls together. When the braces were removed, they drifted apart.)

ELPS 2H

Freewriting

Have students discuss which ideas Nina used from her freewriting. Ask how freewriting helps a writer to generate and gather ideas.

Gather images. Suggest that students use cluster diagrams to gather possible metaphors that might become part of their poems.

TEKS 11.14B

Drafting Your First Draft

Remind students not to focus on grammar and mechanics as they draft their poems; they should look for ways to use rhythm and other literary techniques to express themselves.

Using Rhythm

Read aloud the two sample stanzas to contrast the different rhythms. Demonstrate how the second example can be read with a regular beat that resembles the *chug-chug* of a train.

Tip

Suggest that students read or reread a few poems aloud to hear different rhythms. Remind them that a poem's rhythm can be subtle and not necessarily noticeable to the reader.

Using Line Breaks

Review the different ways that line breaks can be used in poetry to convey particular ideas, moods, or even shapes. Then direct students' attention back to the sample poem on SE page 362, in which the parenthetical lines are indented from the left margin. Ask why the poet might have done this. (Possible answer: indenting, along with the parentheses, gives those lines the feeling of intimate reminders, whispered to the friend.)

Draft your poem. Remind students not to judge their writing at this point. They should allow ideas and images to flow quickly onto the paper, without extensive review or questions.

DIFFERENTIATE INSTRUCTION ↘

⬛ **TEKS** 11.14B

Drafting Your First Draft

Begin to draft your poem. Let your first draft flow freely, without worrying about what's good and what's not so good. Watch for opportunities to use poetic conventions such as rhythm and line breaks. (See conventions on pages 368–369.)

Using Rhythm

While free verse is not locked into a specific meter, rhythm is still important for carrying readers through a poem, and for adding emphasis to particular words and phrases. Compare the rhythm in both versions of the short poem below.

Trains (Version 1)
Like capillaries reaching all through a city,
trains deliver people to workplaces every day
and return them home each night.

> In this version, there is no rhythm; the words read more like prose.

Trains (Version 2)
Vascular system of every metropolis,
daily delivering workers to workplaces,
nightly returning them home.

> In the second version, a definite sense of rhythm carries the reader along.

Tip

Not every poem needs as strong a rhythm as "Trains (Version 2)," but every poem ought to have *some* sense of rhythm. Choose your words and their order carefully to make the rhythm of your poems flow smoothly.

Using Line Breaks

There are no hard-and-fast rules for using line breaks. There are, however, strategies that poets consider when deciding where to break to a new line.

- **Emphasis:** A word at the end of a line gains extra attention. Poets use this to dramatic effect in free verse, breaking a line just after an especially important or interesting word. (Avoid breaking after a weak word, such as a preposition.)
- **Rhythm:** Long lines have a leisurely feel, while short lines tend to have more punch. This affects the overall rhythm of a poem.
- **Shift in ideas:** A line break can separate ideas, even within a sentence.
- **Appearance:** The line breaks of a poem determine its overall appearance on a page.

Draft

Draft your poem. Allow ideas to pour out of you and experiment with poetic images and conventions.

Differentiated Instruction: Struggling Learners

Encourage auditory learners to read each line or phrase in their poem aloud as they write, listening for musical and rhythmic effects. Remind students that in poetry words should create *sound*—as well as convey meaning.

 TEKS **11.14B** Write a poem that reflects an awareness of poetic conventions and traditions within different forms

Considering More Poetic Conventions

Exploring imagery, rhythm, and the use of line breaks will help develop your free-verse poem. Keep in mind that poetry is often meant to be read aloud. Therefore, the way the words sound is another important poetic element.

Poetic conventions like alliteration and assonance emphasize letter sounds. Another poetic convention, repetition, emphasizes entire words.

Alliteration

Alliteration is the repetition of consonant sounds at the beginning of words. Nina recalled that she and her friend Marla both wore braces on their teeth when they were friends. In her poem, she described their braces as "gated guardians," and the repeated initial *g* sound helps the reader focus on the words and the sounds the words make together. Try inserting alliterative elements in your poem to emphasize important ideas through sound.

Assonance

Assonance is the repetition of vowel sounds anywhere in words. In her poem, Nina tells how she and Marla even knew each other's shoe size: "(Mine, size nine; yours, size seven.)" The repeated long *i* sound helps the reader notice this observation.

While you draft your poem, consider reading your words aloud to help you notice vowel sounds.

Repetition

Repetition is the repeating of a word, a phrase, or an idea. In her poem, Nina writes that she and her friend "dreamed the same dreams" to emphasize this important element of friendship. Her use of the words *secretly* and *secrets* points out another thing friends have in common. In her second stanza, Nina uses the word *different* three times to highlight that the girls' relationship has changed.

Alliteration, assonance, and repetition can also be used to add or develop rhythm in poetry. As you write, think of words and sounds that could shape the way your poem might sound.

Try It!

Rewrite the following lines of poetry using either alliteration, assonance, or repetition. Discuss with a partner how these conventions make the poem stronger.

> The night breeze caught the shutters,
> Causing them to bang in the darkness,
> Sending two frightened puppies
> Running for cover.

Creative Writing

Considering More Poetic Conventions

Encourage students to explore different poetic techniques in their free-verse poems. These conventions sometimes occur naturally during writing, so remind students to be open to letting their language roam freely when creating a first draft. ✎ **DIFFERENTIATE INSTRUCTION**

Alliteration

Students may find it useful to freewrite a few alliterative phrases to get them started on their drafts; these combinations of words sometimes result in evocative imagery or ideas that can guide their writing down productive paths.
⭐ **TEKS** 11.14B

Assonance

Remind students that, when looking for alliteration or assonance in their writing, it is important for them to think about how their words *sound* together, and not to rely, for example, on how words are spelled. Reading words aloud will help students hear sounds that "go together" more easily.

Repetition

There are many reasons to employ repetition when writing poetry. Remind students that it isn't always *exact*, word-for-word repetition that conveys the strongest effect; sometimes, repetition is more of an altered echo, lightly drawing the reader or listener back to the central images and ideas the poet wishes to emphasize.

Try It!
Answers

Answers to the Try It! activity will vary but should clearly reflect students' understanding of alliteration, assonance, or repetition.
⭐ **TEKS** 11.14B **ELPS** 2C, 3E, 5B

Differentiated Instruction:
English Language Learners   ⭐ **ELPS** 1C, 2C, 3E, 5B, 5G

Display and read aloud examples of alliteration, assonance, and repetition. Have students write the examples in their notebooks

ELP Level **Beginning**	ELP Level **Intermediate**	ELP Level **Advanced/Advanced High**
• Have students show where each technique is used in each example. • Together, write a new example for each technique.	• Have small groups explain how each technique is used in each example. • Ask groups to write a new example of each technique.	• Have individuals explain how each technique is used in each example. • Have students write examples and read them aloud.

⭐ **TEKS** **11.14B** Write a poem that reflects an awareness of poetic conventions and traditions within different forms; **ELPS** **1C** Use strategic learning strategies to acquire basic and grade-level vocabulary; **2C** Learn new academic vocabulary; **3E** Share information in cooperative learning interactions; **5B** Write using newly acquired basic and content-based grade-level vocabulary; **5G** Describe with increasing specificity and detail

Revising Improving Your Writing

Encourage students to be rigorous with their revisions. Many poets often rewrite their poems entirely before they are satisfied. This is because every word must fit exactly. Suggest that students do the following:

- Read aloud their poem.
- Review every word—is it a cliché, predictable, too vague?
- Review each word image—does it help express the idea? Is it trite or is it vivid?

Revise your writing. Advise students not to feel discouraged if it takes them a while to create the poems they envision.

 11.14B

Revising Checklist

Suggest that students focus on one trait for the entire poem before moving on to the next trait.

Learning Language

Support English learners as they read aloud each other's drafts. As needed, provide accessible examples of each poetic convention being discussed. Help students make suggestions for improvements in each other's work.

ELPS 2C, 3E, 3G

366

 TEKS 11.14B
ELPS 2C, 3E, 3G

Revising Improving Your Writing

 Revise your writing. Read your poem aloud or have someone read it to you. As you revise your poem, use the following questions as a guide.

Revising Checklist

Focus and Coherence

_____ **1.** Does my poem focus on a single relationship in my life?
_____ **2.** Have I made my feelings about this relationship clear?

Organization

_____ **3.** Is my poem written in free verse?
_____ **4.** Have I considered how I use line breaks in my poem?

Development of Ideas

_____ **5.** Have I used poetic conventions to develop or emphasize my ideas?

Voice

_____ **6.** Have I expressed my thoughts in an authentic and genuine voice?
_____ **7.** Have I read my poem aloud and considered how the sounds of my words support important thoughts?

Learning Language

Share your draft with a partner. Read each other's draft aloud. Take turns pointing out how poetic conventions such as line breaks, alliteration, assonance, or repetition have been used. Suggest places where poetic conventions could be used to make the poem even stronger.

 TEKS 11.14B Write a poem that reflects an awareness of poetic conventions and traditions within different forms; **ELPS 2C** Learn new academic vocabulary; **3E** Share information in cooperative learning interactions; **3G** Express ideas

Editing Checking Your Poem

Punctuation is especially important in a poem, since each mark affects the poem's rhythm, readability, or even its meaning. Notice, on page **362**, how Nina used parentheses to set apart lines that emphasize certain ideas and emotions. Use punctuation to enhance the meaning of your poem.

Edit your poem. Don't be afraid to break the rules of punctuation in your poem, but be sure that each mark accomplishes the purpose you intend.

Editing Checklist

Conventions

GRAMMAR

_____ **1.** Do my subjects and verbs agree in number?

_____ **2.** Are my pronouns clearly linked to their antecedents?

SPELLING

_____ **3.** Have I spelled all words correctly?

_____ **4.** Have I double-checked for words that my spell-checker may have missed?

Publishing Sharing Your Poem

Sharing poems can be a fun and enlightening experience. Here are some ways you can share poems you have written.

- **Have a class poetry reading.** Sit on cushions in an informal circle on the floor. Ask each person to read his or her poem out loud.
- **Submit your poem** to a magazine, a Web site, or a contest.
- **Print your poem on a bookmark.** Then make copies and hand them out to friends and family.

Publish your poem. Share your poem with others and discuss the ideas and feelings it presents. Ask your teacher for other publishing ideas.

Creative Writing

Editing Checking Your Poem

Encourage students to be attentive to the effects that punctuation can have in their poetry. Small ways of breaking the rules often have a strong effect on how a reader experiences a poem. Students' close attention to both revising and editing will result in better, stronger poetry.

 TEKS 11.14B

Edit your poem. Encourage students to share their edited poems with a friend or peer.

Editing Checklist

Suggest that students focus on one question for the entire poem and then move to the next one.

✔ DIFFERENTIATE INSTRUCTION

Publishing Sharing Your Poem

Make the class poetry reading a poetry performance event to which others are invited.

Publish your poem. If students submit their poems to outside sources, be sure they review the submission guidelines for that particular forum.

★ Conventions Connections

Grammar: Prepositions and Prepositional Phrases; Phrases
- *Student Edition: Proofreader's Guide* pages 752 (+), 760–761, 762 (+)
- *SkillsBook* pages 128

  ⚡ *Write Source Online* **GrammarSnap**

Grammar: Parts of Speech Review; Adjectives and Adverbs
- *Student Edition: Proofreader's Guide* pages 722 (+), 723–754 (+)
- *SkillsBook* pages 119–120, 108, 113

Grammar: Subjects and Predicates
- *Student Edition: Proofreader's Guide* pages 756 (+), 758 (+)
- *SkillsBook* pages 124–125

Spelling
- *Student Edition: Proofreader's Guide* pages 690–693, 694–695
- *SkillsBook* pages 56–57

 TEKS **11.14B** Write a poem that reflects an awareness of poetic conventions and traditions within different forms; **ELPS** **5C** Spell familiar English words; **5D** Edit writing for standard grammar and usage/subject-verb agreement; **5E** Employ increasingly complex grammatical structures/using correct pronouns/antecedents

---

Differentiated Instruction: English Language Learners

ELPS 5C, 5D, 5E

Read (or reread) the sample free-verse poem aloud; ask students to read parts of it if possible. Discuss it together.

ELP Level **Beginning**	ELP Level **Intermediate**	ELP Level **Advanced/Advanced High**
• Have partners review their drafts together. • Ask them to show where each checklist question can be or needs to be answered.	• Have small groups discuss how to use each checklist. • Ask partners to review their drafts together.	• Have students edit their drafts. • In small groups, have students discuss how they used the checklists and what problems they resolved.

Using Poetic Conventions and Techniques

Have students work together to create a poetry-themed display that illustrates each poetic technique listed on this and the next page. Encourage students to share examples from poems that they enjoy and that will help them remember the meaning of each term. Examples may include song lyrics, as well as poems.

★ **TEKS** 11.14B **ELPS** 2F

Additional items in the display might include the following:
- the poem of the day
- photographs or recordings of poets
- illustrations to accompany the poems on display
- interviews with poets
- examples of different poetic forms, such as sonnets, sestinas, haiku, limericks, ballads, and concrete poems
- original poems
- a recommended reading list

Figures of Speech

Review each figure of speech with students. Ask them to compare and contrast each example sentence and to discuss how each figure of speech creates a different effect or produces a different response in the reader.

Sounds of Poetry

Discuss each type of poetic sound, and ask students to provide new examples of each technique on pages 368 and 369.

DIFFERENTIATE INSTRUCTION ↘

★ **TEKS** 11.14B

Using Poetic Conventions and Techniques

Poets use a variety of poetic conventions and techniques in their work. This page and the next define some of the most important ones.

Figures of Speech

- A **simile** (*sĭm´ə-lē*) compares two unlike things with the word *like* or *as*.
  Her smile was warm as hot cocoa on a cold day.

- A **metaphor** (*mĕt´ə-fôr*) compares two unlike things without using *like* or *as*.
  The leaf was a dancer whirling madly to the wind's wild music.

- **Personification** (*pər-sŏn´ə-fĭ-kā´shən*) is a technique that gives human traits to something that is nonhuman.
  Rocks stubbornly bite the plowshares, leaving ragged teeth marks in the metal.

- **Hyperbole** (*hī-pûr´bə-lē*) is an exaggerated statement, often humorous.
  He lived so near, across the street, a million miles away.

Sounds of Poetry

- **Alliteration** (*ə-lĭt´ə-rā´shən*) is the repetition of consonant sounds at the beginning of words.
  The muck and mire made movement slow.

- **Assonance** (*ăs´ə-nəns*) is the repetition of vowel sounds anywhere in words.
  Blame the day, not the place.

- **Consonance** (*kŏn´sə-nəns*) is the repetition of consonant sounds anywhere in words.
  We drank sparkling water from trickling brooks.

TEKS **11.14B** Write a poem that reflects an awareness of poetic conventions and traditions within different forms; **ELPS** **2F** Listen to and derive meaning from a variety of media/concept and language attainment

- **Line breaks** help control the rhythm of a poem. A reader naturally pauses when he or she comes to the end of a line. The last word in a line also receives added emphasis.

  Branches reaching out,
  stretching,
  as though fingers yearning
  to strum the wind.

- **Onomatopoeia** (ŏn′ə-mät′ə-pē′ə) is the use of words that sound like what they name.

  The plip-plop of the leaky faucet

- **Repetition** (rĕp′i-tĭsh′ən) uses the same word or phrase more than once, for emphasis or for rhythm.

  I wish to fly beyond the world,
  beyond the sun,
  beyond the universe.

- **Rhyme** (rīm) means using words whose endings sound alike.

  - **End rhyme** occurs at the end of lines.

    Through the fog, so thick and pale,
    red lights slice as sirens wail.

  - **Internal rhyme** occurs within lines.

    I stop running and turn,
    To see burning embers pepper the sky.

- **Rhythm** (rĭth′əm) is the pattern of accented and unaccented syllables in a poem.

  - Iambic: an unstressed followed by a stressed syllable (I am′)
  - Trochaic: a stressed followed by an unstressed syllable (la′-ter)
  - Anapestic: two unstressed followed by a stressed syllable (to the moon′)
  - Dactylic: a stressed followed by two unstressed syllables (stealth′-i-ly)

The rhythm of free-verse poetry tends to flow naturally, like speaking. Traditional poetry follows a more regular pattern, as in the following example.

  Moón on snów
  Évening glów

Encourage students to seek out more poetry to read and share with the class. Suggest that interested students form a poetry group and meet regularly to share their own and others' poems.

TEKS 11.14B ELPS 3E, 3J

Bookmark good poetry Web sites on the class computer, or distribute a list of poetry-related URL's for students to explore. The list might include the following:

- The Favorite Poem Project (www.favoritepoem.org), a site established by former poet laureate Robert Pinsky in 1997
- Poetry 180 (www.loc.gov/poetry/180), established by former poet laureate Billy Collins to provide a poem for every school day
- The Academy of American Poets (www.poetry.org), a site with a large database of classic and modern poems
- The Poetry Archive (www. poetryarchive.org), a growing audio database of poets reading their own work

ELPS 2F, 3J

TEKS **11.14B** Write a poem that reflects an awareness of poetic conventions and traditions within different forms; **ELPS 2F** Listen to and derive meaning from a variety of media/concept and language attainment; **3E** Share information in cooperative learning interactions; **3J** Respond orally to information presented/concept and language attainment

Writing a Shakespearean Sonnet

Point out that the form of a sonnet is very specific, at several levels of detail. Ask volunteers to read aloud different lines of the sonnet while the other students listen closely for the syllable pattern (unstressed followed by stressed, ten syllables per line).

Once students understand and can hear the syllable pattern, move on to listening for and analyzing the quatrains and the rhyming scheme across the entire sonnet. Encourage students to recite the sonnet several times, becoming comfortable with its rhythm and language.

DIFFERENTIATE INSTRUCTION ⬆ **DIFFERENTIATE INSTRUCTION** ⬆

 TEKS 11.14B

 Respond to the reading

Answers

Development of Ideas 1. The poet feels he won't be able to fully express the beauty of the person he is writing about; a summer's day, though beautiful, falls short of expressing eternal beauty. **2.** The final couplet resolves the problem by preserving the person's beauty in writing, for eternity.

Voice 3. Answers will vary.

Writing a Shakespearean Sonnet

As you know, poems can be written in a variety of forms. The poetic form known as a *sonnet* became popular in the 13th century. A sonnet consists of fourteen lines written in *iambic pentameter*, which means that each line has ten syllables with a repeated pattern of an unstressed syllable followed by a stressed syllable, as in the following example.

˘ – ˘ – ˘ – ˘ – ˘ –
The sun, once bright, now hides behind a cloud

The term sonnet literally means "little song." William Shakespeare, perhaps the world's best-known playwright, also was famous for his poetry, especially his sonnets. A Shakespearean sonnet consists of three *quatrains* (four lines in each stanza) and a final rhyming *couplet* (two lines). The rhyme pattern for line endings, or *scheme*, is abab, cdcd, efef, gg.

In his sonnets, Shakespeare tended to create strong images by using the ordinary vocabulary of his time. Often, a Shakespearean sonnet sets up a problem or question in the three quatrains and then resolves or answers it in the final couplet. As you read Shakespeare's Sonnet 18, below, think about how he resolves the problem posed in the first three quatrains.

> Shall I compare thee to a summer's day?
> Thou art more lovely and more temperate:
> Rough winds do shake the darling buds of May,
> And summer's lease hath all too short a date:
> 5 Sometime too hot the eye of heaven shines,
> And often is his gold complexion dimm'd;
> And every fair from fair sometime declines,
> By chance, or nature's changing course untrimm'd;
> But thy eternal summer shall not fade,
> 10 Nor lose possession of that fair thou ow'st,
> Nor shall death brag thou wander'st in his shade,
> When in eternal lines to time thou grow'st;
> So long as men can breathe, or eyes can see,
> So long lives this, and this gives life to thee.

 Respond to the reading. Use the following questions to guide your reflection on the sonnet above.

Development of Ideas (1) What is the problem or question in the first three quatrains? (2) How does the final couplet resolve the problem?

Voice (3) Does the iambic pentameter sound natural or forced? Explain.

Differentiated Instruction: Struggling Learners

Have a small group take turns reading the sonnet aloud, two lines per student. Ask them to pause after each *quatrain* (every four lines) to restate what the poet has said and to explain the syllable and rhyme pattern to each other. Some students may find it easier to concentrate on the form if they memorize the sonnet first.

Differentiated Instruction: Advanced Learners

Challenge students to explore the origins of the phrase *iambic pentameter*. Then ask students to look for contemporary songs or poetry that are written in iambic pentameter; encourage them to choose something that's close to the pattern and then adapt it as needed into a Shakespearean sonnet.

TEKS 11.14B

Sample Shakespearean Sonnet

Student writer Luis Harris wrote the following Shakespearean sonnet to describe an important relationship in his life. As you read, notice how Luis follows the conventions of this poetic tradition.

A Lost Friend

Myself alone, a leafless sapling grown,
Fall's fearsome winds have blown and now have left.
Night's curtain drops, no noise, myself, alone.
My friend, you leave no clue, my soul bereft.
Oh friend, on you have I come to depend
For news anew, to break bleak times alone.
Our team of two no more, our games at end.
I hear no cheers of joy, no happy tone.
Did I drop you uncaring, there, or here?
Two friends divide, one searches, one is lost.
But wait! A sound familiar pierce my ear
Amidst the mess in backpack, cruelly tossed?
At last I find you, joy and gladness great!
Set I you now, to ring, not to vibrate.

Luis followed the conventions of a Shakespearean sonnet:

- **Quatrains and Couplets** Fourteen lines made of three quatrains and a final couplet
- **Iambic Pentameter** Written in iambic pentameter, 10 syllables in each line, a pattern of an unstressed syllable followed by a stressed syllable
- **Scheme** A rhyme scheme of abab cdcd efef gg

Luis also used rich images and set up a problem that is resolved in the final couplet.

 Write a Shakespearean sonnet with a partner or small group. Try to follow all of the conventions of this type of sonnet. Once you choose a topic, have one person record possible lines. Be sure to say the lines aloud as you compose your sonnet to help hear stressed and unstressed syllables. When you are finished, share your sonnet with a larger group.

Creative Writing

Sample Shakespearean Sonnet

Ask students to discuss how Luis's sonnet follows the conventions of this poetic form. Have individual students analyze individual lines for the correct syllable pattern, speaking each line aloud to emphasize the unstressed, then stressed pattern of the ten syllables. Then review the three quatrains, one couplet pattern of the entire sonnet, and the rhyme scheme as well.

ELPS 2I, 3E ✔ DIFFERENTIATE INSTRUCTION

Have students look closely at Luis's use of punctuation. Ask how the punctuation guides them when reading the poem, both silently and aloud. Encourage them to make any suggestions they think might improve the sonnet.

Write a Shakespearean sonnet with a partner or small group. Provide additional examples of sonnets for students to refer to as they work together to write their own.

TEKS 11.14B ELPS 2I, 5B

Differentiated Instruction: English Language Learners ELPS 2I, 3E, 5B

With students, create a diagram or grid that shows the pattern of a sonnet. Use colors, letters, and numbers to show each convention.

ELP Level **Beginning**	ELP Level **Intermediate**	ELP Level **Advanced/Advanced High**
• Ask students questions, such as *How many lines does a sonnet have?* • Have them demonstrate the answers to help create the diagram.	• Ask small groups to suggest how to show certain conventions, such as syllable pattern. • Use the suggestions as you create the diagram together.	• Form small groups; have each group create a diagram. • Groups can compare and contrast their finished work.

TEKS **11.14B** Write a poem that reflects an awareness of poetic conventions and traditions within different forms; **ELPS 2I** Demonstrate listening comprehension/collaborating with peers; **3E** Share information in cooperative learning interactions; **5B** Write using newly acquired basic and content-based grade-level vocabulary

Poetic Form: Quatrains

After students have read each sample quatrain aloud, challenge them to identify the sample poems that are the strongest examples of iambic meter (the second and fourth). Note that both of these poems are humorous, and explain that a regular rhythm is often used with lighter subjects. Point out that using this rhythm pattern can easily create a singsong effect that may not be desirable. **DIFFERENTIATE INSTRUCTION ↘**

 TEKS 11.14B

Poetic Form: Quatrains

Quatrains are poem with four lines. They can be rhymed or unrhymed, but if they are rhymed, they most often have a definite rhyme scheme, or pattern. Quatrains got their name in the late 1500s and became an important part of poetic traditions in a number of European countries. Today quatrains are a common poetic form in many global cultures.

Some of the most common quatrain rhyme schemes are modeled below. Read each quatrain out loud to help you hear the rhyming pattern.

- **abcb** The second and fourth lines rhyme.

    As a child, I thought my parents
    Didn't have a clue.
    When I'd grown I was surprised
    By just how much they knew!

- **abab** The first and third lines rhyme, and the second and fourth lines rhyme.

    I love to hear a froggy croak,
    It is a lovely thing.
    It sings of life that's newly woke,
    And of the joy of spring.

- **abba** The first and fourth lines rhyme, as do the second and third.

    Don't smile and say you'll be my friend,
    When all you really want is to be free.
    If you would rather be a *you* than *we*,
    Say honestly our time is at an end.

- **aabb** The first and second lines rhyme, as do the third and fourth. (This sort of rhyme is often used for humorous subjects.)

    I hear the thud
    And think, Oh, crud!
    My car's been hit
    And bent a bit.

Differentiated Instruction: Advanced Learners

Challenge students to design and write greeting cards that contain quatrains. Each card should contain a quatrain that relates to a specific event or occasion. Encourage students to illustrate and publish their cards as a class project.

TEKS 11.14B

Quatrains and Poetic Traditions

Quatrains have been used in poetry throughout the world for centuries and are still commonly used today. This is probably because of the many opportunities for variation within this simple form.

Heroic Quatrains

A quatrain that uses the rhyme scheme abab composed with an iambic meter (an unstressed syllable followed by a stressed syllable) is often referred to as a *heroic quatrain*. Used in epic poetry, like Homer's *Iliad* and *Odyssey*, to celebrate the heroic achievements of a particular person, real or mythological, or a group, the heroic quatrain has a long poetic tradition.

Elegies

Quatrains with the abab rhyme scheme are sometimes called *elegiac stanzas*, used in a verse form known as an *elegy*. Elegies come from a tradition of writing poems on the occasion of someone's death and are written as a memorial to honor that person's life or achievements.

Other Traditions

Using quatrains with distinct rhyme schemes are common in even more poetic traditions, including Shakespearean sonnets (three quatrains followed by a couplet). Many of the poems of the American poet Emily Dickinson are meditations on nature and man's existence, written in quatrains. Note the abcb rhyme scheme that begins her poem *712*:

> Because I could not stop for Death—
> He kindly stopped for me—
> The Carriage held but just Ourselves—
> And Immortality.

Write your own quatrain. **Pick a subject, select a rhyme scheme and rhythm pattern, and write four lines about your topic.**

Creative Writing

Quatrains and Poetic Traditions

Provide, or ask students to find, additional examples of quatrains to share in class. Encourage them to decide whether these examples fit into any of the following categories.

Heroic Quatrains

Explore portions of Homer's *Iliad* or *Odyssey* with students, looking for quatrains that fit this poetic form. Have students recite a few aloud, listening for the rhyme scheme and the syllable stress pattern.

Elegies and Other Traditions

Challenge students to find other quatrains with distinct rhyme schemes in their reading of poetry. Suggest that they also explore song lyrics to find examples of quatrains that they may not have noticed before. Students who are particularly interested in music may also enjoy creating music for the poetry they find or setting their own sonnets or quatrains to music.

Write your own quatrain. Remind students to review the poetic conventions and techniques on SE pages 368–369, including the section on rhythm, for ideas. DIFFERENTIATE INSTRUCTION

TEKS 11.14B ELPS 1E, 5B

Differentiated Instruction: English Language Learners

ELPS 1E, 2A, 5B

Read aloud several quatrains, discussing the rhyme, rhythm, and intonation patterns. Use these ideas to support student writing.

ELP Level **Beginning**	ELP Level **Intermediate**	ELP Level **Advanced/Advanced High**
Write a quatrain together. Ask questions such as *What rhyme scheme will we use?* Have students demonstrate answers.	Provide simple quatrains as examples. Have small groups read them aloud and then use them as models for their own quatrains.	Have partners write quatrains together. Guide their work by asking questions, suggesting useful words, and providing feedback.

TEKS **11.14B** Write a poem that reflects an awareness of poetic conventions and traditions within different forms; ELPS **1E** Internalize new basic and academic language by using and reusing it/writing; **2A** Distinguish intonation patterns of English; **5B** Write using newly acquired basic and content-based grade-level vocabulary

Research Writing

UNIT TEKS

11.13A Plan a first draft by selecting the correct genre for conveying the intended meaning to multiple audiences, determining appropriate topic through a range of strategies, and developing a thesis or controlling idea; **11.13E** Revise final draft in response to feedback from peers and teacher and publish written work for appropriate audiences; **11.15D** Produce a multimedia presentation with graphics, images, and sound that appeals to a specific audience and synthesizes information from multiple points of view; **11.17A** Use and understand the function of different types of clauses and phrases; **11.17B** Use a variety of correctly-structured sentences; **11.18A** Correctly and consistently use conventions of punctuation and capitalization; **11.19** Spell correctly, including using various resources to determine and check correct spellings; **11.20A** Brainstorm, consult with others, decide upon a topic, and formulate a major research question to address the major research topic; **11.20B** Formulate a plan for engaging in in-depth research on a complex, multi-faceted topic; **11.21A** Follow the research plan to gather evidence from experts on the topic and texts written for informed audiences in the field, distinguishing between reliable and unreliable sources, and avoiding over-reliance on one source; **11.21B** Systematically organize relevant and accurate information to support central ideas, concepts, and themes, outline ideas into conceptual maps/timelines, and separate factual data from complex inferences; **11.21C** Paraphrase, summarize, quote, and accurately cite all researched information according to a standard format, differentiating among primary, secondary, and other sources; **11.22A** Modify the major research question as necessary to refocus the research plan; **11.22B** Differentiate between theories and the evidence that supports them and determine whether the evidence found is weak or strong and how that evidence helps create a cogent argument; **11.22C** Critique the research process at each step to implement changes as the need occurs and is identified; **11.23A** Provide an analysis that supports and develops personal opinions, as opposed to simply restating existing information; **11.23B** Use a variety of formats and rhetorical strategies to argue for the thesis; **11.23C** Develop an argument that incorporates the complexities and discrepancies in information from multiple sources and perspectives while anticipating and refuting counter-arguments; **11.23D** Use a style manual to document sources and format written materials; **11.23E** Synthesize research into an oral presentation that is of sufficient length and complexity to address the topic

UNIT ELPS

1B; 1C; 1D; 1E; 1F; 1G; 2A; 2C; 2D; 2E; 2F; 2G; 2H; 2I; 3A; 3B; 3C; 3D; 3E; 3F; 3G; 3H; 3I; 3J; 4A; 4B; 4C; 4D; 4F; 4G; 4I; 4J; 4K; 5B; 5C; 5E; 5F; 5G

Research Skills (pages 375–384)

Students learn about where to find information and how to evaluate its reliability.

MLA Research Paper (pages 385–432)

Through the process of researching and writing a paper, students will learn to study an issue and communicate what they learn to their classmates.

Writing Responsibly (pages 433–440)

Students learn how to paraphrase and properly use quoted materials and cite sources for both.

Documenting Research (pages 441–454)

Students learn about how to properly cite sources both at point of use and by creating a Works Cited page for their Research Paper.

Making Oral Presentations (pages 455–467)

Students explore the preparation and techniques needed to be effective speakers.

Technology Connections

 Write Source Online www.hmheducation.com/tx/writesource
- **Net-text**
- **Writing Network**
- **Portfolio**
- **GrammarSnap**
- **Essay Scoring**
- **File Cabinet**

 Interactive Whiteboard Lessons

Research Writing Unit Scope and Sequence

Day	Writing and Grammar Instruction	Write Source Student Edition			Daily Language Workouts	Skills-Book	iWrite
		Core Unit	Tools of Language	Resource Units			
Week 1 1–5	**Research Skills**	375–384	TL 598–603		94–97		Interactive Whiteboard Lesson
Week 2 6	**MLA Research Paper** Model	385–394	TL 598–603		98–101		Net-text
7–10	Prewriting	395–407		BEW 619–620			Net-text
Week 3 11–15	Drafting	408–414	TL 598–603	BEW 621–631	102–105		Net-text
Week 4 16–18	Revising	415–424	TL 598–603		106–109		Net-text
19–20	Editing, Publishing	425–432		BEW 632–633			Net-text
	Skills Activities: • Parallel Structure					170–172	GrammarSnap
	• Compound, Complex, and Compound-Complex Sentences			PG 766–767		139, 140	GrammarSnap
	• Punctuation and Capitalization of Direct Quotations			PG 660–663		31	GrammarSnap
Week 5 21	**Writing Responsibly**	433–440	TL 598–603		110–113		Net-text
22–23	**Documenting Research**	441–454					Net-text
24–25	**Making Oral Presentations**	455–467					Net-text

Resource Units referenced above are located in the back of the *Student Edition* and *Teacher's Edition*
TL *"The Tools of Language"*   BEW *"Basic Elements of Writing"*   PG *"Proofreader's Guide"*

Writing Focus

- Research Skills
- MLA Research Paper
- Writing Responsibly
- Documenting Research
- Making Oral Presentations

Grammar Focus

- Parallel Structure
- Punctuating Quotations

Learning Language

Read aloud the basic and academic terms, as well as the descriptions and questions. Model for students how to read one question and answer it. For example, *It says that biased information is unfair or incomplete. It's asking me to think about why a TV ad would give biased information. I guess it's because writers would only want to tell you what's good about a product they want you to buy.* Have partners monitor their understanding of the terms by working through the meanings and questions together. DIFFERENTIATE INSTRUCTION ↘

 ELPS 1F, 2C, 3E, 4G

Minilessons

Giving Credit
Writing Responsibly

- Have students **CHOOSE** a topic related to social security and **LOCATE** at least three library books on the subject. Instruct them to also **FIND** two magazine articles and two Internet references. Tell them to **ASSUME** that they have written a paper using material from these sources and **LIST** the sources on a documentation page in MLA style.

Public Speaking
Making Oral Presentations

- Have students **WATCH** a brief clip of a famous speech. Ask them to **ANSWER** questions such as *Where did the speaker seem to be looking? What facial expressions or hand movements did the speaker use? Did the speaker move around or stay in one spot? What could the speaker have done to improve his or her delivery?*

ELPS 1F Use accessible language and learn new and essential language in the process; **2C** Learn new basic and academic vocabulary; **3E** Share information in cooperative learning interactions; **4G** Demonstrate comprehension of increasingly complex English/responding to questions

374 ELPS 1F, 2C, 3E, 4G

Research Writing

Writing Focus

Grammar Focus

Learning Language

Work with a partner. Read the meanings and share answers to the questions.

1. Biased information is unfair or incomplete.
   Why would a TV ad give biased information?
2. Outdated information is old or no longer true.
   Should you use an outdated bus schedule? Why?
3. A reliable source gives information that is true.
   Which is more reliable: a blog or news report?
4. A social issue is a subject the community cares about.
   Which social issue do you care most about?
5. Surfing the Web means means looking at Web sites.
   When is surfing the Web most interesting to you?

Research Writing
Research Skills

"Research" is a strange word. One might think that its meaning is obvious from the prefix *re* ("again") and the root *search* ("to look for"). And in a way, that definition is correct: When you do research, you investigate facts not in just one place but in many. You need to look and look again.

This is why knowing where to find reliable information is so important when writing research papers. You have to discover the facts before you can interpret them. In this chapter, you'll read about finding information on the Internet and in the library. You will also learn that every source needs a critical eye to determine its worth.

- **Primary vs. Secondary Sources**
- **Evaluating Sources of Information**
- **Using the Internet**
- **Using the Library**
- **Using Reference Books**

"Research is formalized curiosity. It is poking and prying with a purpose."

—Zora Neale Hurston

Research Skills

Objectives

- review the distinctions between primary and secondary sources
- evaluate sources for relevancy and accuracy
- use the Internet as a research tool
- use the elements of a dictionary page

Prompt small groups of students to discuss how research skills are used in everyday life. Responses may include the following:

- investigating a product before making a purchase
- reading food labels for nutritional information
- learning about candidates' positions in an election
- finding out how to repair or make something
- filling in background about books or movies; for example, investigating the civil rights movement while reading *To Kill a Mockingbird,* by Harper Lee

⭐ ELPS 3E

 Technology Connections

Use the Interactive Whiteboard lessons to introduce research writing.

🔅 *Interactive Whiteboard Lesson*

Differentiated Instruction:
English Language Learners

⭐ ELPS 2A, 3E, 4A

ELP Level **Beginning**	ELP Level **Intermediate**	ELP Level **Advanced/Advanced High**
Have students repeat the words after you say them. Guide them to distinguish sounds and learn relationships between sounds and letters, such as the /sh/ sound in *social.*	Have students repeat the words with you. Point out accented syllables and guide students to use intonation to decode and pronounce the words.	Have students read aloud *biased, outdated,* and *reliable* and discuss how to decode each word. Have partners identify antonyms and share them with the group.
Use pages 598–603	Use pages 598–603	Use pages 598–603

⭐ **ELPS 2A** Distinguish sounds and intonation patterns of English; **3E** Share information in cooperative learning interactions; **4A** Learn relationships between sounds and letters of English and decode using a combination of skills

Primary vs. Secondary Sources

Remind students that *primary* means "first." Primary sources are firsthand accounts, whereas secondary sources are secondhand accounts.

Primary sources include ...

Discuss the types of information that each primary source might provide for a researcher.

Primary Sources

Ask students to discuss the advantages and disadvantages of a primary source such as an interview with a travel guide.

Secondary Sources

Explain that secondary sources focus on explanation, analysis, or both. Writers, therefore, use reliable secondary sources, such as encyclopedias or works by experts, to get a general overview of a topic.

To help students develop background information, have them work in small groups and together examine examples of primary and secondary sources. Have them answer the following questions:
- Which sources are primary and which are secondary? How can you tell?
- What kinds of information can you get from a primary source?
- What kinds of information can you get from a secondary source?
- Why should you use both primary and secondary sources in a research report?

TEKS 11.21A; **ELPS** 4F

Try It!
Answers

(Possible answers: primary sources—interviews with military personnel; visit to a military base; diaries, letters, or Web sites by members of the military; secondary sources—books, articles, news articles, or documentaries by military experts) DIFFERENTIATE INSTRUCTION ↘

 TEKS 11.21A

Primary vs. Secondary Sources

Primary sources are original sources. These sources (*diaries, people, events, surveys*) inform you directly, not through a second person's explanation or interpretation. Ideally, when you research a topic, you should find as much primary information as possible. (See below.)

Primary sources include . . .
- **Diaries, journals, and letters:** You can often find these in museums, in libraries, or at historic sites.
- **Presentations:** A speaker at a museum or a historic site can give you firsthand information, but be aware of the presenter's own interpretation of events.
- **Interviews:** Talk to an expert on your research topic. You can do this by phone, e-mail, or letter.
- **Surveys and questionnaires:** These tools help you gather a great deal of data from many people.
- **Observation and participation:** Your own observations of a person, a place, or an event provide excellent firsthand information. Participating in an event can give you insights that cannot be discovered through the reports of others.

Secondary sources are third-person accounts found in research done by other people. Much of the news (*television, radio, Internet, books, magazines*) can be considered a secondary source of information, as are texts written for an informed audience in a field. Keep in mind that, by their very nature, secondary sources represent filtered information that may contain biases or misunderstandings.

Primary Sources	Secondary Sources
1. Reading the journal of a travel guide	1. Exploring a Web site about being a travel guide
2. Listening to a presentation by a travel guide	2. Reading a magazine article about a travel guide
3. Interviewing a travel guide	3. Watching a TV documentary about a travel guide

Try It!

List two primary and two secondary sources you might use to learn about life in the military. Be as specific as you can.

Evaluating Sources of Information

You may find a lot of information about your research topic. However, before you use any of it, decide whether or not the information is dependable. Use the following questions to help you decide about the reliability of your sources.

Is the source a primary source or a secondary source?

You can usually trust any information you've collected yourself, but be careful with secondary sources. Although many of them are reliable, others may contain outdated or incorrect information.

Is the source an expert?

An expert knows more about a subject than other people. Using an expert's thoughts and opinions can make your paper more believable. If you aren't sure about a source's authority, ask a teacher or librarian what he or she thinks.

Is the information accurate?

Big-city newspapers and well-known Web sites (CNN or NPR) are usually reliable sources of information. Little-known sources that do not support their facts or that contain errors may not be reliable. Look for authors who are quoted frequently or who appear in most bibliographies on your topic.

Tip

Be especially cautious about the accuracy of information on the Internet. While there is an incredible amount of solid information available on the Net, there is also a lot of misinformation.

Is the information fair and complete?

A reliable source should provide information fairly, covering all sides of a subject or an issue. If a source presents only one side of a subject, its information may not be accurate. To make themselves sound better, politicians and advertisers often present just their side of a subject, hoping readers will infer that the information is complete. Avoid one-sided sources, and look for those that are balanced.

Is the information current?

Usually, you want to have the most up-to-date information about a subject. Sometimes information changes, and sources can become outdated quickly. Check the copyright page in a book, the issue date of a magazine, and the posting date of online information.

Research

Evaluating Sources of Information

Discuss the following topics with students to help them organize and analyze whether the information they find is accurate and relevant.

Is the source a primary source or a secondary source? Point out the limitations of primary sources.

- Because a primary account reveals one person's experience or viewpoint, it will necessarily contain some bias.
- For this reason, primary sources should be compared to each other for accuracy.

Is the source an expert? Remind students to check the biographies and backgrounds of expert authors to determine what makes them qualified to discuss the topic.

Is the information accurate? Remind students to check that the authors of their secondary sources, including Internet sources, have supported their facts and statistics.

Tip

Tell students that Internet sources that end with *.edu, .org,* or *.gov* are generally reliable sources.

Is the information fair and complete? Ask: *Does the source cover both sides of the topic? Does it represent divergent viewpoints? Does it have another agenda other than simply conveying information?*

Is the information current? Some topics may have new or changed information. Remind students to check that they have the most up-to-date information available.

TEKS 11.21A, 11.21B; **ELPS** 4K

TEKS **11.21A** Follow the research plan to gather evidence from experts on the topic and texts written for informed audiences in the field; **11.21B** Systematically organize relevant and accurate information to support central ideas, concepts, and themes; **ELPS** **4F** Use support from peers and teachers to develop background knowledge; **4J** Demonstrate English comprehension and expand reading skills by employing inferential skills; **4K** Demonstrate English comprehension and expand reading skills by employing analytical skills

Using the Internet

Point out that although *.edu, .org,* and *.gov* Web sites are generally considered objective, any Web site may be an advocate for one side of an issue and thus may present and interpret the facts in favor of a particular viewpoint. As they formulate plans for research, advise students that information from all Web sites should be confirmed by checking multiple sources.

Internet Guidelines

Give students the following hints for using search engines.

- Most browsers will search for an exact phrase if the words are enclosed in quotation marks (for example, *"to be or not to be"*).
- Adding carefully chosen keywords will produce more relevant results. For example, adding the name of the playwright (Shakespeare) or play (*Hamlet*) will help you find the right information faster.
- Clicking on the *Advanced* link of a browser pulls up a detailed search form that can help users narrow their results.

 DIFFERENTIATE INSTRUCTION

TEKS 11.20B

Try It!
Answers

Students' answers will vary depending on their topic. Have students share and explain their answers orally to a partner. Have partners give feedback to each other.

TEKS 11.20A; **ELPS** 3J

378

TEKS 11.20A, 11.20B

Using the Internet

Because you can access many resources by surfing the Web, the Internet is a valuable research aid. You can find government publications, encyclopedia entries, business reports, and firsthand observations on the Internet. The increasing speed of computers makes the Internet even more inviting. When researching on the Internet, keep in mind the following points.

Internet Guidelines

- **Use the Internet wisely.** Sites that include *.edu, .org,* and *.gov* in the Web address are often reliable. These sites are from educational, nonprofit, or government agencies. If you have questions about the reliability of a site, consult with others, such as your teacher. (See also page **377**.) Remember to check the date of the Web site. Abandoned Web sites may contain outdated information.

- **Try several search engines.** When you type a term into a search engine's input box, the search engine scans its database for matching sites. Then the engine returns recommendations for you to explore. Because there is an enormous amount of information on the Web, no one search engine can handle it all. So employ at least two search engines when you surf the Web. Enter keywords to start your research or enter specific questions to zero in on your topic.

- **Take advantage of links.** When you read a page, watch for links to other sites. These may offer different perspectives or points of view on your topic.

- **Experiment with keywords.** Sometimes you must ask a number of different questions or use different keywords to find the information you need to formulate a research question for your topic.

- **Ignore Web sites that advertise research papers for sale.** Using these sites is dishonest. Teachers and librarians can recognize and verify when a paper is someone else's work.

- **Learn your school's Internet policy.** Using a computer at school or at home is a privilege. To maintain that privilege, follow your school's Internet policy and any guidelines your parents may have set.

Try It!

Decide on a topic that would be appropriate for a research paper. Come up with at least three keywords to use in a search engine. Which one, in your opinion, provides the best results? Explain in a brief paragraph.

Differentiated Instruction: Struggling Learners

Model how to narrow a search by using different keywords from the memorable phrase from *Hamlet*. For example, demonstrate how to find information about the 1942 film *To Be Or Not to Be,* directed by Ernst Lubitsch and starring Carole Lombard and Jack Benny. Add (+) one of the names to the phrase to narrow the search.

⭐ **TEKS** 11.20A, 11.20B

Using the Library

The Internet may be a good place to initiate your research, but a library is often a more valuable place to continue your research to help you decide on a topic. Most libraries contain the following resources.

Books

- **Reference** books include encyclopedias, almanacs, dictionaries, atlases, and directories, plus resources such as consumer information guides and car repair manuals. Reference books provide a quick review or overview of research topics.

- **Nonfiction** texts are a good source of facts that can serve as a foundation for your research. Check the copyright dates to be sure you are reading reasonably up-to-date information. (Some libraries organize nonfiction using the Library of Congress system, but most libraries use the Dewey decimal system as shown on page **381**.)

- **Fiction** can sometimes aid or enhance your research and help you formulate and fine tune a major research question. For example, a historical novel can reveal people's feelings about a particular time in history. (Fiction books are grouped together in alphabetical order by the authors' last names.)

Periodicals

Periodicals (*newspapers* and *magazines*) are grouped together in a library. Use the *Readers' Guide to Periodical Literature* to find articles in periodicals. (See page **384**.) You will have to consult with the librarian for older issues.

The Media Section

The media section of your library includes DVD's, CD-ROM's, CD's, cassettes, and videotapes. These resources can immerse you in an event. Keep in mind, however, that directors and screenwriters may present events in a way that accommodates their personal views.

Computers

Computers are available in most libraries, and many are connected to the Internet, although there may be restrictions on their use.

Try It!

Consult with a local public librarian to find out whether you may access the library's catalog online. If so, you can check to see if your needed materials are available before you visit the library.

Research

Using the Library

Review the types of resources available in your school or local library. ✔ **DIFFERENTIATE INSTRUCTION**

Books

Explain that if a library doesn't have the book students want, they can often request it through interlibrary loan, which will send the book to students' local library. Encourage students to consult a librarian for this and other research needs.

Periodicals

Many libraries have the *Readers' Guide to Periodical Literature* and other indexes online. Check with the librarian to find out about your library's electronic resources.

The Media Section

Encourage students to explore the media section of their library. Explain that their research paper will be strengthened if they derive meaning from a variety of media types as sources.
⭐ **ELPS** 2F

Computers

Students who do extensive Internet research may encounter promising Web sites and electronic books that require payment of a fee. Tell students that many libraries provide free access to these materials.

Try It!
Answers

To help students ask for information using key words and expressions, have them talk with the librarian before using an online catalog. Suggest that they ask the librarian what information they should note during an online catalog search.

⭐ **TEKS** 11.20A, 11.20B **ELPS** 3F

**Differentiated Instruction:
English Language Learners** 　　　　　⭐ **ELPS** 1D, 2F, 3F, 3J

Arrange a visit with a school or local resource librarian.

ELP Level **Beginning**	ELP Level **Intermediate**	ELP Level **Advanced/Advanced High**
Present examples of various media and resources and explain where they can be found. Ask yes/no questions to confirm understanding of concepts.	Present examples of various media and resources and explain where they can be found. Provide stems that students can use to form questions.	Present examples of various media and resources and explain where they can be found. Invite students to describe how each source might be used in research.
Use pages 598–603	Use pages 598–603	Use pages 598–603

⭐ **TEKS** **11.20A** Brainstorm, consult with others, decide upon a topic, and formulate a major research question to address the major research topic; **11.20B** Formulate a plan for engaging in in-depth research on a complex, multi-faceted topic; **ELPS** **1D** Speak using learning strategies; **2F** Listen to and derive meaning from a variety of media/concept and language attainment; **3F** Ask for information during extended speaking assignments; **3J** Respond orally to information presented/concept and language attainment

Using the Computer Catalog

Suggest that students check with their librarian to make sure they understand the types of information included in the online catalog.

Using a Variety of Search Methods

Have students follow these directions for searching an online catalog.

- If students have a particular topic in mind but aren't sure of the title or the author, they can enter keywords about the topic in the appropriate search field. The resulting list of titles may help them find good sources.
- If students don't have a particular topic in mind, they can do a general subject search and check the list of results for promising titles.
- Instead of working only with the online catalog, suggest that students jot down a few call numbers of books about their topics that interest them and browse that section of the library. DIFFERENTIATE INSTRUCTION ↘

⭐ **TEKS** 11.21A; **ELPS** 2I

Sample Computer Catalog Screen

Suggest that students work with a partner to make sure they understand the types of information available from an online catalog.

Try It!
Answers

Before speaking with the librarian, suggest that students jot down any questions they want to ask. DIFFERENTIATE INSTRUCTION ↘

Using the Computer Catalog

Some libraries still use a card catalog located in a cabinet with drawers. Most libraries, however, have put their entire catalog on computer. Each system varies a bit, so ask for help if you're not sure how the system in your library works. A *computer catalog* lists the books held in your library and affiliated systems.

Using a Variety of Search Methods

When you are using a computer catalog, you can find information about a book with any of the following methods:

- If you know it, enter the **title** of the book.
- If you know the **author** of the book, enter the first and last names.
- A general search of your **subject** will also help you find books by experts on your topic. Enter either the subject or a related keyword.

Sample Computer Catalog Screen

In the illustration below, the key to the right identifies the types of information provided for a particular resource, in this case, a book. Once you locate the book you need, make note of the call number. You will use this to find the book on the shelf.

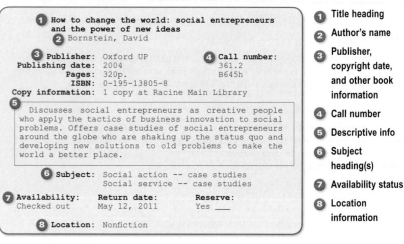

1	Title heading
2	Author's name
3	Publisher, copyright date, and other book information
4	Call number
5	Descriptive info
6	Subject heading(s)
7	Availability status
8	Location information

Try It!

Use the computer catalog to find texts written for informed audiences on a topic of your choice. Ask the librarian if you need help to do this.

Differentiated Instruction: Struggling Learners

Tell students that if they're trying to decide whether it's worthwhile to request a book through interlibrary loan, they can get the information about the book by typing the title into the search box on a commercial bookseller's Web site. These sites often provide thorough descriptions as well as reviews and reader's comments.

TEKS 11.21A

Understanding Call Numbers

All nonfiction books in the library have **call numbers**. The books are arranged on the shelves according to these numbers. Call numbers are usually based on the **Dewey decimal classification** system, which divides nonfiction books into 10 subject categories.

000–099	General Works	500–599	Sciences
100–199	Philosophy	600–699	Technology
200–299	Religion	700–799	Arts and Recreation
300–399	Social Sciences	800–899	Literature
400–499	Languages	900–999	History and Geography

A call number often has a decimal in it, followed by the first letter of an author's name. Note how the following call numbers are ordered on the shelf.

973 M · 973.19 D · 973.2 De · 973.2 Do · 974 F · 974 H · 974.3 B · 974.3 R · 975 R · 975.5 Ry

Try It!

Make up appropriate titles (based on their placement in the Dewey decimal classification system) and authors who are experts on the topic for three of the books on the shelf above.

Identifying the Parts of a Book

Each part of a book provides valuable information. The **title page** includes the title of the book, the author's name, and the publisher's name and city. The **copyright page** follows with the year the book was published. The **preface, foreword,** or **introduction** comes before the table of contents and tells why the book was written. The **table of contents** lists the names and page numbers of sections and chapters in the book. At the end of the book, you may find at least one **appendix,** containing various maps, tables, and lists. Finally, the **index** is an alphabetical list of important topics and their page numbers in the book.

Understanding Call Numbers

Provide students with this additional information about the Dewey decimal classification system:

- Librarian Melvil Dewey created the system in 1876, assigning numbers for all types of subjects in nonfiction and fiction. The system is revised and updated regularly.
- Over time, many libraries removed English-language fiction and biographies from the Dewey classification. These are usually shelved alphabetically by author (fiction) or subject (biography).
- Each digit of a call number has a specific meaning. Refer interested students to the Dewey decimal Web site (www.oclc.org/dewey).

TEKS 11.21A

Try It!
Answers

Answers will vary. Suggest that students do a computer catalog search for the call numbers to find out what subjects their titles should address.

Identifying the Parts of a Book

Give partners a book and direct them to find the title page; copyright page; and, depending on the book, the preface, forward, introduction, table of contents, appendix, and index. (Note: Not all books have all of these parts.)

ELPS 2I

Differentiated Instruction:
English Language Learners   ELPS 2G, 2I

ELP Level **Beginning**	ELP Level **Intermediate**	ELP Level **Advanced/Advanced High**
Choose a specific topic, and guide students to use a variety of search methods to find information on it in a computer catalog.	Choose a specific topic, and have students follow your directions to use a variety of search methods to find information on it in a computer catalog.	Direct students to use a variety of search methods to find information on specified topics in a computer catalog. Discuss their findings as a group.
Use pages 598–603	Use pages 598–603	Use pages 598–603

 TEKS 11.21A Follow the research plan to gather evidence from experts on the topic and texts written for informed audiences in the field, distinguishing between reliable and unreliable sources; **ELPS 2G** Understand general meaning of spoken language/contexts and topics; **2I** Demonstrate listening comprehension/following directions

Using Reference Books

Discuss the variety of reference books that are usually found in the library.

Referring to Encyclopedias

In addition to helping students become familiar with general-purpose encyclopedias such as *Encyclopædia Britannica* and *Encyclopedia Americana*, encourage them to look for subject-specific encyclopedias related to their topics. Examples include:

■ Grove's dictionary series (multivolume sets on such subjects as European and American art and music)

■ Gale encyclopedias (such as the multivolume set on the topic of Native Americans)

To find a topic-specific encyclopedia, suggest that students do a computer catalog search, entering their topic keyword in the subject field and either *encyclopedia* or *dictionary* in the title field.

⭐ **TEKS** 11.21A

Tips for Using Encyclopedias

Suggest that students use these tips as they do their research.

Sample Encyclopedia Index

Have students work with a partner to check that they understand what type of information an encyclopedia index will give them and what parts they need to note in order to find their article.

 ⭐ **TEKS** 11.21A

Using Reference Books

A reference book is a special kind of nonfiction book that contains specific facts or background information from experts on the topic. The reference section includes encyclopedias, dictionaries, almanacs, and so on. Usually, reference books cannot be checked out, so you must use them in the library.

Referring to Encyclopedias

An encyclopedia is a set of books (or a CD-ROM) that contains basic information on topics from A to Z. Topics are arranged alphabetically.

Tips for Using Encyclopedias

■ **At the end of an article, there is often a list of related articles.**
You can read these other articles to learn more about your topic.

■ **The index can help you find out more about your topic.**
The index is usually in a separate volume or at the end of the last volume. It lists every article that contains information about a topic. For example, if you look up "newspapers" in the index, you would find a list of articles—"United States Media," "Freedom of the Press," and so on—that includes information on that topic. (See below.)

■ **Libraries usually have several sets of encyclopedias.**
Review each set and decide which were written for informed audiences on the topic of your choice. (Always check with your teacher first to see if you can use an encyclopedia as a source for your research.)

Sample Encyclopedia Index

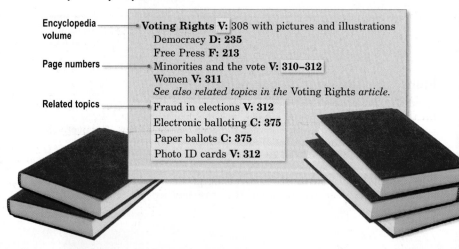

Encyclopedia volume ⟶ **Voting Rights V:** 308 with pictures and illustrations
Democracy **D: 235**
Free Press **F: 213**
Page numbers ⟶ Minorities and the vote **V: 310–312**
Women **V: 311**
See also related topics in the Voting Rights *article.*
Related topics ⟶ Fraud in elections **V: 312**
Electronic balloting **C: 375**
Paper ballots **C: 375**
Photo ID cards **V: 312**

 TEKS **11.21A** Follow the research plan to gather evidence from experts on the topic and texts written for informed audiences in the field, distinguishing between reliable and unreliable sources

★ TEKS 11.21A

Consulting Other Reference Books

Most libraries contain several types of reference books in addition to encyclopedias. The most common ones are listed below.

Almanacs

Almanacs are books filled with facts and statistics from experts about many different subjects. *The World Almanac and Book of Facts* contains celebrity profiles; statistics about politics, business, and sports; plus consumer information.

Atlases

Atlases contain detailed maps of the world, continents, countries, and so on. They also contain statistics and related information. Specialized atlases cover topics such as outer space or oceans especially for informed audiences in those fields.

Dictionaries

Dictionaries contain definitions of words and their origins. Biographical dictionaries focus on famous people. Specialized dictionaries deal with science, history, medicine, and other subjects.

Directories

Directories list information about groups of people, businesses, and organizations. The most widely used directories are telephone books.

Periodical Indexes

Periodical indexes list articles in magazines and newspapers. These indexes are arranged alphabetically by subject.

- The *Readers' Guide to Periodical Literature* lists articles from many publications. (See page **384**.)
- The *New York Times Index* lists articles from the *New York Times* newspaper.

Other Reference Books

Some reference books do not fit into any one category but are recognized by their names:

- *Facts on File* includes thousands of short but informative facts about events, discoveries, people, and places.
- *Facts About the Presidents* presents information about all of the presidents of the United States.
- *Bartlett's Familiar Quotations* lists thousands of quotations from famous people.

Research

Consulting Other Reference Books

If your library allows patrons to access its electronic resources from home, show students how to use this service.

Almanacs

Have students work in small groups and examine an almanac. Have them share information about when an almanac might prove a useful reference for a research paper.
★ ELPS 3E

Atlases

Suggest that students who need geographical information use an atlas.

Dictionaries

Acquaint students with some of the specialized dictionaries available to them such as medical, law, real estate, baseball, math, finance, and biographical dictionaries.

Directories

Point out that there are directories for virtually any contemporary business, topic, or profession and that directories can provide contact information for people they want to interview.

Periodical Indexes

Tell students that some online periodical indexes include abstracts of articles, the full text of articles, or hyperlinks connecting readers to similar articles or articles by the same author.

Other Reference Books

Have students work with a partner and summarize the information available in the various references sources they've studied.
✔ DIFFERENTIATE INSTRUCTION
★ TEKS 11.21A; ELPS 2I

★ TEKS **11.21A** Follow the research plan to gather evidence from experts on the topic and texts written for informed audiences in the field, distinguishing between reliable and unreliable sources; **ELPS 2I** Demonstrate listening comprehension/ retelling or summarizing, collaborating with peers; **3E** Share information in cooperative learning interactions

Using Periodical Guides

Discuss different ways students might access magazine articles in the library.

- Current issues are likely to be shelved in the periodicals section.
- Recent issues are usually bound into volume files or stored in boxes.
- Older periodicals are stored as photographic reproductions on microfilm or microfiche.
- Many articles are available in electronic format and stored in databases that can be accessed through library computers.

Readers' Guide to Periodical Literature

To help students internalize vocabulary, have them work in small groups and summarize how to access magazine articles in a library and how to read an entry in *The Readers' Guide to Periodical Literature.* **DIFFERENTIATE INSTRUCTION ⬎**

 ELPS 3B

Sample *Readers' Guide* Format

Have students work in pairs with an unannotated entry from the *Readers' Guide to Periodical Literature.* Have them label the entry, indicating the type of information given. Ask them to confirm their understanding by explaining their annotations.

 ELPS 2E

Tip

Remind students to focus on authority, accuracy, and currency when evaluating their sources.

 TEKS 11.21A

384

TEKS 11.21A

Using Periodical Guides

Periodical guides are located in the reference or periodical section of the library. These guides alphabetically list topics and articles found in magazines, newspapers, and journals written for informed audiences in a field. Some guides are printed volumes and some are CD's. Many libraries are linking to Web sites for periodical searches. Ask your librarian for the most up-to-date Web site.

Readers' Guide to Periodical Literature

The *Readers' Guide to Periodical Literature* is a well-known periodical reference source and is found in most libraries. The following tips will help you look up your topic in this and other similar resources:

- Articles are always listed alphabetically by author and topic.
- Some topics are subdivided, with each article listed under the appropriate subtopic.
- Cross-references refer to related topic entries where you may find more articles pertinent to your topic.

Sample *Readers' Guide* Format

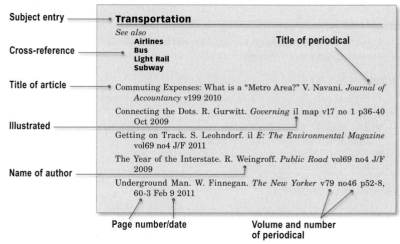

Tip

When you find a listing for your topic, focus on aricles written by experts. Note the magazine name and issue date and the title and page numbers of the article. Your librarian may get the periodical for you, or you may need to find it yourself.

Differentiated Instruction: Advanced Learners

To emphasize that periodicals can be sources for both current and historical topics, challenge students to use the *Readers' Guide to Periodical Literature* to see who can find the earliest and the latest article on a popular topic, such as photography.

Research Writing
MLA Research Paper

Thomas Jefferson once said, "If a nation expects to be ignorant and free, in a state of civilization, it expects what never was and never will be." The point is, maintaining a civilization takes work and requires knowledge. What sort of knowledge? Franklin D. Roosevelt said, "If civilization is to survive, we must cultivate the science of human relationships—the ability of all peoples, of all kinds, to live together, in the same world, at peace." In other words, civilization depends on the social interaction of all sorts of people.

In this chapter, you will learn to write an MLA research paper about an important social issue. In the process, you will study that issue and communicate what you learn to your classmates. In effect, your research paper itself will serve as one small part of the process by which civilization is maintained.

Writing Guidelines

Subject: A solution to a social issue
Purpose: To research and explain a solution to a social issue
Form: MLA research paper
Audience: Classmates

"Civilization is a movement and not a condition, a voyage and not a harbor."
—Arnold Toynbee

MLA Research Paper

MLA Research Paper

Objectives
- demonstrate an understanding of the form and content of a research paper
- learn the process by which a research paper is created
- plan, draft, revise, edit, and publish a research paper

Discuss what is meant by the term *MLA research paper* and have students confirm their understanding by answering questions. Encourage them to seek clarification as needed.

- *MLA* stands for Modern Language Association, a group established in 1883 for the purpose of studying education in the humanities.
- The MLA devised a set of rules for formatting research papers; this is known as "MLA style." Tell students that teachers in other fields may ask them to use the APA (American Psychological Association) style, but in the field of language and literature, MLA is the most commonly used style.
- One important feature of MLA style is its method for acknowledging sources (parenthetical citations in the text and a works-cited page at the end). Students will learn about APA style later in this unit (SE pages 442–444; 453–454).

⭐ **ELPS** 2D, 2G ☑ **DIFFERENTIATE INSTRUCTION**

ELPS **2D** Monitor understanding of spoken language and seek clarification as needed; **2E** Use visual, contextual, and linguistic support to confirm understanding of spoken language; **2G** Understand general meaning of spoken language/topics, language, and contexts; **3B** Expand vocabulary/retelling simple stories and basic information and learning and using routine language needed for classroom communication

Research Paper

Many students find it difficult to plan detailed outlines before they begin writing. Let students know whether or not you require them to submit a formal outline like the one on this page. Explain that a formal outline provides the focus and the scope of the research for the reader.

A working outline, on the other hand, is meant to be a rough guide to their research and writing. Because it is difficult to decide in advance everything students will include in their papers, they may diverge from their working outline whenever better ideas come to mind.

386

Research Paper

Fidel Novielli got excited as he read a magazine article about "social capitalism." He researched the topic further and wrote the following paper. Margin notes point out important features of organization and formatting.

Meeting the Needs of the Future

Fidel Novielli
Ms. Palacek
Language Arts
23 February 2011

Title Page
Center the title one-third of the way down the page. Center author information two-thirds of the way down.

Meeting the Needs of the Future

THESIS STATEMENT: "Social entrepreneurs" have begun to apply business strategies to human problems, with impressive results.

I. The root problem is that social systems are about 300 years behind the times.
   A. The industrial revolution made businesses competitive and innovative.
   B. Government and other social systems remained uncompetitive.
   C. For 300 years, business continued to evolve, while the social systems fell further behind.

II. The industrial revolution brought new challenges.
   A. The Tofflers explained that society had become more urban.
   B. The rural support system, primarily the family, did not carry over to urban life.
   C. Relocation resulted in poverty, crime, and disease.

III. About 25 years ago, this dichotomy began to change dramatically.
   A. Faced with such need and opportunity, social entrepreneurs began to appear.
   B. Bill Drayton founded Ashoka to help foster . . .

Outline
Center the title one inch from the top of the page. Double-space throughout. Include the outline after the title page and before the first page of the report.

Note: If your teacher requires a title page or an outline, follow the guidelines above or any special instructions you are given.

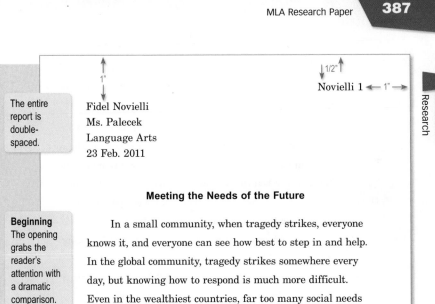

Research

The entire report is double-spaced.

Fidel Novielli
Ms. Palecek
Language Arts
23 Feb. 2011

↓ 1/2" ↑
Novielli 1 ← 1" →

Meeting the Needs of the Future

Beginning
The opening grabs the reader's attention with a dramatic comparison.

In a small community, when tragedy strikes, everyone knows it, and everyone can see how best to step in and help. In the global community, tragedy strikes somewhere every day, but knowing how to respond is much more difficult. Even in the wealthiest countries, far too many social needs remain unmet. In the United States alone, 12 million

← 1" → American children live with hunger (Berg and Freedman). Globally, 25,000 children a day die from malnutrition and disease ("Hunger").

Faced with numbers like these, an individual might be tempted to despair and cry out, "I'm only one person. What can I do?" Fortunately, a new breed of concerned citizenry has begun to demonstrate that one person can do a lot, given a little imagination and determination. In the business world, these qualities have long been recognized as the features of an entrepreneur. <u>Now "social</u>

The beginning part leads up to the thesis statement (underlined).

<u>entrepreneurs"—sometimes called "social capitalists"—</u> <u>have begun to apply business strategies to human</u> <u>problems, with impressive results.</u>

1"

Ask students to read the full model research paper and accompanying margin notes carefully. When they have finished, review each margin note and discuss the information in detail as a group. ☑ **DIFFERENTIATE INSTRUCTION**

Point out that the thesis isn't stated until the end of the second paragraph, and note that in longer papers, more than one paragraph may be needed for the beginning. Explain that because a research paper examines a topic in depth, it is likely to have a more complex thesis. It makes sense that the writer would develop a longer introduction to lead up to the thesis.

Have students identify the purpose of each of the beginning paragraphs.
- The first paragraph states that social problems in the global community are widespread, and it provides statistics to support that assertion.
- The second paragraph focuses on the idea that individuals may feel powerless to help solve the world's problems. It then presents the writer's thesis: social entrepreneurship is a way for individuals to solve problems using business methods.

Draw students' attention to the section headings in the model paper (*The Problem, The Solution, Conclusions*). Remind students that using headings is a good way to let readers know what information they're about to encounter, in the same way that chapter titles give readers clues about what is to come.

Have students work with a partner or in a small group. Ask them to explain how the section headings follow the outline. (The author uses simple headings that match up with sections I, II, and III of the outline.) Discuss other approaches the author could have taken for headings. (Answers will vary. Students might suggest repeating important phrases from the text; summing up the purpose of each section in a creative way by, for example, using a quotation that applies to each section; or asking a question that is answered by the text that follows.)

DIFFERENTIATE INSTRUCTION ↘

Novielli 2

The Problem

According to Bill Drayton, founder of Ashoka, an organization that promotes social entrepreneurship, the root problem is that social systems are about 300 years behind the times. When the industrial revolution started in the early 1700s, the business sector became competitive and innovative. However, government and other social systems remained uncompetitive, supported by taxes or donations and bolstered by tradition. As business continued to evolve over the centuries, social systems fell further and further behind in their cost-effectiveness (Hammonds).

Worse, the Industrial Age brought new challenges that the old social systems were simply not equipped to handle. As futurists Alvin and Heidi Toffler explain, society had become increasingly urban, drawing people away from farms and villages to work in factories. The social support of rural communities, with their multigenerational families, could not carry over into the cities, where many people had relocated, living alone or in a "nuclear family" of father, mother, and a few children (19-24). As any Dickens novel reveals, and every modern metropolitan newspaper repeats, far too often this relocation has resulted in poverty, crime, and disease.

The Solution

Drayton believes that roughly 25 years ago, this situation began to change dramatically. The social sectors

Middle
The first middle paragraphs identify the problem, followed by proposed solutions.

The source of paraphrased information is identified in parentheses.

Headings help guide the reader from section to section.

Research

Novielli 3

started applying the lessons of business. In his words, "It was like hearing the ice breaking up at the end of winter in a lake. Creak, creak, groan, crash! The need was so big, the gap so huge, the opportunity to learn was right before people's eyes" (Hammonds). Faced with such need and opportunity, a new breed of entrepreneur began to emerge, this time in the social sector. Drayton created Ashoka as a means of fostering this social entrepreneurship on a global scale. His goal is literally to change the world.

> If that seems audacious, it is important to understand Drayton's vision and his experience. As one former employer explains, "Everything that Drayton did he focused on the fundamentals." In other words, Drayton believes in attacking the root of a problem. For example, while serving as assistant administrator for the Environmental Protection Agency, he successfully championed a "bubble" method of cheaply and effectively combating pollution. Under this plan, pollution is tackled as a whole, rather than as individual processes. Instead of dictating specific details for reducing emissions, the plan gives each business an emissions target, and that business can determine the most cost-effective way to meet that goal. Businesses can even trade gains at one location against shortfalls at another, to bring the overall level of pollution down. This "bubble and trading" plan quickly became the official policy of the U.S. Since then, it has also been included

A quotation is integrated into the paper for voice and authority.

The writer provides an example to clarify a point.

Work with students to analyze a paragraph in the model using the writing traits. For example, have them focus on the first new paragraph on this page.

Focus and Coherence— How does the first sentence in the paragraph connect to or build on the previous paragraph? (The phrase, "If that seems audacious," refers directly to Drayton's goal to change the world.)

Organization—How is the paragraph organized? (Examples supporting the topic are presented in logical order.)

Development of Ideas—Does the writer offer enough support for the main idea of the paragraph? (Students' answers will vary but should include some of what follows. The writer starts with a quotation about Drayton's personality and approach, and then gives an example of something he did that demonstrates the quotation's accuracy. This leads to an explanation of how the actions Drayton took at the EPA worked, followed by an example of how other organizations adopted his ideas.)

ELPS 4I, 4K

Differentiated Instruction: English Language Learners

ELPS 2E, 4F, 4I

Use visuals and simplified language to provide contextual and linguistic support for ideas about the Industrial Revolution.

ELP Level **Beginning**	ELP Level **Intermediate**	ELP Level **Advanced/Advanced High**
Read the headings *The Problem* and *The Solution* together. Use sentence stems to discuss familiar problems and solutions.	Use basic language to discuss the first two paragraphs. Help students summarize challenges and problems from this time.	As you read SE pages 388–389 together, pause to have students identify and summarize main ideas and supporting details.
Use pages 598–603	Use pages 598–603	Use pages 598–603

ELPS 2E Use visual, contextual, and linguistic support to confirm understanding of spoken language; **4F** Use support from peers and teachers to develop background knowledge; **4I** Demonstrate English comprehension by employing and expanding basic reading skills; **4K** Demonstrate English comprehension and expand reading skills by employing analytical skills

Continue discussing the paragraph on SE page 389 with students. Challenge them to point out the transitional words and phrases used in the paragraph. Ask them to explain how each one works to connect ideas. Answers will vary. Possible answers shown. **DIFFERENTIATE INSTRUCTION ↘**

- *If that seems audacious* is an introductory clause that creates a transition from the previous paragraph by using a pronoun *(that)* that refers to the antecedent at the end of the previous paragraph *(goal . . . to change the world).*

- *In other words* is an introductory phrase to a sentence that clarifies the meaning of the preceding quotation.

- *For example* is an introductory phrase that signals an illustration of Drayton's way of working.

- *Since then* is an introductory phrase that provides readers with a time reference to help them understand the order of events.

✳ For more about using transitions, see SE page 623.

Novielli 4

When a source has page numbers, the appropriate numbers are included in the citation.

Writer develops an argument that incorporates the complexities of various sources of information.

A technical term is defined for the reader.

as a central part of the Kyoto Protocol for international emissions, and the European Parliament has adopted it for their global emissions-trading market (Bornstein 53–58).

It is this sort of "fundamental solution" thinking that characterizes social entrepreneurship and that distinguishes it from traditional social work. Traditional social programs tend to be a one-sided, top-down approach to solving a problem. This approach involves the *have's* handing something down to the *have-not's*. More often than not, a response focuses on a crisis. Social capitalism, on the other hand, seeks to change the situation that causes the need. It looks for opportunities by which the needy can better themselves. In the process, society benefits as well.

Consider the example of Erzsébet Szekeres of Hungary, whose son Tibor was born with microcephalus (an abnormally small skull) and severe mental retardation. Under the strain of caring for Tibor during his early years, Szekeres' marriage and career began to suffer. Friends and family urged the woman to put her son in a state institution and go on with her life. Szekeres saw, however, that these institutions were little more than prisons where the severely handicapped were shut away from public view. She dreamed of a group home where people like Tibor could care for themselves, with assistance, and even have meaningful work.

It took years of determined effort on Szekeres' part to make that dream a reality. Often, the government itself

Research

Novielli 5

opposed her efforts because she was not a member of the
health-care profession. Eventually, however, with two loans
from disability organizations, she purchased an abandoned
farming cooperative and turned it into a community for
the disabled. Today, this facility includes dorm-style rooms,
a cafeteria, a community room where dances are held
and movies are shown, and work facilities where people
like her son earn money by assembling curtain clips
and other such assembly-line jobs. To date, Szekeres has
created 21 institutions across Hungary, where more than
600 multiply-disabled people live and work. Her efforts
are even changing the way the state itself deals with the
handicapped (Bornstein 98–116).

> Perhaps an even clearer example of social capitalism
is shown in the food-bank program created by Wojciech
Onyszkiewicz in Poland. During the years that Soviet
communism ruled Poland, the very existence of poverty
was denied. After the fall of the Soviet Union, it was
estimated that 20 percent of the population lived below
the poverty line, and 31 percent of those in poverty were
multi-child families. While rural communities often had
a surplus of food, there were no systems in place for
getting it to urban populations ("Ashoka"). In addition,
rural citizens were not happy about giving charity
to people they perceived as "parasites" (Bornstein 201).
On the other hand, these same rural people envied the

Each paragraph contains effective supporting details.

An example helps explain "social capitalism."

Draw students' attention to the first new
paragraph on this page. Note that the writer
strengthens his explanation by providing
historical context:
- The need for the food bank is made clearer by
  explaining that Poland was under Soviet rule
  and the Soviet government denied the existence
  of poverty.
- Noting the fall of the Soviet government
  explains how it became possible to establish
  the food bank.

Point out that the writer also could have included
dates to accompany the historical explanations
(the years Poland was under Soviet rule or the
year the government fell).

Differentiated Instruction: English Language Learners

ELPS 1C, 1E

ELP Level **Beginning**	ELP Level **Intermediate**	ELP Level **Advanced/Advanced High**
Use simplified language to summarize and chart the problem a mother in Hungary faced and how she solved it. Guide students to read the chart with you.	Use simplified language to discuss the example. Have partners work together to complete sentence stems about the problem and the solution.	As you read pages 390–391 together, pause to have students write brief summaries to identify the main idea and purpose of each paragraph.
Use pages 598–603	Use pages 598–603	Use pages 598–603

ELPS 1C Use strategic learning strategies to acquire basic and
grade-level vocabulary; **1E** Internalize new basic and academic
language by using and reusing it/writing

Draw students' attention to the dashes used on this page. Point out the two common uses for dashes—to set off parenthetical material (see this page) and to add emphasis (see SE page 393).

■ Remind students that inserting explanatory material in the middle of a sentence, as on this page, requires a pair of dashes, one on each side of the insertion. If the added information falls at the end of the sentence, only the first dash is needed.

■ Commas are also used to set off added information. Point out that the dashes on these two pages could be replaced with commas. Ask students whether their reading of the sentence with commas changes. If so, how?

Ask partners to write one or two sentences using dashes to practice the sentence pattern.

🗣 ELPS 5F

✳ For more about using dashes, see SE page 668.

Novielli 6

opportunities for education and culture that were available to urban citizens.

Onyszkiewicz came up with a plan in which rural communities would donate excess food for urban use, and in exchange, rural children would travel to the cities to help distribute that food, visit museums, attend sessions of parliament, and take part in other such activities ("Ashoka"). Under a similar plan, Onyszkiewicz organized computer training for rural children by recruiting physically disabled computer users from the city. In exchange for their expertise, these city dwellers are able to visit the countryside. Villagers prepare wheelchair ramps and arrange outdoor activities that the urbanites could not otherwise experience (Bornstein 201). In both of these cases, "commodities" are exchanged in a very capitalistic manner, and in both cases, important human needs are met.

Ashoka itself is actually another example of social capitalism at work. The organization's goal is to identify promising social entrepreneurs in the earliest stages of their work and to provide support to help that work flourish. While some of this support is monetary—a small stipend to allow the blossoming entrepreneur to work full-time on the project—most of it is less tangible. Ashoka fellows "get support, ideas, and, quite literally, protection," as in the case of a Brazilian Ashoka fellow whose work in drug rehabilitation resulted in attacks by local police. The

> The writer provides clear explanation throughout the paper.

> Smooth-reading sentences make the paper very "readable."

Research

Novielli 7

organization took the case to the local governor, and the attacks stopped (Hammonds). What makes this support capitalistic is that by applying it early in the work of a social entrepreneur, Ashoka gets the greatest "return" on its investment—the most good from the least assistance.

Conclusion

These are only a few examples from thousands of programs around the world. (Ashoka alone has more than 1,500 fellows.) Social entrepreneurs are tackling problems at all levels, from helping inner-city children fill out college applications to training health-care workers for the millions of AIDS victims in South Africa. It is no exaggeration to say that their efforts often lift entire communities out of poverty. Since 2004, Fast Company and the Monitor Group have given awards recognizing the 25 best social entrepreneurs each year ("25"). The competition is stiff, and the stories of the finalists are every bit as inspiring as those of the award-winners.

Bill Drayton believes that the next step in this social evolution is a partnering of business and social entrepreneurs, which he sees as only natural. It was the splitting of business and social concerns 300 years ago that was unnatural. Eventually, he believes, everyone will be a change-maker, and as a result, everyone will feel that his or her life has meaning.

Ending
The closing paragraphs summarize the main points and leave the reader with a final thought.

Note that, just as the writer created a two-paragraph beginning, he also created a two-paragraph ending. Ask students to analyze each part of the ending and discuss how it is organized. Possible responses:

- The first paragraph refers back to the thesis and supports it by stating that there are many more examples of successful social entrepreneurship in addition to those described.
- Details that support the topic sentence of the first ending paragraph give the number of social entrepreneurs who are Ashoka fellows, and name the two organizations that give awards to social entrepreneurs.
- The last paragraph leaves the reader with an interesting parting thought by suggesting the next step in the development of social entrepreneurship. ✓ **DIFFERENTIATE INSTRUCTION**

⚙ **ELPS** 4K

Differentiated Instruction: English Language Learners

✦ **ELPS** 4K

ELP Level **Beginning**	ELP Level **Intermediate**	ELP Level **Advanced/Advanced High**
Discuss the paper's conclusion. Use visuals, gestures, and simplified language to chart how the writer gives final examples and sums up his ideas.	Together, write sentences that analyze how the writer forms his conclusion, such as *He summarizes his main ideas. He gives more examples.*	Have partners analyze the paper's conclusion by writing answers to questions such as *How does the writer summarize his main points?*
Use pages 598–603	Use pages 598–603	Use pages 598–603

ELPS **4K** Demonstrate English comprehension and expand reading skills by employing analytical skills

Have students work in pairs to find in-text citations that correspond to each source listed on the Works Cited page. Point out that as required by MLA style, in-text citations are in parentheses and consist of the author's last name or the first word of an article title and the page number. Remind students to use the appropriate vocabulary to discuss the citations.

 TEKS 11.23D; **ELPS** 1C, 1D

Offer these tips for citations:

- If two authors have the same last name, include their initials before their last name.
- If two or more works by the same author are used, include the first word of each title with the author's last name.
- For articles starting with the same word, use the first two words of these titles.

Respond to the reading.

You may wish to have students work in small groups to answer questions. Possible answers shown.

Answers

1. **Focus and Coherence** Yes. The opening paragraphs are engaging, include striking statistics, and evoke the frustration people feel when faced with huge problems. Both effectively introduce the author's thesis.

2. **Organization** Examples supporting the thesis are arranged in logical order.

3. **Development of Ideas** Specific examples of social capitalism support the writer's thesis.

4. **Voice** The writer uses rhetorical devices to express his voice: appeals to emotion: *might be tempted to despair* . . . (p. 387); parallel structure: *As any Dickens novel reveals. . .* (p. 388). **DIFFERENTIATE INSTRUCTION**

 ELPS 3E

 TEKS 11.23D

Novielli 8

Works Cited

"Ashoka Fellow Profile—Wojciech Onyszkiewicz." *Ashoka*. 6 Oct. 1995. Web. 12 Jan. 2011

Berg, Joel and Freedman, Tom. "Ending Child Hunger in America." Progressive Policy Institute. 1 Jan. 2009. Web. 15 Jan. 2011.

Bornstein, David. *How to Change the World: Social Entrepreneurs and the Power of New Ideas*. New York: Oxford, 2004. Print.

Hammonds, Keith H. "A Lever Long Enough to Move the World." *Fast Company*. Jan. 2005. Web. 3 July 2010.

"Hunger Facts." United Nations World Food Programme. n.d. Web. 2009.

Toffler, Alvin, and Heidi Toffler. *Creating a New Civilization*. Atlanta: Turner, 1995. Print.

"25 Entrepreneurs Who Are Changing the World." *Fast Company*. 19 Feb. 2006. Web. 21 Oct. 2010.

> A separate page alphabetically lists sources cited in the paper.

> Lines that run over are indented five spaces.

Respond to the reading. Answer the following questions.

Focus and Coherence (1) Is the writer's introduction effective? Explain.

Organization (2) What organizing pattern does the writer use?

Development of Ideas (3) What evidence supports the writer's thesis?

Voice (4) How does the writer express his unique perspective?

MLA Research Paper **395**

Prewriting

Research

Your research paper must start with planning. During this prewriting stage, you will organize your initial thoughts, decide what the type of information you need, and gather that information in preparation for writing your paper.

Keys to Effective Prewriting

1. For your topic, choose a social issue that interests you.

2. Make a list of questions you want to have answered about that subject.

3. Use a gathering grid to organize your research questions and answers. Use note cards to keep track of longer answers. (See pages 399–400.)

4. Be careful to record the sources of any information you summarize or quote.

5. Note the publication details of all your sources, for making a works-cited page later. (See pages 445–454.)

6. Make sure that you find enough to say about your topic, including an explanation of the problem and a discussion of possible solutions.

Prewriting

Keys to Effective Prewriting

Remind students of the purpose of the prewriting stage in the writing process: It is when the writer selects a topic, gathers details, and decides how to organize those details.

The Keys to Effective Prewriting list explains the process students will be guided through on SE pages 396–407.

Note that the prewriting stage for a research paper will require much more time than what students have spent on other writing assignments, such as a personal narrative, because during prewriting the writer does extensive research to gather and sort information. Using this time wisely will help students focus their ideas and organize their writing. ✔ **DIFFERENTIATE INSTRUCTION**

Differentiated Instruction: English Language Learners

⭐ **ELPS** 1B, 1D, 2D, 2I, 3E

Work with students in small, mixed-language-ability groups to have them share ideas and ask for clarification about ideas and concepts.

ELP Level **Beginning**	ELP Level **Intermediate**	ELP Level **Advanced/Advanced High**
Guide students to ask partners questions such as *What is the writer's main idea?* and employ self-corrective techniques as needed.	Help students complete sentence stems such as *I don't understand ____* to ask for specific assistance or clarification.	Have students model using non-verbal cues when asking and answering questions.

ELPS 1B Monitor oral language production and employ self-corrective techniques or other resources; **1D** Speak using learning strategies; **2D** Monitor understanding of spoken language and seek clarification as needed; **2I** Demonstrate listening comprehension/collaborating with peers; **3E** Share information in cooperative learning interactions

Prewriting Selecting a Topic

Explain that a cluster is one way to brainstorm and organize ideas for possible writing topics.

Cluster

Point out that Fidel uses the stages of life as the main categories for his topic cluster. Have partners brainstorm other categories students might use to organize their topic cluster. Responses may include the following:

- Occupational areas—for example: agriculture, manufacturing, education, science
- Media—for example: TV, radio, the Internet, books, periodicals
- Necessities of life—for example: food, housing, health care, education DIFFERENTIATE INSTRUCTION ↘

✳ For information about the basics of life list, see SE page 93.

⬛ **ELPS** 1C

Make a cluster. Once students have completed their clusters, have them work with a partner to get feedback on their topic choice. Partners should look for the interest level of the topic and think about whether it is too broad or too narrow.
DIFFERENTIATE INSTRUCTION ↘

⬛ **TEKS** 11.13A, 11.20A

Prewriting Selecting a Topic

When you brainstorm for a specific topic on a general subject such as "a social issue," you can make a cluster. Fidel made a cluster using stages of life as main categories. He then listed specific examples of social issues for each age category. You can see part of his cluster below.

Cluster

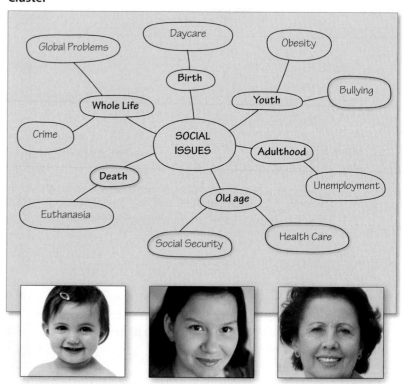

Prewrite

Make a cluster. To find a topic for your research paper, make a cluster. Start by writing the general subject inside a circle. Next, add circles around it with main categories related to social issues. Around those categories, list specific issues. Choose an issue that interests you as the topic for your research paper. Consult with others for their thoughts on interesting topics.

Differentiated Instruction: Struggling Learners

To help students decide on a topic, remind them that choosing a manageable topic will allow them to focus and limit their research. Point out that the cluster method is an effective tool that can help them consider aspects of a topic.

If students find a more compelling focus during research, they should make an appointment with you to discuss the option. For example, a student who begins by researching rising obesity rates in children may decide to focus solely on the obesity rates in preschool-age children.

⬛ **TEKS** **11.13A** Plan a first draft by determining appropriate topics through a range of strategies; **11.20A** Brainstorm, consult with others, decide upon a topic, and formulate a major research question to address the major research topic; **ELPS 1C** Use strategic learning strategies to acquire basic and grade-level vocabulary

TEKS 11.13A, 11.20A

Research

Sizing Up Your Topic

An effective research paper about an important social issue should cover three main areas.

- **The issue:** What is the social issue? Define the problem.
- **The solution:** How can the problem be solved? Explain a likely solution. This might also include a history of solutions that have been tried in the past.
- **The conclusion:** What steps should be taken next? Start with a summary of the issue and the suggested solution. Then include a call to action, or leave the reader with something to think about.

When Fidel prepared his report on social entrepreneurship, he did some quick initial research. He took notes about what he found.

Research Notes

> **What is the issue?**
> - The human race is facing global problems of hunger, disease, overpopulation, and poverty.
> - Current social systems seem unable to address these problems.
>
> **What is the solution?**
> - Social entrepreneurship looks for new ways to solve old problems.
> - Social capitalism makes problem solving cost-effective, not just charity.
> - This approach matches needs with opportunities so that everyone benefits.
> - It tackles the root of a problem rather than treating the symptoms.
>
> **What are the next steps?**
> - Continue to encourage social entrepreneurs.
> - Look for ways that common people can be involved.
> - Match business interests with social needs.

Fidel found sufficient information to know that there would be plenty to write about for his topic. He understood that in order to make his points, he would have to describe specific examples of social capitalism. Finding those examples would require further research.

Prewrite

Size up your topic. Look up your topic on the Internet or use another reliable basic resource. List the key details you find. Consult with others about your research. Are there enough details to support a research paper? If not, consider another topic.

Sizing Up Your Topic

As students work to get a basic grasp of their topic, they may consult many secondary sources because these tend to provide overviews of a subject. Have students review the information about evaluating sources on SE pages 376–378 and discuss how to derive meaning from each one. Point out that reliable secondary sources generally include

- major newspaper and magazine articles, including reviews of books about the topic;
- encyclopedias; and
- film and television documentaries.

ELPS 2F

Research Notes

Tell students they may discover that no real solution has yet been found for their topics. This is to be expected when dealing with complex issues. Suggest that as they consider solutions, instead of using the head "The Answer," they might describe the attempts to find solutions or might uncover or suggest new ways of approaching the problem.

Size up your topic. As students evaluate their topics, remind them to make sure that the topic they focus on is neither too broad nor too narrow.

TEKS 11.13A, 11.20A

TEKS **11.13A** Plan a first draft by determining appropriate topics through a range of strategies; **11.20A** Brainstorm, consult with others, decide upon a topic, and formulate a major research question to address the major research topic; **ELPS 1C** Use strategic learning strategies to acquire basic and grade-level vocabulary; **2F** Listen to and derive meaning from a variety of media/concept and language attainment; **4J** Demonstrate English comprehension and expand reading skills by employing inferential skills

Prewriting Writing Your Research Question

Remind students that their research question must be specific because it will guide their in-depth research process. Point out that this means going beyond a question that is too broad or too narrow. **DIFFERENTIATE INSTRUCTION ↘**

Sample Research Questions

Have students work in pairs to explain, or critique, how each sample research question could guide an in-depth research process.
TEKS 11.20A, 11.20B, 11.22C

Write your major research question. Have students review their notes and formulate a major research question about multi-faceted topic. Point out the question will guide their in-depth research plan. If students have difficulty formulating their questions, remind them to critique their research process and consider whether additional research is needed.
TEKS 11.13A, 11.20A, 11.20B, 11.22C; **ELPS** 2I

 **TEKS** 11.13A, 11.20A, 11.20B, 11.22C

Prewriting Writing Your Research Question

With your research underway, it is time to write a research question. This question will state the main idea of your paper and will guide your writing. The rest of your paper will serve to explain and support this main idea. You can use this formula to help you write your major research question.

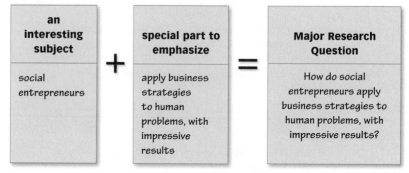

an interesting subject	+	special part to emphasize	=	Major Research Question
social entrepreneurs		apply business strategies to human problems, with impressive results		How do social entrepreneurs apply business strategies to human problems, with impressive results?

Sample Research Questions

Why does the globalization of human civilization (an interesting subject) mean that a threat to one part of the world threatens the well-being of the whole world (a special part to emphasize)?

In the Information Age (an interesting subject), why is wealth no longer a limited commodity to be hoarded by some and denied to others (a special part to emphasize)?

What was the effect of Gandhi's belief in a new type of ethics (an interesting subject) based on empathy rather than rules (a special part to emphasize)?

 Prewrite

Write your major research question. Review your research notes and choose a main point you could make about your topic. Using the formula above, write a major research question.

Differentiated Instruction: Struggling Learners

Have students form small groups to evaluate each research question.

- Will it interest the reader?
- Is its main point clear?
- Does it seem correct and logical?
- Is it easily understood?

Students should make revisions based on classmates' comments.

 TEKS **11.13A** Plan a first draft by determining appropriate topics through a range of strategies, and developing a thesis or controlling idea; **11.20A** Brainstorm, consult with others, decide upon a topic, and formulate a major research question to address the major research topic; **11.20B** Formulate a plan for engaging in in-depth research on a complex, multi-faceted topic; **11.22C** Critique the research process at each step to implement changes as the need occurs and is identified; **ELPS** **2I** Demonstrate listening comprehension/following directions and taking notes

Research

Prewriting Using a Gathering Grid

Fidel used a gathering grid to help him form a research plan for his paper. This grid organizes the information he found during his research on social capitalism. On the left-hand side, Fidel listed questions about the topic. Across the top, he listed sources that answered those questions. For answers too long to fit in the grid, Fidel used note cards. (See the next page.) Part of Fidel's grid is shown below.

Gathering Grid

SOCIAL CAPITALISM	How to Change the World (book)	Berg and Freedman (Web)	"A Lever Long Enough..." (magazine article)
What is the problem?	See card 2.	12 million children in the United States living with hunger	See card 1.
What is a solution?	Apply business entrepreneurship to change the world.		See card 3.
What next steps are needed?	People have to believe the problems can be solved. (282)		Match business needs with public needs.

Prewrite

Create a gathering grid. List questions in the left-hand column of your grid. Across the top, list sources that you will use. Fill in the grid with answers that you find. Use note cards for longer, more detailed answers.

Prewriting Using a Gathering Grid

Suggest that students make a gathering grid template on a computer, using the table-making function of their word processing program. For most programs, the process is as follows:

- Set the page orientation to "landscape" so the table will be arranged lengthwise across the paper.
- Set the page margins to be as small as possible, to provide the maximum amount of space inside the table.
- Create a table or spreadsheet with four rows and with four or five columns, and then adjust the table so that it fills the page, making all the cells as large as possible.
- Type the topic in the upper left-hand cell, and add the three questions in the first cell in each row, as shown in the sample gathering grid.
- Save the document and print several copies to use for research.

Gathering Grid

Discuss how the categories and headings used on the sample gathering grid relate to the model research paper. Elicit that the gathering grid can help them to stay focused on their research plan.

Create a gathering grid If a student's topic does not have an obvious solution, suggest that the student change the third head on the grid from *What is the Solution?* to *What Are Possible Solutions?* Remind students to number their grid pages and keep them with their prewriting work.

✔ DIFFERENTIATE INSTRUCTION

TEKS 11.13A, 11.20A, 11.20B

TEKS **11.13A** Plan a first draft by determining appropriate topics through a range of strategies, and developing a thesis or controlling idea; **11.20A** Brainstorm, consult with others, decide upon a topic, and formulate a major research question to address the major research topic; **11.20B** Formulate a plan for engaging in in-depth research on a complex, multi-faceted topic; **ELPS 2I** Demonstrate listening comprehension/following directions and collaborating with peers; **4G** Demonstrate comprehension of increasingly complex English/taking notes

Prewriting Creating Note Cards

Point out that research involves gathering information from a variety of reliable sources and experts in the field. Explain that creating note cards helps students organize the information, and demonstrates their comprehension of research material through their summaries.

 TEKS 11.21A

Note Cards

Paraphrase Explain that paraphrases will help to get students in the habit of using their own words to express ideas.

List Point out that a list is a useful way to condense information from several sources.

Quotation Remind students to copy any quotations carefully and exactly, and to cite the source.

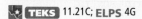 **TEKS** 11.21C; **ELPS** 4G

Create note cards. Suggest practical tips for working with note cards. For example, students can color-code the cards by doing one of the following:

- choose three different colors of cards,
- highlight the top edge of the cards in different colors, or
- use a different color of ink for each question.

Also suggest that students find a method for securing the cards and keeping them together.

Creating Note Cards

Presumably, you have gathered information from experts on your topic and from texts written for informed audiences in the field. Often, these sources will require space for in-depth answers. In such cases, use note cards. Number each new card and write a question at the top. Answer the question with a list, a quotation, or a paraphrase (see page 401). At the bottom, identify the source of the information (including a page number if appropriate).

Note Cards

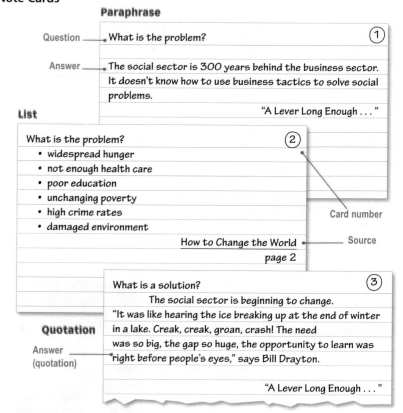

Paraphrase

Question — What is the problem?　①

Answer — The social sector is 300 years behind the business sector. It doesn't know how to use business tactics to solve social problems.

"A Lever Long Enough . . ."

List

What is the problem?　②
- widespread hunger
- not enough health care
- poor education
- unchanging poverty
- high crime rates
- damaged environment

How to Change the World — Source
page 2

Card number

What is a solution?　③
The social sector is beginning to change.
"It was like hearing the ice breaking up at the end of winter in a lake. Creak, creak, groan, crash! The need was so big, the gap so huge, the opportunity to learn was right before people's eyes," says Bill Drayton.

Quotation

Answer (quotation) —

"A Lever Long Enough . . ."

 Prewrite
Create note cards. Make note cards like the examples above whenever your answers are too long to fit on your gathering grid.

TEKS **11.21A** Follow the research plan to gather evidence from experts on the topic and texts written for informed audiences in the field; **11.21C** Paraphrase, summarize, quote, and accurately cite all researched information according to a standard format, differentiating among primary, secondary, and other sources; **ELPS** **4G** Demonstrate comprehension of increasingly complex English/retelling or summarizing

Research

Avoiding Plagiarism

It's always important to give other people credit for their words and ideas. If you don't, that is called **plagiarism,** and it is stealing. As you note facts and ideas during your research, take care to note the source, and to indicate whether your note is a paraphrase or a quotation.

- **Paraphrase:** It's usually best to put ideas you find into your own words, so that your paper sounds like you. This is called paraphrasing. Still, you must give credit to the source of the ideas.

- **Quote exact words:** Sometimes it's best to use the exact words of a source to add authority or interesting color to your report. Be sure to include those words in quotation marks and give credit to the source.

Paraphrase

> What next steps are needed?
>
> Bill Drayton believes that the next step in this social evolution is a partnering of business and social entrepreneurs.
>
>   "A Lever Long Enough . . . "

Quote

> What next steps are needed?
>
> "Next big idea: Global partnerships between social entrepreneurs and business . . . Business must use social networks to reach new markets. And the citizen sector needs the [business] marketplace to gain financial sustainability."
>
> "A Lever Long Enough . . . "

Note: Use ellipses in your quotations to show where you left out words from the original source and square brackets where you added or changed words.

Try It!

The following excerpt is from an article entitled "A New Breed of Champion." Label a note card with the question "What is the solution?" and *paraphrase* the selection.

> Many people assume that wealth and poverty go hand in hand. That is to say, ever since the invention of money, some people have had a lot and others have had little.

ELP Level **Beginning**	ELP Level **Intermediate**	ELP Level **Advanced/Advanced High**
Use simplified language to discuss paraphrasing and quoting. Ask yes/no questions to gauge comprehension and to have students summarize the concepts.	Lead a shared reading of the text on paraphrasing and quoting. Assess comprehension by having students complete sentence stems to summarize the ideas.	Discuss paraphrasing and quoting. Have students summarize each concept orally and explain why they should work to avoid plagiarism.

Avoiding Plagiarism

Have students turn ahead to SE pages 433–440 and read the detailed information about writing responsibly to avoid plagiarism. Point out that it's possible to plagiarize accidentally. This can happen when the writer fails to clearly identify notes that are paraphrases or direct quotations from the source, or forgets to write down the source information on the notes.

Paraphrase

Remind students that paraphrases require source information.

Quote

Emphasize the importance of enclosing word-for-word text in quotation marks. Require that students also underline all quotations on their note cards.

Try It!
Answers

Possible paraphrase:
Since there has always been wealth and poverty, it's often assumed that you can't have one without the other. ☑ **DIFFERENTIATE INSTRUCTION**

★ **TEKS** 11.21A

 TEKS **11.21A** Follow the research plan to gather evidence from experts on the topic and texts written for informed audiences in the field; **ELPS** **4G** Demonstrate comprehension of increasingly complex English/retelling or summarizing

Prewriting Keeping Track of Your Sources

Have students work in pairs and together familiarize themselves with the MLA style for citing resources detailed on SE pages 445–452.

Source Notes

Have partners each write a source note for a book, magazine, newspaper, Internet article, and videocassette or DVD. Have partners review each other's source notes, using appropriate vocabulary to discuss the format.

★ ELPS 1E, 3D, 5B

List sources. Remind students to separate their sources according to type. In other words, place books in one section, magazine articles in another, and so on, as shown in the model on SE page 402.

★ TEKS 11.21B, 11.21C

Keeping Track of Your Sources

As you do your research, keep careful track of the sources of information you find so that you can correctly cite them in your final paper. This will also help to show the reliability of your sources, and will remind you not to rely too much on one source when you begin writing. You'll need to record the following information.

- **Book:** Author's name. Title. Publisher and city. Copyright date.
- **Magazine:** Author's name. Article title. Magazine title. Date published. Page numbers.
- **Newspaper:** Author's name. Article title. Newspaper title. City. Date published. Section. Page numbers.
- **Internet:** Author's name (if listed). Page title. Site title. Date posted or copyright date (if listed). Site sponsor. Date accessed.
- **Videocassette or DVD:** Title. Distributor. Release date. Medium.

Source Notes

Book
David Bornstein. *How to Change the World: Social Entrepreneurs and the Power of New Ideas.* Oxford UP. New York. 2004.

Magazine
Keith H. Hammonds. "A Lever Long Enough to Move the World." *Fast Company.* Jan. 2005. Page 61. 11 Jan. 2011

Newspaper
Andi Atwater. "State Shuts Medicaid Payment System." *The Wichita Eagle.* 11 Feb. 2006. Section E. Page 2.

Internet
Joel Berg and Tom Freedman. "Ending Child Hunger in America." Progressive Policy Institute. Posted in 2009. Accessed 10 Feb. 2010.

Interview
Lu Tribby. E-mail. 31 Jan. 2010.

Television Program
"Delivering the Goods." *Rx for Survival: A Global Health Challenge.* WNET, New York. 13 Feb. 2010.

Prewrite

List sources. Keep a list of each of your sources with the information shown above. Whenever you find a new source, add it to the list.

Differentiated Instruction: Struggling Learners

To help students plan their sentence outline, have them interview one another about their topics. Partners should ask each other the following questions and take notes on the answers:

- What is the thesis?
- What are the main aspects of the social problem?
- What are some details or examples of the problem?
- What are the solutions?

- What still needs to be done to achieve those solutions?

Students can refer to the notes their partners took as they develop their outlines.

★ **TEKS** **11.21B** Systematically organize relevant and accurate information to support central ideas, concepts, and themes; **11.21C** Paraphrase, summarize, quote, and accurately cite all researched information according to a standard fornat, differentiating among primary, secondary, and other sources; **ELPS 1E** Internalize new basic and academic language by using and reusing it/speaking; **3D** Speak using grade-level content-area vocabulary in context/new English words and academic vocabulary; **5B** Write using newly acquired basic and content-based grade-level vocabulary

MLA Research Paper **403**

Outlining Your Ideas

One way to organize and plan your research paper is to make an outline. An outline is like a map of the ideas in your paper. You can list those ideas in either a topic outline that lists ideas as words or phrases or as a sentence outline that lists ideas in full sentences. (Also see page **619**.)

Below is the first part of a sentence outline for the paper on pages **387–394**. Notice that the outline begins with the research question. Next, it lists the topic sentence for each middle paragraph as a major point, with a Roman numeral. Below each topic sentence is a list of supporting details, each identified by a capital letter. Compare this partial outline with the first two paragraphs of the finished paper.

Sentence Outline

Remember, in an outline, if you use the Roman numeral I., you must also use at least the Roman numeral II. Similarly, if you use the letter A, you must also use at least the letter B.

Research question

Major Points (I., II.)

Supporting details (A., B., C.)

> RESEARCH QUESTION: How can we solve big problems like poverty and hunger?
>
> I. The root problem is that social systems are about 300 years behind the times.
>   A. The industrial revolution made businesses competitive and innovative.
>   B. Government and other social systems remained uncompetitive.
>   C. For 300 years, business continued to evolve, while the social systems fell further behind.
> II. The industrial revolution brought new challenges.
>   A. The Tofflers explain that society had become more urban.
>   B. The rural support system, primarily the family, did not carry over to urban life.
>   C. Relocation resulted in poverty, crime, and disease.

Prewrite

Create your outline. Write a sentence outline for your research paper, using the details from your research. Be sure that each topic sentence (I., II., III., . . .) supports the research question and that each detail (A., B., C., . . .) supports its topic sentence. Use your outline as a guide for writing your first draft.

Outlining Your Ideas

Outlining a previously well-written research paper can help students

- understand how that essay was organized,
- practice locating the thesis statement and topic sentences, and
- identify the kinds of supporting details to include in their own papers.

Distribute photocopies of a finished sample essay and work with students to outline it.

✱ For information about outlining ideas, see SE page 619. ⟪ DIFFERENTIATE INSTRUCTION ⟫

Sentence Outline

Remind students that their sentence outline must include a major research question, major points, and supporting details.

Create your outline. Tell students to take time writing sentences for their sentence outlines. Carefully and accurately written sentences will form the base for their final papers.

⟪ DIFFERENTIATE INSTRUCTION ⟫

TEKS 11.21B

Differentiated Instruction: English Language Learners

ELPS 1E, 3D, 3G, 5B

ELP Level **Beginning**	ELP Level **Intermediate**	ELP Level **Advanced/Advanced High**
Use simplified language to examine the sample outline. Have students repeat academic language as you discuss major points and supporting details.	Use the sample to examine how an outline is an aid for writing a research paper. Provide sentence frames for using content-area vocabulary in context.	Have partners write a summary of what is included in a sentence outline. Have them express their ideas about how an outline is useful.

TEKS 11.21B Systematically organize relevant and accurate information to support central ideas, concepts, and themes; **ELPS** 1E Internalize new basic and academic language by using and reusing it/speaking; **3D** Speak using grade-level content-area vocabulary in context/new English words and academic vocabulary; **3G** Express ideas; **5B** Write using newly acquired basic and content-based grade-level vocabulary

Research

Modify Your Research Question

Remind students that as they research they will often find information that causes them to rethink their original ideas. Tell them that this is a natural part of the research process. Encourage them to change or modify their research question based on new information.

DIFFERENTIATE INSTRUCTION ↘

Look Critically at Your Initial Research Question

Have students work in pairs to look critically at their research questions. Have them ask each other: *Is the question too broad? If so, how can it be narrowed? Is the question too narrow? If so, how can it be broadened? Is the question interesting?*

⭐ **TEKS** 11.22A, 11.22C

Fidel's Research Questions

Have students, working in pairs or in small groups, discuss the process Fidel went through to arrive at his final research question.

Refocus Your Research Plan

Remind students that if they change their research question they will need to adjust the information on their sentence outline as well.

Modify your research question. Tell students that changing their research question does not mean that they will have to start their paper from scratch. In most cases, they will be able to use their research by rearranging it to answer their revised research question.

⭐ **TEKS** 11.22A, 11.22C

Modify Your Research Question

As you prepare to modify your research question, consider the amount of time you have and the expected length of your paper. Rethink research questions that are too broad (you won't have the time or space to thoroughly cover your question) or questions that are too narrow (you may not be able to find enough information).

Look Critically at Your Initial Research Question

Fidel's initial research question was "How can we solve big social problems like poverty and hunger?" He looked over his research and realized that his question was too broad to be fully addressed in his paper. He decided that he needed to focus on a question that he could address adequately in a research paper.

As he reread his notes, Fidel noticed that terms like "social captalism" and "social entrepreneurship" came up quite often. He decided to narrow his topic by focusing on social entrepreneurship. Fidel came up with three ideas of ways he could modify his research question. Here are his ideas.

Fidel's Research Questions

> **What is "social entrepreneurship"?**
> This is an interesting question, but it doesn't connect to the things I originally wanted to research.

> **Why is the social sector so far behind the business sector?**
> This is way off my original topic. Also, it is much too broad a question to treat in a research paper.

> **How can "social entrepreneurship" provide solutions for pressing issues?**
> This seems just right. I have answers to this question and some good evidence. It's a topic I can cover in a research paper.

Refocus Your Research Plan

Go back to the Gathering Grid you created on page **399**. Adjust your information, as needed, to address your revised research question.

 Prewrite

Modify your research question. Look at your research question and your research. Is your question too broad? Is it too narrow? Remember that if you revise your research question, you should also revise your Gathering Grid.

Research

Analyzing the Evidence

Just because something has been printed in a book or online doesn't mean it is true. You need to examine the information you find to determine what has been proven true and what has not.

Separating Theories and Evidence

As part of your research, you will find both theories and evidence, and it is important to be able to tell the difference. *Theories* are unproven assumptions or explanations of facts. *Evidence* is factual information that furnishes proof. The table below gives examples of theories and evidence. Theories that you use in your writing always need to be backed up by evidence or factual information.

Theory	Evidence
With imagination and determination, one person can do a lot. To solve problems, you have to attack the root of the problem. The next step in social evolution is a partnering of business and social entrepreneurs.	Bill Drayton created a method for cheaply and effectively combating pollution. Erzsébet Szekeres found a way to get her son help by starting a group home for handicapped people. In Poland, Wojciech Onyszkiewicz created a food-bank program by partnering rural and urban needs.

Is My Evidence Weak or Strong?

Strong evidence is based on facts, facts that directly support your topic. Below are examples of strong and weak evidence.

Topic Sentence: It took years of determined effort from Szekeres to make her dream a reality.	
Strong Evidence	**Weak Evidence**
Often the government opposed her efforts. With two loans, Szekeres purchased an abandoned farming cooperative. To date, Szekeres has created 21 institutions across Hungary.	Szekeres was the oldest of five children. If you try hard enough, you can accomplish anything. The world needs more nurturing places for handicapped children.

Analyzing the Evidence

Remind students to check that their sources are credible and reliable. Suggest that they consult a teacher or librarian if they have questions.

TEKS 11.21A

Separating Theories and Evidence

Have students, working in pairs, analyze the examples of theory and evidence. Have them ask themselves: *How does the content of "Theory" differ from the content of "Evidence"?* (The sentences under "Theory" are persuasive rather than factual. The sentences under "Evidence" are factual and can be proven.)

TEKS 11.22B; **ELPS** 4K

Is My Evidence Weak or Strong?

Remind students that in order for evidence to be strong it must be not only factual but also directly support the topic.

Differentiated Instruction: English Language Learners

ELPS 4K

ELP Level **Beginning**	ELP Level **Intermediate**	ELP Level **Advanced/Advanced High**
Work with students individually to analyze their initial research question and modify it as needed.	Guide individual students to analyze their initial research question and modify it as needed. Provide support as needed.	Have students analyze their initial research question and modify it as needed. Confer with each student to discuss their research questions.

TEKS **11.21A** Follow the research plan to gather evidence from experts on the topic and texts written for informed audiences in the field, distinguishing between reliable and unreliable sources and avoiding over-reliance on one source; **11.22B** Differentiate between theories and the evidence that supports them and determine whether the evidence found is weak or strong and how that evidence helps create a cogent argument; **ELPS** **4K** Demonstrate English comprehension and expand reading skills by employing analytical skills

Writing the Thesis Statement

Suggest that students check that their research question accurately reflects their topic before they begin writing their thesis statement.

Write Your Thesis Statement Carefully

Have students work in small groups to review and comment on each other's thesis statements, using the new academic language to express ideas. Have them use the tips below and on the SE page to guide their discussion. Encourage them to ask questions in addition to stating ideas and opinions.

TEKS 11.13A, 11.20A; **ELPS** 3C, 3G

Mistakes to Avoid

Give students these additional tips on writing a strong thesis statement.

- Think of your thesis statement as a concise answer to your research question.
- Make your thesis specific, covering only material presented in your paper.
- Avoid beginning with *I will show*. What you will show or prove should be obvious from your thesis statement.
- As much as possible, use active voice.

Review your notes and research question. Have students check that their thesis clearly states their topic and position, and uses the evidence they have gathered to create a cogent argument.

TEKS 11.22B; **ELPS** 1E, 5B

 **TEKS** 11.13A, 11.20A, 11.22B

Writing the Thesis Statement

Once your research is complete and you have revised your research question, you are ready to write your thesis statement. Use your revised research question to help create your thesis statement.

Write Your Thesis Statement Carefully

Your thesis statement should be the result of lengthy thinking. You have taken the time to collect and organize information. You have looked for relationships among the facts you collected. Now, take the time to write a clear and compelling thesis statement that can be the foundation for a well-written research report. A clear thesis statement will guide your writing and help you to write a focused and coherent paper.

> Unclear: Social entrepreneurs make money while solving problems.
> Clear: Social entrepreneurs apply business strategies to human problems, with impressive results.

Mistakes to Avoid

Check your thesis statement for these common errors. Ask yourself the following questions.

- **Does my thesis state the obvious?** *(Chronic hunger is not good for children.)* If so, go back and revise.
- **Is my thesis too vague?** *(Social entrepenship is a good thing.)* If so, you need to rewrite it.
- **Does my thesis statement fail to make my position on the topic clear?** *(Ashoka promotes social entrepreneurship.)* Rewrite your thesis statement to include your position on the topic.

 Prewrite **Review your notes and research question.** Carefully write a thesis statement that states your topic and your position.

TEKS **11.13A** Plan a first draft by selecting the correct genre for conveying the intended meaning to multiple audiences, determining appropriate topic through a range of strategies, and developing a thesis or controlling idea; **11.20A** Brainstorm, consult with others, decide upon a topic and formulate a major research question to address the major research topic; **11.22B** Determine how evidence helps create a cogent argument; **ELPS 1E** Internalize new academic language by using and reusing it/writing; **3C** Speak using a variety of sentence types; **3G** Express ideas; **5B** Write using newly acquired basic and content-based grade-level vocabulary

Research

Critiquing the Research Process

If you are the kind of person who likes to make to-do lists and cross off each item as you complete it, the process of writing a research paper can be a daunting task. That is because you can never really cross an item off of your list until your research paper is final!

As with other types of writing, preparing to write a research paper is a recursive process, that is, a process that requires you to go back to work you did earlier and re-evaluate it in terms of new information or insights.

As you've worked through the prewriting stage in this chapter, you have already begun the process of critiquing your work. You have adjusted your initial topic ideas as you gathered more information. You have analyzed the research information you gathered to judge its accuracy, relevance, and completeness. You have re-examined your research question and modified or changed it as needed. Finally, you have written a carefully crafted thesis statement that clearly states the purpose of your paper.

Do a Final Check

Before you begin actually writing your research paper, do a final check. Ask yourself these questions.

- Reread your outline. Is there a logical flow from one idea to another?
- Are all of your topics directly related to your thesis?
- Do you have enough reliable and relevant information to back up your ideas and theories?
- Do you have complete documentation for all of your sources?

After answering these questions, make changes or do additional research as needed.

Prewrite

Do a final check of your notes, outline, evidence, and sources. Make any necessary changes or adjustments. If your evidence is weak or not complete, do additional research.

Critiquing the Research Process

Suggest that students work in pairs or in small groups to summarize their research process and make suggestions as to what the might do differently they next time they are asked to write a research paper.

TEKS 11.22C

Do a Final Check

Remind students about all of the work they've put into writing their papers thus far. Caution them to reread their outlines and documentation carefully and not to race through the final check phase. Making a thorough final check and corrections as needed can make the difference between an adequate paper and a great paper.

Do a final check of your notes, outline, evidence, and sources. Encourage students to read the information they have gathered carefully. If students find that their evidence is weak or lacking, encourage them to find the stronger, more compelling evidence they need and add it to their paper.

TEKS 11.22B; ELPS 4I, 5B

Differentiated Instruction: English Language Learners   ELPS 1E, 3C, 3G, 3H, 5B

ELP Level **Beginning**	ELP Level **Intermediate**	ELP Level **Advanced/Advanced High**
Work with students to form and write thesis statements. Identify examples of academic language and have students repeat these terms.	Use a recording device as students explain what their papers will be about. Review the oral notes and guide them to form and write their thesis statements.	Have students write their thesis statements independently. Then meet with each student to have them present and discuss their ideas.

TEKS **11.22B** Differentiate between theories and the evidence that supports them and determine whether the evidence found is weak or strong and how that evidence helps create a cogent argument; **11.22C** Critique the research process at each step to implement changes as the need occurs and is identified; ELPS **1E** Internalize new academic language by using and reusing it/writing; **3C** Speak using a variety of sentence types; **3G** Express ideas; **3H** Explain with increasing specificity and detail; **4I** Demonstrate English comprehension by employing basic reading skills and expanding reading skills; **5B** Write using newly acquired basic and content-based grade-level vocabulary

Drafting Keys to Effective Writing

Remind students that the drafting stage is when they are able to put their ideas on paper.

The Keys to Effective Writing list explains the process students will be guided through on SE pages 409–414.

In preparation for beginning their drafts, have students make sure they have all their research notes available. Ask them to begin by rereading their thesis statements and by asking these questions:

- Are there special terms in the thesis that should be explained for readers?
- Should background information be provided before making this statement?
- What interesting detail in my notes would provide good support for the thesis?

Note that as students think about their beginnings, they may find that they need to adjust the wording of their thesis statements to express their ideas more clearly. Remind them that they may revise their original thesis statements several times as they write their first drafts. **DIFFERENTIATE INSTRUCTION ↘**

Drafting

Now that you have finished your research and prepared an outline, it's time to begin writing your paper. This is your first attempt at connecting in writing your thoughts and feelings about the topic. Don't worry about getting everything perfect in this first draft; you'll have time to revise your paper later. For now, just get things down on paper in a way that makes sense to you. The following keys will help.

Keys to Effective Writing

1. Use your first paragraph to get your reader's attention, introduce your topic, and present your thesis statement.

2. In the next section, define and explain the social problem.

3. After that, present a solution or solutions, with examples.

4. In the final section, summarize the paper and give the reader something to think about.

5. Remember to cite the sources of any ideas you paraphrase or quote and list those sources alphabetically on a works-cited page.

TEKS 11.23A, 11.23B

Drafting Starting Your Research Paper

The opening paragraphs of your research paper are critical. They must grab your reader's attention, introduce your topic, and present your thesis statement. Here are several effective ways to begin your opening.

- Start with an interesting fact (or question).
  Hunger and disease are not strangers in the United States. Nearly 12 million children live with hunger.
- Start with a quotation.
  "It was like hearing the ice breaking up at the end of the winter . . . " said Drayton.

Beginning Paragraph(s)

The beginning paragraph starts with an interesting observation.

> In a small community, when tragedy strikes, everyone knows it, and everyone can see how best to step in and help. In our global community, tragedy strikes somewhere every day, but knowing how to respond is much more difficult. In the United States alone, 12 million children live with hunger (Berg and Freedman). Globally, 25,000 children a day die from malnutrition and disease ("Hunger").
>
> Faced with numbers like these, we might be tempted to despair and cry out, "I'm only one person. What can I do?" Fortunately, a new breed of social champion has begun to demonstrate that one person can do a lot, given a little imagination and determination. In the business world, these qualities have long been recognized as the features of an entrepreneur. Now "social entrepreneurs"—sometimes called "social capitalists"—have begun to apply business strategies to human problems, with impressive results.

The opening ends with a clear thesis statement.

Draft

Draft your beginning paragraph(s). Using one of these approaches, draft your opening paragraph(s). Be sure to grab the reader's interest at the beginning, then introduce your topic, and end with a clear thesis statement.

Drafting Starting Your Research Paper

Have students browse through nonfiction articles, books, films, or documentaries to find exceptionally strong openings to share with the class. Ask them to briefly describe what the pieces are about and then read aloud or retell the openings. Analyze each opening as a group, addressing questions such as the following:

- What strategy does the author use in this opening?
- Do other openings that have been discussed so far use a similar opening strategy?
- Why is this opening effective?

TEKS 11.23A; **ELPS** 3F, 4K

Beginning Paragraph(s)

Encourage students to try one of the strategies they discovered during the discussion above when they begin writing their papers.

Draft your beginning paragraph(s). Remind students to keep their readers in mind as they draft their opening paragraphs. Suggest that they think about what first interested them about the topic. This may remind them of formats or rhetorical strategies that will help them draft an engaging and interesting opening to argue for the thesis.

TEKS 11.23A, 11.23B

Differentiated Instruction: English Language Learners

ELPS 3B, 3J, 4K

Examine the Keys to Effective Writing to enhance concept attainment and allow practice in using routine classroom language.

ELP Level **Beginning**	ELP Level **Intermediate**	ELP Level **Advanced/Advanced High**
Read the Keys aloud together. Ask yes/no questions to confirm understanding and to expand vocabulary.	Read the Keys aloud together. Have students orally summarize Keys 1–4 and analyze them as steps in a process they will use.	Together, create a flowchart as students analyze Keys 1–4 as steps in a process they will use.

TEKS **11.23A** Provide an analysis that supports and develops personal opinions, as opposed to simply restating existing information; **11.23B** Use a variety of formats and rhetorical strategies to argue for the thesis; **ELPS** **3B** Expand vocabulary/retelling simple stories and basic information; **3F** Give information during speaking assignments; **3J** Respond orally to information presented/concept and language attainment; **4K** Demonstrate English comprehension and expand reading skills by employing analytical skills

Drafting Developing the Middle Part

To help students write the middle part, have them compare their notes.

- First ask them to sort their note cards in stacks according to their outline.
- If students have many details in their gathering grids, suggest that they photocopy the grids and then cut the copies along the lines so they can be sorted with the cards.
- Note that although there is no fixed number of details that must be included in any given paragraph, students should have at least three cards in a stack. If they have fewer than three, they should rethink the paragraph or do additional research.

Middle Paragraphs

Use the callouts to frame the discussion of the writing model. Remind students that they need to provide analysis that supports opinions, rather than simply restating existing information. Point out that returning to research notes instead of working solely with the outline reminds students of important details they may not have put on their outlines. Tell students to be sure to add missing details to their sentence outline so that the information is there when they write the middle part. Also suggest that they think about rhetorical strategies or formats that could support their ideas. **DIFFERENTIATE INSTRUCTION ↘**

☆ TEKS 11.23A, 11.23B

Drafting Developing the Middle Part

In the middle part of your research paper, give details that support your thesis statement. Start by defining the social problem, giving examples, if necessary. Then present one or more possible solutions, again giving examples.

Each middle paragraph should cover one main idea. Near the beginning of the paragraph, include a topic sentence. (Usually, the topic sentence is the first sentence in the paragraph. However, some paragraphs may begin with a sentence that provides a transition from the previous paragraph.) After the topic sentence, include sentences with supporting details. Use your sentence outline as a guide to your writing.

Middle Paragraphs

The first middle paragraph(s) define the problem.

The Problem

According to Bill Drayton, founder of Ashoka, an organization that fosters social entrepreneurship, the root problem is that social systems are about 300 years behind the times. When the industrial revolution started in the early 1700s, the business sector became competitive and innovative. However, government and other social systems remained uncompetitive, supported by taxes or donations and bolstered by tradition. As business continued to evolve in expertise and influence over the centuries, social systems fell further and further behind in their cost-effectiveness (Hammonds).

All the details in each paragraph support the topic sentence (underlined).

Worse, the Industrial Age brought new challenges that the old social systems were simply not equipped to handle. As futurists Alvin and Heidi Toffler explain, society had become increasingly urban, drawing people away from farms and villages to work in factories. The social support of rural communities,

Differentiated Instruction: Struggling Learners

To help students make sure they cover all the important aspects of their topic in their middle paragraphs, have them check their writing to see if it answers the following 5 W and H questions:

- **Who** is affected by the problem and **who** is trying to solve it?
- **What** is the problem?
- **Why** is the problem important?
- **When** does the problem occur and what is its history?
- **Where** does the problem occur?
- **How** can the problem be resolved?

TEKS **11.23A** Provide an analysis that supports and develops personal opinions, as opposed to simply restating existing information; **11.23B** Use a variety of formats and rhetorical strategies to argue for the thesis

Research

> with their multigenerational families, could not carry over into the cities, where many people had relocated, living alone or in a "nuclear family" of father, mother, and a few children (19-24). As any Dickens novel reveals, and every modern metropolitan newspaper repeats, far too often this relocation has resulted in poverty, crime, and disease.
>
> The Solution
>
>   Drayton believes that roughly 25 years ago, this situation began to change dramatically. In his words, "It was like hearing the ice breaking up at the end of winter in a lake. Creak, creak, groan, crash! The need was so big, the gap so huge, the opportunity to learn was right before people's eyes" (Hammonds). Faced with such need and opportunity, a new breed of entrepreneur began to emerge, this time in the citizen sector. Drayton created Ashoka as a means of fostering this social entrepreneurship on a global scale. His goal is literally to change the world.
>
>   If that seems audacious, it is important to understand Drayton's vision and his experience. As one former . . .

The next middle paragraphs present one or more solutions, with examples.

Sentences are arranged so that the reader can easily follow the ideas.

Draft your middle paragraphs. Keep these tips in mind as you write.

1. Use a topic sentence and supporting details in each paragraph.
2. Refer to your outline for direction. (See page 403.)
3. Add parenthetical references to give credit to all sources. (See page 442.)

Draft your middle paragraphs. After students have researched their topic and have thought intensively about the organization of information, they will benefit from following their sentence outline to write the middle part. Suggest that when students are ready to draft the middle, they should

- decide on a time limit for a writing session (for example, two hours);
- choose a comfortable, quiet workspace, one with room to spread out their planning notes;
- follow their outline carefully; and
- cite all sources used.

Encourage students to avoid pausing to correct conventions—but do suggest that they highlight suspected errors to check later. Also suggest that they insert reminders in the draft, such as *Quotation about _____ here* or *Check information paraphrased here.* This will mark the spots where they need to go back to confirm details and insert parenthetical references.

⭐ ELPS 1B

Students should continue to hold writing sessions until they complete the draft.

☑ DIFFERENTIATE INSTRUCTION

Differentiated Instruction: English Language Learners

⭐ ELPS 1B, 5B, 5G

ELP Level **Beginning**	ELP Level **Intermediate**	ELP Level **Advanced/Advanced High**
Have students focus on writing one paragraph at a time. Guide them to use their prewriting materials as they draft.	As students draft one paragraph at a time, guide them to use new and content-based vocabulary in their writing.	Encourage students to write with increasing specificity and detail as they draft. Have them mark sentences or sections that they may revise later.

ELPS 1B Monitor written language production and employ self-corrective techniques or other resources; **5B** Write using newly acquired basic and content-based grade-level vocabulary; **5G** Explain with increasing specificity and detail

Drafting Ending Your Research Paper

Point out that an issue-related research paper can be like persuasive writing if the writer's goal is to persuade readers to agree to a certain solution or a call to action. Encourage students to consider whether a call to action would work as a way to end their topic. Ask them to discuss these questions:

- Is one solution to the problem better than others?
- Does implementing the solution require expert knowledge or special status?
- If experts must enact the solution, what can readers do to inform experts of the problem?

✻ For more information about writing the ending, see SE page 106.

Ending Paragraph(s)

Discuss with students how the ending paragraphs provide a sense of completeness to the essay.

Draft your ending paragraph(s). Remind students to be sure that their ending paragraphs summarize their thesis with specificity and detail, and leave readers with something to think about, rather than simply restating information. Suggest that they consider rhetorical strategies, such as questions or figurative language, to argue for the thesis. DIFFERENTIATE INSTRUCTION ⬎

⭐ **TEKS** 11.23A, 11.23B; **ELPS** 1B, 5G

⭐ **TEKS** 11.23A, 11.23B

Drafting Ending Your Research Paper

Your ending paragraph should sum up your research and bring your paper to a thoughtful close. To accomplish that, you might . . .

- remind the reader of the thesis of the paper.
- give a "call to action" for the future.
- leave the reader with something to think about.

Ending Paragraph(s)

> **Conclusion**
>
>   These are only a few examples from thousands of programs around the world. (Ashoka alone has more than 1,500 fellows.) Social entrepreneurs are tackling problems at all levels, from helping inner-city children fill out college applications, to training workers for the millions of AIDS victims in South Africa. It is no exaggeration to say that their efforts often lift entire communities out of poverty. Since 2004, Fast Company and the Monitor Group have given awards recognizing the twenty-five best social entrepreneurs each year ("25"). The competition is stiff, and the stories of the finalists are every bit as inspiring as those of the award-winners.
>
>   Bill Drayton believes that the next step in this social evolution is a partnering of business and social entrepreneurs, which he sees as only natural. It was the splitting of . . .

The conclusion summarizes the thesis.

The writer points out a next step for people to take.

Draft

Draft your ending paragraph(s). Draft your ending paragraph(s) using the guidelines above.

Note: Review your first draft. Read your draft to make sure it is complete. Check your research notes and outline to make sure you haven't forgotten any important details. In the margins and between the lines, make notes about anything you should add or change.

🔷 **TEKS** **11.23A** Provide an analysis that supports and develops personal opinions, as opposed to simply restating existing information; **11.23B** Use a variety of formats and rhetorical strategies to argue for the thesis; **ELPS** **1B** Monitor written language production and employ self-corrective techniques or other resources; **5G** Explain with increasing specificity and detail

 **TEKS** 11.21C, 11.23D

Research

Creating Your Works-Cited Page

The purpose of a works-cited page is simply to let your readers find and read the sources you used. Work from the notes you have taken and format the sources you used. Then list those sources in alphabetical order. For additional information about the standard format of common types of sources see pages **445–454**. Also review the works-cited page on page **394**.

Book

Bornstein, David. *How to Change the World: Social Entrepreneurs and the Power of New Ideas.* New York: Oxford UP, 2004. Print.

Magazine

Hammonds, Keith H. "A Lever Long Enough to Move the World." *Fast Company* Jan. 2005: 61. Print.

Newspaper

Atwater, Andi. "State Shuts Medicaid Payment System." *The Wichita Eagle* 11 Feb. 2006, sec. E: 2. Print.

Internet

Joel Berg and Tom Freedman. "Ending Childhood Hunger in America." Progressive Policy Institute. Posted 2009. Web. Accessed 10 Feb. 2010.

E-Mail Message

Tribby, Lu. "Interview Questions." Message to the author. 31 Jan. 2010. E-Mail.

Television Program

"Delivering the Goods." *Rx for Survival: A Global Health Challenge.* WNET, New York. 13 Feb. 2010.

 Draft

Format your sources. Check your paper and your list of sources (page 402) to see which sources you actually used. Then follow these directions.

1. Write your sources using the guidelines above. You can write them on a sheet of paper or on note cards.
2. List your sources in alphabetical order.
3. Create your works-cited page. (See the example on page 394.)

Creating Your Works-Cited Page

If students used the proper formatting as they wrote down their resource information (SE page 402), then most of the work of creating their works-cited page is already done. They will save more time if they use a computer to store their resource information.

Review the format for each type of source and point out similarities and differences.

Format your sources. Remind students to check the MLA handbook or website if they have questions about how to format a source.

If students have typed their information into a computer file, they can use features in the word processing program to create the works-cited page. As needed, point out that they can
- adjust the left margin on the page so that it automatically indents every line after the first line in the paragraph, and
- use the program's "sort" function to alphabetize the entries.

TEKS 11.21C, 11.23D

Differentiated Instruction: English Language Learners

ELPS 1B, 5G

ELP Level **Beginning**	ELP Level **Intermediate**	ELP Level **Advanced/Advanced High**
Work together to guide students as they write their endings. Point out opportunities to include more detail, and work together to strengthen their ideas.	Guide students to draft their endings. Provide sentence frames to help them write closing statements that add specificity about why their topic is important.	Have students draft their endings. Then have partners review each other's work and note areas that need more detail or revision for clarity.

TEKS **11.21C** Accurately cite all researched information according to a standard format, differentiating among primary, secondary, and other sources; **11.23D** Use a style manual to document sources and format written materials; **ELPS** **1B** Monitor written language production and employ self-corrective techniques or other resources; **5G** Explain with increasing specificity and detail

Drafting Compiling Your Entries

Suggest the students refer to SE page 402 to be sure that they have formatted their works-cited page correctly. As needed, tell students to check the MLA style guide for correct formatting.

Arranging Your Entries

Remind students that entries that do not include the author's name should be alphabetized by title, ignoring any initial *A, An,* or *The.*

Tip

Suggest that students keep their works-cited page handy as they draft their research papers. Explain that this will allow them to easily insert correctly formatted in-text parenthetical references.

★ **TEKS** 11.21C, 11.23D

★ **TEKS** 11.21C, 11.23D

Compiling Your Entries

Cite only sources you have consulted or read. Sources you were unable to locate or didn't have time to read, no matter how relevant they sound, do not belong on your works-cited list.

It's a good idea to have your works-cited entries complete before you start writing. As you write you will need to give parenthetical citations of works you used. Parenthetical citations within the text should usually include the author's last name and the page number of the work. However, two common instances when you can omit the page number from the parenthetical citation are

- when you are citing a complete work such as a film or a TV program, or a Web publication without page numbering, or
- when you are citing a one-page article.

Having your works-cited information already compiled and easy to reference will save you a lot of time and frustration once you begin to write, and allow you to focus on your primary task: getting your research paper written.

Arranging Your Entries

Arrange the entries in your works-cited list in alphabetical order. In most cases, entries are arranged by the author's last name.

- If two authors have the same last name, use the first name to alphabetize.
- In the case of two or more entries citing coauthors (multiple authors of the same work), alphabetize by the last names of the second author listed.
- If you cite two or more works by the same author, give the author's name only in the first entry and alphabetize the entries using the title of the work.

Examples

MacDonald, Alice
McNally, Jane
Schumer, Frank and Julio Martinez
Schumer, Frank, Ellen Sullivan, and David Cohen
Schumer, Frank and Thomas Vasquez
Polster, Marie. A City's Dark History. Boston: Beacon Press, 1999. Print.
---, Designing for Growth. Princeton: Princeton UP, 2001. Print.
---, Rebuilding Our Communities. New York: Ballantine-Random, 2006. Print.

Tip

As you take notes for your research paper, always include the page numbers for specific references you plan to use in your paper, or note why you have not included a page number.

★ **TEKS** **11.21C** Accurately cite all researched information according to a standard format, differentiating among primary, secondary, and other sources; **11.23D** Use a style manual to document sources and format written materials

Revising

In the first draft of your research paper, you put your thoughts down in a logical order. Now it's time to revise. During revising, you make changes to ensure that you have maintained your focus, your ideas are clear and interesting, your organizational pattern makes sense, and your voice is authentic and original.

Keys to Effective Revising

1. Read your entire draft to get an overall sense of your research paper.

2. Review your thesis statement to be sure that it clearly states your main point about the topic.

3. Be certain that your beginning engages the reader and that your ending offers an insightful final thought.

4. Check that the middle part clearly and completely supports the thesis statement.

5. Check that your organizational pattern makes sense.

6. Review and adjust your voice to sound authentic and interested in the topic.

Revising

Keys to Effective Revising

Remind students that the revising stage is when writers have an opportunity to make improvements to their first draft. Have students read the Keys to Effective Revising list carefully and discuss refinements and improvements they might not have considered when they were drafting their paper.

The Keys to Effective Revising list lays out the process students will be guided through on SE pages 416–424. Suggest that students refer to the more detailed revision sections elsewhere in their book.

- SE pages 175–184 (revising an informative article—expository writing)
- SE pages 233–242 (revising an argumentative essay—persuasive writing)

✔ DIFFERENTIATE INSTRUCTION

Differentiated Instruction: English Language Learners

ELPS 1F, 3B, 3D

Examine the Keys to Effective Revising to enhance concept attainment and allow practice in using academic and routine classroom language.

ELP Level **Beginning**	ELP Level **Intermediate**	ELP Level **Advanced/Advanced High**
Use accessible, simplified language to read the Keys aloud. Have students repeat key terms and ask yes/no questions about each concept.	Read the Keys aloud together. Have students complete sentence frames to define key terms and summarize concepts.	Discuss the Keys together. Have students use complete sentences to summarize why each step is important.

ELPS 1F Use accessible language and learn new and essential language in the process; **3B** Expand vocabulary/retelling simple stories and basic information; **3D** Speak using grade-level content-area vocabulary in context/new English words and academic language

Revising for Focus and Coherence

Explain that developing an argument that incorporates the complexities of information from multiple sources requires focus and coherence. Point out that even though individual sentences in students' essays might be well written, their essays could still lack focus and coherence. To have focus and coherence students' ideas must be clearly connected to each other and to their thesis statement. **DIFFERENTIATE INSTRUCTION ↘**

Are my ideas clearly connected?

Have students demonstrate reading skills by working in pairs or small groups to discuss how well their papers have achieved focus and coherence. Suggest that they follow the suggestions presented on SE page 416 to frame their discussion. Encourage students to explain their ideas with specificity and detail.

⭐ **ELPS** 4I, 5G

Exercise
Answers

Students' rewrites will vary. Deleted sections should include: (lines 3–4) *Imagination and determination … business world;* (lines 4–5) *These qualities … of years.*

Revise for focus and coherence. Remind students that revising for focus and coherence takes time and patience. Suggest that they confer often with peers or their teacher while deciding on revisions that incorporate the complexities of information from multiple sources.

⭐ **TEKS** 11.23C

416

⭐ **TEKS** 11.23C

Revising for Focus and Coherence

When you revise for *focus and coherence*, you make sure that you have maintained your focus throughout your essay. You check your writing to be sure

- that your ideas are clearly connected to each other and to your thesis,
- that you have included an attention-grabbing introduction and a meaningful conclusion,
- that your paper has an overall sense of completeness.

You also analyze how well your paper has incorporated the complexities of and discrepancies in information from multiple sources and whether it anticipates and refutes counter-arguments.

Are my ideas clearly connected?

Reread your opening paragraphs, paying special attention to your thesis statement. Does your thesis statement clearly state the purpose of your essay? Reread the rest of your paper checking that all of your details contribute to or support your thesis. Delete irrelevant or weak details. Check also that you have included enough details to support your major points. Add more details if needed to support your major points. Determine whether all of your ideas are clearly connected to each other and to your thesis statement. Rewrite sentences that do not establish a clear connection between ideas.

Exercise

Read the following paragraph. Delete any details that do not support the thesis statement. Rewrite sentences that do not establish a clear connection between ideas.

1   A new breed of concerned citizenry has begun to demonstrate that one
2 person can do a lot, given a little imagination and determination. Students and
3 others in the community often volunteer their time. Imagination and determination
4 are admired in the the business world. These qualities have operated for hundreds
5 of years. Now "social entrepreneurs"—sometimes called "social capitalists"— have
6 begun to apply business strategies to human problems.

Revise for focus and coherence. Carefully check that you have maintained your focus and made connections between ideas.

TEKS **11.23C** Develop an argument that incorporates the complexities of and discrepancies in information from multiple sources and perspectives; **ELPS** **4I** Demonstrate English comprehension by employing basic reading skills and expanding reading skills; **5G** Explain with increasing specificity and detail

Research

Have I included complexities and addressed ambiguities?

Often, in the course of your research, you will encounter sources that give ambigious or even contradictory information about your topic. Provided your sources are reliable, it's always important to pay attention to new information, even if it appears to contradict your thesis. If you know there are reliable sources that disagree with or question your thesis, be sure that you address their arguments.

Focus and Coherence

In this paragraph, the writer counters the argument that social entrepreneurs are little more than untrained social workers.

> It is this sort of "fundamental solution" thinking that characterizes social entrepreneurship and that distinguishes it from traditional social work . . . In the process, society benefits as well. (p. 390)

Have I created an engaging introduction?

Check that your introduction engages your readers, introduces the topic, and includes a clearly word thesis statement. Consider using a rhetorical device, a forceful quotation, or a dramatic image. Notice how Fidel revised his opening paragraph to make it more compelling.

Focus and Coherence

Using the rhetorical device of parallelism highlights the contrasts and adds interest to the opening paragraph.

> In a small community, when tragedy strikes, everyone knows
> it, and everyone can see how best to step in and help. ~~Globally,~~
> _In the global community_
> _somewhere every day_
> tragedy strikes ~~often,~~ but knowing how to respond is much
> more difficult.

Is my ending powerful?

Reread your concluding paragraphs to be sure that they sum up your major points and leave the reader with something to think about. Your paper should, at this point, have a sense of completeness.

Revise

Revise for focus and coherence. Look for ways to refute possible objections, and to provide a meaningful introduction and conclusion.

Have I incorporated complexities and addressed ambiguities?

Tell students that encountering contradictory information from reliable sources can often feel like setback in the sense that it forces the author to reevaluate all the research done thus far. Remind students that adding, accounting for, or even altering their thesis statement based on new information will only improve the persuasiveness of their paper.

TEKS 11.23C

Have I created an engaging introduction?

Suggest that students review the sentence structure of their introduction, reminding them that varying sentence structure can affect the overall power of their introduction.

ELPS 5F

Is my ending powerful?

Suggest that students reread their introduction, paying close attention to their thesis statement. Have them ask themselves: _Does my ending refer back to my thesis? Does it sum up my major points? Does it leave the reader with something to think about?_

Revise for focus and coherence. Suggest that students work with a partner, with each checking the other's introduction and conclusion for focus and coherence.

Differentiated Instruction: English Language Learners

ELPS 4I, 5F, 5G

ELP Level **Beginning**	ELP Level **Intermediate**	ELP Level **Advanced/Advanced High**
Use gestures and simplified language to read and discuss the goals for revising for focus and coherence. Guide students to revise their writing for this trait.	Together, read the goals for revising for focus and coherence. Work with students to revise their writing for this trait, focusing on one paragraph at a time.	Encourage students to add detail and use a variety of sentence lengths, patterns, and connecting words as they revise for focus and coherence.

 TEKS **11.23C** Develop an agument that incorporates the complexities of and discrepancies in information from multiple sources and perspectives; ELPS **4I** Demonstrate English comprehension by employing basic reading skills and expanding reading skills; **5F** Write using a variety of grade-appropriate sentence lengths, sentence patterns, and connecting words; **5G** Explain with increasing specificity and detail

Revising for Organization

Suggest that students check that they have used transitional words and phrases to connect their ideas.

Have I created an organizational pattern for my paper?

Have students analyze their writing to determine the organizational pattern they used for their essay. Suggest that they use the list on SE page 418 to help them name their organizational pattern. Remind them that a paper can use one pattern or a combination of organizational patterns.

Exercise
Answers

Answers may vary. Accept answers that students can reasonably explain.

1. Name the problem and give examples of solutions
2. Cause and effect
3. Basic information to increasingly complex information

 ELPS 4K

Look for your organizational pattern. Suggest that students work with a partner to be sure that the format used to argue their thesis is logical. Remind students also to check for correct placement and format in any citations used. Suggest that they consult a style manual as needed.

TEKS 11.23B, 11.23D

  TEKS 11.23B, 11.23D

Revising for Organization

When you revise for *organization,* you check the structure of your essay. You make sure that your paragraphs are organized in a clear order, have a logical flow, and are connected by transitional words and phrases. Ask yourself these questions.

Have I created an organizational pattern for my paper?

Below are some organizational patterns you might use for a research paper.

- Cause and effect
- Comparison-contrast
- Basic information to increasingly complex information
- Least persuasive example to most persuasive example
- Name the problem and give examples of solutions

Sometimes writers will use one or a combination of the organizational patterns listed above.

Exercise

Read each of the following passages and decide which organizational pattern is suggested by each one. Be prepared to explain your response.

1. Bill Drayton believes in attacking the root of the problem. For example, while working for the Environmental Protection Agency, he developed a method of cheaply combating pollution by focusing on the whole rather than individual processes.

2. Because businesses need to make money to survive, innovative ideas that can be implemented at minimal cost are encouraged, welcomed, and rewarded.

3. The concept of a home office has taken root in many businesses in order to allow employees flexibility in the hours they work and a savings in time and cost by not traveling to a central office. However, working from home is not effective for those who require a structured environment, or for those whose work requires face-to-face interactions with colleagues.

Look for your organizational pattern. Reread your paper to analyze the flow of information. Revise your paper by using transitional words or phrases to make the organizational pattern clearer.

MLA Research Paper 419

Research

Is my information in an order that makes sense?

As he revised individual paragraphs to check that the order he used makes sense, Fidel moved a sentence that was out of place.

Organization
A sentence is moved to a place where it makes more organizational sense.

> To date, Szekeres has created twenty-one such institutions across Hungary, where more than 600 multiply-disabled people live and work. Today, this facility includes dorm-style rooms, a cafeteria, a community room where dances are held and movies are shown, and work facilities where people like her son earn money by assembling curtain clips and other such assembly-line jobs. Her efforts are even changing the way the state itself deals with the handicapped (Bornstein 98-116).

Have I used transitional words and phrases to connect ideas?

As you move from one idea to another, repeat key words and/or use transitional words and phrases to connect them. Notice how Fidel repeats key words and uses transitional words and phrases to connect his ideas.

Organization
The transitional word *Worse* connects the second paragraph on page 388 with the paragaph that precedes it.

> Worse, the Industrial Age brought new challenges that the old social systems were not equipped to handle. (p. 388) . . .

Revise for organization. Check the structure of your paper. Be sure that it has an overall organizational pattern and that information in individual paragraphs is in an order that makes sense. Check that you have used transitional words and phrases to connect ideas.

Is my information in an order that makes sense?

Suggest that students monitor their writing by consulting with a peer or a teacher if they think they have a sentence that is out of order.
★ ELPS 1B

Have I used transitional words and phrases to connect ideas?

Have students check carefully that they have used transitional words and phrases as needed to connect ideas and to combine phrases, clauses, and sentences. Remind them that each sentence should build on, or connect to, the sentence preceding it. ✓ DIFFERENTIATE INSTRUCTION

★ TEKS 11.23B; ELPS 5F

Revise for organization. Remind students to check that each sentence has a connection to the sentence that precedes it and that all paragraphs and sentences within them have a logical order.

TEKS 11.23B Use a variety of formats and rhetorical strategies to argue for the thesis; **ELPS 1B** Monitor written language production and employ self-corrective techniques or other resources; **5F** Write using a variety of grade-appropriate sentence patterns; **5G** Explain with increasing specificity and detail

Revising for Development of Ideas

Remind students that the major thing they need to look for when they check for development of ideas is that they have offered enough support and details for their major ideas.

Have I provided enough and the right kind of support?

Tell students to check the relevance of their support. Remind them that their analysis should support and develop their opinions, and that all of their support should be relevant, that is, it should directly support the topic sentence of the paragraph and as well as their thesis statement.

TEKS 11.23A; **ELPS** 4I

 TEKS 11.23A

Revising for Development of Ideas

When you revise for *development of ideas*, you check that you have offered enough support and specific details to allow the reader to understand your major points. Check that your analysis develops personal opinions, rather than simply restating existing information. Finally, check that you have brought a unique perspective to your topic, a perspective that adds to the overall quality of your writing. Ask yourself the following questions.

Have I provided enough and the right kind of support?

You must not only provide support for your ideas, but also check that your support is relevant. In the paragraph that follows, Fidel offers five relevant details to support his topic sentence.

> It took years of determined effort on Szekeres' part to make that dream a reality. (1) Often, the government itself opposed her efforts because she was not a member of the health-care profession. (2) Eventually, however, with two loans from disability organizations, she purchased an abandoned farming cooperative and turned it into a community for the disabled. (3) Today, this facility includes dorm-style rooms, a cafeteria, a community room where dances are held and movies are shown, and work facilities where people like her son earn money by assembling curtain clips and other such assembly-line jobs. (4) To date, Szekeres has created 21 institutions across Hungary, where more than 600 multiply-disabled people live and work. (5) Her efforts are even changing the way the state itself deals with the handicapped (Bornstein 98–116). (pp. 390–391)

TEKS **11.23A** Provide an analysis that supports and develops personal opinions, as opposed to simply restating existing information; **ELPS** **4I** Demonstrate English comprehension by employing basic reading skills and expanding reading skills

Does my paper present my viewpoint rather than simply restate existing information?

Almost anyone can collect research, and then repeat the information in a coherent way. What will make your research paper strong is your unique perspective on the information you have gathered. Look for ways to present your viewpoint or opinion on your topic, and make sure that the supporting details that you provide lend credibility to that view.

Fidel did this early in his paper in his thesis statement by pointing out that social entrepreneurs have begun to apply business strategies to social problems "with impressive results." In his concluding paragraphs, Fidel expresses his opinion even more forcefully.

Development of Ideas

Fidel's comment about lifting "entire communities" shows clearly his perspective on the subject.

Development of Ideas

Fidel reinforces his positive take on social entrepreneurship with the phrase "every bit as inspiring."

> These are only a few examples from thousands of programs around the world. (Ashoka alone has more than 1,500 fellows.) Social entrepreneurs are tackling problems at all levels, from helping inner-city children fill out college applications to training health-care workers for the millions of AIDS victims in South Africa. It is no exaggeration to say that their efforts often lift entire communities out of poverty. Since 2004, *Fast Company* and the Monitor Group have given awards recognizing the 25 best social entrepreneurs each year ("25"). The competition is stiff, and the stories of the finalists are every bit as inspiring as those of the award-winners. (p. 393)

Revise

Revise for development of ideas. Check that your analysis supports and develops your personal opinions, and that you have brought a unique perspective to your topic.

Does my paper present my viewpoint rather than simply restate existing information?

Remind students of the importance of stating a personal opinion and expressing this opinion in a unique way. Have them work with a partner or in small groups to explain opinions orally before they revise their writing. Suggest that they use details to answer the following questions during the discussion: *Have I presented my own honest opinion on my topic? Have I carefully chosen details that support my thesis? Have I accounted for divergent viewpoints?*

TEKS 11.23A; ELPS 3H

Revise for development of ideas. To help students explain with increasing specificity and detail, suggest that they work with a partner and together check that their thesis statement accurately reflects their feelings and opinions about their topic. ✓ DIFFERENTIATE INSTRUCTION

ELPS 5G

Differentiated Instruction: English Language Learners

ELPS 3H, 5G

ELP Level **Beginning**	ELP Level **Intermediate**	ELP Level **Advanced/Advanced High**
Work with students to review how they have developed their ideas. Guide them to make revisions to add increasing specificity and detail.	Review drafts with students. Point out opportunities to revise to add details to develop ideas and add increasing specificity and detail.	Have students review their drafts for development of ideas. Have them explain orally how potential revisions will add specificity and detail.

TEKS **11.23A** Provide an analysis that supports and develops personal opinions, as oppposed to simply restating existing information; ELPS **3H** Explain with increasing specificity and detail; **5G** Explain with increasing specificity and detail

Revising for Voice

As students begin to revise for voice, suggest that they read their paper to a friend and ask if their paper sounds like them and if it sounds as if they care about and are engaged with the topic.

Have I engaged my readers?
Remind students that if they are bored reading their papers, their readers will likely be bored as well. If they find their papers boring, suggest that they ask themselves the following questions: *What first interested me or engaged me about this topic? Have I chosen the best, most engaging details? Does my analysis support my opinion or simply restate existing information? Does my argument anticipate and refute counterarguments that readers may have?*

⭐ **TEKS** 1123A, 11.23C

Have I conveyed that I care about the topic?
Tell students that if they don't believe in their point of view, their readers won't either. Remind them that to convey interest, they have to genuinely care about their topic; otherwise, their paper will ring false. Guide students to use rhetorical strategies to help to argue for their thesis.

⭐ **TEKS** 11.23B

Revising for Voice

When you revise for *voice*, you make sure that you have engaged your reader throughout your paper, that you have conveyed that you care about the topic, that you have dealt with divergent viewpoints, and that your writing is authentic and original. Ask yourself the following questions.

Have I engaged my readers?

As you reread your paper, notice if you find yourself bored or distracted. Chances are if you are bored, your readers will be as well. Find parts of your paper that sound dull. Think about varying your sentence structure or adding rhetorical devices to liven up your writing.

> **Voice**
> The writer engages readers and adds authority to his writing by including a powerful quote.

> In his words, "It was like hearing the ice breaking up at the end of winter in a lake. Creak, creak, groan, crash! The need was so big, the gap so huge, the opportunity to learn was right before people's eyes" (Hammonds). (p. 389)

Have I conveyed that I care about the topic?

You convey that you care about your topic by including relevant and carefully selected evidence and by writing about your topic with conviction. Fidel revised his opening sentences to make his passion for the topic clear.

> **Voice**
> The writer's revision evokes the frustration he and others feel when faced with huge but important social problems.

> an individual might be tempted to despair and cry out,
> Faced with numbers like these, ~~people might think I'm~~
> "I'm only one person. What can I do?"
> ~~only one person. There's nothing I can do.~~ Fortunately, a new breed of concerned citizenry has begun to demonstrate that one person can do a lot, given a little imagination and determination.

⭐ **TEKS** **11.23A** Provide an analysis that supports and develops personal opinions, as opposed to simply restating existing information; **11.23B** Use a variety of formats and rhetorical strategies to argue for the thesis; **11.23C** Develop an argument that incorporates the complexities of and discrepancies in information from multiple sources and perspectives while anticipating and refuting counter-arguments

★ **TEKS** 11.22C, 11.23A, 11.23B, 11.23C

Research

Is my writing authentic and original?

Have you ever had a friend or relative comment, "That doesn't sound like you!" Perhaps you made a surprising or unusual comment that didn't reflect your personality. Maybe you used words that are not typically part of your vocabulary. Whatever the reason, someone realized that what you said didn't sound quite right. That is because you have a particular "voice" that family and friends recognize. The same should be true of your writing.

The more you care about your topic, the more your writing will be authentic and original. If you care about your topic, you will want to convince other people to care about it as well. To do this, you need to write in a way that reveals your honest and unique views.. Fidel found his voice in the opening lines of his paper and succeeded in maintaining it throughout his writing.

Voice
The writer conveys an authentic and original voice, both in the structure of this sentence and the inclusion of a reference to the novels of Charles Dickens.

> As any Dickens novel reveals, and every modern metropolitan newspaper repeats, far too often this relocation has resulted in poverty, crime, and disease. (p. 388)

Revise for voice. Check that you have engaged your readers, conveyed that you care about your topic, and written in a style that is authentic and original.

Exercise

Choose one of the following topics and write an introductory statement that conveys your interest in the topic.

professional internships for students   the benefits of fitness

volunteering in the community   gaining driving experience

Is my writing authentic and original?

Remind students that their analysis should support their opinion in a way that sounds like them. Point out that their argument should anticipate and refute in an authentic and original way any counterarguments that readers may have. Suggest that students have someone they know well—a friend or a relative—read their paper to evaluate the presence or absence of the writer's voice. Suggest that readers ask themselves the question, *Does this sound like [author's name]?*

★ **TEKS** 11.23A, 11.23C

Revise for voice. Have students work with a partner or in groups to check that their essays have engaged readers, conveyed interest, and are written in an authentic and original style. Remind them to critique their research process to decide if additional information would create a more authentic voice. ✔ DIFFERENTIATE INSTRUCTION

★ **TEKS** 11.22C; **ELPS** 4K, 5G

Exercise
Answers

Answers will vary but should include an example of an interesting and engaging introductory paragraph that uses rhetorical strategies to argue for a thesis.

★ **TEKS** 11.23B

Differentiated Instruction:
English Language Learners

★ **ELPS** 1B, 1E, 4K, 5G

ELP Level **Beginning**	ELP Level **Intermediate**	ELP Level **Advanced/Advanced High**
Work with students to revise for voice. Point out opportunities to include new and academic language to help convey a knowledgeable voice.	Work with students to read their introductions to analyze whether their voice is engaging. Guide them to strengthen voice by adding specificity and detail.	Have partners read each other's work and analyze whether the voice sounds engaging, authentic, and original. Students can then make revisions as needed.

TEKS **11.22C** Critique the research process at each step to implement changes as the need occurs and is identified; **11.23A** Provide an analysis that supports and develops personal opinions, as opposed to simply restating existing information; **11.23B** Use a variety of formats and rhetorical strategies to argue for the thesis; **11.23C** Develop an argument that incorporates the complexities of and discrepancies in information from multiple sources and perspectives while anticipating and refuting counter-arguments; **ELPS** **1B** Monitor written language production and employ self-corrective techniques or other resources; **1E** Internalize new basic and academic language by using and reusing it/writing; **4K** Demonstrate English comprehension and expand reading skills by employing analytical skills; **5G** Explain with increasing specificity and detail

Revising **Using a Checklist**

Share with students strategies that can help them make better use of the checklist.

- Take some time off before filling out the checklist so you can evaluate the draft with fresh eyes.
- Read the draft aloud to yourself or have someone else read it aloud before going through the checklist.
- Clarify any issue on the checklist by consulting the index of the book to locate additional help.

Revise your writing. Remind students to answer the checklist questions carefully and honestly.

DIFFERENTIATE INSTRUCTION ↘

Revising Checklist

Point out that Question 12 on the checklist is intended to address a common problem in research writing—simply restating information rather than analyzing the way in which the information supports a personal opinion.

TEKS 11.23A; **ELPS** 4I, 4K

424

TEKS 11.23A

Revising **Using a Checklist**

Revise your writing. On a piece of paper, write the numbers 1 to 17. If you can answer "yes" to a question, put a check mark after that number. Continue to revise until you can answer all of the questions with a "yes."

Revising Checklist

Focus and Coherence

     1. Have I written a clearly stated thesis?

     2. Have I maintained my focus throughout my paper?

     3. Do all of my details support my thesis statement?

     4. Have I incorporated the complexities of and discrepancies in information from multiple sources?

     5. Have I included a strong introduction and conclusion?

     6. Does my paper have an overall sense of completeness?

Organization

     7. Have I created an effective beginning, middle, and ending?

     8. Have I chosen a logical order for my main arguments?

     9. Have I used transitional words and phrases to connect my arguments?

Development of Ideas

     10. Have I offered enough support and specific details to allow readers to appreciate my major arguments?

     11. Have I effectively answered significant objections?

     12. Have I developed personal opinions rather than simply restating facts?

     13. Have I brought a unique perspective to my topic?

Voice

     14. Have I engaged my readers throughout my writing?

     15. Does my writing show that I care about the topic?

     16. Have I dealt with divergent opinions?

     17. Is my writing authentic and original?

Editing

When you finish revising your research paper, you edit it by checking for conventions in grammar, sentence structure, mechanics (capitalization and punctuation), and spelling.

Research

Keys to Effective Editing

1. Read your essay out loud and listen for words or phrases that may be incorrect.

2. Use a dictionary, a thesaurus, your computer's spell-checker, and the "Proofreader's Guide" in the back of this book.

3. Look for errors in grammar, punctuation, capitalization, and spelling.

4. Check your paper for proper formatting. (See pages 386–394.)

5. If you use a computer, edit on a printed copy. Then enter your changes on the computer.

6. Use the editing and proofreading marks inside the back cover of this book. Check all citations for accuracy.

company were to ship goods over a fifteen-mile distance, it would be more economical such reason to use a truck rather han a train or a plane automobile

---

Editing

Keys to Effective Editing

Remind students that during the editing stage, they have a chance to find and correct errors in

- grammar,
- sentence structure,
- mechanics (capitalization and punctuation),
- and spelling.

Focus on item 5, which instructs computer users to print out a copy for editing. Students may use their spell-checker and grammar-checker functions before they print out their paper, but caution them that

- suggestions offered by the grammar checker are often—perhaps even usually—incorrect, and
- the checker can completely miss common kinds of errors, such as using the right word.

Tell students that when they use a grammar checker, they should look very critically at each item the grammar checker flags and refer to the Proofreader's Guide (SE pages 634–779) whenever they have a question, and use the checker only as a backup method to help them spot-check their work.

ELPS 2H Understand implicit ideas and information in spoken language; **4I** Demonstrate English comprehension by employing basic reading skills and expanding reading skills; **4K** Demonstrate English comprehension and expand reading skills by employing analytical skills

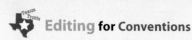 **Editing for Conventions**

Grammar

Remind students that uncorrected grammatical errors can seriously affect the overall quality of their paper.

How can I check my parallel structure?

To help students use different types of phrases and clauses, suggest that they look for parts of their paper where they list three or more words, phrases, or clauses. Have them check that they have correctly punctuated items in a series. Then, have them look for parts of their paper in which they compare or contrast items. Have them check that the second half of the comparison has the same structure as the first half.

TEKS 11.17A; **ELPS** 5E

Grammar Exercise
Answers

Answers may vary. Accept answers that preserve the structure of the first half of the sentence. Possible answers shown below.

1. A dog's hearing is much keener than a human's hearing.
2. A cloudy day is better for a race than a sunny day.
3. The actress had a beautiful face, a lovely voice, and great acting ability.
4. The sight in my right eye is stronger than the sight in my left eye.

Check your use of parallel structure. Have students check their use of punctuation with words, phrases, or clauses in a series.

 Conventions Connections

Grammar: Parallel Structure
- **Student Edition: Proofreader's Guide** pages 770–773
- **SkillsBook** page 172

Write Source Online GrammarSnap

 TEKS 11.17A

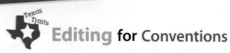 **Editing for Conventions**

Grammar

When you edit for *grammar,* you check to be sure that nouns, verbs, and adjectives are used correctly, and that subjects and predicates agree in number.

How can I check my parallel structure?

Parallel structure refers to a sentence structure that repeats similar word patterns—or grammatical structures—to achieve clarity, rhythm, or emphasis. You can use parallel structure with words, phrases, or clauses in a series. In sentences where you repeat three or more elements, the elements must have a similar structure.

Incorrect:	We needed to know when the trip would start, how long it would take, and our arrival time. (clause, clause, noun phrase)
Correct:	We needed to know when the trip would start, how long it would take, and when we would arrive. (three clauses in a series)

You also need to use parallel structure when you compare and contrast ideas in a sentence. The second half of the comparison or contrast must have the same structure as the first half.

Incorrect:	Monique was praised more for her style than the content of her paper. (prepositional phrase, noun phrase)
Correct:	Monique was praised more for her style than for the content of her paper. (prepositional phrases

Grammar Exercise

Rewrite each sentence, correcting errors in parallel structure.

1. A dog's hearing is much keener than what humans can hear.
2. A cloudy day is better for a race than when the sun is shining brightly.
3. The actress had a beautiful face, a lovely voice, and her acting was great.
4. The sight in my right eye is stronger than my left.

 Check your use of parallel structure. Review your writing to see if you have used word, phrases, or clauses in a series of three. Check that your have used parallel structures correctly.

TEKS 11.17A Use and understand the function of different types of clauses and phrases; **ELPS** 5E Employ increasingly complex grammatical structures

MLA Research Paper **427**

Research

Sentence Structure

One way to vary your *sentence structure* is to use sentences of different lengths. Using compound, complex, and compound-complex sentences with help you vary the length of your sentences.

Are my sentences compound, complex, or compound-complex?

A **compound sentence** expresses two or more complete ideas (independent clauses) joined by the conjunction *and, but,* or *or.* A comma usually separates the parts of a compound sentence.

> **Lisa practiced for three hours, but Melita practiced for six hours.**

A **complex sentence** is composed of an independent and dependent clause. If the dependent clause comes at the beginning of a sentence, it is followed by a comma.

> **When you go to the gym, ask Alex to come home. (dependent clause, followed by independent clause)**

A **compound-complex sentence** has at least two independent clauses and at least one dependent clause.

> **Although Julio trained for months, he did not run well, and he lost the race. (dependent clause, independent clause, independent clause)**

Exercise

Rewrite the sentences to form longer sentences with varied sentence structures. Label your sentences compound, complex, or compound-complex.

1   **Running is hard work. Running is Florita's favorite sport. The big race is a**
2   **month away. Florita ran five miles on Friday. She plans to run seven miles today.**

Check your sentence structures. Review the sentence structures used in your paper. Look for places where you can combine simple sentences to create a compound, complex, or compound-complex sentence.

Learning Language

The words *and, but,* and *or* are used to connect ideas and changing them can sometimes change the meaning of the sentence. Talk with a partner about how the meaning of each sentence below is different.

> **You can walk and we will ride.   You can walk but we will ride.**
>
> **You can walk or we will ride.**

Sentence Structure

Remind students that using different sentence lengths and patterns will make their writing more interesting and easier to read.

Are my sentences compound, complex, or compound-complex?

As needed, review the examples of each sentence type.

Exercise
Answers

Possible answer:
1. Running, Florita's favorite sport, is hard work. Because the race is only a month away, Florita ran five miles on Friday and plans to run seven miles today.

Check your sentence structures. If students can't find compound, complex, and compound-complex sentences in their writing, suggest that they revise to vary sentence lengths and patterns.

TEKS 11.17B; **ELPS** 5E, 5F

Learning Language

Remind students that *and* connects elements of equal importance; *but* implies a contrast between the connected items; and *or* suggests alternatives. ✓ DIFFERENTIATE INSTRUCTION

⭐ Conventions Connections

Grammar: Compound, Complex, and Compound-Complex Sentences
- *Student Edition: Proofreader's Guide* pages 766–767
- *SkillsBook* pages 139, 140

🖈 *Write Source Online* **GrammarSnap**

Differentiated Instruction: English Language Learners

ELPS 5E, 5F

ELP Level **Beginning**	ELP Level **Intermediate**	ELP Level **Advanced/Advanced High**
Read each sentence aloud and have students repeat it with you. Use gestures and visuals to demonstrate the meaning of each connecting word.	Read each sentence aloud together. Ask yes/no questions to confirm understanding of each connecting word. Write sentences together using *and, but,* and *or.*	Have students tell how *and, but,* and *or* influence sentence meaning. Have them write sentences with a variety of lengths and patterns that use these words.

TEKS 11.17B Use a variety of correctly structured sentences; **ELPS** 5E Employ increasingly complex grammatical structures; 5F Write using a variety of grade-appropriate sentence lengths, sentence patterns, and connecting words

Conventions: Mechanics

Remind students that using correct punctuation will help make their paper easier to read. Correct punctuation tells the reader when to pause and when to move ahead without pausing.

How do I punctuate direct quotations?

Have students work in pairs or in small groups. Together have them look for direct quotations in their papers. Then, have them check that they have used correct capitalization and punctuation.

⭐ **TEKS** 11.18A

Exercise
Answers

Brown says that the Civil War "altered forever" the lives of civilians. In the South, people suffered severe food shortages. Food riots broke out in 1863. "Starvation and hunger destroyed southern morale," Brown charges. To make matters worse, as living conditions "worsened by the day" in the South, they steadily improved in the North.

Check your punctuation of quotations. Have students check that they have included a person's exact words within quotation marks, that they have not used a comma to separate quoted material that is only a word, phrase or clause from the rest of the sentence, and that they have placed question marks and exclamation points that are part of the quotation within the quotation marks.

⭐ **Conventions Connections**

Mechanics: Punctuating and Capitalizing Direct Quotations

- **Student Edition: Proofreader's Guide** pages 660–663, 674–679
- **SkillsBook** pages 31, 46

✴ *Write Source Online* **GrammarSnap**

⭐ **TEKS** 11.18A

Conventions: Mechanics

When you edit for *mechanics,* you check for correct use of capitalization and punctuation. To edit for punctuation, look for correct use of periods, question marks, commas, and quotation marks.

How do I punctuate direct quotations?

When you include a direct quotation—a person's exact words—in your paper, you need to begin and end the direct quotation with quotation marks.

- Directly quoted sentences begin with a capital letter.
- Use a comma to separate a quoted sentence from the rest of the sentence.
- Place question marks and exclamation points that are part of the quoted material within the quotation marks.
- If the quoted material is only a word or a phrase, it does not need to be introduced by a comma. It should start with a capital letter only if the quote begins the sentence.

The author warned, "Waiting will only make the problem worse."
Blakely opens with the question, "What can we do to solve the problem of world hunger?"

President Lincoln urged his fellow Americans to dedicate themselves "to the unfinished work" of the country.

Exercise

Rewrite the following sentences, correcting errors in capitalization and punctuation.

1 Brown says that the Civil War, "altered forever" the lives of civilians. In
2 the South, people suffered severe food shortages. Food riots broke out in 1863.
3 "Starvation and hunger destroyed southern morale" Brown charges. To make
4 matters worse, as living conditions "Worsened by the day" in the South, they
5 steadily improved in the North.

 Edit

Check your punctuation of quotations. Review your use of quotations in your paper to make sure they are punctuated correctly and that you have used capital letters only where they are appropriate.

 TEKS **11.18A** Correctly and consistently use conventions of punctuation and capitalization

TEKS 11.19

Research

Conventions: Spelling

When you edit your paper for *spelling,* do not rely exclusively on spell check. Spell check will only alert you to words that are misspelled. It will not tell you, for example, if you have used words incorrectly that sound the same but have different meanings (*two, too,* and *to* or *your* and *you're*). Here are some other tips to keep in mind as you edit your paper for spelling.

Are words spelled consistently?

Some words have more than one spelling listed in the dictionary. In this case, always use the first spelling listed in the dictionary. Once you have used one spelling, continue to use that spelling throughout your paper.

Have I correctly spelled time designations?

Spell out the names of months (January, February) and days of the week (Monday, Tuesday) in your paper. Abbreviate them only in your Works Cited list.

Have I correctly spelled foreign words?

If you use a word, or quote a word from a foreign language, be sure to include all accent marks and any other marks. If you include a foreign word in your paper, put the word in italics unless it is a word that is familiar to most people.

próximo   *a bientôt*   *pantalón*

Have I correctly spelled people's names?

The first time you use a person's name in your paper, state it as fully and as accurately as it appears on your source cards.

First Use	Subsequent Uses
Nathaniel Hawthorne	Hawthorne
Edgan Allan Poe	Poe
Hillary Rodham Clinton	Clinton (not Mrs. Clinton)

Check your spelling. Make sure that any names or dates you have used are spelled out fully and correctly.

Conventions: Spelling

Remind students that spelling errors will detract from the quality of their paper. At best, it will show they are poor spellers; at worst, that they didn't care enough to make corrections.

Are words spelled consistently?

Tell students to check that words are spelled consistently. Remind them to use the first spelling given in the dictionary.

Have I correctly spelled time designations?

If students have used names of days, remind them to check that they have spelled out the name, that is *Monday, Tuesday,* etc., rather than using an abbreviation.

Have I correctly spelled foreign words?

If students have used foreign words, remind them to include accents and other marks.

Have I correctly spelled people's names?

Tell students to state a person's full name the first time they use it, and then refer to the person using only his or her last name.

Check your spelling. Have students give their paper a final check to make sure that all words are spelled consistently, time designations are spelled out, and foreign words and people's names are spelled correctly.

✔ DIFFERENTIATE INSTRUCTION

TEKS 11.19; ELPS 5C

TEKS **11.19** Spell correctly, including various resources to determine and check correct spellings; ELPS **5C** Spell familiar English words and employ English spelling patterns and rules with increasing accuracy

Editing Using a Checklist

Point out that the checklist is a guide, and that students need to review their writing for all types of errors in grammar, usage, and mechanics.

Edit your writing. Remind students to check for correct spelling, capitalization, and punctuation. Prompt students to refer to the Proofreaders Guide on SE pages 634–779 if they have questions about particular grammatical structures, the function of phrases and clauses, or sentence patterns.

TEKS 11.17A, 11.17B; **ELPS** 1B, 5E, 5F

Editing Checklist

Ask students to review the editing changes they made on their draft and to reflect on previous writing assignments. Are there certain conventions errors—not mentioned on the checklist—that trip them up over and over? To help students modify the checklist for their own needs, encourage them to customize the editing checklist by adding questions that will remind them to watch for those types of errors.

TEKS 11.18A, 11.19; **ELPS** 1B

Italics and Underlining in MLA Research Papers

Remind students to check that they have italicized all titles and specialized words.

Editing Using a Checklist

Edit your writing. On a piece of paper, write the numbers 1 to 10. If you can answer "yes" to a question, put a check mark after that number. Continue editing until you can answer all of the questions with a "yes."

Editing Checklist

Conventions

GRAMMAR

_____ 1. Have I corrected any errors in parallel structure?

_____ 2. Have I tried writing compound, complex, and compound-complex sentences?

SENTENCE STRUCTURE

_____ 3. Have I used parallel structure to vary my sentences?

_____ 4. Have I tried using a variety of long and short sentences?

MECHANICS (CAPITALIZATION AND PUNCTUATION)

_____ 5. Do I use end punctuation in all of my sentences?

_____ 6. Have I used correct punctuation and capitalization for all direct quotations?

_____ 7. Have I correctly cited sources in my paper?

SPELLING

_____ 8. Have I spelled all words correctly?

_____ 9. Have I checked for commonly misused pairs?

_____ 10. Have I used the names of persons correctly?

Italics and Underlining in MLA Research Papers

In high school, research papers are commonly written in MLA format. (See pages **386–394**.) MLA stands for Modern Language Association. The MLA suggests that writers of research papers use italics for titles and specialized words. However, always follow your teacher's instructions.

TEKS **11.17A** Use and understand the function of different types of clauses and phrases; **11.17B** Use a variety of correctly structured sentences; **11.18A** Correctly and consistently use conventions of punctuation and capitalization; **11.19** Spell correctly, including various resources to determine and check correct spellings; **ELPS** **1B** Monitor written language production and employ self-corrective techniques or other resources; **5E** Employ increasingly complex grammatical structures; **5F** Write using a variety of grade-appropriate sentence lengths, sentence patterns, and connecting words

★ **TEKS** 11.13E

Publishing

Sharing Your Paper

After you edit and proofread your paper, make a neat final copy to give to your teacher. You may also wish to make extra copies for family and friends.

A research paper can also be presented as a speech, in a multimedia presentation, or on a Web page. (See pages **455–467**.) You worked hard on the report, so find ways to share it with other people.

Publish

Make a final copy. Use the following guidelines to format your paper. Create a clean final copy and share it with your classmates and family.

Focusing on Presentation

- Use blue or black ink and double-space the entire paper.
- Write your name, your teacher's name, the class, and the date in the upper left corner of page 1.
- Skip a line and center your title; skip another line and start your writing.
- Indent every paragraph and leave a one-inch margin on all four sides.
- For a research paper, you should write your last name and the page number in the upper right corner of every page of your paper.
- If your teacher requires a cover page and outline, follow your teacher's requirements. (See page **386**.)

Creating a Title

Take some extra time and thought and give your paper an interesting title. You can try one of the following approaches.

- Be creative: **Social Entrepreneurs, Take a Bow**
- Identify the topic:
  Meeting the Needs of the Future
- Use an idea from your paper:
  Competing to Save the World
- Use compelling words:
  Innovation + Initiative = Impact

Publishing

Sharing Your Paper

Tell students that for all writers, sharing their work and getting feedback from readers is an essential part of the writing process.

✔ **DIFFERENTIATE INSTRUCTION**

Make a final copy. Remind students that it is important, especially considering the effort they've already put into their paper, to be careful about creating their final copy.

Focusing on Presentation

Remind students that the model research paper on SE pages 386–394 is properly formatted in MLA style. Have students compare the model to the bulleted guidelines on this page to clarify their understanding of formatting.

Creating a Title

Before students create their own title, share with them examples of successful essay titles. Discuss why each title is effective. Ask students to recall feedback they received during the writing process about the strengths of their paper before they jot down ideas for their titles. Then, suggest that they work with a partner to brainstorm other suggestions.

★ **TEKS** 11.13E

TEKS **11.13E** Revise final draft in response to feedback from peers and teacher and publish written work for appropriate audiences; **ELPS** **3G** Express opinions, ideas, and feelings; **4B** Recognize directionality of English reading; **4K** Demonstrate English comprehension and expand reading skills by employing analytical skills

Publishing Creating a Multimedia Presentation

Remind students that multimedia presentations can help them reach larger audiences, particularly people who derive meaning more easily from a visual or auditory format.

Investigating Types of Multimedia Presentations

To help students choose a format, explain and, if possible, show examples of the following types of presentations.

- Power presentations and interactive web pages both use computers to create visuals, text, and sound. Interactive web pages also allow audience participation.
- Dramatic presentations use actors, dialogue, and action to tell a story.
- Documentaries and news reports present facts about events and/or people.
- Infomercials are extended advertisements.
- Docudramas are fictionalized dramatizations of actual events or people.

 ELPS 2F

Choosing Your Multimedia Format

Remind students to consider the types of media that they find most effective for learning new concepts, and to get help with their presentation if they need it.

Giving Yourself Enough Time

Caution students that their presentations should reflect the thesis and main ideas presented in their papers.

Prepare your presentation. Suggest that students work with a partner to rehearse giving information with specificity and detail during their multimedia production.

TEKS 11.15D; **ELPS** 3F, 3H

Publishing Creating a Multimedia Presentation

One way to share the work you've done in your research paper is to do a multimedia presentation that synthesizes your information and presents it in a visual and/or auditory format. If you are considering a multimedia presentation, think about your topic and what kind of alternate treatment would best suit it. (See pages **464–467**.)

Investigating Types of Multimedia Presentations

The type of multimedia presentation you choose will depend in large measure on your topic. Here are some types of multimedia presentations you might consider.

- Power presentation
- Interactive Web page
- Dramatic presentation
- Documentary
- Infomercial
- Docudrama
- News report

Choosing Your Multimedia Format

Think about the content and focus of your report and the type of information you would like to present. Ask yourself these questions.

- What is the purpose of my report? Is to inform, to persuade, or to demonstrate?
- Do I have special skills that I could bring to a multimedia presentation, or will I need to get help?
- Which format would best help me to engage my audience and get people interested in my topic?

Giving Yourself Enough Time

An effective multimedia presentation takes time to plan and execute. Give yourself enough time to choose the right media for your paper, plan your project carefully, get help if you need it, and rehearse your presentation.

Publish

Prepare your presentation. Once you begin working with a format for your presentation, make sure that all of the content of your research paper is included. Double check that you have not omitted any important ideas or supporting details.

TEKS **11.15D** Produce a multimedia presentation with graphics, images, and sound that appeals to a specific audience and synthesizes information from multiple points of view; **ELPS** **2F** Listen to and derive meaning from a variety of media/concept and language attainment; **3F** Give information during speaking assignments; **3H** Explain with increasing specificity and detail

Writing Responsibly

A good part of your learning process involves reading and then interpreting or analyzing what you've read. In a research paper, you develop your own ideas while writing knowledgeably about material you've gathered. It's your chance to show that you understand the subject matter. Often, this will entail quoting material as well as paraphrasing—and then identifying the source of the information for your reader.

By citing your sources, you give credit to the authors whose thinking has influenced the ideas you've developed. You also lend integrity to your own ideas by being honest about how you arrived at them.

- Using Sources
- Avoiding Plagiarism
- Writing Paraphrases
- Using Quoted Material

"Rules are not necessarily sacred; principles are."
—Franklin D. Roosevelt

Writing Responsibly

Objectives
- learn how to use research sources responsibly
- understand what constitutes plagiarism and other abuses of sources
- learn to avoid plagiarism through the effective use of paraphrases and quotations

Point out to students that although they sometimes may be tempted to copy a source or use ideas without thinking deeply about them, plagiarism is stealing. In the long run, it undermines their opportunity to learn and improve as a writer.

Explain that the following pages will help them recognize and avoid habits that might lead to plagiarism. Emphasize how important it is to practice and master the techniques they will learn about.

Differentiated Instruction:
English Language Learners　　　　　ELPS　2F, 3F, 3H

Provide guidance as needed to help students prepare presentations.

ELP Level **Beginning**	ELP Level **Intermediate**	ELP Level **Advanced/Advanced High**
Have students practice using key words and expressions as they prepare their multimedia presentations for a small group.	Have students practice their multimedia presentations with an English-proficient peer and focus on explaining their ideas with increasing specificity and detail.	Have students focus on using content-based vocabulary in their presentations. Have listeners ask questions to clarify concepts and language.

 ELPS 2F Listen to and derive meaning from a variety of media/ concept and language attainment; **3F** Give information during extended speaking assignments; **3H** Explain with increasing specificity and detail

Using Sources

Explain that researching is a recursive process. Each new piece of information students find requires that they go back and reexamine their topic and research question.

Beginning Your Research

Tell students to keep their minds as open as possible during this stage of the process and to ask questions that interest them.

Try It!
Answers

Do the **Try It!** activity as a group. Suggest a topic and have students collaborate to pose questions, suggest possible sources, and examine the list of sources for variety and balance (using both primary and secondary sources).

ELPS 2I

Reflecting on Your Research

Remind students that if they do their research with an open mind, they will find information that will prompt them to reevaluate their topic and research question.

TEKS 11.22A, 11.22C

Doing Further Research

Tell students to modify their research question based on new information as needed.

Presenting Your Results

Remind students that a central part of using sources responsibly is to give authors credit for any ideas that are not their own.

Point out that a writer who is investigating many angles while researching must stay organized. Otherwise, information might accidentally make its way, unacknowledged, from the sources into the writing.

 **TEKS** 11.22A, 11.22C

Using Sources

What does *research* mean? Research means "searching out answers to questions."

Beginning Your Research

- **Consider your topic.** What do you already know about your topic? If you had to write your paper right now, what would you write?
- **Begin with the basics.** An encyclopedia or Web search will turn up basic information. Use these sources for an overview of the topic.
- **Ask questions.** What do you wonder about your topic? Make a list of questions; then consider what sources you will search to find answers.

Try It!

Choose a research topic that interests you and do the "Ask questions" activity above.

Reflecting on Your Research

- **Critique your research process.** How has your initial research affected your thinking about the topic? What new questions do you have as a result of your reading?
- **Refine your topic, if necessary.** Should you broaden or narrow your topic? Implement changes in your topic and research as the need occurs.

Doing Further Research

- **Focus your efforts.** Look for answers to your new questions.
- **Use the best sources.** Use trustworthy books, periodicals, Web sites, and other sources to find answers to your questions.
- **Critique your research process again.** If you identify any weak areas, now is the time to make shifts or changes.

Presenting Your Results

- **Make the topic your own.** Your research paper should not just repeat other people's ideas. First and foremost, it should present your own thoughts and understanding of the topic.
- **Paraphrase or quote appropriately.** To support your ideas, paraphrase or quote credible sources. Remember, however, that references to other sources should be used only to enhance or support your own thinking.
- **Credit your sources.** Let your reader know the source of each idea you summarize or quote.

TEKS **11.22A** Modify the major research question as necessary to refocus the research plan; **11.22C** Critique the research process at each step to implement changes as the need occurs and is identified; **ELPS** **2I** Demonstrate listening comprehension/collaborating with peers

Research

Avoiding Plagiarism

You owe it to your sources and your reader to give credit for others' ideas in your research paper. If you don't, you may be guilty of *plagiarism*—the act of presenting someone else's ideas as your own. (See the following pages for examples.) As you gather evidence from experts on your topic, cite every piece of information that you borrow, unless you're sure that it is common knowledge.

Forms of Plagiarism

- **Submitting another writer's paper:** The most blatant form of plagiarism is to put your name on someone else's work (another student's paper, an essay bought from a "paper mill," the text of an article from the Internet, and so on) and turn it in as your own.
- **Using copy-and-paste:** It is unethical to copy phrases, sentences, or larger sections from a source and paste them into your paper without giving credit for the material.
- **Neglecting necessary quotation marks:** Whether it's just a phrase or a larger section of text, if you use the exact words of a source, they must be put in quotation marks and identified with a citation.
- **Paraphrasing without citing a source:** Paraphrasing (rephrasing ideas in your own words) is an important research skill. If you paraphrase or summarize researched information, you must credit the source, even if you reword the material entirely.
- **Confusing borrowed material with your own ideas:** While taking research notes, it is important to identify the source of each idea you record. That way, you won't forget whom to credit as you write your paper.

Other Source Abuses

- **Using sources inaccurately:** Be certain that your quotation or paraphrase accurately reflects the meaning of the original. Do not misrepresent the original author's intent.
- **Overusing source material:** Your paper should be primarily your own words and thoughts, supported by outside sources. If you simply string together quotations and paraphrases, your voice will be lost.
- **"Plunking" source material:** When you write, smoothly incorporate source material. Dropping in or "plunking" a quotation or paraphrased idea without comment creates choppy, disconnected writing.
- **Over-reliance on one source:** If your writing is dominated by one source, the reader may doubt the depth and integrity of your research.

Avoiding Plagiarism

Discuss what is "common knowledge" and how writers can tell when they need to cite a source.

- General factual information such as dates, names, and descriptions of events that are found in many sources are common knowledge.
- Unusual facts uncovered through a scholar's or other expert's research (such as proof that a historical figure was born three years before the year commonly listed in biographies) must be cited. (Such a fact may become common knowledge over time.)
- Statistics gathered by a person or organization must be cited.
- Ideas, opinions, theories, and interpretations of the facts must be cited. ✔DIFFERENTIATE INSTRUCTION

TEKS 11.21A

Forms of Plagiarism

Have students work with a partner or in small groups and discuss the forms of plagiarism. Suggest that they monitor their understanding by asking: *Is the writing in my paper mine? Have I used copy-and-paste without acknowledging my source? Have I paraphrased original ideas without citing my source? Have I confused someone else's ideas with my own?* Encourage students to seek clarification as needed.

ELPS 2D

Other Source Abuses

Have students check that they have not used sources in a way that distorts the author's original meaning, that they have primarily relied on their own words and thoughts in their paper, and that they have not over-relied in a single source.

TEKS 11.21C

 TEKS **11.21A** Follow the research plan to gather evidence from experts on the topic; **11.21C** Paraphrase, summarize, quote, and accurately cite all researched information; **ELPS** **2D** Monitor understanding of spoken language and seek clarification as needed; **2H** Understand implicit ideas and information in spoken language; **3D** Speak using grade-level content area vocabulary in context/new English words and academic language

Original Article

After students have read the original article and the information on SE page 436, note that it is an example of information from an expert.

Point out that for the purposes of illustration, fairly large sections of the original text are used in the examples of plagiarism on SE page 437. Emphasize that the quantity of words used is not important. It would still be plagiarism even if much smaller pieces of the original text were involved. Echoing any distinctive word choices—possibly even a single word, if it is unique enough—can be considered plagiarism.

DIFFERENTIATE INSTRUCTION ↘

 **TEKS** 11.21A, 11.21C

Original Article

The excerpt below about the Ogallala Aquifer is an original-source article. Take note of the examples of plagiarism on the next page.

"Ancient Water for the Future" by James Stator

The Ogallala Aquifer has helped transform the Great Plains states into a great agricultural region. The aquifer is a huge, natural underground reservoir that extends through most of the Plains states. These states experience very little rainfall compared to other parts of the country, and without irrigation, they could not support agriculture. **Thanks to the Ogallala, farmers can make a living in this semiarid region, producing beef and grain in record amounts.** How important is the aquifer to the country? The United States Department of Agriculture estimates that 65 percent of all irrigated land in the country is supplied by that aquifer.

For some time, scientists have worried about the Ogallala Aquifer. This great water system has been tapped beyond its capacity to replenish itself, and as a result, the aquifer has shrunk drastically. According to *Choices,* **a farm magazine, the Ogallala showed significant losses as early as the 1970s, which forced policy makers to figure out how this limited resource can be properly used and conserved.**

The aquifer directly provides water for every aspect of life on the Great Plains. The Docking Institute of Public Affairs in 2001 found that current practices take too much water from the Ogallala. For example, the institute noted that in one year Kansas pumped 2 million more acre-feet from the aquifer than was replaced by rain. The rain and snow that renew the aquifer cannot keep up with the demands of modern irrigation and growing cities.

Farmers are worried. They appreciate how important the aquifer is to life on the Great Plains. Farmers know their livelihood is at risk, so they have found ways to cut back their use of water from the Ogallala. Rotation of crops and new irrigation methods have reduced water loss due to evaporation. The Department of Agriculture has determined that water levels have not dropped as rapidly as was predicted. Unfortunately, conservation is not a simple matter. More and more people are living in the aquifer states, and they need water as well. In addition, demands by other western cities ultimately impact the amount of water available to replenish the Ogallala. A collapse of the . . .

Differentiated Instruction: Struggling Learners

Students may mistake simply changing a few words in a sentence for paraphrasing, when, in fact, it is plagiarizing.

To show the difference, write this line from the sample article on the board: *More and more people are living in the aquifer states, and they need water as well.*

- Ask students to replace three words (for example, *states* becomes *area*).

- Point out that their new sentence plagiarizes the structure and remaining words.

Have students contrast their changes with the following paraphrased line, which alters both word choice and sentence structure: *Demand for aquifer water is, however, increasing as more people move to the area it feeds.*

Research

Examples of Plagiarism

Below are the three common types of plagiarism, sometimes committed on purpose and sometimes by accident. The plagiarized text is shown in bold type.

🚫 Using copy-and-paste

- In this sample, the writer pastes in two sentences from the original article without using quotation marks or a citation.

> The Plains states are typically flat and dry, but **the Ogallala Aquifer has helped transform the Great Plains states into a great agricultural region. Thanks to the Ogallala, farmers can make a living in this semiarid region, producing beef and grain in record amounts.** The aquifer allows farmers in the United States to export food to the world. That's one reason why the Great Plains became known as the nation's breadbasket.

🚫 Paraphrasing without citing a source

- Below, the writer accurately paraphrases (restates) a passage from the original article, but she neglects to accurately cite the source.

> **Since the 1970s, researchers have been concerned about the alarming depletion of the Ogallala. Agricultural experts have scrambled to see how to save the great aquifer. Too many demands on the Ogallala have overwhelmed the capacity to replenish this magnificent reservoir.**

🚫 Neglecting necessary quotation marks

- In the sample below, the writer cites the source of the exact words that she uses from the original article, but she doesn't enclose those words in quotation marks.

> In the early days of irrigation, crops were bountiful, and everyone was pleased. Today, things are different. In "Ancient Water for the Future," James Stator states that **farmers are worried. They appreciate how important the aquifer is to life on the Great Plains. Farmers know their livelihood is at risk, so they have found ways to cut back their use of water from the Ogallala.** These farmers realize that they cannot afford to lose this life-giving source of water.

Examples of Plagiarism

Explain that the rise of the Internet has made the copy-and-paste method of plagiarism more common because it is so easy to transfer text from a Web page to a working document. Often the writer intends to use the source responsibly but fails to do so. ☑ **DIFFERENTIATE INSTRUCTION**

Tell students that they can avoid inadvertent plagiarism if they make a habit of never pasting text from an expert's research into their draft. Instead, they should limit copying and pasting to the following uses:

- To incorporate information into research notes—Students must make sure to enclose the information in quotation marks and to document the source. They can then work from printouts of the notes as they type their draft.
- To obtain URLs for source information—It is best to copy URLs from the browser window into a works-cited page. This ensures there will be no errors in long Web addresses.

Using copy-and-paste Point out to students that although the writer did not copy the entire article, he or she did use parts of the article, word for word, without either citing the source or enclosing material within quotation marks.

Paraphrasing without citing a source Have partners explain to each other why the boldfaced material needs to have sources cited. Remind them to ask for assistance if they need it.

Neglecting necessary quotation marks Tell students that it is not enough to cite the source when directly quoting material. They must enclose the material within quotation marks. Have students review the rules for punctuating direct quotations on SE page 660.

⭐ **TEKS** 11.21A, 11.21C

Differentiated Instruction: English Language Learners

⭐ **ELPS** 1C, 2D, 2E

Provide visual, contextual, and linguistic support as needed to help students confirm their understanding of vocabulary and concepts.

ELP Level **Beginning**	ELP Level **Intermediate**	ELP Level **Advanced/Advanced High**
Display a simple source example to discuss using quotation marks. Guide students to practice pronouncing relevant vocabulary and using the marks.	Use the sample to discuss avoiding copying and pasting. Provide sentence and question stems to help student discuss concepts and seek clarification.	Read and discuss the samples together. Have students take notes to monitor their understanding. Guide them ask questions to seek clarification.

⭐ **TEKS** **11.21A** Follow the research plan to gather evidence from experts on the topic; **11.21C** Paraphrase, summarize, quote, and accurately cite all researched information; **ELPS 1C** Use strategic learning strategies to acquire basic and grade-level vocabulary; **2D** Monitor understanding of spoken language and seek clarification as needed; **2E** Use visual, contextual, and linguistic support to enhance and confirm understanding of spoken language

Writing Paraphrases

Discuss the six steps for writing paraphrases. Elicit ideas from students about why each step is necessary for effective and accurate paraphrases.

FYI

Review the information in the FYI box and note that summarizing and paraphrasing are similar because both are restatements of information. Focus on how they differ.

- In summarizing a passage, the main goal is to present the information in a shortened form.
- In paraphrasing a passage, the main goal is to explain the information clearly. Depending on the complexity of the information, a paraphrase might be longer than the original.

DIFFERENTIATE INSTRUCTION ↘

 **TEKS** 11.21C

 TEKS 11.21C

Writing Paraphrases

There are two ways to share information from another source: (1) quote the source directly or (2) paraphrase the source. When you quote directly, you include the exact words of the author and put quotation marks around them. When you paraphrase, you use your own words to restate someone else's ideas. In either case, you must accurately cite the researched information. To paraphrase, follow the steps below.

1. **Skim the selection first** to get the overall meaning.
2. **Read the selection carefully,** paying attention to key words and phrases.
3. **List the main ideas** on a piece of paper.
4. **Review the selection** again.
5. **Write your paraphrase;** restate the author's ideas using your own words.
   - Stick to the essential information. Drop anecdotes and details.
   - Put quotation marks around key words or phrases taken directly from the source.
   - Arrange the ideas into a smooth, logical order.
6. **Check your paraphrase** for accuracy by asking these questions: *Have I kept the author's ideas and viewpoints clear in my paraphrase? Have I quoted only as necessary? Could another person understand the author's main ideas by reading my paraphrase?*

FYI

A *quotation,* a *paraphrase,* and a *summary* reference a source in different ways.

- **Quoting:** A quotation states the words of a source exactly. Quoting should be used sparingly in a research paper so that your writing doesn't sound like a patchwork of other people's statements. Use a quotation only when the exact words of the source are essential.
- **Paraphrasing:** In a paraphrase, you recast an idea from a source into your own words. Paraphrasing demonstrates that you understand the idea, and it maintains your voice within your paper. Paraphrasing is more commonly used than quoting or summarizing.
- **Summarizing:** A summary is a condensed version of an entire source. In a research paper, there is seldom any need to summarize an entire work unless that work is the subject of the paper. For example, you might summarize the plot of *King Lear* in a research paper about that play.

TEKS 11.21C

Research

Sample Paraphrases

Following the original passage below (from page 26 of a book by Travis Taylor), you'll find two properly and accurately cited paraphrases.

Original Passage

> Kyudo, which means "the way of the bow" in Japanese, is the Zen martial art of archery. It was adapted into traditional Buddhist practice from medieval Japanese archers who used seven-foot asymmetrical bows called yumi. Although kyudo lacks the widespread popularity of karate or judo, it is often regarded as one of the most intensive martial arts in existence, taking 30 years to master.
>
> The standard execution of kyudo involves a series of specific actions, including assuming the proper posture, approaching the intended target, nocking the arrow, drawing it, releasing it, and then repeating the process. After the second arrow has been released, the archer approaches the target, withdraws the arrows, and thus completes the exercise.
>
> There is far more to kyudo, however, than simply shooting arrows. For every movement, the archer must maintain a specific posture, inhaling and exhaling at predetermined points throughout the exercise. The repetitive action and deep breathing greatly relaxes the archer—heightening his alertness and lowering his stress.

Basic Paraphrase

> Kyudo is the Zen martial art of archery. It was adapted from medieval Japanese archery into a spiritual and physical exercise. Through a series of specific actions, the archer prepares and shoots an arrow into a target and then repeats the action one more time. The archer's control comes from focused breathing and balanced posture, which lessen stress and increase the archer's ability to concentrate (Taylor 26).

Basic Paraphrase with Quotation

> Kyudo is the Zen martial art of archery. It was adapted from traditional medieval Japanese archery into a spiritual and physical exercise. "The standard execution of kyudo involves a series of specific actions, including assuming the proper posture, approaching the intended target, nocking the arrow, drawing it, [and] releasing it . . ." (Taylor 26). An archer's control comes from focused breathing and balanced posture, which lessen stress and increase the archer's ability to concentrate (26).

Sample Paraphrases

Tell students that they are going to read an original passage followed by a basic paraphrase and a paraphrase with quotations of the passage.

Original Passage

After students read the original passage, ask them to cover the sample paraphrases and write a paraphrase of the passage on their own, including a quotation. When students have finished writing, have them compare their work to the samples.

TEKS 11.21C

Basic Paraphrase

Ask students to locate parts of the original passage that are not included in the paraphrase. Have them explain why these parts were left out.

Basic Paraphrase with Quotation

Have students work in pairs and compare the basic paraphrase with the paraphrase with the quotation. Have them discuss which version they prefer and explain why.

Discuss the paraphrases as a group to help students monitor their oral and written language production and employ self-corrective techniques.

- Did they focus on the same basic ideas?
- Did they use the same quotation as the one in the sample?
- Invite two or three students to read their paraphrase aloud. Discuss how the paraphrases exhibit slightly different points of view and different voices, even though they are based on the same passage. Point out that those differences show that the paraphrases were written in the writer's own voice and with the writer's own words.

ELPS 1B

Differentiated Instruction: English Language Learners

ELPS 1E, 3B, 4G, 4I, 5B, 5G

ELP Level **Beginning**	ELP Level **Intermediate**	ELP Level **Advanced/Advanced High**
Use an accessible source to model the steps in writing a paraphrase. Have students participate through writing, retelling, and using new vocabulary.	Present a sample source. Work together to write a paraphrase. Use sentence stems to have students infer and summarize ideas and information.	Present a sample source and have students paraphrase it. Discuss paraphrases together and have students revise their work for clarity or to add detail.

TEKS **11.21C** Paraphrase, summarize, quote, and accurately cite all researched information; **ELPS** **1B** Monitor oral and written language production and employ self-corrective techniques or other resources; **1E** Internalize new academic language by using and reusing it/speaking/writing; **3B** Expand vocabulary/retelling simple stories and basic information; **4G** Demonstrate comprehension of increasingly complex English/retelling or summarizing; **4I** Demonstrate English comprehension and expand reading skills by employing basic reading skills; **5B** Write using newly acquired basic vocabulary and content-based grade-level vocabulary; **5G** Describe and explain with increasing specificity and detail

Using Quoted Material

Explain that good researchers often use quotations from experts to support their ideas. Display examples of the different ways of presenting quotations as described on the page.

 DIFFERENTIATE INSTRUCTION ↘

TEKS 11.21A

Short Quotations

Have students check the length of each quotation they have used to determine if it should be worked into the body of the text and enclosed within quotation marks.

Long Quotations

Discuss why longer quotes should be set off from the rest of the writing.

Quoting Poetry

Point out to students that quoting poetry follows the same short quote vs. long quote rules as quoting prose.

Partial Quotations

Remind students that if ellipses indicate part of a sentence or line is omitted, use three periods; if it indicates more, use four points.

Make sure students understand that when they need to insert changes into quotations,

■ bracketed comments are placed within the quotation marks, and

■ comments in parentheses are placed outside of the quotation marks.

Explain that comments in brackets may include the following:

■ clarifications: *"I've always wanted to go [to Paris], but I can't afford it yet."*

■ correction of errors: *"It's a romantic city and is the scene of such momentous events as the storming of the Bastille in 1798 [1789]."*

■ indication that an unusual usage or word is shown as it appears in the original text: This is done by inserting the Latin term *sic* (meaning "thus")—*"The Bastile [sic] prison was demolished soon after the riot, but there is a monument at the site."*

✳ For more about using brackets, see SE page 672.

Using Quoted Material

A quotation can be a single word or an entire paragraph. Choose quotations carefully and keep them as brief as possible. Use them only when they are necessary, and cite them using a standard format. When you do quote material directly, be sure that the capitalization, punctuation, and spelling are the same as that in the original work. Clearly mark changes for your readers: (1) changes within the quotation are enclosed in brackets [like this]; (2) explanations are enclosed in parentheses at the end of the quotation before closing punctuation (like this).

Short Quotations

If a quotation is four typed lines or fewer, work it into the body of your paper and put quotation marks around it.

Long Quotations

Quotations of more than four typed lines should be set off from the rest of the writing by indenting each line one inch from the left margin and double-spacing the material. When quoting two or more paragraphs, indent the first line of each paragraph an additional one-quarter inch. Do not use quotation marks. (See **660.3.**)

Note: Place the parenthetical reference after the final punctuation mark of the quotation. Generally, a colon is used to introduce quotations set off from the text. (See **650.4.**)

Quoting Poetry

When quoting up to three lines of poetry (or lyrics), use quotation marks and work the lines into your writing. Use a diagonal (/) to show where each line of the poem ends. For quotations of four lines or more, indent each line one inch from the left margin and double-space. Do not use quotation marks.

Note: To show that you have left out a line or more of verse in a longer quotation, make a line of spaced periods the approximate length of a complete line of the poem.

Partial Quotations

If you want to leave out part of the quotation, use an ellipsis to signify the omission. An ellipsis (. . .) is three periods with a space before and after each one. (See page **670.**)

Note: Do not take out something that will change the author's original meaning.

 TEKS **11.21A** Follow the research plan to gather evidence from experts on the topic; **11.21C** Paraphrase, summarize, quote, and accurately cite all researched information

Documenting Research

Most academic disciplines have their own manuals of style for research paper documentation. The style manual of the Modern Language Association *(MLA Handbook for Writers of Research Papers),* for example, is widely used in the humanities (literature, philosophy, history, and so on), making it the most popular manual in high school and college writing courses. (For complete information about MLA style, refer to the latest version of the *MLA Handbook.*) For papers in social sciences and social studies, the documentation style of the American Psychological Association (APA) is often used.

This chapter will provide you with guidelines for citing sources in both the MLA and APA styles. (The MLA works-cited list is very extensive; the APA reference listed is abbreviated.) *Remember:* Always follow your teacher's directions, which may include special requirements or exceptions for the use of either documentation style. Because these styles continue to evolve, check the Web site for the style you are using to be sure you have the most up-to-date information about documenting electronic sources.

- **Guidelines for In-Text Citations**
- **MLA Works-Cited List**
- **APA Reference List**

"Research is the process of going up alleys to see if they are blind."

—Marston Bates

Documenting Research

Documenting Research

Objectives

- cite sources in the text of an essay, following MLA and APA style
- format source information for an MLA-style works-cited list
- format source information for an APA reference list

Discuss with students how using a fixed style is helpful to the writer.

- It helps writers make sure they include all the information needed to document their sources.
- It provides ready answers to questions of consistency, such as whether or not to spell out numbers (SE page 429).

Point out that it is important for writers to obey the style rules they've been asked to follow. At the high-school level, their grades may depend on this. In later life, it can affect their professional success. For example, scholars who submit articles to academic journals risk having the editors reject their work without reading it if they fail to follow the specified style.

Guidelines for In-Text Citations

Provided students have done a careful and complete job of compiling their Works Cited list, they should have all the information they need to insert parenthetical references.

Points to Remember

Tell students that if they use several ideas from the same source in succession, it is only necessary to include one parenthetical citation after the last piece of information from that source. For an example of this, refer students to the student model on SE pages 390–391. Point out that the details about the case of Erzsébet Szekeres are distributed over two paragraphs and are covered by one citation *(Bornstein 98–116)*.

MLA/APA

Draw students' attention to the first bullet point for both styles. Make sure they understand that a parenthetical citation should not repeat the author's last name or title information if they have already mentioned it in their text. (Note, however, that students should cite page numbers in parentheses.) **DIFFERENTIATE INSTRUCTION ↘**

★ TEKS 11.21C, 11.23D

Guidelines for In-Text Citations

Whether you paraphrase, summarize, or include a quotation, the simplest way to credit a source is to insert the information in parentheses after the words or ideas taken from that source. These in-text citations (often called "parenthetical references") refer to the "Works Cited" list at the end of an MLA paper or the "References" page at the end of an APA paper.

Points to Remember

- Make sure each in-text citation clearly points to an entry in your reference list or list of works cited. Use the word or words by which the entry is alphabetized.
- Keep citations brief and integrate them into your writing.
- When paraphrasing rather than quoting, make it clear where your borrowing begins and ends. Use stylistic cues to distinguish the source's thoughts ("Kalmbach points out . . . ") from your own ("I believe . . . ").
- Place your parenthetical citation at the end of a sentence, before the end punctuation.
- Do not offer page numbers when citing complete works. If you cite a specific part, give the page number, chapter, or section, using the appropriate abbreviations (p. or pp., chap., or sec.). Do not, however, use p. and pp. in MLA parenthetical citations.

MLA	APA
• Place the **author's last name** (or, if unavailable, the first word or two of the title) and/or **page number** (if available) in parentheses following the cited text, except when these items are included in the text.	• Place the **author** (or title), **date of the source,** and **page number** (if any) in parentheses, separated by commas, following the cited text, unless these items have been included in the text.
• For inclusive **page numbers** larger than 99, give only the two digits of the second number (113–14, not 113–114).	• **Titles** are italicized, but APA style requires that only first words and proper nouns in titles be capitalized.
• For **titles,** use italics.	

Research

Model In-Text Citations

MLA	APA

A Work by One Author

Genetic engineering was dubbed "eugenics" by a cousin of Darwin's, Sir Francis Galton, in 1885 (Bullough 5).	Bush's 2002 budget was based on revenue estimates that "now appear to have been far too optimistic" (Lemann, 2003, p. 48).

A Work by Two or Three Authors

Students learned more than a full year's Spanish in ten days using the complete supermemory method (Ostrander and Schroeder 51).	Love changes not just who we are, but who we can become, as well (Lewis, Amini, & Lannon, 2000, p. 25).

Note: For APA, this format also applies to a work by up to five authors. After the first citation, list only the first author followed by "et al." (meaning "and others").

A Work by Many Authors

This format applies to a work by four or more authors in MLA format or six or more authors in APA format. List only the first author followed by "et al."

Communication on the job is more than talking; it is "inseparable from your total behavior" (Culligan et al. 111).	Among children 13 to 14 years old, a direct correlation can be shown between cigarette advertising and smoking (Lopez et al., 2004, p. 75).

An Anonymous Work

When there is no author listed, give the title or a shortened version of the title as it appears on the works-cited or reference page.

Statistics indicate that drinking water can make up 20 percent of a person's total exposure to lead (*Information* 572).	. . . including a guide to low-impact exercise (*Staying Healthy*, 2004, p. 30).

Model In-Text Citations

Remind students that source information that is in the text does not need to be repeated in the citation. Ask students to rewrite two of the sample sentences, one for each style, incorporating some information from the parenthetical citation into the regular text. As needed, provide the following examples for *A Work by One Author*:

■ Bullough notes that genetic engineering was dubbed "eugenics" by a cousin of Darwin's, Sir Francis Galton, in 1885 (5).

■ In 2003, Lehmann noted that Bush's budget for the previous year had been based on revenue estimates that "now appear to have been far too optimistic" (p. 48).

★ **TEKS** 11.21C, 11.23D

A Work by One Author

Point out to students the basic structure of a parenthetical reference as shown in the examples.

A Work by Two or Three Authors

Remind students that in MLA style there are no commas between elements of a parenthetical reference.

A Work by Many Authors

Tell students that the Latin abbreviation *et al.* means "and others."

An Anonymous Work

Remind students that many reference books do not name an author.

 TEKS **11.21C** Accurately cite all researched information according to a standard format, differentiating among primary, secondary, and other sources; **11.23D** Use a style manual to document sources and format written materials; **ELPS 1E** Internalize new basic and academic language by using and reusing it/writing; **2E** Use visual, contextual, and linguistic support to enhance and confirm understanding of spoken language

Personal Communications

Remind students to include full information for personal communications on their Works Cited page. (See SE page 452.)

A Work Referred to in Another Work

Tell students that citing quoted material correctly requires that they be careful as they are conducting research to note when a quote orginally came from another source.

Quoting Prose

Explain that students who use a word processor can use program tools to help them format longer quotations. Demonstrate these methods, if possible.

- Instead of indenting the text of long quotations manually by using the space bar or tab key, students should select the entire quoted section and adjust its left margin to 2 inches (MLA) or 1.5 inches (APA). This represents an increase in the indent for the quotation of one inch and one half inch respectively.
- Instead of counting words in a quotation for an APA-style report, students can use the word processing program's "word count" function.

Try It!
Answers

Possible answers:

MLA style: People suspected that Jane Goodall was a spy. They couldn't imagine that a young woman would travel from faraway England to study chimpanzees (Goodall 16).

APA style: People suspected that Jane Goodall was a spy. They couldn't imagine that a young woman would travel from faraway England to study chimpanzees (Goodall, 1971, p. 16).

DIFFERENTIATE INSTRUCTION ⬎

⭐ **TEKS** 11.21C, 11.23D

⭐ **TEKS** 11.21C, 11.23D

Personal Communications

For an MLA paper, this parenthetical reference is the same as that for a publication with one author. In an APA paper, cite letters, e-mail messages, phone conversations, and so on as "personal communication" with their full date.

MLA	APA
. . . concern for the wetland frog population (Barzinji).	The management team expects to finish hiring this spring (R. Fouser, personal communication, December 14, 2004).

A Work Referred to in Another Work

In MLA, use the abbreviation *qtd. in* (quoted in) before the source in your reference. For APA, credit the source by adding *as cited in* within the parentheses.

Quoting Prose

In MLA format, when you are quoting any sort of prose that takes more than four typed lines, do not use quotation marks. Instead, indent each line of the quotation one inch, and put the parenthetical citation (the pages and any chapter or other numbers) outside the end punctuation mark of the quotation.

Allende describes the flying machine that Marcos has assembled:

The contraption lay with its stomach on terra firma, heavy and sluggish and looking more like a wounded duck than like one of those newfangled airplanes they were starting to produce in the United States. There was nothing in its appearance to suggest that it could move, much less take flight. (12; ch. 1)

Note: In APA format, quotations of 40 or more words are handled similarly, although the block of lines is indented only one-half inch, and the abbreviation p. or pp. is included in the parenthetical reference.

Try It!

Paraphrase the following passage and refer to the source in a parenthetical citation in both MLA and APA styles.

"He explained that they were all worried and resentful; they could not believe a young girl would come all the way from England just to look at apes, and so the rumor had spread that I was a government spy."

Source: page 16 of *In the Shadow of Man* by Jane Goodall, published 1971

⭐ **TEKS** **11.21C** Accurately cite all researched information according to a standard format, differentiating among primary, secondary, and other sources; **11.23D** Use a style manual to document sources and format written materials

MLA Works-Cited List

The works-cited section of your report lists all of the sources you have referred to in your text. It does not include sources you may have read but did not refer to in your paper. Begin your list on a new page.

List each entry alphabetically by author's last name. If there is no author, use the first word of the title (disregard *A, An, The*). Note that titles are italicized.

List only the city for the place of publication unless it is outside the United States. In that case, add an abbreviation of the country, if necessary, for clarity. If several cities are listed, give only the first.

Additionally, note that publishers' names should be shortened by omitting articles (*a, an, the*), business abbreviations (*Co., Inc.*), and descriptive words (*Books, Press*). Cite the surname alone if the publisher's name includes the name of one person. If it includes the names of more than one person, cite only the first of the surnames. Abbreviate "University Press" as UP. Also use standard abbreviations whenever possible.

Books

Basic Format

Author's last name, First name. *Book Title.* City: Publisher, year of publication. Medium of publication.

Opie, John. *Ogallala: Water for a Dry Land.* Lincoln: U of Nebraska P, 2000. Print.

In the rare instance that a book does not state publication information, use the following abbreviations in place of information you cannot supply:

n.p.	No place of publication given		n.p.	No publisher given
n.d.	No date of publication given		n. pag.	No pagination given

A Book by Two or Three Authors

Haynes, John Earl, and Harvey Klehr. *In Denial: Historians, Communism, & Espionage.* San Francisco: Encounter, 2003. Print.

List the authors in the same order as they appear on the title page. Reverse only the name of the first author.

A Book by Four or More Authors

Schulte-Peevers, Andrea, et al. *Germany.* Victoria, Austral.: Lonely Planet, 2000. Print.

MLA Works-Cited List

Have students note the organization of the information in this section and the APA section on SE pages 453–454. Point out how the SE organization makes the pages easier to use.

- Sources are listed in a hierarchy. Books, the most common resources, are listed first, since all research papers should include books as sources. Periodicals, online sources, and other sources follow.
- At the beginning of each category, a basic format is shown. Students can use this as a model if their resource information is simple.
- After the basic format, more specific examples are grouped according to type and arranged in order of increasing complexity.

Books

Basic Format Have students work in small groups with two or three books that follow the basic format. Together, have them work out how they would cite the books on a Works Cited page.

A Book by Two or Three Authors Make sure that students understand that when they list two or three authors, they only reverse the name of the first author.

A Book by Four or More Authors Remind students that when listing a book with four or more authors, only the name of the first author needs to be cited.

TEKS 11.21C, 11.23D

TEKS **11.21C** Accurately cite all researched information according to a standard format, differentiating among primary, secondary, and other sources; **11.23D** Use a style manual to document sources and format written materials; **ELPS 2E** Use visual, contextual, and linguistic support to confirm understanding of spoken language; **4G** Demonstrate comprehension of increasingly complex English/retelling or summarizing; **4I** Demonstrate English comprehension and expand reading skills by employing basic reading skills

Two or More Books by the Same Author Draw students' attention to the three hyphens that substitute for repeating the author's name. Note that there is a space between each hyphen.

A Book with No Author Tell students that books with no author are alphabetized by the first word in the title, excluding *A, An,* and *The.*

A Single Work from an Anthology Remind students that the abbreviation for editor in an anthology is *Ed.*

An Article in a Familiar Reference Book Tell students that familiar references include well-known names of encyclopedias, dictionaries, or almanacs.

A Government Publication Draw students' attention to the abbreviations used in the example: *GPO* (Government Printing Office) and *Cong. Rec.* (Congressional Record).

A Pamphlet, Brochure, Manual, or Other Workplace Document Have students note the following abbreviations: *n.p.* (no page given) and *n.d.* (no date given). Refer students to the *MLA Handbook* for additional abbreviations, such as *qtd. in* (quoted in), *rev. of* (review of), *trans.* (translator), *UP* (University Press), *vol.* (volume), and *vols.* (volumes). **DIFFERENTIATE INSTRUCTION ↘**

⭐ **TEKS** 11.21C, 11.23D

⭐ **TEKS** 11.21C, 11.23D

Two or More Books by the Same Author

List the books alphabetically according to title. After the first entry, substitute three hyphens for the author's name, followed by a period.

Dershowitz, Alan M. *Rights from Wrongs.* New York: Basic, 2005. Print.

---. *Supreme Injustice: How the High Court Hijacked Election 2000.* Oxford: Oxford UP, 2001. Print.

A Book with No Author

Chase's Calendar of Events 2002. Chicago: Contemporary, 2002. Print.

A Single Work from an Anthology

Follow the format for a book entry, and include the name of the book's editor and the page numbers of the cited piece.

Mitchell, Joseph. "The Bottom of the Harbor." *American Sea Writing.* Print. Ed. Peter Neill. New York: Library of America, 2000. 584–608.

An Article in a Familiar Reference Book

It is not necessary to give full publication information for familiar reference works (encyclopedias, dictionaries). List the edition and publication year. If an article is not initialed, list the title first. If it is initialed, check the index of authors for the author's full name.

Lum, P. Andrea. "Computed Tomography." *World Book.* 2000 ed. Print.

A Government Publication

State the name of the government (country, state, and so on) followed by the name of the agency. Most federal publications are published by the Government Printing Office (GPO).

United States. Dept. of Labor. Bureau of Labor Statistics. *Occupational Outlook Handbook 2000–2001.* Washington: GPO, 2000. Print.

When citing the *Congressional Record,* give the day, month, and year of publication, as well as the page numbers.

Cong. Rec. 5 Feb. 2002: S311–15. Print.

A Pamphlet, Brochure, Manual, or Other Workplace Document

Treat any such publication as you would a book.

Grayson, George W. *The North American Free Trade Agreement.* New York: Foreign Policy Assn., 1993. Print.

Research

If publication information is missing, list as much information as you can. Use square brackets if the country of publication is not listed in the document. Use n.p. and n.d. as for a book.

> *Pedestrian Safety.* [United States]: n.p., n.d. Print.

One Volume of a Multivolume Work

> Cooke, Jacob Ernest, and Milton M. Klein, eds. *North America in Colonial Times.* Vol. 2. New York: Scribner's, 1998. Print.

Note: If you cite two or more volumes in a multivolume work, give the total number of volumes after each title. Offer specific references to volume and page numbers in the parenthetical reference in your text, like this: (8:112–14).

> Salzman, Jack, David Lionel Smith, and Cornel West. *Encyclopedia of African-American Culture and History.* 5 vols. New York: Simon, 1996. Print.

An Introduction, a Preface, a Foreword, or an Afterword

To cite the introduction, preface, foreword, or afterword of a book, list the author of the part first. Then identify the part by type, followed by the title of the book. Next, identify the author of the work, using the word *By.* (If the book author and the part's author are the same person, give just the last name after *By.*) For a book that gives cover credit to an editor instead of an author, identify the editor. Finally, list any page numbers for the part being cited.

> Barry, Anne. Afterword. *Making Room for Students.* By Celia Oyler. New York: Teachers College, 1996. Print.

> Lefebvre, Mark. Foreword. *The Journey Home.* Vol. 1. Ed. Jim Stephens. Madison: North Country, 1989. ix. Print.

Second and Subsequent Edition

An edition refers to the particular publication you are citing, as in the third (3rd) edition.

> Joss, Molly W. *Looking Good in Presentations.* 3rd ed. Scottsdale: Coriolis, 1999. Print.

An Edition with Author and Editor

The term *edition* can refer to the work of one person that is prepared by another person, an editor.

> Shakespeare, William. *A Midsummer Night's Dream.* Ed. Jane Bachman. Lincolnwood: NTC, 1994. Print.

One Volume of a Multivolume Work Have students note than when listing more than one editor, the abbreviation is *eds.*

An Introduction, a Preface, or an Afterword Point out that the author of an introduction, preface, foreword, or afterword may be different from the author of the book. Use the examples and work with students to be sure they understand where and how elements should be placed.

Second and Subsequent Edition Remind students that many books are published in various editions. It is important to include the edition of a book republished after the first edition. If the book does not list the edition, it can usually be assumed that it is the first edition. First editions do not need to be identified as such.

An Edition with Author and Editor Point out that the abbreviations for the terms for *edition (Ed.)* and *editor (Ed.)* are the same. Remind students that readers will have little difficulty figuring out what is meant because of the positioning of the abbreviations within the citation.

★ **TEKS** 11.21C, 11.23D

Periodicals

Basic Format Remind students that the title of the article is listed in quotation marks ("Testing by Design") and the title of the publication is italicized (*Middle Ground*). DIFFERENTIATE INSTRUCTION ⬊

An Article in a Weekly or Biweekly Magazine Draw students' attention to the dates used in MLA-style references and ask how the format is different from what they are accustomed to using. (The day is listed before the month.) Note that no commas are listed in the dates.

An Article in a Monthly or Bimonthly Magazine Work with students to determine how citing a monthly or bimonthy magazine differs from citing a weekly or biweekly magazine. (The listing for the weekly or biweekly publication includes the full date of publication [*Rolling Stone* 6–13 Dec. 2001]; the listing for a monthly or bimonthly magazine does not. [*Scientific American* Dec. 2001])

An Article in a Scholarly Journal Citing scholarly journals can be complicated and difficult. If, after reading the directions, students still have difficulty, suggest that they consult a teacher or librarian for help.

⭐ **TEKS** 11.21C, 11.23D

Periodicals

Basic Format

> Author's last name, First name. "Article Title." *Periodical Title*
> date: page numbers. Medium of publication.

> **Stearns, Denise Heffernan. "Testing by Design."** *Middle Ground*
> Oct. 2000: 21–25. Print.

An Article in a Weekly or Biweekly Magazine

List the author (if identified), article title (in quotation marks), publication title (italicized), full date of publication, page numbers for the article, and the medium of publication. Do not include volume and issue numbers.

> **Goodell, Jeff. "The Uneasy Assimilation."** *Rolling Stone* 6–13 Dec. 2001: 63–66. Print.

An Article in a Monthly or Bimonthly Magazine

As for a weekly or biweekly magazine, list the author (if identified), article title (in quotation marks), publication title (italicized), and the medium of publication. Then identify the month(s) and year of the issue, followed by page numbers for the article. However, do not give volume and issue numbers.

> **"Patent Pamphleteer."** *Scientific American* Dec. 2001: 33. Print.

An Article in a Scholarly Journal

Some scholarly journals are paginated by issues. Most are paginated continuously throughout in a single volume. List the author, then the journal title, and the volume number followed by a period. Then list the issue number, the year of publication (in parentheses), followed by a colon, and the page numbers of the article (not just the pages you used).

> **Chu, Wujin. "Costs and Benefits of Hard-Sell."** *Journal of Marketing Research* 32.2 (1995): 97–102. Print.

Note: For articles that are continued on a nonconsecutive page, regardless of the publication type, add a plus sign (+) after the first page number, for example, 8+.

Research

A Printed Interview

Begin with the name of the person interviewed.

Cantwell, Maria. Interview with Erika Rasmusson. "The New Technocrat." *Working Woman* Apr. 2001: 20–21. Print.

If the interview is untitled, use *Interview* (no italics) in place of the title.

A Newspaper Article

Bleakley, Fred R. "Companies' Profits Grew 48% Despite Economy." *Wall Street Journal* 1 May 1995, Midwest ed.: 1. Print.

If a local paper does not name the city, add it in brackets (not underlined) after the paper's name.

To cite an article in a lettered section of the newspaper, list the section and the page number (A4). If the sections are numbered, however, use a comma after the year (or the edition); then indicate sec. 1, 2, 3, and so on, followed by a colon and the page number (sec. 1: 20). An unsigned newspaper article follows a similar format:

"Bombs—Real and Threatened—Keep Northern Ireland Edgy." *Chicago Tribune* 6 Dec. 2001, sec. 1: 20. Print.

A Newspaper Editorial

If an article is an editorial, put *Editorial* (no italics) after the title.

"Hospital Power." Editorial. *Bangor Daily News* 14 Sept. 2004: A6. Print.

A Review

Begin with the author (if identified) and title of the review. Use the notation *Rev. of* (no italics) between the title of the review and that of the original work. Identify the author of the original work with the word *by* (no italics). Then follow with publication data for the review.

Olsen, Jack. "Brains and Industry." Rev. of *Land of Opportunity,* by Sarah Marr. *New York Times* 23 Apr. 1995, sec. 3: 28. Print.

An Article with a Title or Quotation Within Its Title

Morgenstern, Joe. "Sleeper of the Year: *In the Bedroom* Is Rich Tale of Tragic Love." *Wall Street Journal* 23 Nov. 2001: W1. Print.

Note: Use single quotation marks around the shorter title if it is a title normally punctuated with quotation marks.

A Printed Interview Point out that the format for citing a printed interview is the same as that for citing a magazine article.

A Newspaper Article Remind students that if the newspaper title doesn't include the place of publication, they must insert it. This is important because some newspapers published in different places may have the same title, such as *The Observer* or *The Post.*

A Newspaper Editorial Tell students that the title "Editorial" is not abbreviated.

A Review Point out to students the abbreviation "Rev. of" (Review of).

An Article with a Title or Quotation Within Its Title Review the note at the end of this section. Point out that this instruction holds true not only in reference citations, but also whenever students must present quotations within quotations.

TEKS 11.21C, 11.23D

✳ For more about quotations within quotations see SE page 662.

Differentiated Instruction:
English Language Learners

ELPS 4C, 4F

Use actual examples to provide visual and contextual support as you discuss periodicals.

ELP Level **Beginning**	ELP Level **Intermediate**	ELP Level **Advanced/Advanced High**
Develop new sight vocabulary by pointing out and reading together terms that appear on these pages, such as *article, magazine,* and *newspaper.*	Discuss the concepts, having students identify terms they know. Have them create a word bank of new terms about periodicals and read them with a partner.	Discuss the concepts, having students take notes on new vocabulary and their meanings. They may want to create categories or webs of related words.

TEKS **11.21C** Accurately cite all researched information according to a standard format, differentiating among primary, secondary, and other sources; **11.23D** Use a style manual to document sources and format written materials; **ELPS 4C** Develop basic sight vocabulary; **4F** Use visual and contextual support to develop background knowledge

Online Sources

Suggest that students explore the Web sites for the online sources listed and bookmark them on their Web browsers. These are reliable sites, which students can use as valuable sources of information on topics they might want to research.

Basic Format To help students learn new academic vocabulary, such as *format, medium,* and *online sources*, point out how the format for citing an online article is similar to that for citing a print article. Elicit from students that citing the medium, in this case, *Web,* is key to differentiating the two types of sources.

DIFFERENTIATE INSTRUCTION ↘

ELPS 2C

An Article in an Online Periodical Review with students the abbreviations to use if a Web site is missing information: *n.d.* (no date of publication available) and *n.p.* (no publisher available).

An Article in an Online Reference Work Remind students that online references works often do not identify the author. In these cases, students should begin their entry with the title, followed by the name of the reference source.

TEKS 11.21C, 11.23D

Online Sources

Like with other media, the goal of citing online sources is to document your sources so that they can easily be found by readers.

Basic Format

Author's last name, First name. "Title." *Site Title.* Site publisher or sponsor. Date of publication. Medium of publication. Date of access.

> Tenenbaum, David. "Dust Never Sleeps." *The Why Files.* U of Wisconsin, Board of Regents. Web. 26 April 2010.

If there is no site publisher or sponsor, use n.p. If there is no date of publication, use n.d. Include as much information as you can. If your teacher requires a URL, add it after the date of access in angle brackets followed by a period.

> "Frederica: An 18th-Century Planned Community." *National Register of Historic Places.* National Parks Service. n.d. Web. 27 Feb 2004 <http://www.cr.nps.gov/nr/>.

An Article in an Online Periodical

Begin with the author's name; the article title in quotation marks; the italicized name of the periodical; and date of publication. Add the medium of publication and the date of access.

> Dickerson, John. "Nailing Jello." *Time.com* 5 Nov. 2001. Web. 9 Dec. 2010.

An Article in an Online Reference Work

Unless the author of the entry is identified, begin with the entry name in quotation marks. Follow with the usual online publication information.

> "Eakins, Thomas." *Britannica Concise Encyclopedia.* Encyclopædia Britannica. 2004. Web. 26 Sept. 2011.

Research

A Personal Web Page

For this type of source, include the name of the person who created the site, the title of the Web site or the words *Home page* (no italics), the date of the last update (if given), the medium of publication, and the date you accessed the site.

> Wood, Lloyd. *Lloyd's Satellite Constellations.* 22 Oct 2005. Web. 23 Oct. 2011.

A Podcast

Begin with the title or a description of the podcast, followed by its date and the title of the show. Include the title of the larger site (if it applies), and the date of download.

> "Rhubarb: Reviving a Forgotten Crop." 26 June 2009. "Farm Fresh Foods." *NPR Morning Edition.* 30 Oct. 2011.

An Online Multimedia Resource: Painting, Photograph, Musical Composition, Film or Film Clip, Etc.

After the usual information for the type of work being cited, add the title of the database or Web site, the medium of publication, and the date of access.

> Goya, Francisco de. *Saturn Devouring His Children.* 1819-1823. Museo del Prado, Madrid. *Internet Archive.* Web. 13 Dec. 2010.

An E-Mail Message

Identify the author of the e-mail, then include the title of the message, if any, taken from the Subject line, followed by the words *Message to* (no italics) and the recipient's first and last name, followed by the date of the message and the medium of delivery.

> Barzinji, Atman. "Frog Populations in Wisconsin Wetlands." Message to the author. 1 Jan. 2002. E-mail.

A Personal Web Page Provide visual and contextual support by showing students an example of a personal Web page. Highlight any new or unusual language on the page. Point out that when they cite a personal Web page they need to include the date of its last publication and the date that they accessed the site. Ask questions to confirm understanding.
★ **ELPS** 2E

A Podcast Remind students that when citing a podcast, they must include the title of the larger site and the date they downloaded the podcast.

An Online Multimedia Resource: Painting, Photograph, Musical Composition, Film or Film Clip, Etc. Point out that this type of citation requires the title of the database or Web site and the date the site was accessed.

An E-Mail Message Draw students' attention to the example of a citation for an e-mail communication. Note that when sending e-mail, many people don't use the subject line, either leaving it blank or putting in very general information. Suggest that including a specific, descriptive subject line in their e-mail communications will

- help experts they contact understand at a glance what's being asked of them (making it less likely that they'll delete a message from an unfamiliar sender),
- help students keep their e-mail messages better organized, and
- provide a useful title to list in their references.

✳ For more about composing e-mail messages, see SE pages 544–545.
★ **TEKS** 11.21C, 11.23D

 TEKS **11.21C** Accurately cite all researched information according to a standard format, differentiating among primary, secondary, and other sources; **11.23D** Use a style manual to document sources and format written materials; **ELPS** **1F** Use accessible language and learn new and essential language in the process; **2E** Use visual, contextual, and linguistic support to confirm understanding of spoken language

Other Sources: Primary, Personal, and Multimedia

A Television or Radio Program Have students note that the episode title is enclosed in quotation marks and the series title is underlined. Tell students to use these styles when referring to television or radio programs, even in regular text.

✱ For information about using quotation marks or italics for titles, see SE pages 662 and 664.

A Film Have students note that after the title, citations should include the names of the director, distributor, and medium as well as any other pertinent information.

A Video Recording Remind students to include the medium in their citation.

An Audio Recording Again, remind students to include the specific medium in their citation.

An Interview by the Author (Yourself) Point out that to cite an interview they conducted themselves, students should use the term, "Personal Interview."

A Cartoon or Comic Strip (in Print) Remind students that if they accessed the cartoon online, the source should read "Web."

A Lecture, a Speech, an Address, or a Reading Point out that if the lecture, speech, etc., has no title, they should assign it a descriptive label as shown in the example.

⭐ **TEKS** 11.21C, 11.23D

Other Sources: Primary, Personal, and Multimedia

These examples of works-cited entries illustrate how to cite electronic and digital sources.

A Television or Radio Program

Include the episode and program titles, and the title of the series, if one exists. State the network name, its call letters, and the city of the local station, if needed, followed by a broadcast date and medium of reception.

"Another Atlantis?" *Deep Sea Detectives.* History Channel. 13 June 2005. Television.

A Film

The director, distributor, year of release, and medium of reception follow the title. Other pertinent information may be noted, such as a specific remake.

The Aviator. Dir. Martin Scorsese. Miramax Films, 2004. Film.

A Video Recording

Cite a filmstrip, slide program, videocassette, cartridge, or DVD just as you would a film, but include the specific medium of reception.

Safe Boating is No Accident. JOI Home Video, 2010. DVD.

An Audio Recording

Cite the medium of reception or format, such as CD, LP, MP3 file, Audiocassette, or Audiotape. To cite a specific song, place its title in quotation marks before the title of the recording.

Notkin, Molly. *The Story of a Veil.* Tine Audio Publishers, 2011. MP3 file.

An Interview by the Author (Yourself)

Brooks, Sarah. Personal interview. 15 Oct. 2010.

A Cartoon or Comic Strip (in Print)

Luckovich, Mike. "The Drawing Board." Cartoon. *Time* 17 Sept. 2001: 18. Print.

A Lecture, a Speech, an Address, or a Reading

If there is a title, use it instead of the descriptive label. Include identifying elements such as the place, date and nature of the oral presentation.

Annan, Kofi. *Acceptance of Nobel Peace Prize.* Oslo City Hall, Oslo, Norway. 10 Dec. 2001.Lecture.

Research

APA Reference List

The reference list begins on a separate page and includes all retrievable sources cited in a paper. List the entries alphabetically by author's last name. If no author is given, then list by title (disregarding *A, An,* or *The*).

Leave a single space after all end punctuation marks. Quotation marks are not used for article titles; italicize other titles. Capitalize only the first word (and any proper nouns) of book and article titles; capitalize the names of periodicals in the standard upper- and lowercase manner.

Books

Basic Format

Author's last name, Initials. (year). *Book title.* Location: Publisher.

Guttman, J. (1999). *The gift wrapped in sorrow: A mother's quest for healing.* Palm Springs, CA: JMJ.

Note: Give the city or publication alone if it is well-known. Otherwise, include the state. Include the state or province and the country if outside the United States.

A Book by Two or More Authors

Lynn, J., & Harrold, J. (1999). *Handbook for mortals: Guidance for people facing serious illness.* New York: Oxford.

List up to six authors; abbreviate subsequent authors as "et al." List all authors' names in reverse order. Separate authors' names with commas, and include an ampersand (&) before the last.

An Anonymous Book

If an author is listed as "Anonymous," treat it as the author's name. Otherwise, follow this format:

American Medical Association essential guide to asthma. (2003). New York: American Medical Association.

A Single Work from an Anthology

Nichols, J. (2005). Diversity and stability in language. In B. D. Joseph & R. D. Janda (Eds.), *The handbook of historical linguistics* (pp. 283–310). Malden, MA: Blackwell.

An Article in a Reference Book

Lewer, N. (1999). Non-lethal weapons. In *World encyclopedia of peace* (pp. 279–280). Oxford: Pergamon.

APA Reference List

Ask students to compare the American Psychological Association (APA) documentation style to the MLA style on the previous pages. Suggest that because the styles are fairly similar, students may need to take extra care when working with a less-familiar style to observe the subtle distinctions, such as the placement of the date or whether to spell out the author's first name (MLA) or use initials (APA).

✔ DIFFERENTIATE INSTRUCTION

Books Work with students to compare MLA and APA citations of books.

A Book by Two or More Authors Guide students to compare MLA and APA citations of a book by two or more authors.

An Anonymous Book Have students note that the treatment of an unnamed author differs in MLA and APA styles.

A Single Work from an Anthology Work with students to distinguish how APA style for citing a single work from an anthology differs from MLA style.

An Article in a Reference Book Explain and discuss the format used.

Note that this abbreviated APA style list omits the section on citing primary, personal, and multimedia sources, partly because social sciences reports are less likely to make use of them. However, the APA has created formats for these types of sources. Students can find this information online.

TEKS 11.21C, 11.23D

 TEKS 11.21C Accurately cite all researched information according to a standard format, differentiating among primary, secondary, and other sources; **11.23D** Use a style manual to document sources and format written materials; **ELPS 2D** Monitor understanding of spoken language and seek clarification as needed; **3F** Ask for information during extended speaking assignments

Periodicals

Basic Format Remind students to double-check the information as they first write it down.

If students need to confirm their citation later and no longer have access to the original source, suggest that they look for it on the Internet.

- Many publishers and booksellers' Web sites provide previews of covers and copyright pages which can be used to confirm source information.
- A library computer catalog can provide information for many kinds of sources. The New York Public Library (www.nypl.org) has an especially large collection.
- Periodical information may be available in the archive of the publication's Web site.

TEKS 11.21C, 11.23D

A Journal Article, Two Authors Point out the use of the ampersand (&) between the names.

A Journal Article, More Than Six Authors Remind students that *et al.* means "and others."

A Journal Article, Paginated by Issue Explain that some journals are paginated by issue, while others number continuously from one issue to the next.

A Newspaper Article Provide examples of news articles that are continued in other sections of the newpaper.

Online Sources

Basic Format Suggest that students work in pairs or in small groups to list differences in order and wording for APA and MLA style when citing online sources.

ELPS 4F

 **TEKS** 11.21C, 11.23D

Periodicals
Basic Format

Author's last name, Initials. (year, Month day). Article. *Periodical, vol.* (issue), pages.

Silberman, S. (2001, December). The geek syndrome. *Wired, 9*(12), 174–183.

A Journal Article, Two Authors

Newman, P. A., & Nash, E. R. (2005). The unusual southern hemisphere stratosphere winter of 2002. *Journal of the Atmospheric Sciences, 62*(3), 614–628.

A Journal Article, More Than Six Authors

Watanabe, T., Bihoreau, M-T., McCarthy, L., Kiguwa, S., Hishigaki, H., Tsaji, A., et al. (1999, May 1). A radiation hybrid map of the rat genome containing 5,255 markers. *Nature Genetics, 22,* 27–36.

A Journal Article, Paginated by Issue

When the page numbering of the issue starts with page 1, the issue number (not italicized) is placed in parentheses after the volume number.

Lewer, N. (1999, summer). Nonlethal weapons. *Forum, 14*(2), 39–45.

A Newspaper Article

For newspapers, use "p." or "pp." before the page numbers; if the article is not on continuous pages, give all the page numbers, separated by commas.

Stolberg, S. C. (2002, January 4). Breakthrough in pig cloning could aid organ transplants. *The New York Times,* pp. 1A, 17A.

Online Sources
Basic Format

Author's last name, Initials. (year, Month day). Article. *Periodical, vol.* (issue), pages if available. Retrieved Month day, year, from electronic address

Volz, J. (2000, January). Successful aging: the second 50. *Monitor on Psychology, 31*(1). Retrieved Apr. 26, 2006, from http://www.apa.org/monitor/jan00/cs.html

Note: If you have read an exact duplicate of a print article online, simply use the basic journal reference, but add [Electronic version] after the title of the article.

 TEKS **11.21C** Accurately cite all researched information according to a standard format, differentiating among primary, secondary, and other sources; **11.23D** Use a style manual to document sources and format written materials; **ELPS** **4F** Use visual and contextual support and support from peers and teachers to enhance and confirm understanding and develop background knowledge

Making Oral Presentations

A good public speaker is like a good book. When you read a great book, you get caught up in the ideas, not in the cover or the page design. In the same way, when you listen to an effective speaker, you are drawn to the message, not to the presenter.

Delivering a presentation well takes preparation and practice. It means knowing the information so thoroughly that you don't stumble. It means being comfortable enough to engage and capture the audience with your ideas. This chapter will help you do just that. You'll learn how to organize the material, how to bring it to life with visual aids, and how to practice your way to a smooth, effective delivery.

- Planning Your Presentation
- Creating Note Cards
- Considering Visual Aids
- Practicing Your Speech
- Delivering Your Presentation
- Evaluating a Presentation
- Creating a Multimedia Report

"Make sure you have finished speaking before your audience has finished listening."

—Dorothy Sarnoff

Objectives
- transform a written research report into an oral presentation
- plan, practice, present, and evaluate an oral report
- enhance an oral presentation by adding multimedia elements

Acknowledge that many people feel nervous when they have to speak in front of an audience, but assure students that preparing well and getting plenty of practice is the key to conquering a fear of public speaking. Invite students who enjoy performing in front of audiences (perhaps on a debate team, in theater productions, or as musicians) to talk about their experiences. Why do they enjoy it? What tips do they have for others?

Differentiated Instruction: English Language Learners

ELPS 4F

Present actual examples of sources to provide context and develop background knowledge. Invite students to share what they know about the sources.

ELP Level **Beginning**	ELP Level **Intermediate**	ELP Level **Advanced/Advanced High**
Work together to create citations for the sources. Use the sources to enhance the meaning of key terms such as *volume* and *issue*.	Pair students with an English-proficient peer to create citations. Have them match key terms with information in the sources.	Have partners work together to create citations for the sources. Then have them discuss their work with a group.

ELPS 4F Use visual and contextual support and support from peers and teachers to enhance and confirm understanding and develop background knowledge

Planning Your Presentation

Consider allowing students to choose a research report other than their most recent one to adapt for oral presentation, as long as they still have all their planning notes. If a student's topic is unfamiliar to you, schedule a conference with them to discuss their choice.

DIFFERENTIATE INSTRUCTION ↘

Determining Your Purpose

Remind students that determining their purpose is important because it will infuence whether they narrate, describe, or explain the information they present. Giving a persuasive report, for example, is different from demonstrating how to do something.

ELPS 3H

Considering Your Audience

Tell students to think about their audience and how best to engage them. If students anticipate questions, tell them to answer them in their report.

Reviewing Your Report

Suggest that students practice their presentation with a partner. Each partner should check the other's pronunciation and use of new vocabulary.

ELPS 3A, 3D

Try It!
Answers

Suggest that students share their ideas for their oral presentation with a partner and ask for feedback about incorporating the complexities and discrepancies in information from multiple sources. Remind them to anticipate and refute counter-arguments in their presentations.

DIFFERENTIATE INSTRUCTION ↘

TEKS 11.23C

 TEKS 11.23C

Planning Your Presentation

To transform a research paper into an oral presentation, you need to consider your purpose, your audience, and the content of your paper.

Determining Your Purpose

Your purpose is your reason for giving a presentation.

- **Informative** speeches educate by providing valuable information.
- **Persuasive** speeches argue for or against something.
- **Demonstration** speeches show how to do or make something.

Considering Your Audience

As you think about your specific audience, keep the following points in mind.

- **Be clear.** Listeners should understand your main points immediately.
- **Anticipate questions** the audience might have and answer them. This helps keep the audience connected.
- **Engage your listeners** through thought-provoking questions, revealing anecdotes, interesting details, and effective visuals.

Reviewing Your Report

During an oral report, obviously your audience cannot go back and listen again to earlier statements, so you must be sure to share your ideas clearly from beginning to end. Review your paper to see how the different parts will work in an oral presentation. Use the following questions as a review guide.

- Will my opening grab the listeners' attention?
- What are the main points that listeners need to know? Do I incorporate the complexities of my topic?
- What visual aids can I use to create interest in my topic? (See page **460**.)
- Will the ending have the proper impact on the audience?

Try It!

Identify your purpose. If you were to orally present your most recent research paper, what would your purpose be (to inform, to persuade, or to demonstrate)? List some of your ideas for accomplishing that goal, and think about how you could address discrepanies in the multiple sources and perspectives used to discuss your topic. Consider visual aids that would enhance your presentation.

TEKS 11.23C Develop an argument that incorporates the complexities of and discrepancies in information from multiple sources and perspectives while anticipating and refuting counter-arguments; **ELPS** 3A Practice producing sounds of newly acquired vocabulary to pronounce English words; **3D** Speak using grade-level content-area vocabulary in context/new English words and academic language; **3H** Narrate, describe, and explain with increasing specificity and detail

---

Differentiated Instruction: Struggling Learners

To help students become more comfortable with speaking, provide opportunities for practice. During the week before their presentation, have students give mini-talks such as the following:

- Day 1, in their seat: Tell the class the name of the last book they read.
- Day 2, standing: Name the last movie they saw.
- Day 3, in front of the class: Describe a pet, sibling, or neighbor.
- Day 4, in front of the class: Share the topic of their presentation.
- Day 5, in front of the class: Explain why they chose their topic.

Research

Adapting Your Paper

To create an effective oral presentation, you may need to rewrite certain parts of your paper. The new beginning below grabs the listeners' attention by using short, punchy phrases. The new ending simplifies the complexities of the argument and makes a closer connection to the beginning.

Written Introduction (page 387)

> In a small community, when tragedy strikes, everyone knows it, and everyone can see how best to step in and help. In the global community, tragedy strikes somewhere every day, but knowing how to respond is much more difficult. . . . Faced with numbers like these, an individual might be tempted to despair and cry out, "I'm only one person. What can I do?" . . .

Oral Introduction

> Do you remember when the senior center in town burned down last year? Everyone knew it, and many people stepped in to help. It's a different story with tragedies like hunger, malnutrition, and disease, especially when they're far from home. As individuals, we feel . . .

Written Conclusion (page 393)

> . . . It is no exaggeration to say that their efforts often lift entire communities out of poverty. . . . Bill Drayton believes that the next step in this social evolution is a partnering of business and social entrepreneurs, which he sees as only natural. It was the splitting of business and social concerns 300 years ago . . .

Oral Conclusion

> We see that the efforts of individuals are able to lift entire communities out of poverty. We see that tragedies can be overcome. Businesses will begin to see that they, too, have something to gain by partnering with social entrepreneurs. Everyone benefits, and the world becomes a better place.

Adapting Your Paper

Remind students that engaging readers with an oral presentation requires a different approach than engaging readers in writing. Students' approach needs to be more conversational, while maintaining the formal purpose of an oral presentation. To help students adapt spoken language appropriately for formal and informal purposes, discuss the differences between the written and oral versions of the introduction and conclusion shown on SE page 457.
★ **ELPS** 3i

Remind students that like their written research reports, their oral presentation should incorporate the complexities and discrepancies in information from multiple sources. Elicit that they should also anticipate and refute counter-arguments in their presentations.
★ **TEKS** 11.23C

Written Introduction/Oral Introduction

With partners or in small groups, have students discuss the written and oral introductions. Suggest that students ask themselves *How does the oral presentation immediately engage listeners?* (the speaker starts with an example familiar to the specific audience) *What important points does the oral introduction retain?* (the differences between tragedies in a small community and global tragedies)

Written Conclusion/Oral Conclusion

With partners or in small groups, have students discuss the differences between the written and oral conclusion. Suggest that students ask themselves *How does the writer simplify the message for an oral presentation?* (by using shorter, simpler sentences)

Differentiated Instruction: English Language Learners

★ **ELPS** 3A, 3D, 3H, 3I

ELP Level **Beginning**	ELP Level **Intermediate**	ELP Level **Advanced/Advanced High**
Have students review their research papers and identify new vocabulary and academic language. Guide students to practice pronouncing these words.	Have partners practice reading their research papers to each other. Have them focus on narrating, describing, and explaining their ideas smoothly.	Have partners review their papers and consider different audiences. Have them discuss how they would adapt a spoken report for formal and informal purposes.

 TEKS 11.23C Develop an argument that incorporates the complexities of and discrepancies in information from multiple sources and perspectives while anticipating and refuting counter-arguments; **ELPS** 3A Practice producing sounds of newly acquired vocabulary to pronounce English words; **3D** Speak using grade-level content-area vocabulary in context/new English words and academic language; **3H** Narrate, describe, and explain with increasing specificity and detail; **3I** Adapt spoken language for formal and informal purposes

Creating Note Cards

Before students create their note cards, have them look at the information about visual aids on SE page 460. They should keep this information in mind as they create their note cards.

Note Card Guidelines

Suggest that students refer to their outline as well as to their research paper as they create their cards. Point out that they should follow the bulleted guidelines to systematically organize the note cards for their presentation. Have them adapt and write out word-for-word the introduction and the conclusion to memorize.

 TEKS 11.21B

Three Main Parts to Consider

To help students analyze what to include in the oral presentation, remind them to take into account any teacher comments on their paper. This is a chance to make improvements that were suggested to their focus and coherence, organization, development of ideas, or voice.

ELPS 4K

Try It!
Answers

Suggest that students share their introductions and conclusions with a partner. Partners should give each other feedback regarding how well the introduction and conclusion would work for an oral presentation. **DIFFERENTIATE INSTRUCTION ↘**

ELPS 1B

 TEKS 11.21B

"It usually takes more than three weeks to prepare a good impromptu speech."
—Mark Twain

Creating Note Cards

If you are giving a prepared speech rather than an oral reading of your paper, you should use note cards as a way to systematically organize your central ideas and concepts. The guidelines below will help you make effective cards.

Note Card Guidelines

Write out your entire introduction and conclusion on separate note cards. For the body of your speech, write one point per card, along with specific details. Clearly number your cards.

- Place each main point at the top of a separate note card.
- Write supporting ideas on the lines below the main idea, using key words and phrases to help you remember specific details.
- Number each card.
- Highlight any ideas you want to emphasize.
- Mark the places that call for visual aids.

Three Main Parts to Consider

As you prepare your note cards, keep the following points in mind about the three parts of your oral presentation: the introduction, body, and conclusion.

- **The introduction** should grab the listeners' attention, identify the topic and the focus of your presentation, and provide any essential background information about the topic. (See pages **456–457**.)
- **The body** should contain the central ideas and concepts from your paper and present relevant and accurate details that will hold your listeners' attention. Remember to note the visual aids that you plan to use. (See the bold notes on the sample cards on page **459**.)
- **The conclusion** should restate your focus and leave the listeners with a final thought about your topic. (See pages **456–457**.)

Try It!

Using one of your recent research papers, adapt the introduction and conclusion for an oral report. Write your complete beginning and ending on separate note cards.

TEKS **11.21B** Systematicaly organize relevant information to support central ideas; **ELPS** **1B** Monitor oral language production and employ self-corrective techniques or other resources; **4K** Demonstrate English comprehension and expand reading skills by employing analytical skills

TEKS 11.21B

Making Oral Presentations 459

Sample Note Cards

Below are the note cards Fidel used to systematically organize information for his oral presentation about social entrepreneurs.

Introduction	1
photo: burned family center	

Do you remember when the Baptist church in town burned down last year? Everyone knew it, and lots of people stepped in to help. It's a different story with tragedies like hunger, malnutrition, and disease, especially when they're far

The Problem	2

– early 1700s—business sector is competitive and innovative

– government, other social support systems uncompetitive

– result is slow response to problems

The Solution	3
photo: Bill Drayton, founder Ashoka	

– Ashoka: organization that fosters entrepreneurs

– offers monetary support as well as ideas

– citizen entrepreneurs seek to change situations that cause need

– the needy better themselves, and society benefits as well

Example 1	4

– Erzsébet Szekeres of Hungary—son severely mentally retarded

– instead of institution, she made a group home (assisted living)

– so far she has created 21 group homes

– state's way is changing as a result

Example 2	5
Chart	

– Wojciech Onyszkiewicz, Poland—food-bank program

– rural communities: surplus food that urban people need

– exchanged for education and culture

– disabled urbanites teach computer skills to rural children

Conclusion	6

We see that the efforts of individuals are able to lift entire communities out of poverty. We see that tragedies can be overcome. Businesses will begin to see that they, too, have something to gain by partnering with social entrepreneurs. Everyone benefits, and the world becomes a better place.

Sample Note Cards

Advise students that during their presentation they should use their note cards only as prompts; they should not plan to read directly from them. Give them tips for creating useful note cards.

- Use larger note cards. Advise students not to fill the extra space with more information, but to make their handwriting larger and leave more space between points for easy reference.
- Use different color cards or ink to organize the cards and to remind them when to display their visual aids.
- Print neatly when creating the cards. Illegible writing might cause students to stumble during their presentation.
- Punch a hole in the top left-hand corner of each card and attach a notebook ring to ensure that the cards stay in order.

TEKS 11.21B

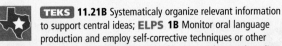

TEKS **11.21B** Systematicaly organize relevant information to support central ideas; ELPS **1B** Monitor oral language production and employ self-corrective techniques or other resources; **4K** Demonstrate English comprehension and expand reading skills by employing analytical skills

Considering Visual Aids

Discuss the types of visual aids listed and the practical issues associated with using them.

- Large posters, charts, and maps can be attached to a wall so that a speaker can point to them during the presentation.
- Smaller visuals might work better as projections (see *computer slides* below).
- Objects require the presenter to speak while showing the piece. Small objects may have to be passed through the audience.
- Using computer slides is the best way to make sure the audience can see all the visual aids. If students plan to use slides, have them turn ahead to the information on SE pages 464– 465. **DIFFERENTIATE INSTRUCTION ↘**

Indicating When to Present Visuals

Suggest that students develop a method to remind themselves when to show a visual, such as the use of a particular color or symbol.

Try It!
Answers

To help students develop expertise in deriving meaning from a variety of media, have them share their ideas for visuals with a partner and ask for feedback.

TEKS 11.23B; **ELPS** 2F

Tip

Have students check the visual aids they plan to use against these bulleted tips and other suggestions on this page.

 TEKS 11.23B

Considering Visual Aids

Consider using visual aids during your speech. They can make your presentation clearer and more meaningful. Here are some examples.

Posters	can include words, pictures, or both.
Photographs	illustrate what you are talking about.
Charts	explain points, compare facts, or give statistics.
Maps	identify or locate specific places being discussed.
Objects	show important items related to your topic.
Computer slides	project your photographs, charts, and maps onto a screen and turn your speech into a multimedia presentation. (See pages 464–467.)

Indicating When to Present Visuals

Write notes on your note cards to indicate where a visual aid would be helpful. Fidel considered the following visuals for his presentation about social entrepreneurs.

- **photo of the local church that burned**
- **photo of Bill Drayton, founder of Ashoka**
- **a chart showing the exchange of goods for services in Poland**

Try It!

Explore a variety of formats for visual aids. Identify two or three visual aids you could use in your presentation. Explain when and how you would use each one.

Tip

When creating visual aids, keep these points in mind.

- **Make them big.** Your visuals should be large enough for everyone in the audience to see.
- **Keep them simple.** Use labels and short phrases rather than full sentences.
- **Make them eye-catching.** Use color, bold lines, and simple shapes to make the contents clear and interesting.

Differentiated Instruction: Struggling Learners

Explain that maintaining eye contact with one's audience during a presentation is crucial. Suggest that students first practice this skill during normal conversations with friends and family (point out that many people don't maintain eye contact, even with people they know well).

Then, to prepare them to speak in front of the class, have students practice in a small group. Have each student make eye contact with three others by looking at each in turn, greeting them, and asking a pre-set question. The student addressed should answer only if eye contact is maintained.

Research

Practicing Your Speech

Practice is the key to giving an effective oral presentation. Knowing what to say and how to say it will help eliminate those butterflies speakers often feel. Here are some hints for an effective practice session.

- **Arrange your note cards in the proper order.** This will eliminate any confusion as you practice.
- **Practice in front of a mirror.** Check your posture and eye contact and be sure your visual aids are easy to see.
- **Practice in front of others.** Friends and family can help you identify parts that need work.
- **Record or videotape a practice presentation.** Do you sound interested in your topic? Are your voice and message clear?
- **Time yourself.** If you have a time limit, practice staying within it. Make sure that the length of your presentation is sufficient to address the complexity of the topic.
- **Speak clearly.** Do not rush your words, especially later when you are in front of your audience.
- **Speak up.** Your voice will sound louder to you than it will to the audience. If you sound too loud to yourself, you are probably sounding just right to your audience.
- **Work on eye contact.** Look down only to glance at a card.
- **Look confident.** This will help engage your listeners.

Practice Checklist

To review each practice session, ask yourself the following questions.

_____ 1. Did I appear at ease?
_____ 2. Could my voice be heard and my words understood?
_____ 3. Did I sound like I enjoyed and understood my topic?
_____ 4. Were my visual aids interesting and used effectively?
_____ 5. Did I avoid rushing through my speech?
_____ 6. Did I include everything I wanted to say?

Try It!

Practice your presentation. Give your speech to family or friends. Consider video recording your speech.

Practicing Your Speech

Have students form small groups to practice their presentations together, taking turns serving as listeners and speakers. Encourage them to use all the practice tips, as well as the checklist, to monitor their oral language production. Provide additional suggestions, such as the following:

- Begin working with the visual aids as early as possible, rather than waiting to practice with them at the last minute.
- Memorize the introduction and conclusion. Students should glance at their note cards occasionally for reminders; they shouldn't plan to read from them.
- Hold dress rehearsals and critique the presentations.

ELPS 1B

Practice Checklist

As needed, point out Question 6, reminding students that their presentation should be of sufficient length and complexity to address the topic. Encourage students to give their audience a copy of the checklist and ask audience members to use it as the basis for an honest evaluation.

TEKS 11.23E

Try It!
Answers

If students have access to a video camera, encourage them to film themselves. Filming provides good practice and will give students valuable information on their presentations.

✔ DIFFERENTIATE INSTRUCTION

TEKS 11.23E Synthesize research into an oral presentation that is of sufficient length and complexity to address the topic; **ELPS 1B** Monitor oral language production and employ self-corrective techniques or other resources; **2A** Distinguish sounds and intonation patterns of English; **3A** Practice producing sounds of newly acquired vocabulary to pronounce English words; **3C** Speak using a variety of grammatical structures, sentence lengths and types, and connecting words; **3H** Narrate, describe, and explain with increasing specificity and detail

Delivering Your Presentation

Remind students that provided they have thoroughly prepared and rehearsed their oral presentation, delivering it should go smoothly.

Controlling Your Voice

Acknowledge that even experienced public speakers sometimes feel nervous facing an audience. It may help students to know that

- relaxation exercises, such as deep breathing, before addressing an audience can help; and
- remembering to speak slowly and clearly will also help students to breathe naturally.

Tip

Tell students that a big part of their task is to engage their audience, rather than rattle off rehearsed material. As they rehearse, remind them to speak as if they were talking to friends while retaining the formal aspect of an oral presentation.

ELPS 3I

Considering Your Body Language

Explain that by staying alert and focused, speakers show their respect, interest, and support for the speaker.

Try It!
Answers

Point out that in an oral format, the speaker is the most important part of the argument for a thesis. Remind students, as they deliver their presentations, to focus on their audience. Suggest that they ask themselves *Is my voice loud enough? I am speaking slowly enough? Am I using tone of voice effectively?*

TEKS 11.23B

462

TEKS 11.23B

Delivering Your Presentation

When you deliver a speech, concentrate on your voice quality and body language. They communicate as much as your words do.

Controlling Your Voice

Use your voice as a rhetorical strategy to help you communicate your ideas. *Volume, tone,* and *pace* are three aspects of your formal speaking voice. If you can control these, your listeners will be able to follow your ideas.

- **Volume** is the loudness of your voice. Imagine that you are speaking to someone in the back of the room and adjust your volume accordingly.
- **Tone** expresses your feelings. Be enthusiastic about your topic and let your voice show that.
- **Pace** is the speed at which you speak. For the most part, speak at a relaxed pace.

Tip

You can make an important point by slowing down, by pausing, by increasing your volume, or by emphasizing individual words.

Considering Your Body Language

Your body language (*posture, gestures,* and *facial expressions*) plays an important role during a speech. Use the strategies suggested below in order to communicate effectively.

- **Assume a straight but relaxed posture.** This tells the audience that you are confident and prepared. If you are using a podium, let your hands rest lightly on the surface.
- **Pause before you begin.** Take a deep breath and relax.
- **Look at your audience.** Try to look toward every section of the room at least once during your speech.
- **Think about what you are saying** and let your facial expressions reflect your true feelings.
- **Point to your visual aids** or use natural gestures to make a point.

Try It!

Deliver your presentation. As you do, be sure to control your voice and exhibit the proper body language.

TEKS 11.23B Use a variety of formats and rhetorical strategies to argue for the thesis; **ELPS** 3I Adapt spoken language for formal and informal purposes

Evaluating a Presentation

Use this form to evaluate an oral presentation, including how well the ideas were developed. Circle the best description for each trait. Then make a positive comment and a helpful suggestion.

Research

Peer Evaluation Sheet

Speaker _____ Evaluator _____

1. **Vocal Presentation**

   Volume:
   Clear and loud   Loud enough   A little soft   Mumbled

   Pace:
   Relaxed   A little rushed or slow   Rushed or slow   Hard to follow

   Comments:
   a. _____
   b. _____

2. **Physical Presentation**

   Posture:
   Relaxed, straight   A bit stiff   Fidgeted a lot   Slumped

   Eye contact:
   Excellent contact   Some contact   Quick glances   None

   Comments:
   a. _____
   b. _____

3. **Information**

   Thought provoking   Interesting   A few points   Not informative

   Comments:
   a. _____
   b. _____

4. **Visual Aids**

   Well used   Easy to follow   Not clear   None

   Comments:
   a. _____
   b. _____

Evaluating a Presentation

As students prepare to evaluate presentations, remind them that presentations should present opinions as well as restate information, and should be of sufficient length and complexity to address the topic. In the interest of time, you may decide not to have students fill out an evaluation sheet for each of their classmates. As an alternative, you could have students fill out a full evaluation for the members of their practice group and give their evaluations to those students at the end of the class; or ask students to take notes during the presentation and be prepared to offer a positive comment and a suggestion to the speaker during the class discussion that follows the presentations. ✔DIFFERENTIATE INSTRUCTION

TEKS 11.23A, 11.23E; **ELPS** 2G, 2I

Differentiated Instruction: English Language Learners		ELPS 2E, 2G
ELP Level **Beginning**	**ELP Level** **Intermediate**	**ELP Level** **Advanced/Advanced High**
Guide listeners to identify key words and ideas. Together, identify visual, contextual, and linguistic support that aided their comprehension.	Have listeners complete sentence stems to identify the topics, ideas, and details in each presentation.	Have listeners take notes to identify and ask questions about topics, language, contexts, main ideas, and details.

TEKS **11.23A** Provide an analysis that supports and develops personal opinions, as opposed to simply restating existing information; **11.23E** Synthesize research into an oral presentation that is of sufficient length and complexity to address the topic; **ELPS** **2E** Use visual, contextual, and linguistic support to confirm understanding of spoken language; **2G** Understand general meaning, main points, and important details of spoken language/topics, language, and contexts; **2I** Demonstrate listening comprehension/collaborating with peers and taking notes

Creating a Multimedia Report

Tell students that *synthesize* means to combine elements to create something new and that a multimedia report synthesizes in the sense that it takes major elements from their original report and combines them in new ways

Choosing a Format for Your Report

Explain that thinking about the main points they want to convey will guide students to choose an appropriate format.

A Power Presentation

Remind students power presentations will allow them to use visuals, text, and sound simultaneously to convey their ideas.

An Interactive Web Page

Tell students that choosing an interactive Web format allows users to respond to their presentation. Have students ask themselves *Does my topic lend itself to audience responses? Do I want my readers/viewers to respond to my topic?*

A Dramatic Presentation

Suggest students consider a dramatic presentation only if their topic has a strong narrative thrust.

Video-based Formats

Tell students that video-based formats work best with news or historical topics for which videos are available.

Try It!
Answers

Remind students that when they create their charts, they should consider how well particular formats will enable them to argue for their thesis and to synthesize information from multiple points of view. `DIFFERENTIATE INSTRUCTION ↘`

TEKS 11.15D, 11.23B

 **TEKS** 11.15D, 11.23B

Creating a Multimedia Report

You can also transform your research paper into a multimedia report, such as a power presentation, an interactive web page, a dramatic presentation, or a video-based format. A multimedia report can be an effective way to synthesize information from multiple points of view.

Choosing a Format for Your Report

To help you choose a format for your report, review your report's content and focus. Ask yourself questions such as the following:

- What types of information do I present in my research paper?
- What is the purpose of my report—to inform or to persuade?
- How do I want to engage my audience?
- What elements might I need to gain access to or learn about to create my report?

Use your answers to these questions as you consider possible formats you might choose for a multimedia report.

A Power Presentation

Modern computer software can help you use visuals, text, and sound to communicate multiple and complex ideas.

An Interactive Web Page

Using modern computer software lets you present a variety of information by incorporating visuals, text, and sound. Additionally, your audience can take an active role in learning about and responding to the ideas you present.

A Dramatic Presentation

Bringing your ideas to life on the stage can help your audience understand multiple viewpoints and ideas.

Video-based Formats

Creating a documentary or a news report can allow an audience to see and hear ideas in real-life situations.

Try It!

Create a chart to help you make a decision about which format would be best for creating a multimedia report from your research paper. List the advantages and disadvantages of each format.

 TEKS **11.15D** Produce a multimedia presentation with graphics, images, and sound that appeals to a specific audience and synthesizes information from multiple points of view;

11.23B Uses a variety of formats and rhetorical strategies to argue for the thesis

★ TEKS 11.15D

Research

Creating a Power Presentation

Plan how you can use and prepare these elements of a power presentation.

Slides

Slides will develop your ideas and shape the flow of your presentation. Plan to prepare slides that:

- introduce the topic
- present your key points with supporting evidence
- present your conclusion

For each slide, write a headline and include two or three bullet points that highlight and summarize the ideas you want to present. Be sure to include information that helps present and synthesize multiple points of view.

Graphics, Images, and Design Elements

Visual elements are a key part of an effective power presentation. Keep these points in mind as you consider graphics, images, and other design elements.

- **Choose effective graphics.** Tables, charts, and graphs can present a lot of information in a way that is easy for your audience to understand. Avoid overly complicated graphics that present too much information and overwhelm your audience.
- **Include useful images.** A picture can indeed be worth a thousand words. Images that support your ideas can communicate meaning far more effectively than huge amounts of text. However, using too many images or using them for filler will weaken your presentation.
- **Use a consistent design.** Design elements like colors, borders, and fonts can enhance your ideas and help focus the audience's attention. Be sure that your choices are consistent, reflect a tone appropriate to your topic, and do not distract from your ideas.

Music, Animation, and Sound Effects

Adding audio or animation to your presentation is a great way to engage your audience. Make choices that support the purpose of your presentation, however. Always use music, animation, and other audio elements in ways that will help your audience consider and remember your ideas.

Delivering a Power Presentation

As you would with any presentation, practice your power presentation. Read your slides aloud, and expand on the ideas you present with each one. Use a relaxed, confident tone, and speak at an appropriate volume and rate. Employ gestures, eye contact, and facial expressions to keep your audience engaged.

Creating a Power Presentation

Slides

Remind students to choose their slides carefully. Tell them to use only slides that add to and support their main ideas.

Graphics, Images, and Design Elements

Tell students, as they choose graphics, images, and design elements for their power presentation, to ask themselves the following questions: *Does this visual element help to synthesize information from multiple points of view? Does it simply and effectively communicate a complicated idea? Does it appeal to a specific audience?*

★ TEKS 11.15D

Music, Animation, and Sound Effects

Caution students about using music that might be inappropriate or might detract from or overwhelm the main points they want to make in their presentation.

Delivering a Power Presentation

Tell students to employ self-corrective techniques as they deliver their power presentation. Remind them not to expect their power presentation to do all of the work. Explain that their delivery and rapport with their audience will be an integral part of the effectiveness of their presentation.

★ ELPS 1B

Differentiated Instruction: English Language Learners

★ ELPS 1G, 3B, 3H

ELP Level **Beginning**	ELP Level **Intermediate**	ELP Level **Advanced/Advanced High**
As you guide students to consider different formats, have them point out key terms they will use to identify and describe their ideas.	Pair students with an English-proficient peer to discuss formats. Have students explain and describe the ideas they want to communicate.	Have partners discuss different formats. Have them determine which might involve using formal and informal English as they consider choices.

TEKS 11.15D Produce a multimedia presentation with graphics, images, and sound that appeals to a specific audience and synthesizes information from multiple points of view; **ELPS** 1B Monitor oral language production and employ self-corrective techniques or other resources; 1G Demonstrate ability to distinguish between formal and informal English and the knowledge of when to use formal and informal English; 3B Expand vocabulary/learning and using high-frequency words for identifying and describing; 3H Describe and explain with increasing specificity and detail

Creating an Interactive Web Page

Remind students planning to create an interactive Web page to ask for help if necessary.

Plan Your Web Page

As students plan their Web page, suggest they consider Web pages that interest or intrigue them. Remind them that a visually boring page will not engage readers.

Create Your Web Page

Tell students that the purpose of their Web page is to convey information about their topic. Caution them about getting sidetracked from their topic.

Present Your Web Page

Suggest that students practice presenting their Web page with several audiences. Have them check that their explanations are clear, their tone is formal enough for the audience, their audience understands what they are trying to do, and their main points have been effectively communicated.

ELPS 3I

Try It!
Answers

Producing a multimedia presentation provides an opportunity for students to give information during an extended speaking assignment. Have students ask for feedback and respond to that feedback. Suggest they have someone take notes for them so they can concentrate on responding to their audience. **DIFFERENTIATE INSTRUCTION ⌄**

TEKS 11.15D; **ELPS** 3F

Creating an Interactive Web Page

As with a power presentation, an interactive Web page uses graphics, images, and sound to present and synthesize information about your research topic.

First, you will need a software program to create a Web page. One program, known as a text editor, is often part of a computer's operating system. Another application, a specialized HTML editor, is commonly used to create Web pages. After you have created a Web page, you will need to determine how to upload the page to a server. Check with your teacher about how to address these issues.

Plan Your Web Page

Start planning your Web page by identifying the basics—your subject, your purpose, your main idea, and the key points and information you want to include. Next, consider questions such as the following:

- **How do you want your Web page to look?** You can create your own original design, or you can use a pre-made Web template. Some of these Web publishing tools will also host your page.

- **How will you make your page interactive?** Links to other sites can help your audience understand the complexities of information from multiple sources or address discrepancies among sources. You can also provide a place for comments from readers to encourage a conversation about the topic.

Create Your Web Page

As you create your page, use graphics, images, and sound in ways that will enhance your ideas and effectively present information on your topic. See page **465** for points to keep in mind as you choose these elements.

Present Your Web Page

As with a power presentation, you need to read some information aloud and expand on your main points. You will also need to demonstrate how your page is interactive and why this is a useful feature for your audience.

To prepare for your presentation, you will need to practice. Rehearsing your presentation before friends or family members will help you anticipate areas that need clarification or improvement. Practicing will also help you become more confident and relaxed.

Try It!

Deliver your presentation of your interactive Web page. Demonstrate how the interactive features help your audience learn about your topic. Speak at an appropriate volume and pace, and use effective body language.

TEKS **11.15D** Produce a multimedia presentation with graphics, images, and sound that appeals to a specific audience and synthesizes information from multiple points of view;
ELPS **3F** Give information during extended speaking assignments; **3I** Adapt spoken language for formal and informal purposes

Creating a Dramatic Presentation

Depending on the topic of your research report, a dramatic presentation can be a powerful medium for getting your ideas across to an audience. Consider the following ideas to help make your topic come alive in a staged production.

- **Choose a dramatic form.** You might want to write a script that presents a scene or scenes about your topic. Another possibility is a seated reading in which actors present a variety of viewpoints and related issues. The actors might interact with each other, or act as single voices to express ideas about your topic.
- **Enlist actors.** Invite friends or classmates to perform in your production. Whether your actors memorize their lines or read from a script, you will need to arrange rehearsal sessions so that they are prepared and comfortable with their roles. Recording a rehearsal will help you and your actors fine-tune the production.
- **Prepare dramatic elements.** Costumes, props, sound, and lighting can all add depth and impact to a dramatic presentation. Be realistic as you consider these aspects of your production, and keep in mind your available resources, the venue for your production, and your potential audience.

Creating a Video-Based Presentation

A video-based format, such as a documentary or a news report, is an excellent way to incorporate real-life information and situations about your research topic. These formats can also allow you to synthesize information from multiple points of view. Keep in mind how you might address some considerations to create a video-based presentation:

- **Equipment** You may need to arrange access to camera, sound, and editing equipment at your school or at a local community access station. Check with your teacher to get more information.
- **Shooting script** Preparing a storyboard or a shooting script is crucial to planning a video-based production. This planning will also help you determine shooting times and locations, for which you will probably need to gain permission in advance.
- **Cast and crew** For a documentary, your "cast" will consist of real people sharing information about topics or situations about which they have first-hand knowledge. You may want to arrange interviews or tours that will communicate the ideas you want to present. For a news report, you might enlist friends or classmates as reporters presenting a news segment in a studio set or from actual locations. Both formats will also require a crew to operate camera, sound, and editing equipment.

Research

Creating a Dramatic Presentation

Remind students that in order to make a dramatic presentation work, their topic needs to be something that actors could act out or re-create. As they create their script, suggest that students focus on the most dramatic, interesting parts of their paper. Tell them to give descriptions of their major characters and the setting of their script. Remind them that even though they need to stay true to the events they are describing, they can and should create believable, compelling dialog for their characters.

Creating a Video-Based Presentation

A documentary or a news report needs to have a story line, but not one as focused on a plot, conflict, and resolution as a dramatic presentation would require. Encourage students to create a storyboard—a series of illustrations or images telling a story, panel by panel—to organize their thoughts, plan out their sequence, and indicate camera position for various scenes.

★ TEKS 11.15D

Differentiated Instruction: English Language Learners

★ ELPS   1B, 1G, 3B, 3F, 3H, 3I

Allow time for students to practice their presentations with a partner. Guide them to adapt their language for formal or informal speaking purposes.

ELP Level **Beginning**	ELP Level **Intermediate**	ELP Level **Advanced/Advanced High**
As students practice, guide them to identify and practice high-frequency words. Have them monitor their speech and use self-corrective techniques.	Have students identify and practice key words and phrases they will use as they narrate, describe, and explain their ideas and present information.	Have speakers narrate, describe, and explain their ideas as they present information. Have listeners note uses of formal and informal English.

★ TEKS **11.15D** Produce a multimedia presentation with graphics, images, and sound that appeals to a specific audience and synthesizes information from multiple points of view; **ELPS 1B** Monitor oral language production and employ self-corrective techniques or other resources; **1G** Demonstrate ability to distinguish between formal and informal English; **3B** Expand vocabulary/learning and using high-frequency words for identifying and describing; **3F** Give information during extended speaking assignments; **3H** Narrate, describe, and explain with increasing specificity and detail; **3I** Adapt spoken language for formal and informal purposes

Writing Across the Curriculum

Recording Your Learning (pages 469–474)

In all curriculum areas, student success is dependent on learning and retaining key information and details. To that end, this section is focused on techniques for taking careful classroom and reading notes and keeping learning logs.

Writing in Science (pages 475–486)

Science writing is about hypotheses, observations, explanations, and conclusions. In this section, students will learn about developing cause-effect essays, creating procedure documents, and, using the STRAP questions, respond to an expository prompt about a scientific concept.

Writing in Social Studies (pages 487–504)

Students learn to respond to topics in different ways by using information gathered from a variety of sources to create a historical skit and write a document-based social studies report.

Writing in Math (pages 505–514)

In order to explore how writing about mathematics can enhance their understanding of the subject, students will analyze a comparison problem, create an argumentative essay, and respond to a math prompt, along with learning about other forms of writing in math.

Writing in the Applied Sciences (pages 515–522)

Students apply their writing skills to real-world situations through creating a classification essay, writing a restaurant review, responding to a test prompt, and by learning about other forms of practical writing.

Writing in the Arts (pages 523–536)

By creating a research report and crafting a performance review, students learn to explore the arts through their writing.

Writing in the Workplace (pages 537–549)

Students learn about the tools and techniques of workplace writing by writing a business letter, a proposal, and an e-mail message; creating an agenda for a business meeting and taking notes at the meeting and publishing them for participants afterward.

Writing Across the Curriculum Reference Guide

Writing Focus

- Recording Your Learning
- Writing in Science
- Writing in Social Studies
- Writing in Math
- Writing in the Applied Sciences
- Writing in the Arts
- Writing in the Workspace

Learning Language

Read aloud the basic and academic terms, as well as the descriptions and questions. Model for students how to read one question and answer it. For example, *It says that phenomena are events that can be observed, so it's asking me what weather events I have observed. The weather event I most remember seeing is a tornado.* Have partners monitor their understanding of the terms by working through the meanings and questions together.

> **DIFFERENTIATE INSTRUCTION ⟶**

✪ ELPS 1F, 2C, 3E, 4G

Minilessons

First ... Then ...   Writing in Science

- Challenge students to **WRITE** detailed directions for a procedure they understand (how to use a computer program, change oil in a car, bake bread, execute a skateboard or snowboard stunt, and so on).

Rules of the Game   Writing in Math

- Have students **CHOOSE** a game or sport that requires a point-scoring system (tennis, cribbage, bridge, football, diving). Tell them to **WRITE** an explanation for the scoring system of the game that a 10-year old could understand. Remind them to **EXPLAIN** the scoring system in a clear, concise manner.

Five Stars   Writing in the Arts

- Discuss a five-star rating system like the one used for movie reviews. Have students use the system to **ANALYZE** a book or story the class read recently. Tell them to **WRITE** a brief, detailed paragraph explaining the rating.

 ELPS **1F** Use accessible language and learn new and essential language in the process; **2C** Learn new language structures, expressions, and basic and academic vocabulary; **3E** Share information in cooperative learning interactions; **4G** Demonstrate comprehension of increasingly complex English/responding to questions

---

TEXAS WRITE SOURCE Online
www.hmheducation.com/tx/writesource

Writing Across the Curriculum

Writing Focus

Learning Language

Work with a partner. Read the meanings and share answers to the questions.

1. A hypothesis is an unproven idea or explanation.
   In what subject would you make a hypothesis?
2. Phenomena are events that can be observed.
   What weather phenomena have you seen?
3. A calculation is an answer based on math.
   What is your calculation of the cost of lunch?
4. If you are feeling the pinch, you are short of money.
   Why would someone to be feeling the pinch?

Recording Your Learning

We've all seen people in a grocery store using a list to remind them of the items they need to buy. Maybe you've even used a list yourself. Just as a list helps shoppers to remember the items they need to buy, good notes help you recall the new information you learn in school.

Whether you are reading, listening, or viewing, taking good notes will help you to recall important information about what you have learned. If you do not take any notes or do not take good notes, you take the chance that you will forget key details.

There's nothing worse than going back over your notes to prepare for a test and discovering that they're incomplete, or worse yet, just don't make much sense. This is why learning how to take notes—notes that will help you weeks after you orginally learned something—is so important. In this chapter you will learn how to take classroom notes, take reading notes, and keep a learning log.

- Taking Classroom Notes
- Taking Reading Notes
- Keeping a Learning Log

"Learning is not attained by chance, it must be sought for with ardor and attended to with diligence."

—Abigail Adams

Recording Your Learning

Objectives
- demonstrate an understanding of the steps involved in taking good classroom and reading notes.
- learn to keep and use a learning log as a study and writing aid.
- use a learning log to track questions, observations, and personal reflections.

The section that follows encompasses various methods and suggestions for taking notes, and for recording thoughts, and observations on classroom and other learning situations. Tips for keeping those notes organized and easy to access are also included.

The lessons in the pages that follow provide models of classroom notes, reading notes, and learning logs. The tips provided will help students
- set up their notes and learning logs,
- know what to do and how to listen as they take notes or fill in a learning log, and
- know what to do with their notes and learning logs after they have completed them.

Taking Classroom Notes

Point out that the tips presented here apply to classroom notes in all content areas. Remind students that they should always adhere to the guidelines established by individual teachers.

Before you take notes ...

Discuss the usefulness of organizing notebooks in the ways suggested.

As you take notes ...

Tell students that they can also use the following learning strategies to monitor understanding of key ideas in a lecture.

- Listen for significant pauses. Speakers often pause before making an important point.
- Listen for language structures, such as repeated ideas. Speakers may repeat key words, phrases, or whole sentences that contain important points.
- Listen for emphasis. Speakers may stress important points by adjusting their speaking rate and volume.
- Watch body language. Speakers often use hand, body, and facial gestures to emphasize key ideas.
- Focus on visuals. Speakers may write ideas on the board and underline key words or phrases for emphasis. They may also refer to a visual or graphic, such as a chart or diagram.

DIFFERENTIATE INSTRUCTION ↘

ELPS 1H, 2C, 2D, 4C, 4G

After you've taken notes ...

Review the sample notes, guiding students to see how the strategies on page 470 were utilized. Have them examine their own notes to see which strategies they have used or might use in the future.

ELPS 1B

 ELPS 1B, 1H, 2C, 2D, 4C, 4G

Taking Classroom Notes

Taking good notes helps you remember key lecture points, understand new material, and prepare for tests and writing assignments. Follow these tips to take good notes in your classes.

Before you take notes ...

- **Set up your notes** in a three-ring binder so that you can insert handouts. A spiral notebook with a folder in the back is another option.
- **Date each entry** in your notebook and write down the topic.
- **Organize each page.** A two-column format with lecture information on the left and questions on the right works well.

As you take notes ...

- **Listen for key words.** Pay attention to information that comes after phrases like *for example, as a result,* or *most importantly.*
- **Use your own words** as much as possible.
- **Write down questions** as they occur to you.
- **Draw pictures** or quick sketches to capture complex ideas.

After you've taken notes ...

- **Reread your notes** after class and add any information needed to make them clearer.
- **Study your notes** to prepare for tests and exams.

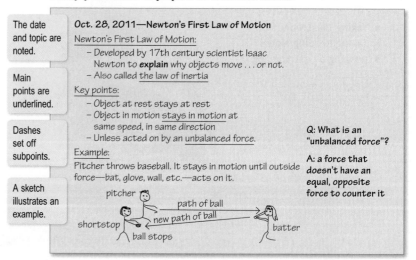

ELPS **1B** Monitor written language production and employ self-corrective techniques or other resources; **1H** Develop and expand repertoire of learning strategies; **2C** Learn new language structures; **2D** Monitor understanding of spoken language; **4C** Comprehend English language structures; **4G** Demonstrate comprehension of increasingly complex English/taking notes

Differentiated Instruction: Struggling Learners

Advise students that they should not try to write down every word a presenter says, and remind them that they do not need to use full sentences in their notes, unless instructed to copy something verbatim. Encourage students to compare their notes with those of a study partner to make sure they have recorded all of the main points.

ELPS 1B, 1H, 2D, 4C, 4D, 4G

Taking Reading Notes

Note taking can increase your understanding of reading assignments. Here are some tips on taking reading notes.

Before you take notes . . .

- **Write the date, chapter, book title, and topic** before each entry.
- **Organize each page.** For a two-column format, put your notes on the left and your thoughts and questions on the right.
- **Quickly skim the assigned text.** Read the title, introduction, headings, and chapter summaries. Examine any graphics, charts, and examples.

As you take notes . . .

- **Write down headings or subtopics** and the most important details under each.
- **Use your own words** to help you understand the material better.
- **Summarize graphics.** Write down or sketch out main ideas.
- **List vocabulary words** and look up definitions later.

After you've taken notes . . .

- **Review your notes.** When you're done reading, write down any other questions you have. Research the answers and add them to your notes.

> Nov. 10, 2011—Today's Physics: Chap. 4, Sec. 5
> Centrifugal and Centripetal Force
>
> **Questions and thoughts are listed in the second column.**
>
> 1. Centripetal means force that causes objects to follow a circular path.
> 2. This force is perpendicular to the line of travel.
> 3. Centrifugal force is the apparent outward force of circular motion.
> 4. This force is an effect of rotation inertia and is not a true force.
>
> Q: How does this fit into the laws of motion?
>
> Example: Whirling a can on a string—the string is the force.
>
> Q: What's the difference between centripetal and centrifugal?
>
> A: Centrifugal means "center fleeing." Centripetal means "center seeking."

Try It!

Use the information above as a guide the next time you take notes for a reading assignment. For the best results, be sure to follow all of the tips.

Notes

Differentiated Instruction: English Language Learners

ELPS 1H, 2I, 4C, 4G

ELP Level **Beginning**	ELP Level **Intermediate**	ELP Level **Advanced/Advanced High**
Model reading a short passage and taking notes on it, having students repeat key language structures after you. Guide partners to take notes on another passage.	Have partners review the strategies, and discuss how they will apply each one. Have them show understanding by working together to apply the strategies as they take notes on another assignment.	Have students work independently to take notes for a current reading assignment. Then have partners analyze the notes to see which tips they could apply more carefully.

Taking Reading Notes

Before reading, ask students who regularly take reading notes to explain how they use their notes and tell what benefits they gain from their notes. Then encourage them to discuss what they find difficult about taking notes about their reading.

ELPS 4D

Before you take notes …

Some students may consider taking reading notes to be too much additional work. Assure them that as they improve their ability to recognize important details, they will find it easier to paraphrase, summarize, or synthesize the main ideas into manageable notes.

As you take notes …

Point out that because note taking forces readers to become involved in their reading material, it can help them pinpoint areas where their comprehension breaks down. As a result, they can seek clarification about those ideas before more complex concepts are introduced in class. Explain that taking notes can also raise questions that reach beyond the scope of the text.

After you've taken notes …

Review the sample notes, guiding students to see how the tips on page 471 were utilized. Have students examine their own notes and ask them to suggest additional tips that they might utilize.

ELPS 1B, 2I

Try It!
Answers

Suggest that students copy the strategies into their notebooks and refer to them as needed until they have internalized them as part of their note-taking process. **✔ DIFFERENTIATE INSTRUCTION**

ELPS 1H, 2D, 4G

 1B Monitor written language production and employ self-corrective techniques or other resources; **1H** Develop and expand repertoire of learning strategies; **2D** Monitor understanding of spoken language; **2I** Demonstrate listening comprehension/taking notes; **4C** Comprehend English language structures; **4D** Use prereading supports to enhance comprehension of written text; **4G** Demonstrate comprehension of increasingly complex English/taking notes

Keeping a Learning Log

Remind students that taking notes is an objective thinking and recording process. Review that classroom notes

- summarize important information from a lecture or reading assignment,
- are often in outline form, and
- do not include personal comments.

Before you make an entry ...

Point out the similarities in organization for taking notes and starting a learning log. Explain that learning log entries differ from classroom notes in that

- entries reflect students' thoughts on topics by making connections to their life and learning experiences, and
- the writing, while based on factual information, is reflective in style.

As you make an entry ...

Tell students that an effective learning log will help them think through and connect concepts and form questions about new material.

After you've made an entry ...

Review the tips, pointing out that some follow-up is required for a learning log.

Tip

Have students work in pairs to practice the "stop and write" technique, sharing and discussing their understanding of the concepts.

DIFFERENTIATE INSTRUCTION ↘ DIFFERENTIATE INSTRUCTION ↘

⭐ ELPS 2H, 2I, 4G, 4I

Try It!
Answers

Have students work in small groups after they have set up their learning log. Have them share their initial entries with and get feedback from the group. DIFFERENTIATE INSTRUCTION ↘

⭐ ELPS 1A, 2H, 2I, 4G, 4I

⭐ ELPS **1A** Use prior knowledge and experiences; **2H** Understand implicit information in spoken language; **2I** Demonstrate listening comprehension/taking notes; **4G** Demonstrate comprehension of increasingly complex English/retelling or summarizing/responding to questions/taking notes; **4I** Demonstrate English comprehension by employing basic reading skills

---

⭐ ELPS 1A, 2H, 2I, 4G, 4I

Keeping a Learning Log

A learning log is a specialized journal you use to reflect on things you are learning. In a learning log, you write about new concepts by connecting them to previous learning or personal experiences. Here are some tips for keeping a learning log.

Before you make an entry ...

- **Set up your learning log** in a binder or notebook.
- **Write the topic and date of each entry** so that you can find it easily.
- **Leave wide margins** so you have room for your own thoughts and questions.

As you make an entry ...

- **Summarize key concepts** and develop meaningful comparisons.
- **Apply new ideas** to things you already know.
- **Think about questions** you may have about the subject.
- **Predict how the new ideas** may prove helpful in the future.
- **Make personal connections** by explaining what the ideas mean to you.

After you've made an entry ...

- **Review your entries** periodically to see how your thoughts have been developing.
- **Research any questions** you have and write down the answers.
- **Continue your reflections** by writing new observations in the margins.

Tip

You can use an approach called "stop and write" for your learning log. Stop in the middle of your reading or at the end of your classroom discussion and immediately write down your thoughts about what you've just learned. This can show how well you understand the topics read or discussed in class. Your learning-log entries can also help you prepare for exams by revealing which concepts were the most difficult for you.

Try It!

Follow the guidelines above to set up your own learning log. When you have a few minutes during class, stop and write, reflecting on what you are learning. Make personal observations about the ideas.

Differentiated Instruction: Struggling Learners

Have small groups review their class notes from a specific date. Then have students use the notes to create their own learning-log entry. Tell them to focus on exploring only the main concepts. Encourage them to make personal connections with ideas that remind them of something they have learned or experienced. ⭐ ELPS 1A

Differentiated Instruction: Advanced Learners

Invite volunteers to take class minutes on a classroom topic or on group work. Students who have been absent can then use the minutes to catch up on the day's topic or discussion, special instructions, and reading assignments.

Recording Your Learning **473**

Learning-Log Entries

Here are three sample learning-log entries from students in an earth science class, a math class, and a social studies class. In each case, the student thinks about the ideas discussed in class, analyzes them, and summarizes key concepts.

March 12, 2011 – Plate Tectonics

Today we discussed plate tectonics, a theory that has changed the way geologists view the earth. Alfred Wegener proposed the theory in 1912, but it wasn't widely accepted until the mid-20th century.

Plate tectonics theory says the earth is made up of large plates, which move and change over time. Where plates meet, volcanoes and earthquakes occur and mountains are likely to form.

Plate tectonics suggests that continents are drifting, and new oceanic crust is being created at mid-ocean ridges, then moving out from there. This is called sea floor spreading.

March 13, 2011 – Earth's Layers

We saw a presentation on plate tectonics. The earth has three layers — the core, the mantle, and the crust. The crust and upper mantle, called the lithosphere, are rigid plates. The softer, lower mantle is called the asthenosphere. Convection from radioactive heat in the earth's core occurs in the asthenosphere, causing plates to move.

Plates move away from each other, toward each other, and over each other. There are 7 major plates and 20 smaller ones.

Notes

Q: Why didn't scientists accept Wegener's theories at first?

A: Scientists couldn't understand what force would be strong enough to move continents.

Q: What evidence supports plate tectonics?

A: New, more precise tools help scientists measure activity at plate boundaries and explore deeper in the earth.

Q: Why is this important?

A: Scientists can more accurately predict earthquakes and tsunamis.

The date and topic are given, and ideas from the class are reviewed.

Questions are listed, and answers from the teacher and from additional reading are added.

Another entry shows growing understanding.

Learning-Log Entries

Use the following questions to guide a discussion about the sample learning-log entries.

- How does the second entry show the student's growing understanding of the topic of plate tectonics? (Possible response: The first entry says the earth's plates move and change over time. The second entry explains why and how the plates move.)
- What do the questions suggest about the student's attitude toward science class? (Possible response: The student takes class seriously, has reflected on the ideas presented, and wants to understand why these ideas should matter to people.)
- How does the writing style of the learning-log entries differ from the style of the notes on SE pages 470 and 471? (Possible response: The notes are factual and objective. They're written in outline form. The learning-log entries use the pronoun *we,* making them more personal and reflective. They're written in paragraph form.)

More Learning-Log Entries

Have students work in small groups to analyze the model learning-log entries. Suggest that they discuss the following.

- In the November 3 model, how does the second half of the entry reinforce the information in the first half of the entry? (Possible response: It shows a drawing that illustrates the math concepts and shows that the student understands the concepts. The drawing will help the student remember the concepts.)
- In the September 15 model, find places where the student's own thoughts and reflections come through. (Possible response: *It's hard to imagine . . . ; I think many good ideas . . .*)
- In the September 15 model, discuss how the student's personal reflections and connections helped him or her generate an intriguing question about the topic. (Possible response: The student thought about women not having the vote and imagined what it must have been like for them, which led him or her to consider how many good ideas might have been lost.)

Try It!
Answers

Have students share their learning-log entries with a partner and ask for feedback.

DIFFERENTIATE INSTRUCTION ↘ **DIFFERENTIATE INSTRUCTION ↘**

⭐ **ELPS** 2I

474

More Learning-Log Entries

A learning log allows you to write about what you are learning, think through new concepts, ask questions, and find answers.

Nov. 3, 2011 – Trig Apps

The sine and cosine functions can help us to find missing sides of right triangles.

We can use the definitions of the functions and patterns for right triangles with angles of "certain" degrees:

30-60-90 degree triangles have sides of lengths x and x · √3 and 2 · x

45-45-90 degree triangles have sides of lengths x and x and x · √2

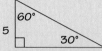

The side opposite the 30° angle is x (5).

Using the pattern, the side opposite 60° is 5 √3 and the side opposite 90° is 2 · 5 = 10.

The size of the angles corresponds to the side length. (The shortest side is always across from the smallest angle.) We could use the definition of cosine to find the other sides (see notes).

September 15, 2011
American Women and the Fight for Suffrage

> Questions and thoughts are listed in the second column.

Today we learned about American women's long battle to win the right to vote. It took decades of hard work and lobbying.

It's hard to imagine that at one time women did not have the same right to vote as men did. That meant that men made every political decision, from passing laws to declaring war. And women had to live under those laws, even though their ideas were not used to create them. I think many good ideas must have been wasted because women thought of them.

One woman who worked hard for suffrage was Elizabeth Cady Stanton. She was a national women's leader from 1848 to 1902. I am interested in her and plan to choose her as the subject of my biographical essay.

How would history be different if women had demanded the vote sooner?

Try It!

Keep a learning log for one of your classes. Concentrate on understanding topics and making a personal connection to what you learn.

Differentiated Instruction: Struggling Learners

Remind students that diagrams or quick sketches can convey information in a quick, easy-to-understand format. Also, encourage visual learners to color-code their entries, using one color ink for definitions or key points, and a different color for their own observations. Explain that this will help them with their studying later on.

475

Writing in Science

Writing is central to science. It allows scientists to express their hypotheses, to record observations, and to communicate their conclusions. Writing gives structure to the scientific method.

In science classes—chemistry, physics, geology, astronomy, and life sciences—you can make discoveries about the natural world and learn ways to explore it further. Writing about the practical applications of science in your everyday life requires thoughtful research skills, accurate observations, and clear explanations.

This chapter covers types of writing that you will encounter in your science classes and in projects that require scientific knowledge. In research papers and responses to prompts, you share what you learn with your teacher and others. Practical writing allows you to apply what you've learned about science to jobs, hobbies, or day-to-day situations.

- **Writing Guidelines: Cause-Effect Essay**
- **Writing Guidelines: Procedure Document**
- **Response to an Expository Prompt**

"Science is the desire to know causes."
—William Hazlitt

Writing in Science

Objective
- apply the writing process and traits of writing to a cause-effect essay, a procedure document, and an expository prompt

The lessons on the following pages provide models of writing students might do in a science class. Assigning these forms of writing will depend on
- the skill level of your students,
- the subject matter they are studying in the field of science, and
- the writing goals of your school, district, or state.

Differentiated Instruction: English Language Learners

ELPS 2!

ELP Level **Beginning**	ELP Level **Intermediate**	ELP Level **Advanced/Advanced High**
Work with students to identify the class for which they will create their learning log. Preview the subject matter and practice pronouncing possible vocabulary terms.	Have partners collaborate to decide on the class for which they will create their learning logs. Have them brainstorm and discuss relevant vocabulary.	Have partners who create learning logs for the same class analyze one another's notes and discuss similarities and differences.

 ELPS 2I Demonstrate listening comprehension/taking notes

Writing Guidelines
Cause-Effect Essay

Tell students that the guidelines on the pages that follow can be applied to any cause-effect essay in any subject area.

Note that the cause-and-effect graphic organizer on SE page 614 shows one cause and multiple effects. Tell students that they can

- easily reverse this graphic organizer to show multiple causes leading to one central effect, or
- make multiple copies of the graphic organizer to show cause-effect relationships related to the topic.

Explain that often an effect becomes a cause that leads to another effect. (For example, in a pile-up on a highway, one vehicle hits another vehicle that then hits another, and so on.) Tell students that this is known as a *causal chain* (a series in which an effect becomes a cause leading to an effect). If students recognize this pattern in their topic, have them make a chart or diagram to show how each cause and effect is linked. Explain that this will help them to create a clear organizational schema for conveying ideas in their essays.

⭐ **TEKS** 11.15A(iv); **ELPS** 2C

Prewriting

Walk through the prewriting guidelines with students, making sure that they understand what they need to do during this stage of the writing process. Remind them that their cause-effect essays should include relevant and substantial evidence and well-chosen details. Guide them to check the validity, reliability, and relevance of the primary and secondary sources they choose.

⭐ **TEKS** 11.15A(v), 11.15A(vi)

⭐ **TEKS** 15A(iv), 15A(v), 15A(vi)

Writing Guidelines Cause-Effect Essay

In your science classes, you might be called on to research the causes and effects of scientific phenomena. Your focus might be on one cause and one main effect, multiple causes and effects, one effect and its many causes, or so on. Follow these guidelines.

Prewriting

- **Select a topic.** If your teacher doesn't assign a specific topic, review your class notes, learning log, and textbook for ideas. Think about topics you have discussed in class. Choose a topic with a number of causes and/or effects.
- **Gather details.** Research your topic so that you understand it thoroughly. List the topic's cause and effects, or the central effect and its causes. (Consider using a graphic organizer. See page **614**.)
- **Outline your essay.** Write a thesis statement that names your topic. Then write down the causes and effects, in order of importance. You can list the most important cause first or last, depending on which works best in your essay. Include any important details explaining the cause and its effects (or the effect and its causes).
- **Use both primary and secondary sources.** Primary sources (such as diaries, journals, or original research) inform you directly, rather than through another person's explanation. Secondary sources (such as newspaper articles, TV and radio news, or magazine articles) are third-person accounts of events as well as scientific or mathematical findings. (See page **376**.)
- **Find other perspectives.** Often, you will find sources that offer divergent or even contradictory views on your topic. Do not make the mistake of discarding sources because they do not support your main idea. In fact, you should seek out such sources. Your research and, ultimately, your writing will only be strengthened by including and rebutting divergent points of view.
- **Check that your sources are reliable.** How can you tell if the sources you use are reliable? First, do not assume something is accurate just because it appears in print or on the Internet. Ask yourself the following questions. *Is the author an expert in the field? Is the information presented clearly and without bias? Are multiple points of view included? Is the source current? Who is the publisher or supporting organization?* If you still have doubts, ask your teacher or librarian for help. (See pages **377–378**.)

⭐ **TEKS** **11.15A(iv)** Write an analytical essay of sufficient length that includes a clear organizational schema for conveying ideas; **11.15A(v)** Write an analytical essay of sufficient length that includes relevant and substantial evidence and well-chosen details; **11.15A(vi)** Write an analytical essay of sufficient length that includes information on multiple relevant perspectives and a consideration of the validity, reliability, and relevance of primary and secondary sources; **ELPS** **2C** Learn new academic vocabulary

Drafting

After you have chosen your topic, researched it, and formulated and revised your research question, you can write your thesis statement. Use your final research question to create your thesis statement.

Write Your Thesis Statement

In most cases, a thesis statement expresses your viewpoint about your topic or about an aspect of your topic. Take time and write your thesis statement carefully. Remember, it is your thesis statement that will shape your information into a coherent whole and help you to stay on track as you write. Keep two things in mind as you write your thesis statement: your purpose and your audience.

- Do I want to explain something?
- Do I want to persuade people to take action or adopt a particular viewpoint?
- Do I want to argue a particular point of view?
- Is my audience a teacher? My classmates? Someone who might not agree with me?

Write an Introduction and Conclusion

Write an introductory paragraph that grabs your readers' attention, introduces the topic, and includes a clearly worded thesis statement. Consider beginning with a startling quote or example, a rhetorical question, or an evocative metaphor or simile. Be sure that you end your essay in a convincing way. Write concluding paragraphs that sum up your main points and leave your readers with something to think about.

Connect Your Ideas

Check that you have chosen a logical pattern that works for your topic and for a cause-effect essay. Be sure that your middle paragraphs list your causes and effects in order of importance. You can list either most important first or most important last depending on what works best for your paper. Use transitional words and phrases (such as *since, due to, thus, as a result, because, therefore, so,* and *consequently*) to connect sections, paragraphs, and sentences within paragraphs. If your writing sounds choppy or if people reading your essay have a hard time following your ideas, a lack of transitional words and phrases are the likely culprits. Transitional words and phrases signal relationships between ideas and help readers move smoothly from one idea to the next.

Tip

Whenever possible, use active voice in your thesis statement. Using active rather than passive voice will help condense, clarify, and strengthen your thesis statement.

Drafting

Suggest that students revisit their research question to make sure that it accurately reflects the topic they want to explore.

Write Your Thesis Statement

Have students use their research question as the starting point for writing their thesis statement. Remind them to determine their purpose and their audience. Finally, caution students about simply summarizing or restating facts in their thesis statement. Remind them that their thesis statement should use specificity and detail to describe their unique point of view on the topic.
TEKS 11.15A(iii); ELPS 5G

Write an Introduction and Conclusion

Tell students that their introductory paragraphs should "hook" their readers, and their concluding paragraphs should convincingly sum up their main points. Model rhetorical devices they might use to open their essays, such as *Clean, fresh water is like breathable air, an essential element of life* (an effective simile).
TEKS 11.15A(i), 11.15A(ii)

Connect Your Ideas

Remind students to check that their organizational pattern is clear and that they have used transitional words and phrases effectively. ✔DIFFERENTIATE INSTRUCTION
TEKS 11.15A(ii)

Tip

Give students examples of active vs. passive voice, such as *Well-managed watersheds are a crucial element in the management of water supplies* (passive), and *Water supplies depend on well-managed watersheds* (active).

ELP Level **Beginning**	ELP Level **Intermediate**	ELP Level **Advanced/Advanced High**
Use visuals, simplified language, and examples to present common cause-effect signal words such as *since, because,* and *as a result.* Have students repeat each example after you.	Have partners complete sentence frames using common cause-effect signal words such as *I ____ because ____,* or *As a result of ____, we had to____.* Remind them to use specificity and detail.	Have students work independently to write sentences using cause-effect signal words. Have partners share and discuss their sentences, and then revise as needed to add specificity and detail.

TEKS **11.15A(i)** Write an analytical essay of sufficient length that includes effective introductory and concluding paragraphs and a variety of sentence structures; **11.15A(ii)** Write an analytical essay of sufficient length that includes rhetorical devices, and transitions between paragraphs; **11.15A(iii)** Write an analytical essay of sufficient length that includes a clear thesis statement or controlling idea; **ELPS 2C** Learn new academic vocabulary; **5G** Describe and explain with increasing specificity and detail

Revising

Have students use the questions provided on SE page 478 and the questions below to evaluate their first draft for focus and coherence, organization, development of ideas, and voice.

Focus and Coherence: Does my thesis statement clearly state the focus of the essay? Are all ideas clearly connected to each other and to the thesis statement? Are the introduction and conclusion effective?

Organization: What is the organizational schema of my essay? Is this schema used consistently? Do transitional words and phrases help the reader move smoothly from one idea to the next?

Development of Ideas: Have I given ample and relevant support for all main ideas? Can I use rhetorical devices to better illustrate my ideas? Have I used specificity and well-chosen detail to explain and describe ideas?

Voice: Does the writing express my unique voice and perspective? Have I used a variety of sentence lengths and patterns to add interest to my writing?

TEKS 11.13C, 11.15A(i), 11.15A(ii),11.15A(iii), 11.15A(iv), 11.15A(v); **ELPS** 5F; 5G

Editing

Have students use the suggestions provided on SE page 478 to evaluate their first draft for correct use of grammar, sentence structure, capitalization, punctuation, and spelling.

Tip

Suggest that students work with a partner to check their essay revisions.

TEKS 13C, 15A(i), 15A(ii), 15A(iii), 15A(iv), 15A(v)

Revising

Review your first draft for focus and coherence, organization, development of ideas, and voice. Ask yourself the following questions:

- Does my essay address the topic or prompt?
- Does my essay focus on causes and effects?
- Have I written an attention-grabbing introduction that includes a clearly worded thesis statement?
- Does my organizational pattern work for my topic and audience?
- Are all my ideas clearly connected to each other and to my thesis statement?
- Do transitional words and phrases connect my ideas?
- Have I included ample support and specific details to support my ideas?
- Does my conclusion sum up my main ideas, add depth to my essay, and leave the reader with something to think about?
- Do I express a unique perspective?
- Is my writing authentic and original?
- Have I engaged my readers throughout my writing?

The revising stage is also the time to improve your style. Include rhetorical devices, when appropriate, for emphasis and to engage your readers. Vary your sentence length to improve smoothness and flow.

Editing

When you edit for conventions, you check your use of grammar, sentence structure, capitalization, punctuation, and spelling. Once you have done that, use the following suggestions:

- Have a classmate or a teacher read your essay to check for convention errors. Correct any the errors you discover.
- Use the holistic scoring guide on pages **36–37** as a final revising guide, and use the Proofreader's Guide on pages **634–779** as an editing guide.
- Prepare a final copy. Make a neat, final copy of your cause-effect essay, and check it once more for errors.

Tip

Careful revising will significantly improve the quality of your essay. Do not rush through this part of the process. Take the time you need to address parts of your essay that do not work or need improvement.

TEKS **11.13C** Revise drafts to clarify meaning; **11.15A(i)** Write an analytical essay of sufficient length that includes effective introductory and concluding paragraphs and a variety of sentence structures; **11.15A(ii)** Write an analytical essay of sufficient length that includes rhetorical devices, and transitions between paragraphs; **11.15A(iii)** Write an analytical essay of sufficient length that includes a clear thesis statement or controlling idea; **11.15A(iv)** Write an analytical essay of sufficient length that includes a clear organizational schema for conveying ideas; **11.15A(v)** Write an analytical essay of sufficient length that includes relevant and substantial evidence and well-chosen details; **ELPS** **5F** Write using a variety of grade-appropriate sentence lengths, patterns, and connecting words; **5G** Describe and explain with increasing specificity and detail

Differentiated Instruction: Struggling Learners

Encourage students to identify the words in the essay that signal cause-and-effect relationships (*cause, affects, As a result*). Point out that these types of transition words are needed when writing about causes and effects of a scientific phenomenon.

Cause-Effect Essay

In this essay, Chan discusses the effects of natural events and human actions on lakes, rivers, streams, and aquifers.

Science

Balancing Nature: How Drought, Floods, and Irrigation Impact Watersheds

Increasingly, water supplies depend on well-managed watersheds, areas that receive precipitation and then hold it as groundwater or as a form of surface water (freshwater lakes and marshes). Extensive woodlands absorb and hold water that would otherwise simply run off into streams and rivers and be lost for local water needs. Various types of vegetation and ground cover, artificial reservoirs, as well as natural lakes and marshes, also serve as vital watersheds. A number of natural conditions and human activities cause the consistent supply of clean, fresh water to be put at risk in this country and around the world.

Drought, an extended period of dramatically below-normal precipitation, directly affects lakes, rivers, and streams. Insufficient rain and snow mean that river flow will decrease and groundwater levels will fall. Such conditions often produce stagnant pools that are breeding grounds for algae, mosquitoes, and other harmful organisms. In addition, wells may not provide enough water or may dry up altogether.

Of course, too much moisture can also cause serious problems. Ground cover can be ripped away, increasing the chances that water will flow violently across the land. Flooding will not only destroy crops and homes, but it can also wash pollutants into lakes and rivers, raising bacteria levels. As a result, authorities have been forced to close beaches and use more chemicals to treat drinking water. Fertilizer, a benefit to crops, becomes a menace when washed into the watershed because it feeds algae. The nutrients in the fertilizer cause this small plant to bloom wildly and cloud the water. If conditions are right, algae blooms can sufficiently deplete the oxygen supply in the water to kill fish. In such extreme cases, recreational use of lakes and streams sharply declines, impacting local communities dependent on tourist trade.

The **beginning** introduces the topic and leads to the thesis statement (underlined).

The **middle** first discusses two major natural causes that affect a watershed. Examples of unwanted effects are identified.

Transitional words and phrases connect ideas.

Cause-Effect Essay

Have students work in pairs or in small groups to evaluate the student model on SE pages 479–480 for focus and coherence and organization. Suggest that students use the Revising questions on SE page 478, as well as the following:

- How do the introductory sentences prepare the reader to understand the author's thesis statement? (Possible response: They give important background information.)
- How is the essay organized? (Possible response: The author lists causes—drought, floods, and irrigation— and examines their effect on watersheds.)
- How does the first sentence of the third paragraph on SE page 479 provide a smooth transition from the paragraph that precedes it? (Possible response: The author reminds readers of the previous discussion of drought and transitions smoothly into a discussion of flooding with the sentence *Of course, too much moisture can also cause serious problems.*)
- How does the first sentence of the first paragraph on SE page 480 connect both to the thesis statement and the paragraph on SE page 479 that precedes it? (Possible response: The phrase *are more likely to be a problem* connects the paragraph both to the thesis and the preceding paragraph.)

✔ **DIFFERENTIATE INSTRUCTION** ✔ **DIFFERENTIATE INSTRUCTION**

Differentiated Instruction: English Language Learners

⭐ ELPS **4F**

ELP Level **Beginning**	ELP Level **Intermediate**	ELP Level **Advanced/Advanced High**
Preteach words such as *drought, irrigation*, and *floods*. Model creating a web to categorize other words in the essay that are related to water.	Preteach vocabulary such as *precipitation, pollutants*, and *fertilizer*. Have partners sort words that are related to nature and those related to human activity.	Have partners identify and define any unfamiliar terms in the essay. After reading have them explain what they learned about each term.

 ELPS 4F Use support from peers and teachers to develop vocabulary

Have students work in pairs or in small groups to evaluate and analyze the student model on SE pages 479 and 480 for development of ideas and voice. Remind students to use specificity and detail as they describe and explain their answers to the following questions.

- In the third paragraph on SE page 479, what support does the author give for the topic sentence? (Possible response: Flooding washes pollutants into lakes and rivers; fertilizer becomes a menace when washed into the watershed)
- In the same paragraph, what specific details does the author provide? (Possible response: authorities forced to close beaches and use chemicals to treat water; algae blooms destroy oxygen supply and destroy fish; recreational use of rivers and lakes declines)
- Find examples that show that the author has engaged the reader and used an authentic voice. (Possible response: third paragraph on SE page 479, last sentence; second paragraph on SE page 480, last two sentences)

ELPS 4K, 5G

Try It!
Answers

Review the topic each student selects to be sure that the subject matter lends itself to a cause-effect organization.

Two major actions that affect watersheds are described, and their effects are listed.

In the western part of the country, irrigation and the rapid growth of cities are more likely to be a problem. Even though farmers are guaranteed consistent yields and cities can increase in size, irrigation and the demand for water in cities draw down the levels of the lakes, rivers, and aquifers (underground water sources). Cities enter into legal battles with farmers to keep irrigation from harming the water supply. In some areas, irrigation increases the likelihood of saline seep, a condition in which salts accumulate in the topsoil, destroying its crop potential. Since the average moisture levels in the West are low, these two phenomena result in watershed levels drastically reduced and rivers almost drained of water.

As towns and cities grow and more people build in rural areas, natural drainage and water collection are changed or destroyed. Trees and other plants are removed during construction. Buildings and roads quickly shed water. This means an important source for replenishing local aquifers is lost. Also, oil, battery acid, and antifreeze (from cars, buses, and trucks) are quickly washed into the water system. Trash thoughtlessly discarded adds to the trouble. These unfortunate by-products of development affect the water quality for other communities downstream.

The **ending** summarizes major points and leaves the reader with something to think about.

Many causes have negative effects on watersheds. Scientists, officials, and the public have a growing awareness of how vital watersheds are to clean, clear water for refreshment, agriculture, industry, and recreation. Well-maintained watersheds can minimize the problems created by drought. Protection of expanses of wetlands produces a natural overflow area to trap water and offsets the damage done by floodwaters. Keeping a "big picture" view of irrigation can reduce draining vital groundwater and avoid inefficient uses of water that rob watersheds. Development must take watershed issues into account by protecting existent watersheds and creating new ones.

Try It!

Write a cause-effect essay. Select a topic that interests you and follow the prewriting and drafting guidelines on pages **476–477**.

Differentiated Instruction: Advanced Learners

Invite students to brainstorm different types of procedure documents they have written recently. Examples may include lab reports, how-to writing, instructions, directions, or guidelines. Have students also discuss the purpose of nonacademic types of procedure documents.

Writing Guidelines Procedure Document

Sometimes you have the opportunity to write about science outside of school. For example, you may be asked to write technical directions for others, based on scientific concepts you've learned in class. While this type of writing is more informal than academic writing, it still requires careful attention to details. The following writing tips will help.

Prewriting

- **Focus on the purpose** of your writing assignment.
- **Jot down key points** you want to make. If you are describing a process, list the key steps.
- **Consider using a graphic organizer** to help order your ideas.
- **Create a clear statement of purpose.**
- **Ask relevant questions.** Consider your readers and what they need to know. What, if anything, do your readers know about the topic?

Drafting

- **Keep your purpose in mind** as you write.
- **Use an organizing pattern** that fits your purpose and audience.
- **Provide details** that support that purpose. Include all the relevant points you listed during your prewriting.
- **Omit points** listed during your prewriting that are irrelevant or not directly related to your topic.
- **If you need more details** or examples, add them.
- **Use examples** where needed to make your key points clear. Be sure the examples you choose will clarify your information rather than confuse readers.
- **Define any technical terms** in easy-to-understand language. Avoid words or terms your readers might not understand.
- **Use transitional words and phrases** to connect ideas between sections, paragraphs, and sentences within paragraphs.
- **Write a conclusion** that sums up your main points, restates your thesis, and leaves readers with something to think about.

Tip

The main purpose of prewriting is to generate as many ideas as possible. Remember, some of your ideas will be relevant and useful while others will be irrelevant. Use the drafting stage to choose your best ideas and eliminate those that do not work well.

Writing Guidelines
Procedure Document

Most students will have had experience writing about a process. Point out that a procedure document explaining how something works or how something is done is basically a process paper. To organize step-by-step details for a procedure document, students can use a time line or a process diagram. ✔ **DIFFERENTIATE INSTRUCTION**

✔ **DIFFERENTIATE INSTRUCTION**

✱ For more about process organization, see SE pages 209 and 615.

Prewriting

Remind students to use the prewriting stage of the process to get all possible ideas and details on paper or note cards.

Drafting

Tell students to keep their purpose in mind as they draft. Keeping that purpose and their viewpoint in mind will help students eliminate unnecessary details, add more details as needed, and structure their essay in a way that works for their readers.

⭐ **TEKS** 11.15B(i),11.15B(iii), 11.15B(v); **ELPS** 5G

Tip

Suggest that students work with a partner to get feedback on what ideas generated in the prewriting stage are not relevant and need to be eliminated.

TEKS **11.15B(i)** Write procedural documents that include a clearly stated purpose combined with a well-supported viewpoint on the topic; **11.15B(iii)** Write procedural documents that include relevant questions that engage readers and consider their needs; **11.15B(v)** Write procedural documents that include appropriate organizational structures supported by facts and details; **ELPS** **5G** Explain with increasing specificity and detail

Revising

Have students use the questions provided on SE page 482 and the questions below to evaluate their first draft for focus and coherence, organization, development of ideas, and voice.

Focus and Coherence: Is my writing clearly and exclusively focused on my purpose?

Organization: Is the organizational pattern of my essay consistent? Have I presented the procedure in logical order and provided supporting facts and details? Have I used appropriate formatting structures, such as headings or numbered lists, that make my ideas clear?

Development of Ideas: Do my examples make sense? Will they help readers understand the procedure? Do I need to be more specific or include more detail? Have I used accessible language to explain technical terms?

Voice: Does my authentic voice come through?

TEKS 11.15B(ii), 11.15B(iv), 11.15B(v); **ELPS** 5G

Editing

Have students use the suggestions provided on SE page 482 to evaluate their first draft for correct use of grammar, sentence structure, capitalization, punctuation, and spelling.

Tip

Suggest that students read their essay aloud to a partner. Have partners give each other feedback. Partners should look for parts of the essay that don't read smoothly and parts where their attention flags, possibly because sentences sound the same. **DIFFERENTIATE INSTRUCTION ⬊**

ELPS 5F

Revising

When you revise your writing, you review your first draft for focus and coherence, organization, development of ideas, and voice. Ask yourself the following questions:

- Does my procedure document address the topic or prompt?
- Have I clearly stated my purpose?
- Have I focused on my purpose throughout the procedure document?
- Does my organizational pattern work for my topic and audience?
- Have I provided details and examples as needed?
- Have I checked that my examples will clarify my ideas rather than confuse readers?
- Are all my ideas clearly connected to each other and to my thesis statement?
- Have I defined technical terms? Is my language accessible?
- Do transitional words and phrases connect my ideas?
- Have I engaged my readers?
- Is my document formatted correctly?

Revising is also a time to improve the style of your procedure document. Use rhetorical devices, when appropriate, for emphasis and to engage your readers, but be careful not to sacrifice the clarity of your document.

Editing

When you edit for conventions, you check for correct grammar, sentence structure, capitalization, punctuation, and spelling. Remember, even a few errors in your writing may decrease the reader's trust in your information. Also consider the following tips:

- **Have a classmate or a teacher read your procedure document** to check for convention errors. Correct any the errors you discover.
- **Use the Proofreader's Guide** on pages **634–779** as a final editing guide.
- **Prepare a final copy** of your procedure document and check it once more for errors.

Tip

Another method for revising and improving your essay is to read it out loud. Reading your work out loud will help you spot parts of your essay that sound the same, do not read smoothly, or need transitional words or phrases.

TEKS **11.15B(ii)** Write procedural documents that include appropriate formatting structures; **11.15B(iv)** Write procedural documents that include accurate technical information in accessible language; **11.15B(v)** Write procedural documents that include appropriate organizational structures supported by facts and details; **ELPS** **5F** Write using a variety of grade-appropriate sentence lengths, patterns, and connecting words; **5G** Explain with increasing specificity and detail

Writing in Science **483**

Procedure Document

Lena, a junior in high school, has been hired for a summer job supervising new lifeguards at her community swimming pool. One of her jobs is to train the lifeguards how to test the pool water and add needed chemicals. Lena knows from her chemistry class how dangerous chemicals can be if used in the wrong way. She prepared the following written guidelines for new workers.

The beginning introduces the topic and leads to the thesis statement (underlined).

Safety Precautions for Pool Cleaning

Test the pool water regularly to measure the chlorine pH (alkalinity/acid) and calcium (hardness and softness) levels. Follow the testing schedule posted on the locked shed where pool chemicals are kept. Before using any of the chemicals for the first time, be sure to view the safety video. Mixing the wrong chemicals together or using them the wrong way can cause dangerous reactions, including the formation of toxic gas and even explosions. <u>Follow all pool cleaning safety precautions carefully and exactly.</u>

Observe the following safety precautions for handling pool chemicals:

The middle provides clear and relevant details.

- Read and follow all directions on the package.
- Observe any precautions on the package. This includes wearing goggles and gloves when handling certain chemicals.
- Store the chemicals only in proper containers.
- Add the chemicals to water. Do not add water to the chemicals.
- Use separate measuring cups for each chemical.
- Wear goggles and gloves when handling the chlorine.
- Wash your hands thoroughly after handling the chemicals.
- Don't touch your eyes, nose, or mouth when using chemicals.
- Keep the pool chemicals in the locked storage shed when not in use.

The ending summarizes the information and reinforces the thesis.

Being sure the pool water is clean is one of the most important regular maintenance procedures. Following these safety precautions will ensure protection while handling pool chemicals.

Science

Procedure Document

Point out that the student model does not explain how to do something or how something works; instead, it offers guidelines for new workers to follow. Ask students why they think the writer presented some guidelines in the beginning paragraph, and other guidelines in a bulleted list. (Possible response: The guidelines in the first paragraph are general and involve lifeguards' duties. The items in the bulleted list are specifically about handling chemicals safely.) Elicit that using a bulleted list emphasizes the importance of these guidelines and makes them more noticeable.

After reading and discussing the student model, provide additional examples of procedure documents written by former students. Try to include some examples that explain steps in a process. Have partners work together to

- point out what makes each paper successful or unsuccessful, and
- suggest ways that the less successful reports could be improved.

ELPS 4F

ELPS **4F** Use support from peers and teachers to read content area text; **5F** Write using a variety of grade-appropriate sentence lengths, patterns, and connecting words; **5G** Explain with increasing specificity and detail

Multimedia Presentation of Procedure Document

Suggest that before they begin creating their multimedia presentation of a procedure document, students take time to analyze their essays to decide what is most important to include for a specific audience. Remind them of the importance of synthesizing, or combining the various elements of their presentation into a cohesive whole.

TEKS 11.15D; **ELPS** 4K

Using Visual Elements

Point out that the mistake novice creators of a multimedia presentation most often make is to include elements that are interesting but not directly related to the information they want to convey. Caution students to double check that all their visual elements help explain and clarify the procedure.

ELPS 5G

Adding Sound

Remind students that if they decide to supplement the visual portion of their multimedia presentation with sound—video, audio, or music—that they will need to practice combining their visual and audio portions to be sure that they work smoothly together.

Sharing Your Video

If students need help putting their video online, suggest that they ask for assistance from a teacher or a librarian.

Multimedia Presentation of Procedure Document

As you probably already know, people have different learning styles. Some people will most easily learn a procedure by reading about it. Others will learn best by viewing or hearing about the procedure.

Assume that the people who need to learn the procedure have, like most of us, different learning styles. What would be the best way to reach people who learn by viewing or listening, rather than by reading? One way to do this is the create a multimedia presentation of your procedure document that synthesizes information from multiple points of view and presents it in a visual and/or auditory format.

Using Visual Elements

Adding visual elements such as graphics, images, animation, slides, or a video can greatly enhance the effectiveness of your procedure document.

- **Choose effective graphics.** Make sure that the visual elements you choose—tables, charts, graphs, or illustrations—are clear and work well with the content you want to present.
- **Include useful images.** Carefully chosen images can communicate complex ideas or steps quickly and effectively.
- **Show your procedure on a video.**

Adding Sound

- **Supplement your video.** If you choose to present your procedure on a video, include an audio portion (a person talking as he or she demonstrates the procedure, for example) in your video.
- **Use music.** Music is a wonderful way to engage your audience. Be sure that the music you choose is more than just background. It should enhance and add to your presentation.

Sharing Your Video

- **Put your video online.** Putting your video online will allow you to share your information with a large audience.
- **An additional advantage of sharing your video online** is that you will most likely get feedback from viewers as to what parts of your video work or do not work.

Differentiated Instruction: Struggling Learners

Remind students of some of the main characteristics of an expository essay:

- a clear thesis statement
- details, facts, and statistics that support the thesis
- an organized plan with smooth transitions
- a knowledgeable and interested voice
- use of specific terms related to the topic

 TEKS **11.15D** Produce a multimedia presentation with graphics, images, and sound that appeals to a specific audience and synthesizes information from multiple points of view; **ELPS** **4K** Demonstrate English comprehension and expand reading skills by employing analytical skills; **5G** Explain with increasing specificity and detail

Response to an Expository Prompt

On a science test, you may be asked to write a response to an expository prompt. This sort of test question is a great way to evaluate your knowledge and understanding of a scientific concept. You may have limited time to answer the question, so prepare using a writing strategy. Make the best of your time.

Before you write . . .

- **Understand the prompt.** Review the STRAP questions listed on page **208**. Remember that an expository prompt asks you to explain something or to share information.
- **Plan your time wisely.** Start by making notes and planning before you write. Save a few minutes at the end of the timed writing to read over what you have written. Spend the main part of your time writing.
- **Make a graphic organizer.** Jot down main points and details for your essay.

As you write . . .

- **Decide on a focus or thesis for your essay.** Keep this main idea or purpose in mind during your writing.
- **Be selective.** Working from your notes, use examples and explanations that directly support your focus.
- **Connect your ideas.** Use transitional words and phrases to connect your ideas.
- **Use rhetorical devices**—figurative language, rhetorical questions, parallel structure, for example—to achieve, clarity, emphasis, and an engaging voice.
- **End in a meaningful way.** Close your essay by restating your main idea in a new way.

After you've written a first draft . . .

- **Check for completeness.** Use the STRAP questions on page **212** as a guide to revision.
- **Check for correctness.** Correct any errors in grammar, sentence structure, mechanics (capitalization and punctuation), and spelling.

Response to an Expository Prompt

As appropriate, discuss the specifics of state or local tests as they apply to writing a response to an expository prompt. ✔ **DIFFERENTIATE INSTRUCTION**

Before you write . . .

Together, review the STRAP questions on SE page 208 to make sure students understand how to use the questions as they analyze a prompt. Encourage students to use graphic organizers to organize their ideas and information before they write Remind them to use their strongest and most relevant details. ✔ **DIFFERENTIATE INSTRUCTION**
★ **ELPS** 1C

As you write . . .

Remind students to use transitional words and phrases to connect key ideas as they write. Point out that because test questions are designed to assess acquired knowledge, students won't be tested on anything that hasn't been covered in class. Explain that students will be prepared to answer an expository prompt if they always

- pay attention in class and take good notes;
- do all the assigned readings, making sure to take notes; and
- review all their notes and ask questions about material that is unclear.
★ **TEKS** 11.13B; **ELPS** 1C, 1E

After you've written a first draft . . .

Discuss the STRAP questions on SE page 208 to help students apply the questions as they revise their response. Remind students to manage their time so that they can carefully check their drafts for errors in grammar, mechanics, and spelling.

✱ For more detailed instruction about responding to expository prompts, see SE pages 207–213.

Differentiated Instruction: **English Language Learners**		★ **ELPS** 1C, 1E
ELP Level **Beginning**	**ELP Level** **Intermediate**	**ELP Level** **Advanced/Advanced High**
Review the words *subject, type, role, audience,* and *purpose* and have students repeat each one after you. Use the words to discuss a simple writing prompt.	Provide a sample prompt and have partners use the STRAP strategy by completing sentence stems such as *The subject is ___* or *My audience is ___*.	Provide a sample prompt and have students use the language of the STRAP strategy to write an explanation of how they would use the strategy to respond.

TEKS **11.13B** Develop drafts in timed and open-ended situations that include transitions; **ELPS** **1C** Use strategic learning strategies to acquire basic and grade-level vocabulary; **1E** Internalize new basic and academic language by using and reusing it/writing

Response to an Expository Prompt

Before discussing the student model, have students work together to analyze the prompt.

Prompt

Have students use the STRAP questions provided on SE page 208 to express ideas about the prompt with specificity and detail.

- **Subject:** an outbreak of salmonellosis in the neighborhood
- **Type:** expository essay
- **Role:** neighborhood resident
- **Audience:** classmates, citizens of the community
- **Purpose:** explain

⭐ ELPS 3G, 3H

Discuss with students how to use the last sentence of the prompt to organize the response into three paragraphs.

- Paragraph 1: Explain the term *salmonellosis*.
- Paragraph 2: Explain why health officials suspect the delicatessen is the source.
- Paragraph 3: Explain how to avoid future outbreaks of salmonellosis.

Try It!
Answers

Make sure students understand that the before-and-after strategy mentioned in the **Try It!** activity includes using the STRAP questions for analyzing the prompt before they write and for revising the response after they write.

DIFFERENTIATE INSTRUCTION ↘

⭐ ELPS 5G

Response to an Expository Prompt

The writer uses scientific knowledge to answer the following prompt. Notice how he responds to each aspect of the prompt.

Prompt

An outbreak of salmonellosis has occurred in your neighborhood. The victims had all eaten at Rob's Delicatessen, a neighborhood restaurant. Explain what salmonellosis is, why health officials might suspect the delicatessen as the source, and how to avoid future outbreaks.

The first part of the prompt is addressed.

Salmonellosis

Salmonellosis is the most common food-borne infection in the United States. Common symptoms of the disease are nausea, vomiting, fever, headache, abdominal cramps, and diarrhea. The condition is caused by salmonella bacteria, which usually enters the human intestines through food, especially undercooked poultry and raw eggs. Unrefrigerated foods containing cooked meat or eggs can also be a source of salmonellosis.

The second part of the prompt is discussed.

Because the infection is a result of improper food care, health officials are often able to track down the source. The fact that victims had eaten at Rob's Delicatessen makes that a likely source for this outbreak. By observing restaurant practices and testing foods served at the restaurant, health officials may be able to determine exactly what food caused the disease.

The final part of the prompt is answered.

Meats and eggs must be fully cooked and properly refrigerated. Raw meats and eggs should always be kept separate from prepared foods. By following these health rules, the staff of Rob's Delicatessen can help avoid another salmonellosis outbreak.

Try It!

Use the before-and-after strategy described on page **485** the next time you respond to an expository prompt in a science class. (See pages **212–213** for more information about responding to a prompt.)

ELPS 3G Express ideas; **3H** Explain with increasing specificity and detail; **5G** Write to explain with increasing specificity and detail

487

Writing in Social Studies

Social studies involves taking a close look at people and their cultures. In order to get a clear picture of a social studies topic, you will often use information from a variety of sources (texts, charts, graphs, maps, and photos for example). Besides gathering the information, you'll need to analyze, summarize, organize, and present it in a compelling fashion.

In social studies, you may be asked to respond to a topic in a number of different ways, including writing a historical skit, responding to an editorial cartoon, or responding to a series of documents. This chapter contains information about how to accomplish all of these writing tasks. In addition, you'll find helpful tips for taking notes and for organizing data.

- **Writing Guidelines:**
  Historical Skit
- **Writing Guidelines:**
  Report on Social Studies

"The power to question is the basis of all human progress."

—Indira Gandhi

Writing in Social Studies

Objective
- apply the writing process and traits of writing to a historical skit and a report on social studies

The lessons on the following pages provide samples of writing students might do in a social studies class. Assigning these forms of writing will depend on
- the skill level of your students,
- the subject matter they are studying in different social studies classes, and
- the writing goals of your school, district, or state.

Differentiated Instruction: English Language Learners

ELPS 3G, 3H, 5G

ELP Level Beginning	**ELP Level** Intermediate	**ELP Level** Advanced/Advanced High
Model using the words *before* and *after* to describe several actions and have students repeat after you. Then guide students to express simple ideas using *before* and *after*.	Have partners express ideas about how to implement the before-and-after strategy. Then ask them to write the ideas in guidelines, using examples and details.	Have students write a brief paragraph to explain how the before-and-after strategy will help them in their next writing assignment, using examples and details.

ELPS 3G Express ideas; **3H** Explain with increasing specificity and detail; **5G** Write to explain with increasing specificity and detail

Writing Guidelines
Historical Skit

Tell students that because a historical skit is based on historical or current events does not necessarily mean that it has to be serious in tone. Point out that comedy shows that feature parodies or satires of current personalities and events are historical skits in the sense that they dramatize real-life events.

Prewriting Select a Topic

Remind students that one of the most important things to consider as they choose their topic is whether it includes a conflict and its resolution. Point out that a dramatic presentation depends on conflict and resolution.

Gathering Details

Tell students to gather much more information than they think they will actually use. Having an abundance of information will allow them to choose the best details for their historical skit.

`DIFFERENTIATE INSTRUCTION ↘` `DIFFERENTIATE INSTRUCTION ↘`

Thinking About the Theme

Remind students that it does not matter whether their theme is stated explicitly—that is, directly by a character or narrator—or indirectly, as long as the theme is clear to the audience. Remind them to consider literary devices such as flashbacks or personification that can help to convey the theme.

⭐ **TEKS** 11.14C

Tip

Remind students that in order to make their dialogue sound authentic they have to research their major characters and thoroughly understand their personalities and speech patterns.

Writing Guidelines Historical Skit

A historical skit is a short play, focused on real people or events from the past. The skit may give a behind-the-scenes look at a historical event, or it may delve into the characters of the people involved.

Prewriting Select a topic.

If a topic has not already been assigned, choose a person from a historical period that interests you. Consider the following before deciding on a topic.

- **Your protagonist** This is the person or persons who are the subject of your historical skit. Choose an interesting and complex person.
- **Your conflict** Your protagonist must face a problem that he or she will solve in the course of your skit.
- **Your tone** The tone of your skit will reflect your feelings about the protagonist and his or her conflict. Your tone could be serious, angry, hopeful, patient, or satiric.

Gathering Details

Learn all you can about your subject. Keep the following in mind as you research your topic.

- Focus on a conflict your protagonist faced. Ask yourself, *Is this a conflict that will engage my audience?*
- Choose characters and a conflict that you can cover adequately.
- Record the exact words of your protagonist and others involved in the conflict. At times you will have to create dialogue to dramatize the event. When you create dialogue, stick as closely as you can to the historical facts.
- Gather information about the setting where the conflict takes place.

Thinking About the Theme

As you gather details, think about the message or lesson you want your skit to convey. Do you want the audience to explore feelings about a war, or perhaps see the cost of a leader's absolute power? Whatever your theme, you need to decide if you will state it explicitly or make it implicit through actions and dialogue.

- An **explicit theme** is stated by one of the characters or by a narrator.
- An **implicit theme** is not ever stated, but characters' behavior, dialogue, and actions all lead an audience to an understanding of the writer's message.

Tip

In cases where you have to make up dialogue, make sure that your dialogue reflects the speaking style of the character. In other words, make sure it sounds authentic and real.

 TEKS 11.14C Write a script with an explicit or implicit theme, using a variety of literary techniques

Social Studies

Drafting

As you create your first draft, follow these steps:
- Write your beginning by listing your characters and, if necessary, who they are. Give your opening stage directions. Set the scene with information the audience needs to know in a way that will interest them. Introduce your characters and the conflict.
- Write your middle. Use dialogue and action to move the plot forward. Present the climax.
- Write your ending. Resolve the climax and end your skit.

Revising

To improve your writing, check your skit for focus and coherence, organization, development of ideas, and voice. Ask yourself the following questions:
- Have I given my audience enough background information?
- Is the conflict in my skit clear?
- Do I have an explicit or implicit theme? Does my tone help convey the theme?
- Does my skit build to a climax?
- Do I have stage directions where they are needed? Are my stage directions clear?
- Do my characters come to life?
- Does my dialogue sound natural and authentic?
- Is my climax successfully resolved?

Editing

When you check for conventions, you look for correct use of grammar, sentence structure, capitalization, punctuation, and spelling. Ask yourself the following questions.
- Does my skit follow correct script form?
- Have I punctuated and used capitalization correctly?
- Have I checked for spelling errors?

Tip

Try reading your script aloud to yourself or to a classmate to check that it has a beginning, middle, and end; an engaging conflict; dialogue that advances the plot and sounds natural; and clear stage directions.

Drafting

Have students create a first draft of their historical skits. Remind them that their skits should include a list of characters and brief description of each one; an introduction that sets the scene, if necessary; a theme; and dialogue and action that move the plot forward.
TEKS 11.14C

Revising

Have students work with a partner or in small groups discuss and analyze their first drafts. Suggest that students use the questions provided on SE page 489 to guide their discussion.
ELPS 1B, 3E

Editing

Suggest that students work with a partner to check their historical skit for conventions. Have them use the questions provided on SE page 489 as a guide.

Tip

As students read their scripts aloud to themselves or to a classmate, suggest that they listen for parts that are awkward to read or where the dialogue does not sound authentic. Remind them to consider whether formal or informal language is more appropriate for the tone of the skit. **DIFFERENTIATE INSTRUCTION**
ELPS 1G

Differentiated Instruction: **English Language Learners**		**ELPS** 1B, 1G, 3E
ELP Level **Beginning**	**ELP Level** **Intermediate**	**ELP Level** **Advanced/Advanced High**
Work together to evaluate the language in students' skits. Model identifying formal or informal language, and help them to revise as needed.	Have partners identify examples of formal or informal language, and discuss whether each example is appropriate in the context of the skit.	Have students identify examples of formal or informal language in their skits, and explain to a partner why each example is appropriate in the context of the skit.

TEKS 11.14C Write a script with an explicit or implicit theme, using a variety of literary techniques; **ELPS 1B** Monitor written language production and employ self-corrective techniques or other resources; **1G** Demonstrate ability to distinguish between formal and informal English and knowledge of when to use formal and informal English; **3E** Share information in cooperative learning interactions

Sample Historical Skit

Have students work in pairs or in small groups to discuss the first page of the historical skit. Guide them to address the questions that follow.

- Why is Kenny O'Donnell the only character for whom a short description is given? (Possible response: The narrator doesn't need a description. Because the other characters are well-known historical figures, no description in necessary for them.)
- The author needed to find a way to introduce both the narrator and Kenny O'Donnell in the first scene without confusing the audience. How did the author accomplish this goal? (Possible response: The author used a stage direction to leave Kenny O'Donnell's desk in the dark while shining the lights on the narrator. The next stage direction calls for dimmed lights on the narrator and adds light on O'Donnell.)
- Give examples of the author's use of effective stage directions. (Possible response: walking into Kenny O'Donnell's . . . ; looks at the photos, puzzled and confused)
- What does the first scene reveal about the theme of the skit? (Possible response: The theme may be related to the causes of war, or to the role of behind-the-scenes events in seemingly public episodes.)

★ TEKS 11.14C

Sample Historical Skit

This historical skit, created by student writer Estaban Rodriquez, dramatizes the 1962 Cuban missile crisis. The side notes identify key points in the development of the play.

OCTOBER CRISIS

Characters: **NARRATOR**

PRESIDENT JOHN F. KENNEDY

PREMIER NIKITA KHRUSHCHEV

KENNY O'DONNELL, top aide and close friend to John F. Kennedy

SCENE 1

(The curtain rises to reveal the narrator. Behind and to the side in the dark is a desk and furniture set up to show an office. O'Donnell is seated behind the desk.)

NARRATOR: It is the fall of 1962. President John F. Kennedy has just been shown reconnaissance photos revealing that the Soviets are placing nuclear weapons in Cuba. These weapons, if operational, could conceivably wipe out the eastern and southern United States. The president shares his concerns with his advisor, Kenny O'Donnell.

(Dim lights on narrator; light desk and Kenny O'Donnell.)

PRESIDENT KENNEDY: *(walking into Kenny O'Donnell's office)*: So, do you still think that all of this fuss about Cuba is unimportant?

O'DONNELL: Absolutely! I'm telling you the voters don't care a whit about Cuba.

KENNEDY: *(laying the photos on Kenny's desk)*: I want to show you something.

O'DONNELL: *(looks at the photos, puzzled and confused)*

KENNEDY: What you're looking at here, Ken, is the beginning of a launching site for a medium-range ballistic missile.

O'DONNELL: I don't believe it.

KENNEDY: Well, you better believe it. And I don't want to be the Commander-in-Chief who looked the

Stage Directions
The opening scene is described.

Background information is given.

Beginning
Characters are introduced and the problem is presented.

★ TEKS 11.14C

Writing in Social Studies **491**

Social Studies

Theme
The discussion of voters' concerns and Kennedy's response suggests the implicit theme.

Middle
Complications are introduced as rising action.

Theme
Kennedy's deliberations and public announcement provide clues to the implicit theme.

other way while the Soviets put missiles 90 miles away from the United States. One more thing, Ken, not a word of this to anyone. We want it to look as though nothing unusual is going on around here. (*Lights go down.*)

SCENE 2

(*The curtain rises with lights on the narrator. Behind the narrator in darkness is a desk. Seated at the desk is Nikita Khrushchev.*)

NARRATOR: Kennedy assembled a team of his most trusted advisors to create a plan for dealing with the missile build-up in Cuba. His advisors were divided. Some recommended bombing or invading Cuba. Others urged a more restrained response: a quarantine of Cuba so that military supplies could not be brought in. With each passing day, tension in the White House grew. Finally, Kennedy decided on the quarantine rather than risk an all-out nuclear war. On October 22, 1962 Kennedy announced the crisis and his decision on national television. Earlier that day, Kennedy sent Nikita Khrushchev a copy of his speech. (*Dim lights on narrator.*)

(*Kennedy replaces narrator in center stage. Lights on Kennedy, as he addresses the nation.*)

KENNEDY: This Government, as promised, has maintained the closest surveillance of the Soviet military buildup on the island of Cuba. Within the past week, unmistakable evidence has established the fact that a series of offensive missile sites is now in preparation on that imprisoned island. The purposes of these bases can be none other than to provide a nuclear strike capability against the Western Hemisphere. . . . This urgent transformation of Cuba into an important strategic base—by the presence of these large, long-range, and clearly offensive weapons of sudden mass destruction—constitutes an explicit threat to the peace and security of all the Americas. (*Lights dim on Kennedy.*)

Discuss SE page 491 of the skit with students. Use the following questions.

- Why does Kennedy tell O'Donnell not to mention the build up of Soviet weapons to anyone? (Possible response: Kennedy does not want to panic the public until he has made a decision.)

- What implicit theme does the line—*And I don't want to be . . . 90 miles away from the United States*—on SE pages 490–491 suggest? (Possible response: Leaders should be perceived as strong and decisive in all situations. Kennedy's concern is that he appear to be strong in relation to the Soviets.)

- Summarize the complications that are introduced in Scene 2. (Possible response: Advisors were divided about how to respond to the missile build-up; Kennedy had to convey his decision to both Khrushchev and the American public)

- Pick out phrases in Kennedy's speech that give clues concerning the implicit theme of the skit. (Possible response: *unmistakable evidence, clearly offensive weapons, explicit threat*)

✓ **DIFFERENTIATE INSTRUCTION**

★ TEKS 11.14C; ELPS 4G

Differentiated Instruction:
English Language Learners   ★ ELPS 3D, 4F

ELP Level **Beginning**	ELP Level **Intermediate**	ELP Level **Advanced/Advanced High**
Use maps to show Cuba's proximity to the U.S. Preteach vocabulary such as *crisis, wipe out, launching site,* and *missile.* Have students repeat each term after you.	Have partners use maps to discuss why missiles in Cuba were a concern. Ask them to use vocabulary such as *advisor, reconnaissance,* and *operational* to discuss the situation.	Have partners identify unfamiliar vocabulary in the skit, and use it as they discuss and develop background knowledge about the Cuban Missile Crisis.

★ TEKS **11.14C** Write a script with an explicit or implicit theme, using a variety of literary techniques; ELPS **3D** Speak using grade-level content area vocabulary in context/new English words and academic language; **4F** Use visual and contextual support and support from peers and teachers to develop background knowledge; **4G** Demonstrate comprehension of increasingly complex English/retelling or summarizing/responding to questions

Have students work with a partner or in small groups to respond to the following questions about SE page 492.

- What implied threat does Khrushchev include in his response to Kennedy? (Possible response: "a catastrophic consequence for world peace" as a result of Kennedy's actions, *i.e.*, the threat of nuclear war)
- How is the conflict between the United States and the Soviet Union resolved? (Khrushchev backs down and dismantles missile installations in Cuba.) **DIFFERENTIATE INSTRUCTION ↘**

 Respond to the reading

Have students work with a partner to share ideas as they respond to the questions.
Answers
Focus and Coherence (1) The conflict revolves around what to do about the missile installations in Cuba.
Organization (2) chronological order
Development of Ideas (3) Possible response: The theme is implicit: as Commander in Chief, Kennedy had to do what was best strategically for the country and to convince the American public that he had made the best decision.
Voice (4) The writer sets the scene with lighting, and uses Khrushchev's words. The resolution is not clear until the final sentence.
TEKS 11.14C; **ELPS** 3G, 4G

 TEKS 11.14C

Climax
Kennedy's internal problem (what decision to make) is solved.

(Lights on Narrator.)

NARRATOR: Kennedy had announced that Cuba would be quarantined, warned that any missile launched from Cuba would be regarded as a Soviet attack on the United States, and demanded that the Soviets remove all of their offensive weapons from Cuba immediately. Khrushchev read the speech and was enfuriated. He replied to Kennedy that night. *(Dim lights on narrator.)*

(Light Khrushchev seated behind a desk, reading aloud his response to Kennedy.)

Falling Action
Results of the action are given.

Khrushchev: I must say frankly that the measures indicated in your statement indicate a serious threat to peace and to the security of nations . . . We reaffirm that the armaments which are in Cuba . . . are intended solely for defensive purposes . . . . I hope the United States government will display wisdom and renounce the actions pursued by you, which may lead to a catastrophic consequence for world peace. *(Dim lights on Khrushchev.)*

(Light narrator.)

Resolution
War has been avoided, and the stand-off is ended.

NARRATOR: For the next five days, the world waited as the United States and the Soviet Union hovered on the brink of war. Finally, On October 27, 1962, Khrushchev agreed to dismantle the installations in Cuba and return the missiles to the Soviet union in exchange for Kennedy's promise that the U.S. would not invade Cuba.

 Respond to the reading. Answer the following questions about the play.

Focus and Coherence (1) What is the conflict of the skit?

Organization (2) What organizational pattern does the writer use?

Development of Ideas (3) What is the theme, or message, of the skit? Is it explicit or implicit?

Voice (4) How does the writer engage the reader?

Differentiated Instruction: Advanced Learners

Invite students to extend the skit by adding a scene or scenes for the events described by the narrator at the beginning of Scene 2. Remind students to research the events and people involved in the discussion. They may also wish to add a scene showing citizens reacting to news about the crisis.

 TEKS **11.14C** Write a script with an explicit or implicit theme, using a variety of literary techniques; **ELPS** **3G** Express ideas; **4G** Demonstrate comprehension of increasingly complex English/responding to questions

Social Studies

Multimedia Presentation of a Historical Skit

In a sense, your historical skit already employs elements of a multimedia presentation. It is visual (actors dramatize events) and auditory (actors speak lines). You can, however, use your research and your imagination to totally recast your historical skit in different media. Depending on the type of information and conflict you present in your historical skit, consider the following. (See also pp. 464–467.)

Using Visual Elements

- Graphics, charts, or tables
- Photographs
- Slides
- Copies of artifacts (original documents, people's handwritten notes, etc.)
- A power presentation
- An interactive Web page
- A video of your historical skit
- Your own Web page, highlighting your topic

Adding Sound

- If, as part of your presentation, you are showing photographs, consider adding a taped audio portion to it.
- Use music if it works with your topic. Music is a wonderful way to engage your audience. Be sure, however, that the music you choose is more than just background. It should enhance and add to your presentation.
- If there are recordings of a person you are researching available, consider using them.

Sharing Your Multimedia Presentation

- Put your video online. This will allow you to share your presentation with a larger audience.
- Give a power presentation for your class.
- Present your Web page, highlighting your topic.

Tip

Don't add multimedia elements for the sake of adding multimedia elements. Be sure you have a clear idea of what you want to present and that all your multimedia elements help clarify that idea.

Multimedia Presentation of a Historical Skit

Tell students that using too many elements in their presentation may blur their major point. Remind them to consider the needs of their audience to help them decide which elements to include.

Using Visual Elements

Tell students that all of their visual elements should directly relate to their topic. If students plan to create a power presentation, an interactive Web page, a video, or a personal Web page, suggest that they get help from a teacher, librarian, or computer specialist with technical aspects of their presentation.

Adding Sound

Tell students who plan to add audio as a separate part of their presentation to practice combining visuals and audio to be sure that both parts work smoothly together.

Sharing Your Multimedia Presentation

Suggest that students deliver their multimedia presentation to a partner or a small group for practice and feedback. Suggest they ask each other *What parts work best? What parts to not work as well? Have I included information from multiple points of view?* ✔ DIFFERENTIATE INSTRUCTION
★ TEKS 11.15D; ELPS 3C, 3D

Tip

When students share their multimedia presentations have them ask each other *Have I included too many elements? Do all parts of my presentation support my topic?*

Differentiated Instruction: English Language Learners   ELPS 3A, 3C, 3D

ELP Level **Beginning**	ELP Level **Intermediate**	ELP Level **Advanced/Advanced High**
Work with students to practice producing sounds in any newly acquired vocabulary prior to sharing their multimedia presentations.	Have partners practice the sounds of newly acquired vocabulary to gain confidence. Tell them to use the new words in context sentences of varying lengths.	Have partners check one another's pronunciation of newly acquired vocabulary. Prompt them to use the new words in a variety of contexts.

 TEKS **11.15D** Produce a multimedia presentation with graphics, images, and sound that appeals to a specific audience and synthesizes information from multiple points of view; **ELPS 3A** Practice producing sounds of newly acquired vocabulary to pronounce English words; **3C** Speak using a variety of grammatical structures, sentence lengths, sentence types, and connecting words; **3D** Speak using grade-level content area vocabulary in context/new English words and academic language

Writing Guidelines Report on Social Studies

Explain that as students develop a plan for engaging in in-depth research and formulate a research question, it is useful to brainstorm and consult with others as they gather information. Give partners time to skim SE pages 495–498 to see the examples of the different kinds of documents they may be asked to write about and the kinds of questions they may be asked to answer about these documents.

Interpreting

Tell students to ask themselves questions such as *Why is this important? How do these ideas relate?*

DIFFERENTIATE INSTRUCTION ↘

Analyzing

Remind students to consult with a teacher or librarian if they need guidance to decide on the reliability and validity of a source.

Evaluating

Tell students to be sure to consider the facts on which divergent views are based when they evaluate documents.

Synthesizing

Explain that synthesizing gives "added value" to research information by combining ideas in an original way.

Tip

Have students work in pairs to discuss the tasks involved in creating a document-based essay: interpreting, analyzing, evaluating, and synthesizing.

TEKS 11.20A, 11.20B; **ELPS** 4F

494

 **TEKS** 11.20A, 11.20B

Writing Guidelines Report on Social Studies

When you research for a report on social studies, you often need to read a series of documents as part of in-depth research on a complex, multi-faceted topic. Text-based documents may include excerpts from books, newspapers, Web pages, diaries, letters, eyewitness accounts, speeches, or other text sources. Visual documents may include maps, charts, works or art, tables, graphs, time lines, editorial cartoons, or photographs.

When you write a report based on the documents, you may also translate information from the documents into a new form, such as placing data into a graph or a table. To complete such an assignment, you need to carefully analyze the documents and develop a major research question that reflects your analysis.

Interpreting

One of your tasks in a report on social studies is to interpret the meaning and significance of primary and secondary sources. To interpret documents you will first have to read them carefully and then assess their meaning in relation to your purpose.

Analyzing

In addition to understanding the documents and relating them to the research question you are answering, writing a report on social studies requires you to assess the validity and reliability of your sources and compare the information you get from each source. In other words, you will need to read the documents in relation to the question you are answering and in relation to each other.

Evaluating

Sometimes the documents you are working with will provide divergent or even contradictory information. In such cases, you will need to evaluate the sources, account for the divergent views, and decide which sources you find most reliable.

Synthesizing

Perhaps the most difficult and important task of writing a report on social studies is to synthesize the information and use it to support your answer to the research question. Synthesizing involves using your sources and combining them to create an original answer to the question you are addressing.

Tip

There is no single correct response to a report on social studies. Instead, there are various possible approaches to the topic, depending on your ability to interpret the documents and judge their significance.

Differentiated Instruction: Struggling Learners

Encourage students to take reading notes on each document that they are asked to analyze. They should list the main ideas and the purpose of each document. For more practice taking reading notes, refer students to SE page 471.

 TEKS **11.20A** Brainstorm, consult with others, decide upon a topic, and formulate a major research question to address the major research topic; **11.20B** Formulate a plan for engaging in in-depth research on a complex, multi-faceted topic; **ELPS** **4F** Use support from peers and teachers to read content area text and to develop background knowledge

Sample Documents

Introduction: The increasing cost of health care has made staying healthy more and more difficult for many people in the United States. In the past decade, health-care costs have risen dramatically, putting both insurance and treatment out of reach for many people.

Social Studies

Document One

The High Cost of Health Care

Ask many people in this country today what worries them most, and sooner or later you'll get to the subject of health care. While today's advanced health-care technologies and procedures offer an unprecedented ability to keep people healthy, the cost of these technologies and procedures is skyrocketing. Because employers are increasingly unwilling to shoulder the burden of health insurance coverage, many people who might benefit from modern health care are unable to afford it.

In the not too distant past, most employers offered their workers health insurance packages that allowed people and their families to maintain their health. However, in an effort to cut costs and increase profits, many businesses have asked their employees to pick up a greater portion of the health insurance tab—or have cut health-care benefits altogether. Workers have few options—pay high premiums on their own, apply for limited benefits issued by the government, or simply live insurance free and hope to stay healthy.

Source: Hill, Ennis. *A System in Crisis*. Health Solutions Press, 2003.

Task: Summarize the relationship between businesses and the health-care crisis.

Many businesses used to pay for health insurance for their employees. Insurance, however, is expensive, and many businesses are cutting or eliminating health benefits. Without insurance from their employers, it is difficult for workers to get the health care they need.

> Only the most important information is included in the summary.

Sample Documents

Explain that all the documents on the following pages include information from experts in the field and were written for well-informed audiences. Point out that there are sample tasks and sample student responses for each one. Consider having students create their own responses for each task before they read the sample response. ✔ DIFFERENTIATE INSTRUCTION

TEKS 11.21A

Document One

Before students read the sample summary at the bottom of the page, have them

- point out the most important ideas in Document One, "The High Cost of Health Care";
- work together to complete the **Task** at the bottom of the page; and then
- compare their summary to the sample response.

ELPS 2I, 3J, 4G

Differentiated Instruction: English Language Learners

ELPS 2I, 3J

ELP Level **Beginning**	ELP Level **Intermediate**	ELP Level **Advanced/Advanced High**
Use visuals and gestures to discuss *skyrocketing* and *shoulder the burden*. Ask yes-no questions to help students respond and show understanding of each concept.	Have students respond orally to questions about the terms *skyrocketing* and *shoulder the burden* to show understanding of each concept.	Have partners ask and answer questions about the terms *skyrocketing* and *shoulder the burden* to show understanding of each concept.

 TEKS 11.21A Follow the research plan to gather evidence from experts on the topic and texts written for informed audiences in the field; **ELPS 2I** Demonstrate listening comprehension/collaborating with peers; **3J** Respond orally to information presented/concept attainment; **4G** Demonstrate comprehension of increasingly complex English/retelling or summarizing

Document Two

Ask students to explain how using a simple chart such as the one at the bottom of the page can help them better understand different views on a topic. Students may suggest that a chart can help them

- recognize the nuances in the different views,
- see at a glance who holds different or opposing views, and
- make inferences and draw conclusions about the reasons and motivations of the individuals or groups that hold opposing views.

Select a topic related to a current domestic or international crisis, and ask students to gather quotations from ordinary citizens, politicians, and public interest groups that express varied views on the topic. Have students work together to make a chart that analyzes the perspectives of these three different groups on the topic.

DIFFERENTIATE INSTRUCTION ↘

⚑ **ELPS** 4K

496

Document Two

Varied Views on the Health-Care Crisis

"We offer an incredibly broad range of medical treatment to those we insure. We are proud that we constantly search for ways to expand coverage while keeping premium costs low."

Estelle Sinclair, Health Insurance Collaborative

"My patients and their needs are very important to me. That being said, my costs are rapidly escalating. Last year I paid over $90,000 in malpractice insurance premiums."

Dr. Joanna Yin, orthopedic surgeon

"I pay $1,900 every month for health insurance for me and my family. I bring home about $500 a week from my full-time job. You do the math."

Bob Miller, security guard

"Sure, we'd like to give our employees better health insurance. But look at the cost of premiums. If I offer everyone health insurance, I may lose my business."

Aurelia Sanchez, bookstore owner

"Technology is the key. We should be using computers, for example, to manage and distribute medical records effectively. That would dramatically cut health-care costs."

Jen McCoy, health insurance claims adjuster

"As doctors our first priority must always be effective treatment for our patients. Never will I turn away a patient simply because he or she has no health insurance."

Dr. Madeline Rivera, general practitioner

Source: Comments from the Regional Health Care Symposium, July 2011

Task: Make a chart showing the perspectives of consumers, doctors, and insurance companies on the health-care crisis.

> A word or two is all that is needed to list answers in a chart.

Consumers	Doctors	Insurance Companies
– forced to choose between health care and other expenses	– pinched by their own insurance costs – dedicated to patient care	– working to cut costs – proud of helping people stay healthy

Differentiated Instruction: Struggling Learners

The disjointed nature of this document may be a challenge. Ask these questions to monitor comprehension:

- How can you tell where each opinion begins and ends? (quotation marks; speaker's name and title)
- How do the quotations relate to each other? (They all address the same issue, the health care crisis.)

ELPS **4K** Demonstrate English comprehension and expand reading skills by employing analytical skills;

Social Studies

Document Three

People Without Health Insurance, United States, 2000-2004

Task: Express the total increase in uninsured people from 2004 to 2008 as a simple number and as a percentage increase.

> The total number of people in the United States who did not have health insurance increased by 1 million from 2004–2008. Reflected as a percentage, the growth of uninsured Americans was 1.38 percent.

Graph information is changed to text form.

Document Four

Task: State how the cartoonist feels about the health-care industry.

> The cartoonist is saying that the health-care industry cares more about money than making people healthy.

An inference is used to interpret the cartoon.

Document Three

Display several examples of labeled graphs from newspapers, news magazines, and other published sources, and have students practice expressing the information in the graph in text form. Students can use the sample response to the task for Document Three as a model.

☑ **DIFFERENTIATE INSTRUCTION**

Document Four

When discussing the sample response for Document Four, remind students that an inference is a logical guess or conclusion based on details provided in the text or, in this case, the cartoon, and their own knowledge about the topic. Have students point out the details in the cartoon that the student writer could have used to infer that the cartoonist has a low opinion of the health-care industry. (The doctor representing the health care industry is shaking money out of the patient by turning him upside down.)

⭐ **ELPS** 4J

Differentiated Instruction: English Language Learners

⭐ **ELPS** 4F

ELP Level **Beginning**	ELP Level **Intermediate**	ELP Level **Advanced/Advanced High**
Point out the base word and affixes in *insurance* and *uninsured*, and then use visuals and gestures to explain the terms. Have students repeat each term after you.	Have partners define and discuss *insurance* and *uninsured*. As needed, point out the base word and affixes in the terms and guide students to develop background knowledge.	Have partners ask and answer questions about the terms *insurance* and *uninsured* to develop vocabulary and background knowledge.

ELPS 4F Use support from peers and teachers to develop vocabulary and background knowledge; **4J** Demonstrate English comprehension and expand reading skills by employing inferential skills

Document Five

In the sample response for Document Five, the writer uses statistics from the map to make generalizations. Explain that a generalization is a statement or a conclusion based on a large number of examples. For a generalization to be valid, it must be based on complete, accurate, and current information. Tell students they can assume that the documents their teachers provide contain reliable information. However, for other types of expository writing assignments—for example, research reports—students must analyze documents to be sure that the statistics they use to form generalizations are reliable and current.

⚡ ELPS 4K

✱ For more on evaluating the reliability of source information, see SE page 377.

Document Six

Guide students to make other inferences about the information in Document Six, such as what crisis the writer is referring to in the second sentence.

⚡ ELPS 4J

498

Document Five

Average Percentage without Health Insurance, 2007-2008

Average Percentage without Health Insurance, 2007-2008.

- 8–11.9%
- 12–15.9%
- 16–19.9%
- 20–25%
- 25 OR MORE

Task: Identify state or regional trends in health insurance coverage.

Statistics are used to make some generalizations.

> Overall, states in the Northeast and Midwest do the best job providing health insurance. In the South and the West, rates of uninsured tend to be higher.

Document Six

The quest to reform the health insurance industry could take years—maybe even decades. Meanwhile, there is plenty we can do to address the crisis. As a nation, by quitting smoking, losing weight, exercising more, and eating balanced diets, Americans can become dramatically healthier and thus reduce health-care costs.

Task: How does the writer propose to reduce health-care costs?

By encouraging Americans to improve their fitness levels.

Social Studies

Prewriting

Reviewing the Assignment

Begin by reviewing the purpose of your assignment and your major research question. Focus first on verbs in the question or assignment, such as *evaluate, establish the validity,* or *assess, compare, explain,* or *define* in order to assess what type of thinking and writing required.

Also, look carefully at any conjunctions in the question, such as *and* and *or.* Be sure, for example, that you understand whether you are being asked to compare *and* contrast or to compare *or* contrast.

Looking at the Evidence

Read all the documents and any introductory material thoroughly. As you read, draw on what you already know about the topic and consider what each document contributes to the topic. Notice documents that present opposing views. As you read, look specifically for things that you might be able to use in your essay.

Be very attentive to details when analyzing a visual document such as a political cartoon. Use what you already know about humor and satire to help you interpret the document and be alert to possible bias in documents.

Organizing Your Facts

Use an outline or other graphic organizer to plan your essay. Write out a preliminary thesis statement. Pull together information from all the documents and from your own prior knowledge. Use an organizational pattern that suits your topic and your audience.

Synthesizing Evidence

Reread your preliminary thesis statement. Revise your thesis statement if indicated by your research or by new ideas. Look at your outline and decide how and in what order you will use your documents. Check that you are using documents in a way that supports your thesis statement. Make sure that you have accounted for divergent or ambiguous viewpoints.

Tip

Notice the author and dates for all of your documents. This will provide you with valuable clues for interpreting documents.

Prewriting

Remind students to read the question or assignment carefully.

Reviewing the Assignment

Suggest that students underline key words such as *evaluate, assess, compare* and *contrast* to be sure they understand exactly what the question is asking them to do.

Looking at the Evidence

Tell students to read each of the documents carefully to differentiate between theories and evidence and to decide if the evidence is strong or weak. Remind them to consider how the evidence will help them create a cogent argument.

⭐ **TEKS** 11.22B

Organizing Your Facts

Encourage students to use an outline or a graphic organizer, such as a Venn diagram, a T-chart, or a web organizer, to plan their essays. Remind students to account for all of their documents as they plan.

⭐ **TEKS** 11.21B; **ELPS** 1C

Synthesizing Evidence

Remind students that summarizing information is not the same as synthesizing it. Tell students that to synthesize is to combine to form a new, more complex product. Have them analyze their thesis statement to be sure it synthesizes information and encourage students to modify their research questions if necessary.

✔ DIFFERENTIATE INSTRUCTION

⭐ **TEKS** 11.22A; **ELPS** 4K

Tip

Remind students to indicate in their notes what kind of document they are referring to—an article, graph, political cartoon, map, etc.

 TEKS **11.21B** Systematically organize relevant and accurate information to support central ideas and concepts; **11.22A** Modify the major research question as necessary to refocus the research plan; **11.22B** Differentiate between theories and the evidence that supports them and determine whether the evidence found is weak or strong and how that evidence helps create a cogent argument; **ELPS** **1C** Use strategic learning strategies to acquire basic and grade-level vocabulary; **4K** Demonstrate English comprehension and expand reading skills by employing analytical skills

Drafting

Remind students that as they get their ideas in writing for their first draft, they may make new connections and that making such unexpected connections can be an exciting part of the writing process. Emphasize to students the importance paying attention to these new connections as these connections will help them develop and support personal opinions, making their analysis of the documents original.

★ TEKS 11.23A

Presenting Your Original Analysis

Remind students that a document-based essay should follow the same guidelines as any expository or informative essay.

- **Beginning Your Essay** Review that the introductory paragraphs should present the topic in an engaging way.
- **Writing Your Middle** Explain that the middle paragraphs should develop and support the thesis statement.
- **Concluding Your Essay** Point out that the concluding paragraphs should sum up major points and leave readers with something to think about.

Using Rhetorical Devices

Suggest that students work with a partner to find parts of their essay where the use of a rhetorical device, such as those suggested on this page, could improve their writing. Suggest that partners also check that sentence patterns in the essay are varied.

★ TEKS 11.23B; **ELPS** 1H, 5F

Drafting

Your task in your first draft is to get down in writing and in an order that makes sense all of your main points. Follow your thesis statement and outline closely. Mistakes in grammar or spelling can be fixed later.

Presenting Your Original Analysis

As you write your first draft you have several tasks that you will need to do simultaneously: address the research question, use documents to support your thesis, and provide an original analysis and interpretation of those documents.

Beginning Your Essay

- Find a way to get your readers' attention.
- Introduce your topic, giving background information as needed.
- Lead in to your thesis statement.

Writing Your Middle

- Follow your outline, but be open to new ideas as you write.
- Refer frequently to your thesis statement to be sure that you are staying on topic.
- Use your documents to support your major points. Develop each main point in a separate paragraph.
- When you use a document, provide enough information for readers to know which document you are referring to.

Concluding Your Essay

- Sum up your major points.
- Restate your thesis statement.
- Leave your readers with something to think about.

Using Rhetorical Devices

Look for places where adding a rhetorical devise might enliven your writing, help readers better understand a major point, or emphasize an important idea. Depending on the content of your essay, consider using these devices below.

- Figurative language, such as metaphor or simile *(The road to effective healthcare reform is full of landmines.)*
- A rhetorical question *(What would you do in this man's position?)*
- Parallel structure *(Wanting only to secure re-election, Senator Giswald voted for the most expensive, least effective, but most popular plan.)*
- Repetition for effect and emphasis *("It was the best of times, it was the worst of times, it was the age of wisdom, it was the age of foolishness . . ."* Charles Dickens, *A Tale of Two Cities)* Note, this is also an example of parallel structure.

TEKS **11.23A** Provides an analysis that supports and develops personal opinions, as opposed to simply restating existing information; **11.23B** Uses a variety of formats and rhetorical strategies to argue for the thesis; **ELPS 1H** Develop and expand repertoire of learning strategies; **5F** Write using a variety of grade-appropriate sentence patterns

Social Studies

Revising for Organization

When you revise for *organization*, you check to be sure you have used an effective organizational pattern throughout your essay. Ask yourself the following questions.

- Do I have a clear organizational pattern that suits my purpose and my audience?
- Have I maintained this organizational pattern throughout my essay?
- Have I layered and fleshed out my ideas so that each sentence adds meaning to the sentence that precedes it?
- Is my support from documents placed where it is most effective?
- Have I actually written an original essay, or have I simply summarized the content of my documents?
- Does my essay have a smooth and logical flow?
- Have I included transitional words and phrases to help the reader easily move from one idea to the next?

Using a Style Manual

Choose a style manual that conforms to the style your instructor wants you to use in your paper. A style manual can answer many questions that may come up as you are revising and checking your writing. Here are some topics a style manual can help you with.

- Multiple spellings of words
- Apostrophes with plurals and words ending in –*s*
- Correct use of colons, semicolons, commas, dashes, and hyphens
- Punctuation of quoted material
- Parentheses and square brackets
- Foreign language terms and names
- Ellipses
- Using words or numerals
- Abbreviations, reference words, and proofreading symbols
- Evaluating sources and determining what needs to be documented
- Paraphrasing sources
- Documentation of sources within text
- Alphabetizing a Works Cited list
- Examples of correct formatting of any type of material you may need to list

Tip

You may feel that you don't have time to plow through a style manual. Neglecting to do so is a serious mistake. Attention to the type of details explained in a style manual can make the difference between an average and outstanding paper.

Revising for Organization

In addition to the questions related to organization on SE page 501, have students use the questions below to evaluate their first draft for focus and coherence, development of ideas, and voice.

Focus and Coherence: Have I included an effective introduction and conclusion? Have I maintained my focus throughout my writing?

Development of Ideas: Is my essay of sufficient length and complexity to address the topic? Do the support and details in my essay help the reader to appreciate my major points? Have I used new content-based vocabulary correctly and effectively?

Voice: Have I engaged my readers throughout the essay? Is my voice authentic and original?

 TEKS 11.23E; **ELPS** 1B, 5B, 5G

Using a Style Manual

Have students go through the list on SE page 501 with a partner to be sure they have addressed all applicable style issues in their essays.

DIFFERENTIATE INSTRUCTION

TEKS 11.23D; **ELPS** 1B

Tip

Students may resist the idea of doing a final style check before passing in their essay because they feel they have already done more than enough work. Use whatever analogies will work best with your students (the final miles of a marathon run, for example) to persuade them to do a thorough final check.

 TEKS 11.23D Uses a style manual to document sources and format written materials; **11.23E** Synthesize the research into an extended written or oral presentation that is of sufficient length and complexity to address the topic; **ELPS 1B** Monitor written language production and employ self-corrective techniques or other resources; **5B** Write using newly acquired basic vocabulary and content-based grade-level vocabulary; **5G** Explain with increasing specificity and detail

Report on Social Studies

Before students complete their final drafts, encourage them to analyze the model essay to see how the writer synthesized information from the six documents on SE pages 495–498 to respond to the prompt and correctly acknowledge all sources. As needed, have students use a style guide to verify that in-text citations are used correctly. Ask them to read silently the anecdote in the first paragraph and elicit that it adds variety and interest to the opening.

TEKS 11.23B, 11.23D; **ELPS** 4H

Ask students to explain the thesis, using the details in the beginning paragraph. Remind them that their thesis should reflect personal opinions on the topic rather than a restatement of facts. (Possible response: Because of rising health-care costs, many people in this country cannot afford to pay for health care at all, or they are suffering great financial burdens to pay for the health care they have; yet the solution to this health-care crisis is not easy to agree upon—or to find.)

TEKS 11.23A

Have students work in pairs or in small groups to locate facts and statistics the author uses to support the thesis statement. (Possible responses: Facts and statistics: increase in number of uninsured from 2004–2008; increase for physicians in malpractice insurance; Theory: Many Americans can not afford heath care; Evidence: employers can't afford health care; examples; statistics) Elicit that the facts and statistics represent information from multiple perspectives and show that the writer has anticipated counterarguments and provided evidence to refute them.

TEKS 11.23C, 11.23E; **ELPS** 4F

 **TEKS** 11.23A, 11.23B, 11.23C, 11.23D, 11.23E

Report on Social Studies

In this sample, a student writes an essay that draws on information presented in the six original documents.

> **Task: Extended Essay**
>
> *Using all six documents and your own knowledge about this topic, write an essay about the health-care crisis in the United States.*

Documents 1, 2, 3, 5, and 6
The opening defines the health-care problem and outlines the thesis.

Facts, statistics, and demographic data from the Documents 3 and 5 support the author's ideas.

Quoted material from Document 2 supports the author's ideas.

The High Cost of Health Care

More and more United States citizens are asking themselves if they can afford to get sick. Faced with rising health-care costs and deprived of the solid insurance packages once offered by employers, many cannot afford health care. Even those who can are struggling under expensive premiums and prescription drugs. Bob Miller, who told his story at the recent Regional Health Care Symposium, is a typical example of those burdened by a health-care system in crisis. He earns $500 a week as a security guard, and his health insurance costs $1900 per month. Miller's plight is common, and a solution to the health-care crisis remains elusive.

Today, more and more U.S. citizens are unable to afford health care. From 2004 to 2008, federal, state, and local governments all worked to address the health-care crisis. Meanwhile, the number of uninsured people rose from 45.3 million to 46.3 million—an increase of 1 million people. The hardest hit areas include the South and West; people in the Northeast and Midwest are more likely to be insured. Even in Minnesota, where the percentage of insured is high, over 8% of people are still not insured.

Health-care consumers aren't the only ones feeling pressured by health-care costs. Physicians have seen dramatic rises in malpractice insurance. Some, like Dr. Joanna Yin, pay over $90,000 in malpractice insurance. To make matters worse, many of these doctors have been forced for economic reasons to pass these increases on to their patients.

TEKS **11.23A** Provides an analysis that supports and develops personal opinions, as opposed to simply restating existing information; **11.23B** Uses a variety of formats and rhetorical strategies to argue for the thesis; **11.23C** Develops an argument that incorporates the complexities of and discrepancies in information from multiple sources and perspectives while anticipating and refuting counter-arguments; **11.23D** Uses a style manual to document sources and format written materials; **11.23E** Synthesize the research into an extended written or oral presentation that is of sufficient length and complexity to address the topic; **ELPS** **4F** Use visual and contextual support to read content area text and to enhance and confirm understanding; **4H** Read silently with increasing ease

Document 2
The problem is viewed from all angles.

The author addresses a divergent view and bias in **Document 4**.

The author uses prior knowledge and information from **Document 6** to advance his or her argument.

Employers like Aurelia Sanchez are feeling the pinch as well. While some employers cut their contribution to employee health insurance to increase their profits, many employers, like Sanchez, still want to provide their workers with good coverage. However, as premium costs rise, business owners are often forced to cut their health-care expenses or risk losing their businesses. Even insurance companies, often portrayed negatively, are struggling. Many are proud to offer quality care but have trouble getting that care to the people who need it.

As the health-care crisis worsens, consumers, legislators, health-care practitioners, and health-care insurance representatives search for solutions. As tempting as it is, on the one hand, to demonize heath insurance companies as the cartoonist does in Document 4 or, on the other hand, to accuse people too poor to afford health insurance of causing their own problems, oversimplifying the problem will not solve it. Potential solutions range from dramatic reforms aimed at scrapping the existing health care system to smaller, incremental changes.

Among the former, the idea of a single national health insurance program, like that in Canada and many European countries, has been one of the most often proposed. Its proponents argue that cutting down the number of insurance providers will dramatically reduce paperwork and streamline operations, saving billions in costs.

Others have suggested more modest reforms. Among these are lowering costs by changing the way healthcare is delivered, clamping down on fraud, selling health insurance across state lines, compelling insurers to compete on efficiency and quality through insurance exchanges, forcing insurance companies to accept people with pre-existing medical problems, reforming Medicare, enacting tort reform, and ending the practice of tying insurance to employment.

At the far end of the spectrum of potentional solutions is one that many say could have dramatic results—making people in this country healthier. Proponents of this solution argue that by forcefully addressing public health issues such as smoking, obesity, nutrition, and physical fitness, the U.S. could dramatically reduce its dependence on the health-care system.

Social Studies

To encourage students to read silently with increasing ease and comprehension for longer periods, have students reread SE page 503 silently. Then have them, working with a partner or in small groups, answer the following questions.

- What different angle does the author examine in the first paragraph on SE page 503? (Possible response: the financial difficulties employers, who want to pay health insurance, face)
- What divergent viewpoint and bias does the author address in the second paragraph? (Possible response: demonizing health insurance companies)
- What potential solutions to the heath care problem does the author list? (Possible response: single national health insurance program, lowering health care costs, making people healthier) ✔ DIFFERENTIATE INSTRUCTION

✪ **ELPS** 4H

Differentiated Instruction: English Language Learners

✪ **ELPS** 3I,

ELP Level **Beginning**	ELP Level **Intermediate**	ELP Level **Advanced/Advanced High**
Using examples from the essay, model adapting spoken language for informal purposes. For example, you might replace *proponents* with *those who believe*.	Have partners discuss the essay, adapting their spoken language for this informal purpose. For example, they might replace *proponents* with *those who believe*.	Have partners discuss the essay, adapting their spoken language for this informal purpose. Ask them to cite examples of ways in which they adapted their language.

ELPS 3I Adapt spoken language for informal purposes; **4H** Read silently with increasing ease and comprehension

Encourage students to include their own knowledge of a subject in a document-based essay, but caution them to avoid allowing their own opinions and feelings to lead them to

- exaggerate to make a point,
- make generalizations that are based on limited examples or on emotions rather than fact,
- use overly emotional language to express their ideas, or
- state opinions and personal beliefs as fact.

Essay Checklist

Have students use the Essay Checklist to evaluate the model essay for focus and coherence, organization, development of ideas, voice, and conventions. Suggest that they use the checklist and the following questions as a guide.

- Check the Task on SE page 502 against the model essay. Has the writer addressed the question completely and used all six documents to support the thesis? (Possible response. Yes, the author has outlined the causes and effects of the high costs of health care and used all six documents in the essay.)
- What personal knowledge does the author add to the topic? (Possible response: *For most Americans, healthcare hits close to home . . . Also of concern to many . . . On the other side of the argument . . .*)
- Find examples where the author correctly punctuates a complicated sentence. (Possible response: SE p. 502, paragraph one: *Bob Miller, who told . . .* ; SE p. 502, paragraph two: *The hardest hit . . .*; SE p. 503, paragraph two: *As the health-care crisis . . .*; SE p. 503, paragraph three: *Among the former . . .*)

DIFFERENTIATE INSTRUCTION ↘

504

> The author uses a rhetorical device (rhetorical question) to engage readers and emphasize a point.

For most Americans, healthcare hits close to home. People want to know that if they or their relatives get sick, they will be given timely and quality medical care. They want assurance they they are not just a job loss away from losing their health insurance. They want to know that if they get a serious illness their insurance will not be revoked. Is it any wonder that the issue has generated such heated debate?

Also of concern to many is the price of meaningful health care reform. Some argue that we should wait until the economy improves before tackling health care. Others worry that we will pass on tremendous debts to our grandchildren. Still others are concerned about unfair tax burdens and penalties for not purchasing insurance,

> Transitional phrases connect this paragraph with the one preceding it.

On the other side of the argument, proponents of sweeping reforms argue that we can't afford not to reform health care. As Document 7 illustrates, health care spending is expected to reach an $2.5 trillion dollars in 2009 and will account for 17.6 percent of our gross domestic spending. Proponents of reform argue that these costs are crippling families, businesses, and our long-range economic outlook.

> A powerful ending summarizes the essay and leaves the reader with something to think about.

Few would argue that the current healthcare system is working. Too many are uninsured or have insurance denied. Health care costs are escalating at an alarming rate. Small businesses, families, and medical professionals all suffer as a result. As our elected officials search for a solution to the health-care crisis, the goal is clear—a system that offers quality care to more of our citizens without bankrupting the country. For those struggling with or locked out of the health-care system, however, the solution may come too late.

Essay Checklist

_____ **1.** Do all the ideas in my essay support my thesis statement?

_____ **2.** Do I fulfill the requirements outlined in the task?

_____ **3.** Do I summarize my main points in conclusion?

_____ **4.** Do I include some of my own knowledge about this topic?

_____ **5.** Have I checked my grammar, sentence structure, mechanics (capitalization and punctuation), and spelling?

Differentiated Instruction: English Language Learners

⬛ ELPS 5D

ELP Level **Beginning**	ELP Level **Intermediate**	ELP Level **Advanced/Advanced High**
Provide extra support for item 5. Model checking for subject-verb agreement, pronoun agreement, and correct tenses, using simplified examples. Prompt students to follow a similar process.	To address item 5, have partners check each other's work for subject-verb agreement, pronoun agreement, and correct tenses. Have them explain their reasoning for any changes.	To address item 5, have students check their essays for subject-verb agreement, pronoun agreement, and correct tenses. Have them explain their reasoning for any changes.

ELPS 5D Edit writing for standard grammar and usage/ subject-verb agreement, pronoun agreement, verb tenses

Writing in Math

As you move through high school, you may choose to take accelerated math courses, or not. No matter what you decide, you will find that it is important to understand mathematics. This is true whether you go to college, enroll in a technical program, or enter directly into the workplace.

Mathematics surrounds us in our daily lives. Balancing a checkbook, understanding loan interest, completing tax forms, and interpreting sports statistics all require knowledge of math. In this chapter, you will learn how writing can enhance your understanding of mathematics, both inside and outside the classroom.

- **Writing Guidelines:
  Analysis of a Comparison Problem**
- **Writing Guidelines:
  Argumentative Essay**
- **Writing Guidelines: Response to a Math Prompt**
- **Other Forms of
  Writing in Math**

"The essence of mathematics is not to make simple things complicated, but to make complicated things simple."

—S. Gudder

Writing in Math

Objectives
- apply the writing process and traits of writing to an analysis of a comparison problem, an argumentative essay, and a response to a math prompt
- learn about other forms of writing in math

The lessons on the following pages provide samples of writing students might do in a math class. Assigning these forms of writing will depend on
- the skill level of your students,
- the subject matter they are studying in different math classes, and
- the writing goals of your school, district, or state.

Writing Guidelines
Analysis of a Comparison Problem

Before asking students to write an analysis of a comparison problem, review the writing process steps shown here and read and discuss the model analysis on SE page 507.

Prewriting

Consider having all students write an analysis of the same comparison problem. Explain that the goal is to help them understand how to apply the traits of writing to a math analysis, not to teach math concepts. Have partners work together to do their prewriting, reviewing their assumptions and helping each other with calculations and math vocabulary terms.

Point out that writing an analysis ensures that they do not skip any of the important steps in the problem-solving process and can help them recognize weaknesses in their problem-solving methods, which they can then address.

ELPS 1C, 4F

Drafting

Suggest that students concentrate on using their expository writing skills to explain the problem in a clear, well-organized, interesting way.

DIFFERENTIATE INSTRUCTION ↘

TEKS 11.13B

Revising

After students have completed their initial revisions, suggest that they check their work with a partner. Have partners use the questions on SE page 506 as a guide for their discussion.

TEKS 11.13C

Editing

Remind students to check their completed essays carefully for errors in conventions.

TEKS **11.13B** Structure ideas in a sustained and persuasive way; **11.13C** Revise drafts to clarify meaning; **ELPS** **1C** Use strategic learning strategies to acquire basic and grade-level vocabulary; **4F** Use support from peers and teachers to read content area text and to develop vocabulary

---

 **TEKS** 11.13B, 11.13C

Writing Guidelines Analysis of a Comparison Problem

You may be asked to analyze a math problem, compare information, and then decide which of two options is better. To do this, you must understand these math concepts.

- **Assumptions** are statements believed to be true.
- **Evaluations** are step-by-step calculations and manipulations.
- **Explanations** clarify any confusing part of the estimate.

Prewriting

- **Select a topic.** If your teacher does not assign a specific mathematical comparison problem, review your learning log or textbook for ideas.
- **Review the assumptions.** Be sure you understand the assignment. Write down any assumptions and write down what you are comparing.
- **Plan the steps.** Break down the process into steps and write each step in the correct order.

Drafting

- **Write your first draft.** First, introduce the problem and explain it step-by-step. Identify what it is you are comparing.
- **Perform the calculations** using the information provided about the comparisons.
- **Take into account that your answer involves choosing the better option.** Explain why it is better, using mathematics to support your conclusion.

Revising

- **Improve your writing.** Review your *focus and coherence, organization, development of ideas,* and *voice.* Ask yourself the following: *Do I identify the assumptions and explain the process clearly? Do I sound knowledgeable?*
- **Improve your style.** Ask yourself the following: *Have I correctly used and defined any math terms readers may be unfamiliar with? Have I varied my sentence structure and length? Do my ideas flow smoothly?*

Editing

- **Check for conventions.** Correct all grammar, sentence structure, mechanics (capitalization and punctuation), and spelling errors.
- **Prepare a final copy.** Make a neat final copy of your work.

Differentiated Instruction: Struggling Learners

Point out that the analysis includes complete sentences, equations, and incomplete phrases. Note how the use of two columns to show comparisons helps to clarify the difference in prices. Also note that numbers from 1 to 10 are not written out in this example because they are being compared and contrasted.

Differentiated Instruction: Advanced Learners

To extend this lesson, have students bring in offers from two or more competing DVD rental programs, long-distance phone plans, cell phone plans, or introductory Internet plans. Have students decide which program would be more cost-effective over a 1-month period, 1-year period, and 5-year period.

Analysis of a Comparison Problem

Writing in Math **507**

When a problem requires you to compare options, it's important to explain what you are comparing and to clearly show the reasons for your choice.

Math

You are charged $20 per month for your cellular phone's calling plan. The first 30 minutes of local calls are free, but then you are charged $1 for each additional minute. You are also charged a roaming fee of $3 for each call that is placed outside of your local calling area, and $2 for each minute the call lasts (when outside of the area).

Last month you placed 32 minutes of local calls and made one three-minute call outside your calling area. Assume that all taxes are included in the prices given. Determine the answers to the following questions.

1. You heard about another calling plan. It would charge you $1 for each minute, local or long distance. Would this have been a better deal for you last month?

> The original plan cost $20 for the first 30 min. and $2 for min. over 30. The long-distance charge was $3 + $2(3 min.) = $9 for a total of 20 + 2 + 9 = $31.
>
> The new plan would cost $32 for the local calls ($1 per min.). The long-distance call would be $3 ($1 per min.). The new plan would cost 32 + 3 = $35. The new plan would not have been a better deal.

2. If you made the one long-distance call described above, how many minutes of local calls would you need to make the new plan a better deal?

> Original plan:
> $20 for 30 min.
> + $9 long distance = $29
>
> New plan:
> $30 for 30 min.
> + $3 long distance = $33
>
> You would need to make fewer than 26 minutes of local calls since the plans are equal at 26 minutes.
>
> Original plan:
> $20 for 26 min.
> + $9 long distance = $29
>
> New plan:
> $26 for 26 min.
> + $3 long distance = $29
>
> As can be seen, the two plans cost the same at 26 minutes. Therefore, the new plan is only a better deal for less than 26 minutes of local calls since the cost will fall below $29 while the original plan's cost will remain the same ($29).

Analysis of a Comparison Problem

Have students read through the model analysis. Then discuss how the writer has applied the traits of writing to the analysis. Include the points below in the discussion.

✔ DIFFERENTIATE INSTRUCTION ✔ DIFFERENTIATE INSTRUCTION

⭐ ELPS 4K

Focus and Coherence

- The writer maintains his or her focus throughout the essay: comparing two cell phone calling plans.
- A clear and meaningful introduction and conclusion frame the essay.

Organization

- The essay has a smooth and logical flow.
- Transitional words and phrases (*Last month, As can be seen, Therefore*) help the reader move from one idea to the next.
- Numbered steps make each part of the problem analysis easy to read and follow.
- The calculations are set off to make them clear.

Development of Ideas

- An assumption (all taxes are included in the prices given) is clearly stated.
- The author offers ample support and specific details (calculations comparing the two plans) to support his or her thesis.

Voice

- The use of the second-person pronoun *you* immediately engages the reader and gives the essay a conversational tone.
- Specialized terms such as *calling area, calling plan,* and *roaming fee* create a knowledgeable voice.

Differentiated Instruction: English Language Learners

⭐ ELPS 4F

ELP Level **Beginning**	ELP Level **Intermediate**	ELP Level **Advanced/Advanced High**
Use simplified language and visuals to present example phrases using comparison signal words such as *both, alike, also, same,* and *better.* Have students repeat each phrase after you.	Have partners practice completing sentence frames such as _____ *and* _____ *are alike because* _____. Then have students create their own comparison sentences.	Have partners create comparison sentences using words such as *both, alike, also, same,* and *better.* Tell them to create two versions of each sentence by varying the signal words.

ELPS 4F Use support from peers and teachers to read content area text and to develop vocabulary; **4K** Demonstrate English comprehension and expand reading skills by employing analytical skills

Writing Guidelines Argumentative Essay

If students have written an argumentative essay, they will understand how to apply the writing traits. Students who have not yet studied and practiced argumentative writing may need additional guidance understanding the following elements of an effective argumentative paper:

- an interesting beginning with a clear thesis statement
- two or three compelling reasons that support the thesis, usually organized in order of importance
- an answer to a valid objection or divergent point of view
- an ending that summarizes the main points of the argument
- serious, fair language that is respectful of opposing views and a range of relevant perspectives

⭐ **TEKS** 11.16B, 11.16D

✳ All students will benefit from a review of the goals for an argumentative essay, presented in the Understanding Your Goal chart on SE page 218 and in the models for an argumentative essay on SE pages 250–255.

Prewriting

Discuss with students each of the bulleted items on SE page 508. Emphasize the importance of evaluating sources and taking good notes as they research.

⭐ **ELPS** 4G

Exercise
Answers

1. expression of commonly held belief
2. fact
3. quotation
4. expert opinion

DIFFERENTIATE INSTRUCTION ↘

⭐ **TEKS** 11.16A

508

⭐ **TEKS** 11.16A, 11.16B, 11.16D

Writing Guidelines Argumentative Essay

Mathematics is the study of numbers and symbols, and the methods of study can spark controversy. One controversial issue is the use of calculators in the classroom. Should students be forced to make calculations in the traditional way, or should they be allowed to use calculators for daily homework, and even on tests? At some point, you may be asked to decide on such an issue and defend your position. Use the guidelines below to help you develop argumentative essays for mathematics.

Prewriting

- **Select a topic that interests you.** Think about problems or issues related to mathematics in your school or your community.
- **Gather information.** Gather and make notes about your own thoughts on the topic. Then consult other sources of information, and take notes. Look for sources that includes precise and relevant information, such as facts, expert opinions, quotations, or expressions of commonly held beliefs. Always remember to evaluate the reliability of your information. Based on your own thoughts and your other sources of information, form your opinion. In your notes, label supporting points "pro" and opposing points "con." Be sure to include divergent views in your notes.
- **Consider your reader.** Think about your readers and how much they know or do not know about your topic. Decide what information your readers need to know in order to understand your argument.
- **Make a list or an outline.** List your major points in an order that makes sense. Use your list or outline as a planning guide.
- **Create a clear and concise thesis statement** that states your argument.

Exercise

Label the following notes *facts, expert opinions, quotations,* or *expressions of commonly held beliefs.*

1. People need to know how to do basic math with or without a calculator.
2. One of the earliest devices used to help people calculate was the abacus.
3. "Math is like love—a simple idea, but it can get complicated." —Albert Einstein
4. "Almost half the the nation's 17-year-olds do not know or understand enough math to qualify for a job requiring even rudimentary calculation." Marisa Faulkner, Cornell University

---

⭐ **TEKS** **11.16A** Write an argumentative essay that includes a clear thesis or position based on logical reasons supported by precise and relevant evidence, including facts, expert opinions, quotations, and/or expressions of commonly accepted beliefs; **11.16B** Write an argumentative essay that includes accurate and honest representation of divergent views; **11.16D** Write an argumentative essay that includes information on the complete range of relevant perspectives; **ELPS** **4G** Demonstrate comprehension of increasingly complex English/taking notes

Math

Drafting

- **Identify your position.** In your opening paragraph, introduce your topic and state your opinion about it.
- **Support your position.** Present the main supporting points and details that advance your argument. Be sure to present your main points in the best possible order.
- **Present and rebut a viewpoint or argument that differs from your own.**
- **Restate your position.** In the closing paragraph, restate your argument and leave the reader with a final key idea.

Revising

Improve your writing. Review your essay for *focus and coherence, organization, development of ideas,* and *voice.* Ask yourself the following questions.

- Have I presented a reasonable argument?
- Do I have a logical order that suits my purpose and my audience?
- Is my essay easy to follow?
- Have I written an engaging introduction and a meaningful conclusion?
- Do all of my supporting points support my argument?
- Have I offered a unique perspective on the topic?
- Have I included and addressed a divergent viewpoint?
- Have I engaged my readers throughout my essay?

Check your style. Review the tone and style of your essay. Ask yourself the following questions.

- Have I defined or explained any specialized words?
- Have I used rhetorical devices, such as appeals to logic, emotions, or ethical beliefs to support my argument?
- Have I used a variety of sentence lengths?

Editing

Check for conventions. Find and correct any errors in grammar, sentence structure, mechanics (capitalization and punctuation), and spelling.

Prepare a final copy. Proofread this copy before sharing it.

Tip

Read your essay aloud, or share it with your teacher or a classmate. Check that your arguments are sound and well supported, that your organizational pattern makes sense, and that your essay reads smoothly.

Drafting

Remind students of the importance of choosing a topic about which reasonable people might disagree. Tell them to state their positions clearly in their opening paragraphs. Remind students to evaluate all of their sources for validity and reliability.

⭐ **TEKS** 11.16E

Revising

After students have revised their essays, suggest that they work with a partner to check their revisions. Have partners use the questions provided on SE page 509 to check their revisions. Remind students to consider their purpose and audience as they revise.

⭐ **TEKS** 11.16C

Editing

Remind students that it is important to check for correct use of conventions in their argumentative essays. Point out that neglecting to correct such errors will detract from the overall quality of their essay.

Tip

Tell students that reading their essay aloud can be a very effective tool for locating parts of the essay that do not read smoothly, parts where the organizational structure breaks down, and parts that could be more clearly or concisely worded. Encourage them to listen to their essays as they read them aloud and note parts that need more work.

⭐ **TEKS** 11.16C; **ELPS** 1B

Differentiated Instruction: English Language Learners		⭐ **ELPS** 1E, 1F
ELP Level Beginning	**ELP Level Intermediate**	**ELP Level Advanced/Advanced High**
Use visuals, gestures, and examples to explain the terms *facts, expert opinions, quotations,* and *commonly held beliefs.* Have students repeat each term after you.	Explain the terms *facts, expert opinions, quotations,* and *commonly held beliefs.* Have partners work together to write sentences about each term.	As needed, explain the terms *facts, expert opinions, quotations,* and *commonly held beliefs.* Have students write sentences that give examples of each term.

TEKS **11.16C** Write an argumentative essay that includes an organizing structure appropriate to the purpose, audience, and context; **11.16E** Write an argumentative essay that includes demonstrated consideration of the validity and reliability of all primary and secondary sources used; **ELPS** **1B** Monitor written language production and employ self-corrective techniques or other resources; **1E** Internalize new basic and academic language by using and reusing it/writing; **1F** Use accessible language and learn new and essential language in the process

Argumentative Essay

After students read the model essay silently, have small groups discuss the the following questions to demonstrate comprehension.

- Explain why the author's opening paragraph is effective. (Possible response: The rhetorical question immediately draws the reader into the discussion.)
- What organizational pattern does the author use? (Possible response: logical order, with each major argument supported by relevant details)
- What relevant and specific facts does the writer use to support his or her argument? (Possible response: number-crunching speed of calculators; graphing calculators can open up whole new worlds of exploration)
- What divergent viewpoint to the author address? (Possible response: Math teachers worry that the use of calculators will negatively impact math learning.)
- How does the author show that he or she has considered the validity and reliability of sources? (Possible response: The author tests his or her sources by successfully addressing a divergent viewpoint.)

ELPS 4H

Try It!
Answers

Have students brainstorm problems or issues connected to the study of mathematics, and then have them choose a topic from the list as the subject for an argumentative essay.

Distribute the reproducible T-chart provided on TE page A95 for use in gathering information. Tell students to label one side of the T-chart *pro* for supporting points, and one side *con* for opposing views.

TEKS 11.16A, 11.16B, 11.16C, 11.16D, 11.16E

TEKS 11.16A, 11.16B, 11.16C, 11.16D, 11.16E

Argumentative Essay

The following persuasive essay explains why one student thinks calculators should be allowed in high school math classes.

It All Adds Up to Yes

The author uses a **rhetorical device** (a rhetorical question) to engage readers.

In mathematics, does taking the fastest and most accurate route to problem-solving undermine rudimentary mathetical understanding? This is the question at the heart of the debate about using calculators in math classes.

Topic is introduced and thesis stated.

Students should be allowed to use calculators in math classes. Because of the number-crunching speed of calculators, calculators allow students to quickly accomplish ordinary tasks such as long division, multiplication, and addition. It simply doesn't make sense to ask students to spend time multiplying 117 times 338 rather than using a calculator. Using a calculator not only saves time, but also encourages students to focus on complex mathematical processes instead of simple calculations.

Relevant and specific facts support the author's arguments.

Calculators, in particular graphing calculators, can open up a whole new world of exploration and understanding to math students. Graphing calculators, designed to help students visualize math and science concepts, are much more than just answer generators. Graphing calculators challenge students to work out problems by visualizing, thus enabling them to develop a deeper understanding of mathematical concepts. Using calculators, students can focus on

Try It!

Think of another issue involving mathematics at your school. Gather information and write an argumentative essay that supports your position on the issue. Follow the guidelines on pages **508–509**.

TEKS **11.16A** Write an argumentative essay that includes a clear thesis or position based on logical reasons supported by precise and relevant evidence, including facts, expert opinions, quotations, and/or expressions of commonly accepted beliefs; **11.16B** Write an argumentative essay that includes accurate and honest representation of divergent views; **11.16C** Write an argumentative essay that includes an organizing structure appropriate to the purpose, audience, and context; **11.16D** Write an argumentative essay that includes information on the complete range of relevant perspectives; **11.16E** Write an argumentative essay that includes demonstrated consideration of the validity and reliability of all primary and secondary sources used; **ELPS** **4H** Read silently with increasing ease and comprehension

Author cites a divergent viewpoint and offers solutions to the problem.

advanced math problems and the process for solving such problems. For example, using a calculator students can quickly see how different values can dramatically change the solution of a problem, as in finding the solution to the number of feet per second a car travels at 70 miles per hour versus 60 miles per hour.

Of course, math teachers worry that calculators may negatively affect math learning. It is possible that students could simply calculate answers without understanding the math process behind the solutions, but a simple test can show which students have mastered basic math skills. Only those students would be allowed to use calculators in class. To keep students' skills sharp, other tests could be given once every three months, or students could be required to do class work every Friday without using a calculator.

Arguments are summarized and the reader is left with something to think about.

Calculators can never replace a thinking and aware human, but they could save students the drudgery of computation, allowing them to reserve their brain power for understanding advanced mathamatics concepts. There is one added benefit. For gadget-loving teenagers, calculators might well entice math-phobic students to give math a serious try. Used judiciously and only after students have mastered basic math concepts, calculators will improve students' effeciency, accuracy, and understanding.

Math

Essay Checklist

_____ **1.** Do all the ideas in my essay support my thesis statement?
_____ **2.** Do I fulfill all the requirements outlined in the task?
_____ **3.** Do I support my argument with specific and relevant details?
_____ **4.** Do I summarize my points in my conclusion?
_____ **5.** Do I cite and answer a divergent viewpoint?
_____ **6.** Have I checked my grammar, sentence structure, mechanics (capitalization and punctuation), and spelling?

Differentiated Instruction: English Language Learners

⭐ **ELPS** 4K

ELP Level **Beginning**	ELP Level **Intermediate**	ELP Level **Advanced/Advanced High**
Use visuals and gestures to explain *drudgery, computation, brain power,* and *phobic.* Have students repeat each term after you and respond to yes-no questions.	Have students sort words such as *drudgery, benefit, computation, brain power,* and *phobic* by analyzing whether each one refers to something positive or something negative.	Have students analyze the essay for terms that imply good or positive things and for terms that imply bad or negative things.

Have students reread silently the last paragraph of the student model on SE page 511. Have small groups or partners analyze the passage, using the following questions to demonstate comprehension:

- As the author sums up his or her main arguments in the conclusion of the essay, what major argument is presented for allowing students to use calculators? (Possible response: Calculators will save students from the drudgery of computation.)
- What additional benefit does the author list? (Possible response: Math-phobic teenagers might be enticed by the calculators to give math a try.)
- What caution does the author suggest about the use of calculators in the classroom? (Possible response: Students need to have mastered basic math concepts before being allowed to use calculators in class.)
- What primary and secondary sources might the writer have used for this essay? How could the validity and reliability of those sources be checked? (Possible responses: interviews with teachers, current and former students, and parents; news articles about how other schools and communities have address the issue; Interviews would provide expert opinions and commonly held beliefs; news articles are based on facts that could be verified.)

✔ **DIFFERENTIATE INSTRUCTION**

⭐ **TEKS** 11.16E; **ELPS** 4H, 4K

Essay Checklist

Have students use the Essay Checklist to evaluate the model essay for focus and coherence, organization, development of ideas, voice, and conventions.

⭐ **TEKS** 11.16A, 11.16B, 11.16C, 11.16D

⭐ **TEKS** **11.16A** Write an argumentative essay that includes a clear thesis or position based on logical reasons supported by precise and relevant evidence, including facts, expert opinions, quotations, and/or expressions of commonly accepted beliefs; **11.16B** Write an argumentative essay that includes accurate and honest representation of divergent views; **11.16C** Write an argumentative essay that includes an organizing structure appropriate to the purpose, audience, and context; **11.16D** Write an argumentative essay that includes information on the complete range of relevant perspectives; **11.16E** Write an argumentative essay that includes demonstrated consideration of the validity and reliability of all primary and secondary sources used; **ELPS** **4H** Read silently with increasing ease and comprehension; **4K** Demonstrate English comprehension and expand reading skills by employing analytical skills

Writing Guidelines Response to a Math Prompt

Explain that writing about a math prompt is a way to share one's thinking process.

Before you write... Encourage students to use the STRAP questions to analyze math prompts before writing. Although the responses for Type, Role, and Audience are not likely to differ from one prompt to another, identifying the subject and the purpose will help students focus their ideas so that they can respond effectively to the prompt. Have students recall the meaning of the letters in the acronym STRAP:

- **S**ubject
- **T**ype
- **R**ole
- **A**udience
- **P**urpose

Provide examples of math prompts, and have students practice using the STRAP questions to analyze them and plan responses. Point out that generally for a math prompt, the **Type** will be paragraph or essay, the **Role** will be student, and the **Audience** will be teacher or peers.

TEKS 11.13A; **ELPS** 1H, 4K

✱ For more about using STRAP questions, see SE page 208.

As you write... Point out that the goal is to demonstrate understanding of mathematical reasoning, and so thought processes must be logically explained as well as calculations.

DIFFERENTIATE INSTRUCTION ↘

TEKS 11.13B

After you've written a first draft... As with other forms of writing, encourage students to check for focus and coherence, organization, development of ideas, voice and conventions.

TEKS 11.13A, 11.13B

Writing Guidelines Response to a Math Prompt

Math prompts propose word problems. You are asked to respond in writing in addition to showing your mathematical calculations and your answers. First you must analyze the prompt and decide what you are supposed to do. Then you respond one step at a time. Follow these guidelines.

Before you write . . .

- **Read the prompt.** Read carefully and watch for key words such as *find, solve, justify, demonstrate,* or *compare.* Carry out only the requested actions. Be aware that some prompts will ask you to do more than one thing.
- **Gather details and data.** Write down any values, assumptions, or variables provided in the prompt.

As you write . . .

- **Build your solution.** Respond to each part of the prompt. Jot down formulas or equations and sketch brief diagrams if they will help solve the problem. Make the necessary calculations to get an answer. Be sure to show all of your work.

After you've written a first draft . . .

- **Improve your response.** Reread the prompt after you do your calculations. If the problem has more than one part, be sure you have answered every part. Work the problem in another way to check that your solution is correct.
- **Check for conventions.** Check your solution for errors in grammar, sentence structure, mechanics (capitalization and punctuation), and spelling.
- **Prepare a final copy.** Make a neat copy of your solution.

Response to a Math Prompt

The following math prompt contains more than one part. The writer answers each part using words, numbers, and diagrams.

> *Compare and contrast the graphs of the sine and cosine functions.*

The sine and cosine functions have graphs that are similar in that they both have a period of 360°. This means they will repeat their pattern every 360°. They also have values that range between -1 and 1.

The graphs are different because the cosine function is really a shifted sine function. The graphs are the same (as explained above), but just shifted 90°.

The similarities and differences described above can be seen in the graph of each.

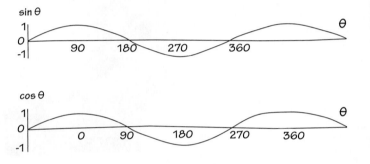

Try It!

Find a math prompt and write a response. Choose a practice prompt from your textbook or one recommended by your teacher. Follow the guidelines on page **512**.

Response to a Math Prompt

To help students internalize the academic vocabulary, have them point out the key words in the prompt that suggest what the writer is supposed to do to answer the prompt completely and effectively.

- The words *graphs of the sine and cosine functions* tell the writer what the subject of the response should be.
- The words *compare and contrast* tell the writer to explain how the graphs of sine and cosine functions are alike and different.
- The word *graphs* suggests that the writer should include a sketch of the graphs in the explanation to support ideas and to make the similarities and differences between the two kinds of graphs clear for the reader.

✔ DIFFERENTIATE INSTRUCTION

⭐ ELPS 1E, 1H, 3D

Try It!
Answers

If you presented sample math prompts for students to analyze earlier (TE page 512), encourage students to write a response for one of these prompts for the **Try It!** activity.

Differentiated Instruction:
English Language Learners   ⭐ ELPS 1E, 1H, 3D

ELP Level **Beginning**	ELP Level **Intermediate**	ELP Level **Advanced/Advanced High**
Use visuals and gestures to explain *graphs, functions, compare,* and *contrast.* Have students repeat each term after you and respond to yes-no questions.	Have partners create separate webs for *graphs, functions, compare,* and *contrast.* Have them present and explain why they chose the terms used in each section of the webs.	Have partners define and discuss *graphs, functions, compare,* and *contrast.* Then have them work together to create a plan to respond to the prompt.

 ELPS 1E Internalize new basic and academic language by using and reusing it/speaking; **1H** Develop and expand repertoire of learning strategies; **3D** Speak using grade-level content area vocabulary in context/academic language

Other Forms of Writing in Math

These assignments provide an excellent opportunity for students to recognize the legitimate application of math to real-world situations and experiences.

Encourage students to choose one of these other forms for writing in math. Then have students who have chosen the same writing form meet in small groups to discuss the directions for writing and to summarize the key elements that need to be included in their essays. **DIFFERENTIATE INSTRUCTION** ↘

DIFFERENTIATE INSTRUCTION ↘
⭐ **ELPS** 2I

Descriptive Writing

✱ For help with the Descriptive Writing assignment, have students review SE pages 61, 609, and 630.

Definition, Classification, and Process Writing

✱ The Definition, Classification, and Process assignments are forms of expository writing. If students choose one of these ideas, suggest that they review the strategies for expository writing on SE pages 157–198.

Narrative Writing

✱ For help with narrative writing, have students skim SE pages 135–155.

Research Writing

✱ For a review of research writing skills and report writing guidelines, students can turn to SE pages 375–454.

514

Other Forms of Writing in Math

Descriptive Writing
Geometry or Trigonometry—Write a description of the water at a beach using geometry and/or trigonometry.

Definition
Trigonometry—Write a detailed expository paragraph on the definition of the word "trigonometry."

Classification
Geometry—Write an essay comparing and contrasting types of triangles.

Narrative
Any Math—Write a narrative essay about how you may be using math in your daily life three years after your high school graduation.

Process
Algebra—Write a process paragraph about the details needed to solve a linear equation.

Research
Any Math—Write a report on a famous mathematician. In your report, explain the historical context of this individual as well as his or her mathematical contribution.

Differentiated Instruction: Struggling Learners

Before students try any of the forms of writing in math listed on this page, have them work in small groups to brainstorm key terms and ideas to include in their chosen form. They should then create an organizer or outline showing how they would express themselves in the clearest way.

⭐ **TEKS** 11.13A

TEKS **11.13A** Plan a first draft by selecting the correct genre for conveying the intended meaning to multiple audiences; **ELPS** **2I** Demonstrate listening comprehension/following directions/retelling or summarizing

515

Writing in the Applied Sciences

You take notes and write essays in school, of course, but writing is also an important part of the world outside of school. As an adult, you may need to write directions for someone, leave a note with instructions for the babysitter, write a letter of complaint for poor service or a faulty product, or compose a letter requesting funds for a PTA project. On your job, you may be asked to write reports, letters, summaries, and e-mail messages. Writing will always be a part of your life, and knowing how to write will allow you to effectively interact with the world around you.

In this chapter you will learn how to write a classification essay, a restaurant review, and a response to a test prompt.

- **Writing Guidelines:**
  Classification Essay
- **Writing Guidelines:**
  Restaurant Review
- **Writing Guidelines:**
  Response to a Prompt
- **Other Forms of**
  Practical Writing

"I learned from watching and
I learned from doing."

—Claire Bloom

Writing in the
Applied Sciences

Objective

- apply the writing process and traits of writing to a classification essay, a restaurant review, and a response to a test prompt

The lessons on the following pages provide samples of writing students might do in a family and consumer science or technical education class. Assigning these forms of writing will depend on

- the skill level of your students,
- the subject matter they are studying in fields of applied science, and
- the writing goals of your school, district, or state.

Writing Guidelines Classification Essay

Point out that using a gathering grid works well for collecting details for a classification essay. Refer students to the sample gathering grids on SE pages 164 and 399 and elicit their ideas about why the grids are effective tools.

⭐ **ELPS** 2E

Prewriting

Tell students that they can choose any sensible pattern of organization for a classification essay, but that a category-by-category pattern generally works best.

Have students refer to the model classification essay on SE page 517, explaining that their opening paragraph should introduce the categories; the middle paragraphs should name the categories and examine each one using relevant evidence and well-chosen details; and the ending paragraph should recall what the categories have in common.

⭐ **TEKS** 11.13A, 11.15A(i), 11.15A(v)

Drafting

Encourage students to use transition words such as *the first type*, and *another type* to create a smooth flow from one category to the next.

⭐ **TEKS** 11.13B, 11.15A(iv)

Revising

Have students share their revised papers with a partner and ask for and discuss feedback.

⭐ **ELPS** 2G

Editing

Remind students that errors in conventions can seriously mar the overall quality of their papers.

Writing Guidelines Classification Essay

A classification essay divides a subject into different parts and proceeds to explain each part in turn. The goal is to completely explain each part.

Prewriting

- **Select a topic.** If your teacher does not assign a specific topic, review your notes, manual, or textbook for ideas. For example, in a metals class you might categorize different tools into groups. In a class on textiles, you could explain different kinds of needlework.
- **Gather details.** Use a graphic organizer to help you arrange your categories and details. Include work techniques, tools, and other materials used for each part.
- **Plan and organize.** Decide in which order to present your categories. How are they related? Decide on a clearly organized schema for conveying ideas as you move from one category or item to the next.

Writing

- **Connect your ideas.** Introduce your points and their connection in the beginning paragraph. Then present each point with relevant and substantial evidence and well-chosen detail, covering one completely before moving on to the next.

Revising

- **Improve your writing.** Examine your work for *focus and coherence, organization, development of ideas,* and *voice.* Rework any ideas that are unclear or incomplete.
- **Improve your style.** Look at your writing to be sure you have used a variety of sentence structures and make any changes necessary to improve clarity and flow.

Editing

- **Check for conventions.** Look for errors in grammar, sentence structure, mechanics (captalization and punctuation), and spelling.
- **Make a neat final copy.**

⭐ **TEKS** **11.13A** Plan a first draft by selecting the correct genre for conveying the intended meaning to multiple audiences; **11.13B** Develop drafts that include transitions and rhetorical devices to convey meaning; **11.15A(i)** Write an analytical essay of sufficient length that includes effective introductory and concluding paragraphs and a variety of sentence structures; **11.15A(iv)** Write an analytical essay of sufficient length that includes a clear organizational schema for conveying ideas; **11.15A(v)** Write an analytical essay of sufficient length that includes relevant and substantial evidence and well-chosen details; **ELPS** **2E** Use visual, contextual, and linguistic support to confirm understanding of spoken language; **2G** Understand the general meaning, main points, and important details of spoken language/contexts

Classification Essay

For his building construction class, Carlo examined and wrote about the different types of windows.

Applied Sciences

The **beginning** introduces the topic and presents the thesis statement (underlined).

The **middle** has a clearly organized schema to examine each type.

The **ending** wraps up the essay and gives a final statement.

Windows on the World

One of the most important parts of new home construction is the type of window used. <u>There are three main types, each with its own advantages and disadvantages.</u>

One type is the double- or single-hung window. This type has two separate sashes that slide up and down on side tracks. In the double-hung window, both sashes move independently. In a single-hung window, only one of the sashes moves while the other is fixed. In both, a screen and/or storm window is usually attached to the outside. Some newer windows are designed to pull out for easy cleaning of both sides.

A second type of window is the casement window, which cranks out. An "awning" window has the hinge at the top. Sky windows—skylights that open—are usually of this type. A casement window can be adjusted to catch a breeze. These windows usually have the screen on the inside, and are cost efficient because of the tight seal they create when closed. However, because they open out, it is more difficult to clean the outside glass.

Sliding windows, or sliders, move sideways and comprise a third type of window. Because of their structure, sliding windows might have a screen either on the inside or outside. Cleaning these windows might be a little difficult, especially if they are located on upper floors.

All three types of windows have advantages and disadvantages. When considering which type of window to install in their homes, homeowners should consider the look desired along with efficiency and ease of care. The right window can certainly improve a home, as well as the homeowner's outlook on the world.

Try It!

Write a classification essay about something you are studying. Select a topic that you can break down into several categories.

Classification Essay

Before students write their own classification essay, have them work together to analyze the model classification essay, breaking it down into outline form, and identifying the introduction, thesis statement, topic sentences for each middle and concluding paragraph, and relevant and substantive details that support the topic sentences.

⭐ **ELPS** 3H, 4K

✱ For more about outlines, see SE pages 226 and 403.

Have students express ideas about how the thesis statement at the end of the first paragraph of the model classification essay controls the ideas and organization of the essay. (It says that there are three main types, each with its own advantages and disadvantages. With this statement as a guide, the body of the essay should contain three middle paragraphs, each one describing a type of window and telling about its advantages and disadvantages.)

⭐ **TEKS** 11.15A(i), 11.15A(iv), 11.15A(v); **ELPS** 3G

Try It!
Answers

Suggest that students limit their classification essay to three or four categories to make the writing manageable. **✓DIFFERENTIATE INSTRUCTION**

Differentiated Instruction: English Language Learners

⭐ **ELPS** 3G, 3H, 4K

ELP Level **Beginning**	ELP Level **Intermediate**	ELP Level **Advanced/Advanced High**
Model creating a web or gathering grid for the model essay, having students point out categories of information. Work together to plan categories for a new topic.	Have partners identify categories for their writing topics and express ideas about specific details that should be included in each one. Have them work together to create gathering grids.	Have partners share and analyze gathering grids for the topics they have chosen. Invite them to express ideas about specific details that should be included.

 TEKS **11.15A(i)** Write an analytical essay of sufficient length that includes effective introductory and concluding paragraphs and a variety of sentence structures; **11.15A(iv)** Write an analytical essay of sufficient length that includes a clear organizational schema for conveying ideas; **11.15A(v)** Write an analytical essay of sufficient length that includes relevant and substantial evidence and well-chosen details; **ELPS** **3G** Express ideas; **3H** Explain with increasing specificity and detail; **4K** Demonstrate English comprehension and expand reading skills by employing analytical skills

Writing Guidelines Restaurant Review

Explain that restaurant reviewers hold a powerful position in many communities. Some reviewers visit restaurants incognito so they won't receive special treatment. Good restaurant reviewers strive to maintain a level of objectivity about the menu, the service, food preparation and presentation, prices, and the physical environment (cleanliness, decor, music and kitchen sounds, proximity of tables, locale, security, parking, and accessibility) of the restaurants they review.

Prewriting

Ask students to bring in restaurant reviews from local newspapers to share with the class. Have students point out common elements in the reviews, discuss how they're organized, and note the specific language reviewers use to praise or criticize different types of restaurants.

⭐ **TEKS** 11.13A; **ELPS** 4F

Drafting

Remind students to include an attention-grabbing introduction, a clear thesis statement, relevant and substantial details to support their major points, and an effective conclusion.

⭐ **TEKS** 11.13B, 11.15A(i), 11.15A(v)

Revising

Have students share their essay with a partner and ask for feedback. Suggest that partners look for a clear organizational scheme that connects the ideas in the review.

⭐ **TEKS** 11.15(iv)

Editing

Remind students to check their writing carefully for errors in conventions.

518

⭐ **TEKS** 11.13A, 11.13B, 11.15A(i), 11.15A(iv), 11.15A(v)

Writing Guidelines Restaurant Review

A restaurant review is a specific type of writing. The review should cover all aspects of a restaurant, not just the food.

Prewriting

- **Pinpoint your purpose.** Explain why you are writing the review. Consider your audience. What will they want to know about the restaurant?
- **Gather details.** A restaurant review should include well-chosen details about the menu, service, prices, and physical environment of the establishment. Include anything that makes the restaurant stand out or fall short.
- **Plan and organize.** Decide on a clear organizational schema. Reviews often use chronological order, as though the writer were taking the reader through the dining experience.

Writing

- **Include a clear beginning.** Present your first impressions or reason for visiting the restaurant.
- **Write the middle.** Describe the experience, noting both positive and negative points.
- **End with a final comment.** Wrap up by suggesting the reader either try or avoid the restaurant.

Revising

- **Improve your writing.** Check your *focus and coherence, organization, development of ideas,* and *voice.* Add sensory details to describe the restaurant and your experience as completely as possible.
- **Improve your style.** Be certain your sentences vary in type and length and read smoothly. Avoid angry or inflammatory language, and keep your tone cool and neutral.

Editing

- **Check for conventions.** Find and correct any errors in grammar, sentence structure, capitalization, punctuation, and spelling.
- **Make a clean final copy.**

⭐ **TEKS** **11.13A** Plan a first draft by selecting the correct genre for conveying the intended meaning to multiple audiences; **11.13B** Develop drafts that include transitions and rhetorical devices to convey meaning; **11.15A(i)** Write an analytical essay of sufficient length that includes effective introductory and concluding paragraphs and a variety of sentence structures; **11.15A(iv)** Write an analytical essay of sufficient length that includes a clear organizational schema for conveying ideas; **11.15A(v)** Write an analytical essay of sufficient length that includes relevant and substantial evidence and well-chosen details; **ELPS** **4F** Use visual and contextual support and support from peers and teachers to develop background knowledge

TEKS 11.15A(i), 11.15A(iv), 11.15A(v)

Restaurant Review

Leona's Foods Service class focuses on running a cafeteria or restaurant. She used what she had learned to write the following restaurant review.

Applied Sciences

Feed Mill Offers Old-Time Flavor

A new restaurant, The Feed Mill, recently opened in the Uptown District, an area greatly in need of new businesses. This restaurant should become an important part of this district for years to come.

Housed in the old Clayton Feed building, the restaurant draws its theme from its historic home. Huge sepia-colored photos of farms line the walls, while rusted farm equipment hangs from the ceiling. Old-time touches such as potbellied stoves and water pumps dot the dining area, which is enhanced by warm wood trim and red leather chairs and booths.

The menu continues the down-on-the-farm feel, with such home-style fare as "Mom's Meatloaf," but each dish boasts a distinctive twist. For example, the meatloaf is spiraled around a sweet potato filling. Even the restaurant's signature dessert, "Apple Brown Delia," is set apart by a hint of fresh ginger.

A nice touch is the huge list of country side dishes available, from "mulled applesauce" to "cheesy broccoli." Warm, crusty sourdough bread accompanies every meal. Prices run in the moderate range, and the a la carte option allows for affordable family meals. This is truly old-school cooking, and patrons will not find much in the way of heart-healthy or low-carb options.

Service is well paced, with attentive waitstaff dressed in butcher aprons, arm garters, and straw hats. The restaurant boasts a completely smoke-free environment.

The Feed Mill provides good, hearty food and is a bridge between cheap fast food and high-priced elegant dining. As such, it is a welcome addition to Clayton.

The **beginning** gives the purpose for the review.

The **middle** covers the atmosphere and service but focuses on the food.

A divergent view (no heart-healthy, low-carb option) is acknowledged and addressed.

The **ending** offers a wrap-up and a final thought.

Try It!

Visit a local restaurant and write a review. Include details about the physical environment, service, menu, and overall quality.

Restaurant Review

Discuss the model restaurant review with students. Use the margin notes to analyze the organization and relevant and substantial details in the review; then discuss these points:

- How does the author introduce the topic? (The author gets readers' attention by reminding them that the Uptown District needs new restaurant business.)
- What sensory details does the writer use to help readers share the experience? (huge sepia-colored photos, rusted farm equipment, potbellied stoves and water pumps, warm wood trim, red leather chairs and booths)
- What does the writer recommend in the concluding paragraph? (that The Feed Mill provides good food and is a welcome addition to Clayton)

TEKS 11.15A(i), 11.15A(iv), 11.15A(v); **ELPS** 4F

Try It!
Answers

Ask students to share their restaurant reviews with the class. Students who review the same restaurant will find it interesting to hear another viewpoint and will enjoy expressing opinions and ideas. Invite students to submit their final reviews to a school or local newspaper.

✓ DIFFERENTIATE INSTRUCTION

TEKS 11.15A(i), 11.15A(iv), 11.15A(v); **ELPS** 3G

Differentiated Instruction: English Language Learners

ELPS 3G, 4F

ELP Level **Beginning**	ELP Level **Intermediate**	ELP Level **Advanced/Advanced High**
Model using simple sentences such as *The food is good/The food is bad.* Help students express opinions by brainstorming additional adjectives to use in the sentence stem.	Have partners create a T-chart to list positive and negative words that describe food. Have them use the words to express feelings and opinions about a restaurant.	Have partners brainstorm lists of words to express opinions and feelings about each aspect of a restaurant. Suggest they consult several reviews for more ideas.

TEKS **11.15A(i)** Write an analytical essay of sufficient length that includes effective introductory and concluding paragraphs and a variety of sentence structures; **11.15A(iv)** Write an analytical essay of sufficient length that includes a clear organizational schema for conveying ideas; **11.15A(v)** Write an analytical essay of sufficient length that includes relevant and substantial evidence and well-chosen details; **ELPS** **3G** Express opinions and feelings; **4F** Use visual and contextual support and support from peers and teachers to read content area text and confirm understanding

Writing Guidelines Response to a Prompt

Discuss with students some effective ways to break down the parts of the writing process into clear chunks of time for a timed response. For example, if students have 45 minutes to write a response, they could break it down into the following segments of time:

- 15 minutes for analyzing the prompt, gathering notes, and planning a response;
- 20 minutes for writing; and
- 10 minutes for revising, editing, and proofreading.

Before you write... Tell students that when they are planning a response, they should allow the most time for writing.

As needed, define and discuss the words *subject, purpose,* and *focus.* Have students explain how the questions provided will help them address each term.

 TEKS 11.13B; **ELPS** 1C, 1F

As you write... Point out that students will not usually have time to make extensive revisions or to copy over their response, so they should write with this in mind. Remind them to include transitions to connect ideas between paragraphs.

After you've written a first draft... Explain that any changes or corrections students make should be neat and legible.

Writing Guidelines Response to a Prompt

Before you write . . .

- **Know your time limit.** Plan your time to accomplish prewriting, writing, and revising.
- **Examine the prompt.** Look for key words that will help you determine the following elements:
  - **Subject** What is the topic of your writing?
  - **Purpose** Will you explain, inform, analyze, or persuade?
  - **Focus** What aspect of the subject should you examine?
- **Plan your response.** Write your thesis or argument and organize details in a brief outline or graphic organizer.

As you write . . .

- **Write an effective opening paragraph.** Grab your reader's attention, provide necessary background information, and include your thesis statement.
- **Develop the middle.** Structure ideas in a sustained and persuasive way. Develop a clear topic sentence for each paragraph. Support each main point with details, including examples and paraphrases. If you are allowed to look at class notes or texts, include quotations and statistics.
- **Write a strong closing paragraph.** Restate your thesis statement and offer a final thought. If you are writing a persuasive piece, include a call to action.

After you've written a first draft . . .

- **Read through your work.** Add, cut, or move your details to make your work stronger and your organizational structure more logical. Look for places where a a rhetorical device can better convey your meaning. Make only the most important changes however, keeping your time limit in mind.
- **Check for conventions.** Find and correct any errors you find in grammar, sentence structure, mechanics (capitalization and punctuation), and spelling.

Differentiated Instruction: Advanced Learners

Challenge students to create a list of writing prompts for expository and persuasive essays. Then, as a class, review each prompt and answer the STRAP questions. Work as a group to create outlines or organizers for each prompt.

TEKS **11.13B** Structure ideas in a sustained and persuasive way and develop drafts in timed and open-ended situations that include transitions and rhetorical devices to convey meaning; **ELPS 1C** Use strategic learning strategies to acquire basic and grade-level vocabulary; **1F** Use accessible language and learn new and essential language in the process

TEKS 11.16A, 11.16B

Response to a Prompt

Mai Li wrote a response to the following prompt.

> *Convince the school board to improve one of your classes.*

The **beginning** supplies background information and presents the thesis statement (underlined).

Real Baby Care

Our parenting class tries to teach students what it's like to care for an infant. We have used eggs and sacks of flour to represent babies, but we need a more accurate feel for taking care of a real baby. The school board should purchase Baby Do All dolls.

The **middle** paragraphs cover the main supporting ideas.

The Baby Do All doll is physically realistic and offers sounds, from a contented sigh to an ear-piercing shriek. A student must feed, change, burp, or cuddle the doll. The baby can also be programmed to cry no matter what, just like a real baby, to help students understand that having a baby can be frustrating.

While students can easily ignore an egg or a flour sack, the Baby Do All doll cannot be ignored. The doll interacts with its "parent" through an electronic wristband. Wireless control units transmit data to the control board, so teachers can monitor care conveniently and accurately grade students on their baby care.

An objection is dealt with.

Although the Baby Do All doll is somewhat expensive, it can present students with the reality of caring for a baby. This may lower the number of teen pregnancies. Statistics support this idea, showing that a realistic doll has much more impact on students than an egg or a sack of flour. The entire experience of child care becomes more intense, more exhausting, and more real.

The **ending** restates the thesis and offers a final statement.

The school board should consider purchasing these dolls for the parenting class. If our students have a real taste of parenting short term, they may think twice before becoming parents for real and always.

Try It!

Choose a writing prompt from those given you by your teacher. Write your response in the time limit your teacher sets.

Response to a Prompt

Have students analyze the model prompt by answering the STRAP questions before they read the response.

- **Subject:** improve a class
- **Type:** persuasive essay
- **Role:** concerned student
- **Audience:** school board
- **Purpose:** persuade

✱ See SE page 266 for more about using the STRAP questions for responding to a persuasive prompt.

To help students analyze the essay, discuss with them the margin notes that accompany the student model. Use the following questions.

- What background information does the author give before stating his or her thesis? (Possible response: information on a typical parenting class)
- What relevant details does the author provide to support the main ideas? (Possible response: The Baby Do All doll cries for no apparent reason; the doll interacts with its "parent"; the doll forces students to experience the exhausting realities of parenthood)
- What objection does the author address? (the doll's high price)

TEKS 11.16A; 11.16B

Try It!
Answers

Have on hand a wide variety of prompts from which students can choose. Select prompts that require students to respond in narrative, expository, or persuasive writing forms.

✔ **DIFFERENTIATE INSTRUCTION** ✔ **DIFFERENTIATE INSTRUCTION**

TEKS **11.16A** Write an argumentative essay to the appropriate audience that includes a clear thesis or position based on logical reasons supported by precise and relevant evidence, including facts,, expert opinions, quotations, and/or expressions of commonly accepted beliefs; **11.16B** Write an argumentative essay to the appropriate audience that includes accurate and honest representation of divergent views; **ELPS** **5B** Write using newly acquired basic and content-based grade-level vocabulary

Other Forms of Practical Writing

The ideas for practical writing suggested on this page apply to specific life science classes. If some of these classes are not available to your students, adapt the ideas to suit classes offered in your school. Ask teachers of applied sciences classes in your district what kinds of practical writing students will be expected to complete.

Process Essay

Suggest other processes as appropriate to your school's curriculum.

Letter of Complaint

Direct students who write a letter of complaint to skim SE pages 538–539 for a refresher on correct business letter format and voice.

Essay of Analysis

Have partners use a T-chart to list and discuss positives and negatives. **DIFFERENTIATE INSTRUCTION** ⌄
✦ **ELPS** 1D, 3B

Persuasive Essay

Remind students to include a response to possible objections in the essay.

Essay of Explanation

Point out that students should include descriptive details in their explanations.

Problem-Solution Essay

Suggest other types of problems and solutions as appropriate to your school's curriculum.

Personal Narrative Essay

Invite students to suggest other relevant topics for this type of essay.

522

Other Forms of Practical Writing

Process Essay

Auto Mechanics Class— Explain the steps necessary for changing a tire. Use imperative sentences with verbs that give commands.

Letter of Complaint

*Living On Your Own Class—*Write a letter of complaint to your landlord, who has put off fixing a leaky faucet in your apartment. Include specific details about why you need it fixed soon. State your case in a cool, neutral tone, and include a call to action.

Essay of Analysis

Food and Nutrition Class— Analyze a popular weight-loss plan, giving both the positives and negatives of the plan. Give specific possible short-term and long-range effects on the body.

Persuasive Essay

Home Construction Class— Persuade a client building a new home to include central air-conditioning. Include details about cost, efficiency, comfort, and value.

Essay of Explanation

Sewing for the Home Class— Explain what fabrics you would use to create a sofa slipcover, a lamp shade, formal draperies, and throw pillows. Give your reasons for choosing each fabric.

Problem-Solution Essay

*Advanced Metals Fabrication Class—*You are suddenly faced with a contaminated electrode while working on a project. Give possible causes of the problem and explain your solution.

Personal Narrative Essay

*Child Care Class—*Remember a time you received a punishment you thought was unfair. Describe how you felt about it then, and explain whether you still feel the same way. Suggest a different punishment that may have been more effective.

ELPS **1D** Speak using learning strategies; **3B** Expand vocabulary/learning and using routine language needed for classroom communication

523

Writing in the Arts

Works of art or music stimulate your mind and trigger questions. Why did a painter use a particular medium? Why does an architect use certain materials? What are the roots of a particular style of music? How do different types of music and styles of art affect people's feelings? How are computer synthesizers and digital cameras changing music and art today?

As you explore the arts, through writing, you can deepen your understanding and enjoyment of these creative expressions. This chapter will help you write essays and reports about the arts. You may even want to try writing reviews of performances to share with others on your blog, on a Web site, or in the school newspaper.

- **Writing Guidelines:
  Research Report**
- **Writing Guidelines:
  Performance Review**

"Treat a work of art like a prince. Let it speak to you first."

—Arthur Schopenhauer

Writing in the Arts

Objective
- apply the writing process and traits of writing to a research report for art or music, a multimedia presentation of a research report, and a performance review

The lessons on the following pages provide samples of writing students might do in an art or music class. Assigning these forms of writing will depend on
- the skill level of your students,
- the subject matter they are studying in different arts classes, and
- the writing goals of your school, district, or state.

**Differentiated Instruction:
English Language Learners**

 ELPS 1D, 3B

ELP Level **Beginning**	ELP Level **Intermediate**	ELP Level **Advanced/Advanced High**
Present words related to the topic, such *food, nutrition, weight, health, exercise,* and *heart* and have students repeat each one. Model sorting the words into categories.	Have partners brainstorm words related to the topic and then discuss how the words could be used in describing positive and negative aspects of the weight-loss plan.	Have partner define and discuss technical language related to a weight-loss plan. Such language might include names of weight-related illnesses or conditions.

ELPS 1D Speak using learning strategies; **3B** Expand vocabulary/learning and using routine language needed for classroom communication

Writing Guidelines Research Report

Tell students to read the writing guidelines and the tips that follow carefully. Remind them to choose a topic that interests them and about which they can find enough information.

Prewriting

Provide students with the following tips for selecting and sizing up a topic for a short research report:

- Create a cluster to explore works of art and artists, films and directors, plays and playwrights, musical trends, and other topics in the arts.
- Circle three ideas in the cluster that you would enjoy writing about. Star the idea that interests you the most.
- Do some preliminary research on your starred topic. Use the Internet as well as other sources to find a focus for your report. List key details.
- If you cannot find enough material to support your research question, explore another topic. If the information available is overwhelming, narrow your focus or choose another topic.
- Once you have settled on a topic, formulate a research plan that will allow you to explore the topic in depth. Remember to gather evidence from experts and from multiple reliable sources.

TEKS 11.20B, 11.21A

✳ For more information on exploring and researching topics for a report, see SE pages 396–402.

Tip

Suggest that students share their topic ideas with a partner. Each partner should try to assess which topic most interests the other.

TEKS 11.20A

Writing Guidelines Research Report

You may be asked to write a research report in your art or music class. You may decide to write about a famous painter or analyze a trend in music. The following guidelines will help you create a research report.

Prewriting

- **Choose a subject.** If your teacher doesn't provide a specific subject, list artworks, artists, musical trends, or other ideas that interest you.
- **Brainstorm possible topics.** Consult with others about your ideas.
- **Pick two or three possible subjects** and make notes on what you already know about them. Jot down any questions you may have.
- **Pick the subject that most interests you** and about which you could write a complex and interesting report.
- **Conduct research on your subject.** Check your school or public library catalogs for books; look through magazines; explore Web sites; consult local experts on your topic. Look for information that includes precise and relevant data, such as facts, expert opinions, quotations, or expressions of commonly held beliefs.
- **As you research, formulate your major research question.** Use both primary and secondary sources, distinguish between reliable and unreliable sources, and avoid relying too much on a single source. Think about your readers and how much they need to know in order to understand your report. Find at least one source that presents an opinion different from yours. Keep good notes on all of your sources, including accurate bibliographical information.
- **Write a thesis statement.** Review your major research question and your notes. Take time to write a statement that accurately expresses the specific topic and focus of your report. Remember that your thesis question will act as a road map for your entire report. A carefully written thesis statement will make writing the rest of your report much easier.
- **Plan and organize.** Outline your paper, putting details in the most appropriate order—for example, you may put key points in spatial order, chronological order, or order of importance.

Tip

Choose a subject that interests you and about which you really want to learn more. It is difficult, if not impossible, to write an engaging report on a topic you don't care about.

TEKS **11.20A** Brainstorm, consult with others, decide upon a topic, and formulate a major research question to address the major research topic; **11.20B** Formulate a plan for engaging in in-depth research on a complex, multi-faceted topic; **11.21A** Follow the research plan to gather evidence from experts on the topic and texts written for informed audiences in the field, distinguishing between reliable and unreliable sources and avoiding over-reliance on one source

TEKS 11.21B, 11.22A, 11.22B

Arts

Prewriting Organizing Information

Once you have done some initial research, you can use a graphic organizer, conceptual map, or outline to organize your ideas.

- Choose an organizational pattern that works well for your topic and audience.
- Consider using spatial order, chronological order, or order of importance.
- Use only information that directly supports your thesis statement.
- Check that you have enough information to support each of your major points.
- If you do not have enough information, do additional research.

Refine Your Research Question

You may find as you research or develop a plan for writing, that you need to refine your research question and/or your thesis statement.

- If, at this point, you find that you would like to alter your focus or adjust your research question, do so.
- Refining and adjusting your research question is an important part of writing a successful essay.
- If you refine or adjust your research question, revise your thesis statement as needed.

Theories and Evidence

As part of your research, you will find both theories and evidence. It is important to be able to tell the difference between the two.

- *Theories* are unproven assumptions used to explain a situation or phenomenon.
- *Evidence* is factual information that furnishes proof.

Exercise

Label each sentence *theory* or *evidence*. Explain your answers.

1. Humor is an important factor in establishing a positive learning environment.
2. The artist Georgia O'Keeffe was born on November 15, 1887 in Sun Prairie, Wisconsin.
3. The function of a work of art is to embody beauty.
4. Pablo Picasso said, "Art washes away from the soul the dust of everyday life."
5. American painter and printmaker Mary Cassatt spent much of her adult life in France.

Prewriting Organizing Information

Have students use a gathering grid to record their information after they have selected a topic and written their major research question. Suggest that they use note cards to record definitions and examples related to unfamiliar vocabulary they encounter during research.

TEKS 11.21B; **ELPS** 1C

Refine Your Research Question

Students may balk at the idea of changing or refining their research question. Remind them that a good research question will serve as the basis for their thesis statement, which will in turn guide the organization and support for their research essay.

TEKS 11.22A

Theories and Evidence

Review the differences between theories and facts. Remind students that theories are assumptions or beliefs that need to be proven. Have students work with a partner. Together, have them find each other's theories and check that each theory is supported by relevant facts and evidence. DIFFERENTIATE INSTRUCTION

TEKS 11.22B; **ELPS** 1E

Exercise
Answers
1. theory
2. fact
3. theory
4. fact
5. fact

ELPS 1E

| Differentiated Instruction: English Language Learners | | ELPS 1C, 1E |

ELP Level **Beginning**	ELP Level **Intermediate**	ELP Level **Advanced/Advanced High**
Use visuals and gestures to explain the terms *theory* and *fact*, and have students repeat each one. Then work together to complete the Exercise.	Define *theory* and *fact*. Have partners work together to write at least two examples of theories and facts. Have them exchange papers with another pair to discuss each other's examples.	Have students write at least two examples of theories and facts. Have them exchange papers with another student to discuss what makes the examples fit each label.

 TEKS **11.21B** Systematically organize relevant and accurate information to support central ideas and concepts; **11.22A** Modify the research question as necessary to refocus the research plan; **11.22B** Differentiate between theories and the evidence that supports them and determine whether the evidence found is weak or strong and how that evidence helps create a cogent argument; **ELPS 1C** Use strategic learning strategies to acquire basic and grade-level vocabulary; **1E** Internalize new basic and academic language by using and reusing it/speaking and writing

Drafting

Remind students that including and accounting for a divergent viewpoint in their paper will strengthen rather than weaken their argument. Suggest that students share their divergent viewpoint with a partner. Partners should check that the divergent viewpoint is clearly stated and that each student's response to it is supported by relevant evidence.

Citing Your Research Materials

Work with students to make sure they understand the differences in format between sources cited within the text and sources listed on the Works-Cited page.

 TEKS 11.21C

How Evidence Shapes Arguments

Remind students that all theories must be supported by relevant and reliable evidence or facts. Have them check their papers to make sure there are no unsupported theories.

TEKS 11.22B

Stating Your Opinions

Have students locate an original idea or opinion in their papers. If they cannot find one, suggest that they go over their research notes with a fresh eye and make connections that add something new and original to their topic.

TEKS 11.23A

 **TEKS** 11.21C, 11.22B, 11.23A

Drafting

Remember that the purpose of your first draft is to get all of your ideas in writing and in an order that makes sense.

- Use your first paragraph to get your reader's attention, introduce your topic, and present your thesis statement.
- Your middle paragraphs should offer specific and reliable evidence that supports your thesis statement and your main ideas.
- Middle paragraphs should include a viewpoint that differs from your own. Explain or refute that viewpoint.
- Use your concluding paragraphs to summarize your main points and leave your reader with something to think about.

Citing Your Research Materials

The purpose of a Works-Cited page and of internal references within your paper is to let the reader easily view the sources of your information. Keep the following in mind when citing sources. (See pages **394**, **413**, and **445–454**.)

- **Your Works-Cited page should list all of the sources you consulted in alphabetical order.** Work from the notes you took as you were doing your research. Format the sources listed in your Works-Cited page in accordance with the instructions given by your teacher. Do not cite sources unless you actually used them.
- **Cite sources within your essay according to instructions given by your teacher.** In-text citations are placed in parentheses after the words or ideas taken from the source. In most cases, in-text citations need only include a word, such as the author's last name, and the page number on which the reference occurs. For example: (Bullough 5).

How Evidence Shapes Arguments

Just as relevant and reliable evidence will strengthen your essay, so irrelevant or unreliable evidence will weaken your essay. Ask yourself the following questions.

- Is my evidence based on facts, expert opinions, or commonly held assumptions?
- Does my evidence support my thesis statement and major points?
- Are my sources reliable? Are they current?

Stating Your Opinions

A good research paper should do more than summarize facts. To make your research interesting and engaging, you need to use your evidence to support an original idea related to your topic. Ask yourself the following questions.

- Have I developed an original idea or argument related to my topic?
- Have I supported my opinion with relevant evidence?

TEKS **11.21C** Paraphrase, summarize, quote, and accurately cite all researched information according to a standard format, differentiating among primary, secondary, and other sources; **11.22B** Differentiate between theories and the evidence that supports them; **11.23A** Synthesize the research into an extended written or oral presentation that provides an analysis that supports and develops personal opinions, as opposed to simply restating existing information

TEKS 11.23C

Revising **for** Focus and Coherence

When you revise for *focus and coherence*, you make sure that you have maintained your focus throughout your essay, and that your ideas are clearly connected to each other and to your thesis statement. You also check that you have included an engaging introduction that clearly states your thesis and a meaningful conclusion, and that your paper has an overall sense of completeness. Check also that your paper incorporates complexities and ambiguities related to your topic, including divergent views. Ask yourself the following questions.

Is my argument focused?

- Reread your opening paragraphs. Pay close attention to your thesis statement. Does it clearly define the focus of year essay?
- Reread the rest of your paper. Do all of your ideas and details support your thesis statement? If not, delete weak or irrelevant details.
- Reread your concluding paragraphs. Do they sum up your main ideas? Do they leave your reader with something to think about?

Do my ideas connect to each other and to my thesis statement?

- Check that all your ideas are clearly connected to and support your thesis statement.
- Rewrite sentences that do not establish a clear connection between ideas.

Do I address counterarguments?

- Check that you have included at least one opinion that differs from your own.
- Make sure that you have explained or rebutted divergent opinions.

Does my essay have an overall sense of completeness?

- Check that your introduction is engaging and adequately introduces your topic.
- Make sure that your concluding paragraphs sum up your main ideas and leave your readers with something to think about.

Tip

Include a divergent viewpoint. Your report will be considerably strengthened if you acknowledge and explain or rebut a viewpoint that differs from your own.

Arts

Revising **for** Focus and Coherence

Is my argument focused?

Have students share their papers with a partner to analyze their work for focus and coherence. Suggest they use the questions provided to guide their discussion. **DIFFERENTIATE INSTRUCTION**

ELPS 3D, 4K

Do my ideas connect to each other and to my thesis statement?

Remind students to use transitional words and phrases to connect ideas and give their essays a smooth and logical flow.

Do I address counterarguments?

Tell students that their research may uncover evidence that contradicts their thesis statement or evidence that adds complexities and ambiguities they had not previously considered. Remind them to account for evidence presented in all reliable sources.

TEKS 11.23C

Does my essay have an overall sense of completeness?

Have students share their concluding paragraphs with a partner to check that their essay ends in a satisfying way.

Tip

Encourage students to use transitional words, phrases, and clauses such as *on the other hand, in contrast,* or *Others disagree,* to introduce a divergent view.

 TEKS 11.23C Synthesize the research into an extended written and oral presentation that develops an argument that incorporates the complexities of and discrepancies in information from multiple sources and perspectives while anticipating and refuting counter-arguments; **ELPS** **3D** Speak using grade-level content-area vocabulary in context/new English words and academic language; **4K** Demonstrate English comprehension and expand reading skills by employing analytical skills

Revising for Organization

Remind students that part of revising for organization is checking that they have formatted in-text and works-cited citations correctly.

⭐ **TEKS** 11.23D

Does my paper have a clear organizational pattern?

Guide students to identify the organization pattern or patterns they have used. Then have partners discuss whether the pattern is used clearly and appropriately.

Does my organization suit my topic and my audience?

Remind students to check that each paragraph focuses on one topic and thoroughly develops the complexities of that topic.

⭐ **TEKS** 11.23E

Is each paragraph and sentence logically connected?

Provide examples, such as former students' papers, to have students analyze the use of repeated key words and ideas to link one paragraph to the paragraph that precedes it.

⭐ **ELPS** 4K

Exercise
Answers
Possible response:

Edgar Degas, a French artist renowned for his work in painting, sculpture, printmaking, and drawing and commonly regarded as one of the founders of French impressionism, is most widely associated with the subject of dance. Almost half of his work is devoted to the subject, and his portraits and drawings of dancers evidence his superb mastery at depicting movement.

DIFFERENTIATE INSTRUCTION ↘
⭐ **ELPS** 5F

 **TEKS** 11.23D, 11.23E

 Revising for Organization

When you revise for *organization*, you check the structure and the organizational pattern of your essay. Make sure that your paragraphs are organized in an order that works for your topic and for your audience. Check that your essay has a logical flow and that your ideas are connected by transitional words and phrases. Ask yourself the following questions.

Does my paper have a clear organizational pattern?

Some organizational patterns you might use for a research paper follow.
- Cause and effect
- Comparison-contrast
- Basic information to increasingly complex information
- Least persuasive evidence to most persuasive evidence
- Name the problem and give examples of solutions

Sometimes writers will use one or a combination of the organizational patterns listed above.

Does my organization suit my topic and my audience?

Reread your middle paragraphs or share them with a classmate. Ask the following questions.
- Have I used a logical organization throughout my essay?
- Are there sentences that are out of place and need to be moved?
- Are ideas connected by transitional words and phrases or repeated key words to connect ideas?

Is each paragraph and sentence logically connected?

- Make sure that each paragraph is linked to the paragraph before it. Repeat key words or ideas as needed to establish the connection.
- Check that none of your sentences are extraneous or repetitive. Delete or rewrite extraneous or repetive sentences.

Exercise

Rewrite the following paragraph to improve its organization by putting sentences in a more logical order or by adding transitional words and phrases to make the logical flow more clear.

Edgar Degas, a French artist renowned for his work in painting, sculpture, printmaking, and drawing, is widely regarded as one of the founders of French impressionism. Over half of his work depicts dancers. His portraits and drawings of dancers evidence his mastery at depicting movement. Degas is most widely associated with the subject of dance.

⭐ **TEKS 11.23D** Synthesize the research into an extended written or oral presentation that uses a style manual to document sources and format written materials; **11.23E** Synthesize the research into an extended written or oral presentation that is of sufficient length and complexity to address the topic; **ELPS 4K** Demonstrate English comprehension and expand reading skills by employing analytical skills; **5F** Write using a variety of grade-appropriate sentence lengths, sentence patterns, and connecting words

Revising for Development of Ideas

When you revise for *development of ideas*, you check that you have provided enough support and specific details to allow readers to understand your major points. You also check that rather than simply restating or summarizing existing information, you have provided an analysis of the topic that reflects your viewpoint. Finally, you look for ways to emphasize important points and clarify your ideas. Ask yourself questions such as the following:

- **Have I provided enough and the right kind of support?** You must not only provide support for your ideas but also check that your support is relevant. Delete support that is not relevant.
- **Have I layered my ideas and sufficiently developed my argument?** You have layered your ideas if each sentence adds meaning to the sentence that precedes it. Such layering makes your development of ideas apparent and adds depth to your overall report.
- **Does my report present my viewpoint rather than simply restate existing information?** Present your own viewpoint on your topic. Check that your viewpoint is something at least slightly controversial. If you state a viewpoint that everyone else would agree with, you will end up with a pretty bland and uninteresting report.

Using Rhetorical Devices

Check that you have used rhetorical devices to emphasize major ideas and to help clarify your thoughts. Consider using a rhetorical question, parallel structure, or an illuminating metaphor or simile.

Developing Your Argument

Review your report to be sure you have sufficiently developed your argument. Ask yourself the following questions.

- Have I created an intriguing thesis?
- Have I provided relevant support?
- Have I layered my ideas?
- Have I presented and answered a divergent viewpoint?
- Have I used rhetorical devices to emphasize or clarify important ideas?

Tip

Check your support. Make sure that you have developed thoroughly each of your major ideas and supported them with relevant details.

Revising for Development of Ideas

Have students work with a partner or in small groups to revise their essays for development of ideas. Suggest that they use the bulleted questions to guide their discussion.

Using Rhetorical Devices

Show examples of the effective use of rhetorical devices. Include examples of a rhetorical question, parallel structure, and an effective metaphor or simile. Tell students to use the examples as models when they revise their essays.

TEKS 11.23B; **ELPS** 5F

Developing Your Argument

Review with students the meaning of "layering ideas" (making sure that each idea builds on and adds to the idea that precedes it) and the importance of incorporating the complexities and ambiguities of multiple sources in their paper. Guide them to analzye the effects of layering ideas in their papers

TEKS 11.23C; **ELPS** 4K

Tip

Remind students to check that all of their details are relevant, that is, that they all directly support their major points.

Differentiated Instruction:
English Language Learners

ELPS 4K, 5F

ELP Level **Beginning**	ELP Level **Intermediate**	ELP Level **Advanced/Advanced High**
List transition or connecting words on the board and have students read them with you. Then model using the words to combine or rewrite sentences in the Exercise.	Have partners analyze and discuss the Exercise paragraph. Then have them work together to revise it, using a variety of sentence lengths and patterns.	Have students complete the Exercise independently, and then work with a partner to analyze and compare their revisions. Have them decide which is better and why.

TEKS **11.23B** Synthesize the research into an extended written or oral presentation that uses a variety of formats and rhetorical strategies to argue for the thesis; **11.23C** Synthesize the research into an extended written or oral presentation that develops an argument that incorporates the complexities of and discrepancies in information from multiple sources and perspectives while anticipating and refuting counter-arguments; **ELPS** **4K** Demonstrate English comprehension and expand reading skills by employing analytical skills; **5F** Write using a variety of grade-appropriate sentence lengths, sentence patterns, and connecting words

Editing

Point out that the editing stage of the writing process is the time to check writing for correct grammar, usage, and mechanics.

Understanding Noun Phrases and Clauses

Remind students that the careful use of noun phrases and noun clauses can help make their writing more concise (saying more with fewer words) and easier to read by helping them vary their sentence structures. Working with the examples on SE page 530, make sure that students understand how the use of noun phrases and clauses makes writing more concise and varies the usual subject-verb-object sentence order. Compare, for example, these sentences with the first sample sentence on SE page 530: *The woman from Georgia won. She won first prize in the contest.* Have students demonstrate understanding by incorporating noun phrases and clauses in their essays.

TEKS 11.17A; **ELPS** 5F

Checking Punctuation in Citations

Remind students that the punctuation they use for in-text citations and works-cited citations differs substantially. Tell them to check their style manuals or sheets to be sure they have cited their sources correctly. Finally, explain that style sheets and style manuals aren't intended to make their lives more difficult. Rather, the function of punctuation is to ease readers' comprehension so they can more easily follow the information in their text.

TEKS 11.18A

Editing

Understanding Noun Phrases and Clauses

A *noun phrase* is a group of words, usually a noun, modifiers, and articles, that together function in a sentence the way nouns do—as subjects and as objects of a verb or preposition. Remember, a phrase is a group of words that does not contain a verb.

> The Georgia woman won first prize in the contest.
>
> Noun phrase functioning as the subject of the sentence
>
> Noun phrase functioning as the direct object of the verb *won*

> The men in the class listened intently to the controversial speaker.
>
> Noun phrase functioning as the subject of the sentence
>
> Noun phrase functioning as the object of the preposition *to*

A *noun clause* is a subordinate or dependent clause that functions in a sentence the way nouns do—as subjects and as objects of a verb or preposition. Remember that a clause is a group of words that includes a subject and a predicate. A subordinate or dependent clause does not express a complete thought and cannot stand alone.

> I don't know when he can be reached.
>
> Noun clause functioning as the object of the verb *know*

> Whoever shows up can audition for a part.
>
> Noun clause functioning as the subject of the verb *can audition*

Checking Punctuation in Citations

Correct punctuation is a very important part of citing references both in your text and in your Works-Cited list. Be sure to use your teacher's preferred formatting method. (See pp. 394, 413, 445–452 for the formatting of an MLA paper.)

- **In-text citations** In-text citations direct readers to an entry in your Works-Cited list. Keep your in-text citations brief, providing the reader with either the author's last name or, if there is no author, a short title of the work. There is no punctuation between the author's name or the title of the work.
- **Works-Cited list** Follow the format indicated by your teacher exactly. Pay particular attention to the order in which information is given and to standard abbreviations and punctuation of various types of entries.

Differentiated Instruction: Struggling Learners

To help students analyze the organization of the report, have them work together to create an outline that Kerrie might have used in her prewriting stage. Remind students to look for the topic sentence of each paragraph.

Writing in the Arts **531**

Research Report

Artists reflect their own culture and background when they create works of art. Kerrie Shiver saw a painting by artist Frida Kahlo in a museum and became interested in her work. After researching this famous Mexican artist, she wrote the following report.

Arts

Frida Kahlo: Pioneering Mexican Artist

Author uses a rhetorical device (rhetorical question) to engage readers.

Looking at Frida Kahlo's paintings one is immediately struck by their direct and uncompromising view of life. Coupled with this starkness is vibrant color, simpicity of style, and a calm serenity that infuses many of her paintings. It is a startling and often confusing combination. Who was Frida Kahlo and what influenced her to create such an unforgettable paintings?

Opening paragraphs introduce the topic and lead in to the author's thesis statement (underlined).

Frida Kahlo was born in Mexico in 1907. Her father was a German immigrant and photographer while her mother was of Mexican and Indian descent. As a child she was influenced both by her dual heritage and by her experiences helping her father touch up photographs with delicate brushstrokes. As important as these early influences were, however, the key to understanding Kahlo's art is appreciating the extent to which her personal experience of physical and emotion pain permeated her work, infusing it with a grim and startling power.

Middle paragraphs detail pivotal events in the painter's life.

When she was only six years old, Kahlo was struck by polio. The disease left her right leg whithered, a deformity she often disguised by wearing colorful, long skirts. When she was eighteen more tragedy struck. Kahlo, at the time a medical student, was seriously injured in a bus accident. An iron railing crashed through her right hip, shattering her spine and right leg (Turner 2). Her injuries resulted in long hospitalizations, multiple surgeries, and a lifetime filled with pain. As would be typical of her throughout her life, Kahlo did everything she could to turn her personal tragedy into the subject matter of art. Recalling when her father took pictures of her after her accident, Kahlo said, "I started looking straight at the lens, unflinching, unsmiling, determined to show I was a good fighter to the end" (Turner 3).

Relevant quotes support the author's argument.

Research Report

Have students read the model research report and then discuss with them the model's margin notes and the following questions to help them recognize why this is a well-written report.

✔ **DIFFERENTIATE INSTRUCTION**

- What rhetoricial device does the author use in the opening paragraphs? (a rhetorical question: *Who was Frida . . . unforgettable paintings.*)
- How do the middle paragraphs support the thesis? (Specific details explain the sources of Kahlo's personal and physical pain and how she expressed this pain in her artwork.)
- What organizational plan does Kerrie use? (logical order—The first two middle paragraphs provide background information explaining how her accident and her later her marriage to Diego Rivera, affected Kahlo's artistic career. The next two paragraphs discuss how Kahlo's personal pain and Mexican culture influenced her art. The last two paragraphs cite and address a divergent viewpoint and then summarize the entire paper.) ✔ **DIFFERENTIATE INSTRUCTION**
- Elicit from students that the author's use of in-text citations is evidence of the use of multiple sources to investigate complexities and discrepancies in information.

TEKS 11.23A, 11.23B, 11.23C, 11.23D, 11.23E

Differentiated Instruction:
English Language Learners

ELPS 1C, 4D, 4F

ELP Level **Beginning**	ELP Level **Intermediate**	ELP Level **Advanced/Advanced High**
Provide prereading support by teaching the words *dual, physical, emotional,* and *subject matter.* Have students repeat each word, and answer yes-no questions to show comprehension.	Preteach words such as *vibrant, serenity,* and *influenced.* Have partners create webs for each word and then use the words in sentences that relate to art.	Have partners identify and define any unfamiliar vocabulary before reading the essay. Have them use the words in sentences that relate to art.

TEKS **11.23A** Synthesize the research into an extended written or presentation that provides an analysis that supports and develops personal opinions, as opposed to simply restating existing information; **11.23B** Synthesize the research into an extended written or presentation that uses a variety of formats and rhetorical strategies to argue for the thesis; **11.23C** Synthesize the research into an extended written or presentation that develops an argument that incorporates the complexities of and discrepancies in information from multiple sources and perspectives while anticipating and refuting counter-arguments; **11.23D** Synthesize the research into an extended written or presentation that uses a style manual to document sources and format written materials; **11.23E** Synthesize the research into an extended written or presentation that is of sufficient length and complexity to address the topic; **ELPS** **1C** Use strategic learning strategies to acquire basic and grade-level vocabulary; **4D** Use prereading supports to enhance comprehension of written text; **4F** Use support from peers and teacher to develop vocabulary and background knowledge

Remind students of the importance of engaging their readers in their report. Have them reread SE pages 531 and 532 silently and then work in pairs to find parts of the essay that they think are likely to engage and interest readers. (Possible response: opening rhetorical question, specific biographical details about Kahlo's injury and marriage, use of Kahlo's direct quotations, descriptions of her paintings)

ELPS 4H

Direct students' attention to the format of in-text citations shown on SE page 532 *(Hubbard 85; Gates 172; Garza 113).*

Had it not been for this tragic accident, Kahlo might have never taken up painting. During her long recuperation, Kahlo began painting, as she put it, "to combat the boredom and the pain" (About Frida 1). Her parents had a mirror fitted onto her hospital bed, and thus Kahlo became her own first painting subject and would eventually do many self-portraits. "I paint myself," she said "because I am so often alone and because I am the subject I know best." (Hubbard 85).

A turbulent marriage to fellow artist Diego Rivera, added more pain and ultimately fueled her art (Herrera 150). For much of her life, Kahlo's art was overshadowed by her husband's work. In fact, when she died in 1954, the *New York Times* described her as the wife of the great Mexican muralist Diego Rivera and only once mentioned that "she also was a painter" (Gates 172).

Kahlo's work is vibrant, provocative, revolutionary, and sometimes disturbing. The strong colors in her paintings reflect the simple, vivid tones popular in her country's folk art and in Mexican clothing and decoration. She frequently adapted folk forms and religious symbols and devices in her work. For example, in one famous self-portrait, she used the form of a retablo, a traditional Mexican folk style that shows saints and miracles. Kahlo identified strongly with Mexico's indigenous people and was deeply influenced by the surge of nationalism that developed in the early twentieth century. She often wore traditional Mexican clothing and braided and decorated her hair with flowers, ribbons, and bows in her self-portraits. Her black hair and strongly marked eyebrows further accentuated her Mexican heritage and add to the vivid impact of her self-portraits (Garza 113).

What most characterizes Kahlo's work, however, is its relationship to her own life. Drawing deeply on her own personal experiences, her work is marked by harsh portrayals of pain. In her self-portraits she painted herself as she was—staring defiantly straight ahead. Often, her pain and physical ailments were symbolized in her paintings—a broken column, for example, in place of her spine.

Relevant biographical details support the author's thesis.

Author addresses cultural influences on Kahlo's art.

Writer adds support for the thesis statement.

ELPS **4H** Read silently with increasing ease and comprehension

Writer cites and rebuts a divergent viewpoint.

Critics who cite the clear autobiographical theme in Kahlo's work as a failing and accuse her of portraying the stereotypical ideal of a quietly suffering woman miss an obvious point: there is nothing quiet or resigned about Kahlo's art. Rather, it is a loud, colorful, and defiant testament by a woman determined to live life to the fullest (Mencimer 5).

Writer concludes with a summary of the impact of Kahlo's work.

Today Kahlo's Casa Azul, or Blue House, in Mexico City is a major tourist attraction. "Mexicans don't lead what you would call an easy life, so in a certain way we see that tragedy reflected in her paintings," said one Mexico City resident in an interview with the *New York Times*. "Although we don't suffer the same exact problems, we can see that she was able to overcome hers . . . and it gives us pride that people in other countries know her and identify with her" (Gates 183).

Note: Here are examples of two of the full references listed in Kerrie's Works-Cited list.

Mencimer, Stephanie. "The Trouble with Frida Kahlo." *Washington Monthly* June 2002: 1–9. Web.

Herrera, Hayden. *Frida: A Biography of Frida Kahlo.* New York: Harper & Row, 1983. Print.

Respond to the reading. Answer the following questions about the report.

Focus and Coherence (1) What is the author's main argument?

Organization (2) What organizational pattern does the author use?

Development of Ideas (3) What kind of details support the author's ideas?

Voice (4) What techniques does the author use to engage readers?

Differentiated Instruction:
English Language Learners

 ELPS 4F

ELP Level **Beginning**	ELP Level **Intermediate**	ELP Level **Advanced/Advanced High**
Provide visuals of Kahlo's art to support understanding of the essay and to build background. Then model using the context of the essay to answer each question.	Have partners build background by analyzing examples of Kahlo's art and relating them to the essay. Have them work together to answer each question.	Have students locate examples of Kahlo's art and relate them to the context of the essay before answering the questions. Have them use the art to support their answers.

Have students work in pairs to examine the first paragraph on SE page 533. Suggest that they analyze and discuss the following questions.

■ What divergent view does the author address? (critics who accuse Kahlo of portraying a stereotypical quietly suffering woman)

■ How does the author address this divergent viewpoint? (with evidence of Kahlo's loud and defiant art) ✓ DIFFERENTIATE INSTRUCTION

✦ ELPS 4G, 4K

The Note at the bottom of the page refers to Kerrie's list of sources at the end of her report. (Call attention to the in-text citations in parentheses in the model research report.) Explain that these citations refer to resources the writer used for specific facts. Tell students to use this as a model for providing source information in their report.

✱ If students are required to turn in a works-cited page with their report, encourage them to take the time to review the guidelines for formatting reference sources on SE pages 394 and 413.

Respond to the reading

Answers

Focus and Coherence 1. that Kahlo's physical and emotional pain permeated her art

Organization 2. logical order

Development of Ideas 3. specific biographical details, descriptions of her art

Voice 4. rhetorical questions, direct quotations, evocative biographical details
✓ DIFFERENTIATE INSTRUCTION

✦ ELPS 4G, 4K

 ELPS 4F Use visual and contextual support to read content area text, enhance and confirm understanding, and develop background knowledge; **4G** Demonstrate comprehension of increasingly complex English/responding to questions; **4K** Demonstrate English comprehension and expand reading skills by employing analytical skills

Multimedia Presentation of Your Research Report

Point out that writing in the arts is especially well-suited for multimedia presentations.

Investigating Types of Multimedia Presentations

Have students work in pairs or in small groups to explore the type of multimedia presentation that would work best with their topic. Suggest that students consider and discuss the following.

- What kinds of multimedia information are readily available for your topic (news reports, graphics, photographs, artifacts, music)?
- As you imagine your report presented in a multimedia format, what would you want to visualize and hear? What should you include?
- If you plan to use visuals, will you use a storyboard (a series of panels representing scenes or visual sequences) to map out ideas?

 TEKS 11.15D; **ELPS** 1D, 3F

Choosing Your Multimedia Format

Tell students to think carefully about their audience and the things that would engage them as they plan their multimedia presentations.

Giving Yourself Enough Time

Tell students that in many ways a multimedia presentation requires more planning than a research paper because it usually requires that several elements to work smoothly together. Remind them to allow for the planning and time needed to coordinate all the elements.

 TEKS 11.15D

Multimedia Presentation of Your Research Report

One way to share the work you've done in your research report is to create a multimedia presentation that synthesizes your information and presents it in a visual and/or auditory format. If you are considering a multimedia presentation, think carefully about your topic and what multimedia formats would best suit it. (See pages **464–467**.)

Investigating Types of Multimedia Presentations

The type of multimedia presentation you choose will depend in large measure on your topic. If, for example, your paper investigates the work of a visual artist as Kerrie's does, you will want to include visual examples of the artist's work. If you analyze the work of a musician, you will want to include recordings of the musician's work. Below are some types of multimedia presentations you might want to consider.

- Power presentation
- Dramatic presentation
- Class newspaper article
- News report
- Audio presentation
- Graphics or images
- Interactive Web page
- Documentary
- Docudrama
- Slide show
- Visual or text parodies

Choosing Your Multimedia Format

Think about the content and focus of your report and the type of information you want to present. Think also about your audience and their interests. Ask yourself the following questions.

- What is the purpose of my report? Is it to inform, persuade, narrate, or demonstrate?
- What about my audience? Is there a particular format that I should use to engage them?
- Do I have special skills that I could bring to a multimedia presentation, or will I need to get help?

Giving Yourself Enough Time

An effective multimedia presentation takes time to plan and execute. Give yourself enough time to let your creative juices flow, choose the most effective media, plan your presentation carefully, get help if you need it, and rehearse your presentation.

TEKS **11.15D** Produce a multimedia presentation with graphics, images, and sound that appeals to a specific audience and synthesizes information from multiple points of view; **ELPS** **1D** Speak using learning strategies; **3F** Give information during extended speaking assignments

---

Differentiated Instruction: Advanced Learners

Point out that review writers strive to convey a strong opinion in an open and often entertaining way. Have students bring in published examples of performance reviews to analyze. Have them determine the tone of each piece; for example, entertaining, witty, wry, serious, or harsh.

TEKS 11.13A, 11.13B, 11.15A(i), 11.15A(iv), 11.15A(v)

Writing Guidelines Performance Review

You may be asked to write about the arts by reviewing a specific performance. On the other hand, you may enjoy a performance so much that you want to share your thoughts with others through a blog, on your own Web site, or in a letter to someone.

While this type of writing is more informal, or personal, than most academic writing, you should follow basic writing guidelines. Readers will respect your evaluation if your writing shows clarity and insight, so be sure to maintain your focus throughout the review.

Prewriting

- **Focus on what you want to say.**
- **Make notes** on your impressions of a painting, show, or concert.
- **Write a thesis statement.** Review your notes and state your focus.
- **Plan and organize.** Outline key points you want to make in your review.

Drafting

- **Write freely,** always keeping your main idea in mind. Use your outline as a basic writing guide.
- **Use examples to support your points.** Whether readers agree with you or not, they will appreciate what you've written if you support your point of view with solid evidence.
- **Keep your audience in mind** in terms of what you might need to explain and what your audience might want to know.
- **Write a strong ending.** Sum up why the topic was important enough for you to write about it.

Revising

- **Improve your writing.** Check your focus and coherence, organization, development of ideas, and voice. Ask these questions: *Have I created a clear thesis? Have I supported it with a variety of details? Are my details in the best order? Do I sound knowledgeable?*
- **Improve your style.** Check that you have used varied sentence structures. Ask these questions: *Have I used varied sentence lengths and structures? Do my sentences flow smoothly?*

Editing

- **Check for conventions.** Look for errors in grammar, sentence structure, mechanics (capitalization and punctuation), and spelling.
- **Prepare your final copy.** Proofread your research paper before turning it in.

Arts

Writing Guidelines Performance Review

Provide several examples of professional reviews of the same performance. Point out that even when reviewers pan a performance, they still use formal language. Have students provide specific details to demonstrate their ability to distinguish between formal and informal English.

✔ **DIFFERENTIATE INSTRUCTION** ✔ **DIFFERENTIATE INSTRUCTION**

ELPS 1G

Prewriting

If students will be attending a performance as part of another class, encourage them to write a review of the performance. Be sure students read the model music review on SE page 536 before writing their own reviews.

Drafting

Remind students that their introduction should engage readers and include a statement reflecting their overall assessment of the performance. Remind them also to support their major points with relevant and specific details and to organize those details in a logical order.

TEKS 11.13A, 11.13B, 11.15A(i), 11.15A(iv), 11.15A(v)

Revising

Suggest that students share their drafts with a partner and ask for feedback, using the questions provided on SE page 535 to guide their discussion.

Editing

Tell students to check the final papers for any errors in conventions: grammar, sentence structure, capitalization, punctuation, and spelling.

Differentiated Instruction:
English Language Learners

ELPS 4F

ELP Level **Beginning**	ELP Level **Intermediate**	ELP Level **Advanced/Advanced High**
Use gestures to discuss words that could describe a performance, such as *exciting, lively, boring,* or *dull.* Model completing sentence stems such as *The show was _____.*	Have partners brainstorm words that could describe a performance. Then have them complete sentence stems such as *The show was____,* or *The part I liked best was _____.*	Have partners list positive or negative words that could be used in describing a performance. Tell them to consult the lists as they write their reviews.

TEKS **11.13A** Plan a first draft by selecting the correct genre for conveying the intended meaning to multiple audiences; **11.13B** Develop drafts in timed and open-ended situations that include transitions and rhetorical devices to convey meaning; **11.15A(i)** Write an analytical essay of sufficient length that includes effective introductory and concluding paragraphs and a variety of sentence structures; **11.15A(iv)** Write an analytical essay of sufficient length that includes a clear organizational schema for conveying ideas; **11.15A(v)** Write an analytical essay of sufficient length that includes relevant and substantial evidence and well-chosen details; **ELPS** **1G** Demonstrate ability to distinguish between formal and informal English and knowledge of when to use formal and informal English; **4F** Use support from peers and teachers to develop vocabulary and background knowledge

Performance Review

Discuss the model music review as a class, or have students discuss the review in small groups. Provide these questions to guide students' discussion of their opinions, ideas, and feelings. Remind students to adjust their spoken language for an informal discussion. **DIFFERENTIATE INSTRUCTION** ↘

- How does Antonio engage readers in the opening paragraph? (Possible response: He recalls the rainy weather, uses vivid verbs and adjectives, and offers an enthusiastic assessment.)
- What is Antonio's opinion of the Lima Beans' performance? (very positive)
- What details does Antonio use to support his opinion? (Possible response: focuses on the performance of specific pieces and specific members of the group)
- How is the essay organized? (logical order, with an introduction that includes a thesis statement; middle paragraphs that provide specific supporting details; and a conclusion that sums up the review and leaves the reader with something to think about)
- Would you trust Antonio's opinion? Explain. (Accept reasonable responses.)
- What part of the review do you like best? Why? (Accept reasonable responses.)

⭐ **TEKS** 11.15A(i) 11.15A(iv), 11.15A(v); **ELPS** 3E, 3G, 3I, 3J

⭐ **TEKS** 11.15A(i), 11.15A(iv), 11.15A(v)

Performance Review

The Lima Beans, the nationally known Lima High School of the Arts jazz ensemble, performed at Antonio's high school. He wrote the following review to post on a jazz fan Web site.

> **Lima Beans Jazz It Up!**
>
> On the cold, rainy evening of March 21, people who attended the Lima Beans in concert at South High School found themselves immersed in a jazzy blast of spring. The Lima Beans dazzled with cool, crisp rhythms and passionate improvisations that lit up the gym. The Ohio-based ensemble from the Lima High School of the Arts proved that young musicians can master the challenges of jazz when they combine creativity and hard work.
>
> The group showcased their knowledge of the fundamentals as they led off with the classic "Satin Doll." The Lima Beans then explored complex and enchanting improvisations of some jazz standards. Igor Liban on the tenor sax did breathtaking displays of that instrument's range. Keyboardist Johnny Black brought power and a satin-smooth touch to his rendition of "Cry Me a River." Later, Juniper Green drummed up a furious compelling beat in "It Don't Mean a Thing (If It Ain't Got that Swing)." Bass player Aldar Winski led the way through some playful improvisations of "April in Paris" and "The Way You Look Tonight." All the musicians exhibit talent and intense energy as they perform, and it's evident they are having fun.
>
> Because of the demands of their academic studies, the Lima Beans don't have a tour schedule. If given the chance, any jazz enthusiast should hear these gifted young musicians on the road to jazz fame.

The beginning clearly states the writer's reaction to the performance.

The middle offers supporting details and demonstrates knowledge of the subject.

The ending summarizes the writer's opinion and invites others to discover this group.

⭐ **TEKS** **11.15A(i)** Write an analytical essay of sufficient length that includes effective introductory and concluding paragraphs and a variety of sentence structures; **11.15A(iv)** Write an analytical essay of sufficient length that includes a clear organizational schema for conveying ideas; **11.15A(v)** Write an analytical essay of sufficient length that includes relevant and substantial evidence and well-chosen details; **ELPS** **3E** Share information in cooperative learning interactions; **3G** Express opinions, ideas, and feelings; **3I** Adapt spoken language for formal and informal purposes; **3J** Respond orally to information presented/concept and language attainment

Writing in the Workplace

Whatever career you're planning—police officer, customer-service representative, nurse, lawyer, executive assistant, video game designer—chances are, writing will be part of your job. Although the forms of writing may be changing—a customer-service representative often writes an e-mail message to a customer rather than a formal, typed letter—the essentials remain the same.

As a student, you will write business letters and e-mail messages to seek information, apply for a job, and deal with problems. You may also use other forms of workplace communication—memos, proposals, and meeting agendas—at school, in a summer or part-time job, or as part of your work with an organization or a club. This chapter shows you some of the tools and techniques that will help you with your workplace writing.

- **Parts of a Business Letter**
- **Writing Guidelines: Proposal**
- **Writing Guidelines: E-Mail Message**
- **Writing Guidelines: How To Conduct a Business Meeting**
- **Writing Guidelines: How To Take Minutes During a Business Meeting**

"Put it before them briefly so they will read it, clearly so they will appreciate it, picturesquely so they will remember it, and above all, accurately so they will be guided by its light."

—Joseph Pulitzer

Writing in the Workplace

Objectives
- learn the proper form for business letters, including a letter of inquiry or request, and a letter of application
- learn how to address an envelope
- apply the writing process and the traits of writing to a proposal, a workplace memo, an e-mail message, a business meeting agenda, and minutes of a business meeting

The lessons on the following pages provide samples of writing students might do in the workplace. Assigning these forms of writing will depend on
- the skill level of your students, and
- the writing goals of your school, district, or state.

Parts of a Business Letter

Share examples of business form letters that do not contain private or sensitive personal information, or black out such content. Discuss the similarities in the format and purpose of each—for example, to request information, to apply for a position, to offer a service, and so forth.

★ **TEKS** 11.15B(i); **ELPS** 4F

Review the parts of a business letter, using the letter on SE page 539 as a model. Point out common formatting structures in the letters you shared.

★ **TEKS** 11.15B(ii)

Elicit from students the differences in tone and language used in a friendly letter and a business letter (friendly letter is informal; business letter is formal, using language suited to the audience). Note that business letters may also include technical language related to the product or service the business provides and that writers must sometimes explain such terms in language that is understandable to all.

DIFFERENTIATE INSTRUCTION ↘

★ **TEKS** 11.15B(iv); **ELPS** 1G

Many students rarely send a letter through the postal service. Emphasize that even if students don't currently have many opportunities to write or send business letters, they will have them in the near future, as they get closer to graduation and write to businesses and colleges. Remind students they can also apply what they learn about the format of a business letter to writing professional e-mail messages.

★ **TEKS** 11.15B(i), 11.15B(ii), 11.15B(iv)

Parts of a Business Letter

Writers use business letters to request information, apply for a job, or file a complaint. The basic format of an effective letter is similar whether it is sent through the regular mail or delivered via e-mail.

- The **heading** includes the writer's complete address, either on company stationery, in a computer template, or typed out manually. The heading also includes the day, month, and year. If the address is part of the letterhead, place only the date in the upper left-hand corner.

- The **inside address** includes the recipient's name and complete address. If you're not sure who should receive the letter or how to correctly spell someone's name, you can call the company to ask. If a person's title is a single word or very short, include it on the same line as the name, preceded by a comma. If the title is longer, put it on a separate line under the name.

- The **salutation** is the greeting. For business letters, use a colon following the recipient's name, not a comma. Use Mr. or Ms. followed by the person's last name, unless you happen to be well acquainted with the person. Do not guess at whether a woman prefers *Miss* or *Mrs*. If the person's gender is not obvious from the name, one acceptable solution is to use the full name in the salutation. For example, *Dear Pat Johnson*. If you don't know the name of the person who will read your letter, use a salutation such as one of these:

  - Dear Manager:
  - Dear Sir or Madam:
  - Attention: Human Resources Department
  - Attention: Personnel Director

- The **body** is the main part of the letter. It is organized in three parts. The beginning states why you are writing, the middle provides the needed details, and the ending focuses on what should happen next. In a business letter, double-space between the paragraphs; do not indent. If the letter is longer than one page, on subsequent pages put the reader's name at the top left, the page number in the center, and the date at the right margin.

- The **complimentary closing** ends the message. Use *Sincerely* or *Yours truly*—followed by a comma. Capitalize only the first word.

- The **signature** makes the letter official. Leave four blank lines between the complimentary closing and your typed name. Write your signature in that space.

- The **notes** tell who authored the letter (uppercase initials and a colon), who typed the letter (lowercase initials), who received a copy (after *cc:*), and what enclosures are included (after *Enclosure* or *Encl:*).

★ **TEKS** **11.15B(i)** Write procedural or work-related documents that include a clearly stated purpose combined with a well-supported viewpoint on the topic; **11.15B(ii)** Write procedural or work-related documents that include appropriate formatting structures; **11.15B(iv)** Write procedural or work-related documents that include accurate technical information in accessible language; **ELPS** **1G** Demonstrate ability to distinguish between formal and informal English; **4F** Use visual and contextual support and support from teachers and peers to develop background knowledge

Differentiated Instruction: Struggling Learners

Discuss the importance of using a formal voice when writing a business letter. Also focus on the length of a business letter, limiting it to one page, if possible. Note that it should be long enough to convey the main point —but short enough that the recipient will read the whole letter attentively.

Letter of Inquiry or Request

The management of a local mall has expressed concern about the number of teenagers gathering there after school. The Irving High School Student Council president, Lucas Haynes, wrote a letter to the mall's manager. A list of recommendations is enclosed, and the school's vice principal is copied.

Workplace

Heading

Irving High School Student Council
512 E. Lincolnview Ave.
Rockwall, TX 75087
November 10, 2011

Four to Seven Spaces

Inside Address

Ms. Alicia Guerrero, Manager
Lincoln Mall
598 E. Lincolnview Ave.
Rockwall, TX 75087

Double Space

Salutation

Dear Ms. Guerrero:

Double Space

The writer explains who he is and why he is writing, provides needed details, and suggests a next step.

I am writing on behalf of the student council of Irving High School. We are aware of your concerns about student behavior after school in the Lincoln Mall. In addition, some students have complained to school administrators and student council members about their treatment by the mall security staff.

Many students enjoy gathering at the mall after school to visit with friends. During the winter, weather makes it difficult to spend much time outside on the school grounds. Of course, many students also enjoy shopping at Lincoln Mall.

We would like to invite you to meet with the student council officers and Mr. Washington, Irving's vice principal, to discuss the situation and work to resolve any problems.

I have enclosed a list of recommendations the student council developed to help solve the problem. If you are willing to meet with us, please contact Ms. Joyce Brown in the school office at 555-4200 ext. 10 to arrange a date and time.

Double Space

Complimentary Closing

Sincerely,

Signature

Lucas Haynes   *Four Spaces*

Lucas Haynes,
Student Council President

Double Space

**Initials
Copies
Enclosure**

LH:jb
cc: Mr. Isaac Washington
Encl: Student Council recommendations

Letter of Inquiry or Request

If students use a classroom or school computer to compose letters, take time to review the business-letter templates that are provided with the computers' word-processing programs. Most templates should conform to the formatting structures shown on SE page 539. If they do not, they can be quickly and easily modified. Most word-processing programs provide a function on the file-saving menu for users to create their own templates or stationery files. Such files cannot be written over accidentally. If this function is available with the computer software your students are using, encourage them to create their own business-letter template that they can use whenever they write a business letter.

⭐ TEKS 11.15B(ii)

Discuss the model letter on SE page 539. Use the margin notes to discuss basic formatting elements. Point out the use of formal language and the content of the writer's letter, in particular his introduction, statement of purpose, and appeal to his audience; the details and practical suggestions that consider the reader's needs provided in the middle two paragraphs, and the information included in the concluding paragraph. ✔DIFFERENTIATE INSTRUCTION

⭐ TEKS 11.15B(i), 11.15B(iii)

TEKS **11.15B(i)** Write procedural or work-related documents that include a clearly stated purpose combined with a well-supported viewpoint on the topic; **11.15B(ii)** Write procedural or work-related documents that include appropriate formatting structures; **11.15B(iii)** Write procedural or work-related documents that include relevant questions that engage readers and consider their needs; **ELPS 1G** Demonstrate ability to distinguish between formal and informal English; **3B** Expand vocabulary/retelling simple stories and basic information and learning and using routine language needed for classroom communication; **4F** Use visual and contextual support and support from peers and teachers to develop background knowledge

Letter of Application

Point out that in order to impress a prospective employer, job applicants sometimes use overblown language or long descriptions of glowing qualifications instead of presenting an honest portrayal of who they are and why they are qualified for the position. Explain that a writer who comes across as pompous may actually lose the reader's interest and the opportunity for employment.

Have students work in small groups to discuss the following tips for writing a successful letter of application. Allow time for each group to summarize their discussion for the class.

- DO follow correct business-letter formatting structures and write with a clear organization.
- DO summarize your background and experience, but provide only those facts related to the purpose of recommending you to the job.
- DO give information about your availability, and provide important contact information.
- DO use respectful language, but let your true personality come through.
- DO provide references.
- DON'T use someone's name as a reference without asking permission ahead of time.
- DON'T use slang or casual language.
- DON'T use language that is exaggerated or artificial.

TEKS 11.15B(i), 11.15B(ii), 11.15B(v); **ELPS** 4G

 **TEKS** 11.15B(i), 11.15B(ii), 11.15B(v)

Letter of Application

Keisha Bingham wrote the following letter to apply for a summer job at a church camp.

Keisha Bingham
148 Helmer St.
Navarro, TX 75151
April 28, 2011

Clara Taylor, Camp Director
Missionary Baptist Church
433 Lehner Ave.
Navarro, TX 75151

Dear Ms. Taylor:

> The opening introduces the writer as well as the purpose of the letter.

My name is Keisha Bingham. I'm completing my junior year in high school. My friend, Kayla Warner, who is a member of your church, mentioned that Camp Wawasee always needs summer help. I am interested in applying for a job as a counselor this summer.

For the past two summers, I have worked as a full-time babysitter for Mr. and Mrs. Joseph Adams, a couple with four children now ages 5, 7, 8, and 11. I have also volunteered in the Sunday School at Grace Baptist Church, helping with crafts.

> The middle paragraphs discuss background and qualifications.

In my paid and volunteer positions, I was responsible for caring for and supervising young children. My future goal is to become a school psychologist, so working at the camp would fit with my interests and career plans. I have taken courses in child care and child development.

> The closing adds information and thanks the reader.

I can supply letters of recommendation from Mr. and Mrs. Adams and from Grace Sanderson, my supervisor at the Sunday School. You may contact me at the address above, by e-mail at Keishabingham@ localmail.com, or by phone at 555-1239. Thank you for considering my application.

Sincerely,

Keisha Bingham

> Signature

Keisha Bingham

TEKS **11.15B(i)** Write procedural or work-related documents that include a clearly stated purpose combined with a well-supported viewpoint on the topic; **11.15B(ii)** Write procedural or work-related documents that include appropriate formatting structures; **11.15B(v)** Write procedural or work-related documents that include appropriate organizational structures supported by facts and details; **ELPS 4G** Demonstrate comprehension of increasingly complex English/ retelling or summarizing

TEKS 11.15B(ii), 11.15B(v)

Preparing the Letter for Mailing

Letters sent through the mail will get to their destinations faster if they are properly addressed and stamped. Always include a ZIP code.

Addressing the Envelope

Place the return address in the upper left corner, the destination address in the center, and the correct postage in the upper right corner. Some word processing programs will automatically format the return and destination address.

KEISHA BINGHAM
148 HELMER ST
NAVARRO, TX 75151

MS CLARA TAYLOR
MISSIONARY BAPTIST CHURCH
433 LEHNER AVE
NAVARRO, TX 75151

There are two acceptable forms for addressing the envelope: the traditional form and the new form preferred by the postal service.

Traditional Form	Postal Service Form
Liam O'Donnell	LIAM O'DONNELL
Macalester College	MACALESTER COLLEGE
Admissions Office	ADMISSIONS OFFICE
1600 N. Grand Ave.	1600 N GRAND AVE
St. Paul, MN 55105-1801	ST PAUL MN 55105-1801

Following U.S. Postal Service Guidelines

The official United States Postal Service guidelines are available at any post office or online at www.usps.org.

- Capitalize everything in the address and leave out commas and periods.
- Use the list of common state and street abbreviations found in the *National ZIP Code Directory* or on page **660** of this book.
- Use numbers rather than words for numbered streets (for example, 42ND AVE or 9TH AVE NW).
- If you know the ZIP + 4 code, use it.

Workplace

Preparing the Letter for Mailing

Emphasize the importance of using a clearly organized form for the correct name (including title), address, and ZIP code information on envelopes sent through the mail.

TEKS 11.15B(v)

Addressing the Envelope

Encourage students to use the envelope-addressing feature that comes with most word-processing programs whenever they send business letters. With some programs, this simply involves highlighting the inside address in the letter and then finding and clicking "Envelope" from the menu bar. The window that comes up automatically shows the highlighted text as the destination address. The return address may also be filled in automatically, or it may have to be added. Creating the final envelope for printing usually involves clicking "OK" or "Enter." Have students research to find a company's full ZIP + 4 code. If they cannot locate it, they can use the five-digit code.

TEKS 11.15B(ii)

Following U.S. Postal Service Guidelines

Have students use prior knowledge to compare and discuss the traditional and postal service forms. Review the abbreviation and punctuation rules for addressing an envelope and confirm that students understand where each type of information belongs on an envelope.

✔ DIFFERENTIATE INSTRUCTION

ELPS 1A

TEKS 11.15B(ii) Write procedural or work-related documents that include appropriate formatting structures; **11.15B(v)** Write procedural or work-related documents that include appropriate organizational structures supported by facts and details; **ELPS 1A** Use prior knowledge; **4B** Recognize directionality of English reading; **4G** Demonstrate comprehension of increasingly complex English/retelling or summarizing

Writing Guidelines Proposal

Explain that including personal opinions in a proposal weakens the persuasive tone, while quotations or favorable recommendations from respected leaders or authorities on the topic, can strengthen the proposal. **DIFFERENTIATE INSTRUCTION ↘**

Prewriting

Remind students that, depending on their audience, they may need to give background information and define terms.

Drafting

Work with students to be sure they understand how to format the heading of their proposal.

Emphasize the importance of using accurate, concrete data including facts, statistics, dollar amounts, and other relevant numbers. Remind students that

- numbers from one to nine are written out,
- numbers over 10 are written as numerals, and
- the word *percent* is written out when it is used with a number in a sentence.

✱ For more about writing numbers, see SE pages 684–685.

⭐ **TEKS** 11.15B(ii)

Revising

Have small groups use the questions provided as a guide for evaluating the clarity and support in their proposals.
⭐ **TEKS** 11.15B(i)

Editing

Emphasize the importance of an error-free proposal. Point out that multiple errors in conventions may result in their proposal not being taken seriously.

⭐ **TEKS** 11.15B(i), 11.15B(ii)

Writing Guidelines Proposal

People write proposals to fix problems, address specific needs, or make improvements. A proposal may be a simple memo suggesting the addition of a microwave to the lunchroom or a complex report recommending establishment of a company day-care center.

Prewriting

- **Consider your audience** by thinking about who will receive your proposal and what you want your audience to understand.
- **Determine your purpose** and jot down what you want your proposal to accomplish. What action are you proposing?
- **Gather details** based on what your audience needs to know in order to make a decision. Gather information to support your viewpoint.

Drafting

- **Format a heading** that includes the following information:
  - *Date:* The month, day, and year
  - *To:* The name(s) of the recipient(s)
  - *From:* Your first and last name
  - *Subject:* A concise summary of the proposal
- **Organize the body** into three parts:
  - *Beginning:* State clearly what you are proposing and why.
  - *Middle:* Provide details such as financial costs and other required resources. Write out key points and information supporting them. Show how the action will benefit the organization.
  - *Ending:* Summarize what actions need to be taken next or what recommendations you are making.

Revising

- **Improve your writing.** Ask yourself these questions related to focus and coherence, organization, development of ideas, and voice. *Is my proposal clear and logical? Is my purpose stated clearly? Have I provided sufficient information and detail to convince the reader that action is needed? Do I have an effective and logical beginning, middle, and ending? Do I provide information to support my recommendations? Have I used a positive, persuasive tone?*

Editing

- **Check for conventions.** Be sure grammar, sentence structure, mechanics (capitalization and punctuation), and spelling are correct.
- **Prepare a final copy.** Proofread the final copy of your proposal.

Differentiated Instruction: Advanced Learners

Have students consider a problem in their community or school. Then, using the information and the model on SE page 543, have them write a proposal to resolve that problem. Students may present their proposals to the class, or they may wish to send their proposals to community leaders or the school principal.

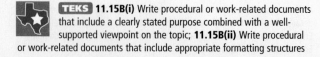

TEKS **11.15B(i)** Write procedural or work-related documents that include a clearly stated purpose combined with a well-supported viewpoint on the topic; **11.15B(ii)** Write procedural or work-related documents that include appropriate formatting structures

Writing in the Workplace **543**

★ **TEKS** 11.15B(i), 11.15B(ii), 11.15B(iii), 11.15B(iv), 11.15B(v)

Proposal

Kim Melchor did a summer internship at Daley Insurance Company. Her boss asked her to research the possibility of opening a day-care center at the company and to draft a proposal for review.

Workplace

> **The proposal includes a complete heading.**

Date: May 5, 2011

To: Pat Stevenson

From: Kim Melchor, summer assistant

Subject: On-Site Day Care

> **Beginning** The purpose is clearly stated.

Employees are interested in having a day-care center at Daley Insurance Company. My research and employee-survey results indicate there is room for a center, and employees would use it.

> **Middle** Accurate information is presented in accessible language.

Daley Insurance is located in an area with few day-care facilities. The employee survey shows that approximately 58 percent of Daley employees have children under the age of five, and 72 percent live within five miles of the work site. Fewer than 10 percent of these employees with children have family in the area to help out with child care. A survey of all employees with children showed that 81 percent preferred on-site day care.

> **Relevant benefits to the organization engage the reader.**

Providing quality, affordable day care at work would help the company attract and retain employees with young children. Having children nearby would allow parents to visit them at noon. It would also improve employee morale and absenteeism and lost productivity caused by child-care issues.

> **An action plan is discussed and documented by facts and details.**

The old employee activity center, which has been empty since the new center was built, meets state codes. The remodeling costs would be minimal (see attached estimate from the chief financial officer).

A quality day-care center could be self-supporting once the initial costs of establishing it are covered. Tax credits may be available to help pay the start-up costs (see attached projections by the CFO).

> **Ending** Recommendations are stated.

Based on my research, I recommend that we complete this proposal for a day-care center and present it to management.

Proposal

Encourage students to use the new and academic vocabulary to express their ideas about the model proposal, using the margin notes and these questions:

- What facts and statistics in the second paragraph support the proposal? (58 percent of employees have children; 72 percent live within five miles; fewer than 10 percent have child care help; 81 percent support on-site day care)
- What benefits does the author highlight? (attract and retain employees with young children; allow parents to visit children at noon; improve morale, reduce absenteeism and lost productivity.)
- What idea does Kim suggest for implementing the plan? (Use the old activity center.)
- How are possible objections to the plan countered? (remodeling costs would be minimal; the day-care center could be self-supporting; and possible tax credits)
- Besides concrete facts and details, how does Kim add credence to the proposal? (She includes attachments from the CFO.)

★ **TEKS** 11.15B(i), 11.15B(ii), 11.15B(iii), 11.15B(iv), 11.15B(v); **ELPS** 1E, 3D, 3E, 3G ✔**DIFFERENTIATE INSTRUCTION**

Differentiated Instruction: English Language Learners

★ **ELPS** 4D, 4F

Use visuals and simplified language to develop background knowledge about workplace daycare centers.

ELP Level **Beginning**	ELP Level **Intermediate**	ELP Level **Advanced/Advanced High**
Use simplified language to summarize the proposal. Ask yes/no questions to clarify ideas and to confirm understanding.	Use simplified language to summarize the proposal. Have students complete sentence stems to clarify terms such as *employee, survey,* and *costs.*	Guide students to summarize the ideas in the proposal. Invite them to discuss and define terms such as *morale, absenteeism,* and *lost productivity.*

★ **TEKS** **11.15B(i)** Write procedural or work-related documents that include a clearly stated purpose combined with a well-supported viewpoint on the topic; **11.15B(ii)** Write procedural or work-related documents that include appropriate formatting structures; **11.15B(iii)** Write procedural or work-related documents that include relevant questions that engage readers and consider their needs; **11.15B(iv)** Write procedural or work-related documents that include accurate technical information in accessible language; **11.15B(v)** Write procedural or work-related documents that include appropriate organizational structures supported by facts and details; **ELPS 1E** Internalize new academic language by using and reusing it/speaking; **3D** Speak using grade-level content-area vocabulary in context/new English words and academic language; **3E** Share information in cooperative learning interactions; **3G** Express ideas; **4D** Use prereading supports to enhance comprehension of written text; **4F** Use support from peers and teachers to develop vocabulary and background knowledge

Writing Guidelines E-Mail Message

Point out that e-mail (electronic mail) is now a standard means of communication throughout the business and academic world.

Prewriting

Guide students to have a clear purpose and to gather relevant details for their e-mails.

⭐ **TEKS** 11.15B(i)

Drafting

Remind students to state a clear subject and to write a beginning, middle, and end with only necessary supporting details included. As needed, explain that readers may miss key details in an overly long or disorganized message.

⭐ **TEKS** 11.15B(ii)

Revising

Have students work in pairs or small groups, using the questions provided to guide their revision of parts of their e-mail that need work.

Editing

Remind students that while e-mail is fast and convenient, it is also permanent. Once it is sent, there is no way to get it back. Caution them to reread carefully before sending it to check for errors and tone.

Tip

Empasize the need to adhere to the rules shown for workplace e-mails or for any other serious communication. Elicit that it is inappropriate to use the type of informal shorthand or icons used in friendly e-mail or text messages.

⭐ **ELPS** 1G

 ⭐ **TEKS** 11.15B(i), 11.15B(ii)

Writing Guidelines E-Mail Message

Electronic mail is a fast, convenient way to communicate in the workplace. It saves paper and allows many people to share information simultaneously.

Prewriting

- **Consider your audience** and your purpose for sending the message.
- **Gather details** based on what the reader needs to know.

Drafting

- **Format and organize the body** in three parts:
  - *Beginning:* Complete your e-mail header, making sure your subject line is clear. Expand on the subject in the first sentences of your message. Get right to the point.
  - *Middle:* Supply all the details of your message while keeping your paragraphs short. Double-space between paragraphs.
  - *Ending:* Let your reader know what follow-up action is needed and when; then end politely.

Revising

- **Improve your writing** by asking yourself these questions concerning focus and coherence, organization, development of ideas, and voice: *Is my message accurate and complete? Have I stated my purpose clearly? Have I included details that support my viewpoint? Do I have an effective beginning, middle, and ending? Is my tone appropriate for the topic and the reader?*
- **Improve your style.** Ask yourself these questions related to sentence structure: *Have I used clear, everyday language? Does my message read smoothly?*

Editing

- **Check for conventions.** Correct any errors in grammar, sentence structure, mechanics (capitalization and punctuation), and spelling before sending your e-mail.

Tip

- Try to be brief. Include long or detailed documents as attachments.
- Never use all capital letters in an e-mail message. People feel you are shouting at them.
- Follow grammar conventions.
- Proofread. Because e-mail is so fast, it's easy to overlook a typo.

⭐ **TEKS** **11.15B(i)** Write procedural or work-related documents that include a clearly stated purpose combined with a well-supported viewpoint on the topic; **11.15B(ii)** Write procedural or work-related documents that include appropriate formatting structures; **ELPS** **1G** Demonstrate knowledge of when to use formal and informal English

TEKS 11.15B(ii), 11.15B(iii), 11.15B(iv), 11.15B(v)

E-Mail Message

Linda Schmid, a high school student working on a research paper about the early days of the civil rights movement, discovered information about a documentary done by students at another school. She wrote this e-mail message to ask for more information.

○ ○ ○	New Message	
To:	office@austinhigh.org	
Cc:		
Subject:	Query About Civil Rights Documentary	

The **heading** includes an address and a subject.

Dear Sir or Madam:

I read the May 2, 2011, story in the *Austin Herald* about the documentary Austin High School students did on little-known heroes of the civil rights movement. I am currently working on a paper for my American History class on the subject, and I would like to view the film as part of my research.

The **beginning** greets the reader and introduces accurate information about the topic.

Would it be possible for me to borrow or buy a copy of the documentary?

The **middle** asks relevant questions and states what the writer needs.

I am willing to buy a copy, or pay a rental fee, if necessary. I would gladly pay postage if you are willing to lend me a copy of the documentary.

Thank you for your help. You can respond via e-mail, or phone me at the number listed below.

The **ending** thanks the reader and offers facts and details for follow-up.

Sincerely,
Linda Schmid
Amarillo Community School
806-555-1234
lindas5956@amarilloschool.org

Workplace

Tip

Most e-mail programs support formatting for titles (bold, italics, and underscore).

E-Mail Message

Discuss with students the model e-mail message and its margin notes. Point out the elements of the heading, the writer's quick statement of the purpose of the e-mail in the opening paragraph, the details and relevant questions included in the middle paragraphs, and the information given in the concluding paragraphs.

TEKS 11.15B(i), 11.15B(ii), 11.15B(iii), 11.15B(iv), 11.15B(v)

Although students have probably written more friendly e-mail than any other form of writing, they will benefit from practice in composing formal e-mail messages. Have them write an e-mail message in response to the model e-mail message on this page. Tell them to create the facts and details they will need to write the response, using the newly acquired vocabulary from the model. DIFFERENTIATE INSTRUCTION

ELPS 5B

Explain that even though most people simply use the "reply" icon to respond to an e-mail, in business e-mail it is standard to include the e-mail address and contact information below the name (signature). Recipients of the e-mail appreciate having all the pertinent contact information in one place.

Tip

If students are using a school computer, alert them regarding the word processing functions its e-mail program does and does not support.

Differentiated Instruction: English Language Learners

ELPS 1B, 1G

ELP Level Beginning	**ELP Level Intermediate**	**ELP Level Advanced/Advanced High**
Guide students to read the e-mail message together. Point out examples of formal English the author uses in its greeting and ending.	Guide students to identify words and phrases that are examples of formal English. Provide sentence stems to have them tell why these choices are appropriate.	Have students compose a reply to the e-mail, proofread it, and correct any errors. Then have partners share their work and identify examples of formal English.

TEKS **11.15B(i)** Write procedural or work-related documents that include a clearly stated purpose combined with a well-supported viewpoint on the topic; **11.15B(ii)** Write procedural or work-related documents that include appropriate formatting structures; **11.15B(iii)** Write procedural or work-related documents that include relevant questions that engage readers and consider their needs; **11.15B(iv)** Write procedural or work-related documents that include accurate technical information in accessible language; **11.15B(v)** Write procedural or work-related documents that include appropriate organizational structures supported by facts and details; **ELPS 1B** Monitor written language production and employ self-corrective techniques or other resources; **1G** Demonstrate ability to distinguish between formal and informal English and knowledge of when to use formal and informal English; **5B** Write using newly acquired basic and content-based grade-level vocabulary

Writing Guidelines
How to Conduct a Business Meeting

Ask students who have had experience heading a school club to share with classmates what they have learned about holding club meetings. Ask them to use relevant vocabulary and expressions to describe their experiences.

 ELPS 2C

Prewriting

Have small groups plan a meeting for a school science club whose purpose is to encourage other students to recycle more. Have groups decide who should attend the meeting and how details suggested for implementing a plan by participants will be recorded and monitored. Remind the members of each group to seek clarification if the ideas presented are not clear.

ELPS 1D, 2D

Drafting

As they draft, remind groups to provide information to address steps 1 through 5 for the meeting.

TEKS 11.15B(i), 11.15B(ii)

Revising

After the initial draft is written, have group members revise as needed for clarity and coherence.

Editing

Using the points provided as a guide, have groups prepare a final agenda as well as a plan for reminding participants about the meeting.

Tip

Remind students to assign a responsible person to distribute any additional information participants of the meeting might need.

 TEKS 11.15B(i), 11.15B(ii)

Writing Guidelines How to Conduct a Business Meeting

Business meetings are conducted for a variety of reasons—to make decisions as a group, to consider proposals, to update staff members, or to address and solve problems. The steps you need to take to conduct a business meeting are similar to those used for the writing process.

Prewriting

- **Determine your purpose** by clearly identifying what you would like the meeting to accomplish.
- **Consider the participants who should attend.** Revisit your purpose. Who can provide information participants will need? Which decision makers need to be present? Who will be affected by the outcome of the meeting?
- **Gather details** based on what participants may need to share or that will be needed to support viewpoints on the topic.

Drafting

- **Step 1:** Clarify the meeting's purpose, and decide who will attend.
- **Step 2:** Set an agenda and share it with participants in advance. Let participants know what information they will need to review or share.
- **Step 3:** Choose a date, place, and time for the meeting.
- **Step 4:** Decide who is responsible for taking minutes of the meeting.
- **Step 5:** Announce the meeting to participants via phone or e-mail.

Revising

- **Make necessary changes.** If you need to make changes regarding the agenda, the participants, or the date, place, and time of the meeting, be certain that participants are updated.

Editing

- **Gather your information.** Check to make sure that you have prepared all the information you will need.
- **Prepare a final agenda.** The agenda should include headings and other formatting, and should be clear and concise. Proofread the final copy and distribute it to participants in advance of the meeting.
- **Remind participants** about the meeting via phone or e-mail.

Tip

If participants are receiving additional information before the meeting, be sure that it is distributed in a timely fashion.

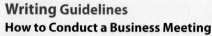 **TEKS** **11.15B(i)** Write procedural or work-related documents that include a clearly stated purpose combined with a well-supported viewpoint on the topic; **11.15B(ii)** Write procedural or work-related documents that include appropriate formatting structures; **ELPS** **1D** Speak using learning strategies; **2C** Learn new expressions and basic vocabulary; **2D** Monitor understanding of spoken language and seek clarification as needed

TEKS 11.15B(ii), 11.15B(iii), 11.15B(iv), 11.15B(v)

Business Meeting Agenda

Jorge Rivas leads a group of high school students who produce a student news program for their local community access cable station. Jorge wrote this business meeting agenda for one of their regular production meetings.

The agenda is formatted so it is easy to read.

Agenda
Production Meeting
March 3, 2011
4:00–5:30 pm

Participants: Jorge Rivas, executive producer
Jessie Marx, segment producer
Graham Jones, segment producer
Marissa Melendez, floor director
Technical crew: Charlie Abrams, Lee Chang,
Nita Harrold, Sanaye Miller

Clear organizational structures are included.

Recording Minutes: Jessie Marx

Purpose of Meeting: Schedule shoots for next episode; report on status of possible upcoming segments; discuss production costs

4:00–4:05: Call to order; welcome/introduce new crew member Nita Harrold

Action words help engage participants.

4:05–4:20: Determine date for production shoot for debate segment; determine date for studio shoot for next episode

4:20–4:40: Report on status of possible segments on soccer team (Jessie) and interview with Principal Henderson (Graham)

Accurate technical information helps participants focus on topics.

4:40–4:55: Report on current production budget (Jorge); discuss revenue sources for set construction costs

4:55–5:00: Schedule next meeting; adjourn

Tip

Make additional copies of the agenda available at the meeting, so that participants are prepared and ready to focus on the topics.

Workplace

Differentiated Instruction:
English Language Learners

ELPS 1D, 2C, 2D, 4F

Use simplified language to develop background knowledge about local cable stations and news programs.

ELP Level **Beginning**	ELP Level **Intermediate**	ELP Level **Advanced/Advanced High**
Point out and have students repeat new terms and expressions such as *minutes, episodes,* and *segment.* Ask yes/no questions to monitor understanding.	Read the minutes together. Have student identify new terms and expressions. Provide question frames to help students seek clarification about the terms.	Have students define the multiple-meaning term *minutes.* Ask them to use complete sentences to summarize and explain why each section of the agenda is useful.

Business Meeting Agenda

Discuss with students the sample business meeting agenda. Use the margin notes and the questions that follow to guide the discussion.

✔ DIFFERENTIATE INSTRUCTION

- What formatting elements are included in the agenda heading? (meeting title, date, and time)
- In addition to names, how are participants listed? (by title or work area)
- What is the purpose of the meeting? (to schedule shoots, report on upcoming segments, and discuss production costs)
- How might assigning specific time limits to each of the main discussion points be helpful? (It will keep participants focused and prevent them from getting off topic.)
- How might the details listed for each time segment engage readers? (Details will keep attention focused on the purpose at hand.)
- What technical language is used? (shoots, segment, budget, production, revenue, adjourn)

TEKS 11.15B(ii); 11.15B(iii), 11.15B(iv), 11.15B(v)

Tip

Remind students that if they are planning a business meeting, they should assign someone to be responsible for bringing extra copies of the agenda.

TEKS **11.15B(ii)** Write procedural or work-related documents that include appropriate formatting structures; **11.15B(iii)** Write procedural or work-related documents that include relevant questions that engage readers and consider their needs; **11.15B(iv)** Write procedural or work-related documents that include accurate technical information in accessible language; **11.15B(v)** Write procedural or work-related documents that include appropriate organizational structures supported by facts and details; **ELPS 1D** Speak using learning strategies; **2C** Learn new basic and academic vocabulary; **2D** Monitor understanding of spoken language and seek clarification of spoken language as needed; **4F** Use visual and contextual support to enhance and confirm understanding and develop background knowledge

Writing Guidelines
How to Take Minutes During a Business Meeting

Discuss the meaning of the term *take minutes* and elicit from students that minutes provide a record so that meeting attendees do not have to rely on their memories.

ELPS 2C

Prewriting

Point out that depending on the complexity of the topics being discussed, it may not be possible for the person taking the minutes to also be an active participant in the meeting.

Drafting

Have students work in pairs or in small groups and retell the purpose and format for recording each type of information mentioned in Steps 1–4.

TEKS 11.15B(i), 11.15B(ii); **ELPS** 3B

Revising

Explain that notes taken during the meeting do not need to be recorded in complete sentences. When the recorder writes up the minutes from his or her notes, however, then they should be entered in complete sentences.

Editing

Remind students to check their minutes, as they would any other formal writing, for errors in conventions.

Tip

Tell students that if they do not write up their minutes as soon as possible after the meeting, they run the risk of forgetting or misstating main points.

548

TEKS 11.15B(i), 11.15B(ii)

Writing Guidelines How to Take Minutes During a Business Meeting

The purpose of taking minutes during a business meeting is to provide a record of what happens during the meeting, including the topics discussed, actions agreed or decided upon, and items for future action or consideration. The minutes can be used for reference as time goes on.

Prewriting

- **Gather necessary materials,** such as a copy of the agenda and a notebook or a laptop computer to record information. A tape recorder can be useful if topics may involve complicated discussions.
- **Focus on the tasks.** Keep in mind that you may be an active participant, but you will also need to record key points about the events of the meeting.

Drafting

- **Step 1:** Record important details, such as the time, date, and place of the meeting, and the names of the attendees. (Circulate a sign-in sheet if more than ten people attend the meeting.)
- **Step 2:** Take notes about each topic on the agenda. You don't need to use complete sentences as you take notes, but aim to fully record important ideas about the main topics of the meeting. If members make formal motions, write down the exact words of each motion, who made it, who seconded it, and whether the motion passed or failed.
- **Step 3:** Record resolutions about actions to be taken. Write down who has been assigned what task and the time frame for the task.
- **Step 4:** Write down the time the meeting adjourned and information about when the next meeting will take place.

Revising

- **Create a revised draft.** Use headings to write complete sentences about each topic, in the order in which they occurred. Avoid using opinion statements, such as *Margo gave an excellent report on finances.*
- **Distribute the draft** to the attendees and solicit their input. Make revisions or clarifications based on the input you receive.

Editing

- **Check for conventions and prepare a final copy.** Distribute the final copy to those who need to know what happened at the meeting.

Tip

Write up the minutes as soon as possible after the meeting so that the events and details are still fresh in your memory.

TEKS **11.15B(i)** Write procedural or work-related documents that include a clearly stated purpose combined with a well-supported viewpoint on the topic; **11.15B(ii)** Write procedural or work-related documents that include appropriate formatting structures; **ELPS** **2C** Learn new expressions; **3B** Expand vocabulary/learning and using high-frequency words for identifying and describing, retelling simple stories and basic information, and learning and using routine language needed for classroom communication

TEKS 11.15B(ii), 11.15B(iii), 11.15B(iv), 11.15B(v)

Minutes of a Business Meeting

Jessie Marx recorded the minutes of a production meeting for a group of high school students who produce a student news program. After getting feedback from other meeting participants, she prepared and distributed this final copy.

Workplace

Teen News: Minutes of Production Meeting

A production meeting of the Teen News team was held on March 3, 2010, at 4 p.m. in Room 5A at Community Cable TV.

Members present: Lee Chang, Nita Harrold, Graham Jones, Jessie Marx, Marissa Melendez, Sanaye Miller, Jorge Rivas

Members absent: Charlie Abrams

Call to Order Jorge Rivas called the meeting to order at 4 p.m. and Jessie Marx recorded the minutes. Nita Harrold was introduced and welcomed as a new member of the technical crew.

Dates for Upcoming Shoots It was agreed that the debate segment on curfews would be shot on Tuesday, March 8 at the cable TV studio. Marissa will reserve studio time.

The full studio shoot for the March 15 episode will take place on Friday, March 11. All Teen News members should arrive by 3:30 p.m. The shoot is expected to end by 6:30 p.m.

Reports on Possible Segments Jessie reported on plans for a segment on the girls' soccer team. Co-captains have agreed to be interviewed. Shooting the segment may have to wait until after the team's final match on May 15.

Graham reported on the status of a possible interview with Principal Henderson. He has an appointment with her on April 2 to discuss the idea.

Report on Current Production Budget Jorge presented a report on the production budget. Teen News has a current balance of $304.80. Jorge asked all members to investigate potential sponsors and to report on these at our next meeting. Jorge reported that the construction costs for the new set are estimated to be about $220 for lumber and other materials. He noted that Wylie Hardware will donate $50 of materials. Lee will solicit additional donations from other vendors, and will provide an update at the next production meeting.

Next Meeting It was agreed that the next production meeting will be scheduled for April 5 at 4 p.m.

The meeting was adjourned at 5:35 p.m.

Respectfully submitted,
Jessie Marx

Appropriate formatting structures are used.

Accurate technical information is clear and understandable.

Facts and details are provided.

Relevant information answers questions readers may have.

Minutes of a Business Meeting

Use the margin notes and the questions below to lead students in a discussion of the model.

⬐ DIFFERENTIATE INSTRUCTION

- What formatting structures does the author use? (title, time, date, and place of meeting; boldfaced heads for major topics; date of next meeting)
- What specific information do the minutes record about dates for upcoming shoots? (debate segment Tuesday, March 8th, first full shoot Friday, March 11th from 3:30 p.m. to 6:30 p.m.)
- What facts and details do the minutes provide on the current production budget? (current balance $304.30, construction cost estimate $220.00, Wylie Hardware donation $50.00 toward material)
- What specific question is addressed at the end of the minutes? (the date of the next meeting)

TEKS 11.15B(ii), 11.15B(iii), 11.15B(iv), 11.15B(v); **ELPS** 3E

Differentiated Instruction: English Language Learners

ELPS 1F, 1G, 2C, 3B

ELP Level **Beginning**	ELP Level **Intermediate**	ELP Level **Advanced/Advanced High**
Use simplified language to discuss the sample. Point out and define descriptive and high-frequency words such as *recorded, reported, agreed,* and *presented.*	Read together sections of the minutes. Have students identify new expressions. Ask yes/no questions to have them retell what happened at the meeting.	Have partners read the minutes together and identify examples of formal English. Together, discuss why formal English is appropriate for minutes.

TEKS 11.15B(ii) Write procedural or work-related documents that include appropriate formatting structures; **11.15B(iii)** Write procedural or work-related documents that include relevant questions that engage readers and consider their needs; **11.15B(iv)** Write procedural or work-related documents that include accurate technical information in accessible language; **11.15B(v)** Write procedural or work-related documents that include appropriate organizational structures supported by facts and details; **ELPS 1F** Use accessible language and learn new and essential language in the process; **1G** Demonstrate ability to distinguish between formal and informal English and the knowledge of when to use formal and informal English; **2C** Learn new expressions; **3B** Expand vocabulary/learning and using high-frequency words for identifying and describing, retelling simple stories and basic information, and learning and using routine language needed for classroom communication; **3E** Share information in cooperative learning interactions

The Tools of Language

Listening and Speaking (pages 551–554)

These pages support all students as they improve their listening and speaking skills.

Using Reference Materials (pages 555–558)

These pages provide information to help all students use reference materials as they write.

Language Strategies (pages 560–561)

These pages provide English language learners with several language-learning strategies for speaking and listening that students can use to develop their academic English.

Language of the Writing Process (pages 562–565)

These pages support English language learners as they delve into The Writing Process (pages 6–32) by giving them a foundation for understanding the process through instruction in key vocabulary and concepts.

Language of the Writing Traits (pages 566–567)

These pages support English language learners as they learn about the writing traits (pages 46–89) by giving them a foundation for understanding the traits through instruction in key vocabulary and concepts.

Language of the Writing Forms (pages 568–603)

This section supports English language learners by introducing them to vocabulary and concepts for each writing form as well as the student writing models.

The Tools of Language Reference Guide

Write Source Student Edition			
The Tools of Language		**Corresponding Core Unit**	
Listening and Speaking	TL 551–554		
Using Reference Materials	TL 555–558		
Learning Language	TL 559–603	**All Core Units**	6–467
•Language Strategies	TL 560–561		
•Language of the Writing Process	TL 562–565	**Using the Writing Process** Exploring the Writing Process	6–32 90–133
•Language of the Writing Traits	TL 566–567	**Understanding the Texas Traits**	46–89
•Language of Narrative Writing	TL 568–573	**Narrative Writing**	134–155
•Language of Expository Writing	TL 574–579	**Expository Writing**	156–213
•Language of Persuasive Writing	TL 580–585	**Persuasive Writing**	214–271
•Language of Writing a Response to Literature	TL 586–591	Interpretive Response	272–337
•Language of Creative Writing	TL 592–597	**Creative Writing**	338–373
•Language of Research Writing	TL 598–603	**Research Writing**	374–467

Learning Language

Read aloud the basic and academic terms, as well as the descriptions and questions. Help students distinguish sounds and recognize elements of English, such as consonant clusters in *strategies* and *clarify*. Then model for students how to read one question and answer it. For example, *It says that* reference materials *are sources of information. It asks what reference materials I have used. I have used a dictionary and the Internet.* Have partners monitor their understanding of the terms by working through the meanings and questions together.

ELPS 1F, 2A, 2B, 2C, 3E, 4G **DIFFERENTIATE INSTRUCTION ↘**

Minilessons

Distracted   Listening and Speaking

- Have one student **READ** a multiple-point paragraph in a normal speaking voice while music is playing, two other students are talking, and TV is on. **ASK** students to **SUMMARIZE** the paragraph, listing at least three important points. **SHARE** results with the class. **DETERMINE** what were the most serious distractions and **DISCUSS** why.

Up Front and Personal   Listening and Speaking

- Have students **LISTEN** as you read a brief story aloud. Students should **OBSERVE** your eye contact, voice, and posture. Then have students **READ** the same (or another) story to a partner. Ask partners to **DISCUSS** the experience and how delivery of the story could be improved.

From Experience   Listening and Speaking

- Have partners **SELECT** a short reading (poem, opening of a short story, or a paragraph from a textbook). Based on the content, have them **LIST** three possible readers (a scientist, an elementary school student, an elderly individual, and so on). Have partners **TAKE TURNS** reading the selection in different voices. Then ask them to **LIST** three possible audiences for the reading. Have them **READ** the selection again for each different audience, varying their voice accordingly.

ELPS 1F Use accessible language and learn new and essential language in the process; **2A** Distinguish sounds and intonation patterns of English; **2B** Recognize elements of the English sound system in newly acquired vocabulary; **2C** Learn new basic and academic vocabulary; **3E** Share information in cooperative learning interactions; **4G** Demonstrate comprehension of increasingly complex English/responding to questions

---

550

ELPS 1F, 2C, 3E, 4G

TEXAS WRITE SOURCE Online
www.hmheducation.com/tx/writesource

The Tools of Language

Learning Language

Work with a partner. Read the meanings and share answers to the questions.

1. When you communicate you share your ideas.
   Writing is one way to communicate. What is another way?

2. Strategies are plans to help you reach a goal.
   What strategies help you to get good grades?

3. When you clarify you tell more to make an idea clear.
   How can you clarify the directions to your home?

4. Reference materials are books or electronic sources of information.
   What reference materials have you used?

5. When you are told to look it up, you search for information in reference materials.
   When do you look up the answer to a question?

551

Listening and Speaking

Strong listening and speaking skills are important to your future. You will use them to interview for colleges and jobs and to communicate well with bosses, co-workers, teachers, and classmates. Listening is the groundwork, or foundation, for all learning. It enables you to understand a speaker's main ideas and to evaluate and organize information. Speaking is just as important. It allows you to explain, argue, persuade, inform, and even entertain.

Each day, you spend 70 percent of your time communicating with others. Three-fourths of that time is spent listening and speaking. In this chapter, you will find strategies to help you become a better listener and speaker. As you practice and master these skills, you will strengthen the foundation of your future.

- Listening in Class
- Speaking in Class
- A Closer Look at Listening and Speaking

"To listen well is as powerful a means of influence as to talk well and is as essential to all true conversation."

—Chinese proverb

Listening and Speaking

Objectives
- learn to become a good listener
- develop skills for participating in a group
- improve speaking skills

Discuss the idea that listening and speaking effectively are skills that students can use in every part of their life, not just at school. As they practice the techniques on the following pages, encourage students to make note of their progress and successes in their writer's notebook.

Direct attention to the Chinese proverb at the bottom of the page. To help students respond to the quotation, ask the following questions:
- How can listening be a powerful means of influence?
- What is meant by the phrase *true conversation*?
- What are some examples of listening *well* and listening *poorly*?

Differentiated Instruction: English Language Learners

ELPS **4A**

ELP Level **Beginning**	ELP Level **Intermediate**	ELP Level **Advanced/Advanced High**
Work with students to decode words such as *communicate* or *strategies* using letter-sound relationships. Then help students write and read the two words on their own.	Have partners work to decode words, such as *communicate, clarify,* and *strategies* using letter-sound relationships. Then have them write and read the words on their own.	Have students decode the words using letter-sound relationships. Then have them use the words in new sentences, both orally and in writing.

 ELPS 4A Learn relationships between sounds and letters of English and decode using a combination of skills

Listening in Class

Focus on the idea that listening takes practice and effort, and acknowledge that there are times when listening can be a challenge. Encourage students to practice using the tips to improve their listening skills. Offer these additional tips for becoming active listeners:

- Sit near the front of the auditorium or lecture hall to make sure you can hear and see the speaker.
- Anticipate avoidable distractions, such as feeling hungry or too warm or too cold.
- Work at keeping attention focused on the speaker. Look at the speaker, take notes, try to anticipate what will be said next, and try to think of a good question to ask.

DIFFERENTIATE INSTRUCTION ⟶

During class, encourage students to monitor their attention level so that they are aware of any lapses in attention. They can compensate for any lapses by meeting with a classmate afterwards to review what was said and supplement their notes.

As needed, encourage students to take a translation dictionary or electronic translator to important presentations. Recommend that they look up only the most important and frequently repeated terms during the presentation; they should write down other terms in the margins of their notes and look them up later.

ELPS 2C, 2D, 2G, 2H, 2I

Try It!
Answers

Responses to the **Try It!** activity will vary. Review the example with students before they begin the activity, and consider having partners or small groups work together to complete it.

552

 ELPS 2C, 2D, 2G, 2H, 2I

Listening in Class

Listening takes practice and effort. The following strategies will help you become a better listener.

- **Know why you are listening.** What is the speaker trying to tell you? Will there be a test? Is this an assignment?
- **Check your understanding.** Ask yourself these six questions as you listen: *Who? What? When? Where? Why? How?* The answers will help you decide what are the speaker's main points.
- **Take notes.** When you hear important details, write them down. Add your questions and comments in the margins. Review, clarify, and complete your notes as soon as possible after the speaker has finished.
- **Put the speaker's ideas into your own words.** Summarize or restate the speaker's key points in your notes. Add your comments.

Try It!

Practice taking notes in class or while listening to a documentary on television. Put the speaker's ideas into your own words. Add your questions and comments in the margins.

The Ring of Fire

- zone of frequent earthquakes and volcanic eruptions
- holds 75% of the world's active and dormant volcanoes
- located at the borders of the Pacific Plate and other major tectonic plates
- forms an arc: New Zealand, around eastern edge of Asia, north across Aleutian Islands, south along coast of N. and S. America (map in textbook)

Subduction
The Pacific Plate is crashing into and sliding under other plates.

Margin notes:
Which volcano has been most active in the Ring of Fire and why?

What do trenches and mountain ranges have to do with plate tectonics?

Subduction: The pushing edge of one plate goes below the edge of another.

Differentiated Instruction: Struggling Learners

Read aloud a short section from a history or science book. Have students take notes, reminding them to write the ideas in their own words. Work with them to ensure that they are not trying to write down every word. Encourage them to add questions and comments in the margins.

ELPS **2C** Learn new basic vocabulary; **2D** Seek clarification of spoken language as needed; **2G** Understand the main points of spoken language/topics; **2H** Understand implicit information in spoken language; **2I** Demonstrate listening comprehension/taking notes

Speaking in Class

Speaking in a group discussion is an important skill to master. A good discussion depends on cooperation and on expressing your ideas, opinions, and feelings clearly. These strategies will help you become a better speaker.

Before you speak . . .

- **Listen** carefully and take notes.
- **Think** about what others are saying.
- **Wait** until it is your turn to speak.
- **Plan** how you can add something positive to the discussion.

As you speak . . .

- **Use a loud, clear voice.**
- **Stick to the topic.**
- **Avoid repeating** what's already been said.
- **Explain ideas** using details such as examples, facts, or anecdotes.
- **Make eye contact** with others in the group or class.

Tips

- Focus your comments on ideas, not on personalities.
- Ask meaningful questions.
- Summarize specific ideas brought up in the discussion.
- Mention another person's comments and expand on them in a helpful way.

Try It!

Warm up your speaking skills using the following talk-show activity. Be sure to express your opinions, ideas, and feelings clearly.

1. Watch excerpts from several talk shows. Notice how the host listens to and interacts with the guest. What questions does the host ask to direct the guest to speak in detail about a topic?
2. Pair up with a classmate for a talk-show interview. Decide who will be the host and who will be the guest.
3. Together, decide on a theme for the interview. Choose a topic, such as a hobby, talent, or sport that the "guest" enjoys, or an interesting event from the "guest's" life.
4. Present a 5-minute interview to the class. Keep the interview on topic and flowing smoothly by using the tips on this page.

(side tab) Listening and Speaking

Speaking in Class

Advise students that they will feel comfortable speaking in class if they keep up-to-date with the subject matter through regular class attendance, active listening, taking good notes, and finishing their homework assignments.

Before you speak... Discuss what students should do before they speak, using the bulleted points shown. Encourage students to observe basic rules of group etiquette, such as waiting one's turn to express ideas, speaking loudly enough to be heard, and listening respectfully to others' ideas.
ELPS 3B, 3G

As you speak... Explain to students that it is important to understand *why* they are speaking so they can choose their vocabulary and style of language carefully. This will ensure that their spoken language supports their purpose, whether it is formal or informal. Work with students to describe some speaking situations in detail and discuss how they might adapt their spoken language to suit each situation.
ELPS 3G, 3H, 3I

Tips

Review the tips shown with students, and provide examples when possible and appropriate.

Try It!
Answers

Responses to the **Try It!** activity will vary. Modify speaking assignments to allow students to practice sharing in smaller groups until they develop the language proficiency and confidence to make whole-class presentations.
✔ DIFFERENTIATE INSTRUCTION
ELPS 3B, 3E, 3F, 3G, 3H

Differentiated Instruction: English Language Learners

ELPS 3B, 3E, 3F, 3G, 3H, 3I

ELP Level **Beginning**	ELP Level **Intermediate**	ELP Level **Advanced/Advanced High**
Have students work with intermediate and advanced students on the Try It! activity. Provide visuals and gestures to use during the interview presentation.	Have small groups work on the Try It! activity. Provide visuals, gestures, and sentence stems that students can use to conduct their interviews.	Have partners work on the Try It! activity. Support them with possible interview questions or outlines as needed. Guide them to find the right tone for their interviews as well.

ELPS 3B Expand vocabulary/learning and using routine language needed for classroom communication; **3E** Share information in cooperative learning interactions; **3F** Ask for and give information during extended speaking assignments; **3G** Express ideas; **3H** Describe with increasing specificity and detail; **3I** Adapt spoken language for formal and informal purposes

A Closer Look at Listening and Speaking

Acknowledge that it's natural to feel nervous about speaking in front of a group. Direct students' attention to the guidelines for good speakers (second column of the chart). Encourage them to practice these points whenever they engage in conversations and discussions. Explain that concentrating on carrying out these specific actions will help them to focus and will increase their confidence. Assure students that the more they practice, the easier it will be for them to participate in group discussions. **DIFFERENTIATE INSTRUCTION ↘**

Remind students that active participation is just as important for listeners as it is for speakers. Maintaining an alert pose and keeping their eyes on the speaker communicates respectful attention and also helps listeners to stay focused. Be mindful that in some cultures, making direct eye contact with elders or people of the opposite sex is considered disrespectful or too bold. Clearly explain that in American culture, eye contact is important and respectful. Have students practice with you.

Try It!
Answers

Responses to the **Try It!** activity will vary. Consider allowing students to practice sharing in smaller groups until they develop high-frequency-word language proficiency and confidence to participate in whole-class discussions. Help partners or small groups summarize the speech and express their feelings about it by reminding them to use the strategies they have learned in this chapter. Remind them to interact, asking for and giving information during the discussion. **DIFFERENTIATE INSTRUCTION ↘**

ELPS 2D, 2E, 3B, 3F, 3G

ELPS **2D** Monitor understanding of spoken language; **2E** Use contextual support to confirm understanding of spoken language; **3B** Expand vocabulary/learning and using high-frequency words for identifying and describing; **3F** Ask for and give information during extended speaking assignments; **3G** Express feelings

ELPS 2D, 2E, 3G

A Closer Look at Listening and Speaking

Improving your listening and speaking skills will help you increase your confidence and effectiveness as a communicator. Follow these guidelines to carry on productive conversations and discussions.

Good Listeners	Good Speakers
■ check their understanding of what the speaker is saying.	■ speak loudly and clearly.
■ stay focused so that they are prepared to respond thoughtfully.	■ make eye contact with their listeners.
■ pay attention to the speaker's tone of voice, gestures, and facial expressions.	■ emphasize their main ideas by changing the tone and volume of their voice.
■ interrupt only when necessary to ask questions or seek clarification.	■ respect their audience by explaining and clarifying information that may be confusing.
	■ use gestures and body language effectively to enhance their message.

Try It!

Use the following activity to practice your listening and speaking skills. As a class, view a video of Dr. Martin Luther King, Jr., delivering his famous "I Have a Dream" speech.

1. Following the speech, participate in a class discussion, using these questions as a guide.
   • What are the main ideas of the speech?
   • What questions would you have wanted to ask Dr. King immediately following the speech?
2. Rate the delivery of the speech using the "Good Speakers" guidelines on this page. Which of the guidelines did you observe while watching and listening to Dr. King's speech?
3. Tell a friend about your feelings about the speech. Summarize Dr. King's main ideas and describe your reaction to his delivery. Use the speaking tips in this chapter to communicate your thoughts effectively.

Differentiated Instruction: Struggling Learners

Read these questions aloud, emphasizing the italic words: Do you want *me* to get that book? Do you want me to get *that* book? Do you want me to get that *book*? Discuss how the changes in volume and emphasis change the meaning of each sentence. Invite students to create their own sentences, varying tone and emphasis to change meanings.

555

Using Reference Materials

Since the late 1980s, the use of computers and the Internet has led people to say that we live in the "Information Age." The term refers to the idea that all sorts of information is easily available to anyone who wants to find it. The key is knowing where to look!

When you need to gather information, knowing which print and electronic reference materials are likely to be helpful can save you time and aggravation. You are probably familiar with some common references such as encyclopedias, newspapers, and atlases. Do you need facts about a specific topic? Do you need to look at maps or read about current events? One of those common references will probably suit your needs.

This chapter will focus on other language resources that may be useful for you. The next two sections provide details about the information found in a dictionary and give a description of other types of language resources you might find useful.

When you are able to use reference materials well, your ability to write clear, engaging, and informative pieces will grow and grow.

- **Using a Dictionary**
- **Other Reference Materials**

"Knowledge is of two kinds. We know a subject ourselves, or we know where we can find information on it."

—Samuel Johnson

Using Reference Materials

Objectives
- understand and practice using the information found in a dictionary
- understand and practice using the information found in other language resources

The following pages provide information about various language resources, including dictionaries, usage guides, thesauruses, and other types of resources that may be of particular use to students who are learning English.

Discuss the Johnson quotation with students. Talk about the importance of knowing how and where to find different types of information on a variety of subjects.

Have students name and discuss any reference materials they are familiar with and have used in the past. Provide examples if possible, both in print and in electronic form, and have students explain how to use them. Then ask students if there are any particular references they would like to understand better. Explain that the next few pages provide information about various language resources they may find useful in their writing and in all their studies.

Differentiated Instruction: English Language Learners

⭐ ELPS 2D, 2E, 3B, 3F, 3G

ELP Level Beginning	ELP Level Intermediate	ELP Level Advanced/Advanced High
Scaffold the Try It! activity by asking students yes-and-no questions, such as *"Did Dr. King explain himself clearly?"* Encourage students to use gestures to show their feelings.	Scaffold the Try It! activity by giving students sentence stems to complete, such as *The main ideas of the speech are ____ and ____.* Also ask students to rate their listening skills.	Have partners write their summaries of Dr. King's ideas and their reactions in a few short paragraphs. Ask them to share their writing with the rest of the group or class.

⭐ **ELPS 2D** Monitor understanding of spoken language; **2E** Use contextual support to confirm understanding of spoken language; **3B** Expand vocabulary/learning and using high-frequency words for identifying and describing; **3F** Ask for and give information during extended speaking assignments; **3G** Express feelings

Using Reference Materials

Using a Dictionary

Review each term and its description, guiding students to use the sample dictionary page (SE page 557) as each term and use of the dictionary is discussed. Also include electronic dictionaries in your discussion of this topic. Provide information such as the following:

- Good electronic dictionaries have the same features as the book versions (except, of course, for guide words).
- In addition to providing pronunciation symbols, many electronic dictionaries include audio files, which give pronunciations.
- Reliable online dictionaries include *American Heritage Dictionary of the English Language, 4th Edition,* at www.bartleby.com/reference. In addition, some public libraries provide online access to the *Oxford English Dictionary,* or *OED,* the most comprehensive English dictionary available.

Try It!
Answers

Answers will vary. The number of definitions will vary according to the dictionary used, but answers should include these three parts of speech: verb, noun, and adjective.

TEKS 11.19; **ELPS** 4C

TEKS 11.19
ELPS 4C

Using Reference Materials

Using a Dictionary

A dictionary gives many types of information. As you read each description, find the information on the sample shown on the next page.

- **Guide words:** These are the first and last words on the dictionary page. You use guide words to find out whether the word you are looking for will be found alphabetically on that page.
- **Entry words:** Each word defined in a dictionary is called an entry word. Entry words are listed alphabetically.
- **Etymology:** Many dictionaries give etymologies (word histories) for some words. An etymology tells what language an English word came from, how the word entered the language, and when it was first used.
- **Syllable divisions:** A dictionary tells you where you may divide a word at the end of a written line of text.
- **Pronunciation and accent marks:** A dictionary tells you how to pronounce a word. It also provides a key to pronunciation symbols, usually at the bottom of each page.
- **Illustrations:** An illustration, photograph, or drawing may be shown.
- **Parts of speech:** A dictionary tells you what part(s) of speech a word is, using these abbreviations:

n.	**noun**	*tr. v.*	**transitive verb**
pron.	**pronoun**	*interj.*	**interjection**
intr. v.	**intransitive verb**	*conj.*	**conjunction**
adj.	**adjective**	*adv.*	**adverb**
prep.	**preposition**		

- **Spelling and capitalization:** Acceptable spelling and capitalization for words are shown. (Some words have more than one spelling.)
- **Definitions:** Some large dictionaries list all of the meanings for a word. Most dictionaries, however, will list only three or four of the most common definitions in the language. Read all of the meanings to be sure that you are using the word correctly.

Try It!

Look up the word *set* in the dictionary. Name the parts of speech that are listed for it and tell how many definitions there are for each.

Sample Dictionary Page

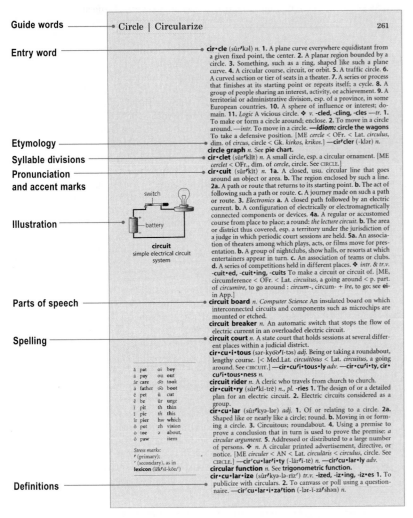

Guide words
Entry word
Etymology
Syllable divisions
Pronunciation and accent marks
Illustration
Parts of speech
Spelling
Definitions

Copyright © 2007 by Houghton Mifflin Company. Adapted and reproduced by permission from *The American Heritage College Dictionary*, Fourth Edition.

Sample Dictionary Page

Review the sample dictionary page with students, focusing on specific parts as needed.

☑ DIFFERENTIATE INSTRUCTION

Pronunciation Symbols Ask students to translate one or two familiar words into phonetic symbols. Remind students that words with more than one syllable will need syllable divisions and accent marks as well. Collect and distribute the words, and have students use the pronunciation symbol key to pronounce the words.

Definitions Students may have difficulty deciding which definition to use if a word has multiple meanings. Guide students to reread the sentence that contains the word they are researching and consider each definition listed to find the one that makes the most sense in the context. Also, context examples of the word are often provided (see definition *4a* under *circuit*) to help clarify meaning.

ELPS 4C

After students have examined the sample page, provide additional information, referring to the sample as necessary. For example:

- When a word relates to a specific field of work or study, this is indicated at the beginning of the definition. See, for example, definition *11* under *circle* and the definition for *circuit board*.
- Variant forms of the entry word are also shown. The sample shows the past tense, present participle, and present tense of verbs (*-cled, -cling, -cles,* for *circle*); adverb forms (*circuitously*); noun forms (*circuitry, circuitousness*); and irregular plurals of nouns (*-ries,* for *circuitry*).

TEKS 11.19; ELPS 4C

 TEKS 11.19 Spell correctly, including using various resources to determine and check correct spellings **ELPS** 4B Recognize directionality of English reading; 4C Comprehend English vocabulary

Other Reference Materials

Review each resource with students, providing actual examples to work with if possible. Discuss the following points regarding each resource:

- What type of information it provides
- When it makes the most sense to use it
- Where to find it
- How to use it

Have partners choose two or three particular resources and work together to answer the above questions about each one. Have them use print or electronic versions to practice. Then have partners provide a tutorial for the group regarding how to use the resources they chose.

Encourage students to ask for assistance as needed, ask each other questions, clarify unclear information, and use synonyms or other familiar words when they don't know the exact English word for something.

⊞ ELPS 1D

Other Reference Materials

As you have seen, dictionaries are an excellent source of information about language. The list below describes other language resources you may find useful.

- **Books of Synonyms, Antonyms, and Homonyms** Thesauruses, or books of synonyms, are probably the most well-known language resource. Synonyms—words that mean the same or almost the same—can be helpful for understanding the meaning of an unfamiliar word, and can add variety to your writing. Many of these resources also include lists of common antonyms (words with opposite meanings) and homonyms (words with the same spelling but different meanings) for thousands of frequently used words.

- **Dictionaries of Idioms** Idioms are used in books, magazines, newspapers, everyday speech—just about anywhere you hear or read language. Phrases that are idioms have a different meaning than the actual words suggest. For example, if you put a project "on the back burner" it means you will work on it later, not that you've placed it on a stove. Learning common English idioms will help you in your reading and your writing; understanding and using them will give you the ability to communicate your thoughts and ideas with expression and imagination.

- **Usage Guides** Usage guides can help you improve your grammar, spelling, and punctuation. Many of these resources also provide guidance about different writing or speaking styles to use for different audiences. Choose a good, multi-purpose guide for general usage issues; for specific types of writing, such as writing for a newspaper, you may want to use a more specific guide as well.

- **Pronunciation Dictionaries** Pronunciation dictionaries allow you to type in or look up a particular word and hear it pronounced, either online or on a CD accompanied by a book. Variations in pronunciation are often included as well.

- **Translation Dictionaries** Translation dictionaries help you take a familiar word in one language and find a word with the same or almost the same meaning in another language. These resources can help you transfer your knowledge in one language into a new language, making your ideas and your writing clearer for your audience.

Learning Language

Writing process, writing traits, narrative writing, expository writing—
these terms are all part of the language of writing. The language of writing
is the vocabulary words and terms that teachers and students use to talk
about writing. Learning the language of writing is just as important as
developing your ability to write well.

Have you ever had to teach a skill to someone? Whether it's how to
solve a math problem or how to bake a cake, teaching a skill often helps
you understand the skill better. The same thing is true for the language of
writing. Using the language of writing to talk about writing will help you
improve your writing, as well as improve your understanding of writing
as a process.

- Language Strategies
- Language of the Writing Process
- Language of the Writing Traits
- Language of the Writing Forms

"The palest ink is better than the
best memory."

—Chinese proverb

Learning Language

Learning Language

Objectives
- learn and use strategies for acquiring basic
  and academic language
- demonstrate basic understanding of the
  writing process and associated vocabulary
- demonstrate basic understanding of the
  writing traits and associated vocabulary
- demonstrate basic understanding of major
  writing forms and associated vocabulary

Discussing the language of writing, including
words that describe the writing process, the
traits of writing, and writing forms, is critical to
students' understanding of these topics as well as
to their overall success in the classroom. Guide
students' understanding by following these steps.

- Explain the words *strategy, process,* and *trait,*
  and write them in a graphic organizer. Discuss
  examples of each term and add the examples
  to the organizer. Model routine classroom
  language during your discussion.
- Have partners work together to come up with
  additional examples. Encourage students to
  use some of the routine language that you
  modeled as they discuss the terms.
- Invite pairs to share their examples with each
  other, and clarify any misunderstandings.
  Have students add their examples to the
  graphic organizer.
- Students can revisit the graphic organizer
  later as a reminder or to add information.

⭐ ELPS 1C, 3B, 3G ✔DIFFERENTIATE INSTRUCTION

Differentiated Instruction: English Language Learners

⭐ ELPS 1C, 3B, 3G

ELP Level **Beginning**	ELP Level **Intermediate**	ELP Level **Advanced/Advanced High**
Have students choose one word and practice saying it after you. Ask them to write the word in the organizer. Then guide them to illustrate and label examples of any terms they choose.	Have partners help fill in the organizer by providing key words such as *plan* or *correct*. During discussion, guide students to respond with phrases and short sentences.	Students may use individual organizers to plan responses. During discussion, guide students to respond in complete sentences and extended descriptions as appropriate.

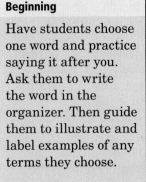

ELPS 1C Use strategic learning strategies to acquire basic
and grade-level vocabulary; **3B** Expand vocabulary/learning and
using routine language needed for classroom communication;
3G Express ideas

Language Strategies

Teach these language-learning strategies, using the examples shown in blue to model as needed.

`DIFFERENTIATE INSTRUCTION ↘` `DIFFERENTIATE INSTRUCTION ↘`

Use Language Patterns

Explain that listening for language patterns, or chunks of language, will help students learn new basic vocabulary and monitor their understanding of spoken language.

Try It!
Answers

Responses will vary, but sentences should include words or phrases that indicate time and sequence of events.
⭐ **ELPS** 2C, 2D

Look for the Context

Explain that by looking around the words on signs, labels, and in sentences, students can discover information that will help them understand the meaning of unfamiliar print.

Try It!
Answers

Responses will vary, but explanations should include recognition of surrounding word parts or symbols, as well as an understanding of how others are or would be using or reacting to the environmental print.
⭐ **ELPS** 4C

Use Academic Language

Explain that students can internalize new basic and academic language by using and reusing it in speech.

Try It!
Answers

Responses will vary, but students should demonstrate an ability to use new academic language in multiple speaking contexts.
⭐ **ELPS** 2C

ELPS 2C Learn new basic and academic vocabulary; **2D** Monitor understanding of spoken language; **4C** Derive meaning of environmental print

---

 ELPS 2C, 2D, 4C

Language Strategies

You hear and read new words every day. Here are some strategies to help you understand, remember, and use this new language.

Use Language Patterns

Listen and look for the repeated words and phrases, or patterns, that others use when they speak and when they write.

You hear: **Today**, Zoe will present her report. You will present **tomorrow**.
You can say: **Tomorrow**, I will present my report.

Try It!

Turn to a partner. Say two or three sentences that tell what will happen. Start with a word that tells *when*.

Look for the Context

Signs, labels, posters, and other print around you can sometimes be unclear. Look for familiar word parts or symbols that might help you discover the meaning of something unfamiliar. Look at where the sign is and how other people are reacting to it. These approaches will help you decide what many kinds of environmental print mean.

Try It!

Work with a partner. Choose two signs or labels around you and explain them to each other. Use the context to help you.

Use Academic Language

Teachers may use words you don't know in class. Repeat and write down these words. When you can, use a dictionary to look them up.

You hear: The U.S. Constitution defines the rights of all American citizens.
You say and write down: **constitution**.

Try It!

Repeat and write down words you don't understand from today's classes. If you are not sure how to write the word, ask a friend.

Struggling Learners

Visual learners may benefit from using different colored pens or highlighting their notes. Have them assign different colors for key phrases, special vocabulary, steps in a process or cycle, important dates, and so forth. This can be helpful when studying later. It will be easier for visual students to access and recall information when they associate it with a specific color.

Say It Again

Your teacher gives an instruction that you do not understand. Ask a classmate to listen as you retell or summarize the instructions in your own words to make sure you understand the information correctly.

You can say: I think we are supposed to write our outline in class and draft an essay for homework. Is that right?

Try It!

Listen carefully to a class message or your teacher's instructions. Work with a partner to retell or summarize what you heard.

Look for Word Parts You Know

Many words share prefixes, suffixes, or roots, even words in different languages. For example, the prefix *bio-* means "life" in many languages, including French, Spanish, and German.

You think: The Spanish word *biología* looks almost the same as the English word *biology*. Maybe they mean the same.

Try It!

If you hear a word you don't know, try writing it down. See if you recognize any of its parts. If so, use that part to help you understand the meaning of the whole word.

Learn New Meanings of Words

You may hear a word that you know used in a way that is unfamiliar to you. Finding the connection to what you know can help you understand the new use of the word.

You think: Suki has to parallel park to pass her driving test. In geometry, parallel lines go in the same direction and never meet. Parallel parking must mean that the car is parallel to the curb, going in the same direction.

Try It!

Listen for familiar words used in unfamiliar ways. Try to find the logical connection between the two uses.

Say It Again

Explain to students that when someone tries to retell or summarize information, the speaker often recognizes the need for clarification of some ideas. Point out that retelling or summarizing instructions or other information will also help them understand and remember the information clearly.

Try It!
Answers

Responses will vary; guide students to retell or summarize accurately as needed.

⭐ ELPS 1D, 2I

Look for Word Parts You Know

Explain that by looking for familiar word parts students can often discover the meanings of unknown words.

Try It!
Answers

Responses will vary; encourage students to build vocabulary by coming up with other examples similar to the one given.

⭐ ELPS 2C

Learn New Meanings of Words

Explain that students can internalize the meanings of new basic and academic words used in new contexts by connecting them to meanings they already know.

Try It!
Answers

Responses will vary; students should show an ability to make connections to between familiar words and words used in new contexts.

⭐ ELPS 2C, 2D

Differentiated Instruction: English Language Learners

⭐ ELPS 1D, 1H

ELP Level **Beginning**	ELP Level **Intermediate**	ELP Level **Advanced/Advanced High**
Focus on the strategies "Use Language Patterns," "Look for the Context," and "Use Academic Language" with students at the beginning level.	Focus on the strategies mentioned in the Beginning column as well as "Say It Again" and "Learn New Meanings of Words" with students at the intermediate level.	Students can benefit from instruction in all the strategies, but you may find that "Say It Again" and "Look for Words Parts You Know" are most appropriate for advanced students.

⭐ **ELPS 1D** Speak using learning strategies; **1H** Develop and expand repertoire of learning strategies; **2C** Learn new expressions and new basic vocabulary; **2D** Monitor understanding of spoken language; **2I** Demonstrate listening comprehension/retelling or summarizing

Language of the Writing Process

Before you begin the unit Using the Writing Process (SE pages 6–32) with English language learners, work through pages 562–565 together. These pages will help build students' familiarity with the writing process and the language used to discuss it.

Work with students to understand each step of the writing process, as follows.

■ Introduce the terms for each step in the writing process.

■ Together, read the explanation for each term.

■ Provide examples of the terms from shared experiences to help students comprehend the English vocabulary.

■ Help students recognize each term quickly and easily on sight, associating it clearly with its meaning and spelling.

■ Identify any words that present difficulties for students. Have them practice reading and saying the difficult words repeatedly so that they will eventually recognize the words in other written classroom materials.

DIFFERENTIATE INSTRUCTION ↘

 ELPS 4C

 ELPS 4C

Language of the Writing Process

Read each of the terms in order, saying them aloud to help you remember them. Write down any unfamiliar words on a separate sheet of paper and look them up in a dictionary.

Prewrite

The first step of the writing process is to prewrite, or plan your writing. During prewriting, you will select a topic and decide what genre, or form of writing, you will use. Next, you will gather your thoughts about that topic and do any research that might be needed to gather information and details about your topic. When you have gathered your ideas and information, you will create a thesis statement. Finally, you will organize or categorize your thoughts, arranging them into a logical sequence that supports your thesis statement.

Draft

When you begin a draft, you start to develop your ideas into a complete, organized piece of writing. You think about your audience and your purpose. Your goal is to create a clear beginning, middle, and ending that clearly communicates and supports your thesis statement and that will interest and excite your readers.

Revise

Now it is time to read your draft and revise it, or make changes. At this step, you review your draft for four of the five writing traits: *focus and coherence, organization, development of ideas,* and *voice.* You read your writing to decide which parts work well, which pieces should be deleted or moved, and which parts need more development. This is also when you might ask a friend or a teacher to give you feedback about your writing.

Edit

When you edit, you are looking at your revised draft to review for the fifth trait, *conventions.* You proofread for correct spelling, grammar, and mechanics (capitalization and punctuation) and correct any errors that you find.

Publish

At this stage, you publish your work by making a neat final copy and deciding how you want to share your writing with others. Publishing should happen when you know that all parts of your writing make sense and feel right to you.

Vocabulary: Writing Process

audience	draft	edit
mechanics	prewrite	proofread
publish	purpose	revise
thesis statement		

1. **Say the word.** Listen to the words as your teacher reads them, and then repeat them aloud. Which of these words have you heard before? Which do you already know?

2. **Discover the meaning.** With a partner, make a three-column chart. List the vocabulary words in the first column, the meanings in the second column, and an example sentence in the third. Start with the words you already know, and discuss how you can fill in the chart as you learn about the other words.

3. **Learn more.** Listen as your teacher explains the meaning of each word. Work with your partner to add new information to your chart.

4. **Think about it.** Use your notebook to answer the questions below.
   - Which step should you do first—create a draft or write a thesis statement?
   - How does your writing change if your audience is a friend instead of a teacher?
   - What is something you might change when you revise your writing?
   - What is something you might change when you edit your writing?

5. **Show your understanding.** Practice explaining how each word in the vocabulary box above fits into the writing process. Share your explanation with a partner. Work together to add specific details in order to create an accurate meaning for each word.

6. **Write about it.** Write a short paragraph explaining the writing process. Use at least three of the vocabulary words above in your paragraph.

Vocabulary: Writing Process

1. Read each word aloud, demonstrating how to pronounce the distinct sounds in each word. Have students repeat the words after you, practicing producing the sounds of the newly acquired vocabulary.
   ELPS 3A

2. Help students create and fill in their vocabulary graphic organizers. Tell students that they will use their charts to help them learn the new academic vocabulary. Partners should share information as they fill in their charts.
   ELPS 3E, 4C

3. Explain what each term means with respect to the steps in the writing process. Help students understand general meanings of the terms by illustrating terms on the board (for example, several stick figures for "audience"). Clarify any misunderstandings. Help students understand the specific meanings by discussing the main points of each term (for example, an audience is a group of people who will read your writing). Partners should work together to add new information to their charts.
   ELPS 2D, 2I, 3E, 4C

4. Have students show that they understand the meanings of the new academic vocabulary by responding to the questions. Model how to answer the first one. Then work with students to answer the remaining questions.
   ELPS 2D, 2I, 3E, 3G, 3H, 4C

5. Have partners practice and share their explanations. Check in with pairs to clarify any misunderstandings.
   ELPS 2D, 2I, 3E, 3G, 3H, 4C

6. Guide individual students as they write their paragraphs.
   ELPS 5B, 5G

Differentiated Instruction: English Language Learners

ELPS 3E, 3G, 3H, 4C

ELP Level **Beginning**	ELP Level **Intermediate**	ELP Level **Advanced/Advanced High**
Students at this level should focus on the steps of the writing process. Provide visuals and gestures, as possible, for each step. Also encourage native-language peer discussion.	Support students at this level by providing phrases and short sentences as well as visuals when you explain the terms.	Students at this level should be able to use extensive language to express ideas and write about terms. Support them by providing flash cards for commonly misunderstood terms.

ELPS 2D Monitor understanding of spoken language; **2I** Demonstrate listening comprehension/collaborating with peers; **3A** Practice producing sounds of newly acquired vocabulary to pronounce English words; **3E** Share information in cooperative learning interactions; **3G** Express opinions and ideas; **3H** Explain with increasing specificity and detail; **4C** Develop basic sight vocabulary and comprehend English vocabulary and language structures; **5B** Write using newly acquired basic vocabulary and content-based grade-level vocabulary; **5G** Explain with increasing specificity and detail

The Writing Process in Action

For each step in the process, use the **Modeled Writing** instruction that follows to model the steps for students. Write in the narrative or expository form, and focus on a familiar topic.

After you have modeled all the steps, go back to **Revisit for Shared Writing** under each step to create a new Shared Writing piece with students. Use the same writing form as your model.

Prewrite

- **Modeled Writing** Think aloud as you choose a topic, focus statement, audience, and writing form for your piece.
- **Revisit for Shared Writing** Begin a new piece together. Tell students that as you work, you will ask them to give you information for the writing piece. They should listen for words such as "Would you please" that signal requests. Remind students of relevant parts of your model as you discuss the questions and request information from students.

Draft

- **Modeled Writing** Think aloud as you draft your writing piece. Discuss how you are organizing your ideas to support your focus statement as you write. You may wish to use a graphic organizer to group ideas together visually before you write.
- **Revisit for Shared Writing** Begin the Shared Writing draft by discussing the questions with students. Invite students to supply ideas for the draft, prompting them as necessary and referring back to your model draft when appropriate.

⭐ **ELPS** 2I, 3E **DIFFERENTIATE INSTRUCTION** ↘

 ⭐ ELPS 2I, 3E

The Writing Process in Action

You've learned the language of the writing process. Now it's time to see and experience the process in action. Your teacher will demonstrate each step of the writing process. Then the class will write together, going through the steps of the writing process. Use the questions below to guide you through the steps.

Prewrite

1. What ideas do you have for a topic? How does the assignment help you choose a topic?
2. What ideas and thoughts do you want to include?
3. How does your audience affect the ideas you have about the writing?
4. What genre, or form, will you use to write?
5. How will you gather ideas for your writing? What information will you need to gather to add to your ideas?
6. Will you try freewriting or brainstorming to add to your ideas?
7. What research materials will you use? Will you need to go online or use print materials from the library? What primary or secondary sources might you use?
8. How will you organize your ideas? What information and ideas will go in each paragraph?
9. What graphic organizers, diagrams, or drawings might help you organize your ideas?

Draft

1. As you draft, are your ideas fitting together well? Is the writing flowing easily or not?
2. Is the beginning clear and focused? Does it communicate well with your audience?
3. Do the ideas in the middle connect to the beginning and to each other? Is the sequence of ideas easy to follow and understand?
4. Have you included everything you think is important?
5. Have you added new details or ideas that came to you as you were writing? Have these improved the writing for your audience?

Learning Language **565**

⭐ ELPS 2I, 3E, 3G

Revise

1. Do you focus on your topic? Which ideas are working well? Which ideas do you need to change or delete?
2. Is everything you included important to your thesis statement?
3. Are there any sentences that are confusing or distracting to your audience?
4. Is the writing in the correct order? Does each sentence and paragraph build on the ones that come before it?
5. Does the tone, or voice, of your writing connect with your audience? Do you need to change some words to create a better voice for your writing?
6. Have you asked someone to read the draft and incorporated any responses that will improve your writing?

Edit

1. Did you follow the rules of grammar and mechanics? Is all the punctuation and capitalization correct?
2. Does each sentence make sense? Are all the words in the correct order? Are any words missing?
3. Are all the words spelled correctly? Do you use the correct form of words with more than one spelling, such as *there, their,* and *they're*?
4. Is there agreement between subjects and verbs? Are the verb tenses correct and consistent?
5. Did you print a clean copy and proofread it?

Publish

1. Have you made a clean copy after proofreading? Are the margins even? Are paragraphs indented?
2. Is your writing neat and easy to read? Are the pages numbered and in the correct order?
3. Are you ready to present your writing with confidence?

 Turn and Talk

Talk with a classmate about the writing you just finished. Share your ideas about what was easy, what was difficult, and what you like or don't like about your writing.

Example: The easiest part was _____. The difficult part was _____. What I like about my writing is _____.

Revise

- **Modeled Writing** Revisit your model draft. Think aloud as you revise to make sure that the text is relevant to the focus statement, that it flows logically, and that it is appropriate for the audience.
- **Revisit for Shared Writing** Return to the shared draft and work together to identify areas of improvement, using the questions as needed.

Edit

- **Modeled Writing** Think aloud as you identify errors in grammar and mechanics, such as inappropriate verb tenses. Model correcting them by using proofreading marks.
- **Revisit for Shared Writing** Return to the shared draft and work together to identify errors in grammar, spelling, and mechanics, including errors in verb tense. Correct errors together.

Publish

- **Modeled Writing** Model how to seek and incorporate feedback from peers. Then think aloud about the best way to publish your piece and begin to create a neat final copy.
- **Revisit for Shared Writing** Return to the shared draft and discuss the Publish questions. Work with students to seek and provide feedback. Invite a volunteer to make a neat final copy.

 Turn and Talk

Model how to listen to a speaker's main points as you turn and talk with a student. Tell students that as they discuss the writing process and the shared writing they just completed, they should listen carefully for their partner's main points.

⭐ ELPS 2I, 3E, 3G

Differentiated Instruction: English Language Learners		⭐ ELPS 2I, 3E, 3G
ELP Level **Beginning**	**ELP Level** **Intermediate**	**ELP Level** **Advanced/Advanced High**
Provide visuals and gestures when possible for students at this level. Post a bank of words related to the shared writing topic so that students can point to words to use in the writing.	Use a graphic organizer for students at this level as you draft, and provide a bank of sentence stems that they can use to supply sentences for shared writing.	Use a graphic organizer as you draft, encouraging students to contribute to the organizer and to add their own creative sentences to the shared writing piece.

 ELPS 2I Demonstrate listening comprehension/collaborating with peers; **3E** Share information in cooperative learning interactions; **3G** Express opinions, ideas, feelings

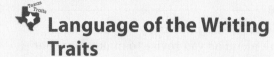

Language of the Writing Traits

Before you begin the section Understanding the Traits of Writing (SE pages 46–89) with English language learners, work through pages 566–567 together. These pages will help build students' familiarity with the writing traits and the language used to discuss each of them.

Work with students to understand each of the writing traits, as follows.

- Introduce the terms for each writing trait.
- Together, read the explanation for each term.
- Provide examples of the terms from shared experiences to help students comprehend the English vocabulary.
- Help students recognize each term or phrase quickly and easily on sight, associating it clearly with its meaning and spelling.
- Identify any words that present difficulties for students. Have them practice reading and saying the difficult words repeatedly so that they will eventually recognize the words in other written classroom materials.

ELPS 4C **DIFFERENTIATE INSTRUCTION**

 ELPS 4C

Language of the Writing Traits

Read each of these terms. Keep a list of any words you don't know.

Focus and Coherence

Writing has focus when it has a thesis statement that can be clearly understood by the audience. Coherence means that the main points and details support this thesis; all the information and the sentences connect and make sense together. Your writing should have focus and coherence to help your audience understand your ideas.

Organization

Your writing should be organized, or put together, to make it easy to follow from beginning to end. The beginning, middle, and ending of the writing should lead the reader easily, step by step, through your ideas. Each sentence and paragraph should logically follow those that come before them.

Development of Ideas

Developing ideas in depth, with interesting and important details, helps readers understand your thesis statement. Each sentence should add meaning to the sentences that have come before it. Choosing your supporting points and details carefully will help you explain your ideas clearly to your readers.

Voice

Your writing should show the way you think and feel, and it should reflect your personality. This is called your writing "voice." Your voice gets readers interested in what you have to say; it helps create a relationship between you and your reader that keeps them reading all the way to the end of the piece.

Conventions

The rules for writing are called conventions. This means that you need to think about grammar, sentence structure, mechanics (capitalization and punctuation), and spelling. Writing that has no mistakes or errors is easier to read and understand.

⭐ ELPS 2D, 3E, 3G, 3H, 4C, 4G, 5B, 5G

Vocabulary: Writing Traits

coherence	conventions	depth
development	focus	organization
voice		

1. **Say the word.** Listen to the words as your teacher reads them, and then repeat them aloud. Which of these words have you heard before? Which do you already know?

2. **Discover the meaning.** Working with a partner, write the vocabulary words and meanings that you already know. Discuss the words with a partner; teach each other the words you know. Some of these words have more than one meaning. If you are not sure of the correct meaning in this context, list the word with the meaning you know.

3. **Learn more.** Listen as your teacher explains each word. Work with your partner to restate the meaning of each one in your own words.

4. **Think about it.** Work with a partner to answer the questions below. Record your answers in your notebook.
   - Why is it important for your writing to have focus and coherence?
   - What are some ways to develop ideas about a trip to a museum?
   - How can you be sure that your writing has depth?

5. **Show your understanding.** Practice explaining how each word in the vocabulary box helps to improve writing. Share your explanation with a partner. Then work together to connect the five traits of writing to the writing process. Create a diagram showing which traits are most important at each step of the writing process.

6. **Write about it.** Write a short paragraph explaining the traits of writing. Use at least three of the vocabulary words above in your paragraph.

Differentiated Instruction: English Language Learners

⭐ ELPS 3E, 4C

ELP Level **Beginning**	ELP Level **Intermediate**	ELP Level **Advanced/Advanced High**
Students at this level should focus on the writing traits terms. Provide visuals and gestures, as possible, for each term. Encourage native-language discussion with peers.	Support students at this level by providing phrases and short sentences as well as visuals when you explain the terms.	Students at this level should be able to use extensive language to discuss and write about the traits. Support them by providing flash cards for any commonly misunderstood terms.

Vocabulary: Writing Traits

1. Read each word aloud, demonstrating how to pronounce the distinct sounds in each word. Have students repeat the words after you, practicing producing the sounds of the newly acquired vocabulary.
   ⭐ ELPS 3A

2. Have students share information with each other as they search for information on meanings of the vocabulary terms. To provide extra support, you can direct them to the first unit in the SE and help them identify relevant information.
   ⭐ ELPS 3E, 4C

3. Explain what each term means with respect to the writing traits. Help students understand general meanings of the terms by illustrating terms on the board (for example, a file folder for "organization"). Clarify any misunderstandings. Help students understand the specific meanings by discussing the main points of each term (for example, *conventions* are the rules of language and include grammar, punctuation, etc.). Partners should add new information to their notebooks.
   ⭐ ELPS 2D, 3E, 4C

4. Have students show that they understand the meanings of the new academic vocabulary by responding to the questions. Model how to answer the first one. Then work with students to answer the remaining questions.
   ⭐ ELPS 2D, 3E, 3G, 3H, 4C, 4G

5. Have partners practice and share their explanations. Check in with pairs to clarify any misunderstandings, and guide students as they create their diagrams.
   ⭐ ELPS 2D, 3E, 3G, 3H, 4C, 4G

6. Guide individual students as they write their paragraphs.
   ⭐ ELPS 5B, 5G

 ELPS 2D Monitor understanding of spoken language; **3A** Practice producing sounds of newly acquired vocabulary to pronounce English words; **3E** Share information in cooperative learning interactions; **3G** Express opinions, ideas; **3H** Explain with increasing specificity and detail; **4C** Develop basic sight vocabulary and comprehend English vocabulary; **4G** Demonstrate comprehension of increasingly complex English/retelling or summarizing; **5B** Write using newly acquired basic vocabulary and content-based grade-level vocabulary; **5G** Explain with increasing specificity and detail

Language of Narrative Writing

Read aloud the explanation of narrative writing with students and discuss the graphic organizer together. Model using a combination of decoding skills to read the text in the organizer. For example, work with students to sound out *controlling* and then discuss *control* as its root. Invite volunteers to read the text in the organizer, using multiple decoding skills such as those you modeled.

 ELPS 4A

 Turn and Talk

As needed, explain that "catch a reader's attention" is an idiom that means "get a reader interested." Model some things you might do to get the group's attention to start a class, such as asking an interesting question. Explain that writers do similar things to get readers interested in a piece of writing. Tell students to turn and talk to a partner about the idiom, and then discuss how to catch a listener's interest when telling a story or describing an experience. Remind them to use detail in their explanations.

ELPS 2C, 3E, 3H, 4C

 ELPS 2C, 3E, 4C

Language of Narrative Writing

A narrative essay is writing that tells about a true experience in the writer's life. The experience might be one that occurred over a period of time and changed the writer in some way. Narrative essays have the same basic organization: a beginning that catches the reader's attention and identifies a main, or controlling idea, middle paragraphs that use sensory details to tell about the experience in chronological order, and an ending paragraph that reflects on what the writer learned from the experience.

Narrative Writing Organization

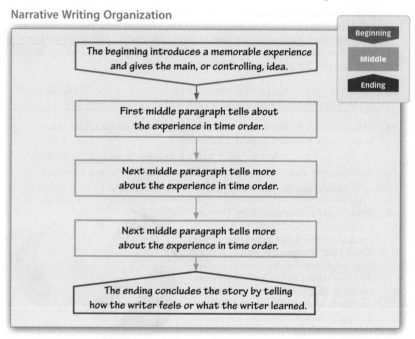

Turn and Talk
Talk with a partner about what the phrase "catch a reader's attention" means.

To catch a reader's attention means to _____.

ELPS 2C Learn new expressions; **3E** Share information in cooperative learning interactions; **3H** Explain with increasing specificity and detail; **4A** Decode using a combination of skills; **4C** Comprehend English vocabulary and language structures

☆ **ELPS** 2C, 2D, 3E, 3H, 4C, 5B, 5G

Vocabulary: Narrative Writing

attention	chronological order	conclude
controlling idea	experience	memorable
narrative	reflect	sensory details

1. **Say the word or phrase.** Listen as your teacher reads the words aloud. Then repeat each word.

2. **Discover the meaning.** Work with a partner to sort the vocabulary words under these three headings: Words I Know, Word Parts I Know, and New Words. Write notes about what you think the familiar words or word parts mean.

3. **Learn more.** Listen as your teacher explains the meaning of each word. Work with your partner to check and correct your earlier notes. Write the meanings for additional words.

4. **Think About it.** Use your notebook to write out answers to the questions below.

   ■ What would make an experience memorable?

   ■ Why do you tell an experience in chronological order?

   ■ Why is the ending of a narrative essay a good place to reflect on your experience?

5. **Show your understanding.** Use details to explain to your partner what each vocabulary word means, but don't say the word. Give clues that are synonyms, or words that mean the same thing. For example, "I use this word to say I finish or end my essay." After your partner identifies the correct word, ask him or her to give clues to you for another vocabulary word.

6. **Write About it.** Write a short paragraph explaining how to write a narrative. Use at least three of the vocabulary words above in your paragraph.

Language

Vocabulary: Narrative Writing

① Read each word aloud, demonstrating how to pronounce its distinct sounds. Have students repeat the words after you, practicing producing the sounds of the newly acquired vocabulary.

② Tell students to create a three-column chart using the suggested headings and to list the vocabulary terms in the appropriate column. Model writing notes about the words and point out familiar word parts. As students share information with each other, they should make notes in their notebooks about the meanings of the terms.

③ Explain what each term means with respect to the narrative form. Help students understand general meaning of the terms by illustrating them on the board (such as a stop sign for "conclude"). Then clarify any misunderstandings. Help students understand the specific meanings by discussing the main points of each term (for example, to conclude a piece of writing means to end it, leaving the reader with a strong impression). Partners should monitor their understanding as they add new information to their notebooks, and seek clarification as needed.

④ Have students show that they understand the meanings of the new academic vocabulary by responding to the questions. Model how to answer the first one. Then work with students to answer the remaining questions.

⑤ Model how to give clues, and then circulate to provide assistance as partners work together.

⑥ Circulate to provide assistance as students develop their paragraphs independently.

☑ **DIFFERENTIATE INSTRUCTION**

☆ **ELPS** 2C, 2D, 3A, 3E, 3H, 4C, 5B, 5G

Differentiated Instruction: English Language Learners

☆ **ELPS** 2C, 3E, 3H, 4C, 5B, 5G

ELP Level **Beginning**	**ELP Level** **Intermediate**	**ELP Level** **Advanced/Advanced High**
Guide students to connect each term to the graphic organizer on page 568. Provide visuals, gestures, and examples, as possible, for each term. Have students repeat each term after you.	Use phrases and short sentences as well as visuals when you explain the terms. Have partners discuss how each term "fits" on the graphic organizer on page 568.	Tell partners to discuss and create a web that shows the relationships between and among the terms. Then have students work independently to write about the terms with detail.

ELPS 2C Learn new basic and academic vocabulary; **2D** Monitor understanding of spoken language during classroom instruction and interactions and seek clarification as needed; **3A** Practice producing sounds of newly acquired vocabulary to pronounce English words; **3E** Share information in cooperative learning interactions; **3H** Explain with increasing specificity and detail; **4C** Develop basic sight vocabulary; **5B** Write using newly acquired basic vocabulary and content-based grade-level vocabulary; **5G** Explain with increasing specificity and detail

Reading the Narrative Model

What Do You Know?

Tell students that the writing model they will listen to shortly is about choices. Explain that the model describes what happens as a result of a bad choice. Discuss the types of choices students make and experiences they have had with the results of a bad choice. Encourage students to use their primary language when necessary.

ELPS 2I, 3H

Build Background

Provide background information about the writing model so that students have knowledge about the topic before they hear the narrative. Use visuals whenever possible as you provide information. **DIFFERENTIATE INSTRUCTION ↘**

Listening

Tell students that they will need to listen carefully and take notes as you read the writing model aloud because you will ask them to identify the controlling, or main, idea of the writing after you have read the first paragraph. After you have finished reading, discuss students' answers to the questions.

ELPS 2I, 3H, 4G

Key Narrative Writing Words

Read aloud the terms in the box as students follow along. Tell students that they will see these terms when they read the writing model. Point out the basic sight words *finally* and *following* and have students repeat them several times. Then help students as they complete the activity. Remind them to use specificity and detail as they describe their experiences.

ELPS 3H, 4C

Reading the Narrative Model

What Do You Know?

Next you will read *The Wrong Club* on pages 136–137. This narrative writing model describes a bad choice and its consequences. You make dozens of choices every day. What happens when you make the wrong choice? How do you live with the results of a bad choice? What can you do to "fix" things when you make a bad choice? Tell what you know.

Build Background

In a debate, a speaker has a certain amount of time to state his or her views on a topic. Then another speaker has the same amount of time to present the opposite opinion. Next, each debater has a second turn to speak in order to rebut, or challenge, the ideas presented by the other speaker. Debaters prepare by studying the topic carefully to find facts and examples that support their views. They try to present their views in a believable and lively way. Judges name the most convincing debater to be the winner.

Listening

Listen as your teacher or a classmate reads *The Wrong Club* aloud. As you listen, take notes about the controlling idea. Be prepared to answer the questions below.

1. What are two ways the writer creates effective images for the reader?
2. How does the writer's description of the photography club reveal his feelings about his choice?
3. What lesson does the writer learn about making choices?

Key Narrative Writing Words

advisor	alternate	argue
belong	choices	convincing
finally	immediately	issue
popular	that season	the following week

Look at the words in the box. You will see these words when you read the writing model. With a partner, use some of the words to describe joining a club or activity in your school or town. Include as many details as you can. Discuss whether the club or activity was a good choice for you.

Read Along

Now it's your turn to read. Turn to pages **136–137**. Read the writing model as your teacher or a classmate reads it aloud.

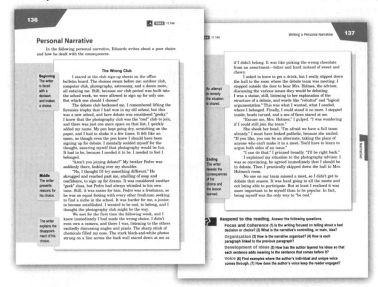

After Reading

Copy the following chart on a sheet of paper and fill it in with information about the writing model. Use your chart to summarize the writing model with a partner.

Action or Event	Sensory Details	Your Thoughts
First		
Next		
Next		
Last		

Read Along

Have students read the writing model silently as you read it aloud. As appropriate, have students track the print to demonstrate their understanding of the directionality of English text. You may wish to have students refer back to visuals you provided earlier to support their comprehension of the text.

⭐ ELPS 4B, 4G

After Reading

Draw the chart from SE page 571 on the board and model finding information from the personal narrative to fill in the chart. Have partners find additional information and fill in the chart on their own paper. Then model using one row of the chart to summarize part of the personal narrative and have students follow your lead with the remaining rows. Invite a volunteer to use his or her chart to summarize the model for the group.

⭐ ELPS 2I, 4G

ELPS 2I Demonstrate listening comprehension/collaborating with peers; **3H** Narrate with increasing specificity and detail; **4B** Recognize directionality of English reading; **4D** Use prereading supports to enhance comprehension of written text; **4G** Demonstrate comprehension of increasingly complex English/shared reading/retelling or summarizing

Oral Language: Narrative Writing

Read through the text at the top of the page with students. Then provide an example of varying a story for different audiences. For example, you might model telling a four-year-old a funny story about how you trained a puppy to sit, versus narrating the same story on a television show about dog training. Point out the differences in the way you narrated the story. Then provide other examples, asking students to express their ideas about the differences in the narrations. Explain that it is also important to adjust the way you write for different audiences.

⭐ **ELPS** 3G, 4G

Try It!
Answers

Students' responses to the activity will vary widely, but partners should demonstrate an ability to narrate stories with specificity and detail that is appropriate for different audiences.

⭐ **ELPS** 3E, 3H, 4G

Oral Language: Narrative Writing

The person or people who will listen to you or read your writing are called the audience. When you speak or write, it is important to choose just the right words that will convey your ideas to the right audience. In writing, the tone, or the way you write, will be different for each audience.

Try It!

Read about the situation below. Then choose two audiences from the list. With a partner, discuss how the words you choose to tell your story might be different for each audience.

Situation

You tried out for a school play because a friend was also trying out. You both got roles in the play, but you feel uncomfortable when you rehearse and you didn't realize that you would have to learn so many lines. You wish you could quit but no one can take your part. Tell your story.

Audiences

- The director of the play
- Your favorite teacher
- A brother or sister

Effective Talk

When you answer a question, you might use a few words, a sentence, or a few sentences. When you use more details to tell about something, the other person will have a better understanding.

Read the question and the answers below. In the first box, there are only two words. In the second box, there is a short sentence that answers the question. The third answer contains more detail and does a better job answering the question.

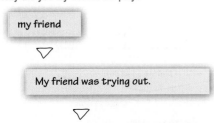

Why did you try out for the play?

> my friend

▽

> My friend was trying out.

▽

> My friend was trying out and he asked me to go to the try-outs with him so he wouldn't be so nervous. I've never done anything like that, but I agreed. I never thought that I would get a role in the play too, but I did.

Try It!

Choose a question to talk about with a partner. Write two or three ideas for answering the question. Next add details that will help your partner understand your ideas. Finally, use your notes as you and your partner describe your answers to the questions.

Here are some ideas to get you started.

1. Have you ever tried a new school activity to help a friend? Tell why and what happened.

2. Tell about a new experience, like trying out for a play for the first time, that taught you an important lesson.

Language

Effective Talk

Read the information at the top of the page aloud as students follow along. Write the question in blue on the board and discuss what it is asking. Then talk about how the three answers provided contain varying degrees of detail, with the third answer providing the most detail.

Try It!
Answers

Discuss the **Try It!** activity and model providing an answer to one of the questions. Invite students to match the level of detail in your answer with one of the example answers shown above. Talk together about how you could add more detail to your response in order to more clearly communicate your message.

Answers will vary widely, but partners should demonstrate an understanding of how to add specificity and detail to make their retelling of the stories more complete. ✔ DIFFERENTIATE INSTRUCTION

⭐ ELPS 2I, 3E, 3G, 3H

Differentiated Instruction: **English Language Learners**		⭐ ELPS 2I, 3B, 3E, 3G, 3H
ELP Level **Beginning**	**ELP Level** **Intermediate**	**ELP Level** **Advanced/Advanced High**
Allow students to create drawings or comic strips to illustrate their experiences. Ask them to explain their drawings using one or two high-frequency words.	Have students create drawings or comic strips. Provide sentence frames such as *I joined the____club with _____because____* to describe their experience with greater detail.	Suggest that partners brainstorm ideas together. Remind students that their responses should include rich detail and examples.

ELPS 2I Demonstrate listening comprehension/collaborating with peers; **3B** Expand vocabulary/learning and using high-frequency words for identifying and describing and retelling simple stories and basic information; **3E** Share information in cooperative learning interactions; **3G** Express ideas; **3H** Describe with increasing specificity and detail

Language of Expository Writing

Read aloud the explanation of expository writing with students and discuss the graphic organizer together. Model using a combination of decoding skills to read the text in the organizer. For example, guide students to sound out *introduction* and *conclusion*, pointing out the similarity in the *-tion* and *-sion* suffixes. Have students identify and pronounce other common suffixes (*-ing, -ment*) in the organizer. Invite volunteers to read the text in the organizer, using multiple decoding skills such as those you modeled.

 ELPS 4A

 Turn and Talk

As needed, explain that background is information that helps to explain what something is like or why something is happening. Provide an example, such as the rules of a popular school sport or activity, to show how background increases understanding of a topic. Tell students to use the vocabulary and language structures you modeled when they turn and talk to a partner about why background is important when explaining information. Remind them to use detail to express their ideas.

 ELPS 3E, 3G, 4C

574

ELPS 3E, 3G, 4C

Language of Expository Writing

Expository writing provides and explains information to the writer's audience. Also called informative writing, this type of writing might explain one subject, or it might compare two subjects. Most often, expository essays have the same basic organization: an introduction with a thesis statement, middle paragraphs that give supporting details, and a conclusion.

Expository Essay Organization

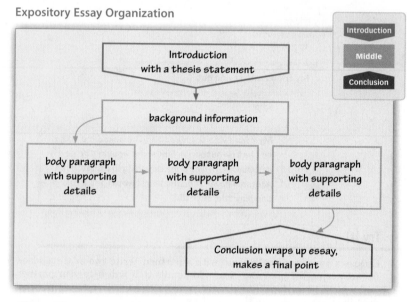

Turn and Talk

Talk with a partner about why an expository essay might include background information.

Readers may need background information because _____.

ELPS **3E** Share information in cooperative learning interactions; **3G** Express ideas; **4A** Decode using a combination of skills; **4C** Comprehend English vocabulary and language structures

⭐ ELPS 2C, 2I, 3E, 3H, 4C, 5B, 5G

Language

Vocabulary: Expository Writing

background	body paragraph	compare
conclusion	expository	introduction
supporting detail	thesis statement	

1. **Say the word or phrase.** Listen as your teacher reads the words aloud. Then repeat each word.

2. **Discover the meaning.** Work with a partner to find an example of each vocabulary word in the writing model on pages **161–162**. For example, which paragraph is a conclusion? Which is an introduction? Write notes about what you think the words mean.

3. **Learn more.** Listen as your teacher explains the meaning of each word. Work with your partner to check and correct your earlier notes. Write the meanings for additional words.

4. **Think about it.** Use your notebook to answer the questions below.
   - Which two vocabulary words are opposites?
   - Where should a thesis statement appear? Why?
   - Which is a better supporting detail, a fact or an opinion?

5. **Show your understanding.** Now that you know more about the vocabulary words, talk to your partner about ways to sort the words. For example, you might sort the words as nouns, verbs, or adjectives. You might choose to sort the words according to which part of an essay they relate to, beginning, middle or ending. Try to sort the words in at least two different ways. Be prepared to explain your sorting methods.

6. **Write about it.** Write a short paragraph explaining how to write an expository essay. Use at least three of the vocabulary words above in your paragraph.

Vocabulary: Expository Writing

1. Read each term aloud, demonstrating how to pronounce its distinct sounds. Have students repeat the terms after you, practicing producing the sounds of the newly acquired vocabulary.

2. Model writing notes about the terms. As students share information with each other, they should take notes in their notebooks about the meanings of the terms.

3. Explain what each term means with respect to the expository form. Help students understand general meaning of the terms by illustrating them on the board (such as a Venn diagram for "compare"). Then clarify any misunderstandings. Help students understand the specific meanings by discussing the main points of each term (for example, to compare two things means to tell how they are similar). Partners should monitor their understanding as they add new information to their notebooks, and seek clarification as needed.

4. Have students take time to think about the meanings of the new academic vocabulary by responding to the questions in their notebooks. Model how to answer the first question. Then work with students to answer the remaining questions.

5. Model one method of sorting the words, and then circulate to provide assistance as partners work together.

6. Circulate to provide assistance as students develop their paragraphs independently.

✔ DIFFERENTIATE INSTRUCTION

⭐ ELPS 2C, 2I, 3A 3E, 3H, 4C, 5B, 5G

Differentiated Instruction: English Language Learners

⭐ ELPS 2C, 2I, 3E, 3H, 4C, 5B, 5G

ELP Level **Beginning**	ELP Level **Intermediate**	ELP Level **Advanced/Advanced High**
Guide students to connect each term to the graphic organizer on page 574. Provide visuals, gestures, and examples, as possible, for each term. Have students repeat each term after you.	Provide support by using short sentences as well as visuals to explain the terms. Have partners explain how each term relates to or describes a section of the graphic organizer on page 574.	Tell partners to discuss and create a web that shows the relationships between and among the terms. Then have students work independently to write about the terms with detail.

⭐ **ELPS 2C** Learn new basic and academic vocabulary; **2I** Demonstrate listening comprehension/collaborating with peers; **3A** Practice producing sounds of newly acquired vocabulary to pronounce English words; **3E** Share information in cooperative learning interactions; **3H** Explain with increasing specificity and detail; **4C** Develop basic sight vocabulary; **5B** Write using newly acquired basic vocabulary and content-based grade-level vocabulary; **5G** Explain with increasing specificity and detail

Reading the Expository Model

What Do You Know?

Tell students that the writing model they will listen to shortly is about the sport of ice climbing. Provide photographs of ice climbers to support students' comprehension. Model describing one aspect of a photo. Then ask students to describe what they know about this and other winter sports. Encourage them to use their primary language when necessary.

ELPS 3H

Build Background

Provide background information about the topic of the report so that students have knowledge about it before they hear the writing model. Use visuals whenever possible as you provide information. DIFFERENTIATE INSTRUCTION ↘

Listening

Tell students that they will need to listen carefully and take notes as you read the writing model aloud because you will ask them to identify the thesis statement, or main idea, of the writing after you have read the first paragraph. After you have finished reading, discuss students' answers to the questions.

ELPS 2I, 3H, 4G

Key Words

Read aloud the terms in the box as students follow along. Tell students that they will see these terms when they read the writing model. Discuss the antonyms *experienced* and *inexperienced,* pointing out the prefix *in-* and the base word *experience.* Have students repeat the words several times and distinguish the difference in sounds. Then help students as they complete the activity.

ELPS 2A, 2I, 3H, 4G

Reading the Expository Model

What Do You Know?

Next you will read the writing model called *Life on Ice* on pages **161–162**. It is an expository essay about ice climbing. From the name, what do you think ice climbing is? Have you, or anyone you know, ever tried ice climbing? Where might you see ice climbers? Tell what you know.

Build Background

Some ice climbers head for an icy mountainside, while others like the challenge of a frozen waterfall. Climbers may create a place to step to or to hold by using an small ax to chip away ice. Climbers also attach crampons over their boots. Crampons have sharp metal points at the front and sides that climbers can jab into the ice, giving them a way to step their way up a slippery surface.

Listening

Listen as your teacher or a classmate reads *Life on Ice* aloud. As you listen, take notes about the thesis statement. Be prepared to answer the questions below.
1. What is the writer's thesis statement?
2. What does the writer mean by the phrase "living on the edge"?
3. With what final thought does the writer leave the reader?

Key Words

accomplishment	bold	experienced
inexperienced	risky	scaling
training grounds	unique	vertical
veteran	viable	

Look at the words in the box. You will see these words when you read the writing model. With a partner, use the words to talk about a new or challenging activity you have tried. Use as many details as you can to describe what makes the activity fun as well as any challenges or difficulties involved.

ELPS **2A** Distinguish sounds of English; **2I** Demonstrate listening comprehension/responding to questions and requests/ taking notes; **3H** Describe with increasing specificity and detail; **4G** Demonstrate comprehension of increasingly complex English/ responding to questions/ taking notes

Read Along

Now it's your turn to read. Turn to pages **161–162**. Read the writing model as your teacher or a classmate reads it aloud.

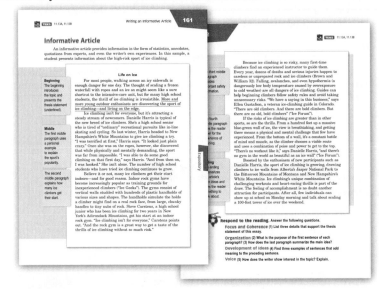

After Reading

Copy the following chart on a sheet of paper and fill it in with the thrills and dangers involved in ice climbing. Use your chart to summarize the writing model with a partner.

Thrills	Dangers

Read Along

Have students read the expository essay silently as you read it aloud. As appropriate, have students track the print to demonstrate their understanding of the directionality of English text. You may wish to have students refer back to visuals you provided earlier to support their comprehension of the text.

 ELPS 4B

After Reading

Draw the chart from SE page 577 on the board and model finding information from the expository essay to fill in the chart. Have partners find additional information and fill in the chart on their own paper. Then model using one row of the chart to summarize part of the expository essay and have students follow your lead with the remaining rows. Invite a volunteer to use his or her chart to summarize the expository essay for the group.

ELPS 2I, 4G

ELPS 2I Demonstrate listening comprehension/collaborating with peers; **3H** Explain with increasing specificity and detail; **4B** Recognize directionality of English reading; **4D** Use prereading supports to enhance comprehension of written text; **4G** Demonstrate comprehension of increasingly complex English/shared reading/retelling or summarizing

Oral Language: Expository Writing

Read through the text at the top of the page with students. Then provide an example of changing an explanation for different audiences. For example, you might model explaining to a four-year-old how to make a sandwich, versus explaining the same process on a television cooking show. Point out differences in the two examples. Then provide other examples, inviting students to identify the differences. Explain that it is also important to adjust the way you write for different audiences.

Try It!
Answers

Students' responses to the activity will vary widely, but partners should demonstrate an ability to express and explain ideas with specificity and detail that is appropriate for different audiences.

⭐ **ELPS** 3E, 3G, 3H, 4G

578

⭐ ELPS 3E, 3G, 3H, 4G

Oral Language: Expository Writing

The person or people who will listen to you or read your writing are called the audience. When you speak or write, it is important to choose just the right words that will reach your audience. In writing, the tone, or the way you write, will be different for each audience.

Try It!

Read about the situation below. Then choose two audiences from the list. With a partner, discuss how the words you use to explain your feelings might be different for each audience.

Situation

Your school offers an after-school class for new or inexperienced drivers. The class will provide instruction in how to avoid skidding, how to drive in rain or snow, and how to protect yourself from accidents. You will explain why the class is both important and popular.

Audiences

- A group of new drivers
- School principal
- A parent

Language

Effective Talk

When you answer a question, you might use a few words, a sentence, or a few sentences. When you use more details to explain something, the other person will have a better understanding.

Read the question and the answers below. In the first box, there is only one word. In the second box, there is a short sentence that answers the question. The third answer contains more detail and does a better job answering the question.

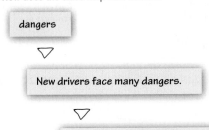

How does the class help new drivers?

dangers

▽

New drivers face many dangers.

▽

New drivers face many dangers for the first time. Knowing how to handle dangers such as skidding, bad weather, or situations where an accident could occur can mean the difference between life and death.

Try It!

Choose a question to talk about with a partner. Write two or three ideas for answering the question. Next add details that will help your partner understand your ideas. Finally, use your notes as you and your partner explain and discuss your answers to the questions.

Here are some ideas to get you started.

1. What kinds of road signs give the most useful information to drivers?

2. Which sport do you think is the most challenging or difficult to learn? Explain your choice.

Effective Talk

Read the information at the top of the page aloud as students follow along. Write the question in blue on the board and discuss what it is asking. Then talk about how the three answers provided contain varying degrees of detail, with the third answer providing the most detail.

Try It!
Answers

Discuss the **Try It!** activity and model providing an answer to one of the questions. Invite students to match the level of detail in your answer with one of the example answers in the book. Talk together about how you could add more detail to your response in order to more clearly communicate your message.

Answers will vary widely, but partners should demonstrate an understanding of how to add specificity and detail to make their responses more complete. ✔ DIFFERENTIATE INSTRUCTION

⭐ ELPS 2I, 3E, 3G, 3H

ELPS 2I Demonstrate listening comprehension/ collaborating with peers; **3B** Expand vocabulary/learning and using high-frequency words for identifying and describing; **3E** Share information in cooperative learning interactions; **3G** Express ideas; **3H** Explain with increasing specificity and detail; **4C** Derive meaning of environmental print

Language of Persuasive Writing

Read aloud the explanation of persuasive writing with students and discuss the graphic organizer together. Model using a combination of decoding skills to read the text in the organizer. For example, point out the similarity of the *-tion* and *-sion* suffixes as you sound out *introduction, position, objection, conclusion,* and *action.* Guide students to identify other common endings (*-ed, -s*) in the graphic organizer. Invite volunteers to read the text in the organizer, using multiple decoding skills such as those you modeled.

 ELPS 4A

 Turn and Talk

Provide examples of common situations in which partners might want to persuade one another, such as choosing a movie to see or discussing which school activity to join. Model using the vocabulary and language structures you might use to persuade someone to agree with you in those situations. Explain that writers do similar things to get readers to agree with an opinion in writing. Tell students to use the vocabulary and language structures you modeled to turn and talk to a partner about their experiences with persuading someone to agree with them. Remind them to use detail in their explanations.

 ELPS 3E, 3H, 4C

580

 ELPS 3E, 4C

Language of Persuasive Writing

Persuasive writing presents ideas in order to convince the writer's audience to share his or her opinion, or position, about a controversy. Details that support the opinion are the writer's argument. Persuasive writing usually has the same basic organization: an introduction in which the writer states a position, middle paragraphs that include reasons to support the position as well as a response to possible objections, and a conclusion that restates the position and gives a call to action.

Persuasive Writing Organization

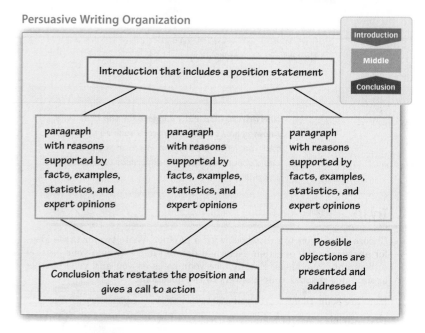

 Turn and Talk
Talk with a partner about one way to help someone agree with your ideas or opinions.

When I want someone to agree with my ideas I _____.

⭐ ELPS 2I, 3A, 3G, 3H, 4C, 5B, 5G

Vocabulary: Persuasive Writing

argument	call to action	controversy
convince	expert opinion	fact
objection	position	statistics

1. **Say the word or phrase.** Listen as your teacher reads the words aloud. Then practice saying each word aloud.

2. **Discover the meaning.** Work with a partner to find some of the vocabulary words in the blue boxes next to the writing model on pages **219–220**. Write notes about what you think the words mean.

3. **Learn more.** Listen as your teacher explains the meaning of each word. Work with your partner to check and correct your earlier notes. Write the meanings for additional words.

4. **Think about it.** Use your notebook to answer the questions below.
   - Why are there likely to be different opinions about a controversy?
   - Why does it make sense to state your position at the beginning of an essay?
   - Which is the better support for your argument: facts or expert opinions? Why do you think so?

5. **Show your understanding.** Talk to your partner about a recent controversy in your school or community. Use the vocabulary words to explain the different positions people had on the issue, the reasons given for each position, and which arguments were most persuasive.

6. **Write about it.** Write a short paragraph explaining how to write a persuasive essay. Use at least three of the vocabulary words above in your paragraph.

Vocabulary: Persuasive Writing

1. Read each word or phrase aloud, demonstrating how to pronounce its distinct sounds. Have students repeat the terms after you, practicing producing the sounds of the newly acquired vocabulary.

2. Help students to locate the call-out boxes in the margins of the writing model and to find information about some of the vocabulary terms. Model writing notes about the words. As students share information with each other, they should take notes in their notebooks about the meanings of the terms.

3. Explain what each term means with respect to the persuasive form. Help students understand general meaning of the terms by using visuals and gestures. Then clarify any misunderstandings. Help students understand the specific meanings by discussing the main points of each term (for example, in persuasive writing an argument is a statement of a position). Partners should monitor their understanding as they add new information to their notebooks, and seek clarification as needed.

4. Have students show that they understand the meanings of the new academic vocabulary by responding to the questions. Model how to answer the first question. Then work with students to answer or express opinions about the remaining questions.

5. As needed, suggest recent controversies with which students are familiar, and then circulate to provide assistance as partners work together to express opinions.

6. Circulate to provide assistance as students develop their paragraphs independently.

✓ DIFFERENTIATE INSTRUCTION

⭐ ELPS 2I, 3A, 3E, 3G, 3H, 4C, 5B, 5G

Differentiated Instruction: English Language Learners

⭐ ELPS 2C, 3E, 3H, 4C, 5B, 5G

ELP Level **Beginning**	ELP Level **Intermediate**	ELP Level **Advanced/Advanced High**
Guide students to connect each term to the graphic organizer on page 580. Provide visuals, gestures, and examples, as possible, for each term. Have students repeat each term after you.	Use phrases and short sentences as well as visuals to explain the terms. Have partners explain how each term connects to the graphic organizer on page 580.	Tell partners to discuss and create a web that shows the relationships between and among the terms. Then have students work independently to write about the terms with detail.

⭐ **ELPS 2C** Learn new basic and academic vocabulary; **2I** Demonstrate listening comprehension/responding to questions and requests/collaborating with peers/taking notes; **3A** Practice producing sounds of newly acquired vocabulary to pronounce English words; **3E** Share information in cooperative learning interactions; **3G** Express opinions; **3H** Explain with increasing specificity and detail; **4C** Comprehend English vocabulary and language structures; **5B** Write using newly acquired basic vocabulary and content-based grade-level vocabulary; **5G** Explain with increasing specificity and detail

Reading the Persuasive Model

What Do You Know?

Tell students that the writing model they will listen to shortly is about sanctions, an action that one government may take against another. As needed, prompt students to suggest online and print resources that might discuss sanctions. Encourage students to use their primary language when necessary.

Build Background

Provide background information about the writing model so that students have knowledge about the topic before they hear the argumentative essay. Use visuals whenever possible as you provide information.

DIFFERENTIATE INSTRUCTION ↘

Listening

Tell students that they will need to listen carefully and take notes as you read the writing model aloud because you will ask them to identify the position statement, or main idea, of the writing after you have read the first paragraph. After you have finished reading, discuss students' answers to the questions.

★ ELPS 2I, 4G

Key Persuasive Writing Words

Read aloud the terms in the box as students follow along. Tell students that they will see these terms when they read the writing model. Point out the basic sight words *begin, with, another, important* and *most* and have students repeat them several times. Then help students to express their opinions as they complete the activity.

★ ELPS 2C, 3G, 4G

★ ELPS 2I, 3G, 4G

Reading the Persuasive Model

What Do You Know?

Next you will read the writing model called *Sanctions Won't Solve Political Problems* on pages **219–220**. It is an persuasive essay about the usefulness of sanctions. Have you read or heard reports about the use of sanctions? How could you learn more about the use of sanctions? Tell what you know.

Build Background

When countries have strong disagreements they may go to war. However, most countries want to avoid war. Instead, governments may impose sanctions to try force leaders of other countries to change their actions. For example, if the United States decides to sanction Country "A," we do not sell American products to Country "A" and we do not buy products from Country "A." This will cause Country "A" to have less money and will cause shortages of some products it needs or wants. If this creates a problem for Country "A's" leaders, they may decide to change their actions.

Listening

Listen as your teacher or a classmate reads *Sanctions Won't Solve Political Problems* aloud. As you listen, take notes about the writer's position statement. Be prepared to answer the questions below.

1. What is the writer's position on sanctions?
2. What are two examples the writer uses to show that sanctions do not work?
3. What does the writer believe countries should do when they disagree?

Key Persuasive Writing Words

another reason	common ground	dialogue
dispute	ineffective	one reason
most important reason	to begin with	

Look at the words in the box. You will see these words when you read the writing model. With a partner, use the words to express your opinions about what countries or friends can do when they disagree with one another.

ELPS 2C Learn new basic vocabulary; **2I** Demonstrate listening comprehension/responding to questions and requests/taking notes; **3G** Express opinions; **4G** Demonstrate comprehension of increasingly complex English/responding to questions/ taking notes

⭐ **ELPS** 2D, 4G

Learning Language **583**

Read Along

Now it's your turn to read. Turn to pages **219–220.** Read the sample essay as your teacher or a classmate reads it aloud.

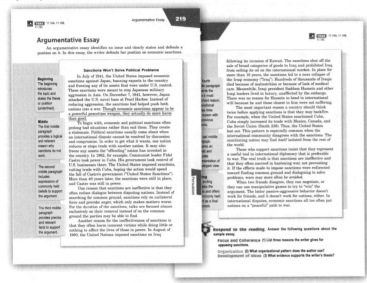

After Reading

Copy the following chart on a sheet of paper and fill it in with the writer's reasons for opposing sanctions, along with the details used to support each reason. Use your chart to summarize the writing model with a partner.

	Reasons	Supporting Facts, Examples, Statistics
Reason 1:		
Reason 2:		
Reason 3:		

Read Along

Have students read the persuasive essay silently as you read it aloud. As appropriate, have students track the print to demonstrate their understanding of the directionality of English text. You may wish to have students refer back to visuals you provided earlier to support their comprehension of the text. Encourage students to monitor their understanding as they listen, and to seek clarification as needed.

⭐ **ELPS** 2D, 4B, 4G

After Reading

Draw the chart from SE page 583 on the board and model finding information from the persuasive essay to fill in the chart. Have partners find additional information and fill in the chart on their own paper. Then model using one row of the chart to summarize part of the persuasive essay and have students follow your lead with the remaining rows. Invite a volunteer to use his or her chart to summarize the persuasive essay for the group.

⭐ **ELPS** 2I, 4G

ELPS 2D Monitor understanding of spoken language and seek clarification as needed; **2I** Demonstrate listening comprehension/collaborating with peers; **3H** Explain with increasing specificity and detail; **4B** Recognize directionality of English reading; **4D** Use prereading supports to enhance comprehension of written text; **4G** Demonstrate comprehension of increasingly complex English/ shared reading/retelling or summarizing

Oral Language: Persuasive Writing

Read through the text at the top of the page with students. Then provide an example of how you would vary an argument for different audiences. For example, you might model persuading a student to perform in a school play versus convincing an administrator to allow the play to be performed. Point out the differences in the way you presented the arguments. Then provide other examples, inviting students to identify the differences in tone and language. Explain that it is also important to adjust the way you write for different audiences.

⭐ **ELPS** 4G

Try It!
Answers

Students' responses to the activity will vary widely, but students should demonstrate an ability to express opinions with specificity and detail that is appropriate for different audiences.

⭐ **ELPS** 3E, 3G, 3H, 4G

⭐ **ELPS** 3E, 3G, 3H, 4G

Oral Language: Persuasive Writing

The person or people who will listen to you or read your writing are called the audience. When you speak or write, it is important to choose just the right words that will reach your audience. In writing, the tone, or the way you write, will be different for each audience.

Try It!

Read about the situation below. Then choose two audiences from the list. With a partner, discuss how the words you choose might be different for each audience.

Situation

> The leaders of your school district are considering whether students should be required to wear uniforms in school. Some students in your school are in favor of the idea, while others are not. You will explain your position on the issue.

Audiences

- ■ A classmate with a different position
- ■ A classmate with the same position
- ■ School principal

🏴 **ELPS 3E** Share information in cooperative learning interactions; **3G** Express opinions; **3H** Explain with increasing specificity and detail; **4G** Demonstrate comprehension of increasingly complex English/responding to questions

ELPS 2I, 3E, 3G, 3H

Effective Talk

When you answer a question, you might use a few words, a sentence, or a few sentences. When you use more details to tell about something, the other person will have a better understanding.

Read the question and the answers below. In the first box, there are only three words. In the second box, there is a short sentence that answers the question. The third answer contains more detail and does a better job answering the question.

What is your position on school uniforms?

> agree with it

▽

> I agree with the idea of wearing school uniforms.

▽

> I believe that wearing uniforms in school is a good idea. Uniforms would allow students to focus on school subjects rather than on what others are wearing. Students who have less money could dress as well as those who have more money.

Try It!

Choose a question to talk about with a partner. Write two or three ideas for answering the question. Next add details that will help your partner understand your ideas. Finally, use your notes as you and your partner explain your opinions about the questions.

Here are some ideas to get you started.

1. Should school cafeteria menus be changed so that only healthy foods are available?

2. Should high school students be required to do volunteer work in their community?

Language

Effective Talk

Read the information at the top of the page aloud as students follow along. Write the question in blue on the board and discuss what it is asking. Then talk about how the three answers provided contain varying degrees of detail, with the third answer providing the most detail

Try It!
Answers

Discuss the **Try It!** activity and model providing an answer to one of the questions. Invite students to match the level of detail in your answer with one of the example answers shown above. Talk together about how you could add more detail to your response in order to more clearly communicate your message.

Answers will vary widely, but partners should demonstrate an understanding of how to add specificity and detail to express their opinions more completely. ✔DIFFERENTIATE INSTRUCTION

⭐ **ELPS** 2I, 3E, 3G, 3H

Differentiated Instruction: English Language Learners

⭐ **ELPS** 2I, 3B, 3E, 3G, 3H

ELP Level **Beginning**	ELP Level **Intermediate**	ELP Level **Advanced/Advanced High**
Allow students to create drawings or comic strips to present their opinions. Ask them to explain their drawings using one or two high-frequency words.	Have students create drawings or comic strips. Provide sentence frames such as *I agree with the idea that____ because ____* to help them express opinions to their partners.	Suggest that partners brainstorm ideas together. Remind students that their responses should include rich detail and examples.

ELPS 2I Demonstrate listening comprehension/ collaborating with peers; **3B** Expand vocabulary/learning and using high-frequency words for identifying and describing and retelling simple stories and basic information; **3E** Share information in cooperative learning interactions; **3G** Express opinions; **3H** Explain with increasing specificity and detail

Language of Writing a Response to Literature

Read aloud the explanation of a response to literature with students and discuss the graphic organizer together. Model using a combination of decoding skills to read the text in the organizer. For example, point out the CVC*e* pattern as you pronounce the long vowel sound in *introduce, state, theme, describe* and *restate*. Invite volunteers to read the text in the organizer, using multiple decoding skills such as those you modeled.

 ELPS 4A

 Turn and Talk

Model stating the theme of a familiar story, emphasizing that other readers may interpret the theme of that story differently. Encourage students to monitor their understanding of the theme concept and seek clarification as needed. Then tell students to turn and talk to a partner about the theme or message of story that they have enjoyed. Remind them to use detail in their explanations.

ELPS 2D, 3E, 3H, 4C

Language of Writing a Response to Literature

A response to literature is writing that tells about a book or story you have read. In a response to literature essay, a writer interprets a book's main theme, or message, using paraphrases and quotations to support the interpretation. This type of essay has a beginning, a middle, and an ending. The graphic organizer below shows the purpose of each part.

Response to Literature Organization

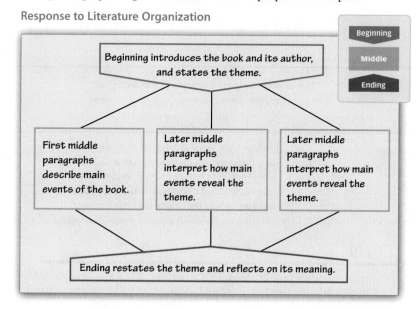

Turn and Talk

Check your understanding of a response to literature essay by talking with a partner about the theme, or message, of a favorite book or story.

One theme, or message, in my favorite book is _____.

ELPS 2D Monitor understanding of spoken language during classroom instruction and interactions and seek clarification as needed; **3E** Share information in cooperative learning interactions; **3H** Explain with increasing specificity and detail; **4A** Decode using a combination of skills; **4C** Comprehend English vocabulary and language structures

Learning Language 587

★ ELPS 2C, 2I, 3E, 3G, 3H, 4C

Vocabulary: Response to Literature

interpret	literature	message
paraphrase	quotation	reflect
response	restate	theme

Language

1. **Say the word.** Listen as your teacher reads the words aloud. Then, pratice saying each word aloud.

2. **Discover the meaning.** Work with a partner to find some of the vocabulary words in the blue boxes next to the writing model on pages 277–278. Write notes about what you think the words mean.

3. **Learn more.** Listen as your teacher explains the meaning of each word. Work with your partner to check and correct your earlier notes. Write the meanings for additional words.

4. **Think about it.** Use your notebook to answer the questions below.
   - What are some examples of literature you have read?
   - What is the difference between a paraphrase and a quotation?
   - Why might the way you interpret a theme be different from someone else's?

5. **Show your understanding.** Talk to your partner about a book or story you read recently. Use the vocabulary words to describe the type of literature and your opinions about the book's theme, or message. Work together to decide whether you would suggest that a friend read the book.

6. **Write about it.** Write a short paragraph explaining how to write a response to literature. Use at least three of the vocabulary words above in your paragraph.

Differentiated Instruction: English Language Learners

★ ELPS 2C, 2I, 3E, 3G, 3H, 4C, 5B, 5G

ELP Level **Beginning**	**ELP Level** **Intermediate**	**ELP Level** **Advanced/Advanced High**
Guide students to connect each term to the graphic organizer on page 586. Provide visuals, gestures, and examples, as possible, for each term. Have students repeat each term after you.	Use phrases and short sentences as well as visuals to explain the terms. Have partners describe how each term relates to the graphic organizer on page 586.	Tell partners to discuss and create a web that shows the relationships between and among the terms. Then have students work independently to write about the terms with detail.

Vocabulary: Response to Literature

1 Read each word aloud, demonstrating how to pronounce its distinct sounds. Have students repeat the words after you, practicing producing the sounds of the newly acquired vocabulary.

2 Help students to locate the call-out boxes in the margins of the writing model on SE pp. 277–278 and to find information about some of the vocabulary terms. Model writing notes about the words. As students share information with each other, they should take notes in their notebooks about the meanings of the terms.

3 Explain what each term means with respect to a response to literature. Help students understand general meaning of the terms by illustrating them on the board (such as a set of books for "literature"). Then clarify any misunderstandings. Help students understand the specific meanings by discussing the main points of each term (for example, a quotation is a repetition of an author's exact words from a literature selection). Partners should monitor their understanding as they add new information to their notebooks, and seek clarification as needed.

4 Have students show that they understand the meanings of the new academic vocabulary by responding to the questions with specificity and detail. Model how to answer the first question. Then work with students to answer the remaining questions.

5 Prompt discussion by suggesting several pieces of literature, and then circulate to provide assistance as partners express their opinions.

6 Circulate to provide assistance as students develop their paragraphs independently.

☑ DIFFERENTIATE INSTRUCTION

★ ELPS 2C, 2I, 3A 3E, 3G, 3H, 4C, 5B, 5G

 ELPS 2C Learn new basic and academic vocabulary; **2I** Demonstrate listening comprehension/responding to questions and requests/ collaborating with peers/ taking notes; **3A** Practice producing sounds of newly acquired vocabulary to pronounce English words; **3E** Share information in cooperative learning interactions; **3G** Express opinions and ideas; **3H** Describe with increasing specificity and detail; **4C** Comprehend basic sight and English vocabulary; **5B** Write using newly acquired basic vocabulary and content-based grade-level vocabulary; **5G** Explain with increasing specificity and detail

Reading the Response to Literature Model

What Do You Know?

Tell students that the writing model they will listen to shortly is a response to a classic piece of literature, *Walden, or Life in the Woods*. Explain that the model interprets one theme of the book. Discuss why someone might choose to try living a simple life in the woods. Encourage students to use their primary language when necessary.

Build Background

Provide background information about the writing model so that students have knowledge about the topic before they hear the response to literature. Use visuals whenever possible as you provide information. **DIFFERENTIATE INSTRUCTION ↘**

Listening

Tell students that they will need to listen carefully and take notes as you read the writing model aloud because you will ask them to identify the thesis statement, or main idea, of the writing, after you have read the first paragraph. After you have finished reading, have partners discuss their answers to the questions.

★ ELPS 2I, 4G

Key Words

Read aloud the terms in the box as students follow along. Tell students that they will see these terms when they read the writing model. Have students repeat the words several times and guide them to create word families (*value, values, valued, valuable*) for as many words as possible. Then help partners as they complete the activity.

★ ELPS 2C

Reading the Response to Literature Model

What Do You Know?

Next you will read the writing model called *A Search for Harmony* on pages **277–278**. It is a response to literature essay about Henry David Thoreau's book *Walden, or Life in the Woods*. What do you know about this book or its author? What does the title of the essay suggest to you about the topic of the book? What might a life in the woods be like? Tell what you know.

Build Background

Henry David Thoreau (1817–1862) was an American author and poet who is best known for his books *Walden, or Life in the Woods* and *Civil Disobedience*. His observations about nature in *Walden* and other books were early versions of some modern methods used to study ecology and the environment. Thoreau's ideas about civil disobedience influenced modern-day leaders such as Mahatma Gandhi and Martin Luther King, Jr.

Listening

Listen as your teacher or a classmate reads *A Search for Harmony* aloud. As you listen, take notes about the thesis statement. Be prepared to answer the questions below.

1. What theme does the writer interpret?
2. Why does Thoreau decide to live in a cabin near Walden Pond?
3. How does the writer use quotations to support the interpretation?

Key Words

individuality	insight	nature
observer	purpose	self-reliant
simply	solitude	valued

Look at the words in the box. You will see these words when you read the writing model. Write a sentence for each word using the meaning from the essay. Trade your sentences with a partner. Discuss how your understandings of each word are the same or different. Consider another meaning for some of the words. Write sentences to reflect those meanings.

ELPS 2C Learn new basic and academic vocabulary; **2I** Demonstrate listening comprehension/responding to questions and requests/collaborating with peers/taking notes; **3H** Explain with increasing specificity and detail; **4G** Demonstrate comprehension of increasingly complex English/responding to questions/taking notes

⭐ ELPS 2I, 4G

Learning Language **589**

Read Along

Now it's your turn to read. Turn to pages **277–278**. Read the writing model as your teacher or a classmate reads it aloud.

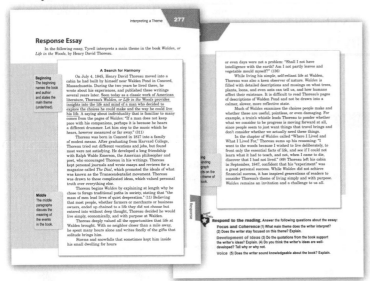

After Reading

Copy the following chart on a sheet of paper and fill it in with events that the writer used to interpret a theme of *Walden, or Life in the Woods*. Use your chart to summarize the writing model with a partner.

Event	How It Shows the Theme	Paraphrase or Quotation

Read Along

Have students read the response to literature silently as you read it aloud. As appropriate, have students track the print to demonstrate their understanding of the directionality of English text. You may wish to have students refer back to visuals you provided earlier to support their comprehension of the text.

⭐ ELPS 4B, 4G

After Reading

Draw the chart from SE page 589 on the board and model finding information from the response to literature to fill in the chart. Have partners find additional information and fill in the chart on their own paper. Then model using one row of the chart to summarize part of the response to literature and have students follow your lead with the remaining rows. Invite a volunteer to use his or her chart to summarize the response to literature for the group.

⭐ ELPS 2I, 4G

Differentiated Instruction: English Language Learners

⭐ ELPS 2I, 4D

ELP Level **Beginning**	ELP Level **Intermediate**	ELP Level **Advanced/Advanced High**
Provide prereading support using visuals and gestures. Preview terms such as *cabin, woods, means,* and *nature.* Ask yes-no questions to confirm students' understanding.	Have partners scan the writing model to identify unfamiliar vocabulary. Then discuss the terms and and have students respond to simple questions to confirm understanding.	Preview and discuss unfamiliar terms. Have students interpret the familiar quotations in the writing model. Remind them to include as much detail as possible.

ELPS 2I Demonstrate listening comprehension/responding to questions and requests/collaborating with peers; **4B** Recognize directionality of English reading; **4D** Use prereading supports to enhance comprehension of written text; **4G** Demonstrate comprehension of increasingly complex English/shared reading/retelling or summarizing

Oral Language: Response to Literature

Read through the text at the top of the page with students. Then provide an example of varying a story for different audiences. For example, you might model telling a younger student about the theme of a popular fairy tale versus interpreting the theme of the same tale for high school students. Point out the differences in your language and tone. Then provide other examples, inviting students to state their opinions about the differences. Explain that it is also important to adjust the way you write for different audiences.

ELPS 3G, 3H

Try It!
Answers

Students' responses to the activity will vary widely, but partners should demonstrate an ability to express opinions about themes with specificity and detail that is appropriate for different audiences.

ELPS 3E, 3G, 3H, 4G

590

ELPS 3E, 3G, 3H, 4G

Oral Language: Response to Literature

The person or people who will listen to you or read your writing are called the audience. When you speak or write, it is important to choose just the right words that will reach your audience. In writing, the tone, or the way you write, will be different for each audience.

Try It!

Read about the situation below. Then choose two audiences from the list. With a partner, discuss how the words you choose might be different for each audience.

Situation

You have read the biography of one of your favorite authors and you want to explain how a significant moment in the author's life is reflected in the theme of one of his or her books. You will interpret how the theme is revealed and provide examples to support your opinion.

Audiences

- A younger student
- A teacher
- A librarian in your city or town

Language

Effective Talk

When you answer a question, you might use a few words, a sentence, or a few sentences. When you use more details to tell about something, the other person will have a better understanding.

Read the question and the answers below. In the first box, there are only two words. In the second box, there is a short sentence that answers the question. The third answer contains more detail and does a better job answering the question.

How is the book similar to the author's life?

> story events

▽

> The author's life is shown in story events.

▽

> The events in the author's life are very similar to the events the character in the story experiences. The character has the same doubts and struggles as the author had in real life, and the character's behavior changes as a result.

Try It!

Choose a question to talk about with a partner. Write two or three ideas for answering the question. Next add details that will help your partner understand your ideas. Finally, use your notes as you and your partner discuss your answers to the questions.

Here are some ideas to get you started.

1. What theme or lesson from your life could you use to tell a great story?
2. What is a theme you would like to read more about?

Effective Talk

Read the information at the top of the page aloud as students follow along. Write the question in blue on the board and discuss what it is asking. Then talk about how the three answers provided contain varying degrees of detail, with the third answer providing the most detail.

Try It!
Answers

Discuss the **Try It!** activity and model providing an answer to one of the questions. Invite students to match the level of detail in your answer to one of the example answers in the book. Talk together about how you could add more detail to your response in order to more clearly communicate your message.

Answers will vary widely, but partners should demonstrate an understanding of how to add specificity and detail to make their responses more complete. ✔ DIFFERENTIATE INSTRUCTION

⭐ ELPS 2I, 3E, 3G, 3H

Differentiated Instruction: English Language Learners
⭐ ELPS 2I, 3B, 3E, 3G, 3H

ELP Level **Beginning**	ELP Level **Intermediate**	ELP Level **Advanced/Advanced High**
Allow students to create drawings or comic strips to discuss a story or theme. Ask them to narrate and explain their drawings using one or two high-frequency words.	Provide sentence frames such as *A lesson that would make a good story is___* to help students narrate and explain to their partners.	Suggest that partners brainstorm ideas together. Remind students to express their ideas with rich, specific detail and examples.

ELPS 2I Demonstrate listening comprehension/ collaborating with peers; **3B** Expand vocabulary/learning and using high-frequency words for identifying and describing and retelling simple stories and basic information; **3E** Share information in cooperative learning interactions; **3G** Express ideas; **3H** Narrate and explain with increasing specificity and detail

Language of Creative Writing

Read aloud the explanation of creative writing with students and discuss the graphic organizer together. Model using a combination of decoding skills to read the text in the organizer. For example, point out the consonant blends as you sound out *conflict (fl, ct)*, *complications (pl)*, *crisis (cr)*, and *climax (cl)*. Invite volunteers to read the text in the organizer, using multiple decoding skills such as those you modeled.

 ELPS 4A

 Turn and Talk

Prompt discussion by reminding students of familiar stories and literature that they read recently in class. Model completing the sentence starter in several ways, using phrases such as "includes a surprise" or "reminds me of something that happened to me." Tell students to turn and talk to a partner about the types of stories that interest them. Remind them to use detail in their explanations.

ELPS 3E, 4C

592

 ELPS 3E, 4C

Language of Creative Writing

Creative writing is writing that tells a fictional story. This type of writing can take the form of a story, a play, and even poetry. Most often, creative writing has the same basic organization: an exposition that introduces the character, conflict, and setting; rising action that reaches a climax and then falls; and a resolution. This graphic organizer shows the parts found in most creative writing.

Creative Writing Organization

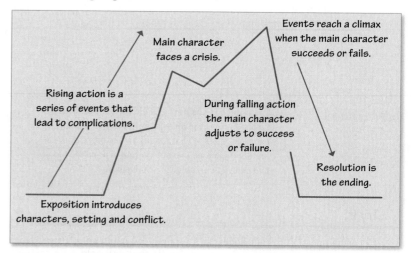

Main character faces a crisis.

Events reach a climax when the main character succeeds or fails.

Rising action is a series of events that lead to complications.

During falling action the main character adjusts to success or failure.

Resolution is the ending.

Exposition introduces characters, setting and conflict.

 Turn and Talk

Talk with a partner about what makes a story interesting to you.

I think a story is really interesting when it _____.

 ELPS 3E Share information in cooperative learning interactions; **4A** Decode using a combination of skills; **4C** Comprehend English vocabulary and language structures

ELPS 3A, 3E, 3G, 3H, 4C, 5B, 5G

Vocabulary: Creative Writing

character	climax	conflict
crisis	exposition	falling action
fictional	resolution	rising action

1. **Say the word or phrase.** Listen as your teacher reads the words aloud. Then, practice saying each word aloud. Pay special attention to words like *character* that might have a silent letter.

2. **Discover the meaning.** Work with a partner to find some of the vocabulary words in the blue boxes next to the writing model on pages 341–343. Write notes about what you think the words mean.

3. **Learn more.** Listen as your teacher explains the meaning of each word. Work with your partner to check and correct your earlier notes. Write the meanings for additional words.

4. **Think about it.** Use your notebook to answer the questions below.
   - What do you learn from a story's exposition?
   - Which two terms are opposites?
   - What makes a story more interesting: the character's conflict or the crisis?
   - What happens in the resolution of a story?

5. **Show your understanding.** Talk to your partner about the kind of music that might go through your mind as you read a story. Use the vocabulary words to discuss your opinion about the type of music that might go with each part of a story.

6. **Write About it.** Write a short paragraph explaining how to write a story. Use at least three of the vocabulary words above in your paragraph.

Vocabulary: Creative Writing

1. Read each term aloud, demonstrating how to pronounce its distinct sounds. Have students repeat the terms after you, practicing producing the sounds of the newly acquired vocabulary.

2. Help students to locate the call-out boxes in the margins of the writing model and to find information about some of the vocabulary terms. Model writing notes about the words. As students share information with each other, they should make notes in their notebooks about the meanings of the terms.

3. Explain what each term means with respect to the creative form. Help students understand the general meaning of the terms by illustrating them on the board (such as an upward arrow for "rising" and a downward arrow for "falling"). Then clarify any misunderstandings. Help students understand the specific meanings by discussing the main points of each term (for example, the conflict is the problem the main character faces). Partners should monitor their understanding as they add new information to their notebooks, and seek clarification as needed.

4. Have students show that they understand the meanings of the new academic vocabulary by responding to the questions. Model how to answer the first question. Then work with students to answer the remaining questions.

5. Model describing the type of music that might go with one part of a story, and then circulate to provide assistance as partners work together to express their own opinions.

6. Circulate to provide assistance as students develop their paragraphs independently.

✔ DIFFERENTIATE INSTRUCTION

ELPS 2C, 2D, 2I, 3A, 3E, 3G, 4C, 5B, 5G

ELPS **2C** Learn new basic and academic vocabulary; **2D** Monitor understanding of spoken language and seek clarification as needed; **2I** Demonstrate listening comprehension/responding to questions and requests and collaborating with peers; **3A** Practice producing sounds of newly acquired vocabulary to pronounce English words; **3E** Share information in cooperative learning interactions; **3G** Express opinions; **3H** Describe with increasing specificity and detail; **4C** Develop basic sight vocabulary and comprehend English vocabulary; **5B** Write using newly acquired basic and content-based grade-level vocabulary; **5G** Explain with increasing specificity and detail

---

Differentiated Instruction: English Language Learners

ELPS 2C, 3E, 3H, 4C, 5B, 5G

ELP Level **Beginning**	ELP Level **Intermediate**	ELP Level **Advanced/Advanced High**
Guide students to connect each term to the graphic organizer on page 592. Provide visuals, gestures, and examples, as possible, for each term. Have students repeat each term after you.	Use phrases and short sentences as well as visuals when you explain the terms. Have partners discuss how each term applies to the graphic organizer on page 592.	Tell partners to discuss and create a web that describes the relationships between and among the terms. Then have students work independently to write about the terms with detail.

Reading the Creative Model

What Do You Know?

Tell students that they will listen to a writing model about a family conflict. Explain that the model is about a girl trying to come to terms with her parents' decision to separate. Encourage students to express the feelings a young person might have in that situation.

ELPS 3G

Build Background

Provide background information about the writing model so that students have knowledge about the topic before they hear the story. Use visuals whenever possible as you provide information. DIFFERENTIATE INSTRUCTION ↘

Listening

Tell students that they will need to listen carefully and take notes as you read the writing model aloud because you will ask them to identify the main conflict in the story after you have read the first few paragraphs. After you have finished reading, have partners collaborate to discuss ideas about the conflict and their answers to the questions.

ELPS 2I, 3G, 4G

Key Words

Read aloud the terms in the box as students follow along. Tell students that they will see these terms when they read the writing model. Guide students to identify and discuss the words that describe feelings or emotions: *bitter, forgive, rejected, hurt, understand,* and *pleading.* Then help students as they complete the activity. Remind them to use specificity and detail as they express their ideas.

ELPS 2C, 3G, 4C

 ELPS 2C, 2I, 3G, 4G

Reading the Creative Writing Model

What Do You Know?

Next you will read the writing model called *Small Steps* on pages **341–343.** It is a story about a girl who reconnects with her father after nearly a year apart. What are some reasons that family members might be separated from one another? What might cause a child to be angry with a parent? What can family members do to move forward when feelings have been hurt? Tell what you know.

Build Background

Many lawyers who work in large law firms are paid according to their billable hours, the amount of time they spend actively working for a particular client. For this reason, law firms often require lawyers to work a certain number of billable hours each year to help the firm make money. Time spent in training, department meetings, or dealing with the general business does not count toward billable hours. This often means that lawyers have to work many hours beyond a typical work week.

Listening

Listen as your teacher or a classmate reads *Small Steps* aloud. As you listen, take notes about the conflict in the story. Be prepared to answer the questions below.
1. What is Hannah's conflict?
2. What complication does Hannah face as she spends more time with her father?
3. What happens during the resolution of the story?

Key Words

bitter	family	find himself
forgive	hurt	lawyer
office	payment	pleading
rejected	understand	work

Look at the words in the box. You will see these words when you read the writing model. With a partner, use the words to talk about how a child might feel when a parent has to work long hours or be away for a long period of time. Compare your ideas with your classmates' ideas.

ELPS **2C** Learn new basic vocabulary; **2I** Demonstrate listening comprehension/responding to questions and requests/collaborating with peers/taking notes; **3G** Express ideas and feelings; **4C** Develop basic sight vocabulary; **4G** Demonstrate comprehension of increasingly complex English/responding to questions and taking notes

Read Along

Now it's your turn to read. Turn to pages **341–343**. Read the sample essay as your teacher or a classmate reads it aloud.

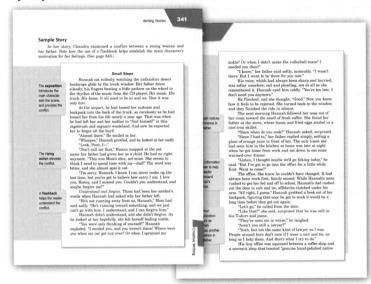

After Reading

Copy the following chart on a sheet of paper and fill it in with key events from the story's plot. Use your chart to retell the writing model with a partner.

Exposition:	
Rising Action and Conflict:	
Climax:	
Falling Action and Resolution:	

Read Along

Have students read the model story silently as you read it aloud. As appropriate, have students track the print to demonstrate their understanding of the directionality of English text. You may wish to have students refer back to visuals you provided earlier to support their comprehension of the text.

ELPS 4B, 4G

After Reading

Draw the chart from SE page 595 on the board and model finding information from the story to fill in the chart. Have partners find additional information and fill in the chart on their own paper. Then model using one row of the chart to retell part of the story and have students follow your lead with the remaining rows. Invite a volunteer to use his or her chart to retell the story for the group.

ELPS 2I, 4G

ELPS 2I Demonstrate listening comprehension/retelling or summarizing/ collaborating with peers; **3H** Narrate with increasing specificity and detail; **4B** Recognize directionality of English reading; **4D** Use prereading supports to enhance comprehension of written text; **4G** Demonstrate comprehension of increasingly complex English/shared reading/retelling or summarizing

Oral Language: Creative Writing

Read through the text at the top of the page with students. Then provide an example of varying a story for different audiences. For example, you might model telling a kindergartner a story about a new student in a school versus narrating the same story to a group of high school students. Point out the differences in the way you told the story. Then provide other examples, asking students to express their ideas about the differences in language and tone. Explain that it is also important to adjust the way you write for different audiences.

ELPS 3G, 4G

Try It!
Answers

Students' responses to the activity will vary widely, but students should demonstrate an ability to narrate stories with specificity and detail that is appropriate for different audiences.

ELPS 3E, 3H, 4G

 ELPS 3E, 3G, 3H, 4G

Oral Language: Creative Writing

The person or people who will listen to you or read your writing are called the audience. When you speak or write, it is important to choose just the right words that will reach your audience. In writing, the tone, or the way you write, will be different for each audience.

Try It!

Read about the situation below. Then choose two audiences from the list. With a partner, discuss how the words you choose to express ideas might be different for each audience.

Situation

Jed is looking forward to sharing his senior year of high school with many long-time friends. His mother is offered a major promotion at work, but must move to another state to accept the position. Jed's father and sister are willing to move, but he is not. You will retell Jed's story.

Audiences

- A high school student
- A friend's parent
- A favorite grandparent

Language

Effective Talk

When you answer a question, you might use a few words, a sentence, or a few sentences. When you use more details to tell about something, the other person will have a better understanding.

Read the question and the answers below. In the first box, there are only two words. In the second box, there is a short sentence that answers the question. The third answer contains more detail and does a better job answering the question.

How will Jed react to the idea of moving?

be angry

▽

Jed will be angry if his family decides to move.

▽

Jed is looking forward to sharing his senior year with friends he's had all through school. He will be upset and angry if he misses out on the experience, and knows that in another state he will only have a short time to make new friends.

Try It!

Choose a question to talk about with a partner. Write two or three ideas for answering the question. Next add details that will help your partner understand your ideas. Finally, use your notes as you and your partner discuss your answers to the questions.

Here are some ideas to get you started.

1. What would school be like if a favorite or trusted teacher was unable to finish out the year?

2. What might happen if, instead of you, a best friend got a role in a play or was chosen to be on a sports team?

Effective Talk

Read the information at the top of the page aloud as students follow along. Write the question in blue on the board and discuss what it is asking. Then talk about how the three answers provided contain varying degrees of detail, with the third answer providing the most detail.

Try It!
Answers

Discuss the **Try It!** activity and model providing an answer to one of the questions. Invite students to compare the level of detail in your answer to the example answers in the book. Talk together about how you could add more detail to your response in order to more clearly communicate your message.

Answers will vary, but students should demonstrate an understanding of how to add specificity and detail to make their responses more complete. ✔ DIFFERENTIATE INSTRUCTION

★ ELPS 2I, 3E, 3G, 3H

Differentiated Instruction:
English Language Learners

★ ELPS 2I, 3B, 3E, 3G, 3H

ELP Level **Beginning**	ELP Level **Intermediate**	ELP Level **Advanced/Advanced High**
Allow students to create drawings or comic strips to tell their stories. Ask them to use one or two high-frequency words to explain their drawings.	Have students create drawings or comic strips. Provide sentence frames such as *Without ____, school would be ____* to tell their stories with greater detail.	Suggest that partners brainstorm ideas together. Remind students that their responses should include rich detail and examples.

 ELPS 2I Demonstrate listening comprehension/collaborating with peers; **3B** Expand vocabulary/learning and using high-frequency words for identifying and describing and retelling simple stories and basic information; **3E** Share information in cooperative learning interactions; **3G** Express ideas; **3H** Narrate with increasing specificity and detail

Language of Research Writing

Read aloud the explanation of research writing with students and discuss the graphic organizer together. Model using a combination of decoding skills to read the text in the organizer. For example, pronounce the long vowel sounds in *introduces, provides, summarize, statement, details, leaves, reader,* and *sheet,* pointing out the different ways to spell the long vowel sound as needed. Invite volunteers to read the text in the organizer, using multiple decoding skills such as those you modeled.

 ELPS 4A

 Turn and Talk

Remind students that supporting details may include facts, statistics, examples, and expert opinions. Model completing the sentence starter in several ways, using phrases such as "it shows the writer is knowledgeable about the topic" or "it proves the writer's thesis statement." Tell students to turn and talk to a partner about the types of supporting details often found in research writing, and about why these details are important. Remind them to use detail in their explanations.

ELPS 3E, 4C

598

 ELPS 3E, 4C

Language of Research Writing

Research writing presents information from multiple resources about a topic of interest to an audience. Good research writing follows certain style rules, such as those of the Modern Language Association (MLA). MLA research reports have an introduction that involves the reader and provides a thesis statement, a middle section with supporting details, and a conclusion that sums up the paper and leaves the reader with a final thought about the topic. Sections are often separated by headings. Sources are listed at the end on a separate sheet of paper.

Research Report Organization

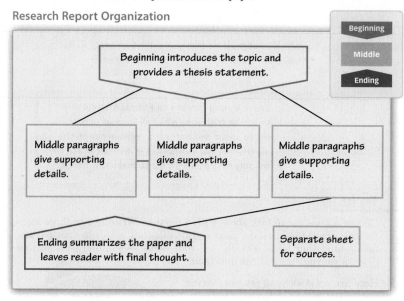

Beginning introduces the topic and provides a thesis statement.

Middle paragraphs give supporting details.

Middle paragraphs give supporting details.

Middle paragraphs give supporting details.

Ending summarizes the paper and leaves reader with final thought.

Separate sheet for sources.

Beginning | Middle | Ending

Turn and Talk

Talk with a partner about why it is important for a research paper to include several sections of supporting details.

Research papers should include many supporting details because _____.

Vocabulary: Research Writing

headings	multiple	report
research	resources	section
sources	style	sums up

1. **Say the word or phrase.** Listen as your teacher reads the words aloud. Then, practice saying each word aloud.

2. **Discover the meaning.** Work with a partner to find some of the vocabulary words in the blue boxes next to the writing model on pages 386–394. Write notes about what you think the words mean.

3. **Learn more.** Listen as your teacher explains the meaning of each word. Work with your partner to check and correct your earlier notes. Write the meanings for additional words.

4. **Think about it.** Use your notebook to answer the questions below.
   - What is one reason to use multiple resources when you gather information?
   - Why do you think headings are used in longer research reports?
   - What do you do when you sum up your report?

5. **Show your understanding.** Talk to your partner about the tasks you have to do before you begin to write a research report. Use the vocabulary words to describe the steps you might follow when you are preparing to write your report.

6. **Write about it.** Write a short paragraph explaining how to write a research paper. Use at least three of the vocabulary words above in your paragraph.

Language

Differentiated Instruction: English Language Learners

ELPS 2C, 3E, 3H, 4C, 5B, 5G

ELP Level Beginning	ELP Level Intermediate	ELP Level Advanced/Advanced High
Guide students to connect each term to the graphic organizer on page 598. Provide visuals, gestures, and examples, as possible, for each term. Have students repeat each term after you.	Use phrases and short sentences as well as visuals when you explain the terms. Have partners discuss how each term "fits" on the graphic organizer on page 598.	Tell partners to discuss and create a web that describes the relationships between and among the terms. Then have students work independently to write about the terms with detail.

Vocabulary: Research Writing

1 Read each word aloud, demonstrating how to pronounce its distinct sounds. Have students repeat the words after you, practicing producing the sounds of the newly acquired vocabulary.

2 Help students to locate the call-out boxes in the margins of the writing model and to find information about some of the vocabulary terms. Model writing notes about the words. As students share information with each other, they should make notes in their notebooks about the meanings of the terms.

3 Explain what each term means with respect to research writing. Help students understand the general meaning of the terms by illustrating them on the board (such as a whole-part drawing for "section"). Then clarify any misunderstandings. Help students understand the specific meanings by discussing the main points of each term (for example, headings are used to identify the main topic of each section of a report). Partners should monitor their understanding as they add new information to their notebooks, and seek clarification as needed.

4 Have students show that they understand the meanings of the new academic vocabulary by responding to the questions. Model how to answer the first one. Then work with students to answer the remaining questions.

5 Model describing some tasks involved in research reports and then circulate to provide assistance as partners work together to describe their preparation for writing a research report.

6 Circulate to provide assistance as students develop their paragraphs independently.
✔ DIFFERENTIATE INSTRUCTION

ELPS 2C, 2D, 2I, 3A, 3E, 4C, 5B, 5G

 ELPS 2C Learn new expressions, and basic and academic vocabulary; **2D** Monitor understanding of spoken language and seek clarification as needed; **2I** Demonstrate listening comprehension/responding to questions and requests/ collaborating with peers; **3A** Practice producing sounds of newly acquired vocabulary to pronounce English words; **3E** Share information in cooperative learning interactions; **3H** Describe with increasing specificity and detail; **4C** Develop basic sight vocabulary and comprehend English vocabulary; **5B** Write using newly acquired basic and content-based grade-level vocabulary; **5G** Explain with increasing specificity and detail

Reading the Research Model

What Do You Know?

Tell students that the writing model they will listen to shortly is about developing businesses that address social problems. Ask students to describe local businesses or groups that focus on dealing with issues such as poverty, hunger, or health concerns. Encourage students to use their primary language when necessary.

Build Background

Provide background information about the writing model so that students have knowledge about the topic before they hear the report. Use visuals whenever possible as you provide information. DIFFERENTIATE INSTRUCTION ↘

Listening

Tell students that they will need to listen carefully and take notes as you read the writing model aloud because you will ask them to identify the thesis statement after you have read the first few paragraphs. After you have finished reading, collaborate to discuss students' answers to the questions.

⭐ ELPS 2I, 3G, 4G

Key Words

Read aloud the terms in the box as students follow along. Tell students that they will see these terms when they read the writing model. Point out the antonyms *problem/solution* and *urban/rural* and have students repeat them several times. Then help students as they complete the activity. Remind them to use specificity and detail as they express their ideas.

⭐ ELPS 2C, 3G, 4C

⭐ ELPS 2C, 2I, 3G, 4G

Reading the Research Model

What Do You Know?

Next you will read the writing model called *Meeting the Needs of the Future* on pages **386–394**. It is a research report about efforts to solve the some of the world's social problems. What are some ways that people in your community try to help others? What jobs or businesses are involved with helping people who face hunger, disabilities, or illnesses? Tell what you know.

Build Background

An entrepreneur is someone who starts a new business, most often by offering a product or a service that was not available before. Entrepreneurs run the risk of failure, losing the money invested in their business. A social entrepreneur is someone whose business is focused on solving a problem such as hunger, poverty, pollution, or lack of medical care.

Listening

Listen as your teacher or a classmate reads *Meeting the Needs of the Future* aloud. As you listen, take notes about the thesis statement. Be prepared to answer the questions below.
1. According to the report, what are two examples of social entrepreneurship?
2. How does Ashoka help social entrepreneurs?
3. What is one way a social entrepreneur addressed the cause of a problem?

Key Words

business	community	competitive
organization	opportunity	problem
rural	social	solution
strategies	systems	urban

Look at the words in the box. You will see these words when you read the writing model. With a partner, use the words to talk about some businesses that help people in your commuity. Then discuss ideas for new businesses to help your community.

ELPS 2C Learn new basic vocabulary; **2I** Demonstrate listening comprehension/responding to questions and requests/ collaborating with peers/taking notes; **3G** Express ideas; **4C** Develop basic sight vocabulary and comprehend English vocabulary; **4G** Demonstrate comprehension of increasingly complex English/responding to questions/ taking notes

Read Along

Now it's your turn to read. Turn to pages **386–394**. Read the writing model as your teacher or a classmate reads it aloud.

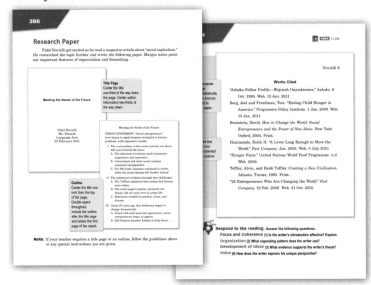

After Reading

Copy the following chart on a sheet of paper and fill it in with examples of social entrepreneurs mentioned in the report. Use your chart to summarize the writing model with a partner.

	Who and Where	What They Did
Example 1		
Example 2		
Example 3		

Read Along

Have students read the research report silently as you read it aloud. As appropriate, have students track the print to demonstrate their understanding of the directionality of English text. You may wish to have students refer back to visuals you provided earlier to support their comprehension of the text.

ELPS 4B, 4G

After Reading

Draw the chart from SE page 601 on the board and model finding information from the research report to fill in the chart. Have partners find additional information and fill in the chart on their own paper. Then model using one row of the chart to summarize part of the research report and have students follow your lead with the remaining rows. Invite a volunteer to use his or her chart to summarize the model for the group.

ELPS 2I, 4G

ELP Level **Beginning**	ELP Level **Intermediate**	ELP Level **Advanced/Advanced High**
Use visuals and gestures to provide prereading support for students. Preview terms such as *business, poverty, global, society,* and *goal* and have students repeat each one after you.	Have partners scan the writing model to identify unfamiliar vocabulary. Then discuss the terms and ask yes-no questions to confirm students' understanding.	Have partners discuss *entrepreneur* and other unfamiliar terms before reading the model. Have them explain examples of entrepreneurs in other fields, such as technology.

 ELPS 2I Demonstrate listening comprehension/retelling or summarizing/ collaborating with peers; **3H** Explain with increasing specificity and detail; **4B** Recognize directionality of English reading; **4D** Use prereading supports to enhance comprehension of written text; **4G** Demonstrate comprehension of increasingly complex English/shared reading/retelling or summarizing

Oral Language: Research Writing

Read through the text at the top of the page with students. Then provide an example of varying a report for different audiences. For example, you might model reporting on the effects of a new law to teenagers versus explaining the same law to a group of adults. Point out the differences in the way you gave the information. Then provide other examples, asking students to express their ideas about the differences in language and tone. Explain that it is also important to adjust the way you write for different audiences.

⭐ **ELPS** 3G, 4G

Try It!
Answers

Students' responses to the activity will vary widely, but students should demonstrate an ability to explain how they would report with specificity and detail that is appropriate for different audiences.

⭐ **ELPS** 3E, 3H, 4G

602

⭐ ELPS 3E, 3G, 3H, 4G

Oral Language: Research Writing

The person or people who will listen to you or read your writing are called the audience. When you speak or write, it is important to choose just the right words that will reach your audience. In writing, the tone, or the way you write, will be different for each audience.

Try It!

Read about the situation below. Then choose two audiences from the list. With a partner, discuss how the words you choose might be different for each audience.

Situation

You will research a problem in your community to find out how it has been handled in other cities or towns. You will look at solutions as well as ideas that did not work out. You will use your research to explain how your community can use these ideas and experiences.

Audiences

- Classmates who want to solve the problem
- Your town or city's mayor
- A person who has experienced the problem

Effective Talk

When you answer a question, you might use a few words, a sentence, or a few sentences. When you use more details to tell about something, the other person will have a better understanding.

Read the question and the answers below. In the first box, there are only two words. In the second box, there is a short sentence that answers the question. The third answer contains more detail and does a better job answering the question.

How will you find ideas about how to solve the problem?

> other towns

▽

> I will find out what other towns have done.

▽

> Our town isn't the only one that has to deal with this problem. I will research to find out what other towns have done, and report on their successes as well as on ideas that didn't work out. We can learn from their experiences.

Try It!

Choose a question to talk about with a partner. Write two or three ideas for answering the question. Next add details that will help your partner understand your ideas. Finally, use your notes as you and your partner discuss your answers to the questions.

Here are some ideas to get you started.

1. How can you learn more about local businesses that help the environment?

2. How might a partnership between a local business and our school be good for our town?

Effective Talk

Read the information at the top of the page aloud as students follow along. Write the question in blue on the board and discuss what it is asking. Then talk about how the three answers provided contain varying degrees of detail, with the third answer providing the most detail.

Try It!
Answers

Discuss the **Try It!** activity and model providing an answer to one of the questions. Invite students to compare the level of detail in your answer to the example answers shown above. Talk together about how you could add more detail to your response in order to more clearly communicate your message.

Answers will vary, but partners should demonstrate an understanding of how to add specificity and detail to make their responses more complete. ✔ DIFFERENTIATE INSTRUCTION

⬡ ELPS 2I, 3E, 3G, 3H

Differentiated Instruction: English Language Learners		⬡ ELPS 2I, 3B, 3E, 3G, 3H
ELP Level Beginning	**ELP Level** Intermediate	**ELP Level** Advanced/Advanced High
Allow students to create drawings or use photographs to share their ideas. Ask them to use one or two high-frequency words to explain the drawing or photograph.	Have students create drawings or use photographs. Provide sentence frames such as *A business that helps the environment is ____* to help them share their ideas with greater detail.	Suggest that partners brainstorm ideas together. Remind students that their responses should include rich detail and examples.

ELPS 2I Demonstrate listening comprehension/collaborating with peers; **3B** Expand vocabulary/learning and using high-frequency words for identifying and describing and retelling simple stories and basic information; **3E** Share information in cooperative learning interactions; **3G** Express ideas; **3H** Describe and explain with increasing specificity and detail

Resource Units

BEW *"Basic Elements of Writing"* **PG** *"Proofreader's Guide"*

Basic Elements of Writing

Basic Paragraph Skills (pages 605–616)

Students learn about the parts of a paragraph, types of paragraphs, patterns of organization, and how writing effective paragraphs helps them gain control of their writing.

Basic Essay Skills (pages 617–633)

After learning about the parts of an essay and exploring the skills of outlining ideas, writing thesis statements, creating effective beginnings, middles, and endings, students will have a solid foundation for most academic writing assignments.

Proofreader's Guide

★ UNIT TEKS

11.17A Use/understand the function of different types of clauses, phrases; **11.17B** Use a variety of correctly structured sentences; **11.18A** Correctly/consistently use conventions of punctuation, capitalization; **11.19** Spell correctly, including using various resources to determine/check spellings

★ UNIT ELPS

1F Use accessible language; learn new/essential language in the process; **1G** Demonstrate ability to distinguish between/knowledge of when to use formal/informal English; **2A** Distinguish sounds/intonation patterns of English; **2B** Recognize elements of the English sound system; **2C** Learn new expressions, basic/academic vocabulary; **2D** Monitor understanding of spoken language; **2G** Understand general meaning of spoken language; **2I** Demonstrate listening comprehension; **3A** Practice producing sounds of vocabulary to pronounce English words; **3D** Speak using grade-level content-area vocabulary in context; **3E** Share information in cooperative learning interactions; **3G** Express ideas, feelings; **3H** Describe, explain with increasing specificity/detail; **4A** Learn relationships between sounds/letters of English; **4C** Develop basic sight vocabulary, derive meaning of environmental print, comprehend English vocabulary; **4G** Demonstrate comprehension of increasingly complex English; **5B** Write using basic/content-based vocabulary; **5C** Spell familiar English words; employ English spelling patterns, rules with increasing accuracy; **5D** Edit writing for standard grammar, usage; **5E** Employ increasingly complex grammatical structures

Marking Punctuation

(pages 635–673)

A reference guide for the correct use of punctuation, along with practice exercises.

Checking Mechanics

(pages 674–695)

In this section, students explore rules for capitalization, plurals, numbers, abbreviations, acronyms and initialisms, and spelling and practice correct usage by editing paragraphs for mechanics.

Understanding Idioms

(pages 696–701)

A guide to common American English idioms and their meanings.

Using the Right Word

(pages 702–721)

Students explore commonly confused words and phrases and practice their correct usage.

Parts of Speech **(pages 722–755)**

Students learn about the eight parts of speech and practice editing sentences and paragraphs for proper usage.

Understanding Sentences

(pages 756–779)

Through practice exercises, students learn about sentence construction, variety, arrangement, structure, and subject-verb agreement.

Writing Paragraphs

Day	Writing and Grammar Instruction	Basic Elements of Writing	Proofreader's Guide	SkillsBook	Write Source Online
1–2	**Basic Paragraph Skills** The Parts of a Paragraph	605–607			
	Skills Activities: • Spelling		690–695	51–52, 55–59	
	• Understanding Idioms		696–701		
	• Using the Right Word		702–721	61–66	
	• Verb Tense Consistency				GrammarSnap
	• Parallel Structure				GrammarSnap
3	Types of Paragraphs	608–611			
4–5	Patterns of Organization	612–616			

WEEK 1

ELPS 1F, 2C, 3E, 4G

Basic Elements of Writing

Writing Focus

Learning Language

Work with a partner. Read the meanings and share answers to the questions.

1. Something logical has a sequence that makes sense.
   Explain a logical way to do your schoolwork.
2. To contradict means to say or do the opposite.
   When might you need to contradict someone?
3. Something revealing tells something new or unknown.
   What can be revealing in a conversation?
4. Similarities are ways that things are the same.
   Tell three similarities between cats and dogs.
5. When you "wrap up" an activity, you finish it.
   Name three activities you will wrap up this week.

Basic Paragraph Skills

A paragraph is a concise unit of thinking and writing. It is typically organized around a controlling idea stated in a topic sentence. The main part of a paragraph consists of sentences that support the controlling idea. The final sentence usually summarizes the content of the paragraph and, if the paragraph is part of an essay, prepares the reader for the next main point.

Paragraphs are often called "mini-essays" because they can describe, narrate, explain, or defend an opinion. The form will depend upon your topic and the types of details you have gathered. Whatever form it takes, a paragraph must contain enough information—enough supporting details—to give the reader a clear picture of the topic. Being able to write effective paragraphs can certainly help you gain control of all of your academic writing—essays, reports, analyses, research papers, and so on.

- The Parts of a Paragraph
- Types of Paragraphs: Narrative, Descriptive, Expository, and Persuasive
- Patterns of Organization: Classification, Comparison-Contrast, Cause-and-Effect, Process, and Logical Order

"Good writing is clear thinking made visible."

—Bill Wheeler

Writing Focus

- Basic Paragraph Skills
- Basic Essay Skills

Learning Language

Read aloud the basic and academic terms, as well as the descriptions and questions. Point out elements of the English sound system, such as the different spellings for the long *e* sound in *revealing* and *similarities*. Have students practice producing the sounds of the newly acquired vocabulary. Then model for students how to read one question and answer it. For example, *It says that* contradict *means to say or do the opposite, and it asks when I might need to contradict someone. I would contradict someone who gave the wrong directions to a place by giving the correct directions.* Have partners monitor their understanding of the terms by working through the meanings and questions together.

ELPS 1F Use accessible language and learn new and essential language in the process; **2B** Recognize elements of the English sound system in newly acquired vocabulary; **2C** Learn new basic and academic vocabulary; **3A** Practice producing sounds of newly acquired vocabulary to pronounce English words; **3E** Share information in cooperative learning interactions; **4A** Learn relationships between sounds and letters of the English language and decode words using a combination of skills; **4G** Demonstrate comprehension of increasingly complex English/responding to questions

The Parts of a Paragraph

A basic paragraph contains three parts: a topic sentence, body sentences, and a closing sentence. The following expository paragraph provides information about an annual rodeo called the Calgary Stampede. Each detail in the body supports the topic sentence.

Topic Sentence

Body

Closing Sentence

The Calgary Stampede

The Calgary Stampede in Alberta, Canada, has grown to become the largest and most exciting rodeo in the world. It began in 1912, when Guy Weadick thought of celebrating the Old West with a show modeled after those he had seen in the United States. The stampede included six days of cowboy competitions and shows and was a huge success, drawing thousands of visitors. Eventually, the stampede merged with Calgary's annual Industrial Exhibition, and by 1968, the 10-day event was being billed as "The Greatest Outdoor Show on Earth." New buildings sprang up. Tourist numbers skyrocketed. Today, purses offer more than a million dollars in prize money for bareback riding, bull riding, barrel racing, roping, steer wrestling, and so on. Each July, the Stampede begins with a two-hour parade followed by rodeo events, grandstand shows, and many other special features. One of the most popular features is the daily Rangeland Derby Chuckwagon Race, called "The Chucks" in which four-horse teams pull chuckwagons on a figure-eight track. The Chucks is followed by more entertainment and a fireworks display. The Stampede also includes a midway, free shows, and agricultural exhibits, as well as a First Nations village offering native foods and exhibits. More than a million people visit the stampede annually to enjoy a brief trip back in time to the Canadian Old West.

 Respond to the reading. What is the main idea of this paragraph? What specific details in the body support this idea? Name two or three of them.

A Closer Look at the Parts

Most paragraphs, whether written to stand alone or to be part of a longer piece of writing, have three parts.

The Topic Sentence

Every topic sentence should do two things: **(1)** give the specific topic of the paragraph and **(2)** present a specific feature or feeling about the topic. When writing your topic sentence, use the following formula as a guide.

a specific topic

+ a particular feature or feeling about the topic

= an effective topic sentence

the Calgary Stampede in Alberta, Canada

+ has grown to become the largest and most exciting rodeo in the world

= **The Calgary Stampede in Alberta, Canada, has grown to become the largest and most exciting rodeo in the world.**

Tip

The topic sentence is usually the first sentence in a paragraph. However, it can also be located elsewhere. For example, you can present details that build up to an important summary topic sentence at the end of a paragraph.

The Body

Each sentence in the body of the paragraph should support the topic sentence. These sentences should add new details about the topic.

- Use specific details to make your paragraph interesting.
  Eventually, the stampede merged with Calgary's annual Industrial Exhibition, and by 1968, the 10-day event was being billed as "The Greatest Outdoor Show on Earth."

- Use the method of organization that best suits your topic: classification, order of importance, chronological order, and so on.

The Closing Sentence

The closing sentence ends the paragraph and may restate the topic, summarize the paragraph, or provide a link to the next paragraph.

More than a million people visit the stampede annually to enjoy a brief trip back in time to the Canadian Old West.

Basic Elements

 Answers

Respond to the reading.

Have students employ basic reading skills to identify the main idea and details.

Main idea: The Calgary Stampede in Canada has grown to be the most exciting rodeo in the world.

Details:

- by 1968 the stampede was a 10-day event that had combined with the Industrial Exhibition

- prize purses amounting to a million dollars are available to event winners

- the Calgary Stampede now includes chuckwagon racing events, fireworks, a midway, free shows, agricultural exhibits, and First Nations foods and exhibits

⭐ Conventions Connections

Dashes, Colons, Commas, Exclamation Points
- ***Proofreader's Guide*** pages 668 (+), 650 (+), 635 (+), 646 (+)
- ***SkillsBook*** page 39

Capitalization, Numbers, Abbreviations
- ***Proofreader's Guide*** pages 674 (+), 676–677, 678–679, 686–687, 688–689
- ***SkillsBook*** pages 44, 48, 49, 50

Sentence Review
- ***SkillsBook*** pages 183–184

Proofreading
- ***Proofreader's Guide*** pages 635–695 (+)
- ***SkillsBook*** pages 67–68

 ELPS 4I Demonstrate English comprehension by employing basic reading skills

TEKS 11.14A

Types of Paragraphs

There are four basic types of paragraphs: *narrative, descriptive, expository,* and *persuasive.*

Narrative Paragraph

A **narrative paragraph** tells a story. It may draw from the writer's personal experience or from other sources of information. A narrative paragraph is almost always organized chronologically, or according to time.

A Leap of Faith

Topic Sentence

When I applied to work on a mail boat last summer, I went through an unusual application process. Surprisingly, there was no interview for this job. Instead, I had to show that I could leap from boat to pier and back again. On "audition" day, all of the job hopefuls were loaded onto the huge, flat mail boat, which motored away from the dock to start its circle

Body

around the large lake. At the first pier, the driver shouted a name. A girl with a long ponytail stepped up, and was handed a fake packet of mail and instructed to make the delivery. She mistimed her jump and hit the water with a loud splash. We pulled her in, laughing and sputtering, and the boat continued to the next pier. One by one, we each had to make the jump from boat to pier. Some of us made it, and some of us didn't. I didn't time my return jump quite right and fell into the cold water. Those in the group who made the leap both ways became mail deliverers. I ended up working for a boat

Closing Sentence

rental business, instead. That wasn't too bad, but it wasn't as exciting as working on the mail boat. So next year I will again leap at the chance to deliver mail.

 Respond to the reading. What is the tone of the story (sad, humorous, angry)? What details help make the story interesting?

 Write a narrative paragraph. Write a narrative paragraph in which you share your first job interview or your first tryout for an activity.

 TEKS 11.15A

Basic Paragraph Skills　**609**

Descriptive Paragraph

A **descriptive paragraph** gives the reader a detailed picture of a person, a place, an object, or an event. This type of paragraph should contain a variety of sensory details—specific sights, sounds, smells, tastes, and textures.

Queen of the Bus

Topic Sentence

The new passenger made herself known. She stomped up each stair onto the bus, one hand gripping the steel side bar, the other hand firmly pressed on her cane, a thick walking stick with a worn silver duck's head for a handle. She nodded regally to the driver as her coins clattered into the fare box, then surveyed the bus for the likeliest seat. She started slowly down the center aisle, her wizened hand flitting from the back of one seat to the next. The scent of stale lilacs mingled with a trace of fried onions followed her down the aisle. Finally, she stopped in front of a young girl whose ear was dotted with piercings. The old woman

Body

tapped her cane against the girl's booted foot, nudging it aside. The girl wordlessly moved over to the window seat. Leaning on her cane, the old woman sat down gingerly, swinging her legs in after her. She smoothed the front of her coat, made of an expensive fabric that had seen better days. Wrapping the coat tightly about her thin frame, she wiggled over slightly as her seat partner pulled closer to the window. Head erect, cloudy

Closing Sentence

black eyes bright with defiant victory, the old woman stared straight ahead, her left hand, adorned with only a worn gold band, gently caressing the silver duck head. Her highness had claimed her kingdom.

Basic Elements

 Respond to the reading. Is there a clear picture of the woman being described? Which two or three details are particularly effective?

 Write a descriptive paragraph. Write a paragraph that describes someone you know or have observed. Use sensory details to let the reader know your exact feeling about that person, but do not be overly critical or negative.

 Answers

Respond to the reading.

Have students demonstrate comprehension by responding to the questions.

The tone of the story is both humorous and informative. Interesting details:

- hopefuls loaded onto a huge, flat boat
- girl missed the pier and went into the water
- laughing and sputtering
- the writer ended up in the cold water
- the writer will try again next year

Write a narrative paragraph.

Remind students to use specificity and detail to write an engaging narrative paragraph that includes a conflict and resolution related to an interview or tryout.

 Answers

Respond to the reading.

Have students demonstrate comprehension by responding to the questions.

Yes, there is a clear picture of a woman. Details:

- the silver duck's head for a cane handle
- the scent of stale lilacs mingled with a trace of fried onions

Write a descriptive paragraph.

Point out that relevant, well-chosen sensory details will help students to write an effective descriptive paragraph about the person they have observed.

 TEKS **11.14A** Write an engaging story with a well-developed conflict and resolution; **11.15A** Write an analytical essay of sufficient length that includes relevant and substantial evidence and well-chosen details; **ELPS 4G** Demonstrate comprehension of increasingly complex English/responding to questions; **5G** Narrate and describe with increasing specificity and detail

TEKS 11.15A

Expository Paragraph

An **expository paragraph** shares information about a specific topic. Expository writing is informative. It might present facts, give directions, define terms, explain a process, and so on. Some ways to organize expository writing include logical order, classification, comparison-contrast, cause-effect, problem/solution, and time order.

 Topic Sentence

 Body

Closing Sentence

Roundabout Cartoonist

The name Rube Goldberg has become synonymous with convoluted cartoon inventions, yet the artist gave much more to the world. After being awarded his degree in engineering from the University of California, Berkeley, Goldberg followed his love of cartooning to work for several newspapers, first in California and later in New York. In New York, he developed a character known as Professor Lucius Gorgonzola Butts, whose crazy inventions included such gems as the self-operating napkin. But Goldberg's drawings went beyond the merely amusing because in 1948 he was awarded a Pulitzer Prize for his political cartoons. Goldberg was also awarded the Gold T-Square Award by the National Cartoonist Society. After retiring from cartooning in 1964, he created bronze sculptures, presenting them in several one-man shows, including one at the National Museum of American History. In 1970, Rube Goldberg was inducted posthumously into the Cartoonist Hall of Fame. The intellectual descendants of his absurd inventions can be seen today in many films, from the *Back to the Future* series to animated features such as *Wallace and Gromit*. Goldberg's talent was obvious and his contributions many, yet he is best known—and best loved—for his crazy cartoon inventions.

 Respond to the reading. What is the focus of this paragraph? Name three details that support this focus.

Write an expository paragraph. Write a paragraph that shares information about a topic that truly interests you. Include plenty of details.

  TEKS 11.16

Basic Paragraph Skills

Persuasive Paragraph

A **persuasive paragraph** expresses an opinion and tries to convince the reader that the opinion is valid. To be persuasive, a writer must include effective supporting reasons and facts.

 Topic Sentence

 Body

Closing Sentence

Violence Begets Violence

Capital punishment should be abolished for three major reasons. First of all, common sense says that two wrongs don't make a right. To kill someone convicted of murder contradicts the reasoning behind the law that taking another's life is wrong. The state, however, is committing the same violent, dehumanizing act it is condemning. In addition, the death penalty is not an effective deterrent. Numerous studies show that murder is usually the result of complex psychological and sociological problems and that most murderers do not contemplate the consequences of their acts; or, if they do, any penalty is seen as a far-off possibility. The offense, on the other hand, supposedly solves an immediate problem or crisis. Most importantly, death is final and cannot be altered. Errors in deciding guilt or innocence will always be present in a system of trial by jury. There is too great a risk that innocent people will be put to death. Official records show that it has happened in the past. For these reasons, capital punishment should be replaced with a system that puts all doubt on the side of life—not death.

 Respond to the reading. What are the three main points that support the writer's opinion? Which of these points is the most important?

Write a persuasive paragraph. Write a paragraph presenting your opinion. Include at least three strong reasons to support your opinion.

Basic Elements

Answers

Respond to the reading.

Have students employ basic reading skills to demonstrate comprehension.

Focus: Rube Goldberg was a great cartoonist, and also made other contributions to society. Details:

- his famous cartoon character, Gorgonzola Butts, winning a Pulitzer Prize
- being awarded the Gold T-Square Award from the National Cartoonist Society
- exhibiting his sculptures at the National Museum of American History

Write an expository paragraph.

Remind students to use relevant, well-chosen details to explain the topic.

Answers

Respond to the reading.

Have students employ basic reading skills to demonstrate comprehension.

Three main points that support the writer's opinion:

1. two wrongs don't make a right
2. the death penalty is not an effective deterrent
3. some innocent people may be put to death, and that cannot be reversed

The final point is the most important.

Write a persuasive paragraph.

Remind students to support their thesis or position with logical reasons.

 TEKS **11.15A** Write an analytical essay that includes relevant and substantial evidence and well-chosen details; **11.16** Write an argumentative essay that includes a clear thesis or position based on logical reasons; **ELPS** **4I** Demonstrate English comprehension by employing basic reading skills; **5G** Describe and explain with increasing specificity and detail

TEKS 11.13B, 11.13C

Patterns of Organization

On the following pages, sample paragraphs demonstrate a variety of basic patterns of organization.

Classification Order

You organize by classification when you need to break a topic down into categories. The following paragraph classifies the different types of automobile passengers. The writer used a line diagram to help plan his writing.

Line Diagram

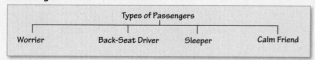

Types of Passengers

Worrier   Back-Seat Driver   Sleeper   Calm Friend

Topic Sentence

Body

Closing Sentence

Along for the Ride

The quality of a road trip really depends on the type of passenger riding along. Perhaps the worst passenger is the worrier who is certain that nothing is more dangerous than riding with you in a car. Ironically, the worrier's gasps and shrieks could be enough to startle you into an accident. Another troublesome passenger is the back-seat driver. This person constantly points out all of the things that the driver does wrong, from driving too fast to not checking your mirrors enough. Just as annoying is the sleeper. The minute the car is started, this person passes out, totally oblivious to anything until the destination is reached. So much for stimulating conversation! If a driver is lucky, he or she will share the trip with the best type of passenger, the calm friend. This person talks, keeping the driver alert and entertained throughout the entire trip. In the end, a passenger can make or break a road trip. A successful road trip begins and ends with a good traveling companion.

 Respond to the reading. Which details did you find most amusing or interesting in the above paragraph? Name three you found particularly engaging.

TEKS 11.13B, 11.13C

Comparison-Contrast Order

You organize by comparison when you want to show the similarities or differences between two subjects. To compare two styles of Japanese theater, one student used a Venn diagram to organize her details. In her paragraph, the writer focused most of her attention on the differences between the two styles.

Venn Diagram

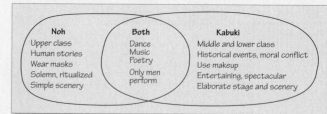

Noh
Upper class
Human stories
Wear masks
Solemn, ritualized
Simple scenery

Both
Dance
Music
Poetry
Only men perform

Kabuki
Middle and lower class
Historical events, moral conflict
Use makeup
Entertaining, spectacular
Elaborate stage and scenery

Topic Sentence

Body

Closing Sentence

Noh and Kabuki

Japan's two main styles of theater, Noh and Kabuki, are quite different. Both styles incorporate dance, music, poetry, and drama and are performed only by men. Performances in both theaters can last five hours or longer. The similarities end there. Noh is the older of the two, having begun in the 14th century as entertainment for royalty and the upper class. Kabuki started in the 17th century, and its style, more entertaining than enlightening, became popular with the common class. Noh plays deal with human failings and dilemmas performed on a simple platform with little scenery or props. Kabuki concentrates on spectacularly produced plays about historical events or dramatic moral conflicts. Noh uses masks to portray women and other characters, but Kabuki actors use makeup to make the transformation. Despite their differences, the two traditional forms of Japanese theater offer theatergoers a choice between two excellent forms of entertainment.

 Respond to the reading. How is the above paragraph organized? What different way might it have been arranged?

Basic Elements

Answers

Discuss the categories used to create a logical organization in the paragraph.

Respond to the reading.

Guide students to express opinions about which details are most amusing and engaging. Possible answers:

- "worrier's" gasps and shrieks
- observations about back-seat drivers
- the person who "passes out," unaware of everything that is going on

---

Answers

Have students identify how the ideas from the Venn diagram were used to create a logical organization in the paragraph. Elicit examples of comparison and contrast signal words used to make connections between ideas.

Respond to the reading.

Have students demonstrate comprehension by analyzing the reading. They should note that the paragraph is organized by comparing and contrasting Noh and Kabuki point by point. Sentences and paragraphs could be rearranged to cover all of Noh's characteristics first before covering Kabuki's characteristics.

 TEKS **11.13B** Structure ideas in a sustained and persuasive way; **11.13C** Revise drafts to clarify meaning and achieve logical organization by rearranging the words, sentences, and paragraphs, and by adding transitional words and phrases; **ELPS** **3G** Express opinions; **4K** Demonstrate English comprehension and expand reading skills by employing analytical skills

Cause-and-Effect Order

You organize by cause and effect when you want to discuss one cause followed by its specific effects or an effect followed by its specific causes. The paragraph below discusses one cause (dehydration) and its effects.

Cause-Effect Organizer

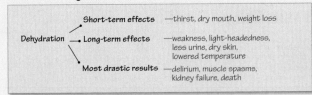

Topic Sentence

Body

Closing Sentence

Dangerous Effects of Dehydration

An individual who does not get enough fluid each day runs the risk of dehydration. In the short term, dehydration creates general thirst—an easy reminder to drink some water. Surprisingly, it may also lead to a rapid drop in weight. In the long term (more than several days), the sufferer may begin to feel weak and light-headed. With the lack of water, the skin loses its elasticity and becomes dry and crinkly. Continued dehydration can lead to a drop in body temperature, causing the sufferer to feel cold. At this point, dehydration could also affect mental functioning and lead to a feeling of general apathy. If the dehydration continues, an individual could experience muscle spasms and delirium. The kidneys could also shut down, and if the condition continues, the entire body could shut down. While the consequences of dehydration are severe, the solution is simple: Be sure to drink enough water, a minimum of 32 ounces every day.

 Respond to the reading. What are the three levels of dehydration? Give one supporting detail for each.

 TEKS 11.13B, 11.13C

Basic Paragraph Skills **615**

Process Organization

You organize step-by-step when you want to explain a process. The following paragraph explains the process of eutrophication, which essentially kills a freshwater lake.

Process Diagram

| The Process of Eutrophication |
| phase 1: oligotrophic |
| ↓ |
| phase 2: mesotrophic |
| ↓ |
| phase 3: eutrophic |
| ↓ |
| phase 4: hypereutrophic |
| ↓ |
| phase 5: dystrophic |

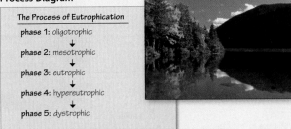

Topic Sentence

Body

Closing Sentence

Eutrophication

Perhaps the biggest threat to the nation's freshwater lakes is the process of eutrophication, caused by an excess of nutrients. The process begins at the **oligotrophic** phase, when water is clear with little aerobic activity. In the second phase, the **mesotrophic** phase, fertilizers are washed into the water through rain runoff. Rich with nitrates and phosphates, the fertilizers stimulate the growth of algae and other water plants, creating an algal "bloom." By phase three, the **eutrophic** phase, the bloom has grown to affect the oxygen level in the water in two ways. First, it prevents the water from absorbing light needed for oxygen generation. Second, the algae is broken down by aerobic bacteria that further deplete the oxygen in the water. Left unchecked, the process moves to the **hypereutrophic** phase, when algae chokes and kills living organisms. The final stage is the **dystrophic** phase, where water becomes hypoxic, or lacking in enough oxygen to sustain life, and the body of water becomes officially "dead." People in this country must find a way to counteract this process or face losing the nation's clean freshwater supply.

Answers

Guide students to recognize the logical organization of the cause-effect paragraph. Elicit examples of cause-effect signal words used to make connections between ideas. Follow a similar procedure with the Process Organization paragraph.

Respond to the reading.

Have students demonstrate comprehension by responding to the questions. They should infer that the three levels of dehydration are short-term, long-term, and severe.

Answers (cont'd)

Details:

- Short-term dehydration can cause rapid weight loss.

- Long-term dehydration can cause the skin to lose elasticity and the mind to be affected.

- Severe dehydration can cause the kidneys and all body functions to shut down.

 TEKS **11.13B** Structure ideas in a sustained and persuasive way; **11.13C** Revise drafts to clarify meaning and achieve logical organization by rearranging the words, sentences, and paragraphs, and by adding transitional words and phrases; **ELPS 4G** Demonstrate comprehension of increasingly complex English/responding to questions; **4J** Demonstrate English comprehension and expand reading skills by employing inferential skills

TEKS 11.13B, 11.13C

Logical Order

You organize by logical order when your main points are of equal importance and can be placed in any order in your paragraph. Move logically from one point to the next so your writing flows well and is not confusing. In the paragraph below, transitional words and phrases help the writer move from point to point.

Logical Order List (partial)

Braille

- developed by Louis Braille
- alphabetic code of raised dots
- read by running fingers across the page
- basic unit of code is the "cell"
- books in Braille longer than regular books

Topic Sentence

Body

Closing Sentence

Braille

Braille is a system of communication used by the blind. It was developed by Louis Braille, a blind French student, in 1824. The code consists of an alphabet using combinations of small raised dots. The dots are imprinted on paper and can be felt, and thus read, by running the fingers across the page. The basic unit of the code is called a "cell," which is two dots wide and three dots high. Each letter is formed by different combinations of these dots. Numbers, punctuation marks, and even a system for writing music are also expressed by using different arrangements. Books written in Braille require many more pages than a print book, and one novel might require many different volumes. The Braille system is used for different languages all over the world and is used for many things other than books. Braille is commonly used in elevators to indicate floors, and some restaurants even provide menus in Braille. There are also Braille codes that are used to read math symbols and music! Special Braille equipment includes typewriters and even a Braille embosser that can be attached to a computer. The small Braille dots, which may seem insignificant to the sighted, have opened up the entire world of books and reading for the blind.

? **Respond to the reading.** This paragraph provides many key details. Which ones do you find the most revealing? Name two.

Basic Essay Skills

At this point in your life, most of your academic writing is essay writing. You take essay tests; you write procedure (how-to) papers; you respond to the books that you read. All of these are essays—writing in which you explain, argue, or describe your thinking on a particular topic. The way you develop an essay depends on the guidelines established by your instructor and on your own good judgment about a particular writing idea. For some essays, a straightforward, traditional approach might be best; for others, a more creative approach might be more effective.

No matter what approach you take, keep in mind that developing an essay can be challenging. You must have a good understanding of your topic, have confidence in your position, and then develop it so that your readers can clearly share in your thinking. The information in this chapter serves as a basic guide to essay writing. (Also see the specific essay-writing chapters earlier in the book.)

- **Understanding the Basic Parts**
- **Outlining Your Ideas**
- **Writing Thesis Statements**
- **Creating Great Beginnings**
- **Developing the Middle Part**
- **Using Transitions**
- **Shaping Great Endings**
- **Key Terms, Techniques, and Forms**

"Essays are how we speak to one another in print."

—Edward Hoagland

? ## Answers

Respond to the reading.

Guide students analyze the paragraph's logical organization and to identify transitional words and phrases. Then encourage them to express ideas and opinions about which details are most revealing. Answers will vary.

⭐ **TEKS** **11.13B** Structure ideas in a sustained and persuasive way; **11.13C** Revise drafts to clarify meaning and achieve logical organization by rearranging the words, sentences, and paragraphs, and by adding transitional words and phrases; **ELPS 3G** Express opinions and ideas; **4K** Demonstrate English comprehension and expand reading skills by employing analytical skills

TEKS 11.13A, 11.13B

Understanding the Basic Parts

Each part of an essay—the beginning, middle, and ending—plays an important role. To develop your writing, refer to the suggestions below and to the sample essays earlier in this book.

Beginning Your opening paragraph should capture the reader's attention and state your thesis. Here are some ways to capture your reader's attention:

- Tell a dramatic or exciting story (anecdote) about the topic.
- Ask an intriguing question or two.
- Provide a few surprising facts or statistics.
- Provide an interesting quotation.
- Explain your personal experience or involvement with the topic.

> Beginning
> Middle
> Ending

Middle The middle paragraphs should support your thesis statement. They provide information that fully explains the thesis statement. For example, in an essay about safety measures in Grand Prix racing, each middle paragraph could focus on one main aspect of improved safety. Follow your own outline while writing this section.

> Beginning
> Middle
> Ending

Ending Your closing paragraph should summarize your thesis and leave the reader with something to think about. Here are some strategies for creating a strong closing:

- Review your main points.
- Emphasize the special importance of one main point.
- Answer any questions the reader may still have.
- Draw a conclusion and put the information in perspective.
- Provide a significant final thought for the reader.

> Beginning
> Middle
> Ending

 TEKS 11.21B

Outlining Your Ideas

Once you've established a general pattern of development, you're ready to organize the information (main points, supporting details, etc.) that you will cover in your essay. It may work to jot down a brief list of ideas to follow. Then again, you may find it helpful to organize your ideas in a topic or sentence outline.

Topic Outline

An outline is an orderly listing of related ideas. In a **topic outline**, each new idea is stated as a word or phrase rather than in complete sentences. Before you start, write your working thesis statement at the top of your paper to keep you focused on the subject of your essay. Do not attempt to outline your opening and closing paragraphs unless specifically asked to do so.

> Introduction
> I. The technology of genetic engineering
>   A. Gene manipulation
>   B. Gene copying and transferring
>   C. Gene recombining and cloning
> II. The uses of genetic engineering
>   A. Unpredictable in past
>   B. More predictable now
>   C. More potential in future
> III. The fears about genetic engineering
>   A. Release of dangerous organisms
>   B. Lack of trust in scientists
> Conclusion

Sentence Outline

A **sentence outline** naturally contains more detail than a topic outline because each new idea is expressed as a complete sentence. It is often required for longer essays or a research paper.

> Introduction
> I. Genetic engineering is a form of biotechnology.
>   A. Scientists can manipulate genes.
>   B. Genes can be copied and moved to cells in other species.
>   C. Scientists can recombine genes and clone entire organisms.
> II. Genetic engineering affects animal and plant breeding.
>   A. Past species improvement efforts proved unpredictable.
>   B. Now development time is cut dramatically with better results.
>   C. Animals are potential chemical factories, and new animals can be created and patented.
> III. Genetic engineering is feared by some.
>   A. Dangerous organisms could be released.
>   B. Public confidence in scientists has been undermined.
> Conclusion

Basic Elements

Understanding the Basic Parts

Discuss with students how understanding the basic parts of an essay can help them structure their ideas in a sustained and persuasive way as they write. Point out that the beginning/middle/ending structure can be applied to almost all types of writing. Remind them that their thesis statement should appear in the beginning section of the essay.

Outlining Your Ideas

Draw attention to the similarities and differences in the topic outline and sentence outline. Elicit from students that both formats will help them to systematically organize information to support central ideas, concepts, and themes.

 TEKS **11.13A** Plan a first draft by developing a thesis or controlling idea; **11.13B** Structure ideas in a sustained and persuasive way; **11.21B** Systematically organize relevant and accurate information to support central ideas, concepts, and themes/outline ideas

TEKS 11.13A

Writing Thesis Statements

In most cases, a thesis statement takes a stand or expresses a specific feeling about, or feature of, your topic. An effective thesis statement gives you the necessary direction to develop your essay.

Using a Formula

a specific topic *(the Harlem Renaissance)*

+ **a particular feature or feeling about the topic** *(helped the African American intellectual community gain acceptance in mainstream America)*

= **an effective topic sentence** *(The Harlem Renaissance helped the African American intellectual community gain acceptance in mainstream America.)*

Sample Thesis Statements

Writing Assignment: Examine a political theme in a novel.
Specific Topic: *All Quiet on the Western Front*
Thesis Statement: In *All Quiet on the Western Front*, by Erich Maria Remarque, **(topic)** idealistic views of nationalism are brought into question **(particular feeling)**.

Writing Assignment: Explore a current water resource in the area.
Specific Topic: Recreational fishing on Lake Michigan
Thesis Statement: Recreational fishing on Lake Michigan **(topic)** needs more oversight **(particular stand)**.

Writing Assignment: Research on human growth and development.
Specific Topic: Personality traits
Thesis Statement: An individual's peer group **(particular feature)** shapes certain personality traits **(topic)**.

Thesis Checklist

Be sure that your thesis statement . . .

_____ **identifies** a limited, specific topic,

_____ **focuses** on a particular feature or feeling about the topic,

_____ **can be supported** with convincing facts and details, and

_____ **meets the requirements** of the assignment.

TEKS 11.13B

Creating Great Beginnings

The opening paragraph of an essay should grab the reader's attention, introduce your topic, and present your thesis. Try one of these approaches to start an opening paragraph.

- **Start with an interesting fact.**
  In the period between world wars, the Harlem Renaissance thrust African American culture into the United States mainstream.
- **Ask an interesting question.**
  Did you know that the civil rights movement really began with the Harlem Renaissance in the 1920s?
- **Start with a quotation.**
  "As one who loves literature, art, music, and history, I've been deeply rooted in the Harlem Renaissance for many years." So states Debbie Allen, a well-known actress of film and television fame.

Beginning Strategies

If you have trouble coming up with a good opening paragraph, follow the step-by-step example below.

First sentence—Grab the reader's attention.

Start with a sentence that catches your reader's attention (see above).
In the period between world wars, the Harlem Renaissance thrust African American culture into the United States mainstream.

Second sentence—Give some background information.

Provide some information about the topic.
It became a precursor to the civil rights movement, creating an environment of awareness of the black culture.

Third sentence—Introduce the specific topic of the essay.

Introduce the topic in a way that builds up to the thesis statement.
The period was a time of growth in African American literature and art.

Fourth sentence—Give the thesis statement.

Write the thesis statement of the paper (see page 620).
As such, the Harlem Renaissance helped the African American intellectual community gain acceptance in mainstream America.

Basic Elements

Writing Thesis Statements

Discuss the formula for writing a thesis statement, encouraging students to use the academic language to help them internalize it. Remind them that the time to formulate a thesis statement is when they are planning their first draft. Point out that an effective thesis statement will help to guide them to structure ideas in a sustained and persuasive way. Encourage them to use the Thesis Checklist as a resource to monitor the effectiveness of the thesis statements that they write.

Creating Great Beginnings

Elicit from students that the strategies provided will help them to structure ideas in their writing. Suggest that they use the strategies to monitor the organization of their writing. Have students use the strategies to write an analysis of a recent piece of writing, using the academic language to describe their work.

TEKS **11.13A** Plan a first draft by developing a thesis or controlling idea; **11.13B** Structure ideas in a sustained and persuasive way; **ELPS** **1B** Monitor written language production and employ self-corrective techniques or other resources; **1E** Internalize new basic and academic language by using and reusing it/writing

TEKS 11.13B

TEKS 11.13B, 11.13C

Developing the Middle Part

The middle part of an essay is where you do most of the work. In this part, you develop the main points that support your thesis statement.

Use your outline or other planning notes as a guide when you write this section. However, new ideas may pop into your head as you go along. Make note of these ideas in case you may want to explore them further later on.

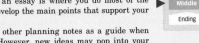

Advancing Your Thesis

Keep these points in mind as you explain and develop your thesis statement.

- **Cover your main points.** Develop each main point in a paragraph or series of paragraphs.
- **Give background information.** If necessary, provide some history of your topic to help you put it in context.
- **Define terms.** Clarify any terms that your reader is not likely to know.
- **Sort out the main points.** Present the main ideas in a logical order (according to your outline).

Testing Your Ideas

When you write the middle part of an essay, you're testing your first thoughts about your topic. Here are some ways to test your line of thinking as you write.

- **Raise questions.** Anticipate what questions the reader may have about your topic.
- **Consider alternative ideas.** Take inventory of your thesis as you go along: Do you need to strengthen or rethink it? Also look at your main points from different angles.
- **Answer objections.** Address different points of view about your topic.

Building a Coherent Structure

Each middle paragraph should include main points and details that logically develop your thesis.

- **Develop one paragraph at a time.** Start a new paragraph whenever a shift or change in the essay takes place.
- **Connect your main points.** Use transitional phrases to link each new paragraph with the preceding one. (See page **623**.)

Using Transitions

Transitions can be used to connect one sentence to another sentence within a paragraph, or to connect one paragraph to another within a longer essay or report. The lists below show a number of transitions and how they are used. Each colored list is a group of transitions that could work well together in a piece of writing.

Words used to show location

above	around	between	inside	outside
across	behind	by	into	over
against	below	down	near	throughout
along	beneath	in back of	next to	to the right
among	beside	in front of	on top of	under

Above	In front of	On top of
Below	Beside	Next to
To the left	In back of	Beneath
To the right		

Words used to show time

about	during	yesterday	until	finally
after	first	meanwhile	next	then
at	second	today	soon	as soon as
before	to begin	tomorrow	later	in the end

First	To begin	Now	First	Before
Second	To continue	Soon	Then	During
Third	To conclude	Eventually	Next	After
Finally			In the end	

Words used to compare things

likewise	as	in the same way	one way
like	also	similarly	both

In the same way	One way
Also	Another way
Similarly	Both

Basic Elements

Developing the Middle Part

Remind students that the middle part of an essay is key to providing reasons, examples, and details that support their thesis statements. Draw attention to the suggestions under "Building a Coherent Structure" and elicit that using transitional words and phrases to connect ideas also helps to guide readers to understand and appreciate the point the writer is trying to make.

Using Transitions

Explain that many of the words listed on SE page 623 are high-frequency words that are often used to identify or describe. Review each category of transition words and have students work in small groups to identify a scenario in which the words might be used (for example, describing a new store's location). Challenge them to use as many of the transition words as possible.

TEKS **11.13B** Develop drafts in open-ended situations that include transitions; **11.13C** Revise drafts by adding transitional words; **ELPS 3B** Expand vocabulary/learning and using high-frequency words for identifying and describing

Words used to contrast (show differences)

| but | still | although | on the other hand |
| however | yet | otherwise | even though |

On the other hand	Although
Even though	Yet
Still	Nevertheless

Words used to emphasize a point

| again | truly | especially | for this reason |
| to repeat | in fact | to emphasize | |

| For this reason | Truly | In fact |
| Especially | To emphasize | To repeat |

Words used to conclude or summarize

| finally | as a result | to sum it up | in conclusion |
| lastly | therefore | all in all | because |

| Because | As a result | To sum it up | Therefore |
| In conclusion | All in all | Because | Finally |

Words used to add information

again	another	for instance	for example
also	and	moreover	additionally
as well	besides	along with	other
next	finally	in addition	

For example	For instance	Next	Another
Additionally	Besides	Moreover	Along with
Finally	Next	Also	As well

Words used to clarify

| in other words | for instance | that is | for example |

| For instance | For example |
| In other words | Equally important |

Shaping Great Endings

The closing paragraph of a paper should summarize your thesis and leave the reader with something to think about. When writing your closing paragraph, use two or more of the following approaches:

- Review your main points.
- Emphasize the special importance of one main point.
- Answer any questions the reader may still have.
- Draw a conclusion and put the information in perspective.
- Provide a significant final thought for the reader.

Ending Strategies

If you have trouble coming up with an effective closing paragraph, follow the step-by-step example below.

First sentence—Reflect on the topic.

Start by reflecting on the material presented previously about the topic.

> Although the Harlem Renaissance lasted a brief time, its influence is still felt.

Second sentence—Add another point.

Include a final point of interest that you didn't mention before.

> Some argue that the movement failed in its goal of equality, stating the ongoing existence of racism as proof.

Third sentence—Emphasize the most important point.

Stress the importance of one or more key points that support the thesis.

> While that may be true, the fact remains that the black voice is strong throughout the creative world. African American writers, artists, and philosophers are heard and their ideas respected.

Fourth sentence—Wrap up the topic or draw a conclusion.

Add one final thought about the topic, or draw a conclusion from the points you've presented in the writing.

> Philosopher Alaine Hock says that the Harlem Renaissance gave African Americans their first chance for "group expression and self-determination," and the writers and artists clearly made the most of their opportunities.

Basic Elements

Using Transitions (cont'd)

Remind students that many of the words listed on SE page 624 are high-frequency words that are often used to identify or describe. Ask students to describe situations in which each set of transition words or phrases might be used.

Shaping Great Endings

Review each of the strategies for writing an effective concluding paragraph or paragraphs and ask students to describe writing assignments in which they have used each one. Suggest that they list the strategies in their writing notebooks and internalize the academic language by using it to explain how and when they should be used.

 TEKS **11.13B** Develop drafts in open-ended situations that include transitions; **11.13C** Revise drafts by adding transitional words; **11.15A(i)** Write an analytical essay of sufficient length that includes effective concluding paragraph(s); **ELPS** **1E** Internalize new basic and academic language by using and reusing it/writing; **3B** Expand vocabulary/learning and using high-frequency words for identifying and describing

Learning Key Writing Terms

The next two pages include important terms related to writing. Refer to these pages whenever you have a question about the vocabulary associated with any part of the writing process.

Balance   Arranging words or phrases in a way to give them equal importance

Body   The main part of a piece of writing, containing details that support or develop the thesis statement

Brainstorming   Collecting ideas by thinking freely about all the possibilities; used most often with groups

Central idea   The main point of a piece of writing, often stated in a thesis statement or a topic sentence

Closing sentence   The summary or final part in a piece of writing

Coherence   The logical arranging of ideas so they are clear and easy to follow

Dialogue   Written conversation between two or more people

Emphasis   Giving great importance to a specific idea in a piece of writing

Exposition   Writing that explains and informs

Figurative language   Language that goes beyond the normal meaning of the words used, often called "figures of speech"

Focus (thesis)   The specific part of a topic that is written about in an essay

Generalization   A general statement that gives an overall view, rather than focusing on specific details

Grammar   The rules that govern the standard structure and features of a language

Idiom   A phrase or an expression that means something different from what the words actually say

The answer was really out in left field. (This means the answer was not even close to being correct.)

Next year you'll sing a different tune. (This means you'll think differently.)

Jargon   The special language of a certain group or occupation

The weaver pointed out the fabric's unique warp and woof.

Computer jargon: byte   icon   server   virus

Limiting the subject   Narrowing a general subject to a more specific one

Literal   The actual dictionary meaning of a word; language that means exactly what it appears to mean

Loaded words   Words slanted for or against the subject

The ignorant politicians think we're all illiterate.

Logic   Correctly using facts, examples, and reasons to support a point

Modifiers   Words, phrases, or clauses that limit or describe another word or group of words

Objective   Writing that gives factual information without adding feelings or opinions (See *subjective*.)

Poetic license   A writer's freedom to bend the rules of writing to achieve a certain effect

Point of view   The position or angle from which a story is told (See page 348.)

Prose   Writing in standard sentence form

Purpose   The specific goal of the writing

Style   The author's unique choice of words and sentences

Subjective   Writing that includes the writer's feelings, attitudes, and opinions (See *objective*.)

Supporting details   Facts or ideas used to sustain the main point

Syntax   The order and relationship of words in a sentence

Theme   The main point or unifying idea of a piece of writing

Thesis statement   A statement of the purpose, or main idea, of an essay

Tone   The writer's attitude toward the subject

Topic   The specific subject of a piece of writing

Topic sentence   The sentence that carries the main idea of a paragraph

Transitions   Words or phrases that connect or tie ideas together

Unity   A sense of oneness in writing in which each sentence helps to develop the main idea

Usage   The way in which people use language (*Standard language* follows the rules; *nonstandard language* does not.)

Voice   A writer's unique personal tone or feeling that comes across in a piece of writing

Basic Elements

Learning Key Writing Terms

Have students work in small groups to categorize the writing terms according to their function in writing or in the writing process. Students might create webs or charts to show the categories they choose. Students could sort according to the stages of the writing process, language (or author's craft), or other categories of their choosing. Tell students to be prepared to explain their rationale for sorting.

ELPS 1C Use strategic learning strategies to acquire basic and grade-level vocabulary

Using Writing Techniques

Experiment with some of these techniques in your own essays and stories.

Allusion A reference to a familiar person, place, thing, or event
Mario threw me my mitt. "Hey, Babe Ruth, you forgot this!"

Analogy A comparison of similar ideas or objects to help clarify one of them
There is no frigate like a book, to take us lands away.
—Emily Dickinson

Anecdote A brief story used to illustrate or make a point
It is said that the last words John Adams uttered were "Thomas Jefferson survives." Ironically, Jefferson had died just a few hours earlier. Both deaths occurred on July 4, 1826—the 50th anniversary of the Declaration of Independence shepherded by the two great men. (This ironic anecdote intensifies the importance of both men in our nation's history.)

Colloquialism A common word or phrase suitable for everyday conversation but not for formal speech or writing
"Cool" and "rad" are colloquialisms suggesting approval.

Exaggeration An overstatement or a stretching of the truth to emphasize a point (See *hyperbole* and *overstatement*.)
We opened up the boat's engine and sped along at a million miles an hour.

Flashback A technique in which a writer interrupts a story to go back and relive an earlier time or event
I stopped at the gate, panting. Suddenly I was seven years old again, and my brother was there, calling me "chicken" from the edge of the stone well. Then I opened my eyes and heard only the crickets chirping. The years, the well, and my brother were gone. I turned back to the road, determined to get home before nightfall.

Foreshadowing Hints about what will happen next in a story
As Mai explained why she had to break their date, she noticed Luke looking past her. Turning, she saw Meg smiling—at Luke.

Hyperbole (hi-púr-bə-lē) Exaggeration used to emphasize a point
The music was loud enough to make your ears bleed.

Irony An expression in which the author says one thing but means just the opposite
As we all know, there's nothing students love more than homework.

Juxtaposition Putting two words or ideas close together to create a contrasting of ideas or an ironic meaning
Ah, the sweet smell of fuel emissions!

Local color The use of details that are common in a certain place

Metaphor A figure of speech that compares two things without using the words *like* or *as*
The sheep were dense, dancing clouds scuttling across the road.

Overstatement An exaggeration or a stretching of the truth (See *exaggeration* and *hyperbole*.)
If I eat one more piece of turkey, I will burst!

Oxymoron Connecting two words with opposite meanings
small fortune   cruel kindness   original copy

Paradox A true statement that says two opposite things
As I crossed the finish line dead last, I felt a surge of triumph.

Parallelism Repeating similar grammatical structures (words, phrases, or sentences) to give writing rhythm
We cannot undo, we will not forget, and we should not ignore the pain of the past.

Personification A figure of speech in which a nonhuman thing is given human characteristics
The computer spit out my disk.

Pun A phrase that uses words that sound the same in a way that gives them a funny effect
I call my dog Trousers because he pants so much.

Simile A figure of speech that compares two things using *like* or *as*
Her silent anger was like a rock wall, hard and impenetrable.

Slang Informal words or phrases used by a particular group of people
cool it   hang out   shoot the curl

Symbol A concrete object used to represent an idea

Understatement The opposite of exaggeration; using very calm language to call attention to an object or an idea
"... except for an interruption caused by my wife falling out of the car, the journey went very well."
—E. B. White

Basic Elements

Using Writing Techniques

Allow time for students to read through the listing of writing techniques. Then ask them to identify one or two techniques they have used effectively in the past, and write a reflection on the experience in their writer's notebooks. Remind them to narrate, describe, and explain with detail.

Knowing the Different Forms

Finding the right form for your writing is just as important as finding the right topic. When you are selecting a form, be sure to ask yourself who you're writing for (your *audience*) and why you're writing (your *purpose*).

Anecdote	A brief story that helps to make a point
Autobiography	A writer's story of his or her own life
Biography	A writer's story of someone else's life
Book review	An essay offering an opinion about a book, not to be confused with *literary analysis*
Cause and effect	A paper examining an event, the forces leading up to that event, and the effects following the event
Character sketch	A brief description of a specific character showing some aspect of that character's personality
Descriptive writing	Writing that uses sensory details that allow the reader to clearly visualize a person, a place, a thing, or an idea
Editorial	A letter or an article offering an opinion, an idea, or a solution
Essay	A thoughtful piece of writing in which ideas are explained, analyzed, or evaluated
Expository writing	Writing that explains something by presenting its steps, causes, or kinds
Eyewitness account	A report giving specific details of an event or a person
Fable	A short story that teaches a lesson or moral, often using talking animals as the main characters
Fantasy	A story set in an imaginary world in which the characters usually have supernatural powers or abilities
Freewriting	Spontaneous, rapid writing to explore your thoughts about a topic of interest
Historical fiction	An invented story based on an actual historical event
Interview	Writing based on facts and details obtained through speaking with another person
Journal writing	Writing regularly to record personal observations, thoughts, and ideas

Literary analysis	A careful examination or interpretation of some aspect of a piece of literature
Myth	A traditional story intended to explain a mystery of nature, religion, or culture
Novel	A book-length story with several characters and a well-developed plot, usually with one or more subplots
Personal narrative	Writing that shares an event or experience from the writer's personal life
Persuasive writing	Writing intended to persuade the reader to follow the writer's way of thinking about something
Play	A form that uses dialogue to tell a story, usually meant to be performed in front of an audience
Poem	A creative expression that may use rhyme, rhythm, and imagery
Problem-solution	Writing that presents a problem followed by a proposed solution
Process paper	Writing that explains how a process works or how to do or make something
Profile	An essay that reveals an individual or re-creates a time period
Proposal	Writing that includes specific information about an idea or a project that is being considered for approval
Research report	An essay that shares information about a topic that has been thoroughly researched
Response to literature	Writing that is a reaction to something the writer has read
Science fiction	Writing based on real or imaginary science and often set in the future
Short story	A short fictional piece with only a few characters and one conflict or problem
Summary	Writing that presents the most important ideas from a longer piece of writing
Tall tale	A humorous, exaggerated story about a character or an animal that does impossible things
Tragedy	Literature in which the hero fails or is destroyed because of a serious character flaw

Basic Elements

Knowing the Different Forms

Ask students to list the forms of writing with which they have experience. Then have them work in small groups to describe the audiences for which particular forms are appropriate. Ask each group to choose a form and write a description of at least two possible audiences. Tell them to include an explanation of their choices.

TEKS 11.13A Plan a first draft by selecting the correct genre for conveying the intended meaning to multiple audiences; **ELPS** 5G Narrate, describe, and explain with increasing specificity and detail

Editing and Proofreading Marks

Once you have revised a piece of writing, you will need to reread it carefully for grammar and mechanics issues. The marks shown on the next page will help you quickly and clearly proofread and edit your work. Think of these marks as a special shorthand, making your editing work efficient and easily understood by both you and your teacher.

Insertions and Deletions

Insertions are indicated with a small, arrowlike mark, called a caret (see chart, rows 6–9). Keep these points in mind:
- **Carets pointing upward** indicate punctuation marks that align at the bottom of the text line.
- **Carets pointing downward** indicate punctuation marks that align with the top of the text line.
- **To make long insertions**, write the new text in the margin or on a separate piece of paper. Label both the caret and the insertion (for example, "Insert A") so that it is easy to match the new text with the point at which you want to insert it.
- **Inserting a period** is done with a special mark (see chart, row 3). Because a period is hard to see, circling it makes the correction clearer.

Deletions are marked using a special delete mark (see row 5). If you are deleting a word or phrase and replacing it with new text, use a delete mark to show all the text that is being deleted. Then add an insert mark to show where the new text should be placed.

Capitalization, Spelling, and Other Corrections

Rows 1, 2, and 4 of the chart show correction marks for capitalization and spelling errors. For spelling errors, you may want to write the correct spelling above the incorrect word. (This is useful if you have had to check the spelling and do not want to have to look it up again.) Row 10 shows how to indicate a new paragraph; row 11 shows the mark for switching words or letters.

The corrections shown in the chart are the most common you will find while editing and proofreading your work. Learning these marks will improve your ability to edit and proofread your work quickly and well.

Editing and Proofreading Marks

Use the symbols and letters below to show where and how your writing needs to be changed. Your teachers may also use these symbols to point out errors in your writing.

Symbols	Meaning	Example	Corrected Example
≡	Capitalize a letter.	F. Scott Fitzgerald wrote the Great Gatsby.	F. Scott Fitzgerald wrote The Great Gatsby.
/	Make a capital letter lowercase.	The book tells the story of a young Middle-class man.	The book tells the story of a young middle-class man.
⊙	Insert (add) a period.	The focus is the American Dream⊙ Gatsby recently . . .	The focus is the American Dream. Gatsby recently . . .
◯ or sp.	Correct spelling.	Nick Caraway, Gatsby's friend, tells the story.	Nick Carraway, Gatsby's friend, tells the story.
⌿	Delete (take out) or replace.	Jay Gatsby is a fabulously wealthy.	Jay Gatsby is fabulously wealthy.
∧	Insert here.	Gatsby is Nick's mysterious neighbor.	Gatsby is Nick's mysterious neighbor.
∧ ∧ ∧	Insert a comma, a colon, or a semicolon.	He is madly in love with Nick's cousin Daisy.	He is madly in love with Nick's cousin, Daisy.
∨ ∨̈ ∨̈	Insert an apostrophe or quotation marks.	"She saw something awful in the very simplicity she failed to understand.	"She saw something awful in the very simplicity she failed to understand."
? ! ∧ ∧	Insert a question mark or an exclamation point.	What was Jay Gatsby's fatal flaw	What was Jay Gatsby's fatal flaw?
¶	Start a new paragraph.	¶Gatsby dreams the dream, but . . .	Gatsby dreams the dream, but . . .
∼	Switch words or letters.	He was not enough sensible.	He was not sensible enough.

Basic Elements

Editing and Proofreading Marks

Review and discuss the editing and proofreading marks. Guide students to use the new basic vocabulary to discuss situations in which each type of mark is used. Encourage students to use the list of marks as a resource whenever they self-correct their writing or that of a peer.

ELPS 1B Monitor written language production and employ self-corrective techniques or other resources; **2C** Learn new basic vocabulary

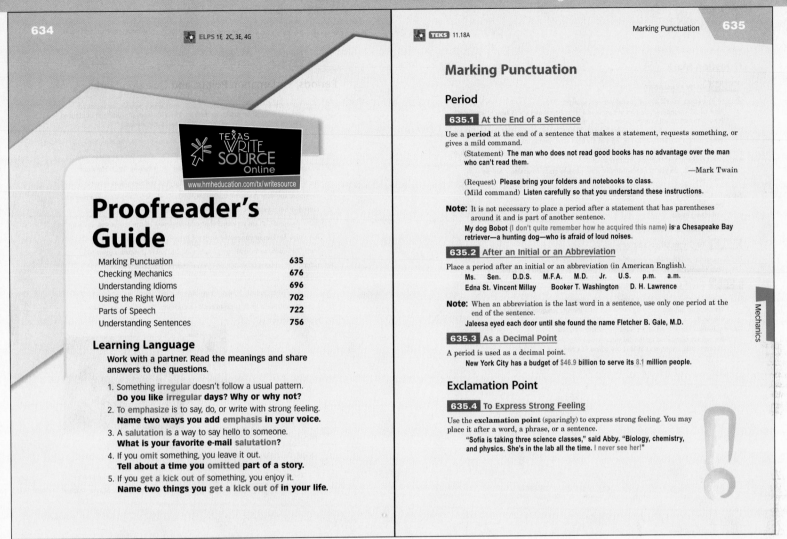

Proofreader's Guide

Learning Language

Work with a partner. Read the meanings and share answers to the questions.

1. Something *irregular* doesn't follow a usual pattern.
   Do you like irregular days? Why or why not?

2. To *emphasize* is to say, do, or write with strong feeling.
   Name two ways you add emphasis in your voice.

3. A *salutation* is a way to say hello to someone.
   What is your favorite e-mail salutation?

4. If you *omit* something, you leave it out.
   Tell about a time you omitted part of a story.

5. If you *get a kick out of* something, you enjoy it.
   Name two things you get a kick out of in your life.

Marking Punctuation

Period

635.1 At the End of a Sentence

Use a **period** at the end of a sentence that makes a statement, requests something, or gives a mild command.

(Statement) The man who does not read good books has no advantage over the man who can't read them.

—Mark Twain

(Request) Please bring your folders and notebooks to class.

(Mild command) Listen carefully so that you understand these instructions.

Note: It is not necessary to place a period after a statement that has parentheses around it and is part of another sentence.

My dog Bobot (I don't quite remember how he acquired this name) is a Chesapeake Bay retriever—a hunting dog—who is afraid of loud noises.

635.2 After an Initial or an Abbreviation

Place a period after an initial or an abbreviation (in American English).

Ms.   Sen.   D.D.S.   M.F.A.   M.D.   Jr.   U.S.   p.m.   a.m.
Edna St. Vincent Millay   Booker T. Washington   D. H. Lawrence

Note: When an abbreviation is the last word in a sentence, use only one period at the end of the sentence.

Jaleesa eyed each door until she found the name Fletcher B. Gale, M.D.

635.3 As a Decimal Point

A period is used as a decimal point.

New York City has a budget of $46.9 billion to serve its 8.1 million people.

Exclamation Point

635.4 To Express Strong Feeling

Use the **exclamation point** (sparingly) to express strong feeling. You may place it after a word, a phrase, or a sentence.

"Sofía is taking three science classes," said Abby. "Biology, chemistry, and physics. She's in the lab all the time. I never see her!"

Mechanics

Learning Language

Read aloud the basic and academic terms, as well as the descriptions and questions. Point out the *r*-controlled vowel sound that begins *irregular*, and other common sounds, and have students practice producing the sounds in the newly acquired vocabulary. Then model how to read one question and answer it. For example, *It says that* emphasize *means to say, do or write with strong feelings. It asks how to add emphasis to my voice. One way is to say certain words in a stronger voice.* Have partners monitor their understanding of the terms by working through the meanings and questions together.

Marking Punctuation

Point out that the explanations and examples provided will help students to correctly and consistently use the conventions of punctuation.

Related Skills Activities

■ *SkillsBook*
Pretest: Punctuation, pp. 3–4
End Punctuation, p. 5

TEKS 11.18A Correctly and consistently use conventions of punctuation and capitalization; **ELPS 1F** Use accessible language and learn new and essential language in the process; **2A** Distinguish sounds and intonation patterns of English; **2B** Recognize elements of the English sound system in newly acquired vocabulary; **2C** Learn new basic and academic vocabulary; **3A** Practice producing sounds of newly acquired vocabulary to pronounce English words; **3E** Share information in cooperative learning interactions; **4G** Demonstrate comprehension of increasingly complex English/responding to questions

TEKS 11.18A

Question Mark

636.1 Direct Question

Place a **question mark** at the end of a direct question.

> **Now what? I wondered. Do I go out and buy a jar of honey and stand around waving it? How in the world am I supposed to catch a bear?**
>
> —Ken Taylor, "The Case of the Grizzly on the Greens"
>
> **When did the fire alarm stop ringing and my ears start ringing instead?**

When a question ends with a quotation that is also a question, use only one question mark, and place it within the quotation marks.

> **On road trips, do you remember driving your parents crazy by asking, "Are we there yet?"**

Note: Do not use a question mark after an indirect question.

> **Once the train had left the station, Miguel and I asked the conductor where we could get something to eat.**
>
> **Marta asked me if I finished my calculus homework yet.**

636.2 To Show Uncertainty

Use a question mark within parentheses to show uncertainty.

> **This summer marks the 20th season (?) of the American Players Theatre.**

636.3 Short Question Within a Sentence

Use a question mark for a short question within parentheses.

> **We crept so quietly** (had they heard us?) **past the kitchen door and back to our room.**

Use a question mark for a short question within dashes.

> **We quickly clambered up the old willow tree**—what teenager wouldn't?—**but even gazing out from that height, we couldn't see where Rex had gone.**

 TEKS 11.18A

Practice

Periods, Exclamation Points, and Question Marks

For each line in the paragraphs below, write where periods, exclamation points, or question marks are needed. Write the word preceding or containing each mark, as well. (Write "none" if no marks are needed.)

1.   Joaquin had an appointment with his podiatrist, Dr Marston,
2. because of chronic foot pain When he got to the office, he was surprised
3. to see a different name on the door instead—K R Green, M D. He went
4. in, thinking he had the wrong office, and asked the receptionist about the
5. name on the door Then he understood—she had recently gotten married and
6. changed her name. Dr. Marston *was* Dr. Green
7.   Joaquin's exam revealed that misalignment of his bones was causing
8. his pain. Dr Green suggested surgery to move the bone a fraction of an
9. inch (125 inch) to relieve the pressure on the nerve Joaquin requested
10. information about other options (wasn't surgery supposed to be a last
11. resort) and considered them.
12.   Dr Green asked, "Do you have any further questions" Joaquin asked
13. if he could take a little time to make a decision. The doctor emphatically
14. replied, "Please do"

Model

Model the following sentence to practice using question marks for short questions within parentheses.

> **Todd knew he had seen her before** (hadn't he?), **but he simply could not recall the woman's name.**
>
> —C. Marie, "Skins"

Mechanics

Related Skills Activities

■ **SkillsBook**
End Punctuation, p. 5

 ## Answers

Have students demonstrate their ability to correctly use the conventions of punctuation by completing the Practice activity.

line 1   Dr.
line 2   pain.
line 3   K.R.
          M.D.
line 4   none
line 5   door.
line 6   Green.
line 7   none
line 8   Dr.
line 9   .125
          nerve.
line 10 none
line 11 resort?
line 12 Dr.
          questions?"
line 13 none
line 14 do!"

TEKS 11.18A

Comma

638.1 Between Two Independent Clauses

Use a **comma** between two independent clauses that are joined by a coordinating conjunction (and, but, or, nor, for, yet, so).

> I wanted to knock on the glass to attract attention, but I couldn't move.
> —Ralph Ellison, *Invisible Man*

Note: Do not confuse a sentence containing a compound verb for a compound sentence.

> Jake had to mow the lawn and then use clippers to trim around the trees.

638.2 To Separate Adjectives

Use commas to separate two or more adjectives that *equally* modify the same noun. (Note: Do not use a comma between the last adjective and the noun.)

> Bao's eyes met the hard, bright lights hanging directly above her.
> —Julie Ament, student writer

A Closer Look

To determine whether adjectives modify equally—and should, therefore, be separated by commas—use these two tests:

1. Shift the order of the adjectives; if the sentence is clear, the adjectives modify equally. (In the example below, *hot* and *smelly* can be shifted and the sentence is still clear; *usual* and *morning* cannot.)

2. Insert *and* between the adjectives; if the sentence reads well, use a comma when the *and* is omitted. (The word *and* can be inserted between *hot* and *smelly*, but *and* does not make sense between *usual* and *morning*.)

> Matty was tired of working in the hot, smelly kitchen and decided to take her usual morning walk.

638.3 To Separate Contrasted Elements

Use commas to separate contrasted elements within a sentence. Often the word or phrase that is set off is preceded by *not*.

> The posted warnings were about moose, and not grizzly bears, but we still felt safer hanging our food high up in a tree, out of reach of any hungry animals.

Practice

Commas 1

- Between Two Independent Clauses
- To Separate Adjectives
- To Separate Contrasted Elements

Indicate where commas are needed in the following lines by writing the commas along with the words that surround them. (If no commas are needed, write "none" next to the line.)

1   You see a big hairy spider and your first inclination is to step back.
2   The fact is that a common spider should be afraid of you not the other way
3   around. Of the world's 40,000 spider species, less than 0.1 percent (that's one
4   species out of a thousand) have venom that's harmful to humans. A spider
5   bite may be painful but it's almost always harmless.
6   The only time a spider would bite a human is in self-defense not for
7   blood. Spiders do not feed on the blood of mammals. A spider's prey consists
8   mainly of smaller weaker insects, whose soft tissues are broken down by
9   digestive juices that the spider injects into their bodies. Then the spiders
10 suck everything up for a tasty satisfying meal.
11 So the next time you come upon an eight-legged four-eyed creature
12 from a web, remember the good that spiders do: They eat lots of pests
13 such as mosquitoes and their webs are truly beautiful objects. In addition,
14 researchers have actually found in venom chemicals that may be helpful to
15 humans. Go ahead and step back but don't step on a spider.

Model

Model the following sentences to practice using commas to separate contrasted elements.

> I must govern the clock, not be governed by it.
> —Golda Meir

> It is our responsibilities, not ourselves, that we should take seriously.
> —Peter Ustinov

Mechanics

Related Skills Activities

- **Sentence Fluency**
  Combining Sentences, p. 87

- **SkillsBook**
  Commas Between Independent Clauses, p. 7
  Commas in a Series and to Separate
  Equal Adjectives, p. 9
  Commas to Set Off Contrasted Elements
  and Appositives, p. 13

Answers

Have students demonstrate their ability to correctly use the conventions of punctuation by completing the Practice activity.

line 1   big, hairy spider, and
line 2   you, not
line 3   none
line 4   none
line 5   painful, but
line 6   self-defense, not
line 7   none
line 8   smaller, weaker
line 9   none
line 10 tasty, satisfying
line 11 eight-legged, four-eyed
line 12 none
line 13 mosquitoes, and
line 14 none
line 15 back, but

TEKS 11.18A Correctly and consistently use conventions of punctuation and capitalization

Comma (continued)

640.1 To Set Off Appositives

A specific kind of explanatory word or phrase called an **appositive** identifies or renames a preceding noun or pronoun.

> **Benson,** our uninhibited and enthusiastic Yorkshire terrier, **joined our family on my sister's fifteenth birthday.**
> —Chad Hockerman, student writer

Note: Do not use commas with *restrictive appositives*. A restrictive appositive is essential to the basic meaning of the sentence.

> Sixteen-year-old student Ray Perez **was awarded an athletic scholarship.**

640.2 Between Items in a Series

Use commas to separate individual words, phrases, or clauses in a series. (A series contains at least three items.)

> **Grandma makes** cider, applesauce, and jelly **from the apples in her orchard.** (words)
> **Clara** does the long jump, runs the hurdles, and throws the shotput **on the track team.** (phrases)

Note: Do not use commas when all the words in a series are connected with *or, nor,* or *and.*

> **Her fingernails are pointed** and **manicured** and **painted a shiny red.**
> —Carson McCullers, "Sucker"

640.3 After Introductory Phrases and Clauses

Use a comma after an introductory participial phrase.

> **Determined to finish the sweater by Friday, my grandmother knit night and day.**

Use a comma after a long introductory prepositional phrase or after two or more short ones.

> In the oddest places and at the strangest times, **my grandmother can be found knitting madly away.**

Note: You may omit the comma if the introductory phrase is short.

> Before breakfast **my grandmother knits.**

Use a comma after an introductory adverb (subordinate) clause.

> After the practice was over, **Tina walked home.**

Note: A comma is not used if an adverb clause *follows* the main clause and is needed to complete the meaning of the sentence.

> **Tina practiced hard** because she feared losing.

However, a comma is used if the adverb clause following the main clause begins with *although, even though, while,* or another conjunction expressing a contrast.

> **Tina walked home,** even though it was raining very hard.

Practice

Commas 2

- To Set Off Appositives
- Between Items in a Series
- After Introductory Phrases and Clauses

Indicate where commas are needed in the following lines by writing the commas along with the words that surround them. (If no commas are needed, write "none" next to the line.)

1   Health officials have recently become concerned about avian flu a viral
2   infection in birds. Avian flu can affect virtually every kind of bird, including
3   ducks geese turkeys and chickens. No one is certain where flu viruses
4   originate, but most doctors realize that people living close to barnyard
5   animals are at risk as well. In some parts of the world people live so close
6   to their farm animals that sometimes the flu makes the jump to humans.
7   Although scientists have studied the problem for many years they are still
8   trying to figure out how the virus mutates to affect humans. Once an avian
9   flu virus is able to infect humans trouble begins. The flu can become a
10   pandemic an epidemic that spans the globe when people transmit the disease
11   to other people.

Model

Model the following sentence to practice using commas between items in a series.

> **The country is the real thing, the substantial thing, the eternal thing; it is the thing to watch over and care for and be loyal to . . .**
> —Mark Twain, *A Connecticut Yankee in King Arthur's Court*

Mechanics

Related Skills Activities

- **Voice**
  Selecting Specific Adjectives, p. 80

- **Conventions**
  Combining Sentences, p. 87

- *SkillsBook*
  Commas in a Series and to Separate
    Equal Adjectives, p. 8
  Commas After Introductory Phrases and Clauses
    1 and 2, pp. 9–11
  Commas to Set Off Contrasted Elements
    and Appositives, p. 13

 ## Answers

Have students demonstrate their ability to correctly use the conventions of punctuation by completing the Practice activity.

line 1   flu, a
line 2   none
line 3   ducks, geese, turkeys, and
line 4   none
line 5   world, people
line 6   none
line 7   years, they
line 8   none
line 9   humans, trouble
line 10   pandemic, an
              globe, when
line 11   none

 TEKS 11.18A Correctly and consistently use conventions of punctuation and capitalization

Comma *(continued)*

642.1 To Enclose Parenthetical Elements

Use commas to separate parenthetical elements, such as an explanatory word or phrase, within a sentence.

Caleb's parents looked toward him, beyond the mangled fence and the broken window, concerned but relieved that he was on his feet and unhurt.

Allison meandered into class, late as usual, and sat down.

642.2 To Set Off Nonrestrictive Phrases and Clauses

Use commas to set off **nonrestrictive** (unnecessary) clauses and participial phrases. A nonrestrictive clause or participial phrase adds information that is not necessary to the basic meaning of the sentence. For example, if the clause or phrase (in red) were left out in the two examples below, the meaning of the sentences would remain clear. Therefore, commas are used to set them off.

The Altena Fitness Center and Visker Gymnasium, which were built last year, are busy every day. (nonrestrictive clause)

Students and faculty, improving their health through exercise, use both facilities throughout the week. (nonrestrictive phrase)

Do not use commas to set off a **restrictive** (necessary) clause or participial phrase, which helps to define a noun or pronoun. It adds information that the reader needs to know in order to understand the sentence. For example, if the clause and phrase (in red) were dropped from the examples below, the meaning wouldn't be the same. Therefore, commas are *not* used.

The handball court that has a sign-up sheet by the door must be reserved. The clause identifies which handball court must be reserved. (restrictive clause)

Individuals wanting to use this court must sign up a day in advance. (restrictive phrase)

A Closer Look

Use *that* to introduce restrictive (necessary) clauses; use *which* to introduce nonrestrictive (unnecessary) clauses. When the two words are used in this way, the reader can quickly distinguish necessary and unnecessary information.

The treadmill that monitors heart rate is the one you must use. (The reader needs the information to find the right treadmill.)

This treadmill, which we got last year, is required for your program. (The main clause tells the reader which treadmill to use; the other clause gives additional, unnecessary information.)

 ## Practice

Commas 3

- To Enclose Parenthetical Elements
- To Set Off Nonrestrictive Phrases and Clauses

Indicate where commas are needed in the following sentences by writing the commas along with the words that surround them. (Write "none" if no commas are needed.)

1. This lipliner which I sometimes apply as eyeliner is my favorite makeup.

2. Dave Grohl who is the lead singer and guitarist for the Foo Fighters previously played drums for Nirvana.

3. We saw the teacher who subbed for Mr. Planey at the store yesterday.

4. Dakota's handwriting normally illegible was quite neat for last week's poetry assignment.

5. *Harmonia axyridis* also known as Asian lady beetles were first seen in the United States in 1988.

6. They are despite their bothersome nature beneficial as aphids eaters.

7. My friend Judi who has multiple sclerosis asks me to join her in the MS Walk every year.

8. She wept with regret realizing the ring that her husband had given her had slipped down the drain.

9. The radio station's morning DJ's whom we love to listen to as we get ready for school are now syndicated to other stations as well.

10. The driver of the car that hit mine as I turned left was not hurt.

Model

Model the following sentences to practice using commas to enclose parenthetical elements and to set off nonrestrictive clauses.

All adventures, especially into new territory, are scary.   —Sally Ride

Human beings, who are almost unique in having the ability to learn from the experience of others, are also remarkable for their apparent disinclination to do so.
                                        —Douglas Adams, *Last Chance to See*

Mechanics

Related Skills Activities

- *SkillsBook*
  Commas with Nonrestrictive Phrases and Clauses 1 and 2, pp. 14–15

 ## Answers

Have students demonstrate their ability to correctly use the conventions of punctuation by completing the Practice activity.

1. lipliner, which
   eyeliner, is
2. Grohl, who
   Fighters, previously
3. none
4. handwriting, normally illegible, was
5. *axyridis*, also
   beetles, were
6. are, despite
   nature, beneficial
7. Judi, who
   sclerosis, asks
8. regret, realizing
9. DJ's, whom
   school, are
10. none

TEKS 11.18A

Comma *(continued)*

644.1 To Set Off Dates

Use commas to set off items in a date.

> On September 30, 1997, my little sister entered our lives.
> He began working out on December 1, 2005, but quit by May 1, 2006.

However, when only the month and year are given, no commas are needed.

> He began working out in December 2005 but quit by May 2006.

When a full date appears in the middle of a sentence, a comma follows the year.

> On June 7, 1924, my great-grandfather met his future wife.

644.2 To Set Off Items in Addresses

Use commas to set off items in an address. (No comma is placed between the state and ZIP code.)

> Mail the box to Friends of Wildlife, Box 402, Spokane, Washington 20077.

When a city and state (or country) appear in the middle of a sentence, a comma follows the last item in the address.

> Several charitable organizations in Juneau, Alaska, pool their funds.

644.3 In Numbers

Use commas to separate numerals in large numbers in order to distinguish hundreds, thousands, millions, and so forth.

> 1,101   25,000   7,642,020

644.4 To Enclose Titles or Initials

Use commas to enclose a title or initials and names that follow a surname (a last name).

> Letitia O'Reilly, M.D., is our family physician.
> Hickok, J. B., and Cody, William F., are two popular Western heroes.

644.5 Before Tags

Use a comma before a tag, which is a short statement or question at the end of a sentence.

> He's the candidate who lost the election, isn't he?
> You're not going to like this casserole, I know.

644.6 Following Conjunctive Adverbs and Transitional Phrases

Use a comma following conjunctive adverbs such as *however, instead,* and *nevertheless,* and transitional phrases such as *for example, in fact,* and *as a result.* (Also see 648.2.)

> Jaleel is bright and studies hard; however, he suffers from test anxiety.
> Pablo was born in the Andes; as a result, he loves mountains.

Practice

Commas 4

- To Set Off Dates
- To Set Off Items in Addresses
- In Numbers
- To Enclose Titles or Initials

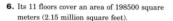 Indicate where commas are needed in the following sentences by writing the commas along with the words or numbers that surround them.

1. According to the *Guinness Book of World Records,* the oldest human footprints were discovered 60 miles north of Cape Town South Africa.

2. The geologist who found them estimates they are 117000 years old.

3. An American woman who was born on August 15 1890 lived until December 11 2006—she was 116 years old!

4. The first heart transplant was performed on December 3 1967 by Christiaan Barnard M.D.

5. ABIOMED, Inc., maker of an artificial heart, is located at 22 Cherry Hill Drive Danvers Massachusetts.

6. Its 11 floors cover an area of 198500 square meters (2.15 million square feet).

7. In July 1999, a participant in an auction in London England paid $3001294 for a Louis XVI clock.

8. Richard Mascola D.D.S. is the president of the American Dental Association, the world's largest association with 155400 members.

Model

Model the following sentence to practice using commas to set off items in addresses.

> Born in Chicago Heights, Illinois, Jacobs attended St. Kieran School for his first four years of formal education.

Mechanics

Related Skills Activities

- **SkillsBook**
  Other Uses of Commas 1 and 2, pp. 16–17

Answers

Have students demonstrate their ability to correctly use the conventions of punctuation by completing the Practice activity. After they have completed the activity, have partners take turns reading the sentences aloud with appropriate pauses. Ask them to cite the relevant rule in the Proofreader's Guide to explain their reasons to adding commas.

1. Town, South
2. 117,000
3. 15, 1890, lived
   11, 2006
4. 3, 1967, by
   Barnard, M.D.
5. Drive, Danvers, Massachusetts.
6. 198,500
7. London, England, paid $3,001,294
8. Mascola, D.D.S., is
   155,400

 TEKS 11.18A Correctly and consistently use conventions of punctuation and capitalization; **ELPS** 2G Understand general meaning of spoken language/topic and contexts; **3D** Speak using grade-level content-area vocabulary in context/new English words and academic language

TEKS 11.18A

Comma (continued)

646.1 To Set Off Dialogue

Use commas to set off the speaker's exact words from the rest of the sentence. (It may be helpful to remember that the comma is always to the left of the quotation mark.)

"I don't understand why we can't form our own committee," exclaimed Tamara, a junior at Lakemont High.

646.2 To Set Off Interjections

Use a comma to separate an interjection or a weak exclamation from the rest of the sentence.

Hey, when will we be able to pick up our new uniforms?

646.3 To Set Off Interruptions

Use commas to set off a word, a phrase, or a clause that interrupts the movement of a sentence. Such expressions usually can be identified through the following tests: (1) They may be omitted without changing the meaning of a sentence. (2) They may be placed nearly anywhere in the sentence without changing its meaning.

For me, well, it's just a good job gone!
—Langston Hughes

The safest way to cross this street, as a general rule, is with the light.

646.4 In Direct Address

Use commas to separate a noun of direct address from the rest of the sentence. A *noun of direct address* is the noun that names the person(s) spoken to.

"You can't pick up the car, Sam, because the license plates haven't arrived yet."

646.5 For Clarity or Emphasis

You may use a comma for clarity or for emphasis. There will be times when none of the traditional rules call for a comma, but one will be needed to prevent confusion or to emphasize an important idea.

The longest working day may be short, to those who work with passion. (emphasis)

What the crew does, does affect our voyage. (clarity)

TEKS 11.18A

Practice

Commas 5

- To Set Off Interjections
- To Set Off Interruptions
- In Direct Address
- For Clarity or Emphasis

Indicate where commas are needed in the following sentences by writing the commas along with the words that surround them.

1. Darn it I can't get these wires untangled!

2. Hey where did this mess come from?

3. Don't ask me because if you must know I just got here.

4. You just got here here in the cafeteria or here to this planet?

5. That's uh very funny Mr. Clean.

6. The song that this band plays plays too much on the radio.

7. Do you know which one I'm talking about Will?

8. Yeah I know the one—it's on at least once an hour.

9. It seems like we hear new music only once a day if that.

10. Will why don't you call the radio station?

11. I hmm never thought of that.

Model

Model the following sentences to practice using commas to set off interruptions and for emphasis.

I loved to spend time at Thimbleberry's, listening to his rhythmic, even if somewhat nasal, intonations.
—Robert Fox, "The Year of the Dog"

She felt angry enough to scream, angry enough to say that the dog had grown up in the apartment and had the right to walk around.
—Ann Beattie, "Distant Music"

Mechanics

Related Skills Activities

- **SkillsBook**
  Other Uses of Commas 1 and 2, pp. 16–17

Answers

Have students demonstrate their ability to correctly use the conventions of punctuation by completing the Practice activity.

1. Darn it, I
2. Hey, where
3. me, because, if
   know, I
4. here, here
   cafeteria, or
5. That's, uh, very funny, Mr.
6. plays, plays
7. about, Will?
8. Yeah, I
9. day, if
10. Will, why
11. I, hmm, never

TEKS 11.18A

Semicolon

648.1 To Join Two Independent Clauses

Use a **semicolon** to join two or more closely related independent clauses that are not connected with a coordinating conjunction. (Independent clauses can stand alone as separate sentences.)

> I did not call myself a poet; I told people I wrote poems.
> —Terry McMillan, "Breaking Ice"

> Steam swirled around the locomotive like a coat of gauze; the passengers emerged as if into a humid summer's day.

Note: When independent clauses are especially long or contain commas, a semicolon may punctuate the sentence, even though a coordinating conjunction connects the clauses.

> We waited all day in that wide line, tired travelers pressing in from all sides; and when we needed drinks or sandwiches, I would squeeze my way to the cafeteria and back.

648.2 With Conjunctive Adverbs and Transitional Phrases

A semicolon is used *before* a conjunctive adverb or transitional phrase (with a comma after it) when the word connects two independent clauses in a compound sentence.

> Mia found that she didn't enjoy running five miles every day; therefore, she decided not to begin training for the marathon.

Common conjunctive adverbs

also, besides, finally, however, indeed, instead, meanwhile, moreover, nevertheless, next, still, then, therefore, thus

Common transitional phrases

after all, as a matter of fact, as a result, at any rate, at the same time, even so, for example, for instance, in addition, in conclusion, in fact, in other words, in the first place, on the contrary, on the other hand

---

648.3 To Separate Groups That Contain Commas

A semicolon is used to separate groups of words that already contain commas.

> Every Saturday night my little brother gathers up his things—goggles, shower cap, and snorkel; bubble bath, soap, and shampoo; tapes, stereo, and rubber duck—and heads for the tub.

TEKS 11.18A

Practice

Semicolons

- To Join Two Independent Clauses
- With Conjunctive Adverbs
- To Separate Groups That Contain Commas

Indicate where a semicolon is needed in the following sentences by writing the semicolon along with the words that surround it.

1. When Jean-Paul was young, he lived in the countryside of southern France his current residence is a tiny apartment in Detroit.

2. Jean-Paul likes space-saving items such as pot racks, under-cabinet appliances, and recessed shelves for canned foods a Murphy bed and an over-the-door ironing board and a wall-mounted TV, a pocket shoe organizer, and under-bed storage boxes.

3. His apartment is nothing like his childhood home nevertheless, he makes the best of it.

4. My older brother uses a wheelchair he is partially paralyzed.

5. He does not feel limited by it indeed, he feels it gives him some freedom.

6. On our backyard deck we have a table, benches, and chairs potted plants, torches, and solar lights and a portable outdoor fire pit.

7. Mom and Dad enjoy the deck a great deal it's like an extra room in the house to them.

8. I like the deck, too however, my friends and I usually hang out in the basement.

Model

Model the following sentences to practice using a semicolon with a conjunctive adverb and to join independent clauses.

> It is forbidden to kill; therefore, all murderers are punished unless they kill in large numbers and to the sound of trumpets.
> —Voltaire

> I believe in getting into hot water; it keeps you clean.
> —G. K. Chesterton

Mechanics

Semicolon

Encourage students to review the lists of common conjunctive adverbs and common transitional phrases to be sure they are familiar with most of this basic sight vocabulary.

Related Skills Activities

- **SkillsBook**
  Semicolons, p. 19
  Conjunctive Adverbs, p. 110

Answers

Have students demonstrate their ability to correctly use the conventions of punctuation by completing the Practice activity.

1. France; his
2. foods; a
   board; and
3. home; nevertheless
4. wheelchair; he
5. it; indeed
6. chairs; potted
   lights; and
7. deal; it's
8. too; however

TEKS 11.18A

Colon

650.1 After a Salutation

Use a **colon** after the salutation of a business letter.

Dear Judge Parker: **Dear Governor Whitman:**

650.2 Between Numerals Indicating Time

Use a colon between the hours, minutes, and seconds of a number indicating time.

8:30 p.m. **9:45 a.m.** **10:24:55**

650.3 For Emphasis

Use a colon to emphasize a word, a phrase, a clause, or a sentence that explains or adds impact to the main clause (also see **676.3**).

His guest lecturers are local chefs who learn a lesson themselves: Homeless people are worth employing.

—Beth Brophy, "Feeding Those Who Are Hungry"

650.4 To Introduce a Quotation

Use a colon to formally introduce a quotation, a sentence, or a question.

Directly a voice in the corner rang out wild and clear: "I've got him! I've got him!"

—Mark Twain, *Roughing It*

650.5 To Introduce a List

A colon is used to introduce a list.

Ms. Sherman found all the supplies we needed: old rags, scrub brushes, several pairs of rubber gloves, dishwashing soap, and a big tub to fill with hot water.

A Closer Look

Do not use a colon between a verb and its object or complement or between a preposition and its object.

Incorrect: Min has: a snowmobile, an ATV, and a canoe.
Correct: Min has plenty of toys: a snowmobile, an ATV, and a canoe.
Incorrect: I watch a TV show about: cooking wild game.
Correct: I watch a TV show about a new subject: cooking wild game.

650.6 Between a Title and a Subtitle

Use a colon to distinguish between a title and a subtitle, volume and page, and chapter and verse in literature.

***Encyclopedia Americana* IV: 211** **Psalm 23:1–6**

TEKS 11.18A

Practice

Colons

- After a Salutation
- Between Numerals Indicating Time
- To Introduce a Quotation
- Between a Title and a Subtitle

Indicate where a colon is needed in the following letter by writing the line number, the colon, and the word that precedes it.

1 Dear Ms. Grey

2   I am excited that you have decided to teach history this year. I

3 believe in the words of Robert Heinlein "A generation that ignores history

4 has no past and no future." Educating young people about history is an

5 important job.

6   As for my reading recommendations for your history class, my first

7 suggestion is *Warriors Portraits from the Battlefield* by Max Hastings. I

8 think your students will find it appealing. Another title you might look into

9 is *A Different Mirror A History of Multicultural America* by Ronald Takaki.

10   If you would like to meet for discussion, I am free between 200 and 400

11 p.m. this coming Tuesday. Please feel free to call.

12 Sincerely,

13 Cameron Neitler

Model

Model the following sentences to practice using a colon for emphasis.

I'm not fond of fish, let alone seaweed, but I like them together: sushi!

—Rob King

Appreciate your mistakes for what they are: precious life lessons that can only be learned the hard way.

—Al Franken

Mechanics

Related Skills Activities

- ***SkillsBook***
  Colon, p. 20

Answers

Have students demonstrate their ability to correctly use the conventions of punctuation by completing the Practice activity.

line 1   Grey:
line 3   Heinlein:
line 7   *Warriors:*
line 9   *Mirror:*
line 10 2:00
line 11 4:00

Hyphen

652.1 In Compound Words

Use the **hyphen** to make some compound words.

great-great-grandfather   maid-in-waiting   three-year-old

652.2 To Create New Words

Use a hyphen to form new words beginning with the prefixes *self-, ex-, all-,* and *half-*. Also use a hyphen to join any prefix to a proper noun, a proper adjective, or the official name of an office. Use a hyphen before the suffix *-elect*.

self-contained   ex-governor   all-inclusive   half-painted
pre-Cambrian   mid-December   president-elect

Use a hyphen to join the prefix *great-* only to the names of relatives.

great-aunt, great-grandfather (correct)   great-hall (incorrect)

652.3 To Form an Adjective

Use a hyphen to join two or more words that serve as a single adjective (a single-thought adjective) before a noun.

Jem's mother is a tan, small-boned woman with a smiling, brown-eyed face.

Use common sense to determine whether a compound adjective might be misread if it is not hyphenated. Generally, hyphenate a compound adjective that is composed of . . .

- a phrase   heat-and-serve **meal**   off-and-on **relationship**
- a noun + adjective   oven-safe **handles**   book-smart **student**
- a noun + participle (*ing* or *ed* form of a verb)   bone-chilling **story**

652.4 To Join Letters and Words

Use a hyphen to join a capital letter or lowercase letter to a noun or participle. (Check your dictionary if you're not sure of the hyphenation.)

T-shirt   Y-turn   G-rated   x-axis

A Closer Look

When words forming the adjective come after the noun, do not hyphenate them.

Jem's mother is tan and small boned.

When the first of these words is an adverb ending in *-ly*, do not use a hyphen.

delicately prepared **pastry**

Also, do not use a hyphen when a number or a letter is the final element in a single-thought adjective.

class B **movie**

Practice

Hyphens 1

- To Create New Words
- To Form an Adjective
- To Join Letters and Words

 For each sentence below, write the words that should be hyphenated. Some sentences contain more than one hyphenated word.

1. My friend's mom is still friends with her exhusband.

2. Many financial advisors are promoting the value of T bills for investment.

3. Dane was getting frustrated with the slow moving traffic.

4. The governor elect held a reception for an elite group of supporters.

5. Please email the file right away; it is a very time sensitive document.

6. The neighbors are vacationing at an all inclusive resort in Mexico.

7. Most television sets purchased today have V chip technology.

8. Macy claims she had an out of body experience during her surgery.

9. Such mass produced items are quite easy to acquire.

10. The general population finds a gforce greater than that experienced on a roller coaster extremely uncomfortable.

Model

Model the following sentences to practice using hyphens to create new words and to form an adjective.

It has always been the prerogative of children and half-wits to point out that the emperor has no clothes.
—Neil Gaiman, *Sandman*

It is only possible to live happily ever after on a day-to-day basis.
—Margaret Bonnano

Mechanics

Related Skills Activities

- **SkillsBook**
  Hyphens, p. 22

Answers

Have students demonstrate their ability to correctly use the conventions of punctuation by completing the Practice activity.

1. ex-husband
2. T-bills
3. slow-moving
4. governor-elect
5. e-mail
   time-sensitive
6. all-inclusive
7. V-chip
8. out-of-body
9. mass-produced
10. g-force

Hyphen *(continued)*

654.1 Between Numbers and Fractions

Use a hyphen to join the words in compound numbers from *twenty-one* to *ninety-nine* when it is necessary to write them out (see 658.3).

Use a hyphen between the numerator and denominator of a fraction, but not when one or both of those elements are already hyphenated.

> **four-tenths**   **five-sixteenths**   **(7/32) seven thirty-seconds**

654.2 In a Special Series

Use hyphens when two or more words have a common element that is omitted in all but the last term.

> **The ship has lovely two-, four-, or six-person cabins.**

654.3 To Join Numbers

Use a hyphen to join numbers indicating the life span of a person or the score in a contest or a vote.

> **We can thank Louis Pasteur (1822–1895) for pasteurized milk.**
>
> **In the 2007 Rose Bowl, USC defeated Michigan 32–18.**

654.4 To Prevent Confusion

Use a hyphen with prefixes or suffixes to avoid confusion or awkward spelling.

> **re-create (not *recreate*) the image**   **re-cover (not *recover*) the sofa**

654.5 To Divide a Word

Use a hyphen to divide a word, only between its syllables, at the end of a line of print. Always place the hyphen after the syllable at the end of the line—never before a syllable at the beginning of the following line.

Guidelines for Dividing with Hyphens

1. Always divide a compound word between its basic units: **sister-in-law,** not **sis-ter-in-law.**

2. Avoid dividing a word of five or fewer letters: **paper, study, July.**

3. Avoid dividing the last word in a paragraph.

4. Never divide a one-syllable word: **rained, skills, through.**

5. Never divide a one-letter syllable from the rest of the word: **omit-ted,** not **o-mitted.**

6. When a vowel is a syllable by itself, divide the word after the vowel: **epi-sode,** not **ep-isode.**

7. Never divide abbreviations or contractions: **shouldn't,** not **should-n't.**

8. Never divide the last word in more than two lines in a row.

 Practice

Hyphens 2

- In a Special Series
- To Prevent Confusion

In the paragraphs below, find the words that should be hyphenated and write them, along with the line number, correctly on your paper.

1   It was the first time I had enrolled in a multiinstructor course. We'd

2   have different teachers for lectures and labs. To further complicate my

3   schedule, the labs would be either one or two hour sessions, depending on

4   the particular experiment.

5   The first lab was a bit strange. The teacher, a balding man with a

6   thin, pencillike mustache perched on his lip, entered the room. He arranged

7   a bunch of equipment: test tubes, Bunsen burners, 50 and 250 ml beakers,

8   petri dishes, and so on. After he talked about all of them, he resorted them

9   before putting them away.

10   Then he donned latex gloves and a surgical

11   mask and said, "You'll want to wear these to

12   prevent infection from any labborne pathogens."

13   The class was dumbstruck. Some jaws actually

14   dropped . . . but then he said, "Just kidding."

Model

Model the following sentences to practice using hyphens to prevent confusion and in a special series.

> **The sow bug cannot manage [to curl into a ball], but it does have two tail-like appendages the pill bug lacks.**
>   —William Olkowski and Sheila Daar,
>   *The Gardener's Guide to Common-Sense Pest Control*

> **The hardware includes two one-eighth- and two three-quarter-inch Phillips head screws.**

Mechanics

Related Skills Activities

- ***SkillsBook***
  Hyphens, p. 22

 Answers

Have students demonstrate their ability to correctly use the conventions of punctuation by completing the Practice activity.

line 1	multi-instructor
line 3	one- or two-hour
line 6	pencil-like
line 7	50- and 250-ml
line 8	re-sorted
line 12	lab-borne

TEKS 11.18A

Apostrophe

656.1 In Contractions

Use an **apostrophe** to show that one or more letters have been left out of a word group to form a contraction.

hadn't – *o* is left out   they'd – *woul* is left out   it's – *i* is left out

Note: Use an apostrophe to show that one or more numerals or letters have been left out of numbers or words in order to show special pronunciation.

class of '09 – *20* is left out   g'day – *ood* is left out

656.2 To Form Singular Possessives

Add an apostrophe and *s* to form the possessive of most singular nouns.

Spock's **ears**   Captain Kirk's **singing**   the ship's **escape plan**

Note: When a singular noun ends with an *s* or a *z* sound, you may form the possessive by adding just an apostrophe. When the singular noun is a one-syllable word, however, you usually add both an apostrophe and an *s* to form the possessive.

San Carlos' **government** (or) San Carlos's **government** (two-syllable word)

Ross's **essay** (one-syllable word)   The class's **field trip** (one-syllable word)

656.3 To Form Plural Possessives

The possessive form of plural nouns ending in *s* is usually made by adding just an apostrophe.

students' **homework**   bosses' **orders**

For plural nouns not ending in *s*, an apostrophe and *s* must be added.

children's **book**   men's **department**

A Closer Look

It will help you punctuate correctly if you remember that the word immediately before the apostrophe is the owner.

girl's **guitar** (*girl* is the owner)   boss's **order** (*boss* is the owner)

girls' **guitars** (*girls* are the owners)   bosses' **order** (*bosses* are the owners)

656.4 To Show Shared Possession

When possession is shared by more than one noun, use the possessive form for the last noun in the series.

Hoshi, Linda, and Nakiva's **water skis** (All three own the same skis.)

Hoshi's, Linda's, and Nakiva's **water skis** (Each owns her own skis.)

Practice

Apostrophes 1

- To Form Singular Possessives
- To Form Plural Possessives
- To Show Shared Possession

 For each sentence, write the possessive form of the word or words in parentheses.

1. "Is that (*Joaquin and Juan*) car over there?" asked Marinda.

2. Fire was coming from the (*car*) exhaust pipe.

3. Their (*parents*) insurance company might not cover the cost to fix it.

4. I will be pet-sitting for (*Ms. Gedraitis*) cats this weekend.

5. She said I will find the (*cats*) food in the cabinet by the telephone.

6. The sound of the (*mice*) feet skittering over our heads was getting annoying.

7. (*Junji and Padma*) overdue library books are going to cost them $8.00 each.

8. My (*shoes*) laces just won't stay tied!

9. You would not believe the size of the (*women*) room here—it's huge!

10. The newscaster continued, "The full measure of (*agribusiness*) effect on the economy is at stake."

11. The (*actresses*) agents were politely notified that their talents would not be required for this movie.

12. Grandma marveled at the ancient (*dish*) patina.

Model

Model the following sentences to practice using apostrophes to form singular and plural possessives.

You can tell a lot about a fellow's character by his way of eating jellybeans.
—Ronald Reagan

My parents' home holds reminders of all their children's triumphs and disappointments; Kara's trophies, Mike's drawings, and my manuscripts fill the attic with all of childhood's tears, fears, and dreams.

Mechanics

Related Skills Activities

- **SkillsBook**

  Apostrophes in Contractions and Plurals, p. 25

  Apostrophes to Form Possessives 1, 2, and 3, pp. 26–29

Answers

Have students complete the Practice activity to demonstrate understanding of the use of the apostrophe to form the possessive case and other conventions of punctuation.

1. Joaquin and Juan's
2. car's
3. parents'
4. Ms. Gedraitis's
5. cats'
6. mice's
7. Junji's and Padma's
8. shoes'
9. women's
10. agribusinesses's
11. actresses'
12. dish's

TEKS 11.18A

Apostrophe (continued)

658.1 To Show Possession with Indefinite Pronouns

Form the possessive of an indefinite pronoun by placing an apostrophe and an *s* on the last word (see 726.1 and 728.3).

> everyone's   anyone's   somebody's
>
> It is everybody's responsibility to keep his or her locker orderly.

In expressions using *else*, add the apostrophe and *s* after the last word.

> This is somebody else's mess, not mine.

658.2 To Show Possession in Compound Nouns

Form the possessive of a compound noun by placing the possessive ending after the last word.

> the secretary of the interior's (singular) agenda
>
> her lady-in-waiting's (singular) day off

If forming a possessive of a plural compound noun creates an awkward construction, you may replace the possessive with an *of* phrase. (All four forms below are correct.)

> their fathers-in-law's (plural) birthdays
>
> or the birthdays of their fathers-in-law (plural)
>
> the ambassadors-at-large's (plural) plans
>
> or the plans of the ambassadors-at-large (plural)

658.3 To Express Time or Amount

Use an apostrophe and an *s* with an adjective that is part of an expression indicating time or amount.

> a penny's worth   two cents' worth   this morning's meeting
>
> yesterday's news   a day's wage   six months' pay

658.4 To Form Certain Plurals

Use an apostrophe and *s* to form the plural of a letter, a number, a sign, or a word discussed as a word.

> B – B's   C – C's   8 – 8's   + – +'s   *and* – *and*'s
>
> Ms. D'Aquisto says our conversations contain too many *like*'s and *no way*'s.

Note: If two apostrophes are called for in the same word, omit the second one.

> Follow closely the *do*'s and *don't*s (not *don't*'s) on the checklist.

TEKS 11.18A

Practice

Apostrophes 2

- To Show Possession with Indefinite Pronouns
- To Show Possession in Compound Nouns
- To Express Time or Amount
- To Form Certain Plurals

Write the underlined words from the following paragraphs, correctly placing the apostrophe in each.

I had about three **(1)** <u>weeks</u> laundry with me when I finally made it to the crowded laundromat. After sorting it into piles, I checked for open machines. Although **(2)** <u>someone elses</u> clothes filled most of the other washers, I was able to load two of my piles. I poured a **(3)** <u>dollars</u> worth of detergent (from the vending machine) into each, and then I got out my quarters from **(4)** <u>yesterdays</u> trip to the bank. All of the **(5)** <u>1s</u> and **(6)** <u>$s</u> had been scratched off the **(7)** <u>washing machines</u> slots long ago; each washer now wanted six quarters or more.

When I took out my first load, a "little" surprise was waiting for me: My favorite wool blazer had shrunk! I forgot about this **(8)** <u>dry-clean-onlys</u> need for special treatment—and it was **(9)** <u>nobodys</u> fault but mine. That trip to the laundromat ended up costing me a **(10)** <u>months</u> pay from my part-time job!

Model

Model the following sentence to practice using apostrophes to express time or amount.

> Space isn't remote at all. It's only an hour's drive away if your car could go straight up.
>
> —Fred Hoyle

Mechanics

Related Skills Activities

- **SkillsBook**

  Apostrophes in Contractions and Plurals, p. 25

  Apostrophes to Form Possessives 1, 2, and 3, pp. 26–29

Answers

Have students complete the Practice activity to demonstrate understanding of the use of the apostrophe to form the possessive case and other conventions of punctuation.

1. weeks'
2. someone else's
3. dollar's
4. yesterday's
5. 1's
6. $'s
7. washing machines'
8. dry-clean-only's
9. nobody's
10. month's

TEKS 11.18A Correctly and consistently use conventions of punctuation and capitalization; **ELPS** 5E Employ increasingly complex grammatical structures/using possessive case

TEKS 11.18A

Quotation Marks

660.1 To Set Off Direct Quotations

Place **quotation marks** before and after the words in direct quotations.

> "Take the magazine with you," she cried. "I know you'll want to read that article soon."

In a quoted passage, put brackets around any word or punctuation mark that is not part of the original quotation. (See 672.1.)

If you quote only part of the original passage, be sure to construct a sentence that is both accurate and grammatically correct.

> Much of the restructuring of the Postal Service has involved "turning over large parts of its work to the private sector."

660.2 Placement of Punctuation

Always place periods and commas inside quotation marks.

> "You're early, Abby," Mr. Chang said quickly. "Please take a seat. We'll be ready to start your make-up exam in a few minutes."

Place an exclamation point or a question mark *inside* quotation marks when it punctuates the quotation and *outside* when it punctuates the main sentence.

> "Am I dreaming?"   Had she heard him say, "Here's the key to your new car"?

Always place semicolons or colons outside quotation marks.

> I wrote about James Joyce's "The Dead"; I found it thought provoking.

660.3 For Long Quotations

If you quote more than one paragraph, place quotation marks before each paragraph and at the end of the last paragraph (Example A). If a quotation has more than four lines on a page, you may set it off from the text by indenting 10 spaces from the left margin (block form). Do not use quotation marks either before or after the quoted material, unless they appear in the original (Example B).

Example A

> "_____
> _____
> _____.
> "_____
> _____
> _____.
> "_____."

Example B

> _____.
> _____
> _____
> _____
> _____
> _____
> _____.

TEKS 11.18A   Marking Punctuation   **661**

Practice

Quotation Marks 1

- To Set Off Direct Quotations
- Placement of Punctuation
- For Long Quotations

Indicate where quotation marks are needed in the following paragraphs by writing the line number and the quotation marks, along with the words and other punctuation after or before them. (Use an ellipsis to show omitted words in your answers.)

1   Hey, Gerardo, I said. Take a look at this.

2   At what? he asked as he headed my way.

3   I was reading an article that I found particularly interesting. I showed
4   him the following text, hoping he'd get a kick out of it.

5   Do dreams have anything to do with reality? Many online dream
6   interpreters think so and are only too willing to take your money
7   to show you how. A Web site called DreamOn.com charges $25 for
8   an initial consultation and offers a money-back guarantee if their
9   interpretations can be proved wrong.

10   Uh-huh . . . proving a dream interpretation wrong can be pretty sticky
11   business, Gerardo said. But here are some ways.

12   Let's say my dream was about a brown dog
13   that kept following me everywhere I went, and the
14   interpreter said that it obviously means that I am
15   thinking of some social activity. Actually, the brown
16   dog is Hunter, my dog, and I'm dreaming about him
17   because he is staring at me while I sleep.

18   Or how about this: You dream about a
19   mansion with the numbers 377 on it. This is
20   interpreted as wealth gained via a trilogy (the
21   three) of music and art (the sevens). You, however,
22   know that it is your great-great-uncle's old family
23   home in Nagelschmidt, Germany, that you dream of
24   returning to someday.

25   Yeah—I want my money back! I laughed.

Model

Model the following sentence to practice correct placement of punctuation with quotation marks.

> Together, Tom and that wild mustang were a "violent destructive whirling wind": a tornado of rider and horse, swirling dust in our faces.

Mechanics

Related Skills Activities

- ### *SkillsBook*
  Quotation Marks with Dialogue, p. 30
  Quotation Marks with Direct Quotations, p. 31

Answers

Have students demonstrate their ability to correctly use the conventions of punctuation for using quotation marks by completing the Practice activity.

line 1   "Hey, Gerardo,"
            "Take . . . this."
line 2   "At what?"
line 10   "Uh-huh . . .
line 11   business,"
            "But
line 12   "Let's . . .
line 18   "Or . . .
line 24   someday."
line 25   "Yeah . . . back!"

Quotation Marks (continued)

662.1 Quotation Marks Within Quotations

Use single quotation marks to punctuate a quotation within a quotation. Use double quotation marks if you need to distinguish a quotation within a quotation within a quotation.

> "For tomorrow," said Mr. Botts, "read 'Unlighted Lamps.'"
> Sue asked, "Did you hear Mr. Botts say, 'Read "Unlighted Lamps"'?"

662.2 For Special Words

You may use quotation marks (1) to distinguish a word that is being discussed, (2) to indicate that a word is unfamiliar slang, or (3) to point out that a word is being used in a special way.

> (1) A commentary on the times is that the word "honesty" is now preceded by "old-fashioned."
> —Larry Wolters
>
> (2) The senator called his opponent's objections "argle-bargle," claiming that the trivial arguments would harm the voters.
>
> (3) Tom pushed the wheelchair across the street, showed the lady his "honest" smile . . . and stole her purse.

Note: You may use italics (underlining) in place of quotation marks in each of these three situations. (See 664.3.)

662.3 To Punctuate Titles

Use **quotation marks** to punctuate titles of songs, poems, short stories, one-act plays, lectures, episodes of radio or television programs, chapters of books, unpublished works, electronic files, and articles found in magazines, newspapers, encyclopedias, or online sources. (For punctuation of other titles, see 664.2.)

> "Santa Lucia" (song)
> "The Chameleon" (short story)
> "Twentieth-Century Memories" (lecture)
> "Affordable Adventures" (magazine article)
> "Dire Prophecy of the Howling Dog" (chapter in a book)
> "Dancing with Debra" (television episode)
> "Miss Julie" (one-act play)

Note: Punctuate one title within another title as follows:

> "Clarkson's 'Breakaway' Hits the Waves"
> (title of a song in title of an article)

Practice

Quotation Marks 2

- Quotation Marks Within Quotations
- For Special Words
- To Punctuate Titles

 Write the word or words that should be enclosed in quotation marks in the following sentences.

1. Dr. Polk called his lecture on hybrid engines Green Machines.

2. Martin asked, Did you hear the part when he read directly from the *Times* article Hybrid Sales Rise with Gas Prices?

3. He was upset that many women perceived him as just handsome when he had so much more to offer than just his good looks.

4. In some English-speaking countries, words such as color, theater, and license have different spellings.

5. Reading the book's fifth chapter, New World, New Name, reminded me of my great-grandparents' experience coming into this country.

6. People often use the term whatsername to identify someone whose name's been forgotten.

7. Mr. Cornwall is a repo man, hired by a financial institution to take back cars when people default on their car payments.

8. Corinna said, Poe's Annabelle Lee is one of my favorite poems.

Model

Model the following sentence to practice using quotation marks within quotations.

> In a *Rolling Stone* review, Rob Sheffield wrote, "Even the Swedish guys who wrote 'Since U Been Gone' admit they were just trying to copy the Strokes."

Related Skills Activities

- **SkillsBook**
  Italics (Underlining) and Quotation Marks, p. 32
  Punctuation for Research Papers 1 and 2, pp. 34–35

Answers

Have students demonstrate their ability to correctly use the conventions of punctuation for using quotation marks by completing the Practice activity.

1. "Green Machines."
2. "Did . . . 'Hybrid Sales Rise with Gas Prices'?"
3. "handsome"
4. "color," "theater," and "license"
5. "New World, New Name,"
6. "whatsername"
7. "repo man"
8. "Poe's 'Annabelle Lee' . . . poems."

Italics (Underlining)

664.1 Handwritten and Printed Material

Italics is a printer's term for a style of type that is slightly slanted. In this sentence, the word *happiness* is printed in italics. In material that is handwritten or typed on a machine that cannot print in italics, underline each word or letter that should be in italics.

> *My Ántonia* is the story of a strong and determined pioneer woman.
> (printed)

> Willa Cather's <u>My Ántonia</u> describes pioneer life in America.
> (typed or handwritten)

664.2 In Titles

Use italics to indicate the titles of magazines, newspapers, pamphlets, books, full-length plays, films, videos, radio and television programs, book-length poems, ballets, operas, paintings, lengthy musical compositions, sculptures, cassettes, CD's, legal cases, and the names of ships and aircraft. (For punctuation of other titles, see 662.3.)

Newsweek (magazine)	*Cold Sassy Tree* (book)
Pride and Prejudice (film)	*Law & Order* (television program)
Caring for Your Kitten (pamphlet)	*Hedda Gabler* (full-length play)
Chicago Tribune (newspaper)	*The Thinker* (sculpture)

664.3 For Special Uses

Use italics for a number, letter, or word that is being discussed or used in a special way. (Sometimes quotation marks are used for this reason. See 662.2.)

> I hope that this letter *I* on my report card stands for *incredible* and not *incomplete*.

664.4 For Foreign Words

Use italics for foreign words that have not been adopted into the English language; also use italics for scientific names.

> The voyageurs—tough men with natural *bonhomie*—discovered the shy *Castor canadensis*, or North American beaver.

664.5 For Emphasis

Use italics for words that require particular emphasis.

> I guess it really *was* worth it to put in extra study time.

Italics (Underlining)

- In Titles
- For Special Uses
- For Foreign Words

 Write and underline the word or words that should be italicized in the following sentences. If there aren't any, write "none."

1. The letter e is the most common in the English language.

2. We recently saw an off-Broadway production of Phantom of the Opera.

3. The sans serif typeface Verdana is recommended for Web pages.

4. If a coffee has a foreign flavor, it denotes imperfect flavor due to some kind of contamination.

5. Helena was embarrassed at her faux pas and vowed she would know better next time.

6. Napoleon Dynamite was a surprise hit for the film's producers.

7. The Olympic hopeful was elated to see a big 10 on one of her scorecards.

8. Florentina began writing for the Bingham Bugle, her small city's newspaper, when she was in high school.

9. The first article she had published was "Storm Damages Concession Stand."

10. Noah said he'd have to go mano a mano with Cheung over the cheating incident.

Model

Model the following sentences to practice using italics (underlining) for emphasis.

> "Oh, not *now*," said Buffie, scandalized. "We can't do that . . ."
> —Frederik Pohl, "Punch"

> And I had imagined my sisters now being ten or eleven, jumping up and down, holding hands, their pigtails bouncing, excited that their mother—*their* mother—was coming, whereas my mother was dead.
> —Amy Tan, *The Joy Luck Club*

Mechanics

Related Skills Activities

- **SkillsBook**
  Italics (Underlining) and Quotation Marks, p. 32
  Punctuation for Research Papers 1 and 2, pp. 34–35

Answers

Have students complete the Practice activity to demonstrate understanding of the conventions for the use of italics.

1. <u>e</u>
2. <u>Phantom of the Opera</u>
3. none
4. none
5. <u>faux pas</u>
6. <u>Napoleon Dynamite</u>
7. <u>10</u>
8. <u>Bingham Bugle</u>
9. none
10. <u>mano a mano</u>

⭐ **TEKS** 11.18A

Parentheses

666.1 To Set Off Explanatory Material

You may use **parentheses** to set off explanatory or added material that interrupts the normal sentence structure.

> **Benson** (our dog) **sits in on our piano lessons** (on the piano bench)**, much to the teacher's surprise and amusement.**
> —Chad Hockerman, student writer

Note: Place question marks and exclamation points within the parentheses when they mark the added material.

> **Ivan at once concluded** (the rascal!) **that I had a passion for dances, and . . . wanted to drag me off to a dancing class.**
> —Fyodor Dostoyevsky, "A Novel in Nine Letters"

666.2 With Full Sentences

When using a full sentence within another sentence, do not capitalize it or use a period inside the parentheses.

> **And, since your friend won't have the assignment** (he was just thinking about calling you)**, you'll have to make a couple more calls to actually get it.**
> —Ken Taylor, "The Art and Practice of Avoiding Homework"

When the parenthetical sentence comes after the period of the main sentence, capitalize and punctuate it the same way you would any other complete sentence.

> **Shelley insisted that we redo our science experiment today.** (She thinks we used the wrong amount of saline solution.)

Note: For unavoidable parentheses within parentheses (. . . [. . .] . . .), use brackets. Avoid overuse of parentheses by using commas instead.

Diagonal

666.3 To Show a Choice

Use a **diagonal** (also called a *slash* or forward *slash*) between two words, as in *and/or*, to indicate that either is acceptable.

> **Press the** load/eject **button.**
> **Don't worry; this is** indoor/outdoor **carpet.**

666.4 When Quoting Poetry

When quoting more than one line of poetry, use a diagonal to show where each line of poetry ends. (Insert a space on each side of the diagonal.)

> **The brain is wider than the sky, / For, put them side by side, / The one the other will include / With ease, and you beside.**
> —Emily Dickinson

 Practice

Parentheses and Diagonals

 Write the word or words that should be enclosed in parentheses or divided by a diagonal. Use the correct punctuation.

1. Nona slurped her *tom yum* hot and sour soup at the Thai restaurant.

2. Kirsten Dunst she was in the Spider-Man movies is one of my favorite actresses.

3. Don't forget to change the cable antenna switch on the remote when you want to watch regular TV.

4. Marion Morrison was the given name of John Wayne star of many old Western movies.

5. For Spirit Day, we're supposed to wear red and or blue our school colors.

6. Dave our blue parakeet was always very noisy whenever the phone rang.

7. Larry Bird he was a rookie at the same time Magic Johnson was played for only one team during his 13-year professional career: the Boston Celtics.

8. Catina said she learned all about the fastest search engine from Donnell the walking encyclopedia.

Model

Model the following sentence to practice using parentheses with full sentences.

> **From the time we landed, Zeus 7** (I'll never understand why they didn't call the project *Mars*) **was considered a success, but we didn't hit the headlines until the third day.**
> —Paul Bond, "The Mars Stone"

Write the lyrics to a song to practice using diagonals when quoting poetry.

> **Oh give me a home, where the buffalo roam / And the deer and the antelope play, / Where seldom is heard a discouraging word / And the skies are not cloudy all day.**
> —American folksong

■ Related Skills Activities

■ *SkillsBook*
Brackets and Parentheses, p. 40

 Answers

Have students complete the Practice activity to demonstrate understanding of the conventions for the use of parentheses and diagonals.

1. (hot and sour soup)
2. (she was in the Spider-Man movies)
3. cable/antenna
4. (star of many old Western movies).
5. and/or
   (our school colors)
6. (our blue parakeet)
7. (he was a rookie . . . was)
8. (the walking encyclopedia).

TEKS 11.18A

Dash

668.1 To Indicate a Sudden Break

Use a **dash** to indicate a sudden break or change in the sentence.

Near the semester's end—and this is not always due to poor planning—**some students may find themselves in a real crunch.**

Note: Dashes are often used in place of commas. Use dashes when you want to give special emphasis; use commas when there is no need for emphasis.

668.2 To Set Off an Introductory Series

Use a dash to set off an introductory series from the clause that explains the series.

A good book, a cup of tea, a comfortable chair—these things always saved my mother's sanity.

668.3 To Set Off Parenthetical Material

You may use a dash to set off parenthetical material—material that explains or clarifies a word or a phrase.

A single incident—a tornado that came without warning—**changed the face of the small town forever.**

668.4 To Indicate Interrupted Speech

Use a dash to show interrupted or faltering speech in dialogue.

Sojourner: Mama, why are you—
Mama: Isabelle, do as I say!
—Sandy Asher, *A Woman Called Truth*

668.5 For Emphasis

Use a dash to emphasize a word, a series, a phrase, or a clause.

After years of trial and error, Belther made history with his invention—the unicycle.

After several hours of hearing the high-pitched yipping, Petra finally realized what it was—coyote pups.

Practice

Dashes

- To Indicate a Sudden Break
- To Set Off an Introductory Series
- To Set Off Parenthetical Material
- To Indicate Interrupted Speech
- For Emphasis

A word, a phrase, or a clause follows each sentence below. Write the sentences to include those words, set off by one or two dashes.

1. The words she used made her appear intelligent, even if she was not. *(infinitesimal, querulous)*

2. Until recently, not many people knew that this man was plagued by depression. *(Abraham Lincoln)*

3. At that moment, he finally came to accept something he'd been hiding from for years. *(the truth)*

4. All of these are necessary for a winter day spent outdoors in northern Minnesota. *(long underwear, a hat, gloves, and a heavy coat)*

5. Nearby, the lead singer of the band made his way to the stage. *(but not as near as I wished)*

6. Macintosh High School senior Taneka Reeves has been accepted at Princeton. *(winner of this year's corporate scholarship)*

7. Yasin wanted that car stereo for his own wheels. *(the one he first heard in Grady's car)*

8. These were some of the most popular progressive rock bands of the seventies. *(Genesis, Yes, and Pink Floyd)*

Model

Model the following sentences to practice using a dash to indicate interrupted speech.

"I—uh—Mrs. Ferman? I got your name from a friend, Bill Seavers? I understand you—" his voice dropped low, "—rent rooms."
—Ray Russell, "The Room"

Before she realized her mom was right behind her, Nastasia shouted, "Mom, tele—"
—Alicia Kimball, "The Nightstand"

Mechanics

Related Skills Activities

- **SkillsBook**
Dashes, p. 23
Punctuation to Add Emphasis, p. 39

Answers

Have students complete the Practice activity to demonstrate their understanding of the correct use of the conventions of punctuation for dashes.

1. The words she used—infinitesimal, querulous—made her appear intelligent, even if she was not.

2. Until recently, not many people knew that this man—Abraham Lincoln—was plagued by depression.

Answers (continued)

3. At that moment, he finally came to accept something he'd been hiding from for years—the truth.

4. All of these—long underwear, a hat, gloves, and a heavy coat—are necessary for a winter day spent outdoors in northern Minnesota.

5. Nearby—but not as near as I wished—the lead singer of the band made his way to the stage.

6. Macintosh High School senior Taneka Reeves—winner of this year's corporate scholarship—has been accepted at Princeton.

7. Yasin wanted that car stereo—the one he first heard in Grady's car—for his own wheels.

8. These—Genesis, Yes, and Pink Floyd—were some of the most popular progressive rock bands of the seventies.

 TEKS 11.18A Correctly and consistently use conventions of punctuation and capitalization

TEKS 11.18A

Ellipsis

670.1 To Show Omitted Words

Use an **ellipsis** (three periods with one space before and after each period) to show that one or more words have been omitted in a quotation.

(Original)

We the people of the United States, in order to form a more perfect Union, establish justice, insure domestic tranquility, provide for the common defense, promote the general welfare, and secure the blessings of liberty to ourselves and our posterity, do ordain and establish this Constitution for the United States of America.

—Preamble, U.S. Constitution

(Quotation)

"We the people . . . in order to form a more perfect Union . . . establish this Constitution for the United States of America."

670.2 At the End of a Sentence

If words from a quotation are omitted at the end of a sentence, place the ellipsis after the period that marks the conclusion of the sentence.

"We have come to dedicate a portion of that field, as a final resting place for those who here gave their lives that that nation might live. . . . But, in a larger sense, we can not dedicate — we can not consecrate — we can not hallow — this ground. The brave men, living and dead, who struggled here, have consecrated it, far above our poor power to add or detract."

—Abraham Lincoln, "The Gettysburg Address"

Note: If the quoted material is a complete sentence (even if it was not complete in the original), use a period, then an ellipsis.

(Original)

I am tired; my heart is sick and sad. From where the sun now stands I will fight no more forever.

—Chief Joseph of the Nez Percé

(Quotation)

"I am tired. . . . From where the sun now stands I will fight no more forever."

or

"I am tired. . . . I will fight no more. . . ."

670.3 To Show a Pause

Use an ellipsis to indicate a pause.

I brought my trembling hand to my focusing eyes. It was oozing, it was red, it was . . . it was . . . a tomato!

—Laura Baginski, student writer

TEKS 11.18A

Practice

Ellipses

- To Show Omitted Words
- At the End of a Sentence
- To Show a Pause

For the following paragraph, select the least important information to replace with ellipses. Write the shortened paragraph on your own paper.

1   Globe artichokes are delicious as an appetizer or as part of a nutritious
2   dinner. Prepare each artichoke for cooking by removing most of the stem.
3   Then cut off about a quarter of each leaf, removing the thorns that make
4   eating the leaves difficult. Now boil the artichokes for 15–45 minutes,
5   depending on their sizes and how many you're cooking. You may also steam
6   them until tender. After cooking, let them cool off a bit. Use your hands to
7   pull off a leaf, and use your teeth to pull off the soft bottom part. You may
8   want to try dipping it first into a sauce or some mayonnaise. (You don't eat
9   the rest of the leaf; put it aside to discard later.) Continue eating the leaves
10   until you get to the really small ones, which you cut off. You'll see a layer
11   of feathery thistle; cut that off, too. You've reached the heart of the
12   artichoke—the best part! Remove it from the stem with a knife and
13   savor its unique flavor.

Exercise

Respond to each of the following situations by writing a sentence or two in which you use an ellipsis to show a pause.

1. Aunt Daphne is wondering where you buy such stylish clothes.
2. You are surprised when something turns out other than how you thought it would.

Mechanics

Related Skills Activities

- ***SkillsBook***
  Punctuation to Add Emphasis, p. 39

Answers

Have students complete the Practice and Exercise activities to demonstrate their understanding of the correct use of the conventions of punctuation for ellipses.

Answers will vary.

TEKS **11.18A** Correctly and consistently use conventions of punctuation and capitalization

TEKS 11.18A

Brackets

672.1 To Set Off Clarifying Information

Use **brackets** before and after words that are added to clarify what another person has said or written.

"I could feel it [the ocean] wash over my feet, grabbing the sand, carrying it back to itself in a great tug-of-war with the land."

Note: The brackets indicate that the words *the ocean* are not part of the quotation but were added for clarification.

672.2 Around an Editorial Correction

Place brackets around an editorial correction inserted within quoted material.

"Brooklyn alone has 8 percent of lead poisoning [victims] nationwide," said Marjorie Moore.

—Donna Actie, student writer

Note: The brackets indicate that the word *victims* replaced the author's original word. Place brackets around the letters *sic* (Latin for "as such"); the letters indicate that an error appearing in the material being quoted was made by the original speaker or writer.

"'When I'm queen,' mused Lucy, 'I'll show these blockheads whose [*sic*] got beauty and brains'."

672.3 To Set Off Added Words

Place brackets around comments that have been added to a quotation.

"Congratulations to the astronomy club's softball team, which put in, shall we say, a 'stellar' performance." [groans]

Punctuation Marks

´	Accent, acute	,	Comma	( )	Parentheses
`	Accent, grave	†	Dagger	.	Period
'	Apostrophe	—	Dash	?	Question mark
*	Asterisk	/	Diagonal/Slash	" "	Quotation marks
{ }	Brace	¨ (ü)	Dieresis	§	Section
[ ]	Brackets	. . .	Ellipsis	;	Semicolon
^	Caret	!	Exclamation point	~	Tilde
(ç)	Cedilla	·	Hyphen	__	Underscore
^	Circumflex	...	Leaders		
:	Colon	¶	Paragraph		

TEKS 11.18A

Practice

Brackets

■ To Set Off Clarifying Information
■ Around an Editorial Correction

 Follow the directions for each activity below.

1. In the following quotation, the speaker is talking about *tsunamis*. Rewrite the quotation, using the word in brackets to clarify the quotation.

   "The term 'tidal wave' is incorrect," explained Dr. Crabo, "since they are not related to tides at all. They are caused by earthquakes, volcanic eruptions, and the like."

2. Quote the following statement and show that the error was made by Carl Braun, the original writer of a letter to the editor.

   Isn't the seperation of church and state part of our great country's constitution?

3. In the following quotation, replace the speaker's words *Mach 1* with *the speed of sound*. Place brackets around your editorial correction.

   According to David Scott and Alexei Leonov, "Until Yeager beat it, Mach 1 was regarded as an insuperable barrier, which no human being could cross and emerge alive."

4. In the following quotation from *Big-Leaf Mahogany*, the speaker is talking about mahogany. Clarify the quotation using brackets.

   "The natural range is vast, and although the species is not on the verge of extinction, genetic erosion has been alleged," Mr. Colon explains.

Model

Model the following sentence to practice using brackets to set off clarifying information.

It [security] does not exist in nature, nor do the children of men as a whole experience it.

—Helen Keller, *Let Us Have Faith*

Mechanics

Related Skills Activities

■ **SkillsBook**
Brackets and Parentheses, p. 40

Answers

Have students complete the Practice activity to demonstrate their understanding of the correct use of the conventions of punctuation for brackets.

1. . . . "since they [tsunamis] are not. . ."
2. In a letter to the editor, Carl Braun wrote, "Isn't the seperation [sic] of . . ."
3. ". . . beat it, [the speed of sound] was regarded . . ."
4. ". . . the species [mahogany] is not. . ."

TEKS 11.18A

Checking Mechanics

Capitalization

674.1 Proper Nouns and Adjectives

Capitalize proper nouns and proper adjectives (those derived from proper nouns). The chart below provides a quick overview of capitalization rules. The pages following explain some specific rules of capitalization.

Capitalization at a Glance

Names of people	Alice Walker, Matilda, Jim, Mr. Roker
Days of the week, months	Sunday, Tuesday, June, August
Holidays, holy days	Thanksgiving, Easter, Hanukkah
Periods, events in history	Middle Ages, the Battle of Bunker Hill
Official documents	Declaration of Independence
Special events	Elgin Community Spring Gala
Languages, nationalities, religions	French, Canadian, Islam
Political parties	Republican Party, Socialist Party
Trade names	Oscar Mayer hot dogs, Pontiac Sunbird
Official titles used with names	Mayor John Spetler, Senator Feinstein
Formal epithets	Alexander the Great
Geographical names	
Planets, heavenly bodies	Earth, Jupiter, the Milky Way
Continents	Australia, South America
Countries	Ireland, Grenada, Sri Lanka
States, provinces	Texas, Utah, Nova Scotia
Cities, towns, villages	El Paso, Burlington, Wonewoc
Streets, roads, highways	Park Avenue, Route 66, Interstate 90
Landforms	the Rocky Mountains, the Sahara Desert
Bodies of water	Yellowstone Lake, Pumpkin Creek
Buildings, monuments	Elkhorn High School, Gateway Arch
Public areas	Times Square, Sequoia National Park

TEKS 11.18A | 675 | Checking Mechanics

Practice

Capitalization 1

■ Proper Nouns and Adjectives

 For each sentence below, write the word or words that should be capitalized.

1. Hattie Wyatt Caraway of Arkansas was the first woman elected to the united states senate.

2. A giant red spot on jupiter is thrice the diameter of planet earth.

3. Mayor j. b. mcDonald opened this year's winter carnival in colby county.

4. The aswan dam provides egypt with hydroelectric power.

5. About two-thirds of the korean peninsula is composed of precambrian metamorphic and granitic rocks.

6. Anne's roommate at college is from alaska.

7. The petronas twin towers, the world's tallest office buildings, are located in kuala lumpur, malaysia.

8. The main artery of transportation through the salt lake city metropolitan area is interstate 15.

9. David cobb and patricia LaMarche represented the green party in the 2004 u.s. presidential election.

10. The chang jiang, china's longest river, is also known as the yangtze.

Model

Model this sentence to practice capitalizing proper nouns and adjectives.

Clearly, the Arabs served as a conduit, but the math laid on the doorstep of Renaissance Europe cannot be attributed solely to ancient Greece.
—Dick Teresi, *Lost Discoveries: The Ancient Roots of Modern Science*

Mechanics

Checking Mechanics: Capitalization

Review the use of capitalization, eliciting from students categories of words that are capitalized as well as other conventions of capitalization. Ask students to suggest contexts in which it is important to understand these conventions.

Related Skills Activities

■ **SkillsBook**
Pretest: Capitalization pp. 41–42
Capitalization 1, 2, and 3, pp. 43–45

Answers

Have students demonstrate their ability to correctly use the conventions of capitalization by completing the Practice activity.

1. United States Senate
2. Jupiter, Earth
3. J. B. McDonald, Colby County
4. Aswan Dam, Egypt
5. Korean, Precambrian
6. Alaska
7. Petronas Twin Towers, Kuala Lumpur, Malaysia
8. Salt Lake City, Interstate 15
9. Cobb, Patricia, Green Party, U.S.
10. Chang Jiang, China's, Yangtze

TEKS 11.18A

Capitalization *(continued)*

676.1 First Words

Capitalize the first word of every sentence, including the first word of a full-sentence direct quotation.

> **The crowd was quiet. A girl whispered, "I hope it's not Nancy," and the sound of her whisper reached the edges of the crowd.**
>
> —Shirley Jackson, "The Lottery"

676.2 Sentences in Parentheses

Capitalize the first word in a sentence enclosed in parentheses, but do not capitalize the first word if the parenthetical appears within another sentence.

> **Confidentially she took my hand and whispered in my ear. (What did she whisper? That will remain secret between just the two of us.)**
>
> **Damien's aunt (she's a wild woman) plays bingo every Saturday night.**

676.3 Sentences Following Colons

Capitalize the first word in a complete sentence that follows a colon when (1) you want to emphasize the sentence or (2) the sentence is a quotation.

> **When we quarreled and made horrible faces at one another, Mother knew what to say: "Your faces will stay that way, and no one will marry you."**

676.4 Sections of the Country

Capitalize words that indicate particular sections of the country; do not capitalize words that simply indicate direction.

> **Mr. Johnson is from the Southwest.** (section of the country)
>
> **After moving north to Montana, he had to buy winter clothes.** (direction)

676.5 Certain Religious Words

Capitalize nouns that refer to the Supreme Being, the word *Bible,* the books of the Bible, and the names for other holy books.

> **God   Jehovah   the Lord   the Savior   Allah   Bible   Genesis**

676.6 Titles

Capitalize the first word of a title, the last word, and every word in between except articles (*a, an, the*), short prepositions, and coordinating conjunctions. Follow this rule for titles of books, newspapers, magazines, poems, plays, songs, articles, films, works of art, photographs, and stories.

> ***Washington Post***   **"The Diary of a Madman"**   ***Nights of Rain and Stars***

Practice

Capitalization 2

- First Words
- Sentences in Parentheses
- Sentences Following Colons
- Titles

For each of the following sentences, correctly write any word or word groups that are incorrectly capitalized.

1. Mr. Vance had an announcement: our next play would be *steel magnolias.*

2. Robert Harling authored that play as well as the screenplay for *sister act* (this is a film starring Whoopi Goldberg).

3. *Steel magnolias* opened off-Broadway in 1987 (It ran for 1,126 performances) before it finally opened on Broadway in 2005.

4. in the film version, Shirley MacLaine plays Ouiser. (she is a woman you love to hate.)

5. Ouiser is well-to-do and mean spirited: she annoys everyone in the small Louisiana town where she lives.

6. this production should be even better than our last one, *You can't take it with you.*

7. That play was about a crazy family during the Depression: it affirms that money isn't everything.

8. Our plays always get great reviews in the *mortontown centennial times.*

Model

Model the following sentence to practice capitalizing a sentence following a colon.

> **[M]y mother had held him up to us as a sort of ogre with which to frighten us into obedience: Don't stray on the mountain, don't play by the river, or Iida will get you!**
>
> —Lian Hearn, *Across the Nightingale Floor: Tales of the Otori*

Mechanics

Related Skills Activities

- ***SkillsBook***
  Capitalization 1, 2, and 3, pp. 43–45

Answers

Have students demonstrate their ability to correctly use the conventions of capitalization by completing the Practice activity.

1. Our
   Steel Magnolias
2. *Sister Act*
3. *Magnolias*
   it
4. In
   She
5. She
6. This
   You Can't Take It with You
7. It
8. *Mortontown Centennial Times*

Capitalization (continued)

678.1 Words Used as Names

Capitalize words like *father*, *mother*, *uncle*, and *senator* when they are used as titles with a personal name or when they are substituted for proper nouns (especially in direct address).

We've missed you, Aunt Lucinda! (*Aunt* is part of the name.)
I hope Mayor Bates arrives soon. (*Mayor* is part of the name.)

A Closer Look

To test whether a word is being substituted for a proper noun, simply read the sentence with a proper noun in place of the word. If the proper noun fits in the sentence, the word being tested should be capitalized; otherwise, the word should not be capitalized.

Did Mom (Sue) say we could go? (*Sue* works in this sentence.)
Did your mom (Sue) say you could go? (*Sue* does not work here.)

Note: Usually the word is not capitalized if it follows a possessive—*my*, *his*, *your*—as it does in the second sentence above.

678.2 Letters

Capitalize the letters used to indicate form or shape.

U-turn   I-beam   S-curve   T-shirt   V-shaped

678.3 Organizations

Capitalize the name of an organization, an association, or a team.

Lake Ontario Sailors   American Indian Movement   Democratic Party

678.4 Abbreviations

Capitalize abbreviations of titles and organizations. (Some other abbreviations are also capitalized. See pages 686–688.)

AAA   CEO   NAACP   M.D.   Ph.D.

678.5 Titles of Courses

Capitalize words like *sociology* and *history* when they are used as titles of specific courses; do not capitalize these words when they name a field of study.

Who teaches History 202? (title of a specific course)
It's the same professor who teaches my sociology course. (a field of study)

Note: The words *freshman*, *sophomore*, *junior*, and *senior* are not capitalized unless they are part of an official title.
Rosa is a senior this year and is in charge of the Senior Class Banquet.

Practice

Capitalization 3

- Words Used as Names
- Letters
- Organizations
- Abbreviations
- Titles of Courses

Write the line number along with the words that should be capitalized.

1 Date: September 15, 2006

2 **To:**   principal Sosa

3 **From:**   Darcella White, president of the junior class

4 **Subject:**   Fundraiser for Danville children's hospital

5 Here is the latest update from the valley high student volunteer committee

6 regarding the dance to benefit Danville children's hospital.

7 • Mr. Baden, who teaches english 101, will serve as our faculty advisor.

8 • The valley high art club has agreed to be in charge of decorations.

9 • Richard Dole, sr., an instructor in electrical engineering at Valley View Tech,

10 will supervise installation of specialty lighting in the gym.

11 • Tomas Rosero, ceo of citywide catering, will donate food and beverages.

12 • Money donations will be handled by superintendent Hayek.

13 • The volunteer committee has ordered 250 t-shirts to sell at the dance.

14 • Next Wednesday, we will meet with members of the Danville children's

15 hospital auxiliary (dcha) to finalize our plans.

16 Please inform me of any questions or comments you may have. Thank you!

Model

Model the following sentence to practice capitalizing abbreviations and the names of organizations.

The National Football League (NFL) estimated that in 2001 43 percent of its total fan base was female.

—Teena Spencer, *The Girlfriend's Guide to Football*

Capitalization (continued)

Have partners work together to discuss the suggestion in "A Closer Look," using the content-area vocabulary to explain which words should be capitalized. Then have them create similar examples to challenge another pair of students.

Related Skills Activities

- *SkillsBook*
  Capitalization 1, 2, and 3, pp. 43–45

Answers

Have students demonstrate their ability to correctly use the conventions of capitalization by completing the Practice activity.

line 2   Principal
line 4   Children's Hospital
line 5   Valley High Student Volunteer Committee
line 6   Children's Hospital
line 7   English
line 8   Valley High Art Club
line 9   Sr.
line 11   CEO, Citywide Catering
line 12   Superintendent
line 13   T-shirts
line 14   Children's
line 15   Hospital Auxiliary (DCHA)

680

Plurals

680.1 Most Nouns

Form the **plurals** of most nouns by adding *s* to the singular.

cheerleader – cheerleaders
sign – signs   crate – crates

680.2 Nouns Ending in *sh, ch, x, s,* and *z*

Form the plurals of nouns ending in *sh, ch, x, s,* and *z* by adding *es* to the singular.

lunch – lunches   dish – dishes   mess – messes   fox – foxes

Exception: When the final *ch* sounds like *k*, add an *s* (*monarchs*).

680.3 Nouns Ending in *y*

The plurals of common nouns that end in *y* (preceded by a consonant) are formed by changing the *y* to *i* and adding *es*.

fly – flies   jalopy – jalopies

Form the plurals of nouns that end in *y* (preceded by a vowel) by adding only an *s*.

donkey – donkeys   monkey – monkeys

Note: Form the plurals of all proper nouns ending in *y* by adding *s* (*Kathys*).

680.4 Nouns Ending in *o*

The plurals of nouns ending in *o* (preceded by a vowel) are formed by adding an *s*.

radio – radios   rodeo – rodeos   studio – studios   duo – duos

The plurals of most nouns ending in *o* (preceded by a consonant) are formed by adding *es*.

echo – echoes   hero – heroes   tomato – tomatoes

Exception: Musical terms always form plurals by adding *s*.

alto – altos   banjo – banjos   solo – solos   piano – pianos

680.5 Nouns Ending in *ful*

Form the plurals of nouns that end in *ful* by adding an *s* at the end of the word.

two tankfuls   three pailfuls   four mouthfuls

Note: Do not confuse these examples with *three pails full* (when you are referring to three separate pails full of something) or *two tanks full*.

680.6 Compound Nouns

Form the plurals of most compound nouns by adding *s* or *es* to the important word in the compound.

brothers-in-law   maids of honor   secretaries of state

---

681   Checking Mechanics

Practice

Plurals 1

- Most Nouns
- Nouns Ending in *sh, ch, x, s,* and *z*
- Nouns Ending in *y*
- Nouns Ending in *o*
- Nouns Ending in *ful*
- Compound Nouns

 Write the correct plural of the underlined words or phrases in each sentence.

1. Some chemical <u>mix</u> will react violently, generate a lot of heat, or produce toxic <u>gas</u>.

2. Band members heard <u>buzz</u> and <u>echo</u> from Manny's electric guitar, especially during his <u>solo</u>.

3. Erosion is one of the most alarming <u>threat</u> to regional, national, and international <u>beach</u>.

4. Salt <u>marsh</u> are found on the edges of <u>estuary</u> where rivers flow into the ocean.

5. Take two <u>spoonful</u> every four to six <u>hour</u>.

6. Several <u>travel agency</u> are offering low-cost winter <u>getaway</u>.

7. The American Association of <u>Physics Teacher</u> was established in 1930.

8. Rosh Hashana and Yom Kippur are Jewish <u>holiday</u>.

9. There are two <u>McCarthy</u> in my afternoon class.

10. Zack downed two <u>glassful</u> of water after the race.

11. Phan's <u>brother-in-law</u> drive beat-up <u>auto</u> in the demolition derby.

12. The pond near the park is swarming with <u>mosquito</u>.

Exercise

Write the plurals of the following words or phrases. Then use as many of them as you can in one sentence.

hobby, sister-in-law, radio, search, antique shop, dress, latchkey

---

Mechanics

Plurals

Read aloud the examples provided in each category, guiding students to note the letters that represent the sounds for /s/, /z/, and /ez/. Have students practice producing the sounds as they say each word. Then have partners complete the Practice and Exercise activities to demonstrate that they can apply the spelling rules correctly. Encourage them to use a dictionary as needed, and to use the academic language to explain which rule applies in each case.

Related Skills Activities

- ***SkillsBook***
  Pretest: Plurals and Spelling, pp. 51–52
  Plurals 1, p. 53

Answers

1. mixes
   gases
2. buzzes
   echoes
   solos
3. threats
   beaches
4. marshes
   estuaries
5. spoonfuls
   hours
6. travel agencies
   getaways
7. Physics Teachers
8. holidays
9. McCarthys
10. glassfuls
11. brothers-in-law
    autos
12. mosquitoes

Exercise ## Answers

Sentences will vary but should use as many of these words as possible: hobbies, sisters-in-law, radios, searches, antique shops, dresses, latchkeys

---

TEKS 11.19 Spell correctly, including using various resources to determine and check correct spellings; **ELPS 3A** Practice producing sounds of newly acquired vocabulary to pronounce English words; **3D** Speak using grade-level content-area vocabulary in context/new English words and academic language; **4A** Learn relationships between sounds and letters of English; **5C** Employ English spelling rules with increasing accuracy

TEKS 11.19

Plurals (continued)

Form the plurals of nouns that end in *f* or *fe* in one of two ways: If the final *f* sound is still heard in the plural form of the word, simply add *s;* but if the final *f* sound becomes a *v* sound, change the *f* to *ve* and add *s.*

> **Plural ends with f sound:** roof – roofs; chief – chiefs
> **Plural ends with v sound:** wife – wives; loaf – loaves

Note: Several words are correct with either ending.
> **Plural ends with either sound:** hoof – hooves/hoofs

682.2 **Irregular Spelling**

A number of words form a plural by taking on an irregular spelling.

> crisis – crises   child – children   radius – radii
> criterion – criteria   goose – geese   die – dice

Note: Some of these words are acceptable with the commonly used *s* or *es* ending.

> index – indices/indexes   cactus – cacti/cactuses

Some nouns remain unchanged when used as plurals.

> deer   sheep   salmon   aircraft   series

682.3 **Words Discussed as Words**

The plurals of symbols, letters, numbers, and words being discussed as words are formed by adding an apostrophe and an *s.*

> Dad yelled a lot of *wow's* and *yippee's* when he saw my A's and B's.

Note: You may omit the apostrophe if it does not cause any confusion.

> the three R's or Rs   YMCA's or YMCAs

682.4 **Collective Nouns**

A collective noun may be singular or plural depending upon how it's used. A collective noun is singular when it refers to a group considered as one unit; it is plural when it refers to the individuals in the group.

> **The class was on its best behavior.** (group as a unit)
> **The class are preparing for their final exams.** (individuals in the group)

If it seems awkward to use a plural verb with a collective noun, add a clearly plural noun such as *members* to the sentence, or change the collective noun into a possessive followed by a plural noun that describes the individuals in the group.

> **The class members are preparing for their final exams.**
> **The class's students are preparing for their final exams.**

 TEKS 11.19   Checking Mechanics **683**

Practice

Plurals 2

- Nouns Ending in *f* or *fe*
- Irregular Spellings
- Words Discussed as Words
- Collective Nouns

For each sentence below, write the plural form of the words or letters in parentheses.

1. The *(thief)* did not know they were stealing equipment containing radioactive material.

2. The book chronicles the everyday *(life)* of colonial *(person)*.

3. Male baboons somehow recognize their own genetic *(offspring)*.

4. The sample experiment contained four different *(stimulus)*.

5. Jack thought the password had two *(7)* and a couple of *(F)*.

6. While sailing on the ocean last summer, we saw *(tuna)* and *(shark)*.

7. There were lots of *(hurray)* when the class saw their new *(PC)*.

8. There is a strange theory that the Great Pyramids of Giza are actually huge *(antenna)*.

For each sentence below, choose the correct word in parentheses.

9. The football team has *(its, their)* own bus for away games.

10. After a long day in school, the class finished *(its, their)* essays at home.

Exercise

Write sentences using plurals of these words.

> *vertebra, alumnus, self, belief, moose*

Mechanics

Plurals (continued)

Have students complete the Practice and Exercise activities to demonstrate that they can apply the spelling rules correctly. Encourage them to note the spelling patterns and to be prepared to explain which rule applies in each case. Suggest that students use a dictionary as needed.

Related Skills Activities

- ***SkillsBook***
  Plurals 2, p. 54

 ## Answers

1. thieves	6. tuna
2. lives	sharks
people	7. hurray's
3. offspring	PC's
4. stimuli	8. antennae
5. 7's	9. its
F's	10. their

Exercise **Answers**

Sentences will vary but should use these words: vertebrae, alumni, selves, beliefs, moose.

684

Numbers

684.1 Numerals or Words

Numbers from one to nine are usually written as words; numbers 10 and over are usually written as numerals. However, numbers being compared or contrasted should be kept in the same style.

    8 to 11 years old   eight to eleven years old

You may use a combination of numerals and words for very large numbers.

    1.5 million   3 billion to 3.2 billion   6 trillion

If numbers are used infrequently in a piece of writing, you may spell out those that can be written in no more than two words.

    ten   twenty-five   two hundred   ten thousand

684.2 Numerals Only

Use numerals for the following forms: decimals, percentages, chapters, pages, addresses, phone numbers, identification numbers, and statistics.

26.2	8 percent	Highway 36	chapter 7
pages 287–89	July 6, 1945	44 B.C.E.	a vote of 23 to 4

Always use numerals with abbreviations and symbols.

    8%   10 mm   3 cc   8 oz   90° C   24 mph   6' 3"

684.3 Words Only

Use words to express numbers that begin a sentence.

    Fourteen students "forgot" their assignments.

Note: Change the sentence structure if this rule creates a clumsy construction.

    Clumsy: *Six hundred thirty-nine teachers were laid off this year.*

    Better: This year, 639 teachers were laid off.

Use words for numbers that come before a compound modifier if that modifier includes a numeral.

    They made twelve 10-foot sub sandwiches for the picnic.

684.4 Time and Money

If time is expressed with an abbreviation, use numerals; if it is expressed in words, spell out the number.

    4:00 a.m. (or) four o'clock

If an amount of money is spelled out, so is the currency; use a numeral if a symbol is used.

    twenty dollars (or) $20

Practice

Numbers

- Numerals or Words
- Numerals Only
- Words Only
- Time and Money

 For each sentence below, write the underlined numbers the correct way. If a number is already correctly presented, write "correct."

1. In <u>two thousand five</u>, Hurricane Katrina caused <u>$one hundred twenty-five billion</u> worth of damage.

2. <u>20</u> basketball teams make it to the playoffs every year.

3. An <u>Fthree</u> tornado packs winds up to <u>206</u> mph.

4. James Michener's book *Hawaii* has more than a <u>thousand</u> pages.

5. Neptune's moon, Larissa, orbits <u>73,550</u> km from the center of Neptune and measures about <u>one hundred four</u> by <u>eighty-nine</u> km.

6. Many students get up around <u>five</u> A.M.

7. Voters age <u>eighteen</u> to <u>twenty-nine</u> made up <u>17</u> percent of all November <u>two</u>, 2004, voters.

8. My brother's new desktop computer cost <u>$879</u>.

9. The Airbus <u>Athree-eighty</u> is capable of carrying <u>8 hundred</u> passengers.

10. The library's main number is <u>626- five-five-three-zero</u>.

11. CNN was the first news agency to air the special report at <u>two o'clock</u>.

12. Aristotle (<u>three hundred eighty-four</u> – <u>322</u> B.C.E.) was a Greek philosopher.

Model

Complete this sentence using your own numbers.

    The girls' varsity basketball team won _____ percent of its games but ended the season with a _____ – _____ loss.

Related Skills Activities

■ *SkillsBook*
   Numbers 1 and 2, pp. 47–48

Answers

1. 2005
   $125 billion
2. Twenty
3. F3
   correct
4. correct
5. correct
   104
   89
6. 5:00
7. 18
   29
   correct
   2
8. correct
9. A380
   800 *or* eight hundred
10. correct
    5530
11. correct
12. 384
    correct

Abbreviations

686.1 Formal and Informal Abbreviations

An **abbreviation** is the shortened form of a word or phrase. Some abbreviations are always acceptable in both formal and informal writing:

Mr.   Mrs.   Jr.   Ms.   Dr.   a.m. (A.M.)   p.m. (P.M.)

Note: In most of your writing, you do not abbreviate the names of states, countries, months, days, or units of measure. However, you may use the abbreviation *U.S.* after it has been spelled out once. Do not abbreviate the words *Street, Company,* and similar words, especially when they are part of a proper name. Also, do not use signs or symbols (%, &, #, @) in place of words. The dollar sign, however, is appropriate with numerals ($325).

686.2 Correspondence Abbreviations

United States

	Standard	Postal
Alabama	Ala.	AL
Alaska	Alaska	AK
Arizona	Ariz.	AZ
Arkansas	Ark.	AR
California	Calif.	CA
Colorado	Colo.	CO
Connecticut	Conn.	CT
Delaware	Del.	DE
District of Columbia	D.C.	DC
Florida	Fla.	FL
Georgia	Ga.	GA
Guam	Guam	GU
Hawaii	Hawaii	HI
Idaho	Idaho	ID
Illinois	Ill.	IL
Indiana	Ind.	IN
Iowa	Iowa	IA
Kansas	Kan.	KS
Kentucky	Ky.	KY
Louisiana	La.	LA
Maine	Maine	ME
Maryland	Md.	MD
Massachusetts	Mass.	MA
Michigan	Mich.	MI
Minnesota	Minn.	MN
Mississippi	Miss.	MS
Missouri	Mo.	MO
Montana	Mont.	MT
Nebraska	Neb.	NE
Nevada	Nev.	NV
New Hampshire	N.H.	NH
New Jersey	N.J.	NJ
New Mexico	N.M.	NM
New York	N.Y.	NY
North Carolina	N.C.	NC
North Dakota	N.D.	ND
Ohio	Ohio	OH
Oklahoma	Okla.	OK
Oregon	Ore.	OR
Pennsylvania	Pa.	PA
Puerto Rico	P.R.	PR
Rhode Island	R.I.	RI
South Carolina	S.C.	SC
South Dakota	S.D.	SD
Tennessee	Tenn.	TN
Texas	Texas	TX
Utah	Utah	UT
Vermont	Vt.	VT
Virginia	Va.	VA
Virgin Islands	V.I.	VI
Washington	Wash.	WA
West Virginia	W.Va.	WV
Wisconsin	Wis.	WI
Wyoming	Wyo.	WY

Canadian Provinces

	Standard	Postal
Alberta	Alta.	AB
British Columbia	B.C.	BC
Labrador	Lab.	NL
Manitoba	Man.	MB
New Brunswick	N.B.	NB
Newfoundland	N.F.	NL
Northwest Territories	N.W.T.	NT
Nova Scotia	N.S.	NS
Nunavut		NU
Ontario	Ont.	ON
Prince Edward Island	P.E.I.	PE
Quebec	Que.	QC
Saskatchewan	Sask.	SK
Yukon Territory	Y.T.	YT

Addresses

	Standard	Postal
Apartment	Apt.	APT
Avenue	Ave.	AVE
Boulevard	Blvd.	BLVD
Circle	Cir.	CIR
Court	Ct.	CT
Drive	Dr.	DR
East	E.	E
Expressway	Expy.	EXPY
Freeway	Fwy.	FWY
Heights	Hts.	HTS
Highway	Hwy.	HWY
Hospital	Hosp.	HOSP
Junction	Junc.	JCT
Lake	L.	LK
Lakes	Ls.	LKS
Lane	Ln.	LN
Meadows	Mdws.	MDWS
North	N.	N
Palms	Palms	PLMS
Park	Pk.	PK
Parkway	Pky.	PKY
Place	Pl.	PL
Plaza	Plaza	PLZ
Post Office Box	P.O. Box	PO BOX
Ridge	Rdg.	RDG
River	R.	RV
Road	Rd.	RD
Room	Rm.	RM
Rural	R.	R
Rural Route	R.R.	RR
Shore	Sh.	SH
South	S.	S
Square	Sq.	SQ
Station	Sta.	STA
Street	St.	ST
Suite	Ste.	STE
Terrace	Ter.	TER
Turnpike	Tpke.	TPKE
Union	Un.	UN
View	View	VW
Village	Vil.	VLG
West	W.	W

687.1 Other Common Abbreviations

abr. abridged; abridgment
AC, ac alternating current
ack. acknowledge; acknowledgment
acv actual cash value
A.D. in the year of the Lord (Latin *anno Domini*)
AM amplitude modulation
A.M., a.m. before noon (Latin *ante meridiem*)
ASAP as soon as possible
avg., av. average
BBB Better Business Bureau
B.C. before Christ
B.C.E. before the Common Era
bibliog. bibliographer; bibliography
biog. biographer; biographical; biography
C 1. Celsius 2. centigrade 3. coulomb
c. 1. circa (about) 2. cup
cc 1. cubic centimeter 2. carbon copy
CDT, C.D.T. central daylight time
C.E. of the Common Era
chap. chapter
cm centimeter
c.o., c/o care of
COD, C.O.D. 1. cash on delivery 2. collect on delivery
co-op. cooperative
CST, C.S.T. central standard time
cu., c cubic
D.A. district attorney
d.b.a. doing business as
DC, dc direct current
dec. deceased
dept. department
DST, D.S.T. daylight saving time
dup. duplicate
DVD digital video disc
ea. each
ed. edition; editor
EDT, E.D.T. eastern daylight time
e.g. for example (Latin *exempli gratia*)
EST, E.S.T. eastern standard time
etc. and so forth (Latin *et cetera*)
ex. example
F Fahrenheit
FM frequency modulation
F.O.B., f.o.b. free on board
ft foot
g 1. gram 2. gravity
gal. gallon
gloss. glossary
GNP gross national product
hdqrs, HQ headquarters
HIV human immunodeficiency virus

Hon. Honorable (title)
hp horsepower
HTML hypertext markup language
Hz hertz
ibid. in the same place (Latin *ibidem*)
id. the same (Latin *idem*)
i.e. that is (Latin *id est*)
illus. illustration
inc. incorporated
IQ, I.Q. intelligence quotient
IRS Internal Revenue Service
ISBN International Standard Book Number
Jr., jr. junior
K 1. kelvin (temperature unit) 2. Kelvin (temperature scale)
kc kilocycle
kg kilogram
km kilometer
kn knot
kW kilowatt
l liter
lat. latitude
lb, lb. pound (Latin *libra*)
l.c. lowercase
lit. literary; literature
log logarithm
long. longitude
Ltd., ltd. limited
m meter
M.A. master of arts (Latin *Magister Artium*)
Mc, mc megacycle
M.C., m.c. master of ceremonies
M.D. doctor of medicine (Latin *medicinae doctor*)
mdse. merchandise
mfg. manufacturing
mg milligram
mi. 1. mile 2. mill (monetary unit)
misc. miscellaneous
ml milliliter
mm millimeter
mpg, m.p.g. miles per gallon
mph, m.p.h. miles per hour
MS 1. manuscript 2. Mississippi 3. multiple sclerosis
Ms., Ms title of courtesy for a woman
MST, M.S.T. mountain standard time
neg. negative
N.S.F., n.s.f. not sufficient funds
oz, oz. ounce
PA 1. public-address system 2. Pennsylvania
pct. percent
pd. paid

PDT, P.D.T. Pacific daylight time
PFC, Pfc. private first class
pg., p. page
P.M., p.m. after noon (Latin *post meridiem*)
P.O. 1. personnel officer 2. purchase order 3. postal order; post office 4. (also p.o.) petty officer
pop. population
POW, P.O.W. prisoner of war
pp. pages
ppd. 1. postpaid 2. prepaid
PR, P.R. 1. public relations 2. Puerto Rico
P.S. post script
psi, p.s.i. pounds per square inch
PST, P.S.T. Pacific standard time
PTA, P.T.A. Parent-Teacher Association
qt. quart
RF radio frequency
RN registered nurse
R.P.M., rpm revolutions per minute
R.S.V.P., r.s.v.p. please reply (French *répondez s'il vous plaît*)
SASE self-addressed stamped envelope
SCSI small computer system interface
SOS 1. international distress signal 2. any call for help
Sr. 1. senior (after surname) 2. sister (religious)
ST standard time
St. 1. saint 2. strait 3. street
std. standard
syn. synonymous; synonym
TBA to be announced
tbs, tbsp tablespoon
TM trademark
tsp teaspoon
UHF, uhf ultra high frequency
UPC universal product code
UV ultraviolet
V 1. *Physics:* velocity 2. *Electricity:* volt 3. volume
V.A., VA Veterans Administration
VHF, vhf very high frequency
VIP *Informal:* very important person
vol. 1. volume 2. volunteer
vs. versus
W 1. *Electricity:* watt 2. *Physics:* (also w) west 3. west
whse., whs. warehouse
wkly. weekly
w/o without
wt. weight
yd yard (measurement)

Mechanics

Abbreviations

As needed before discussing the abbreviations, guide students to develop basic sight vocabulary such as *street, road, lane, park, company,* and *page.* Then have students demonstrate knowledge of when to use formal and informal abbreviations by describing situations in which each type might be used.

Related Skills Activities

■ *SkillsBook*
Abbreviations, p. 49

Acronyms and Initialisms

688.1 Acronyms

An **acronym** is a word formed from the first (or first few) letters of words in a phrase. Even though acronyms are abbreviations, they require no periods.

    radar radio detecting and ranging
    CARE   Cooperative for American Relief Everywhere
    NASA   National Aeronautics and Space Administration
    VISTA Volunteers in Service to America
    LAN   local area network

688.2 Initialisms

An **initialism** is similar to an acronym except that the initials used to form this abbreviation are pronounced individually.

    CIA Central Intelligence Agency
    FBI Federal Bureau of Investigation
    FHA Federal Housing Administration

688.3 Common Acronyms and Initialisms

ADD	attention deficit disorder	**LLC**	limited liability company
AIDS	acquired immunodeficiency syndrome	**MADD**	Mothers Against Drunk Driving
AKA	also known as	**MRI**	magnetic resonance imaging
ATM	automatic teller machine	**NASA**	National Aeronautics and Space Administration
BMI	body mass index	**NATO**	North Atlantic Treaty Organization
CD	compact disc; certificate of deposit	**OPEC**	Organization of Petroleum-Exporting Countries
DMV	Department of Motor Vehicles	**OSHA**	Occupational Safety and Health Administration
ETA	estimated time of arrival		
FAA	Federal Aviation Administration	**PAC**	political action committee
FCC	Federal Communications Commission	**PDF**	portable document format
FDA	Food and Drug Administration	**PETA**	People for the Ethical Treatment of Animals
FDIC	Federal Deposit Insurance Corporation	**PIN**	personal identification number
FEMA	Federal Emergency Management Agency	**PSA**	public service announcement
FTC	Federal Trade Commission	**ROTC**	Reserve Officers' Training Corps
FYI	for your information		
GPS	global positioning system	**SADD**	Students Against Destructive Decisions
HDTV	high-definition television	**SUV**	sport utility vehicle
IRS	Internal Revenue Service	**SWAT**	special weapons and tactics
IT	information technology	**TDD**	telecommunications device for the deaf
JPEG	Joint Photographic Experts Group		
LCD	liquid crystal display		

Practice

Abbreviations, Acronyms, and Initialisms

For each of the following sentences, write the correct abbreviation for the underlined word or words.

1. Several students from <u>Mister</u> Chang's class participated in a mock trial at the <u>district attorney's</u> office.

2. Satellite radio is quickly becoming as popular as <u>frequency modulation</u> radio.

3. Dred Scott <u>versus</u> John Sandford was a famous pre-Civil War Supreme Court case.

4. Chuck enjoys reading technical books (<u>that is</u>, books about repairing cars and electronics).

5. The <u>gross national product</u> might be the most important indicator of the status of an economy.

6. The senator's flight arrives in New York at 4:38 <u>post meridiem</u>.

7. Several of Dominick's family members work for True-Line <u>Manufacturing</u>.

8. My cousin's wedding invitation said to <u>please reply</u> by March 20.

9. Winter vacation packages include snow sports: skiing, snowboarding, snowshoeing, <u>and so forth</u>.

10. Euripides (485–408 <u>before the Common Era</u>) was the first modern dramatist.

11. My dad is Raul K. Martinez, <u>Junior</u>.

12. Use a meat thermometer to make sure a burger's internal temperature reaches 160 degrees <u>Fahrenheit</u>.

Model

Model the following acronyms and initialisms to come up with your own abbreviations. (Write at least one acronym and one initialism.)

    CHAC – Canaan High Astronomy Club
    WYSIWYG – what you see is what you get
    IV – intravenous
    BLT – bacon, lettuce, tomato

Mechanics

Acronyms and Initialisms

As needed before discussing the acronyms and initialisms, guide students to develop the basic sight vocabulary used in terms such as *also known as* and *for your information*. Then have students complete the Practice activity.

Related Skills Activities

■ *SkillsBook*
Abbreviations, p. 49

Answers

1. Mr.
   D.A.'s
2. FM
3. *Dred Scott v. John Sandford*
4. i.e.,
5. GNP
6. p.m.
7. Mfg.
8. R.S.V.P. *or* r.s.v.p.
9. etc.
10. B.C.E.
11. Jr.
12. 160° F

ELPS 4C Develop basic sight vocabulary

TEKS 11.19

Spelling Rules

690.1 Write *i* before *e*

Write *i* before *e* except after *c*, or when sounded like *a* as in *neighbor* and *weigh*.

relief   receive   perceive   reign   freight   beige

Exceptions: There are a number of exceptions to this rule, including these: *neither, leisure, seize, weird, species, science.*

690.2 Words with Consonant Endings

When a one-syllable word *(bat)* ends in a consonant *(t)* preceded by one vowel *(a)*, double the final consonant before adding a suffix that begins with a vowel *(batting)*.

sum—summary   god—goddess

Note: When a multisyllabic word *(control)* ends in a consonant *(l)* preceded by one vowel *(o)*, the accent is on the last syllable *(con trol')*, and the suffix begins with a vowel *(ing)*—the same rule holds true: Double the final consonant *(controlling)*.

prefer—preferred   begin—beginning
forget—forgettable   admit—admittance

690.3 Words with a Silent *e*

If a word ends with a silent *e*, drop the *e* before adding a suffix that begins with a vowel. Do not drop the *e* when the suffix begins with a consonant.

state—stating—statement   like—liking—likeness
use—using—useful   nine—ninety—nineteen

Exceptions: *judgment, truly, argument, ninth*

690.4 Words Ending in *y*

When *y* is the last letter in a word and the *y* is preceded by a consonant, change the *y* to *i* before adding any suffix except those beginning with *i*.

fry—fries—frying   hurry—hurried—hurrying   lady—ladies
ply—pliable   happy—happiness   beauty—beautiful

When *y* is the last letter in a word and the *y* is preceded by a vowel, do not change the *y* to *i* before adding a suffix.

play—plays—playful   stay—stays—staying
employ—employed

Important reminder: Never trust your spelling even to the best spell-checker. Use a dictionary for words your spell-checker does not cover.

 TEKS 11.19

Practice

Spelling 1

Find the 10 words that are misspelled in the following paragraph and write them correctly. (Each misspelled word is in the "Commonly Misspelled Words" list on pages 692–693.)

1   A summer job can be an excellent oportunity to learn how a business
2 works from the inside out. If you work in a fast-food restaurant, for example,
3 gather knowlege as you work. Talk to the manager and the owner, if
4 possible, and ask questions about things like hygeine requirements, cash
5 flow, staffing, and health department standards. Pondar how the business
6 meets the needs of the cunsumer. Find out what it takes to buy a franchise,
7 and learn what skills a qualifyed owner should possess. Finally, look around
8 you and investagate the responsibilty of each employe. You can learn an
9 incredable amount about business and human nature while working in a
10 fast-food restaurant.

Exercise

Write the words that result by combining the following base words and suffixes. Then write sentences that include them.

lucky + er   excite + ing   love + able   beauty + ful

Mechanics

Spelling Rules

Have students demonstrate their ability to employ spelling rules by completing the Practice and Exercise activities. Encourage students to use print or online dictionaries to check their spelling as needed.

Related Skills Activities

■ *SkillsBook*
Pretest: Plurals and Spelling, pp. 51–52
Spelling 1, p. 55

 ## Answers

line 1   opportunity
line 3   knowledge
line 4   hygiene
line 5   Ponder
line 6   consumer
line 7   qualified
line 8   investigate
          responsibility
          employee
line 9   incredible

Exercise ## Answers

luckier, exciting, lovable, beautiful

Commonly Misspelled Words

A

abbreviate
abrupt
absence
absolute (ly)
absurd
abundance
academic
accelerate
accept (ance)
accessible
accessory
accidentally
accommodate
accompany
accomplish
accumulate
accurate
accustom (ed)
ache
achieve (ment)
acknowledge
acquaintance
acquired
across
address
adequate
adjustment
admissible
admittance
adolescent
advantageous
advertisement
advisable
aggravate
aggression
alcohol
alleviate
almost
alternative
although
aluminum
amateur
analysis
analyze
anarchy
ancient
anecdote
anesthetic
annihilate
announce
annual
anonymous
answer
anxious
apologize
apparatus
apparent (ly)
appearance
appetite
applies
appreciate
appropriate
approximately
architect
arctic
argument
arithmetic
arrangement
artificial
ascend
assistance
association
athlete
attendance
attire
attitude
audience
authority
available

B

balance
balloon
bargain
basically
beautiful
beginning
believe
benefit (ed)
biscuit
bought
boycott
brevity
brilliant
Britain
bureau
business

C

cafeteria
caffeine
calculator
calendar
campaign
canceled
candidate
catastrophe
category
caught
cavalry
celebration
cemetery
certificate
changeable
chief
chocolate
circuit
circumstance
civilization
colonel
colossal
column
commercial
commitment
committed
committee
comparative
comparison
competitively
conceivable
condemn
condescend
conference
conferred
confidential
congratulate
conscience
conscientious
conscious
consequence
consumer
contaminate
convenience
cooperate
correspondence
cough
coupon

courageous
courteous
creditor
criticism
criticize
curiosity
curious
cylinder

D

dealt
deceitful
deceive
decision
defense
deferred
definite (ly)
definition
delicious
descend
describe
description
despair
desperate
destruction
development
diameter
diaphragm
diarrhea
dictionary
dining
disagreeable
disappear
disappoint
disastrous
discipline
discrimination
discuss
dismissal
dissatisfied
dissect
distinctly
dormitory
doubt
drought
duplicate
dyeing
dying

E

earliest
efficiency
eighth
elaborate
eligible
eliminate
ellipse
embarrass
emphasize
employee
enclosure
encourage
endeavor
English
enormous
enough
enrichment
enthusiastic
entirely
entrance
environment
equipment
equipped
equivalent
especially
essential
eventually
exaggerate
examination
exceed
excellent
excessive
excite
executive
exercise
exhaust (ed)
exhibition
exhilaration
existence
expensive
experience
explanation
exquisite
extinguish
extraordinary
extremely

FG

facilities
familiar
fascinate
fashion
fatigue (d)
feature
February
fiery
financially
flourish
forcible
foreign
forfeit
fortunate
forty
fourth
freight
friend
fulfill
gauge
generally
generous
genuine
glimpse
gnarled
gnaw
government
gradual
grammar
gratitude
grievous
grocery
guard
guidance

H

happiness
harass
harmonize
height
hemorrhage
hereditary
hindrance
hoping
hopping
hospitable
humorous

IJ

ignorance
illiterate
illustrate
imaginary
immediately
immense
incidentally
inconvenience
incredible
indefinitely
independence
indispensable
industrial
industrious
inevitable
infinite
inflation
innocence
inoculation
inquiry
installation
instrumental
intelligence
interesting
interfere
interrupt
investigate
irregular
irresistible
issuing
itinerary
jealous (y)
jewelry
journal
judgment

KL

knowledge
laboratory
laugh
lawyer
league
legacy
legalize
legitimate
leisure

hygiene
hymn
hypocrisy

liaison
license
lightning
likable
liquid
literature
loneliness

MN

maintenance
maneuver
manufacture
marriage
mathematics
medieval
memento
menagerie
merchandise
merely
mileage
miniature
miscellaneous
mischievous
misspell
moat
mobile
mortgage
multiplied
muscle
musician
mustache
mutual
mysterious
naive
nauseous
necessary
neither
neurotic
nevertheless
ninety
nighttime
noticeable
nuclear
nuisance

OP

obstacle
obvious
occasion
occupant
occupation

occurred
occurrence
official
often
omitted
opinion
opponent
opportunity
opposite
optimism
ordinarily
organization
original
outrageous
pamphlet
parallel
paralyze
partial
particularly
pastime
patience
peculiar
pedestal
performance
permanent
permissible
perseverance
personal (ly)
personality
perspiration
persuade
petition
phenomenon
physical
physician
picnicking
planned
playwright
plead
pneumonia
politician
ponder
positively
possession
practically
precede
precious
preference
prejudice
preparation
presence
prevalent
primitive

privilege
probably
proceed
professional
professor
prominent
pronounce
pronunciation
protein
psychology
puny
purchase
pursuing

QR

qualified
quality
quantity
questionnaire
quiet
quite
quizzes
recede
receipt
receive
recipe
recognize
recommend
reference
referred
regard
regimen
religious
repel
repetition
residue
responsibility
restaurant
rheumatism
rhythm
ridiculous
robot
roommate

S

sacrifice
salary
sandwich
satisfactory
scarcely
scenic

schedule
scholar
science
secretary
seize
separate
sergeant
several
severely
sheriff
shrubbery
siege
signature
signify
silhouette
similar
simultaneous
sincerely
skiing
skunk
society
solar
sophomore
souvenir
spaghetti
specific
specimen
statue
stomach
stopped
strength
strictly
submission
substitute
subtle
succeed
success
sufficient
supersede
suppose
surprise
suspicious
symbolism
sympathy
synthetic

TU

tariff
technique
temperature
temporary
tendency

thermostat
thorough (ly)
though
throughout
tongue
tornado
tortoise
tragedy
transferred
tremendous
tried
trite
truly
unanimous
undoubtedly
unfortunately
unique
unnecessary
until
urgent
usable
usher
usually

V

vacuum
vague
valuable
variety
vengeance
versatile
vicinity
villain
visibility
visual

W

waif
Wednesday
weird
wholly
width
women
wrath
wreckage

Y

yesterday
yield
yolk

Mechanics

Commonly Misspelled Words

Have partners review the list of commonly
misspelled words to identify spelling rules and
patterns that will help them to spell the words
correctly. Encourage students to use print
or online dictionaries to check their spelling
accuracy as needed.

Related Skills Activities

■ *SkillsBook*
Spelling 2, 3, and 4, pp. 56–58

ELPS 5C Spell familiar English words and employ English spelling patterns and rules with increasing accuracy

TEKS 11.19

Steps to Becoming a Better Speller

1. Be patient.
Becoming a good speller takes time.

2. Check the correct pronunciation of each word you are attempting to spell.
Knowing the correct pronunciation of a word can help you remember its spelling.

3. Note the meaning and history of each word as you are checking the dictionary for pronunciation.
Knowing the meaning and history of a word provides you with a better notion of how the word is properly used, and this can help you remember its spelling.

4. Before you close the dictionary, practice spelling the word.
Look away from the page and try to "see" the word in your mind. Then write it on a piece of paper. Check your spelling in the dictionary; repeat the process until you are able to spell the word correctly.

5. Learn some spelling rules.
For four of the most useful rules, see page 690.

6. Make a list of the words that you often misspell.
Select the first 10 and practice spelling them.

STEP A: Read each word carefully; then write it on a piece of paper. Check to see that you've spelled it correctly. Repeat this step for the words that you misspelled.

STEP B: When you have finished your first 10 words, ask someone to read them to you as you write them again. Then check for misspellings. If you find none, congratulations! (Repeat both steps with your next 10 words, and so on.)

7. Write often.

Practice

Spelling 2

For each sentence below, fill in the blank with the correct word from the list of "Commonly Misspelled Words" (pages 692–693).

1. There is no s_____u__e for experience.

2. A graphing c_____r can help a student be more effective while taking the SAT test.

3. Planes were unable to land at LaGuardia due to poor v_____.

4. The best s____v_____ I ever got was a postcard from the Taj Mahal.

5. Seth watched the hot-air balloon slowly d_____d upon the wheat field.

6. The rates listed include all taxes and s_____rs_____ all previous rates.

7. Lightning is a p_____v_____t weather event in the Upper Klamath Basin.

8. Mr. Penski consulted a l_____ about preparing his will.

9. The c_____y is a good place to gather information about a particular family's genealogy.

10. Malik's name was a_____d_____y omitted from the list.

Exercise

Write the words that result by combining the following base words and suffixes. Then write sentences that include them.

occur + ed   stub + ing   permit + ed

Mechanics

Steps to Becoming a Better Speller

Have students demonstrate the ability to employ spelling rules and patterns by completing the Practice and Exercise activities. Encourage students to use print or online dictionaries to check their spelling accuracy as needed.

 Answers

1. substitute
2. calculator
3. visibility
4. souvenir
5. descend
6. supersede
7. prevalent
8. lawyer
9. cemetery
10. accidentally

Exercise   Answers

occurred
stubbing
permitted

Understanding Idioms

Idioms are phrases that are used in a special way. You can't understand an idiom just by knowing the meaning of each word in the phrase. You must learn it as a whole. For example, the idiom *bury the hatchet* means "to settle an argument," even though the individual words in the phrase mean something much different. This section will help you learn some of the common idioms in American English.

apple of his eye	Eagle Lake is the apple of his eye. (something he likes very much)
as plain as day	The mistake in the ad was as plain as day. (very clear)
as the crow flies	New London is 200 miles from here as the crow flies. (in a straight line)
at a snail's pace	My last hour at work passes at a snail's pace. (very, very slowly)
axe to grind	The manager has an axe to grind with that umpire. (disagreement to settle)
bad apple	There are no bad apples in this class. (bad influences)
beat around the bush	Don't beat around the bush; answer the question. (avoid getting to the point)
benefit of the doubt	Everyone has been given the benefit of the doubt at least once. (another chance)
beyond the shadow of a doubt	Beyond the shadow of a doubt, this is my best science project. (for certain)
blew my top	When I saw the broken statue, I blew my top. (showed great anger)
bone to pick	Alison had a bone to pick with the student who copied her paper. (problem to settle)
brain drain	Brain drain is a serious problem in some states. (the best students moving elsewhere)
break the ice	The nervous ninth graders were afraid to break the ice. (start a conversation)
burn the midnight oil	Devon had to burn the midnight oil to finish his report. (work late into the night)

bury the hatchet	My sisters were told to bury the hatchet immediately. (settle an argument)
by the skin of her teeth	Sumey avoided an accident by the skin of her teeth. (just barely)
champing at the bit	The skiers were champing at the bit to get on the slopes. (eager, excited)
chicken feed	The prize was chicken feed to some people. (not worth much money)
chip off the old block	Frank's just like his father. He's a chip off the old block. (just like someone else)
clean as a whistle	My boss told me to make sure the place was as clean as a whistle before I left. (very clean)
cold shoulder	I wanted to fit in with that group, but they gave me the cold shoulder. (ignored me)
crack of dawn	Ali delivers his papers at the crack of dawn. (first light of day, early morning)
cry wolf	If you cry wolf too often, no one will believe you. (say you are in trouble when you aren't)
dead of night	Hearing a loud noise in the dead of night frightened Bill. (middle of the night)
dirt cheap	A lot of clothes at that store are dirt cheap. (inexpensive, costing very little money)
doesn't hold a candle to	That award doesn't hold a candle to a gold medal. (is not as good as)
drop in the bucket	The contributions were a drop in the bucket. (a small amount compared to what's needed)
everything from A to Z	That catalog lists everything from A to Z. (a lot of different things)
face the music	Todd had to face the music when he broke the window. (deal with the punishment)
fish out of water	He felt like a fish out of water in the new math class. (someone in an unfamiliar place)
fit for a king	The food at the athletic banquet was fit for a king. (very special)

Idioms

Understanding Idioms

Allow time for students to read the introduction, and then ask questions to confirm their understanding of the term *idiom*. Have partners work together to discuss the example and explanation of each idiom. Tell partners to choose a situation and correctly use three or four idioms in a conversation about that situation.

ELPS 2C Learn new expressions

flew off the handle	Bill flew off the handle when he saw a reckless driver near the school. (became very angry)
floating on air	Celine was floating on air at the prom. (feeling very happy)
food for thought	The boys' foolish and dangerous prank gave us food for thought. (something to think about)
get down to business	After sharing several jokes, Mr. Sell said we should get down to business. (start working)
get the upper hand	The wrestler moved quickly on his opponent in order to get the upper hand. (gain the advantage)
give their all	Student volunteers give their all to help others. (work as hard as they can)
go fly a kite	Charlene stared at her nosy brother and said, "Go fly a kite." (go away)
has a green thumb	Talk to Mrs. Smith about your sick plant. She has a green thumb. (is good at growing plants)
has a heart of gold	Joe has a heart of gold. (is very kind and generous)
hit a home run	Rhonda hit a home run with her speech. (succeeded, or did well)
hit the ceiling	When my parents saw my grades, they hit the ceiling. (were very angry)
hit the hay	Exhausted from the hike, Jamal hit the hay without eating supper. (went to bed)
in a nutshell	Can you, in a nutshell, tell us your goals for this year? (in summary)
in one ear and out the other	Sharl, concerned about her pet, let the lecture go in one ear and out the other. (without really listening)
in the black	My aunt's gift shop is finally in the black. (making money)
in the nick of time	Janelle caught the falling vase in the nick of time. (just in time)
in the red	Many businesses start out in the red. (in debt)
in the same boat	The new tax bill meant everyone would be in the same boat. (in a similar situation)

iron out	Joe will meet with the work crew to iron out their complaints. (solve, work out)
it goes without saying	It goes without saying that saving money is a good idea. (it is clear)
it stands to reason	It stands to reason that your stamina will increase if you run every day. (it makes sense)
keep a stiff upper lip	Keep a stiff upper lip when you visit the doctor. (be brave)
keep it under your hat	Keep it under your hat about the pop quiz. (don't tell anyone)
knock on wood	My uncle knocked on wood after he said he had never had the flu. (did something for good luck)
knuckle down	After wasting half the day, we were told to knuckle down. (work hard)
learn the ropes	It takes every new employee a few months to learn the ropes. (get to know how things are done)
leave no stone unturned	The police plan to leave no stone unturned at the crime scene. (check everything)
lend someone a hand	You will feel good if you lend someone a hand. (help someone)
let the cat out of the bag	Tom let the cat out of the bag during lunch. (told a secret)
let's face it	Let's face it. You don't like rap. (let's admit it)
look high and low	We looked high and low for Jan's dog. (looked everywhere)
lose face	In some cultures, it is very bad to lose face. (be embarrassed)
needle in a haystack	Trying to find a person in New York is like trying to find a needle in a haystack. (something impossible to find)
nose to the grindstone	With all of these assignments, I have to keep my nose to the grindstone. (work hard)
on cloud nine	After talking to my girlfriend, I was on cloud nine. (feeling very happy)
on pins and needles	Emiko was on pins and needles during the championship game. (feeling nervous)

Idioms

Understanding Idioms (continued)

Have partners work together to discuss the example and explanation of each idiom. Tell partners to choose a situation and correctly use three or four idioms in a conversation about that situation.

out the window	Once the rain started, our plans were out the window. (ruined)
over and above	Over and above the required work, Will cleaned up the lab. (in addition to)
pain in the neck	Franklin knew the report would be a pain in the neck. (very annoying)
pull your leg	Cary was only pulling your leg. (telling you a little lie as a joke)
put his foot in his mouth	Lane put his foot in his mouth when he answered the question. (said something embarrassing)
put the cart before the horse	Tonya put the cart before the horse when she sealed the envelope before inserting the letter. (did something in the wrong order)
put your best foot forward	When applying for a job, you should put your best foot forward. (do the best that you can do)
red-letter day	Sovann had a red-letter day because she did so well on her math test. (very good day)
rock the boat	I was told not to rock the boat. (cause trouble)
rude awakening	Jake will have a rude awakening when he sees the bill for his computer. (sudden, unpleasant surprise)
save face	His gift was clearly an attempt to save face. (fix an embarrassing situation)
see eye to eye	We see eye to eye about the need for a new school. (are in agreement)
shake a leg	I told Mako to shake a leg so that we wouldn't be late. (hurry)
shift into high gear	Greg had to shift into high gear to finish the test in time. (speed up, hurry)
sight for sore eyes	My grandmother's smiling face was a sight for sore eyes. (good to see)
sight unseen	Liz bought the coat sight unseen. (without seeing it first)
sink or swim	Whether you sink or swim in school depends on your study habits. (fail or succeed)

spilled the beans	Suddenly, Kesia realized that she had spilled the beans. (revealed a secret)
spring chicken	Although Mr. Gordon isn't a spring chicken, he sure knows how to talk to kids. (young person)
stick to your guns	Know what you believe, and stick to your guns. (don't change your mind)
sweet tooth	Chocolate is often the candy of choice for those with a sweet tooth. (a love for sweets, like candy and cake)
take a dim view	My sister will take a dim view of that movie. (disapprove)
take it with a grain of salt	When you read that advertisement, take it with a grain of salt. (don't believe everything)
take the bull by the horns	It's time to take the bull by the horns so the project gets done on time. (take control)
through thick and thin	Those two girls have remained friends through thick and thin. (in good times and in bad times)
time flies	Time flies as you grow older. (time passes quickly)
time to kill	Grace had time to kill, so she read a book. (extra time)
to go overboard	The class was told not to go overboard. A $50.00 donation was fine. (to do too much)
toe the line	The new teacher made everyone toe the line. (follow the rules)
tongue-tied	He can talk easily with friends, but in class he is usually tongue-tied. (not knowing what to say)
turn over a new leaf	He decided to turn over a new leaf in school. (make a new start)
two peas in a pod	Ever since kindergarten, Lil and Eve have been like two peas in a pod. (very much alike)
under the weather	Guy was feeling under the weather this morning. (sick)
wallflower	Cho knew the other girls thought she was a wallflower. (a shy person)
word of mouth	Joseph learns a lot about his favorite team by word of mouth. (talking with other people)

Idioms

Understanding Idioms (continued)

Have partners work together to discuss the example and explanation of each idiom. Tell partners to choose a situation and correctly use three or four idioms in a conversation about that situation. Remind them to monitor their understanding of the conversation and to seek clarification as needed.

ELPS 2C Learn new expressions; **2D** Monitor understanding of spoken language and seek clarification as needed

TEKS 11.19

Using the Right Word

a lot ■ *A lot* (always two words) is a vague descriptive phrase that should be used sparingly.

After watching a lot of movies, Brayden felt ready to write one of his own.

accept, except ■ The verb *accept* means "to receive" or "to believe"; the preposition *except* means "other than."

The principal accepted the boy's story about the broken window, but she asked why no one except him saw the ball accidentally slip from his hand.

adapt, adopt ■ *Adapt* means "to adjust or change to fit"; *adopt* means "to choose and treat as your own" (a child, an idea).

After a lengthy period of study, Malcolm X adopted the Islamic faith and adapted to its lifestyle.

affect, effect ■ The verb *affect* means "to influence"; the verb *effect* means "to produce, accomplish, complete."

Ming's hard work effected an A on the test, which positively affected her semester grade.

The noun *effect* means the "result."

Good grades have a calming effect on parents.

aisle, isle ■ An *aisle* is a passage between seats; an *isle* is a small island.

Many airline passengers on their way to the Isle of Capri prefer an aisle seat.

all right ■ *All right* is always two words (not *alright*).

allusion, illusion ■ *Allusion* is an indirect reference to someone or something; *illusion* is a false picture or idea.

My little sister, under the illusion that she's movie-star material, makes frequent allusions to her future fans.

already, all ready ■ *Already* is an adverb meaning "before this time" or "by this time." *All ready* is an adjective meaning "fully prepared."

Note: Use *all ready* if you can substitute *ready* alone in the sentence.

Although I've already had some dessert, I am all ready for some ice cream from the street vendor.

TEKS 11.19 Using the Right Word **703**

Practice

Using the Right Word 1

accept, except; adapt, adopt; affect, effect; allusion, illusion

 If an underlined word in the following paragraphs is used incorrectly, write the correct word. If it's correct as is, write "OK."

As my thirteenth birthday approached, my parents asked me what I'd like. "I don't want anything **(1)** accept a dog," I replied. I knew it was pointless to say, for I'd been saying it since I was five years old and had never gotten one. Although I *could* **(2)** except that I would never have a dog, I persisted in bringing it up.

Well, my efforts to wear them down must finally have had an **(3)** affect. The morning of December 19, Mom told me to get my coat on; they had a surprise for me. When we pulled into the lot of the animal shelter, I thought it was some kind of **(4)** allusion. I was in utter disbelief that, after so many years of badgering, we were really going to **(5)** adopt a dog!

The handlers at the shelter warned us that it might take several weeks for our chosen dog to **(6)** adopt to her new surroundings. Though she was a fairly young dog, this period of adjustment might **(7)** affect her training somewhat. At this point, Mom and Dad made a thinly veiled **(8)** illusion to books at the library about training dogs. The new dog was going to be *my* responsibility, and they were showing me that they now trusted me enough to indulge my longing for my very own dog. It was the best birthday gift in the world.

Model

Model the following sentences to practice using the words *accept* and *except* correctly.

If you don't accept responsibility for your own actions, then you are forever chained to a position of defense.
—Holly Lisle, *Fire in the Mist*

Use what talents you possess: The woods would be very silent if no birds sang there except those that sang best.
—Henry Van Dyke

Using the Right Word

Allow time for partners to discuss and differentiate the words in each set, using the examples provided. Remind students to monitor their understanding and encourage them to seek clarification as needed. Then have students demonstrate their ability to spell correctly by completing the Practice activity independently. Remind them to check a print or online dictionary as needed to help them spell accurately.

Related Skills Activities

■ **SkillsBook**
Using the Right Word, p. 61
Troublesome Verbs, p. 102
Using the Right Word 1, p. 62

Answers

1. except
2. accept
3. effect
4. illusion
5. OK
6. adapt
7. OK
8. allusion

TEKS 11.19

altogether, all together ■ *Altogether* means "entirely." The phrase *all together* means "in a group" or "all at once."

"There is altogether too much gridlock," complained the Democrats. All together, the Republicans yelled, "No way!"

among, between ■ *Among* is typically used when speaking of more than two persons or things. *Between* is used when speaking of only two.

between   among

The three of us talked among ourselves to decide between going out or eating in.

amount, number ■ *Amount* is used for bulk measurement. *Number* is used to count separate units. (See also *fewer, less*.)

A substantial amount of honey spilled all over a number of my CD's.

annual, biannual, semiannual, biennial, perennial ■ An *annual* event happens once every year. A *biannual* or *semiannual* event happens twice a year. A *biennial* event happens every two years. A *perennial* event is one that is persistent or constant.

Dad's annual family reunion gets bigger every year.
We're going shopping at the department store's semiannual white sale.
Due to dwindling attendance, the county fair is now a biennial celebration.
A perennial plant persists for several years.

anyway ■ Do not add an *s* to *anyway*.

ascent, assent ■ *Ascent* is the act of rising or climbing; *assent* is "to agree to something after some consideration" (or such an agreement).

We completed our ascent of the butte with the assent of the landowner.

bad, badly ■ *Bad* is an adjective. *Badly* is an adverb.

This apple is bad, but one bad apple doesn't always ruin the whole bushel.
In today's game, Sumey passed badly.

base, bass ■ *Base* is the foundation or the lower part of something. *Bass* (pronounced like *base*) is a deep sound. *Bass* (pronounced like *class*) is a fish.

A car's wheel base is the distance between the centers of the front and rear wheels.
Luther is the bass player in his bluegrass band.

beside, besides ■ *Beside* means "by the side of." *Besides* means "in addition to."

Mother always grew roses beside the trash bin. Besides looking nice, they also gave off a sweet smell that masked odors.

TEKS 11.19
ELPS 3A, 4C, 5B

Practice

Using the Right Word 2

among, between; amount, number; ascent, assent; bad, badly; base, bass

Write the correct word from each choice given in parentheses.

1. The choir director placed Dario, a *(base, bass)*, *(among, between)* two altos.

2. "I will give my *(ascent, assent)* to your sneaky little plan," snorted the troll, "provided that my share is the greatest *(amount, number)* of your haul."

3. Maya wanted to reach the summit so *(bad, badly)* that her *(ascent, assent)* did not seem difficult at all.

4. A good *(amount, number)* of my shoes look *(bad, badly)* from walking on snowy and salt-strewn sidewalks.

5. Ms. Sawyer selected the trophy with the heaviest *(base, bass)* from *(among, between)* the half-dozen in the display case.

6. I don't think I did too *(bad, badly)* on today's test, but my grade will depend on the *(amount, number)* of others who did well.

7. Several largemouth *(base, bass)* were swimming in the aquarium *(among, between)* catfish, bream, and bluegill.

8. Grandmother Hughes would never *(ascent, assent)* to selling her property—for any *(amount, number)* of money.

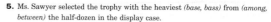

ascent

assent

Learning Language

Discuss your Practice responses with a partner. Take turns telling how you decided which word was correct in each sentence. Tell which clues (spelling, pronunciation, sentence context) helped you make your choices. Then write sentences using *bad, badly, base, bass* (the voice), and *bass* (the fish) correctly. Read each other's sentences aloud, and explain why each word is used correctly.

Right Word

Using the Right Word (continued)

Allow time for partners to discuss and differentiate the words in each set, using the examples provided. As needed, point out and discuss sight vocabulary such as *all, bad,* and *beside*. Have students demonstrate their ability to spell correctly by completing the Practice activity independently. Remind them to check a print or online dictionary as needed to help them spell accurately.

Related Skills Activities

■ *SkillsBook*
Using the Right Word 1, p. 62

Answers

1. bass, between
2. assent, amount
3. badly, ascent
4. number, bad
5. base, among
6. badly, number
7. bass, among
8. assent, amount

Learning Language

Have students practice producing the sounds of the newly acquired vocabulary before they begin writing their sentences. Remind them to be prepared to explain the spelling they choose.

 TEKS 11.19 Spell correctly, including using various resources to determine and check spellings; **ELPS** 3A Practice producing sounds of newly acquired vocabulary to produce English words; 4C Develop basic sight vocabulary and comprehend English vocabulary; 5B Write using newly acquired basic and content-based grade-level vocabulary

board, bored ■ *Board* is a piece of wood. *Board* is also an administrative group or council.

> The school board approved the purchase of fifty 1- by 6-inch pine boards.

Bored is the past tense of the verb "bore," which may mean "to make a hole by drilling" or "to become weary out of dullness."

> Watching television bored Joe, so he took his drill and bored a hole in the wall where he could hang his new clock.

brake, break ■ *Brake* is a device used to stop a vehicle. *Break* means "to separate or to destroy."

> I hope the brakes on my car never break.

bring, take ■ *Bring* suggests the action is directed toward the speaker; *take* suggests the action is directed away from the speaker.

> Bring home some garbage bags so I can take the trash outside.

can, may ■ *Can* suggests ability while *may* suggests permission.

> "Can I go to the mall?" means "Am I physically able to go to the mall?"

> "May I go to the mall?" asks permission to go.

capital, capitol ■ The noun *capital* refers to a city or to money. The adjective *capital* means "major or important." *Capitol* refers to a building.

> The state capital is home to the capitol building for a capital reason. The state government contributed capital for its construction.

cent, sent, scent ■ *Cent* is a coin; *sent* is the past tense of the verb "send"; *scent* is an odor or a smell.

> For forty-four cents, I sent my girlfriend a mushy love poem in a perfumed envelope. She adored the scent but hated the poem.

cereal, serial ■ *Cereal* is a grain, often made into breakfast food. *Serial* relates to something in a series.

> Mohammed enjoys reading serial novels while he eats a bowl of cereal.

chord, cord ■ *Chord* may mean "an emotion" or "a combination of musical tones sounded at the same time." A *cord* is a string or a rope.

> The guitar player strummed the opening chord to the group's hit song, which struck a responsive chord with the audience.

chose, choose ■ *Chose (chōz)* is the past tense of the verb *choose (chōōz)*.

> Last quarter I chose to read Chitra Divakaruni's *The Unknown Errors of Our Lives*—a fascinating book about Indian immigrants.

Practice

Using the Right Word 3

bring, take; *capital, capitol;* **cereal, serial;** *chose, choose*

Select the correct word from the list above to complete each sentence.

1. Veterinarians recommend pet foods without a lot of _____ fillers.

2. "Regina, dear, will you please _____ me an aspirin?" Grandpa asked.

3. Ignacio _____ an electric blue tuxedo for prom.

4. Amber wanted to _____ my black rain umbrella to the beach.

5. A _____ cause of traffic backups in this town is the preponderance of one-way streets.

6. You must have your product's _____ number on hand before talking to the service department personnel.

7. Between 1926 and 1929, Cuba's _____ was built by 8,000 specialized workers.

8. In the near future, you may have to _____ between fingerprint and iris identification rather than a government-issued ID.

Model

Model the following sentences to practice using the words *can* and *may* correctly.

> My spoon is poised over my just-poured-the-milk-in bowl of cereal as she asks if I can go over a few revisions.
>
> —Peter Bowerman, *The Well-Fed Writer*

> I can start working on my research paper tomorrow if I may borrow your in-line skates to get to the library.

Right Word

Using the Right Word (continued)

Allow time for partners to discuss and differentiate the words in each set, using the examples provided. As needed, point out and discuss sight vocabulary such as *brake, break, can,* and *may.* Have students demonstrate their ability to spell correctly by completing the Practice activity independently. Remind them to check a print or online dictionary as needed to help them spell accurately.

Related Skills Activities

■ *SkillsBook*
Using the Right Word 1, p. 62

Answers

1. cereal
2. bring
3. chose
4. take
5. capital
6. serial
7. capitol
8. choose

---

coarse, course ■ *Coarse* means "rough or crude"; *course* means "a path or direction taken." *Course* also means "a class or a series of studies."

> Fletcher, known for using coarse language, was barred from the golf course until he took an etiquette course.

complement, compliment ■ *Complement* refers to that which completes or fulfills. *Compliment* is an expression of admiration or praise.

> Kimberly smiled, thinking she had received a compliment when Carlos said that her new Chihuahua complemented her personality.

continual, continuous ■ *Continual* refers to something that happens again and again with some breaks or pauses; *continuous* refers to something that keeps happening, uninterrupted.

> Sunlight hits Iowa on a continual basis; sunlight hits Earth continuously.

counsel, council ■ When used as a noun, *counsel* means "advice"; when used as a verb, it means "to advise." *Council* refers to a group that advises.

> The student council counseled all freshmen to join a school club. That's good counsel.

desert, dessert ■ The noun *desert* (dĕz'ərt) refers to barren wilderness. *Dessert* (dĭ zûrt') is food served at the end of a meal.

> The scorpion tiptoed through the moonlit desert, searching for dessert.

The verb *desert* (dĭ zûrt') means "to abandon"; the noun *desert* (dĭ zûrt') means "deserved reward or punishment."

> The burglar's hiding place deserted him when the spotlight swung his way; his subsequent arrest was his just desert.

die, dye ■ *Die* (dying) means "to stop living." *Dye* (dyeing) is used to change the color of something.

different from, different than ■ Use *different from* in a comparison of two things. *Different than* should be used only when followed by a clause.

> Yassine is quite different from his brother.
> Life is different than it used to be.

farther, further ■ *Farther* refers to a physical distance; *further* refers to additional time, quantity, or degree.

> Alaska extends farther north than Iceland does. Further information can be obtained in an atlas.

fewer, less ■ *Fewer* refers to the number of separate units; *less* refers to bulk quantity.

> Because we have fewer orders for cakes, we'll buy less sugar and flour.

Using the Right Word 4

coarse, course; complement, compliment; **continual, continuous**; different from, different than; **farther, further**

 If an underlined word is used incorrectly, write the correct word. If it's correct as is, write "OK."

1. Studies show that a woman accepts a <u>compliment</u> with more ease than a man does.

2. Kure Island, Hawaii, and Elliot Key, Florida, are <u>further</u> from each other than any other United States locations.

3. "You will be punished for the use of any <u>course</u> language in this classroom," the new teacher warned.

4. "At this factory, we use a secret process <u>different from</u> anyone else uses," the line manager boasted.

5. The <u>continual</u> revisions that software undergoes makes it hard to keep up with the latest versions.

6. Upon <u>further</u> investigation, the detectives discovered that Mr. Dall was not the man they thought he was.

7. I think au gratin potatoes are the perfect <u>compliment</u> to roast pork.

8. Have you ever run an obstacle <u>coarse</u> (besides the one in your room)?

9. The <u>continual</u> tinkling of the chimes was an indicator of the wind's staying power that stormy afternoon.

10. Though they appear similar, this pen is quite <u>different than</u> that one.

Learning Language

With a partner, compare the spellings of the word pairs on pages 706 and 708. Focus on quickly recognizing the small differences in spelling between the words in each pair; this will improve your sight recognition of these words and also increase your ability to use them accurately in your writing. Then review your responses to exercises 1–10 together, explaining your choices.

Using the Right Word (continued)

Allow time for partners to discuss and differentiate the words in each set, using the examples provided. As needed, point out and discuss sight vocabulary such as *from, than, fewer,* and *less.* Have students demonstrate their ability to spell correctly by completing the Practice activity independently. Remind them to check a print or online dictionary as needed to help them spell accurately.

Related Skills Activities

■ *SkillsBook*
Using the Right Word 2, p. 63

Answers

1. OK
2. farther
3. coarse
4. different than
5. OK
6. OK
7. complement
8. course
9. continuous
10. different from

Learning Language

As partners discuss their responses to items 1–10, remind them to monitor their understanding and to seek clarification as needed. Ask them to use specificity and detail as they express ideas about their choices.

TEKS 11.19 Spell correctly, including using various resources to determine and check spellings; **ELPS 2D** Monitor understanding of spoken language and seek clarification as needed; **3G** Express ideas; **3H** Describe with increasing specificity and detail; **4C** Develop basic sight vocabulary and comprehend English vocabulary

flair, flare ■ *Flair* refers to style or natural talent; *flare* means "to light up quickly" or "burst out" (or an object that does so).

> Ronni was thrilled with Jorge's flair for decorating—until one of his strategically placed candles flared, marring the wall.

good, well ■ *Good* is an adjective; *well* is nearly always an adverb. (When *well* is used to describe a state of health, it is an adjective: He was happy to be *well* again.)

> The CD player works well.
> Our team looks good this season.

heal, heel ■ *Heal* means "to mend or restore to health." A *heel* is the back part of a foot.

> Achilles died because a poison arrow pierced his heel and caused a wound that would not heal.

healthful, healthy ■ *Healthful* means "causing or improving health"; *healthy* means "possessing health."

> Healthful foods build healthy bodies.

hear, here ■ You *hear* with your ears. *Here* means "the area close by."

hear

heard, herd ■ *Heard* is the past tense of the verb "hear"; *herd* is a large group of animals.

hole, whole ■ A *hole* is a cavity or hollow place. *Whole* means "complete."

idle, idol ■ *Idle* means "not working." An *idol* is someone or something that is worshipped.

> The once-popular actress, who had been idle lately, wistfully recalled her days as an idol.

DON'T EVEN THINK OF PARKING HERE

immigrate, emigrate ■ *Immigrate* means "to come into a new country or environment." *Emigrate* means "to go out of one country to live in another."

> Martin Ulferts immigrated to this country in 1882. He was only three years old when he emigrated from Germany.

imply, infer ■ *Imply* means "to suggest or express indirectly"; *infer* means "to draw a conclusion from facts." (A writer or speaker implies; a reader or listener infers.)

> Dad implied by his comment that I should drive more carefully, and I inferred that he was concerned for both me and his new car.

 Practice

Using the Right Word 5

flair, flare; good, well; healthful, healthy; immigrate, emigrate; imply, infer

Write the correct choice from those given in parentheses.

One of my neighbors, Mr. Blagovitch, **(1)** *(immigrated, emigrated)* from his native Ukraine when he was only three years old, so he doesn't remember it at all. His parents worked hard to provide a good life for their family in Chicago. His mother had a **(2)** *(flair, flare)* for cooking **(3)** *(healthful, healthy)*, stick-to-the-ribs food and found work in a local ethnic restaurant. His father was **(4)** *(good, well)* at making things grow and began his own landscaping company.

At one point, Mr. Blagovitch was not doing **(5)** *(good, well)* in school. His mother admonished, "We did not **(6)** *(emigrate, immigrate)* to this country to see you fail!" His father's temper **(7)** *(flaired, flared)*. In terse sentences, he **(8)** *(implied, inferred)* that his son had better shape up . . . or else.

Mr. Blagovitch did not even attempt to **(9)** *(imply, infer)* what his father meant by "or else"; he knew from experience it would not be **(10)** *(good, well)*. It took just that one vague threat from his **(11)** *(healthful, healthy)*, muscled father to get Mr. Blagovitch back on track. He improved his grades and even discovered his **(12)** *(flair, flare)* for music, which ultimately led him to make a career of it.

Model

Model the following sentences to practice using the words *flair* and *flare* correctly.

> I have long thought that her flair for melodrama has been wasted on her usual audience, a family that has more often called for the hook than begged for an encore.
> —Jan Burke, *Liar*

> The sailor dropped the flare to the deck, and almost instantly it began to shine with a tremendous light, the heat radiating out to unbearable levels, and toxic fumes spewing forth.
> —Gregory A. Freeman, *Sailors to the End*

Right Word

Using the Right Word (continued)

Allow time for partners to discuss and differentiate the words in each set, using the examples provided. As needed, point out and discuss sight vocabulary such as *good, well, hear,* and *here*. Have students demonstrate their ability to spell correctly by completing the Practice activity independently. Remind them to check a print or online dictionary as needed to help them spell accurately.

Related Skills Activities

■ *SkillsBook*
Using the Right Word 2, p. 63

Answers

1. emigrated
2. flair
3. healthful
4. good
5. well
6. immigrate
7. flared
8. implied
9. infer
10. good
11. healthy
12. flair

TEKS 11.19

insure, ensure ■ *Insure* means "to secure from financial harm or loss." *Ensure* means "to make certain of something."

To ensure that you can legally drive that new car, you'll have to insure it.

it's, its ■ *It's* is the contraction of "it is." *Its* is the possessive form of "it."

It's hard to believe, but the movie *Shrek* still holds its appeal for many kids.

later, latter ■ *Later* means "after a period of time." *Latter* refers to the second of two things mentioned.

Later that year we had our second baby and adopted a stray kitten. The latter was far more welcomed by our toddler.

lay, lie ■ *Lay* means "to place." *Lay* is a transitive verb. (See 736.1.)

Lay your books on the big table.

Lie means "to recline," and *lay* is the past tense of *lie*. *Lie* is an intransitive verb. (See 736.1.)

In this heat, the children must lie down for a nap. Yesterday they lay down without one complaint. Sometimes they have lain in the hammocks to rest.

lead, led ■ *Lead* (lēd) is the present tense of the verb meaning "to guide." The past tense of the verb is *led* (lĕd). The noun *lead* (lĕd) is a metal.

We were led along the path that leads to an abandoned lead mine.

learn, teach ■ *Learn* means "to acquire information." *Teach* means "to give information."

I learn better when people teach with real-world examples.

leave, let ■ *Leave* means "to allow something to remain behind." *Let* means "to permit."

Would you let me leave my bike at your house?

lend, borrow ■ *Lend* means "to give for temporary use." *Borrow* means "to receive for temporary use."

I told Mom I needed to borrow $18 for a CD, but she said she could lend only money for school supplies.

She lends.

He borrows.

like, as ■ When *like* is used as a preposition meaning "similar to," it can be followed only by a noun, pronoun, or noun phrase; when *as* is used as a subordinating conjunction, it introduces a subordinate clause.

You could become a gymnast like her, as you work and practice hard.

medal, meddle ■ *Medal* is an award. *Meddle* means "to interfere."

Some parents meddle in the awards process to be sure that their kids get medals.

Practice

Using the Right Word 6

insure, ensure; it's, its; lay, lie; leave, let; like, as; medal, meddle

 Write the correct choice from those given in each set of numbered parentheses.

Last weekend I got in a little fender-bender accident on my way home. My great-grandmother, an ancient religious woman, told me, "**(1)** *(It's, Its)* not just luck that it wasn't worse. The St. Christopher **(2)** *(medal, meddle)* that I gave you **(3)** *(insured, ensured)* your safety."

"Oh," I replied. "I was going to ask you why you would **(4)** *(leave, let)* something **(5)** *(like, as)* that in my car. Well, thanks, Grandma. I'm exhausted. I'm going to go **(6)** *(lay, lie)* down now."

Then my dad said, "You better start praying that you find another company to **(7)** *(insure, ensure)* your car. We're not going to keep somebody who drives **(8)** *(like, as)* you do on our policy anymore."

"The accident wasn't my fault, Dad! The car's not damaged badly; there's just a dent in **(9)** *(it's, its)* rear panel," I said. "I won't even file a claim."

My mom entered the fray. "That sounds reasonable, Tom. **(10)** *(Leave, Let)* her drive around in a dented car."

"I'd rather you didn't **(11)** *(medal, meddle)* in this conversation, Dee," he fumed. "We need to **(12)** *(lay, lie)* down some rules now!" And, just like that, I'm in the market for my own insurance. Got any advice?

Learning Language

Work with a partner. Compare your Practice responses and read the short narrative aloud. Discuss the situation in the narrative. Then write a short response to answer the question, "Got any advice?" Tell how you would feel if you were the girl who had the accident. Offer advice about what she might do next. Use at least three words from the list at the top of the page.

Right Word

Using the Right Word (continued)

Allow time for partners to discuss and differentiate the words in each set, using the examples provided. Suggest that partners practice producing the sounds of the newly acquired vocabulary. As needed, point out and discuss sight vocabulary such as *it's, its, learn, teach, like,* and *as.* Have students demonstrate their ability to spell correctly by completing the Practice activity independently. Remind them to check a print or online dictionary as needed to help them spell accurately.

Related Skills Activities

■ *SkillsBook*
Using the Right Word 3, p. 64

Answers

1. It's
2. medal
3. ensured
4. leave
5. like
6. lie
7. insure
8. as
9. its
10. Let
11. meddle
12. lay

Learning Language

Invite partners to express their feelings about the driver and the advice they might offer before they begin writing.

metal, mettle ■ *Metal* is a chemical element like iron or gold. *Mettle* is "strength of spirit."

Grandad's mettle during battle left him with some metal in his shoulder.

miner, minor ■ A *miner* digs for valuable ore. A *minor* is a person who is not legally an adult. A *minor* problem is one of no great importance.

moral, morale ■ A *moral* is a lesson drawn from a story; as an adjective, it relates to the principles of right and wrong. *Morale* refers to someone's attitude.

Ms. Ladue considers it her moral obligation to go to church every day.
The students' morale sank after their defeat in the forensics competition.

passed, past ■ *Passed* is a verb. *Past* can be used as a noun, an adjective, or a preposition.

That old pickup truck passed my sports car! (verb)
Many senior citizens hold dearly to the past. (noun)
Tilly's past life as a circus worker must have been . . . interesting. (adjective)
Who can walk past a bakery without looking in the window? (preposition)

peace, piece ■ *Peace* means "tranquility or freedom from war." *Piece* is a part or fragment.

Grandma sits in the peace and quiet of the parlor, enjoying a piece of pie.

peak, peek, pique ■ A *peak* is a high point. *Peek* means "brief look" (or "look briefly"). *Pique*, as a verb, means "to excite by challenging"; as a noun, it is a feeling of resentment.

The peak of Dr. Fedder's professional life was his ability to pique children's interest in his work. "Peek at this slide," he said to the eager students.

pedal, peddle, petal ■ A *pedal* is a foot lever; as a verb, it means "to ride a bike." *Peddle* means "to go from place to place selling something." A *petal* is part of a flower.

Don Miller paints beautiful petals on his homemade birdhouses. Then he pedals through the flea market every weekend to peddle them.

personal, personnel ■ *Personal* means "private." *Personnel* are people working at a particular job.

plain, plane ■ *Plain* means "an area of land that is flat or level"; it also means "clearly seen or clearly understood."

It's plain to see why settlers of the Great Plains had trouble moving west.
Plane means "flat, level"; it is also a tool used to smooth the surface of wood.
I used a plane to make the board plane and smooth.

Practice

Using the Right Word 7

metal, mettle; moral, morale; **peace, piece**; peak, peek, pique; **plain, plane**

Select the correct word from the list above to complete each sentence. (One word is used twice.)

1. The _____ and quiet of the isolated meadow made her worries dissolve.

2. Each _____ on an electrocardiogram shows a specific electrical activity of the heart.

3. I could see that Jay's _____ was low by his slow gait and sagging shoulders.

4. "Ferrous" means "containing iron"; please give an example of a nonferrous _____.

5. The group of kids near his new school seemed unfriendly, so Jerry was careful not to _____ them.

6. The choir director told us to wear _____ white shirts for the concert.

7. The dog proved its _____ as it chased the burglar from the house.

8. I hate it when the doctor says, "Let's take a _____ in your ear."

9. Is the study of medical ethics a purely _____ issue?

10. Funding has been cut, and every agency wants its _____ of the pie.

11. In the story of the prodigal son, did the son who had remained at home show any _____ at the father's lavish treatment of the other?

12. By definition, a pebble-textured tabletop does not have a _____ surface.

Model

Model these sentences to practice using *moral* and *morale* correctly.

It is curious that physical courage should be so common in the world and moral courage so rare.
—Mark Twain

Eating well gives a spectacular joy to life and contributes immensely to goodwill and happy companionship. It is of great importance to the morale.
—Elsa Schiaparelli, *Shocking Life*

Right Word

Using the Right Word (continued)

Allow time for partners to discuss and differentiate the words in each set, using the examples provided. Explain that they should monitor their understanding of the discussion and seek clarification as needed. Have students demonstrate their ability to spell correctly by completing the Practice activity independently. Remind them to check a print or online dictionary as needed to help them spell accurately.

Related Skills Activities

■ **SkillsBook**
Using the Right Word 3, p. 64

Answers

1. peace
2. peak
3. morale
4. metal
5. pique
6. plain
7. mettle
8. peek
9. moral
10. piece
11. pique
12. plane

 TEKS 11.19 Spell correctly, including using various resources to determine and check spellings; **ELPS** 2D Monitor understanding of spoken language and seek clarification as needed

poor, pour, pore ■ *Poor* means "needy or pitiable." *Pour* means "to cause to flow in a stream." A *pore* is an opening in the skin.

Tough exams on late spring days make my poor pores pour sweat.

principal, principle ■ As an adjective, *principal* means "primary." As a noun, it can mean "a school administrator" or "a sum of money." *Principle* means "idea or doctrine."

His principal concern is fitness. (adjective) The principal retired. (noun)
During the first year of a loan, you pay more interest than principal. (noun)
The principle of *caveat emptor* is "Let the buyer beware."

quiet, quit, quite ■ *Quiet* is the opposite of "noisy." *Quit* means "to stop." *Quite* means "completely or entirely."

quote, quotation ■ *Quote* is a verb; *quotation* is a noun.

The quotation I used was from Woody Allen. You may quote me on that.

real, really, very ■ Do not use *real* in place of the adverbs *very* or *really*.

Mother's cake is usually very (not *real*) tasty, but this one is really stale!

right, write, wright, rite ■ *Right* means "correct or proper"; it also refers to that which a person has a legal claim to, as in *copyright*. *Write* means "to inscribe or record." A *wright* is a person who makes or builds something. *Rite* refers to a ritual or ceremonial act.

Write this down: It is the right of the shipwright to perform the rite of christening—breaking a bottle of champagne on the stern of the ship.

ring, wring ■ *Ring* means "encircle" or "to sound by striking." *Wring* means "to squeeze or twist."

At the beach, Grandma would ring her head with a large scarf. Once, it blew into the sea, so she had me wring it out.

scene, seen ■ *Scene* refers to the setting or location where something happens; it also may mean "sight or spectacle." *Seen* is a form of the verb "see."

Serena had seen her boyfriend making a scene; she cringed.

seam, seem ■ *Seam* (noun) is a line formed by connecting two pieces. *Seem* (verb) means "to appear to exist."

The ragged seams in his old coat seem to match the creases in his face.

set, sit ■ *Set* means "to place." *Sit* means "to put the body in a seated position." *Set* is transitive; *sit* is intransitive. (See 736.1.)

How can you just sit there and watch as I set all these chairs in place?

Practice

Using the Right Word 8

quote, quotation; real, really, very; right, write, rite; set, sit

 If an underlined word is used incorrectly, write the correct word. If it's correct as is, write "OK."

1. If I <u>sit</u> the monitor on this shelf, there's no room for the tower.

2. My dad is fond of this Yogi Berra <u>quote</u>: "You can observe a lot just by watching."

3. The bristlecone pines of California's White Mountains are <u>really</u> ancient trees.

4. Lissa is definitely <u>rite</u> when she says she needs a vacation.

5. If you <u>quote</u> a source in a research paper, you must include a reference to that source.

6. Dwayne tried to tell his little sister that the "monster" under her bed was not <u>real</u>.

7. Some college students see a trip to some place that's warm as an annual <u>right</u> of spring.

8. Dr. Levine had a <u>real</u> rough night in the emergency room.

9. When you receive unsatisfactory service from a company, often the best tactic is to <u>write</u> a letter of complaint.

10. "Please have a seat in the waiting room" loosely translates to "<u>Set</u> and wait for a long time."

Learning Language

Review several of the word pairs on page 716 with a partner. Explain the meanings in your own words. Then take turns using each pair of words in oral sentences. Check each other's pronunciation, paying close attention to short and long vowel sounds. If you have questions about meanings or pronunciations, check with your teacher, another student, or in the dictionary.

Right Word

Using the Right Word (continued)

Allow time for partners to discuss and differentiate the words in each set, using the examples provided. As needed, point out and discuss sight vocabulary such as *poor, real, really, very, right, write, seen, seem, set,* and *sit.* Have students demonstrate their ability to spell correctly by completing the Practice activity independently. Remind them to check a print or online dictionary to help them spell accurately.

Related Skills Activities

■ *SkillsBook*
Using the Right Word 3, p. 64

Answers

1. set
2. quotation
3. OK
4. right
5. OK
6. OK
7. rite
8. really *or* very
9. OK
10. Sit

Learning Language

Have partners practice producing the sounds of the newly acquired vocabulary before they explain the meanings in their own words. Remind them to include specific details in their explanations.

 TEKS 11.19 Spell correctly, including using various resources to determine and check spellings; **ELPS 3A** Practice producing sounds of newly acquired vocabulary to produce English words; **3H** Explain with increasing specificity and detail; **4C** Develop basic sight vocabulary and comprehend English vocabulary

718

sight, cite, site ■ *Sight* means "the act of seeing"; a *sight* is what is seen. *Cite* means "to quote" or "to summon," as before a court. *Site* means "location."

> In her report, the general contractor cited several problems at the downtown job site. For one, the loading area was a chaotic sight.

sole, soul ■ *Sole* means "single, only one"; *sole* also refers to the bottom surface of the foot. *Soul* refers to the spiritual part of a person.

> As the sole inhabitant of the island, he put his heart and soul into his farming.

stationary, stationery ■ *Stationary* means "not movable"; *stationery* refers to the paper and envelopes used to write letters.

steal, steel ■ *Steal* means "to take something without permission"; *steel* is a type of metal.

> It takes nerves of steel to brazenly steal another's possessions in broad daylight.

than, then ■ *Than* is used in a comparison; *then* tells when.

> Abigail shouted that her big brother was bigger than my big brother. Then she ran away.

their, there, they're ■ *Their* is a possessive personal pronoun. *There* is an adverb used to point out location. *They're* is the contraction for "they are."

> They're a well-dressed couple. Do you see them there, with their matching jackets?

threw, through ■ *Threw* is the past tense of "throw." *Through* means "from beginning to end."

> Through seven innings, Daisha threw just seven strikes.

to, too, two ■ *To* is a preposition that can mean "in the direction of." *To* is also used to form an infinitive. (See 746.2) *Too* means "also" or "very." *Two* is a number.

vain, vane, vein ■ *Vain* means "valueless or fruitless"; it may also mean "holding a high regard for oneself." *Vane* is a flat piece of material set up to show which way the wind blows. *Vein* refers to a blood vessel or a mineral deposit.

> The vain prospector, boasting about the vein of silver he'd uncovered, paused to look up at the turning weather vane.

vary, very ■ *Vary* means "to change." *Very* means "to a high degree."

> Though the weather may vary from day to day, generally, it is very pleasant.

Practice

Using the Right Word 9

sight, cite, site; sole, soul; than, then; vain, vane, vein; vary, very

Write the correct choice from those given in parentheses.

1. Kris has a *(vain, vein)* in her temple that begins to throb when she is angry.

2. A neighbor was *(sighted, cited)* for disturbing the peace after a loud party.

3. The air is *(vary, very)* cold, but the ice on the lake hasn't frozen solid yet.

4. Some people who've had near-death experiences report seeing their *(soles, souls)* as balls of bright light.

5. Turn left and *(than, then)* take an immediate right onto Hayes Road.

6. Decorative weather *(vanes, veins)* sell well at county fairs.

7. The ship's captain was alerted by the lookout who had *(sighted, sited)* land.

8. Anyone who thinks all fashion models are *(vain, vane)* hasn't met Kat Stevens.

9. On a long car trip, I would rather listen to a book on CD *(than, then)* to music or talk radio.

10. Jacinda's nervousness at being the *(sole, soul)* presenter at the awards ceremony was evident.

11. Although your mileage may *(vary, very)*, this model typically gets about 30 mpg on the highway.

12. Pete and his friends chose a grassy, level *(sight, site)* to pitch their tent.

Model

Model the following sentences to practice using the words *sole* and *soul* correctly.

> **The keenest sorrow is to recognize ourselves as the sole cause of all our adversities.**
> —Sophocles

> **Nothing contributes so much to tranquilizing the mind as a steady purpose—a point on which the soul may fix its intellectual eye.**
> —Mary Wollstonecraft Shelley

Right Word

Using the Right Word (continued)

Allow time for partners to discuss and differentiate the words in each set, using the examples provided. Explain that they should monitor their understanding of the discussion and seek clarification when necessary. As needed, point out and discuss sight vocabulary such as *than, then, to, too,* and *two*. Have students demonstrate their ability to spell correctly by completing the Practice activity independently. Remind them to check a print or online dictionary as needed to help them spell accurately.

Related Skills Activities

■ **SkillsBook**
Using the Right Word 3, p. 64

Answers

1. vein
2. cited
3. very
4. souls
5. then
6. vanes
7. sighted
8. vain
9. than
10. sole
11. vary
12. site

 TEKS 11.19 Spell correctly, including using various resources to determine and check spellings; **ELPS 2D** Monitor understanding of spoken language and seek clarification as needed; **4C** Develop basic sight vocabulary

TEKS 11.19

vial, vile ■ A *vial* is a small container for liquid. *Vile* is an adjective meaning "foul, despicable."

It's a vile job, but someone has to clean these lab vials.

waste

waist, waste ■ *Waist* is the part of the body just above the hips. The verb *waste* means "to spend or use carelessly" or "to wear away or decay"; the noun *waste* refers to material that is unused or useless.

Her waist is small because she wastes no opportunity to exercise.

waist

wait, weight ■ *Wait* means "to stay somewhere expecting something." *Weight* refers to a degree or unit of heaviness.

ware, wear, where ■ *Ware* refers to a product that is sold; *wear* means "to have on or to carry on one's body"; *where* asks "in what place?" or "in what situation?"

The designer boasted, "Where can anybody wear my wares? Anywhere."

way, weigh ■ *Way* means "path or route." *Weigh* means "to measure weight" or "to have a certain heaviness."

My dogs weigh too much. The best way to reduce is a daily run in the park.

weather, whether ■ *Weather* refers to the condition of the atmosphere. *Whether* refers to a possibility.

Due to the weather, the coach wondered whether he should cancel the meet.

which, that ■ Use *which* to refer to objects or animals in a nonrestrictive clause (set off with commas). Use *that* to refer to objects or animals in a restrictive clause. (For more information about these types of clauses, see 642.2.)

The birds, which stay in the area all winter, know where the feeders are located.
The food that attracts the most birds is sunflower seed.

who, whom ■ Use *who* to refer to people. *Who* is used as the subject of a verb in an independent clause or in a relative clause. *Whom* is used as the object of a preposition or as a direct object.

To whom do we owe our thanks for these pizzas? And who ordered anchovies?

who's, whose ■ *Who's* is the contraction for "who is." *Whose* is a pronoun that can show possession or ownership.

Cody, whose car is new, will drive. Who's going to read the map?

your, you're ■ *Your* is a possessive pronoun. *You're* is the contraction for "you are."

Take your boots if you're going out in that snow.

Practice

Using the Right Word 10

vial, vile; weather, whether; **which, that**; who, whom; **your, you're**

 First decide which pair of words from above belongs in each sentence. Then write them in the correct order to fill in the blanks.

1. Alonzo had to go to Class China Replacements, _____ was about a hundred miles away, to get a replacement for the valuable teacup _____ he had broken last week.

2. The small _____ in Dr. Brown's lab, despite its size, gave off a _____ odor that wafted into the hall.

3. My mom's sister and brother-in-law, _____ live in New Jersey, are the family members _____ we enjoy the most.

4. "I don't care _____ it's raining now or not," Bailee's stern mother said. "The _____ report predicts rain, so you are taking a raincoat."

5. Since _____ going to the store anyway, you can get _____ own hair gel.

Learning Language

Work with a partner. Review your responses to the Practice activity. Then choose three different pairs of words from page **720**. Together, write sentences that use each pair of words correctly, leaving blanks for each word choice. Exchange your sentences with another pair of students. Complete each other's sentences and discuss your answers, explaining why each word choice is used correctly.

Using the Right Word (continued)

Allow time for partners to discuss and differentiate the words in each set, using the examples provided. As needed, point out and discuss sight vocabulary such as *wait, where, way, that, who,* and *your.* Have students demonstrate their ability to spell correctly by completing the Practice activity independently. Remind them to check a print or online dictionary as needed to help them spell accurately.

Related Skills Activities

■ *SkillsBook*
Using the Right Word 4, p. 65

Answers

1. which, that
2. vial, vile
3. who, whom
4. whether, weather
5. you're, your

Learning Language

Remind partners to help the other pair decide on the correct answers by providing context clues in the sentences that they write. Tell them to use specificity and detail when they explain their choices.

TEKS **11.19** Spell correctly, including using various resources to determine and check spellings; **ELPS** **3H** Explain with increasing specificity and detail; **4C** Develop basic sight vocabulary and comprehend English vocabulary; **5B** Write using newly acquired basic and content-based grade-level vocabulary

722

Parts of Speech

Words in the English language are used in eight different ways. For this reason, there are eight parts of speech.

722.1 Noun

A word that names a person, a place, a thing, or an idea
Governor Smith-Jones   Oregon   hospital   religion

722.2 Pronoun

A word used in place of a noun
**I   you   she   him   who   everyone   these   neither
theirs   themselves   which**

722.3 Verb

A word that expresses action or state of being
float   sniff   discover   seem   were   was

722.4 Adjective

A word that describes a noun or a pronoun
young   big   grim   Canadian   longer

722.5 Adverb

A word that describes a verb, an adjective, or another adverb
briefly   forward   regally   slowly   better

722.6 Preposition

The first word or words in a prepositional phrase (which functions as an adjective or an adverb)
away from   under   before   with   for   out of

722.7 Conjunction

A word that connects other words or groups of words
and   but   although   because   either, or   so

722.8 Interjection

A word that shows strong emotion or surprise
Oh no!   Yipes!   Good grief!   Well, . . .

Noun

A **noun** is a word that names something: a person, a place, a thing, or an idea.
governor   Oregon   hospital   Buddhism   love

Classes of Nouns

The five classes of nouns are *proper, common, concrete, abstract,* and *collective.*

723.1 Proper Noun

A **proper noun** names a particular person, place, thing, or idea. Proper nouns are always capitalized.

Jackie Robinson	Brooklyn	World Series
Christianity	Ebbets Field	Hinduism

723.2 Common Noun

A **common noun** does not name a particular person, place, thing, or idea. Common nouns are not capitalized.
person   woman   president   park   baseball   government

723.3 Concrete Noun

A **concrete noun** names a thing that is tangible (can be seen, touched, heard, smelled, or tasted). Concrete nouns are either proper or common.

child	Grand Canyon	music
aroma	fireworks	Becky

723.4 Abstract Noun

An **abstract noun** names an idea, a condition, or a feeling—in other words, something that cannot be touched, smelled, tasted, seen, or heard.

New Deal   greed   poverty   progress   freedom   awe

723.5 Collective Noun

A **collective noun** names a group or a unit.

United States   Portland Cementers   team   crowd   community

---

Related Skills Activities

■ **Voice**
Using Effective Modifiers, p. 80
Including Sensory Details, p. 81
Choosing Vivid Verbs, p. 82

■ *SkillsBook*
Pretest: Nouns, p.71
Types of Nouns 1, p. 72
Specific Nouns, p. 76

Forms of Nouns

Nouns are grouped according to their *number, gender,* and *case.*

724.1 Number of a Noun

Number indicates whether the noun is singular or plural.

A **singular noun** refers to one person, place, thing, or idea.
actor stadium Canadian bully truth child person

A **plural noun** refers to more than one person, place, thing, or idea.
actors stadiums Canadians bullies truths children people

724.2 Gender of a Noun

Gender indicates whether a noun is masculine, feminine, neuter, or indefinite.

Masculine:
uncle brother men bull rooster stallion

Feminine:
aunt sister women cow hen filly

Neuter (without gender):
tree cobweb flying fish closet

Indefinite (masculine or feminine):
president plumber doctor parent

724.3 Case of a Noun

Case tells how nouns are related to other words used with them. There are three cases: *nominative, possessive,* and *objective.*

■ A **nominative case** noun can be the subject of a clause.
> Danny's feet were tapping nervously under the table; that heavy-set man in the corner owed an explanation to the boy he had left behind.

A nominative noun can also be a predicate noun (or predicate nominative), which follows a "be" verb (*am, is, are, was, were, be, being, been*) and renames the subject. In the sentence below, *style* renames *house.*
> The Grangers's house was a different style than those they had lived in before.

■ A **possessive case** noun shows possession or ownership.
> Like the spider's claw, a part of him touches a world he will never enter.
> —Loren Eiseley, "The Hidden Teacher"

■ An **objective case** noun can be a direct object, an indirect object, or an object of the preposition.
> Marna always gives Mylo science fiction books for his birthday.
> (*Mylo* is the indirect object and *books* is the direct object of the verb "gives." *Birthday* is the object of the preposition "for.")

Grammar Practice

Nouns

■ Classes
■ Number
■ Case

 For each numbered noun, classify it as *proper or common* and *concrete or abstract.* Also indicate whether it is a *collective* noun. Then write whether it is *singular* or *plural* and identify its case as *nominative, possessive,* or *objective.*

My extended **(1)** family is having a reunion in **(2)** July. **(3)** Invitations went out almost a year in advance. Before the last **(4)** time we tried to get together, a hurricane forced us to cancel.

This time, we've reserved the **(5)** Cantwell Grove Picnic Area in our county park. Even if it rains, we will have **(6)** shelter. We are using my brother **(7)** Dean's stereo system. My nieces and **(8)** nephews from **(9)** Alaska will attend. My **(10)** aunt's husband, a chef, will be whipping up some incredible **(11)** food for us. I'm looking forward to this **(12)** party!

Model

Model the following sentences to practice using an abstract noun in the objective case.

> For a list of all the ways technology has failed to improve the quality of life, please press three.
> —Alice Kahn

> Education is a progressive discovery of our own ignorance.
> —Will Durant

Related Skills Activities

■ *SkillsBook*
Types of Nouns, p. 73
Function of Nouns, p. 74
Nominative, Possessive, and Objective Cases of Nouns, p. 75

Answers

1. common, concrete, collective, singular, nominative
2. proper, abstract, singular, objective
3. common, concrete, plural, nominative
4. common, abstract, singular, objective
5. proper, concrete, singular, objective
6. common, abstract, singular, objective
7. proper, concrete, singular, possessive
8. common, concrete, plural, nominative
9. proper, concrete, singular, objective
10. common, concrete, singular, possessive
11. common, concrete, singular, objective
12. common, abstract, singular, objective

Pronoun

A **pronoun** is a word used in place of a noun.

> I, you, she, it, which, that, themselves, whoever, me, he, they, mine, ours

The three types of pronouns are *simple, compound,* and *phrasal.*

> **Simple:** I, you, he, she, it, we, they, who, what
> **Compound:** myself, someone, anybody, everything, itself, whoever
> **Phrasal:** one another, each other

All pronouns have **antecedents**. An antecedent is the noun that the pronoun refers to or replaces.

> Charlie is completely immersed in his family's decisions. His brothers seldom make a move without consulting him first, and he continually offers advice to his parents on a variety of topics.
> (*Charlie* is the antecedent of *his, him,* and *he.*)

Note: Each pronoun must agree with its antecedent. (See page 774.)

726.1 **Classes of Pronouns**

The six classes of pronouns are *personal, reflexive and intensive, relative, indefinite, interrogative,* and *demonstrative.*

Personal
I, me, my, mine / we, us, our, ours
you, your, yours / they, them, their, theirs
he, him, his, she, her, hers, it, its

Reflexive and Intensive
myself, yourself, himself, herself, itself, ourselves, yourselves, themselves

Relative
what, who, whose, whom, which, that

Indefinite

all	both	everything	nobody	several
another	each	few	none	some
any	each one	many	no one	somebody
anybody	either	most	nothing	someone
anyone	everybody	much	one	something
anything	everyone	neither	other	such

Interrogative
who, whose, whom, which, what

Demonstrative
this, that, these, those

Grammar Practice

Pronouns 1

■ Antecedents

 For the sentences below, write each pronoun followed by its antecedent.

1. Two friends have their own cars.

2. Louis Braille, inventor of the Braille reading and writing system, died when he was only 35 years old.

3. The gray squirrel that always tries to get the birdseed is getting rather round.

4. The chorus members sang an anthem as they entered the auditorium.

5. Bryce was upset with Tomás when he fumbled the football.

6. The planning committee granted its permission to build an ice rink on the vacant lot.

7. Yasin insists the MP3 player is his.

8. Julian and Terry blame themselves for the team's loss.

9. The dilapidated log shed, which was built during the Depression, should be dismantled carefully.

10. Grandma Moses based much of her painting on childhood memories.

Model

Model the following sentences to practice using phrasal pronouns.

> Let us make one point, that we meet each other with a smile when it is difficult to smile.
> —Mother Teresa

> Talent hits a target no one else can hit; genius hits a target no one else can see.
> —Arthur Schopenhauer

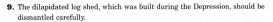

Pronoun

Have students demonstrate their ability to recognize and use pronouns and their antecedents by completing the Grammar Practice activity.

Related Skills Activities

■ **SkillsBook**
Pretest: Pronouns, p. 78
Personal Pronouns, p. 79
Reflexive and Intensive Pronouns, p. 83
Relative Pronouns, p. 84
Indefinite, Interrogative, and Demonstrative Pronouns, p. 86

Answers

1. their, friends
2. he, Louis Braille
3. that, squirrel
4. they, members
5. he, Tomás
6. its, committee
7. his, Yasin
8. themselves; Julian, Terry
9. which, shed
10. her, Grandma Moses

TEKS 11.17A

Pronoun *(continued)*

728.1 Personal Pronouns

A **personal pronoun** can take the place of any noun.

Our coach made her point loud and clear when she raised her voice.

- A **reflexive pronoun** is formed by adding *-self* or *-selves* to a personal pronoun. A reflexive pronoun can be a direct object, an indirect object, an object of the preposition, or a predicate nominative.

    Miss Sally Sunshine loves herself. (direct object of *loves*)

    Tomisha does not seem herself today. (predicate nominative)

- An **intensive pronoun** is a reflexive pronoun that intensifies, or emphasizes, the noun or pronoun it refers to.

    Leo himself taught his children to invest their lives in others.

728.2 Relative Pronouns

A **relative pronoun** relates or connects an adjective clause to the noun or pronoun it modifies.

Students who study regularly get the best grades. Surprise!

The dance, which we had looked forward to for weeks, was canceled.

(The relative pronoun *who* relates the adjective clause to *students; which* relates the adjective clause to *dance*.)

728.3 Indefinite Pronouns

An **indefinite pronoun** refers to unnamed or unknown people or things.

Is there anybody you can remember, anybody you would want to call, anybody who should come looking for you if you were lost?

(The antecedent of *anybody* is unknown.)

728.4 Interrogative Pronouns

An **interrogative pronoun** asks a question.

"What is your name? Where is your house? Who can I call to come and pick you up?"

728.5 Demonstrative Pronouns

A **demonstrative pronoun** points out people, places, or things without naming them.

This shouldn't be too hard   That looks about right.

These are the best ones.   Those ought to be thrown out.

Note: When one of these words precedes a noun, it functions as an adjective, not a pronoun. (See 748.1.)

That movie bothers me. (*That* is an adjective.)

Grammar Practice

Pronouns 2

- Indefinite Pronouns
- Interrogative Pronouns
- Demonstrative Pronouns

 In the sentences below, identify each underlined pronoun as *indefinite, interrogative,* or *demonstrative.*

1. Quan wants to buy those from you.

2. All of the people were asked to leave the stadium aisles.

3. What is that, over there behind the desk?

4. This has been a very positive semester for our junior class.

5. Who thought that anyone in our school would participate in the Olympics?

6. Each season another of the teams tries to break our long-standing record.

7. Neither of us believed a word Claire said.

8. Whose computer just crashed?

9. These look a lot better than the ones you showed me yesterday.

10. A few of the students asked to be excused early.

11. Which is your brother's car?

12. Whom did Denyce choose to travel with her to Washington?

Model

Model the following sentences to practice using indefinite, interrogative, and demonstrative pronouns.

Everybody knows that if you are too careful, you are so occupied in being careful that you are sure to stumble over something.
—Gertrude Stein

Where is the bicycle that you were riding yesterday?

That which is not good for the beehive cannot be good for the bees.
—Marcus Aurelius

Parts of Speech

Pronoun (continued)

Have students suggest additional examples in which a relative pronoun connects an adjective clause to a noun or pronoun. After completing the Grammar Practice activity, have partners discuss their responses using the content-area vocabulary terms *indefinite, interrogative,* and *demonstrative.*

Related Skills Activities

- **Conventions**
    Combining Sentences, p. 87
    Expanding Sentence, p. 88

- *SkillsBook*
    Personal Pronouns, p. 78
    Reflexive and Intensive Pronouns, p. 83
    Relative Pronouns, p. 84
    Indefinite, Interrogative, and Demonstrative
        Pronouns, p. 86

Answers

1. demonstrative
2. indefinite
3. interrogative, demonstrative
4. demonstrative
5. interrogative, indefinite
6. indefinite
7. indefinite
8. interrogative
9. demonstrative
10. indefinite
11. interrogative
12. interrogative

 TEKS **11.17A** Use and understand the function of different types of clauses and phrases; **ELPS 3D** Speak using grade-level content-area vocabulary in context/new English words

Forms of Personal Pronouns

The form of a personal pronoun indicates its *number* (singular or plural), its *person* (first, second, third), its *case* (nominative, possessive, or objective), and its *gender* (masculine, feminine, or neuter).

730.1 Number of a Pronoun

Personal pronouns are singular or plural. The singular personal pronouns include *my, him, he, she, it.* The plural personal pronouns include *we, you, them, our.* (*You* can be singular or plural.) Notice in the caption below that the first *you* is singular and the second *you* is plural.

"Larry, you need to keep all four tires on the road when turning. Are you still with us back there?"

730.2 Person of a Pronoun

The **person** of a pronoun indicates whether the person, place, thing, or idea represented by the pronoun is speaking, is spoken to, or is spoken about.

- **First person** is used in place of the name of the speaker or speakers.

   "I drove the car yesterday," said Peter. "We took a slow trip around the lake, and I didn't make any mistakes!"

- **Second-person** pronouns name the person or persons spoken to.

   "You went to the movies yesterday, and you didn't call me? You need to check your messages more often."

- **Third-person** pronouns name the person or thing spoken about.

   She had hardly realized the news, further than to understand that she had been brought . . . face to face with something unexpected and final. It did not even occur to her to ask for any explanation.
   —Joseph Conrad, "The Idiots"

Grammar Practice

Pronouns 3

- Number of a Pronoun
- Person of a Pronoun

 Identify the person and number of each underlined pronoun.

1. "You better get up!" Tia Rose said when she noticed that I had hit the "snooze" button one more time.

2. We don't know how long it will take to get to Utah.

3. She ran down the hallway shouting, "Help! Fire!"

4. Whistles and exclamations arose when they saw the motorcycle that Jack bought.

5. I am ordering pizzas to celebrate the end of exams.

6. "Where are you taking them?" Mom asked the boys.

7. It never occurred to him to ask where she had been.

8. I can't understand why Gina won't talk to them.

9. I lost my biology homework.

10. "Will you please try to visit us more often?" Grandpa asked Rob.

Model

Model the following sentences to practice using first-person pronouns.

   Call me Ishmael. Some years ago—never mind how long precisely—having little or no money in my purse, and nothing particular to interest me on shore, I thought I would sail about a little and see the watery part of the world.
   —Herman Melville, *Moby Dick*

Forms of Personal Pronouns

As needed, point out and discuss sight vocabulary such as the personal pronouns *I, we, you, he, she,* and *it,* as well as *my, you,* and *them.* Guide students to understand the terms *first person, second person,* and *third person* in the context of grammar.

Related Skills Activities

- **SkillsBook**
   Number and Person of a Pronoun, p. 80

Answers

1. second person singular
2. first person plural
3. third person singular
4. third person plural
5. first person singular
6. second person plural, third person plural
7. third person singular, third person singular, third person singular
8. first person singular, third person plural
9. first person singular, first person singular
10. second person singular, first person plural

732

732.1 Case of a Pronoun

The **case** of each pronoun tells how it is related to the other words used with it. There are three cases: *nominative, possessive,* and *objective.*

- A **nominative case** pronoun can be the subject of a clause. The following are nominative forms: *I, you, he, she, it, we, they.*

  I like life when things go well. You must live life in order to love life.

A nominative pronoun is a *predicate nominative* if it follows a "be" verb (*am, is, are, was, were, be, being, been*) or another linking verb (*appear, become, feel,* etc.) and renames the subject.

  "Oh, it's only she who scared me just now," said Mama to Papa, glancing over her shoulder.
  "Yes, it is I," said Mai in a superior tone.

- **Possessive case** pronouns show possession or ownership. Apostrophes, however, are not used with personal pronouns. (Pronouns in the possessive case can also be classified as adjectives.)

  But as I placed my hand upon his shoulder, there came a strong shudder over his whole person.
  —Edgar Allan Poe, "The Fall of the House of Usher"

- An **objective case** pronoun can be a direct object, an indirect object, or an object of the preposition.

  The kids loved it! We lit a campfire for them and told them old ghost stories. (*It* is the direct object of the verb *loved. Them* is the object of the preposition *for* and the indirect object of the verb *told.*)

Number, Person, and Case of Personal Pronouns

	Nominative	Possessive	Objective
First Person Singular	I	my, mine	me
Second Person Singular	you	your, yours	you
Third Person Singular	he	his	him
	she	her, hers	her
	it	its	it
	Nominative	Possessive	Objective
First Person Plural	we	our, ours	us
Second Person Plural	you	your, yours	you
Third Person Plural	they	their, theirs	them

732.2 Gender of a Pronoun

Gender indicates whether a pronoun is masculine, feminine, or neuter.

  Masculine: **he him his**   Feminine: **she her hers**
  Neuter (without gender): **it its**

Grammar Practice

Pronouns 4

- Case of a Pronoun
- Gender of a Pronoun

Identify each underlined pronoun as *nominative, possessive,* or *objective.* If the pronoun is gender specific, write its gender.

Maddie, **(1)** my best friend, and I were sitting in **(2)** our school's cafeteria and talking about **(3)** her recent visit to Texas A&M University. **(4)** She wants to go there after graduation.

(5) "We went to Aggieland on Saturday," Maddie told me. **(6)** "It was so cool! A student guide took **(7)** us on a tour of the campus. **(8)** He showed us **(9)** their classrooms, the library, and other campus buildings. Then, one of the girls took **(10)** me to see the dorms."

"What were **(11)** they like?" I asked.

"The only room I saw was **(12)** hers," Maddie answered. "It was about as big as **(13)** your bedroom at home, and it had **(14)** its own bathroom. I wanted it to be **(15)** mine!"

"I wish I could have gone with **(16)** you," I said.

(17) "I do, too," Maddie replied. "All of **(18)** you can visit me there someday."

Model

Model the following sentences to practice using objective case pronouns.

Dreams are illustrations . . . from the book your soul is writing about you.
—Marsha Norman

There are two ways of spreading light: to be the candle or the mirror that reflects it.
—Edith Wharton

Forms of Personal Pronouns (continued)

As needed, point out and discuss sight vocabulary for personal pronouns listed in the blue chart on SE page 732.

Related Skills Activities

- **SkillsBook**
Nominative, Possessive, and Objective Cases of Pronouns, p. 82

ELPS 4C Develop basic sight vocabulary

Answers

1. possessive
2. possessive
3. possessive, feminine
4. nominative, feminine
5. nominative
6. nominative, neuter
7. objective
8. nominative, masculine
9. possessive
10. objective
11. nominative
12. possessive, feminine
13. possessive
14. possessive, neuter
15. possessive
16. objective
17. nominative
18. objective

Verb

A **verb** is a word that expresses action (*run, carried, declared*) or state of being (*is, are, seemed*).

Classes of Verbs

734.1 Linking Verbs

A **linking verb** links the subject to a noun or an adjective in the predicate.

> In the outfield, the boy felt confident.
> He was the best fielder around.

Common Linking Verbs						
is	are	was	were	be	been	am

Additional Linking Verbs					
smell	seem	grow	become	appear	sound
taste	feel	get	remain	stay	look	turn

Note: The verbs listed as "additional linking verbs" function as linking verbs when they do not show actual action. An adjective usually follows these linking verbs. (When they do show action, an adverb or a direct object may follow them. In this case, they are action verbs.)

LINKING: This fruit smells rotten.
ACTION: Maya always smells fruit carefully before eating it.

734.2 Auxiliary Verbs

Auxiliary verbs, or helping verbs, are used to form some of the **tenses** (738.3), the **mood** (744.1), and the **voice** (742.2) of the main verb. (In the example below, the auxiliary verbs are in red; the main verbs are in blue.)

> The long procession was led by white-robed priests, their faces streaked with red and yellow and white ash. By this time the flames had stopped spurting, and the pit consisted of a red-hot mass of burning wood, which attendants were leveling with long branches.
> —Leonard Feinberg, "Fire Walking in Ceylon"

Common Auxiliary Verbs						
is	was	being	did	have	would	shall	might
am	were	been	does	had	could	can	must
are	be	do	has	should	will	may	

Grammar Practice

Verbs 1

- Linking Verbs
- Auxiliary Verbs

Write whether each underlined word is a linking verb or an auxiliary verb.

Some "truths" **(1)** are not worth taking too seriously. For example, perhaps you have **(2)** been told that chewing gum stays in your digestive system for seven years. In reality, your body processes it at the same rate as it does other food. **(3)** Do you believe that you use only 10 percent of your brain? That's another tall tale. Electronic images of the human brain **(4)** appear so colorful because of all the activity going on (even when its host **(5)** is sleeping!).

On the other hand, you **(6)** can learn something from other "legends" that are actually true. One **(7)** is the unfortunate death of a certain cowboy who hawked cigarettes—he died of lung cancer. Perhaps you've **(8)** become smart as a result of eating fish—a "brain food" that contains nutrients very important for brain function. And if you **(9)** are watching your weight, eating celery really does burn more calories than you consume. In general, it would **(10)** be smart for people to verify stories they hear.

Learning Language

Work with a partner. Create a T-chart; label one column "Linking Verbs" and one column "Auxiliary Verbs." Complete the above activity together, explaining to each other why each verb is a linking or an auxiliary verb. Then, individually, write two pairs of sentences that show the difference between a linking verb and an action verb. Exchange and read each other's sentences, explaining why each example is correct.

Related Skills Activities

- **Voice**
  Choosing Vivid Verbs, p. 82

- **SkillsBook**
  Pretest: Verbs, p. 88
  Main Verbs and Auxiliary Verbs, p. 89
  Linking Verbs, Predicate Nouns and Predicate Adjectives, p. 90
  Using Adverbs vs. Alternatives, p. 112

Answers

1. linking
2. auxiliary
3. auxiliary
4. linking
5. auxiliary
6. auxiliary
7. linking
8. linking
9. auxiliary
10. linking

Learning Language

Display environmental print such as a T-chart showing the common linking and auxiliary verbs to help students incorporate these verbs into their sight vocabulary. Suggest that students refer to the chart to help them as they write their sentences and explain their use of linking and auxiliary verbs.

736

736.1 Action Verbs: Transitive and Intransitive

An **intransitive verb** communicates an action that is complete in itself. It does not need an object to receive the action.

> The boy flew on his skateboard. He jumped and flipped and twisted.

A **transitive verb** (red) is an action verb that needs an object (blue) to complete its meaning.

> The city council passed a strict noise ordinance.
> Raul takes pictures for the student paper.

While some action verbs are only transitive *or* intransitive, some can be either, depending on how they are used.

> He finally stopped to rest. (intransitive)
> He finally stopped the show. (transitive)

736.2 Objects with Transitive Verbs

- A **direct object** receives the action of a transitive verb directly from the subject. Without it, the transitive verb's meaning is incomplete.

> The boy kicked his skateboard forward. (*Skateboard* is the direct object.)
> Then he put one foot on it and rode like a pro.

- An **indirect object** also receives the action of a transitive verb, but indirectly. An indirect object names the person *to whom* or *for whom* something is done. (An indirect object can also name the thing *to what* or *for what* something is done.)

> Ms. Oakfield showed us pictures of the solar system.
> (*Us* is the indirect object.)
> She gave Tony an A on his project.

Note: When the word naming the indirect receiver of the action is in a prepositional phrase, it is no longer considered an indirect object.

> Ms. Oakfield showed pictures of the solar system to us.
> (*Us* is the object of the preposition *to*.)

Grammar Practice

Verbs 2

- Transitive and Intransitive Verbs
- Direct and Indirect Objects

 Write whether each underlined verb is transitive or intransitive. For a transitive verb, also write its direct object. If there is an indirect object, write it and label it "IO."

Health insurance companies **(1)** exist to pay the medical costs of the people they insure. An insurer **(2)** charges customers a monthly fee—say $200—for coverage. Some members of a group **(3)** will not use $2,400 for medical services in a particular year, and others will use more. In this way, the costs of medical care are spread out among a certain population, and no one who gets sick **(4)** will have unmanageable expenses.

A problem **(5)** arises, however, when an insurance company **(6)** deems its corporate profits more important than the welfare of the people who **(7)** apply for coverage. In cases where an insurance company knows that it **(8)** will pay considerable benefits (for instance, for a person with a chronic disease such as diabetes), the company **(9)** can deny coverage in the first place. Therefore, the people who **(10)** need insurance the most have the hardest time getting it. It's a controversial issue that demands more attention.

Model

Model the following sentences to practice writing sentences with direct and indirect objects.

> Those two won't even give you the time of day unless you have something to trade.
> —Sue Grafton, *M Is for Malice*

> Show me a sane man and I will cure him for you.
> —C. G. Jung

Related Skills Activities

- **SkillsBook**
  Transitive and Intransitive Verbs, p. 97
  Direct and Indirect Objects, p. 98

Answers

1. intransitive
2. transitive, fee, IO customers
3. transitive, $2,400
4. transitive, expenses
5. intransitive
6. transitive, profits
7. intransitive
8. transitive, benefits
9. transitive, coverage
10. transitive, insurance

Forms of Verbs

A verb has different forms depending on its *number, person, tense, voice,* and *mood.*

738.1 Number of a Verb

Number indicates whether a verb is singular or plural. In a clause, the verb (in blue below) and its subject (in red) must both be singular or both be plural.

- **Singular**
  One large island floats off Italy's "toe."
  Italy's northern countryside includes the truly spectacular Alps.

- **Plural**
  Five small islands float inside Michigan's "thumb."
  The Porcupine Mountains rise above the shores of Lake Superior.

738.2 Person of a Verb

Person indicates whether the subject of the verb is first, second, or third person (is speaking, is spoken to, or is spoken about). The form of the verb usually changes only when a present-tense verb is used with a third-person singular subject.

	Singular	Plural
First Person	I sniff	we sniff
Second Person	you sniff	you sniff
Third Person	he/she/it sniffs	they sniff

738.3 Tense of a Verb

Tense indicates time. Each verb has three principal parts: the *present, past,* and *past participle.* All six tenses are formed from these principal parts. The past and past participle of regular verbs are formed by adding *ed* to the present form. For irregular verbs, the past and past participle are usually different words; however, a few have the same form in all three principal parts (see 740.2).

738.4 Simple Tenses

- **Present tense** expresses action that is happening at the present time, or action that happens continually, regularly.
  In September, sophomores smirk and joke about the "little freshies."

- **Past tense** expresses action that was completed at a particular time in the past.
  They forgot that just ninety days separated them from freshman status.

- **Future tense** expresses action that will take place in the future.
  They will recall this in three years when they will be freshmen again.

Grammar Practice

Verbs 3

- Number of a Verb
- Person of a Verb
- Simple Tenses

 Write the person and number of each underlined verb. Also write its tense.

1. Tahi <u>will start</u> college next fall.

2. We <u>listen</u> to books on CD whenever Dad <u>drives</u> us to Michigan.

3. Peter Gabriel <u>played</u> in the band Genesis in the 1970s.

4. Darnell, please <u>vacuum</u> the stairs before you leave.

5. A garbled message <u>popped</u> onto the computer screen; then the computer crashed.

6. Bachelor's buttons <u>are</u> not true perennial flowers, but they <u>will return</u> year after year.

7. Turning onto Cuba Road, I <u>reached</u> for the map in the glove box.

8. The moon <u>has</u> an orange halo tonight.

9. Giraffes <u>have</u> the same number of vertebrae as humans do.

10. Keisha's dog <u>wore</u> spotted pajamas in the animal shelter parade.

Model

Model the following sentences to practice using the correct present-tense verb form with third-person singular subjects.

Asking a working writer what he thinks about critics is like asking a lamppost how it feels about dogs.
—Christopher Hampton

The time to stop talking is when the other person nods his head affirmatively but says nothing.
—Henry S. Haskins

Forms of Verbs

Have students complete the Grammar Practice activity to demonstrate their understanding of verb tenses. Remind students to edit for consistent use of verb tenses whenever they write.

Related Skills Activities

- ***SkillsBook***
  Present, Past, and Future Tense Verbs, p. 93
  All Six Verb Tenses, p. 95

Answers

1. third person singular, future tense
2. first person plural, present tense; third person singular, present tense
3. third person singular, past tense
4. second person singular, present tense
5. third person singular, past tense
6. third person plural, present tense; third person plural, future tense
7. first person singular, past tense
8. third person singular, present tense
9. third person plural, present tense
10. third person singular, past tense

ELPS 5D Edit writing for standard grammar and usage/verb tenses

Forms of Verbs (continued)

740.1 Perfect Tenses

- **Present perfect tense** expresses action that began in the past but continues in the present or is completed in the present.
  > Our boat has weathered worse storms than this one.

- **Past perfect tense** expresses an action in the past that occurred before another past action.
  > They reported, wrongly, that the hurricane had missed the island.

- **Future perfect tense** expresses action that will begin in the future and be completed by a specific time in the future.
  > By this time tomorrow, the hurricane will have smashed into the coast.

740.2 Irregular Verbs

Common Irregular Verbs and Their Principal Parts

Present Tense	Past Tense	Past Participle	Present Tense	Past Tense	Past Participle	Present Tense	Past Tense	Past Participle
am, be	was, were	been	go	went	gone	shrink	shrank	shrunk
begin	began	begun	grow	grew	grown	sing	sang, sung	sung
bite	bit	bitten	hang	hanged	hanged	sink	sank, sunk	sunk
blow	blew	blown	(execute)			sit	sat	sat
break	broke	broken	hang	hung	hung	slay	slew	slain
bring	brought	brought	(suspend)			speak	spoke	spoken
buy	bought	bought	hide	hid	hidden, hid	spring	sprang,	sprung
catch	caught	caught	know	knew	known		sprung	
choose	chose	chosen	lay	laid	laid	steal	stole	stolen
come	came	come	lead	led	led	strive	strove	striven
dive	dove	dived	leave	left	left	swear	swore	sworn
do	did	done	lie	lay	lain	swim	swam	swum
draw	drew	drawn	(recline)			swing	swung	swung
drink	drank	drunk	lie	lied	lied	take	took	taken
drive	drove	driven	(deceive)			teach	taught	taught
eat	ate	eaten	lose	lost	lost	tear	tore	torn
fall	fell	fallen	make	made	made	throw	threw	thrown
fight	fought	fought	ride	rode	ridden	wake	waked,	waked,
flee	fled	fled	ring	rang	rung		woke	woken
fly	flew	flown	rise	rose	risen	wear	wore	worn
forsake	forsook	forsaken	run	ran	run	weave	weaved,	weaved,
freeze	froze	frozen	see	saw	seen		wove	woven
get	got	gotten	shake	shook	shaken	wring	wrung	wrung
give	gave	given	show	showed	shown	write	wrote	written

These verbs are the same in all principal parts: *burst, cost, cut, hurt, let, put, set,* and *spread.*

Grammar Practice

Verbs 4

- Perfect Tenses
- Irregular Verbs

For each sentence, copy the verb phrase in parentheses, using the past participle of the irregular verb that appears in italics. Then label the tense of each verb (present perfect, past perfect, or future perfect).

1. After Ahmed worked on the car, it was really no surprise to see that the oil pan (had *spring*) a leak.

2. You (will have *spread*) the lawn fertilizer by this weekend, right?

3. I thought I (had *lay*) the blanket over the back of the couch, but it's gone now.

4. The refugees (have *flee*) their country for political reasons.

5. Rebels (had *slay*) family members in a nearby town.

6. Ladonna (has *come*) to my house after school since we were in fifth grade.

7. I hope the pond (will have *freeze*) by the time we return next month.

8. Either your sweaters (have *shrink*) lately, or you are growing really fast.

9. I would (have *go*) to the mall with you if you had asked.

10. My dog never (has *bite*) anyone, but I think she would if she were provoked.

11. In Inez's opinion, a pass to the local pool shouldn't (have *cost*) that much.

12. As soon as he (had *lie*) on the sofa, he started snoring.

Model

Model the following sentences to practice using past and present perfect-tense verbs.

> When I took office, only high energy physicists had ever heard of what is called the World Wide Web . . . now even my cat has its own page.
> —Bill Clinton

> My passport photo is one of the most remarkable photographs I have ever seen—no retouching, no shadows, no flattery—just stark me.
> —Anne Morrow Lindbergh

Forms of Verbs (continued)

Have students complete the Grammar Practice activity to demonstrate their understanding of verb tenses. Remind students to edit for consistent use of verb tenses whenever they write.

Related Skills Activities

- **SkillsBook**
  Perfect Tense Verbs, p. 94
  All Six Verb Tenses, p. 95
  Irregular Verbs 1 and 2, pp. 100–101

Answers

1. had sprung, past perfect
2. will have spread, future perfect
3. had laid, past perfect
4. have fled, present perfect
5. had slain, past perfect
6. has come, present perfect
7. will have frozen, future perfect
8. have shrunk, present perfect
9. have gone, present perfect
10. has bitten, present perfect
11. have cost, present perfect
12. had lain, past perfect

ELPS 5D Edit writing for standard grammar and usage/verb tenses

742.1 Continuous Tenses

- A **present continuous tense** verb expresses action that is not completed at the time of stating it. The present continuous tense is formed by adding *am, is,* or *are* to the *-ing* form of the main verb.

  Scientists are learning a great deal from their study of the sky.

- A **past continuous tense** verb expresses action that was happening at a certain time in the past. This tense is formed by adding *was* or *were* to the *-ing* form of the main verb.

  Astronomers were beginning their quest for knowledge hundreds of years ago.

- A **future continuous tense** verb expresses action that will take place at a certain time in the future. This tense is formed by adding *will be* to the *-ing* form of the main verb.

  Someday astronauts will be going to Mars.

  This tense can also be formed by adding a phrase noting the future *(are going to)* plus *be* to the *-ing* form of the main verb.

  They are going to be performing many experiments.

742.2 Voice of a Verb

Voice indicates whether the subject is acting or being acted upon.

- **Active voice** indicates that the subject of the verb is, has been, or will be doing something.

  For many years Lou Brock held the base-stealing record.

Active voice makes your writing more direct and lively.

- **Passive voice** indicates that the subject of the verb is being, has been, or will be acted upon.

  For many years the base-stealing record was held by Lou Brock.

Note: With a passive verb, the person or thing creating the action is not always stated.

The ordinance was overturned. (Who did the overturning?)

Tense	Active Voice Singular	Plural	Passive Voice Singular	Plural
Present	I see you see he/she/it sees	we see you see they see	I am seen you are seen he/she/it is seen	we are seen you are seen they are seen
Past	I/he saw you saw	we/they saw you saw	I/it was seen you were seen	we/they were seen you were seen
Future	I/you/he will see	we/you/they will see	I/you/it will be seen	we/you/they will be seen

---

Grammar Practice

Verbs 5

- Active and Passive Verbs

In the following paragraphs, if any sentence or part of a sentence is in the passive voice, rewrite it in the active voice. Write "active" if it is already in the active voice.

(1) Few realize the importance that knots and cordage have played in the world's history. **(2)** If it had not been for these simple and everyday things, which as a rule are given far too little consideration, the human race could never have developed beyond savages. **(3)** Indeed, I am not sure, but it would be safe to state that the real difference between civilized and savage man consists largely in the knowledge of knots and rope work. **(4)** No cloth could be woven, no net or seine knitted, no bow strung, and no craft sailed on lake or sea without numerous knots and proper lines or ropes. **(5)** Columbus himself would have been far more handicapped without knots than without a compass.

(6) History abounds with mention of knots, and in the eighth book of *The Odyssey,* Ulysses is represented as securing various articles of raiment by a rope fastened in a "knot closed with Circean art." **(7)** As further proof of the prominence the ancients gave to knots, the famous Gordian Knot may be mentioned. **(8)** Probably no one will ever learn just how this fabulous knot was tied. **(9)** Like many modern knots, it was doubtless far easier for Alexander to cut it than to untie it.

From *Knots, Splices, and Rope Work,* by A. Hyatt Verrill

Learning Language

Choose a piece of your own writing. Read it aloud to a partner, discussing the sentences one-by-one to decide if they are in the active or the passive voice. Repeat with a piece of your partner's writing. Then work together to rewrite any sentences that might be better if restated in the active voice. Finally, review your responses to the Practice activity above, comparing and explaining your answers together.

Related Skills Activities

- **Voice**
  Choosing Vivid Verbs, p. 82

- ***SkillsBook***
  Active and Passive Voice, p. 92

Answers

1. active
2. . . . things, to which people give too little consideration, . . .
3. active
4. No one could weave cloth, knit net or seine, string a bow, or sail on a lake or sea without numerous knots and proper lines or ropes.
5. active
6. . . . Ulysses secures various articles . . . by fastening a rope in . . .

Answers (continued)

7. The famous Gordian Knot gives further proof of the prominence the ancients gave to knots.
8. Probably no one will ever learn how someone tied this fabulous knot.
9. active

Learning Language

Circulate as partners analyze and discuss their use of active and passive voice, reminding them to express ideas with specificity and detail. Provide help as needed to guide students to rewrite sentences using an active voice. Remind them to edit for consistent use of verb tenses whenever they write.

744.1 Mood of a Verb

The **mood** of a verb indicates the tone or attitude with which a statement is made.

- **Indicative mood** is used to state a fact or to ask a question.

  I shouted across the canyon sometimes, hoping to hear a voice whisper to me across the emptiness. Only the echo of my voice came back.

- **Imperative mood** is used to give a command.

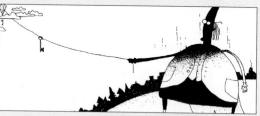

"Whatever you do, don't fly your kite during a storm."
—Mrs. Abiah Franklin

- **Subjunctive mood** is used to express several conditions.

  Use the subjunctive *were* to express a condition that is contrary to fact.
  If I were finished with my report, I could go to the movie.

  Use the subjunctive *were* after *as though* or *as if* to express an unreal condition.
  Mrs. Young acted as if she were sixteen again.

  Use the subjunctive *be* in "that" clauses to express necessity, legal decisions, or parliamentary motions.
  "It is moved and supported that no more than 6 million quad be used to explore the planet Earth."

  "Ridiculous! Knowing earthlings is bound to help us understand ourselves! Therefore, I move that the sum be amended to 12 million quad."

  "Stupidity! I move that all missions be postponed until we have living proof of life on Earth."

Grammar Practice

Verbs 6

- Mood of a Verb

 Write whether each statement shows indicative, imperative, or subjunctive mood.

1. He talks about Yale as if he were already a student there.
2. The first show starts at 6:45 this Friday night.
3. Take a seat in the front section of the auditorium.
4. Do research to find out what happened on the day you were born.
5. What's the name of that new CD you bought?
6. Read chapter 8 before the test on Friday.
7. I move that the meeting be postponed until next month.
8. The answer to the last question was perfectly clear.
9. That game was the best one we've played all year!
10. Notice how my grades have improved this semester.
11. It looked as though she were floating in midair.
12. My parents love music by the Grateful Dead.

Model

Model the following sentences to practice using the imperative mood.

Always behave like a duck—keep calm and unruffled on the surface but paddle like the devil underneath.
—Jacob Braude

Have the courage to act instead of react.
—Earlene Larson Jenks

Answers

1. subjunctive
2. indicative
3. imperative
4. imperative
5. indicative
6. imperative
7. subjunctive
8. indicative
9. indicative
10. imperative
11. subjunctive
12. indicative

746

Verbals

A **verbal** is a word that is derived from a verb but does not function as a verb in a sentence. Instead, a verbal acts as another part of speech—noun, adjective, or adverb. There are three types of verbals: *gerunds, infinitives,* and *participles.* Each is often part of a verbal phrase.

746.1 Gerunds

A **gerund** is a verb form that ends in *ing* and is used as a noun.

Swimming **is my favorite pastime.** (subject)
I began swimming **at the age of six months.**
(direct object)
The hardest part of swimming **is the resulting sore muscles.**
(object of the preposition *of*)
Swimming **in chlorinated pools makes my eyes red.**
(gerund phrase used as a subject)

746.2 Infinitives

An **infinitive** is a verb form that is usually introduced by *to;* the infinitive may be used as a noun, an adjective, or an adverb.

Most people find it easy to swim. (adverb modifying an adjective)
To swim the English Channel **must be a thrill.** (infinitive phrase as noun)
The urge to swim in tropical waters **is more common.** (infinitive phrase as adjective)

746.3 Participles

A **participle** is a verb form ending in *ing* or *ed* that acts as an adjective.

The workers raking leaves **are tired and hungry.**
(participial phrase modifies *workers*)
The bags full of raked **leaves are evidence of their hard work.**
(participle modifies *leaves*)
Smiling **faces greeted my father when he returned from a business trip.**
(participle modifying *faces*)

Note: The past participle of an irregular verb can also act as an adjective:
That rake is obviously broken.

747

ELPS 3A, 3G, 3H, 5B

Parts of Speech   **747**

Grammar Practice

Verbals

■ Verbals

Find and write the verbal in each sentence below. Identify it as a *gerund*, a *participle*, or an *infinitive*.

1. Falling temperatures will result in icy roads this afternoon.
2. Tyrell likes to experiment with the color of his hair.
3. Avoid watering the plants too much during the winter months.
4. It's a known fact that Leah has been accepted at Princeton.
5. Dan dreams of making money with his photography.
6. Feeling defeated, Jacinda dragged herself to the locker room.
7. To succeed in sales, knowledge of and belief in the product are essential.
8. You must cross the bridge over the Des Plaines River to get there.
9. Going to the mall is Shawn's therapy when she feels down.
10. I was driving Mom's car when, rounding the curve, I saw an accident that had just happened.

Learning Language

Review your responses to the Practice activity with a partner. Explain your responses together. Then choose one example of each verbal—gerund, participle, infinitive—and write a new sentence using each one. Read your sentences aloud to each other, explaining why each one is correct.

Related Skills Activities

■ **Conventions**
Combining Sentences, p. 87
Expanding Sentences, p. 88

■ *SkillsBook*
Verbals: Gerund, Infinitives, and Participles, p. 99

Answers

1. falling, participle
2. to experiment, infinitive
3. watering, gerund
4. known, participle
5. making, gerund
6. feeling, participle
7. To succeed, infinitive
8. to get, infinitive
9. Going, gerund
10. rounding, participle

Learning Language

Before partners begin their discussion, read aloud the terms *gerund, participle,* and *infinitive* and work with students to practice producing the sounds of these newly acquired vocabulary words. Remind partners to use the terms as they express their ideas about the Grammar Practice activity. Tell students to be prepared to use specificity and detail to explain their use of verbals in the sentences they write.

 ELPS 3A Practice producing sounds of newly acquired vocabulary to pronounce English words; **3G** Express ideas; **3H** Describe with increasing specificity and detail; **5B** Write using newly acquired basic and content-based grade-level vocabulary

Adjective

An **adjective** describes or modifies a noun or a pronoun. The articles *a, an,* and *the* are also adjectives.

The young **driver** peeked through the big
steering wheel.

(*The* and *young* modify *driver;* the and *big* modify *steering wheel.*)

748.1 Types of Adjectives

A **proper adjective** is created from a proper noun and is capitalized.

In Canada (proper noun), **you will find many cultures and climates.**

Canadian (proper adjective) **winters can be harsh.**

A **predicate adjective** follows a form of the "be" verb (or other linking verb) and describes the subject.

Late autumn seems grim **to those who love summer.** (*Grim* modifies *autumn.*)

Note: Some words can be either adjectives or pronouns (*that, these, all, each, both, many, some,* and so on). These words are adjectives when they come before the nouns they modify; they are pronouns when they stand alone.

Jiao made both **goals.** (*Both* modifies *goals;* it is an adjective.)

Both **were scored in the final period.** (*Both* stands alone; it is a pronoun.)

748.2 Forms of Adjectives

Adjectives have three forms: *positive, comparative,* and *superlative.*

■ The **positive form** describes a noun or a pronoun without comparing it to anyone or anything else.

The first game was long **and** tiresome.

■ The **comparative form** (*-er, more,* or *less*) compares two persons, places, things, or ideas.

The second game was longer **and** more tiresome **than the first.**

■ The **superlative form** (*-est, most,* or *least*) compares three or more persons, places, things, or ideas.

The third game was the longest **and** most tiresome **of all.**

Note: Use *more* and *most* (or *less* and *least*)—instead of adding a suffix—with many adjectives of two or more syllables.

Positive	Comparative	Superlative
big	bigger	biggest
helpful	more helpful	most helpful
painful	less painful	least painful

Grammar Practice

Adjectives

- Types of Adjectives
- Forms of Adjectives

 Write the adjectives (not including articles) in each of the following sentences. Label predicate adjectives, comparative adjectives, and superlative adjectives.

1. This Seattle market offers some of the freshest fish I've ever had.

2. They sell two types of sole from Africa: the slender Agulhas sole and the round West Coast sole.

3. You will also find snoek there, an oily fish that is popular with South African people.

4. Norwegian sardines are young herrings that are smaller than full-grown ones.

5. Along with other varieties caught along the North American West Coast, salmon is a favorite treat for Seattlites.

6. Thomas Beecham said, "Movie music is noise . . . even more painful than my sciatica."

7. Upgrading the ancient computers is the most problematic issue on the agenda.

8. In the dead of gray winter, frequent dreams of cloudless blue skies and lush green grass keep me sane.

Model

Model the following sentences to practice using adjectives well.

Small and slightly plump, she had the perfect skin and apple cheeks of a picture poster.

—Maeve Binchy, *Firefly Summer*

Life, for all its raw talent, has little sense of structure. It creates amazing textures, but it can't be counted on for snappy beginnings or good endings either.

—Larry McMurtry

Related Skills Activities

■ **Voice**
Using Effective Modifiers, p. 80

■ *SkillsBook*
Pretest: Adjectives and Adverbs, p. 104
Adjectives (Article), p. 105
Forms of Adjectives, p. 106
Effective Adjectives, p. 107

Answers

1. This, Seattle, freshest—superlative
2. two, slender, Agulhas, round, West Coast
3. oily, popular—predicate, South African
4. Norwegian, young, smaller—comparative and predicate, full-grown
5. other, North American, West, favorite
6. Movie, more painful—comparative
7. ancient, most problematic—superlative
8. gray, frequent, cloudless, blue, lush, green, sane

Adverb

An **adverb** describes or modifies a verb, an adjective, or another adverb.

She sneezed loudly. (*Loudly* modifies the verb *sneezed*.)

Her sneezes are really **dramatic**. (*Really* modifies the adjective *dramatic*.)

The sneeze exploded very **noisily**. (*Very* modifies the adverb *noisily*.)

An adverb usually tells *when, where, how,* or *how much.*

750.1 Types of Adverbs

Adverbs can be cataloged in four basic ways: *time, place, manner,* and *degree.*

Time (These adverbs tell *when, how often,* and *how long.*)

today, yesterday   daily, weekly   briefly, eternally

Place (These adverbs tell *where, to where,* and *from where.*)

here, there   nearby, beyond   backward, forward

Manner (These adverbs often end in *ly* and tell *how* something is done.)

precisely   effectively   regally   smoothly   well

Degree (These adverbs tell *how much* or *how little.*)

substantially   greatly   entirely   partly   too

Note: Some adverbs can be written with or without the *ly* ending. When in doubt, use the *ly* form.

slow, slowly   loud, loudly   fair, fairly   tight, tightly   quick, quickly

750.2 Forms of Adverbs

Adverbs of manner have three forms: *positive, comparative,* and *superlative.*

■ The **positive form** describes a verb, an adjective, or another adverb without comparing it to anyone or anything else.

Model X vacuum cleans well **and runs** quietly.

■ The **comparative form** (*-er, more,* or *less*) compares how two things are done.

Model Y vacuum cleans better **and runs** more quietly **than model X does.**

■ The **superlative form** (*-est, most,* or *least*) compares how three or more things are done.

Model Z vacuum cleans best **and runs** most quietly **of all.**

Irregular Forms		
Positive	Comparative	Superlative
well	better	best
fast	faster	fastest
remorsefully	more remorsefully	most remorsefully

Grammar Practice

Adverbs

■ Types of Adverbs
■ Forms of Adverbs

 Write the 18 adverbs you'll find in the following paragraphs. Identify each as an adverb of time, place, manner, or degree. For an adverb of manner, also identify it as positive, comparative, or superlative.

Direction on food safety is badly needed in underdeveloped countries. There, diarrhea caused by contaminated food and water is a leading cause of death. With that in mind, the World Health Organization (WHO) recently revised a poster, available in 32 languages, to more clearly show some simple rules for safe food handling and preparation.

The cardinal rule, of course, involves cleanliness. Dangerous germs (widely found in soil, water, animals, and people) can be transmitted quite easily to food via unwashed hands. In addition, dishrags, utensils, and cutting boards need frequent washing. WHO also pushes for the use of safe water and raw materials.

Temperature is the next concern. Proper cooking kills dangerous microorganisms the best—but it's also important to keep cooked and raw food at a safe temperature. Never leave cooked food unrefrigerated for longer than two hours, and do not thaw frozen food at room temperature.

Finally, do not handle raw food and cooked food together. Meat, poultry, and seafood can be especially dangerous; they should always be separated from other foods during their preparation. These simple steps can dramatically reduce food- and water-borne illness here and around the world.

Model

Model these sentences to practice using comparative and superlative adverbs.

It was one of those perfect English autumnal days that occur more frequently **in memory than in life.**

—P. D. James

Those who are urged to feel afraid, very **afraid, have both the greatest sense of independence and the** most **finely honed skepticism about government.**

—Ellen Goodman

Adverb

Have students demonstrate understanding of the types and forms of adverbs by completing the Grammar Practice activity. Have them work with partners to check their responses. Remind them to monitor their understanding of the discussion and to seek clarification as needed.

Related Skills Activities

■ **Voice**
Using Effective Modifiers, p. 80

■ *SkillsBook*
Adverbs, p. 109
Forms of Adverbs, p. 111

Answers

1. badly, manner—positive
2. There, place
3. recently, time
4. more clearly, manner—comparative
5. widely, degree
6. quite, degree
7. easily, manner—positive
8. best, manner—superlative
9. also, degree
10. Never, time
11. not, degree
12. Finally, time
13. not, degree
14. together, manner—positive
15. especially, degree
16. always, time
17. dramatically, manner—positive
18. here, place

Preposition

A **preposition** is the first word (or group of words) in a prepositional phrase. It shows the relationship between its object (a noun or a pronoun that follows the preposition) and another word in the sentence. The first noun or pronoun following a preposition is its object.

> To make a mustache, Natasha placed the hairy caterpillar **under** her nose.
> (*Under* shows the relationship between the verb, *placed*, and the object of the preposition, *nose*.)

> The drowsy insect clung obediently **to** the girl's upper lip.
> (The first noun following the preposition *to* is *lip; lip* is the object of the preposition.)

752.1 Prepositional Phrases

A **prepositional phrase** includes the preposition, the object of the preposition, and the modifiers of the object. A prepositional phrase functions as an adverb or as an adjective.

> Some people **run** away from caterpillars.
> (The phrase functions as an adverb and modifies the verb *run*.)

> However, little **kids** with inquisitive minds **enjoy their company**.
> (The phrase functions as an adjective and modifies the noun *kids*.)

Note: A preposition is always followed by an object; if there is no object, the word is an adverb, not a preposition.

> Natasha never **played** with caterpillars **before**. (The word *before* is not followed by an object; therefore, it functions as an adverb that modifies *played*, a verb.)

Common Prepositions

aboard	before	from	of	save
about	behind	from among	off	since
above	below	from between	on	subsequent to
according to	beneath	from under	on account of	through
across	beside	in	on behalf of	throughout
across from	besides	in addition to	onto	to
after	between	in back of	on top of	together with
against	beyond	in behalf of	opposite	toward
along	by	in front of	out	under
alongside	by means of	in place of	out of	underneath
along with	concerning	in regard to	outside of	until
amid	considering	inside	over	unto
among	despite	inside of	over to	up
apart from	down	in spite of	owing to	upon
around	down from	instead of	past	up to
aside from	during	into	prior to	with
at	except	like	regarding	within
away from	except for	near	round	without
because of	for	near to	round about	

Grammar Practice

Prepositions

■ Prepositional Phrases

 For each underlined prepositional phrase, indicate whether it functions as an adjective or an adverb.

1. The sleeping dog's legs twitched as he dreamed <u>of the bothersome squirrel</u> <u>at the bird feeder</u>.

2. All the animals at the zoo <u>except for the polar bears</u> stayed huddled <u>inside their enclosures</u>.

3. <u>In spite of the frigid temperatures</u>, the white bears seemed comfortable.

4. Create a memo <u>regarding the dress code</u> <u>for all employees</u>.

5. Coach Walters had us run <u>around the block</u> ten times.

6. The child standing <u>beside her mother</u> looked quite forlorn.

7. Bonita dances <u>in an uninhibited way</u> when she hears her favorite music.

8. The spiderweb <u>between the ceiling and wall</u> looks like a bit <u>of fuzz</u>.

Model

Model the following sentences to practice using prepositional phrases as adverbs.

> To confine our attention to terrestrial matters would be to limit the human spirit.
> —Stephen Hawking

> To stay ahead, you must have your next idea waiting in the wings.
> —Rosabeth Moss Kanter

Preposition

Before students begin the Grammar Practice activity, review the list of Common Prepositions together. Provide context sentences for any prepositions with which students are not familiar to help them develop their basic sight vocabulary.

Related Skills Activities

■ **Conventions**
Expanding Sentences, p. 88

■ *SkillsBook*
Pretest: Prepositions, Conjunctions, and Interjections, p. 114
Prepositions and Interjections, p. 115

 Answers

1. adverb, adjective
2. adjective, adverb
3. adverb
4. adjective, adjective
5. adverb
6. adverb
7. adverb
8. adjective, adjective

 ELPS 4C Develop basic sight vocabulary

Conjunction

A **conjunction** connects individual words or groups of words. There are three kinds of conjunctions: *coordinating, correlative,* and *subordinating.*

754.1 Coordinating Conjunctions

Coordinating conjunctions usually connect a word to a word, a phrase to a phrase, or a clause to a clause. The words, phrases, or clauses joined by a coordinating conjunction are equal in importance or are of the same type.

I knew that my niece Kailee *was excited* and *wanted to ride the biggest roller coaster,* but *her dad was a little worried about it.*

(*And* connects the two parts of a compound predicate; *but* connects two independent clauses that could stand on their own.)

754.2 Correlative Conjunctions

Correlative conjunctions are conjunctions used in pairs.

They were not only exhausted by the day's journey but also sunburned.

754.3 Subordinating Conjunctions

Subordinating conjunctions connect two clauses that are *not* equally important, thereby showing the relationship between them. A subordinating conjunction connects a dependent clause to an independent clause in order to complete the meaning of the dependent clause.

A brown trout will study the bait before he eats it. (The clause *before he eats it* is dependent. It depends on the rest of the sentence to complete its meaning.)

Kinds of Conjunctions

Coordinating: and, but, or, nor, for, yet, so
Correlative: either, or; neither, nor; not only, but also; both, and; whether, or
Subordinating: after, although, as, as if, as long as, as though, because, before, if, in order that, provided that, since, so that, that, though, till, unless, until, when, where, whereas, while

---

Note: Relative pronouns (see **728.2**) and conjunctive adverbs (see **648.2**) can also connect clauses.

Interjection

An **interjection** communicates strong emotion or surprise. Punctuation—a comma or an exclamation point—sets off an interjection from the rest of the sentence.

Oh no! The TV broke. Good grief! I have nothing to do! Yipes, I'll go mad!

Grammar Practice

Conjunctions

Number your paper from 1 to 7. Write the conjunctions you find in the following paragraph and label them coordinating, subordinating, or correlative. (Write both correlative conjunctions as one answer.)

1 Most people know Georgia O'Keeffe as a celebrated artist, but few
2 people know that she almost gave up on her talent. In the early twentieth
3 century, O'Keeffe studied at the Art Institute of Chicago, where she learned
4 imitative realism. Although she had won awards for paintings she had
5 done in this style, she felt the technique did not suit her. Discouraged, she
6 quit making art until she took a course at the University of Virginia in
7 Charlottesville, four years later. There she found the freedom to incorporate
8 her own personal ideas into her art. O'Keeffe not only experimented with
9 new techniques in line, color, and light, but she also discovered her own
10 personal style. She created abstract charcoal drawings that were among
11 the most innovative of the time. She is probably best known for her large-
12 scale paintings of flowers. Before she died in 1986, Georgia O'Keeffe
13 was awarded the Medal of
14 Freedom and the National
15 Medal of Arts.

Model

Model the following sentences to practice using interjections effectively.

An apology? Bah! Disgusting! Cowardly! It is beneath the dignity of any gentleman, however wrong he might be.
—Baroness Orczy Emmuska

The most exciting phrase to hear in science, the one that heralds new discoveries, is not "Eureka!" (I found it!) but "That's funny . . . "
—Isaac Asimov

Conjunction

Before students begin the Grammar Practice activity, review together the conjunctions listed in the blue Kinds of Conjunctions box. Provide context sentences for any conjunctions with which students are not familiar to help them develop their basic sight vocabulary.

Related Skills Activities

■ **Conventions**
Combining Sentences, p. 87
Revising Run-On Sentences, p. 89

■ *SkillsBook*
Pretest: Prepositions, Conjunctions, and Interjections, p. 114
Coordinating Conjunctions, p. 116
Correlative and Subordinating Conjunctions, p. 117

Answers

1. but—coordinating
2. where—subordinating
3. Although—subordinating
4. until—subordinating
5. not only . . . , but . . . also—correlative
6. Before—subordinating
7. and—coordinating

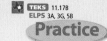

Understanding Sentences

Constructing Sentences

A **sentence** is made up of one or more words that express a complete thought. Sentences begin with a capital letter; they end with a period, a question mark, or an exclamation point.

What should we do this afternoon? We could have a picnic. No, I hate the ants!

Using Subjects and Predicates

A sentence usually has a subject and a predicate. The subject is the part of the sentence about which something is said. The predicate, which contains the verb, is the part of the sentence that says something about the subject.

We write from aspiration and antagonism, as well as from experience.

—Ralph Waldo Emerson

756.1 The Subject

The **subject** is the part of the sentence about which something is said. The subject is always a noun; a pronoun; or a word, clause, or phrase that functions as a noun (such as a gerund or a gerund phrase or an infinitive).

Wolves **howl.** (noun)
They **howl for a variety of reasons.** (pronoun)
To establish their turf **may be one reason.** (infinitive phrase)
Searching for "lost" pack members **may be another.** (gerund phrase)
That wolves and dogs are similar animals **seems obvious.** (noun clause)

- A **simple subject** is the subject without its modifiers.
  Most wildlife **biologists** disapprove of crossbreeding wolves and dogs.

- A **complete subject** is the subject with all of its modifiers.
  Most wildlife biologists disapprove of crossbreeding wolves and dogs.

- A **compound subject** is composed of two or more simple subjects.
  Wise **breeders** and **owners** know that wolf-dog puppies can display unexpected, destructive behaviors.

756.2 Delayed Subject

In sentences that begin with *there* or *it* followed by a form of the "be" verb, the subject comes after the verb. The subject is also delayed in questions.

There was **nothing** in the refrigerator. (The subject is *nothing;* the verb is *was.*)
Where is my **sandwich**? (The subject is *sandwich;* the verb is *is.*)

Sentences

Practice

Constructing Sentences 1

- Simple, Complete, and Compound Subjects
- Delayed Subjects

 Write the complete subject of each sentence (and of each dependent clause in a complex sentence). Circle the simple subject or subjects.

(1) One summer long ago, some people took a boat from the northern tip of Wisconsin to Madeline Island in Lake Superior. **(2)** Those hardy souls liked it so much that they decided to build homes and businesses there. **(3)** And then winter came. **(4)** Chequamegon Bay, the body of water between the island and the mainland, froze. **(5)** The islanders were in for a long winter.

(6) There were those who had sleds and dogs to get back to Wisconsin. **(7)** But the time came when another question begged an answer: **(8)** Would the ice hold something heavier, like a car? **(9)** (And who wanted to be the one to find out?)

(10) Fortunately, ice roads are no longer a questionable possibility but a scientific reality. **(11)** Numerous companies and government agencies in frozen climates build and maintain these winter roads to deliver goods to remote locations. **(12)** They use sophisticated equipment to measure the ice thickness and mark the route. **(13)** The dedicated workers keep it solid and plow it as needed. **(14)** Now areas that cannot be reached by road in the summer can be reached in the winter.

Learning Language

With a partner, work together to complete the first paragraph of the Practice activity. Discuss your answers and compare them with another pair of students. Then continue through the next two paragraphs. After you finish, write a paragraph expressing how it might feel to drive on the ice roads described in the activity. Try to include some complex sentences in your writing. Read your paragraph aloud to a partner.

Related Skills Activities

- ***SkillsBook***
  Pretest: Subjects and Predicates, p. 123
  Subjects and Predicates, p. 124

Learning Language

Before partners begin the activity, work together to practice producing the sounds of the terms *simple, complete, compound subjects* and *delayed subject.* Suggest that partners discuss their feelings about driving on icy roads before they begin to write their paragraphs. Encourage students to include vocabulary from the Practice passage. Remind them to check that they have used a variety of correctly structured sentences.

Answers

Students will circle the boldface words below.

1. some **people**
2. Those hardy **souls; they**
3. **winter**
4. **Chequamegon Bay,** the body . . .
5. The **islanders**
6. **those who**
7. the **time;** another **question**
8. the **ice**
9. **who**
10. ice **roads**
11. Numerous **companies** and government **agencies** in frozen climates
12. **They**
13. The dedicated **workers**
14. **areas that**

758.1 Predicates

The **predicate** is the part of the sentence that shows action or says something about the subject.

Giant squid do exist.

- A **simple predicate** is the verb without its modifiers.
  One giant squid measured **nearly 60 feet long**.
- A **complete predicate** is the simple predicate with all its modifiers.
  One giant squid measured nearly 60 feet long.
  (*Measured* is the simple predicate; *nearly 60 feet long* modifies *measured*.)
- Compound and complex sentences have more than one predicate.
  The sperm whale has an enormous head **that** is approximately a third of its entire length.
  A whale is a mammal, **but a squid** is a mollusk.
- A **compound predicate** is composed of two or more simple predicates.
  A squid grasps **its prey with tentacles and** bites **it with its beak.**

Note: A sentence can have a **compound subject** and a **compound predicate**.
  Both sperm whales **and** giant squid live **and occasionally** clash **in the deep waters off New Zealand's South Island.**

- A **direct object** is part of the predicate and receives the action of the verb. (See 736.2.)
  Sperm whales sometimes eat **giant squid.**
  (The direct object *giant squid* receives the action of the verb *eat* by answering the question *whales eat what?*)

Note: The **direct object** may be compound.
  In the past, whalers harvested **oil,** spermaceti, **and** ambergris **from slain sperm whales.**

758.2 Understood Subjects and Predicates

Either the subject or the predicate may be "missing" from a sentence, but both must be clearly **understood**.

Who is in the hot-air balloon?
(*Who* is the subject; *is in the hot-air balloon* is the predicate.)

No one.
(*No one* is the subject; the predicate *is in the hot-air balloon* is understood.)

Get out of the way!
(The subject *you* is understood; *get out of the way* is the predicate.)

Practice

Constructing Sentences 2

- Simple, Complete, and Compound Predicates

 Write the complete predicate of each sentence (and of each dependent clause in a complex sentence). Circle the simple predicate or predicates. Underline any direct objects.

1. Cole and his sister Marlene survived the hurricane by going to a public shelter.
2. Julio gave his customized car another coat of wax.
3. Julio and his brothers have been working on the car for almost two years.
4. Service club members who packed boxes to send to troops in Iraq also loaded them into the truck.
5. My cousin chose mint green, lavender, and mauve for her wedding bouquet.
6. Either Alando or Tucker will come by and take me to work.
7. The students who had arrived at the prom relaxed and enjoyed the music and dancing.
8. Who is taking Alisha to the dance?
9. The new telephone system at work has several cool features.
10. A bonobo is a kind of chimpanzee that lives mostly in the Democratic Republic of Congo.

Model

Model the following sentences to practice using a compound predicate.

A person travels the world over in search of what he needs and returns home to find it.
—George Moore

He stepped behind a thick-boled pine tree and peered out at the man in the tree stand seventy yards away.
—Chet Williamson, "First Kill"

Sentences

Predicates/Subjects and Predicates

Before students begin the Practice activity, discuss how using simple, complete, and compound predicates can help them to use a variety of sentence structures.

Related Skills Activities

- *SkillsBook*
  Subjects and Predicates, p. 124

Answers

The boldface words below will be circled.

1. **survived** the hurricane by going to a public shelter
2. **gave** his customized car another coat of wax
3. **have been working** on the car for almost two years
4. **packed** boxes to send to troops in Iraq also **loaded** them into a truck
5. **chose** mint green, lavender, and mauve for her wedding bouquet
6. **will come** by and **take** me to work
7. **had arrived** at the prom **relaxed** and **enjoyed** the music and dancing
8. **is taking** Alisha to the dance
9. **has** several cool features
10. **is** a kind of chimpanzee **lives** mostly in the Democratic Republic of Congo

11.17A

Using Phrases

A **phrase** is a group of related words that function as a single part of speech. The sentence below contains a number of phrases.

Finishing the race will require biking up some steep slopes.

finishing the race (This gerund phrase functions as a subject noun.)

will require (This phrase functions as a verb.)

biking up some steep slopes (This gerund phrase acts as an object noun.)

760.1 Types of Phrases

■ An **appositive phrase**, which follows a noun or a pronoun and renames it, consists of a noun and its modifiers. An appositive adds new information about the noun or pronoun it follows.

The Trans-Siberian Railroad, the world's longest railway, stretches from Moscow to Vladivostok. (The appositive phrase renames *Trans-Siberian Railroad* and provides new information.)

■ A **verbal phrase** is a phrase based on one of the three types of verbals: *gerund, infinitive,* or *participle.* (See 746.1, 746.2, and 746.3.)

■ A **gerund phrase** consists of a gerund and its modifiers. The whole phrase functions as a noun.

Spotting the tiny mouse **was easy for the hawk.**
(The gerund phrase is used as the subject of the sentence.)

Dinner escaped by ducking under a rock.
(The gerund phrase is the object of the preposition *by.*)

■ An **infinitive phrase** consists of an infinitive and its modifiers. The whole phrase functions either as a noun, an adjective, or an adverb.

To shake every voter's hand **was the candidate's goal.**
(The infinitive phrase functions as a noun used as the subject.)

Your efforts to clean the chalkboard **are appreciated.**
(The infinitive phrase is used as an adjective modifying *efforts.*)

Please watch carefully to see the difference.
(The infinitive phrase is used as an adverb modifying *watch.*)

■ A **participial phrase** consists of a past or present participle and its modifiers. The whole phrase functions as an adjective.

Following his nose, **the beagle took off like a jackrabbit.**
(The participial phrase modifies the noun *beagle.*)

The raccoons, warned by the rustling, took cover.
(The participial phrase modifies the noun *raccoons.*)

 11.17A

Practice

Constructing Sentences 3

■ Appositive Phrases
■ Verbal Phrases

Identify each underlined group of words as an *appositive, gerund, infinitive,* or *participial phrase.*

1. Rance decided that rappelling over the side of the cliff was unsafe.

2. The stars arriving at the red-carpet event smiled and waved for the cameras.

3. Most teachers believe their students' parents are willing to vote in favor of the referendum.

4. My grandfather, an avid reader and U.S. historian, will review the article before it is published.

5. Distracted by the shouts, Linc was unable to sink the putt.

6. Surfing in the ocean when the waves are so high seems a little risky.

7. Dyann must decide whether she wants to be part of the debate team.

8. Steve Fossett, a bold adventurer, is known for his long-distance flights.

9. Mr. Geissman pursued his campaign to prevent the city from limiting free parking.

10. Rising before dawn, Jen hit the road early to avoid the crowds at the beach.

Model

Model the following sentences to practice using gerund phrases.

Besides the noble art of getting things done, there is a nobler art of leaving things undone.
—Lin Yutang

He always enjoyed showing people the ropes, fascinating them with his abilities, and teaching them to do the same kind of thing.
—Chet Williamson, "Mushrooms"

Sentences

Using Phrases

Have students complete the Practice activity to demonstrate their understanding of the use and function of different types of phrases.

Related Skills Activities

■ **Conventions**
Combining Sentences, p. 87
Expanding Sentences, p. 88

■ *SkillsBook*
Pretest: Phrases, p. 126
Verbal Phrases, p. 127
Prepositional and Appositive Phrases, p. 128
Effective Phrases, p. 130
Sentence Combining 1 and 2, pp. 156–157

Answers

1. gerund phrase
2. participial phrase
3. infinitive phrase
4. appositive phrase
5. participial phrase
6. gerund phrase
7. infinitive phrase
8. appositive phrase
9. gerund phrase
10. participial phrase

 TEKS 11.17A Use and understand the function of different types of clauses and phrases

TEKS 11.17A

Using Phrases (continued)

- A **verb phrase** consists of a main verb preceded by one or more helping verbs.
  Snow **has been falling** for days. (*Has been falling* is a verb phrase.)

- A **prepositional phrase** is a group of words beginning with a preposition and ending with a noun or a pronoun. Prepositional phrases function mainly as adjectives and adverbs.

  Reach for that catnip ball **behind the couch.** (The prepositional phrase *behind the couch* is used as an adjective modifying *catnip ball.*)

  Zach won the wheelchair race **in record time.** (*In record time* is used as an adverb modifying the verb *won.*)

- An **absolute phrase** consists of a noun and a participle (plus the participle's object, if there is one, and any modifiers). An absolute phrase functions as a modifier that adds information to the entire sentence. Absolute phrases are always set off with commas.

  Its wheels clattering rhythmically over the rails, **the train rolled into town.** (The noun *wheels* is modified by the present participle *clattering.* The entire phrase modifies the rest of the sentence.)

Using Clauses

A **clause** is a group of related words that has both a subject and a predicate.

762.1 Independent and Dependent Clauses

An **independent clause** presents a complete thought and can stand alone as a sentence; a **dependent clause** (also called a *subordinate clause*) does not present a complete thought and cannot stand alone as a sentence.

Sparrows make nests in cattle barns (independent clause) **so that they can stay warm during the winter** (dependent clause).

762.2 Types of Dependent Clauses

There are three basic types of dependent clauses: *adverb*, *noun*, and *adjective*.

- An **adverb clause** is used like an adverb to modify a verb, an adjective, or an adverb. Adverb clauses begin with a subordinating conjunction. (See 754.3.)
  If I study hard, **I will pass this test.** (The adverb clause modifies the verb *will pass.*)

- A **noun clause** is used in place of a noun.
  However, the teacher said **that the essay questions are based only on the last two chapters.** (The noun clause functions as a direct object.)

- An **adjective clause** modifies a noun or a pronoun.
  Tomorrow's test, **which covers the entire book, is half essay and half short answers.** (The adjective clause modifies the noun *test.*)

Sentences

Practice

Constructing Sentences 4

- Absolute Phrases
- Independent Clauses
- Dependent Clauses

 Identify each underlined group of words as an *absolute phrase*, an *independent clause*, or a *dependent clause*. For dependent clauses, also identify their type.

1. Did I tell you about the Olympic skier <u>who spoke at the conference?</u>

2. If everyone cooperates, <u>we can make up the time</u> that we lost yesterday.

3. Adam wanted to leave the party <u>because none of his friends were there.</u>

4. <u>His heart pounding and his legs trembling,</u> he crossed the finish line.

5. Many writers agree <u>that the story contains enough truth to sway even the most skeptical reader.</u>

6. This is the stadium <u>where the Steelers and the Seahawks played in the Super Bowl.</u>

7. The game was over for almost an hour <u>before all the fans left the stadium.</u>

8. Brian climbed the ladder to the burning roof, <u>the fire hose held firmly under his arm.</u>

9. At the beginning of the ceremony, <u>line up at the doors</u> while the principal makes her opening remarks.

10. It is important to ask <u>which chapters will be covered on the exam.</u>

Model

Model the following sentence to practice using adverb and adjective clauses.

On the way, Lida and Petra had talked about their discoveries while I observed the countryside, which was still covered with trackless, uninhabited forests.
—Ivan Klima, "Archeology"

Using Phrases/Using Clauses

Have students complete the Practice activity to demonstrate their understanding of the use and function of different types of clauses and phrases.

Related Skills Activities

- **Conventions**
  Expanding Sentences, p. 88

- **SkillsBook**
  Prepositional and Appositive Phrases, p. 128
  Absolute Phrases, p. 129
  Effective Phrases, p. 130
  Pretest: Clauses, p. 132
  Independent and Dependent Clauses, p. 133
  Adverb Clauses, p. 134
  Adjective Clauses, p. 135

Answers

1. dependent clause, adjective
2. independent clause
3. dependent clause, adverb
4. absolute phrase
5. dependent clause, noun
6. dependent clause, adjective
7. dependent clause, adverb
8. absolute phrase
9. independent clause
10. dependent clause, noun

Using Sentence Variety

A **sentence** may be classified according to the type of statement it makes, the way it is constructed, and its arrangement of words.

764.1 Kinds of Sentences

The five basic kinds of sentences are *declarative, interrogative, imperative, exclamatory,* and *conditional.*

- **Declarative sentences** make statements. They tell us something about a person, a place, a thing, or an idea. Although declarative sentences make up the bulk of most academic writing, there are overwhelmingly diverse ways in which to express them.

  The Statue of Liberty stands in New York Harbor.

  For over a century, it has greeted immigrants and visitors to America.

- **Interrogative sentences** ask questions.

  Did you know that the Statue of Liberty is made of copper and stands more than 150 feet tall?

  Are we allowed to climb all the way to the top?

- **Imperative sentences** make commands.

  You must purchase a ticket.

  They often contain an understood subject *(you)* as in the examples below.

  Go see the Statue of Liberty.

  After a few weeks of physical conditioning, climb its 168 stairs.

- **Exclamatory sentences** communicate strong emotion or surprise.

  Climbing 168 stairs is not a dumb idea!

  Just muster some of that old pioneering spirit, that desire to try something new, that never-say-die attitude that made America great!

- **Conditional sentences** express wishes ("if . . . then" statements) or conditions contrary to fact.

  If I could design a country's flag, I would use six colors behind a sun, a star, and a moon.

  I would feel as if I were representing many cultures in my design.

Practice

Kinds of Sentences

 Write the kind of each sentence below: *declarative, interrogative, imperative, exclamatory,* or *conditional.*

1. Do you know where Burkina Faso is?

2. It is a small, landlocked country in West Africa.

3. Try to find it on a globe.

4. The whole country is only slightly larger than Colorado!

5. Burkina Faso's official language is French, but 90 percent of the population speak native African languages.

6. Less than 3 percent of the population is older than 65.

7. If AIDS didn't have such a major impact on its people, the average life expectancy would probably be greater than the present 48 years.

8. About three-quarters of Burkina Faso's people are illiterate, and 45 percent live below the poverty line.

9. It is almost as if the country has been forgotten by the rest of the world.

10. What can be done?

Learning Language

Work with a partner. Compare your answers to the Practice activity. Then, on separate pieces of paper, write one sentence of each type. Exchange sentences with each other, and identify each sentence type on your partner's paper. Explain your answers to each other. Finally, choose a piece of your own writing and identify the sentence types you find in it.

Using Sentence Variety

Have students complete the Practice activity to demonstrate their ability to recognize a variety of correctly structured sentences. Remind them to use the terms *declarative, interrogative, imperative, exclamatory,* and *conditional* in their responses.

Related Skills Activities

- *SkillsBook*
  Pretest: Sentences, p. 137
  Kinds of Sentences, p. 138

Answers

1. interrogative	6. declarative
2. declarative	7. conditional
3. imperative	8. declarative
4. exclamatory	9. conditional
5. declarative	10. interrogative

Learning Language

Tell partners to use the academic language *declarative, interrogative, imperative, exclamatory,* and *conditional* as they discuss the sentences they have written. Remind them to express their ideas with specificity and detail.

TEKS 11.17B

766.1 Types of Sentence Constructions

A sentence may be *simple, compound, complex,* or *compound-complex.* It all depends on the relationship between independent and dependent clauses.

- A **simple sentence** can have a single subject or a compound subject. It can have a single predicate or a compound predicate. However, a simple sentence has only one independent clause, and it has no dependent clauses.

   My back aches.
   (single subject; single predicate)
   My teeth **and my** eyes hurt.
   (compound subject; single predicate)
   My throat **and** nose feel **sore and** look **red.**
   (compound subject; compound predicate)
   I must have caught the flu **from the sick kids in class.**
   (independent clause with two phrases: *from the sick kids* and *in class*)

- A **compound sentence** consists of two independent clauses. The clauses must be joined by a comma and a coordinating conjunction or by a semicolon.

   I usually don't mind missing school, but **this is not fun.**
   I feel too sick to watch TV; I feel too sick to eat.

Note: The comma can be omitted when the clauses are very short.
   I wept and **I wept.**

- A **complex sentence** contains one independent clause (in black) and one or more dependent clauses (in red).

   When I get back to school, **I'm actually going to appreciate it.**
   (dependent clause; independent clause)
   I won't even complain about math class, although I might be talking out of my head because I'm feverish.
   (independent clause; two dependent clauses)

- A **compound-complex sentence** contains two or more independent clauses (in black) and one or more dependent clauses (in red).

   Yes, I have a bad flu, and because I need to get well soon, **I won't think about school just yet.**
   (two independent clauses; one dependent clause)
   The best remedy for those who suffer with flu symptoms **is plenty of rest and fluids, but the chicken soup** that Grandma makes for me **always helps, too.**
   (two independent clauses; two dependent clauses)

TEKS 11.17B

Practice

Types of Sentence Constructions

Identify each of the following sentences as *simple, compound, complex,* or *compound-complex.*

1. If you are like the average high school junior, you are eager to register to vote and to enjoy the privilege of voting in local, state, and national elections.

2. You must be 18 years old to vote, and you must be a United States citizen.

3. States have varying registration requirements, so you should check to see what your state requires.

4. It is important to register, and because you are almost of voting age, you should find out about the registration process.

5. In most states, you register by going to the county clerk's office.

6. You may be able to register using a mail-in form.

7. Once you are registered, you will be notified of the location of your polling place.

8. Voting allows you to participate in the political process, and it gives you a voice in issues of great importance.

Model

Model the following sentence to practice forming a compound-complex sentence.

   We often told Luke to pay more attention—especially during rehearsals when he didn't seem to hear or see the other actors—but he couldn't seem to concentrate on anything other than his own lines.

Types of Sentence Constructions

Read aloud the directions for the Practice activity and have students restate them in their own words. Then tell students to complete the Practice activity to demonstrate their ability to recognize a variety of correctly structured sentences.

Related Skills Activities

- ***SkillsBook***
   Simple and Compound Sentences, p. 39
   Complex and Compound-Complex Sentences, p. 140

 ## Answers

1. complex
2. compound
3. compound
4. compound-complex
5. simple
6. simple
7. complex
8. compound

 TEKS 11.17B Use a variety of correctly structured sentences; **ELPS 2I** Demonstrate listening comprehension/following directions

TEKS 11.17B

768.1 Arrangements of Sentences

Depending on the arrangement of the words and the placement of emphasis, a sentence may also be classified as *loose, balanced, periodic,* or *cumulative.*

- **A loose sentence** expresses the main thought near the beginning and adds explanatory material as needed.

  We hauled out the boxes of food and set up the camp stove, **all the time battling the hot wind that would not stop, even when we screamed into the sky.**

  Melody gives confidence to every team member—**knows all the plays the team has practiced, finds the open player on the court every time.**

- **A balanced sentence** is constructed so that it emphasizes a similarity or a contrast between two or more of its parts (words, phrases, or clauses).

  The wind in our ears drove us crazy **and** pushed us on.
  (The similar wording emphasizes the main idea in this sentence.)

  Happiness is not found in what comes to you; **it is found in** what you give to others.

- **A periodic sentence** is one that postpones the crucial or most surprising idea until the end.

  Following my mother's repeated threats to ground me for life, I decided it was time to propose a compromise.

  Jemma didn't know what the next moment held—a close-up encounter with Tesla crater or her very last view of the glorious Moon.

- **A cumulative sentence** places the general idea in the middle of the sentence with modifying clauses and phrases coming before and after.

  With careful thought and extra attention to detail, I wrote out my plan for being a model teenager, **a teen who cared about neatness and reliability.**

  Not too long ago, architects who planned college classrooms and dormitories were advised against making the furnishings too pleasant or comfortable **lest the students become distracted or fall asleep.**
  —Robert Sommer, "Hard Architecture"

Practice

Arrangements of Sentences

 Classify each of the following sentences as *loose, balanced, periodic,* or *cumulative.*

(1) Despite going through training and tryouts each year, Jamaal had never made the team. (2) Last fall, however, he finally aced his tryout. (3) He had changed over the summer; he'd grown several inches and put on a few pounds of muscle.

(4) With more than a little envy, the other guys watched him kick the ball over the goalpost from the opposing 47-yard line, something none of them had ever done. (5) Jamaal was ecstatic; his teammates weren't sure what to think. (6) By now, with two seasons behind them, they were used to playing with Antoine as their kicker. (7) They worried that Jamaal was about to bump Antoine out of that role.

(8) In spite of that rocky start with his teammates, Jamaal was soon accepted as one of the guys. (9) He and Antoine played together in most of the games, as it turned out, leading the team to an 8–2 winning season. (10) They had high hopes for the following season.

Model

Model the following balanced sentences.

The lamps are going out all over Europe: we shall not see them lit again in our lifetime.
—Viscount Grey of Fallodon

It doesn't matter who my father was; it matters who I remember he was.
—Anne Sexton

Arrangements of Sentences

Read aloud the directions for the Practice activity and have students restate them in their own words. Then have students complete the Practice activity to demonstrate their ability to recognize a variety of correctly structured sentences.

Related Skills Activities

- ***SkillsBook***
  Simple and Compound Sentences, p. 39
  Sentence Modeling 1, 2, and 3, pp. 141–143

Answers

1. periodic
2. periodic
3. balanced
4. cumulative
5. balanced
6. periodic
7. loose
8. periodic
9. loose
10. loose

Getting Sentence Parts to Agree

Agreement of Subject and Verb

A verb must agree in number (singular or plural) with its subject.
The student was proud of her quarter grades.

Note: Do not be confused by words that come between the subject and verb.
The manager, as well as the players, is required to display good sportsmanship. (*Manager,* not *players,* is the subject.)

770.1 Compound Subjects

Compound subjects joined by *or* or *nor* take a singular verb.
Neither Bev nor Kendra goes to the street dances.

Note: When one of the subjects joined by *or* or *nor* is singular and one is plural, the verb must agree with the subject nearer the verb.
Neither Yoshi nor his friends sing in the band anymore. (The plural subject *friends* is nearer the verb, so the plural verb *sing* is correct.)
Compound subjects connected with *and* require a plural verb.
Strength and balance are necessary for gymnastics.

770.2 Delayed Subjects

Delayed subjects occur when the verb comes before the subject in a sentence. In these inverted sentences, the delayed subject must agree with the verb.
There are many hardworking students in our schools.
There is present among many young people today a will to succeed.
(*Students* and *will* are the true subjects of these sentences, not *there.*)

770.3 "Be" Verbs

When a sentence contains a form of the "be" verb—and a noun comes before and after that verb—the verb must agree with the subject, not the *complement* (the noun coming after the verb).
The cause of his problem was the bad brakes.
The bad brakes were the cause of his problem.

770.4 Special Cases

Some nouns that are **plural in form but singular in meaning** take a singular verb: *mumps, measles, news, mathematics, economics, gallows, shambles.*
Measles is still considered a serious disease in many parts of the world.

Some nouns that are plural in form but singular in meaning take a plural verb: *scissors, trousers, tidings.*
The scissors disappear whenever I need them.

 Grammar Practice

Agreement of Subject and Verb 1

 For each sentence, write the correct verb from the choice given in parentheses.

1. Neither his brothers nor Todd *(have, has)* a driver's license.
2. On the wall *(was, were)* several of Karyn's paintings.
3. Artisans from Indonesia *(was, were)* making decorative drums.
4. *(Is, Are)* you in Kendra's physics class?
5. There *(go, goes)* Malik's stepsister, Melissa.
6. There *(is, are)* a mynah bird at the pet store.
7. There *(is, are)* many qualified applicants for the summer internship.
8. *(Were, Was)* Emily embarrassed when the waiters sang to her?
9. The police *(is, are)* sponsoring this weekend's safety seminar.
10. Arnie, Josh, or Ted *(have, has)* the best chance of winning.
11. I can't believe that those statistics *(are, is)* correct.
12. Current band members, as well as a recent graduate, *(was, were)* invited to play in the winter concert.

Model

Model the following sentences to practice subject-verb agreement.
The surest way to make a monkey out of a man is to quote him.
—Robert Benchley

People with bad consciences always fear the judgement of children.
—Mary McCarthy

Getting Sentence Parts to Agree

As needed, review the answer choices in the Grammar Practice activity to help students develop their basic sight vocabulary. Then have students complete the Grammar Practice activity to demonstrate their ability to employ complex grammatical structures.

Related Skills Activities

■ *SkillsBook*
Pretest: Subject and Verb Agreement, p. 145
Subject and Verb Agreement 1, 2, and 3, pp. 146–148

Answers

1. has
2. were
3. were
4. Are
5. goes
6. is
7. are
8. Was
9. are
10. has
11. are
12. were

 ELPS 4C Develop basic sight vocabulary; **5E** Employ increasingly complex grammatical structures

Agreement of Subject and Verb *(continued)*

772.1 Collective Nouns

Collective nouns *(faculty, committee, team, congress, species, crowd, army, pair, squad)* take a singular verb when they refer to a group as a unit; collective nouns take a plural verb when they refer to the individuals within the group.

> The favored **team is losing**, and the **crowd is getting ugly**. (Both *team* and *crowd* are considered units in this sentence, requiring the singular verb *is*.)
> The **pair reunite after 20 years apart**.
> (Here, *pair* refers to two individuals, so the plural verb *reunite* is required.)

772.2 Indefinite Pronouns

Some **indefinite pronouns** are singular: *each, either, neither, one, everybody, another, anybody, everyone, nobody, everything, somebody,* and *someone*. They require a singular verb.

> **Everybody is invited to the cafeteria for refreshments.**

Some **indefinite pronouns** are plural: *both, few, many,* and *several*.

> **Several like trail-mix bars. Many ask for frozen yogurt, too.**

Some **indefinite pronouns** are singular or plural: *all, any, most, none* and *some*.

Note: Do not be confused by words or phrases that come between the indefinite pronoun and the verb.

> **One of the participants is** (not *are*) going to have to stay late to clean up.

A Closer Look

Some **indefinite pronouns** can be either singular or plural: *all, any, most, none,* and *some*. These pronouns are singular if the number of the noun in the prepositional phrase is singular; they are plural if the noun is plural.

> **Most of the food complaints are coming from the seniors.**
> (*Complaints* is plural, so *most* is plural.)
> **Most of the tabletop is sticky.**
> (*Tabletop* is singular, so *most* is singular.)

772.3 Relative Pronouns

When a **relative pronoun** *(who, which, that)* is used as the subject of a clause, the number of the verb is determined by the antecedent of the pronoun. (The antecedent is the word to which the pronoun refers.)

> **This is one of the books that are required for geography class.** (The relative pronoun *that* requires the plural verb *are* because its antecedent, *books*, is plural.)

Note: To test this type of sentence for agreement, read the "of" phrase first.

> **Of the books that are required for geography class, this is one.**

Grammar Practice

Agreement of Subject and Verb 2

For each numbered sentence, write the correct verb from the choice given in parentheses.

(1) One of the important themes in Arthur Miller's play *Death of a Salesman (is, are)* abandonment. **(2)** It's a matter that *(arise, arises)* from a traumatic time in the life of the main character, Willy Loman. **(3)** As young boys, he and his brother, Ben, *(were, was)* left with nothing when their father abandoned them.

(4) Willy's fear of abandonment and loss *(cause, causes)* him to set high standards for himself and his family. **(5)** He believes that he can attain the American Dream, which *(lead, leads)* to his inflated sense of self-importance.

(6) He talks as if he were a success, but his family *(is, are)* aware that he is a failure. **(7)** This is one of the character traits that *(lead, leads)* Willy to estrangement with his sons, Biff and Happy.

The theme of abandonment continues. Ben has recently died. He was a wealthy man, a fact that intensifies Willy's underlying sense of failure. **(8)** He feels that none of his accomplishments *(is, are)* enough. **(9)** The day when Willy loses his job as a traveling salesman *(make, makes)* him face reality and, ultimately, his own death.

Learning Language

Review pages **770** and **772** with a small group, reading the example sentences aloud to one another. Listen carefully to the correct verb in each example. Then work through the first paragraph of the Practice activity together, discussing each choice. Complete the activity on your own, and then share your responses with a partner. Take turns reading the complete activity aloud with the group, reading along for clarity.

Related Skills Activities

■ **Conventions**
Combining Sentences, p. 87
Expanding Sentences, p. 88

Answers

1. is
2. arises
3. were
4. causes
5. leads
6. is
7. lead
8. are
9. makes

Learning Language

After students review SE pages 770 and 772, have them discuss the example sentences. Ask them to express ideas about which types of agreement are most challenging. Remind them to explain their ideas with specificity and detail. As needed, review the answer choices in the Grammar Practice activity to help students develop their basic sight vocabulary. Then have students complete the Grammar Practice activity to demonstrate their ability to use verbs correctly.

ELPS 3G Express ideas; **3H** Explain with increasing specificity and detail; **4C** Develop basic sight vocabulary and comprehend English vocabulary; **5E** Employ increasingly complex grammatical structures/using correct verbs

Agreement of Pronoun and Antecedent

A pronoun must agree in number, person, and gender with its *antecedent*. (The *antecedent* is the word to which the pronoun refers.)

> Cal **brought** his **gerbil to school.** (The antecedent of *his* is *Cal*. Both the pronoun and its antecedent are singular, third person, and masculine; therefore, the pronoun is said to "agree" with its antecedent.)

774.1 Agreement in Number

Use a **singular pronoun** to refer to such antecedents as *each, either, neither, one, anyone, anybody, everyone, everybody, somebody, another, nobody,* and *a person.*

> **Neither** of the brothers **likes** his (not their) **room.**

Two or more singular antecedents joined by *or* or *nor* are also referred to by a **singular pronoun.**

> **Either** Connie or Sue **left** her **headset in the library.**

If one of the antecedents joined by *or* or *nor* is singular and one is plural, the pronoun should agree with the nearer antecedent.

> **Neither the** manager **nor the** players **were crazy about** their **new uniforms.**

Use a **plural pronoun** to refer to plural antecedents as well as compound subjects joined by *and.*

> **Jared and** Carlos **are finishing** their **assignments.**

774.2 Agreement in Gender

Use a **masculine** or **feminine pronoun** depending upon the gender of the antecedent.

> **Tristan would like to bring** his **dog along on the trip.**
> **Claire is always complaining that** her **feet are cold.**

Use a **neuter** pronoun when the antecedent has no gender.

> **The ancient** weeping willow **is losing many of** its **branches.**

When *a person* or *everyone* is used to refer to both sexes or either sex, you will have to choose whether to offer optional pronouns or rewrite the sentence.

> **A person should be allowed to choose** her or his **own footwear.**
> (optional pronouns)
> **People should be allowed to choose** their **own footwear.**
> (rewritten in plural form)

Grammar Practice

Agreement of Pronoun and Antecedent

 For each sentence, write the correct pronoun from the choice given in parentheses.

1. J. W. and Marcus hung out and played *(his, their)* video games.

2. Latisha and Corinne submitted *(her, their)* editorials to the local newspaper.

3. Each of the students sent *(his or her, their)* essay with an application.

4. Emily or Trisha works at *(their, her)* parents' restaurant.

5. Monique's scissors were missing, and nobody knew where *(they, it)* were.

6. Most of the cars in the lot had small dents in *(its, their)* hoods from last night's hailstorm.

7. Most of the cake had little Tommy's fingerprints on *(it, them)*.

8. Devon or his brothers are rebuilding *(his, their)* grandfather's '68 Mustang.

9. I told everyone to bring *(his or her, their)* favorite CD's to my party.

10. One of these plants is rapidly losing *(its, their)* leaves.

Model

> Model the following sentences to practice making a pronoun and its antecedent agree.

> **People can no more be judged by their looks than the sea can be measured in bushels.**
> —Chinese proverb

> **Just as the sweetest words in the language to a given person are his or her own name, so too are his or her opinions.**
> —Gary O. Bosley, *Campaigning to Win*

Sentences

Agreement of Pronoun and Antecedent

As needed, review the answer choices in the Grammar Practice activity to help students develop their basic sight vocabulary. Then have students complete the Grammar Practice activity to demonstrate their ability to use pronouns and antecedents correctly.

Related Skills Activities

■ **SkillsBook**
Pretest: Pronoun-Antecedent Agreement, p. 150
Pronoun-Antecedent Agreement 1 and 2, pp. 151–152
Pronoun References, p. 153

Answers

1. their
2. their
3. his or her
4. her
5. they
6. their
7. it
8. their
9. his or her
10. its

Diagramming Sentences

A **graphic diagram** of a sentence is a picture of how the words in that sentence are related and how they fit together to form a complete thought.

776.1 Simple Sentence with One Subject and One Verb

Chris fishes.

subject	verb

776.2 Simple Sentence with a Predicate Adjective

Fish are delicious.

subject	verb	predicate adjective

776.3 Simple Sentence with a Predicate Noun and Adjectives

Fishing is my favorite hobby.

subject	verb	predicate noun

adjective
adjective

Note: When possessive pronouns (*my, his, their,* and so on) are used as adjectives, they are placed on a diagonal line under the word they modify.

776.4 Simple Sentence with an Indirect and Direct Object

My grandpa gave us a trout.

subject	verb	direct object

adjective
indirect object
adjective

Note: Articles (*a, an, the*) are adjectives and are placed on a diagonal line under the word they modify.

Grammar Practice

Sentence Diagramming 1

Diagram the following sentences.

1. Danae reads many magazines.
2. The old brick house is a day care center.
3. This fudge torte tastes incredible!
4. Mom showed her nephew a card trick.
5. Martha Washington was the true First Lady.
6. The yellow tulips are gorgeous.
7. Isaiah vacuumed the carpeted stairs.
8. Darcy's dad made us some cookies.
9. David typed.
10. That restaurant serves some tasty food.

Model

Model the following sentences to practice writing simple sentences with direct objects.

The flowers learn their colored shapes.

—Maria Konopnicka

A teacher affects eternity.

—Henry Brooks Adams

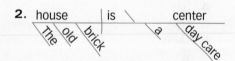

Answers for page 777

1. Danae | reads | magazines
   many

2. house | is \ center
   The, old, brick, a, day care

3. torte | tastes \ incredible
   This, fudge

4. Mom | showed | trick
   nephew, a, card
   her

5. Martha Washington | was \ First Lady
   the, true

6. tulips | are \ gorgeous
   The, yellow

7. Isaiah | vacuumed | stairs
   the, carpeted

8. dad | made | cookies
   Darcy's, us, some

9. David | typed

10. restaurant | serves | food
    That, some, tasty

Sentences

Diagramming Sentences *(continued)*

778.1 Simple Sentence with a Prepositional Phrase

I like fishing by myself.

(diagram: I | like | fishing; by myself)

(diagram: subject | verb | direct object; preposition / object of preposition)

778.2 Simple Sentence with a Compound Subject and Verb

The team and fans clapped and cheered.

(diagram: The team and fans | clapped and cheered)

(diagram: subject, adjective, conjunction, verb)

778.3 Compound Sentence

The team scored, and the crowd cheered wildly.

(diagram: The team | scored, and the crowd | cheered wildly)

(diagram: subject, adjective, conjunction, verb, adverb)

778.4 Complex Sentence with a Subordinate Clause

Before Erin scored, the crowd sat quietly.

(diagram: the crowd | sat quietly; Before Erin scored)

(diagram: subject, adjective, Before, conjunction, verb, adverb)

Grammar Practice

Sentence Diagramming 2

Diagram the following sentences.

1. Marette enjoyed her first trip to Paris.

2. She stayed near the Louvre and ate at sidewalk cafes.

3. In our neighborhood, the Kellmans have the biggest yard.

4. The postal worker who delivers our mail always wears shorts.

5. A truck driver can earn a good living, but it is hard work.

6. I will be happy when I graduate from high school.

7. Robin and Darita went to the library and got some DVD's.

8. Many radio stations are not independent, so they do not have control over their playlists.

9. The fire that destroyed the Bergs' house started in their basement.

10. Jeron and I saw the movie yesterday and bought the sound track today.

Model

Diagram the following model complex sentences.

All men are prepared to accomplish the incredible if their ideals are threatened.

—Hermann Hesse

Success is often achieved by those who don't know that failure is inevitable.

—Coco Chanel

Answers for page 779

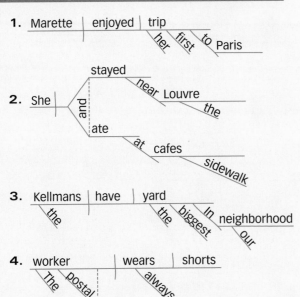

1. Marette | enjoyed | trip; her, first, to Paris

2. She | stayed and ate; near Louvre the; at cafes sidewalk

3. Kellmans | have | yard; the, the, biggest, In neighborhood our

4. worker | wears | shorts; The, postal, always; who | delivers | mail our

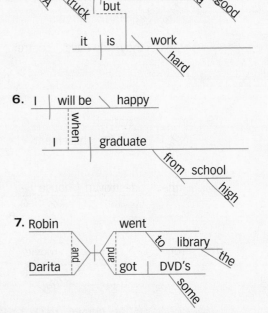

5. driver | can earn | living; A, truck, a, good, but; it | is | work hard

6. I | will be \ happy; when I | graduate; from school high

7. Robin and Darita | went and got; to library the; DVD's some

Answers 8–10 are on page 780.

(continued from page 778–779)

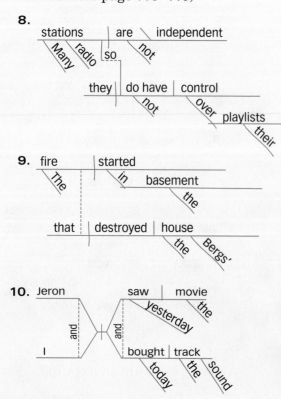

Appendix

Professional Development for Writing

Language Transfer Support

Reading-Writing Connection

Scope and Sequence

Getting Started

Benchmark Papers

Graphic Organizers

Credits

Index

How Does *Texas Write Source* Teach the Forms of Writing?

Texas Write Source provides numerous models and assignments for each major form of writing: **descriptive**, **narrative**, **expository**, **persuasive**, **interpretive response**, **creative**, and **research**.

Writing Assignments

Each integrated core writing unit provides students with a comprehensive, research-based exploration of a particular form. Every unit includes the following writing lessons:

- a **start-up paragraph assignment**—complete with a writing sample and step-by-step writing guidelines;

- two or more **multiparagraph essay assignments**—complete with writing samples, in-depth step-by-step guidelines, and integration of Texas traits and grammar instruction;

- one **assessment writing assignment**—complete with a sample response to a prompt plus writing tips.

- **Writing Across the Curriculum** provides students with authentic writing assignments from the major content areas and the world of work. Each assignment includes step-by-step instruction and models.

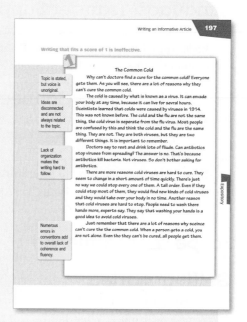

Writing Skills and Strategies

As students develop the writing in each unit, they will gain valuable experience working with the following skills or strategies:

- reading and responding to literature (writing models)
- **working with the writing process integrated with the Texas traits**
- using graphic organizers
- developing beginnings, middles, and endings
- **practicing grammar skills in context**
- publishing (presenting) writing
- reflecting on writing
- **responding to a prompt for assessment**

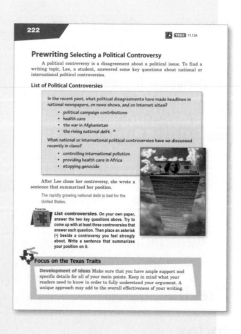

How Does the Program Integrate the Writing Process and the Traits of Writing?

Throughout each core writing unit, the Texas traits of writing are integrated into the steps of the writing process. As students develop their writing in each unit, they will develop an understanding of and appreciation for each trait of writing. In addition, checklists, guidelines, and activities are used to ensure that each piece of writing is completely traits based.

The Process and the Texas Traits in the Core Units

Understanding Your Goal

The beginning of each core essay assignment helps students understand the goal of their writing. A chart listing the traits of writing helps students meet that goal.

Focus on the Traits

As students develop their essays, they will find valuable discussions of the Texas traits at different points during the writing process.

Revising and Editing for the Traits

When students are ready to revise and edit, they will find step-by-step instruction, guidelines, and strategies to help them improve their writing for each of the traits of writing.

Model Essays and Holistic Scoring

Each core unit contains example essays for each score on the Holistic Scoring Guide, from 4 ("highly effective") to 1 ("not effective"). These annotated examples will help students gauge the effectiveness of their own writing and better understand how holistic scoring works.

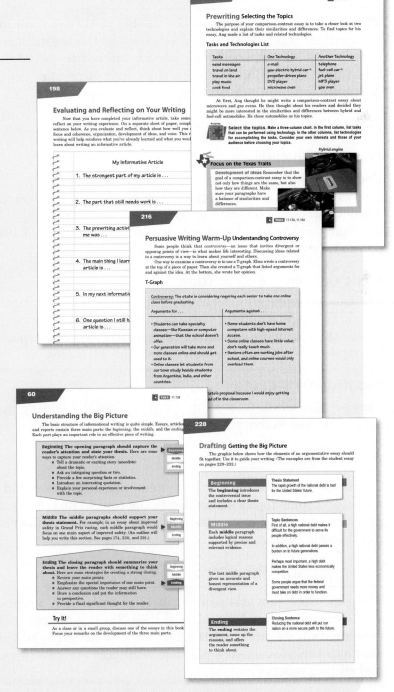

How Is Grammar Presented?

If you follow the suggested yearlong timetable, you will cover all the key grammar skills, including those listed in the TEKS. The program includes grammar instruction integrated into the core writing units. This allows students to learn about grammar in context when they are working on their own writing. If students have trouble with a particular concept, you can refer to a wealth of print and online resources for additional support.

Grammar in the Teacher's Edition

The yearlong timetable provides the big picture of grammar integration, and the scope and sequence at the beginning of each unit shows specifically what grammar to use while teaching writing. Conventions connections at point of use pinpoint the time to present each new concept.

Grammar in the Student Edition

Forms of Writing

Each core unit includes grammar instruction integrated into the revising and editing steps in the development of the main essay or story. Instruction on grammar skills includes examples and practice and application activities, and it links to students' writing.

Basic Grammar and Writing

For more grammar in the context of writing, turn to "Basic Paragraph Skills" and "Basic Essay Skills." Use these minilessons to workshop specific grammar and style issues that students can apply to their writing. These pages include instruction and examples of each skill, as well as practice activities.

Proofreader's Guide

This section serves as a complete grammar and editing guide, providing rules, examples, and activities.

Write Source Online

The *Write Source* **Net-text** offers interactive instruction and practice for the grammar and conventions topics embedded in the core writing units. *Write Source* **GrammarSnap** provides additional instruction, practice, and basic skills reinforcement through videos, minilessons, games, and quizzes.

Grammar in Other Program Components

The *SkillsBook* provides more than 130 punctuation, mechanics, spelling, usage, sentence, and parts-of-speech activities. *Texas Assessment Preparation* contains pretests, benchmark tests, and post-tests for basic writing and editing skills. *Daily Language Workouts* includes a year's worth of sentences (daily) and paragraphs (weekly) for writing and editing practice.

Planning Grammar Instruction

Should I implement *all* of the suggested basic grammar activities?

In the course of the year, if you assigned every grammar exercise listed in the daily lesson schedules (located in the unit overviews of your TE), your students would complete **all** of the "Basic Elements of Writing," "Proofreader's Guide," *SkillsBook*, and GrammarSnap activities.

Because the most effective grammar instruction happens in context, daily lesson schedules call for these exercises at appropriate times during revising and editing in the core writing units. As the teacher, you must choose the type and number of exercises that will best meet the needs of your students.

How are all the grammar resources related?

Texas Write Source SkillsBook activities parallel and expand on the rules and exercises found in the "Proofreader's Guide." In "Basic Elements of Writing," the brief exercises function well as minilessons and may be assigned on an as-needed basis. GrammarSnap offers additional support for key editing topics in an engaging, interactive format.

How do I use the unit scope and sequence chart?

The sample below from the "Persuasive Writing" unit is followed by three points that explain how to read and use the daily lesson schedules.

Persuasive Writing Unit Scope and Sequence

		Write Source Student Edition			Daily Language Workouts	Skills-Book	Write Source Online
Day	Writing and Conventions Instruction	Core Unit	Tools of Language	Resource Units			
1–2	**Argumentative Paragraph** Model	215–217	TL 580–585	BEW 611	42–45		Interactive Whiteboard Lesson
	Skills Activities: • Shifts in Verb Tenses					176–178	GrammarSnap
3–5	**Argumentative Essay** Model, Prewriting ⏵ Literature Connection *Anti-Federalist Letter* by Centinel	218–226		BEW 617–620			Net-text

(Left side vertical label: **WEEK 1**)

 Resource Units referenced above are located in the back of the *Student Edition* and *Teacher's Edition*
TL *"The Tools of Language"*   BEW *"Basic Elements of Writing"*   PG *"Proofreader's Guide"*

1. The Resource Units column indicates the SE pages that cover rules, examples, and exercises for each "Skills Activity" item.
2. The *Daily Language Workouts*, *SkillsBook*, and *Write Source* Online columns indicate pages and information from those particular resources, not from the SE.
3. A (+) following a page number means the exercise or practice is called for elsewhere and may have been completed already. You may review the exercise orally if this is the case.

How do I use *Daily Language Workouts*?

Daily Language Workouts is a teacher resource that provides a high-interest sentence for each day of the year and weekly paragraphs for additional editing and proofreading practice. This regular practice helps students develop the objectivity they need to effectively edit their own writing.

How is Writing Across the Curriculum Addressed?

*T*exas *Write Source* program provides a wide variety of writing across the curriculum activities and assignments. It promotes *writing to show learning, writing to learn new concepts,* and *writing to reflect on learning.*

Writing to Show Learning

Writing to show learning is the most common type of writing that content-area teachers assign. The following forms of writing covered in the program are commonly used for this purpose.

- Narrative paragraph and essay
- Expository paragraph and essay
- Persuasive paragraph and essay
- Response paragraph and book review
- Response to nonfiction
- Summary paragraph
- Research report

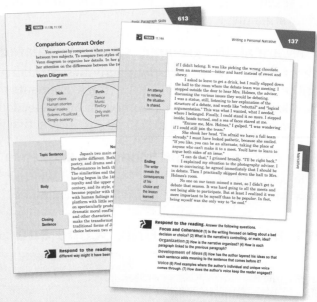

Specific Writing Across the Curriculum Assignments

Specific content-area assignments let students show learning.

Writing in Science
Cause-Effect Essay
Procedure Document

Writing in Social Studies
Historical Skit
Report on Social Studies
Multimedia Presentation

Writing in Math
Analysis of a Comparison Problem
Argumentative Essay
Response to a Math Prompt

Writing in the Applied Sciences
Classification Essay
Restaurant Review
Response to a Prompt

Writing in the Arts
Research Report
Performance Review

Writing in the Workplace
Proposal
E-Mail Message
How to Conduct a Business Meeting
How to Take Minutes During a Business Meeting

How Does *Texas Write Source* Incorporate Technology?

*T*exas Write Source includes a number of digital resources to help you provide each student the scaffolding—and challenges—he or she needs.

Interactive Whiteboard Lessons

Interactive Whiteboard Lessons provide an engaging means of introducing the major forms of writing. Whether used for whole class or small group instruction, these interactive lessons help you generate interest, promote discussion, and build background in the foundational concepts needed for success in writing.

Net-text

Designed as a digital worktext, the **Net-text** serves as an online alternative to key instruction found in the core print units. The **Net-text** features interactive instruction, online document creation, peer-to-peer commenting, additional grammar support, and more—all supported by simple yet powerful tools that help you monitor progress and give feedback.

GrammarSnap

GrammarSnap offers a suite of flexible resources that reinforce and extend the applied grammar instruction embedded in the core units of Write Source. Videos, practice exercises, and games make learning about parts of speech, sentences, and mechanics fun. Follow-up quizzes measure understanding.

Online Portfolio

The *Write Source* **Online Portfolio** gives students an authentic resource for publication, reflection, and discussion. In addition, it provides you with a flexible vehicle for ongoing, formative assessment as well as a handy tool for parent-teacher conferences.

Assignment Manager

How Can I Implement a Writing Workshop?

Texas Write Source complements implementation of a writing workshop through both print and technology resources. The program includes minilessons for instruction, high-quality models to encourage individual writing, support for whole-class sharing, and much more.

Integrated Minilessons

As a starting point, **Interactive Whiteboard Lessons** provide short, focused teaching opportunities designed to lay a foundation in key concepts. Students build on this foundation as they move through the core units, where each step in the writing process presents additional opportunities for minilessons targeting individual need. Both the print book and the **Net-text** lessons teach students to:

- preview the Texas trait-based goal of a writing project
- select a topic and gather details using a graphic organizer
- create a focus (thesis) statement
- organize details using a list or an outline
- create a strong beginning, a coherent middle, and an effective ending
- receive (and provide) peer responses
- revise for the Texas traits
- edit and proofread for conventions
- publish a finished piece
- use Texas traits-based rubrics

Mon	Tues	Wed	Thurs	Fri
Writing Minilessons (10 minutes as needed)				
Status Checks (2 minutes) Find out what students will work on for the day.				
Individual Work (30 minutes) Drafting, Revising, Editing, Conferencing, or Publishing				
Whole-Class Sharing Session (5 minutes)				

Graphic Organizers

Texas Write Source contains a wealth of graphic organizers that can serve as the subject of minilessons. The graphic organizers modeled in print and technology include the following:

Pie graph	Sensory chart	Process diagram	"Why" chart	Topic list
Web	Plot chart	Venn diagram	Basics of life list	Character chart
Cluster	Storyboard	Circle graph	5 W's chart	Picture diagram
T-chart	Bar graph	Cycle diagram	Cause-effect chart	Comparison-contrast chart
Outline	KWL chart	Gathering grid	Problem-solution chart	Time line

High-Quality Models

Each core unit begins with a high interest model, complete with annotations pointing out key features. The **Net-text** provides additional tools for exploring each model, including the ability for students to interact with their classroom peers online as they rate and comment on the model. Once students have read and analyzed each model, they will be ready—and excited—to begin their own writing. Other models and examples throughout each unit offer specific techniques that students can use in their own writing.

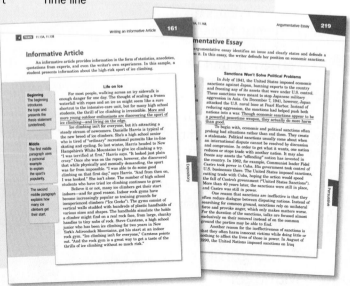

Individual Writing

Texas Write Source makes it easy for writing-workshop students to work on their own. It also provides specific help whenever students have questions about their writing. Here are some of the areas that are addressed:

- catching the reader's interest
- providing background information
- developing strong paragraphs
- elaborating on ideas
- organizing ideas by time, location, importance, logic
- quoting, paraphrasing, and summarizing
- using transitions
- drawing conclusions
- calling the reader to act

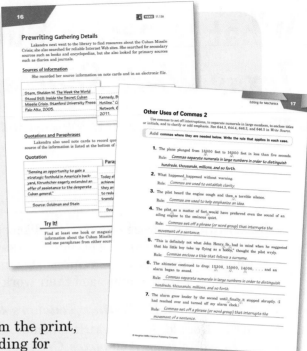

In addition to supporting these and other key concepts from the print, the *Write Source* **Net-text** provides an extra layer of scaffolding for independent writing, including exercises with immediate feedback; at-a-click support for grammar and conventions concepts; ready access to resources such as a dictionary and thesaurus; and an application for creating and managing work online.

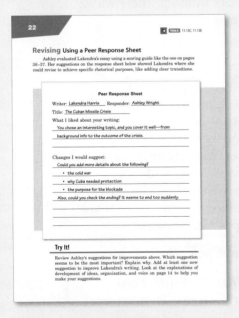

Peer and Teacher Response

Texas Write Source reviews peer responding and provides a peer response sheet. Consistent integration of the traits in the writing process allows students and teachers to speak a common language as they conduct responding sessions. Traits-based checklists and rubrics help pinpoint just what is working—and what could work better—in each piece of writing. The *Write Source* **Net-text** provides additional support for teacher-to-student and student-to-student response, including a commenting tool and notifications.

Whole-Class Sharing

Texas Write Source helps students complete their work, preparing it for whole-class sharing—whether in a traditional presentation or in the public section of the **Online Portfolio**. In addition, the program provides a wealth of suggestions for publishing student work in a variety of forms and for a variety of audiences.

Every writing unit ends with evaluation using traits-based rubrics. Even the evaluation process is modeled with sample essays and assessments. A reflection sheet also helps students think about what they have learned and internalize the lessons to use in the future.

What Research Supports
Texas Write Source?

Texas *Write Source* reflects the best thinking and research on writing instruction.

Applying the Process Approach to Writing

Research: The process approach, discussed by educators Donald M. Murray and Donald H. Graves, among others, breaks writing down into a series of steps—prewriting through publishing. Research has shown that students write more effectively, and more thoughtfully, if they approach their work as a process rather than as an end product.

Graves, Donald. H. *Writing: Teachers & Children at Work.* Heinemann, 2003.

Murray, Donald. M.; Newkirk, Thomas; Miller, Lisa C. *The Essential Don Murray Lessons from America's Greatest Writing Teacher.* Boynton/Cook Heinemann, 2009.

Texas Write Source: All writing units and assignments are arranged according to the steps in the writing process. This arrangement helps students manage their work, especially in the case of longer essay or research report assignments.

Sequencing Assignments

Research: Writing instructor and researcher James Moffett developed a sequence of writing assignments—known as the "Universe of Discourse"—that has, over the years, served countless English/language arts classrooms. Moffett sequences the modes of writing according to their connection or immediacy to the writer. Moffett suggests that students first develop descriptive and narrative pieces because the students have an immediate, personal connection to this type of writing. Next, they should develop informational pieces that require some investigation before moving on to more challenging, reflective writing, such as persuasive essays and position papers.

Moffett, James. *Teaching the Universe of Discourse.* Boynton/Cook, 1987.

Related Title: Fleischer, Cathy; Andrew-Vaughn, Sarah. *Writing Outside Your Comfort Zone: Helping Students Navigate Unfamiliar Genres.* Heinemann, 2009.

Texas Write Source: The writing units and assignments in the *Texas Write Source* texts are arranged according to the "Universe of Discourse," starting with descriptive and narrative writing, moving on to expository writing, and so on. These assignments are designed to be used in a sequence that supports an existing writing curriculum or integrated reading/language arts program.

Implementing a Writing Workshop

Research: Countless respected writing instructors and researchers have touted the importance of establishing a community of writers in the classroom. Teachers can establish such a community by implementing a writing workshop. In a writing workshop, students are immersed in all aspects of writing, including sharing their work with their peers.

Atwell, Nancie. *In the Middle: New Understandings About Writing, Reading, and Learning.* Heinemann, 1998.

Texas Write Source: The units in *Texas Write Source* are so clearly presented that most students can work independently on their writing in a workshop. In addition, the core units contain innumerable opportunities for workshop minilessons.

Producing Writing with Detail

Research: Rebekah Caplan learned through her teaching experience that students don't automatically know how to add details to their personal, informational, and persuasive writing. She discovered with her students that adding detail to writing is a skill that must be practiced regularly. To address this problem, Caplan came up with the "show-me" sentence strategy in which students begin with a basic idea—"My locker is messy"—and create a brief paragraph that shows rather than tells the idea.

Caplan, Rebekah. *Writers in Training: A Guide to Developing a Composition Program.* Dale Seymour Publications, 1984.

Related Title: Bernabi, Gretchen S.; Hover, Jayne; Candler, Cynthia. *Crunchtime: Lessons to Help Students Blow the Roof Off Writing Tests—and Become Better Writers in the Process.* Heinemann, 2009.

Texas Write Source: *Daily Language Workouts* contain a series of show-me sentences that teachers can implement as a regular classroom warm-up.

Meeting Students' Diverse Needs

Research: Many students in today's classrooms struggle with writing and learning. For struggling students, following the writing process is not enough. According to the research done by James L. Collins, struggling students need specific strategies and aids to help them become better writers. Collins found that these students benefit from the following: *skills instruction integrated into the process of writing, color coding and signposts in the presentation of instructional material, the use of graphic organizers, instructions presented in discreet chunks of copy,* and so on.

Collins, James L. *Strategies for Struggling Writers.* Guilford Press, 1998.

Related Title: Cruz, M. Colleen; Calkins, Lucy; *A Quick Guide to Researching Struggling Writers, K–5.* FirstHand/Heinemann, 2008.

Texas Write Source: The core writing units contain all the key features from Collins's work. As a result, the units are well suited for struggling learners and English language learners.

Language Transfer Support

Introduction

Students learning English come to us with myriad backgrounds, both culturally and linguistically. These backgrounds serve as marvelous resources for learning another language. For instance, all spoken languages are made up of sounds that comprise words that comprise sentences that comprise communication. We use the wealth of knowledge provided to us by our first language as a roadmap for interpreting all aspects of a second language—grammar (syntax), phonics (sounds and writing symbols), and vocabulary. This knowledge is an asset and a valuable tool in accelerating the acquisition of a second language. Just think how much harder language learning would be if a learner didn't know to look for words among the endless string of babble!

Because English language learners rely on their primary language experiences to guide their acquisition of English, transfer issues—language learning areas in which the primary language influences English production—arise. There are three types of transfer between languages.

The first is **positive transfer.** Cognates are an excellent example of positive transfer. If a student speaks Spanish and knows the word *teléfono,* he or she will have little trouble learning the word *telephone* in English. The two words sound similar and even have a similar spelling to a certain extent. The transfer from Spanish to English, in this case, has a positive effect. Another example of positive transfer can occur in the realm of phonics. If a student speaks Spanish and has learned that the letter *m* represents /m/, that knowledge will transfer readily to English phonics, in which the letter represents the same sound.

The second type of language transfer is **zero transfer.** Zero transfer occurs when something is encountered in English that is not present in the primary language. For some languages, such as Chinese, the writing system of English is a zero transfer situation. Because these languages rely on different writing systems, a student from one of these language backgrounds will not mistake the letter *j* for another sound because he or she has never encountered that writing symbol in the primary language. In a sense, the slate is clean, and while there is no assistance from the primary language as in positive transfer, there is no impediment either.

The last type of language transfer is **negative transfer.** In these situations, an element of the primary language conflicts with an element of English and causes difficulty in acquiring that specific element of English. A simple example is that Spanish speakers who know the word *librería* might be tempted to use their knowledge to interpret the English word *library* as a bookstore instead of as an institution that lends books to the public. In the realm of grammar, that same Spanish speaker might be tempted to place an adjective after the noun (*house big* as in *casa grande*) when constructing English sentences. And when he or she encounters the letter *j* while learning to read, the reader with a Spanish language background might substitute /h/ for the English *j* sound because that is the Spanish letter-sound correspondence.

Because each primary language has unique characteristics, there are unique language transfer issues for all of the languages represented in our classrooms. This resource guide focuses on providing teachers valuable information about zero and negative Language Transfer Support that affect the English acquisition of our students. As part of this introduction, background information for the ten languages highlighted in this guide is provided. The first chart that follows provides grammar transfer issues for the top ten primary languages found among English language learners in U.S. schools. The second chart provides phonics transfer issues for the top seven primary languages. A final section highlights word study transfer issues for five languages.

Teachers should use this wealth of information to help them identify possible areas of difficulty for students in their classrooms during instruction and to modify expectations accordingly. For instance, when teaching third-person agreement to Vietnamese students, it's helpful to know that the group may not be able to produce a final *s* sound. Therefore, while they might be able to listen to and absorb the grammar lesson passively, the teacher should be aware that Vietnamese speakers may have difficulty producing the sentence *That hurts me* with accurate third-person agreement.

> Because each primary language has unique characteristics, there are unique language transfer issues for all of the languages represented in our classrooms.

The phonics transfer chart is divided into two sections: sound transfer (phonology) and sound-symbol transfer (phonics). Acquiring the sound-symbol system of English phonics relies on two elements for an English language learner—first, the learner's ability to produce the English sound accurately and second, his or her ability to associate the sound produced with the correct symbol. Therefore, both the sound system and the writing system of the primary language can affect a student's English language acquisition. The sound-symbol correspondence chart includes only those languages that use the Roman alphabet because other languages have zero transfer for the entire English writing system.

Best instructional practice proceeds from the known to the unknown. Therefore, with a group of language learners with a single language background, elements of positive transfer are taught first, followed by zero transfer elements, and finally by negative transfer elements.

When encountering an element of negative transfer in a young learner's ability to produce the sounds of English, teachers often find that overt correction can raise children's anxiety, resulting in an overall negative effect for language learning. Because children who learn a second language before the age of 12 will generally acquire the sound system perfectly over time, spending instructional time on pronunciation is not necessary. Rather, modeling correct pronunciation back to students while validating their English approximations is the best course to follow.

It can also be beneficial to use knowledge about negative transfer issues to inform an instructional approach to a specific language element. For instance, when teaching the letters *b* and *v* to Spanish-speaking students (these two sounds are variants of a single phoneme, or distinctive sound, in Spanish), an approach that contrasts the English sounds and symbols of these two letters will probably yield the best results. Similarly, raising the awareness of intermediate language learners to the cause of their errors can help them learn to self-correct. For example, a teacher might say, "Lupita, I see that you wrote *country large* in this assignment. I know that's how you say it in Spanish, but we always say *large country* in English. Next time you write a paper, maybe you can proofread for that type of mistake." Metacognitive language learning strategies, those in which students are actively engaged in analyzing and improving their learning process, can accelerate language learning.

> **Best instructional practice proceeds from the known to the unknown.**

Good instruction is anchored in a well-rounded knowledge of students and their learning needs. Because teachers of English language learners cannot possibly speak all the primary languages that represent the backgrounds of each of their students, we have brought together expert language consultants in order to provide important information that can inform classroom instruction.

Background Information for Ten Primary Languages

The following background information is provided to help you understand the linguistic and cultural heritage of the students in your classroom. The list is ordered according to size of population in U.S. schools.

Spanish

The largest group of English language learners in the United States is comprised of Spanish-speaking students whose families have come from Mexico, Central America, South America, and the Caribbean. Immigrants come to the United States seeking economic opportunity, education, or refuge from political unrest. Spanish colonial conquest led to the dominance of Spanish as the official language in much of the Americas. Over 70 percent of Spanish-speaking immigrants come to the United States from Mexico. Other Spanish-speaking countries and territories are Argentina, Bolivia, Chile, Colombia, Costa Rica, Cuba, Dominican Republic, Ecuador, El Salvador, Guatemala, Honduras, Nicaragua, Panama, Paraguay, Peru, Puerto Rico, Spain, Uruguay, and Venezuela. This great diversity is reflected in the different regional variations of Spanish spoken by different groups. There can be several different words (lexical variants) to refer to the same thing or express the same action. However, Spanish speakers from different regions can still communicate with each other. Given that Spanish is a language derived from Latin and that English also contains many words of Latin origin, English and Spanish share many cognates with a common Latin root. These cognates are words with a common origin that have a similar meaning and spelling in both languages.

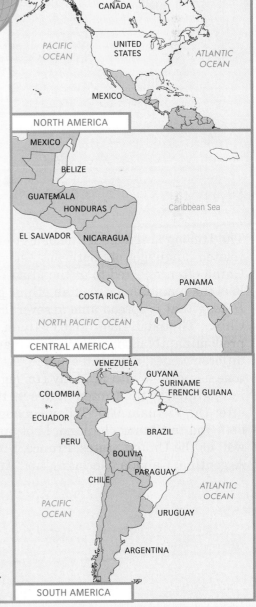

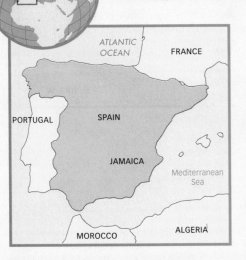

Vietnamese

Vietnamese is one of approximately 150 languages belonging to the Austro-Asiatic family of languages. It is spoken in Vietnam, on the eastern portion of the Indo-Chinese Peninsula in Southeast Asia. The official language of Vietnam, Vietnamese, is a tonal language made up of six distinct tones. Vietnamese is written with the Roman alphabet and employs diacritical markings to depict tones. Many Vietnamese speakers immigrated to the United States in 1975 after the end of the Vietnam War and the reunification of North and South Vietnam, and, most recently, from 1985 to 1991 through family reunification programs.

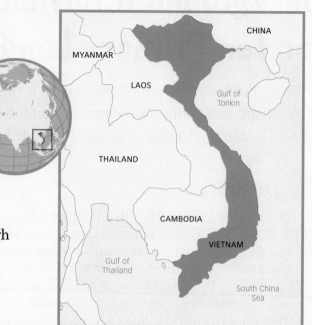

Hmong

The Hmong language is one of a group of closely related languages of Southeast Asia and Southern China often referred to as the Miao-Yao languages. It is the tonal language of an ethnic group called *Hmong* that is spread among several countries: China, Thailand, Laos, and Vietnam. Hmong is predominantly monosyllabic. It is made up of eight different tones, and each syllable has a particular tone associated with it. Many Hmong speakers immigrated to the United States in 1975 as refugees after the Vietnam War. Today Hmong people can be found in China, Thailand, Laos, and Vietnam as well as the United States, France, French Guiana, Argentina, Canada, Germany, and Australia.

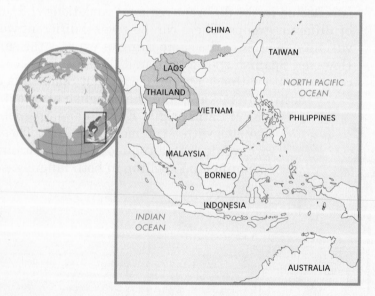

Cantonese

Cantonese is a tonal language belonging to the Sino-Tibetan language family. It is one of the major dialects of Chinese spoken in both the Zhujiang delta, in South China's Guangdong Province, and in Hong Kong. Other major dialects of Chinese include Mandarin, Hakka, Wu, and Min. Although these Chinese dialects share a common writing system, speakers of the various dialects cannot necessarily understand one another. Chinese is traditionally written top to bottom rather than left to right, and text starts from what we usually consider the back of a book. Mandarin, the official language of the People's Republic of China, is used in education in Guangdong rather than Cantonese. An influx of Cantonese speakers came into the United States after World War II and again in the late 1960s after the passage of the Immigration and Naturalization Act of 1965. A further impetus occurred in the 1970s, when the United States offered educational opportunities to Chinese immigrants.

Korean

Korean is a non-tonal Asian language spoken in the Korean Peninsula in Northeast Asia. There are seven Korean dialects: Ham-Kyung, Pyung-Yang, Choong-Chung, Kyung-Sang, Chul-La, Che-Joo, and Central, which is spoken in Seoul and Kyung-Gui. Korean speakers can be found in both North and South Korea, China, Japan, and Russia. Many immigrated to the United States after the liberation of Korea from Japanese colonization in 1945 and again after the passage of the 1965 Immigration and Naturalization Act. Koreans continue to immigrate to the United States seeking a higher standard of living, better educational opportunities, and political stability.

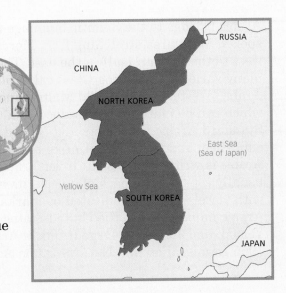

Haitian Creole

An official language of Haiti and the sole language of much of the population of Haiti, Haitian Creole is a language that developed out of contact between the French colonists and West African languages of the plantation workers. As a result, it contains elements of all of these languages. While much of its vocabulary is similar to French, other elements of the language, such as grammar, differ dramatically. Since 1940 three different writing systems, all based on the Roman alphabet, have been introduced for the language, resulting in widespread use of hybrid elements of each of these systems despite the Haitian government's adoption of a standard writing system in 1979. Speakers of Haitian Creole come to the United States seeking economic opportunity. Between 1981 and 1996, almost one million people left Haiti.

Arabic

Arabic belongs to the Semitic language family. It is spoken in an area stretching from Morocco in the west to the Persian Gulf in the east. There are many varieties, including Classical Arabic, Eastern Arabic, Western Arabic, and Maltese, not all of which can be mutually understood. A Modern Standard Arabic also exists and is used in literature, education, and the media. Unlike most European languages, Arabic is written from right to left, and text starts from what we usually consider the back of a book. Its alphabet consists of 28 letters, mainly consonants, with vowels that are indicated by marks above or below the letters. Most speakers of Arabic immigrated to the United States from the nations of Syria, Lebanon, Egypt, Yemen, and Jordan. A large influx of Arabic speakers occurred after the passage of the 1965 Immigration and Naturalization Act.

Russian

As a member of the Indo-European language family, the same language family as English, Russian shares some cognates with English. Cognates are words of similar meaning that sound similar between two languages. Russian is written in a left-to-right format, with the Cyrillic alphabet, however, not the Roman one. The first influx of Russian-speaking immigrants to the United States occurred during the first decades of the last century and consisted of those seeking religious and political freedom and an escape from war. A second wave of immigration to the United States from Russia occurred in the 1970s, when dissidents were exiled from the Soviet Union, many of them choosing the United States as their new country of residence. After the demise of the Soviet Union in the 1990s, more Russian immigrants have come to the United States seeking better economic opportunities and social stability.

Tagalog

Tagalog (pronounced tah-GAH-lug) is one of over 300 languages that belong to the Malayo-Polynesian family of languages spoken in the Philippines, a set of islands off the southeast coast of mainland China. Tagalog (also called *Filipino*) and English have been the two official languages of the Philippines since 1973, while Tagalog remains the sole national language of the Philippines. There is a great diversity of languages in the Philippines. Some of the major languages other than Tagalog include Cebuano, Ilocano, Hiligaynon, Bicol, and Waray. Tagalog speakers immigrated to the United States mainly after 1946, when they achieved independence after being a U.S. territory for 46 years.

Khmer (Cambodian)

The word *Khmer* (pronounced kuh-MIE, rhymes with *pie*) refers to both the national language and the people of Cambodia, located in Southeast Asia. Khmer, a non-tonal language, is spoken by 90 percent of the population in Cambodia and also by many people in northeast Thailand and southern Vietnam. Cambodian Americans arrived in the United States in two waves. The first wave consisted of a small number who escaped Cambodia just before the Khmer Rouge takeover in 1975. The second wave consisted of a much larger number of refugees who fled the country after the 1979 invasion of Cambodia by Vietnam, ending the reign of the Khmer Rouge. Between 1975 and 1987, over 140,000 Cambodian refugees resettled in the United States. Refugee resettlement came to an end in the late 1980s, but Cambodian immigrants continue to arrive as Cambodian Americans sponsor family members who had been left behind.

Grammar Transfer Support

The following chart identifies areas in which speakers of various primary languages may have some difficulty in acquiring English grammar (syntax). The type of transfer error and its cause is outlined for each grammatical category.

NOUNS

Grammar Point	Type of Transfer Error in English	Language Background	Cause of Transfer Difficulty
Plural forms	omission of plural marker –s *I have 5 book.*	Cantonese, Haitian Creole, Hmong, Khmer, Korean, Tagalog, Vietnamese	Nouns do not change form to show the plural in the primary language.
Possessive forms	avoidance of *'s* to describe possession *the children of my sister* instead of *my sister's children*	Haitian Creole, Hmong, Khmer, Spanish, Tagalog, Vietnamese	The use of a prepositional phrase to express possession reflects the only structure or a more common structure in the primary language.
	no marker for possessive forms *house my friend* instead of *my friend's house*	Haitian Creole, Khmer, Vietnamese	A noun's owner comes after the object in the primary language.
Count versus noncount nouns	use of plural forms for English noncount nouns *the furnitures, the color of her hairs*	Haitian Creole, Russian, Spanish, Tagalog	Nouns that are count and noncount differ between English and the primary language.

ARTICLES

Grammar Point	Type of Transfer Error in English	Language Background	Cause of Transfer Difficulty
Placement of articles	omission of article *He has job.* *His dream is to become lawyer, not teacher.*	Cantonese, Haitian Creole, Hmong, Khmer, Korean, Russian, Tagalog, Vietnamese	Articles are either lacking or the distinction between *a* and *the* is not paralleled in the primary language.
	omission of articles in certain contexts, such as to identify a profession *He is teacher.*	Spanish	The article is not used in Spanish in this context, but it is needed in English.
Use of articles	overuse of articles *The honesty is the best policy.* *This food is popular in the Japan.* *I like the cats.*	Arabic, Haitian Creole, Hmong, Spanish, Tagalog	The article is used in the primary language in places where it isn't used in English.
	use of *one* for *a/an* *He is one engineer.*	Haitian Creole, Hmong, Vietnamese	Learners sometimes confuse the articles *a/an* with *one* since articles either do not exist in the primary language or serve a different function.

PRONOUNS

Grammar Point	Type of Transfer Error in English	Language Background	Cause of Transfer Difficulty
Personal pronouns, gender	use of pronouns with inappropriate gender *He is my sister.*	Cantonese, Haitian Creole, Hmong, Khmer, Korean, Tagalog	The third person pronoun in the primary language is gender free. The same pronoun is used where English uses masculine, feminine, and neuter pronouns, resulting in confusion of pronoun forms in English.
	use of pronouns with inappropriate gender *He is my sister.*	Spanish	In Spanish, subject pronouns are dropped in everyday speech and the verb conveys third-person agreement, effectively collapsing the two pronouns and causing transfer difficulty for subject pronouns in English.
	use of inappropriate gender, particularly with neuter nouns *The house is big. She is beautiful.*	Russian, Spanish	Inanimate nouns have feminine and masculine gender in the primary language, and the gender may be carried over into English.
Personal pronoun forms	confusion of subject and object pronoun forms *Him hit me.* *I like she.* *Let we go.*	Cantonese, Hmong, Khmer	The same pronoun form is used for *he/him, she/her,* and in some primary languages for *I/me* and *we/us.*
	use of incorrect number for pronouns *I saw many yellow flowers. It was pretty.*	Cantonese, Korean	There is no number agreement in the primary language.
	omission of subject pronouns *Michael isn't here. Is in school.*	Korean, Russian, Spanish	Subject pronouns may be dropped in the primary language and the verb ending supplies information on number and/or gender.
	omission of object pronouns *That man is very rude, so nobody likes.*	Korean, Vietnamese	Direct objects are frequently dropped in the primary language.
	omission of pronouns in clauses *If not have jobs, they will not have food.*	Cantonese, Vietnamese	A subordinate clause at the beginning of a sentence does not require a subject in the primary language.
	use of pronouns with subject nouns *This car it runs very fast.* *Your friend he seems so nice.* *My parents they live in Vietnam.*	Hmong, Spanish, Vietnamese	This type of redundant structure reflects the popular "topic-comment" approach used in the primary language: The speaker mentions a topic and then makes a comment on it.

PRONOUNS *continued*

Grammar Point	Type of Transfer Error in English	Language Background	Cause of Transfer Difficulty
Pronoun use	avoidance of pronouns by repetition of nouns *Sara visits her grandfather every Sunday, and Sara makes a meal.*	Korean, Vietnamese	It is common in the primary language to repeat nouns rather than to use pronouns.
Pronoun *one*	omission of the pronoun *one* *I saw two nice cars, and I like the small.*	Russian, Spanish, Tagalog	Adjectives can be used on their own in the primary language, whereas English often requires a noun or *one*.
Possessive forms	confusion of possessive forms *The book is my.*	Cantonese, Hmong, Vietnamese	Cantonese and Hmong speakers tend to omit final *n*, creating confusion between *my* and *mine*.

ADJECTIVES

Grammar Point	Type of Transfer Error in English	Language Background	Cause of Transfer Difficulty
Placement of adjective	position of adjectives after nouns *I read a book interesting.*	Haitian Creole, Hmong, Khmer, Spanish, Vietnamese	Adjectives commonly come after nouns in the primary language.
	position of adjectives before certain pronouns *This is interesting something.*	Cantonese, Korean	Adjectives always come before words they modify in the primary language.
Comparison	omission of markers for comparison *She is smart than me.*	Khmer	Since there are no suffixes or inflections in Khmer, the tendency is to omit them in English.
	avoidance of *-er* and *-est* endings *I am more old than my brother.*	Hmong, Khmer, Korean, Spanish	Comparative and superlative are usually formed with separate words in the primary language, the equivalent of *more* and *most* in English.
Confusion of *-ing* and *-ed* forms	confusion of *-ing* and *-ed* forms *The movie was bored.* *I am very interesting in sports.*	Cantonese, Khmer, Korean, Spanish	The adjective forms in the primary language that correspond to the ones in English do not have active and passive meanings. In Korean, for many adjectives, the same form is used for both active and passive meanings, such as *boring* versus *bored*.

VERBS

Grammar Point	Type of Transfer Error in English	Language Background	Cause of Transfer Difficulty
Present tense	omission of *s* in present tense, third person agreement *She go to school every day.*	Cantonese, Haitian Creole, Hmong, Khmer, Korean, Tagalog, Vietnamese	There is no subject-verb agreement in the primary language.
	problems with irregular subject-verb agreement *Sue and Ed has a new house.*	Cantonese, Hmong, Khmer, Korean, Tagalog	Verb forms do not change to indicate the number of the subject in the primary language.
Past tense	omission of tense markers *I study English yesterday.* *I give it to him yesterday.*	Cantonese, Haitian Creole, Hmong, Khmer, Korean, Tagalog, Vietnamese	Verbs in the primary language do not change form to express tense.
	confusion of present form and simple past of irregular verbs *I give it to him yesterday.*	Cantonese, Spanish	Speakers of the primary language have difficulty recognizing that merely a vowel shift in the middle of the verb, rather than a change in the ending of the verb, is sufficient to produce a change of tense in irregular verbs.
	incorrect use of present for the future *I come tomorrow.*	Cantonese, Korean	The primary language allows the use of present tense for the future.
In negative statements	omission of helping verbs in negative statements *I no understand.* *I not get into university.*	Cantonese, Korean, Russian, Spanish, Tagalog	Helping verbs are not used in negative statements in the primary language.
Perfect tenses	avoidance of present perfect where it should be used *I live here for two years.*	Haitian Creole, Russian, Tagalog, Vietnamese	The verb form either doesn't exist in the primary language or has a different function.
	use of present perfect where past perfect should be used *Yesterday I have done that.*	Khmer, Korean	In the primary language a past marker, e.g., *yesterday*, is inserted to indicate a completed action and no other change is necessary. In English when a past marker is used, the verb form must change to past perfect instead of present perfect.
Past continuous	use of past continuous for recurring action in the past *When I was young, I was studying a lot.*	Korean, Spanish, Tagalog	In the primary language, the past continuous form can be used in contexts in which English uses the expression *used to* or the simple past.
Verb as a noun	omission of infinitive marker *to* *Criticize people is not good.*	Cantonese	Unlike English, Cantonese does not require an infinitive marker when using a verb as a noun.

VERBS *continued*

Grammar Point	Type of Transfer Error in English	Language Background	Cause of Transfer Difficulty
Two verbs in a sentence	Use of two or more main verbs in one clause without any connectors *I took a book studied at the library.*	Hmong	In Hmong verbs can be connected without *and* or any other conjunction (serial verbs).
Linking verbs	Omission of linking verb *He hungry.*	Cantonese, Haitian Creole, Hmong, Khmer, Russian, Vietnamese	The verb *be* is not required in all sentences. In some primary languages, it is implied in the adjectival form. In others, the concept is expressed as a verb.
Passive voice	Omission of helping verb *be* in passive voice *The food finished.*	Cantonese, Vietnamese	Passive voice in the primary language does not require a helping verb.
	Avoidance of passive constructions *They speak Creole here.* *One speaks Creole here.* avoiding the alternate *Creole is spoken here.*	Haitian Creole	Passive constructions do not exist in Haitian Creole.
Transitive verbs versus intransitive verbs	confusion of transitive and intransitive verbs *He married with a nice girl.*	Cantonese, Korean, Russian, Spanish, Tagalog	Verbs that do and do not take a direct object differ between English and the primary language.
Phrasal verbs	confusion of related phrasal verbs *I look after the word in the dictionary.* instead of *I look up the word in the dictionary.*	Korean, Russian, Spanish	Phrasal verbs do not exist in the primary language. There is often confusion over their meaning in English.
have **versus** *be*	use of *have* instead of *be* *I have hunger.* *I have right.*	Spanish	Some Spanish constructions use *have* where English uses *be*.

ADVERBS

Grammar Point	Type of Transfer Error in English	Language Background	Cause of Transfer Difficulty
Use of adverbs	use of adjective form where adverb form is needed *Walk quiet.*	Haitian Creole, Hmong, Khmer	There are no suffix-derived adverb forms in the primary language, and the adjective form is used after the verb.
Placement of adverbs	placement of adverbs before verbs *At ten o'clock this morning my plane landed.* avoiding the alternate, *My plane landed at ten o'clock this morning.*	Cantonese, Korean	Adverbs usually come before verbs in the primary language, and this tendency is carried over into English.

PREPOSITIONS

Grammar Point	Type of Transfer Error in English	Language Background	Cause of Transfer Difficulty
Preposition use	omission of prepositions *Money does not grow trees.*	Cantonese	There are no exact equivalents of English prepositions in Cantonese although there are words to mark location and movement.

COMPLEX SENTENCES

Grammar Point	Type of Transfer Error in English	Language Background	Cause of Transfer Difficulty
Relative clauses	omission of relative pronouns *My grandfather was a generous man helped everyone.*	Vietnamese	Relative pronouns are not required in Vietnamese.
	incorrect pronoun used to introduce a relative clause *the house <u>who</u> is big*	Hmong	Hmong uses the same forms of relative pronouns for both personal and inanimate antecedents.
Adverbial clauses	inclusion of additional connecting word *Because he was reckless, <u>so</u> he caused an accident.* *Although my parents are poor, <u>but</u> they are very generous.*	Cantonese, Korean, Vietnamese	The primary language sometimes uses a "balancing word" in the main clause.
	use of inconsistent tenses in sentences with multiple clauses *She <u>speaks</u> French before she <u>studied</u> English.* *After she <u>comes</u> home, it <u>was</u> raining.* *We <u>will go</u> to the beach if the weather <u>will be</u> nice.*	Cantonese, Hmong, Tagalog, Vietnamese	The primary language lacks tense markers so that matching the tenses of two verbs in one sentence correctly can be difficult. Learners may also try to analyze the tense needed in English according to meaning, which in some cases can result in the use of an incorrect tense.
If versus when	Confusion of *if* and *when* *If you get there, call me!* instead of *When you get there, call me!*	Korean	The primary language has one expression that covers the use of English *if* and *when* for the future.

INFINITIVES AND GERUNDS

Grammar Point	Type of Transfer Error in English	Language Background	Cause of Transfer Difficulty
Infinitive and gerund use	use of present tense verbs in places where gerunds or infinitives are used in English *Stop* <u>*walk*</u>. *I want* <u>*go*</u> *there.*	Haitian Creole, Khmer, Korean	Either the *–ing* form does not exist in the primary language, or learners tend to use present tense verbs instead of gerunds even if they do exist [Haitian Creole].
	use of *for* in infinitive phrases *They went* <u>*for*</u> *to see the movie.*	Spanish	Spanish uses a prepositional form in similar constructions, which is carried over into English and translated as *for*.

SENTENCE STRUCTURE

Grammar Point	Type of Transfer Error in English	Language Background	Cause of Transfer Difficulty
Objects	omission of object *He dyed [his hair].* *Yes, I want [some].*	Korean	Korean tends to omit objects and noun phrases after verbs.
Variety	lack of variety in the position of clauses *Because you weren't at home and I couldn't find you, I left.* avoiding the alternate, *I left because you weren't at home and I couldn't find you.*	Korean	Since main clauses always come last in Korean, there is a tendency to put the main clause last in English. This is not an error in English, but it leads to a lack of sentence variety.
Sequential action	clauses that describe earlier actions come first *After I finish my homework, I will watch TV.* avoiding the alternate, *I will watch TV after I finish my homework.*	Cantonese, Korean	The pattern in the primary language is to describe what happens first while later occurrences follow. This is not an error in English, but it leads to a lack of sentence variety.
Placement issues	placement of phrase with the indirect object before the direct object *They gave* <u>*to the girl*</u> *the book.*	Spanish	The phrase with the indirect object can come before the direct object in Spanish.
	placement of modifiers between verb and direct object *She speaks* <u>*very well*</u> *English.*	Korean, Spanish	Word order, including the placement of adverbials, is freer in the primary language than in English.
Usage issues	use of double negatives *I* <u>*no*</u> *see* <u>*nobody*</u>.	Spanish	Spanish requires double negatives in many sentence structures.
	use of clauses for other structures *I want* <u>*that you help me.*</u>	Russian, Spanish	Verbs that take direct objects versus those that require clauses differ in the primary language and English.

QUESTIONS

Grammar Point	Type of Transfer Error in English	Language Background	Cause of Transfer Difficulty
Subject-verb order	lack of subject-verb inversion in questions with helping verbs *When she will be home?* *Where you are going?*	Cantonese, Hmong, Russian, Tagalog	In the primary language, word order is the same in some questions and statements, depending on the context.
Do **and** *did*	omission of *do* or *did* in questions *Where you went?*	Haitian Creole, Hmong, Khmer, Korean, Russian, Spanish, Tagalog	In the primary language, there is no exact counterpart to the *do/did* verb in questions.
Yes/no questions	avoidance of English inverted question forms in yes/no questions in favor of tag questions or intonation *You come tomorrow, OK?* *He goes to school with you?*	Cantonese, Haitian Creole, Khmer, Korean, Russian, Tagalog, Vietnamese	The primary language doesn't use subject-verb inversion in questions.
	incorrect answer form for yes/no questions *A: Do you want more food?* *B: I want.* *A: Do you have a pen?* *B: I not have.*	Cantonese, Hmong, Khmer, Korean, Russian	In the primary language, learners tend to answer *yes* by repeating the verb in the question. They tend to say *no* by using *not* and repeating the verb.
	positive answer to negative question *A: Aren't you going?* *B: Yes. (when the person is not going)*	Cantonese, Korean, Russian	The appropriate response pattern differs between the primary language and English.
Tag questions	incorrect tag questions *You want to go home, are you?*	Cantonese, Khmer, Korean, Vietnamese	The primary language has no exact counterpart to a tag question, forms them differently, or does not add *do/did* to questions.

Phonics Transfer Support for Seven Languages

Sound Transfer (Phonology)

The symbol ■ identifies areas in which these primary language speakers may have some difficulty pronouncing and perceiving spoken English. The sound may not exist in the primary language, may exist but be pronounced somewhat differently, or may be confused with another sound. Sound production and perception issues affect phonics instruction.

CONSONANTS

Sound	Spanish	Vietnamese	Hmong	Cantonese	Haitian Creole	Korean	Khmer
/b/ as in bat			■	■		■	
/k/ as in cat and kite			■				
/d/ as in dog				■		■	
/f/ as in fan						■	
/g/ as in goat			■	■		■	■
/h/ as in hen					■		
/j/ as in jacket	■	■	■	■		■	
/l/ as in lemon						■	
/m/ as in money							
/n/ as in nail							
/p/ as in pig			■				
/r/ as in rabbit	■		■	■	■	■	
/s/ as in sun			■				
/t/ as in teen		■	■				
/v/ as in video	■			■		■	■
/w/ as in wagon	■		■				■
/y/ as in yo-yo							
/z/ as in zebra	■		■	■		■	■
/kw/ as in queen			■				
/ks/ as in X ray			■	■			

SHORT VOWELS

Sound	Spanish	Vietnamese	Hmong	Cantonese	Haitian Creole	Korean	Khmer
short a as in hat	■	■		■		■	
short e as in set	■		■	■	■	■	
short i as in sit	■	■	■	■	■	■	
short o as in hot	■		■			■	
short u as in cup	■		■	■	■	■	

LONG VOWELS

Sound	Spanish	Vietnamese	Hmong	Cantonese	Haitian Creole	Korean	Khmer
long a as in d<u>a</u>te			■	■			
long e as in b<u>e</u>				■		■	
long i as in <u>i</u>ce				■			
long o as in r<u>oa</u>d			■	■			
long u as in tr<u>ue</u>				■		■	

VOWEL PATTERNS

Sound	Spanish	Vietnamese	Hmong	Cantonese	Haitian Creole	Korean	Khmer
oo as in b<u>oo</u>k	■	■	■		■	■	■
aw as in s<u>aw</u>	■					■	

DIPHTHONGS

Sound	Spanish	Vietnamese	Hmong	Cantonese	Haitian Creole	Korean	Khmer
oy as in b<u>oy</u>			■				
ow as in h<u>ow</u>	■						

R-CONTROLLED VOWELS

Sound	Spanish	Vietnamese	Hmong	Cantonese	Haitian Creole	Korean	Khmer
ir as in b<u>ir</u>d	■	■	■	■	■	■	■
ar as in h<u>ar</u>d	■	■	■	■	■	■	■
or as in f<u>or</u>m	■	■	■	■	■	■	■
air as in h<u>air</u>	■	■	■	■	■	■	■
ear as in h<u>ear</u>	■	■	■	■	■	■	■

CONSONANT DIGRAPHS

Sound	Spanish	Vietnamese	Hmong	Cantonese	Haitian Creole	Korean	Khmer
sh as in <u>sh</u>oe	■*	■		■			■
ch as in <u>ch</u>ain		■	■				
th as in <u>th</u>ink	■	■		■	■	■	■
ng as in si<u>ng</u>	■			■	■		

CONSONANT BLENDS

Sound	Spanish	Vietnamese	Hmong	Cantonese	Haitian Creole	Korean	Khmer
bl, tr, dr, etc. (start of words) as in <u>bl</u>ack, <u>tr</u>ee, <u>dr</u>ess		■	■	■		■	
ld, nt, rt, etc. (end of words) as in co<u>ld</u>, te<u>nt</u>, sta<u>rt</u>		■	■	■	■	■	■

* Spanish speakers from Mexico or Central America who also speak Nahuatl or a Mayan language will be familiar with this sound, written as an x in words like *mixteca* (pronounced *mishteca*).

Sound-Symbol Transfer (Phonics)

The following chart identifies sound-symbol transfer issues for four languages that use the roman alphabet. (The remaining three do not.) The symbol ■ identifies symbols which do not represent the corresponding sound in the writing system of the primary language.

CONSONANTS

Sound	Spanish	Vietnamese	Hmong	Haitian Creole
b as in <u>b</u>at			■	
c as in <u>c</u>at		■	■	■
as in <u>c</u>ent		■	■	
d as in <u>d</u>og				
f as in <u>f</u>ish				
g as in <u>g</u>oat			■	
as in <u>g</u>iant	■		■	
h as in <u>h</u>en	■			
j as in <u>j</u>acket	■	■	■	
k as in <u>k</u>ite			■	
l as in <u>l</u>emon				
m as in <u>m</u>oon				
n as in <u>n</u>ice				
p as in <u>p</u>ig				
qu as in <u>qu</u>een	■		■	■
r as in <u>r</u>abbit	■		■	
s as in <u>s</u>un			■	
t as in <u>t</u>een			■	
v as in <u>v</u>ideo	■			
w as in <u>w</u>agon		■	■	
x as in <u>X</u> ray		■	■	■
y as in <u>y</u>o-<u>y</u>o	■			
z as in <u>z</u>ebra	■	■	■	

CONSONANT DIAGRAPHS

Sound	Spanish	Vietnamese	Hmong	Haitian Creole
sh as in <u>sh</u>oe	■			
ch as in <u>ch</u>air				■
th as in <u>th</u>ink as in <u>th</u>at	■			■

VOWELS AND VOWEL PATTERNS

Sound	Spanish	Vietnamese	Hmong	Haitian Creole
a as in bat	■		■	
aCe as in date	■	■		
ai as in rain	■	■	■	■
ay as in day	■		■	■
au as in author	■	■	■	■
aw as in saw	■	■	■	■
e as in bet	■		■	■
ee as in seed	■	■	■	■
ea as in tea	■	■	■	■
ew as in few	■	■	■	■
i as in sit	■		■	■
iCe as in pipe	■	■	■	■
o as in hot	■		■	■
o as in rode	■	■	■	■
oo as in moon	■	■	■	■
oo as in book	■		■	■
oa as in boat	■	■	■	■
ow as in row	■	■	■	■
ow as in how	■	■	■	■
ou as in sound	■	■	■	■
oi as in boil			■	■
oy as in boy		■	■	■
u as in cup	■	■	■	■
uCe as in June	■	■		
ui as in suit	■	■	■	■
ue as in blue	■	■	■	■
y as in try	■	■		■
ar as in star			■	■
er as in fern	■		■	■
ir as in bird	■		■	■
or as in torn	■		■	
ur as in burn	■		■	

Word Study Transfer Support

Spanish

English and Spanish share some basic linguistic characteristics, such as using word parts like prefixes and suffixes and changing verb forms. The example words below are not intended to be cognates, but words that illustrate the similar meaning of the word parts Note that Haitian Creole, Cantonese, Hmong, and Vietnamese do not use word parts to construct new words in the same way that English does.

PREFIXES

English Word Part or Parts	English Example Words	Spanish Word Part or Parts	Spanish Example Words	Word Part Purpose
un-, non-, in-, dis-	unhappy nonstop incorrect dislike	*in-, des-/dis-* *no* plus the verb *sin* plus the noun or verb	infeliz, incorrecto desconocido disparejo no gustar sin parar	Means "not"
re-	redo	*re-*	rehacer	Means "again"
pre-	preteen	*pre-*	preescolar	Means "before"

SUFFIXES

English Word Part or Parts	English Example Words	Spanish Word Part or Parts	Spanish Example Words	Word Part Purpose
-ful	powerful	*-oso/a*	poderoso/a	Means "with"; turns a noun into an adjective
-able	readable likeable	*-ible* *-able*	legible agradable	Turns a verb into an adjective
-less	fearless careless	*sin* plus the noun prefix *des-*	sin miedo descuidado	Means "without"; turns a noun into an adjective
-ness	happiness	*-idad*	felicidad	Turns an adjective into a noun
-ion/-tion, -ment	reaction payment amazement	*-ción/-sión* verb stem + *-o*	reacción conclusión pago asombro	Turns a verb into a noun
-ly	quickly	*-mente*	rápidamente	Turns an adjective into an adverb

Reading-Writing Connection

The literary works listed on pages TE 36–43 provide high-interest **mentor texts** that you can use to inspire your students as you teach the different forms of writing. Use these texts to accentuate **writer's craft**:

- Read **strong beginnings** or **strong endings** to inspire students as they create their own beginnings and endings.
- Read paragraphs that **develop deas** or demonstrate **strong organization**.
- Read from two different examples to **contrast voice** and **word choice**.
- Read from different authors to examine their **sentence style**.

Narrative Books for Grades 11–12

The Perks of Being a Wallflower
Stephen Chbosky, 1999

The Body of Christopher Creed
Carol Plum-Ucci, 2001

A Door Near Here
Heather Quarles, 1998

Crazy as Chocolate
Elizabeth Hyde, 2002

Diamond Dogs
Alan Watt, 2000

A Long Way Gone: Memoirs of a Boy Soldier
Ishmael Beah, 2007

Born Again
Kelly Kerney, 2006

Fruit of the Lemon
Andrea Levy, 2007

The Discomfort Zone: A Personal History
Jonathan Franzen, 2006

The Syringa Tree
Pamela Gien, 2006

The Marsh Birds
Eva Sallis, 2006

Perfect, Once Removed: When Baseball Was All the World to Me
Phillip Hoose, 2006

Holdup
Terri Fields, 2007

A Novel Idea
Aimee Friedman, 2006

Monkey Town: The Summer of the Scopes Trial
Ronald Kidd, 2006

The Book Thief
Markus Zusak, 2006

Saint Iggy
K. L. Going, 2006

The Braid
Helen Frost, 2006

Harlem Hustle
Janet McDonald, 2006

A Summer Life
Gary Soto, 1990

Growing Up
Russell Baker, 1982

Story of a Girl
Sara Zarr

I Know Why the Caged Bird Sings
Maya Angelou, 1969

The Awakening
Kate Chopin, 1899

The Bean Trees
Barbara Kingsolver, 1997

Tuesdays with Morrie
Mitch Albom, 1997

Angela's Ashes
Frank McCourt, 1996

A Yellow Raft in Blue Water
Michael Dorris, 1987

A Tree Grows in Brooklyn
Betty Smith, 1943

Survival in Auschwitz
Primo Levi, 1961

Rocket Boys
Homer Hickam, 1998

Long Walk to Freedom: The Autobiography of Nelson Mandela
Nelson Mandela, 1994

The First Part Last
Angela Johnson, 2003

A River Runs Through It
Norman Maclean, 1976

Black Like Me
John H Griffin, 1969

Oldest Living Confederate Widow Tells All: A Novel
Allan Gurganus, 1989

In the Time of the Butterflies
Julia Alvarez, 1994

The Last Shot: City Streets, Basketball Dreams
Darcy Frey, 1994

Travels with Charley
John Steinbeck, 1962

The Beet Queen
Louise Erdrich, 1986

Expository Books for Grades 11–12

Electric Universe
David Bodnis, 2005

Silent Snow: The Slow Poisoning of the Arctic
Marla Cone, 2005

And Still We Rise
Miles Corwin, 2001

Chronicles: Volume One
Bob Dylan, 2004

Nickle and Dimed: On (Not) Getting by in America
Barbara Enrenreich, 2001

The Tipping Point: How Little Things Can Make a Difference
Malcolm Gladwell, 2002

The Modern American Presidency
Lewis Gould, 2003

Will in the World: How Shakespeare Became Shakespeare
Stephen Greenblatt, 2004

A Brief History of Time: From the Big Bang to Black Holes
Stephen Hawking, 1998

On Writing: A Memoir of the Craft
Stephen King, 2000

Founding Mothers: The Women Who Raised Our Nation
Cokie Roberts, 2004

Fast Food Nation
Eric Schlosser, 2001

Scourge: The Once and Future Threat of Smallpox
Jonathan B. Tucker, 2001

The Future of Life
Edward O. Wilson, 2002

Think
Simon Blackburn, 1999

Influenza: The Next Pandemic?
Connie Goldsmith, 2006

Extrasolar Planets
Ron Miller, 2002

The Gatekeepers: Inside the Admissions Process of a Premier College
Jacques Steinberg, 2002

Patterns of Culture
Ruth Benedict, 1989

The Sea Around Us
Rachel Carson, 1953

Requiem
Horst Faas, Tim Page, 1997

Gideon's Trumpet
Anthony Lewis, 1964

Moneyball: The Art of Winning an Unfair Game
Michael Lewis, 2003

The Rise of the Indian Rope Trick: How a Spectacular Hoax Became History
Peter Lamont, 2004

Finding Atlantis: A True Story of Genius, Madness, and an Extraordinary Quest for a Lost World
David King, 2005

There Are No Children Here: The Story of Two Boys Growing Up in the Other America
Alex Kotlowitz, 1991

Last Days of Democracy: How Big Media and Power-Hungry Government Are Turning America into a Dictatorship
Elliott D. Cohen, Bruce W. Fraser, 2007

Island of the Lost
Joan Druett, 2007

Webslinger: SF and Comic Writers on Your Friendly Neighborhood Spider-Man
Glenn Yeffeth, 2007

The Secret Family: Twenty-four Hours Inside the Mysterious Worlds of Our Minds and Bodies
David Bodanis, 1997

School of Dreams: Making the Grade at a Top American High School
Edward Humes, 2003

Freedom Writers Diary: How a Teacher and 150 Teens Used Writing to Change Themselves and the World Around Them
The Freedom Writers, 1999

With Their Eyes: September 11th -- The View from a High School at Ground Zero
Annie Thoms, 2002

What Color Is Your Parachute? For Teens
Richard Nelson Bolles, Carol Christen, 2006

Rock the SAT
Michael Moshan, 2006

Teenage Investor: How to Start Early, Invest Often, and Build Wealth
Timothy Olsen, 2003

Harriers: The Making of a Championship Cross Country Team
Joseph P. Shivers, Paul Shivers, 2006

Firestarters: 100 Job Profiles to Inspire Young Women
Kelly Beatty, 2006

The 7 Simple Truths of Acting for the Teen Actor
Larry Silverberg, 2006

High School Journalism
Homer L. Hall, 2002

Persuasive Books for Grades 11–12

Examples of Satire:

Animal Farm
George Orwell, 1946

Cat's Cradle
Kurt Vonnegut, 1963

Fahrenheit 451
Ray Bradbury, 1953

American Satire: An Anthology of Writings from Colonial Times to the Present
Nicholas Bakalar, 1997

Thank You for Smoking
Christopher Buckley, 1994

The View from the Upper Deck: Sportspickle Presents the Funniest Collection of Sports Satire Ever
D. J. Gallo

Devil's Dictionary
Ambrose Bierce, 2006 (reprint)

Santa Lives! Five Conclusive Arguments for the Existence of Santa Claus
Ellis Weiner, 2005

Ever Wonder Why? And Other Controversial Essays
Thomas Sowell, 2006

Our Endangered Values: America's Moral Crisis
Jimmy Carter, 2005

The JFK Assassination Debates: Lone Gunman versus Conspiracy
Michael L. Kurtz, 2006

The Unaborted Socrates: A Dramatic Debate on the Issues Surrounding Abortion
Peter. Kreeft, 1983

Debating the Death Penalty
Hugo Adam Bedau, 2005

Four Arguments for the Elimination of Television
Jerry Mander, 1978

The Vaccine Controversy: The History, Use, and Safety of Vaccinations
Kurt Link, 2005

Garbage and Waste (Current Controversies Series)
Charles P. Cozic, 1997

Censorship (Current Controversies Series)
Laura K. Egendorf, 2000

Civil Liberties (Current Controversies Series)
James D. Torr, 2003

Afghanistan (Current Controversies Series)
Jann Einfeld, 2005

Team Spirits: The Native American Mascots Controversy
C. Richard King, 2001

The Extreme Future: The Top Trends That Will Shape the World for the Next 5, 10, and 20 Years
James M. Canton, 2006

Clicking: 17 Trends That Drive America
Faith Popcorn, 1998

Gun Control (Opposing Viewpoints)
Tamara L. Roleff, 2002

Ethics (Opposing Viewpoints)
Laurie Dimauro, 2006

The Patriot Act (Opposing Viewpoints)
Louise I. Gerdes, 2005

Books About Responding to Literature—Grades 11–12

Understanding Of Mice and Men
Bradley Steffens, 2002

Understanding The Canterbury Tales
Clarice Swisher, 2003

Understanding Literature: An Introduction to Reading and Writing
Walter Kalaidjian, 2004

Understanding Frankenstein
Don Nardo, 2003

Understanding The Adventures of Huckleberry Finn
Gary Wiener, 2001

Understanding Pride and Prejudice: A Student Casebook to Issues, Sources, and Historical Documents
Debra Teachman, 1997

Understanding The Tempest: A Student Casebook to Issues, Sources, and Historical Documents
Faith Nostbakken, 2004

A Student's Guide to F. Scott Fitzgerald
Eva Weisbrod, 2004

Young Adult Poetry: A Survey and Theme Guide
Rachel Schwedt, Janice DeLong, 2001

When Text Meets Text: Helping High School Readers Make Connections in Literature
Barbara King-Shaver, 2005

Theme-Sets for Secondary Students: How to Scaffold Core Literature
Jeannine D. Richison, Anita C. Hernandez, Marcia J. Carter, 2006

A Student's Guide to Robert Frost
Connie Ann Kirk, 2006

A Student's Guide to Emily Dickinson
Audrey Borus, 2005

How to Read a Poem: And Fall in Love with Poetry
Edward Hirsch, 2000

Sleeping on the Wing: An Anthology of Modern Poetry with Essays on Reading and Writing
Kenneth Koch, Kate Farrell, 1982

A Grain of Poetry: How to Read Contemporary Poems and Make Them A Part of Your Life
Herbert R. Kohl, 2000

Born Storytellers: Readers Theatre Celebrates the Lives and Literature of Classic Authors
Ann N. Black, 2005

Novels into Film: The Encyclopedia of Movies Adapted from Books
John C. Tibbetts, James Michael Welsh, 1999

The Book Lover's Cookbook: Recipes Inspired by Celebrated Works of Literature, and the Passages That Feature Them
Shaunda Kennedy Wenger, Janet Jensen, 2005

Making Books by Hand
Peter Thomas, Donna Thomas, 2005

The Ideals Guide to Literary Places in the U.S.
Michelle Prater Burke, 1998

The Book That Changed My Life: 71 Remarkable Writers Celebrate the Books That Matter Most to Them
Roxanne J. Coady, Joy Johannessen, 2006

The Young Actor's Book of Improvisation: Dramatic Situations Based on Literature, Plays, and Films : Ages 12-16
Sandra Caruso, Susan Kosoff, 1998

Books About Creative Writing—Grades 11–12

Twice Told: Original Stories Inspired by Original Artwork
Scott Hunt, 2006

Teen Ink: Written in the Dirt: A Collection of Short Stories, Poetry, Art and Photography
Stephanie H. Meyer, John Meyer, 2004

The Struggle to Be Strong: True Stories by Teens About Overcoming Tough Times
Al Desetta, Sybil Wolin, 2000

On the Fringe: Stories
Various authors, 2003

Blood on the Forehead: What I Know About Writing
M. E. Kerr, 1998

Turning Life into Fiction: Finding Character, Plot, Setting and Other Elements of Novel and Short Story Writing in the Everyday World
Robin Hemley, 1997

Points of View: An Anthology of Short Stories (Revised Edition)
James Moffett, Kenneth R. McElheny, 1995

Kennedy Center Presents: Award-Winning Plays from the American College Theater Festival
Gary Garrison, 2006

Stage Writing: A Practical Guide
Val Taylor, 2002

Twenty 10-Minute Plays for Teens (Volume I)
Kristen Dabrowski, 2004

Take Ten: More Ten-Minute Plays
Eric Lane, 2003

Scenes for Young Actors
Lorraine Cohen, 1990

Doodlebug: A Selection of Plays Written by Wahoo High School Students for the Enersen Playwriting Contest 1995-2001
Larry Fangman, 2001

Just People & Paper/Pen/Poem: A Young Writer's Way to Begin
Kathi Appelt, Kenneth Appelt, 1997

Paint Me Like I Am: Teen Poems from WritersCorps
Bill Aguado, 2003

Shifting Sands
Weslynn McCallister, 2004

Complete Collected Poems of Maya Angelou
Maya Angelou, 1995

The Complete Sonnets and Poems (Oxford World's Classics)
William Shakespeare, Colin Burrow, 2002

Writing Sonnets for Your Friends and Soul Mates
Vee Bdosa, 2001

Sonnets: 150 Contemporary Sonnets
William Baer, 2005

A Teen's Guide to Getting Published: Publishing for Profit, Recognition and Academic Success
Jessica Dunn, Danielle Dunn, 2006

Luna, Luna: Creative Writing Ideas from Spanish & Latino Literature
Julio Marzan, 1997

Making a Winning Short: How to Write, Direct, Edit, and Produce a Short Film
Edmond Levy, 1994

The Practice of Poetry: Writing Exercises from Poets Who Teach
Robin Behn, 1992

Reference Books for Grades 11–12

The American Heritage High School Dictionary (Fourth Edition)
Houghton Mifflin, 2007

The American Heritage Essential Student Thesaurus
Houghton Mifflin, 2003

100 Research Topic Guides for Students
Barbara Wood Borne, 1996

100 More Research Topic Guides for Students
Dana McDougald, 1999

Encyclopedia of Genocide and Crimes Against Humanity
Dinah Sheltonm, 2005

The Greenhaven Encyclopedia of Capital Punishment
Bruce E. R. Thompson, 2005

Tobacco in History and Culture: An Encyclopedia
Jordan Goodman, 2005

Encyclopedia of Science, Technology and Ethics
Carl Mitcham, 2005

Encyclopedia of the American Presidency
Michael A. Genovese, 2004

Major Acts of Congress
Brian K. Landsberg (editor), 2003

Historical Encyclopedia of U.S. Presidential Use of Force, 1789-2000
Karl R. DeRouen, 2000

My Fellow Americans: Presidential Addresses That Shaped History
James C. Humes, 1992

Social Issues in America: An Encyclopedia (8-Volume Set)
James Ciment, 2006

Encyclopedia of American Civil Rights & Liberties
Otis H. Stephens, 2006

The Executive Branch of State Government: People, Process, and Politics
Margaret R. Ferguson, 2006

Writing Research Papers 2001: Your Complete Guide to the Process of Writing a Research Paper, from Finding a Topic to Preparing the Final Manuscript
Houghton Mifflin, 2000

The Facts on File Guide to Research
Jeff Lenburg, 2005

Internet Research Illustrated, Third Edition (Illustrated Series)
Donald I. Barker, Carol D Terry, 2006

Words You Should Know in High School: 1000 Essential Words to Build Vocabulary, Improve Standardized Test Scores, and Write Successful Papers
Burton Jay Nadler, Jordan Nadler, Justin Nadler, 2005

National Geographic Atlas of the World
National Geographic, 2005

Scientific American Inventions and Discoveries: All the Milestones in Ingenuity - From the Discovery of Fire to the Invention of the Microwave Oven
Rodney P. Carlisle, 2004

The Facts on File Dictionary of Proverbs
Martin H. Manser, Rosalind Fergusson, David Pickering, 2007

Scope and Sequence

Grades	2	3	4	5	6	7	8	9	10	11	12
FORMS OF WRITING											
Descriptive Writing											
paragraph	X	X	X	X	X	X	X				
essay		X	X	X	X	X	X				
Narrative Writing											
paragraph	X	X	X	X	X	X	X				
personal narrative	X	X	X	X	X	X	X	X	X	X	X
biographical narrative					X		X	X			
phase autobiography						X			X		
historical narrative									X		
reflective narrative										X	
college entrance essay											X
Expository Writing											
paragraph	X	X	X	X	X	X	X				
letter	X										
essay		X	X	X							
classification essay					X		X				
how-to/process essay					X			X			
cause-and-effect essay						X			X		
comparison-contrast essay						X	X			X	
comparison essay								X			
concept definition essay								X			
informative article										X	
opposing ideas essay											X
analysis essay											X
Persuasive Writing											
paragraph	X	X	X	X	X	X	X				
letter	X	X					X				
essay				X	X	X					
promote a cause						X					
problem-solution essay							X		X		

	Grades	2	3	4	5	6	7	8	9	10	11	12
Persuasive Writing (continued)												
editorial							■			■	■	■
personal commentary								■				
argumentative essay									■	■	■	■
Response to Texts												
paragraph		■	■	■	■	■	■	■				
book review		■	■	■	■	■	■					
respond to a poem		■	■		■				■	■	■	
respond to a nonfiction article				■	■					■		
respond to a biography				■								
respond to a textbook				■								
respond to a tall tale				■								
respond to a quotation					■							
respond to an anecdote					■							
respond to a magazine article						■						
respond to an expository text							■	■				■
analysis of a theme								■		■	■	■
respond to an essay									■			
respond to a short story									■		■	
respond to a novel												■
Creative Writing												
story		■	■	■	■	■	■	■	■	■	■	■
poem		■	■	■	■	■	■	■	■	■	■	■
play/script		■	■		■				■	■	■	■
Research Writing												
research report		■	■	■	■	■	■	■				
MLA research paper									■	■	■	■
multimedia presentation			■	■	■	■	■	■	■	■	■	■
oral presentation		■	■	■	■	■	■	■	■	■	■	■
Writing for Assessment												
narrative writing		■	■	■	■	■	■	■	■	■	■	■
expository writing		■	■	■	■	■	■	■	■	■	■	■
persuasive writing		■	■	■	■	■	■	■	■	■	■	■
response writing							■	■	■	■	■	■

	Grades	2	3	4	5	6	7	8	9	10	11	12

THE WRITING PROCESS

Prewriting

Select a Topic

	2	3	4	5	6	7	8	9	10	11	12
make a list	■	■	■	■	■	■	■	■	■	■	■
create a cluster/web	■	■	■	■	■	■	■	■	■	■	
brainstorm	■	■	■	■	■	■	■	■		■	■
use sentence starters		■	■	■	■	■	■	■	■	■	
freewrite		■	■	■	■	■	■	■	■	■	■
create a line diagram				■	■		■				
take notes				■	■		■				
create a people chart					■				■		■
create a media grid					■		■				

Gather Details

	2	3	4	5	6	7	8	9	10	11	12
draw	■	■									
use sentence starters	■		■			■					
create a sensory/details chart	■	■	■	■	■	■	■	■			
use a map	■	■								■	
create a time line	■	■	■	■	■	■	■	■	■	■	
create a 5 Ws chart/list	■	■	■	■	■	■	■	■	■	■	■
answer questions	■	■	■	■	■	■	■	■	■	■	■
create a T-chart	■	■		■				■		■	■
create a gathering grid/chart	■	■	■	■		■	■	■	■	■	■
create a chart/cluster	■	■	■	■	■	■	■	■	■		
list topics/ideas	■	■	■	■	■	■	■	■	■	■	■
create a character chart		■	■			■		■			
freewrite			■	■		■		■	■	■	
take notes			■	■	■	■	■	■	■	■	■
create a table diagram			■	■	■	■	■				
create a cause-effect chart						■		■	■		
create a problem-solution chart						■		■			
create a before-and-after chart							■	■	■		

Use Research Skills

Grades	2	3	4	5	6	7	8	9	10	11	12
understand the parts of a book	■	■	■	■	■	■	■	■	■	■	■
use diagrams, charts, time lines, maps	■	■	■	■	■	■	■	■	■	■	■
take notes/summarize	■	■	■	■	■	■	■	■	■	■	■
use computer catalogs	■	■	■	■	■	■	■	■	■	■	■
use periodicals	■	■	■	■	■	■	■	■	■	■	■
interview experts	■	■	■	■	■	■	■	■	■	■	■
conduct online research	■	■	■	■	■	■	■	■	■	■	■
use reference texts	■	■	■	■	■	■	■	■	■	■	■
use a library	■	■	■	■	■	■	■	■	■	■	■
formulate open-ended questions	■	■	■	■	■	■	■	■	■	■	■
create a works cited list/bibliography	■	■	■	■	■	■	■	■	■	■	■
evaluate sources	■	■	■	■	■	■	■	■	■	■	■
use primary vs. secondary sources					■	■	■	■	■	■	■

Organize Details

Grades	2	3	4	5	6	7	8	9	10	11	12
create a sequence chart	■	■				■					
create a cluster/details web	■	■			■					■	■
list topics/ideas	■	■	■	■	■	■	■	■	■	■	■
outline topics/ideas	■	■	■	■	■	■	■	■	■	■	■
create a chart	■	■	■	■	■	■	■	■	■	■	■
put events/ideas in time order	■	■	■	■	■	■	■	■	■	■	■
create a plot/setting/character chart		■	■	■			■		■		
create a Venn diagram		■				■	■	■		■	■
create a story/plot line		■						■	■	■	
create a sensory chart				■		■					
create a collection sheet/grid				■	■				■	■	
use note cards				■	■	■	■	■	■	■	■
create a table diagram					■	■	■				
create a line diagram					■			■			

Drafting

Beginning Paragraphs

Grades	2	3	4	5	6	7	8	9	10	11	12
connect with the reader	■	■	■	■	■	■	■	■	■	■	■
write a main idea/topic sentence	■	■	■	■	■	■	■	■	■	■	■
write a position statement	■	■	■	■	■	■	■	■	■	■	■

Grades	2	3	4	5	6	7	8	9	10	11	12
Beginning Paragraphs (continued)											
incorporate dialogue	■	■	■	■	■	■	■	■	■	■	■
write a focus statement		■	■	■	■	■	■	■	■	■	■
write a thesis statement		■	■	■	■	■	■	■	■	■	■
incorporate a quotation						■	■	■	■		
ask a question	■	■	■	■	■	■	■	■	■	■	
include an interesting fact	■		■	■		■	■	■	■		■
specify time and place	■			■		■	■		■		■
include background information		■				■	■	■	■	■	■
begin with a surprising statement			■	■				■	■	■	■
include an anecdote				■		■		■	■	■	■
Middle Paragraphs											
make comparisons	■	■	■	■	■	■	■	■	■	■	■
incorporate dialogue	■	■	■	■	■	■	■	■	■	■	■
include supporting details/reasons	■	■	■	■	■	■	■	■	■	■	■
include sensory details	■	■	■	■	■	■	■	■	■	■	■
incorporate personal feelings/details	■	■	■	■	■	■	■	■	■	■	■
include specific details	■	■	■	■	■	■	■	■	■	■	■
write topic sentences	■	■	■	■	■	■	■	■	■	■	■
use action words	■	■	■	■	■	■	■	■	■	■	■
use transitions	■	■	■	■	■	■	■	■	■	■	■
include facts	■	■	■	■		■		■	■	■	■
include a point-by-point discussion		■		■		■	■	■	■		
counter objections		■		■		■	■	■	■	■	■
paraphrase information			■	■	■	■	■	■		■	■
build to a climax/high point		■	■	■	■	■	■	■	■	■	■
incorporate quotations			■	■	■	■	■	■	■	■	■
show, don't tell		■				■	■	■			
explain terms							■	■			
include anecdotes							■	■	■	■	■
build suspense								■	■	■	■
incorporate statistics								■	■	■	■

	Grades	2	3	4	5	6	7	8	9	10	11	12

Ending Paragraphs

	2	3	4	5	6	7	8	9	10	11	12
include interesting facts	■		■	■		■	■	■			
include a call to action	■	■	■	■	■	■	■		■	■	
write a concluding statement	■	■	■	■	■	■	■	■	■	■	■
add a final thought/insight	■	■	■	■	■	■	■	■	■	■	■
reflect on experiences	■	■	■	■	■	■	■	■	■	■	■
restate a thesis/focus statement		■	■	■	■	■	■	■	■	■	■
revisit a theme		■					■	■			
refer to the beginning		■				■	■		■	■	
include a direct quotation		■	■	■	■	■	■	■	■	■	
restate a position		■	■	■	■	■	■	■	■	■	
summarize ideas		■	■	■	■	■	■	■	■	■	■
propose a solution					■	■	■	■	■		
include a final scene						■	■	■		■	
emphasize a key idea						■	■		■		■
add new information							■	■			

Revising

Focus and Coherence

	2	3	4	5	6	7	8	9	10	11	12
focus on one main idea	■	■	■	■	■	■	■	■	■	■	■
eliminate unnecessary information	■	■	■	■	■	■	■	■	■	■	■
connect ideas		■	■	■	■	■	■	■	■	■	■
clarify supporting information			■	■	■	■	■	■	■	■	■
improve coherence		■	■	■	■	■	■	■	■	■	■
revise the thesis statement			■	■	■	■	■	■	■	■	■
include a clear introduction/conclusion			■	■	■	■	■	■	■	■	■

Organization

	2	3	4	5	6	7	8	9	10	11	12
order ideas/details	■	■	■	■	■	■	■				
check time order	■	■	■	■	■	■	■				
check order of importance	■	■	■	■	■	■	■	■			
check logical order	■	■	■	■	■	■	■	■	■		■
check overall organization	■	■	■	■	■	■	■	■	■	■	■
use transitional words and phrases	■	■	■	■	■	■	■	■	■	■	■
include a clear beginning/middle/ending	■	■	■	■	■	■	■	■	■	■	■
include line breaks/indents		■						■	■	■	

	Grades	2	3	4	5	6	7	8	9	10	11	12
Organization (continued)												
use clear topic sentences			■				■	■		■	■	■
build to a high point								■	■	■	■	■
use key ideas										■	■	■
Development of Ideas												
write clear topic sentences		■	■	■	■	■	■	■				
add supporting details		■	■	■	■	■	■	■				
add sensory details		■	■	■	■	■	■	■	■	■	■	
add dialogue			■	■	■	■	■	■				
delete unnecessary details			■	■	■	■	■	■				
show, don't tell			■				■	■	■	■		
add specific reasons			■				■			■	■	■
write clear focus statements				■	■	■	■	■				
write a clear thesis statement								■		■	■	■
use sources							■	■	■			
include a conflict							■	■	■	■	■	■
Voice												
sound confident		■	■				■					
use formal/informal language		■		■	■	■	■	■				
match voice to writing purpose		■		■	■	■	■	■	■	■		
sound interested		■	■	■	■	■	■	■	■	■		
sound convincing		■	■	■	■	■	■	■	■	■	■	■
sound natural		■	■	■	■	■	■	■	■	■	■	■
sound knowledgeable			■	■	■	■	■	■	■	■	■	■
add dialogue			■	■	■	■	■	■	■	■	■	■
engage readers			■				■	■	■	■	■	■
match voice to topic					■		■	■	■	■	■	
Editing												
use correct grammar rules		■	■	■	■	■	■	■	■	■	■	■
use correct usage rules		■	■	■	■	■	■	■	■	■	■	■
use correct punctuation rules		■	■	■	■	■	■	■	■	■	■	■
use correct capitalization rules		■	■	■	■	■	■	■	■	■	■	■
use correct sentence structure		■	■	■	■	■	■	■	■	■	■	■

	Grades	2	3	4	5	6	7	8	9	10	11	12
Editing (continued)												
use spelling rules		X	X	X	X	X	X	X	X	X	X	X
use rubrics		X	X	X	X	X	X	X	X	X	X	X
Publishing												
create a final copy		X	X	X	X	X	X	X	X	X	X	X
use a self assessment		X	X	X	X	X	X	X	X	X	X	X
create a portfolio		X	X	X	X	X	X	X	X	X	X	X
evaluate writing models			X	X	X	X	X	X	X	X	X	X

WRITING ACROSS THE CURRICULUM

Descriptive Writing

	Grades	2	3	4	5	6	7	8	9	10	11	12
math		X					X	X	X		X	
practical/workplace		X					X	X	X		X	
science		X		X	X	X	X	X				
social studies			X	X	X	X	X	X	X			

Narrative Writing

	Grades	2	3	4	5	6	7	8	9	10	11	12
art			X									
math			X	X	X	X	X					
music		X										
practical/workplace		X	X	X	X	X	X	X				
science				X		X	X	X				
social studies		X	X		X	X	X	X				

Expository Writing

	Grades	2	3	4	5	6	7	8	9	10	11	12
math				X	X	X	X	X	X	X	X	X
music/arts			X							X	X	X
practical/workplace		X	X	X	X	X	X	X	X	X	X	X
science		X	X		X		X	X	X	X	X	X
social studies			X		X	X	X	X	X	X	X	X

Persuasive Writing

	Grades	2	3	4	5	6	7	8	9	10	11	12
health			X									
math				X		X	X	X	X	X	X	X
practical/workplace			X	X	X	X	X	X	X			
science		X	X	X	X	X	X	X	X			
social studies		X			X	X	X	X	X			

Grades	2	3	4	5	6	7	8	9	10	11	12
Response to Texts											
art								■	■		■
math									■	■	■
practical/workplace					■	■	■				
science					■	■	■	■			
social studies					■	■	■				
TOOLS OF LANGUAGE											
language strategies	■	■	■	■	■	■	■	■	■	■	■
language of writing	■	■	■	■	■	■	■	■	■	■	■
informal/formal language	■	■	■	■	■	■	■	■	■	■	■
listening/speaking skills	■	■	■	■	■	■	■	■	■	■	■
idioms	■	■	■	■	■	■	■	■	■	■	■
shared reading	■	■	■	■	■	■	■	■	■	■	■
reference materials	■	■	■	■	■	■	■	■	■	■	■
GRAMMAR											
Understanding Sentences											
word order	■	■									
run-on sentence	■	■	■	■	■	■	■				
simple subject/predicate	■	■	■	■	■	■	■				
compound sentence	■	■	■	■	■	■	■				
complete subject/predicate	■	■	■	■	■	■	■				
prepositional phrase	■	■	■	■	■	■	■				
subject-verb agreement	■	■	■	■	■	■	■	■	■	■	■
complete sentence	■	■	■	■	■	■	■	■	■	■	■
sentence variety	■	■	■	■	■	■	■	■	■	■	■
declarative/exclamatory/ interrogative/imperative sentence	■	■	■	■	■	■	■	■	■	■	■
compound subject/predicate		■	■	■	■	■	■				
modeling		■	■	■	■	■	■	■	■	■	■
appositive phrase			■	■	■	■					
direct object			■	■	■	■	■				
indirect object			■	■	■	■	■				
double negative			■	■	■	■	■				
independent clause			■	■	■	■	■				
dependent clause			■	■	■	■	■				

	Grades	2	3	4	5	6	7	8	9	10	11	12

Understanding Sentences (continued)

	2	3	4	5	6	7	8	9	10	11	12
complex sentence				■	■	■	■	■	■	■	■
noun/verb phrase				■	■	■	■	■	■	■	■
sentence diagramming						■				■	■

Understanding the Parts of Speech

Nouns

	2	3	4	5	6	7	8	9	10	11	12
possessive	■	■	■	■	■	■	■				
specific	■	■	■	■	■	■	■				
singular/plural	■	■	■	■	■	■	■	■	■	■	■
common/proper	■	■	■	■	■	■	■	■	■	■	■
singular/plural possessive	■	■	■	■	■	■	■	■	■	■	■
appositive			■	■	■	■	■				
compound			■	■	■	■	■				
object			■	■	■	■	■				
predicate			■	■	■	■	■				
subject			■	■	■	■	■				
abstract/concrete			■	■	■	■	■	■	■	■	■
collective		■	■	■	■	■	■	■	■	■	■
case								■	■	■	■

Verbs

	2	3	4	5	6	7	8	9	10	11	12
contractions with *not*	■	■	■	■	■	■	■				
subject-verb agreement	■	■	■	■	■	■	■				
helping	■	■	■	■	■	■	■				
past, present, future tense	■	■	■	■	■	■	■	■	■	■	■
action	■	■	■	■	■	■	■	■	■	■	■
linking	■	■	■	■	■	■	■	■	■	■	■
singular/plural	■	■	■	■	■	■	■	■	■	■	■
irregular	■	■	■	■	■	■	■	■	■	■	■
simple tense			■	■	■	■	■				
perfect tense			■	■	■	■	■				
transitive/intransitive			■	■	■	■	■	■	■	■	■
active/passive voice			■	■	■	■	■	■	■	■	■
participle				■	■	■					
continuous tense					■		■				

Grades	2	3	4	5	6	7	8	9	10	11	12
Verbs (continued)											
gerund					■	■	■				
infinitive					■	■	■				
auxiliary							■	■	■	■	■
verbal							■	■	■	■	■
complex tense							■	■	■	■	■
mood								■	■	■	■
person								■	■	■	■
Pronouns											
possessive	■	■	■	■	■	■	■				
personal	■	■	■	■	■	■	■	■	■	■	■
antecedent	■	■	■	■	■	■	■	■	■	■	■
singular/plural	■	■	■	■	■	■	■	■	■	■	■
subject/object	■	■	■	■	■	■	■	■	■	■	■
intensive/reflexive			■	■	■	■	■	■	■	■	■
demonstrative/interrogative			■	■	■	■	■	■	■	■	■
indefinite			■	■	■	■	■	■	■	■	■
relative			■	■	■	■	■	■	■	■	■
gender			■		■	■	■	■	■	■	■
person	■						■	■	■	■	■
case							■	■	■	■	■
Adjectives											
comparative/superlative	■	■	■	■	■	■	■	■	■	■	■
article	■	■	■	■	■	■	■	■	■	■	■
compound		■	■	■	■	■	■	■	■	■	■
positive		■	■	■	■	■	■	■	■	■	■
proper		■	■	■	■	■	■	■	■	■	■
demonstrative			■	■	■	■	■	■	■	■	■
equal			■	■	■	■	■				
indefinite			■	■	■	■	■				
predicate			■	■	■	■	■	■	■	■	■
Interjections	■	■	■	■	■	■	■	■	■	■	■

Grades	2	3	4	5	6	7	8	9	10	11	12
Adverbs											
of manner	X	X	X	X	X	X	X	X	X	X	X
of place	X	X	X	X	X	X	X	X	X	X	X
of time	X	X	X	X	X	X	X	X	X	X	X
to modify verbs	X	X	X	X	X	X	X	X	X	X	X
of degree			X	X	X	X	X	X	X	X	X
to modify adjectives/adverbs			X	X	X	X	X	X	X	X	X
comparative/superlative			X	X	X	X	X	X	X	X	X
positive			X	X	X	X	X	X	X	X	X
Conjunctions											
coordinating	X	X	X	X	X	X	X	X	X	X	X
correlative			X	X	X	X	X	X	X	X	X
subordinating			X	X	X	X	X	X	X	X	X
Prepositions											
common	X	X	X	X	X	X	X	X	X	X	X
prepositional phrase	X	X	X	X	X	X	X	X	X	X	X

Mechanics

Grades	2	3	4	5	6	7	8	9	10	11	12
Capitalization											
pronoun I	X	X				X	X	X			
beginning of a quotation	X	X	X	X	X	X	X				
name of a day, month, holiday	X	X	X	X	X	X	X	X	X	X	X
first word of a sentence	X	X	X	X	X	X	X	X	X	X	X
name of a person	X	X	X	X	X	X	X	X	X	X	X
proper noun	X	X	X	X	X	X	X	X	X	X	X
title used with a name	X	X	X	X	X	X	X	X	X	X	X
title	X	X	X	X	X	X	X	X	X	X	X
geographical name/place	X	X	X	X	X	X	X	X	X	X	X
abbreviation, acronym	X	X	X	X	X	X	X	X	X	X	X
proper adjective		X	X	X	X	X	X	X	X	X	X
word used as a name		X	X	X	X	X	X	X	X	X	X
name of a historical event or period		X	X	X	X	X	X	X	X	X	X
name of a religion, nationality			X	X	X	X	X	X	X	X	X
name of an organization			X	X	X	X	X	X	X	X	X
particular section of a country			X	X	X	X	X	X	X	X	X

Grades	2	3	4	5	6	7	8	9	10	11	12
Capitalization (continued)											
trade name/official name			■	■	■	■	■	■	■	■	■
names of a language, ethnicity		■	■				■	■	■	■	■
letter to indicate form or direction					■	■	■	■	■	■	■
specific course name					■	■	■	■	■	■	■
sentence following a colon							■	■	■	■	■
sentence in parentheses							■	■	■	■	■
Plurals											
common noun	■	■	■	■	■	■	■				
noun with irregular spelling	■	■	■	■	■	■	■	■	■	■	■
noun ending with sh, ch, x, s, or z	■	■	■	■	■	■	■	■	■	■	■
noun ending in y	■	■	■	■	■	■	■	■	■	■	■
adding 's			■	■	■	■	■	■	■	■	■
compound noun			■	■	■	■	■	■	■	■	■
noun ending with f or fe			■	■	■	■	■	■	■	■	■
noun ending with ful			■	■	■	■	■	■	■	■	■
noun ending with o			■	■	■	■	■	■	■	■	■
word discussed as a word							■	■	■	■	■
collective noun								■	■	■	■
Abbreviations											
day and month	■	■	■	■	■	■	■				
title of a person	■	■	■	■	■	■	■				
address	■	■	■	■	■	■	■				
state postal abbreviation		■	■	■	■	■	■				
acronym/initialism			■	■	■	■	■	■	■	■	■
correspondence abbreviation							■	■	■	■	■
Numbers											
numbers 1 to 9		■	■	■	■	■	■				
sentence beginning		■	■	■	■	■	■				
numeral only		■	■	■	■	■	■	■	■	■	■
very large number		■	■	■	■	■	■	■	■	■	
time/money				■		■	■	■	■	■	■
in a compound modifier					■	■	■	■	■	■	■
word only							■	■	■	■	■
numeral or word							■	■	■	■	■

	Grades	2	3	4	5	6	7	8	9	10	11	12
Punctuation												
Periods												
after an initial or abbreviation		■	■	■	■	■	■	■	■	■	■	■
end of a sentence		■	■	■	■	■	■	■	■	■	■	■
as a decimal point			■	■	■	■	■	■	■	■	■	■
after an indirect question						■	■	■				
Question Marks												
end of a question		■	■	■	■	■	■	■				
after a tag question				■	■	■	■	■				
to show doubt						■	■	■	■	■	■	■
end of a direct/indirect question									■	■	■	
short question within a sentence								■	■	■		
Exclamation Points												
for a word, phrase, sentence		■	■	■	■	■	■	■				
for an interjection			■	■	■	■	■	■				
to express strong feelings		■	■	■	■	■	■	■	■	■	■	■
Commas												
in greeting of friendly letter		■	■	■	■	■	■	■				
after an introductory word or phrase		■	■	■	■	■	■					
in a series		■	■	■	■	■	■	■	■	■	■	■
in a date and address			■	■	■	■	■	■	■	■	■	■
with an interjection		■	■	■	■	■	■	■	■	■	■	■
in a compound sentence		■	■	■	■	■	■	■	■	■	■	■
to set off dialogue		■	■	■	■	■	■	■	■	■	■	■
in a direct address		■	■	■	■	■	■	■	■	■	■	■
in a number			■	■	■	■	■	■				
to separate equal adjectives			■	■	■	■	■	■	■	■	■	■
to set off a phrase						■	■	■	■	■		
to set off an appositive			■	■	■	■	■	■	■	■	■	■
to set off an interruption			■	■	■	■	■	■	■	■	■	■
to separate nonrestrictive/ introductory clauses and phrases						■			■	■	■	■
to set off a title of person					■	■	■	■	■	■	■	
to enclose parenthetical elements									■	■	■	■
to separate contrasted elements								■	■	■	■	■

Grades	2	3	4	5	6	7	8	9	10	11	12
Apostrophes											
in a contraction	■	■	■	■	■	■	■	■	■	■	■
to form a plural possessive noun	■	■	■	■	■	■	■	■	■	■	■
to form a singular possessive noun	■	■	■	■	■	■	■	■	■	■	■
to form certain plurals			■	■	■	■	■	■	■	■	■
to replace an omitted number/letter			■	■	■	■	■	■	■	■	■
with an indefinite pronoun			■	■	■	■	■	■	■	■	■
to show shared possession			■	■	■	■	■	■	■	■	■
in a possessive with compound nouns					■	■	■				
to express time or amount					■	■	■	■	■	■	■
Quotation Marks											
for a direct quotation	■	■	■	■	■	■	■			■	■
for a title		■	■	■	■	■	■	■	■	■	■
for a special word			■	■	■	■	■	■	■	■	■
for a quotation within a quotation					■	■	■	■	■	■	■
Colons											
after a salutation of business letter		■	■	■	■	■	■	■	■	■	■
between hour and minutes		■	■	■	■	■	■	■	■	■	■
to introduce a list of items		■	■	■	■	■	■	■	■	■	■
to introduce a quotation					■						
to introduce a sentence					■	■	■	■	■	■	■
for emphasis						■	■	■	■	■	■
between a title and a subtitle						■		■	■	■	■
Hyphens											
in word division		■	■	■	■	■	■	■	■	■	■
in a compound word			■	■	■	■	■	■	■	■	■
in a fraction			■	■	■	■	■	■	■	■	■
to create a new word			■	■	■	■	■	■	■	■	■
to join letters and words			■	■	■	■	■	■	■	■	■
to avoid confusion or awkward spelling					■	■	■	■	■	■	■
to make an adjective					■	■	■	■	■	■	■
Parentheses											
to add information		■	■	■	■	■	■	■	■	■	■

	Grades	2	3	4	5	6	7	8	9	10	11	12
Dashes												
for emphasis				■	■	■	■	■	■	■	■	■
to show a sentence break				■	■	■	■	■	■	■	■	■
to show interrupted speech				■	■	■	■	■	■	■	■	■
Ellipses												
to show a pause				■	■	■	■	■	■	■	■	■
to show omitted words				■	■	■	■	■	■	■	■	■
Semicolons												
in a compound sentence				■		■	■	■	■	■	■	■
to separate groups (that have commas) in a series				■	■	■	■	■	■	■	■	■
to join two independent clauses						■	■	■	■	■	■	■
with a conjunctive adverb						■	■	■	■	■	■	■
Brackets												
to set off clarifying information						■		■	■	■	■	■
to set off added words						■		■	■	■	■	■
around an editorial correction								■	■	■	■	■
Underlining and Italics												
for a title		■	■	■	■	■	■	■	■	■	■	■
for a special word				■	■	■	■	■				
for special uses					■			■	■	■	■	■
in handwritten and printed material								■	■	■	■	■
for scientific and foreign words						■	■	■	■	■	■	■
Using the Right Word		■	■	■	■	■	■	■	■	■	■	■
Improving Spelling		■	■	■	■	■	■	■	■	■	■	■

Scavenger Hunt 1: Find It!

Directions   Find the following information in your handbook by turning to the pages listed in parentheses.

1. Types of details you can include in your writing to support your topic (pages 57–58)

_____

_____

2. What STRAP stands for (page 212)

_____

3. How to check subject-verb agreement (page 186)

_____

4. What the idiom _doesn't hold a candle to_ means (page 697)

_____

5. Three ways a Style Manual can help you (page 501)

_____

_____

6. Graphic organizers you can use to plan your writing (pages 612–616)

_____

_____

7. Common types of plagiarism (page 437)

_____

_____

8. A formula for writing an editorial thesis statement (page 261)

_____

_____

9. Two things to do when submitting your writing for publication (page 129)

_____

10. Classifications of sentences according to word arrangement (page 768)

_____

Scavenger Hunt 2: What Is It?

 **Directions** Find the answers to the following questions using the index in the back of the book.

1. What is a protagonist?

_____

2. What does the word "sonnet" literally mean?

_____

_____

3. What is OAQS?

_____

_____

4. What are the types of sentence construction?

_____

5. What is the "Rule of Threes"?

_____

6. What is irony?

_____

7. What is the complimentary closing of a business letter?

_____

8. What is a vivid verb?

_____

9. What is a works-cited page?

_____

10. What does the acronym LAN stand for?

_____

11. What is the past participle of *lie* (recline)?

_____

12. What is the subjunctive mood?

_____

Getting to Know *Write Source*

> **Directions** Locate the pages in *Write Source* where answers to the following learning tasks can be found. Both the index and the table of contents can help you.

_____ **1.** Your teacher reminds you to focus on the traits of writing in your next writing assignment. You need to make sure you understand the traits.

_____ **2.** Your teacher suggests you keep a learning log. You need to know how to use a learning log in class.

_____ **3.** Your assignment is to write an editorial. You need to see a model of one before you begin to write.

_____ **4.** Your teacher tells you to use a scoring guide to model your writing, as well as to assess it. You need to know how to use a scoring guide for these purposes.

_____ **5.** You are supposed to create a multimedia presentation of your research report. You need to know what steps to take to create this.

_____ **6.** Before you begin to write a quatrain, your teacher reminds you to choose a rhyme scheme. You need to know some common rhyme schemes.

_____ **7.** You are writing an essay on immigration and aren't sure whether people *immigrate* or *emigrate* from the country they are leaving. You need to know which is the right word to use.

_____ **8.** You find it difficult to organize and write a response to a prompt in an on-demand situation. You need some tips for budgeting your time.

_____ **9.** Some classmates get permission to set up a Web site for publishing students' writing and ask you to help. You need to know how to create a Web site.

_____ **10.** Your teacher rates your expository essay "2" in part because some of your sentences are run-on sentences. You need to know how to fix run-on sentences.

Getting Started Activity Answers

Scavenger Hunt 1: Find It!

1. Details you can include in your writing to support your topic are facts, statistics, examples, anecdotes, quotations, definitions, reasons, and comparisons.

2. STRAP stands for Subject, Type, Role, Audience, and Purpose.

3. Check subject-verb agreement by making sure singular subjects have singular verbs and plural subjects have plural verbs.

4. The idiom doesn't hold a candle to means "is not as good as."

5. Accept any three of the examples on page 501

6. Several graphic organizers you can use to plan your writing include line diagrams, Venn diagrams, cause-effect organizers, process diagrams, and logical order lists.

7. There are three common types of plagiarism: using copy-and-paste, paraphrasing without citing a source, and neglecting necessary quotation marks.

8. This is a formula for writing a satirical position statement: local or school controversy + research results = thesis statement.

9. Two things to do when submitting your writing for publication are sending it to school publications and local publications.

10. According to word arrangement, there are four classifications of sentences: loose, balanced, periodic, and cumulative.

Scavenger Hunt 2: What Is It?

1. A protagonist is the main character of a story or play. The word literally means "first contender (p. 353).

2. The word "sonnet" literally means "little song" (p. 370).

3. OAQS is a four-step strategy used in peer responding. It stands for Observe, Appreciate, Question, and Suggest (p. 120).

4. There are four types of sentence construction: simple, compound, complex, and compound-complex (p. 766).

5. The "Rule of Threes" says that you must have three main arguments each supported by three or more relevant details (p. 238).

6. Irony is an expression in which the author says one thing but means just the opposite (p. 628).

7. The complimentary closing ends the message. Use Sincerely or Yours truly—followed by a comma. Capitalize only the first word (p. 538).

8. Vivid verbs help create a clear word picture. Vivid verbs usually show rather than tell (p. 82).

9. A works-cited page is a separate page that alphabetically lists sources cited in the paper (p. 394).

10. The acronym LAN stands for local area network (p. 688.1).

11. The past participle of lie (recline) is lain (p. 740.2).

12. The subjunctive mood is used to express conditions contrary to fact, unreal conditions, necessity, legal decisions, or parliamentary motions (p. 744).

Getting to Know *Write Source*

1. 48	6. 372
2. 472	7. 710
3. 258-259	8. 213
4. 36-37	9. 133
5. 534	10. 89

Narrative Writing

Happy Days

1   "You're listening to Oldies 104. It's now 7:45 and time for the

2 news." I peel back my covers and stumble out of bed. Just like every

3 morning, I wonder why I need a summer job that starts so early, and

4 just like every morning, I mechanically pull on my paint-speckled

5 work jeans, old summer rec T-shirt, and running shoes. I live by a

6 system. Up at 7:45, get dressed, twist my hair into a ponytail, shove

7 in my contacts, grab a toaster pastry, and steal some money from

8 my brother's cupboard for break time. By 7:56 I am in my car, Oldies

9 cranked, and on my way to the maintenance shed—the headquarters

10 for my summer job. Another day has begun—another day of caring for

11 the parks in my little Iowa town.

12   I pull into my regular parking place. As I munch on my pastry,

13 I trudge to the shed, shoelaces flopping about. I enter the dark,

14 cluttered shed, and there he sits. "You know, you're supposed to be

15 dressed before you get here," he says. It's old Ben, otherwise known

16 as "Bendable," who's early as usual and seated on the tailgate of the

17 pickup, legs swinging about. Ben "baby-sits" the workers, but he's

18 more of a grandfather to me than a boss. A retired trucker in his early

19 seventies, skin darkened and worn by hours in the sun, Ben is a man

20 of many, many words.

21   I smile, shrug, and head to my seat behind the wheel of Big Red,

22 the tractor that pulls our fold-out, three-deck mower. Here I finish

Narrative Writing *(cont.)*

23 breakfast, tie my shoes, and soak in my surroundings as I shake off

24 the last of my sleepiness. It's at this point as my companions slowly

25 trickle in that I'm reminded why I bother having a summer job.

26   Todd is the first to rumble up on his motorcycle. At six foot ten,

27 Todd is supported by size-18 feet. He nods a welcome to Ben and me

28 as he enters, quietly going right to his work, checking the oil in the

29 mowers and filling them with gas.

30   A commotion outside tells me that Derek and Steve have arrived.

31 These two are joined at the hip or something. They saunter in,

32 comparing their tans and their sun-bleached hair and discussing the

33 movie they saw the night before.

34   Behind them follows Nicole, looking sleepy. Nicole is Ben's

35 granddaughter and a good friend of mine. As usual, her attire looks

36 almost identical to mine. She too has to tie her shoes and we receive

37 our instructions for the day. As usual, Nicole and I are sent on trash

38 and bathrooms run while the boys begin a different mission. We load

39 up the pickup, fight over the driver's seat, and head out to do our

40 duties.

41   It's amazing how much fun you can have cleaning bathrooms,

42 sweeping shelter houses, and checking garbage cans. Nicole and I

43 discuss many things as we work, from friend problems to guys in

44 general, from pickups to weekend car races. We take great pleasure in

45 belting out our favorite oldies.

46   Working with the guys is never boring either. One afternoon

Narrative Writing *(cont.)*

47   while trimming crab apple trees, a war broke out. I don't know whho

48   threw the first "bullet," but I went home with quite a few welts. Of

49   course, *I* was hard at work and threw very few.

50   Somehow, I always seem to end up as the butt of everyone's jokes.

51   I locked up the brakes on the pickup ONE TIME to avoid hitting

52   a reckless biker, and my driving days have never been the same.

53   Anytime my foot even grazes the brake pedal, everyone flies forward

54   and hits the dash like I am some sort of maniac.

55   I guess I do have a slight problem with machines. One morning, I

56   was mowing at the pool and removed my jacket when the sun peeked

57   out. I tied my jacket to my seat, and forgot about it. But when I hoped

58   off the mower to move a picnic table blocking my path, the mower

59   started screeching behind me. I turned around to find my jacket gone

60   white smoke and puffs of cotton spewing from the back of the mower.

61   The sleeve of the jacket had gotten sucked into the moving parts of

62   the mower, which had torn it to shreds. The mower was repairable,

63   but sad to say, my jacket was not.

64   Some of the best parts of my summer job, however, come during

65   break time. We take a 15-minute break in the morning and another in

66   the afternoon. The local grocery store employees know us all by name,

67   as well as our own special purchases: Steve and Derek each have a

68   huge candy bar, Nicole and I share a bag of chips, and Todd devours

69   a huge stack of cake donuts (six to be exact). We all sit together in

70   the back booth, sharing the latest gossip (guys are much worse than

Narrative Writing *(cont.)*

71   girls), reading the paper, and joking around. The 15 minutes always

72   fly by.

73   I arrived at the maintenance shed on the first day of work a

74   timid, shy person, afraid of what summer would bring. I left with

75   friends who accepted me and let me by myself. Although I cringe at

76   some of the minor disasters of that time, I couldn't have asked for a

77   better crew with whom to form those summer memories.

Narrative Writing
Benchmark Paper Comments

Title: Happy Days   Holistic Score: **4**

The writer of this highly effective narrative focuses on the people and events that made a summer job memorable. This response engages the reader from the radio voice opening sentences, (*"You're listening to Oldies 104. It's now 7:45 and time for the news."*), and maintains the connection throughout. The strength of conventions, colorful descriptions (*paint-speckled work jeans, shoelaces flopping about*) and entertaining anecdotes (the crabapple fight, break time) allow the reader to enjoy the writer's unique perspective.

	Focus and Coherence	Organization	Development of Ideas	Voice	Conventions
4	focused and connected	**flows smoothly**	**ideas deeply supported**	**highly engaging and original**	**strong command of conventions**
3	**mostly focused and connected**	generally flows smoothly	ideas thoughtfully supported	mostly engaging and original	few errors
2	somewhat focused	flows somewhat smoothly	ideas adequately supported	somewhat engaging and original	some errors
1	unfocused, disconnected	does not flow	ideas unsupported	not engaging or original	major errors

Narrative Writing

My First Skateboard

1   When I was in the fifth grade I wanted to go skateboarding so

2 bad and I nagged my parents so much that they finally got one for my

3 birthday just to shut me up. So luckily I lived close to a skateboard

4 park so I got to practice all the time.

5   The first couple of times I went with my friends were great all of

6 us were shouting and laughing and having the time of our life. But

7 then one time about a week or two later I went off this ramp and fell

8 off my board and came down way to hard on my ankel and I knew

9 right away that it was bad. By the time I got home I was crying. I was

10 in so much pain!

11   After coming home from the hospital I was still in a lot of pain

12 that first night home and I asked my dad if I could sleep on the couch

13 so that if I needed something I could call to him and mom since there

14 room was on the first floor too. Plus I really didn't want to take those

15 stairs too often.

16   At school I had fun at first from all the attention I got because of

17 my cast and crutches and al but then it just got old real fast and was

18 pretty much a colosal pain. That only part that was really fun was

19 racing kids down the hall on my crutches. It was fun until I fell down,

20 even so it was pretty funny. And when I finally did get the cast off I

21 was pretty happy. But in all it was a good learning experience because

22 I know not to take simple things like walking and running so much

Narrative Writing *(cont.)*

23 for granted like I used to. I really no now to apreciate what I've got

24 each day.

Narrative Writing
Benchmark Paper Comments

Title: My First Skateboard   Holistic Score: **2**

In this somewhat effective composition, the writer describes the consequences of a skateboarding accident. The events are effectively organized in chronological order (getting skateboard, injury, using crutches) and the conclusion states a life lesson learned (*I really no now to appreciate what I've got each day.*). However, the overall superficial development of events and weak command of conventions, especially multiple run-on sentences, limit the effectiveness of this response.

	Focus and Coherence	Organization	Development of Ideas	Voice	Conventions
4	focused and connected	flows smoothly	ideas deeply supported	highly engaging and original	strong command of conventions
3	mostly focused and connected	generally flows smoothly	ideas thoughtfully supported	mostly engaging and original	few errors
2	**somewhat focused**	**flows somewhat smoothly**	ideas adequately supported	**somewhat engaging and original**	some errors
1	unfocused, disconnected	does not flow	**ideas unsupported**	not engaging or original	**major errors**

Expository Writing

Hot Dogs: This Is No Bologna!

1   Can you name a food that one of every three children claim is

2   their favorite food for outdoor activities? According to a poll taken by

3   the National Hot Dog Council, that food is the hot dog. Given that

4   twenty billion hot dogs are steam, grilled, boiled or microwaved in

5   the United States each year, it would seem that children are not the

6   only hot-dog lovers. One can only wonder if this would be the case if

7   unsuspecting consumers knew more about the contents of an average

8   hot-dog. For these tasty little tubes are actually storage bins for a

9   wealth of unhealthy ingredients.

10   According to Bruce Friedrich, head of PETA (People for the

11   Ethical Treatment of Animals), an average hot dog consists of about

12   16 grams of artery-clogging fat. But fat is certainly not the only

13   unappetizing ingredient in hot dogs. Hot dogs are pretty much the

14   leftovers of the meat processing line. The remains of cows and pigs are

15   the essential ingredients of this highly processed meat, but you never

16   know the complete list of additives that can be found in hot dogs. This

17   vital information is "accidentally" hidden from view! Brenda Shoss,

18   director of an animal rights group in St. Louis, states that, "Every

19   time you bite into a hot dog, you are biting into pesticides, animal

20   feces, ground-up animal parts, and antibiotics that have been pumped

21   into animals."

22   Yet, every second, 634 hot dogs are served to consumers.

Expository Writing *(cont.)*

23 Ballparks account for 9 percent of all the hot-dog consumption in the

24 United States. It is estimated that 26 million hot dogs are consumed

25 each year in American ballparks; enough to be lined up from Shea

26 Stadium in New York to Dodger Stadium in L.A.!

27 Perhaps the link between hot dogs and ballparks can be traced

28 to the origin of this fast food. When the St. Louis Browns were a very

29 popular baseball team in the United States, sodas and ice cream were

30 often a quenching summertime beverage and snack at the ballpark.

31 But as the weather turned cooler, the sales of soda and ice cream

32 declined. Concessionaire Harry Stevens was one of the many who

33 were losing money on sales at the ballpark. He told his venders to go

34 find as many skinny dachshund sausages they could find at all the

35 local butcher shops. Harry then boiled the dachshund sausages in

36 the hot water tanks and sold them to a craving crowd. He shouted up

37 and down the aisles, "Get your red hot dachshund!" Ted Dorgan wrote

38 about the event the next day in the local sports page, only he didn't

39 know how to spell dachshund, so he called them hot dogs. The name

40 stuck.

41 Obviously, the ingredients of hot dogs are rarely a concern of the

42 fans or of adults who serve them to children. They see hot dogs as a

43 quick meal or easy way to feed the kids. This is typical society today.

44 Hot dogs are certainly easy to fix. Because they are precooked, all

45 they need is to be removed from the package and eaten raw, as many

46 little children do; or they can be heated quickly in any manner. An

Expository Writing *(cont.)*

47   open flame is the preference of many, including myself. Like most

48   people, I just try not to think about what's in these tender little tubes

49   of highly processed meat. As they say, ignorance is bliss.

Expository Writing
Benchmark Paper Comments

Title: Hot Dogs: This Is No Bologna!   Holistic Score: **3**

The writer of this well-organized expository piece presents many interesting facts about the hot dog supported by statistics and expert sources (*According to a poll taken by the National Hot Dog Council . . . According to Bruce Friedrich, head of PETA*). However, it is not quite clear if the topic is dangerous ingredients (*storage bins for . . . unhealthy ingredients*) or an overview (*the origin of this fast food*). The writer has few convention errors and excellent knowledge of the subject, but the switch to first person in the last paragraph (*I just try not to think about*) is awkward and contributes to the generally effective rating instead of a higher score.

	Focus and Coherence	Organization	Development of Ideas	Voice	Conventions
4	focused and connected	flows smoothly	**ideas deeply supported**	**highly engaging and original**	strong command of conventions
3	**mostly focused and connected**	**generally flows smoothly**	ideas thoughtfully supported	mostly engaging and original	**few errors**
2	somewhat focused	flows somewhat smoothly	ideas adequately supported	somewhat engaging and original	some errors
1	unfocused, disconnected	does not flow	ideas unsupported	not engaging or original	major errors

Expository Writing

Recycling

1   Recycling means to make something new again or reuse

2   them instead of throwing them away. Its definitly good. Help the

3   environment. Their are lots of reason why. Lots of materials can be

4   recycled now. Like aluminum cans and steel. Glass, botles, paper,

5   palastic, old oil like form cars, tires. Recycled paper can be made

6   into new soda cans and other metal products. Paper is also used

7   for new card board and sometimes in plaster for houses and other

8   buildings and glass for new glass containers and sometimes in road

9   construction.

10   There are many ways to recycle. They are: buy-back deals, drop

11   off centers, curb side pick up. The centers, though are open for such

12   short times that people do not have time to get there when their open,

13   so thats an area that needs improvement. For pick up, people have to

14   be better about sorting. Pick up may be dropped. Then these products

15   are taken to a place for converting them into usable objects.

16   Recycling is so good. It keeps stuff out of landfills. Reduces costs

17   for manufacterers. How? By saving money on materials they need

18   to make their products. Plus when we recycle we save our natural

19   resources because we use the same ones instead of using ups more

20   of what we have left. It also saves water and clean air by reducing

21   pollution casue waste products don't have to be burned. Which keeps

22   smog down. The best part is it conserves energy. Because it takes less

Expository Writing *(cont.)*

23 energy to recycle products than make new ones.

24   All community should start there own program. We need to

25 because landfills are filling up and then what. Also, some natural

26 resources are getting used up. Another big problem. It costs less to

27 recycle than to make new products, so we also save ourselves money.

28 So get started. Ask for curb side collection. Start a buy back center.

29 Take advantage of it. Do your part to save nature, because landfills is

30 taking away our forests and animals are pushed out of there homes.

31 Do your part and recycling can work.

Expository Writing
Benchmark Paper Comments

Title: Recycling   Holistic Score: **1**

In this ineffective expository composition, the writer discusses the broad topic of recycling. Even though the voice shows genuine concern for the topic (*We need to because landfills are filling up and then what.*) and some specific knowledge (*buy-back deals, drop-off centers*), the essay lacks focus and does not show any clear organizational pattern. Frequent errors in conventions, such as rambling sentences and fragments (*Another big problem.*), as well as in basic spelling (*botles, palastic*), punctuation (*dont, thats*), and grammar interfere with effective communication of the writer's ideas.

	Focus and Coherence	Organization	Development of Ideas	Voice	Conventions
4	focused and connected	flows smoothly	ideas deeply supported	highly engaging and original	strong command of conventions
3	mostly focused and connected	generally flows smoothly	ideas thoughtfully supported	mostly engaging and original	few errors
2	somewhat focused	flows somewhat smoothly	**ideas adequately supported**	**somewhat engaging and original**	some errors
1	**unfocused, disconnected**	**does not flow**	ideas unsupported	not engaging or original	**major errors**

Persuasive Writing

Secondhand Smoke: A Silent Killer

1   In our legal system, it is considered a crime to harm anyone

2   else without a legitimate reason. Smokers should carefully examine

3   these words the next time they decide to light up a cigarette in a

4   public place. Secondhand smoke is becoming a rising problem in our

5   society today. The more we learn about it, the more we realize just

6   how dangerous it is. Smoking not only directly harms the smoker, but

7   it also harms the innocent bystanders. In order for the people of San

8   Diego to be able to breathe healthier air, something drastic must be

9   done. Namely, smoking should be banned from public places.

10   What the smoker does to himself may be his own business,

11   but what the smoker does to the nonsmoker is everyone's business.

12   According to health care professionals, secondhand smoke is the third

13   leading cause of preventable death in this country, killing 53,000

14   nonsmokers in the United States each year. These innocent victims

15   did not choose to smoke. Rather, they happened to be in the vicinity of

16   smokers and they paid for this contact with their health. Why should

17   people who have chosen not to smoke be indirectly forced into this

18   situation? No one should have to suffer the consequences of other

19   people's actions. It is proven that secondhand smoke contains twice

20   as much tar and nicotine per unit volumes as does smoke inhaled

21   from the cigarette. That means by choosing not to smoke, we are

22   being punished more severely than a person who does smoke. That is

Persuasive Writing *(cont.)*

23 quite unjust. Critics of this issue will often argue that people have the

24 right to smoke anywhere they please; and by not allowing them to do

25 so, they are being denied those rights. What about the rights of the

26 nonsmoker? Don't we deserve the right to decide if we want to smoke

27 or not? Apparently our health is irrelevant.

28   Everyone who has ever inhaled secondhand smoke should defend

29 their right to a healthy environment. Communicate your concerns

30 with public officials. Urge them to protect you from the abundant

31 toxins contained in secondhand smoke by banning smoking from

32 public places.

Persuasive Writing[gr 11 p. A83]
Benchmark Paper Comments

Title: Secondhand Smoke: A Silent Killer   Holistic Score: **4**

The writer of this focused persuasive essay suggests that smoking should be prohibited in public places because of the dangers of secondhand smoke. Specific details (*secondhand smoke is the third leading cause of preventable death in this country*), strong opinions (*No one should have to suffer the consequences of other people's actions*), and refuting an opposing view contribute to the development of ideas. Although a sarcastic statement might offend the reader (*Apparently our health is irrelevant*), the solid organizational plan, precise word choice (*legitimate, unjust*) and good command of conventions make this a highly effective composition.

	Focus and Coherence	Organization	Development of Ideas	Voice	Conventions
4	focused and connected	flows smoothly	ideas deeply supported	highly engaging and original	strong command of conventions
3	mostly focused and connected	generally flows smoothly	ideas thoughtfully supported	mostly engaging and original	few errors
2	somewhat focused	flows somewhat smoothly	ideas adequately supported	somewhat engaging and original	some errors
1	unfocused, disconnected	does not flow	ideas unsupported	not engaging or original	major errors

Persuasive Writing

High Insurance for Teens

1   Insurance is too high these days. Especialy for us teenagers.

2   Insurance rates need to be lower for teen drivers. Here's

3   why. Insurance rates for teenagers are crazy! The rates are

4   disproportionatly high for teen drivers. Especially for those who are

5   just driving to school or elsewhere. Teenagers who have sport cars pay

6   even more. Like around $400 to $500 every six months in most cases.

7   Parents go off the deep end when they see those insurance bills. I

8   don't blame them!

9   Teenagers can't afford to pay for this high insurance so they go

10   out and drive without it just encourages them to do something like

11   that, but what else are they supposed to do when parents can't afford

12   this kind of expence and the rates are too high for them to pay and

13   keep up their school work. Most parents can't pay for the extra every

14   month. Or even help their kids out. Insurance rates should definitely

15   drop.

16   Plus the fact that insurance companies make a ton of money off

17   teenage drivers, huge profits that go right into their own pockets and

18   let them drive around their big fancy cars with no though for the

19   struggling teens who pay for the extra stuff teenage drivers should

20   pay the same rates as other drivers. Because insurance companies

21   make this huge profit off drivers who are just learning to drive.

22   Is that fair? No matter what kind of car you drive or what color it

Persuasive Writing *(cont.)*

23 happens to be painted. You should pay the same as everybody else.

24 Insurance people shouldn't just get rich off poor teenage drivers.

25 Why are teenage drivers penalized by insurance companies the

26 way we are. If we are old enough to drive and responsible enough to

27 own a car, we should get the same rates as adults. Come on, let's be

28 fair!

Persuasive Writing
Benchmark Paper Comments

Title: High Insurance for Teens   Holistic Score: **2**

In this somewhat effective persuasive response, the writer argues that car insurance for teens is unfairly expensive. The writer's voice is evident and sincere throughout (*If we are old enough to drive and responsible enough to own a car, we should get the same rates as adults.*) but the progression of ideas is unorganized and the development is superficial (*Insurance rates for teenagers are crazy!*). General statements that are unsupported (*insurance companies make a ton of money off teenage drivers*) along with some errors in conventions interfere with the effective communication of ideas.

	Focus and Coherence	Organization	Development of Ideas	Voice	Conventions
4	focused and connected	flows smoothly	ideas deeply supported	highly engaging and original	strong command of conventions
3	mostly focused and connected	generally flows smoothly	ideas thoughtfully supported	mostly engaging and original	few errors
2	**somewhat focused**	flows somewhat smoothly	ideas adequately supported	**somewhat engaging and original**	**some errors**
1	unfocused, disconnected	**does not flow**	**ideas unsupported**	not engaging or original	major errors

Interpretive Response

The Source of Horror in "The Lottery"

1   "The Lottery" is a frightening story. Like any good scary story, it

2 has monsters; but the monsters don't appear in the shape of vampires

3 and werewolves. The monsters in "The Lottery" are the monsters that

4 can be found in nice, average, decent people. People like you and me.

5   There isn't much action in the story. The people in a small

6 village gather together on a beautiful summer day, men, women, and

7 children. The children play and the grown-ups gossip or talk about

8 their crops. With the arrival of Mr. Summers, ". . . who had time and

9 energy to devote to civic activities," preparations for the lottery begin.

10 Names of families are placed in the "black box" and following an

11 abbreviated version of what apparently was once a more complicated

12 ritual, the heads of the families draw a slip from the box. The

13 "winner" is the family representative who draws the slip with a black

14 dot.

15   Blank slips of paper for each "winning" family member are put in

16 the box. The slip with the black dot is used in place of one blank slip.

17 Each family member then draws a slip. The one drawing the black

18 dot is then stoned to death by the others. Everyone in the village

19 participates in the murder. This includes the victim's family members.

20 The lottery is concluded in time for the villagers to get home for

21 lunch.

22   The full horror of the story comes through the juxtaposition of

Interpretive Response *(cont.)*

23 the revelation of the true nature of the lottery and the manner in

24 which it is regarded by the participants and presented by the author.

25 The narrative is presented flatly, with no interior probing of the

26 characters. Everything appears quite matter-of-fact and normal.

27 The lottery is seen as just another annual civic event like a

28 Halloween program. The focus of the villagers' concern is on the

29 details of the procedure to be followed, on questions like whether a

30 new box should be made for the drawing. There is no real indication

31 that anyone has any serious moral objections to stoning some village

32 member to death.

33 Someone does mention tentatively that other villages have

34 stopped their lotteries, but Old Man Warner, the oldest surviving

35 participant, scoffs at this notion, suggesting that soon "They'll be

36 wanting to go back to living in caves." Given the nature of the lottery,

37 Warner's defense of the lottery—that discounting it would be a step

38 backward—is clearly ironic.

39 The original reason for the lottery is obscure. Warner's mention

40 of "Lottery in June, corn be heavy soon" hints that it may have been

41 some kind of sacrificial rite, but the real reason and indeed most of

42 the ritual have been forgotten. What remains is the ritual murder

43 repeated each year, tradition carried to its ugliest extreme.

44 At first the only emotion displayed by the villagers seems to be

45 relief at not being the victim. Even the children of Mrs. Hutchinson,

46 the woman to be stoned, smile when they discover they have not

Interpretive Response *(cont.)*

47   drawn the black dot. Worse, however, is the positive glee with which

48   the villagers join in the stoning. It almost seems as if a blood lust

49   is inherent in each villager. There is more here then just ignorance

50   or an unquestioning acceptance of tradition. "The Lottery" calls

51   into question the very nature of the human heart, and focuses our

52   attention on the evil (or the monsters) lurking beneath the surface of

53   civilized life.

Interpretive Response
Benchmark Paper Comments

Title: The Source of Horror in "The Lottery"   Holistic Score: **4**

This highly effective composition discusses the horror of the stoning in "The Lottery" and an engaging premise (*The monsters . . . can be found in nice, average, decent people*). The writer presents a good summary and uses direct quotations from the text for a smooth progression of thought. The maturity of sentence structure (*Given the nature . . . is clearly ironic.*) and word choice (*abbreviated version, complicated ritual, obscure, inherent*), are enhanced by the nearly flawless control of conventions. The conclusion connecting the author's ideas to real life helps make this essay powerful and effective.

	Focus and Coherence	Organization	Development of Ideas	Voice	Conventions
4	focused and connected	flows smoothly	ideas deeply supported	highly engaging and original	strong command of conventions
3	mostly focused and connected	generally flows smoothly	ideas thoughtfully supported	mostly engaging and original	few errors
2	somewhat focused	flows somewhat smoothly	ideas adequately supported	somewhat engaging and original	some errors
1	unfocused, disconnected	does not flow	ideas unsupported	not engaging or original	major errors

Interpretive Response

O Sweet Spontaneous

1   Sometimes poems do more than just sound great. They have a

2   deeper meaning. Here is a look at some of the possible meanings in

3   the poem by a e.e. cummings "o sweet spontaneous".

4   This poem is about a man destroying the earth. It also showed

5   that the earth can survive in spite of what we do to mess it up. The

6   scientists that create nuclear weapons, strip mines, steal, this all

7   takes away the natural resources and cause nature a lot of problems

8   and also, philosophers and religious people that take hundreds of

9   lives. So I think cummings is trying to say that we need to stop before

10 its too late and man is no longer able to survive on earth.

11 I think that the tone of this poem is that man is basically

12 destroying the earth. Nature keeps trying to deal with it by having

13 spring, When nature gets to blooms and be fresh and new. So the title

14 was about this too. About being spring and spring overcoming all of

15 the bad things man comes up with to mess it up.

16 There are a lot of poetic divices used in this poem, like

17 alliteration (three times, once in the title, once in the 6th line and also

18 in the 1st line). Also assonance. It is used in lines 15–17. I also saw

19 some personification in that earth is compared to a human being who

20 speaks. Nature is also an example of personification.

Interpretive Response *(cont.)*

21   This poem doesn't rhyme and isn't rhythmic at all. It does have

22   some weird uses of punctuation and no capitals. I guess the poet

23   didn't like them because he does even use them in his own name!

24   It was written in 1920. It wasn't published until 1923 with some

25   of his other works. I don't think the year affected this poem too much,

26   or the poet. I can't think of much that was going on in history during

27   this time that would have any affect on it. It's not like he wrote

28   during the end of World War II when everyone was worried about

29   the bomb droping on their heads. How that would make sense, for

30   this poem to have been written then but during this time, no one was

31   thinking about that. So I don't think the history has any baring on

32   this poem at all.

33   I also don't thing that cummings life has much to do with this

34   poem. Some of the other poem we studied by him definitely did,

35   though. Like The Enormous Room, which was written about being

36   a prisoner of war. That really happened to him. During the Spanish

37   Civil war. He may be sort of pesemistic because of that time. I know

38   I would be! Maybe that's why a lot of his writing seems so sad and

39   confusing. Maybe that's how he was feeling at the time.

40   I always get the feeling from this poem that I agree with

41   cummings, man is really messing up the planet. And I don't think

42   that we can count on spring always baling us out every year, like in

43   this poem. Someday we'll be out of luck. Then what.

Interpretive Response *(cont.)*

44   I do like this poem even though its very depressing because

45   I agree with it and the poet was good at making his point here.

46   Everyone should read this poem before they go on pulluting and

47   thinking their not hurting anything.

Interpretive Response
Benchmark Paper Comments

Title: O Sweet Spontaneous   Holistic Score: **2**

The writer of this somewhat effective response to literature analyzes the possible meanings of the poem "O Sweet Spontaneous." The writer attempts an organization plan and has a sense of voice, but repetition (*man . . . destroying the earth*) and references to poetic devices without explaining them (*alliteration three times*) slow the progression of ideas. Although a few points (spring overcomes man's bad things, history does not affect the poem) are somewhat developed and supported, and the conclusion connects the poem to real life, the superficial ideas and frequent usage and agreement errors (*Some of the other poem we studied by him definitely did*) limit the reader's understanding and appreciation.

	Focus and Coherence	Organization	Development of Ideas	Voice	Conventions
4	focused and connected	flows smoothly	ideas deeply supported	highly engaging and original	strong command of conventions
3	mostly focused and connected	generally flows smoothly	ideas thoughtfully supported	mostly engaging and original	few errors
2	**somewhat focused**	**flows somewhat smoothly**	**ideas adequately supported**	**somewhat engaging and original**	**some errors**
1	unfocused, disconnected	does not flow	ideas unsupported	not engaging or original	major errors

Time Line

Topic: _____

5 W's Chart

Topic: _____

Who?	
What?	
When?	
Where?	
Why?	
How?	

T-Chart

Topic:

Venn Diagram

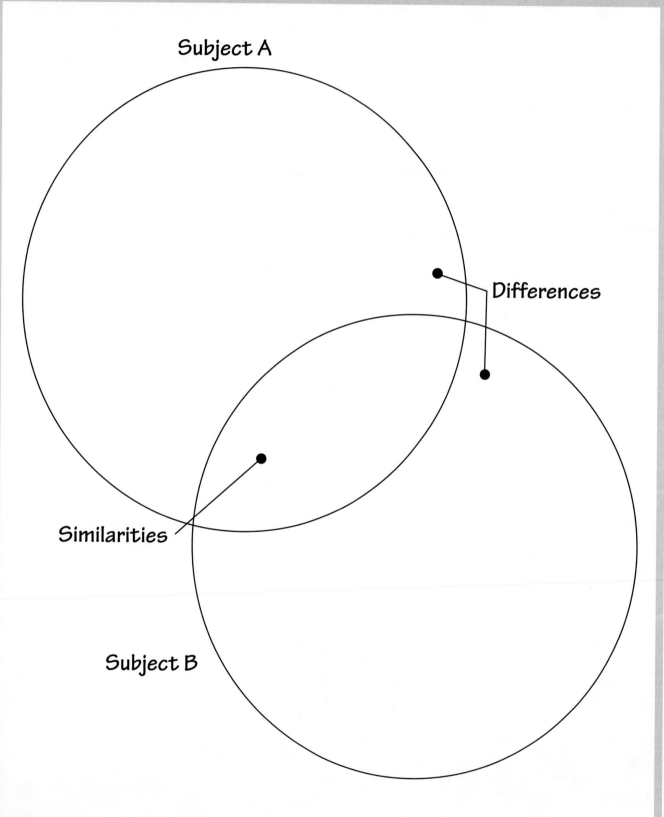

Subject A

Differences

Similarities

Subject B

Sensory Chart

Subject: _____

Sights	Sounds	Smells	Tastes	Textures

Details Chart

Quick List

1. First Point:

    ■

    ■

2. Second Point:

    ■

    ■

3. Third Point:

    ■

    ■

Credits

Credits

Photo Acknowledgements P. A9 ©Mike Kemp/Getty Images; TE8-9 ©Andrzej Tokarski/ Alamy.

Index